"No other guide has as much to o[...] a pleasure to read."   Gene Shalit

". . . Excellently organized for the casual traveler who is looking for a mix of recreation and cultural insight."
Washington Post

★ ★ ★ ★ ★ (5-star rating) "Crisply written and remarkably personable. Cleverly organized so you can pluck out the minutest fact in a moment. Satisfyingly thorough."
Réalités

"The information they offer is up-to-date, crisply presented but far from exhaustive, the judgments knowledgeable but not opinionated."   *New York Times*

"The individual volumes are compact, the prose succinct, and the coverage up-to-date and knowledgeable . . . The format is portable and the index admirably detailed."
John Barkham Syndicate

". . . An abundance of excellent directions, diversions, and facts, including perspectives and getting-ready-to-go advice — succinct, detailed, and well organized in an easy-to-follow style."   *Los Angeles Times*

"They contain an amount of information that is truly staggering, besides being surprisingly current."
Detroit News

"These guides address themselves to the needs of the modern traveler demanding precise, qualitative information . . . Upbeat, slick, and well put together."
Dallas Morning News

". . . Attractive to look at, refreshingly easy to read, and generously packed with information."   *Miami Herald*

"These guides are as good as any published, and much better than most."   *Louisville* (Kentucky) *Times*

Stephen Birnbaum Travel Guides

Acapulco
Bahamas, Turks & Caicos
Barcelona
Bermuda
Boston
Canada
Cancun, Cozumel, and Isla Mujeres
Caribbean
Chicago
Disneyland
Eastern Europe
Europe
Europe for Business Travelers
Florence
France
Great Britain
Hawaii
Ireland
Italy
Ixtapa & Zihuatanejo
London
Los Angeles
Mexico
Miami
New York
Paris
Portugal
Rome
San Francisco
South America
Spain
United States
USA for Business Travelers
Venice
Walt Disney World
Western Europe

CONTRIBUTING EDITORS

Carmen Anthony
David Baird
F. Lisa Beebe
Frederick H. Brengelman
Kevin Causey
Dwight V. Gast
Judith Glynn
Arline Inge
Donald A. Jeffrey
David Cemlyn-Jones
Emily Kadin
Robert Latona
Charles Leocha
Howell Llewellyn

Jan S. McGirk
Erica Meltzer
Jeanne Muchnick
Joan Kane Nichols
Clare Pedrick
Mark Potok
Allan Seiden
Frank Shiell
Richard Slovak
Melinda Tang
Paul Wade
David Wickers
Mark Williams

MAPS B. Andrew Mudryk
SYMBOLS Gloria McKeown

A Stephen Birnbaum Travel Guide

Birnbaum's
SPAIN
1992

Stephen Birnbaum
Alexandra Mayes Birnbaum
EDITORS

Lois Spritzer
EXECUTIVE EDITOR

Laura L. Brengelman
Managing Editor

Mary Callahan
Ann-Rebecca Laschever
Beth Schlau
Dana Margaret Schwartz
Associate Editors

Gene Gold
Assistant Editor

HarperPerennial
A Division of HarperCollins*Publishers*

FIRST EDITION

ISSN: 0749-2561 (Stephen Birnbaum Travel Guides)
ISSN: 1055-565X (Spain)
ISBN: 0-06-278012-3 (pbk.)

91 92 93 94 95 96 CC/WP 10 9 8 7 6 5 4 3 2 1

Contents

PERSPECTIVES

A cultural and historical survey of Spain's past and present, its people, politics, and heritage.

THE CITIES

Thorough, qualitative guides to each of the 13 cities most often visited by vacationers and businesspeople. Each section, a comprehensive report of the city's most appealing attractions and amenities, is designed to be used on the spot. Directions and recommendations are immediately accessible because each guide is presented in a consistent form.

DIVERSIONS

A selective guide to 19 active and cerebral vacations, including the places to pursue them where your quality of experience is likely to be highest.

For the Experience

For the Body

For the Mind

DIRECTIONS

The most spectacular routes and roads; most arresting natural wonders; and most magnificent castles, manor houses, and gardens — all organized into 13 specific driving tours.

Spain

A Word from the Editor

I was a little slow in getting around to running away from home — to tell the truth, I waited until the summer after my 20th birthday — but when I finally decided to hit the road, I made up for lost time. Rather than head across town to Aunt Maude's, I decided to sulk along the southern coast of Spain, a decision that was among the very best I ever made.

One of the major contributors to the joys of that very special summer was the limited amount of cash I had in my pocket. I'd been traveling very much on the cheap (remind me to tell you about the several nights spent snoozing on the beach), so my first views of Spain were often from the wrong side of a dining room tray.

I have the impression that in the course of the nearly 3 months I walked from Málaga (actually Torremolinos) to Barcelona I really saw the country. The truth is, I hitchhiked more often than not, took the bus when I felt I could spare the change, and worked as everything from a bartender (I often served as vice president in charge of making dirty glasses clean) to a fisherman (my highest rank was second net puller).

Above all, I developed a fondness for Spain that I have never lost, and must say that I have waited with some extra eagerness to finally focus on a guide to that country. Spain is at once a part of Europe, and yet very distinctive and distinct from the other members of the European community. The country offers a combination of cultures and historic influences that have molded it in ways very different from its continental neighbors.

Just a brief turning of the pages of this guide will demonstrate the diversity that thrives in Spain between the Pyrenees and the Strait of Gibraltar. The idea that Spain is a single, homogeneous nation is one of travel's least justifiable assertions, and the atmosphere and ambience that thrive across this extremely variegated country are, in themselves, among the prime magnets that draw visitors. At least half a dozen distinct "nations" co-exist under the Spanish flag — each demanding strict attention — and one of the joys of traveling to and through Spain is the constant feeling of surprise and discovery. And during 1992, the surfeit of special events in Spain makes exploring the nation a singular pleasure.

Once again, the opportunity to present a single corner of the European continent in great detail has been part of the pleasure of preparing this guide. It gives us the opportunity to deal with Spanish destinations in the sort of detail that they truly deserve, and to provide a modern traveler with the perspectives and insights that are required to do more than just superficially see one of Europe's most intriguing countries.

Such thorough treatment only mirrors an increasingly pervasive trend among travelers — the frequent return to treasured foreign travel spots. Once upon a time, even the most dedicated travelers would visit distant parts of the world no more than once in a lifetime — usually as part of that fabled Grand Tour. But greater numbers of would-be sojourners are now availing themselves of the opportunity to visit favored parts of the world over and over again.

So where once it was routine to say you'd "seen" a particular country after a very superficial, once-over-lightly encounter, the more perceptive travelers of today recognize that it's entirely possible to have only skimmed the surface of a specific destination even after having visited that place more than a dozen times. Similarly, repeated visits to a single site permit true exploration of special interests, whether they be sporting, artistic, or intellectual in nature.

For those of us who spent several years working out the special system under which we present information in this series, the luxury of being able to devote nearly as much space as we'd like to just a single country is as close to paradise for guide writers and editors as any of us expects to come. But clearly this is not the first guide to the glories of Spain — guides of one sort or another have existed for centuries, so a traveler might logically ask why a new one is suddenly necessary.

Our answer is that the nature of travel to Spain — and even of the travelers who now routinely make the trip — has changed dramatically. For the past 2,000 years or so, travel to and through Spain was an extremely elaborate undertaking, one that required extensive advance planning. Even as recently as the 1950s, a person who had actually been to Madrid, Barcelona, or the Costa Brava could dine out on his or her experiences for years, since such adventures were quite extraordinary and usually the province of the privileged alone.

With the advent of jet air travel in the late 1950s, however, and of increased-capacity, wide-body aircraft during the late 1960s, travel to and around these once distant lands became extremely common. In fact, in more than 2 decades of nearly unending inflation, airfares may be the only commodity in the world that has actually gone down in price.

Attitudes, as well as costs, also have changed significantly in the last couple of decades. Beginning with the so-called flower children of the 1960s, international travel lost much of its aura of mystery. Whereas their parents might have been happy with just a superficial sampling of Seville or Granada, these young people simply picked up and settled in various parts of Europe for an indefinite stay. While living as inexpensively as possible, they adapted to the local lifestyle, and generally immersed themselves in things European.

Thus began an explosion of travel to and through Spain. And over the years, the development of inexpensive charter flights and packages fueled the new American interest in and appetite for more extensive exploration.

Now, in the 1990s, those same flower children who were in the forefront of the modern travel revolution have undeniably aged. While it may be impolite to point out that they are probably well into their untrustworthy 30s and (some) 40s, their original zeal for travel remains undiminished. For them it's hardly news that the way to get from western Europe to the Costa del Sol is to head toward the Mediterranean, make a right, and then watch for the outline of the Rock of Gibraltar. Such experienced and knowledgeable travelers know precisely where they want to go, and are more often searching for ideas and insights to expand their already sophisticated travel consciousness.

Obviously, any new guidebook to Spain must keep pace with and answer the real needs of today's travelers. That's why we've tried to create a guide that's specifically organized, written, and edited for this more demanding modern audience, one for whom qualitative information is infinitely more desirable than mere quantities of unappraised data. We think that this book and the other guides in our series represent a new generation of travel guides, one that is especially responsive to modern needs and interests.

For years, dating back as far as Herr Baedeker, travel guides have tended to be encyclopedic, seemingly much more concerned with demonstrating expertise in geography and history than with a real analysis of the sorts of things that actually concern a typical tourist. But today, when it is hardly necessary to tell a traveler where the Pyrenees are (in many cases, the traveler has been there nearly as often as the guidebook editors), it becomes the responsibility of those editors to provide new perspectives and to suggest new directions in order to make the guide genuinely valuable.

That's exactly what we've tried to do in this series. I think you'll notice a different, more contemporary tone to the text, as well as an organization and focus that are distinctive and more functional. And even a random reading of what follows will demonstrate a substantial departure from the standard guidebook orientation, for we've not only attempted to provide information of a more compelling sort, but we also have tried to present the data in a context that makes it particularly accessible.

Needless to say, it's difficult to decide precisely what to include in a guidebook of this size — and what to omit. Early on, we realized that giving up the encyclopedic approach precluded our listing every single route and restaurant, a realization that helped define our overall editorial focus. Similarly, when we discussed the possibility of presenting certain information in other than strict geographic order, we found that the new format enabled us to arrange data in a way that we feel best answers the questions travelers typically ask.

Large numbers of specific questions have provided the real editorial skeleton for this book. The volume of mail I regularly receive emphasizes that modern travelers want very precise information, so we've tried to address these needs and have organized our material in the most responsive way possible. Readers who want to know the most evocative sights around Salamanca or the best places to dine in Valencia will have no trouble whatever extracting that data from this guide.

Travel guides are, understandably, reflections of personal taste, and putting one's name on a title page obviously puts one's preferences on the line. But I think I ought to amplify just what "personal" means. I don't believe in the sort of personal guidebook that's a palpable misrepresentation on its face. It is, for example, hardly possible for any single travel writer to visit thousands of restaurants (and nearly as many hotels) in any given year and provide accurate appraisals of each. And even if it were physically possible for one human being to survive such an itinerary, it would of necessity have to be done at a dead sprint and the perceptions derived therefrom would probably be less valid than those of any other intelligent individual visiting the same establishments. It is, therefore, impossible (especially in a large, annually revised guidebook *series* such as we offer) to have only one person provide all the data on the entire world.

I also happen to think that such individual orientation is of substantially less value. Visiting a single hotel for just one night or eating one hasty meal in a random restaurant hardly equips anyone to provide appraisals that are of more than passing interest. No amount of doggedly alliterative or oppressively onomatopoetic text can camouflage a technique that is essentially specious. We have, therefore, chosen what I like to describe as the "thee and me" approach to restaurant and hotel evaluation and, to a somewhat more limited degree, to the sites and sights in the other sections of our text. What this really reflects is a personal sampling tempered by intelligent counsel from informed local sources, and these additional friends-of-the-editors are almost always residents of the city and/or area about which they are consulted.

Despite the presence of several editors, writers, researchers, and local correspondents, very precise editing and tailoring keeps our text fiercely subjective. So what follows is the gospel according to the Birnbaums, and represents as much of our own taste and instinct as we can manage. It is probable, therefore, that if you like your cities stylish and your mountainsides uncrowded, prefer small hotels with personality to huge high-rise anonymities, and won't tolerate paella or fresh fish that's been relentlessly overcooked, we're likely to have a long and meaningful relationship. Readers with dissimilar tastes may be less enraptured.

I also should point out something about the person to whom this guidebook is directed. Above all, he or she is a "visitor." This means that such elements as restaurants have been specifically picked to provide the visitor with a representative, enlightening, stimulating, and above all, pleasant experience. Since so many extraneous considerations can affect the reception and service accorded a regular restaurant patron, our choices can in no way be construed as an exhaustive guide to resident dining. We think we've listed all the best places, in various price ranges, but they were chosen with a visitor's enjoyment in mind.

Other evidence of how we've tried to tailor our text to reflect modern travel habits is most apparent in the section we call DIVERSIONS. Where once it was common for travelers to spend a foreign visit nailed to a single spot, the emphasis today is more on pursuing some athletic enterprise or special interest while seeing the surrounding countryside. So we've organized every activity we could reasonably evaluate and organized the material in a way that is especially accessible to activists of either athletic or cerebral bent. It is no longer necessary, therefore, to wade through a pound or two of superfluous prose just to find the very best crafts shop or the most picturesque *parador* within a reasonable distance of your destination.

If there is a single thing that best characterizes the revolution in and evolution of current holiday habits, it is that most travelers now consider travel a right rather than a privilege. No longer is a trip to the far corners of the country — or to Europe or the Orient — necessarily a once-in-a-lifetime thing; nor is the idea of visiting exotic, faraway places in the least worrisome. Travel today translates as the enthusiastic desire to sample all of the world's opportunities, to find that elusive quality of experience that is not only enriching but comfortable. For that reason, we've tried to make what follows not only helpful and enlightening but the sort of welcome companion of which every traveler dreams.

Finally, I also should point out that every good travel guide is a living enterprise; that is, no part of this text is carved in stone. In our annual revisions, we refine, expand, and further hone all our material to serve your travel needs better. To this end, no contribution is of greater value to us than your personal reaction to what we have written, as well as information reflecting your own experiences while using the book. We earnestly and enthusiastically solicit your comments about this guide *and* your opinions and perceptions about places you have recently visited. In this way, we will be able to provide the most current information — including the actual experiences of recent travelers — to make those experiences more readily available to others. Please write to us at 60 E. 42nd St., New York, NY 10165.

We sincerely hope to hear from you.

STEPHEN BIRNBAUM

How to Use This Guide

 A great deal of care has gone into the organization of this guide-book, and we believe it represents a real breakthrough in the presentation of travel material. Our aim is to create a new, more modern generation of travel books, and to make this guide the most useful and practical travel tool available today.

Our text is divided into five basic sections, in order to best present information in the best way on every possible aspect of a vacation in Spain. This organization itself should alert you to the vast and varied opportunities available, as well as indicating all the specific data necessary to plan a successful visit. You won't find much of the conventional "swaying palms and shimmering sands" text here; we've chosen instead to deliver more useful and practical information. Prospective itineraries tend to speak for themselves, and with so many diverse travel opportunities, we feel our main job is to highlight what's where and to provide basic information — how, when, where, how much, and what's best — to assist you in making the most intelligent choices possible.

Here is a brief summary of the five sections of this book, and what you can expect to find in each. We believe that you will find both your travel planning and en route enjoyment enhanced by having this book at your side.

GETTING READY TO GO

This mini-encyclopedia of practical travel facts is meant to be a sort of know-it-all companion with all the precise information necessary to create a successful trip to and through Spain. There are entries on more than 2 dozen separate topics, including how to get where you're going, what preparations to make before leaving, what to expect in the different parts of the country, what the trip is likely to cost, and how to avoid prospective problems. The individual entries are specific, realistic, and, where appropriate, cost-oriented.

We expect you to use this section most in the course of planning your trip, for its ideas and suggestions are intended to simplify this often confusing period. Entries are intentionally concise, in an effort to get to the meat of the matter, with the least extraneous prose. These entries are augmented by extensive lists of specific sources from which to obtain even more specialized data, plus some suggestions for obtaining travel information on your own.

PERSPECTIVES

Any visit to an unfamiliar destination is enhanced and enriched by understanding the cultural and historical heritage of that area. We have, therefore, provided just such an introduction to Spain, its past and present, people and politics, architecture, literature, music and dance, and food and drink.

THE CITIES

Individual reports on the 13 Spanish cities most visited by travelers have been prepared with the assistance of researchers, contributors, professional journalists, and other experts on the spot. Although useful at the planning stage, THE CITIES is really designed to be taken along and used on the spot. Each report offers a short-stay guide within a consistent format: an essay introduces the city as a historic entity and a contemporary place to live and visit; *At-a-Glance* material is actually a site-by-site survey of the most important, interesting, and sometimes unusual sights to see and things to do; *Sources and Resources* is a concise listing of pertinent tourism information, meant to answer myriad potentially pressing questions as they arise such as the address of the local tourist office, how to get around, which sightseeing tours to take, when special events occur, where to find the best nightspot or hail a taxi, which shops have the finest merchandise or the more irresistable bargains, and where the best local skiing, golf, tennis, fishing, and swimming are to be found; and *Best in Town* lists our cost-and-quality choices of the best places to eat and sleep on a variety of budgets.

DIVERSIONS

This section is designed to help travelers find the best places in which to pursue a wide range of physical and cerebral activities, without having to wade through endless pages of unrelated text. This very selective guide lists the broadest possible range of activities, including all the best places to pursue them.

We start with a list of possibilities that offer various places to stay and eat, and move to those that require some perspiration — sports preferences and other rigorous pursuits — and go on to report on a number of more cerebral and spiritual vacation opportunities. In every case, our suggestion of a particular location — and often our recommendation of a specific resort — is intended to guide you to that special place where the quality of experience is likely to be highest. Whether you opt for shopping or skiing, attending theater festivals or country fairs, the most stylish hotels or most esoteric museums, or tours of spectacular resorts, each entry is the equivalent of a comprehensive checklist of the absolute best in Spain.

DIRECTIONS

Here are 13 itineraries that range all across Spain, along the most beautiful routes and roads, past the most spectacular natural wonders, through the most historic cities and countrysides and the most idyllic islands. DIRECTIONS is the only section of the book that is organized geographically, and its itineraries cover the touring highlights of Spain in short, independent journeys of 3 to 5 days' duration. Itineraries can be "connected" for longer trips or used individually for short, intensive explorations.

Each entry includes a guide to sightseeing highlights; a qualitative guide to accommodations and food along the road (small inns, castle hotels, country hotels); and suggestions for activities.

Although each of this book's sections has a distinct format and a special function, they have all been designed to be used together to provide a complete inventory of travel information. To use this book to full advantage, take a few minutes to read the table of contents and random entries in each section to give you an idea of how it all fits together.

Pick and choose needed information. Assume, for example, that you always have wanted to take that typically Spanish vacation, a walking tour through rural Iberia, but you never really knew how to organize it or where to go. Turn first to the hiking section of GETTING READY TO GO, as well as the chapters on planning a trip, accommodations, and climate and clothes. These short, informative entries provide plenty of practical information. But where to go? Turn next to DIRECTIONS. Routes and desirable detours are all clearly set forth. Your trip will likely begin or end in Madrid, and for a complete rundown on this remarkable city, you should read the Madrid chapter of THE CITIES. Finally, turn to DIVERSIONS to peruse the chapters on sports, hotels, antiques, and other activities in which you are especially interested, to make sure you don't miss anything along your chosen route.

In other words, the sections of this book are building blocks to help you put together the best possible trip. Use them selectively as a tool, a source of ideas, a reference work for accurate facts, and a guide to the best buys, the most exciting sights, the most pleasant accommodations, the tastiest food — *the best travel experience* that you can have in Spain.

GETTING READY TO GO

When and How to Go

What's Where

Spain comprises the major portion of what is most often referred to as the Iberian Peninsula, a 230,436-square-mile rectangle jutting out from Europe to the southwest. Spain shares the peninsula with Portugal and its western boundaries with this smaller nation are marked less by rivers and mountains than by lack of people: For much of its length the Spanish-Portuguese border is a wasteland. The rugged Pyrenees separate the peninsula from France and Andorra, its most immediate neighbors to the northeast, and the slender Strait of Gibraltar separates it from North Africa to the south. Spain's possessions in the Mediterranean, to the east, are the Balearic Islands, and in the Atlantic, to the west, are the Canary Islands.

In shape, Spain, the second-largest country in Western Europe, resembles an armless torso. Of the 50 provinces in its 17 autonomous regions, many have their own distinct language and culture. In all, Spain covers some 194,883 square miles and has a population of 39 million people.

Running north to south, Spain comprises three main regions: the green and mountainous north, the dry, windswept *meseta,* or tableland, of the center, and the sultry, romantic south. Second only to Switzerland as Europe's most mountainous country, Spain — with an average altitude of about 2,000 feet above sea level — contains many of the continent's highest roads and villages. Mountains spring almost straight up from the coasts, leaving only narrow strips or estuaries along the shoreline. Much of the country is dry, and, since people cluster near water, wide empty spaces separate one inhabited area from another. The sharpest boundaries in Spain are those that set off dry land from damp.

The green and mountainous north stretches from the province of Galicia on Spain's western shoulder to the province of Catalonia on the east. The misty coastal region, with the North Atlantic on two sides, brings to mind Ireland, Wales, or the Scottish Highlands. It extends from the Basque mountain range — which abuts the foothills of the Pyrenees — west to the reaches above Portugal. In the Middle Ages, pilgrims from Europe crossed the Pyrenees over this shoulder of the Spanish torso to the holy city of Santiago de Compostela, a pilgrimage still made today. The heavily industrialized Basque region lies east of the coast and occupies part of the Cantabrian Mountains. The fiercely independent Basques, with their unique language and customs, are quite possibly the oldest surviving ethnic group in Europe, predating the ancient Iberian tribes of Spain. In the Basque region are the caves of Altamira, famous for their 13,000-year-old paintings. Nearby, in Navarre, is the town of Pamplona, famous for its yearly "running of the bulls." Farther east, Aragon is close to the tiny, snow-capped country of Andorra.

Catalonia, on Spain's eastern shoulder, borders the Mediterranean. Its coast, the Costa Brava (Wild Coast), forms Spain's twisted, tortuous northeastern shoreline. Unquestionably the country's most rugged coast, as well as its shortest, the Costa Brava's jagged granite cliffs rise from the sea as though chewed out of the earth by some gigantic sea monster with serrated teeth. These cliffs shelter a plethora of bays, coves, inlets, beaches, and traditional whitewashed villages. Catalonia as a whole differs in character and history from the other regions of Spain. The Catalans, who have their own Provençal-like language and culture, are a progressive, vigorous, and businesslike breed whose efforts have made their region Spain's chief economic center and the most up-to-date and densely populated part of the peninsula. Barcelona, its cosmopolitan capital, is a major European commercial and industrial city.

The 2,000-foot-high *meseta,* its brown earth sometimes awash with golden wheat, dominates central Spain — to many people the real Spain. Here, in the geographic center of the country, is the *comunidad,* or province, of Madrid, surrounded by the expansive regions of New and Old Castile. It was on this austere, windswept plateau that the character of the traditional Spaniard was formed; here, under vast skies, the fictional Don Quixote, the Man of La Mancha, tilted at windmills. Its considerable altitude makes for a continental climate, with hot summers, cold winters, and a continual wind. The names of its cities evoke splendors — Madrid, the nation's capital; old-fashioned Toledo; Avila, city of soldiers and St. Teresa; Salamanca, with its university; the Roman aqueduct and fabulous castle of Segovia. On Spain's western edge is the province of Extremadura, which despite its wealth of wildflowers is a harsh land. Many have emigrated from here, beginning with Cortés and Pizarro, Balboa and de Soto. To the east is the Levante, the Mediterranean coast where the Phoenicians traded, and the city of Valencia, famous for its rice fields and its wonderful rice dish, paella. Surrounding the city is the most fertile land in Europe, a densely populated agricultural region where the aroma of orange trees is overwhelming. Murcia, a little farther south along the coast, is on the fringe of a desert.

There also are those who claim that the real Spain is Andalusia. The warm, romantic south of Spain has everything most people think of as Spanish: snow-capped mountains and massive coastal dunes; the flamenco, a flamboyant music and dance identified with the Gypsies of Granada and Seville; Spain's many famous matadors; the traditional whitewashed cottages, draped with orange blossoms, clinging precariously to rocky hillsides; and the stunning Moorish palace and garden complex, the Alhambra. Mountain ranges occupy large sections of the region. Much of the land is given over to the cultivation of olives, oranges, sunflowers, and grapes. The Costa del Sol, which extends along the Mediterranean coast on Andalusia's southeast, is Spain's answer to Acapulco and Rio de Janeiro. Formerly a dry, hilly land sprinkled with whitewashed cottages, the Costa del Sol has become one of Europe's most developed (some say overdeveloped) and most popular beach resort areas, a traditional retreat of the British from their damp, cold winters. The Costa del Sol extends from Almería, on the easternmost part of the southern Mediterranean coast, to Algeciras, 236 miles to the west. The 84 miles between Málaga, an important southern port, and Algeciras is the most developed (and crowded) resort area. Along this stretch, Swedish, German, French, Arabic, and English are more widely spoken than Spanish. Near Algeciras, at the very tip of Spain, is Gibraltar, which is not Spanish but British. From Algeciras, a ferry sails across the Straits to Ceuta, which is not Moroccan but Spanish.

CANARY ISLANDS: A cluster of seven major and six minor islands in the Atlantic Ocean, the Canary Islands lie about 65 miles off the northwest coast of Africa. The major islands are Gran Canaria, Tenerife, Fuerteventura, La Palma, Gomera, and Hierro. The charming villages of white cottages with red roofs sprinkled throughout the mountainous interior of these volcanic formations make the Canary Island archipelago inviting to travelers seeking unusual places of distinctive character.

BALEARIC ISLANDS: The Balearic Islands lie 90 miles southeast of Barcelona in the Mediterranean Sea. The major section of this archipelago consists of two pairs of islands: Majorca and Minorca, Formentera and Ibiza. Many smaller islands complete the archipelagic structure. The Balearic Mountains are thick with ancient fig and olive trees; the beaches are shaded by evergreens. The surrounding seas are exceptionally calm and clear despite the prevailing winds.

When to Go

 There really isn't a "best" time to visit Spain. For North Americans, as well as Europeans, the period from mid-May to mid-September has long been — and remains — the peak travel period, traditionally the most popular vacation time.

It is important to emphasize that Spain is hardly a single-season destination; more and more vacationers who have a choice are enjoying the substantial advantages of off-season travel. Though lesser tourist attractions may close during the off-season — roughly November to *Easter* — the major ones remain open and tend to be less crowded, as are some cities and other parts of the country. During the off-season, people relax and Spanish life proceeds at a more leisurely pace. What's more, travel generally is less expensive.

For some, the most convincing argument in favor of off-season travel is the economic one. Getting there and staying there is less expensive during less popular travel periods, as airfares, hotel rooms, and car rental rates go down and less expensive package tours become available; the independent traveler can go farther on less, too. Keep in mind, however, that Spain is unlike the Caribbean, where high and low seasons are precisely defined and rates drop automatically on a particular date. In Spain, the general tourism off-season is high season for skiers in the Pyrenees, the Picos de Europa, the Sierra de Guadarrama, and the Sierra Nevada, meaning higher prices and crowds everywhere there is snow. And traveling in the dead of winter is not for everyone. While most of Spain does not suffer freezing temperatures, the rain, fog, and cold gray skies in some regions are not always conducive to relaxed sightseeing.

A definite bonus to visiting during the off-season is that even the most basic services are performed more efficiently. In theory, off-season service is identical to that offered during high season, but the fact is that the absence of demanding crowds inevitably begets much more thoughtful and personal attention. The very same staff that barely can manage to get fresh towels onto the racks during the height of summer at coastal resort areas has the time to chat pleasantly in the spring or fall. And it is not only hotel service that benefits from the absence of the high-season mobs.

Even during the off-season, high-season rates also may prevail because of an important local event (and in 1992 Spain is hosting numerous special events, see below). Particularly in the larger cities, special events and major trade show or conferences held at the time of your visit are sure to affect not only the availability of discounts on accommodations, but the basic availability of a place to stay. Although smaller establishments in some areas may close during the off-season in response to reduced demand, there still are plenty of alternatives, and, in cities, cut-rate "mini-break" packages for stays of more than 1 night, especially over weekends (when business travelers traditionally go home), are more common.

It also should be noted that the months immediately before and after the peak summer months — what the travel industry refers to as shoulder seasons — often are sought out because they offer fair weather and somewhat smaller crowds. But be aware that very near high-season prices can prevail, notably in certain popular resort areas such as the Costa del Sol

In short, like many other popular places, Spain's vacation appeal has become multi-seasonal. But the noted exceptions notwithstanding, most travel destinations are decidedly less trafficked and less expensive during the winter.

CLIMATE: The basic distinction in climate in Spain is the amount of rainfall, which varies among the northern, central, and southern regions. Contrary to a popular "weather report," the rain in Spain, *does not* fall mainly on the plain. Precipitation is not uncommon in any region. Snow is common in the mountains of Spain, but in other areas frosts are rare.

Those planning on traveling during the high season should note that Spain's Costa del Sol and Costa Blanca can be extremely hot throughout the summer. During July and August, stores and shops in Madrid, Seville, and Córdoba often close for the day in the early afternoon, when the heat becomes too intense. If sightseeing is a priority, the months of May, June, and September may offer more comfortable weather. In the coastal regions, mild weather is not uncommon during February and November. Although winters on the Spanish *meseta* can be piercingly cold and windy, in the summer the weather resembles that of the drier parts of the southwestern US.

The following chart lists average low and high temperatures in major Spanish cities at different times of the year to help in planning. *(Please note that although temperatures usually are recorded on the Celsius scale in Spain, for purposes of clarity we use the more familiar Fahrenheit scale throughout this guide.)*

Travelers can get current readings and 3-day Accu-Weather forecasts through *American Express Travel Related Services'* Worldwide Weather Report number. By dialing 900-WEATHER and punching in either the area code for most major cities in the US or an access code for numerous travel destinations worldwide, an up-to-date recording will provide current temperature, sky conditions, wind speed and direction, heat index, relative humidity, local time, highway reports, and beach and boating reports or ski conditions (where appropriate). For the weather in Spain, punch in BAR for Barcelona, GRA for Granada, MAD for Madrid, MAL for Málaga, SEV for Seville, or VAL for Valencia. This 24-hour service can be accessed from any touch-tone phone in the US or Canada and costs 75¢ per minute. The charge will show up on your phone bill. For a free list of the areas covered, send a self-addressed, stamped envelope to *1-900-WEATHER*, 261 Central Ave., Farmingdale, NY 11735.

SPECIAL EVENTS: Many travelers may want to schedule a trip to Spain to coincide

AVERAGE TEMPERATURES (in °F)

	January	April	July	October
Alicante	43–61	52–70	62–88	57–77
Barcelona	43–55	52–64	70–82	59–70
Burgos	30–43	39–50	54–74	45–61
Cádiz	48–59	55–68	68–81	54–72
Córdoba	41–55	50–73	68–99	55–77
Madrid	36–48	45–64	63–88	50–66
Málaga	46–63	55–77	70–84	61–73
Majorca, Balearic Islands	43–57	50–65	66–83	57–79
Pamplona	34–46	43–61	57–81	46–66
Salamanca	32–46	39–63	57–86	45–66
Santiago de Compostela	41–50	46–64	55–75	52–70
Seville	43–59	52–75	68–97	57–79
Tenerife, Canary Islands	57–68	61–73	68–82	65–79
Toledo	36–50	46–66	66–91	50–70
Valencia	43–59	50–68	68–84	55–73
Zaragoza	36–50	46–66	64–88	52–68

with some special event. For a music lover, a concert in a great cathedral or in a splendid natural setting may be an especially thrilling experience, and much more memorable than seeing the same place on an ordinary sightseeing itinerary. Golf enthusiasts may derive as much pleasure following Severiano Ballesteros and other international superstars from tee to green during a Spanish golf tournament as they would if they were actually playing on one of the country's championship courses. A folklore or harvest festival can bring nearly forgotten traditions alive or underscore their continuing significance in modern life.

Spain has literally hundreds of fiestas or festivals each year, particularly from *Easter* through October. City and town squares are festooned with brightly colored arches and lanterns, houses are adorned with flags, and people of all ages dress in folk costumes handed down for generations to take part in parades, folk dances, singing, and fantastic fireworks displays. No one is a stranger and everyone is drawn into the merriment. Spanish fiestas include *gigantes y cabezudos* (giants and bigheads), pasteboard figures symbolizing rulers (giants) and the conquered (bigheads); the flower-strewn *Corpus Christi* processions held on the second Thursday after *Whitsunday* (also known as *Trinity Sunday*); *ferias,* traditional fairs honoring past gatherings of Gypsies and dealers who traded horses, donkeys, and mules; and *romerías* (pilgrimages), religious processions usually honoring a city's or town's patron saint.

And this year, Spain presents a triple-header of special events: The world's fair Columbus celebration, *Expo '92,* centered in Seville, and the *1992 Summer Olympics* in Barcelona. In addition, Madrid has been chosen by the European Economic Community as the 1992 Cultural Capital of Europe — an honor that is bound to spark a plethora of special events celebrating the arts throughout the year. (For detailed information on these happenings, see the *Barcelona, Madrid,* and *Seville* chapters in THE CITIES.)

The events that follow are the major regularly scheduled ones, listed according to the months in which they usually occur. Where possible, we have indicated the exact dates for the festivities this year. However, for those events for which specific dates were not yet available as we went to press, and to guard against inevitable scheduling changes, it is best to check with the National Tourist Office of Spain for the exact dates of anything that may be of interest and for current schedules of festivals, fairs, and other events. Also keep in mind that some events, particularly festivals, may vary by a few days to several weeks from town to town and region to region; again, it's best to check with the tourist authorities for the most up-to-date information (see *Tourist Information Offices,* in this section, for addresses).

January
Epiphany: The day Spanish children traditionally receive their *Christmas* gifts. January 6.

Día de los Reyes: The Procession of the Three Kings. January 7.

La Puebla: Parades, bonfires, dancing, and the blessing of the herd in honor of St. Anthony. Majorca, Madrid, and Burgos. January 17.

Tamborrada de San Sebastián: One of Spain's great undiscovered festivals, highlighted by colorful parades, including the marches of the Basque pipe and drum corps in honor of the city's patron saint. January 20 is *St. Sebastián's Day,* and for 24 hours, beginning at midnight on the 19th, the Old Town is filled with young and old dressed as 19th-century soldiers, bakers, and chefs, all banging *tambores* (drums) in a surprisingly orderly fashion. San Sebastián.

February
Bocairente Festival of Moors and Christians: One week of parades, costumes, fireworks, and reenactments of the epic struggles between Moors and Christians, some of which are the most colorful, exuberant fiestas to be found anywhere in

the world — the first of many similar celebrations held throughout the year. Lasting several days (the exact dates vary from town to town), these fiestas usually feature the "Moors" capturing a "Christian" stronghold, only to be ousted amid a deafening fusillade of "gunfire."

Fiestas de Santa Agueda: Ancient "women's liberation" festival. Women parade through the streets in traditional costumes, culminating in "wheel dancing" and the burning of male effigies. February 5. Zamarramala.

Carnavales de Cádiz: Spain's oldest and most popular carnival; the singing, wild music and dancing, and other madness goes on day and night. A fireworks display signals the end of the celebrations, and the next morning all that remains — besides a citywide hangover — are several tons of confetti and empty wine bottles. Held the week before *Lent:* February 8–12, this year. Cádiz.

La Endiablada: A pre-Christian religious celebration featuring dancing and parades of "devils" dressed in floral outfits carrying huge metal bells. Almonacid del Marquesado.

March

Barcelona to Sitges Antique Car Rally: A 13-mile "race" held in early March that features an international assembly of colorful antique automobiles. De Dion–Boutons and Daimlers, Panhards and Bugattis, Fords, Hispanos, and Rolls-Royces compete as ladies and gentlemen, dressed in the style of the respective eras, "put-put" their way from Barcelona to Sitges.

Fallas de San José: One of Spain's great festivals, featuring a week of flower-bedecked processions, bullfights, and all-out partying. Beginning on March 12, it ends at midnight on *St. Joseph's Day* (March 19), when a fantastic array of huge papier-mâché and wooden caricatures are set afire. The fiesta dates from the Middle Ages, when on the day of its patron saint the carpenters' guild burned the wood shavings accumulated during the year. Today, no one is immune to the papier-mâché lampooning — politicians, the church, the rich, and the poor all are fair game. Valencia.

April

Semana Santa: Nationwide *Holy Week* celebrations. Seville features more than 100 parades and the singing of *saetas* (strange laments); Cuenca offers a week-long festival of religious music and candlelight processions; and Chinchón stages a reenactment of the Passion of Christ in the Plaza Mayor. Bridges the months of March and April (March 30 through about April 6).

Feria de Sevilla: This week-long fair began in the 19th century as a rural livestock market, but it has gussied itself up considerably since then: Andalusia's high-stepping horses, in tassels and bells, go through their paces, and brightly costumed groups parade around town in flower-decked coaches. Through mid-April there are nightly *corridas* (bullfights), fireworks, amusements, and dancing in the streets. Seville.

Expo '92: The center of Spain's celebration of the 500th anniversary of Columbus's discovery of America will be the international exhibition held in Seville (from April 20 through October 12), following the theme "The Age of Discoveries."

St. Jordi's Day: On April 23, flower stands overflow with roses and bookstalls on Las Ramblas are bustling; this is the day for lovers, and the traditional gifts are a rose and a book, associated with St. Jordi, patron saint of Catalonia. Barcelona.

May

Fiesta de los Patios: This famous festival fills the city with visitors during the first 2 weeks of May, when everyone goes from one private patio to another admiring walls literally covered with gorgeously planted flowerpots; at the same time, public plazas are decked with flowers and flowered crosses. Prizes are awarded for the best displays. Córdoba.

Fiestas de San Isidro: Ten days (starting on May 10) of nonstop street fairs, festivals, concerts, special daily bullfights, and numerous theater, cultural, and sports events, all celebrating the *Day of St. Isidro,* Madrid's patron saint, on May 15. The fiesta also helps usher in Madrid's bullfighting season and features some of Spain's best bullring exhibitions. Madrid.

Salamanca Celebration of Assumption: Parade featuring traditional costumes followed by an assembly in Plaza Mayor and the performance of the mystery play *Loa* in front of the town church. May 24. La Alberca.

Feria de Nuestra Señora de la Salud: Feria for short, this annual fair follows the *Fiesta de los Patios* during the last week of May and is especially festive because of its location in the heart of town. *Casetas,* or the little private tents for entertaining, and the midway Ferris wheel, merry-go-round, and snack stands run the length of the Jardines de la Victoria. Flamenco contests, pop and classical concerts, ballets, parades, fireworks, and displays of Cordoban horsemanship also fill the streets with action. Córdoba.

Romería del Rocía: Whitsunday pilgrimage (Andalusia's most famous) to the shrine of El Rocía features decorated carts and wagons, singing, and the sounds of drums, flutes, and tambourines. On Monday, 50 men carry the Virgin's statue 9 miles to Almonte for consecration. El Rocía and Almonte. May 19–20.

Corpus Christi: Since 1950, beautiful woven carpets of carnations line the streets in Sitges during this annual celebration. The *National Carnation Show* is held on the same day, with over 2,000 pots containing nearly 300 varieties from various countries. Awards also are given to the most artistically decorated street. Also celebrated elsewhere throughout Spain with traditional processions, mystery plays, bullfights, and other festivities. May 30.

June

Festival of the Virgen del Carmen: Celebration honoring the patroness of sailors and fishermen. Murcia and Málaga. June 16.

Festival International de Música y Danza: Three weeks of first-rate performances featuring classical music, jazz, and ballet by international stars in the *Auditorio Manuel de Falla* and the gardens of the magnificent Alhambra. Granada.

Hogueras de San Juan: Nine-day festival featuring bonfires, the burning of effigies, parades, religious services, and fireworks. Alicante.

July

Festival of Spanish Classic Drama: Dramatic performances staged in a historic theater throughout the month. Almagro.

Festival of Medieval Theater: Excellent medieval plays, food, dancing, and bullfights during the first 2 weeks of July. Hita.

Fiesta de San Fermín: Spain's most popular celebration (made famous by Ernest Hemingway in *The Sun Also Rises*), in which over 100,000 natives and foreigners take part in wild parades and celebrations, wine tasting, bullfights, fireworks, and the much-acclaimed *encierros,* or "running of the bulls," through the town's streets. Pamplona.

San Benitiño de Lérez Festival: Regional celebration featuring Galician music and singing. Pontevedra.

Festival of St. James: Two-week celebration highlighted by the pilgrimage to the tomb of St. James the Apostle, Galecian folkloric shows and competitions, parades, concerts, fireworks, and the swinging of the *botafumerio,* the giant incense burner, in the great cathedral. Santiago de Compostela.

San Sebastián International Jazz Festival: A gathering of top international jazz musicians, held during the last 2 weeks in July in the pavilion at the *Anoeta Sports Complex* and the open-air Plaza de Trinidad in the Old Town. San Sebastián.

1992 Summer Olympics From July 25 to August 9, Barcelona will be the season's host to world class athletes participating in the summer games.

August

International Music and Dance Festival: Month-long annual event featuring symphony and choral concerts, chamber music, recitals, and classical and Spanish ballet. Santander.

Festival of the White Virgin: Seven days of parades, music, dances, and fireworks, highlighted by the *Dawn Rosary Procession* on the morning of August 5. Vitoria.

Asturias Day: This pilgrimage is colorfully highlighted by a parade of decorated floats accompanied by lively folk music. Gijón.

Semana Grande: The week-long celebration includes sporting and cultural events, fireworks, regattas, outstanding bullfights, and the running of "cardboard bulls." San Sebastián.

September

Grape Harvest Fairs and Festivals: These festivals are well noted for great merriment and massive consumption, not necessarily in that order. Usually held in mid-September (sometimes later, depending on the harvest) in the following towns and regions: Jumilla (in Murcia), Montilla (in Córdoba), and Requena (in Valencia).

Cádiz Grape Harvest Festival: Spain's top wine festival, dedicated to a country that exports the world-famous sherry of Jerez, featuring 5 days of parades, a livestock show, a flamenco festival, bullfights, and sherry drinking. Mid-September. Jerez de la Frontera.

San Sebastián International Film Festival: Week-long screenings of international films, during the second half of September, and one of the premier events of its type in Europe. San Sebastián.

Fiesta Nuestra Señora de la Merced: Festival honoring Barcelona's patroness, complete with parades and floats, cavalry bands, *sardana* dancing, swimming races across the Port of Barcelona, men building human pyramids and towers, theater, film, concerts, and bullfights. Barcelona.

October

Fiestas del Pilar: Decorated float parades, sporting events, and dance contests honoring the Virgin of the Pillar. October 12. Zaragoza.

St. Teresa Week: Evening carnivals (*verbenas*), parades of "giants," dancing, singing, and other appropriate merriment. Avila.

The Saffron Rose Festival: Celebrates local folklore and the gathering of the "saffron rose," from which comes the famous spice used in dishes such as paella. Consuegra, Toledo.

December

Alava Nativity Parade: Christmas Eve midnight mass and a bonfire. Labastida.

New Year's Eve: Crowds gather at the Puerta del Sol and eat a grape on the stroke of midnight to ensure a new year of good luck. Madrid.

Traveling by Plane

Flying is the most efficient way to get to Spain, and it is the quickest, most convenient means of travel between different parts of the country once you are there. (Cruise ships that call at Spanish ports generally function more as hotels for passengers cruising European waters, rather than as especially efficient transportation between individual destinations.)

The air space between North America and Europe is the most heavily trafficked in the world. It is served by dozens of airlines, almost all of which sell seats at a variety of prices under a vast spectrum of requirements and restrictions. You probably will spend more for your airfare than for any other single item in your travel budget, so try to take advantage of the lowest fares offered by either scheduled airlines or charter companies. You should know what kinds of flights are available, the rules under which air travel operates, and all the special package options.

GATEWAYS: At present, nonstop flights to Spain leave from Boston, Chicago, Dallas/Ft. Worth, Los Angeles, Miami, Newark, and New York. Additional connecting flights depart from some of the above cities and a few others as well. Nonstop or direct, nearly all of these flights land in major Spanish destinations.

SCHEDULED AIRLINES: *Iberia Airlines of Spain* operates nonstop flights to Barcelona from New York, and to Madrid from Chicago, Los Angeles, Miami, and New York. *TWA* flies nonstop from New York to Barcelona and Madrid. *American* flies nonstop from Dallas/Ft. Worth to Madrid. *United* flies daily from Washington, DC, to Madrid. At press time, *Delta* was scheduled to add service from Atlanta to Barcelona and Madrid; *Pan American's* Spanish routes, however, were in question.

In addition, *British Airways* offers connecting flights from the US through London's Heathrow Airport to Barcelona, Bilboa, Madrid, and Málaga. *Air France* also offers connections through Paris, where, after changing planes, travelers may proceed to Madrid or other Spanish cities. *KLM* offers connecting flights from Atlanta, Anchorage, Baltimore, Chicago, Houston, Los Angeles, New York, and Orlando, via Amsterdam to Barcelona, Madrid, and Málaga. *Tap Air* flies from Boston and New York via Lisbon. *Sabena* flies from a variety of US gateways, with connections made in Brussels for flights to Barcelona, Madrid, and Málaga.

Tickets – When traveling on one of the many regularly scheduled flights, a full-fare ticket provides maximum travel flexibility (although at considerable expense) because there are no advance booking requirements. A prospective passenger can buy a ticket for a flight right up to the minute of takeoff — if a seat is available. If your ticket is for a round trip, you can make the return reservation whenever you wish — months before you leave or the day before you return. Assuming foreign immigration requirements are met, you can stay at your destination for as long as you like. (Tickets generally are good for a year and can be renewed if not used.) You also can cancel your flight at any time without penalty. However, while it is true that this category of ticket can be purchased at the last minute, it is advisable to reserve well in advance during popular vacation periods and around holiday times.

Fares – Airfares continue to change so rapidly that even experts find it difficult to keep up with them. This ever-changing situation is due to a number of factors, including airline deregulation, volatile labor relations, increasing fuel costs, and vastly increased competition.

Perhaps the most common misconception about fares on scheduled airlines is that the cost of the ticket determines how much service will be provided on the flight. This is true only to a certain extent. A far more realistic rule of thumb is that the less you pay for your ticket, the more restrictions and qualifications are likely to come into play before you board the plane (as well as after you get off). These qualifying aspects relate to the months (and the days of the week) during which you must travel, how far in advance you must purchase your ticket, the minimum and maximum amount of time you may or must remain away, your willingness to decide on a return date at the time of booking — and your ability to stick to that decision. It is not uncommon for passengers sitting side by side on the same wide-body jet to have paid fares varying by hundreds of dollars, and all too often the traveler paying more would have been equally willing (and able) to accept the terms of the far less expensive ticket.

In general, the great variety of fares between the US and Spain can be reduced to four basic categories, including first class, coach (also called economy or tourist class), and excursion or discount fares. A fourth category, called business class, has been added by many airlines in recent years. In addition, Advance Purchase Excursion (APEX) fares offer savings under certain conditions.

In a class by itself is the *Concorde,* the supersonic jet developed jointly by France and Great Britain, which cruises at speeds of 1,350 miles an hour (twice the speed of sound) and makes transatlantic crossings in half the time (3½ hours from New York to Paris) of conventional, subsonic jets. *Air France* offers *Concorde* service to Paris from New York; *British Airways* flies from Miami, Washington, DC, and New York to London. Service is "single" class (with champagne and caviar all the way), and the fare is expensive, about 20% more than a first class ticket on a subsonic aircraft. Some discounts have been offered, but time is the real gift of the *Concorde.* For travelers to Spanish destinations, this "gift" may be more or less valuable as compared to a direct flight when taking connections from London or Paris into account.

A **First Class** ticket is your admission to the special section of the aircraft — larger seats, more legroom, sleeperette seating on some wide-body aircraft, better (or more elaborately served) food, free drinks and headsets for movies and music channels, and, above all, personal attention. First class fares are about twice those of full-fare economy, although both first class passengers and those paying full-fare economy fares are entitled to reserve seats and are sold tickets on an open reservation system. An additional advantage of a first class ticket is that if you're planning to visit several cities within Spain or elsewhere in Europe, you may include any number of stops en route to or from your most distant destination, provided that restrictions regarding certain set maximum permitted mileage limits and flight routes are respected.

Not too long ago, there were only two classes of air travel, first class and all the rest, usually called economy or tourist. Then **business class** came into being. At first, business class passengers were merely curtained off from the other economy passengers. Now a separate cabin or cabins — usually toward the front of the plane — is the norm. While standards of comfort and service are not as high as in first class, they represent a considerable improvement over conditions in the rear of the plane, with roomier seats, more leg and shoulder space between passengers, and fewer seats abreast. Free liquor and headsets, a choice of meal entrées, and a separate counter for speedier check-in are other inducements. As in first class, a business class passenger may travel on any scheduled flight he or she wishes, may buy a one-way or round-trip ticket, and have the ticket remain valid for a year. There are no minimum or maximum stay requirements, no advance booking requirements, and no cancellation penalties, and the fare allows the same free stopover privileges as first class. Airlines often have their own names for their business class service — such as Preference Class on *Iberia,* Medallion Class on *Delta,* and Ambassador Class on *TWA.*

The terms of the **coach** or **economy** fare may vary slightly from airline to airline, and in fact from time to time airlines may be selling more than one type of economy fare. Coach or economy passengers sit more snugly, as many as 10 in a single row on a wide-body jet, behind the first class and business class sections. Normally alcoholic drinks are not free, nor are the headsets (except on *British Airways,* which does offer these free of charge). If there are two economy fares on the books, one (often called "regular economy") still may include a number of free stopovers. The other, less expensive fare (often called "special economy") may limit stopovers to one or two, with a charge (typically $25) for each one. Like first class passengers, however, passengers paying the full coach fare are subject to none of the restrictions that usually are attached to less expensive excursion and discount fares. There are no advance booking requirements, no minimum stay requirements, and no cancellation penalties. Tickets are sold on an open reservation system: They can be bought for a flight right up to the minute of takeoff (if seats are available), and if the ticket is round-trip, the return reservation can be made anytime you wish. Both first class and coach tickets generally are good for a year, after which they can be renewed if not used, and if you ultimately decide not to fly at all, your money will be refunded. The cost of economy and business class tickets does not vary much in the course of the year between the US and Spain, though on some transatlantic routes they vary from a basic (low-season) price in effect most of the year to a peak (high-season) price during the summer.

Excursions and other **discount** fares are the airlines' equivalent of a special sale and usually apply to round-trip bookings only. These fares generally differ according to the season and the number of travel days permitted. They are only a bit less flexible than full-fare economy tickets, and are, therefore, often useful for both business and holiday travelers. Most round-trip excursion tickets include strict minimum and maximum stay requirements and can be changed only within prescribed time limits. So don't count on extending a ticket beyond the prescribed time of return or staying less time than required. Different airlines may have different regulations concerning the number of stopovers permitted, and sometimes excursion fares are less expensive during midweek. The availability of these reduced-rate seats is most limited at busy times, such as holidays. Discount or excursion fare ticket holders sit with the coach passengers, and, for all intents and purposes, are indistinguishable from them. They receive all the same basic services, even though they may have paid anywhere between 30% and 55% less for the trip. Obviously, it's wise to make plans early enough to qualify for this less expensive transportation if possible.

These discount or excursion fares may masquerade under a variety of names, they may vary from city to city (from the East Coast to the West Coast, especially), but they invariably have strings attached. A common requirement is that the ticket be purchased a certain number of days — usually no fewer than 7 or 14 days — in advance of departure, though it may be booked weeks or months in advance (it has to be "ticketed," or paid for, shortly after booking, however). The return reservation usually has to be made at the time of the original ticketing and cannot be changed later than a certain number of days (again, usually 7 or 14 days) before the return flight. If events force a passenger to change the return reservation after the date allowed, the difference between the round-trip excursion rate and the round-trip coach rate probably will have to be paid, though most airlines allow passengers to use their discounted fares by standing by for an empty seat, even if they don't otherwise have standby fares. Another common condition is a minimum and maximum stay requirement — for example, 6 to 14 days or 1 to 6 days (but including at least a Saturday night). Last, cancellation penalties of up to 50% of the full price of the ticket have been assessed — check the specific penalty in effect when you purchase your discount/excursion ticket — so careful planning is imperative.

Of even greater risk — and bearing the lowest price of all the current discount fares — is the ticket where no change at all in departure and/or return flights is permitted, and where the ticket price is totally nonrefundable. If you do buy a nonrefundable ticket, you should be aware of a new policy followed by many airlines that may make it easier to change your plans if necessary. For a fee — set by each airline and payable at the airport when checking in — you *may* be able to change the time or date of a return flight on a nonrefundable ticket. However, if the nonrefundable ticket price for the replacement flight is higher than that of the original (as often is the case when trading in a weekday for a weekend flight), you will have to pay the difference. Any such change must be made a certain number of days in advance — in some cases as little as 2 days — of either the original or the replacement flight, whichever is earlier; restrictions are set by the individual carrier. (Travelers holding a nonrefundable or other restricted ticket who must change their plans due to a family emergency should know that some carriers may make special allowances in such situations; for further information, see *Medical and Legal Aid and Consular Services,* in this section.)

In the past, some excursion fares offered for travel to Spain came unencumbered by advance booking requirements and cancellation penalties, permitted one stopover (though not a free one) in each direction, and had "open jaws," meaning that you could fly to one city and depart from another, arranging and paying for your own transportation between the two. Although, for the most part, such excursion fares are no longer offered on flights between the US and the majority of European destinations, they still exist on flights between the US and Spain, where they cost about a third less than economy — during the off-season. High-season prices may be less attractive. The ticket currently is good for a minimum of 7 days and a maximum of 6 months abroad.

There also is a newer, often less expensive, type of excursion fare, the **APEX,** or **Advanced Purchase Excursion** fare. (In the case of flights to Europe, this type of fare also may be called a "Eurosaver" fare.) As with traditional excursion fares, passengers paying an APEX fare sit with and receive the same basic services as any other coach or economy passengers, even though they may have paid up to 50% less for their seats. In return, they are subject to certain restrictions. In the case of flights to Spain, the ticket usually is good for a minimum of 7 days abroad and a maximum, currently, of 2 months (depending on the airline and the destination); and as its name implies, it must be "ticketed," or paid for in its entirety, a certain period of time before departure — usually 21 days, although in the case of Spain it may be as little as 14 days.

The drawback to an APEX fare is that it penalizes travelers who change their minds — and travel plans. The return reservation must be made at the time of the original ticketing, and if for some reason you change your schedule, you will have to pay a penalty of $100 or 10% of the ticket value, whichever is greater, as long as you travel within the validity period of your ticket. But, if you change your return to a date less than the minimum stay or more than the maximum stay, the difference between the round-trip APEX fare and the full round-trip coach rate will have to be paid. There also is a penalty of anywhere from $75 to $125 or more for canceling or changing a reservation *before* travel begins — check the specific penalty in effect when you purchase your ticket. No stopovers are allowed on an APEX ticket, but it is possible to create an open-jaw effect by buying an APEX on a split ticket basis; for example, flying to Barcelona and returning from Madrid. The total price would be half the price of an APEX to Barcelona plus half the price of an APEX to Madrid. APEX tickets to Spain are sold at basic and peak rates (peak season is around May through September) and may include surcharges for weekend flights.

There also is a Winter or Super APEX, which may go under different names for different carriers. Similar to the regular APEX fare, it costs slightly less but is more restrictive. Depending on the airline and destination, it usually is available only for off-peak winter travel and is limited to a stay of between 7 and 21 days. Advance purchase still is required (currently, 30 days prior to travel), and ticketing must be completed within 48 hours of reservation. The fare is nonrefundable, except in cases of hospitalization or death.

Note that Winter or Super APEX sometimes is confusingly called Super PEX by *Iberia.* At the time of this writing, *Iberia* offered Super APEX (or Super PEX) on transatlantic flights to most destinations in Spain during the off-season; this fare also may be available to some destinations during the high season.

Another type of fare that sometimes is available is the youth fare. At present, most airlines flying to Spain are using a form of APEX fare as a youth fare for those through age 24. The maximum stay is extended to a year, and the return booking must be left open. Seats can be reserved no more than 3 days before departure, and tickets must be purchased when the reservation is made. The return is booked from Spain in the same manner, no more than 3 days before flight time. On most airlines (including *Iberia*), there is no cancellation penalty, but the fare is subject to availability, so it may be difficult to book a return during peak travel periods, and as with the regular APEX fare, it may not even be available for travel to or from Spain during high season and may be offered only on selected routes. For instance, *Iberia* offers this type of fare only on flights from the US to Madrid or Barcelona.

Standby fares, at one time the rock-bottom price at which a traveler could fly to Europe, have become rather elusive. At the time of this writing, most major scheduled airlines did not regularly offer standby fares on direct flights to Spain. Because airline fares and their conditions constantly change, bargain hunters should not hesitate to ask if such a fare exists at the time they plan to travel. Travelers to Spain also should inquire about the possibility of connecting flights through other European countries that may be offered on a standby basis.

While the definition of standby varies somewhat from airline to airline, it generally means that you make yourself available to buy a ticket for a flight (usually no sooner than the day of departure), then literally stand by on the chance that a seat will be empty. Once aboard, however, a standby passenger has the same meal service and frills (or lack of them) enjoyed by others in the economy class compartment.

Something else to check is the possibility of qualifying for a **GIT** (Group Inclusive Travel) fare, which requires that a specified dollar amount of ground arrangements be purchased, in advance, along with the ticket. The requirements vary as to the number of travel days and stopovers permitted, and the minimum number of passengers required for a group. The actual fares also vary, but the cost will be spelled out in brochures distributed by the tour operators handling the ground arrangements. In the past, GIT fares were among the least expensive available from the established carriers, but the prevalence of discount fares has caused group fares to all but disappear from some air routes. Travelers reading brochures on group package tours to Spain will find that, in almost all cases, the applicable airfare given as a sample (to be added to the price of the land package to obtain the total tour price) is the same discount fare available to the independent traveler.

The major airlines serving Spain from the US also may offer individual excursion fare rates similar to GIT fares, which are sold in conjunction with ground accommodation packages. Previously called ITX, and sometimes referred to as individual tour-basing fares, these fares generally are offered as part of "air/hotel/car/transfer packages," and can reduce the cost of an economy fare by more than a third. The packages are booked for a specific amount of time, with return dates specified; rescheduling and cancellation restrictions and penalties vary from carrier to carrier. At the time of this writing, this type of fare was offered to popular destinations throughout Spain by *Iberia Airlines of Spain*. Note that their offering may or may not represent substantial savings over standard economy fares, so check at the time you plan to travel. (For further information on package options, see *Package Tours*, in this section.)

Travelers looking for the least expensive possible airfares should, finally, scan the travel pages of their hometown newspapers (especially the Sunday travel sections) for announcements of special promotional fares. Most airlines traditionally have offered their most attractive special fares to encourage travel during slow seasons, and to inaugurate and publicize new routes. Even if none of these factors apply, prospective passengers can be fairly sure that the number of discount seats per flight at the lowest price is strictly limited, or that the fare offering includes a set expiration date — which means it's absolutely necessary to move fast to enjoy the lowest possible price.

Among other special airline promotional deals for which you should be on the lookout are discount or upgrade coupons, sometimes offered by the major carriers and found in mail order merchandise catalogues. For instance, airlines sometimes issue coupons that typically cost around $25 and are good for a percentage discount or an upgrade on an international airline ticket — including flights to Spain. The only requirement beyond the fee generally is that a coupon purchaser must buy at least one item from the catalogue. There usually are some minimum airfare restrictions before the coupon is redeemable, but in general these are worthwhile offers. Restrictions often include certain blackout days (when the coupon cannot be used at all), usually imposed during peak travel periods. These coupons are particularly valuable to business travelers who tend to buy full-fare tickets, and while the coupons are issued in the buyer's name, they can be used by others who are traveling on the same itinerary.

It's always wise to ask about discount or promotional fares and about any conditions that might restrict booking, payment, cancellation, and changes in plans. Check the prices from other neighboring cities. A special rate may be offered in a nearby city but not in yours, and it may be enough of a bargain to warrant your leaving from that city. Ask if there is a difference in price for midweek versus weekend travel, or if there is a further discount for traveling early in the morning or late at night. Also be sure to investigate package deals, which are offered by virtually every airline. These may include a car rental, accommodations, and dining and/or sightseeing features in addition to the basic airfare, and the combined cost of packaged elements usually is considerably less than the cost of the exact same elements when purchased separately.

If in the course of your research you come across a deal that seems too good to be true, keep in mind that logic may not be a component of deeply discounted airfares — there's not always any sane relationship between miles to be flown and the price to get there. More often than not, the level of competition on a given route dictates the degree of discount, and don't be dissuaded from accepting an offer that sounds irresistible just because it also sounds illogical. Better to buy that inexpensive fare while it's being offered and worry about the sense — or absence thereof — while you're flying to your desired destination.

When you're satisfied that you've found the lowest possible price for which you can conveniently qualify (you may have to call the airline more than once, because different airline reservations clerks have been known to quote different prices), make your booking. Then, to protect yourself against fare increases, purchase and pay for your ticket as soon as possible after you've received a confirmed reservation. Airlines generally will honor their tickets, even if the operative price at the time of your flight is higher than the price you paid; if fares go up between the time you *reserve* a flight and the time you *pay* for it, you likely will be out of luck. Finally, with excursion or discount fares, it is important to remember that when a reservation clerk says that you must purchase a ticket by a specific date, this is an absolute deadline. Miss it and the airline may automatically cancel your reservation without telling you.

■ **Note:** Another wrinkle on the airfare scene is that if the fares go *down* after you purchase your ticket, you *may* be entitled to a refund of the difference. However, this is possible only in certain situations — availability and advance purchase restrictions pertaining to the lower rate are set by the airline. If you suspect that you may be able to qualify for such a refund, check with your travel agent or the airline.

Frequent Flyers – The leading carriers serving Spain — including *American, British Airways, Delta, Iberia,* and *TWA* — offer a bonus system to frequent travelers. After the first 10,000 miles, for example, a passenger might be eligible for a first class seat for the coach fare; after another 10,000 miles, he or she might receive a discount on his or her next ticket purchase. The value of the bonuses continues to increase as more miles are logged.

Bonus miles also may be earned by patronizing affiliated car rental companies or hotel chains, or by using one of the credit cards that now offers this reward. In deciding whether to accept such a credit card from one of the issuing organizations that tempt you with frequent flyer mileage bonuses on a specific airline, first determine whether the interest rate charged on the unpaid balance is the same as (or less than) possible alternate credit cards, and whether the annual "membership" fee also is equal or lower. If these charges are slightly higher than those of competing cards, weigh the difference against the potential value in airfare savings. Also ask about any bonus miles awarded just for signing up — 1,000 is common, 5,000 generally the maximum.

For the most up-to-date information on frequent flyer bonus options, you may want to send for the monthly newsletter *Frequent.* Issued by Frequent Publications, it provides current information about frequent flyer plans in general, as well as specific data about promotions, awards, and combination deals to help you keep track of the profusion — and confusion — of current and upcoming availabilities. For a year's subscription, send $33 to Frequent Publications, 4715-C Town Center Dr., Colorado Springs, CO 80916 (phone: 800-333-5937).

There also is a monthly magazine called *Frequent Flyer,* but unlike the newsletter mentioned above, its focus is primarily on newsy articles of interest to business travelers and other frequent flyers. Published by Official Airline Guides (PO Box 58543, Boulder, CO 80322-8543; phone: 800-323-3537), *Frequent Flyer* is available for $24 for a 1-year subscription.

Low-Fare Airlines – Increasingly, the stimulus for special fares is the appearance of airlines associated with bargain rates. On these airlines, all seats on any given flight generally sell for the same price, which is somewhat below the lowest discount fare offered by the larger, more established airlines. It is important to note that tickets offered by the smaller airlines specializing in low-cost travel frequently are not subject to the same restrictions as the lowest-priced ticket offered by the more established carriers. They may not require advance purchase or minimum and maximum stays, may involve no cancellation penalties, and may be available one way or round trip. A disadvantage to low-fare airlines, however, is that when something goes wrong, such as delayed baggage or a flight cancellation due to equipment breakdown, their smaller fleets and fewer flights mean that passengers may have to wait longer for a solution than they would on one of the equipment-rich major carriers.

At press time, one of the few airlines offering a consistently low fare to Europe was *Virgin Atlantic* (phone: 800-862-8621 or 212-242-1330), which flies daily from New York (Newark) to London's Gatwick Airport. The airline sells tickets in several categories, including business or "upper" class, economy, APEX, and nonrefundable variations on standby. Fares from New York to London include Late Saver fares — which must be purchased not less than 7 days prior to travel — and Late Late Saver fares — which are purchased no later than 1 day prior to travel. Travelers to Spain will have to take a second flight from London to Spain, but still may save money. To determine the potential savings, add the cost of these transatlantic fares and the cost of connecting flights to come up with the total ticket price. Remember, too, that since Spain is such a popular holiday destination with the British, ultra-low-priced package programs are frequently available from British-based tour operators and bucket shops.

In a class by itself is *Icelandair,* which always has been a scheduled airline but long has been known as a good source of low-cost flights to Europe. *Icelandair* flies from Baltimore/Washington, DC, New York, and Orlando to Copenhagen (Denmark), Glasgow and London (Great Britain), Gothenburg and Stockholm (Sweden), Helsinki (Finland), Luxembourg (in the country of the same name), Oslo (Norway), Paris (France), and Reykjavik (Iceland). In addition, the airline increases the options for its passengers by offering "thru-fares" on connecting flights to other European cities. (The price of the intra-European flights — aboard Luxembourg's *Luxair* — is included in the price *Icelandair* quotes for the transatlantic portion of the travel to these additional destinations.)

Icelandair sells tickets in a variety of categories, from unrestricted economy fares to a sort of standby "3-days-before" fare (which functions just like the youth fares described above but has no age requirement). Travelers should be aware, however, that most *Icelandair* flights stop in Reykjavik for 45 minutes — a minor delay for most, but one that further prolongs the trip for passengers who will wait again to board connecting flights to their ultimate destination in Spain. (At the time of this writing, *Icelandair* did not offer connecting flights to Spain; however, connecting flight options are available through other carriers.) It may be a better choice for travelers intending to visit other destinations on the Continent when taking both this delay and the cost of connections into account. For reservations and tickets, contact a travel agent or *Icelandair* (phone: 800-223-5500 or 212-967-8888).

Intra-European Fares – The cost of the round trip across the Atlantic is not the only expense to consider, for flights between European cities can be quite expensive. But discounts have recently been introduced on routes between some European cities, and other discounts do exist.

Recent Common Market moves toward airline deregulation are expected to lead gradually to a greater number of budget fares. In the meantime, however, the high cost of fares between most European cities can be avoided by careful use of stopover rights on the higher-priced transatlantic tickets — first class, business class, and full-fare economy. If your ticket doesn't allow stopovers, ask about excursion fares such as PEX and Super PEX, APEX for round trips, and other excursion fares for one-way trips. If you are able to comply with applicable restrictions and can use them, you may save as much as 35% to 50% off full-fare economy. Note that these fares, which once could be bought only after arrival in Europe, now are sold in the US and can be bought before departure.

It is not easy to inform yourself about stopover possibilities by talking to most airline reservations clerks. More than likely, an inquiry concerning any projected trip will prompt the reply that a particular route is nonstop aboard the carrier in question, thereby precluding stopovers completely, or that the carrier does not fly to all the places you want to visit. It may take additional inquiries, perhaps with the aid of a travel agent, to determine the full range of options regarding stopover privileges.

Travelers might be able to squeeze in visits to Amsterdam, Dublin, London, or Paris on a first class ticket to Madrid, for instance; and Madrid might only be the first of many free European stopovers possible on a one-way or round-trip ticket to a city in Eastern Europe or points beyond. The airline that flies you on the first leg of your trip across the Atlantic issues the ticket, though you may have to use several different airlines in order to complete your journey. First class tickets are valid for a full year, so there's no rush.

Both *Iberia* and its subsidiary, *Aviaco* (the Spanish domestic airline), offer PEX-like fares for round-trip travel within Spain. They usually cannot be bought more than 3 days before the flight, are available only on certain flights, and have varying minimum and maximum stay requirements, depending on the route. *Iberia* also offers discounted thru-fares between Spanish and other European cities; these thru-fares must be bought in the US and the restrictions are the same as those for an APEX fare.

For travel within Spain, *Iberia* offers the "Visit Spain" airpass, which allows purchasers to fly *Iberia* or *Aviaco* to as many as 30 Spanish destinations on the mainland or in the Balearic Islands — and gives these passengers 60 days to complete the travel — all for one price. The pass must be bought in the US in conjunction with a transatlantic round-trip ticket to Spain (of which at least the eastbound portion must be aboard *Iberia*). Although the pass holders must choose the Spanish cities to be visited at the time of purchase (with an option to skip any city as long as the original sequence of remaining cities is maintained), reservations for specific flight dates need not be made in advance and pass holders have the flexibility to spend as much time as they wish (within the 60-day validity period) at each destination. For further information and current pass prices, contact *Iberian Airlines of Spain* (phone: 800-772-4642).

Taxes and Other Fees – Travelers who have shopped for the best possible flight at the lowest possible price should be warned that a number of extras will be added to that price and collected by the airline or travel agent who issues the ticket. These taxes *usually* (but not always) are included in the prices quoted by airline reservations clerks.

The $6 International Air Transportation Tax is a departure tax paid by all passengers flying from the US to a foreign destination. A $10 US Federal Inspection Fee is levied on all air and cruise passengers who arrive in the US from outside North America (those arriving from Canada, Mexico, the Caribbean, and US territories are exempt). Still another fee is charged by some airlines to cover more stringent security procedures, prompted by recent terrorist incidents. The 8% federal US Transportation Tax applies to travel within the US or US territories, as well as to passengers flying between US cities en route to a foreign destination if the trip includes a stopover of more than 12 hours at a US point. Someone flying from Los Angeles to New York and stopping in New York for more than 12 hours before boarding a flight to Spain, for instance, would pay the 8% tax on the domestic portion of the trip.

Reservations – For those who don't have the time or patience to investigate personally all possible air departures and connections for a proposed trip, a travel agent can be of inestimable help. A good agent should have all the information on which flights go where and when, and which categories of tickets are available on each. Most have computerized reservation links with the major carriers, so that a seat can be reserved and confirmed in minutes. An increasing number of agents also possess fare-comparison computer programs, so they often are very reliable sources of detailed competitive price data. (For more information, see *How to Use a Travel Agent,* in this section.)

When making reservations through a travel agent, ask the agent to give the airline your home phone number, as well as your daytime business phone number. All too often the agent uses the agency number as the official contact for changes in flight plans. Especially during the winter, weather conditions hundreds or even thousands of miles away can wreak havoc with flight schedules. Aircraft are constantly in use, and a plane delayed in the Orient or on the West Coast can miss its scheduled flight from the East Coast the next morning. The airlines are fairly reliable about getting this sort of information to passengers if they can reach them; diligence does little good at 10 PM if the airline has only the agency's or an office number.

Reconfirmation is strongly recommended for all international flights (though it is not usually required on US domestic flights) and in the case of flights to Spain, it is a good idea to confirm your round-trip reservations — especially the return leg — as well as any point-to-point flights within Europe. Some (though increasingly fewer) reservations to and from international destinations are automatically canceled after a required reconfirmation period (typically 72 hours) has passed — even if you have a confirmed, fully paid ticket in hand. It always is wise to call ahead to make sure that the airline did not slip up in entering your original reservation, or in registering any changes you may have made since, and that it has your seat reservation and/or special meal request in the computer. If you look at the printed information on the ticket, you'll see the airline's reconfirmation policy stated explicitly. Don't be lulled into a false sense of security by the "OK" on your ticket next to the number and time of the return flight. This only means that a reservation has been entered; a reconfirmation still may be necessary. If in doubt — call.

If you plan not to take a flight on which you hold a confirmed reservation, by all means inform the airline. Because the problem of "no-shows" is a constant expense for airlines, they are allowed to overbook flights, a practice that often contributes to the threat of denied boarding for a certain number of passengers (see "Getting Bumped," below).

Seating – For most types of tickets, airline seats usually are assigned on a first-come, first-served basis at check-in, although some airlines make it possible to reserve a seat at the time of ticket purchase. Always check in early for your flight, even with advance seat assignments. A good rule of thumb for international flights is to arrive at the airport *at least* 2 hours before the scheduled departure to give yourself plenty of time in case there are long lines.

Most airlines furnish seating charts, which make choosing a seat much easier, but there are a few basics to consider. You must decide whether you prefer a window, aisle, or middle seat. On flights where smoking is permitted, you also should specify if you prefer the smoking or nonsmoking section.

The amount of legroom provided (as well as chest room, especially when the seat in front of you is in a reclining position) is determined by pitch, a measure of the distance between the back of the seat in front of you and the front of the back of your seat. The amount of pitch is a matter of airline policy, not the type of plane you fly. First class and business class seats have the greatest pitch, a fact that figures prominently in airline advertising. In economy class or coach, the standard pitch ranges from 33 to as little as 31 inches — downright cramped.

The number of seats abreast, another factor determining comfort, depends on a combination of airline policy and airplane dimensions. First class and business class have the fewest seats per row. Economy generally has 9 seats per row on a DC-10 or an L-1011, making either one slightly more comfortable than a 747, on which there normally are 10 seats per row. Charter flights on DC-10s and L-1011s, however, often have 10 seats per row and can be noticeably more cramped than 747 charters, on which the seating normally remains at 10 per row.

Airline representatives claim that most aircraft are more stable toward the front and midsection, while seats farthest from the engines are quietest. Passengers who have long legs and are traveling on a wide-body aircraft might request a seat directly behind a door or emergency exit, since these seats often have greater than average pitch, or a seat in the first row of a given section, which offers extra legroom — although these seats are increasingly being reserved for passengers who are willing (and able) to perform certain tasks in the event of emergency evacuation. It often is impossible, however, to see the movie from these seats, which are directly behind the plane's exits. Be aware that the first row of the economy section (called a "bulkhead" seat) on a conventional aircraft (not a widebody) does *not* offer extra legroom, since the fixed partition will not permit passengers to slide their feet under it, and that watching a movie from this first-row seat can be difficult and uncomfortable. These bulkhead seats do, however, provide ample room to use a bassinet or safety seat and often are reserved for families traveling with children.

A window seat protects you from aisle traffic and clumsy serving carts, and also provides a view, while an aisle seat enables you to get up and stretch your legs without disturbing your fellow travelers. Middle seats are the least desirable, and seats in the last row are the worst of all, since they seldom recline fully. If you wish to avoid children on your flight or if you find that you are sitting in an especially noisy section, you usually are free to move to any unoccupied seat — if there is one.

If you are overweight, you may face the prospect of a long flight with special trepidation. Center seats in the alignments of wide-body 747s, L-1011s, and DC-10s are about 1½ inches wider than those on either side, so larger travelers tend to be more comfortable there.

Despite all these rules of thumb, finding out which specific rows are near emergency exits or at the front of a wide-body cabin can be difficult because seating arrangements on two otherwise identical planes vary from airline to airline. There is, however, a quarterly publication called the *Airline Seating Guide* that publishes seating charts for most major US airlines and many foreign carriers as well. Your travel agent should have a copy, or you can buy the US edition for $39.95 per year and the international edition for $44.95. Order from Carlson Publishing Co., Box 888, Los Alamitos, CA 90720 (phone: 800-728-4877 or 213-493-4877).

Simply reserving an airline seat in advance, however, actually may guarantee very little. Most airlines require that passengers arrive at the departure gate at least 45 minutes (sometimes more) ahead of time to hold a seat reservation. *Iberia* for example, may cancel seat assignments and may not honor reservations of passengers not "checked in" 45 minutes before the scheduled departure time, and they *ask* travelers to check in at least 2 hours before all international flights. It pays to read the fine print on your ticket carefully and plan ahead.

A far better strategy is to visit an airline ticket office (or one of a select group of travel agents) to secure an actual boarding pass for your specific flight. Once this has been issued, airline computers show you as checked in, and you effectively own the seat you have selected (although some carriers may not honor boarding passes of passengers arriving at the gate less than 10 minutes before departure). This also is good — but not foolproof — insurance against getting bumped from an overbooked flight and is, therefore, an especially valuable tactic at peak travel times.

Smoking – One decision regarding choosing a seat has been taken out of the hands of many travelers who smoke. Effective February 25, 1990, the US government imposed a ban that prohibits smoking on all flights scheduled for 6 hours or less within the US and its territories. The new regulation applies to both domestic and international carriers serving these routes.

In the case of flights to Spain, these rules do not apply to nonstop flights going directly from the US to Europe, or those with a *continuous* flight time of over 6 hours between stops in the US or its territories. Smoking is not permitted on segments of international flights where the time between US landings is under 6 hours — for instance, flights that include a stopover (even with no change of plane) or connecting flights. To further complicate the situation, several individual carriers are banning smoking altogether on certain routes. (As we went to press, this ban had not yet extended to carriers flying between the US and Spain — for instance, *Iberia* allows smoking on all transatlantic flights.)

On those flights that do permit smoking, the US Department of Transportation has determined that nonsmoking sections must be enlarged to accommodate all passengers who wish to sit in one. The airline does not, however, have to shift seating to accommodate nonsmokers who arrive late for a flight or travelers flying standby, and in general not all airlines can guarantee a seat in the nonsmoking section on international flights. Cigar and pipe smoking are prohibited on all flights, even in the smoking sections.

For a wallet-size guide, which notes in detail the rights of nonsmokers according to these regulations, send a self-addressed, stamped envelope to ASH (Action on Smoking and Health), Airline Card, 2013 H St. NW, Washington, DC 20006 (phone: 202-659-4310).

Meals – If you have specific diet requirements, be sure to let the airline know well before departure time. The available meals include vegetarian, seafood, kosher, Muslim, Hindu, high-protein, low-calorie, low-cholesterol, low-fat, low-sodium, diabetic, bland, and children's menus. There is no extra charge for this option. It usually is necessary to request special meals when you make your reservations — check-in time is too late. It's also wise to reconfirm that your request for a special meal has made its way into the airline's computer — the time to do this is 24 hours before departure. (Note that special meals generally are not available on intra-European flights on small local carriers. If this poses a problem, try to eat before you board, or bring a snack with you.)

Baggage – Travelers from the US face two different kinds of rules. When you fly on a US airline or on a major international carrier, US baggage regulations will be in effect. Though airline baggage allowances vary slightly, in general all passengers are allowed to carry on board, without charge, one piece of luggage that will fit easily under a seat of the plane or in an overhead bin and whose combined dimensions (length, width, and depth) do not exceed 45 inches. A reasonable amount of reading material, camera equipment, and a handbag also are allowed. In addition, all passengers are allowed to check two bags in the cargo hold: one usually not to exceed 62 inches when length, width, and depth are combined, the other not to exceed 55 inches in combined dimensions. Generally no single bag may weigh more than 70 pounds.

Note that *Iberia* does not make a distinction between the measurements of the two bags, although the standard weight restriction applies. The weight restriction, however, may vary on transatlantic flights of other European airlines, ranging from as much as 88 pounds permitted for first class passengers to as little as 50 pounds for economy class — so check with the specific carrier in advance.

On many intra-European flights, including domestic service in Spain, baggage allowances may be subject to the old weight determination, under which each economy or discount passenger is allowed only a total of 44 pounds of luggage without additional charge. First class or business passengers are allowed a total of 66 pounds. (If you are flying from the US to Europe and connecting to a domestic flight, you generally will be allowed the same amount of baggage as on the transatlantic flight. If you break your trip and then take a domestic flight, the local carrier's weight restrictions apply.)

Charges for additional, oversize, or overweight bags usually are made at a flat rate; the actual dollar amount varies from carrier to carrier. If you plan to travel with any special equipment or sporting gear, be sure to check with the airline beforehand. Most have specific procedures for handling such baggage, and you may have to pay for transport regardless of how much other baggage you have checked. Golf clubs and skis may be checked through as luggage (most airlines are accustomed to handling them), but tennis rackets should be carried onto the plane. Some airlines require that bicycles be partially dismantled and packaged (see *Camping and Caravanning, Hiking and Biking,* in this section).

Airline policies regarding baggage allowances for children vary and usually are based on the percentage of full adult fare paid. Although on many US carriers children who are ticket holders are entitled to the same baggage allowance as a full-fare passenger, some carriers allow only one bag per child, which sometimes must be smaller than an adult's bag (around 39 to 45 inches in combined dimensions). Often there is no luggage allowance for a child traveling on an adult's lap or in a bassinet. Particularly for international carriers, it's always wise to check ahead. (For more information, see *Hints for Traveling with Children,* in this section.)

To reduce the chances of your luggage going astray, remove all airline tags from previous trips, label each bag inside and out — with your business address rather than your home address on the outside, to prevent thieves from knowing whose house might be unguarded. Lock everything and double-check the tag that the airline attaches to make sure that it is coded correctly for your destination: MAD for Barajas Airport in Madrid, for instance.

If your bags are not in the baggage claim area after your flight, or if they're damaged, report the problem to airline personnel immediately. Keep in mind that policies regarding the specific time limit within which you have to make your claim vary from carrier to carrier. Fill out a report form on your lost or damaged luggage and keep a copy of it and your original baggage claim check. If you must surrender the check to claim a damaged bag, get a receipt for it to prove that you did, indeed, check your baggage on the flight. If luggage is missing, be sure to give the airline your destination and/or a telephone number where you can be reached. Also, take the name and number of the person in charge of recovering lost luggage.

Most airlines have emergency funds for passengers stranded away from home without their luggage, but if it turns out that your bags are truly lost and not simply delayed, do not then and there sign any paper indicating you'll accept an offered settlement. Since the airline is responsible for the value of your bags within certain statutory limits ($1,250 per passenger for lost baggage on a US domestic flight; $9.07 per pound or $20 per kilo for checked baggage and up to $400 per passenger for unchecked baggage on an international flight), you should take some time to assess the extent of your loss (see *Insurance,* in this section). It's a good idea to keep records indicating the value of the contents of your luggage. A wise alternative is to take a Polaroid picture of the most valuable of your packed items just after putting them in your suitcase.

Considering the increased incidence of damage to baggage, it's now more than ever a good idea to keep the sales slips that confirm how much you paid for your bags. These are invaluable in establishing the value of damaged baggage and eliminate any arguments. A better way to protect your precious gear from the luggage-eating conveyers is to try to carry it on board wherever possible.

Be aware that airport security increasingly is an issue all over Europe, and the Spanish take it very seriously. Heavily armed police patrol the airports, and unattended luggage of any description may be confiscated and quickly destroyed. Passengers checking in at a European airport may undergo at least two separate inspections of their tickets, passports, and luggage by courteous but serious airline personnel — who ask passengers if their baggage has been out of their possession between packing and the airport or if they have been given gifts or other items to transport — before checked items are accepted.

Airline Clubs – US carriers often have clubs for travelers who pay for membership. These clubs are not solely for first class passengers, although a first class ticket *may* entitle a passenger to lounge privileges. Membership (which, by law, requires a fee) entitles the traveler to use the private lounges at airports along their route, to refreshments served in these lounges, and to check-cashing privileges at most of their counters. Extras include special telephone numbers for individual reservations, embossed luggage tags, and a membership card for identification. Airlines serving Spain that offer membership in such clubs include the following:

American: The *Admiral's Club.* Single yearly membership $175 for the first year; $125 yearly thereafter; spouse an additional $70 per year.

Delta: The *Crown Club.* Single yearly membership $150; spouse an additional $50 per year.

TWA: The *Ambassador Club.* Single yearly membership $150; spouse an additional $25; lifetime memberships also available.

Note that such companies do not have club facilities in all airports. Other airlines also offer a variety of special services in many airports.

Getting Bumped – A special air travel problem is the possibility that an airline will accept more reservations (and sell more tickets) than there are seats on a given flight. This is entirely legal and is done to make up for "no-shows," passengers who don't show up for a flight for which they have made reservations and bought tickets. If the airline has oversold the flight and everyone does show up, there simply aren't enough seats. When this happens, the airline is subject to stringent rules designed to protect travelers.

In such cases, the airline first seeks ticket holders willing to give up their seats voluntarily in return for a negotiable sum of money or some other inducement, such as an offer of upgraded seating on the next flight or a voucher for a free trip at some other time. If there are not enough volunteers, the airline may bump passengers against their wishes.

Anyone inconvenienced in this way, however, is entitled to an explanation of the criteria used to determine who does and does not get on the flight, as well as compensation if the resulting delay exceeds certain limits. If the airline can put the bumped passengers on an alternate flight that is *scheduled to arrive* at their original destination within 1 hour of their originally scheduled arrival time, no compensation is owed. If the delay is more than an hour but less than 2 hours on a domestic US flight, they must be paid denied-boarding compensation equivalent to the one-way fare to their destination (but not more than $200). If the delay is more than 2 hours beyond the original arrival time on a domestic flight or more than 4 hours on an international flight, the compensation must be doubled (not more than $400). The airline also may offer bumped travelers a voucher for a free flight instead of the denied-boarding compensation. The passenger may be given the choice of either the money or the voucher, the dollar value of which may be no less than the monetary compensation to which the passenger would be entitled. The voucher is not a substitute for the bumped passenger's original ticket; the airline continues to honor that as well.

Keep in mind that the above regulations and policies are for flights leaving the US only, and do *not* apply to charters or to inbound flights originating abroad, even on US carriers. Airlines carrying passengers between foreign destinations are free to determine what compensation they will pay to passengers who are bumped because of overbooking. They generally spell out their policies on airline tickets. Some foreign airline policies are similar to the US policy; however, don't assume all carriers will be as generous.

To protect yourself as best you can against getting bumped, arrive at the airport early, allowing plenty of time to check in and get to the gate. If the flight is oversold, ask immediately for the written statement explaining the airline's policy on denied-boarding compensation and its boarding priorities. If the airline refuses to give you this information, or if you feel they have not handled the situation properly, file a complaint with both the airline and the appropriate government agency (see "Consumer Protection," below).

Delays and Cancellations – The above compensation rules also do not apply if the flight is canceled or delayed, or if a smaller aircraft is substituted because of mechanical problems. Each airline has its own policy for assisting passengers whose flights are delayed or canceled or who must wait for another flight because their original one was overbooked. Most airline personnel will make new travel arrangements if necessary. If the delay is longer than 4 hours, the airline may pay for a phone call or telegram, a meal, and, in some cases, a hotel room and transportation to it.

■ **Caution:** If you are bumped or miss a flight, be sure to ask the airline to notify other airlines on which you have reservations or connecting flights. When your name is taken off the passenger list of your initial flight, the computer usually cancels all of your reservations automatically, unless *you* take steps to preserve them.

CHARTER FLIGHTS: By booking a block of seats on a specially arranged flight, charter operators offer travelers air transportation for a substantial reduction over the full coach or economy fare. These operators may offer air-only charters (selling transportation alone) or charter packages (the flight plus a combination of land arrangements such as accommodations, meals, tours, or car rentals). Charters are especially attractive to people living in smaller cities or out-of-the-way places, because they frequently leave from nearby airports, saving travelers the inconvenience and expense of getting to a major gateway.

From the consumer's standpoint, charters differ from scheduled airlines in two main respects: You generally need to book and pay in advance, and you can't change the itinerary or the departure and return dates once you've booked the flight. In practice, however, these restrictions don't always apply. Today, although most charter flights still require advance reservations, some permit last-minute bookings (when there are unsold seats available), and some even offer seats on a standby basis.

Though charters almost always are round-trip, and it is unlikely that you would be sold a one-way seat on a round-trip flight, on rare occasions, one-way tickets on charters are offered. Although it may be possible to book a one-way charter in the US, giving you more flexibility in scheduling your return, note that US regulations pertaining to charters may be more permissive than the charter laws of other countries. For example, if you want to book a one-way foreign charter back to the US, you may find advance booking rules in force.

Some things to keep in mind about the charter game:

1. It cannot be repeated often enough that if you are forced to cancel your trip, you can lose much (and possibly all) of your money unless you have cancellation insurance, which is a *must* (see *Insurance,* in this section). Frequently, if the cancellation occurs far enough in advance (often 6 weeks or more), you may forfeit only a $25 or $50 penalty. If you cancel only 2 or 3 weeks before the flight, there may be no refund at all unless you or the operator can provide a substitute passenger.
2. Charter flights may be canceled by the operator up to 10 days before departure for any reason, usually underbooking. Your money is returned in this event, but there may be too little time for you to make new arrangements.
3. Most charters have little of the flexibility of regularly scheduled flights regarding refunds and the changing of flight dates; if you book a return flight, you must be on it or lose your money.
4. Charter operators are permitted to assess a surcharge, if fuel or other costs warrant it, of up to 10% of the airfare up to 10 days before departure.
5. Because of the economics of charter flights, your plane almost always will be full, so you will be crowded, though not necessarily uncomfortable. (There is, however, a new movement among charter airlines to provide flight accommodations that are more comfort-oriented, so this situation may change in the near future.)

To avoid problems, *always* choose charter flights with care. When you consider a charter, ask your travel agent who runs it and carefully check the company. The Better Business Bureau in the company's home city can report on how many complaints, if any, have been lodged against it in the past. Protect yourself with trip cancellation and interruption insurance, which can help safeguard your investment if you or a traveling companion is unable to make the trip and must cancel too late to receive a full refund from the company providing your travel services. (This is advisable whether you're buying a charter flight alone or a tour package for which the airfare is provided by charter or scheduled flight.)

Bookings – If you do take a charter, read the contract's fine print carefully and pay particular attention to the following:

Instructions concerning the payment of the deposit and its balance and to whom the check is to be made payable. Ordinarily, checks are made out to an escrow account, which means the charter company can't spend your money until your flight has safely returned. This provides some protection for you. To ensure the safe handling of your money, make out your check to the escrow account, the number of which must appear by law on the brochure, though all too often it is on the back in fine print. Write the details of the charter, including the destination and dates, on the face of the check; on the back, print "For Deposit Only." Your travel agent may prefer that you make out your check to the agency, saying that it will then pay the tour operator the fee minus commission. It is perfectly legal to write the check as we suggest, however, and if your agent objects too vociferously (he or she should trust the tour operator to send the proper commission), consider taking your business elsewhere. If you don't make your check out to the escrow account, you lose the protection of that escrow should the trip be canceled. Furthermore, recent bankruptcies in the travel industry have served to point out that even the protection of escrow may not be enough to safeguard a traveler's investment. More and more, insurance is becoming a necessity. The charter company should be bonded (usually by an insurance company), and if you want to file a claim against it, the claim should be sent to the bonding agent. The contract will set a time limit within which a claim must be filed.

Specific stipulations and penalties for cancellations. Most charters allow you to cancel up to 45 days in advance without major penalty, but some cancellation dates are 50 to 60 days before departure.

Stipulations regarding cancellation and major changes made by the charterer. US rules say that charter flights may not be canceled within 10 days of departure except when circumstances — such as natural disasters or political upheavals — make it impossible to fly. Charterers may make "major changes," however, such as in the date or place of departure or return, but you are entitled to cancel and receive a full refund if you don't wish to accept these changes. A price increase of more than 10% at any time up to 10 days before departure is considered a major change; no price increase at all is allowed during the last 10 days immediately before departure.

At the time of this writing, the following companies regularly offered charter flights to Spain:

> *Air Europa* (136 E. 57th St., Suite 1602, New York, NY 10022; phone: 212-888-7010).
>
> *American Trans Air* (PO Box 51609, Indianapolis, IN 46251; phone: 317-243-4150).
>
> *Club de Vacaciones* (775 Park Ave., Suite 200, Huntington, NY 11743; phone: 516-424-9600 in New York State; 800-648-0404 elsewhere in the US).

For the full range of possibilities at the time you plan to travel, you may want to subscribe to the travel newsletter *Jax Fax*, which regularly features a list of charter companies and packagers offering seats on charter flights and may be a source for other charter flights to Spain. For a year's subscription send a check or money order for $12 to *Jax Fax* (397 Post Rd., Darien, CT 06820; phone: 203-655-8746).

DISCOUNTS ON SCHEDULED FLIGHTS: Promotional fares often are called discount fares because they cost less than what used to be the standard airline fare — full-fare economy. Nevertheless, they cost the traveler the same whether they are bought through a travel agent or directly from the airline. Tickets that cost less if bought from some outlet other than the airline do exist, however. While it is likely that the vast majority of travelers flying to Spain in the near future will be doing so on a promotional fare or charter rather than on a "discount" air ticket of this sort, it still is a good idea for cost-conscious consumers to be aware of the latest developments in the budget airfare scene. Note that the following discussion makes clear-cut distinctions among the types of discounts available based on how they reach the consumer; in actual practice, the distinctions are not nearly so precise.

Courier Travel – There was a time when traveling as a courier was a sort of underground way to save money and visit otherwise unaffordable destinations, but more and more this once exotic idea of traveling as a courier is becoming a very "establishment" exercise. Courier means no more than a traveler who accompanies freight of one sort or another, and typically that freight replaces what otherwise would be the traveler's checked baggage. Be prepared, therefore, to carry all your own personal travel gear in a bag that fits under the seat in front of you. In addition, the so-called courier usually pays only a portion of the total airfare — the freight company pays the remainder — and the courier also may be assessed a small registration fee. Note that many courier flights can be booked in advance (sometimes as much as 3 months) and that flights usually are round trip.

There are dozens of courier companies operating actively around the globe, and several publications provide information on courier opportunities:

A Simple Guide to Courier Travel, by Jesse L. Riddle, is a particularly good reference guide to courier travel. Published by the Carriage Group (PO Box 2394, Lake Oswego, OR 97035; phone: 800-344-9375), it's available for $14.95, including postage and handling.

Travel Secrets (PO Box 2325, New York, NY 10108; phone: 212-245-8703). Provides information useful to those considering traveling as a courier and often lists specific US and Canadian courier companies. Monthly; a year's subscription costs $33.

Travel Unlimited (PO Box 1058, Allston, MA 02134-1058; no phone). Lists courier companies and agents worldwide. Monthly; for a year's subscription send $25.

World Courier News (PO Box 77471, San Francisco, CA 94107; no phone). Provides information on courier opportunities, as well as useful tips. Each issue highlights a different destination. Monthly; for a year's subscription send $20.

Companies that regularly send couriers to Spain include *Discount Travel International* (152 W. 72nd Street, Suite 223, New York, NY 10023; phone: 212-655-5151) and *Courier Travel Service* (530 Central Ave., Cedarhurst, NY 11516; phone: 800-922-2FLY or 516-374-2299). Travelers to Spain also may want to consider contacting *Excaliber International Courier Inc.*, as this company often sends couriers to London (where you can catch a connecting flight to Spain). For information, contact *Excaliber*'s representative, *Way to Go Travel* (3317 Barham Blvd., Hollywood, CA 90068; phone: 213-851-2572). In addition, *Now Voyager* (74 Varick St., Suite 307, New York, NY 10013; phone: 212-431-1616) is a referral agency that matches would-be couriers up with courier companies.

Net Fare Sources – The newest notion for reducing the costs of travel services comes from travel agents who offer individual travelers "net" fares. Defined simply, a net fare is the bare minimum amount at which an airline or tour operator will carry a prospective traveler. It doesn't include the amount that normally would be paid to the travel agent as a commission. Traditionally, such commissions amount to about 10% on domestic fares and from 10% to 20% on international fares — not counting significant additions to these commission levels that are paid retroactively when agents sell more than a specific volume of tickets or trips for a single supplier. At press time, at least one travel agency in the US was offering travelers the opportunity to purchase tickets and/or tours for a net price. Instead of making its income from individual commissions, this agency assesses a fixed fee that may or may not provide a bargain for travelers; it requires a little arithmetic to determine whether to use the services of a net travel agent or those of one who accepts conventional commissions. One of the potential drawbacks of buying from agencies selling travel services at net fares is that some airlines refuse to do business with them, thus possibly limiting your flight options.

Travel Avenue is a fee-based agency that rebates its ordinary agency commission to the customer. For domestic flights, they will find the lowest retail fare, then rebate 7% to 10% (depending on the airline selected) of that price minus a $10 ticket-writing charge. The rebate percentage for international flights varies from 5% to 16% (again depending on the airline), and the ticket-writing fee is $25. The ticket-writing charge is imposed per ticket; if the ticket includes more than eight separate flights, an additional $10 or $25 fee is charged. Customers using free flight coupons pay the ticket-writing charge, plus an additional $5 coupon processing fee.

Travel Avenue will rebate its commissions on all tickets, including heavily discounted fares and senior citizen passes. Available 7 days a week, reservations should be made far enough in advance to allow the tickets to be sent by first class mail, since extra charges accrue for special handling. It's possible to economize further by making your own airline reservation, then asking *Travel Avenue* only to write/issue your ticket. For travelers outside the Chicago area, business may be transacted by phone and purchases charged to a credit card. For further information, contact *Travel Avenue* at 641 W. Lake St., Suite 201, Chicago, IL 60606-1012 (phone: 312-876-1116 in Illinois; 800-333-3335 elsewhere in the US).

Consolidators and Bucket Shops – Other vendors of travel services can afford to sell tickets to their customers at an even greater discount because the airline has sold the tickets to them at a substantial discount (usually accomplished by sharply increasing commissions to that vendor), a practice in which many airlines indulge, albeit discreetly, preferring that the general public not know they are undercutting their own "list" prices. Airlines anticipating a slow period on a particular route sometimes sell off a certain portion of their capacity to a wholesaler, or consolidator. The wholesaler sometimes is a charter operator who resells the seats to the public as though they were charter seats, which is why prospective travelers perusing the brochures of charter operators with large programs frequently see a number of flights designated as "scheduled service." As often as not, however, the consolidator, in turn, sells the seats to a travel agency specializing in discounting. Airlines also can sell seats directly to such an agency, which thus acts as its own consolidator. The airline offers the seats either at a net wholesale price, but without the volume-purchase requirement that would be difficult for a modest retail travel agency to fulfill, or at the standard price, but with a commission override large enough (as high as 50%) to allow both a profit and a price reduction to the public.

Travel agencies specializing in discounting sometimes are called "bucket shops," a term fraught with connotations of unreliability in this country. But in today's highly competitive travel marketplace, more and more conventional travel agencies are selling consolidator-supplied tickets, and the old bucket shops' image is becoming respectable. Agencies that specialize in discounted tickets exist in most large cities, and usually can be found by studying the smaller ads in the travel sections of Sunday newspapers.

Before buying a discounted ticket, whether from a bucket shop or a conventional, full-service travel agency, keep the following considerations in mind: To be in a position to judge how much you'll be saving, first find out the "list" prices of tickets to your destination. Then, do some comparison shopping among agencies. Also bear in mind that a ticket that may not differ much in price from one available directly from the airline may, however, allow the circumvention of such things as the advance purchase requirement. If your plans are less than final, be sure to find out about any other restrictions, such as penalties for canceling a flight or changing a reservation. Most discount tickets are non-endorsable, meaning that they can be used only on the airline that issued them, and they usually are marked "nonrefundable" to prevent their being cashed for a list price refund.

A great many bucket shops are small businesses operating on a thin margin, so it's a good idea to check the local Better Business Bureau for any complaints registered against the one with which you're dealing — before parting with any money. If you still do not feel reassured, consider buying discounted tickets only through a conventional travel agency, which can be expected to have found its own reliable source of consolidator tickets — some of the largest consolidators, in fact, sell only to travel agencies.

A few bucket shops require payment in cash or by certified check or money order, but if credit cards are accepted, use that option. Note, however, if buying from a charter operator selling seats for both scheduled and charter flights, that the scheduled seats are not protected by the regulations — including the use of escrow accounts — governing the charter seats. Well-established charter operators, nevertheless, may extend the same protections to their scheduled flights, and when this is the case, consumers should be sure that the payment option selected directs their money into the escrow account.

Among the numerous consolidators offering discount fares to Spain (and Europe in general) are the following:

Bargain Air (655 Deep Valley Dr., Suite 355, Rolling Hills, CA 90274; phone: 800-347-2345 or 213-377-2919).

Maharaja/Consumer Wholesale (393 Fifth Ave. 2nd Floor, New York, NY 10016 (phone: 212-391-0122 in New York; 800-223-6862 elsewhere in the US).

TFI Tours International (34 W. 37th St., 12th Floor, New York, NY 10001; phone: 212-736-1140).

Travac Tours and Charters (989 Sixth Ave., New York, NY 10018; phone: 212-563-3303).

25 West Tours (2490 Coral Way, Miami, FL 33145; phone: 305-856-0810; 800-423-6954 in Florida; 800-252-5025 elsewhere in the US).

Unitravel 1177 N. Warson Rd., St. Louis, MO 63132; phone: 314-569-0900 in Missouri; 800-325-2222 elsewhere in the US).

■**Note:** Although rebating and discounting are becoming increasingly common, there is some legal ambiguity concerning them. Strictly speaking, it is legal to discount domestic tickets, but not international tickets. On the other hand, the law that prohibits discounting, the Federal Aviation Act of 1958, consistently is ignored these days, in part because consumers benefit from the practice and in part because many illegal arrangements are indistinguishable from legal ones. Since the line separating the two is so fine that even the authorities can't always tell the difference, it is unlikely that most consumers would be able to do so, and in fact it is not illegal to *buy* a discounted ticket. If the issue of legality bothers you, ask the agency whether any ticket you're about to buy would be permissible under the above-mentioned act.

OTHER DISCOUNT TRAVEL SOURCES: An excellent source of information on economical travel opportunities is the *Consumer Reports Travel Letter,* published monthly by Consumers Union. It keeps abreast of the scene on a wide variety of fronts, including package tours, rental cars, insurance, and more, but it is especially helpful for its comprehensive coverage of airfares, offering guidance on all the options from scheduled flights on major or low-fare airlines to charters and discount sources. For a year's subscription, send $37 ($57 for 2 years) to *Consumer Reports Travel Letter* (PO Box 53629, Boulder, CO 80322-3629; phone: 800-999-7959). For information on other travel newsletters, see *Sources and Resources,* in this section.

Last-Minute Travel Clubs – Still another way to take advantage of bargain airfares is open to those who have a flexible schedule. A number of organizations, usually set up as last-minute travel clubs and functioning on a membership basis, routinely keep in touch with travel suppliers to help them dispose of unsold inventory at discounts of between 15% and 60%. A great deal of the inventory consists of complete tour packages and cruises, but some clubs offer air-only charter seats and, occasionally, seats on scheduled flights.

Members pay an annual fee and receive a toll-free hotline number to call for information on imminent trips. In some cases, they also receive periodic mailings with information on bargain travel opportunities for which there is more advance notice. Despite the suggestive names of the clubs providing these services, last-minute travel does not necessarily mean that you cannot make plans until literally the last minute. Trips can be announced as little as a few days or as much as 2 months before departure, but the average is from 1 to 4 weeks' notice.

Among the organizations regularly offering such discounted travel opportunities to Spain are the following:

Discount Club of America (61-33 Woodhaven Blvd., Rego Park, NY 11374; phone: 800-321-9587 or 718-335-9612). Annual fee: $39 per family.

Discount Travel International (Ives Building, 114 Forrest Ave., Suite 205, Narberth, PA 19072; phone: 800-334-9294 or 215-668-7184). Annual fee: $45 per household.

Encore Short Notice (4501 Forbes Blvd., Lanham, MD 20706; phone: 301-459-8020; 800-638-0930 for customer service). Annual fee: $48 per family.

Last Minute Travel (1249 Boylston St., Boston MA 02215; phone: 800-LAST-MIN or 617-267-9800). No fee.

Moment's Notice (425 Madison Ave., New York, NY 10017; phone: 212-486-0503). Annual fee: $19.95 per family.

Spur-of-the-Moment Tours and Cruises (10780 Jefferson Blvd., Culver City, CA 90230; phone: 213-839-2418 in California; 800-343-1991 elsewhere in the US). No fee.

Traveler's Advantage (3033 S. Parker Rd., Suite 1000, Aurora, CO 80014; phone: 800-548-1116). Annual fee: $49 per family.

Vacations to Go (2411 Fountain View, Suite 201, Houston, TX 77057; phone: 800-338-4962). Annual fee: $19.95 per family.

Worldwide Discount Travel Club (1674 Meridian Ave., Miami Beach, FL 33139; phone: 305-534-2082). Annual fee: $40 per person; $50 per family.

Generic Air Travel – Organizations that apply the same flexible-schedule idea to air travel only and sell tickets at literally the last minute also exist. The service they provide sometimes is known as "generic" air travel, and it operates somewhat like an ordinary airline standby service, except that the organizations running it offer seats on not one but several scheduled and charter airlines.

One pioneer of generic flights is *Airhitch* (2790 Broadway, Suite 100, New York, NY 10025; phone: 212-864-2000), which arranges flights to Spain from various US gateways. Prospective travelers register by paying a fee (applicable toward the fare) and stipulate a range of acceptable departure dates and their desired destination, along with alternate choices. The week before the date range begins, they are notified of at least two flights that will be available during the time period, agree on one, and remit the balance of the fare to the company. If they do not accept any of the suggested flights, they lose their deposit; if, through no fault of their own, they do not ultimately get on any agreed-on flight, all of their money is refunded. Return flights are arranged the same way.

BARTERED TRAVEL SOURCES: Suppose a hotel buys advertising space in a newspaper. As payment, the hotel gives the publishing company the use of a number of hotel rooms in lieu of cash. This is barter, a common means of exchange among hotels, airlines, car rental companies, cruise lines, tour operators, restaurants, and other travel service companies. When a bartering company finds itself with empty airline seats (or excess hotel rooms, or cruise ship cabin space, and so on) and offers them to the public, considerable savings can be enjoyed.

Bartered-travel clubs often offer discounts of up to 50% to members who pay an annual fee (approximately $50 at press time) which entitles them to select from the flights, cruises, hotel rooms, or other travel services that the club obtained by barter. Members usually present a voucher, club credit card, or scrip (a dollar-denomination voucher negotiable only for the bartered product) to the hotel, which in turn subtracts the dollar amount from the bartering company's account.

Selling bartered travel is a perfectly legitimate means of retailing. One advantage to club members is that they don't have to wait until the last minute to obtain flight or room reservations.

Among the companies specializing in bartered travel, several that frequently offer members travel services to and in Spain include the following:

IGT (In Good Taste) Services (1111 Lincoln Rd., 4th Floor, Miami Beach, FL 33139; phone: 800-444-8872 or 305-534-7900). Annual fee: $48 per family.

Travel Guide (18210 Redmond Way, Redmond, WA 98052; phone: 206-885-1213). Annual fee: $48 per family.

Travel World Leisure Club (225 W. 34th St., Suite 2203, New York, NY 10122; phone: 800-444-TWLC or 212-239-4855). Annual fee: $50 per family.

CONSUMER PROTECTION: Consumers who feel that they have not been dealt with fairly by an airline should make their complaints known. Begin with the customer service representative at the airport where the problem occurs. If he or she cannot resolve your complaint to your satisfaction, write to the airline's consumer office. In a businesslike, typed letter, explain what reservations you held, what happened, the names of the employees involved, and what you expect the airline to do to remedy the situation. Send copies (never the originals) of the tickets, receipts, and other documents that back your claims. Ideally, all correspondence should be sent via certified mail, return receipt requested. This provides proof that your complaint was received.

Passengers with consumer complaints — lost baggage, compensation for getting bumped, smoking and nonsmoking rules, deceptive practices by an airline, charter regulations — who are not satisfied with the airline's response should contact the Department of Transportation (DOT), Consumer Affairs Division (400 Seventh St. SW, Room 10405, Washington, DC 20590; phone: 202-366-2220). DOT personnel stress, however, that consumers initially should direct their complaints to the airline that provoked them.

Travelers with an unresolved complaint involving a foreign carrier also can contact the US Department of Transportation. DOT personnel will do what they can to help resolve all such complaints, although their influence may be limited.

Although Spain does not have a specific government bureau that deals with airline complaints, consumers with complaints against a Spanish airline or other travel-related service company can write to the tourist authority in the area of Spain where the problem occurred (see *Sources and Resources*, in this section, for addresses). Outline the specifics *in Spanish* in as much detail as possible. (Keep in mind, if a translator is required, that this correspondence could get expensive.) The agency will try to resolve the complaint or, if it is out of their jurisdiction, will refer the matter to the proper authorities, and will notify you in writing (probably in Spanish) of the result of their inquires and/or any action taken.

Remember, too, that the federal Fair Credit Billing Act permits purchasers to refuse payment for credit card charges where services have not been delivered, so the onus of dealing with the receiver for a bankrupt airline falls on the credit card company. Do not rely on another airline to honor the ticket you're holding, since the days when virtually all major carriers subscribed to a default protection program that bound them to do so are long gone. Some airlines may voluntarily step forward to accommodate the stranded passengers of a fellow carrier, but this now is an entirely altruistic act.

The deregulation of US airlines has meant that a traveler must find out for himself or herself what he or she is entitled to receive. The Department of Transportation's informative consumer booklet *Fly Rights* is a good place to start. To receive a copy, send $1 to the Superintendent of Documents (US Government Printing Office, Washington, DC 20402-9325; phone: 202-783-3238). Specify its stock number, 050-000-00513-5, and allow 3 to 4 weeks for delivery.

■ **Note:** Those who tend to experience discomfort due to the change in air pressure while flying may be interested in the free pamphlet *Ears, Altitude and Airplane Travel;* for a copy send a self-addressed, stamped, business-size envelope to the *American Academy of Otolaryngology* (One Prince St., Alexandria, VA 22314; phone: 703-836-4444). And for when you land, *Overcoming Jet Lag* offers some helpful tips on minimizing post-flight stress; it is available from Berkeley Publishing Group (PO Box 506, Mail Order Dept., East Rutherford, NJ 07073; phone: 800-631-8571) for $6.95, plus shipping and handling.

Traveling by Ship

 There was a time when traveling by ship was extraordinarily expensive, time-consuming, utterly elegant, and was utilized almost exclusively for getting from one point to another. Alas, the days when steamships reigned as the primary means of transatlantic transportation are gone, days when Italy, France, Sweden, Germany, Norway, the Netherlands, and England — and the US — had fleets of passenger liners that offered week-plus trips across the North Atlantic. Only one ship (*Cunard*'s *Queen Elizabeth 2*) continues to offer this kind of service between the US and Europe with any degree of regularity; others make "positioning" cruises a few times a year at most. At the same time, the possibility of booking passage to Europe on a cargo ship is becoming less practical. Fewer and fewer travelers, therefore, set foot on Spanish soil with sea legs developed during an ocean voyage.

Although fewer travelers to Europe are choosing sea travel as the means of transport to their original specific destination, more and more people are cruising *around* Europe. No longer primarily pure transportation, cruising currently is riding a wave of popularity as a leisure activity in its own right, and the host of new ships (and dozens of rebuilt old ones) testifies dramatically to the attraction of vacationing on the high seas. And due to the growing popularity of travel along coastal and inland waterways, more and more travelers — particularly repeat travelers — are climbing aboard some kind of waterborne conveyance once they've arrived in Europe, and seeing Spanish ports while cruising around the Mediterranean or taking a ferry to one of the Spanish islands.

Many modern-day cruise ships seem much more like motels-at-sea than the classic liners of a couple of generations ago, but they are consistently comfortable and passengers often are pampered. Cruise prices are quite reasonable, and since the single cruise price covers all the major items in a typical vacation — transportation, accommodations, all meals, entertainment, and a full range of social activities, sports, and recreation — a traveler need not fear any unexpected assaults on the family travel budget.

When selecting a cruise, your basic criteria should be where you want to go, the time you have available, how much you want to spend, and the kind of environment that best suits your style and taste (in which case price is an important determinant). Rely on the suggestions of a travel agent — preferably one specializing in cruises (see "A final note on picking a cruise," below) — but be honest with the agent (and with yourself) in describing the type of atmosphere you're seeking. Ask for suggestions from friends who have been on cruises; if you trust their judgment, they should be able to suggest a ship on which you'll feel comfortable.

There are a number of moments in the cruise-planning process when discounts are available from the major cruise lines, so it may be possible to enjoy some diminution of the list price almost anytime you book passage on a cruise ship. For those willing to commit early — say 4 to 6 months before sailing — most of the major cruise lines routinely offer a 10% reduction off posted prices, in addition to the widest selection of cabins. For those who decide to sail rather late in the game — say, 4 to 6 weeks before departure — savings often are even greater — an average of 20% — as steamship lines try to fill up their ships. The only negative aspect is that the choice of cabins tends to be limited, although it is possible that a fare upgrade will be offered to make this limited cabin selection more palatable. In addition, there's the option of buying from a discount travel club or a travel agency that specializes in last-minute bargains; these discounters and other discount travel sources are discussed at the end of *Traveling by Plane*, above.

Most of the time, the inclusion of air transportation in the cruise package costs significantly less than if you were to buy the cruise separately and arrange your own air transportation to the port. If you do decide on one of these economical air/sea packages, be forewarned that it is not unusual for the pre-arranged flight arrangements to be less than convenient. The problems often arrive with the receipt of your cruise ticket, which also includes the airline ticket for the flight to get you to and from the ship dock. This is normally the first time you see the flights on which you have been booked and can appraise the convenience of the departure and arrival times. The cruise ship lines generally are not very forthcoming about altering flight schedules, and your own travel agent also may have difficulty in rearranging flight times or carriers. That means that the only remaining alternative is to ask the line to forget about making your flight arrangements and to pay for them separately by yourself. This may be more costly, but it's more likely to give you an arrival and departure schedule that will best conform to the sailing and docking times of the ship on which you will be cruising.

Cruise lines promote sailings to and around Europe as "get away from it all" vacations. But the prospective cruise ship passenger will find that the variety of cruises is tremendous, and the quality, while generally high, varies depending on shipboard services, the tone of shipboard life, the cost of the cruise, and operative itineraries. Although there are less expensive ways to see Europe, the romance and enjoyment of a sea voyage remain irresistible for many, so a few points should be considered by such sojourners before they sign on for a seagoing vacation (after all, it's hard to get off in mid-ocean). Herewith, a rundown on what to expect from a cruise, a few suggestions on what to look for and arrange when purchasing passage on one, and some representative sailings to and around Spain.

CABINS: The most important factor in determining the price of a cruise is the cabin. Cabin prices are set according to size and location. The size can vary considerably on older ships, less so on newer or more recently modernized ones, and may be entirely uniform on the very newest vessels.

Shipboard accommodations utilize the same pricing pattern as hotels. Suites, which consist of a sitting room–bedroom combination and occasionally a private small deck that could be compared to a patio, cost the most. Prices for other cabins (interchangeably called staterooms) usually are more expensive on the upper passenger decks, less expensive on lower decks; if a cabin has a bathtub instead of a shower, the price probably will be higher. The outside cabins with portholes cost more than inside cabins without views and generally are preferred — although many experienced cruise passengers eschew the more expensive accommodations for they know they will spend very few waking hours in their cabins. As in all forms of travel, accommodations are more expensive for single travelers. If you are traveling on your own but want to share a double cabin to reduce the cost, some ship lines will attempt to find someone of the same sex willing to share quarters (see *Hints for Single Travelers*, in this section).

FACILITIES AND ACTIVITIES: You may not use your cabin very much — organized shipboard activities are geared to keep you busy. A standard schedule might consist of swimming, sunbathing, and numerous other outdoor recreations. Evenings are devoted to leisurely dining, lounge shows or movies, bingo and other organized games, gambling, dancing, and a midnight buffet. Your cruise fare includes all of these activities — except the cost of drinks.

Most cruise ships have at least one major social lounge; a main dining room, several bars, an entertainment room that may double as a discotheque for late dancing, an exercise room, indoor games facilities, at least one pool, and shopping facilities, which can range from a single boutique to an arcade. Still others have gambling casinos and/or slot machines, card rooms, libraries, children's recreation centers, indoor pools (as well as one or more on open decks), separate movie theaters, and private meeting rooms. Open deck space should be ample, because this is where most passengers spend their days at sea.

Usually there is a social director and staff to organize and coordinate activities. Evening entertainment is provided by professionals. Movies are mostly first-run and drinks are moderate in price (or should be) because a ship is exempt from local taxes when at sea.

■ **Note:** To be prepared for possible illnesses at sea, travelers should get a prescription from their doctor for medicine to counteract motion sickness. All ships with more than 12 passengers have a doctor on board, plus facilities for handling sickness or medical emergencies.

Shore Excursions – These side trips almost always are optional and available at extra cost. Before you leave, do a little basic research about the Spanish ports you'll be visiting and decide what sights will interest you. If several of the most compelling of these are some distance from the pier where your ship docks, chances are that paying for a shore excursion will be worth the money.

Shore excursions usually can be booked through your travel agent at the same time you make your cruise booking, but this is worthwhile only if you can get complete details on the nature of each excursion being offered. If you can't get these details, better opt to purchase your shore arrangements after you're on board. Your enthusiasm for an excursion may be higher once you are on board because you will have met other passengers with whom to share the excitement of "shore leave." And depending on your time in port, you may decide to eschew the guided tour and venture out on your own.

Meals – All meals on board almost always are included in the basic price of a cruise, and the food generally is abundant and quite palatable. Evening meals are taken in the main dining room, where tables are assigned according to the passengers' preferences. Tables usually accommodate from 2 to 10; specify your preference when you book your cruise. If there are two sittings, you also can specify which one you want at the time you book or, at the latest, when you board the ship. Later sittings usually are more leisurely. Breakfast frequently is available in your cabin, as well as in the main dining room. For lunch, many passengers prefer the buffet offered on deck, usually at or near the pool, but again, the main dining room is available.

DRESS: Most people pack too much for a cruise on the assumption that their daily attire should be chic and every night is a big event. Comfort is a more realistic criterion. Daytime wear on most ships is decidedly casual. Evening wear for most cruises is dressy-casual. Formal attire probably is not necessary for 1-week cruises, optional for longer ones. (For information on choosing and packing a basic wardrobe, see *How to Pack,* in this section.)

TIPS: Tips are a strictly personal expense, and you *are* expected to tip — in particular, your cabin and dining room stewards. The general rule of thumb (or palm) is to expect to pay from 10% to 20% of your total cruise budget for gratuities — the actual amount within this range is based on the length of the cruise and the extent of personalized services provided. Allow $2 to $5 a day for each cabin and dining room steward (more if you wish), and additional sums for very good service. (*Note:* Tips should be paid by and for each individual in a cabin, whether there are one, two, or more.) Others who may merit tips are the deck steward who sets up your chair at the pool or elsewhere, the wine steward in the dining room, porters who handle your luggage (tip them individually at the time they assist you), and any others who provide personal service. On some ships you can charge your bar tab to your cabin; throw in the tip when you pay it at the end of the cruise. Smart travelers tip twice during the trip: about midway through the cruise and at the end; even wiser travelers tip a bit at the start of the trip to ensure better service throughout.

Although some cruise lines do have a no-tipping policy and you are not penalized by the crew for not tipping, naturally, you aren't penalized for tipping, either. If you can restrain yourself, it is better not to tip on those few ships that discourage it. However, never make the mistake of not tipping on the majority of ships, where it is a common, expected practice. (For further information on calculating gratuities, see *Tipping,* in this section.)

SHIP SANITATION: The US Public Health Service (PHS) currently inspects all passenger vessels calling at US ports, so very precise information is available on which ships meet its requirements and which do not. The further requirement that ships immediately report any illness that occurs on board adds to the available data.

The problem for a prospective cruise passenger is to determine whether the ship on which he or she plans to sail has met the official sanitary standard. US regulations require the PHS to publish actual grades for the ships inspected (rather than the old pass or fail designation), so it's now easy to determine any cruise ship's status. Nearly 4,000 travel agents, public health organizations, and doctors receive a copy of each monthly ship sanitation summary, but be aware that not all travel agents fully understand what this ship inspection program is all about. The best advice is to deal with a travel agent who specializes in cruise bookings, for he or she is most likely to have the latest information on the sanitary conditions of all cruise ships (see "A final note on picking a cruise," below). To receive a copy of the most recent summary or a particular inspection report, contact Chief, Vessel Sanitation Program, Center for Environmental Health and Injury Control, 1015 N. America Way, Room 107, Miami, FL 33132 (phone: 305-536-4307).

TRANSATLANTIC CROSSINGS: There are several cruise lines that sail between the US and Europe. Some include Spanish ports as part of their European itineraries, while on others passengers may disembark at other ports on the Continent and sail, fly, or drive to Spain.

For seagoing enthusiasts, *Cunard*'s *Queen Elizabeth 2* is one of the largest and most comfortable vessels afloat and each year the *QE2* schedules approximately a dozen round-trip transatlantic crossings between June and, usually, December. The *QE2* normally sets its course from New York to Southampton, England (a 5-day trip), and then sails directly back to the US, although on a few of the crossings it proceeds from Southampton to Cherbourg, France, or to other European ports before turning back across the Atlantic. (Similarly, on some crossings, the ship calls at various East Coast US ports in addition to New York, thus giving passengers a choice of where to embark or disembark.) For instance, last year the *QE2* made a Mediterranean cruise that included Spanish ports — Barcelona, Málaga, and Palma de Mallorca — before returning to Southampton and then continuing on its usual return trip.

If Spanish ports are not included in the applicable itinerary, travelers can take an intra-European flight from Southampton or Cherbourg to Spain, and from there take a transatlantic flight home. For those sailing to Europe on the *QE2* and flying home, another option for travel to Spain is based on the validity period of the return ticket. Following the transatlantic crossing, passengers have a specified time — up to 35 days for first class passengers and 15 days for the less expensive fares — during which they can take a trip to Spain via a separate round-trip ticket on *British Airways* from London to Barcelona, Bilbao, Madrid, or Málaga. The intra-European round-trip fare is subject to the availability of discounts, and the traveler must return to London in time to leave for home within the 15 or 35 days specified. Usually the included transatlantic flight must be to selected US gateways served by *British Airways,* although passengers may return to other gateways by paying a supplement. Those who want to splurge can apply the air allowance included in such air/sea packages towards a ticket aboard *British Airways'* supersonic *Concorde,* although the difference between the basic allowance and the *Concorde* fare is substantial. For further information on current air/sea offerings, check with your travel agent, call *British Airways* (phone: 800-AIRWAYS), or contact *Cunard* (555 Fifth Ave., New York, NY 10017; phone: 800-221-4770 or 800-5-CU-NARD).

Positioning Cruises – Another interesting possibility for those who have the time is what the industry calls a positioning cruise. This is the sailing of a US- or Caribbean-based vessel from its winter berth to the city in Europe from which it will be offering summer cruise programs. Eastbound positioning cruises take place in the spring; westbound cruises return in the fall. Since ships do not make the return trip until they need to position themselves for the next cruise season, most lines offering positioning cruises have some air/sea arrangement that allows passengers to fly home economically — though the cruises themselves are not an inexpensive way to travel.

Typically, the ships set sail from Florida or San Juan, Puerto Rico, and cross the Atlantic to any one of a number of European ports where the trip may be broken — including Spanish ports — before proceeding to cruise European waters (for example, the Mediterranean, the Baltic Sea, the Black Sea, the Norwegian fjords). Passengers can elect to stay aboard for the basic transatlantic segment alone or for both the crossing and the subsequent European cruise. Ports of call on such crossings and subsequent itineraries may vary substantially from year to year. For the most current information on operative itineraries, ask your travel agent or contact the cruise lines directly.

Among the ships that offer positioning cruises to Spain are the following:

> *Cunard* (555 Fifth Ave., New York, NY 10017; phone: 800-221-4770). The *Princess* makes a positioning cruise from Ft. Lauderdale to Málaga. Passengers have the option to continue on additional sailings (such as a 10-day Canary Island cruise, including as many as nine ports of call) or to add on land-vacation extensions (such as a 2-night land package in Málaga, with excursions to Granada or Ronda). *Cunard*'s luxurious *Sea Goddess I* also makes a positioning cruise from St. Thomas in the Caribbean to Málaga in April, returning to St. Thomas in October.

> *Royal Cruise Line* (One Maritime Plaza, Suite 1400, San Francisco, CA 94111; phone: 800-227-5628 or 415-956-7200). Offers a 19-day transatlantic positioning cruise aboard the *Golden Odyssey* from San Juan, Puerto Rico, to Venice — travelers to Spain can disembark at Málaga. This year, *Royal Cruise Line*'s *Crown Odyssey* also will make a 20-day trip from Buenos Aires that calls at Cádiz.

> *Royal Viking Line* (95 Merrick Way, Coral Gables, FL 33134; phone: 800-422-8000). The *Royal Viking Sea*'s westbound crossing is a 20-day trip from Rome to Ft. Lauderdale, via Barcelona and Gibraltar. Included in the price are a 2-day pre- or post-cruise land package in either Rome or Ft. Lauderdale, airfare; optional golf packages also are available.

> *Sun Line* (1 Rockefeller Plaza, Suite 315, New York, NY 10020; phone: 800-445-6400 or 212-397-6400). The *Stella Solaris* makes a 12-day positioning cruise between Ft. Lauderdale and Piraeus, Greece, that includes Minorca among the

Mediterranean ports of call. One-way fares include return airfare from Piraeus to New York.

MEDITERRANEAN CRUISES: The Mediterranean Sea is one of the world's most popular and picturesque cruising grounds, busy with ships offering sailings of varying lengths from spring through fall. The Atlantic Ocean southwest of the Iberian Peninsula, where it laps Spain's Canary Islands, attracts almost as much pleasure-seeking cruise traffic. Thus, it's not difficult to find a cruise ship calling at Barcelona, Málaga, Las Palmas on Gran Canaria, or some other Spanish port. Less easy to find is a cruise devoting its time exclusively to Spanish territory. Many Mediterranean cruises may begin in a Spanish port, but end elsewhere — Genoa or Venice or even farther afield. (The reverse itinerary also is common.) And many Canary Islands cruises call at a number of Moroccan ports or, even when cruising the islands alone, sail from and to a home base as far away as Southampton.

Commodore Cruise Line (800 Douglas Rd., Suite 700, Coral Gables, FL 33135; phone: 800-237-5361). The *Eurosun* makes 7-day cruises around the Canary Islands. Departing from Las Palmas, the cruise also visits Morocco. A post-cruise 2-night stay in Barcelona or Seville is included in the package price.

Costa Cruises (PO Box 019614, Miami, FL 33101-9865; phone: 305-358-7330). Offers several cruises that include Spanish ports of call, such as a 10-day cruise aboard the *Eugenio Costa* that sails from Genoa (Italy) and stops in Cádiz, Málaga, and Palma de Mallorca.

Crystal Cruises (2121 Ave. of the Stars, Los Angeles, CA 90067; phone 800-446-6645). Offers several trips (generally 12 or 13 days in length) aboard the *Crystal Harmony* that stop in Barcelona, Málaga, and Palma de Mallorca.

Cunard (555 Fifth Ave., New York, NY 10017; phone: 800-221-4770). *Cunard*'s *Sea Goddess I,* a sleek, luxurious, yacht-like vessel, makes 5- to 12-day cruises stopping in Gibraltar, Ibiza, Málaga, and Puerto José Banús. Its shallow draft allows it to visit Spanish village ports, with access to little-known beaches, as well as even more exotic ports of call. The *Sea Goddess I*'s equally luxurious and exclusive sister ship, the *Sea Goddess II,* also offers several cruises, including a 7-day Riviera cruise departing from Monte Carlo which includes Ibiza and other Mediterranean ports of call.

P&O Cruises (c/o *Express Travel Services,* Empire State Building, Suite 7718, 350 Fifth Ave., New York, NY 10118; phone: 212-629-3630 in New York State; 800-223-5799 elsewhere in the US). Offers several Mediterranean cruises that include Spanish ports in their itineraries, such as a 13-day Best of the Mediterranean trip aboard the *Canberra* that stops in Barcelona and Vigo. Also offered is an Indian Summer cruise aboard the *Sea Princess* that stops in Tenerife and Vigo.

Paquet French Cruises (1510 SE 17th St., Ft. Lauderdale, FL 33316; phone: 800-556-8850 or 800-999-0555). From Le Havre, France, the *Mermoz* makes a 10-day cruise taking in Barcelona and Cádiz. Wine is spotlighted and besides shore excursions visiting wine cellars of various regions, there may be lectures, wine tastings, and wine-related contests aboard ship.

Princess Cruises (10100 Santa Monica Blvd., Los Angeles, CA 90067; phone: 800-421-0522). Offers a 13-day cruise aboard either the *Royal Princess* or the *Crown Princess* between Barcelona and Venice. The *Royal Princess* also makes a 13-day cruise from Barcelona to London, stopping in Vigo en route.

Royal Cruise Line (One Maritime Plaza, Suite 1400, San Francisco, CA 94111; phone: 800-227-5628 or 415-956-7200). The *Crown Odyssey* makes a 12-day Great Capitals of Europe cruise from Venice to London that stops in Barcelona. The smaller *Golden Odyssey* departs on a 12-day cruise from Lisbon, Portugal, that stops in Málaga. The *Golden Odyssey* also offers a Magnificent Odyssey cruise, a 21-day cruise calling at Santa Cruz de Tenerife, Palma de Mallora, and Barcelona, as well as Gibraltar. Other itineraries stopping at Spanish ports include Mediterranean Highlights and Gala Mediterranean cruises.

Royal Viking Line (95 Merrick, Coral Gables, FL 33134; phone: 800-422-8000). The *Royal Viking Sun* makes 13-day sailings between Lisbon and Rome that stop in Barcelona and Cádiz, as well other Mediterranean ports.

In addition, the *International Cruise Center* (250 Old Country Rd., Mineola, NY 11501; phone: 516-747-8880 in New York State; 800-221-3254 elsewhere in the US), general sales agent for several European lines, offers Canary Islands cruises (to and from Tilbury, England). It also runs a ferry twice a week from Plymouth, England, to Santander, in northern Spain.

FREIGHTERS: An alternative to conventional cruise ships is travel by freighter. These are cargo ships that also take a limited number of passengers (usually about 12) in reasonably comfortable accommodations. The idea of traveling by freighter has long appealed to romantic souls, but there are a number of drawbacks to keep in mind before casting off. Once upon a time, a major advantage of freighter travel was its low cost, but this is no longer the case. Though freighters usually are less expensive than cruise ships, the difference is not as great as it once was. Accommodations and recreational facilities vary, but freighters were not designed to amuse passengers, so it is important to appreciate the idea of freighter travel itself. Schedules are erratic, and the traveler must fit his or her timetable to that of the ship. Passengers have found themselves waiting as long as a month for a promised sailing, and because freighters follow their cargo commitments, it is possible that a scheduled port could be omitted at the last minute or a new one added.

Anyone contemplating taking a freighter from a US port across the Atlantic to Spain should be aware that at press time, no freighter line made regular stops at Spanish ports. Nevertheless, it pays to check at the time you plan to travel. The following specialists deal only (or largely) in freighter travel and may be able to provide information on current freighter passage to Spain. They provide information, schedules, and, when you're ready to sail, booking services.

Freighter World Cruises, Inc. (180 S. Lake Ave., Suite 335, Pasadena, CA 91101; phone: 818-449-3106). A freighter travel agency that acts as general agent for several freighter lines. Publishes the twice-monthly *Freighter Space Advisory,* listing space available on sailings worldwide. A subscription costs $27 a year, $25 of which can be credited toward the cost of a cruise.

Pearl's Travel Tips (9903 Oaks Lane, Seminole, FL 34642; phone: 813-393-2919). Run by Ilse Hoffman, who finds sailings for her customers and sends them off with all kinds of valuable information and advice.

TravLtips Cruise and Freighter Travel Association (PO Box 188, Flushing, NY 11358; phone: 718-939-2400 in New York; 800-872-8584 elsewhere in the US). A freighter travel agency and club ($15 per year or $25 for 2 years) whose members receive the bimonthly *TravLtips* magazine of cruise and freighter travel.

Those interested in freighter travel also may want to subscribe to *Freighter Travel News,* a publication of the *Freighter Travel Club of America.* A year's subscription to this monthly newsletter costs $18. To subscribe, write to the club at 3524 Harts Lake Rd., Roy, WA 98580.

Another monthly newsletter that may be of interest to those planning to cruise Spanish waters is *Ocean and Cruise News,* which offers comprehensive coverage of the latest on the cruise ship scene. A year's subscription costs $24. Contact *Ocean and Cruise News,* PO Box 92, Stamford, CT 06904 (phone: 203-329-2787).

■ **A final note on picking a cruise:** A "cruise-only" travel agency can best help you choose a cruise ship and itinerary. Cruise-only agents are best equipped to tell you about a particular ship's "personality," the kind of person with whom you'll likely be traveling on a particular ship, what dress is appropriate (it varies from ship to ship), and much more. Travel agencies that specialize in booking cruises usually are members of the *National Association of Cruise Only Agencies (NACOA).* For a listing of the agencies in your area (requests are limited to three states), send a self-addressed, stamped envelope to *NACOA,* PO Box 7209, Freeport, NY 11520, or call 516-378-8006.

FERRIES: Numerous ferries link the Spanish mainland with the Balearic and Canary Islands and with Morocco. Nearly all of them carry both passengers and cars, and nearly all of the routes are in service year-round. Some operators may offer reduced rates for round-trip excursions, midweek travel, or off-season travel. While the trip across the Strait of Gibraltar is relatively brief, trips to the islands tend to be long, so a good many of the ferries travel overnight. Cabins as well as space for cars should be booked as early as possible, especially for crossings from June through September, when the boats can be crowded despite their greater frequency.

Spain's major steamship company, *Trasmediterránea,* services most of the routes, operating in conjunction with other companies on some of them. Its ferries to the Balearics operate from Barcelona and Valencia to Palma de Mallorca, Ibiza, and Mahón, Minorca, and also from Cádiz and Málaga to Palma. In addition, there is hydrofoil service between Altea on the Costa Blanca and Ibiza and Formentera. Ferries to the Canary Islands operate from Cádiz or Málaga (via Cádiz) to Tenerife, Las Palmas, and Morocco. The trip from Cádiz to Tenerife takes a full day and a half and means spending 2 nights at sea, since it departs at 2 PM on Thursdays and Saturdays in summer (Saturdays only the rest of the year), and arrives at 8 AM on Saturdays and Mondays. A trip direct from Cádiz to Las Palmas (not offered during the off-season) is only an hour shorter.

The same company provides most of the inter-island ferry transportation in the Canaries, serving Puerto Rosario on the island of Fuerteventura, Valverde on El Hierro, Santa Cruz de la Palma on the island of La Palma, and La Gomera, besides Las Palmas on Grand Canary, Tenerife, and Arrecife on Lanzarote. The company also runs a year-round, passengers-only hydrofoil service between Las Palmas on Grand Canary and Santa Cruz de Tenerife on Tenerife. Inter-island service in the Balearics is between Palma de Mallorca and Ibiza and between Palma and Mahón. *Trasmediterránea* also provides a *Hydrojet* service from Palma to Ibeza and back; travel time is about 2 hours. The ferry departs twice daily from Palma, at 9 AM and 4 PM, and Ibiza at noon and 7 PM.

Trasmediterránea also is the major ferry operator to Morocco, connecting Algeciras with Tangier, Morocco (2½ hours), and with the Spanish enclave of Ceuta (1½ hours), farther east along the Moroccan coast; Almería and Málaga with Melilla, another Spanish outpost in Morocco; and Tarifa with Tangier.

For schedule and fare information, reservations, and tickets, contact your travel agent or *Trasmediterránea* (2 Calle P. Muñoz Seca, Madrid 28011; phone: 1-431-0700; or 2 Via Laietana, Barcelona 08003; phone: 3-319-8212). Reservations can be made for individual seats, 2- to 4-person cabins (singles are placed in double cabins for only a bit less than the double-occupancy price), and car space. Book at least 6 weeks before your projected trip, and much earlier if possible, although how far in advance reservations are accepted depends on the route and ferry in question.

Other, smaller ferry lines can be found plying the seas from mainland Spain to and among the islands and to Morocco. The National Tourist Office of Spain can provide information on some of them, although they generally do not have US representatives. One to be aware of is *Flebasa,* which operates from approximately mid-March through mid-November from the resort town of Denia, in the province of Alicante, and from Valencia to San Antonio Abad on Ibiza. Travel time is only 3 hours. The company also provides bus transportation from Alicante or Valencia to Denia at no extra charge.

Traveling by Train

Perhaps the most economical, and often the most satisfying, way to see a lot of a foreign country in a relatively short time is by rail. It certainly is the quickest way to travel between two cities up to 300 miles apart (beyond that, a flight normally would be quicker, even counting the time it takes to get to and from the airport). But time isn't always the only consideration. Traveling by train is a way to keep moving and to keep seeing at the same time. The fares usually are reasonable, and with the special discounts available to visitors, it can be an almost irresistible bargain. You only need to get to a station on time; after that, put your watch in your pocket and relax. You may not get to your destination exactly at the appointed hour, but you'll have a marvelous time looking out the window and enjoying the ride.

TRAINS AND ROUTES: While North Americans have been raised to depend on their cars, Europeans have long been able to rely on public transportation. As in other countries on the Continent, the Spanish railway system is relatively extensive; however, the track used in Spain is broad gauge, not the narrow gauge used elsewhere in Europe (due to British influence and construction in the early days). Travelers crossing the Spanish border (to destinations other than Portugal, which uses the same gauge tracks) generally must change to another train. The exception is the specially equipped *Talgos* trains, which can adjust their wheel base automatically to the standard narrow gauge and, therefore, may operate beyond the border into France. (As we went to press, the trains that run only on narrow-gauge tracks were gradually being replaced with these convertible models, and international-gauge track was being laid to allow other European trains to extend service into Spain.)

In Spain, the government-owned and -operated *Red Nacional de los Ferrocarriles Españoles (RENFE),* known to the English-speaking world as *Spanish National Railways,* operates an 8,000-mile railway system. Most main lines radiate from Madrid, at the center of the country, like spokes of a wheel, so travel between the capital and large provincial cities, or between two smaller cities on the same spoke, is fast and frequent. In the case of towns on different spokes, it is sometimes faster and easier to go from one to the other by taking the long way around — via Madrid.

Most Spanish cities and towns have one train station, with the exception of Madrid, which has three, and Barcelona, which has four. In Madrid, the stations are Chamartín (the main station), Príncipe Pío (Norte) — also sometimes called Estación del Norte by residents — and Atocha. In Barcelona, the train stations are Barcelona Central Sants (the main station), Barcelona Terme-França, Plaça de Catalunya, and Plaça d'España.

Unlike in many other countries, Spanish railway tickets are not purchased in the train station but in sales offices (some of which *may* be in a station, but not necessarily).

RENFE sales offices (see below for more details) usually are centrally located in towns and cities. There also are auxiliary sales offices throughout Spain; tickets can be purchased at these offices, but other services, such as travel information, maps, and the like, will be more limited than at the main sales offices. Electronic vending machines dispensing tickets are increasingly common, particularly at auxiliary sales offices.

Although the main sales office in Madrid is closed for renovation until this summer, there is a *RENFE* sales office at the Madrid airport (Aeropuerto de Barajas; phone: 1-429-0202 for information; 1-501-3333 for reservations) with convenient hours: 8 AM to 8 PM, except Sundays and holidays, when it is open from 8 AM to 2 PM. The main sales office in Barcelona is at the main train station, Estación Barcelona Central Sants (phone: 3-490-0202). For information on other main and auxiliary sales offices in Spain, as well as locations for purchasing tickets in the US, see "Further Information," below.

Some of the special trains you may encounter in Spain and elsewhere in Europe (excluding neighboring Portugal) include the *EuroCity (EC)* trains, which have ushered in a new phase of European train service. Introduced in May 1987, the *EC* network has by now all but replaced the *Trans-Europe Express (TEE)* trains, which provided the European Economic Community with fast, efficient, and luxurious train service between major cities since the 1950s. *EC*s currently are the prestige trains of Europe and maintain high standards. They use modern, air conditioned coaches, are punctual and clean, and travel at a minimum speed of 54 miles per hour (the average includes time for station stops). All *EC* trains also have dining facilities and bilingual personnel on board. Both first and second class service is offered, and supplements must be paid for all departures. The supplement includes the price of a reserved seat, which is obligatory on any *EC* border crossing but not on trips within one country. The *EC* network includes 200 connections within the 12 participating countries, including Spain.

If there are no *EC*s on a route, the next best trains are likely to be *Inter-City (IC)* trains, which are similar to *EC*s in that they provide a high standard of service, have both first and second class cars, and generally require payment of a supplement. There are both national and international *IC* trains. Some, in fact, are former *TEE*s to which second class cars have been added in recent years to help curb high operating costs, a problem aggravated by low ridership. A great many more *IC*s already existed as part of the local rail network. Supplements must be paid to ride most continental *IC* trains, while reservations are obligatory only on those crossing borders. Another train of the same high quality is the *Trans-Europe Night (TEN),* an overnight train with sleeping quarters. And joining other European countries in the addition of high-speed rail service, the *Spanish National Railways* will be offering a speedy new service starting in April of this year — called *Alta Velocidad Español (AVE)* — between Seville and Madrid — which will run at 186 mph (298 kph). Future plans include the addition of high-speed lines between Madrid, Barcelona, and the French border, between Madrid and Lisbon, Portugal, and northwest connections to the French border at Irún.

These special trains are but a small part of Europe's highly developed rail service. International trains enter Spain from France at Perpignan-Figueres and Biarritz–San Sebastián. Express service from Paris to Madrid or Barcelona leaves every evening, arriving in the morning. The best of these trains are the *Talgos* (similar to the Europe-wide *EC*s) and *Electrotren* (similar to *IC*s elsewhere in Europe). These generally have first and second class cars and meal service. Those that make overnight trips also offer various sleeping facilities, which must be reserved well in advance during peak travel periods.

Hundreds of towns across Spain are served by "regular" express and local trains. For travel within Spain, again the finest trains are the *Talgos, Electrotren,* and "expresos" (overnight trains with couchettes), which are somewhat slower. *Motorail* service connects Madrid with most major cities. Automobiles also can be transported by train between Madrid and many provincial cities (see "Auto-Expreso," below). Eurailpasses are accepted for travel in Spain, though advance seat reservations are necessary (and must be made once in Spain, as the US offices can't book these particular reservations).

ACCOMMODATIONS, FARES, AND SERVICES: Fares on European trains are based on the quality of accommodations the passenger enjoys. You pay on the basis of traveling first class or second class, and on *EC, IC,* and other expresses such *Talgos* and *Electrotren* in Spain, first or second class, plus a supplement. Traditionally, seating is arranged in compartments, with three or four passengers on one side facing a like number on the other side, but increasingly, in the newer cars, compartments have been replaced by a central-aisle design.

Tickets can be purchased at *RENFE* sales offices in Spain (see the end of this section for a list of some of their major offices). *RENFE* sales offices have both tickets and schedules, and the ticket agent will tell you the station from which your train leaves. In Spain, domestic and international tickets usually are sold separately.

In order to save time, you may want to buy your rail tickets before leaving the US from travel agents or *Rail Europe,* the North American representative of the *Spanish National Railways* (also see below for addresses). *Rail Europe* will make reservations for short, local trips, as well as overnight excursions; bookings require a minimum of 7 days for confirmation.

Most of the international ticket and reservations systems are computerized and efficient. Fares vary from route to route, but short hauls always are more expensive per mile than longer runs. There is a $3 fee for European reservations made in the US (plus a $5 telex fee). Normally, reservations can be made up to 2 months prior to the travel date, and when making a reservation, you can ask for a window seat, as well as for a smoking or nonsmoking section. Reservations reduce flexibility, but they are advisable during the summer on popular routes. They also are advisable at any time of the year if it is imperative that you be on a particular train.

Spanish trains, like others in Europe, carry two basic kinds of sleeping quarters: "couchettes," the coach seats of a compartment converted to sleeping berths, and "wagon-lits," or sleepers, individual individual single or double bedrooms that compare favorably with the slumber coaches on transcontinental American trains. Second class couchettes have six berths per compartment (first class couchettes, which have four, are available only in France and Italy). The berth is narrow, with a pillow, blanket, and sheet provided. Single travelers generally — but not always — are booked into couchettes with others of the same sex; if it matters to you, make a specific request.

Couchettes have a standard charge (around $20 per person if bought in the US) added to the basic first or second class fare. A private or semiprivate wagon-lit or sleeper is more expensive (anywhere from $30 and up, depending on your destination).

The wide range of dining facilities runs the gamut from prix fixe menus served in dining cars or at your seat to self-service cafeteria-style cars and mobile vendors dispensing snacks, sandwiches, and beverages. In-seat and dining car lunch and dinner reservations either are made in advance or after boarding by visiting the dining car or through the train steward. If you're sure you will want to eat en route, it's a good idea to inquire beforehand exactly what meal service is offered on the train you'll be taking and whether advance dining reservations are required.

A standardized pictorial code has been designed to indicate the various amenities offered at many train stations. These may include showers, as well as restaurants, post and telegraph offices, exchange bureaus, and diaper changing facilities. In those cities that have two or more stations (see above), make sure you know the name of the station for your train.

Baggage often can be checked through to your destination or can be checked overnight at most stations. Some stations also provide 24-hour luggage lockers where you can temporarily free yourself of surplus bags, but these are becoming less common throughout Europe, as lockers are being eliminated due to bomb threats. It always is a good idea to travel as light as possible: Porters are in short supply at most stations, and self-service carts frequently are scarce as well.

Those planning driving routes should be aware that all European railways have some form of auto ferry. In Spain, it is called *Auto-Expreso* and is available throughout the country. *Note:* The *Auto-Expreso* can be booked only in Europe, and it is quite popular with Europeans, especially during the peak summer months. Your best bet is to make reservations as soon as you get to Europe, the earlier the better.

RENFE's *Auto-Expreso* is available in three categories; the price is based on the length of the vehicle, the distance to be traveled, the route taken, and the number of passenger tickets purchased. Charges for trailers also are based on length, and motorcycles are transported at half the cost of mid-size cars. *Auto-Expreso* users can travel on a train other than the one transporting their car, which can be checked in and shipped up to 10 days before or 10 days after the travelers' rail trip, with the limitation that the starting point of car transport must be the same as that of the driver. Delivery and pickup of the vehicle usually is at the train stations, which have special areas for this purpose. Vehicles must be at the station 2 hours before the train departs, and delivery is made approximately 1 hour after arrival. Pickup and delivery of the vehicle can be arranged at other locations (such as your hotel) for an additional charge; this service must be requested at least 24 hours in advance. To take advantage of the reduced prices on "Blue Days" (see "Passes," below), the passenger's ticket and automobile ticket should be purchased at the same time. Fares also can be reduced if two or more successive routes or a round trip are made on Blue Days.

PASSES: Rail passes are offered by most European railroad companies. They allow unlimited train travel within a set time period, frequently include connecting service via other forms of transportation, and they can save the traveler a considerable amount of money as well as time. The only requirement is the validation of the pass by an information clerk on the day of your first rail trip; thereafter, there is no need to stand in line — and lines can be very long during peak travel periods — to buy individual tickets for subsequent trips. Designed primarily for foreign visitors, these passes often must be bought in the US (or some other foreign location) prior to arrival in Europe. Although these passes can be among the best bargains around, be sure to look into the comparable cost of individual train tickets which — depending on the number of days you plan to travel — may work out to be less expensive.

The Eurailpass, the first and best known of all rail passes, is valid for travel through Spain and 16 other countries — Austria, Belgium, Denmark, Finland, France, Germany, Greece, Holland, Hungary, Ireland, Italy, Luxembourg, Norway, Portugal, Sweden, and Switzerland. It entitles holders to 15 or 21 days or 1, 2, or 3 months of unlimited first class travel, plus many extras, including some ferry crossings, river trips, lake steamers, and transportation by bus and private railroads, as well as scheduled *Europabus* services, and airport to city center rail connections. Since the Eurailpass is a first class pass, Eurail travelers can ride just about any European train they wish, including special express trains, without paying additional supplements. The only extras are the nominal reservation fee and sleeper and couchette costs.

A Eurailpass for children under 12 is half the adult price (children under 4 travel free) but includes the same features. The Eurail Youthpass, for travelers under 26 years of age, is slightly different, in that it is valid for travel in second class only.

The Eurail Saverpass resembles the basic Eurailpass, except that it provides 15 days of unlimited first class travel for three people traveling together during peak season; two people traveling together qualify if travel takes place entirely between October 1 and March 31. It provides savings of approximately $100 per ticket as compared to the price of a 15-day Eurailpass.

Another option is the Eurail Flexipass, which can be used for first class travel on any 5 days within a 15-day period, 9 days within a 21-day period, or 14 days within a 30-day period. All of these passes must be bought before you go, either from a travel agent or from the US offices of the French, German, Italian, or Swiss railway companies. A Eurail Aid Office in Europe will replace lost passes when proper documentation is provided; a reissuance fee is charged.

Both the 7-day Eurailpass and the 9-day Eurail Flexipass can be combined with 3 to 8 days of car rental in Spain through *Hertz*. The program, marketed under the name *Hertz* EurailDrive Escape, includes a car rental with unlimited mileage, basic insurance, and taxes, as well as some drop-off options within most of the countries of rental. Reservations must be made in the US at least 7 days in advance by calling *Hertz* at 800-654-3001.

The Eurailpass is a bargain for those who are combining a visit to Spain with sightseeing elsewhere on the Continent. But for those traveling strictly within Spain, a pass that allows unlimited travel for defined periods of time over this country's national transportation network is more economical.

RENFE offers a Tourist Pass (also called a Spanish Rail Pass), which is good for either 8 or 15 days of unlimited travel, and is issued in first and second class versions. *Días Azules,* or Blue Days, are discount days for rail travel in Spain. There are presently 300 Blue Days a year, with up to 25% discounts on round-trip travel, 50% discounts for senior citizens and children age 7 to 14, as well as discounts on the *Auto Expreso* (see above). *RENFE* also offers a Spain Flexipass, which is valid for any 4 days in an 8-day period, which also may be bought for either first or second class travel. As with the Eurailpass, these passes must be bought in the US.

TOURS: Special trains providing full-day or weekend sightseeing excursions for tourists are a very popular *RENFE* enterprise. In operation from May through October in most cases, these trains are an enjoyable way for travelers based in Madrid to visit several interesting Spanish towns. The *Tren Murallas de Avila* (Walls of Avila Train), for instance, leaves Madrid's Chamartín Station early on Sundays and holidays bound for Avila, 70 miles northwest, where passengers take a guided motorcoach tour of the city, are left free for lunch and browsing, and then tour the walls before boarding the train back to Madrid for an evening return. Other trains offering day trips are the *Doncel de Sigüenza* (Page of Sigüenza), which travels 80 miles northeast of Madrid to Sigüenza, a town in Guadalajara known for its cathedral, and the *Tren de la Fresa* (Strawberry Train), which follows the route once taken by the royal family to reach the country palace at Aranjuez, 30 miles south of Madrid in the midst of an area known for its strawberries.

Weekend trips (departing on Saturday mornings and returning Sunday evenings) range farther afield. The excursion aboard the *Ciudad Monumental de Cáceres* (Monumental City of Cáceres), visiting the Extremadura region, includes a stop at the Monastery of Guadalupe and a sightseeing tour of Trujillo and continues on to Cáceres for night sightseeing and an overnight stay, then a tour of the Carvajal Palace. (An alternate route takes in other towns of Extremadura, but both itineraries include a guided sightseeing tour of Cáceres.) The *Plaza Mayor de Salamanca,* named for the main square of the old university town that is its destination 125 miles northwest of Madrid, and the *Ciudad Encantada* (Enchanted City), which visits Cuenca, 100 miles east of Madrid, are other tourist trains that include overnight trips. These excursions can be booked in Madrid at travel agencies or *RENFE* offices, and their prices are quite reasonable and include round-trip transportation, sightseeing tours, and hotel accommodations (double occupancy) but no lunches or dinners (a picnic is included on the Cuenca excursion).

Two other tourist trains function as hotels on wheels and are thus in a class by themselves. The more famous one is the *Al Andalús Express,* or *Andalusian Express,* a luxury train made up of refurbished cars of the 1920s, with all the polished wood, decorative ground glass, damask drapes, and plush upholstery that its vintage implies in addition to the comforts of air conditioning, single and double sleeping compartments, shower rooms, a pub, piano bar, restaurant, gameroom, video collection, and discotheque.

This year, there are several itineraries offered aboard this historic train: In May, June, September, and October, the Southern Journey travels from Madrid to Seville, Córdoba, Granada, and Málaga, and back to Madrid; the trip will last 4 days. The price — which is rather expensive — includes a reception, meals aboard the train, and sightseeing visits led by multilingual guides, as well as entry to *Expo '92* in Seville. Slightly less pricey is the overnight trip from Málaga to Seville, which includes dinner, breakfast, and on-board accommodations, but no touring on arrival. Northern Journey packages, offered in July and August, range from 3 to 10 days and visit such cities as Barcelona, Pamplona, Burgos, León, and Santiago de Compostela.

The most recent addition to these itineraries this year is a combined trip: Starting in April, passengers will have the option of taking Spain's new high-speed train from Madrid to Seville (described above), where they can transfer to the *Andalusian Express* for one of the Northern Journey itineraries. Information on current tours and departure dates and reservations are available in the US through any of the three *Marsans International* offices in the US: 3325 Wilshire Blvd., Suite 508, Los Angeles, CA 90010 (phone: 213-738-8016); 1680 Michigan Ave., Suite 1140, Miami Beach, FL 33139 (phone: 305-531-0444); 19 W. 34th St., Suite 302, New York, NY 10001 (phone: 212-239-3880).

The second hotel on wheels is the *El Transcantábrico,* which also uses veteran, although less swank, rolling stock and operates on the narrow-gauge tracks of the *Ferrocariles Españoles de Vías Estrechas (FEVE)* line across the north of Spain. Excursions on this tourist train run twice a month from May through September and are 14 days in length, leaving from San Sebastián and crossing nearly the entire Cantabrian coast before terminating at Santiago de Compostela. En route, stops are made at historic landmarks, tiny Cantabrian fishing ports, cities such as Santander and Oviedo, and in areas of outstanding scenic beauty, such as the Picos de Europa, at 8,700 feet the highest range in the Cordillera Cantábrica, yet only 20 miles from the sea. The fare for this journey includes meals and sightseeing with multilingual guides; round-trip airfare between the US and Spain is available for a supplement. For information and reservations, contact *Marsans International* (address above).

RENFE also offers a variety of SpainRail Tours aboard modern, first class *Talgo* trains. Tour groups are accompanied by English-speaking guides and the tours generally last around 8 days; for current offerings, contact *RENFE.*

FURTHER INFORMATION: Particularly if Spain is only a part of a more extensive trip through Europe or even farther afield, you may want to consult additional sources before finalizing plans. Both the *Eurail Traveler's Guide* (which contains a railroad map) and the *Eurail Timetable* are free from Eurailpass (Box 10383, Stamford, CT 06904-2383), as well as from the Eurail Distribution Centre (Box 300, Succursale R, Montreal, Quebec H2S 3K9, Canada). The *Eurail Guide* by Kathryn Turpin and Marvin Saltzman is available in most travel bookstores; it also can be ordered from Eurail Guide Annuals (27540 Pacific Coast Hwy., Malibu, CA 90265: phone; 213-457-7286) for $14.95, plus shipping and handling. *Europe by Eurail* by George Wright Ferguson is available from Globe Pequot Press (PO Box Q, Chester, CT 06412; phone: 203-526-9571) for $13.95, plus shipping and handling. Both of the latter two guides discuss train travel in general, contain information on the countries included in the Eurail network (the Saltzman book also discusses Eastern Europe and the rest of the world), and suggest numerous sightseeing excursions by rail from various base cities.

You also may want to buy the *Thomas Cook European Timetable,* a weighty and detailed compendium of European international and national rail services that constitutes the most revered and accurate railway reference in existence. The *Timetable* comes out monthly, but because most European countries switch to summer schedules at the end of May (and back to winter schedules at the end of September), the June edition is the first complete summer schedule (and October the first complete winter schedule). The February through May editions, however, contain increasingly more definitive supplements on upcoming summer schedules, which can be used to plan a trip. The *Thomas Cook European Timetable* is available in some travel bookstores or can be ordered from the *Forsyth Travel Library* (PO Box 2975, Shawnee Mission, KS 66201-1375; phone: 800-367-7984 or 913-384-0496) for $21.95, plus shipping and handling; phoned in credit card orders are accepted.

Rail Europe is the North American representative of the *Spanish National Railways* or *RENFE (Red Nacional de los Ferrocarriles Españoles)*. The following offices sell tickets and passes and make reservations for Spanish trains:

California: 360 Post St., San Francisco, CA 94108 (phone: 415-982-1993).
Florida: 800 Corporate Dr., Suite 108, Ft. Lauderdale, FL 33334 (phone: 305-776-2729).
Illinois: 11 E. Adams St., Suite 906, Chicago, IL 60603 (phone: 312-427-8691).
New York State: 226-230 Westchester Ave., White Plains, NY 10604 (phone: 914-682-5172).
Texas: 6060 N. Central Ave., Suite 220, Dallas, TX 75206 (phone: 214-691-5573).
Canada: 2087 Dundas East, Suite 204, Mississauga, Ontario L4X 1M2, Canada (phone: 416-602-4195); 643 Notre Dame Ouest, Suite 200, Montreal, Quebec HC3 1H8 Canada (phone: 514-392-1311); 409 Granville St., Suite 452, Vancouver, British Columbia B6C 1T2, Canada (phone: 604-688-6707).

Following are *RENFE*'s main sales offices in Spain:

Algeciras: 12 Augustín Balsamo (phone: 56-664164 or 56-651155).
Alicante: 1 Explanada de España (phone: 65-212441 or 65-219867).
Almería: 1 Alcalde Muñoz (phone: 51-231822).
Barcelona:
- Barcelona Central Sants (phone: 3-490-0202).
- 617 Avenida Diagonal(phone: 3-322-9953).
- 318 Calle Balmes (phone: 3-209-6165).
- Additional branch offices are located throughout Barcelona.

Gijón: 3 Asturias (phone: 85-347313).
Huelva: Avenida de Italia (phone: 55-246666).
Irún: At the train station, Estación *RENFE,* (phone: 43-612515).
Madrid:
- 44 Alcalá. (At press time, this office was closed but due to reopen this summer.)
- 63 Paseo de las Delicias (phone: 1-528-6083).
- Aeroperto de Barajas (phone: 1-429-0202 for information; 1-501-3333 for reservations).
- 8 Avenida Ciudad de Barcelona (phone: 1-501-3333).
- Additional branch offices are located throughout Madrid.

Málaga: 2-4 Strachan (phone: 52-213122).
Murcia: 4 Barrionuevo (phone: 68-212842).
Palma de Mallorca: 9 Plaza de España (phone: 71-758817).
Salamanca: 11 Plaza de la Libertad (phone: 23-212454).
San Sebastián: 1 Camino (phone: 43-283599).
Santander: 25 Paseo de Pereda (phone: 42-212387).

Seville: 29 Zaragoza (phone: 5-421-7998).
Valencia: 24 Calle Javita (phone: 63-514874).
Valladolid: Estación de Valladolid–Campo Grande (phone: 83-301217).

Additional offices can be found in, among other towns, Aranjuez, Avilés, Benidorm, Burgos, Cádiz, Cartagena, Córdoba, La Coruña, Granada, Lugo, Pamplona, Pontevedra, Tarragona, Toledo, and Zaragoza. For a list of these and other branch offices, contact the Spanish National Tourist Board (see *Tourist Information Offices,* in this section).

Finally, although any travel agent can assist you in making arrangements to tour Spain by rail, you may want to consult a train travel specialist, such as *Accent on Travel,* 1030 Curtis St., Suite 201, Menlo Park, CA 94025 (phone: 415-326-7330 in California; 800-347-0645 elsewhere in the US).

Traveling by Bus

Going from place to place by bus may not be the fastest way to get from here to there, but that (and, in some cases, a little less comfort) is the primary drawback to bus travel. A persuasive argument in its favor is its cost: Short of walking, it is the least expensive way to cover a long distance and at the same time enjoy the scenic view.

Buses also reach outposts remote from railroad tracks, for those so inclined. While train service in Spain is more limited than it is in some other European countries, a map of the bus routes is not much different from a road map: If the way is paved, it's certain that a bus — some bus — is assigned to travel it. The network of express buses — those traveling long distances with few stops en route — is only slightly less extensive. Therefore Spain is particularly well suited to bus travel.

The public bus service in Spain is well developed, but is best for short day trips. Buses go from Madrid to many cities and towns throughout the country. In Spain, the buses are run by several privately owned companies, and tickets are purchased in the bus station. There are bus stations in all major cities, including several in Madrid; the busiest are Estación Sur de Autobuses at 17 Calle Canarias; 11 Paseo de la Florida; 18 Avenida de América; Estación del Norte; and 29 Paseo de la Florida. There are three stations in Barcelona; the busiest is Plaça de l'Universidad.

For schedule information, purchase the government-sponsored *Horario Guía,* a guide listing routes and timetables for buses, as well as trains and airlines in Spain. Updated monthly, it is available at newsstands. Although printed in Spanish, essential destination, arrival, and departure information is quite clear.

BOOKING: Reservations are not usually necessary on most local bus routes, which run on established and published schedules. As many rural lines are very crowded (since buses usually are the main form of transport for local residents), you may want to inquire about the possibility of making a reservation in order to ensure a seat. Tickets usually are bought on the bus and are valid for only that day and that ride. For long journeys, however, travelers must purchase tickets at the bus station before they leave. When you buy your ticket, ask about any discounts available.

SERVICES: Buses are not equipped for food service, but on long trips, as in the US, they do make meal and rest stops. If you plan to spend some time traveling around Spain by bus, it's not a bad idea to bring some food aboard, although you're probably better off waiting until you reach a stop in a town or city where you can eat more comfortably at a restaurant. Toilet facilities are likely to be provided only on the newer buses on long-distance trips, and air conditioning is the exception rather than the rule — particularly on rural routes. If taking a motorcoach *tour,* however, you can expect special amenities such as air conditioning, toilets, upholstered and adjustable seats, and reading lamps.

FOR COMFORTABLE TRAVEL: Dress casually in loose-fitting clothes. Be sure you have a sweater or jacket (even in the summer) and, for when you disembark, a raincoat or umbrella is a must, particularly during the winter (December through March). Passengers are allowed to listen to radios or cassette players, but must use earphones. Choose a seat in the front near the driver for the best view or in the middle between the front and rear wheels for the smoothest ride.

BUS TOURS: Many American tour operators offer motorcoach tours, however, one company *Gray Line,* an affiliate of *Rodoviaria Nacional, EP (RN;* address above) specializes in bus tours of Spain. Among the itineraries offered are 1-day trips between Madrid and Toledo; 4-day tours visiting Avila, Madrid, Salamanca, and Segovia; 4-day tours visiting Córdoba, Granada, and Seville; and other tours of southern Spain in the Costa del Sol. For further information on all-inclusive motorcoach tours offered by US tour operators, see *Package Tours,* in this section.

Traveling by Car

Driving certainly is the most flexible way to explore out-of-the-way regions of Spain. The privacy, comfort, and convenience of touring by car can't be matched by any other form of transport. Trains often whiz much too fast past too many enticing landscapes, tunnel through or pass between hills and mountains rather than climb up and around them for a better view, frequently deposit passengers in an unappealing part of town, and skirt some areas of the country altogether. Buses have a greater range, but they still don't permit many spur-of-the-moment stops and starts. In a car you go where you want when you want, and can stop along the way as often as you like for a meal, a photograph, or a particularly appealing view.

Spain is ideally suited for driving tours. Distances between major cities usually are reasonable, and the historical and cultural density is such that the flexibility of a car can be used to maximum advantage. A visitor can cover large amounts of territory, visit major cities and sites, or motor from one small village to another while exploring the countryside. (See DIRECTIONS for our choices of the most interesting driving itineraries.)

Travelers who wish to cover Spain from end to end can count on a good system of highways to help them make time. Travelers who wish to explore only one region will find that the secondary and even lesser roads are well surfaced and generally in good condition, although farther off the beaten track, this may not always be the case. Either way, there is plenty of satisfying scenery en route.

But driving isn't an inexpensive way to travel. Gas prices are far higher in Spain than in North America, and car rentals seldom are available at bargain rates. Keep in mind, however, that driving becomes more economical with more passengers. Because the price of getting wheels abroad will be more than an incidental expense, it is important to investigate every alternative before making a final choice. Many travelers find this expense amply justified when considering that rather than just the means to an end, a well-planned driving route also can be an important part of the adventure.

Before setting out, make certain that everything you need is in order. If possible, discuss your intended trip with someone who already has driven the route to find out about road conditions and available services. If you can't speak to someone personally, try to read about others' experiences. Automobile clubs (see below) and the Spanish national tourist offices in the US can be a good source of travel information, although when requesting brochures and maps, be sure to specify the areas you are planning to visit. (See "Roads and Maps," below.)

DRIVING: A valid driver's license from his or her own state of residence is required for a US citizen to drive in Spain. In addition, an International Driving Permit (IDP), which is a translation of the US license in 9 languages, is required in a number of countries, including Spain, where a US citizen is required to have an IDP in order to drive a rented car. While Spanish regulations are not always enforced and foreign drivers have driven in Spain without incident using just their regular license, it's not recommended.

You can obtain your IDP before you leave from most branches of the *American Automobile Association (AAA)*. Applicants must be at least 18 years old, and the application must be accompanied by two passport-size photos (some *AAA* branches have a photo machine available), a valid US driver's license, and a fee of $10. The IDP is good for 1 year and must be accompanied by your US license to be valid.

Proof of liability insurance also is required and is a standard part of any car rental contract. (To be sure of having the appropriate coverage, let the rental staff know in advance about the national borders you plan to cross.) If buying a car and using it abroad, the driver must carry an International Insurance Certificate, known as a Green Card (called a *Carta Verde* in Spain). Your insurance agent or carrier at home can arrange for a special policy to cover you in Europe, and automatically will issue your Green Card.

Contrary to first impressions, Spanish drivers tend to be skillful and disciplined. Also contrary to first impressions, rules of the road do exist. Driving in Spain is on the right side of the road, as in most of Europe. Passing is on the left; the left turn signal must be flashing throughout the entire process and the right indicator must be used when pulling back to the right; it's also a common practice to flash your headlights to signal the driver in front what you're doing. On mountain roads, get used to flashing your headlights at night and beeping your horn when rounding blind curves during the day; traffic going up usually has priority over traffic coming down, though signposts may indicate who has the right of way and at what times. In most larger cities, honking is forbidden (except to avoid accidents); flash your headlights instead. Also, don't be intimidated by tailgaters — everyone does it.

According to law, those coming from the right at intersections have the right of way, as in the US, and pedestrians, provided they are in marked crosswalks, have priority over all vehicles. Unfortunately, however, this is not always the case. Exceptions are priority roads, marked by a sign with a yellow diamond on it; these have the right of way until the diamond reappears with a black bar and the right of way reverts to those coming from the right. In many areas, though, signposting is meager, and traffic at intersections converge from all directions, resulting in a proceed-at-your-own-risk flow.

Pictorial direction signs, generally found on the newer roads in Spain, are standardized under the International Roadsign System, and their meanings are indicated by their shapes: Triangular signs indicate danger; circular signs give instructions; and rectangular signs are informative. Driving in European cities can be a tricky proposition, since many of them do not have street signs at convenient corners, but instead identify their byways with plaques attached to the walls of corner buildings. These often are difficult to spot until you've passed them, and since most streets don't run parallel to one another, taking the next turn can lead you astray. Fortunately, most European cities and towns post numerous signs pointing the way to the center of the city, and plotting a course to your destination from there may be far easier. In Spain, look for the signs that read CENTRO. Also note that highway signs showing the distance from point to point are in kilometers rather than miles (1 mile equals approximately 1.6 kilometers; 1 kilometer equals approximately .62 mile). And speed limits are in kilometers per hour, so think twice before hitting the gas when you see a speed limit of 100. That means 62 miles per hour.

In Spanish towns, speed limits usually are 60 kph (about 38 mph). Outside town, the speed limit is 120 kph (75 mph) on *autopistas,* or toll highways (designated by the letter A), 100 kph (about 62 mph) on *nacional,* or main roads (designated by the letter N), and 90 kph (56 mph) elsewhere unless otherwise marked.

Keep in mind, when touring along scenic roadways, that it is all too easy to inch up over the speed limit. And use alcohol sparingly prior to getting behind the wheel. Spain has specific laws pertaining to drinking and driving and, as in other European countries, the Spanish authorities are most zealous in prosecuting those who commit infractions under the influence. Police also have the power to levy on-the-spot fines for other violations such as speeding, failure to stop at a red light, and failure to wear seat belts (required by law).

Traffic congestion is at its worst on main roads, particularly those radiating from major cities. Look for signs pointing out detours or alternative routes to popular holiday destinations. Service stations, information points, and tourist offices often distribute free maps of the alternate routes, which may be the long way around but probably will get you to your destination faster in the end.

■**Note:** Pay particular attention to parking signs in large cities, especially those indicating "control zones," where an unattended parked car presents a serious security risk. If you park in a restricted zone, unlike in the US (where you chance only a ticket or being towed), you may return to find that the trunk and doors have been blown off by overly cautious security forces. It's more likely, however, that you'll return to find one of the car's wheels "clamped," a procedure that renders your car inoperable and involves a tedious (and costly) process to get it freed.

Roads and Maps – Western Europe's network of highways is as well maintained as any in North America, with a system comparable to the American highway system: expressways, first class roads, and well-surfaced secondary roads. Three decades ago, a pan-European commission established standards for international European routes, called E roads. Most European maps note E route numbers together with national route numbers. Single-country maps generally use only a national number.

Spain maintains its own highway system. In general, the majority of main roads throughout the country have recently been widened and repaved, and a lot of money currently is being spent on overall road improvements. In areas of ongoing roadwork, be prepared for substantial delays.

Except for stretches of free autoroutes in the vicinity of cities, most of the autoroutes (designated by A on pan-European maps) are toll roads, and they are fairly expensive. They save time, gas, and wear and tear on the car, but they obviously are not the roads to take if you want to browse and linger along the way. The other main roads (designated by N) and the secondary, or regional (designated by D), are free, well maintained, and much more picturesque, while minor roads have their own charm.

Be aware that in recent years, numerous changes have been taking place in the numbering of European roads. Many N roads have become D roads, some merely changing their prefix from N to D, some changing numbers as well. Another recent development is a new Europe-wide road numbering system. The European designations, prefaced by an E, appear together with the individual country's road numbers; so, for example, autoroute A1 in Spain could also be called E5, but another country's A1 would have a different E number. Both designations appear on Michelin's newest maps, but expect discrepancies between the old and new numbers to appear on maps and in guidebooks and brochures for some time to come.

All Michelin publications — the red and green guides, as well as road maps (by far the best for visitors touring) — are available in bookstores and map shops throughout the US and all over Europe, and also can be ordered from Michelin Guides and Maps (PO Box 3305, Spartanburg, SC 29304-3305; phone: 803-599-0850 in South Carolina; 800-423-0485 elsewhere in the US). A new edition of each Michelin map appears every year; if you're not buying directly from the publisher, make sure that the edition you buy is no more than 2 years old by opening one fold and checking the publication date, given just under the black circle with the map number. A particularly good map of Spain is Michelin's *No. 990,* which is on a scale of 1 cm:10 km. It outlines scenic routes in green, highlights national parks and interesting sights, and includes insets of both the Canary and Balearic islands.

Freytag & Berndt's excellent series of 28 road maps ($8.95 each) cover most major destinations throughout Europe, including a map of the Iberian Peninsula. As the publisher is Austrian, this series is best ordered from the travel sources listed in *Books, Magazines, Newspapers, and Newsletters,* in this section.

Another good source for the maps mentioned above, and just about any other kind of map of just about anywhere in the world, is *Map Link* (25 E. Mason St., Santa Barbara, CA 93101; phone: 805-965-4402). You may want to order their excellent guide to maps worldwide, *The World Map Directory* ($29.95). If they don't have the map you want in stock — they have over 20 maps of Spain — they will do their best to get it for you.

Road maps also are sold at gas stations throughout Europe. Stateside, some free maps can be obtained from the national tourist offices. The National Tourist Office of Spain distributes a smaller, free map of Spain, with insets of Bilbao, Barcelona, Madrid, Seville, Valencia, and Zaragoza. *Avis,* the car rental company (see below), offers "Personally Yours," a travel packet complete with maps and interesting places to see and things to do while driving through Spain.

The *American Automobile Association (AAA)* also provides some useful reference sources, including an overall Europe planning map, several regional maps of Spain, the 600-page *Travel Guide to Europe* (the price varies from branch to branch), and the 64-page *Motoring Europe* ($5.95). All are available through local *AAA* offices (see below). Another invaluable guide, *Euroad: The Complete Guide to Motoring in Europe,* is available for $8.80, including postage and handling, from *VLE Limited,* PO Box 444, Fort Lee, NJ 07204 (phone: 201-585-5080).

Automobile Clubs and Breakdowns – Most European automobile clubs offer emergency service to any breakdown victim, whether a club member or not; however, only members of these clubs or affiliated clubs may have access to certain information services and receive discounted or free towing and repair services.

Members of the *American Automobile Association (AAA)* often are entitled automatically to a number of services from foreign clubs. With over 31 million members in chapters throughout the US and Canada, the *AAA* is the largest automobile club in North America. *AAA* affiliates throughout the US provide a variety of travel services to members, including a travel agency, trip planning, fee-free traveler's checks, and reimbursement for foreign roadside assistance. They will help plan an itinerary, send a map with clear routing directions, and even make hotel reservations. These services apply to travel in both the US and Europe. Although *AAA* members receive maps and other brochures for no charge or at a discount, non-members also can order from an extensive selection of highway and topographical maps. You can join the *AAA* through local chapters (listed in the telephone book under *AAA*) or contact the national office, 1000 AAA Dr., Heathrow, FL 32746-5063 (phone: 407-444-8544).

Through its association with the *International Touring Organization* (in France) the *AAA* is affiliated with automobile clubs throughout Europe that supply travel information, road maps, touring and restaurant information, towing, and limited emergency road service to members with a valid *AAA* membership card. In Spain, contact the *Real Automóvil Club de España,* 10 General Sanjourjo, Madrid 28003 (phone: 1-447-3200).

If you break down on the road, the first emergency procedure is to get the car off the road. If the road has a narrow shoulder, try to get all the way off, even if you have to hang off the shoulder a bit. Better yet, try to make it to an area where the shoulder is wider — if you are crawling along well below the speed limit, use your emergency flashers to warn other drivers. Once you've pulled off, raise the hood as a signal that help is needed, and tie a white handkerchief or rag to the door handle or radio antenna. Don't leave the car unattended, and don't try any major repairs on the road. Note that motor patrols in Spain usually drive small cars painted white with blue trim, and emergency call boxes are located on many major routes. On secondary roads in Spain, emergency phones may be posted with phone numbers of local garages providing towing and basic repair services, although on rural routes, these boxes are rare.

For breakdown assistance in Spain, motorists also can call the *Real Automóvil Club de España* at 1-447-3200; they will direct you to the nearest service station. The National Tourist Office of Spain also can provide a map of garages throughout Spain.

Aside from these options, a driver in distress will have to contact the nearest service center by pay phone. And, although English is spoken in Spain, if language is a barrier in explaining your dilemma, the local operator should be able to connect you to an English-speaking international operator for assistance. (For further information on calling for help, see *Mail, Telephone, and Electricity* and *Medical and Legal Aid and Consular Services,* both in this section.) Car rental companies also make provisions for breakdowns, emergency service, and assistance; ask for a number to call when you pick up the vehicle.

Gasoline – In Spain, gasoline is sold by the liter, which is slightly more than 1 quart; approximately 3.8 liters equal 1 US gallon. Regular or leaded gas generally is sold in two grades — called *gasolina normal* or *gasolina super.* Diesel (called diesel) also is widely available, but unleaded fuel (*gasolina sin plomo*) is only now being introduced in Europe and may be difficult (or even impossible) to find. At least until all European gas stations sell unleaded, your safest bet is to rent a car that takes leaded gasoline.

Gas prices everywhere rise and fall depending on the world supply of oil, and an American traveling overseas is further affected by the prevailing rate of exchange, so it is difficult to say exactly how much fuel will cost when you travel. It is not difficult to predict, however, that gas prices will be substantially higher in Spain than you are accustomed to paying in the US.

Particularly when traveling in rural areas, fill up whenever you come to a gas station. It may be a long way to the next open station. (Even in more populated areas, it may be difficult to find an open station on Sundays or holidays.) You don't want to get stranded on an isolated stretch — so it is a good idea to bring along an extra few gallons in a steel container. (Plastic containers tend to break when a car is bouncing over rocky roads. This, in turn, creates the danger of fire should the gasoline ignite from a static electricity spark. Plastic containers also may burst at high altitudes.)

Considering the cost of gas in Spain relative to US prices, gas economy is of particular concern. The prudent traveler should plan an itinerary and make as many reservations as possible in advance in order not to waste gas figuring out where to go, stay, or eat. Drive early in the day, when there is less traffic. Then leave your car at the hotel and use local transportation whenever possible after you arrive at your destination.

Although it may be as dangerous to drive at a speed much below the posted limit as it is to drive above it — particularly on major highways, where the speed limit is 75 mph — at 88 kph (55 mph) a car gets 25% better mileage than at 112 kph (70 mph). The number of miles per liter or gallon also is increased by driving smoothly.

RENTING A CAR: Although there are other options, such as leasing or outright purchase, most travelers who want to drive in Europe simply rent a car. Travelers to Spain can rent a car through a travel agent or international rental firm before leaving home, or from a local company once they are in Europe. Another possibility, also arranged before departure, is to rent the car as part of a larger travel package (see "Fly/Drive," below, as well as *Package Tours,* in this section).

Renting a car in Spain is not inexpensive, but it is possible to economize by determining your own needs and then shopping around among the car rental companies until you find the best deal. As you comparison shop, keep in mind that rates vary considerably, not only from city to city, but also from location to location within the same city. For instance, it might be less expensive to rent a car in the center of a city rather than at the airport. Ask about special rates or promotional deals, such as weekend or weekly rates, bonus coupons for airline tickets, or 24-hour rates that include gas and unlimited mileage.

Rental car companies operating in Europe can be divided into three basic categories: large international companies; national or regional companies; and smaller local companies. Because of aggressive local competition, the cost of renting a car can be less expensive once a traveler arrives in Europe, compared to the prices quoted in advance from the US. Local companies usually are less expensive than the international giants.

Given this situation, it's tempting to wait until arriving to scout out the lowest-priced rental from the company located the farthest from the airport high-rent district and offering no pick-up services. But if your arrival coincides with a holiday or a peak travel period, you may be disappointed to find that even the most expensive car in town was spoken for months ago. Whenever possible, it is best to reserve in advance, anywhere from a few days in slack periods to a month or more during the busier seasons.

Renting from the US – Travel agents can arrange foreign rentals for clients, but it is just as easy to call and rent a car yourself. Listed below are some of the major international rental companies represented in Spain that have information and reservations numbers that can be dialed toll-free from the US:

Avis (phone: 800-331-1084). Has 150 locations in Spain.

Budget (phone: 800-527-0700). Has over 30 locations in Spain.

Dollar Rent-a-Car (known in Europe as *Eurodollar;* phone: 800-421-6878). Has 4 locations, one each in Barcelona, Madrid, Málaga, and Seville.

Hertz (phone: 800-654-3001). Has 140 locations in Spain.

***National* (known in Europe as *Europcar;* phone: 800-CAR-EUROPE). Has 110 locations in Spain.**

Also note that *Avis* also offers two helpful free services for customers traveling in Spain, as well as in other European countries: the "Know Before You Go" US hotline (phone: 914-355-AVIS); and a Europe Message Center, which will take messages for customers traveling in Europe. The first service provides travelers with tourist information on Spain (as well as Austria, Belgium, Denmark, France, Germany, Great Britain, Holland, Ireland, Italy, Luxembourg, Portugal, and Switzerland). Topics may range from questions about driving (distances, gasoline prices, and license requirements) to queries about currency, customs, tipping, and weather. (Callers then receive a personal letter confirming the information discussed.)

Avis's Europe Message Center operates like any answering service in that it will take phone messages any time day or night for *Avis* customers. *Avis* renters are given a telephone number in Europe that they can leave with anyone who wants to contact them while they are touring; if your rental car comes with a car phone, *Avis* will give this number to callers (with your permission). The tourers themselves can call a toll-free number to pick up messages or leave word for family, friends, or business colleagues. To utilize the service, a renter picks up his or her car at an *Avis* outlet in Europe, and then simply calls the Message Center and registers with the rental agreement number.

It's even possible to leave an itinerary — which can be altered later if necessary — making messages easy to leave and/or pick up.

It also is possible to rent a car before you go by contacting any number of smaller or less well known US companies that do not operate worldwide. These organizations specialize in European auto travel, including leasing and car purchase in addition to car rental, or actually are tour operators with a well-established European car rental programs. These firms, whose names and addresses are listed below, act as agents for a variety of European suppliers, offer unlimited mileage almost exclusively, and frequently manage to undersell their larger competitors by a significant margin.

There are legitimate bargains in car rentals if you shop for them. Call all the familiar car rental names whose toll-free numbers are given above (don't forget to ask about their special discount plans), and then call the smaller companies listed below. In the recent past, the latter have tended to offer significantly lower rates, but it always pays to compare. Begin your comparison shopping early, because the best deals may be booked to capacity quickly and may require payment 14 to 21 days or more before picking up the car.

Auto Europe (PO Box 1097, Camden, ME 04843; phone: 207-236-8235; 800-223-5555 throughout the US; 800-458-9503 in Canada). Offers rentals at over 15 locations in Spain.

Europe by Car (One Rockefeller Plaza, New York, NY 10020; phone: 212-581-3040 in New York State; 800-223-1516 elsewhere in the US; and 9000 Sunset Blvd., Los Angeles, CA 90069; phone: 800-252-9401 or 213-272-0424). Offers rentals in over 20 Spanish cities.

European Car Reservations (349 W. Commercial St., Suite 2950, East Rochester, NY 14445; phone: 800-535-3303). Offers rentals in 13 Spanish cities.

Foremost Euro-Car (5430 Van Nuys Blvd., Suite 306, Van Nuys, CA 91401; phone: 818-786-1960 or 800-272-3299 in California; 800-423-3111 elsewhere in the US). Offers rentals in Barcelona, Madrid, Málaga, and Seville.

Kemwel Group Inc. (106 Calvert St., Harrison, NY 10528; phone: 800-678-0678 or 914-835-5555). Offers rentals at 18 locations in Spain.

Meier's World Travel, Inc. (6033 W. Century Blvd., Suite 1080, Los Angeles, CA 90045; phone: 800-937-0700). In conjunction with major car rental companies arranges economical rentals throughout Spain.

One of the ways to keep the cost of car rentals down is to deal with a car rental consolidator, such as *Connex International* (23 N. Division St., Peekskill, NY 10566; phone: 800-333-3949 or 914-739-0066). *Connex*'s main business is negotiating with virtually all of the major car rental agencies for the lowest possible prices for its customers. This company arranges rentals throughout Europe, including Barcelona, Madrid, Málaga, Seville, and Torremolinos in Spain.

Local Rentals – It long has been common wisdom that the least expensive way to rent a car is to make arrangements in Europe. This is less true today than it used to be. Many medium to large European car rental companies have become the overseas suppliers of stateside companies such as those mentioned previously, and often the stateside agency, by dint of sheer volume, has been able to negotiate more favorable rates for its US customers than the European firm offers its own. Still lower rates may be found by searching out small, strictly local rental companies overseas, whether at less than prime addresses in major cities or in more remote areas. But to find them you must be willing to invest a sufficient amount of vacation time comparing prices on the scene. You also must be prepared to return the car to the location that rented it; drop-off possibilities are likely to be limited.

Once overseas, local branches of the National Tourist Office of Spain may be able to supply the names of Spanish car rental companies. The local yellow pages is another good place to begin. (For further information on local rental companies, see the individual reports in THE CITIES.)

In Spain, *Atesa* is a national car rental company with offices throughout the country. For information, contact *Atesa* (18 Rosario Piño, Madrid; phone: 1-572-0151; or 18 Calle Nicolas Estebañez, Las Palmas; phone: 28-277308), or look for locations at airports and metropolitan centers throughout Spain.

Also bear in mind that *Hertz* offers a rail-and-drive pass, called EurailDrive Escape, which is valid throughout all the countries that are included in the Eurail network, including Spain. (For further information on rail-and-drive packages, see *Traveling by Train,* above.)

Requirements – Whether you decide to rent a car in advance from a large international rental company with European branches or wait to rent from a local company, you should know that renting a car is rarely as simple as signing on the dotted line and roaring off into the night. If you are renting for personal use in Spain, you must have a valid driver's license, as well as an International Driving Permit (IDP), and will have to convince the renting agency that (1) you are personally creditworthy, and (2) you will bring the car back at the stated time. This will be easy if you have a major credit card; most rental companies accept credit cards in lieu of a cash deposit, as well as for payment of your final bill. If you prefer to pay in cash, leave your credit card imprint as a "deposit," then pay your bill in cash when you return the car.

If you are planning to rent a car once in Spain, *Avis, Budget, Hertz,* and other US rental companies usually *will* rent to travelers paying in cash and leaving either a credit card imprint or a substantial amount of cash as a deposit. This is not necessarily standard policy, however, some of the other international chains, and a number of local and regional European companies will *not* rent to an individual who doesn't have a valid credit card. In this case, you may have to call around to find a company that accepts cash.

Also keep in mind that although the minimum age to drive a car in Spain is 18 years, the minimum age to rent a car is set by the rental company. (Restrictions vary from company to company, as well as at different locations.) Many firms have a minimum age requirement of 21 years, some raise that to 23 or 25 years, and for some models of cars it rises to 30 years. The upper age limit at many companies is between 69 and 75; others have no upper limit or may make drivers above a certain age subject to special conditions.

Costs – Finding the most economical car rental will require some telephone shopping on your part. As a *general* rule, expect to hear lower prices quoted by the smaller, strictly local companies than by the well-known international names, with those of the national Spanish companies falling somewhere between the two.

Comparison shopping always is advisable, however, because the company that has the least expensive rentals in one country or city may not have the least expensive in another, and even the international giants offer discount plans whose conditions are easy for most travelers to fulfill. For instance, *Budget* and *National* offer discounts of anywhere from 10% to 30% off their usual rates (according to the size of the car and the duration of the rental), provided that the car is reserved a certain number of days before departure (usually 7 to 14 days, but it can be less), is rented for a minimum period (5 days or, more often, a week), is paid for at the time of booking, and, in most cases, is returned to the same location that supplied it or to another in the same country. Similar discount plans include *Hertz*'s Affordable Europe and *Avis*'s Supervalue Rates Europe.

If driving short distances for only a day or two, the best deal may be a per-day, per-mile (or per-kilometer) rate: You pay a flat fee for each day you keep the car, plus a per-mile (or per-kilometer) charge. An increasingly common alternative is to be granted a certain number of free miles or kilometers each day and then be charged on a per-mile or per-kilometer basis over that number.

A better alternative for touring the countryside may be a flat per-day rate with unlimited free mileage; this certainly is the most economical rate if you plan to drive over 100 miles (160 km). Make sure that the low, flat daily rate that catches your eye, however, is indeed a per-day rate: Often the lowest price advertised by a company turns out to be available only with a minimum 3-day rental — fine if you want the car that long, but not the bargain it appears if you really intend to use it no more than 24 hours for in-city driving. Flat weekly rates also are available, as are some flat monthly rates that represent a further saving over the daily rate. (*Note:* When renting a car in Spain, the term "mileage" may refer either to miles or kilometers.)

Another factor influencing cost is the type of car you rent. Rentals generally are based on a tiered price system, with different sizes of cars — variations of budget, economy, regular, and luxury — often listed as A (the smallest and least expensive) through F, G, or H, and sometimes even higher. Charges may increase by only a few dollars a day through several categories of subcompact and compact cars — where most of the competition is — then increase by great leaps through the remaining classes of full-size and luxury cars and passenger vans. The larger the car, the more it costs to rent and the more gas it consumes, but for some people the greater comfort and extra luggage space of a larger car (in which bags and sporting gear can be safely locked out of sight) may make it worth the additional expense. Be warned, too, that relatively few European cars have automatic transmissions, and those that do are more likely to be in the F than the A group. Similarly, cars with air conditioning are likely to be found in the more expensive categories only. Most expensive are sleek sports cars, but, again, for some people the thrill of driving such a car — for a week or a day — may be worth it.

Electing to pay for collision damage waiver (CDW) protection will add considerably to the cost of renting a car. You may be responsible for the *full value* of the vehicle being rented, but you can dispense with the possible obligation by buying the offered waiver at a cost of about $11 to $13 a day. Before making any decisions about optional collision damage waivers, check with your own insurance agent and determine whether your personal automobile insurance policy covers rented vehicles; if it does, you probably won't need to pay for the waiver. Be aware, too, that increasing numbers of credit cards automatically provide CDW coverage if the car rental is charged to the appropriate credit card. However, the specific terms of such coverage differ sharply among individual credit card companies, so check with the credit card company for information on the nature and amount of coverage provided. Business travelers also should be aware that, at the time of this writing, *American Express* had withdrawn its automatic CDW coverage from some corporate *Green* card accounts — watch for similar cutbacks by other credit card companies.

Overseas, the amount renters may be liable for should damage occur has not risen to the heights it has in the US. In addition, some European car rental agreements include collision damage coverage. In this case, the CDW supplement frees the renter from liability for the *deductible* amount — as opposed to the standard CDW coverage, described above, which releases the driver from liability for the full value of the car. In Spain, this deductible typically ranges from $1,500 to $2,500 at present, but can be more for some luxury car groups. As with the full collision damage waiver, the cost of waiving this liability — which be as high as $25 a day — is far from negligible, however. Drivers who rent cars in the US are often able to decline the CDW because many personal automobile insurance policies (subject to their own deductibles) extend to rental cars; unfortunately, such coverage usually does not extend to cars rented for use outside the US and Canada. Similarly, CDW coverage provided by some credit cards if the rental is charged to the card may be limited to cars rented in the US or Canada.

When inquiring about CDW coverage and costs, you should be aware that a number of the major international car rental companies now automatically are including the cost of this waiver in their quoted prices. This does not mean that they are absorbing this cost and you are receiving free coverage — total rental prices have increased to include the former CDW charge. The disadvantage of this inclusion is that you probably will not have the option to refuse this coverage, and will end up paying the added charge — even if you already are adequately covered by your own insurance policy or through a credit card company.

Additional costs to be added to the price tag include drop-off charges or one-way service fees. The lowest price quoted by any given company may apply only to a car that is returned to the same location from which it was rented. A slightly higher rate may be charged if the car is to be returned to a different location (even within the same city), and a considerably higher rate may prevail if the rental begins in one country and ends in another.

A further consideration: Don't forget that all car rentals are subject to Value Added Tax (VAT — known in Spain as IVA). This tax rarely is included in the rental price that's advertised or quoted, but it always must be paid — whether you pay in advance in the US or pay it when you drop off the car. In Spain, the VAT rate on car rentals is 12%; there is a wide variation in this tax from country to country.

One-way rentals bridging two countries used to be exempt from tax, but that is no longer the case. In general, the tax on one-way rentals is determined by the country in which the car has been rented, so if your tour plans include several countries, you should examine your options regarding the pick-up and drop-off points. Even if you intend to visit only one country, you still might consider a nearby country as a pick-up point if it will provide substantial savings.

Some rental agencies that do not maintain their own fleets use a contractor whose country of registration determines the rate of taxation. An example is *Kemwel Car Rental Europe,* whose one-way rentals from *most* countries are taxed at the Danish rate, 22% (rentals in Spain are taxed at the standard 12% rate). *Kemwel's* special programs offer savings to clients planning on touring throughout Europe (particularly where the tax rate is higher). The SuperSaver Plus and UniSaver Plus tariffs offer inclusive rentals in some 35 cities across Europe, including Barcelona and Madrid. These programs offer full insurance coverage (with a $100 deductible) and all European VAT, plus unlimited mileage. If part of a fly/drive package (see below) booked through *Kemwel,* rates may be even lower. Bookings must be reserved and paid for at least 7 days before delivery of the car, and the vehicle must be returned to the *Kemwel* station from which it originally was rented. For further information, contact *Kemwel Group Inc.,* 106 Calvert St., Harrison, NY 10528 (phone: 800-678-0678 or 914-835-5555).

Also, don't forget to factor in the price of gas. Rental cars usually are delivered with a full tank of gas. (This is not always the case, however, so check the gas gauge when picking up the car, and have the amount of gas noted on your rental agreement if the tank is not full.) Remember to fill the tank before you return the car or you will have to pay to refill it, and gasoline at the car rental company's pump always is much more expensive than at a service station. This policy may vary for smaller local and regional companies; ask when picking up the vehicle. Before you leave the lot, also check to be sure the rental car has a spare tire and jack in the trunk.

Finally, currency fluctuation is another factor to consider. Most brochures quote rental prices in US dollars, but these dollar amounts frequently are only guides; that is, they represent the prevailing rate of exchange at the time the brochure was printed. The rate may be very different when you call to make a reservation, and different again when the time comes to pay the bill (when the amount owed may be paid in cash in foreign currency or as a charge to a credit card, which is recalculated at a still later date's rate of exchange). Some companies guarantee rates in dollars (often for a slight surcharge), but this is an advantage only when the value of the dollar is steadily declining overseas. If the dollar is growing stronger in Spain, you may be better off with rates guaranteed in Spanish pesetas.

Fly/Drive Packages – Airlines, charter companies, car rental companies, and tour operators have been offering fly/drive packages for years, and even though the basic components of the package have changed somewhat — return airfare, a car waiting at the airport, and perhaps a night's lodging all for one inclusive price used to be the rule — the idea remains the same. You rent a car *here* for use *there* by booking it along with other arrangements for the trip. These days, the very minimum arrangement possible is the result of a tie-in between a car rental company and an airline, which entitles customers to a rental car for less than the company's usual rates, provided they show proof of having booked a flight on that airline.

Slightly more elaborate fly/drive packages are listed under various names (go-as-you-please, self-drive, or, simply, car tours) in the independent vacations sections of tour catalogues. Their most common ingredients are the rental car plus some sort of hotel voucher plan, with the applicable airfare listed separately. You set off on your trip with a block of prepaid accommodations vouchers, a list of hotels that accept them (usually members of a hotel chain or association), and a reservation for the first night's stay, after which the staff of each hotel books the next one for you or you make your own reservations. Naturally, the greater the number of establishments participating in the scheme, the more freedom you have to range at will during the day's driving and still be near a place to stay for the night. Less flexible car tours provide a rental car, a hotel plan, and a set itinerary that permits no deviation because the hotels all are reserved in advance.

The cost of these combination packages generally varies according to the size of the car and the quality of the hotels; there usually is an additional drop-off charge if the car is picked up in one city and returned in another. Most packages are offered at several different price levels, ranging from a standard plan covering stays in hotels to a budget plan using accommodations such as small inns or farmhouses. Airlines also have special rental car rates available when you book their flights, often with a flexible hotel voucher program. For information on available packages, check with the airline or your travel agent; also see *Package Tours,* in this section.

LEASING: Anyone planning to be in Europe for 3 weeks or more should compare the cost of renting a car with the cost of leasing one for the same period. While the money saved by leasing — rather than renting for a 23-day (the minimum) or 30-day period — may not be great, what is saved over the course of a long-term lease — 45, 60, 90 days, or more — amounts to hundreds, even thousands, of dollars. Part of the saving is due to the fact that leased cars are exempt from the stiff taxes applicable to rented cars. In addition, leasing plans provide for collision insurance with no deductible amount, so there is no need to add the daily cost of the collision damage waiver protection (an option offered by rental car companies — see above). A further advantage of a car lease — actually, a financed purchase/repurchase plan — is that you reserve your car by specific make and model rather than by group only, and it is delivered to you fresh from the factory.

Unfortunately, leasing as described above is offered only in Belgium and France, and the savings it permits can be realized to the fullest only if the cars are picked up and returned in these countries. While leased cars can be delivered to other countries there is a charge for this service, which can be as high as $350 in the case of Spanish cities, to which must be added an identical return charge. If you don't intend to keep the car very long, the two charges could nullify the amount saved by leasing rather than renting, so you will have to do some arithmetic.

It is possible to lease a car in countries other than Belgium and France, but most of the plans offered are best described as long-term rentals at preferential rates. They differ from true leasing in that you will pay tax and collision damage waiver protection (though it may be included in the quoted price), and the cars usually are late-model used cars rather than brand-new.

One of the major car leasing companies is *Renault,* offering leases of new cars for 23 days to 6 months. The cars are exempt from tax, all insurance is included, and there is no mileage charge. *Renault* offers free pick-up/drop-off in a number of French cities; substantial pick-up/drop-off charges apply to other selected European cities — including Madrid. For further information and reservations, ask your travel agent or contact *Renault USA,* 650 First Ave., New York, NY 10016 (phone: 212-532-1221 in New York State; 800-221-1052 elsewhere in the US).

Peugeot also offers a similar arrangement, called the Peugeot Vacation Plan. In accordance with the standard type of financed purchase/repurchase plan, travelers pick up the car in France, paying at the time of pick-up to use the car for a specific period of time (anywhere between 22 and 175 days), and at the end of this pre-arranged period return it to *Peugeot.* The tax-free temporary "purchase" includes unlimited mileage, factory warranty, full collision damage waiver coverage (no deductible), and 24-hour towing and roadside assistance. Pick-up and drop-off locations and charges are similar to *Renault*'s. *Peugeot*'s European Delivery program is a full-purchase program, including shipment of the car to the US, as discussed below. For further information, contact *Peugeot Motors of America* (1 Peugeot Plaza, Lyndhurst, NJ 07071; phone: 201-935-8400). Some of the car rental firms listed above — *Auto-Europe, Foremost Euro-Car,* and *Kemwel Group* — also arrange European car leases.

BUYING A CAR: If your plans include both buying a new car of European make and a driving tour of Europe, it's possible to combine the two ventures and save some money on each. By buying the car abroad and using it during your vacation, you pay quite a bit less for it than the US dealer would charge and at the same time avoid the expense of renting a car during your holiday. There are two basic ways to achieve this desired end, but one, factory delivery, is far simpler than the other, direct import.

Factory delivery means that you place an order for a car in the US, then pick it up in Europe, often literally at the factory gate. It also means that your new car is built to American specifications, complying with all US emission and safety standards. Because of this, only cars made by manufacturers who have established a formal program for such sales to American customers can be bought at the factory. At present, the list includes Audi, BMW, Jaguar, Mercedes-Benz, Peugeot, Porsche, Saab, Volkswagen, and Volvo, among others (whose manufacturers generally restrict their offerings to those models they ordinarily export to the US). The factory delivery price, in US dollars, usually runs about 5% to 15% below the sticker price of the same model at a US dealership and includes the cost of shipping the car home. All contracts include US customs duty, but the cost of the incidentals and the insurance necessary for driving the car around Europe are extra except in BMW's plan, where those costs are included.

One of the few disadvantages of factory delivery is that car manufacturers make only a limited number of models available each year, and for certain popular models you may have to get in line early in the season. Another is that you must take your trip when the car is ready, not when you are, although you usually will have 8 to 10 weeks' notice. The actual place of delivery can vary; it is more economical to pick up the car at the factory, but arrangements sometimes — but not always — can be made to have it delivered elsewhere for an extra charge. For example, Jaguars must be ordered through a US dealer and picked up at the factory in Coventry, England, although they also can be dropped off for shipment home in any number of European cities. For information, write to *Jaguar Cars,* 555 MacArthur Blvd., Mahwah, NJ 07430 (phone: 201-818-8500).

Cars for factory delivery usually can be ordered either through one of the manufacturer's authorized dealers in the US or through companies — among them *Europe by Car, Foremost Euro-Car,* and *Kemwel Group* (see above for contact information) —

that specialize in such transactions. (Note that *Foremost Euro-Car* serves all of the US for rentals and leasing, but they arrange *sales* only for California residents.) Another company arranging car sales abroad is *Ship Side Tax Free World on Wheels BV,* 600B Lake St., Suite A, Ramsey, NJ 07446 (phone: 201-818-0400).

Occasionally an auto manufacturer offers free or discounted airfare in connection with a European delivery program. This year, Mercedes-Benz has a program including discounted round-trip airfare ($500 for two economy fare seats or one business class seat) from any US gateway served by *Delta, Lufthansa,* or *Swissair* to Stuttgart (where the buyer picks up the car), plus a 2-night stay at the local *Ramada* or *Hilton* hotel, and 15 days' free comprehensive road insurance. For details, contact *Mercedes-Benz of North America,* 1 Mercedes Dr., Montvale, NJ 07645 (phone: 800-458-8202).

The other way to buy a car abroad, **direct import**, sometimes is referred to as "gray market" buying. It is perfectly legal, but not totally hassle-free. Direct import means that you buy abroad a car that was meant for use abroad, not one built according to US specifications. It can be new or used and may even include — if made for use in Ireland or Great Britain — a steering wheel on the right side. The main drawback to direct import is that the process of modification to bring the car into compliance with US standards is expensive and time-consuming: It typically costs from $5,000 to $7,000 in parts and labor and takes from 2 to 6 months. In addition, the same shipping, insurance, and miscellaneous expenses (another $2,000 to $5,000, according to estimates) that would be included in the factory delivery price must be added to the purchase price of the car, and the considerable burden of shepherding it on its journey from showroom to home garage usually is borne by the purchaser. Direct-import dealers do exist (they are not the same as your local, factory-authorized foreign car dealer, with whom you are now in competition), but even if you use one, you still need to do a great deal of paperwork yourself.

Once upon a time, the main advantage of the direct import method — besides the fact that it can be used for makes and models not available on factory delivery programs — was that much more money could be saved importing an expensive car. Given today's exchange rates, however, the method's potential greater gain is harder to realize and must be weighed against its greater difficulties. Still, if direct importing interests you, you can obtain a list of those makes and models approved for conversion in this country, and of the converters licensed to bring them up to US specifications, by contacting the Environmental Protection Agency, Manufacturers' Operations Division, EN-340-F, Investigations/Imports Section, 401 M St. SW, Washington, DC 20460 (phone: 202-382-2505).

If you have special problems getting your car into the US, you might consider contacting a specialist in vehicle importation, such as Daniel Kokal, a regulatory consultant with *Techlaw,* 14500 Avion Parkway, Suite 300, Chantilly, VA 22021 (phone: 703-818-1000).

Package Tours

If the mere thought of buying a package for travel to and through Spain conjures up visions of a race through ten cities in as many days in lockstep with a horde of frazzled fellow travelers, remember that packages have come a long way. For one thing, not all packages necessarily are escorted tours, and the one you buy does not have to include any organized touring at all — nor will it necessarily include traveling companions. If it does, however, you'll find that people of all sorts — many just like yourself — are taking advantage of packages today because they are economical and convenient, save you an immense amount of planning time, and exist in such variety that it's virtually impossible not to find one that suits at least the majority of your travel preferences. Given the high cost of travel these days, packages have emerged as a particularly wise buy.

In essence, a package is just an amalgam of travel services that can be purchased in a single transaction. A package (tour or otherwise) to and through Spain may include any or all of the following: round-trip transatlantic transportation, local transportation (and/or car rentals), accommodations, some or all meals, sightseeing, entertainment, transfers to and from the hotel at each destination, taxes, tips, escort service, and a variety of incidental features that might be offered as options at additional cost. In other words, a package can be any combination of travel elements, from a fully escorted tour offered at an all-inclusive price to a simple fly/drive booking allowing you to move about totally on your own. Its principal advantage is that it saves money: The cost of the combined arrangements invariably is well below the price of all of the same elements if bought separately, and particularly if transportation is provided by charter or discount flight, the whole package could cost less than just a round-trip economy airline ticket on a regularly scheduled flight. A package provides more than economy and convenience: It releases the traveler from having to make individual arrangements for each separate element of a trip.

Tour programs generally can be divided into two categories — "escorted" (or locally hosted) and "independent." An escorted tour means that a guide will accompany the group from the beginning of the tour through to the return flight; a locally hosted tour means that the group will be met upon arrival at each location by a different local host. On independent tours, there generally is a choice of hotels, meal plans, and sightseeing trips in each city, as well as a variety of special excursions. The independent plan is for travelers who do not want a totally set itinerary, but who do prefer confirmed hotel reservations. Whether choosing an escorted or independent tour, always bring along complete contact information for your tour operator in case a problem arises, although US tour operators often have European affiliates who can give additional assistance or make other arrangements on the spot.

To determine whether a package — or, more specifically, *which* package — fits your travel plans, start by evaluating your interests and needs, deciding how much and what you want to spend, see, and do. Gather whatever package tour information is available for your schedule. Be sure that you take the time to read the brochure *carefully* to determine precisely what is included. Keep in mind that travel brochures are written to entice you into signing up for a package tour. Often the language is deceptive and devious. For example, a brochure may quote the lowest prices for a package tour based on facilities that are unavailable during the off-season, undesirable at any season, or just plain nonexistent. Information such as "breakfast included" (as it often is in packages to Spain) or "plus tax" (which can add up) should be taken into account. Note, too, that the prices quoted in brochures almost always are based on double occupancy: The rate listed is for each of two people sharing a double room, and if you travel alone, the supplement for single accommodations can raise the price considerably (see *Hints for Single Travelers,* in this section).

In this age of erratic airfares, the brochure most often will *not* include the price of an airline ticket in the price of the package, though sample fares from various gateway cities usually will be listed separately, to be added to the price of the ground arrangements. Before figuring your actual cost, check the latest fares with the airlines, because the samples invariably are out of date by the time you read them. If the brochure gives more than one category of sample fares per gateway city — such as an individual tour-basing fare, a group fare, an excursion, APEX, or other discount ticket — your travel agent or airline tour desk will be able to tell you which one applies to the package you choose, depending on when you travel, how far in advance you book, and other factors. (An individual tour-basing fare is a fare computed as part of a package that includes land arrangements, thereby entitling a carrier to reduce the air portion almost to the absolute minimum. Though it always represents a savings over full-fare coach or economy, lately the individual tour-basing fare has not been as inexpensive as the excursion and other discount fares that also are available to individuals. The group fare usually is the least expensive fare, and it is the tour operator, not you, who makes up the group.) When the brochure does include round-trip transportation in the package price, don't forget to add the cost of round-trip transportation from your home to the departure city to come up with the total cost of the package.

Finally, read the general information regarding terms and conditions and the responsibility clause (usually in fine print at the end of the descriptive literature) to determine the precise elements for which the tour operator is — and is not — liable. Here the tour operator frequently expresses the right to change services or schedules as long as equivalent arrangements are offered. This clause also absolves the operator of responsibility for circumstances beyond human control, such as floods, or injury to you or your property. While reading, ask the following questions:

1. Does the tour include airfare or other transportation, sightseeing, meals, transfers, taxes, baggage handling, tips, or any other services? Do you want all these services?
2. If the brochure indicates that "some meals" are included, does this mean a welcoming and farewell dinner, two breakfasts, or every evening meal?
3. What classes of hotels are offered? If you will be traveling alone, what is the single supplement?
4. Does the tour itinerary or price vary according to the season?
5. Are the prices guaranteed; that is, if costs increase between the time you book and the time you depart, can surcharges unilaterally be added?
6. Do you get a full refund if you cancel? If not, be sure to obtain cancellation insurance.
7. Can the operator cancel if too few people join? At what point?

One of the consumer's biggest problems is finding enough information to judge the reliability of a tour packager, since individual travelers seldom have direct contact with the firm putting the package together. Usually, a retail travel agent is interposed between customer and tour operator, and much depends on his or her candor and cooperation. So ask a number of questions about the tour you are considering. For example:

- Has the travel agent ever used a package provided by this tour operator?
- How long has the tour operator been in business? Check the Better Business Bureau in the area where the tour operator is based to see if any complaints have been filed against it.
- Is the tour operator a member of the *United States Tour Operators Association* (*USTOA;* 211 E. 51st St., Suite 12B, New York, NY 10022; phone: 212-944-5727)? The *USTOA* will provide a list of its members upon request; it also offers a useful brochure, *How to Select a Package Tour.*
- How many and which companies are involved in the package?
- If air travel is by charter flight, is there an escrow account in which deposits will be held; if so, what is the name of the bank?

This last question is very important. US law requires that tour operators place every charter passenger's deposit and subsequent payment in a proper escrow account. Money paid into such an account cannot legally be used except to pay for the costs of a particular package or as a refund if the trip is canceled. To ensure the safe handling of your money, make your check payable to the escrow account — by law, the name of the depository bank must appear in the operator-participant contract and usually is found in that mass of minuscule type on the back of the brochure. Write the details of the charter, including the destination and dates, on the face of the check; on the back, print "For Deposit Only." Your travel agent may prefer that you make your check out to the agency, saying that it will then pay the tour operator the fee minus commission. But it is perfectly legal to write your check as we suggest, and if your agent objects too strongly (the agent should have sufficient faith in the tour operator to trust him to send the proper commission), consider taking your business elsewhere. If you don't make your check out to the escrow account, you lose the protection of that escrow should the trip be canceled or the tour operator or travel agent fail. Furthermore, recent bankruptcies in the travel industry have served to point out that even the protection of escrow may not be enough to safeguard your investment. Increasingly, insurance is becoming a necessity (see *Insurance,* in this section), and payment by credit card has become popular since it offers some additional safeguards if the tour operator defaults.

■ **A word of advice:** Purchasers of vacation packages who feel they're not getting their money's worth are more likely to get a refund if they complain in writing to the operator — and bail out of the whole package immediately. Alert the tour operator or resort manager to the fact that you are dissatisfied, that you will be leaving for home as soon as transportation can be arranged, and that you expect a refund. They may have forms to fill out detailing your complaint; otherwise, state your case in a letter. Even if the availability of transportation home detains you, your dated, written complaint should help in procuring a refund from the operator.

SAMPLE PACKAGES TO SPAIN: There are so many packages available to Spain that it's probably safe to say that just about any arrangement anyone might want is available for as long as it is wanted. The keynote is flexibility. Some packages tour the country, while others explore only a selected region or visit only major cities.

Escorted Tours – Those seeking the maximum in structure will find that the classic sightseeing tour by motorcoach, fully escorted and all-inclusive (or nearly), has withstood the test of time and still is well represented among the programs of major tour operators. Typically, these tours begin in a major city and last from 1 to 2 weeks. A good many tour operators also offer at least one package that rounds out a visit to Spain with a trip across the Strait of Gibraltar to Morocco, sometimes exploring that country in depth, sometimes going no farther than the port city of Tangier. Others offer such tours of Spain in combination with Portugal and/or other European destinations.

Andalusia and its Mediterranean shore, the Costa del Sol, are by far the areas most frequently visited on escorted tours of Spain, a good many of which take in these popular areas alone, either making a long, narrow loop starting and ending in Madrid or beginning in Madrid and ending in Málaga, where participants board a plane for their flight home. Tours with more time to spare may broaden the loop to include such cities as Barcelona and Valencia en route to or from Andalusia. Some packages avoid Andalusia entirely, however, and focus their attention elsewhere.

Andalusia and the Costa del Sol also figure prominently on combined Spain-Portugal trips, which frequently begin in Madrid, turn south and make their way around Andalusia to Seville, and cross the Spanish border and Portugal's Alentejo Plains to Lisbon. The same itinerary in reverse — Lisbon to Madrid — also is common, as is a full circle, Madrid to Madrid or Lisbon to Lisbon. In this case, the northern link generally is via the cities of Salamanca and Avila, the Beira Mountains, and the Portuguese city of Coimbra.

Hotel accommodations in these packages usually are characterized as first class or better, with private baths or showers accompanying all rooms, although more than a few tour packagers offer less expensive alternatives by providing more modest lodgings. These packages tend to be all-inclusive, although the number of included meals may vary considerably. Among such packages are the following:

Abercrombie & Kent (1420 Kensington Rd., Oak Brook, IL 60521; phone: 708-954-2944 in Illinois; 800-323-7308 elsewhere in the US). Offers all-inclusive package tours that take care of just about everything — right down to a traveling bellhop to handle your baggage. These tours, which are grouped under the heading Great Britain and Europe Express Tours, include packages to Spain, and as the name implies transportation is mainly via rail.

Abreu Tours (317 E. 34th St., New York, NY 10016; phone: 800-223-1580 or 212-661-0555). Offers 6- or 15-day escorted motorcoach tours throughout Spain. Other packages tour both Spain and Portugal.

AIB Tours (3798 Flagler, Coral Gables, FL 33134; phone: 305-442-0246; 800-232-0242 in Florida; 800-242-8687 elsewhere in the US). Their 7-day tour visits Andalusia (as well as destinations in Portugal).

American Express Travel Related Services (offices throughout the US; phone: 800-241-1700 for information and local branch offices). On their motorcoach tours of Europe, travelers can choose from a number of different itineraries, such as the Iberian Sun Seeker 14-day, 7-city package (which visits Granada, Madrid, and Seville) and the Moroccan Fiesta 17-day, 11-city tour (which also visits Córdoba).

Globus-Gateway **and** *Cosmos* (95-25 Queens Blvd., Rego Park, NY 11374; phone: 800-221-0090; or 150 S. Los Robles Ave., Pasadena, CA 91101; phone: 818-449-2019 or 800-556-5454). These affiliated agencies offer numerous tours of Europe, including a 12-day Best of Spain and Portugal package; a 14-day Spain-Portugal-Tangier itinerary; a 15-day Spain-Portugal-Morocco tour; and a 23-day Treasures of France, Spain, and Portugal tour. (Bookings for both agencies must be made through travel agents; however, both can be contacted for information.)

Maupintour (PO Box 807, Lawrence, KS 66044; phone: 800-255-4266). Offers several round-trip tours from Lisbon that visit Spanish destinations, such as Granada, Madrid, and Seville. Their Majorca, Spain, and Portugal Tour visits these cities, plus Barcelona and Palma de Mallorca, and the Pousadas and Paradores tour deviates from the norm by scheduling the majority of overnights in these government-run establishments.

Melia International (450 Seventh Ave., Suite 1805, New York, NY 10103; phone: 212-967-6565 in New York State; 800-848-2314 elsewhere in the US). Offers 7- and 14-day tours of the Iberian Peninsula that visit La Coruña, Lugo, Madrid, Rías Bajas, and Vigo.

Olson Travelworld (100 N. Sepulveda Blvd., Suite 1010, El Segundo, CA 90245; phone: 213-615-0711; 800-421-5785 in California; 800-421-2255 elsewhere in the US). Offers escorted, highly structured packages to Spain, including a 22-day Casbah and Castinets tour that takes in Córdoba, Costa del Sol, Madrid, Seville, Tangier, and Toledo, and a 17-day deluxe Connoisseur's Iberia tour of Spain, Portugal, and Gibraltar.

Skyline Travel Club (666 Old Country Rd., Suite 205, Garden City, NY 11530; phone 516-222-9090 or 800-645-6198). Offers a variety of 11- to 13-day motorcoach itineraries, including a tour of Andalusia and Madrid, and a package visting Barcelona, Málaga, and Madrid.

Thomas Cook (Headquarters: 45 Berkeley St., Piccadilly, London W1A 1EB; phone: 44-71-499-4000). The best known of all British tour operators, its name is practically synonymous with the Grand Tour of Europe, but *Cook*'s wide range of itineraries spans the world. Among the packages to Spain are a 14-day escorted motorcoach tour visiting Costa del Sol, Madrid, Málaga, Salamanca, and Seville. Other tour and stay-put packages also are offered. (Note that although this company is a wholesaler, you can book a tour directly through any of its offices in major cities in North America or through travel agents.)

Trafalgar Tours (21 E. 26th St., New York, NY 10010; phone: 212-689-8977 in New York City; 800-854-0103 elsewhere in the US). Offers numerous first class (as well as some budget) motorcoach itineraries of the Continent. Among the regular itineraries is a 14-day, 8-city, Highlights of Spain and Portugal motorcoach tour. (As this operator is a wholesaler, bookings must be made through a travel agent.)

Travcoa (PO Box 2630, Newport Beach, CA 92658; phone: 714-476-2800; 800-992-2004 in California; 800-992-2003 elsewhere in the US). Offers a lineup of escorted motorcoach tours, including 18-, 26-, or 29-day packages in Spain that include all meals.

TWA Getaway Tours (phone: 800-GETAWAY). Offers a wide variety of escorted motorcoach tours throughout Europe, including Spain.

Independent Tours – Less restrictive arrangements for travelers who prefer more independence than that found on escorted tours are listed in the semi-escorted and hosted sections of tour catalogues. These may combine some aspects of an escorted tour, such as moving from place to place by motorcoach, with longer stays in one spot, where participants are at liberty but where a host or hostess — that is, a representative of the tour company — is available at a local office or even in the hotel to answer questions and assist in arranging activities and optional excursions.

Another equally common type of package to Spain is the car tour or fly/drive arrangement, often described in brochures as a self-drive or go-as-you-please tour. These are independent vacations, geared to travelers who want to cover as much ground as they might on an escorted group sightseeing tour but who prefer to do it on their own. The most flexible plans include no more than a map, a rental car, and a block of as many prepaid hotel vouchers as are needed for the length of the stay (the packages typically are 4 or 7 days long, extendable by individual extra days or additional package segments), along with a list of participating hotels at which the vouchers are accepted. In most cases, only the first night's accommodation is reserved; from then on, travelers book their rooms one stop ahead as they drive from place to place, creating their own itinerary as they go. When the hotels are members of a chain or association — which they usually are — the staff of the last hotel will reserve the next one for you. In other cases, there may be a choice of reserving all accommodations before departure — usually for a fee. Operators offering these packages usually sell vouchers in more than one price category; travelers may have the option of upgrading accommodations by paying a supplement directly to more expensive establishments. Another type of fly/drive arrangement is slightly more restrictive in that the tour packager supplies an itinerary that must be followed day by day, with a specific hotel to be reached each night. Often these plans are more deluxe as well.

AutoVenture (425 Pike St., Suite 502, Seattle, WA 98101; phone: 206-624-6033 in Washington State; 800-426-7502 elsewhere in the US). Their deluxe car tours feature overnight stays in hotels that are elegant converted castles or manor houses or old and distinctive country inns. Some itineraries, which range from 6 to 14 days in length, cover Spain and can be bought in either a self-drive or chauffeured version.

Cavalcade Tours (450 Harmon Meadow Blvd., Secaucus, NJ 07094; phone: 800-356-2405). In conjunction with international car rental companies, offers a variety of European fly/drive programs, including Spain. (As this tour operator is a wholesaler, bookings must be made through a travel agent.)

Extra Value Travel (683 S. Collier Blvd., Marco Island, FL 33937; phone: 800-255-2847). In conjunction with international car rental companies, arranges custom self-drive tours throughout Spain.

Ibero Travel (109-21 72nd Rd., Forest Hills, New York, NY 11375; phone: 800-654-2376 in New York State; 800-882-6678 elsewhere in the US). Offers packages featuring accommodations in *paradores,* primarily in metropolitan locations.

Marsans International Travel (90 W. 34th St., Suite 302, New York, NY 10001; phone: 212-239-3880 in New York State; 800-777-9110 elsewhere in the US). Packages 3- to 7-day car rental packages that can be booked along with airfare and accommodations for a custom fly/drive package.

Stay-Put City and Resort Packages – A further possibility for independent travelers is a "stay-put" package, such as the popular Spanish city packages. These appeal to travelers who want to be on their own and remain in one place for the duration of their vacation, although it is not unusual for travelers to buy more than one package at a time. Basically the city package — no matter what the city — includes round-trip transfer between airport and hotel, a choice of hotel accommodations (usually including breakfast) in several price ranges, plus any number of other features you may not need or want but would lose valuable time arranging if you did. Common package features are 1 or 2 half-day guided tours of the city; a boat cruise; passes for unlimited local travel by bus or train; discount cards for shops, museums, and restaurants; temporary membership in and admission to clubs, discotheques, or other nightspots; and car rental for some or all of your stay. Other features may include anything from a souvenir travel bag to a tasting of local wines, dinner, and a show. The packages usually are a week long — although 4-day and 14-day packages also are available, and most packages can be extended by extra days — and often are hosted; that is, a representative of the tour company may be available at a local office or even in the hotel to answer questions, handle problems, and assist in arranging activities and option excursions. A similar stay-put resort package generally omits the sightseeing tour and may offer some sort of daily meal plan if accommodations are in hotels; accommodations in apartment hotels with kitchenettes are a common alternative.

Among the stay-put packages offered in Spain are the following:

Abreu Tours (317 E. 34th St., New York, NY 10016; phone: 800-223-1580 or 212-661-0555). Offers 3- to 6-night packages of Barcelona and Madrid.

American Express Travel Related Services (offices throughout the US; phone: 800-241-1700 for information and local branch offices). Offers 3- to 6-night city packages in Barcelona, Córdoba, Madrid, and Seville.

Marsans International (19 W. 34th St., Suite 302, New York, NY 10001; phone: 212-239-3880 in New York State; 800-223-6114 elsewhere in the US). Offers 3- to 6-night packages in Barcelona, Granada, Madrid, and Seville.

Mill-Run Tours (20 E. 49th St., New York, NY 10017; phone: 212-486-9840 in New York State, 800-MILL-RUN elsewhere). Offers 3-night packages in Barcelona and Madrid.

Petrabax Tours (97-45 Queens Blvd., Suite 505, Rego Park, NY 11374; phone: 718-897-7272 in New York State, 800-367-6611 elsewhere). Offers 3-night packages in Madrid and Seville.

Spanish Heritage Tours (116-47 Queens Blvd., Forest Hills, NY 11375; phone: 718-520-1300 or 800-221-2580). Offers 6-night packages in Barcelona, Madrid, and Seville.

TWA Getaway Tours (phone: 800-GETAWAY). Offers numerous city packages throughout Europe, including Madrid.

The Spanish resort areas most frequently found on combination city/resort packages are on the Costa del Sol, particularly Torremolinos and Marbella, and the islands of Majorca (the capital, Palma de Mallorca, is the usual choice for hotels) and Ibiza in the Balearics and Gran Canaria and Tenerife in the Canary Islands (where Las Palmas and Puerto de la Cruz, respectively, are the main hotel sites). A third island of the Canaries, Lanzarote, is available on some programs. Besides the tour operators mentioned above, so many others offer packages to one or more of these resorts (often in combination with cities or other resorts) that it's best to consult a travel agent or, since many of these packages are run in conjunction with *Iberia Airlines,* deal directly with that airline.

A good example of a stay-put vacation is the resort package offered by *Club Med* (40 W. 57th St., New York, NY 10019; phone: 800-CLUB-MED), which operates its own resort villages around the world and has five resorts in Spain — one each in Barcelona, Cádiz, Ibiza, Marbella, and Palma de Mallorca.

Special-Interest Packages – Special-interest tours are a growing sector of the travel industry. Programs focusing on food and wine are prominent among the packages of this sort. Note, though, that they tend to be quite structured arrangements rather than independent ones, and they rarely are created with the budget traveler in mind. Also note that inclusive as they may be, few food and wine tours include *all* meals in the package price. This is not necessarily a cost-cutting technique on the part of the packager; rather, because of the lavishness of some of the meals, others may be left to the discretion of the participants, not only to allow time for leisure, but also to allow for differing rates of metabolism. Similarly, even on wine tours that spend entire days in practically full-time tasting, unlimited table wine at meals may not always be included in the package price. The brochures usually are clear about what comes with the package and when.

Among the various food and wine tours are *Bacchants' Pilgrimages'* tours of vineyards and wine cellars. Included are winery-hosted luncheons, picnics, dinners in world class restaurants, and other luncheons and dinners in restaurants of lesser renown. This year's itineraries will include a tour to Spain, in combination with Portugal. Bookings are through travel agents or *Bacchants' Pilgrimages* (475 Sansome St., Suite 850, San Francisco, CA 94111; phone: 415-981-8518). And for groups of 10 or more travelers, *Travel Concepts* (62 Commonwealth Ave., Suite 3, Boston, MA 02116; phone: 617-266-8450) offers a variety of custom-designed food and wine tours throughout Europe. Although there is no pre-planned itinerary in Spain, they can design one for individuals or groups.

There also are special-interest packages catering to travelers particularly interested in the arts and/or cultural studies. Among these are the packages for music and opera lovers offered by *Dailey-Thorp* (315 W. 57th St., New York, NY 10019; phone: 212-307-1555), which focus on European musical events and often visit Spanish cities such as Barcelona, Madrid, and Seville. *Prospect Art Tours* (454-458 Chiswick High Rd., London W45TT, England; phone: 44-81-995-2151 or 44-81-995-2163) offers 5- to 11-day packages visiting key museums, private galleries, and art collections throughout Europe, including Spain.

The prehistoric cave art of northern Spain can be explored on *Past Time Tours'* 14-day package. The tour includes educational lectures and a look at some of the world's most intriguing prehistoric ritual art and symbols. For information, contact *Past Time Tours,* 800 Larch La., Sacramento, CA 95864-5042 (phone: 916-485-8140).

Although there are resorts in northern Spain where it is possible to enjoy a skiing holiday, actual ski packages (other than those offered by the individual resorts) usually are not available. Those interested in such a trip will have to do some investigation and book through a knowledgeable travel agent or on their own. (For a start see *Sensational Spanish Skiing,* DIVERSIONS.)

Golf courses in many European countries are a fairly new addition; however, the courses in Spain have been around for quite some time. Among the companies offering golf tours to Spain are the following:

Adventure Golf Holiday (815 North Rd., Westfield, MA 01085; phone: 800-628-9655 or 413-568-2855). Offers packages to Spain's Costa del Sol.

Adventures in Golf (29 Valencia Dr., Nashua, NH 03062; phone: 603-882-8367). Offers custom-designed golf holidays in Spain.

Fourth Dimension Tours (1150 NW 72nd Ave., Miami, FL 33126; phone: 800-343-0020 or 305-477-1525). Arranges group tours (for 20 or more) to the Costa del Sol.

Golf Intercontinental/Marsans (19 W. 34 St., New York, NY 10001; phone: 212-239-3880 in New York State; 800-223-6114 elsewhere in the US). Offers a 7-day self-drive tour through Spain — for serious golfers only.

Golfing Holidays (231 E. Millbrae Ave., Millbrae, CA 94030; phone: 415-697-0230). Arranges customized golf tours to the Costa del Sol and in the vicinity of Madrid.

InterGolf (1980 Sherbrooke St. W., Suite 210, Montreal, Quebec H3H 1E8, Canada; phone: 514-933-2772). Offers self-drive golf tours throughout Spain.

ITC Golf Tours (Box 5144, Long Beach, CA 90805; phone: 800-257-4981 or 213-595-6905). Arranges custom golf packages anywhere and any way you want it — including in Spain.

Perry Golf (8302 Dunwoodie Pl., Suite 305, Atlanta, GA 30350; phone: 800-344-5257 or 404-641-9696). Has fly/drive golf packages to the Costa del Sol.

Petrabax (97-45 Queens Blvd., Rego Park, NY 11374; phone: 800-367-6611 or 718-897-7272). Offers individual or group packages to Spain's Costa del Sol.

Value Holidays (10224 N. Port Washington Rd., Mequon, WI 53092; phone: 800-558-6850). Offers golf packages to the Costa del Sol.

Wide World of Golf (PO Box 5217, Su Vecino Court, Carmel, CA 93921; phone: 408-624-6667). Offers a 10-day golf package to the Costa del Sol.

Horseback riding holidays are the province of *FITS Equestrian* (2011 Alamo Pintado Rd., Solvang, CA 93463; phone: 800-666-FITS or 805-688-9494), which offers 8-day riding packages that tour the Costa del Sol. *Equitour* (Bitterroot Ranch, Rte. 66, Box 1042, Dubois, WY 82513; phone: 307-455-3363 in Wyoming; 800-545-0019 elsewhere in the US) also offers packages — not for beginners — that include 8 days of riding in Guadalupe with accommodations in a hunting lodge. Most rides are on spirited Andalusian steeds.

Fisherfolk might enjoy the opportunity to fish for salmon in Spain that's offered by *Fishing International* (Hilltop Estate, 4010 Montecito Ave., Santa Rosa CA 95404; phone: 800-950-4242 or 707-542-4242). These week-long packages include accommodations in a small country inn and breakfast daily, and the opportunity to exchange fish stories about the one that got away. This company also designs custom fishing packages.

And for marksmen interested in trying their hands at shooting red-legged partridge in Spain, *Frontiers International* (PO Box 161, Pearce Mill Rd., Wexford, PA 15090; phone: 412-935-1577 in Pennsylvania; 800-245-1950 elsewhere in the US) offers two deluxe 3- and 4-day shooting packages in La Mancha. Accommodations are in a gracious manor house; all meals, cocktails, tips, and even shotgun shells are included. Assistants clean, carry, and load your gun, and guests also can enjoy riding the estate's fine Spanish mounts.

Special-interest tours for practitioners and spectators of other sports include many biking and hiking tours at varying levels of difficulty. For the names and addresses of their organizers, see below.

Sports enthusiasts may want to attend the *1992 Summer Olympics,* which will be hosted by Barcelona. *Olson Travelworld* (address above) is the official tour operator for this year's *Summer Olympics* and will be offering packages including in-city accommodations and tickets to individual sporting events. Other companies, such as *Melia International* (address above) also will be offering similar packages. If you are considering attending the *Olympics,* check with a travel agent well in advance.

Another special event that will be drawing travelers to Spain this year is *Expo 92',* the world's fair being held in Seville and the main event of Spain's year-long celebration of the 500th anniversary of Columbus's discovery of America. Among the tour packagers planning to offer a package tour including local accommodations, admission to the exhibitions, and other features, are *Maupintour, Melia International, Olson Travelworld, Thomas Cook* (again, for addresses, see above). If you are planning to attend *Expo* or stay anywhere in the vicinity of Seville around April 20 through October 12, make plans as early as possible.

Camping and Caravanning, Hiking and Biking

CAMPING AND CARAVANNING: Spain welcomes campers, whether they come alone or with a group, with tents or in recreational vehicles — generally known in Europe as "caravans" (a term that technically refers to towable campers as opposed to fully motorized vehicles, known as "minibuses" or "minivans"). Camping probably is the best way to enjoy the countryside. And, fortunately, campgrounds in Spain are plentiful.

Where to Camp – Caravanning is extremely popular with European vacationers, and many parks cater more to the caravanner than to the tent dweller. Some campgrounds have minimal facilities, and others are quite elaborate, with a variety of amenities on the premises. Most sites are open from about *Easter* through October.

Directors of campgrounds often have a great deal of information about their region, and some even will arrange local tours or recommend sports facilities or attractions in the immediate area. Campgrounds also provide the atmosphere and opportunity to meet other travelers and exchange useful information. Too much so, sometimes — the popularity of European campgrounds causes them to be quite crowded during the summer, and campsites can be so close together that any attempt at privacy or getting away from it all is sabotaged. As campgrounds fill quickly throughout the season, and the more isolated sites always go first, it's a good idea to arrive early in the day and reserve your chosen spot — which leaves you free to explore the area for the rest of the day. (Whenever possible, try to call ahead and arrange a "pitch" in advance. At the height of the season, however, if you do not have advance reservations, you may be lucky to get even a less desirable site.)

In some communities, it is possible to camp free on public grounds. As the local police or local tourism information office about regulations. To camp on private property you first must obtain the permission of the landowner or tenant — and assume the responsibility of leaving the land exactly as it was found in return for the hospitality.

Spanish campgrounds generally are well marked. Still, it's best to have a map or check the information available in one of the numerous comprehensive guides to sites across the Continent. It may not be easy to find camping facilities open before June or after September, so a guide that gives this information comes in particularly handy off-season.

In the US, maps, brochures, and other information for campers are distributed by the National Tourist Office of Spain, including a comprehensive guide, *Guía de Campings* (which is available in English). A variety of useful publications also are available from American and European automobile clubs and other associations.

The *American Automobile Association (AAA)* offers a number of useful resources, including its 600-page *Travel Guide to Europe* and the 64-page *Motoring Europe,* as well as a variety of useful maps; contact the nearest branch of *AAA* or the national office (see *Traveling by Car,* in this section). In addition, the *Automobile Association of Great Britain (AA)* publishes a comprehensive guide, *Camping and Caravanning in Europe* ($12.95), which lists about 4,000 sites throughout Europe, inspected and rated by the *AA,* and provides other information of interest to campers. It is available from the *AA* (Farnum House, Basingstoke, Hampshire RG21 2EA, England). Another useful book, *Camper's Companion to Southern Europe,* which gives camping information for Spain, is out of print. Look for it in your local library.

The French international camping organization *Fédération Internationale de Camping et Caravaning* issues a pass, called a *carnet,* that entitles the bearer to a modest discount at many campgrounds throughout Europe, including Spain. It is available in the US from the *National Campers and Hikers Association* (4804 Transit Rd., Bldg. 2, Depew, NY 14043; phone: 716-668-6242) for a fee of $23, which includes membership in the organization as well as camping information.

Most experienced campers prefer to bring their own tried and true equipment, but camping equipment is available for sale or rent throughout Spain. For information on outfitters, consult the above-mentioned guides to camping and caravanning or contact the national tourist offices in the US which may be able to refer you to reliable Spanish dealers.

Keep in mind that accessible food will lure scavenging wildlife, which may invade tents and vehicles. Also, even if you are assured that the campground where you are staying provides potable water, it is safer to use bottled, purified, or boiled water for drinking. To purify tap water, either use a water purification kit (available at most camping supply stores) or bring the water to a full, *rolling,* boil over a campstove. Unless deep in the wilderness, it is inadvisable to use water from streams, rivers, or lakes — even purified.

Organized Camping Trips – A packaged camping tour abroad is a good way to have your cake and eat it, too. The problems of advance planning and day-to-day organizing are left to someone else, yet you still reap the benefits that shoestring travel affords and can enjoy the insights of experienced guides and the company of other campers. Be aware, however, that these packages usually are geared to the young, with ages 18 to 35 as common limits. Transfer from place to place is by bus or van (as on other sightseeing tours), overnights are in tents or shelters, and meal arrangements vary. Often there is a kitty that covers meals in restaurants or in the camps; sometimes there is a chef, and sometimes the cooking is done by the participants themselves. When considering a package tour to the wilderness, be sure to find out if equipment is included and what individual participants are required to bring.

The *Specialty Travel Index* (305 San Anselmo Ave., Suite 217, San Anselmo, CA 94960; phone: 415-459-4900 in California; 800-442-4924 elsewhere in the US) is a directory to special-interest travel and an invaluable resource. Listings include tour operators specializing in camping, as well as myriad other interests that combine nicely with a camping trip, such as biking, motorcycling, horseback riding, ballooning, and boating. The index costs $5 per copy, $8 for a year's subscription of two issues.

Among such packages are the camping tours of Europe offered by *Autotours* (20 Craven Ter., London W2, England; phone: 44-71-258-0272), which range from 3 to 10 weeks. Recent itineraries included camping in Spain, as part of a 33-day Western

Europe camping tour. All their packages depart from London. *Himalayan Travel* (PO Box 481, Greenwich, CT 06836; phone: 800-225-2380) also offers a variety of camping tours throughout Europe, including Spain. In addition, a number of packagers listed below under "Hiking" and "Biking" may offer these pursuits in combination with camping — it pays to call and ask when planning a trip.

Recreational Vehicles – Known in Europe as caravans (or minibuses or minivans), recreational vehicles (RVs) will appeal most to the kind of person who prefers the flexibility in accommodations — there are countless campgrounds throughout Spain and a number of them provide RV hookups — and enjoys camping with a little extra comfort.

An RV undoubtably saves a traveler a great deal of money on accommodations; in-camp cooking saves money on food as well. However, it is important to remember that renting an RV is a major expense; also, any kind of RV increases gas consumption considerably.

Although the term "recreational vehicle" is applied to all manner of camping vehicles, whether towed or self-propelled, generally the models available for rent in Spain and nearby countries are either towable campers (caravans) or motorized RVs. The motorized models usually are minivans or minibuses — vans customized in various ways for camping, often including elevated roofs — and larger, coach-type, fully equipped homes on wheels, requiring electrical hookups at night to run the TV set, air conditioning, and kitchen appliances. Although most motorized models are equipped with standard shifts, occasionally automatic shift vehicles may be available for an additional charge.

Towed vehicles can be hired overseas, but usually are not offered by US or international companies. At present, however, the only type of motorized caravan rented in Spain is a van or minibus with an elevated roof. These are available from international and regional car rental companies in the major cities (see *Traveling by Car,* earlier in this section), although you will probably have to do some calling around to find one. You can rent other types of RVs in other European countries and drive them across the border into Spain (see list below). In this event, inform the rental company of your plans.

If you are planning to caravan all over Europe, make sure that whatever vehicle you choose is equipped to deal with the electrical and gas standards of all the countries on your itinerary. You should have either a sufficient supply of the type the camper requires or equipment that can use more than one type. When towing a camper, note that nothing towed is covered automatically by the liability insurance of the primary vehicle, so the driver's Green Card must carry a specific endorsement that covers the towed vehicle. (For further information, see *Traveling by Car,* above.)

Whether driving a camper or towing, it is essential to have some idea of the terrain you'll be encountering en route. Only experienced drivers should drive large campers, particularly in northern Spain, where the terrain can be quite steep.In fact, grades sometimes can be too steep for certain vehicles to negotiate, and some roads are off limits to towed caravans. Also be aware that mountain passes and tunnels crossing the borders into France and Andorra sometimes are closed in the winter, depending on altitude, road grade, and severity of the weather. Your best source of information on these routes are Spanish and French automobile clubs. Car tunnels, or "piggyback" services on trains, usually bypass those summits too difficult to climb, but they also impose dimension limitations and often charge high fees. The *AAA* guides noted above provide detailed information on principal European passes and tunnels, as do tourist offices.

As mentioned above, only customized vans (minibuses or minivans) are available in Spain; however, rentals of RVs in neighboring France (or other nearby countries for those planning to do more extensive touring in addition to visiting Spain) are available. Among companies offering minivan and/or RV rentals for Spanish camping are the following:

Auto-Europe (PO Box 1907, Camden, ME 04843; phone: 207-236-8235 in Maine; 800-223-5555 elsewhere in the US). Offers minibus rentals in over 15 cities in Spain.

Avis Rent-A-Car (6128 E. 38th St., Tulsa, OK 74135; phone: 800-331-1084, ext. 7719). Offers minibus rentals at over 150 locations in Spain; larger RVs also can be rented at locations in France, the Netherlands, and Switzerland and driven into Spain. Arrangements must be made through the US office.

Connex (23 N. Division St., Peekskill, NY 10566; phone: 800-333-3949). Rents minibuses in Spain and motorized RVs in Germany, Great Britain, and the Netherlands.

Europe by Car (One Rockefeller Plaza, New York, NY 10020, or 9000 Sunset Blvd., Los Angeles, CA 90069; phone: 800-223-1516 or 213-272-0424). Rents RVs in Germany, and minibuses in Austria, Belgium, Denmark, France, Germany, Greece, Hungary, Ireland, Italy, Luxembourg, Portugal, and Switzerland, which can be driven over the border into Spain.

Kemwel Group (106 Calvert St., Harrison, NY 10528; phone: 800-678-0678 or 914-835-5555). Offers minibus rental in 18 cities in Spain.

The general policy with the above agencies is to make reservations far enough in advance to receive a voucher that will be used to pick up the vehicle at the designated location in Europe. (Early reservations also are advisable as the supply of RVs is limited and the demand great.)

Among the French companies offering RV rentals in France — which by special arrangement may be driven over the border into Spain — are the following:

FCI Location (Zone Industrielle de Saint-Brendan, Quentin 22800, France; phone: 33-96-74-08-36). Rents motorized RVs in France.

Trois Soleils (Maison Trois Soleils, 2 Route de Paris, 67117 Ittenheim, France; phone: 33-88-69-17-17 for reservations). Rents motorized RVs, as well as some basic campers in France; a number of pick-up and drop-off locations are offered.

As in the US, numerous smaller, local companies that rent both motorized and towable campers are to be found throughout Europe. For minivan and minibus rentals in Spain, ask at local car rental companies and tourism offices.

Useful information on RVs is available from the following sources:

Living on Wheels by Richard A. Wolters. Provides useful information on how to choose and operate a recreational vehicle. As it's currently out of print, check your library.

Recreational Vehicle Industry Association (*RVIA;* PO Box 2999, Reston, VA 22090-2999). Issues a useful complimentary package of information on RVs, as well as a 24-page magazine-size guide, *Set Free in an RV* ($3), and a free catalogue of RV sources and consumer information. Write to the association for these and other publications.

Recreational Vehicle Rental Association (*RVRA;* 3251 Old Lee Hwy., Suite 500, Fairfax, VA 22030; phone: 800-336-0355 or 703-591-7130). This RV dealers group publishes an annual rental directory, *Who's Who in RV Rentals* ($7.50).

TL Enterprises (29901 Agoura Rd., Agoura, CA 91301; phone: 818-991-4980) publishes two monthly magazines for RV enthusiasts: *Motorhome* and *Trailer Life.* A year's subscription to either costs $22; a combined subscription to both costs $44. Members of the *TL Enterprises' Good Sam Club* can subscribe for half price and also receive discounts on a variety of other RV services; membership costs $19 per year.

Trailblazer (1000 124th Ave. NE, Bellevue, WA 98005; phone: 206-455-8585). A recreational-vehicle and motorhome magazine. A year's subscription costs $24.

Although most RV travelers head off independently, traveling in a "caravan" where several RVs travel together offers the best of both worlds for an RV trip: Since caravan members are provided with detailed itineraries and directions, they can, if they wish, travel independently — or with one or two other RVs — to and from pre-arranged destinations, yet when the full caravan convenes, they can enjoy the fellowship of the group and participate in planned activities. Caravans usually include from 20 to 40 vehicles, which are lead by a "wagonmaster," who functions as tour escort, keeping things running smoothly and on schedule. His assistant, the "tailgunner," brings up the rear and handles any mechanical problems. The caravan tour operator takes care of trip planning and routing, insurance, campground reservations and fees, and so forth. Besides the planned sightseeing, social activities can include group dinners, shows and other entertainment, cookouts at campsites, and more, but again, caravan members always have the option of spending as much time by themselves as they wish. One operator of such RV caravan trips is *Creative World Rallies and Caravans* (606 N. Carrollton Ave., New Orleans, LA 70119; phone: 800-732-8337 or 504-486-7259) which arranges trips throughout Europe, including Spain.

HIKING: If you would rather eliminate all the gear and planning and take to the outdoors unencumbered, park the car and go for a day's hike. By all means, cover as much area as you can by foot; you'll see everything in far more detail than you would from the window of any conveyance. For information on suggested hikes throughout Spain, see *Great Walks and Mountain Rambles* in DIVERSIONS.

Trails abound in Spain. Preliminary information on where to hike is available from the Spanish tourist offices in the US, and local tourist authorities often distribute information sheets on popular trails in their respective regions upon request. (Even those tourist offices that do not have literature on hand — or have little in English — may be able to direct you to associations in their areas that supply maps, guides, and further information.) There are other sources for those intent on getting about on their own steam; however, as material on hiking in these countries may be difficult to find in the US, you may want to contact international hiking organizations for information.

One particularly useful set of guidebooks is the *Walking Through* series, which covers ten different European cities, including Barcelona, Madrid, and Seville. These guides are available from VLE Limited (PO Box 444, Ft. Lee, NJ 07024; phone: 201-585-5080), for $3 each, or $2.50 each if ordering two or more, and also may be found at select bookstores. Also for those wandering Spanish byways is *Trekking in Spain* (Lonely Planet; $11.95) by Marc Dubin. This book is available from travel and major bookstores.

For those who are hiking on their own, without benefit of a guide or group, a map of the trail is a must. Particularly helpful for those heading out afoot are the Topographical Series maps, which are on a detailed scale of 1:200,000. There are 102 of these maps for Spain and they are available for $10 each from *Map Link* (25 E. Mason St., Santa Barbara, CA 93101; phone: 805-965-4402).

Organized Hiking Trips – Those who who prefer to travel as part of an organized group should contact the following organizations:

Alternative Travel Groups (1-3 George St., Oxford, England 0X1 2AZ; phone: 800-527-5997). The motto of this company is "The best way to see a country is on foot." Among their numerous itineraries worldwide are walking tours in Spain.

American Youth Hostels (PO Box 37613, Washington, DC 20013-7613; phone:

202-783-6161). Their itineraries vary from year to year, but hiking tours of Spain occasionally are offered.

Exodus (9 Weir Rd., London, England SW2 OLT; For information, contact their US representative, *Force 10 Expeditions,* PO Box 30506, Flagstaff, AZ 86003; phone: 800-922-1491). This adventure specialist offers inn-to-inn walking tours throughout Spain.

Himalayan Travel (PO Box 481, Greenwich, CT 06836; phone: 800-225-2380). Offers hotel-to-hotel walking tours throughout Spain.

Mountain Travel (6420 Fairmont Ave., El Cerrito, CA 94530; phone: 415-527-8100 in California; 800-227-2384 elsewhere in the US). This adventure trip specialist offers a wide variety of hiking trips throughout Europe, including tours of the Pyrenees, the Picos de Europa, and a taste of the Basque Country. Their tours range from leisurely hikes that can be taken by anyone in good health to tours only for experienced (and very fit) hikers/climbers.

Sierra Club (Outing Department, 730 Polk St., San Francisco, CA 94109; phone: 415-776-2211). Offers a selection of trips each year, including both walking tours and trips that combine hiking and biking. Some are backpacking trips, moving to a new camp each day; others make day hikes from a base camp. Recent itineraries included hiking tours of southern Spain (and the Balearic Islands).

Wilderness Travel (801 Allston Way, Berkeley, CA 94710; phone: 415-548-0420 or 800-247-6700). Offers a wide range of hiking tours throughout Europe, including Spain.

An alternative to dealing directly with the above companies is to contact *All Adventure Travel,* a specialist in hiking and biking trips worldwide. This company, which acts as a representative for numerous special tour packagers offering such outdoor adventures, can provide a wealth of detailed information about each packager and programs offered. They also will help you design and arrange all aspects of a personalized itinerary. This company operates much like a travel agency, collecting commissions from the packagers. Therefore, there is no additional charge for these services. For information, contact *All Adventure Travel,* PO Box 4307, Boulder, CO 80306 (phone: 800-537-4025 or 303-939-8885).

BIKING: For young and/or fit travelers, the bicycle offers a marvelous tool for exploring. Throughout Spain there is an abundance of secondary roads that thread through picturesque stretches of countryside. Biking does have its drawbacks: Little baggage can be carried, travel is slow, and cyclists are exposed to the elements. However, should a cyclist need rest or refuge from the weather, there always is a welcoming tavern or comfortable inn around the next bend.

Besides being a viable way to tour Spain — and to burn calories to make room for larger portions of regional food — biking is a great way to meet people. Remember, however, that although many residents of Spain do speak some English, this is less likely to be true in rural areas, so pack a good copy of a foreign phrase book if your command of Spanish is not up to par. (For a list of helpful terms and basic expressions, see *Useful Words and Phrases,* in this section.)

A good book to help you plan a trip is *Bicycle Touring in Europe,* by Karen and Gary Hawkins (Random House; $11.95); it offers information on buying and equipping a touring bike, useful clothing and supplies, and helpful techniques for the long-distance biker. Another good general book is *Europe by Bike,* by Karen and Terry Whitehall (Mountaineers Books; $10.95). The *International Youth Hostel Handbook, Volume One: Europe and the Mediterranean* ($13.95) is a guide to all the hostels of Europe to which *AYH* members have access; a map of their locations is included. (For information on joining *American Youth Hostels,* see *Hints for Single Travelers,* in this section.)

Detailed maps will infinitely improve a biking tour and are available from a number of sources. Detailed Michelin maps (1:400,000) covering Europe, including Spain, are available from Michelin Guides and Maps, PO Box 3305, Spartanburg, SC 29304-3305 (phone: 803-599-0850).

One of the best sources for detailed topographical maps and just about any other type of map (of just about anywhere in the world) is *Map Link* (25 E. Mason St., Santa Barbara, CA 93101; phone: 805-965-4402). Their comprehensive guide *The World Map Directory* ($29.95) includes a wealth of sources for travelers afoot, and if they don't stock a map of the area in which you are interested (or the type of map best suited to your outdoor exploration), they will order it for you. But it is likely that they'll have something to suit your needs — they stock numerous maps of Spain.

An additional source of maps and other information useful to cyclists is the local tourist authorities (see *Tourist Information Offices,* in this section, for addresses), which can often offer recommendations on popular scenic and historical routes.

Choosing, Renting, and Buying a Bike – Although many bicycling enthusiasts choose to take along their own bikes, bicycles can be rented throughout Europe. Long and short rentals are available; however, in Spain, particularly in rural areas, it is recommended that you check ahead. Almost all European trains have facilities for bike transport at nominal fees.

As an alternative to renting, you might consider buying a bicycle in Europe. Bicycle shops that rent bikes often also sell them and buying a used bike might be even less expensive than a long-term rental. If you do buy a bike and plan on taking it home, remember that it will be subject to an import duty by US Customs if its price (or the total of all purchases made abroad) exceeds $400. (A European bicycle purchased in the US should have proof-of-purchase papers to avoid potential customs problems.) Bicycle shops exist in most metropolitan areas, so you should be able to replace or add to gear; however, because tires and tubes are sized to metric dimensions in Spain, when riding your own bike, bring extras from home.

Airlines going from the US (or elsewhere) to Europe generally allow bicycles to be checked as baggage and require that the pedals be removed, handlebars be turned sideways, and the bike be in a shipping carton (which some airlines provide, subject to availability — call ahead to make sure). If buying a shipping carton from a bicycle shop, check the airline's specifications and also ask about storing the carton at the destination airport so that you can use it again for the return flight. Although some airlines charge only a nominal fee, if the traveler already has checked two pieces of baggage, there may be an additional excess baggage charge of $70 to $80 for the bicycle. As regulations vary from carrier to carrier, be sure to call well before departure to find out your airline's specific regulations. As with other baggage, make sure that the bike is thoroughly labeled with your name, a business address and phone number, and the correct airport destination code.

Biking Tours – A number of organizations offer bike tours in Spain. Linking up with a bike tour is more expensive than traveling alone, but with experienced leaders, an organized tour often becomes an educational, as well as a very social, experience.

One of the attractions of a bike tour is that shipment of equipment — the bike — is handled by the organizers, and the shipping fee is included in the total tour package. Travelers simply deliver the bike to the airport, already disassembled and boxed; shipping cartons can be obtained from most bicycle shops with little difficulty. Bicyclists not with a tour must make their own arrangements with the airline, and there are no standard procedures for this (see above). Although some tour organizers will rent bikes, most prefer that participants show up with a bike with which they are already familiar. Another attraction of *some* tours is the existence of a "sag wagon" to carry extra luggage, fatigued cyclists, and their bikes, too, when pedaling another mile is impossible.

Most bike tours are scheduled from May to October, last 1 or 2 weeks, are limited to 20 or 25 people, and provide lodging in inns or hotels, though some use hostels or even tents. Tours vary considerably in style and ambience, so request brochures from several operators in order to make the best decision. When contacting groups, be sure to ask about the maximum number of people on the trip, the maximum number of miles to be traveled each day, and the degree of difficulty of the biking; these details should determine which tour you join and can greatly affect your enjoyment of the experience. Planning ahead is essential because trips often fill up 6 months or more in advance.

Among the companies offering biking tours to Spain are the following:

Butterfield & Robinson (70 Bond St., Suite 300, Toronto, Ontario M5B 1X3, Canada; phone: 416-864-1354). Offers a number of first class, sophisticated bike trips throughout Europe, including an 8-day biking tour of northern Spain (and Portugal). Tours are rated at four levels of difficulty.

Cycle Portugal (PO Box 877, San Antonio, FL 33576; phone: 904-588-4132 or 800-245-4226). Although most of this company's itineraries focus on Portugal, they offer a number of packages to Spain, including tours of Andalusia, the Bay of Biscay, and the Pyrenees.

Easy Rider Tours (PO Box 1384, E. Arlington, MA 02174; phone: 617-643-8332). Offers a 14-day tour of northern Spain (and central Portugal).

Eurobike (PO Box 40, DeKalb, IL 60115; phone: 815-758-8851). Offers a 14-day hotel-to-hotel biking tour from Porto, Portugal, to Santiago de Compostela.

Other useful sources of information on bicyling in Spain include the following:

American Youth Hostels (PO Box 37613, Washington, DC 20013-7613; phone: 202-783-6161). A number of biking tours are sponsored annually by this non-profit organization and its local chapters. Membership is open to all ages and departures are geared to various age groups and levels of skill and frequently feature accommodations in hostels — along with hotels for adults and camp-grounds for younger participants.

Cyclists' Touring Club (*CTC;* Cotterell House, 69 Meadrow, Godalming, Surrey GU7 3HS, England; phone: 44-0483-41-7217). Britain's largest cycling associa-tion, this group organizes tours of numerous countries, including Spain. *CTC* has a number of planned routes available in pamphlet form for bikers on their own and helps members plan their own tours. The club also publishes a yearly handbook, as well as magazines.

International Bicycle Touring Society (*IBTS;* PO Box 6979, San Diego, CA 92106-0979; phone: 619-226-TOUR). This nonprofit organization regularly sponsors low-cost bicycle tours led by member volunteers. Participants must be over 21. For information, send $2 plus a self-addressed, stamped envelope.

League of American Wheelmen (6707 Whitestone Rd., Suite 209, Baltimore, MD 21207; phone: 301-944-3399). This organziation publishes *Tourfinder,* a list of organizations that sponsor bicycle tours worldwide. The list is free with mem-bership ($25 individual, $30 family) and can be obtained by non-members who send $5. The *League* also can put you in touch with biking groups in your area.

Preparing

Calculating Costs

$ A realistic appraisal of your travel expenses is the most crucial bit of planning you will undertake before any trip. It also is, unfortunately, one for which it is most difficult to give precise, practical advice.

After several years of living relatively high on the hog, travel from North America to Europe dropped off precipitously in 1987 in response, among other considerations, to the relative weakness of the US dollar on the Continent. Many Americans, who had enjoyed bargain prices while touring through Europe only a couple of years before, found that disadvantageous exchange rates really put a crimp in their travel planning. But even though the halcyon days of dollar domination seem over for the present, discount fares and the availability of charter flights can greatly reduce the cost of a European vacation. Package tours can even further reduce costs, as European providers of travel services try to win back their American clients in the 1990s.

Although most travelers have to plan carefully before they go and manage their travel funds prudently, in general, a holiday in Spain still is a good value. Even though the major cities — like our own — suffer from a relatively high cost of living, travel in the countryside still can be very reasonable (and sometimes even inexpensive) as compared to other destinations in Europe. Spain always has been popular with both the first-time and the seasoned traveler, and the competition for American visitors often works to inspire surprisingly affordable travel opportunities.

In Spain, estimating travel expenses depends on the mode of transportation you choose, the part or parts of the country you plan to visit, how long you will stay, and in some cases, what time of year you plan to travel. In addition to the basics of transportation, hotels, meals, and sightseeing, you have to take into account seasonal price changes that apply on certain air routings and at popular vacation destinations, as well as the vagaries of currency exchange.

In general, it's usually also a good idea to organize your trip so that you pay for as much of it as you can in Spain, using pesetas purchased from Spanish banks (which, barring interim variations, generally offer a more advantageous rate of exchange than US sources). That means minimizing the amount of advance deposits paid in US greenbacks and deferring as many bills as possible until you arrive in Europe, although the economies possible through prepaid package tours and other special deals may offset the savings in currency exchange. (For further information on managing money abroad, see *Credit and Currency,* in this section.)

When calculating costs, start with the basics, the major expenses being transportation, accommodations, and food. However, don't forget such extras as local transportation, shopping, and such miscellaneous items as laundry and tips. The reasonable cost of these items usually is a positive surprise to your budget. Ask about special discount passes that provide unlimited travel by the day or the week on regular city transportation. Entries in the individual city reports in THE CITIES give helpful information on local transportation options.

Other expenses, such as the cost of local sightseeing tours, will vary from city to city. Tourist information offices are plentiful throughout Spain, and most of the better hotels will have someone at the front desk to provide a rundown on the costs of local tours and full-day excursions in and out of the city. Travel agents or railway booking offices (see *Traveling by Train,* in this section) can provide information on rail tours.

Package programs can reduce the price of a vacation in Spain, because the group rates obtained by the tour packager usually are lower than the tariffs for someone traveling on a free-lance basis; that is, paying for each element — airfare, hotel, meals, car rental — separately. And keep in mind, particularly when calculating the major expenses, that costs vary according to fluctuations in the exchange rate — that is, how much of a given foreign currency a dollar will buy.

Budget-minded families can take advantage of some of the more economical accommodations options to be found in Spain (see our discussion of accommodations in *On the Road,* in this section). Campgrounds are particularly inexpensive and they are located throughout the country (see *Camping and Caravanning, Hiking and Biking,* in this section). Picnicking is another excellent way to cut costs, and Spain abounds with well-groomed parks and idyllic pastoral settings, particularly along the coast. A stop at a local market can provide a feast of regional specialties at a surprisingly economical price compared to the cost of a restaurant lunch. (Do, however, read our warnings about seafood in *Staying Healthy,* in this section.)

In planning any travel budget, it also is wise to allow a realistic amount for both entertainment and recreation. Are you planning to spend time sightseeing and visiting local museums? Do you intend to spend your days sailing or horseback riding? Is daily golf or tennis a part of your plan? Will your children be disappointed if they don't take a guided tour of a Moorish castle? Finally, don't forget that if haunting clubs, discotheques, or other nightspots is an essential part of your vacation, or you feel that one performance at the *Auditorio Nacional* in Madrid may not be enough, allow for the extra cost of nightlife.

If at any point in the planning process it appears impossible to estimate expenses, consider this suggestion: The easiest way to put a ceiling on the price of all these elements is to buy a package tour. A totally planned and escorted one, with almost all transportation, rooms, meals, sightseeing, local travel, tips, and a dinner show or two included and prepaid, provides a pretty exact total of what the trip will cost beforehand, and the only surprise will be the one you spring on yourself by succumbing to some irresistible, expensive souvenir.

Also note that a sales tax or VAT (value added tax, known as IVA in Spain) is added to both goods and services in many European countries. In Spain, the rate ranges from lows of 6% on food to a high of 33% on luxury articles. The VAT is buried in the prices of hotel rooms and restaurant meals, so you won't even notice it. It also is included in the amount shown on the price tag of retail goods. There is no escaping the tax on services, but for foreigners the tax on purchases frequently can be reimbursed. Another alternative is to have the goods sent directly to your home address — if the store is willing to do so. For a full discussion of VAT refunds, see *Duty-Free Shopping and Value Added Tax,* in this section.

■ **Note:** The volatility of exchange rates means that between the time you originally make your hotel reservations and the day you arrive, the price in US dollars may vary substantially from the price originally quoted. To avoid paying more than you expected, it's wise to confirm rates by writing directly to hotels or by calling their representatives in the US.

Planning a Trip

123 Travelers fall into two categories: those who make lists and those who do not. Some people prefer to plot the course of their trip to the finest detail, with contingency plans and alternatives at the ready. For others, the joy of a voyage is its spontaneity; exhaustive planning only lessens the thrill of anticipation and the sense of freedom.

For most travelers, however, any week-plus trip to Spain can be too expensive for an "I'll take my chances" type of attitude. Even perennial gypsies and anarchistic wanderers have to take into account the time-consuming logistics of getting around, and even with minimal baggage, they need to think about packing. Hence, at least some planning is crucial.

This is not to suggest that you work out your itinerary in minute detail before you go; but it's still wise to decide certain basics at the very start: where to go, what to do, and how much to spend. These decisions require a certain amount of consideration. So before rigorously planning specific details, you might want to establish your general travel objectives:

1. How much time will you have for the entire trip, and how much of it are you willing to spend getting where you're going?
2. What interests and/or activities do you want to pursue while on vacation? Do you want to visit one, a few, or several different places?
3. At what time of year do you want to go?
4. What kind of geography or climate would you prefer?
5. Do you want peace and privacy or lots of activity and company?
6. How much money can you afford to spend for the entire vacation?

You now can make almost all of your own travel arrangements if you have time to follow through with hotels, airlines, tour operators, and so on. But you'll probably save considerable time and energy if you have a travel agent make arrangements for you. The agent also should be able to advise you of alternate arrangements of which you may not be aware. Only rarely will a travel agent's services cost a traveler any money, and they may even save you some (see *How to Use a Travel Agent,* below).

If it applies to your schedule and destination, pay particular attention to the dates when off-season rates go into effect. In major tourism areas, accommodations may cost less during the off-season (and the weather often is perfectly acceptable at this time). Off-season rates frequently are lower for car rentals and other facilities, too. In general, it is a good idea to be aware of holiday weeks, as rates at hotels generally are higher during these periods and rooms normally are heavily booked.

Make plans early. During the summer season and other holiday periods, make hotel reservations at least a month in advance in all major cities. If you are flying at peak times and want to benefit from savings of discount fares or charter programs, purchase tickets as far ahead as possible. Many Spanish hotels require deposits before they will guarantee reservations, and this most often is the case during peak travel periods. (Be sure you have a receipt for any deposit or use a credit card.) Religious and national holidays also are times requiring reservations well in advance in Spain.

Before your departure, find out what the weather is likely to be at your destination. Consult *When to Go,* in this section, for information on climatic variations and a chart of average temperatures. See *How to Pack,* in this section, for some suggestions on how to decide what clothes to take. Also *When to Go,* as well as the individual city reports in THE CITIES for information on special events that may occur during your stay. The city chapters also provide essential information on local transportation and other services and resources.

Make a list of any valuable items you are carrying with you, including credit card numbers and the serial numbers of your traveler's checks. Put copies in your purse or pocket and leave other copies at home. Put a label with your name and home address on the inside of your luggage for identification in case of loss. Put your name and business address — *never your home address* — on a label on the outside of your luggage. (Those who run businesses from home should use the office address of a friend or relative.)

Review your travel documents. If you are traveling by air, check that your ticket has been filled in correctly. The left side of the ticket should have a list of each stop you will make (even if you are only stopping to change planes), beginning with your departure point. Be sure that the list is correct, and count the number of copies to see that you have one for each plane you will take. If you have confirmed reservations, be sure that the column marked "status" says "OK" beside each flight. Have in hand vouchers or proof of payment for any reservation for which you've paid in advance; this includes hotels, transfers to and from the airport, sightseeing tours, car rentals, and tickets to special events.

Although policies vary from carrier to carrier, it's still smart to reconfirm your flight 48 to 72 hours before departure, both going and returning. Reconfirmation is particularly recommended for point-to-point flights within Europe. If you will be driving while in Spain, bring your driver's license, International Driver's Permit (also required), and any other necessary documentation — such as proof of insurance.

Before traveling to Spain, you should consider learning some basic Spanish. Although you can get by in Spain without speaking Spanish — particularly if you stick to the major resort areas and other popular tourist destinations — your trip will be much more rewarding and enjoyable (and, in some instances, safer) if you can communicate with the people who live in the areas you will be visiting. Spaniards will not make you feel silly or stupid if you don't pronounce words properly — in fact they will openly appreciate your efforts if you do try to converse.

Most adult education programs and community colleges offer courses in Spanish. Berlitz, among others, has a series of teach-yourself language courses on records or audiocassette tapes, which are available for $14.95 (plus postage and handling) from Macmillan Publishing Co. (100 Front St., Riverside, NJ 08075; phone: 800-257-5755). For information on pronunciation and a list of common travel terms, see *Useful Words and Phrases,* in this section; an introduction to a number of native drinks and dishes that you may encounter can be found in *Food and Drink,* PERSPECTIVES.

Finally, you always should bear in mind that despite the most careful plans, things do not always occur on schedule. If you maintain a flexible attitude and try to accept minor disruptions as less than cataclysmic, you will enjoy yourself a lot more.

How to Use a Travel Agent

A reliable travel agent remains the best source of service and information for planning a trip abroad, whether you have a specific itinerary and require an agent only to make reservations or you need extensive help in sorting through the maze of airfares, tour offerings, hotel packages, and the scores of other arrangements that may be involved in a trip to Spain.

Know what you want from a travel agent so that you can evaluate what you are getting. It is perfectly reasonable to expect your agent to be a thoroughly knowledgeable travel specialist, with information about your destination and, even more crucial, a command of current airfares, ground arrangements, and other wrinkles in the travel scene.

Most travel agents work through computer reservations systems (CRS). These are used to assess the availability and cost of flights, hotels, and car rentals, and through them they can book reservations. Despite reports of "computer bias," in which a computer may favor one airline over another, the CRS should provide agents with the entire spectrum of flights available to a given destination, as well as the complete range of fares, in considerably less time than it takes to telephone the airlines individually — and at no extra charge to the client.

Make the most intelligent use of a travel agent's time and expertise; understand the economics of the industry. As a client, traditionally you pay nothing for the agent's services; with few exceptions, it's all free, from hotel bookings to advice on package tours. Any money the travel agent makes on the time spent arranging your itinerary — booking hotels or flights, or suggesting activities — comes from commissions paid by the suppliers of these services — the airlines, hotels, and so on. These commissions generally run from 10% to 15% of the total cost of the service, although suppliers often reward agencies that sell their services in volume with an increased commission, called an override. In most instances, you'll find that travel agents make their time and experience available to you at no cost, and you do not pay more for an airline ticket, package tour, or other product bought from a travel agent than you would for the same product bought directly from the supplier.

Exceptions to the general rule of free service by a travel agent are the agencies beginning to practice net pricing. In essence, such agencies return their commissions and overrides to their customers and make their income by charging a flat fee per transaction instead (thus adding a charge after a reduction for the commissions has been made). Net fares and fees are a growing practice, though hardly widespread.

Even a conventional travel agent sometimes may charge a fee for special services. These chargeable items may include long-distance telephone or cable costs incurred in making a booking, for reserving a room in a place that does not pay a commission (such as a small, out-of-the-way hotel), or for special attention such as planning a highly personalized itinerary. A fee also may be assessed in instances of deeply discounted airfares.

Choose a travel agent with the same care with which you would choose a doctor or lawyer. You will be spending a good deal of money on the basis of the agent's judgment, so you have a right to expect that judgment to be mature, informed, and interested. At the moment, unfortunately, there aren't many standards within the travel agent industry to help you gauge competence, and the quality of individual agents varies enormously.

At present, only nine states have registration, licensing, or other forms of travel agent–related legislation on their books. Rhode Island licenses travel agents; Florida, Hawaii, Iowa, and Ohio register them; and California, Illinois, Oregon, and Washington have laws governing the sale of transportation or related services. While state licensing of agents cannot absolutely guarantee competence, it can at least ensure that an agent has met some minimum requirements.

Perhaps the best-prepared agents are those who have completed the CTC Travel Management program offered by the *Institute of Certified Travel Agents* and carry the initials CTC (Certified Travel Counselor) after their names. This indicates a relatively high level of expertise. For a free list of CTCs in your area, send a self-addressed, stamped, #10 envelope to *ICTA*, 148 Linden St., Box 82-56, Wellesley, MA 02181 (phone: 617-237-0280 in Massachusetts; 800-542-4282 elsewhere in the US).

An agent's membership in the *American Society of Travel Agents (ASTA)* can be a useful guideline in making a selection. But keep in mind that *ASTA* is an industry organization, requiring only that its members be licensed in those states where required; be accredited to represent the suppliers whose products they sell, including airline and cruise tickets; and adhere to its Principles of Professional Conduct and Ethics code. *ASTA* does not guarantee the competence, ethics, or financial soundness of its members, but it does offer some recourse if you feel you have been dealt with unfairly. Complaints may be registered with *ASTA* (Consumer Affairs Dept., PO Box 23992, Washington, DC 20026-3992; phone: 703-739-2782). First try to resolve the complaint directly with the supplier. For a list of *ASTA* members in your area, send a self-addressed, stamped, #10 envelope to *ASTA,* Public Relations Dept., at the address above.

There also is the *Association of Retail Travel Agents (ARTA),* a smaller but highly respected trade organization similar to *ASTA.* Its member agencies and agents similarly agree to abide by a code of ethics, and complaints about a member can be made to *ARTA*'s Grievance Committee, 1745 Jeff Davis Hwy., Arlington, VA 22202-3402 (phone: 800-969-6069 or 703-553-7777).

Perhaps the best way to find a travel agent is by word of mouth. If the agent (or agency) has done a good job for your friends over a period of time, it probably indicates a certain level of commitment and competence. Always ask not only for the name of the company, but for the name of the specific agent with whom your friends dealt, for it is that individual who will serve you, and quality can vary widely within a single agency. There are some superb travel agents in the business, and they can facilitate vacation or business arrangements.

Entry Requirements and Documents

 A valid US passport is the only document a US citizen needs to enter Spain, and that same passport also is needed to reenter the US. If while touring Catalonia, you decide to visit the principality of Andorra, again, a valid passport is the only requirement for entry. As a general rule, a US passport entitles the bearer to remain in Spain for up to 6 months as a tourist. Resident aliens of the US should inquire at the nearest Spanish consulate (see *Tourist Information Offices,* in this section, for addresses) to find out what documents they need to enter Spain; similarly, US citizens intending to work, study, or reside in Spain should address themselves to the consulate.

Vaccination certificates are required only if the traveler is entering from an area of contagion as defined by the World Health Organization, and as the US is considered an area "free from contagion," an international vaccination certificate no longer is required for entering Spain for a short period of time. Because smallpox is considered eradicated from the world, only a few countries continue to require visitors to have a smallpox vaccination certificate. You certainly will not need one to travel to Spain or return to the US.

VISAS: Visas are required, however, for study, residency, or work, and US citizens should address themselves to the the Spanish embassy or consulate, well in advance of a proposed trip. Visas of this type are available for stays in Spain of up to 1 year. Note that although visas for study often are issued, it is much more difficult to get a visa permitting you to work in the country. The ready processing of a visa application also may be based on the duration of the visa you are requesting — visas for studying in Spain for several months are likely to be processed more quickly than residency visas good for 1 year or longer. Proof of substantial means of independent financial support during the stay also is pertinent to the acceptance of any long-term–stay application.

At least two items are necessary to apply for a visa: a valid passport and a completed visa form. (These forms may be obtained by sending a self-addressed, stamped envelope to any Spanish consulate with a written request.) Depending on the type of visa you are requesting, additional documentation may be required. There is no charge for the issuance of visas. Application can be made through the mail or in person at the Spanish embassy or a consulate (see *Tourist Information Offices,* in this section, for addresses). If applying in person, it is a good idea to call ahead to check during what hours and days visa requests are accepted.

PASSPORTS: While traveling in Spain, carry your passport with you at all times (for an exception to this rule, see our note "When Checking In," below). If you lose your passport while abroad, immediately report the loss to the nearest US consulate or embassy (see *Medical and Legal Aid and Consular Services,* in this section, for locations in Spain). You can get a 3-month temporary passport directly from the consulate, but you must fill out a "loss of passport" form and follow the same application procedure — and pay the same fees — as you did for the original (see below). It's likely to speed things up if you have a record of your passport number and the place and date of its issue (a photocopy of the first page of your passport is perfect). Keep this information separate from your passport — you might want to give it to a traveling companion to hold or put it in the bottom of your suitcase.

US passports now are valid for 10 years from the date of issue (5 years for those under age 18). The expired passport itself is not renewable, but must be turned in along with your application for a new and valid one (you will get it back, voided, when you receive the new one). Normal passports contain 24 pages, but frequent travelers can request a 48-page passport at no extra cost. Every individual, regardless of age, must have his or her own passport. Family passports no longer are issued.

Passports can be renewed by mail with forms obtained at designated locations only if the expired passport was issued no more than 12 years before the date of application for renewal and if it was not issued before the applicant's 16th birthday. The rules regarding teens under 16 and younger applicants vary depending on age and when their previous passport was issued. Those who are eligible to apply by mail must send the completed form with the expired passport, two photos (see description below), and $35 (no execution fee required) to the nearest passport agency office. Delivery can take as little as 2 weeks or as long as 6 weeks during the busiest season — from approximately mid-March to mid-September.

Adults applying for the first time and younger applicants who must apply for a passport in person (as well as those who cannot wait for mail application turnaround) can do so at one of the following places:

1. The State Department has passport agencies in Boston, Chicago, Honolulu, Houston, Los Angeles, Miami, New Orleans, New York City, Philadelphia, San Francisco, Seattle, Stamford, CT, and Washington, DC.
2. A federal or state courthouse.
3. Any of the 1,000 post offices across the country with designated acceptance facilities.

Application blanks are available at all these offices and must be presented with the following:

1. Proof of US citizenship. This can be a previous passport or one in which you were included. If you are applying for your first passport and were born in the United States, an original or certified birth certificate is the required proof. If you were born abroad, a Certificate of Naturalization, a Certificate of Citizenship, a Report of Birth Abroad of a Citizen of the United States, or a Certification of Birth is necessary.

2. Two 2-by-2-inch, front-view photographs in color or black and white, with a light, plain background, taken within the previous 6 months. These must be taken by a photographer rather than a machine.

3. A $42 passport fee ($27 for travelers under 16), which includes a $7 execution fee. *Note:* Your best bet is to bring the exact amount in cash (no change is given), or a separate check or money order for each passport. (Note that families usually can combine several passport fees on one check or money order.)

4. Proof of identity. Again, this can be a previous passport, a Certificate of Naturalization or of Citizenship, a driver's license, or a government ID card with a physical description or a photograph. Failing any of these, you should be accompanied by a blood relative or a friend of at least 2 years' standing who will testify to your identity. Credit cards or social security cards do not suffice as proof of identity — but note that since 1988, US citizens *must* supply their social security numbers.

As getting a passport — or international visa — through the mail can mean waiting as much as 6 weeks or more, a new mini-industry has cropped up in those cities where there is a US passport office. The yellow pages currently list quite a few organizations willing to wait on line to expedite obtaining a visa or passport renewal; there's even one alternative for those who live nowhere near the cities mentioned above. In the nation's capital there's an organization called the *Washington Passport and Visa Service.* It may be the answer for folks in need of special rapid action, since this organization can get a passport application or renewal turned around in a single day. What's more, their proximity to an embassy or consulate of every foreign country represented in the US helps to speed the processing of visa applications as well. The fee for a 5- to 7-day turnaround is $30; for next-day service the charge is $50; for same-day service they charge $90. For information, application forms, and other prices, contact *Washington Passport and Visa Service,* 2318 18th St. NW, Washington, DC 20009 (phone: 800-272-7776).

If you need an emergency passport, it also is possible to be issued a passport in a matter of hours by going directly to your nearest passport office (there is no way, however, to avoid waiting in line). Explain the nature of the emergency, usually as serious as a death in the family; a ticket in hand for a flight the following day also will suffice. Should the emergency occur outside of business hours, all is not lost. There's a 24-hour telephone number in Washington, DC (phone: 202-634-3600), that can put you in touch with a State Department duty officer who may be able to expedite your application.

■**When Checking In:** It is not at all unusual for a Spanish hotel to ask you to surrender your passport for 24 hours. While we all get a little nervous when we're parted from our passports, the US State Department's passport division advises that it's a perfectly acceptable procedure. The purpose usually is a local requirement to check the validity of the passport and ascertain whether the passport holder is a fugitive or has a police record. Many hotels merely will ask that you enter your passport number on your registration card. If a hotel does take your passport, make sure it's returned to you the next day.

DUTY AND CUSTOMS: As a general rule, the requirements for bringing the majority of items *into Spain* is that they must be in quantities small enough not to imply commercial import. Among the items that may be taken into Spain duty-free are 200 cigarettes or 250 grams of tobacco, 1 bottle of wine, and 1 bottle of liquor. Personal effects and sports equipment appropriate for a pleasure trip also are allowed.

If you are bringing along a computer, camera, or other electronic equipment for your own use that you will be taking back to the US, you should register the item with the US Customs Service in order to avoid paying duty both entering and returning from

Spain. (Also see *Customs and Returning to the US,* in this section.) For information on this procedure, as well as for a variety of pamphlets on US customs regulations, contact the local office of the US Customs Service or the central office, PO Box 7407, Washington, DC 20044 (phone: 202-566-8195).

Additional information regarding customs regulations is available from the National Tourist Office of Spain. See *Tourist Information Offices,* in this section, for addresses of offices in the US.

■**One rule to follow:** When passing through customs, it is illegal not to declare dutiable items; penalties range from stiff fines and seizure of the goods to prison terms. So don't try to sneak anything through — it just isn't worth it.

Insurance

It is unfortunate that most decisions to buy travel insurance are impulsive and usually are made without any real consideration of the traveler's existing policies. Therefore, the first person with whom you should discuss travel insurance is your own insurance broker, not a travel agent or the clerk behind the airport insurance counter. You may discover that the insurance you already carry — homeowner's policies and/or accident, health, and life insurance — protects you adequately while you travel and that your real needs are in the more mundane areas of excess value insurance for baggage or trip cancellation insurance.

TYPES OF INSURANCE: To make insurance decisions intelligently, however, you first should understand the basic categories of travel insurance and what they cover. Then you can decide what you should have in the broader context of your personal insurance needs, and you can choose the most economical way of getting the desired protection: through riders on existing policies; through onetime short-term policies; through a special program put together for the frequent traveler; through coverage that's part of a travel club's benefits; or with a combination policy sold by insurance companies through brokers, automobile clubs, tour operators, and travel agents.

There are seven basic categories of travel insurance:

1. Baggage and personal effects insurance
2. Personal accident and sickness insurance
3. Trip cancellation and interruption insurance
4. Default and/or bankruptcy insurance
5. Flight insurance (to cover injury or death)
6. Automobile insurance (for driving your own or a rented car)
7. Combination policies

Baggage and Personal Effects Insurance – Ask your insurance agent if baggage and personal effects are included in your current homeowner's policy, or if you will need a special floater to cover you for the duration of a trip. The object is to protect your bags and their contents in case of damage or theft anytime during your travels, not just while you're in flight and covered by the airline's policy. Furthermore, only limited protection is provided by the airline. Baggage liability varies from carrier to carrier, but generally speaking, on domestic flights, luggage usually is insured to $1,250 — that's per passenger, not per bag. For most international flights, including domestic portions of international flights, the airline's liability limit is approximately $9.07 per pound or $20 per kilo (which comes to about $360 per 40-pound suitcase) for checked baggage and up to $400 per passenger for unchecked baggage. These limits should be specified on your airline ticket, but to be awarded any amount, you'll have to provide an itemized list of lost property, and if you're including new and/or expensive items, be prepared for a request that you back up your claim with sales receipts or other proof of purchase.

If you are carrying goods worth more than the maximum protection offered by the airline, bus, or train company, consider excess value insurance. Additional coverage is available from airlines at an average, currently, of $1 to $2 per $100 worth of coverage, up to a maximum of $5,000. This insurance can be purchased at the airline counter when you check in, though you should arrive early enough to fill out the necessary forms and to avoid holding up other passengers.

Major credit card companies also provide coverage for lost or delayed baggage — and this coverage often is over and above what the airline will pay. The basic coverage usually is automatic for all cardholders who use the credit card to purchase tickets, but to qualify for additional coverage, cardholders generally must enroll.

American Express: Provides $500 coverage for checked baggage; $1,250 for carry-on baggage; and $250 for valuables, such as cameras and jewelry.

Carte Blanche and Diners Club: Provide $1,250 free insurance for checked or carry-on baggage that's lost or damaged.

Discover Card: Offers $500 insurance for checked baggage and $1,250 for carry-on baggage — but to qualify for this coverage cardholders first must purchase additional flight insurance (see "Flight Insurance," below).

MasterCard and Visa: Baggage insurance coverage set by the issuing institution.

Additional baggage and personal effects insurance also is included in certain of the combination travel insurance policies discussed below.

■ **A note of warning:** Be sure to read the fine print of any excess value insurance policy; there often are specific exclusions, such as cash, tickets, furs, gold and silver objects, art, and antiques. And remember that insurance companies ordinarily will pay only the depreciated value of the goods rather than their replacement value. The best way to protect the items you're carrying in your luggage is to take photos of your valuables and keep a record of the serial numbers of such items as cameras, typewriters, laptop computers, radios, and so on. This will establish that you do, indeed, own the objects. If your luggage disappears or is damaged en route, deal with the situation immediately. If an airline loses your luggage, you will be asked to fill out a Property Irregularity Report before you leave the airport. If your property disappears at other transportation centers, tell the local company, but also report it to the police (since the insurance company will check with the police when processing the claim). When traveling by train, if you are sending excess luggage as registered baggage, remember that some trains may not have provisions for extra cargo; if your baggage does not arrive when you do, it may not be lost, just on the next train!

Personal Accident and Sickness Insurance – This covers you in case of illness during your trip or death in an accident. Most policies insure you for hospital and doctor's expenses, lost income, and so on. In most cases, it is a standard part of existing health insurance policies, though you should check with your broker to be sure that your policy will pay for any medical expenses incurred abroad. If not, take out a separate vacation accident policy or an entire vacation insurance policy that includes health and life coverage.

Two examples of such comprehensive health and life insurance coverage are the travel insurance packages offered by *Wallach & Co:*

HealthCare Global: This insurance package, which can be purchased for periods of 10 to 180 days, is offered for two age groups: Men and women up to age 75

receive $25,000 medical insurance and $50,000 accidental injury or death benefit; those from ages 76 to 84 are eligible for $12,500 medical insurance and
$25,000 injury or death benefit. For either policy, the cost for a l0-day period
is $25.

HealthCare Abroad: This program is available to individuals up to age 75. For $3
per day (minimum 10 days, maximum 90 days), policy holders receive $100,000
medical insurance and $25,000 accidental injury or death benefit.

Both of these basic programs also may be bought in combination with trip cancella-
tion and baggage insurance at extra cost. For further information, write to *Wallach &
Co.,* 243 Church St. NW, Suite 100-D, Vienna, VA 22180 (phone: 703-281-9500 in
Virginia; 800-237-6615 elsewhere in the US).

Trip Cancellation and Interruption Insurance – Most charter and package tour
passengers pay for their travel well before departure. The disappointment of having to
miss a vacation because of illness or any other reason pales before the awful prospect
that not all (and sometimes none) of the money paid in advance might be returned. So
cancellation insurance for any package tour is a must.

Although cancellation penalties vary (they are listed in the fine print of every tour
brochure, and before you purchase a package tour you should know exactly what they
are), rarely will a passenger get more than 50% of this money back if forced to cancel
within a few weeks of scheduled departure. Therefore, if you book a package tour or
charter flight, you should have trip cancellation insurance to guarantee full reimbursement or refund should you, a traveling companion, or a member of your immediate
family get sick, forcing you to cancel your trip or *return home early.*

The key here is *not* to buy just enough insurance to guarantee full reimbursement
for the cost of the package or charter in case of cancellation. The proper amount of
coverage should be sufficient to reimburse you for the cost of having to catch up with
a tour after its departure or having to travel home at the full economy airfare if you
have to forgo the return flight of your charter. There usually is quite a discrepancy
between a charter fare and the amount charged to travel the same distance on a
regularly scheduled flight at full economy fare.

Trip cancellation insurance is available from travel agents and tour operators in two
forms: as part of a short-term, all-purpose travel insurance package (sold by the travel
agent); or as specific cancellation insurance designed by the tour operator for a specific
charter tour. Generally, tour operators' policies are less expensive, but also less inclusive. Cancellation insurance also is available directly from insurance companies or their
agents as part of a short-term, all-inclusive travel insurance policy.

Before you decide on a policy, read each one carefully. (Either type can be purchased
from a travel agent when you book the charter or package tour.) Be certain that your
policy includes enough coverage to pay your fare from the farthest destination on your
itinerary should you have to miss the charter flight. Also, be sure to check the fine print
for stipulations concerning "family members" and "pre-existing medical conditions,"
as well as allowances for living expenses if you must delay your return due to bodily
injury or illness.

Default and/or Bankruptcy Insurance – Although trip cancellation insurance
usually protects you if *you* are unable to complete — or begin — your trip, a fairly
recent innovation is coverage in the event of default and/or bankruptcy on the part of
the tour operator, airline, or other travel supplier. In some travel insurance packages,
this contingency is included in the trip cancellation portion of the coverage; in others,
it is a separate feature. Either way, it is becoming increasingly important. Whereas
sophisticated travelers long have known to beware of the possibility of default or
bankruptcy when buying a charter flight or tour package, in recent years more than
a few respected airlines unexpectedly have revealed their shaky financial condition,

sometimes leaving hordes of stranded ticket holders in their wake. Moreover, the value of escrow protection of a charter passenger's funds lately has been unreliable. While default/bankruptcy insurance will not ordinarily result in reimbursement in time to pay for new arrangements, it can ensure that you will get your money back, and even independent travelers buying no more than an airplane ticket may want to consider it.

Flight Insurance – Airlines have carefully established limits of liability for injury to or the death of passengers on international flights. For all international flights to, from, or with a stopover in the US, all carriers are liable for up to $75,000 per passenger. For all other international flights, the liability is based on where you purchase the ticket: If booked in advance in the US, the maximum liability is $75,000; if arrangements are made abroad, the liability is $10,000. But remember, these liabilities are not the same thing as insurance policies; every penny that an airline eventually pays in the case of injury or death may be subject to a legal battle.

But before you buy last-minute flight insurance from an airport vending machine, consider the purchase in light of your total existing insurance coverage. A careful review of your current policies may reveal that you already are amply covered for accidental death, sometimes up to three times the amount provided for by the flight insurance you're buying at the airport.

Be aware that airport insurance, the kind typically bought at a counter or from a vending machine, is among the most expensive forms of life insurance coverage, and that even within a single airport, rates for approximately the same coverage vary widely. Often policies sold in vending machines are more expensive than those sold over the counter, even when they are with the same national company.

If you buy your plane ticket with a major credit card, you generally receive automatic insurance coverage at no extra cost. Additional coverage usually can be obtained at extremely reasonable prices, but a cardholder must sign up for it in advance. (Note that rates vary slightly for residents of some states.) As we went to press, the travel accident and life insurance policies of the major credit cards were as follows:

> *American Express:* Automatically provides $100,000 in insurance to its *Green, Gold,* and *Optima* cardholders, and $500,000 to *Platinum* cardholders. With *American Express,* $4 per ticket buys an additional $250,000 worth of flight insurance; $6.50 buys $500,000 worth; and $13 provides an added $1 million worth of coverage.
>
> *Carte Blanche:* Automatically provides $150,000 flight insurance. An additional $250,000 worth of insurance is available for $4; $500,000 costs $6.50.
>
> *Diners Club:* Provides $350,000 free flight insurance. An additional $250,000 worth of insurance is available for $4; $500,000 costs $6.50.
>
> *Discover Card:* Provides $500,000 free flight insurance. An additional $250,000 worth of insurance is available for $4; $500,000 costs $6.50.
>
> *MasterCard and Visa:* Insurance coverage set by the issuing institution.

Automobile Insurance – Public liability and property damage (third-party) insurance is compulsory in Europe, and whether you drive your own or a rental car you must carry insurance. Car rentals in Spain usually include public liability, property damage, fire, and theft coverage and, sometimes (depending on the car rental company), collision damage coverage with a deductible.

In your car rental contract, you'll see that for about $11 to $13 a day, you may buy optional collision damage waiver (CDW) protection. (If partial coverage with a deductible is included in the rental contract, the CDW will cover the deductible in the event of an accident, and can cost as much as $25 per day.) If you do not accept the CDW coverage, you may be liable for as much as the full retail value of the rental car, and by paying for the CDW you are relieved of all responsibility for any damage to the car. Before agreeing to this coverage, however, check with your own broker about your existing personal auto insurance policy. It very well may cover your entire liability exposure without any additional cost, or you automatically may be covered by the credit card company to which you are charging the cost of your rental. To find out the amount of rental car insurance provided by major credit cards, contact the issuing institutions.

You also should know that an increasing number of the major international car rental companies automatically are including the cost of the CDW in their basic rates. Car rental prices have increased to include this coverage, although rental company ad campaigns may promote this as a new, improved rental package "benefit." The disadvantage of this inclusion is that you may not have the option to turn down the CDW — even if you already are adequately covered by your own insurance policy or through a credit card company.

Your rental contract (with the appropriate insurance box checked off), as well as proof of your personal insurance policy, if applicable, are required as proof of insurance. If you will be driving your own car in Spain, you must carry an International Insurance Certificate (called a Green Card — *Carta Verde* in Spain), available through insurance brokers in the US.

Combination Policies – Short-term insurance policies, which may include a combination of any or all of the types of insurance discussed above, are available through retail insurance agencies, automobile clubs, and many travel agents. These combination policies are designed to cover you for the duration of a single trip.

Policies of this type include the following:

Access America International: A subsidiary of the Blue Cross/Blue Shield plans of New York and Washington, DC, now available nationwide. Contact *Access America,* 600 Third Ave., PO Box 807, New York, NY 10163 (phone: 800-284-8300 or 212-490-5345).

Carefree: Underwritten by The Hartford. Contact *Carefree Travel Insurance,* Arm Coverage, PO Box 310, Mineola, NY 11501 (phone: 800-645-2424 or 516-294-0220).

NEAR Services: In addition to a full range of travel services, this organization offers a comprehensive travel insurance package. An added feature is coverage for lost or stolen airline tickets. Contact *NEAR Services,* 450 Prairie Ave., Suite 101, Calumet City, IL 60409 (phone: 708-868-6700 in the Chicago area; 800-654-6700 elsewhere in the US and Canada).

Tele-Trip: Underwritten by the Mutual of Omaha Companies. Contact *Tele-Trip Co.,* PO Box 31685, 3201 Farnam St., Omaha, NE 68131 (phone: 402-345-2400 in Nebraska; 800-228-9792 elsewhere in the US).

Travel Assistance International: Provided by Europ Assistance Worldwide Services, and underwritten by Transamerica Occidental Life Insurance. Contact *Travel Assistance International,* 1333 15th St. NW, Suite 400, Washington, DC 20005 (phone: 202-331-1609 in Washington, DC; 800-821-2828 elsewhere in the US).

Travel Guard International: Underwritten by the Insurance Company of North America, it is available through authorized travel agents, or contact *Travel Guard International,* 1145 Clark St., Stevens Point, WI 54481 (phone: 715-345-0505 in Wisconsin; 800-826-1300 elsewhere in the US).

Travel Insurance PAK: Underwritten by The Travelers. Contact *The Travelers Companies,* Ticket and Travel Plans, One Tower Sq., Hartford, CT 06183-5040 (phone: 203-277-2319 in Connecticut; 800-243-3174 elsewhere in the US).

WorldCare Travel Assistance Association: This organization offers insurance packages underwritten by Transamerica Occidental Life Insurance Company and Transamerica Premier Insurance Company. Contact *WorldCare Travel Assist-*

ance Association, 605 Market St., Suite 1300, San Francisco, CA 94105 (phone: 800-666-4993 or 415-541-4991).

How to Pack

No one can provide a completely foolproof list of precisely what to pack, so it's best to let common sense, space, and comfort guide you. Keep one maxim in mind: Less is more. You simply won't need as much clothing as you think, and you are far more likely to need a forgotten accessory — or a needle and thread or scissors — than a particular piece of clothing.

As with almost anything relating to travel, a little planning can go a long way.

1. Where are you going — city, country, or both?
2. How many total days will you be gone?
3. What's the average temperature likely to be during your stay?

The goal is to remain perfectly comfortable, neat, clean, and fashionable, but to pack as little as possible. Learn to travel light by following two firm packing principles:

1. Organize your travel wardrobe around a single color — blue or brown, for example — that allows you to mix, match, and layer clothes. Holding firm to one color scheme will make it easy to eliminate items of clothing that don't harmonize.
2. Never overpack to ensure a supply of fresh clothing — shirts, blouses, underwear — for each day of a long trip. Use hotel laundries to wash and clean clothes. If these are too expensive, there are self-service laundries (called *las lavanderías*) in most towns of any size.

CLIMATE AND CLOTHES: Exactly what you pack for your trip will be a function of where you are going and when and the kinds of things you intend to do. A few degrees can make all the difference between being comfortably attired and very real suffering, so your initial step should be to find out what the general weather conditions are likely to be in the areas you will visit.

Spain is roughly parallel with the US; Madrid (sitting astride latitude 40°) is about even with Washington, DC. The climate varies among Spain's three principal regions, north, central, and southern — primarily in amounts of rainfall, depending on the time of year. It most often is moderate to hot, although in winter it can be damp and chilly, and even cold and snowy in the Pyrenees. Residents of the US will find that the same wardrobe they would wear in the southern United States will, with a few adjustments, also be appropriate for most parts of Spain in the same season.

Anyone going to Spain from the late fall through the early spring, however, should take into account that while central heating is prevalent, interiors usually are not heated to the same degree they would be in the US. Thus, although there is no need to prepare for sub-zero winters, most people probably will feel more comfortable wearing heavier clothing indoors than they might at home — for instance, sweaters rather than light-weight shirts and blouses.

Especially in northern Spain, where precipitation can be heavy during the winter months, rain gear also is advisable. A raincoat with a zip-out lining — and a hood or rain hat — is a versatile choice. If you do decide to take an umbrella, a compact telescoping model is best.

More information about the climate in Spain, along with a chart of average low and high temperatures for different cities, is given in *When to Go,* in this section; other sources of information are airlines and travel agents.

Keeping temperature and climate in mind, consider the problem of luggage. Plan on one suitcase per person (and in a pinch, remember it's always easier to carry two small suitcases than to schlepp one that is roughly the size of downtown Detroit). Standard 26- to 28-inch suitcases can be made to work for 1 week or 1 month, and unless you are going for no more than a weekend, never cram wardrobes for two people into one suitcase. Hanging bags are best for dresses, suits, and jackets.

Before packing, lay out every piece of clothing you think you might want to take. Select clothing on the basis of what can serve several functions (whenever possible, clothes should be chosen that can be used for both daytime and evening wear). Pack clothes that have a lot of pockets for traveler's checks, documents, and tickets. Eliminate items that don't mix, match, or interchange within your color scheme. If you can't wear it in at least two distinct incarnations, leave it at home. Accessorize everything beforehand so you know exactly what you will be wearing with what.

Layering is the key to comfort — particularly when touring in parts of the countryside where mornings and evenings can be chilly even when the days are mild. No matter where you are traveling in Spain, however, layering is a good way to prepare for atypical temperatures or changes in the weather, and even in a heat wave, an extra layer will be welcome for exploring cathedrals and wine cellars. Recommended basics are T-shirts and lightweight cotton shirts or sweaters, which can be worn under another shirt and perhaps a third layer, such as a pullover sweater, jacket, or windbreaker. In cooler weather, substitute a lightweight wool or heavier cotton turtleneck for the lighter layers. As the weather changes, you can add or remove clothes as required.

And finally — since the best touring of Spain's monuments, churches, and countryside is done on foot — it is essential to bring comfortable shoes (often this means an old pair, already broken in). Sneakers or other rubber-soled shoes are good for walking up and down stairs, up and down hills, and to distant archaeological sites and back. And even in the evening, when walking no farther than to the nearest restaurant, women should avoid spike heels. Cobblestones are ubiquitous, and chunkier heels have a better chance of not getting caught — and ruined.

Your carry-on luggage should contain a survival kit with the basic things you will need in case your luggage gets lost or stolen: a toothbrush, toothpaste, all medications, a sweater, nightclothes, and a change of underwear. With these essential items at hand, you will be prepared for any sudden, unexpected occurrence that separates you from your suitcase. If you have many 1- or 2-night stops, you can live out of your survival case without having to unpack completely at each hotel.

Sundries – If you are traveling in the heat of summer and will be spending a lot of time outdoors, pack special items so that you won't spend your entire vacation horizontal in a hotel room (or hospital) because of sunburn. Be sure to take a sun hat (to protect hair as well as skin), sunscreen, and tanning lotion. Also, if you are heading for a vacation on skis, do not underestimate the effect of the sun's glare off snowy slopes, especially in higher altitudes — your face and neck are particularly susceptible to a burning.

Other items you might consider packing are a a pocket-size flashlight with extra batteries, a small sewing kit, a first-aid kit (see *Staying Healthy,* in this section, for recommended components), binoculars, and a camera or camcorder (see *Cameras and Equipment,* in this section).

■**Note:** For those on the go, *Travel Mini Pack* offers numerous products — from toilet articles to wrinkle remover spray — in handy travel sizes, as well as travel accessories such as money pouches, foreign currency calculators, and even a combination hair dryer/iron. For a catalog, contact *Travel Mini Pack,* PO Box 571, Stony Point, NY 10980 (phone: 914-429-8281).

PACKING: The basic idea of packing is to get everything into the suitcase and out again with as few wrinkles as possible. Simple, casual clothes — shirts, jeans and slacks, permanent press skirts — can be rolled into neat, tight sausages that keep other packed items in place and leave the clothes themselves amazingly unwrinkled. However, for items that are too bulky or delicate for even careful rolling, a suitcase can be packed with the heaviest items on the bottom, toward the hinges, so that they will not wrinkle more perishable clothes. Candidates for the bottom layer include shoes (stuff them with small items to save space), a toilet kit, handbags (stuff them to help keep their shape), and an alarm clock. Fill out this layer with things that will not wrinkle or will not matter if they do, such as sweaters, socks, a bathing suit, gloves, and underwear.

If you get this first, heavy layer as smooth as possible with the fill-ins, you will have a shelf for the next layer — the most easily wrinkled items, like slacks, jackets, shirts, dresses, and skirts. These should be buttoned and zipped and laid along the whole length of the suitcase with as little folding as possible. When you do need to make a fold, do it on a crease (as with pants), along a seam in the fabric, or where it will not show (such as shirttails). Alternate each piece of clothing, using one side of the suitcase, then the other, to make the layers as flat as possible. Make the layers even and the total contents of your bag as full and firm as possible to keep things from shifting around during transit. On the top layer put the things you will want at once: nightclothes, a bathing suit, an umbrella or raincoat, a sweater.

With men's two-suiter suitcases, follow the same procedure. Then place jackets on hangers, straighten them out, and leave them unbuttoned. If they are too wide for the suitcase, fold them lengthwise down the middle, straighten the shoulders, and fold the sleeves in along the seam.

While packing, it is a good idea to separate each layer of clothes with plastic cleaning bags, which will help preserve pressed clothes while they are in the suitcase. Unpack your bags as soon as you get to your hotel. Nothing so thoroughly destroys freshly cleaned and pressed clothes as sitting for days in a suitcase. Finally, if something is badly wrinkled and can't be professionally pressed before you must wear it, hang it for several hours in a bathroom where the bathtub has been filled with very hot water; keep the door closed so the room becomes something of a steamroom. It really works miracles.

SOME FINAL PACKING HINTS: Apart from the items you pack as carry-on luggage (see above), always keep all necessary medicines, valuable jewelry, and travel or business documents in your purse, briefcase, or carry-on bag — *not in the luggage you will check.* Tuck a bathing suit into your handbag or briefcase, too; in the event of lost baggage, it's frustrating to be without one. And whether in your overnight bag or checked luggage, cosmetics and any liquids should be packed in plastic bottles or at least wrapped in plastic bags and tied.

Golf clubs and skis may be checked through as luggage (most airlines are accustomed to handling them), but tennis rackets should be carried onto the plane. Some airlines require that bicycles be partially dismantled and packaged (see *Camping and Caravanning, Hiking and Biking,* in this section). Check with the airline before departure to see if there is a specific regulation concerning any special equipment or sporting gear you plan to take.

Hints for Handicapped Travelers

From 40 to 50 million people in the US alone have some sort of disability, and over half this number are physically handicapped. Like everyone else today, they — and the uncounted disabled millions around the world — are on the move. More than ever before, they are demanding facilities they can use comfortably, and they are being heard.

Spain, a country of many hills and steps, has been comparatively slow in developing access for the handicapped. Generally, only the best or newest hotels and restaurants are easily accessible to a person in a wheelchair, and unless you are on a special tour for the handicapped, you will need to rely mostly on taxis for transportation. Nevertheless, with ingenuity and the help of an able-bodied traveling companion, you can get around Spain well enough to thoroughly enjoy its varied delights. What the Spanish lack in facilities for the handicapped they more than make up for in willingness to help.

PLANNING: Collect as much information as you can about your specific disability and facilities for the disabled in Spain. Make your travel arrangements well in advance and specify to all services involved the exact nature of your condition or restricted mobility, as your trip will be much more comfortable if you know that there are accommodations and facilities to suit your needs. The best way to find out if your intended destination can accommodate a handicapped traveler is to write or call the local tourist authority or hotel and ask specific questions. If you require a corridor of a certain width to maneuver a wheelchair or if you need handles on the bathroom walls for support, ask the hotel manager. A travel agent or the local chapter or national office of the organization that deals with your particular disability — for example, the *American Foundation for the Blind* or the *American Heart Association* — will supply the most up-to-date information on the subject. The following organizations offer general information on access:

ACCENT on Living (PO Box 700, Bloomington, IL 61702; phone: 309-378-2961). This information service for persons with disabilities provides a free list of travel agencies specializing in arranging trips for the disabled; for a copy send a self-addressed, stamped envelope. Also offers a wide range of publications, including a quarterly magazine ($8 per year; $14 for 2 years) for persons with disabilities.

Information Center for Individuals with Disabilities (Fort Point Pl., 1st Floor, 27-43 Wormwood St., Boston, MA 02210; phone: 800-462-5015 in Massachusetts; 617-727-5540/1 elsewhere in the US; both numbers provide voice and TDD — telecommunications device for the deaf). The center offers information and referral services on disability-related issues, publishes fact sheets on travel agents, tour operators, and other travel resources, and can help you research your trip.

Mobility International USA (*MIUSA;* PO Box 3551, Eugene, OR 97403; phone: 503-343-1284; both voice and TDD). This US branch of *Mobility International,* a nonprofit British organization with affiliates worldwide, offers members advice and assistance — including information on accommodations and other travel services, and publications applicable to the traveler's disability. It also offers a quarterly newsletter and a comprehensive sourcebook, *A World of Options for the 90s: A Guide to International Education Exchange, Community Service and Travel for Persons with Disabilities* ($14 for members; $16 for non-members). Membership includes the newsletter and is $20 a year; subscription to the newsletter alone is $10 annually.

The National Institute of Social Services (Ministry of Labour, Health and Social Security, Nuevos Ministerios, Paseo de la Castellana, Madrid 28071, Spain; phone: 1-253-6000, 1-253-7600, or 1-233-7995). Information and escort services.

National Rehabilitation Information Center (8455 Colesville Rd., Suite 935, Silver Spring, MD 20910; phone: 301-588-9284). A general information, resource, research, and referral service.

Paralyzed Veterans of America (*PVA;* PVA/ATTS Program, 801 18th St. NW, Washington, DC 20006; phone: 202-416-7708 in Washington, DC; 800-424-8200 elsewhere in the US). The members of this national service organization all are veterans who have suffered spinal cord injuries, but it offers advocacy services and information to all persons with a disability. *PVA* also sponsors *Access to the Skies,* a program that coordinates the efforts of the national and international air travel industry in providing airport and airplane access for the disabled. Members receive several helpful publications, as well as regular notification of conferences on subjects of interest to the disabled traveler.

Royal Association for Disability and Rehabilitation (*RADAR;* 25 Mortimer St., London W1N 8AB, England; phone: 44-71-637-5400). Offers a number of publications for the handicapped. Their comprehensive guide, *Holidays and Travel Abroad 1991/92 — A Guide for Disabled People,* focuses on international travel. This publication can be ordered by sending payment in British pounds to *RADAR.* As we went to press, it cost just over £6; call for current pricing before ordering.

Society for the Advancement of Travel for the Handicapped (*SATH;* 26 Court St., Penthouse, Brooklyn, NY 11242; phone: 718-858-5483). To keep abreast of developments in travel for the handicapped as they occur, you may want to join *SATH,* a nonprofit organization whose members include consumers, as well as travel service professionals who have experience (or an interest) in travel for the handicapped. For an annual fee of $45 ($25 for students and travelers who are 65 and older) members receive a quarterly newsletter and have access to extensive information and referral services. *SATH* also offers two useful publications: *Travel Tips for the Handicapped* (a series of informative fact sheets) and *The United States Welcomes Handicapped Visitors* (a 48-page guide covering domestic transportation and accommodations that includes useful hints for travelers with disabilities abroad); to order, send a self-addressed, #10 envelope and $1 per title for postage.

Travel Information Service (Moss Rehabilitation Hospital, 1200 W. Tabor Rd., Philadelphia, PA 19141-3099; phone: 215-456-9600 for voice; 215-456-9602 for TDD). This service assists physically handicapped people in planning trips and supplies detailed information on accessibility for a nominal fee.

Blind travelers should contact the *American Foundation for the Blind* (15 W. 16th St., New York, NY 10011; phone: 212-620-2147 in New York State; 800-232-5463 elsewhere in the US) and *The Seeing Eye* (Box 375, Morristown, NJ 07963-0375; phone: 201-539-4425); both provide useful information on resources for the visually impaired. *Note:* In Spain, Seeing Eye dogs must be accompanied by a certificate of inoculation against rabies, issued within the previous year and certified by the attending veterinarian. These certificates must be authorized by a Spanish consul (for a fee of about $3 at press time). *The American Society for the Prevention of Cruelty to Animals* (*ASPCA,* Education Dept., 441 E. 92 St., New York, NY 10128; phone: 212-876-7700) offers a useful booklet, *Traveling With Your Pet,* which lists inoculation and other requirements by country. It is available for $5 (including postage and handling).

In addition, there are a number of publications — from travel guides to magazines — of interest to handicapped travelers. Among these are the following:

Access to the World, by Louise Weiss, offers sound tips for the disabled traveler. Published by Facts on File (460 Park Ave. S., New York, NY 10016; phone: 212-683-2244 in New York State; 800-322-8755 elsewhere in the US; 800-443-8323 in Canada), it costs $16.95. Check with your local bookstore; it also can be ordered by phone with a credit card.

The Diabetic Traveler (PO Box 8223 RW, Stamford, CT 06905; phone: 203-327-5832) is a useful quarterly newsletter. Each issue highlights a single destination or type of travel and includes information on general resources and hints for diabetics. A 1-year subscription costs $15. When subscribing, ask for the free fact sheet including an index of special articles; back issues are available for $4 each.

Guide to Traveling with Arthritis, a free brochure available by writing to the Upjohn Company (PO Box 307-B, Coventry, CT 06238), provides lots of good, commonsense tips on planning your trip and how to be as comfortable as possible when traveling by car, bus, train, cruise ship, or plane.

Handicapped Travel Newsletter is regarded as one of the best sources of information for the disabled traveler. It is edited by wheelchair-bound Vietnam veteran Michael Quigley, who has traveled to 93 countries around the world. Issued every 2 months (plus special issues), a subscription is $10 per year. Write to *Handicapped Travel Newsletter,* PO Box 269, Athens, TX 75751 (phone: 214-677-1260).

Handi-Travel: A Resource Book for Disabled and Elderly Travellers, by Cinnie Noble, is a comprehensive travel guide full of practical tips for those with disabilities affecting mobility, hearing, or sight. To order this book, send $12.95, plus shipping and handling, to the *Canadian Rehabilitation Council for the Disabled,* 45 Sheppard Ave. E., Suite 801, Toronto, Ontario M2N 5W9, Canada (phone: 416-250-7490; both voice and TDD).

The Itinerary (PO Box 2012, Bayonne, NJ 07002-2012; phone: 201-858-3400). This bimonthly travel magazine for people with disabilities includes information on accessibility, listings of tours, news of adaptive devices, travel aids, and special services, as well as numerous general travel hints. A subscription costs $10 a year.

The Physically Disabled Traveler's Guide, by Rod W. Durgin and Norene Lindsay, rates accessibility of a number of travel services and includes a list of organizations specializing in travel for the disabled. It is available for $9.95, plus shipping and handling, from Resource Directories, 3361 Executive Pkwy., Suite 302, Toledo, OH 43606 (phone: 419-536-5353 in the Toledo area; 800-274-8515 elsewhere in the US).

Ticket to Safe Travel offers useful information for travelers with diabetes. A reprint of this article is available free from local chapters of the *American Diabetes Association.* For the nearest branch, contact the central office at 505 Eighth Ave., 21st Floor, New York, NY 10018 (phone: 212-947-9707 in New York State; 800-232-3472 elsewhere in the US).

Travel for the Patient with Chronic Obstructive Pulmonary Disease, a publication of the George Washington University Medical Center, provides some sound practical suggestions for those with emphysema, chronic bronchitis, asthma, or other lung ailments. To order, send $2 to Dr. Harold Silver, 1601 18th St. NW, Washington, DC 20009 (phone: 202-667-0134).

Traveling Like Everybody Else: A Practical Guide for Disabled Travelers, by Jacqueline Freedman and Susan Gersten, offers the disabled tips on traveling by car, cruise ship, and plane, as well as lists of accessible accommodations, tour operators specializing in tours for disabled travelers, and other resources. It is available for $11.95, plus postage and handling, from Modan Publishing, PO Box 1202, Bellmore, NY 11710 (phone: 516-679-1380).

Travel Tips for Hearing-Impaired People, a free pamphlet for deaf and hearing-impaired travelers, is available from the *American Academy of Otolaryngology* (One Prince St., Alexandria, VA 22314; phone: 703-836-4444). For a copy, send a self-addressed, stamped, business-size envelope to the academy.

Travel Tips for People with Arthritis, a free 31-page booklet published by the *Arthritis Foundation,* provides helpful information regarding travel by car, bus, train, cruise ship, or plane, planning your trip, medical considerations, and ways to conserve your energy while traveling. It also includes listings of helpful resources, such as associations and travel agencies that operate tours for disabled travelers. For a copy, contact your local *Arthritis Foundation* chapter, or write to the national office, PO Box 19000, Atlanta, GA 30326 (phone: 404-872-7100).

A few more basic resources to look for are *Travel for the Disabled,* by Helen Hecker ($9.95), and by the same author, *Directory of Travel Agencies for the Disabled* ($19.95). *Wheelchair Vagabond,* by John G. Nelson, is another useful guide for travelers confined to a wheelchair (hardcover, $14.95; paperback, $9.95). All three are published by Twin Peaks Press, PO Box 129, Vancouver, WA 98666 (phone: 800-637-CALM or 206-694-2462).

Another good sources of information are branches of the National Tourist Office of Spain, although brochures specifically for the handicapped may not be in English. (For the US addresses of these government tourist authorities, see *Tourist Information Offices,* in this section.)

Two organizations based in Great Britain offer information for handicapped persons traveling throughout Europe, including Spain. *Tripscope* (63 Esmond Rd., London W4 1JE, UK; phone: 44-81-994-9294) is a telephone-based information and referral service (not a booking agent) that can help with transportation options for journeys throughout Europe. It may, for instance, be able to recommend outlets leasing small family vehicles adapted to accommodate wheelchairs. *Tripscope* also provides information on cassettes for blind or visually-impaired travelers, and accepts written requests for information from those with speech impediments. And for general information, there's *Holiday Care Service* (2 Old Bank Chambers, Station Rd., Horley, Surrey RH6 9HW, UK; phone: 44-293-774535), a first-rate, free advisory service on accommodations, transportation, and holiday packages throughout Europe for disabled visitors.

Regularly revised hotel and restaurant guides use the symbol of access (person in a wheelchair; see the symbol at the beginning of this section) to point out accommodations suitable for wheelchair-bound guests. The red *Michelin Guide to Spain and Portugal* (Michelin; $19.95), found in general and travel bookstores, is one such publication.

PLANE: The US Department of Transportation (DOT) has ruled that US airlines must accept all passengers with disabilities. As a matter of course, US airlines were pretty good about accommodating handicapped passengers even before the ruling, although each airline has somewhat different procedures. Foreign airlines also generally are good about accommodating the disabled traveler, but again, policies vary from carrier to carrier. Ask for specifics when you book your flight.

Disabled passengers always should make reservations well in advance and should provide the airline with all relevant details of their condition. These details include information on mobility and equipment that you will need the airline to supply — such as a wheelchair for boarding or portable oxygen for in-flight use. Be sure that the person to whom you speak fully understands the degree of your disability — the more details provided, the more effective help the airline can give you.

On the day before the flight, call back to make sure that all arrangements have been prepared, and arrive early on the day of the flight so that you can board before the rest of the passengers. It's a good idea to bring a medical certificate with you, stating your specific disability or the need to carry particular medicine.

Because most airports have jetways (corridors connecting the terminal with the door of the plane), a disabled passenger usually can be taken as far as the plane, and sometimes right onto it, in a wheelchair. If not, a narrow boarding chair may be used to take you to your seat. Your own wheelchair, which will be folded and put in the baggage compartment, should be tagged as escort luggage to assure that it's available at planeside upon landing rather than in the baggage claim area. Travel is not quite as simple if your wheelchair is battery-operated: Unless it has non-spillable batteries, it might not be accepted on board, and you will have to check with the airline ahead of time to find out how the batteries and the chair should be packaged for the flight. Usually people in wheelchairs are asked to wait until other passengers have disembarked. If you are making a tight connection, be sure to tell the attendant.

Passengers who use oxygen may not use their personal supply in the cabin, though it may be carried on the plane as cargo when properly packed and labeled. If you will need oxygen during the flight, the airline will supply it to you (there is a charge) provided you have given advance notice — 24 hours to a few days, depending on the carrier.

Useful information on every stage of air travel, from planning to arrival, is provided in the booklet *Incapacitated Passengers Air Travel Guide.* To receive a free copy, write to the *International Air Transport Association* (Publications Sales Department, 2000 Peel St., Montreal, Quebec H3A 2R4, Canada; phone: 514-844-6311). Another helpful publication is *Air Transportation of Handicapped Persons,* which explains the general guidelines that govern air carrier policies. For a copy of this free booklet, write to the US Department of Transportation (Distribution Unit, Publications Section, M-443-2, Washington, DC 20590) and ask for "Free Advisory Circular #AC-120-32." *Access Travel: A Guide to the Accessibility of Airport Terminals,* a free publication of the *Airport Operators Council International,* provides information on more than 500 airports worldwide — including major airports throughout Europe — and offers ratings of 70 features, such as accessibility to bathrooms, corridor width, and parking spaces. For a copy, contact Consumer Information Center (Pueblo, CO 81009; phone: 719-948-3334).

Among the major carriers serving Spain, the following airlines have TDD toll-free lines in the US for the hearing-impaired:

American: 800-582-1573 in Ohio; 800-543-1586 elsewhere in the US
Delta: 800-831-4488
TWA: 800-252-0622 in California; 800-421-8480 elsewhere in the US

SHIP: Among the ships calling at Spanish ports, *Cunard's Queen Elizabeth 2, Crystal Cruises' Crystal Harmony,* and *Royal Cruise Line's Crown Odyssey* are considered the best-equipped vessels for the handicapped. Handicapped travelers are advised to book reservations at least 90 days in advance to reserve specially equipped cabins.

For those in wheelchairs or with limited mobility, one of the best sources for evaluating a ship's accessibility is the free chart issued by the *Cruise Lines International Association* (500 Fifth Ave., Suite 1407, New York, NY 10110; phone: 212-921-0066). The chart lists accessible ships and indicates whether they accommodate standard-size or only narrow wheelchairs, have ramps, wide doors, low or no doorsills, handrails in the rooms, and so on. (For information on ships cruising around Spain, see *Traveling by Ship,* in this section.)

GROUND TRANSPORTATION: Perhaps the simplest solution to getting around is to travel with an able-bodied companion who can drive. Another alternative in Spain is to hire a driver/translator with a car — be sure to get a recommendation from a reputable source. The organizations listed above may be able to help you make arrangements — another source is your hotel concierge.

If you are accustomed to driving your own hand-controlled car and are determined to rent one, you may have to do some extensive research, as in Spain it is difficult to find rental cars fitted with hand controls. If agencies do provide hand-controlled cars, they are apt to be offered only on a limited basis in major metropolitan areas and usually are in high demand. *Hertz,* for instance, rents hand-controlled cars in Madrid and Barcelona only; you need to call at least 7 days in advance (much earlier preferably), and the selection of vehicles is very limited. The best course is to contact the major car rental agencies listed in *Traveling by Car,* in this section, well before your departure, but be forewarned, you still may be out of luck. Other sources for information on vehicles adapted for the handicapped are the organizations discussed above.

The *American Automobile Association (AAA)* publishes a useful booklet, *The Handicapped Driver's Mobility Guide.* Contact the central office of your local *AAA* club for availability and pricing, which may vary at different branch offices.

Although taxis and public transportation also are available in Spain, accessibility for the disabled varies and may be limited in rural areas, as well as in some cities. Check with a travel agent or the Spanish tourist authorities for information.

TRAIN: Train travel in Spain is not well adapted to wheelchairs, although timetables may specify which, if any, departures are accessible. For information on accessible trains and timetables, contact *Rail Europe,* the Spanish rail service representative in the US (addresses are listed in *Traveling by Train,* in this section), or ask for information at regional rail offices abroad.

BUS: In general, bus travel is not recommended for travelers who are totally wheelchair-bound, unless they have someone along who can lift them on and off or they are members of a group tour designed for the handicapped and are using a specially outfitted bus. If you have some mobility, however, you'll find local personnel usually quite happy to help you board and exit.

TOURS: Programs designed for the physically impaired are run by specialists who have researched hotels, restaurants, and sites to be sure they present no insurmountable obstacles. The following travel agencies and tour operators specialize in making group and individual arrangements for travelers with physical or other disabilities.

Access: The Foundation for Accessibility by the Disabled (PO Box 356, Malverne, NY 11565; phone: 516-887-5798). A travelers' referral service that acts as an intermediary with tour operators and agents worldwide, and provides information on accessibility at various locations.

Accessible Tours/Directions Unlimited (720 N. Bedford Rd., Bedford Hills, NY 10507; phone: 914-241-1700 in New York State; 800-533-5343 elsewhere in the continental US). Arranges group or individual tours for disabled persons traveling in the company of able-bodied friends or family members. Accepts the unaccompanied traveler if completely self-sufficient.

Dialysis at Sea Cruises (611 Barry Place, Indian Rocks Beach, FL 34635; phone: 813-596-7604 or 800-544-7604). Offers cruises that include the medical services of a nephrologist (a specialist in kidney disease) and a staff of dialysis nurses. Family, friends, and companions are welcome to travel on these cruises, but the number of dialysis patients usually is limited to roughly ten travelers per trip.

Evergreen Travel Service (4114 198th St. SW, Suite 13, Lynnwood, WA 98036-6742; phone: 206-776-1184 or 800-435-2288 throughout the continental US and Canada). Offers worldwide tours and cruises for the disabled (Wings on Wheels Tours), sight-impaired/blind (White Cane Tours), and hearing-impaired/deaf (Flying Fingers Tours). Most programs are first class or deluxe, and include a trained escort.

Flying Wheels Travel (143 W. Bridge St., Box 382, Owatonna, MN 55060; phone: 507-451-5005 or 800-535-6790). Handles both tours and individual arrangements.

Handi-Travel (First National Travel Ltd., Thornhill Sq., 300 John St., Suite 405, Thornhill, Ontario L3T 5W4, Canada; phone: 416-731-4714). Handles tours and individual arrangements.

USTS Travel Horizons (11 E. 44th St., New York, NY 10017; phone: 800-487-8787 or 212-687-5121). Travel agent and registered nurse Mary Ann Hamm designs trips for individual travelers requiring all types of kidney dialysis and handles arrangements for the dialysis.

Whole Person Tours (PO Box 1084, Bayonne, NJ 07002-1084; phone: 201-858-3400). Handicapped owner Bob Zywicki travels the world with his wheelchair and offers a lineup of escorted tours (many conducted by him) for the disabled. *Whole Person Tours* also publishes *The Itinerary,* a bimonthly newsletter for disabled travelers (see the publication source list above).

Travelers who would benefit from being accompanied by a nurse or physical therapist also can hire a companion through *Traveling Nurses' Network,* a service provided by Twin Peaks Press (PO Box 129, Vancouver, WA 98666; phone: 800-637-CALM or 206-694-2462). For a $10 fee, clients receive the names of three nurses, whom they can then contact directly; for a $125 fee, the agency will make all the hiring arrangements for the client. Travel arrangements also may be made in some cases — the fee for this further service is determined on an individual basis.

A similar service is offered by *MedEscort International* (ABE International Airport, PO Box 8766, Allentown, PA 18105; phone: 800-255-7182 in the continental US; elsewhere, call 215-791-3111). Clients can arrange to be accompanied by a nurse, paramedic, respiratory therapist, or physician through *MedEscort.* The fees are based on the disabled traveler's needs. *MedEscort* also can assist in making travel arrangements.

Hints for Single Travelers

Just about the last trip in human history on which the participants were neatly paired was the voyage of Noah's Ark. Ever since, passenger lists and tour groups have reflected the same kind of asymmetry that occurs in real life, as countless individuals set forth to see the world unaccompanied (or unencumbered, depending on your outlook) by spouse, lover, friend, or relative.

The truth is that the travel industry is not very fair to people who vacation by themselves. People traveling alone almost invariably end up paying more than individuals traveling in pairs. Most travel bargains, including package tours, accommodations, resort packages, and cruises, are based on *double-occupancy* rates. This means that the per-person price is offered on the basis of two people traveling together and sharing a double room (which means they each will spend a good deal more on meals and extras). The single traveler will have to pay a surcharge, called a single supplement, for exactly the same package. In extreme cases, this can add as much as 30% to 55% to the basic per-person rate.

Don't despair, however. Throughout Spain, there are scores of smaller hotels and other hostelries where, in addition to a cozier atmosphere, prices still are quite reasonable for the single traveler. Some ship lines have begun to offer special cruises for singles, and some resorts cater to the single traveler.

The obvious, most effective alternative is to find a traveling companion. Even special "singles' tours" that promise no supplements usually are based on people sharing double rooms. Perhaps the most recent innovation along these lines is the creation of organizations that "introduce" the single traveler to other single travelers, somewhat like a dating service. Some charge fees, others are free, but the basic service offered is the same: to match an unattached person with a compatible travel mate, often as part of the company's own package tours. Among such organizations are the following:

Jane's International (2603 Bath Ave., Brooklyn, NY 11214; phone: 718-266-2045). This service puts potential traveling companions in touch with one another. No age limit, no fee.

Odyssey Network (118 Cedar St., Wellesley, MA 02181; phone: 617-237-2400).

Originally founded to match single women travelers, this company now includes men in its enrollment. *Odyssey* offers a quarterly newsletter for members who are seeking a travel companion, and occasionally organizes small group tours. A newsletter subscription is $50.

Partners-in-Travel (PO Box 491145, Los Angeles, CA 90049; phone: 213-476-4869). Members receive a list of singles seeking traveling companions; prospective companions make contact through the agency. The membership fee is $40 per year and includes a chatty newsletter (6 issues per year).

Travel Companion Exchange (PO Box 833, Amityville, NY 11701; phone: 516-454-0880). This group publishes a newsletter for singles and a directory of individuals looking for travel companions. On joining, members fill out a lengthy questionnaire and write a small listing (much like an ad in a personal column). Based on these listings, members can request copies of profiles and contact prospective traveling companions. It is wise to join well in advance of your planned vacation so that there's enough time to determine compatibility and plan a joint trip. Membership fees, including the newsletter, are $36 for 6 months or $60 a year for a single-sex listing; $66 and $120, respectively, for a complete listing. Subscription to the newsletter alone costs $24 for 6 months or $36 per year.

Also note that certain cruise lines offer guaranteed share rates for single travelers, whereby cabin mates are selected on request. For instance, two cruise lines that provide guaranteed share rates are *Cunard* (phone: 800-221-4770) and *Royal Cruise Line* (phone: 415-956-7200 or 800-622-0538 in California; 800-227-4534 elsewhere in the US).

In addition, a number of tour packagers cater to single travelers. These companies offer packages designed for individuals interested in vacationing with a group of single travelers or in being matched with a traveling companion. Among the better established of these agencies are the following:

Contiki Holidays (1432 E. Katella Ave., Anaheim, CA 92805; phone: 714-937-0611; 800-624-0611 in California; 800-626-0611 elsewhere in the continental US). Specializes in vacations for 18- to 35-year-olds. Packages to Spain frequently are offered. As this packager is a wholesaler, reservations must be booked through a travel agent.

Cosmos: This tour operator offers budget motorcoach tours of Europe — including Spain — with a guaranteed-share plan whereby singles who wish to share rooms (and avoid paying the single supplement) are matched by the tour escort with individuals of the same sex and charged the basic double-occupancy tour price. Contact the firm at one of its three North American branches: 95-25 Queens Blvd., Rego Park, NY 11374 (phone: 800-221-0090 from the eastern US); 150 S. Los Robles Ave., Pasadena, CA 91101 (phone 818-449-0919 or 800-556-5454 from the western US); 1801 Eglinton Ave. W., Suite 104, Toronto, Ontario M6E 2H8, Canada (phone: 416-787-1281).

Grand Circle Travel (347 Congress St., Boston, MA 02210; phone: 617-350-7500 or 800-221-2610). Arranges extended vacations, escorted tours and cruises for the over-50 traveler, including singles. Membership, which is automatic when you book a trip through *Grand Circle,* includes travel discounts and other extras, such as a Pen Pals service for singles seeking traveling companions.

Insight International Tours (745 Atlantic Ave., Boston MA 02111; phone: 800-582-8380 or 617-482-2000). Offers a matching service for single travelers. Several tours are geared for travelers in the 18 to 35 age group.

Saga International Holidays (120 Boylston St., Boston MA 02116; phone: 617-451-6808 or 800-343-0273). A subsidiary of a British company specializing in older travelers, many of them single, *Saga* offers a broad selection of packages for people age 60 and over or those 50 to 59 traveling with someone 60 or older. Although anyone can book a *Saga* trip, a $15 club membership includes a subscription to their newsletter, as well as other publications and travel services — such as a matching service for single travelers.

Singleworld (401 Theodore Fremd Ave., Rye, NY 10580; phone: 914-967-3334 or 800-223-6490 in the continental US). For a yearly fee of $25, this club books members on its tours and cruises, and arranges shared accommodations, allowing individual travelers to avoid the single supplement charge; members also receive a quarterly newsletter. *Singleworld* offers package tours for singles with departures categorized by age group — for those 35 or younger, and for all ages.

Singles in Motion (545 W. 236th St., Suite 1D, Riverdale, NY 10463; phone: 212-884-4464). Offers a number of packages for single travelers, including tours, cruises, and excursions focusing on outdoor activities such as hiking and biking.

Solo Flights (127 S. Compo Rd., Westport, CT 06880; phone: 203-226-9993). Represents a number of packagers and cruise lines and books singles on individual and group tours.

STI (8619 Reseda Blvd., Suite 103, Northridge, CA 91324; phone: 800-525-0525). Specializes in travel for 18- to 30-year-olds. Offers multi-country escorted tours ranging from 2 weeks to 2 months, including itineraries in Spain.

Travel in Two's (239 N. Broadway, Suite 3, N. Tarrytown, NY 10591; phone: 914-631-8409). This company books solo travelers on packages offered by a number of companies (at no extra cost to clients), offers its own tours, and matches singles with traveling companions. Many offerings are listed in their quarterly *Singles Vacation Newsletter,* which costs $7.50 per issue or $20 per year.

A good book for single travelers is *Traveling On Your Own* by Eleanor Berman, which offers tips on traveling solo and includes information on trips for singles, ranging from outdoor adventures to educational programs. Available in bookstores, it also can be ordered by sending $12.95, plus postage and handling, to Random House, Order Dept., 400 Hahn Rd., Westminster, MD 21157 (phone: 800-733-3000).

Single travelers also may want to subscribe to *Going Solo,* a newsletter that offers helpful information on going on your own. Issued eight times a year, a subscription costs $36. Contact Doerfer Communications, PO Box 1035, Cambridge, MA 02238 (phone: 617-876-2764).

An attractive alternative for the single traveler who is particularly interested in meeting the Spanish is *Club Med,* which operates scores of resorts in more than 37 countries worldwide and caters to the single traveler, as well as couples and families. Though the clientele often is under 30, there is a considerable age mix: the average age is 37. *Club Med* has five Spanish resorts (one each in Barcelona, Cádiz, Ibiza, Marbella, and Palma de Mallorca) and most of the guests at its resorts are European. *Club Med* offers single travelers package-rate vacations including airfare, food, wine, lodging, entertainment, and athletic facilities. The atmosphere is relaxed, the dress informal, and the price reasonable. For information, contact *Club Med,* 3 E. 54th St., New York, NY 10022 (phone: 800-CLUB-MED).

Other possibilities that include an opportunity to visit with the Spanish are *pensiones,* which often are family-run, and home stays. See our discussion of accommodations in *On the Road,* in this section, for information on these and other accommodations alternatives suitable for single travelers. And there's always camping. Many areas along the coast, as well as some sites around the countryside, have a place to pitch a tent and enjoy the scenery. (For more information, see *Camping and Caravanning, Hiking and Biking,* in this section.)

WOMEN AND STUDENTS: Two specific groups of single travelers deserve special mention: women and students. Countless women travel by themselves in Spain, and such an adventure need not be feared. One lingering inhibition many female travelers still harbor is that of eating alone in public places. The trick here is to relax and enjoy your meal and surroundings; while you may run across the occasional unenlightened waiter, a woman dining solo is no longer uncommon.

Studying Abroad – A large number of single travelers are students. Travel *is* education. Travel broadens a person's knowledge and deepens his or her perception of the world in a way no media or "armchair" experience ever could. In addition, to study a country's language, art, culture, or history in one of its own schools is to enjoy the most productive method of learning.

By "student" we do not necessarily mean a person who wishes to matriculate at a foreign university to earn a degree. Nor do we necessarily mean a younger person. A student is anyone who wishes to include some sort of educational program in a trip to Spain.

There are many benefits for students abroad, and the way to begin to discover them is to consult the *Council on International Educational Exchange (CIEE).* This organization, which runs a variety of well-known work, study, and travel programs for students, is the US sponsor of the International Student Identity Card (ISIC). Reductions on airfare, other transportation, and entry fees to most museums and other exhibitions are only some of the advantages of the card. To apply for it, write to *CIEE* at one of the following addresses: 205 E. 42nd St., New York, NY 10017 (phone: 212-661-1414); 312 Sutter St., Suite 407, San Francisco, CA 94108 (phone: 415-421-3473); and 919 Irving St., Suite 102, San Francisco, CA 94122 (phone: 415-566-6222). Mark the letter "Attn. Student ID." Application requires a $14 fee, a passport-size photograph, and proof that you are a matriculating student (this means either a transcript or a letter or bill from your school registrar with the school's official seal; high school and junior high school students can use their report cards). There is no maximum age limit, but participants must be at least 12 years old. The *ID Discount Guide,* which gives details of the discounts country by country, is free with membership. Another free publication of *CIEE* is the informative, annual, 64-page *Student Travel Catalog,* which covers all aspects of youth-travel abroad for vacation trips, jobs, or study programs, and also includes a list of other helpful publications. You can order the catalogue from the Information and Student Services Department at the New York address given above.

Another card of value in Europe, and also available through *CIEE,* is the Federation of International Youth Travel Organizations (FIYTO) card, which provides many of the benefits of the ISIC card. In this case, cardholders need not be students, merely under age 26. To apply, send $14 with a passport-size photo and proof of birth date to *CIEE* at one of the addresses above.

CIEE also sponsors charter flights to Europe that are open to students and nonstudents of any age. Flights between New York and Barcelona, Madrid and Málaga (with budget-priced add-ons available from Chicago, Cleveland, Miami, Minneapolis, Phoenix, Portland, Salt Lake City, San Diego, Seattle, and Spokane) arrive and depart at least three times a week from Kennedy (JFK) Airport during the high season. Youth fares also may be offered by some scheduled airlines offering transatlantic service to Spain. To find out about current discounts and restrictions, contact the individual carriers. (Also see *Traveling by Plane,* in this section.)

For extensive travel throughout Europe, there is a version of the Eurailpass restricted to travelers (including non-students) under 26 years of age. The Eurail Youthpass entitles the bearer to either 1 or 2 months of unlimited second class rail travel in 17 countries, including Spain. In addition, it is honored on many European steamers and ferries and on railroad connections between the airport and the center of town in various cities. The pass also entitles the bearer to reduced rates on some bus lines in several countries. The Eurail Youthpass can be purchased only by those living outside Europe or North Africa, and it must be purchased before departure. Eurailpasses can be bought from a US travel agent or from the national railway offices of the countries in the Eurail network (for further information and addresses, see *Traveling by Train,* in this section).

Students and singles in general should keep in mind that youth hostels exist in many cities throughout Spain. They always are inexpensive, generally clean and well situated, and they are a sure place to meet other people traveling alone. Hostels are run by the hosteling associations of 68 countries that make up the *International Youth Hostel Federation (IYHF);* membership in one of the national associations affords access to the hostels of the rest. To join the American affiliate, *American Youth Hostels (AYH)*, contact the national office (PO Box 37613, Washington, DC 20013-7613; phone: 202-783-6161), or the local *AYH* council nearest you. As we went to press, the following membership rates were in effect: $25 for adults (between 18 and 54), $10 for youths (17 and under), $15 for seniors (55 and up), and $35 for family membership. The *AYH Handbook,* which lists hostels in the US, comes with your *AYH* card (non-members can purchase the handbook for $5, plus postage and handling; the *International Youth Hostel Handbooks,* which list hostels worldwide, must be purchased ($10.95 each, plus postage and handling).

Those who go abroad without an *AYH* card may purchase a youth hostel International Guest Card (for the equivalent of about $18), and obtain information on local youth hostels by contacting *Red Española de Albergues Juveniles* (71 Calle José Ortega y Gasset, Madrid 28006, Spain; phone 1-401-1300). This association also provides information on hostels throughout Spain. Another source of information is the tourist boards, which may provide information sheets on hostels in their areas (see the individual city reports in THE CITIES for locations).

Opportunities for study range from summer or academic-year courses in the language and civilization of Spain designed specifically for foreigners (including those whose school days are well behind them) to long-term university attendance by those intending to take a degree.

Complete details on more than 3,000 courses available abroad (including at Spanish universities) and suggestions on how to apply are contained in two books published by the *Institute of International Education* (IIE Books, 809 UN Plaza, New York, NY 10017; phone 212-883-8200): *Vacation Study Abroad* ($24.95, plus shipping and handling) and *Academic Year Abroad* ($31.95, plus shipping and handling). A third book, *Teaching Abroad,* costs $21.95, plus shipping and handling. IIE Books also offers a free pamphlet called *Basic Facts on Study Abroad.*

The *National Registration Center for Study Abroad (NRCSA;* PO Box 1393, Milwaukee, WI 53201; phone: 414-278-0631) also offers a publication called *Worldwide Classroom: Study Abroad and Learning Vacations in 40 Countries: 1991-1992,* available for $8, which includes information on over 160 schools and cultural centers that offer courses for Americans, with the primary focus on foreign language and culture.

Those who are interested in a a "learning vacation" abroad also may be interested in *Travel and Learn* by Evelyn Kaye. This guide to educational travel discusses a wide range of opportunities — everything from archaeology to whale watching — and provides information on organizations that offer programs in these areas of interest. The book is available in bookstores for $23.95; or you can send $26 (which includes shipping charges) to Blue Penguin Publications (147 Sylvan Ave., Leonia, NJ 07605; phone: 800-800-8147 or 201-461-6918). *Learning Vacations* by Gerson G. Eisenberg also provides extensive information on seminars, workshops, courses, and so on — in a wide variety of subjects. Available in bookstores, it also can be ordered from Peterson's Guides (PO Box 2123, Princeton, NJ 08543-2123; phone: 609-243-9111) for $11.95, plus shipping and handling.

Work, Study, Travel Abroad: The Whole World Handbook, issued by the *Council on International Educational Exchange (CIEE),* is an informative, chatty guide on study programs, work opportunities, and travel hints, with a particularly good section on Spain. It is available for $10.95, plus shipping and handling, from CIEE (address above).

AFS Intercultural Programs (313 E. 43rd St., New York, NY 10017; phone 800-AFS-INFO or 212-949-4242) sets up exchanges between US and foreign high school students on an individual basis for a whole academic year or a semester.

National Association of Secondary School Principals (*NASSP;* 1904 Association Dr., Reston, VA 22091; phone: 703-860-0200), an association of administrators, teachers, and state education officials, sponsors *School Partnership International,* a program in which secondary schools in the US are linked with partner schools abroad for an annual short-term exchange of students and faculty.

If you are interested in a home-stay travel program, in which you learn about . European culture by living with a family, contact the *Experiment in International Living* (PO Box 676, Brattleboro, VT 05302-0676; phone: 802-257-7751 in Vermont; 800-345-2929 elsewhere in the continental US), which sponsors home-stay educational travel in more than 40 countries, including locations throughout Spain. The organization aims its programs at high school or college students.

Another organization specializing in travel as an educational experience is the *American Institute for Foreign Study (AIFS)* (102 Greenwich Ave., Greenwich, CT 06830; phone: 800-727-AIFS, 203-869-9090, or 203-863-6087). Students can enroll for the full academic year or for any number of semesters. *AIFS* caters primarily to bona fide high school or college students, but its non-credit international learning programs are open to independent travelers of all ages (approximately 20% of *AIFS* students are over 25).

WORKING ABROAD: Jobs for foreigners in Spain are not easy to come by and in general do not pay well enough to cover all the expenses of a trip. They do provide an invaluable learning experience, however, while helping to make a trip more affordable.

For a complete list of programs administered by Spanish institutions, contact the National Tourist Office of Spain in North America (see *Tourist Information Offices,* in this section, for addresses).

Hints for Older Travelers

Special discounts and more free time are just two factors that have given Americans over age 65 a chance to see the world at affordable prices. Senior citizens make up an ever-growing segment of the travel population, and the trend among them is to travel more frequently and for longer periods of time.

PLANNING: When planning a vacation, prepare your itinerary with one eye on your own physical condition and the other on a topographical map. Keep in mind variations in climate, terrain, and altitudes, which may pose some danger for anyone with heart or breathing problems.

Older travelers may find the following publications of interest:

The Discount Guide for Travelers Over 55, by Caroline and Walter Weintz, is an excellent book for budget-conscious older travelers. It is available by sending $7.95, plus shipping and handling, to Penguin USA (Att. Cash Sales, 120

Woodbine St., Bergenfield, NJ 07621); when ordering, specify the ISBN number: 0-525-48358-6.

Going Abroad: 101 Tips for the Mature Traveler offers tips on preparing for your trip, commonsense precautions en route, and some basic travel terminology. This concise, free booklet is available from *Grand Circle Travel,* 347 Congress St., Boston, MA 02210 (phone: 800-221-2610 or 617-350-7500).

The International Health Guide for Senior Citizen Travelers, by Dr. W. Robert Lange, covers such topics as trip preparations, food and water precautions, adjusting to weather and climate conditions, finding a doctor, motion sickness, jet lag, and so on. Also includes a list of resource organizations that provide medical assistance for travelers. It is available for $4.95 postpaid from Pilot Books, 103 Cooper St., Babylon, NY 11702 (phone: 516-422-2225).

The Mature Traveler is a monthly newsletter that provides information on travel discounts, places of interest, useful tips, and other topics of interest for travelers 49 and up. To subscribe, send $21.95 to GEM Publishing Group, PO Box 50820, Reno, NV 89513 (phone: 702-786-7419).

Travel Easy: The Practical Guide for People Over 50, by Rosalind Massow, discusses a wide range of subjects — from trip planning, transportation options, and preparing for departure to avoiding and handling medical problems en route. It's available for $6.50 to members of the *American Association of Retired Persons (AARP),* and for $8.95 to non-members; call about current charges for postage and handling. Order from *AARP* Books, c/o Customer Service, Scott, Foresman & Company, 1900 E. Lake Ave., Glenview, IL 60025 (phone: 708-729-3000).

Travel Tips for Older Americans is a useful booklet that provides good, basic advice. This US State Department publication (stock number: 044-000-02270-2) can be ordered by sending a check or money order for $1 to the Superintendent of Documents (US Government Printing Office, Washington, DC 20402) or by calling 202-783-3238 and charging the order to a credit card.

Unbelievably Good Deals & Great Adventures That You Absolutely Can't Get Unless You're Over 50, by Joan Rattner Heilman, offers travel tips for older travelers, including discounts on accommodations and transportation, as well as a list of organizations for seniors. It is available for $7.95, plus shipping and handling, from Contemporary Books, 180 N. Michigan Ave., Chicago, IL 60601 (phone: 312-782-9181).

HEALTH: Health facilities in Spain generally are excellent; however, an inability to speak the language can pose a serious problem, not in receiving treatment at large hospitals, where many doctors and other staff members will speak English, but in getting help elsewhere or in getting to the place where help is available. A number of organizations help travelers avoid or deal with a medical emergency overseas. For information on these services, see *Medical and Legal Aid and Consular Services,* in this section.

Pre-trip medical and dental checkups are strongly recommended. In addition, be sure to take along any prescription medication you need, enough to last *without a new prescription* for the duration of your trip; pack all medications with a note from your doctor for the benefit of airport authorities. If you have specific medical problems, bring prescriptions and a "medical file" composed of the following:

1. A summary of your medical history and current diagnosis.
2. A list of drugs to which you are allergic.
3. Your most recent electrocardiogram, if you have heart problems.
4. Your doctor's name, address, and telephone number.

DISCOUNTS AND PACKAGES: Since guidelines change from place to place, it is a good idea to inquire in advance about discounts for accommodations, transportation, tickets to theater performances, concerts, and movies, entrance fees to museums, national monuments, and other attractions.

Many hotel chains, airlines, cruise lines, bus companies, car rental companies, and other travel suppliers offer discounts to older travelers. For instance, *American* and *TWA* offer those age 62 and over (and one traveling companion per qualifying senior citizen) discounts on flights from the US to Spain. Other airlines also offer discounts for passengers age 60 (or 62) and over, which also may apply to one traveling companion. For information on current prices and applicable restrictions, contact the individual carriers.

Some discounts, however, are extended only to bona fide members of certain senior citizens organizations. Because the same organizations frequently offer package tours to both domestic and international destinations, the benefits of membership are twofold: Those who join can take advantage of discounts as individual travelers and also reap the savings that group travel affords. In addition, because the age requirements for some of these organizations are quite low (or nonexistent), the benefits can begin to accrue early. In order to take advantage of these discounts, you should carry proof of your age (or eligibility). A driver's license, membership card in a recognized senior citizens organization, or a Medicare card should be adequate. Among the organizations dedicated to helping older travelers see the world are the following:

American Association of Retired Persons (*AARP;* 1909 K St. NW, Washington, DC 20049; phone: 202-872-4700). The largest and best known of these organizations. Membership is open to anyone 50 or over, whether retired or not; dues are $5 a year, $12.50 for 3 years, or $35 for 10 years, and include spouse. The *AARP* Travel Experience Worldwide program, available through *American Express Travel Related Services,* offers members tours, cruises, and other travel programs worldwide designed exclusively for older travelers. Members can book these services by calling *American Express* at 800-927-0111 for land and air travel, or 800-745-4567 for cruises.

Mature Outlook (Customer Service Center, 6001 N. Clark St., Chicago, IL 60660; phone: 800-336-6330). Through its *Travel Alert,* tours, cruises, and other vacation packages are available to members at special savings. Hotel and car rental discounts and travel accident insurance also are available. Membership is open to anyone 50 years of age or older, costs $9.95 a year, and includes a bimonthly newsletter and magazine, as well as information on package tours.

National Council of Senior Citizens (1331 F St., Washington, DC 20005; phone: 202-347-8800). Here, too, the emphasis is on keeping costs low. This nonprofit organization offers members a different roster of package tours each year, as well as individual arrangements through its affiliated travel agency *(Vantage Travel Service).* Although most members are over 50, membership is open to anyone (regardless of age) for an annual fee of $12 per person or couple. Lifetime membership costs $150.

Certain travel agencies and tour operators offer special trips geared to older travelers. Among them are the following:

Evergreen Travel Service (4114 198th St. SW, Suite 13, Lynnwood, WA 98036-6742; phone: 206-776-1184 or 800-435-2288 throughout the continental US and Canada). This specialist in trips for persons with disabilities recently introduced Lazybones Tours, a program offering leisurely tours for older travelers. Most programs are first class or deluxe, and include an escort.

Grand Circle Travel (347 Congress St., Boston, MA 02210; phone: 800-221-2610 or 617-350-7500). Caters exclusively to the over-50 traveler and packages a large variety of escorted tours, cruises, and extended vacations. Membership, which is automatic when you book a trip through *Grand Circle,* includes discount certificates on future trips and other travel services, such as a matching service for single travelers and a helpful free booklet, *Going Abroad: 101 Tips for Mature Travelers* (see the source list above).

Insight International Tours (745 Atlantic Ave., Boston, MA 02111; phone: 800-582-8380 or 617-482-2000). Offers a matching service for single travelers. Several tours are geared for mature travelers.

OmniTours (1 Northfield Plaza, Northfield, IL 60093; phone: 800-962-0060 or 708-441-5250). Offers combination air and rail group tours designed for travelers 50 years and older.

Saga International Holidays (120 Boylston St., Boston MA 02116; phone: 617-451-6808 or 800-343-0273). A subsidiary of a British company catering to older travelers, *Saga* offers a broad selection of packages for people age 60 and over or those 50 to 59 traveling with someone 60 or older. Although anyone can book a *Saga* trip, a $15 club membership includes a subscription to their newsletter, as well as other publications and travel services.

Sun Holidays (26 Sixth St., Suite 603, Stamford, CT 06905; phone: 203-323-1166 in Connecticut; 800-243-2057 elsewhere in the US). This company specializes in extended-stay packages for senior citizens, including stays on the Costa del Sol.

Many travel agencies, particularly the larger ones, are delighted to make presentations to help a group of senior citizens select destinations. A local chamber of commerce should be able to provide the names of such agencies. Once a time and place are determined, an organization member or travel agent can obtain group quotations for transportation, accommodations, meal plans, and sightseeing. Larger groups usually get the best breaks.

Another choice open to older travelers is a trip that includes an educational element. *Elderhostel,* a nonprofit organization, offers programs at educational institutions worldwide, including Barcelona, Catalonia, and Madrid in Spain. The foreign programs generally last about 2 weeks, and include double-occupancy accommodations in hotels or student residence halls and all meals. Travel to the programs usually is by designated scheduled flights, and participants can arrange to extend their stay at the end of the program. Elderhostelers must be at least 60 years old (younger if a spouse or companion qualifies), in good health, and not in need of special diets. For a free catalogue describing the program and current offerings, write to *Elderhostel* (75 Federal St., Boston, MA 02110; phone: 617-426-7788). Those interested in the program also can borrow slides at no charge or purchase an informational videotape for $5.

Interhostel, a program sponsored by the Division of Continuing Education of the University of New Hampshire, sends travelers back to school at cooperating institutions in 25 countries on 4 continents. Participants attend lectures on the history, economy, politics, and cultural life of the country they are visiting, go on field trips to pertinent points of interest, and take part in activities meant to introduce them to their foreign contemporaries. In Spain, there are two programs, one that travels to Granada, the other to Madrid and Toledo. Trips are for 2 weeks; accommodations are on campus in university residence halls or off campus in modest hotels (double occupancy). Groups are limited to 35 to 40 participants who are at least 50 years old (or at least 40 if a participating spouse is at least 50), physically active, and not in need of special diets. For further information or to receive the three free seasonal catalogues, contact *Interhostel,* UNH Division of Continuing Education, 6 Garrison Ave., Durham, NH 03824 (phone: 800-733-9753 or 603-862-1147).

Hints for Traveling with Children

 What better way to encounter the world's variety than in the company of the young, wide-eyed members of your family? Their presence does not have to be a burden or an excessive expense. The current generation of discounts for children and family package deals can make a trip together quite reasonable.

A family trip will be an investment in your children's future, making geography and history come alive to them, and leaving a sure memory that will be among the fondest you will share with them someday. Their insights will be refreshing to you; their impulses may take you to unexpected places with unexpected dividends. The experience will be invaluable to them at any age.

PLANNING: Here are several hints for making a trip with children easy and fun.

1. Children, like everyone else, will derive more pleasure from a trip if they know something about their destination before they arrive. Begin their education about a month before you leave. Using maps, travel magazines, and books, give children a clear idea of where you are going and how far away it is.

2. Children should help to plan the itinerary, and where you go and what you do should reflect some of their ideas. If they already know something about the sites they'll visit, they will have the excitement of recognition when they arrive.

3. Children also will enjoy learning some Spanish phrases — a few basics like *"hola!"* ("hello"), *"adiós"* ("good-bye"), and *"gracias"* ("thanks").

4. Familiarize your children with pesetas. Give them an allowance for the trip, and be sure they understand just how far it will or won't go.

5. Give children specific responsibilities: The job of carrying their own flight bags and looking after their personal things, along with some other light chores, will give them a stake in the journey.

6. Give each child a diary or scrapbook to take along.

One useful resource to which you may want to refer is the *Berlitz Jr. Spanish* instructional series for children. The series combines an illustrated storybook with a lively 60-minute audiocassette. Each book features a character, Teddy, who goes to school and learns to count and spell and speak Spanish phrases. The book/cassette package is available for $19.95, plus shipping and handling, from Macmillan Publishing Company, Front and Brown Sts., Riverside, NJ 08075 (phone: 800-257-5755).

Children's books about Spain provide an excellent introduction to the country and its culture. Some particularly good titles include the following:

Castle, by David Macaulay (Houghton Mifflin; $14.95 hardcover; $6.95 paperback), uses text and drawings to show how castles were built in the 13th century, and is particularly suited to helping children learn about the castles they may see in Spain.

Cathedral: The Story of Its Construction, by the same author (Houghton Mifflin; $14.95 hardcover; $6.95 paperback), also is interesting and informative.

City of Marvels, by Eduardo Mendoza and translated by Bernard Molloy (Harcourt Brace Jovanovich; $19.95), for older children, is the enthralling story of a Catalonian boy who travels to Barcelona in 1886 and is caught up in a web of intrigue.

Let's Learn About Spain, by Sacha de Nisching and illustrated by Sylvie Rainard (Passport Books; $3.95), includes games and puzzles for very young children.

The Story of Ferdinand, by Munro Lest (Penguin; $3.95), is a nicely illustrated version of the charming tale of Ferdinand the Bull.

Take a Trip to Spain, by Jonathan Rutland (Franklin Watts; $10.95) is a book of photographs for slightly older children covering, among other things, bullfighting, fiestas, homes, money, and schools.

Welcome to Spain, by Heather and John Leigh (Passport Books; $4.95), is beautifully illustrated by Joseph McEwan and covers things to watch for at festivals, music, dancing, and other fun in Spain.

These and other children's books can be found at many general bookstores and in libraries. Bookstores specializing in children's books include the following:

Books of Wonder (132 7th Ave., New York, NY 10011; phone: 212-989-3270; or 464 Hudson St., New York, NY 10014; phone: 212-645-8006). Carries both new and used books for children.

Cheshire Cat (5512 Connecticut Ave. NW, Washington, DC 20015; phone: 202-244-3956). Specializes in books for children of all ages.

Eeyore's Books for Children (2212 Broadway, New York, NY 10024; phone: 212-362-0634; or 25 E. 83rd St., New York, NY 10028; phone: 212-988-3404). Carries an extensive selection of children's books; features a special travel section.

Reading Reptile, Books and Toys for Young Mammals (4120 Pennsylvania, Kansas City, MO 64111; phone: 816-753-0441). Carries books for children and teens to age 15.

Red Balloon (891 Grand Ave., St. Paul, MN 55105; phone: 612-224-8320). Carries both new and used books for children.

White Rabbit Children's Books (7755 Girard Ave., La Jolla, CA 92037; phone: 619-454-3518). Carries books and music for children (and parents).

Another source of children's books perfect to take on the road is *The Family Travel Guides Catalogue.* This detailed booklet contains informative and amusing titles focusing on numerous countries, including Spain. For instance, the *Travel Papers,* a series of short articles full of useful facts for families, covers Spain. The *Travel Papers* and the catalogue are available from Carousel Press (PO Box 6061, Albany, CA 94706; phone: 415-527-5849), which also is the mail-order supplier of all titles listed in the catalogue.

In addition to books, audiocassettes may make Spain come alive for children. The infectious rhythms of Spanish music are a lively introduction to these vibrant cultures. Be sure to include some flamenco music — after listening to the thrilling tones, children will particularly enjoy clapping along to a performance by dashing dancers.

And for parents, *Travel With Your Children* (TWYCH; 80 Eighth Ave., New York, NY 10011; phone: 212-206-0688) publishes a newsletter, *Family Travel Times,* that focuses on families with young travelers and offers helpful hints. An annual subscription (10 issues) is $35 and includes a copy of the "Airline Guide" issue (updated every other year), which focuses on the subject of flying with children. This special issue is available separately for $10.

Another newsletter devoted to family travel is *Getaways.* This quarterly publication provides reviews of family-oriented literature, activities, and useful travel tips. To subscribe, send $25 to *Getaways,* Att. Ms. Brooke Kane, PO Box 11511, Washington, DC 20008 (phone: 703-534-8747).

Also of interest to parents traveling with their children is *How to Take Great Trips With Your Kids,* by psychologist Sanford Portnoy and his wife, Joan Flynn Portnoy. The book includes helpful tips from fellow family travelers, tips on economical accommodations and touring by car, recreational vehicle, and train, as well as over 50 games to play with your children en route. It is available for $8.95, plus shipping and handling, from Harvard Common Press, 535 Albany St., Boston, MA 02118 (phone: 617-423-5803).

Another book on family travel, *Travel with Children* by Maureen Wheeler, offers a wide range of practical tips on traveling with children, and includes accounts of the author's family travel experiences. It is available for $10.95, plus shipping and handling, from Lonely Planet Publications, Embarcadero West, 112 Linden St., Oakland, CA 94607 (phone: 415-893-8555).

Also look for the Spain volume of the "Kidding Around" series, published by John Muir Publications. This book starts with an overview of the country, along with some interesting background information, and then is divided into areas, with descriptions of the various attractions in the general order in which you might encounter them. It can be ordered directly from the publisher by sending $9.95, plus shipping, to John Muir Publications, PO Box 613, Santa Fe, NM 87504, or by calling 800-888-7504 or 505-982-4087.

GETTING THERE AND GETTING AROUND: Begin early to investigate all available family discounts and charter flights, as well as any package deals and special rates offered by the major airlines.

PLANE: When you make your reservations, tell the airline that you are traveling with a child. Children ages 2 through 12 generally travel at about a half to two-thirds of the regular full-fare adult ticket prices on most international flights. This children's fare, however, usually is much higher than the excursion fare, which is applicable to any traveler regardless of age. On many international flights, children under 2 travel at about 10% of the adult fare if they sit on an adult's lap. A second infant without a second adult would pay the fare applicable to children ages 2 through 11.

Although some airlines will, on request, supply bassinets for infants, most carriers encourage parents to bring their own safety seat on board, which then is strapped into the airline seat with a regular seat belt. This is much safer — and certainly more comfortable — than holding the child in your lap. If you do not purchase a seat for your baby, you have the option of bringing the infant restraint along on the off-chance that there might be an empty seat next to yours — in which case some airlines will let you use that seat at no charge for your baby and infant seat. However, if there is no empty seat available, the infant seat no doubt will have to be checked as baggage (and you may have to pay an additional charge), since it generally does not fit under the seat or in the overhead racks.

The safest bet is to pay for a seat — this usually will be the same as fares applicable to children ages 2 through 11. It usually is cheaper to pay for an adult excursion rate than the discounted children's fare.

Be forewarned: Some safety seats designed primarily for use in cars do not fit into plane seats properly. Although nearly all seats manufactured since 1985 carry labels indicating whether they meet federal standards for use aboard planes, actual seat sizes may vary from carrier to carrier. At the time of this writing, the FAA was in the process of reviewing and revising the federal regulations regarding infant travel and safety devices — it was still to be determined if children should be *required* to sit in safety seats and whether the airlines will have to provide them.

If using one of these infant restraints, you should try to get bulkhead seats which will provide extra room to care for your child during the flight. You also should request a bulkhead seat when using a bassinet — again, this is not as safe as strapping the child in. On some planes bassinets hook into a bulkhead wall; on others it is placed on the floor in front of you. (Note that bulkhead seats often are reserved for families traveling with children.) As a general rule, babies should be held during takeoff and landing.

Request seats on the aisle if you have a toddler or if you think you will need to use the bathroom frequently. Carry onto the plane all you will need to care for and occupy your children during the flight — formula, diapers, a sweater, books, favorite stuffed animals, and so on. Dress your baby simply, with a minimum of buttons and snaps, because the only place you may have to change a diaper is at your seat or in a small lavatory. The flight attendant can warm a bottle for you.

On US carriers, such as *American* and *TWA,* you also can ask for a hot dog or hamburger instead of the airline's regular dinner if you give at least 24 hours' notice. Some, but not all, airlines have baby food aboard. While you should bring along toys from home, also ask about children's diversions. Some carriers have terrific free packages of games, coloring books, and puzzles.

When the plane takes off and lands, make sure your baby is nursing or has a bottle, pacifier, or thumb in its mouth. This sucking will make the child swallow and help to clear stopped ears. A piece of hard candy will do the same thing for an older child.

Parents traveling by plane with toddlers, children, or teenagers may want to consult *When Kids Fly,* a free booklet published by Massport (Public Affairs Department, 10 Park Plaza, Boston, MA 02116-3971; phone: 617-973-5600), which includes helpful information on airfares for children, infant seats, what to do in the event of overbooked or cancelled flights, and so on.

■**Note:** Newborn babies, whose lungs may not be able to adjust to the altitude, should not be taken aboard an airplane. And some airlines may refuse to allow a pregnant woman in her 8th or 9th month to fly. Check with the airline ahead of time, and carry a letter from your doctor stating that you are fit to travel — and indicating the estimated date of birth.

SHIP, TRAIN, AND BUS: Some shipping lines offer cruises that feature special activities for children, particularly during periods that coincide with major school holidays like *Christmas, Easter,* and the summer months. On such cruises, children may be charged special cut-rate fares, and there are youth counselors to organize activities. Occasionally, a shipping line even offers free passage during the summer months for children under age 16 occupying a stateroom with two (full-fare) adult passengers. Your travel agent should know which cruise lines offer such programs.

If you plan to travel by train when abroad, note that on some Spanish railways children under 4 (accompanied by an adult) travel free, provided they do not occupy a seat; children under 4 occupying a seat and from ages 4 through 11 also often travel at a lower fare. The Eurailpass, which is good for unlimited train travel throughout Europe, including Spain, is half price for children ages 4 through 12. It must be bought before leaving the US, so plan ahead. Some regional bus lines also may have lower fares for children or family rates. For more information, see *Traveling by Ship, Traveling by Train,* and *Traveling by Bus,* all in this section.

CAR: Traveling by car allows greater flexibility in traveling and packing. You may want to stock the car with a variety of favorite snacks or provisions so that you can stop for picnics. Games and simple toys, such as magnetic checkerboards or drawing pencils and pads, also provide a welcome diversion. Frequent stops so that children can run around make car travel much easier.

ACCOMMODATIONS AND MEALS: Often a cot for a child will be placed in a hotel room at little or no extra charge. If you wish to sleep in separate rooms, special rates sometimes are available for families; some places do not charge for children under a certain age. In many of the larger chain hotels, the staffs are more used to children. These hotels also are likely to have swimming pools or gamerooms — both popular with most youngsters. Many large resorts also have recreation centers for children. Cabins, bungalows, condominiums, and other rental options offer families privacy, flexibility, some kitchen facilities, and often lower costs.

You might want to look into accommodations along the way that will add to the color of your trip. For instance, the many *paradores* and *pensiones* in Spain provide a delightful experience for the whole family and permit a view of Spanish life different from that gained by staying in a conventional hotel. Children will love them.

Among the least expensive options is a camping facility; many are situated in beautiful, out-of-the-way spots, and generally are good and well equipped, and less expensive than any hotel. For further information on accommodations options for the whole family, see our discussions in *On the Road,* and for information on camping facilities, see *Camping and Caravanning, Hiking and Biking,* both in this section.

Although it is difficult to find adequate baby-sitting services in most Spanish cities, most better hotels will try to arrange for a sitter for the times you will want to be without the children — for an evening's entertainment or a particularly rigorous stint of sightseeing. Whether the sitter is hired directly or through an agency, ask for and check references and keep in mind that the candidates may not speak much, if any, English.

At mealtime, don't deny yourself or your children the delights of a new style of cooking. Children like to know what kind of food to expect, so it will be interesting to look up Spanish dishes before leaving. Encourage your children to try new things. In metropolitan and resort areas, you may be able to find American-style food, but you probably will have to settle for local fare everywhere else.

Things to Remember

1. If you are spending your vacation touring many places, pace the days with children in mind. Break the trip into half-day segments, with running around or "doing" time built in. Keep travel time on the road to a maximum of 4 to 5 hours a day.
2. Don't forget that a child's attention span is far shorter than an adult's. Children don't have to see every sight or all of any sight to learn something from their trip; watching, playing with, and talking to other children can be equally enlightening.
3. Let your children lead the way sometimes; their perspective is different from yours, and they may lead you to things you would never have noticed on your own.
4. Remember the places that children love to visit: aquariums, zoos, amusement parks, beaches, nature trails, and so on. Among the activities that may pique their interest are bicycling, snorkeling, boat trips, horseback riding, visiting children's museums, and viewing natural habitat exhibits.

Staying Healthy

The surest way to return home in good health is to be prepared for medical problems that might occur on vacation. Below, we've outlined some things you need to think about before you go.

Older travelers or anyone suffering from a chronic medical condition, such as diabetes, high blood pressure, cardiopulmonary disease, asthma, or ear, eye, or sinus trouble should consult a physician before leaving home. Those with conditions requiring special consideration when traveling should think about seeing, in addition to their regular physician, a specialist in travel medicine. For a referral in a particular community, contact the nearest medical school or ask a local doctor to recommend such a specialist. Dr. Leonard Marcus, a member of the *American Committee on Clinical Tropical Medicine and Travelers' Health,* provides a directory of more than 100 travel doctors across the country. For a copy, send a 9-by-12-inch self-addressed, stamped envelope to Dr. Marcus at 148 Highland Ave., Newton, MA 02165 (phone: 617-527-4003).

FIRST AID: Put together a compact, personal medical kit including Band-Aids, first-aid cream, antiseptic, nose drops, insect repellent, aspirin, an extra pair of prescription glasses or contact lenses (and a copy of your prescription for glasses or contact lenses), sunglasses, over-the-counter remedies for diarrhea, indigestion, and motion sickness, a thermometer, and a supply of those prescription medicines you take regularly.

In a corner of your kit, keep a list of all the drugs you have brought and their purpose, as well as duplicate copies of your doctor's prescriptions (or a note from your doctor). As brand names may vary in different countries, it's a good idea to ask your doctor for the generic name of any drugs you use so that you can ask for their equivalent should you need a refill.

It also is a good idea to ask your doctor to prepare a medical identification card that includes such information as your blood type, your social security number, any allergies or chronic health problems you have, and your medical insurance information. Considering the essential contents of your medical kit, keep it with you, rather than in your checked luggage.

SUNBURN: The burning power of the sun can quickly cause severe sunburn or sunstroke. To protect yourself against these ills, wear sunglasses, take along a broad-brimmed hat and cover-up, and use a sunscreen lotion.

WATER SAFETY: Spain is famous for its beaches, but it is important to remember that the sea can be treacherous. A few precautions are necessary. Beware of the undertow, that current of water running back down the beach after a wave has washed ashore; it can knock you off your feet and into the surf. Even more dangerous is the rip tide, a strong current of water running against the tide, which can pull you out to sea. If you get caught offshore, don't panic or try to fight the current, because it only will exhaust you; instead, ride it out while waiting for it to subside, which usually happens not too far from shore, or try swimming away parallel to the beach.

Sharks are sometimes sighted, but they usually don't come in close to shore, and they are well fed on fish. Should you meet up with one, just swim away as quietly and smoothly as you can, without shouting or splashing. Although not aggressive, eels can be dangerous when threatened. If snorkeling or diving in coastal waters or freshwater lakes or streams, beware of crevices where these creatures may be lurking.

The tentacled Portuguese man-of-war and other jellyfish drift in quiet salt waters for food and often wash up onto the beach; the long tentacles of these creatures sting whatever they touch. Specialists recommend carrying a small bottle of household vinegar and a container of unseasoned meat tenderizer in your beach bag. If stung, do not wash the area or rub with sand. Instead, pour vinegar over the irritation to neutralize the effect of the sting and then apply a paste made of vinegar and meat tenderizer to break down the residual venom.

Spain's coral reefs are not extensive, but they are razor-sharp. Treat all coral cuts with an antiseptic and then watch carefully since coral is a living organism with bacteria on its surface which may cause an infection. If you step on a sea urchin, you'll find that the spines are very sharp, pierce the skin, and break off easily. Like splinters, the tips left embedded in the skin are difficult to remove, but they will dissolve in a week or two; rinsing with vinegar may help to dissolve them more quickly. To avoid these hazards, keep your feet covered whenever possible.

If complications, allergic reactions (such as breathlessness, fever, or cramps), or signs of serious infection result from any of the above circumstances, *see a doctor.*

INSECTS AND OTHER PESTS: Flies and mosquitoes can be troublesome, so it is a good idea to use some form of topical insect repellent — those containing DEET (N,N-diethyl-m-toluamide) are among the most common and effective. The US Environmental Protection Agency (EPA) stresses that you should not use any pesticide that has not been approved by the EPA (check the label) and that all such preparations should be used in moderation. If picnicking or camping, burn mosquito coils or candles containing allethrin, pyrethrin, or citronella, or use a pyrethrum-containing flying-insect spray. For further information about active ingredients in repellents, call the *National Pesticide Telecommunications Network*'s 24-hour hotline number: 800-858-7378.

If you do get bitten — by mosquitoes, horse or black flies, or other bugs — the itching can be relieved with baking soda, topical first-aid cream, or antihistamine tablets. Should a bite become infected, treat it with a disinfectant or antibiotic cream.

Though rarer, bites from scorpions, snakes, or spiders can be serious. If possible, always try to catch the villain for identification purposes. If bitten by these creatures or *any* wild animal, the best course of action may be to head directly to the nearest emergency ward or outpatient clinic of a hospital. Cockroaches, waterbugs, and termites thrive in warm climates, but pose no serious health threat.

FOOD AND WATER: Tap water generally is clean and potable throughout most of Spain. Ask if water is meant for drinking, but if you're at all unsure, bottled water is readily available in stores. In general, it is a good idea to drink bottled water at least at the beginning of the trip. This is not because there is something wrong with the water as far as the residents are concerned, but new microbes in the digestive tract to which you have not become accustomed may cause mild stomach or intestinal upsets. Particularly in rural areas, the water supply may not be thoroughly purified, and residents either have developed immunities to the natural bacteria or boil it for drinking. You also should avoid swimming in or drinking water from freshwater streams, rivers, or pools, as they may be contaminated with leptospira, which causes a bacterial disease called leptospirosis (the symptoms resemble influenza). In campgrounds, water usually is indicated as drinkable or for washing only — if you're not sure, ask.

Milk is pasteurized throughout Spain, and dairy products are safe to eat, as are fruit, vegetables, meat, poultry, and fish. Because of Mediterranean Sea pollution, however, fish and shellfish should be eaten cooked, and make sure it is *fresh,* particularly in the heat of the summer, when inadequate refrigeration is an additional concern.

Following all these precautions will not guarantee an illness-free trip, but should minimize the risk. As a final hedge against economic if not physical problems, make sure your health insurance will cover all eventualities while you are away. If not, there are policies designed specifically for travel. Many are worth investigating. As with all insurance, they seem like a waste of money until you need them. For further information, also see *Insurance* and *Medical and Legal Aid and Consular Services,* both in this section.

HELPFUL PUBLICATIONS: Practically every phase of health care — before, during, and after a trip — is covered in *The New Traveler's Health Guide,* by Drs. Patrick J. Doyle and James E. Banta. It is available for $4.95, plus postage and handling, from Acropolis Books Ltd., 13950 Park Center Rd., Herndon, VA 22071 (phone: 800-451-7771 or 703-709-0006).

The *Traveling Healthy Newsletter,* which is published six times a year, also is brimming with health-related travel tips. For a year's subscription, which costs $24, contact Dr. Karl Neumann (108-48 70th Rd., Forest Hills, NY 11375; phone: 718-268-7290). Dr. Neumann also is the editor of the useful free booklet *Traveling Healthy,* which is available by writing to the *Travel Healthy Program* (PO Box 10208, New Brunswick, NJ 08906-9910; phone: 215-732-4100).

For more information regarding preventive health care for travelers, contact the *International Association for Medical Assistance to Travelers (IAMAT;* 417 Center St., Lewiston, NY 14092; phone: 716-754-4883). The Centers for Disease Control also publishes an interesting booklet, *Health Information for International Travel.* To order send a check or money order for $5 to the Superintendent of Documents (US Government Printing Office, Washington, DC 20402), or charge it to your credit card by calling 202-783-3238. For information on vaccination requirements, disease outbreaks, and other health information pertaining to traveling abroad, you also can call the Centers for Disease Control's 24-hour International Health Requirements and Recommendations Information Hotline: 404-332-4559.

On the Road

Credit and Currency

It may seem hard to believe, but one of the greatest (and least understood) costs of travel is money itself. So your one single objective in relation to the care and retention of travel funds is to make them stretch as far as possible. When you do spend money, it should be on things that expand and enhance your travel experience, with no buying power lost due to carelessness or lack of knowledge. This requires more than merely ferreting out the best airfare or the most charming budget hotel. It means being canny about the management of money itself. Herewith, a primer on making money go as far as possible overseas.

CURRENCY: The basic unit of Spanish currency is the *peseta* (abbreviated pta.). This is distributed in coin denominations of 1, 5, 10, 25, 50, 100, 200, and 500 pesetas. Paper money is issued in bills of 100, 200, 500, 1,000, 2,000, 5,000, and 10,000 pesetas. The value of Spanish currency in relation to the US dollar fluctuates daily, affected by a wide variety of phenomena.

Although US dollars may be accepted in Spain (particularly at points of entry), you certainly will lose a percentage of your dollar's buying power if you do not take the time to convert it into pesetas. By paying for goods and services in the local currency, you save money by not negotiating invariably unfavorable exchange rates for every small purchase, and avoid difficulty where US currency is not readily — or happily — accepted. *Throughout this book, unless specifically stated otherwise, prices are given in US dollars.*

There is no limit to the amount of US currency that can be brought into Spain. To avoid problems anywhere along the line, it's advisable to fill out any customs forms provided when leaving the US on which you can declare all money you are taking with you — cash, traveler's checks, and so on. US law requires that anyone taking more than $10,000 into or out of the US must report this fact on customs form No. 4790, which is available from US Customs. If taking over $10,000 out of the US, you must report this *before* leaving the US; if returning with such an amount, you should include this information on your customs declaration. Although travelers usually are not questioned by customs officials about currency when entering or leaving, the sensible course is to observe all regulations just to be on the safe side.

FOREIGN EXCHANGE: Because of the volatility of exchange rates, be sure to check the current value of the Spanish peseta before finalizing any travel budget. And before you actually depart on your trip, be aware of the most advantageous exchange rates offered by various financial institutions — US banks, currency exchange firms (at home or abroad), or Spanish banks.

For the best sense of current trends, follow the rates posted in the financial section of your local newspaper or in such international newspapers as the *International Herald Tribune*. It also is possible to check with your own bank. *Harold Reuter and Company*, a currency exchange service in New York City (200 Park Ave., Suite 332 E., New York, NY 10166; phone: 212-661-0826), also is particularly helpful in determining current trends in exchange rates; or check with *Thomas Cook Foreign Exchange* (for the nearest location, call 800-972-2192 in Illinois; 800-621-0666 elsewhere in the US). *Ruesch International* also offers up-to-date foreign currency information and currency-related services (such as converting foreign currency checks into US dollars; see *Duty-Free Shopping and Value-Added Tax,* in this section). *Ruesch* also offers a pocket-size *Foreign Currency Guide* (good for estimating general equivalents while planning) and a helpful brochure, *6 Foreign Exchange Tips for the Traveler.* Contact *Ruesch International* at one of the following addresses: 3 First National Plaza, Suite 2020, Chicago, IL 60602 (phone: 312-332-5900); 1925 Century Park E., Suite 240, Los Angeles, CA 90067 (phone: 213-277-7800); 608 Fifth Ave., "Swiss Center," New York, NY 10020 (phone: 212-977-2700); or 1350 Eye St. NW, 10th Floor and street level, Washington, DC 20005 (phone: 800-424-2923 or 202-408-1200).

In Spain, you will find the official rate of exchange posted in banks, airports, money exchange houses, and some shops. As a general rule, expect to get more local currency for your US dollar at banks than at any other commercial establishment. Exchange rates do change from day to day, and most banks offer the same (or very similar) exchange rates. (In a pinch, the convenience of cashing money in your hotel — sometimes on a 24-hour basis — *may* make up for the difference in the exchange rate.) Don't try to bargain in banks or hotels — no one will alter the rates for you.

Money exchange houses *(casas de cambio)* are financial institutions that charge a fee for the service of exchanging dollars into local currency. When considering alternatives, be aware that although the rate again varies among these establishments, the rates of exchange offered are bound to be slightly less favorable than the terms offered at nearby banks — again, don't be surprised if you get fewer pesetas for your dollar than the rate published in the papers.

That said, however, the following rules of thumb are worth remembering:

Rule number one: Never (repeat: *never*) exchange dollars for foreign currency at hotels, restaurants, or retail shops. If you do, you are sure to lose a significant amount of your US dollar's buying power. If you do come across a storefront exchange counter offering what appears to be an incredible bargain, there's too much counterfeit specie in circulation to take the chance. (See Rule number three, below.)

Rule number two: Estimate your needs carefully; if you overbuy you lose twice — buying and selling back. Every time you exchange money, someone is making a profit, and rest assured it isn't you. Use up foreign notes before leaving, saving just enough for last-minute incidentals, and tips.

Rule number three: Don't buy money on the black market. The exchange rate may be better, but it is a common practice to pass off counterfeit bills to unsuspecting foreigners who aren't familiar with the local currency. It's usually a sucker's game, and you almost always are the sucker; it also can land you in jail.

Rule number four: Learn the local currency quickly and keep abreast of daily fluctuations in the exchange rate. These are listed in the English-language *International Herald Tribune* daily for the preceding day, as well as in every major newspaper in Europe. Rates change to some degree every day. For rough calculations, it is quick and safe to use round figures, but for purchases and actual currency exchanges, carry a small pocket calculator to help you compute the exact rate. Inexpensive calculators specifically designed to convert currency amounts quickly for travelers are widely available.

When changing money, don't be afraid to ask how much commission you're being charged, and the exact amount of the prevailing exchange rate. In fact, in any exchange of money for goods or services, you should work out the rate before making any payment.

TIP PACKS: It's not a bad idea to buy a *small* amount of Spanish coins and banknotes before your departure. But note the emphasis on "small," because, for the most part, you are better off carrying the bulk of your travel funds to Spain in US dollar traveler's checks (see below). Still, the advantages of tip packs are threefold:

1. You become familiar with the currency (really the only way to guard against making mistakes or being cheated during your first few hours in a new country).
2. You are guaranteed some money should you arrive when a bank or exchange counter isn't open or available.
3. You don't have to depend on hotel desks, porters, or taxi drivers to change your money.

A "tip pack" is the only foreign currency you should buy before you leave. If you do run short upon arrival, US dollars often are accepted at points of entry. In other areas, they either *may* be accepted, or someone may accommodate you by changing a small amount — though invariably at a less than advantageous rate.

TRAVELER'S CHECKS: It's wise to carry traveler's checks while on the road instead of (or in addition to) cash, since it's possible to replace them if they are stolen or lost; you usually can receive partial or full replacement funds the same day if you have your purchase receipt and proper identification. Issued in various denominations and available in both US dollars and Spanish pesetas, with adequate proof of identification (credit cards, driver's license, passport), traveler's checks are as good as cash in most hotels, restaurants, stores, and banks. Don't assume, however, that restaurants, small shops, and other establishments are going to be able to change checks of large denominations. Worldwide, more and more establishments are beginning to restrict the amount of traveler's checks they will accept or cash, so it is wise to purchase at least some of your checks in small denominations — say, $10 and $20. Also, don't expect to change them into US dollars except at banks and international airports.

Although traveler's checks are available in foreign currencies such as Spanish pesetas, the exchange rates offered by the issuing companies in the US generally are far less favorable than those available from banks both in the US and abroad. Therefore, it usually is better to carry the bulk of your travel funds abroad in US dollar–denomination traveler's checks.

Every type of traveler's check is legal tender in banks around the world and each company guarantees full replacement if checks are lost or stolen. After that the similarity ends. Some charge a fee for purchase, others are free; you can buy traveler's checks at almost any bank, and some are available by mail. Most important, each traveler's check issuer differs slightly in its refund policy — the amount refunded immediately, the accessibility of refund locations, the availability of a 24-hour refund service, and the time it will take for you to receive replacement checks. For instance, *American Express* guarantees replacement of lost or stolen traveler's checks in under 3 hours at any *American Express* office — other companies may not be as prompt. (Note that *American Express*'s 3-hour policy is based on the traveler's being able to provide the serial numbers of the lost checks. Without these numbers, refunds can take much longer.)

We cannot overemphasize the importance of knowing how to replace lost or stolen checks. All of the traveler's check companies have agents around the world, both in their own name and at associated agencies (usually, but not necessarily, banks), where refunds can be obtained during business hours. Most of them also have 24-hour toll-free telephone lines, and some will even provide emergency funds to tide you over on a Sunday.

Be sure to make a photocopy of the refund instructions that will be given to you by the issuing institution at the time of purchase. To avoid complications should you need to redeem lost checks (and to speed up the replacement process), keep the purchase receipt and an accurate list, by serial number, of the checks that have been spent or cashed. You may want to incorporate this information in an "emergency packet," also including your passport number and date of issue, the numbers of the credit cards you are carrying, and any other bits of information you shouldn't be without. Always keep these records separate from the checks and the original records themselves (you may want to give them to a traveling companion to hold).

Although most people understand the desirability of carrying funds in the form of traveler's checks as protection against loss or theft, an equally good reason is that US dollar traveler's checks invariably get a better rate of exchange than cash does — usually by at least 1%. The reasons for this are technical, but potential savings exist and it is a fact of travel life that should not be ignored.

That 1% won't do you much good, however, if you already have spent it buying your traveler's checks. Several of the major traveler's check companies charge 1% for the acquisition of their checks. To receive fee-free traveler's checks you may have to meet certain qualifications — for instance, *Thomas Cook* checks issued in US currency are free if you make your travel arrangements through its travel agency; *American Express* traveler's checks are available without charge to members of the *American Automobile Association.* Holders of some credit cards (such as the *American Express Platinum* card) also may be entitled to free traveler's checks. The issuing institution (e.g., the particular bank at which you purchase them) may itself charge a fee. If you purchase traveler's checks at a bank in which you or your company maintains significant accounts (especially commercial accounts of some size), the bank may absorb the 1% fee as a courtesy.

American Express, Bank of America, Citicorp, Thomas Cook, MasterCard, and *Visa* all offer traveler's checks. Here is a list of the major companies issuing traveler's checks and the numbers to call in the event that loss or theft makes replacement necessary:

American Express: To report lost or stolen checks in the US, call 800-221-7282. In Europe, *American Express* advises travelers to call 44-273-571600 (in Brighton, England), collect. Another (slower) option is to call 801-968-8300 (in the US), collect; or contact the nearest *American Express* office.

Bank of America: To report lost or stolen checks in the US, call 800-227-3460. In Spain and elsewhere worldwide, call 415-624-5400 or 415-622-3800, collect.

Citicorp: To report lost or stolen checks in the US, call 800-645-6556. In Spain and elsewhere worldwide, call 813-623-1709 or 813-626-4444, collect.

MasterCard: To report lost or stolen checks in the US, call 800-223-9920. In Spain, call the New York office at 212-974-5696, collect.

Thomas Cook MasterCard: To report lost or stolen checks in the US, call 800-223-9920. In Spain, call 609-987-7300 (in the US) or 44-733-502995 (in England), collect, and they will direct you to the nearest branch of *Thomas Cook* or *Wagons-Lits,* their European agent.

Visa: To report lost or stolen checks in the continental US, call 800-227-6811. In Spain, call 415-574-7111, collect. In Europe, you also can call this London number collect: 44-71-937-8091.

CREDIT CARDS: Some establishments you encounter during the course of your travels may not honor any credit cards and some may not honor all cards, so there is a practical reason to carry more than one. Most US credit cards, including the principal bank cards, are honored in Spain; however, keep in mind that some cards may be issued under different names in Europe. For example, *MasterCard* may go under the name *Access* or *Eurocard,* and *Visa* often is called *Carte Bleue* — wherever these equivalents are accepted, *MasterCard* and *Visa* may be used. The following is a list of credit cards that enjoy wide domestic and international acceptance:

American Express: Cardholders can cash personal checks for traveler's checks and cash at *American Express* or its representatives' offices in the US up to the following limits (within any 21-day period): $1,000 for *Green* and *Optima* cardholders; $5,000 for *Gold* cardholders; and $10,000 for *Platinum* cardholders. Check cashing also is available to cardholders who are guests at participating hotels (up to $250), and for holders of airline tickets, at participating airlines (up to $50). Free travel accident, baggage, and car rental insurance if ticket or rental is charged to card; additional insurance also is available for additional cost. For further information or to report a lost or stolen *American Express* card, call 800-528-4800 throughout the continental US; in Spain, contact a local *American Express* office or call 212-477-5700, collect.

Carte Blanche: Free travel accident, baggage, and car rental insurance if ticket or rental is charged to card; additional insurance also is available at additional cost. For medical, legal, and travel assistance worldwide, call 800-356-3448 throughout the US; in Spain, call 214-680-6480, collect. For further information or to report a lost or stolen *Carte Blanche* card, call 800-525-9135 throughout the US; in Spain, call 303-790-2433, collect.

Diners Club: Emergency personal check cashing for cardholders staying at participating hotels and motels (up to $250 per stay). Free travel accident, baggage, and car rental insurance if ticket or rental is charged to card; additional insurance also is available for an additional fee. For medical, legal, and travel assistance worldwide, call 800-356-3448 throughout the US; in Spain, call 214-680-6480, collect. For further information or to report a lost or stolen *Diners Club* card, call 800-525-9135 throughout the US; in Spain, call 303-790-2433, collect.

Discover Card: Offered by a subsidiary of Sears, Roebuck & Co., it provides cardholders with cash advances at numerous automatic teller machines and *Sears* stores throughout the US. For further information and to report a lost or stolen *Discover* card, call 800-DISCOVER throughout the US; in Spain, call 302-323-7652, collect.

MasterCard: Cash advances are available at participating banks worldwide. Check with your issuing bank for information. *MasterCard* also offers a 24-hour emergency lost card service; call 800-826-2181 throughout the US; 314-275-6690, collect, from abroad.

Visa: Cash advances are available at participating banks worldwide. Check with your issuing bank for information. *Visa* also offers a 24-hour emergency lost card service; call 800-336-8472 throughout the US. In Spain, call 415-574-7700, collect.

One of the thorniest problems relating to the use of credit cards abroad concerns the rate of exchange at which a purchase is charged. Be aware that the exchange rate in effect on the date that you make a foreign purchase or pay for a foreign service has nothing at all to do with the rate of exchange at which your purchase is billed to you when you get the invoice (sometimes months later) in the US. The amount which the credit card company charges is either a function of the exchange rate at which the establishment's bank processed it or the rate in effect on the day your charge is received at the credit card center. (There is a 1-year limit on the time a business can take to forward its charge slips.)

The principle at work in this credit card–exchange rate roulette is simple, but very hard to predict. You make a purchase at a particular dollar versus local currency exchange rate. If the dollar gets stronger in the time between purchase and billing, your purchase actually costs you less than you anticipated. If the dollar drops in value during the interim, you pay more than you thought you would. There isn't much you can do about these vagaries except to follow one very broad, very clumsy rule of thumb: If the dollar is doing well at the time of purchase, its value increasing against the local currency, use your credit card on the assumption that it still will be doing well when billing takes place. If the dollar is doing badly, assume it will continue to do badly and pay with traveler's checks or cash. If you get too badly stuck, the best recourse is to complain, loudly. Be aware, too, that most credit card companies charge an unannounced, un-itemized 1% fee for converting foreign currency charges to US dollars.

SENDING MONEY ABROAD: If you have used up your traveler's checks, cashed as many emergency personal checks as your credit card allows, drawn on your cash advance line to the fullest extent, and still need money, have it sent to you via one of the following services:

> *American Express* (phone: 800-543-4080). Offers a service called "Moneygram" completing money transfers in anywhere from 15 minutes to 5 days. The sender can go to any *American Express* office in the US and transfer money by presenting cash, a personal check, money order, or credit card — *Discover, MasterCard, Visa,* or *American Express Optima Card* (no other *American Express* or other credit cards are accepted). *American Express Optima* cardholders also can arrange for this transfer over the phone. The minimum transfer charge is $25, which rises with the amount of the transaction; the sender can forward funds of up to $10,000 per transaction (credit card users are limited to the amount of pre-established credit line). To collect at the other end, the receiver must show identification (passport, driver's license, or other picture ID) at an *American Express* office in Barcelona, Madrid, or Marbella and present a passport as identification. For further information on this service, call 800-543-4080.

> *Western Union Telegraph Company* (phone: 800-325-4176 throughout the US). A friend or relative can go, cash in hand, to any *Western Union* office in the US, where, for a *minimum* charge of $13 (it rises with the amount of the transaction), plus a $25 surcharge, the funds will be transferred to a participating *Banco Español de Credito. Western Union*'s correspondent bank in Spain. (The Spanish cities to which money can be wired via *Western Union* are Barcelona, Bilboa, Córdoba, Granada, Madrid, Málaga, Palma de Mallorca, Santa Cruz de Tenerife, Seville, and Valencia.) When the money arrives, you will not be notified — you must go to the bank to inquire. Transfers generally take anywhere from 2 to 5 business days, although the wait may be much longer, particularly in remote areas. The funds will be turned over in local currency, based on the rate of exchange in effect on the day of receipt. For a higher fee, the US party to this transaction may call *Western Union* with a *MasterCard* or *Visa* number to send up to $2,000, although larger transfers will be sent to a predesignated location.

If you are literally down to your last peseta, the nearest US consulate (see *Medical and Legal Aid and Consular Services,* in this section) will let you call home to set these matters in motion.

CASH MACHINES: Automatic teller machines (ATMs) are increasingly common worldwide. If your bank participates in one of the international ATM networks (most do), the bank will issue you a "cash card" along with a personal identification code or number (also called a PIC or PIN). You can use this card at any ATM in the same electronic network to check your account balances, transfer monies between checking and savings accounts, and — most important for a traveler — withdraw cash instantly. Network ATMs generally are located in banks, commercial and transportation centers, and near major tourist attractions.

Some financial institutions offer exclusive automatic teller machines for their own customers only at bank branches. At the time of this writing, ATMs which *are* connected generally belong to one of two international networks, *Cirrus* (phone: 800-4-CIRRUS) or *Plus System* (phone: 800-THE-PLUS). As we went to press, these companies both had plans to add Spanish locations, although no machines had yet been installed. There also was an agreement pending between these two companies to join their networks, which, when finalized, will allow users of either system to withdraw funds from any *Cirrus* or *Plus System* ATM.

Accommodations

From elegant, centuries-old castle resorts to modern, functional high-rises and modest, inexpensive inns, it's easy to be comfortable and well cared for on almost any budget in Spain. Admittedly, the coast is full of deluxe establishments providing expensive services to people with money to burn, but more affordable alternatives have always been available, particularly in the countryside.

In fact, those watching their wallets will be pleased to find a larger selection of accommodations in their price range than is the case either at home or in most other countries in Europe. Spain has long been one of the European destinations where the cost of living is lowest, and it still is relatively affordable, despite inflation and the recent decline in the strength of the US dollar. At the lower end of the price scale, you will not necessarily have to forgo charm. While a fair number of inexpensive establishments are simply no-frills, "generic" places to spend the night, even the sparest room may have the cachet of once having been the nightly retreat of a monk or nun. And some of the most delightful places to stay are the smaller, less expensive, often family-run small inns, *hostales* and *pensiones*.

Once upon a time, such things as the superiority of New World plumbing made many of the numerous, less expensive accommodations alternatives unacceptable for North Americans. Today, the gap has closed considerably, and in Spain the majority of the hostelries catering to the tourist trade are likely to be at least adequate in their basic facilities.

The annual *Guía de Hoteles,* issued by Spain's Secretaría General de Turismo, lists most of the hotels in the country (except for those that are not officially graded according to the government's star system of classification). Hotels are classified from 5 stars (the highest rating) through 1 star (the lowest) on the basis of the tangible facilities they possess — such things as the proportion of rooms with private baths and telephones, the number of elevators, public rooms, and bars, the existence of air conditioning, and so on. Since the rating does not take into account the quality of those facilities or such intangibles as the warmth of the welcome or the sprightliness of the service, it should be considered only a guide in choosing a hotel.

A very few superlatively appointed five-star properties, such as the *Ritz* and the *Villa Magna* in Madrid and the *Meliá Don Pepe* in Marbella, have earned the equivalent of a sixth star and carry the designation *gran lujo* (great luxury). Hotels listed as *residencias* are without restaurants, generally offering breakfast only, although some may have cafeteria service. Classified separately, from 3 stars through 1 star, but also listed in the guide, are *hostales,* more modest accommodations that translate as inns or "hostels," but should not be confused with youth hostels, however, and *pensiones,* which are fewer in number and somewhat like boardinghouses. Both *hostales* and *pensiones* tend to be unassuming places, often run by a family that has inherited a large apartment or the entire floor of a building and converted it for this purpose. Hostels, too, will be listed as *residencias* if they do not serve meals other than breakfast; pensions may require guests to take full or half board.

Also listed in the guide are the *paradores,* a special group of state-owned inns discussed more fully below; motels, although the country has comparatively few; and numerous *hotel apartamentos* and *residencia apartamentos,* or apartment hotels (see "Rental Options" below for more information). Not listed are such accommodations for the shoestring traveler as *casas de huéspedes,* or guesthouses, and *fondas,* which are primarily eating places that also may have rooms for rent. Local tourist offices should have information on these, as they may on the many *camas* (beds), *habitaciones* (rooms), and *casas particulares* (private houses with rooms for rent — similar to bed and breakfast accommodations elsewhere on the Continent) that can be found in smaller towns and the countryside.

Also ask local tourist offices (or, in the US, the National Tourist Office of Spain) for information on staying in a monastery or convent. More than a few, particularly in the region of Castile-León (Old Castile) and along the pilgrimage route to Santiago de Compostela, open their doors to guests (men only or women only, and sometimes married couples), charging very low rates or, occasionally, a voluntary donation. (These are not to be confused with other monasteries, no longer functioning as religious houses, that have been turned into *paradores;* see below.)

The *Guía de Hoteles* can be bought in bookstores in Spain, but regional versions with the same information can be obtained in the US by visiting or writing the nearest branch of the National Tourist Office of Spain (where the full guide also can be consulted) and specifying the city or area of interest (e.g., Barcelona, Balearic Islands, Andalusia). The listing for each hotel includes its star category, address and telephone number, number of rooms, and amenities, along with the prices of double rooms with or without bath and of breakfast and other meals, if offered.

Even without a guide in hand, however, it is not difficult for visitors in Spain to figure out where a particular hotel fits in the scheme of things. A blue plaque by the door of any establishment that has been classified clearly reveals what it is — H means a hotel, HR a *hotel residencia,* Hs a hostel, HsR a *hostal residencia,* P a *pensión* — as well as the number of stars attained. Inside, room prices appear by law in the individual rooms and sometimes are posted by the reception desk as well. The posted prices include service (which generally ranges from 10% to 15%) and Value Added Tax (6%, except in 4- and 5-star hotels, where it is 12%), so that receiving the bill at the end of a stay rarely is a shock. Breakfast may or may not be included in the posted rate, and if it is, there may be no reduction if it is not taken (ask, if this is not clear).

Note that many Spanish hotels keep complaint forms — *hojas de reclamaciones* — handy should guests require them. Because any written complaints must be filed with the proper authorities, most hoteliers are eager to resolve disputes before they are put into writing.

In Spain, a single room is a *habitación sencilla;* a double room is a *habitación doble,* and it has either *camas gemelas* (two twin beds) or *una cama de matrimonio* (one double bed). A room with a private bath is *con baño,* but anyone traveling on a shoestring should note that all rooms in the officially graded accommodations have a sink with hot and cold running water, so it's possible to forgo the luxury of a private bathroom and still not be totally without convenience. Single rooms are in short supply, but if a person traveling alone is given a double because no single is available, the charge should be 80% of its normal price. A third bed placed in a double room increases its price by 35%.

Rates in many hotels vary according to high and low seasons, and some have an intermediate season — known in travel parlance as the "shoulder season." The definition of high season varies according to the hotel and the locality, but remember that in the Canary Islands and in mountain ski resorts on the mainland, winter — generally November through April — is high season, whereas elsewhere on the mainland and in the Balearics, high season corresponds more conventionally to summer. *Christmas, Easter,* and any local festivals also command high season rates. (See *When to Go,* at the beginning of this section, for further information on seasonal variations.)

For those who prefer to reserve in advance, a number of well-known hotel chains or associations have properties in Spain, particularly in major cities. Among these are the following (along with toll-free reservation numbers to call in the US):

Best Western (phone: 800-528-1234). Has over 200 properties in Spain.

Hilton International (phone: 800-445-8667). Owned by the Ladbroke's gambling group of Great Britain, there is no proprietary connection with the US *Hilton* chain. Has 1 property each in Barcelona and the Canary Islands.

Holiday Inn (phone: 800-465-4329). Has 1 property in Spain.

Inter-Continental (phone: 800-327-0200). Has 1 property in Madrid.

Minotels Europe (phone: 800-336-4668). Has 33 properties in Spain.

Sheraton (phone: 800-325-3535). Has 1 property in Palma de Mallorca.

Trusthouse Forte (phone: 800-225-5843). Has 1 property in Madrid.

Among the better-known Spanish chains are *Sol Hotels* with 25 properties in Spain and *Meliá Hotels* with 16 Spanish properties. Note that the *Meliá* and *Sol* chains offer a special voucher program, which guarantees rooms at three-, four-, and five-star hotels. A double room in these establishments usually costs as much as $275 per night for a double room and the vouchers come in booklets good for 3 nights for $378. For these voucher books and reservations, contact *Petrabax Tours* (97-45 Queens Blvd., Suite 505, Rego Park, NY 11374; phone: 718-897-7272 in New York State, 800-367-6611 elsewhere in the US). Reservations also can be made through these hotel chains' US representative, *Utell International* (10605 Burt Circle, Omaha, NE 68114; phone: 800-44-UTELL).

Among other large European chains which have a US office that will provide information and take reservations is *Pullman International,* a group of approximately 200 hotels, with 1 property in Madrid. *Pullman* has a US representative (200 W. 57th St., New York, NY 10019; phone: 800-223-9862 or 212-719-9363). Reservations for all *Pullman* properties also can be made through *Utell International* (address above). *Novotel,* with approximately 238 3-star hotels throughout Europe, has 5 properties in Spain. The *Hoteles Tryp* has a number of properties in Madrid and is represented in the US by *Bravo Tours* (182 Main St., Ridgefield Park, NJ 07660; phone: 201-641-0655 in New Jersey; 800-272-8674 elsewhere in the US). Note, finally, that *Marketing Ahead* (433 Fifth Ave., New York, NY 10016; phone: 212-686-9213) represents numerous independent hotels in Spain, and also makes reservations for Spain's *paradores* (see below). There are several other stateside reservations services for individual Spanish hotels. The Spanish tourist offices should be able to tell you who in the US represents a particular property.

PARADORES: Spain boasts a network of state-owned inns — *paradores* — that are among the most interesting hostelries in Europe. Spain's system was born in 1926, when the country's Royal Tourist Commissioner came up with the idea of providing hotel accommodations in out-of-the-way areas where private investment lagged. The first *parador* opened in 1928 and occupied built-for-the-purpose premises in the Gredos Mountains of Castile. But it wasn't long before the need to create hotels merged with another item on the government's agenda — that of reclaiming abandoned castles, palaces, convents, and other historic structures and converting them to new uses. Thus, today's traveler can sleep in a 15th-century castle where Cortés lived before he left for Mexico or in another occupied by King Carlos V, stay at a monastery in the Pyrenees or in a convent within the confines of the Alhambra, choose the elegance of a Renaissance palace or the rusticity of a Muslim fortress. About half of the 86 *paradores* now in existence are in such old buildings, furnished with antiques or fine reproductions but complete with modern conveniences, while the rest are modern establishments that, however, can be anything from a mountain chalet to a house in the typically tile-roofed, whitewashed style of an Andalusian village.

All *paradores* are set in picturesque, though no longer necessarily remote, locations, and all have restaurants, many of them excellent, specializing in regional cuisine. Yet prices are reasonable. In the Spanish system of grading hotels, *paradores* are mainly

3- and 4-star establishments (a few 2- and 5-star places exist), with prices for a double room varying very little year-round. They can be exceedingly intimate, with as few as 6 rooms, or comparatively large, with as many as 100; the largest, *Parador de San Marcos,* in León, has 258 rooms.

The above-mentioned publication, *Guía de Hoteles,* includes *paradores* among its listings, but the Spanish tourist authority also distributes an illustrated booklet — *Visiting the Paradores* — that provides a somewhat better view of the background and attractions of the individual inns and details of the facilities at each. Prices are omitted, however, so ask for a rate sheet giving the average prices for inns in each category. Since *paradores* are very popular, reservations are strongly recommended, particularly during the high season. In the US, they can be made through travel agents or *Marketing Ahead* (433 Fifth Ave., New York, NY 10016; phone: 212-686-9213). Note that some travel agents will make reservations only for stays of 3 or more nights per establishment; for shorter stays you may want to contact the *parador* directly. In addition, several tour operators offer fly/drive packages featuring accommodations in *paradores* (see *Package Tours,* in this section).

RELAIS & CHÂTEAUX: Most members of this association are in France, but the group has grown to include dozens of establishments in many other countries, including, currently, 12 in Spain.

Relais & Châteaux members are of particular interest to travelers who wish lodgings reflecting the ambience, style, and frequently the history of the places they are visiting. Some properties actually are ancient castles or palaces — dating back more than 1,000 years — which have been converted into hotels. Others — the *relais* — are old inns, manor houses, even converted mills, convents, and monasteries. A few well-known city and resort establishments are included, such as the *Marbella Club* in Spain, but most are in quiet country settings, and freqently are graced with parks, ponds, and flowering gardens.

Another group of members, *Relais Gourmands,* is composed of exceptionally fine restaurants. These establishments also may have rooms for rent, but the establishments are *not* rated on the basis of their accommodations (unless they also are designated as *Relais & Châteaux*), so they may not match (or even come close to) the standards of room quality maintained by other *Relais* hotel members. Four *Gourmand* members in Spain also are *Relais & Châteaux* hotel members and offer both fine food and elegant accommodations.

Members of the *Relais & Châteaux* group often are expensive, though no more than you would pay for deluxe, authentically elegant accommodations and service anywhere in the world (and many are not all that costly). Prices include service and tax; some include breakfast and dinner, but if meals are not included they can add to the cost considerably. Accommodations and service from one *relais* or château to another can range from simple but comfortable to elegantly deluxe, but they all maintain very high standards in order to retain their memberships, as they are appraised annually.

An illustrated catalogue of all the *Relais & Châteaux* properties is published annually and is available for $5 from *Relais & Châteaux* (2200 Lazy Hollow, Suite 152D, Houston, TX 77063) or from *David B. Mitchell & Company* (200 Madison Ave., New York, NY 10016; phone: 800-372-1323 or 212-696-1323). The association also can provide information on member properties. Reservations can be made directly with the establishments, through *David B. Mitchell & Company,* or through a travel agency.

RENTAL OPTIONS: An attractive alternative for the visitor content to stay in one spot for a week or more is to rent one of the numerous properties available throughout Spain. These offer a wide range of luxury and convenience, depending on the price you want to pay. One of the advantages to staying in a house, apartment (usually called a "flat" overseas), or other rented vacation home is that you will feel much more like a visitor than a tourist.

Known to Europeans as a "holiday let" or a "self-catering holiday," a vacation in a furnished rental has both the advantages and disadvantages of living "at home" abroad. It can be less expensive than staying in a first class hotel, although very luxurious and expensive rentals are available, too. It has the comforts of home, including a kitchen, which means potential saving on food. Furthermore, it gives a sense of the country that a large hotel often cannot. On the other hand, a certain amount of housework is involved because if you don't eat out, you have to cook, and though some rentals (especially the luxury ones) include a cleaning person, most don't. (If the rental doesn't include daily cleaning, arrangements often can be made with a maid service.)

For a family, two or more couples, or a group of friends, the per-person cost — even for a luxurious rental — can be quite reasonable. Weekly and monthly rates are available to reduce costs still more. But best of all is the amount of space that no conventional hotel room can equal. As with hotels, the rates for properties in some areas are seasonal, rising during the peak travel season, while for others they remain the same year-round. To have your pick of the properties available, you should begin to make arrangements for a rental at least 6 months in advance.

There are several ways of finding a suitable rental property. Some of the possibilities are listed in the accommodations guides published by the Spanish tourist authority. These include *hotel apartamentos* and *residencia apartamentos,* that is, apartment hotels with or without restaurants and with the facilities and services of hotels, including maid service, but with guestrooms equipped with kitchenettes; and *apartamentos turísticos,* or tourist apartments (more like the "holiday let" arrangements found elsewhere on the Continent), which are furnished rentals geared expressly to the short-term vacationer. Both tourist apartments (rated from 4 keys through 1 key) and apartment hotels are listed in the regional hotel guides available from the National Tourist Office of Spain in the US, whereas the larger *Guía de Hoteles* lists only apartment hotels.

Many tour operators regularly include rental packages among their offerings; these generally are available through a travel agent. In addition, a number of companies specialize in rental vacations. Their plans typically include rental of the property (or several properties, but usually for a minimum stay per location), a rental car, and airfare.

The companies listed below rent a wide range of properties. They handle the booking and confirmation paperwork and can be expected to provide more information about the properties than that which might ordinarily be gleaned from a short listing in an accommodations guide.

At Home Abroad (405 E. 56th St., Apt. 6H, New York, NY 10022; phone: 212-421-9165). Modest to luxurious houses (some with pools) and a few apartments on the Costa del Sol. Photographs of properties and a newsletter are available for a $50 registration fee.

Blake's Vacations (49-39 Dempster St., Skokie, IL 60077; phone: 800-628-8118). Rents small villas on the Costa Brava.

Coast to Coast Resorts (860 Solar Building, 1000 16th St. NW, Washington, DC 20036; phone: 800-368-5721 or 202-293-8000). Handles modest properties throughout Spain.

Eastone Overseas Accommodations (198 Southampton Dr., Jupiter, FL 33458; phone: 407-575-6991/2). Handles a few apartments, but mostly villas and houses on the Costa del Sol.

Europa-Let, Inc. (PO Box 3537, Ashland, OR 97520; phone: 800-462-4486 or 503-482-5806). Rentals range from modest apartments to luxurious villas along the southern coast.

Hideaways International (15 Goldsmith St., PO Box 1270, Littleton, MA 01460;

phone: 800-843-4433 or 508-486-8955). Rents apartments, private homes, and villas throughout Spain.

International Lodging Corp. (300 1st Ave., Suite 7C, New York, NY 10009; phone: 212-228-5900). Flats, villas, and some country homes along the Costa Brava and Costa del Sol, and in the vicinity of Marbella.

Rent a Vacation Everywhere (*RAVE;* 328 Main St. E., Suite 526, Rochester, NY 14604; phone: 716-454-6440). Moderate to luxurious villas and apartments on the Costa del Sol, plus a variety of properties along the Costa Brava, Costa Dorada, and Costa del Azahar, and on the island of Minorca.

Villas International (71 W. 23rd St., New York, NY 10010; phone: 212-929-7585 in New York State; 800-221-2260 elsewhere in the US). Besides apartments in Madrid and Barcelona and a few in Seville and Granada, the choices range from simple and moderate houses and apartments to more luxurious properties along the Costa del Sol and other coastal areas.

In addition, a useful publication, the *Worldwide Home Rental Guide,* lists properties throughout Spain, as well as the managing agencies. Issued twice annually, single copies may be available at newsstands for $10 an issue. For a year's subscription, send $18 to *Worldwide Home Rental Guide,* PO Box 2842, Sante Fe, NM 87504 (phone: 505-988-5188).

When considering a particular vacation rental property, look for answers to the following questions:

- How do you get from the airport to the property?
- If the property is on the shore, how far is the nearest beach? Is it sandy or rocky and is it safe for swimming?
- What size and number of beds are provided?
- How far is the property from whatever else is important to you, such as a golf course or nightlife?
- If there is no grocery store on the premises (which may be comparatively expensive, anyway), how far is the nearest market?
- Are baby-sitters, cribs, bicycles, or anything else you may need for your children available?
- Is maid service provided daily?
- Is air conditioning and/or a phone provided?
- Is a car rental part of the package? Is a car necessary?

Before deciding which rental is for you, make sure you have satisfactory answers to all your questions. Ask your travel agent to find out or call the company involved directly.

HOME EXCHANGES: Still another alternative for travelers who are content to stay in one place during their vacation is a home exchange: The Smith family from St. Louis moves into the home of the Alemán family in Valencia, while the Alemáns enjoy a stay in the Smiths' home. The home exchange is an exceptionally inexpensive way to ensure comfortable, reasonable living quarters with amenities that no hotel possibly could offer; often the trade includes a car. Moreover, it allows you to live in a new community in a way that few tourists ever do: For a little while, at least, you will become something of a resident.

Several companies publish directories of individuals and families willing to trade homes with others for a specific period of time. In some cases, you must be willing to list your own home in the directory; in others, you can subscribe without appearing in it. Most listings are for straight exchanges only, but each directory also has a number of listings placed by people interested in either exchanging or renting (for instance, if they own a second home). Other arrangements include exchanges of hospitality while owners are in residence or youth exchanges, where your teenager is put up as a guest in return for your welcoming their teenager at a later date. A few house-sitting opportunities also are available. In most cases, arrangements for the actual exchange take place directly between you and the foreign host. There is no guarantee that you will find a listing in the area in which you are interested, but each of the organizations given below includes Spanish homes among its hundreds or even thousands of foreign listings.

Home Base Holidays (7 Park Ave., London N13 5PG England; phone: 44-81-886-8752). For $42 a year, subscribers receive four listings, with an option to list in all four.

Intervac US/International Home Exchange Service (Box 190070, San Francisco, CA 94119; phone: 415-435-3497). For $45 (plus postage) subscribers receive copies of the three directories published yearly, and are entitled to list their home in one of them; a black-and-white photo may be included with the listing for an additional $10. A $5 discount is given to travelers over age 62.

Loan-A-Home (2 Park Lane, Apt. 6E, Mt. Vernon, NY 10552; phone: 914-664-7640). Specializes in long-term (4 months or more — excluding July and August) housing arrangements worldwide for students, professors, businesspeople, and retirees, although its two annual directories (with supplements) carry a small list of short-term rentals and/or exchanges. $35 for a copy of one directory and one supplement; $45 for two directories and two supplements.

Vacation Exchange Club (PO Box 820, Haleiwa, HI 96712; phone: 800-638-3841). Some 10,000 listings. For $50, the subscriber receives two directories — one in late winter, one in the spring — and is listed in one. For $35, the subscriber receives both directories but no listing.

World Wide Exchange (1344 Pacific Ave., Suite 103, Santa Cruz, CA 95060; phone: 408-476-4206). The $45 annual membership fee includes one listing (for house, yacht, or motorhome) and three guides.

Worldwide Home Exchange Club (45 Hans Place, London SW1X OJZ, England; phone: 44-71-589-6055; or 806 Brantford Ave., Silver Spring, MD 20904; no phone). Handles over 1,500 listings a year worldwide, including homes throughout Spain. For $20 a year, you will receive two listings yearly, as well as supplements.

Better Homes and Travel (formerly *Home Exchange International*), with offices in New York, Los Angeles, London, Paris, and Milan, functions in a somewhat different manner since it publishes no directory and shepherds the exchange process most of the way. Interested parties supply the firm with photographs of themselves and their homes, information on the type of home they want and where, and a registration fee of $50. The company then works with its other offices to propose a few possibilities, and only when a match is made do the parties exchange names, addresses, and phone numbers. For this service, *Better Homes and Travel* charges a closing fee, which ranges from $150 to $450 for switches from 2 weeks to 3 months in duration, and from $275 to $525 for longer switches. Contact *Better Homes and Travel* at 185 Park Row, New York, NY 10038-0272 (phone: 212-349-5340).

HOME STAYS: If the idea of actually staying in a private home as the guest of a Spanish family appeals to you, check with the *United States Servas Committee,* which maintains a list of hosts throughout the world (at the time of this writing, there were about 310 listings in Spain) willing to throw open their doors to foreigners, entirely free of charge.

The aim of this nonprofit cultural program is to promote international understanding and peace, and every effort is made to discourage freeloaders. *Servas* will send you an application form and the name of the nearest of some 200 interviewers around the US for you to contact. After the interview, if you're approved, you'll receive documentation certifying you as a *Servas* traveler. There is a membership fee of $45 per person and there also is a deposit of $15 to receive the host list, refunded on its return. The list gives the name, address, age, occupation, and other particulars of the hosts, including languages spoken. From then on, it is up to you to write to prospective hosts directly, and *Servas* makes no guarantee that you will be accommodated.

Servas stresses that you should choose only people you really want to meet, and that during your stay (which normally lasts between 2 nights and 2 weeks) you should be interested mainly in your hosts, not in sightseeing. It also suggests that one way to show your appreciation once you've returned home is to become a host yourself. The minimum age of a *Servas* traveler is 18 (however, children under 18 may accompany their parents), and though quite a few are young people who have just finished college, there are travelers (and hosts) in all age ranges and occupations. Contact *Servas* at 11 John St., Room 706, New York, NY 10038 (phone: 212-267-0252).

You also might be interested in a publication called *International Meet-the-People Directory,* published by the *International Visitor Information Service.* It lists several agencies in a number of foreign countries (37 worldwide, 18 in Europe) that arrange home visits for Americans, either for dinner or overnight stays. To order a copy, send $5.95 to the *International Visitor Information Service* (733 15th St. NW, Suite 300, Washington, DC 20005; phone: 202-783-6540). For other local organizations and services offering home exchanges, contact the local tourist authority.

Time Zones, Business Hours, and Public Holidays

TIME ZONES: The countries of Europe fall into three time zones. Greenwich Mean Time — the time in Greenwich, England, at longitude 0°0′ — is the base from which all other time zones are measured. Areas in zones west of Greenwich have earlier times and are called Greenwich Minus; those to the east have later times and are called Greenwich Plus. For example, New York City — which falls into the Greenwich Minus 5 time zone — is 5 hours earlier than Greenwich, England.

Spain (including the Canary Islands) is in the the Greenwich Plus 1 time zone (or Central European Time) — which means that the time is 1 hour later than it is in Greenwich, England, and when it is noon in Madrid, it is 6 AM in New York.

Like most Western European nations, Spain moves its clocks ahead an hour in late spring and an hour back in the fall, although the date of the change tends to be about a week earlier (in spring) and a week later (in fall) than the dates we have adopted in the US. For about 2 weeks a year, then, the time difference between the US and Spain is 1 hour more or less than usual.

Spanish and other European timetables use a 24-hour clock to denote arrival and departure times, which means that hours are expressed sequentially from 1 AM. By this method, 9 AM is recorded as 0900, noon as 1200, 1 PM as 1300, 6 PM as 1800, midnight as 2400, and so on. For example, the departure of a train at 7 AM will be announced as "0700"; one leaving at 7 PM will be noted as "1900."

BUSINESS HOURS: Throughout Spain, most businesses and shops are open Mondays through Fridays from 9 AM to 1 or 2 PM, and then from 3 or 4 PM until 7 or 8 PM. Many shops also are open on Saturdays from 9 AM to 1 PM. In small towns and villages, shops may close on one weekday at 1 PM; others may skip the early closing and simply not open on Mondays (or another day of the week). Larger stores in shopping centers generally stay open through midday and may close as late as 9 PM.

In Spain, weekday banking hours are from 9 AM to 2 PM, usually without a break for lunch. Certain banks may remain open until 1 PM on Saturdays, although Saturday hours are less common during the summer. Most banks are closed on Sundays and public holidays, although major airport banks may be open 7 days a week.

Restaurant hours are similar to those in the US. Most restaurants are open all week during the high season and close 1 day each week during the off-season — the day varies from restaurant to restaurant. Hours in general also tend to be a bit later in summer, and they vary from city to city; check local listings in THE CITIES and DIRECTIONS.

PUBLIC HOLIDAYS: In Spain, the public holidays are as follows:

New Year's Day (January 1)
Epiphany (January 6)
St. Joseph's Day (March 19)
Maundy Thursday (March 28)
Good Friday (April 17)
Labor Day or May Day (May 1)
Feast of Santiago (July 25)
Assumption Day (August 15)
Spain's National Day (October 12)
All Saints' Day (November 1)
Constitution Day (December 6)
Immaculate Conception (December 8)
Christmas Day (December 25)

Note that although *Corpus Christi* (June 21) no longer is an official public holiday in Spain, many businesses still may close for religious observances. For further information on holidays celebrated throughout Spain, see "Special Events" in this section, as well as in each of THE CITIES.

Mail, Telephone, and Electricity

 MAIL: Post offices in Spain are open weekdays from 9 AM to 1 PM and from 4 PM to 8 PM. Some branches also are open on Saturdays from 9 AM to 12:30 or 1 PM. Mail rates change frequently following the upward trend of everything else; stamps *(sellos)* can be bought at the post office and at authorized tobacconists *(estanco)*. As in the US, letters can be mailed in letter boxes found on the street (these are mustard yellow with a red stripe), but it is better to mail them (and certainly packages) directly from post offices. Mailing a letter or package, however, is not as straightforward as in the US. Post offices have different windows for each step in the procedure (one window to buy stamps, another to weigh a package, and so on), and standing in line for service may take a while. Another possibility is that some of the better stores in Spain can arrange to mail your purchases directly for you.

Be advised that delivery from Spain can be slow (especially if you send something any distance by surface mail) and erratic (postcards often are given lowest priority, so don't use them for important messages). Send your correspondence via air mail if it's going any distance, and to ensure or further speed delivery of important letters, send them registered mail or express or special delivery.

If your correspondence is important, you may want to send it via one of the special courier services: *Federal Express, DHL,* and other international services are available in Spain. The cost is considerably higher than sending something via the postal services — but the assurance of its timely arrival is worth it.

If you're mailing to an address within Spain, another way to ensure or speed delivery is to use the postal code. And since small towns in Spain may have similar names, the postal code always should be specified — delivery of a letter may depend on it. If you do not have the correct postal code, call the National Tourist Office of Spain (see *Tourist Information Offices,* in this section, for telephone numbers) — they should be able to look it up for you. Alternatively, you could call the addressee directly — if you have the telephone number — and although this will be costly, it may be worth it to ensure delivery of your correspondence.

There are several places that will receive and hold mail for travelers in Spain. Mail sent to you at a hotel and clearly marked "Guest Mail, Hold for Arrival" is one safe approach. Spanish post offices also will extend this service to you if the mail is addressed to the equivalent of US general delivery — called *Lista de Correos.* This probably is the best way for travelers to have mail sent if they do not have a definite address. Have your correspondents print your last name in big block letters on the envelope (lest there be any doubt as to which is your last name), and as there often are several post office locations in major cities, it is important that the address and/or specific name of the office be indicated (not just the name of the city), in addition to the words *Lista de Correos.* Be sure to call at the correct office when inquiring about mail. Also, don't forget to take your passport with you when you go to collect it. Most Spanish post offices require formal identification before they will release anything; there also may be a small charge for picking up your mail.

If you are an *American Express* customer (a cardholder, a carrier of *American Express* traveler's checks, or traveling on an *American Express Travel Service* tour) you can have mail sent to its offices in cities along your route. Letters are held free of charge — registered mail and packages are not accepted. You must be able to show an *American Express* card, traveler's checks, or a voucher proving you are on one of the company's tours to avoid paying for mail privileges. Those who aren't clients must pay a nominal charge each time they inquire if they have received mail, whether or not they actually have a letter. There also is a forwarding fee, for clients and non-clients alike. Mail should be addressed to you, care of *American Express,* and should be marked "Client Mail Service." Additional information on its mail service and addresses of *American Express* offices in Spain are contained in the pamphlet *Services and Offices,* available from any US branch of *American Express.*

While US embassies and consulates abroad will not under ordinary circumstances accept mail for tourists, they *may* hold mail for US citizens in an emergency situation, especially if the papers sent are important. It is best to inform them either by separate letter or cable, or by phone (particularly if you are in the country already), that you will be using their address for this purpose.

TELEPHONE: The Spanish telephone system is not too different from our own. It includes direct dialing, operator-assisted calls, collect calls, reduced rates for certain times of the day and days of the week, and so on. The number of digits vary considerably within the country, and to further confuse matters, a city code may be included in the digits quoted as the "local" number. If you dial a number directly and your call does not go through, either the circuits are busy or you may need to add or delete one or several digits. If you have tried several times and are sure that you have the correct number, have an international operator place the call — however, this will be more expensive than dialing directly. (To reach an international operator in the US, dial "0" for a local operator and ask him or her to connect you.)

It is easy enough to call Spain from the US: Just dial 011 (the international access code) + 34 (the country code) + the city code (if you don't know this, ask the international operator) + the local number. For example, to place a call from anywhere in the US to Madrid, dial 011 + 34 + 1 (the city code for Madrid) + the local number.

The procedure for making a station-to-station call from Spain to the US (usually a more expensive proposition) is similar to the procedure described above: dial 07 (the international access code) + 1 (the US country code) + the US area code + the local number. For instance, to call a number in New York City from Spain, dial 07 + 1 + 212 + the local number.

For calling from one Spanish city to another, dial 9 + the city code + the local number; and for calls within the same city code coverage area, simply dial the local number. Note that Spanish telephone directories and other sources may include the preceeding 9, which should be used only for dialing within the country; when dialing from the US, follow the procedure described above, *leaving off the 9.*

If you don't know the city code, check the front of a telephone book (if calling within Spain) or ask an operator. What you dial to reach an operator in Spain depends on the type of operator assistance you require:

- To reach a local operator to assist in making a local call or for local information, dial 003. (This operator also can connect you to regional and international operators.)
- To reach an operator to assist in making a call to another city code coverage area within Spain, dial 009.
- To reach an international operator to assist with intra-European calls (to any country outside Spain), dial 008.
- For assistance with international calls to the US (or other non-European countries), dial 005.

Throughout Spain, you can dial the following toll-free number for assistance in the event of an emergency: 091. For further information, see *Medical and Legal Aid and Consular Services,* in this section.

Making connections in Europe sometimes can be hit or miss — all exchanges are not always in operation on the same day. If the number dialed does not go through, try later or the next day. So be warned: Those who have to make an important call — to make a hotel reservation in another city, for instance — should start to do so a few days ahead.

Pay telephones in Spain are located much as in the US — in restaurants, hotel lobbies, booths on the street, and at most tourist centers. A useful tip: Coins are fed into a slot at the top of the phone box and automatically drop down as the price of your call increases. It pays to use more coins than you think you may need to avoid being cut off during your conversation; when you are done with the call, the unused amount will be returned.

Although the majority of Spanish pay phones still take coins, as we went to press, phones that take specially designated phone cards had recently been introduced in Spain. Instituted to cut down on vandalism, the phone cards free callers from the necessity of carrying around a pocketful of change, and are sold in various peseta denominations. The units per card, like message units in US phone parlance, are a combination of time and distance. To use such a card, insert it into a slot in the phone and dial the number you wish to reach. A display gradually will count down the value that remains on your card. When you run out of units on the card, you can insert another. These cards are available at post offices and at branch offices of *Telefónica,* the Spanish national phone company.

Although you can use a telephone company credit card number on any phone, pay phones that take major credit cards (*American Express, MasterCard, Visa,* and so on) are increasingly common, particularly in transportation and tourism centers. Also now available is the "affinity card," a combined telephone calling card/bank credit card that can be used for domestic and international calls. Cards of this type include the following:

AT&T/Universal (phone: 800-662-7759). Cardholders can charge calls to the US from overseas.

Executive Telecard International (phone: 800-950-3800). Cardholders can charge calls to the US from overseas, as well as between most European countries.

Sprint Visa (phone: 800-446-7625). Cardholders can charge calls to the US from overseas.

Similarly, *MCI VisaPhone* (phone: 800-866-0099) can add phone card privileges to the services available through your existing *Visa* card. This service allows you to use your *Visa* account number, plus an additional code, to charge calls on any touch-tone phone in the US and Europe.

Hotel Surcharges – A lot of digits may be involved once a caller starts dialing beyond national borders, but avoiding operator-assisted calls can cut costs considerably and bring rates into a somewhat more reasonable range — except for calls made through hotel switchboards. One of the most unpleasant surprises travelers encounter in many foreign countries is the amount they find tacked on to their hotel bill for telephone calls, because foreign hotels routinely add on astronomical surcharges. (It's not at all uncommon to find 300% or 400% added to the actual telephone charges.)

Until recently, the only recourse against this unconscionable overcharging was to call collect when phoning from abroad or to use a telephone credit card — available through a simple procedure from any local US phone company. (Note, however, that even if you use a telephone credit card, some hotels still may charge a fee for line usage). Now *American Telephone and Telegraph (AT&T)* offers *USA Direct,* a service that connects users, via a toll-free number, with an *AT&T* operator in the US, who then will put a call through at the standard international rate. A new feature of this service is that travelers abroad can reach US toll-free (800) numbers by calling a *USA Direct* operator, who will connect them. Charges for all calls made through *USA Direct* appear on the caller's regular US phone bill. (As we went to press, this service was available in Spain only when calling from special *USA Direct* telephones that can be found at some airports, hotels, and phone centers.) For a brochure and wallet card listing toll-free numbers by country, contact International Information Service, *AT&T Communications,* 635 Grand St., Pittsburgh, PA 15219 (phone: 800-874-4000).

It's wise to ask about surcharge rates *before* calling from a hotel. If the rate is high, it's best to use a telephone credit card, or the direct-dial service described above (where it is available); make a collect call; or place the call and ask the party to call right back. If none of these choices is possible, make international calls from the local post office or special telephone center to avoid surcharges. Another way to keep down the cost of telephoning from Spain is to leave a copy of your itinerary and telephone numbers with people in the US so that they can call you instead.

Frequent business travelers to Spain may want to look into corporate membership in *AT&T*'s Language Line Service. By calling a US toll-free number, employees of member companies will be connected with an interpreter in any one of 143 languages and dialects, who will provide on-line interpretive services for $3.50 a minute. From the US, this service is particularly useful for booking travel services in Europe where English is not spoken or not fluently spoken — such as Spain. Once in Europe — this number can be reached by using the USA Direct toll-free (800) number connection feature described above. As we went to press, *AT&T* had no plans to open membership to individual travelers, however, if you require such a service, it may be worth contacting them at the time you plan to travel. For further information, contact *AT&T* at the address above.

■**Note:** An excellent resource for planning your trip is *AT&T*'s *Toll-Free 800 Directory,* which lists thousands of companies with 800 numbers, both alphabetically (white pages) and by category (yellow pages), including a wide range of travel services — from travel agents to transportation and accommodations. Issued in a consumer edition for $9.95 and a business edition for $14.95, both are available from *AT&T Phone Centers* or by calling 800-426-8686. Other useful directories for use before you leave and on the road include the *Toll-Free Travel & Vacation Information Directory* ($4.95 postpaid from Pilot Books, 103 Cooper St., Babylon, NY 11702; phone: 516-422-2225) and *The Phone Booklet* (send $2 to *Scott American Corporation,* Box 88, West Redding, CT 06896).

ELECTRICITY: The US runs on 110-volt, 60-cycle alternating current; Spain runs on 220- or 240-volt, 50-cycle alternating current. (Some large tourist hotels also *may* offer 110-volt currency for your convenience — but don't count on it.) The difference between US and Spanish voltage means that, without a converter, at 220 volts the motor of a US appliance used overseas would run at twice the speed at which it's meant to operate and would quickly burn out.

Travelers can solve the problem by buying a lightweight converter to transform foreign voltage into the US kind (there are two types of converters, depending on the wattage of the appliance) or by buying dual-voltage appliances, which convert from one to the other at the flick of a switch (hair dryers of this sort are common). The difference between the 50- and 60-cycle currents will cause no problem — the American appliance simply will run more slowly — but it still will be necessary to deal with differing socket configurations before plugging in. To be fully prepared, bring along an extension cord (in older or rural establishments the electrical outlet may be farther from the sink than the cord on your razor or hair dryer can reach), and a wall socket adapter kit with a full set of plugs to ensure that you'll be able to plug in anywhere.

One good source for sets of plugs and adapters for use worldwide is the *Franzus Company* (PO Box 142, Beacon Falls, CT 06403; phone: 203-723-6664). *Franzus* also publishes a useful brochure, *Foreign Electricity Is No Deep Dark Secret,* which provides information about converters and adapter plugs for electric appliances to be used abroad but manufactured for use in the US. To obtain a free copy, send a self-addressed, stamped envelope to *Franzus* at the above address; a catalogue of other travel accessories is available on request.

Medical and Legal Aid and Consular Services

MEDICAL AID ABROAD: Nothing ruins a vacation or business trip more effectively than sudden injury or illness. You will discover, in the event of an emergency, that most tourist facilities — transportation companies, hotels, and resorts — are equipped to handle the situation quickly and efficiently. Most towns and cities of any size have a public hospital, and even the tiniest of villages has a medical clinic or private physician nearby. All hospitals are prepared for emergency cases, and many hospitals also have walk-in clinics to serve people who do not really need emergency service, but who have no place to go for immediate medical attention. The level of medical care in Spain, especially in the larger cities, generally is quite good, providing the same basic specialties and services that are available in the US.

Before you go, be sure to check with your insurance company about the applicability of your hospitalization and major medical policies while you're abroad; many policies do not apply, and others are not accepted in Spain. Older travelers should know that Medicare does not make payments outside the US. If your medical policy does not protect you while you're traveling, there are comprehensive combination policies specifically designed to fill the gap. (For a discussion of medical insurance and a list of inclusive combination policies, see *Insurance,* in this section.)

If a bona fide emergency occurs, the fastest way to get attention may be to take a taxi to the emergency room of the nearest hospital. An alternative is to dial the free national "emergency" number used to summon the police, fire trucks, and ambulances — 091 in Spain.

Most emergency services send out well-equipped and well-staffed ambulances, although ambulances in Spain may not be equipped with the advanced EMS technology found in the US and may provide only basic medical attention and be used mainly for transportation. Since ambulance dispatchers often are accustomed to taking calls from doctors only, state immediately that you are a foreign tourist and then describe the nature of your problem and your location. In Spain, however, the ambulance dispatcher probably will not be bilingual, and unless you speak Spanish, he or she will be unable to determine the nature of the emergency, what equipment will be needed, or even where to send the ambulance. Travelers with little or no foreign language ability should try to get someone else to make the call. If the situation is desperate, dial 005 (throughout Spain) for an international operator who should be able to place the call to the local emergency service and stay on the line as interpreter.

Spain has socialized medicine and there are two types of hospitals: public and private. Medical services at *policlinicas,* or clinics which are for less serious medical matters, are free (or relatively inexpensive) for Spanish citizens, but foreign travelers will have to pay full fees for such service. There may not be an English-speaking health worker there, however, and you can't just walk in off the streets; you need to make an appointment. Although private local services are the preferred option, in an extreme medical emergency, US military hospitals on bases in Rota, Torrejón de Ardez, and Zaragoza in Spain, may treat travelers (of any nationality) who are seriously ill or injured until their conditions are stabilized — assuming that the US hospital has the facilities for the treatment required — and then transfer the patient to other hospitals.

If a doctor is needed for something less than an emergency, there are several ways to find one. If you are staying in a hotel or at a resort, ask for help in reaching a doctor or other emergency services, or for the house physician, who may visit you in your room or ask you to visit an office. Travelers staying at a hotel of any size probably will find that the doctor on call speaks at least a modicum of English — if not, request one who does. When you register at a hotel, it's not a bad idea to include your home address and telephone number; this will facilitate the process of notifying friends, relatives, or your own doctor in case of an emergency.

Dialing the nationwide emergency number (091) also may be of help in locating a physician. It also usually is possible to obtain a referral through a US consulate (see addresses and phone numbers below) or directly through a hospital, especially if it is an emergency. If you already are at the hospital, you may see the doctor there, or you may make an appointment to be seen at his or her office.

There should be no problem finding a 24-hour drugstore *(la farmacia)* in any major city. In Spain, a pharmacy is identified by a red cross and is part of a network within a city, so that there always should be a drugstore somewhere that is open. In many areas, night duty rotates among pharmacies; closed pharmacies generally will have a sign in the window telling you the location of the pharmacy staying open for 24 hours on that day — the name and address follow the words *farmacia du servicos.* A call to the emergency room of the local hospital also may produce this information. In small towns, where none may be open after normal business hours, you may be able to have one open in an emergency situation — such as a diabetic needing insulin — although you may be charged a fee for this off-hour service.

Bring along a copy of any prescription you may have from your doctor in case you should need a refill. In the case of minor complaints, Spanish pharmacists may do some prescribing and *may* fill a foreign prescription; however, do not count on this. In most cases, you will need a local doctor to rewrite the prescription. Even in an emergency, a traveler will more than likely be given only enough of a drug to last until a local prescription can be obtained.

Americans also will notice that some drugs sold only by prescription in the US are sold over the counter in Spain (and vice versa). Though this can be very handy, be aware that common cold medicines and aspirin that contain codeine or other controlled substances will not be allowed back into the US.

Emergency assistance also is available from the various medical programs designed for travelers who have chronic ailments or whose illness requires them to return home:

International Association of Medical Assistance to Travelers (*IAMAT;* 417 Center St., Lewiston, NY 14092; phone: 716-754-4883). Entitles members to the services of participating doctors around the world, as well as clinics and hospitals in various locations. Participating physicians agree to adhere to a basic charge of around $40 to see a patient referred by *IAMAT.* To join, simply write to *IAMAT;* in about 3 weeks you will receive a membership card, the booklet of members, and an inoculation chart. A nonprofit organization, *IAMAT* appreciates donations; with a donation of $25 or more, you will receive a set of worldwide climate charts detailing weather and sanitary conditions. (Delivery can take up to 5 weeks, so plan ahead.)

International SOS Assistance (PO Box 11568, Philadelphia, PA 19116; phone: 800-523-8930 or 215-244-1500). Subscribers are provided with telephone access — 24 hours a day, 365 days a year — to a worldwide, monitored, multilingual network of medical centers. A phone call brings assistance ranging from a telephone consultation to transportation home by ambulance or aircraft, or, in some cases, transportation of a family member to wherever you are hospitalized. Individual rates are $35 for 2 weeks of coverage ($3.50 for each additional day), $70 for 1 month, or $240 for 1 year; couple and family rates also are available.

Medic Alert Foundation (2323 N. Colorado, Turlock, CA 95380; phone: 800-ID-ALERT or 209-668-3333). If you have a health condition that may not be readily perceptible to the casual observer — one that might result in a tragic error in an emergency situation — this organization offers identification emblems specifying such conditions. The foundation also maintains a computerized central file from which your complete medical history is available 24 hours a day by phone (the telephone number is clearly inscribed on the emblem). The onetime membership fee (between $25 and $45) is based on the type of metal from which the emblem is made — the choices range from stainless steel to 10K gold-filled.

TravMed (PO Box 10623, Baltimore, MD 21204; phone: 800-732-5309 or 301-296-5225). For $3 per day, subscribers receive comprehensive medical assistance while abroad. Major medical expenses are covered up to $100,000, and special transportation home or of a family member to wherever you are hospitalized is provided at no additional cost.

■**Note:** Those who are unable to take a reserved flight due to personal illness or who must fly home unexpectedly due to a family emergency should be aware that airlines may offer a discounted airfare (or arrange a partial refund) if the traveler can demonstrate that his or her situation is indeed a legitimate emergency. Your inability to fly or the illness or death of an immediate family member usually must be substantiated by a doctor's note or the name, relationship, and funeral home from which the deceased will be buried. In such cases, airlines often will waive certain advance purchase restrictions or you may receive a refund check or voucher for future travel at a later date. Be aware, however, that this bereavement fare may not necessarily be the least expensive fare available and, if possible, it is best to have a travel agent check all possible flights through a computer reservations system (CRS).

LEGAL AID AND CONSULAR SERVICES: There is one crucial place to keep in mind when outside the US, namely, the American Services section of the US Consulate. If you are injured or become seriously ill, the consulate will direct you to medical assistance and notify your relatives. If, while abroad, you become involved in a dispute that could lead to legal action, the consulate, once again, is the place to turn.

It usually is far more alarming to be arrested abroad than at home. Not only are you alone among strangers, but the punishment can be worse. Granted, the US Consulate can advise you of your rights and provide a list of lawyers, but it cannot interfere with local legal process. Except for minor infractions of the local traffic code, there is no reason for any law-abiding traveler to run afoul of immigration, customs, or any other law enforcement authority.

The best advice is to be honest and law-abiding. If you get a traffic ticket, pay it. If you are approached by drug hawkers, ignore them. The penalties for possession of marijuana, cocaine, and other narcotics are even more severe abroad than in the US. (If you are picked up for any drug-related offense, do not expect US foreign service officials to be sympathetic. Chances are they will notify a lawyer and your family and that's about all. See "Drugs," below.)

In the case of minor traffic accidents (such as a fender bender), it often is most expedient to settle the matter before the police get involved. If, however, you are involved in a serious accident, where an injury or fatality results, the first step is to contact the nearest US consulate (for addresses, see below) and ask the consul to locate a lawyer to assist you. If you have a traveling companion, ask him or her to call the consulate (unless either of you has a local contact who can help you quickly). Competent English-speaking lawyers practice throughout Europe, and it is possible to obtain good legal counsel on short notice.

The US Department of State in Washington, DC, insists that any US citizen who is arrested abroad has the right to contact the US embassy or consulate "immediately," but it may be a while before you are given permission to use a phone. Do not labor under the illusion, however, that in a scrape with foreign officialdom the consulate can act as an arbitrator or ombudsman on a US citizen's behalf. Nothing could be farther from the truth. Consuls have no power, authorized or otherwise, to subvert, alter, or contravene the legal processes, however unfair, of the foreign country in which they serve. Nor can a consul oil the machinery of a foreign bureaucracy or provide legal advice. The consul's responsibilities do encompass "welfare duties," including providing a list of lawyers and information on local sources of legal aid, informing relatives in the US, and organizing and administrating any defense monies sent from home. If a case is tried unfairly or the punishment seems unusually severe, the consul can make a formal complaint to the authorities. For questions about US citizens arrested abroad, how to get money to them, and other useful information, call the *Citizens' Emergency Center* of the Office of Special Consular Services in Washington, DC, at 202-647-5225. (For further information about this invaluable hotline, see below.)

Other welfare duties, not involving legal hassles, cover cases of both illness and destitution. If you should get sick, the US consul can provide names of doctors and dentists, as well as the names of all local hospitals and clinics; the consul also will contact family members in the US and help arrange special ambulance service for a flight home. In a situation involving "legitimate and proven poverty" of an US citizen stranded abroad without funds, the consul will contact sources of money (such as family or friends in the US), apply for aid to agencies in foreign countries, and in a last resort — which is *rarely* — arrange for repatriation at government expense, although this is a loan that must be repaid. And in case of natural disasters or civil unrest, consulates around the world handle the evacuation of US citizens if it becomes necessary.

The consulate is not occupied solely with emergencies and is certainly not there to aid in trivial situations, such as canceled reservations or lost baggage, no matter how important these matters may seem to the victimized tourist. The main duties of any consulate are administrating statutory services, such as the issuance of passports and visas; providing notarial services; distributing VA, social security, and civil service benefits to US citizens; taking depositions; handling extradition cases; and reporting to Washington the births, deaths, and marriages of US citizens living within the consulate's domain.

We hope that none of the information in this section will be necessary during your stay in Spain. If you can avoid legal hassles altogether, you will have a much more pleasant trip. If you become involved in an imbroglio, the local authorities may spare you legal complications if you make clear your tourist status. And if you run into a confrontation that might lead to legal complications developing with a citizen or with local authorities, the best tactic is to apologize and try to leave as gracefully as possible. Do not get into fights with residents, no matter how belligerent or provocative they are in a given situation.

Following are the US embassy and consulates in Spain. If you are not in any of the cities mentioned when a problem arises, contact the nearest office. (If you are not a US citizen, contact the consulate of your own nation.) Note that mailing addresses may be different — so call before sending anything to these offices. Note that we have included the phone number prefix (9) as you are most likely to dial these numbers once in Spain; if calling from the US, leave off the 9.

   Barcelona: US Consulate, 33 Via Layetana, Barcelona 08003 (phone: 93-319-9550).
   Bilboa: US Consulate, 11-3 Avenida del Ejercito, Bilboa 48014 (phone: 94-475-8300).
   Madrid: US Embassy, 75 Calle Serrano, Madrid 28006 (phone: 91-577-4000).

You also can obtain a booklet with addresses of most US embassies and consulates around the world by writing to the Superintendent of Documents (US Government Printing Office, Washington, DC 20402) and asking for publication #78-77, *Key Offices of Foreign Service Posts.*

As mentioned above, the US State Department operates a *Citizens' Emergency Center,* which offers a number of services to US citizens abroad and their families at home. In addition to giving callers up-to-date information on trouble spots, the center will contact authorities abroad in an attempt to locate a traveler or deliver an urgent message. In case of illness, death, arrest, destitution, or repatriation of an US citizen on foreign soil, it will relay information to relatives at home if the consulate is unable to do so. Travel advisory information is available 24 hours a day to people with touch-tone phones (phone: 202-647-5225). Callers with rotary phones can get information at this number from 8:15 AM to 10 PM (Eastern Standard Time) on weekdays; 9 AM to 3 PM Saturdays. In the event of an emergency, this number also may be called during these hours. For emergency calls only, at all other times, call 202-634-3600 and ask for the Duty Officer.

Drinking and Drugs

 DRINKING: It is more than likely that some of the warmest memories of a trip to Spain will be moments of conviviality shared over a drink in a neighborhood bar or sunlit café. Visitors will find that liquor, wine, and brandies in Spain are distilled to the same proof and often are the same labels as those found at home. However, Spanish beer tends to be about 5% higher in alcoholic content than beer brewed in the US.

You'll want to try the country's specialties. Spanish beer and wine are favorites in bars and cafés. Spanish beer *(cerveza)* is served ice cold in three varieties; regular, light *(dorada),* and dark *(negra).* Most Spanish bars, cafés, and *cervecerías* (taverns specializing in beer and wine) serve beer in bottles and on tap. San Miguel and Aguila are popular national brands, while others (Cruz Campo in Seville and Alhambra in Grenada) are sold regionally. Draft beer is *cerveza de barril.*

Spanish wines are as world-renowned as they are varied, with each region boasting its own specialty. The most famous Spanish wine is *jerez* (sherry), served either *manzanillas* (very dry) or *amontillados* (sweet) as an aperitif; or *fino* (dry) or *olorosos* (very sweet) as an after-dinner drink. (For a more thorough discussion of Spanish beverages, see *Food and Drink,* PERSPECTIVES, and *Visitable Vineyards,* DIVERSIONS.)

Spanish bars and cafés open at 8:30 AM or earlier to serve coffee and breakfast, although alcohol generally is not served until at least 10 AM. Most remain open until midnight, but others may stay open until as late as 4 AM. In Spain, there is no established minimum drinking age. The rule of thumb generally is at the discretion of the establishment — in some cases, the bartender.

As in the US, national taxes on alcohol affect the prices of liquor in Spain, and, as a general rule, mixed drinks — especially imported liquors such as whiskey and gin — are more expensive than at home. If you like a drop before dinner, a good way to save money is to buy a bottle of your favorite brand at the airport before leaving the US and enjoy it in your hotel before setting forth.

Visitors to Spain may bring in 1 bottle of wine and 1 bottle of liquor per person duty-free. If you are buying any quantity of alcohol (such as a case of wine) in Spain and traveling through other European countries on your route back to the US, you will have to pass through customs and pay duty at each border crossing, so you might want to arrange to have it shipped home. Whether bringing it with you or shipping, you will have to pay US import duties on any quantity over the allowed 1 liter (see *Customs and Returning to the US,* in this section).

DRUGS: Illegal narcotics are as prevalent in Spain as in the US, but the moderate legal penalties and vague social acceptance that marijuana has gained in the US have no equivalents in Spain. Due to the international war on drugs, enforcement of drug laws is becoming increasingly strict throughout the world. Local European narcotics officers and customs officials are renowned for their absence of understanding and lack of a sense of humor — especially where foreigners are involved.

Opiates and barbiturates, and other increasingly popular drugs — "white powder" substances like heroin and cocaine, and "crack" (the cocaine derivative) — continue to be of major concern to narcotics officials. Most European countries — including Spain — have toughened laws regarding illegal drugs and narcotics, and it is important to bear in mind that the type or quantity of drugs involved is of minor importance. Particularly for foreigners, the maximum penalties may be imposed for possessing even *traces* of illegal drugs. There is a high conviction rate in these cases, and bail for foreigners is rare. Persons arrested are subject to the laws of the country they are visiting, and there isn't much that the US consulate can do for drug offenders beyond providing a list of lawyers. The best advice we can offer is this: Don't carry, use, buy, or sell illegal drugs.

Those who carry medicines that contain a controlled drug should be sure to have a current doctor's prescription with them. Ironically, travelers can get into almost as much trouble coming through US customs with over-the-counter drugs picked up abroad that contain substances that are controlled in the US. Cold medicines, pain relievers, and the like often have codeine or codeine derivatives that are illegal, except by prescription, in the US. Throw them out before leaving for home.

■ **Be forewarned:** US narcotics agents warn travelers of the increasingly common ploy of drug dealers asking travelers to transport a "gift" or other package back to the US. Don't be fooled into thinking that the protection of US law applies abroad — accused of illegal drug trafficking, you will be considered guilty until you prove your innocence. In other words, do not, under any circumstances, agree to take anything across the border for a stranger.

Tipping

 Throughout Spain (as in most of the rest of Europe), you will find the custom of including some kind of service charge as part of a meal more common than in North America. This can confuse Americans not familiar with the custom. On the one hand, many a traveler, unaware of this policy, has left many a superfluous tip. On the other hand, travelers aware of this policy may make the mistake of assuming that it takes care of everything. It doesn't. While "service included" in theory eliminates any question about how much and whom to tip, in practice there still are occasions when on-the-spot tips are appropriate. Among these are tips to show appreciation for special services, as well as tips meant to say "thank you" for services rendered. So keep a pocketful of 100 peseta bills (or coins) ready, and hand these out like dollar bills.

In Spanish restaurants, the service charge (called *servicio incluido*) may appear in one of two ways: It either already is calculated in the prices listed or will be added to the final bill. For the most part, if you see a notation at the bottom of the menu without a percentage figure, the charge should be included in the prices; if a percentage figure is indicated, the service charge has not yet been added. To further confuse the issue, not every restaurant notes if its policy is to include service and at what point the charge is added. If you are at all unsure, you should feel no embarrassment about asking a waiter.

This service charge generally ranges from 15% to 20%. In the rare instance where it isn't added, a 15% tip to the waiter — just as in the US — usually is a safe figure, although one should never hesitate to penalize poor service or reward excellent and efficient attention by leaving less or more. If the tip has been added, no further gratuity is expected — though it's a common practice in Europe to leave a few extra coins on the table. The emphasis is on *few*, and the current equivalent of $1 usually is quite adequate.

Although it's not necessary to tip the maître d' of most restaurants — unless he has been especially helpful in arranging a special party or providing a table (slipping him something in a crowded restaurant *may* get you seated sooner or procure a preferred table) — when tipping is desirable or appropriate, the least amount should be the local equivalent of $5. In the finest restaurants, where a multiplicity of servers are present, plan to tip 5% to the captain. The sommelier (wine waiter) is entitled to a gratuity of approximately 10% of the price of the bottle.

In allocating gratuities at a restaurant, pay particular attention to what has become the standard credit card charge form, which now includes separate places for gratuities for waiters and/or captains. If these separate boxes are not on the charge slip, simply ask the waiter or captain how these separate tips should be indicated. Be aware, too, of the increasingly common, devious practice of placing the amount of an entire restaurant bill (in which service already has been included) in the top box of a charge slip, leaving the "tip" and "total" boxes ominously empty. Don't be intimidated: Leave the "tip" box blank and just repeat the total amount next to "total" before signing. In some establishments, tips indicated on credit card receipts may not be given to the help, so you may want to leave tips in cash.

As in restaurants, visitors usually will find a service charge of 10% to 15% included in their final bill at most Spanish hotels. No additional gratuities are required — or expected — beyond this billed service charge. It is unlikely, however, that a service charge will be added to bills in small family-run guesthouses or other modest establishments. In these cases, guests should let their instincts be their guide; no tipping is expected by members of the family who own the establishment, but it is a nice gesture to leave something for others — such as a dining room waiter or a maid — who may have been helpful. A gratuity of around $1 per night is adequate in most cases.

If a hotel does not automatically add a service charge, it is perfectly proper for guests to ask to have an extra 10% to 15% added to their bill, to be distributed among those who served them. This may be an especially convenient solution in a large hotel, where it's difficult to determine just who out of a horde of attendants actually performed particular services.

For those who prefer to distribute tips themselves, a chambermaid generally is tipped at the rate of approximately $1 per day. Tip the concierge or hall porter for specific services only, with the amount of such gratuities dependent on the level of service provided. For any special service you receive in a hotel, a tip is expected — the current equivalent of $1 being the minimum for a small service.

Bellhops, doormen, and porters at hotels and transporation centers generally are tipped at the rate of $1 per piece of luggage, along with a small additional amount if a doorman helps with a cab or car. Once upon a time, taxi drivers in Europe would give you a rather odd look if presented with a tip for a fare, but times have changed, and 10% to 15% of the amount on the meter is now a standard gratuity.

Miscellaneous tips: Tipping ushers in a movie house, theater, or concert hall used to be the rule, but is becoming less common — the best policy is to check what other patrons are doing and follow suit. Most of the time, the program is not free, and in lieu of a tip it is common practice to purchase a program from the person who seats you. Sightseeing tour guides also should be tipped. If you are traveling in a group, decide together what you want to give the guide and present it from the group at the end of the tour. If you have been individually escorted, the amount paid should depend on the degree of your satisfaction, but it should not be less than 10% of the total tour price. Museum and monument guides also usually are tipped, and it is a nice touch to tip a caretaker who unlocks a small church or turns on the lights in a chapel for you in some out-of-the-way town.

In barbershops and beauty salons, tip as you would at home, keeping in mind that the percentages vary according to the type of establishment — 10% in the most expensive salons; 15% to 20% in less expensive establishments. (As a general rule, the person who washes your hair should get an additional small tip.) The washroom attendants in these places, or wherever you see one, should get a small tip — they usually set out a little plate with a coin already on it indicating the suggested denomination. Don't forget service station attendants, for whom a tip of around 50¢ for cleaning the windshield or other attention is not unusual.

Tipping always is a matter of personal preference. In the situations covered above, as well as in any others that arise where you feel a tip is expected or due, feel free to express your pleasure or displeasure. Again, never hesitate to reward excellent and efficient attention and to penalize poor service. Give an extra gratuity and a word of thanks when someone has gone out of his or her way for you. Either way, the more personal the act of tipping, the more appropriate it seems. And if you didn't like the service — or the attitude — don't tip.

Duty-Free Shopping and Value Added Tax

DUTY-FREE SHOPS: Note that at the time of this writing, because of the newly integrated European economy, there was some question as to the fate and number of duty-free shops that would be maintained at international airports in member countries of the European Economic Community (EEC). It appears, however, that those traveling between EEC countries and any country *not* a member of the Common Market will still be entitled to buy duty-free items. Since the United States is not a Common Market member, duty-free purchases by US travelers will, presumably, remain as is even after the end of 1992.

If common sense says that it always is less expensive to buy goods in an airport duty-free shop than to buy them at home or in the streets of a foreign city, travelers should be aware of some basic facts. Duty-free, first of all, does not mean that the goods travelers buy will be free of duty when they return to the US. Rather, it means that the shop has paid no import tax acquiring goods of foreign make because the goods are not to be used in the country where the shop is located. This is why duty-free goods are available only in the restricted, passengers-only area of international airports or are delivered to departing passengers on the plane. In a duty-free store, travelers save money only on goods of foreign make because they are the only items on which an import tax would be charged in any other store. There usually is no saving on locally made items, although in countries such as Spain that impose Value Added Taxes (see below) that are refundable to foreigners, the prices in airport duty-free shops are minus this tax, sparing travelers the often cumbersome procedures they otherwise have to follow to obtain a VAT refund.

Beyond this, there is little reason to delay buying locally made merchandise and/or souvenirs until reaching the airport (for information on local specialties, see the individual city chapters in THE CITIES, and *Shopping Spree,* in DIVERSIONS). In fact, because airport duty-free shops usually pay high rents, the locally made goods sold in them may well be more expensive than they would be in downtown stores. The real bargains are foreign goods, but — let the buyer beware — not all foreign goods automatically are less expensive in an airport duty-free shop. You can get a good deal on even small amounts of perfume, costing less than the usually required minimum purchase, tax-free. Other fairly standard bargains include spirits, smoking materials, cameras, clothing, watches, chocolates and other food and luxury items — but first be sure to know what these items cost elsewhere. Terrific savings do exist (they are the reason for such shops, after all), but so do overpriced items that an unwary shopper might find equally tempting. In addition, if you wait to do your shopping at airport duty-free shops, you will be taking the chance that the desired item is out of stock or unavailable.

Duty-free shops are located in most major international airports throughout Europe. In Spain, there duty-free shops at airports in Alicante, Barcelona, Girona, Ibiza, Madrid, Mahón, Málaga, Palma de Mallorca, Seville, and Valencia.

VALUE ADDED TAX: Commonly abbreviated as VAT, this is a tax levied by various European countries, including Spain, and added to the purchase price of most goods and services. The standard VAT (known as IVA in Spain and ITE in the Canary Islands) is 12% on most purchases and 6% on food, with the higher rate of 33% applying to luxury goods such as watches, jewelry, furs, glass, and cameras.

The tax is intended for residents (and already is included in the price tag), but visitors are required to pay it, too, unless they have purchases shipped directly to an address abroad by the store. If visitors pay the tax and take purchases with them, however, they generally are entitled to a refund under a retail export scheme that has been in operation in both countries for several years. In the past, returning travelers have complained of delays in receiving the refunds and of difficulties in converting checks written in foreign currency into dollars, but a new service — called *Exencion del Inpuesto* in Spain — has recently been introduced that greatly streamlines the procedure.

In order to qualify for a refund, you must purchase a minimum of 53,000 pesetas (about $486 US at press time) at one store — purchases from several stores cannot be combined. In most cases, stores will provide the appropriate refund forms on request. If the store does not have this form, it can be obtained at the refund office at the airport, which also can provide information on the procedure for submitting the paperwork to obtain the refund. Visitors leaving Spain must have all of their receipts for purchases and refund vouchers stamped by customs; as customs officials may well ask to see the merchandise, it's a good idea not to pack it in the bottom of your suitcase. Refund checks are sent out within about 1 month of receipt of the vouchers, and refunds by credit card also generally appear on the cardholder's statement within 1 month of receipt.

A VAT refund by dollar check or by credit to a credit card account is relatively hassle-free. If it arrives in the form of a foreign currency check and if the refund is less than a significant amount, charges imposed by US banks for converting foreign currency refund checks — which can run as high as $15 or more — could make the whole exercise hardly worth your while.

Far less costly is sending your foreign currency check (after endorsing it) to *Ruesch International,* which will covert it to a check in US dollars for a $2 fee (deducted from the dollar check). Other services include commission-free traveler's checks and foreign currency which can be ordered by mail. Contact *Ruesch International* at one of the following address: 191 Peachtree St., Atlanta, GA 30303 (phone: 404-222-9300); 3 First National Plaza, Suite 2020, Chicago, IL 60602 (phone: 312-332-5900); 1925 Century Park E., Suite 240, Los Angeles, CA 90067 (phone: 213-277-7800); 608 Fifth Ave., "Swiss Center," New York, NY 10020 (phone: 212-977-2700); and 1350 Eye St. NW, 10th Floor and street level, Washington, DC 20005 (phone: 800-424-2923 or 202-408-1200).

■ **Buyer Beware:** You may come across shops *not* at airports that call themselves duty-free shops. These require shoppers to show a foreign passport but are subject to the same rules as other stores, including paying import duty on foreign items. What "tax-free" means in the case of these establishments is something of an advertising strategy: They are announcing loud and clear that they do, indeed, offer the VAT refund service — sometimes on the spot (minus a fee for higher overhead). Prices may be no better at these stores and could be even higher due to the addition of this service.

Religion on the Road

 Spain is predominantly Catholic and every town, right down to the most isolated village, has its own church. In larger, more heavily populated areas, some amount of religious variety is reflected in the churches of other denominations, synagogues, and an occasional mosque or temple.

The surest source of information on English-language religious services in an unfamiliar country is the desk clerk of the hotel or guesthouse in which you are staying; the local tourist information office, a US consul, or a church of another religious affiliation also may be able to provide this information. If you aren't in an area with services held in your own denomination, you might find it interesting to attend the service of another religion. You also might enjoy attending a service in a foreign language — even if you don't understand all the words. There are many beautiful churches throughout Spain, and whether in a stately cathedral or a small village chapel, visitors are welcome.

Customs and Returning to the US

 Whether you return to the United States by air or sea, you must declare to the US Customs official at the point of entry everything you have bought or acquired while in Europe. The customs check can go smoothly, lasting only a few minutes, or can take hours, depending on the officer's instinct. To speed up the process, keep all your receipts handy and try to pack your purchases together in an accessible part of your suitcase. It might save you from unpacking all your belongings.

DUTY-FREE ARTICLES: In general, the duty-free allowance for US citizens returning from abroad is $400. This duty-free limit is based on the provision that your purchases accompany you and are for personal use. This limit includes items used or worn while abroad, souvenirs for friends, and gifts received during the trip. A flat 10% duty based on the "fair retail value in country of acquisition" is assessed on the next $1,000 worth of merchandise brought in for personal use or gifts. Amounts over the basic allotment and the 10% dutiable amount are dutiable at a variety of rates. The average rate for typical tourist purchases is about 12%, but you can find out rates on specific items by consulting *Tariff Schedules of the United States* in a library or at any US Customs Service office.

Families traveling together may make a joint declaration to customs, which permits one member to exceed his or her duty-free exemption to the extent that another falls short. Families also may pool purchases dutiable under the flat rate. A family of three, for example, would be eligible for up to a total of $3,000 at the 10% flat duty rate (after each member had used up his or her $400 duty-free exemption) rather than three separate $1,000 allowances. This grouping of purchases is extremely useful when considering the duty on a high-tariff item, such as jewelry or a fur coat.

Personal exemptions can be used once every 30 days; in order to be eligible, an individual must have been out of the country for more than 48 hours. If any portion of the exemption has been used once within any 30-day period or if your trip is less than 48 hours long, the duty-free allowance is cut to $25.

There are certain articles, however, that are duty-free only up to certain limits. The $25 allowance includes the following: 10 cigars (not Cuban), 60 cigarettes, and 4 ounces of perfume. Individuals eligible for the full $400 duty-free limit are allowed 1 carton of cigarettes (200), 100 cigars, and 1 liter of liquor or wine if the traveler is over 21. Alcohol above this allowance is liable for both duty and an Internal Revenue tax. Antiques, if they are 100 or more years old and you have proof from the seller of that fact, are duty-free, as are paintings and drawings if done entirely by hand.

To avoid paying duty twice, register the serial numbers of foreign-made watches and electronic equipment with the nearest US Customs bureau before departure; receipts of insurance policies also should be carried for other foreign-made items. (Also see the note at the end of *Entry Requirements and Documents,* in this section.)

Gold, gold medals, bullion, and up to $10,000 in currency or negotiable instruments may be brought into the US without being declared. Sums over $10,000 must be declared in writing.

The allotment for individual "unsolicited" gifts mailed from abroad (no more than one per day per recipient) is $50 retail value per gift. These gifts do not have to be declared and are not included in your duty-free exemption (see below). Although you should include a receipt for purchases with each package, the examiner is empowered to impose a duty based on his or her assessment of the value of the goods. The duty owed is collected by the US Postal Service when the package is delivered (also see below). More information on mailing packages home from abroad is contained in the US Customs Service pamphlet *Buyer Beware, International Mail Imports* (see below for where to write for this and other useful brochures).

CLEARING CUSTOMS: This is a simple procedure. Forms are distributed by airline or ship personnel before arrival. (Note that a $5-per-person service charge — called a user fee — is collected by airlines and cruise lines to help cover the cost of customs checks, but this is included in the ticket price.) If your purchases total no more than the $400 duty-free limit, you need only fill out the identification part of the form and make an oral declaration to the customs inspector. If entering with more than $400 worth of goods, you must submit a written declaration.

Customs agents are businesslike, efficient, and not unkind. During the peak season, clearance can take time, but this generally is because of the strain imposed by a number of jumbo jets simultaneously discharging their passengers, not because of unwarranted zealousness on the part of the customs people.

Efforts to streamline procedures used to include the so-called Citizens' Bypass Program, which allowed US citizens whose purchases were within their duty-free allowance to go to the "green line," where they simply showed their passports to the customs inspector. Although at the time of this writing this procedure still is being followed at some international airports in the US, most airports have returned to an earlier system. US citizens arriving from overseas now have to go through a passport check by the Immigration & Naturalization Service (INS) prior to recovering their baggage and proceeding to customs. (US citizens will not be on the same line as foreign visitors, however, though this additional wait does delay clearance on re-entry into the US.) Although all passengers have to go through this passport inspection, those entering with purchases within the duty-free limit may be spared a thorough customs inspection, although inspectors still retain the right to search any luggage they choose — so don't do anything foolish.

It is illegal not to declare dutiable items; not to do so, in fact, constitutes smuggling, and the penalty can be anything from stiff fines and seizure of the goods to prison sentences. It simply isn't worth doing. Nor should you go along with the suggestions of foreign merchants who offer to help you secure a bargain by deceiving customs officials in any way. Such transactions frequently are a setup, using the foreign merchant as an agent of US customs. Another agent of US customs is TECS, the Treasury Enforcement Communications System, a computer that stores all kinds of pertinent information on returning citizens. There is a basic rule to buying goods abroad, and it should never be broken: *If you can't afford the duty on something, don't buy it.* Your list or verbal declaration should include all items purchased abroad, as well as gifts received abroad, purchases made at the behest of others, the value of repairs, and anything brought in for resale in the US.

Do not include in the list items that do not accompany you, i.e., purchases that you have mailed or had shipped home. As mentioned above, these are dutiable in any case, even if for your own use and even if the items that accompany your return from the same trip do not exhaust your duty-free exemption. It is a good idea, if you have accumulated too much while abroad, to mail home any personal effects (made and bought in the US) that you no longer need rather than your foreign purchases. These personal effects pass through US Customs as "American goods returned" and are not subject to duty.

If you cannot avoid shipping home your foreign purchases, however, the US Customs Service suggests that the package be clearly marked "Not for Sale," and that a copy of the bill of sale be included. The US Customs examiner usually will accept this as indicative of the article's fair retail value, but if he or she believes it to be falsified or feels the goods have been seriously undervalued, a higher retail value may be assigned.

FORBIDDEN ITEMS: Narcotics, plants, and many types of food are not allowed into the US. Drugs are totally illegal, with the exception of medication prescribed by a physician. It's a good idea not to travel with too large a quantity of any given prescription drug (although, in the event that a pharmacy is not open when you need it, bring along several extra doses) and to have the prescription on hand in case any question arises either abroad or when reentering the US.

Any sculpture that is part of an architectural structure, any authentic archaeological find, or other artifacts may not be exported from Spain without the permission of the Spanish Ministry of the Interior; for information on items that might fall into this category, contact the Spanish customs office in Madrid (5 Paseo de la Castellana, Madrid 28071; phone: 1-254-3200). If you do not obtain prior permission of the proper regulatory agencies, such items will be confiscated at the border, and you will run the risk of being fined or imprisoned.

Tourists have long been forbidden to bring into the US foreign-made US trade-marked articles purchased abroad (if the trademark is recorded with customs) without written permission. It's now permissable to enter with one such item in your possession as long as it's for personal use.

The US Customs Service implements the rigorous Department of Agriculture regulations concerning the importation of vegetable matter, seeds, bulbs, and the like. Living vegetable matter may not be imported without a permit, and everything must be inspected, permit or not. Approved items (which do not require a permit) include dried bamboo and woven items made of straw; beads made of most seeds (but not jequirity beans — the poisonous scarlet and black seed of the rosary pea); cones of pine and other trees; roasted coffee beans; most flower bulbs; flowers (without roots); dried or canned fruits, jellies, or jams; polished rice, dried beans and teas; herb plants (not witchweed); nuts (but not acorns, chestnuts, or nuts with outer husks); dried lichens, mushrooms, truffles, shamrocks, and seaweed; and most dried spices.

Other processed foods and baked goods usually are okay. Regulations on meat products generally depend on the country of origin and manner of processing. As a rule, commercially canned meat, hermetically sealed and cooked in the can so that it can be stored without refrigeration, is permitted, but not all canned meat fulfills this requirement. Be careful when buying European-made pâté, for instance. Goose liver pâté in itself is acceptable, but the pork fat that often is part of it, either as an ingredient or a rind, may not be. Even canned pâtés may not be admitted for this reason. (The imported ones you see in US stores have been prepared and packaged according to US regulations.) So before stocking up on a newfound favorite, it pays to check in advance — otherwise you might have to leave it behind.

The US Customs Service also enforces federal laws that prohibit the entry of articles made from the furs or hides of animals on the endangered species list. Beware of shoes, bags, and belts made of crocodile and certain kinds of lizard, and anything made from tortoiseshell; this also applies to preserved crocodiles, lizards, and turtles sometimes sold in gift shops. And if you're shopping for big-ticket items, beware of fur coats made from the skins of spotted cats. They are sold in Europe, but they will be confiscated upon your return to the US, and there will be no refund. For information about other animals on the endangered species list, contact the Department of the Interior, US Fish and Wildlife Service (Publications Unit, 4401 N. Fairfax Dr., Room 130, Arlington, VA 22203; phone: 703-358-1711), and ask for the free publication *Facts About Federal Wildlife Laws*.

Also note that some foreign governments prohibit the export of items made from certain species of wildlife, and the US honors any such restrictions. Before you go shopping in any foreign country, check with the US Department of Agriculture (G110 Federal Bldg., Hyattsville, MD 20782; phone: 301-436-8413) and find out what items are prohibited by the country you will be visiting.

The US Customs Service publishes a series of free pamphlets with customs information. It includes *Know Before You Go,* a basic discussion of customs requirements pertaining to all travelers; *Buyer Beware, International Mail Imports; Travelers' Tips on Bringing Food, Plant, and Animal Products into the United States; Importing a Car; GSP and the Traveler; Pocket Hints; Currency Reporting; Pets, Wildlife, US Customs; Customs Hints for Visitors (Nonresidents);* and *Trademark Information for Travelers.* For the entire series or individual pamphlets, write to the US Customs Service (PO Box 7407, Washington, DC 20044) or contact any of the seven regional offices — in Boston, Chicago, Houston, Long Beach (California), Miami, New Orleans, and New York. The US Customs Service has a tape-recorded message whereby callers using Touch-Tone phones can get more information on various topics; the number is 202-566-8195. These pamphlets provide great briefing material, but if you still have questions when you're in Europe, contact the nearest US consulate.

Sources and Resources

Tourist Information Offices

North American branches of the National Tourist Office of Spain generally are the best sources of travel information, and most of their many, varied publications are free for the asking. For the best results, request general information on specific provinces or cities, as well as publications relating to your particular areas of interest: accommodations, restaurants, special events, sports, guided tours, and facilities for specific sports. There is no need to send a self-addressed, stamped envelope with your request, unless specified.

The best places for tourist information in Spanish cities are listed in the individual reports in THE CITIES. The following North American tourist information offices are best equipped to handle written or telephone inquiries from potential visitors on this side of the Atlantic.

Chicago: Water Tower Place, 845 N. Michigan Ave., Suite 915E, Chicago, IL 60611 (phone: 312-642-1992).

Los Angeles: San Vincente Plaza Bldg., 8383 Wilshire Blvd., Suite 938, Beverly Hills, CA 90211 (phone: 213-658-7188).

Miami: 1221 Brickell Ave., Suite 1850, Miami, FL 33131 (phone: 305-358-1992).

New York: 665 Fifth Ave., New York, NY 10022 (phone: 212-759-8822).

Canada: 102 Bloor St. W., 14th Floor, Toronto, Ontario M5S 1M8, Canada (phone: 416-961-3131 or 416-961-4079).

As we went to press, the *Association of the Institute for Tourism Promotion of Spain (TURESPAÑA), Iberia Airlines of Spain,* and *American Express* had jointly introduced a telephone information service for US travelers. By calling 900-73-SPAIN, you can order a free 48-page travel guide to Spain and obtain information on package tours (especially those offered by *American Express*). This hotline is staffed by experts, and is open from 9 AM to 9 PM Eastern Standard Time, Mondays through Fridays. Note that there is a 75¢ per minute charge for all calls; this charge will appear on your telephone bill. In addition, there's a toll-free telephone number *in Spain,* staffed by bilingual operators, that's open during the same hours 7 days a week; the number is 900-10-9090.

The Spanish Embassy and Consulates in the US

The Spanish government maintains an embassy and a number of consulates in the US. One of their primary functions is to provide visas for certain resident aliens (depending on their country of origin) and for Americans planning to visit for longer than 6 months, or to study, reside, or work in Spain. Consulates also are empowered to sign official documents and to notarize copies or translations of US documents, which may be necessary for those papers to be considered legal abroad.

Listed below are the Spanish embassy and consulates in the US.

Embassy: 2700 15th St. NW, Washington, DC 20009 (phone: 202-265-0190).
Consulates:
- 545 Boylston St., Suite 803, Boston, MA 02116 (phone: 617-536-2506).
- 180 N. Michigan Ave., Suite 1500, Chicago, IL 60601 (phone: 312-782-4588).
- 151 Sevilla Ave., 2nd Floor, Coral Gables, FL 33134 (phone: 305-446-5511).
- 1800 Bering Dr., Suite 660, Houston, TX 77057 (phone: 713-783-6200).
- 6300 Wilshire Blvd., Suite 1434, Los Angeles, CA 90048 (phone: 213-658-6050).
- 2102 World Trade Center, 2 Canal St., New Orleans, LA 70130 (phone: 504-525-4951).
- 150 E. 58th St., 16th Floor, New York, NY 10155 (phone: 212-355-4080).
- 2080 Jefferson St., San Francisco, CA 94123 (phone: 415-922-2995).

Theater and Special Event Tickets

In more than one section of this book you will read about events that spark your interest — everything from music festivals and special theater seasons to sporting championships — along with telephone numbers and addresses to which to write for descriptive brochures, reservations, or tickets. The National Tourist Office of Spain can supply information on these and other special events and festivals that take place in Spain, though they cannot in all cases provide the actual program or detailed information on ticket prices.

Since many of these occasions often are fully booked well in advance, think about having your reservation in hand before you go. In some cases, tickets may be reserved over the phone and charged to a credit card, or you can send an international money order or foreign draft. If you do write, remember that any request from the US should be accompanied by an International Reply Coupon to ensure a response (send two of them for an airmail response). These international coupons, money orders, and drafts are available at US post offices.

For further information, write for the *European Travel Commission*'s extensive list of events scheduled for the entire year for its 24 member countries (including Spain). For a free copy, send a self-addressed, stamped, business-size (4 x 9½) envelope, to "European Events," *European Travel Commission,* PO Box 1754, New York, NY 10185.

Books, Newspapers, Magazines, and Newsletters

BOOKS: Throughout GETTING READY TO GO, numerous books and brochures have been recommended as good sources of further information on a variety of topics.

Suggested Reading – The list below comprises books we have seen and think worthwhile; it is by no means complete — but meant merely to start you on your way. These titles include some informative guides to special interests, solid fictional tales, and books that call your attention to things you might not notice otherwise.

Food & Wine
Food of Spain and Portugal by Elizabeth Ortiz (Morrow; $25).
Foods and Wines of Spain by Penelope Casas (1982; Random House; $25).
Tapas: The Little Dishes of Spain by Penelope Casas (1982; Knopf; $16.95).

Art and Culture
Lives of the Artists by Giorgio Vasari (Penguin Classics; published in two volumes, $5.95 each).
Spain by Dennis Gunton (Mallard Press/Bantam Doubleday Dell; $29.98).
Spanish Painting by Jonathan Brown (Cambridge University Press; $75).
Spanish Style by Suzanne Slesin (Crown; $45).
The Story of Art by E. H. Gombrich (Prentice Hall; $36.67).

General Travel & Adventure
Birnbaum's Barcelona 1992 edited by Stephen Birnbaum and Alexandra Mayes Birnbaum (HarperCollins; $9.95).
Don Fernando by W. Somerset Maughan (Paragon House; $10.95).
Homage to Catalonia by George Orwell (Harcourt Brace Jovanovich; $5.95).
Marching Spain by V. S. Prichett (Hogarth Press, London; $19.88).
Spain by Jan Morris (Prentice Hall Press; $24.95).
The Spanish Temper by V. S Prichett (Ecco Press; $8.95).
Two Middle-Aged Ladies in Andalusia by Penelope Chetwode (Century, London; $8.95).
Voices of the Old Sea by Norman Lewis (Penguin; $7.95).

Outdoors
Trekking in Spain by Marc Dublin (Lonely Planet Publications; $11.95).
Wild Spain: A Traveler's and Naturalist's Guide by Frederic V. Grunfeld (Prentice Hall; $13.95).

Biography
Dalí by Ignacio G. De Liano (Rizzoli International; $22.50).
Franco: A Biography by J. P. Fusi, translated by Felipe Fernandez-Armesto (HarperCollins; $25).
Goya's Last Portrait: The Painter Played Today by John Berger and Nells Bielski (Faber & Faber, London; $9.95).
Goya, The Phantasmal Vision by Jacqueline and Maurice Guillard (Clarkson N. Potter Press; $100).
Picasso: His Life and Works by Roland Penrose (University of California Press; $12.95).
Segovia: An Celebration of the Man and His Music by Graham Wade (Schocken; $6.95).
Velasquez by Emma Micheletti (Thames Hudson; $4.95).

History
Alhambra Decree by David Raphael (Carmi House Press; $18).
Blood of Spain by Ronald Fraser (Pantheon; $12.95).
The Conquest of New Spain by Bernal Díaz (Penguin; $5.95).
The European Discovery of America (Oxford University Press, published in two volumes; $35 each),
Inquisition by Edward Peters (University of California Press; $12.95).

> *The Life of St. Teresa of Avila by Herself* translated by John M. Cohen (Penguin; $3).
>
> *Mohammed and Charlemagne* by Henri Pirenne (B&N Imports; $17.95).
>
> *The Spanish Armada: The Experience of War in 1588* by Felipe Fernandez-Armesto (Oxford University Press; $12.95).

Fiction

> *El Cid* edited by Geraldine McCaughrean (Oxford University Press; $17.95).
>
> *Death in the Afternoon* by Ernest Hemingway (MacMillan; $16.95).
>
> *Don Quioxte* by Miguel Cervantes de Saavedra, translated by J. M. Cohen (Penguin; $5.95).
>
> *For Whom the Bell Tolls* by Ernest Hemingway (MacMillan; $9.95).
>
> *Iberia* by James Michener (Random House; $6.95).
>
> *The Poem of El Cid* translated by Rita Hamilton and Janet Perry (Penguin; $5.95).
>
> *The Sun Also Rises* by Ernest Hemingway (MacMillan; $8.95).

In addition, *Culturgrams* is a handy series of pamphlets that provides a good sampling of information on the people, cultures, sights, and bargains to be found in over 90 countries around the world. Each four-page, newsletter-size leaflet covers one country, and Spain is included in the series. The topics included range from customs and courtesies to lifestyles and demographics. These fact-filled pamphlets are published by the David M. Kennedy Center for International Studies at Brigham Young University; for an order form contact the group c/o Publication Services (280 HRCB, Provo, UT 84602; phone: 801-378-6528). When ordering from 1 to 5 *Culturgrams,* the price is $1 each; 6 to 49 pamphlets cost 50¢ each; and for larger quantities, the price per copy goes down proportionately.

Another source of cultural information, is *Do's and Taboos Around the World,* compiled by the Parker Pen Company and edited by Roger E. Axtell. It focuses on protocol, customs, etiquette, hand gestures and body language, gift giving, the dangers of using US jargon, and so on, and can be fun to read even if you're not going anyplace. It's available for $10.95 in bookstores or through John Wiley & Sons, 1 Wiley Dr., Somerset, NJ 08875 (phone: 212-850-6418).

Sources – The books listed above may be ordered directly from the publishers or found in the travel section of any good general bookstore or any sizable public library. If you still can't find something, the following stores and/or mail-order houses also specialize in travel literature. They offer books on the US along with guides to the rest of the world, and in some cases, even an old Baedeker or two.

> *Book Passage* (51 Tamal Vista Blvd., Corte Madera, CA 94925; phone: 415-927-0960 in California; 800-321-9785 elsewhere in the US). Travel guides and maps to all areas of the world. A free catalogue is available.
>
> *The Complete Traveller* (199 Madison Ave., New York, NY 10016; phone: 212-685-9007). Travel guides and maps. A catalogue is available for $2.
>
> *Forsyth Travel Library* (PO Box 2975, Shawnee Mission, KS 66201-1375; phone: 800-367-7984 or 913-384-3440). Travel guides and maps, old and new, to all parts of the world, including Spain. Ask for the "Worldwide Travel Books and Maps" catalogue.
>
> *Gourmet Guides* (2801 Leavenworth Ave., San Francisco, CA 94133; phone: 415-771-3671). Travel guides and maps, along with cookbooks. Mail-order lists available on request.
>
> *Phileas Fogg's Books and Maps* (87 *Stanford Shopping Center,* Palo Alto, CA 94304; phone: 800-533-FOGG or 415-327-1754). Travel guides, maps, and language aids.
>
> *Tattered Cover* (2955 E. First Ave., Denver, CO 80206; phone: 800-833-9327 or

303-322-7727). The travel department alone of this enormous bookstore carries over 7,000 books, as well as maps and atlases. No catalogue is offered (the list is too extensive), but a newsletter, issued three times a year, is available on request.

Thomas Brothers Maps & Travel Books (603 W. Seventh St., Los Angeles, CA 90017; phone: 213-627-4018). Maps (including road atlases, street guides, and wall maps), guidebooks, and travel accessories.

Traveller's Bookstore (22 W. 52nd St., New York, NY 10019; phone: 212-664-0995). Travel guides, maps, literature, and accessories. A catalogue is available for $2.

Librairie de France/Libreria Hispanica (French and Spanish Book Corporation), which specializes in language dictionaries and French and Spanish fiction and nonfiction, carries some guidebooks published in Spain. Of the company's two stores in New York, the one at 610 Fifth Ave., New York, NY 10020 (phone: 212-581-8810), has the greatest selection of travel material; the other is at 115 Fifth Ave., New York, NY 10003 (212-673-7400). *Lectorum* (137 W. 14th St., New York, NY 10011; phone: 212-929-2833) also specializes in Spanish books (although none in translation), including a variety of travel books and Spanish classics.

NEWSPAPERS AND MAGAZINES: A subscription to the *International Herald Tribune* is a good idea for dedicated travelers. This English-language newspaper is written and edited mostly in Paris and is *the* newspaper read most regularly and avidly by Americans abroad to keep up with world news, US news, sports, the stock market (US and foreign), fluctuations in the exchange rate, and an assortment of help-wanted ads, real estate listings, and personals, global in scope. Published 6 days a week (no Sunday paper), it is available at newsstands throughout the US and in cities worldwide. Although you may have some difficulty finding it on newsstands in Spain, larger hotels may have copies in the lobby for guests — if you don't see a copy, ask the hotel concierge if it is available. A 1-year's subscription in the US costs $349. To subscribe, write or call the Subscription Manager, *International Herald Tribune,* 850 Third Ave., 10th Floor, New York, NY 10022 (phone: 800-882-2884 or 212-752-3890).

Among the major US publications that can be bought (generally a day or two after distribution in the US) in many of the larger cities and resort areas, at hotels, airports, and newsstands, are the *Los Angeles Times, The New York Times, USA Today,* and the *Wall Street Journal.* As with other imports, expect these and other US publications to cost considerably more in Spain than in the US.

As sampling the regional fare is likely to be one of the highlights of any visit, you will find reading about local edibles worthwhile before you go or after you return. *Gourmet,* a magazine specializing in food, now and then features articles on Spanish cooking and touring, although its scope is much broader. It is available at newsstands throughout the US for $2.50 an issue or for $18 a year from *Gourmet* (PO Box 2886, Boulder, CO 80322-2886; phone: 800-365-2454). There are numerous additional magazines for every special interest available; check at your library information desk for a directory of such publications, or look over the selection offered by a well-stocked newsstand.

NEWSLETTERS: Throughout GETTING READY TO GO we have mentioned specific newsletters which our readers may be interested in consulting for further information. One of the very best sources of detailed travel information is *Consumer Reports Travel Letter.* Published monthly by Consumers Union (PO Box 53629, Boulder, CO 80322-3629; phone: 800-999-7959), it offers comprehensive coverage of the travel scene on a wide variety of fronts. A year's subscription costs $37; 2 years, $57.

In addition, the following travel newsletters provide useful up-to-date information on travel services and bargains:

Entree (PO Box 5148, Santa Barbara, CA 93150; phone: 805-969-5848). This newsletter caters to a sophisticated, discriminating traveler with the means to explore the places mentioned. Subscribers have access to a 24-hour hotline providing information on restaurants and accommodations around the world. Monthly; a year's subscription costs $59.

The Hideaway Report (Harper Assocs., PO Box 50, Sun Valley, ID 83353; phone: 208-622-3193). This monthly source highlights retreats — including Spanish idylls — for sophisticated travelers. A year's subscription costs $90.

Romantic Hideaways (217 E. 86th St., Suite 258, New York, NY 10028; phone: 212-969-8682). This monthly newsletter leans toward those special places made for those traveling in twos. A year's subscription costs $65.

Travel Smart (Communications House, 40 Beechdale Rd., Dobbs Ferry, NY 10522; phone: 914-693-8300 in New York; 800-327-3633 elsewhere in the US). This monthly covers a wide variety of trips and travel discounts. A year's subscription costs $37.

■**Computer Services:** Anyone who owns a personal computer and a modem can subscribe to a database service providing everything from airline schedules and fares to restaurant listings. Two such services of particular use to travelers are *CompuServe* (5000 Arlington Center Blvd., Columbus, OH 43220; phone: 800-848-8199 or 614-457-8600; $39.95 to join, plus usage fees of $6 to $12.50 per hour) and *Prodigy Services* (445 Hamilton Ave., White Plains, NY 10601; phone: 800-822-6922 or 914-993-8000; $12.95 per month's subscription, plus variable usage fees). Before using any computer bulletin-board services, be sure to take precautions to prevent downloading of a computer "virus." First install one of the programs designed to screen out such nuisances.

Genealogy Hunts

 Some of the most extensive pedigrees in the world are to be found in Spain, where many nobles or "grandees" can trace their genealogies to Roman times. Over the years, Spain has suffered a succession of invaders and civil uprisings, and these, plus the country's isolation on the Iberian Peninsula between the Pyrenees and the sea have produced a unique race, proud, brave, and with a passion for exploration and conquering lands beyond the horizon.

Spain has been inhabited since the earliest times, and there has been little immigration into the country since the Christian kingdoms defeated and expelled the Muslim Moors in the 13th century after more than 400 years of domination by these North African warriors. At the time of the invasion, about AD 711, Spain was a collection of small kingdoms: León, Navarre, Aragon, Castile, and so on. It wasn't until 1492, under King Ferdinand and Queen Isabel, that Spain became a unified kingdom. Three hundred years later, Spain was a dominant world power and established numerous colonies, encouraging emigration to the southern, central, and western Americas.

It was only during the 20th century that those choosing to leave Spain were no longer content with settling in present or former colonies, and immigration to the United States became substantial. Unfortunately, due to the tragic Civil War from 1936 to 1939, many records were destroyed, but far fewer than would be imagined in proportion to the overall destruction, even in areas of the fiercest fighting. Of the 19,000 parishes in Spain, only a handful lost their registers.

Happily for contemporary ancestor-worshipers, the Spanish have kept pretty good records, beginning as far back as the 14th century in some cases, and legitimate evidence of Iberian forebears — no matter how humble their origins — usually is yours for the searching. With a little digging around, you'll probably at least be able to visit the church where your great-uncle Julio married your great-aunt Celina before leaving for America, or the port where your grandfather waved good-bye to the Old Country, or the cemetery where your mother's family has been resting quietly for centuries.

While there is not much written on how to conduct research in Iberia, if dig you must, try to do as much preliminary research as possible before your trip. One of the challenges of this sort of project is the need for creativity, since most people don't have convenient pedigree charts they can consult. Family Bibles are a good source, as are old letters, documents, photographs, or heirlooms, even anecdotes from the oldest members of your family (that's how Alex Haley began when he traced his own *Roots*). What follows is, hopefully, a helpful primer on how to tackle what may at first appear to be a daunting project.

To begin with, check your library and state offices for local published records, regional archives, and local history. The *US Library of Congress* (Local History and Genealogy Room, Jefferson Building, Washington, DC 20540; phone: 202-707-5537) and the *New York Public Library* (Division of US History, Local History and Genealogy, Room 315N, 42nd St. & Fifth Ave., New York, NY 10018; phone: 212-930-0828) both have extensive facilities for personal research; however, you may want to call ahead to find out if they have material relevant to your particular search.

There is a wealth of archival information in Spain to help you trace your family, though you'll probably run into a few dead ends in the process, particularly in regions where war-related destruction obliterated church and civil records. Time and patience are the keys where the information is neither centralized nor indexed. As more Mexicans, South and Central Americans, and others of Spanish descent become interested in learning about their origins, a praiseworthy attempt is being made to organize this information and make it more accessible.

Another source of Spanish information is the *Genealogical Society of the Church of Jesus Christ of Latter-Day Saints,* which has thousands of reels of genealogical records on microfilm, available for consultation in person at its headquarters, the Family History Library (35 NW Temple St., Salt Lake City, UT 84150; phone: 801-240-2331; open Mondays through Saturdays), or through any of its branch libraries. Ruth Gomez de Scheirmacher (phone: 801-240-2881) will guide anyone who asks through the first steps to be taken in a search. Using the Mormons' index reels, you can, for a small fee, order from Salt Lake City the microfilm records of almost any Iberian town. The film should arrive at the branch library in about 6 to 8 weeks, and loans are renewable for 2-week periods up to 6 months. There is no charge for reviewing a film at the headquarters in Salt Lake City.

An indispensable resource found in most libaries is the scholarly reference guide, *The World of Learning* (Europa Publications), which lists libraries and archives throughout Spain. Also look in your library for T. Beard's and D. Demong's comprehensive *How to Find Your Family Roots* (McGraw-Hill, 1977), which contains an excellent list of available genealogical resources. *In Search of Your European Roots* by Angus Baxter (Genealogical Publishing Co., 1985) has chapters on Spain, as does Noel Currer-Briggs's *Worldwide Family History* (Routledge & Kegan Paul, 1982). For general information, take a look at Jeane Eddy Westin's *Finding Your Roots* (J. P. Tarcher, distributed by St. Martin's Press). Another book of particular relevance to genealogical studies in Spain is *Tracing Your Hispanic Heritage,* by George R. Ryskamp (Hispanic

Family History Research, 1984). You also may want to subscribe to the excellent *Ancestry Newsletter,* edited by Robb Barr and published bimonthly by Ancestry Incorporated (PO Box 476, Salt Lake City, UT 84110; phone: 800-531-1790); a yearly subscription costs $12.

Constructing a family tree is a backward process: You need to start with your parents' dates and places of birth, their parents' dates and places, and so on, as far back as you can. It should be a considerable stretch since it's quite possible to trace back several hundred years. To obtain the relevant documents, make sure you have the exact names of each ancestor (remember, many immigrants' surnames were irrevocably, if unwittingly, changed through clerical misspellings at Ellis Island and other ports of entry), as well as the names of any family members closely related to the ancestor you are researching. You can request many different types of documents that contain information about a previous generation: for example, birth and death certificates, marriage licenses, emigration and immigration records, and baptism and christening records.

Records of baptisms, marriages, and burials in Spain may precede 1570, while in the diocese of Solsona, near Saragossa, there are records as far back as 1394. The Spanish National Archives is a good place to start. It's crucial that you know beforehand the birthplaces of your ancestors, not just the port from which they left Spain. There are a number of different National Archives, based mainly on the divisions of what is now a united country. They are included in a list of sources at the end of this section.

REQUESTING RECORDS: Before about 1870, personal records — baptism, confirmation, marriage, and death — were kept, for the most part, only by parish churches. Thus, to obtain information on your family before 1865, you should begin by writing either to the parish priest or to the bishop holding territorial jurisdiction. Since about 1865, birth, marriage, death, and citizenship records have been kept by municipalities, so, after discovering where your ancestors came from, you must write to the local authorities. There are important archives *(Archivo Municipal)* in all the major centers, as well as in smaller towns and villages and in Mahón, in the Balearic Islands. Again, on the local level you will find civil registration *(registros civiles)* as well as church registers *(registros de parroquia).*

DIGGING DEEPER: Once you've done your basic research, you might want to turn to some older records or even use them as duplicates to verify information you've already accumulated. The following are some of the most readily available records by mail or in person.

Certificates of Family Genealogy – Write to the archives office in the town where your family member lived to obtain a certificate of your family genealogy, giving names, relationships, birth dates, and birthplaces of all living family members at the time of recording.

Emigration Records – Passenger lists *(listas de pasajeros),* passports *(pasaportes),* and other emigration records also can be helpful. Again, try the local archives of the province of the emigrant's birthplace or port of departure to obtain documentation of emigration.

Lists of passengers on sailings from the port of Seville, Spain (a major emigration port), to the Americas in 1509–1701 also are available. Unfortunately, these records may be of limited value, as most of the people on the list were functionaries of government or private business and eventually returned to Spain. These records can be found in the *Archivo General de Indias* in Seville.

Records of 20th-century Spanish passports list name, date, place of birth, date of the voyage, and destination. This information is kept by the *Archiva de Gobernación* in Madrid.

Draft Records – Military records *(cartilla militar),* dating from the 1600s, contain the complete personal records of every Spanish soldier and sailor. The lists have been published and indexed, and can be found at the Archives of the *Archivo Central del Ministerio de Marina* (Ministry of the Navy) and the *Archivo del Museo Naval* (Naval Museum).

Clerical Surveys – Catholic parish records in Spain go back to about 1650. A guide to the existing Spanish parishes was published in 1954 *(Guía de la Iglesia en España, Vol. 4)*. Try the archives of the diocese in which the parish is located; duplicate records usually are kept by the bishop. If you don't know the exact diocese, write to the Spanish headquarters of the Catholic church (Conference Episcopal Española, Oficina de Estadística y Sociología, 4 Calle Alfonso XI, Madrid 28014). Be sure to give the name and province of the village in question and ask for the name of the diocese and the address of the diocesan office.

Census Registers and other Municipal Records – Civil censuses have been held frequently in Spain since the 1500s, though there is no official list. The most comprehensive census was called *Catastro del Marqués de la Ensenada,* completed in 1752. These records contain so-called real estate records (actually tax records; census takers were no fools even then) of heads of households, subtenants, or taxpayers and their residences along with the amount of tax assessed. Most of the records are in the various local archives in Spain. For information, write to the local municipal offices *(ayuntamientos)*.

Among the main archives are *Archivo Diocesano* (5 Calle Obispo, Barcelona); *Archivo Histórico Nacional* (115 Calle Serrano, Madrid); *Archivo General de Indias* (Avenida de la Constitución, Seville); *Archivo General de Simancas* in Valladolid; *Archivo de la Corona de Aragón* in Zaragoza; *Archivo del Reino de Valencia* (22 Calle Alameda, Valencia); *Archivo General de Navarra* in Pamplona, Navarre; *Archivo Regional de Galicia* (San Carlos, La Coruña, Galicia); *Archivo del Reino de Mallorca* (3 Calle Ramón Llull, Palma de Mallorca); *Archivo de la Real Chancillería* in Valladolid; *Archivo de la Real Chancellería* (17 Plaza Suárez, Granada); and *Archivo General del Ministerio de Asuntos Exteriores* in Madrid.

For those who would rather leave the digging to others, reputable genealogical societies in Spain will do it for you for a fee. The *Instituto de Genealogía y Heráldica y Federación de Corporaciones* (Apartado de Correos, Madrid 12079) will provide those researching their ancestry in Spain with a list of qualified local genealogists for hire; a copy of the society's catalogue also may be found in many libraries. In the US, contact *Lineage* (PO Box 417, Salt Lake City, UT 84110; phone: 801-531-9297).

With the above information and a little patience, you should have a firm grasp for a lengthy climb up your family tree.

In the Works – This year, the Spanish-government-run *Spain '92 Foundation* (which was formed to encourage cultural exchange between Spain and the US as part of this year's celebration of Columbus's discovery of America) will be offering the public access to the data it has collected on Spanish immigrants to the US. The program — called *Raíces: In Search of One's Hispanic Heritage* — will allow those of Spanish descent to enter their surnames on an interactive computer-video system that will provide information on their ancestral origins in Spain, as well as where their ancestors are likely to have settled in the US. At the time of this writing, the foundation was planning a US tour starting early this year. For further information on the project, including when it will be visiting your area, contact *Spain '92 Foundation,* 1821 Jefferson Pl. NW, Washington, DC 20036 (phone: 202-775-1992).

And later this year, the Library of Congress Archival Survey Office will be releasing a book titled *The Hispanic World: A Guide to Photoreproduced Manuscripts from Spain in the Collections of the United States, Guam and Puerto Rico,* by Guadalupe Jiménez. This work should be a major reference source of Spanish documents available for research in the US and its territories. For further information on this project, call the survey office at 202-707-1992.

Weights and Measures

 When traveling in Spain, you'll find that just about every quantity, whether it is length, weight, or capacity, will be expressed in unfamiliar terms. In fact, this is true for travel almost everywhere in the world, since the US is one of the last countries to make its way to the metric system. Your trip to Spain may serve to familiarize you with what one day may be the weights and measures at your grocery store.

There are some specific things to keep in mind during your trip. Fruits and vegetables at a market generally are recorded in kilos (kilograms), as are your luggage at the airport and your body weight. (This latter is particularly pleasing to people of significant size, who, instead of weighing 220 pounds, hit the scales at a mere 100 kilos.) A kilo equals 2.2 pounds and 1 pound is .45 kilo. Body temperature usually is measured in degrees centigrade or Celsius rather than on the Fahrenheit scale, so that a normal body temperature is 37C, not 98.6F, and freezing is 0 degrees C rather than 32F.

Gasoline is sold by the liter (approximately 3.8 liters to 1 gallon). Tire pressure gauges and other equipment measure in kilograms per square centimeter rather than pounds per square inch. Highway signs are written in kilometers rather than miles (1 mile equals 1.6 kilometers; 1 kilometer equals .62 mile). And speed limits are in kilometers per hour, so think twice before hitting the gas when you see a speed limit of 100. That means 62 miles per hour.

The tables and conversion factors listed below should give you all the information you will need to understand any transaction, road sign, or map you encounter during your travels.

APPROXIMATE EQUIVALENTS		
Metric Unit	**Abbreviation**	**US Equivalent**
LENGTH		
meter	m	39.37 inches
kilometer	km	.62 mile
millimeter	mm	.04 inch
CAPACITY		
liter	l	1.057 quarts
WEIGHT		
gram	g	.035 ounce
kilogram	kg	2.2 pounds
metric ton	MT	1.1 ton
ENERGY		
kilowatt	kw	1.34 horsepower

CONVERSION TABLES
METRIC TO US MEASUREMENTS

Multiply:	by:	to convert to:
LENGTH		
millimeters	.04	inches
meters	3.3	feet
meters	1.1	yards
kilometers	.6	miles
CAPACITY		
liters	2.11	pints (liquid)
liters	1.06	quarts (liquid)
liters	.26	gallons (liquid)
WEIGHT		
grams	.04	ounces (avoir.)
kilograms	2.2	pounds (avoir.)

US TO METRIC MEASUREMENTS

LENGTH		
inches	25.	millimeters
feet	.3	meters
yards	.9	meters
miles	1.6	kilometers
CAPACITY		
pints	.47	liters
quarts	.95	liters
gallons	3.8	liters
WEIGHT		
ounces	28.	grams
pounds	.45	kilograms

TEMPERATURE

$$°F = (°C \times 9/5) + 32 \qquad °C = (°F - 32) \times 5/9$$

Cameras and Equipment

 Vacations are everybody's favorite time for taking pictures and home movies. After all, most of us want to remember the places we visit — and show them off to others. Here are a few suggestions to help you get the best results from your travel photography or videography.

BEFORE THE TRIP

If you're taking your camera or camcorder out after a long period in mothballs, or have just bought a new one, check it thoroughly before you leave to prevent unexpected breakdowns or disappointing pictures.

1. Still cameras should be cleaned carefully and thoroughly, inside and out. If using a camcorder, run a head cleaner through it. You also may want to have your camcorder professionally serviced (opening the casing yourself will violate the manufacturer's warranty). Always use filters to protect your lens while traveling.
2. Check the batteries for your camera's light meter and flash, and take along extras just in case yours wear out during the trip. For camcorders, bring along extra Nickel-Cadmium (Ni-Cad) batteries; if you use rechargeable batteries, a recharger will cut down on the extras.
3. Using all the settings and features, shoot at least one test roll of film or one videocassette, using the type you plan to take along with you.

EQUIPMENT TO TAKE ALONG

Keep your gear light and compact. Items that are too heavy or bulky to be carried comfortably on a full-day excursion will likely remain in your hotel room.

1. Invest in a broad camera or camcorder strap if you now have a thin one. It will make carrying the camera much more comfortable.
2. A sturdy canvas, vinyl, or leather camera or camcorder bag, preferably with padded pockets (not an airline bag), will keep your equipment organized and easy to find. If you will be doing much shooting around the water, a waterproof case is best.
3. For cleaning, bring along a camel's hair brush that retracts into a rubber squeeze bulb. Also take plenty of lens tissue, soft cloths, and plastic bags to protect equipment from dust and moisture.

■ **Note:** If you are planning on using your camcorder in Europe, note that most European countries (including Spain) operate on a different electrical current than the US, so you should make sure that the battery charger that comes with your camcorder is compatible with the current in the countries you're visiting. You'll also need a plug adapter kit to cope with the variations in plug configurations found in Europe. And don't expect to be able to play back your tape through a European TV set or VCR. The US and Canada use a different television standard than most European countries; these systems are incompatible with each other and multiple-standard TV sets are rare.

FILM AND TAPES: If you are concerned about airport security X-rays damaging undeveloped film (X-rays do not affect processed film) or tapes, store them in one of the lead-lined bags sold in camera shops. This possibility is not as much of a threat as it used to be, however. In the US and Canada, incidents of X-ray damage to unprocessed film (exposed or unexposed) are few because low-dosage X-ray equipment is used virtually everywhere. However, when crossing international borders, travelers should know that foreign X-ray equipment used for carry-on baggage may deliver higher levels of radiation and that even more powerful X-ray equipment may be used for checked luggage, so it's best to carry your film on board. If you're traveling without a protective bag, you may want to ask to have your photo equipment inspected by hand. In the US, Federal Aviation Administration regulations require that if you request a hand inspection, you get it, but overseas the response may depend on the humor of the inspector.

One type of film that should never be subjected to X-rays is the very high speed ASA

1000; there are lead-lined bags made especially for it — and, in the event that you are refused a hand inspection, this is the only way to save your film. The walk-through metal detector devices at airports do not affect film, though the film cartridges may set them off. Because cassettes have been favorite carriers for terrorist explosives over the years, airport officials probably will insist that you put these through the X-ray machine as well. If you don't have a choice, put them through and hope for the best.

You should have no problem finding film or tapes throughout Europe. When buying film, tapes, or photo accessories the best rule of thumb is to stick to name brands with which you are familiar. Different countries have their own ways of labeling camcorder tapes, and although the variations in recording and playback standards won't affect your ability to use the tape, they will affect how quickly you record and how much time you actually have to record on the tape. The availability of film processing labs and equipment repair shops will vary from area to area.

■ **A note about courtesy and caution:** When photographing individuals in Spain (and anywhere else in the world), ask first. It's common courtesy. Furthermore, some governments have security regulations regarding the use of cameras and will not permit the photographing of certain subjects, such as particular government and military installations. When in doubt, ask.

Useful Words and Phrases

Unlike the French, who tend to be a bit brusque if you don't speak their language perfectly, the Spanish do not expect you to speak their native tongue — but are very flattered when you try. In many circumstances, you won't have to, because the staffs at most hotels, as well as at a fair number of restaurants, speak serviceable English, or at least a modicum of it, which they usually are eager to try — and that means practicing with you. If you find yourself in a situation where your limited Spanish turns out to be the only means of communication, take the plunge. Don't be afraid of misplaced accents or misconjugated verbs — in most cases you will be understood.

Although there are several languages spoken throughout Spain, including *Gallego* (in the Galician region), *Catalan* (in Catalonia), and *Euskera* (in the Basque Country), the majority of the population is fluent in the most common language, Castilian Spanish. Castilian Spanish represents sounds quite predictably; pronunciation is straightforward, with only some minor dialect variations.

The list that follows is a selection of commonly used words and phrases to speed you on your way. Note that in Spanish, nouns either are masculine or feminine, as well as singular or plural, and that the adjectives that modify them must agree in both gender and quantity. Most nouns ending in *o* in the singular are masculine; the *o* becomes *os* in the plural. Most nouns ending in *a* in the singular are feminine; the *a* becomes *as* in the plural. Nouns may have other endings.

In Spanish, the letter *a* is pronounced as in *father*. The *e* is pronounced as in *egg* or *get*. The *i* is pronounced like the *ee* of *beet*. The *o* is pronounced as in *note*. The *u* is pronounced as in *lute*. The combination *ei* is pronounced like *ey* in *they; ai* is pronounced like *y* in *by; au* is pronounced like *ou* in *house*. In Spanish words, if there is no accent mark the vowel before the last consonant is stressed, with the exception of words ending in *n* or *s,* which are stressed on the second-to-last vowel (or syllable).

Spanish consonants are pronounced approximately as in English with these exceptions: The consonant *b* when beginning a word is pronounced somewhat like the English *b* with the lips slightly open for a softer sound; between vowels, it is pronounced like *v* in *lever*. The *h* always is silent, as in *hola* pronounced *ola*. The *j* is pronounced somewhat like the breathy *h* in *ha!* The consonant *c* preceding *e, i* or *y* in standard Castilian Spanish is generally pronounced *th* as in *then*. The same rule applies to the letter *z*, which is also pronounced as *th*. The *ll* in Spanish is pronounced *lya*, as in the English *million*. The letter *ñ* is pronounced like the *ny* in *canyon*.

These are only the most basic rules, and even they may seem daunting at first, but they shouldn't remain so for long. Nevertheless, if you can't get your mouth to speak Spanish, try your hands at it: With a little observation, you'll pick it up quickly and be surprised at how often your message will get across.

Greetings and Everyday Expressions

Good morning! (also, Good day)	*Buenos días!*
Good afternoon/ evening! (when arriving)	*Buenas tardes/noches!*
Hello!	*Hola!*
How are you?	*Cómo está usted?*
Pleased to meet you. (How do you do?)	*Mucho gusto en concerle.*
Good-bye!	*Adiós!*
So long!	*Hasta luego!*
Goodnight! (when leaving)	*Buenas noches!*
Yes	*Sí*
No	*No*
Please	*Por favor*
Thank you	*Gracias*
You're welcome	*De nada*
I beg your pardon (Excuse me)	*Perdón*
I don't speak Spanish.	*No hablo Español.*
Do you speak English?	*Habla usted inglés?*
I don't understand.	*No comprendo.*
Do you understand?	*Comprende?/Entiende?*
My name is . . .	*Me llamo . . .*
What is your name?	*Cómo se llama?*
miss	*señorita*
madame	*señora* (married)
	doña (unmarried)
mister	*señor*
open	*abierto/a*
closed	*cerrado/a*
entrance	*entrada*
exit	*salida*
push	*empujar*
pull	*tirar*
today	*hoy*
tomorrow	*mañana*
yesterday	*ayer*

Checking In

I would like . . .	*Quisiera . . .*
I have a reservation	*He hecho una reserva*
a single room	*una habitación sencilla*
a double room	*una habitación doble*
a quiet room	*una habitación tranquila*
with bath	*con baño*
with shower	*con ducha*
with a sea view	*con vista al mar*
with air conditioning	*con aire acondicionado*
with balcony	*con balcón*
overnight only	*sólo una noche*
a few days	*algunos días*
a week (at least)	*una semana (por lo menos)*
with full board	*con pensión completa*
with half board	*con media pensión*

Does that price include	*Está incluido en el precio*
breakfast	*el desayuno*
taxes	*los impuestos*
VAT (Value Added Tax)	*IVA*

It doesn't work.	*No funciona*
Do you accept traveler's checks?	*Acepta usted cheques de viajero?*
Do you accept credit cards?	*Acepta tarjetas de crédito?*

Eating Out

ashtray	*un cenicero*
bottle	*una botella*
(extra) chair	*una silla (adicional)*
cup	*una taza*
fork	*un tenedor*
knife	*un cuchillo*
napkin	*una servilleta*
plate	*un plato*
spoon	*una cuchara*
table	*una mesa*

beer	*una cerveza*
hot cocoa	*un chocolate caliente*
black coffee	*un café expreso*
coffee with milk	*café con leche*
cream	*crema*
milk	*leche*
tea	*un té*
fruit juice	*un zumo de fruta*
lemonade	*una limonada*
water	*agua*
mineral water	*agua mineral*
(carbonated/ not carbonated)	*(con gas/sin gas)*

orangeade	*una naranjada*
port	*oporto*
sherry	*jerez*
red wine	*vino tinto*
white wine	*vino blanco*
cold	*frío/a*
hot	*caliente*
sweet	*dulce*
(very) dry	*(muy) seco/a*
bacon	*tocino*
bread	*pan*
butter	*mantequilla*
eggs	*huevos*
hard-boiled	*huevo duro*
fried	*huevos fritos*
omelette	*tortilla*
soft-boiled	*huevo cocido pasado por agua*
scrambled	*huevos revueltos*
honey	*miel*
jam/marmalade	*mermelada*
orange juice	*zumo de naranja*
pepper	*pimienta*
salt	*sal*
sugar	*azúcar*
Waiter	*Camarero*
I would like	*Quisiera*
a glass of	*un vaso de*
a bottle of	*una botella de*
a half bottle of	*una media botella de*
a carafe of	*una garrafa de*
a liter of	*un litro de*
The check, please.	*La cuenta, por favor.*
Is a service charge included?	*Está el servicio incluido?*
I think you made a mistake in this bill.	*Creo que hay un error en la cuenta.*

Shopping

bakery	*la panadería*
bookstore	*la librería*
butcher shop	*la carnicería*
camera shop	*la tienda de fotografía*
delicatessen	*ultramarinos*
department store	*almacén*
grocery	*la tienda de comestibles*
jewelry store	*la joyería*
newsstand	*el quiosco de periódicos*
pastry shop	*la pastelería*
perfume (and cosmetics) store	*perfumería*

pharmacy/drugstore	*la farmacia*
shoestore	*la zapatería*
supermarket	*el supermercado*
tobacconist	*el estanco*
inexpensive	*barato/a*
expensive	*caro/a*
large	*grande*
larger	*más grande*
too large	*demasiado grande*
small	*pequeño/a*
smaller	*más pequeño/a*
too small	*demasiado pequeño/a*
long	*largo/a*
short	*corto/a*
old	*viejo/a*
new	*nuevo/a*
used	*usado/a*
handmade	*hecho/a a mano*
Is it machine washable?	*Es lavable a máquina?*
How much does it cost?	*Cuánto cuesta esto?*
What is it made of?	*De qué está hecho?*
camel's hair	*pelo de camello*
cotton	*algodón*
corduroy	*pana*
filigree	*filigrana*
lace	*encaje*
leather	*cuero*
linen	*lino*
silk	*seda*
suede	*ante*
synthetic	*sintético/a*
tile	*azulejo*
wool	*lana*
brass	*latón*
copper	*cobre*
gold	*oro*
gold plate	*lámina de oro*
silver	*plata*
silver plate	*plata chapada*
stainless steel	*acero inoxidable*
wood	*madera*

Colors

beige	*beige*
black	*negro/a*
blue	*azul*
brown	*marrón*
green	*verde*
gray	*gris*
orange	*naranjo/a*
pink	*roso/a*
purple	*morado/a*

red	*rojo/a*
white	*blanco/a*
yellow	*amarillo/a*
dark	*oscuro/a*
light	*claro/a*

Getting Around

north	*norte*
south	*sur*
east	*este*
west	*oeste*
right	*derecho/a*
left	*izquierdo/a*
Go straight ahead	*Siga todo derecho*
far	*lejos*
near	*cerca*
gas station	*gasolinera*
train station	*la estación de ferrocarril*
bus stop	*la parada de autobuses*
subway station	*estación de metro*
airport	*aeropuerto*
tourist information	*información turística*
map	*mapa*
one-way ticket	*un billete de ida*
round-trip ticket	*un billete de ida y vuelta*
track/platform	*la vía/el andén*
first class	*primera clase*
second class	*segunda clase*
no smoking	*no fumadores*
gasoline	*gasolina*
normal leaded	* gasolina normal*
super leaded	* gasolina super*
unleaded	* gasolina sin plomo*
diesel	* diesel*
tires	*los neumáticos*
oil	*el aceite*
Fill it up, please.	*Llénelo, por favor.*
Where is . . . ?	*Dónde está . . . ?*
Where are . . . ?	*Dónde están . . . ?*
How far is it to . . . from here?	*Qué distancia hay desde aquí hasta . . . ?*
Does this bus go to . . . ?	*Va este autobús a . . . ?*
What time does it leave?	*A qué hora sale?*

Danger	*Peligro*
Caution	*Precaución*
Detour	*Desvío*
Do Not Enter	*Paso Prohibido*
No Parking	*Estacionamento Prohibido*
No Passing	*Prohibido Adelantar*
One Way	*Dirección Unica*
Pay Toll	*Peaje*
Pedestrian Zone	*Peatones*

Reduce Speed	*Despacio*
Steep Incline	*Fuerte Declive*
Stop	*Alto*
Use Headlights	*Encender los faros*
Yield	*Ceda el Paso*

Personal Items and Services

barbershop	*la peluquería*
beauty shop	*el salón de belleza*
dry cleaner	*la tintorería*
hairdresser (salon)	*la peluquería*
launderette or laundry	*la lavandería*
post office	*el correo*

aspirins	*aspirinas*
Band-Aids	*tiritas*
condoms	*preservativos*
sanitary napkins	*unos paños higiénicos*
shampoo	*un champú*
shaving cream	*espuma de afeitar*
soap	*el jabón*
stamps	*sellos*
tampons	*unos tampones higiénicos*
tissues	*unos pañuelos de papel*
toilet paper	*papel higiénico*
toothbrush	*un cepillo de dientes*
toothpaste	*pasta de dientes*

Where is the bathroom?	*Dónde está el baño?*
The bathroom door will say:	
for the men's room	*Caballeros*
for the women's room	*Señoras*

Days of the Week

Monday	*Lunes*
Tuesday	*Martes*
Wednesday	*Miércoles*
Thursday	*Jueves*
Friday	*Viernes*
Saturday	*Sábado*
Sunday	*Domingo*

Months

January	*Enero*
February	*Febrero*
March	*Marzo*
April	*Abril*
May	*Mayo*
June	*Junio*
July	*Julio*
August	*Agosto*
September	*Septiembre*

October	*Octubre*
November	*Noviembre*
December	*Diciembre*

Numbers

zero	*cero*
one	*uno*
two	*dos*
three	*tres*
four	*cuatro*
five	*cinco*
six	*seis*
seven	*siete*
eight	*ocho*
nine	*nueve*
ten	*diez*
eleven	*once*
twelve	*doce*
thirteen	*trece*
fourteen	*catorce*
fifteen	*quince*
sixteen	*dieciséis*
seventeen	*diecisiete*
eighteen	*dieciocho*
nineteen	*diecinueve*
twenty	*veinte*
thirty	*treinta*
forty	*cuarenta*
fifty	*cincuenta*
sixty	*sesenta*
seventy	*setenta*
eighty	*ochenta*
ninety	*noventa*
one hundred	*cien*
one thousand	*mil*

PERSPECTIVES

History

According to the old saying, "Europe ends at the Pyrenees," and it's true that throughout modern history, Spain has often found itself the "odd man out" among European nations. Yet once, for a brief, glorious period, it outshone every other nation in the West. Fresh from the Reconquest against the Moors, Spain emerged at the end of the 15th century to straddle the diplomatic stage like some new colossus: discovering a new world, becoming the greatest power on earth, and creating a breathtaking golden age of culture. Within 150 years, however, her empire was breaking up and her domestic affairs were a shambles. No wonder, then, if today Spain seems to live in the shadow of a great, and oft-remembered past.

As the cave paintings at Altamira and elsewhere attest, people have lived on the Iberian Peninsula since the Stone Age. (Scientists believe that the enigmatic Basques of northern Spain, with their unique language, may be direct descendants of prehistoric Pyrenean cave dwellers.) Early in its recorded history, the peninsula began to exert the special allure it has always held for foreigners. The first to arrive — probably from North Africa sometime around 3000 BC — were the people for whom the peninsula is named: the Iberians. Joining them, about 2000 years later, were Celts from northern Europe, the same people who inhabited Ireland, Scotland, and Wales.

In the course of time, remote Iberia became a final destination for many expanding Mediterranean civilizations, at least for those whose ships dared to pass through the Pillars of Hercules (the Straits of Gibraltar) and brave the certain dangers of the "Sea of Darkness" — the Atlantic Ocean. One people who dared were the seafaring Phoenicians. Around 1100 BC, they established trading cities along the coast, including Gadir (Cádiz) — Europe's oldest continuously inhabited city. Greek colonizers arrived about 5 centuries later, bringing with them the olive and the vine, which would become the two indispensable items of Spanish life.

A misguided invitation brought the Carthaginians. The Phoenicians had asked Carthage, then an emerging power, to assist them against Tartessos, a mysterious native civilization that — from a capital near the mouth of the Guadalquivir River — controlled most of present-day Andalusia. The Carthaginians not only agreed to help, they decided to stay and in no time were entrenched along the coast. Eventually, they took over the peninsula, which they named *Spania,* or the "land of rabbits." The Carthaginians, in turn, lost their hold to Rome in 218 BC, during the Second Punic War.

It took Rome 2 centuries to subdue the bellicose inhabitants of the newly named *Hispania;* one tribe, the Numantians, burned their own city and perished in its flames rather than surrender. In 147 BC, Viriatus the shepherd, one of Spain's (and Portugal's) great heroes, united neighboring tribes and managed to reconquer and control much of western and central Spain for 8 years. But Rome's legions eventually triumphed, and by 19 BC they had the peninsula firmly under control.

Hispania remained a vital colony for 4 centuries, providing Rome with minerals and food, as well as the emperors Trajan and Hadrian. In return, Rome gave the peninsula its first taste of political and cultural unity, an efficient administration, and a code of law. Commerce flourished. Córdoba became a center of intellectual life. Rome built aqueducts, bridges, and roads to serve other prosperous cities such as Itálica and Mérida. It gave its language, Latin, from which the languages of the peninsula — except the enigmatic Basque — derive, and eventually it gave its religion — Christianity.

Roman rule lasted until the arrival of the barbarians during the 5th century. Vandals and others invaded from the north in 409. Five years later, the Visigoths — semi-civilized and Christian — arrived, supposedly to help Rome fend off other barbarian groups. Like so many others, however, they remained — and ruled Iberia for the next 3 centuries, gradually assimilating with the Hispano-Roman population. Though originally followers of Arianism — a heretical form of Christianity — by 589 the Visigoths had converted to Roman Catholicism and adopted it as the state religion.

What eventually brought about the Visigoths' demise was their tradition of elective kingship, which encouraged a steady stream of pretenders to the throne. One such challenger, early in the 8th century, seems to have petitioned North African Muslims for help against his king, Rodrigo. As a result, an Arab-Berber army landed at Gebel-Tarik (Tarik's Rock — eventually corrupted to Gibraltar) on Spain's southern coast and smashed Rodrigo's army. Within a few years the Moors, as they came to be known, had swept across most of the peninsula.

Moorish Spain, called Al-Andalus (today's Andalusia) and centered at the caliphate of Córdoba, endured for nearly 800 years, reaching its height at the end of the 10th century. During that time, it made a profound impact, bringing a new culture, language, and religion to the European continent. While the rest of Europe thrashed about in feudal chaos, Moorish Spain flourished, becoming the most powerful and civilized kingdom in the West. Among its triumphs were new crops — such as oranges and figs — an efficient irrigation system, and expanded commerce. It also had the largest merchant marine in the Mediterranean.

The Moors were a cultivated people. Their scholars preserved and transmitted the wisdom of the ancients, and their architects left behind a wealth of beautiful buildings, including the one immortalized for Americans in Washington Irving's *Tales from the Alhambra.* They also were remarkably tolerant. Many Christians converted to Islam, though there was little pressure to do so. Those who didn't convert but did adopt Arab ways were known as Mozarabs. Jews, too, who had been persecuted under the Visigoths, could now live freely and prosper. The professions were opened to them, and some Jews rose to fill the state's highest offices. Others became scholars, like the great Hebrew philosopher Moses Maimonides.

The one serious mistake the Moors made was neglecting to conquer the northern kingdom of Asturias. From this stronghold, in 722, the Visigothic noble Pelayo and his followers began the *reconquista* (the Reconquest). For the next 7 centuries, the defenders of Christian Spain waged a desultory and meandering war against the Moors, gradually regaining the land they had lost. In the process, they began to unify their country. They claimed St. James (Sant Iago) the Apostle as their patron; his shrine at Santiago de Compostela became the goal of Europe's greatest pilgrimage. Great romantic stories developed out of the Reconquest — of the Crusaders and especially El Cid, Spain's magnificent legendary hero, who captured Valencia in 1094.

Piece by piece, the kingdom of the Moors began to fall apart. In 1002, after the death of Al-Mansur, the last great Cordoban caliph, the caliphate shattered into some 20 small kingdoms. Then, in 1212, the Moors suffered their most stinging defeat yet at Las Navas de Tolosa. They were driven from Córdoba and Seville about 25 years later. By the middle of the 13th century, and for another 200 years, Moorish power was limited to the kingdom of Granada.

During this same period, the small Spanish states began to consolidate. By the end of the 11th century, for example, Alfonso VI was sole ruler of León, Castile, Navarre, and Aragon. Two centuries later, Aragon and Castile were the two largest and most important kingdoms. Aragon — which, turning outward to the Mediterranean, had set up a wealthy commercial empire — was quite different from crusading Castile. But then, in 1469, Castile's Isabella married Aragon's Ferdinand I and united the two kingdoms — creating a nation in one marital swoop. Each kingdom, however, continued to operate autonomously, and no one yet used the term *España* to designate the country as a whole.

For good or ill, the reign of the Catholic Monarchs (so called because of their religious fervor) was the pivotal point in Spanish history. Between them, Isabella and Ferdinand unified the country, instituted the Spanish Inquisition, expelled the Moors and the Jews, discovered a new world, and began an empire.

Their first significant act, in 1478, was to set up an institution to enforce the nation's religious "purity" — a dreaded court with one of history's most odious names: the Spanish Inquisition. Headed by the Dominican monk Tomás de Torquemada, its main victims were insincere Muslim and Jewish converts to Christianity. The Inquisition was to remain a feature of Spanish government for more than 350 years.

One year in the reign of the Catholic Monarchs stands out — 1492. In that year the kingdom of Granada — the Moors' final bastion and a dreamy remnant of Al-Andalus, complete with its fairy-tale palace, the Alhambra — finally surrendered. In the same year, the Catholic Monarchs gave both Muslims and Jews a choice — convert or leave, an edict that sent hundreds of thousands of skilled and able residents fleeing at a time when Spain needed them most. Another of that year's momentous events was the arrival at court of an adventurer named Christopher Columbus. After convincing the queen to sponsor his expedition, he set sail west for a shortcut to the Indies and found, instead, a new world. Within a few years, men like Vasco Núñez de Balboa, Ferdinand Magellan, and Hernando de Soto joined the ranks of explorers financed by the Spanish court.

The Catholic Monarchs were eventually succeeded, in 1516, by their grandson Carlos I of Spain, who was also the Holy Roman Emperor Charles V, heir to the Low Countries, Austria, and much of present-day Germany. He was the first of the Hapsburgs, a line that was destined to rule for nearly 2 centuries — and lead Spain from the pinnacle of power to the depths of despair.

Carlos's reign was the Age of the Conquistadores; Cortés landed in Mexico in 1519, Pizarro in Peru in 1532. Spain eventually laid claim to all of present-day Latin America (except Brazil), the southern part of the present-day United States from Florida to California, and the Philippines. Spanish fleets ruled the seas. Accompanying the explorers and conquistadores were Jesuit priests, members of a religious order founded in 1539 by Ignatius of Loyola to ignite the Counter-Reformation (a movement meant to keep Spain free from Protestantism, which was sprouting all over contemporary Europe) and to make converts, especially in the New World.

During his 40-year reign, Carlos spent just 16 years in Spain. Self-appointed defender of the Catholic faith against Protestants and Turks, he spent more on war than his treasure galleons could garner from the Americas. When he retired, the imperial crown went to his brother, and control of Spain and the Netherlands to his son, Felipe.

Felipe (Philip II), a much-maligned monarch, ruled from 1556 to 1598. He oversaw many of Spain's greatest triumphs and its most ignominious failures — victory over the Turks at Lepanto, the conquest of Portugal, the establishment of the capital at Madrid, and construction of the Escorial palace, as well as chronic warfare in the Netherlands and the disastrous defeat of the Spanish Armada in 1588, which put an end to Spain's hopes of remaining a great world power.

Ironically, just at the time Spain began to slip from political ascendency, its cultural Golden Age bloomed, with El Greco, Velázquez, Ribera, and other such artists, as well as immortal writers such as Cervantes, Lope de Vega, and Tirso de Molina. Their styles were unmistakably Spanish, from the picaresque in literature to the brooding mysticism of religious art.

This cultural explosion peaked in the 17th century, but European wars and a calvalcade of economic setbacks and weak kings left Spain in a pitiful condition. To make matters worse, this was the era of Francis Drake and other "seadogs" who delighted in "singeing the beard" of the Spanish king by capturing his treasure galleons. When the feeble-minded Carlos II became king at the end of the century, everyone knew the Hapsburgs' days were numbered.

Although Carlos had willed the throne to a grandson of Louis XIV, most of Europe spent years fighting the War of the Spanish Succession before the Bourbon dynasty, in the person of Felipe (Philip) V, settled in. Comparatively modern by Hapsburg standards, the new rulers finished the process started by Ferdinand and Isabella: unification of Spain. Hated by the provinces, the Bourbons crushed regionalism and centralized with a passion in favor of Castile, especially Madrid, made Castilian the official language, and built grand avenues and imposing buildings.

New ideas, born of the Enlightenment, trickling in from France found their champion in Carlos III, whose reign (1759–88) offered hope for a revitalized

Spain. But when the French Revolution erupted in 1789, Spanish nationalism was suddenly on a collision course with its proselytizing neighbor. Spain's hostility toward France deepened a few years later when the Spanish king was forced to step aside for Napoleon's brother, Joseph Bonaparte. This usurpation proved intolerable to Spaniards. On *dos de mayo*, May 2, 1808, they rose up against the French to launch the War of Independence (also known as the Peninsular War), a scene movingly depicted in Goya's magnificent painting *The Second of May*. Spanish guerrillas joined with British troops under the future Duke of Wellington to drive out the French.

After a brief flirtation with constitutional government in 1812, Spain reestablished the monarchy 2 years later in the person of the highly reactionary Ferdinand VII. For the remainder of the 19th century, Spanish politics were a continuing clash between the traditional ideas of aristocrats and peasants and the new, more liberal ideas of the emerging middle class. Both Carlist Wars — the first beginning in 1833, the second in 1874 — were expressions of this deep division. The army, which often sided with the liberals, became the ultimate arbiter of power, and so the great question became not who would control Spain, but who would control the army. Shifts in power were often brought about by the *pronunciamiento* (the Spanish version of the coup d'état).

The Spanish-American War in 1898 led to another crisis, for it meant the swift and humiliating loss of the last vestiges of empire. Spain had begun to lose its colonial grip during the Napoleonic Wars. Venezuela had declared its independence in 1811, and other South American countries soon followed its example. Yet Spain somehow held onto a belief in its imperial greatness. The economic and psychological malaise of the war's aftermath found bitter expression in the cultural movement known as the Generation of 1898. Some of modern Spain's great names belonged to it: Baroja, Unamuno, Machado, and Ortega y Gasset.

When the army suffered another disaster in 1921, this time at the hands of the Moroccan Berbers, General Primo de Rivera led a coup to prop up the wilting monarchy. His "benign" dictatorship lasted until 1930. A year later, the king was forced into exile and the Second Republic proclaimed. This unfortunate government — born amid mass enthusiasm — slowly disintegrated into near anarchy.

The stage now was set for the tragedy of the Spanish Civil War. In July 1936, right-wing generals, who had been plotting a revolt for months, decided to act. Led by a young general named Francisco Franco, the Nationalist rebels rose throughout Spain and captured about half the nation. Their supporters included most of the military and police, the Catholic church, landowners and other conservative groups, and the Falange, Spain's Fascist party. Supporters of the Republic, or Loyalists, included a larger slice of the general population: most of the workers and peasants, regional parties from Catalonia and the Basque region, anti-clericals, socialists, Communists, and anarchists.

Unique to the Civil War (1936–39) was the passionate interest it aroused internationally (British statesman Anthony Eden nicknamed it the War of the Spanish Obsession). The Francoists received crucial aid from Germany and Italy, including combat units, and in 1937 a German bombing raid devastated

Guernica, a town that had symbolized Basque independence for over 400 years. Left-wing groups and individuals from around the world rallied to the cause of the Loyalists. American writers, journalists, and intellectuals flocked to Spain to participate in the war and to report on it, among them Ernest Hemingway, who wrote about the conflict in his novel *For Whom the Bell Tolls.* The Loyalists also could count on the famed International Brigades, volunteers from a score of nations, including America's Abraham Lincoln Brigade.

Largely due to foreign aid and the Republic's internal strife, the Nationalists won in 1939. Generalísimo Francisco Franco had been named head of the Nationalist Government the previous year. During World War II, Spain remained neutral, much to Hitler's chagrin. Later, however, in the diplomatic world of postwar Europe, Spain was something of a Fascist pariah to the victorious nations. In reality, Franco's reign was essentially an old-fashioned military dictatorship that looked more to the glories of 16th-century Spain than to any Fascist ideology.

Spain's emergence from the diplomatic boycott began with an agreement allowing American military bases on Spanish soil. The United States exchanged ambassadors with Spain and granted it a large loan. By 1955, Spain was finally accepted into the United Nations. Now Franco — in theory just a guardian until the restoration of the monarchy — could concentrate on shoring up his regime and rebuilding a devastated economy.

Prior to 1969, the question on everyone's mind had been "After Franco, what?" Then, in that year, Franco named Juan Carlos, grandson of deposed King Alfonso XIII and heir to the throne, as his successor, not to assume power, however, until after Franco's death. The old general finally died in November 1975, and a nation eager for change began its great experiment with democracy.

Today, Spain is ruled by a parliamentary monarchy, but King Juan Carlos has proved to be no mere figurehead. In July of 1976, the new king named Adolfo Suárez as prime minister. Suárez swiftly introduced a political reform bill that was just as swiftly endorsed by parliament and the people, and in October 1978, a new liberal constitution was installed. When Suárez resigned in January 1981, the king presented him with a dukedom.

The following month, a group of army officers burst into parliament — the Cortes — and held it at gunpoint for almost 24 hours. The calm decisiveness of King Juan Carlos helped to cut short this attempted coup. Despite this ominous event, Felipe González, a socialist, was elected prime minister on November 28, 1982 — peacefully and with the army's acquiescence. Under González's leadership, the Partido Socialista Obrero Español (PSOE) is in reality a European-style social democratic party, short on ideology and long on social programs.

The most far-reaching recent change has been the acceptance of regionalism. Spain, which began as a land of distinct regions, was not yoked into one nation until the 15th century; in many places strong regional feelings remain — often accompanied by distinct languages — as in the Basque areas, Catalonia, and Galicia. Now the development of the Autonomous Communities — a semi-federal arrangement — gives each of these regions a degree of self-government.

For one group, however, this may not be enough. The Basques have always been a fiercely independent people. These inhabitants of northern Spain and southern France share a language unlike any other in Europe and a history that goes back, many believe, to the Stone Age. Many Basques want complete independence, a country of their own to be named Euskadi ("collection of the Basques"). For the past 30 years, a terrorist organization, ETA (Euskadi Ta Askatasuna — "Euskadi and Freedom"), has been ferociously seeking this goal.

Paradoxically, along with this regional tendency, Spain also has been rekindling its romance with Europe, as shown by its membership in NATO and the Common Market. Now that the country is a full-fledged member of the European Community, it is no longer accurate to say that "Europe ends at the Pyrenees."

Nor is it accurate to look on Spain as an impoverished nation. During the 1960s and 1970s, the country experienced a rapid, dramatic upsurge of economic growth — an "economic miracle," albeit one accompanied by extensive urbanization that aggravated the problem of an already sparsely populated countryside.

Today, looking forward to the immediate future, Spain is approaching new heights of optimism. With Madrid living up to its EEC designation as 1991's Cultural Capital of the Year, the *1992 Summer Olympic Games* slated for Barcelona, a world's fair, *Expo '92,* taking over Seville, and the whole country set to join in commemorations of the quincentenary of Christopher Columbus's discovery of the New World, it would be hard to envision a nation tuned to a greater pitch of collective celebration. As far as the Spanish are concerned, this year finds their country poised on the brink of a new era — just as it was 500 years ago, when Columbus set sail to meet and greet the world.

Literature

From the beginning, Spanish literature has exhibited certain characteristics that have stayed with it through the centuries: a fierce individualism, a stern philosophy of life, a love for the tragic, tempered by lyricism, and the humorous, often satirical, rendition of everyday life. Spain takes its literature seriously; from Seneca to Lorca, Spanish writers have been paid the dubious compliment of paying for their opinions with their lives.

Spanish literature and language began with the Romans, who ruled Spain for 6 centuries after defeating the Carthaginians in 206 BC. One of Roman Spain's most famous writers was the philosopher and dramatist Lucius Annaeus Seneca (ca. 4 BC–AD 65). Born in Córdoba, Seneca advocated the Roman philosophy of Stoicism, which counseled strength of will and calm acceptance of both pain and pleasure. He left Spain early in life to become the tutor and then principal adviser to Nero, the infamous emperor. Learning that Nero had ordered his death for taking part in an alleged conspiracy, Seneca committed suicide. Seneca's forte was melodramatic, bloodthirsty tragedy, written to be read aloud before the emperor's court. *Phaedra* and *Oedipus,* which are based on Greek legends, are among his most exciting works. His ethical essays, however, have proved more influential than his plays. In poetry, the master was Martial (ca. AD 40–104), born in Bilbilis, Spain. Sharp, witty satiric epigrams are his claim to fame.

Later, under Moorish rule the Spanish city of Córdoba became, after Byzantium, the second-most-important center of culture in the Western world. Many scholars believe that the Moorish *zejels* — brief love lyrics in colloquial Arabic — may have spawned the ballads of the troubadors of southern France, whose 12th-century creations underpin modern European poetry and even, perhaps, our whole concept of romantic love.

A truly Spanish national literature began during the medieval period (ca. 1000–1500) with folk epics — popular narratives in verse called *cantares de gesta* — that may have sprung from the Goths' love of epic songs. The most famous — *El cantar del mío cid* (ca. 1140) — celebrates El Cid, the great hero of the Christian Reconquest of Spain from the Moors.

Most medieval poetry consists of either the stories and songs of the minstrels or the devotional and didactic works of the clergy. Gonzalo de Berceo (1180–1246), the earliest Spanish poet of record, wrote in a learned lyrical form of the lives of the saints and the miracles of the Virgin. The most important prose work of the period, *La crónica general* (The General Chronicle — 1270, 1289), author or authors unknown, fuses world history with prose versions of the epics.

A dissolute genius and Spain's first humorist, Juan Ruiz, Archpriest of Hita (ca. 1280–1351), was the 14th century's literary giant. His poetic masterpiece,

Libro de buen amor (Book of Spiritual Love), consists of both narrative and lyrical verses. The extent of its spirituality, however, can be deduced from the activities of its most famous character, Trotaconventos — a go-between for the archpriest's love affairs. The story is told in the first person; its author's distinctive personality suffuses this realistic view of Castilian life.

Due to Spain's geographic isolation and its peoples' fierce individualism, the Renaissance didn't arrive here until late in the 15th century. Some date it from 1469, when Ferdinand of Aragon married Isabella of Castile, a great patron of the arts. The century's greatest poet, Jorge Manrique (ca. 1440–79), wrote *Coplas por la muerte de su padre* (Verses on the Death of His Father), widely known through Longfellow's translation. A priest, Juan del Encina (1469–1529), earned the epithet "father of Spanish drama" for his plays on religious themes.

The century's best literary work, however, may be the prose drama *Celestina* (1499). It is attributed to Fernando de Rojas, a converted Jew who wished for anonymity because of the Inquisition's persecution. Celestina, a sagacious crone whom Calisto enlists to aid him in his suit for Melibea, is one of Spain's great literary characters.

Spain's Golden Age began in the 16th century. As the conquistadores seized gold from the New World, writers mined the spirit of the Renaissance. Garcilaso de la Vega (1501–36) — a nobleman who died fighting in France — commandeered Italian poetic forms, made them Spanish, and composed sublime sonnets to his dead beloved.

During the same century, Spain gave European literature the picaresque novel. The anonymously written *Lazarillo de Tormes* (1554), about a boy and his adventures serving various hardhearted masters, was the first of a genre that realistically depicts peripatetic rogues (*pícaros*) in the underworld.

The most important novelist, however — the master genius of Spanish literature — is Miguel de Cervantes Saavedra (1547–1616). The fourth child of a failed physician, Cervantes was rather a picaresque hero himself. At 22 he left home for Italy, and entered military service a year later. His left hand was crippled in a battle. In 1575, he was captured by pirates and sold into slavery in Algiers. After numerous attempts at escape, he was ransomed 5 years later. In 1584 he married and, needing money, began to write.

Cervantes's first novel, *La Galatea,* was published in 1585. Neither it nor his dramatic works were successful. After taking such jobs as purchasing agent and tax collector, he eventually wound up in debtor's prison. There he conceived and began to write his masterpiece, *Don Quijote de la Mancha* (Don Quixote). By 1603 he was living with his family in Valladolid. The first part of the book, published in 1605, was an enormous success. Unfortunately, Cervantes had sold all his rights to it for a paltry sum.

Don Quixote begins as a satire on the overblown romances of chivalry that were then so popular in Spain. Addicted to these romances, the impoverished nobleman Don Quixote sets forth with his materialistic servant Sancho Panza on a series of adventures; his aim is to revive the glorious ideals of honor and chivalry. Part Two, published 10 years after the first part, is an even richer work: Don Quixote has become more majestic and Sancho wiser.

Although some critics consider *Don Quixote* the quintessence of the picaresque, it is actually far more sophisticated than that simple genre. It has been called the first modern novel — a new fictional form that blends the real with the ideal, poetry with prose, romantic adventures with incisive literary criticism. Cervantes disliked the cynicism of the picaresque. Suffused throughout his work is faith in humanity. Cervantes's other major work is *Novelas ejemplares* (Exemplary Tales), a collection of stories, some of which are picaresque. In the dedication and prologue to his posthumously published *Persiles y Sigismunda* is the artist's moving farewell to the world. He died 4 days after completing it.

Félix Lope de Vega Carpio (1562–1635) is the Golden Age's dramatic giant. An orphan of modest means and little schooling, Lope wrote his first play at the age of 12. He chose to write drama because it was the only remunerative form of writing at the time. Lope wrote prodigiously — an estimated 2,000 plays of which 400 have survived. Many show the weaknesses that come with hasty writing. One of his best is *El caballero de Olmedo* (The Gentleman from Olmedo), about a nobleman who continues to visit his beloved despite repeated warnings that he may be killed. One of Lope's followers was Fray Gabriel Téllez, known as Tirso de Molina (ca. 1584–1648), who, in 1630, gave the world *El burlador de Sevilla* (The Seducer of Seville), the earliest known dramatic version of the Don Juan legend.

Literary critics call the 17th century the Age of Affectation. As Spain declined in power under incompetent Hapsburgs, the Renaissance style evolved into the baroque. Writers practiced *culteranismo,* a pretentious and obscure style and vocabulary designed for the elite. The champions of the worldly priest Luis de Góngora y Argote (1561–1627) changed the name of the style to Gongorism. Although for hundreds of years his poetry was scorned as too mannered, today Góngora has been revived and elevated to the rank of major Spanish poet.

The other well-known dramatist of the Golden Age is Pedro Calderón de la Barca (1600–1681). Although schooled in Gongorism, the well-educated Calderón knew that this type of literary subtlety would not work on stage. His play *La vida es sueño* (Life Is a Dream) is about a Polish prince who is imprisoned in chains by a fearful father. Its hero, Segismondo, now has become a symbol of moral choice.

The 18th century was the Age of Reason. French neo-classicism was the style in Europe and French Bourbon kings ruled Spain. Pedantry rather than artistry ruled Spanish literature. The best novel was the picaresque autobiography (1743) of a mathematics professor and soothsayer, *Vida de Don Diego de Torres Villaroel* (The Life of Don Diego de Torres Villaroel). In poetry and drama, the important figures were Juan Meléndez Valdés (1754–1817) and Leandro Fernández de Moratín (1760–1828), poet and playwright respectively.

During the first half of the 19th century, Europe turned from the objectivity and reason of classicism to the subjectivity and emotionalism of Romanticism. In Spain, Romanticism began in 1833 when Isabella II took the throne, ending the repression of the previous reign and allowing artists to return from exile. A popular literary movement — *costumbrismo* — dealt with local customs and expressed itself in satirical newspaper and magazine essays. Particularly outstanding were those written by the melancholic Mariano José de Larra (1809–37), who committed suicide. In drama, José Zorrilla (1817–93) achieved fame with *Don Juan Tenorio,* which added new touches to the old legend. Critics — and Zorrilla himself — condemned the play for its loose structure, but its popularity has not waned; it is still staged annually in Spain on *All Saints' Day.*

The leading Romantic poet was José de Espronceda (1808–42), a fighting political liberal and exile who once was jailed for his writings. His best work, *El estudiante de Salamanca* (The Student of Salamanca), is also based on the Don Juan legend. Another writer of the period, the post-Romantic dramatist José Echegaray (1832–1916), was the first Spaniard ever to win the Nobel Prize for literature (1904).

Around mid-century, the sketches of *costumbrismo* expanded into a new form of fiction, the regional novel. Countess Emilia Pardo Bazán (1852–1921) introduced the naturalism of Zola to Spain with a pair of novels about the degeneration of a noble Galician family. The Spanish novelist best known to Americans is Vicente Blasco Ibáñez (1867–1928), whose most popular works, *Blood and Sand* and *The Four Horsemen of the Apocalypse,* are not his best. His masterpiece is a regional novel of Valencia, *La barraca* (The Cabin). The greatest novelist of the century, however, was not a regional writer. Benito Pérez Galdós (1843–1920), considered by many to be the Charles Dickens of Spain, composed a 46-volume series of historical romances, *Episodios nacionales* (National Episodes), on 18th-century Spanish life.

A crisis at the close of the century led to a new renaissance in the arts in Spain. After prolonged political and spiritual drifting, the country lost its colonies to the United States in the Spanish-American War of 1898. This loss of prestige brought artists together in a loose coalition called the Generation of 1898. One major prose stylist of the time was Ramón del Valle Inclán (1866–1936), whose four *Sonatas* are novels named for the seasons. Another great novelist was Pío Baroja (1872–1956), a Basque who wrote about life on the road. An important novel was *A.M.D.G.,* a violent attack by Ramón Pérez de Ayala (1881–1962) on Jesuit boarding schools, which he attended.

Many Spanish writers of the time gained international reputations. The author best known outside Spain was the Basque philosopher Miguel de Unamuno (1864–1936), whose greatest work is *Del sentimiento trágico de la vida en los hombres y los pueblos* (The Tragic Sense of Life in Men and Nations). The most important dramatist was Jacinto Benavente (1866–1954). His tour de force, *Los intereses creados* (Bonds of Interest), is based on Italian masqued comedy. In 1922, Benavente became the second Spaniard ever to win the Nobel Prize for literature.

This century's major literary figure, however, was Federico García Lorca (1898–1936), an Andalusian whose haunting blood-and-death poetry mirrored his life right up to its end, when Franco sympathizers dragged him from his home and murdered him in a cemetery. His most compelling work was *Romancero gitano* (Gypsy Romance). His drama is world famous, especially *Bodas de sangre* (Blood Wedding) and *La casa de Bernarda Alba* (The House of Bernarda Alba). The leading dramatist since the Spanish Civil War has been Antonio Buero Vallejo (b. 1916), who was imprisoned several years after the war. Originally a painter, two of his plays are about the lives of the great Spanish artists Goya and Velázquez.

An important Spanish literary style of the 20th century has been *modernismo,* a worldwide movement that focused on the nature of expression. An important modernist — and 1956 Nobel winner — was the poet Juan Ramón Jiménez (1881–1958), who also wrote a notable work of prose, *Platero y yo* (Silver and I), about his Andalusian wanderings with his donkey. Another Nobel-winning poet (1977) was Vicente Aleixandre (1898–1984), a romantic, sometimes surrealistic, writer whose works exhibit great stylistic freedom. The outstanding modernist philosopher was José Ortega y Gasset (1883–1955). He wrote *La rebelión de las masas* (The Revolt of the Masses) in 1930.

The outstanding novelist living today may be Camilo José Cela (b. 1916), the 1989 recipient of the Nobel Prize for Literature, whose *La colmena* (The Hive) captures the truth of gray, post–Civil War Madrid. Two contemporary novelists who have expertly described the spiritual emptiness of the times are Carmen Laforet (b. 1921) and Miguel Delibes (b. 1920). Laforet's first novel, *Nada* (Nothing), about a lonely girl at the University of Barcelona, is the earliest Spanish existentialist narrative. Delibes's best novel is *Cinco horas con Mario* (Five Hours with Mario), a vulgar woman's interior monologue over her husband's dead body.

The years under Franco had a deadening effect on Spanish literature. With the coronation of King Juan Carlos and the end of censorship, many looked for a literary renaissance. It has been slow in coming. The first signs have appeared in poetry; the *novisimos* are a group of poets who deliberately have turned their backs on the social realism of the Franco years. In fiction, the most exciting news has been the work of young women novelists, such as Monserrat Roig. Drama, too, is beginning to experience a rebirth. Hopes are high that the long-awaited renaissance in literature is taking shape at last.

Painting and Sculpture

Spanish painting and sculpture are rooted in the traditions of the Moors who ruled Spain from the 8th to 11th centuries. The Moorish domination and the resulting Catholic resistance to it left an inventory of art that contains a fanatical strain of religiosity and a strong flavor of individuality.

Subjects and styles have varied over the years. Illuminated manuscripts and church paintings are among the earliest works. Romanesque art shaped the 12th and 13th centuries and first showed the world Spain's expressive style and maturity. In Castile, many artists painted scenes from everyday life; in Catalonia, subjects were mostly Byzantine — portraying Christ and the Virgin in majesty. Altar fronts of wood — more economical than gold or silver — were either painted on a single panel or carved in relief.

Spanish sculptors have used various mediums. Polychrome (decorated in several colors) wood sculpture remained the traditional Spanish medium for altar reliefs and statues from the 15th to 20th centuries; unpainted wood (chiefly oak, walnut, cedar, or mahogany) served for choir stalls and lecterns. Alabaster was used for altars and tombs from the late Gothic to Mannerist periods. Marble was popular during the Renaissance and the 18th century. Stucco had a vogue during the 16th and 18th centuries because its ease of modeling appealed to mannerist sensitivities.

In contrast to the balance and elegance of French art or the physical beauty and technical perfection of Italian, Spanish art is characterized by its realistic and expressive details. Spanish artists are famous for expressing both their philosophical and political views, as well as their personalities, on canvas. Spain has fostered some of Europe's most original artists: El Greco, Diego Rodríguez de Silva y Velázquez, Francisco José de Goya, Joan Miró, Salvador Dalí, and Pablo Picasso.

Each region of Spain has its own style — Moorish arches and cheerful hand-painted tiles in Andalusia, Roman remnants and ceramics in Castile-León; lovely fountains and landscaped public gardens in Valencia; enchanting *modernista* buildings and sculptures in Catalonia. But the greatest works of art are in the *Prado Museum* in Madrid. Here the visitor can wander for hours through the various stages of Spanish painting and sculpture, and drink in their glorious history.

PREHISTORY TO ROMANESQUE

Art history in Spain goes back earlier than it does almost anywhere else, to the prehistoric paintings found deep within the Altamira Caves near the city of Santander. Dating from the Upper Paleolithic era (20,000–8,000 BC), these inspired works of art depict bulls and other animals so realistic that they seem to leap from the walls. A later group of Mesolithic (10,000–3,000 BC) paintings in which human figures appear were discovered in the Remigia Cave near Castellon de la Plana.

Successive waves of invaders inundated the Iberian Peninsula and each left samples of their art. Such remains include a Phoenician sarcophagus now in the *Cadiz Museum,* baked clay figurines in a Carthaginian necropolis, a marble statue of the Greek god Aesculapius, and Celtic stone statues of warriors and animals, including the famous Guisando Bulls in Avila.

Native Iberian art is primarily represented through stone sculptures. The reliefs from the Osuna area, on display in the *National Archaeological Museum* in Madrid, are a good example of this style, as are a number of small bronzes, and some murals in the burial chamber at Galera (in Granada). But the masterpiece is the magnificent *Lady of Elche,* now housed in the *Prado Museum.* In this gray limestone bust, the nobly severe features of the lady contrast with her ornate headdress. It is one of the world's finest pieces of sculpture, a fusion of the austere and the extravagant.

Spain is rich in mosaics left behind by the Romans. Some especially fine pieces include the *Sacrifice of Iphigenia* at Ampuras, the *Medusa* at Tarragona, and the chariot racing scenes in a circus, located in the museum in Barcelona. The Romans also left a wealth of sculpture behind, primarily busts of noblemen, statues of the gods, and elaborate sarcophagi.

The next invaders, the Visigoths, left behind little but metalwork. The Moors, however, who first appeared in AD 711 have left an inheritance that influences Spanish art even today. Islamic art, primarily an art of ornamentation, demonstrates its influence in the paucity of traditional European-style painting and sculpture. However, there are some interesting paintings of hunters and soldiers in the Alhambra's Hall of Kings. The Alhambra also is noted for some rare Islamic sculpture such as the lions surrounding the fountain in the Court of the Lions. Ivory carvings make up some of the finest Moorish sculpture, such as the casket from Zamora's cathedral now in the *Archaeological Museum* in Madrid.

The Moorish influence, however, has reached us most strongly in the art of the Mozarabs — Christians who converted to Islam. The chief center for this art was in León and the surrounding areas of north and central Spain. Mozarabic art reached its zenith during the 9th and 10th centuries, survived into the 12th century, and left a strong influence on Romanesque art.

During the 11th century, medieval craftsmen, traveling the pilgrimage roads that joined one religious center to another, carried the Romanesque style to various parts of Europe. The Spanish Romanesque is characterized by a certain expressiveness, although, in both painting and sculpture, aesthetics and form take second place to sentiment. The pieces, however, are additionally notable for their austerity and strength, while simultaneously fulfilling the purposes for which they were created — to adorn churches and teach the faithful the tenets of their religion. Some of the great pieces of Spanish Romanesque sculpture are in the Cathedral of Santiago de Compostela. In the 12th century, panels — mainly altar frontals — were created in the school that flourished in Catalonia. These naive, almost primitive, panels decorated small chapels and village churches.

THE GOTHIC PERIOD

During the 13th century, the French were the predominant influence on Gothic sculpture in Spain, and both French and Sienese works were used as models for painting. Artists of the 14th century cultivated Spain's Gothic style. They painted slender, spiritualized forms on great polyptychs and altarpieces, carved delicate, fantastic scenes, and sculpted fine work in cathedrals' porticoes and sepulchres. Thanks to French and English influence, they enlivened paintings with halftones and shading to add the illusion of a third dimension. Along with the usual subjects of Christ and the Virgin, so common to Romanesque art, they introduced scenes from the lives of the saints.

Under the influence of the Flemish painter Jan van Eyck, Gothic painting around the mid-1400s took on a slightly different form. His style, based on a refined glazing technique that made figures more realistic, inspired a generation of artists in the states attached to the kingdom of Aragon (Catalonia, Valencia, and the Balearic Islands). Works by two van Eyck-inspired painters, Luis Dalmau (1400–1445) and Bartolomé Bermejo (d. ca. 1490) are in Barcelona and Valencia museums. Another van Eyck pupil, Rogier van der Weyden (ca. 1399–1464), is often credited with Spain's complete entry into the Flemish sphere.

Artists flourished during this time; more and more names were added to the lists of masters. By the late 15th century, Fernando Gallego (ca. 1440–1507) had become one of the main figures in the Hispano-Flemish movement. Although at first look, his paintings seem to resemble the Flemish style, on closer scrutiny it is apparent that he also applied a sense of drama to his works. Two painters who worked for Queen Isabella, Juan de Flandes (1465–1514) and Michael Sittow (1469–1525), also stand out. Together they painted the *Polyptych of the Catholic Queen,* preserved in part in Madrid's Royal Palace.

It was at the end of the 15th century that the influence of the Italian Renaissance truly penetrated the Iberian Peninsula. Some artists, such as Fernando Yáñez de la Almedina, Luis de Vargas, Pedro Machuca, and Gaspar Becerra, copied the forms of their Italian masters. Oil on wood was the most common technique at first, then oil on canvas. Though religious works continued to remain popular, the end of the century also marked the beginning of great portrait work, inspired by the reign of Philip II.

After Spain's effective unification under Ferdinand and Isabella in 1469, the country underwent unparalleled expansion and material progress. The reconquest of Granada (the last Arab kingdom) and the voyages of Columbus were reflected in art. Spain was ready to snap its medieval bonds and fully absorb the achievements of the Italian Renaissance — its study of perspective, clarity of composition, and glorification of the human body.

THE SIXTEENTH CENTURY

The Italian influence, which began to appear around 1500, was brought to Spain by sculptors from Italy, and by Spanish, Flemish, and French sculptors who trained there. It first manifested itself in the funeral monuments of cardinals and kings, and initially found its greatest inspiration in the work of Leonardo da Vinci. Its effect was deepest in Valencia, a city that for geographic, political, and economic reasons maintained close ties with Italy. Donatello and Michelangelo were strong influences on such outstanding Spanish sculptors as Alonso Berruguete, Juan de Juni, and Gregorio Fernández.

In 1506, in Valencia, two of Spain's great masters, Fernando Yáñez de la Almedina and Fernando de Llanos, began to paint the 12 panels on the wings of the cathedral retable, or altarpiece. Yáñez was the foremost Spanish painter of the High Renaissance. Known for treating sacred themes in a novel and imaginative way, he used his Italian training and his Spanish personality to transform his work into an expression of vital energy, as shown by his *St. Catherine, St. Damian,* and *Holy Family* paintings.

During the second third of the century, it was the Italian artist Raphael who stimulated Valencian painting. Spanish Raphaelism was headed by Vicente Juan Macip (1475–1550), whose masterpiece is the *Segorbe Retable* (1530). As in the Yáñez/Llanos style, he used sharp, vivid lines and concentrated on filling his canvas with massive figures that block out the background. His son, Juan de Juánes (1500–1579), also used lines like those of Raphael but became famous for his sweeter, more delicate forms, as evidenced by *The Last Supper,* his most popular work.

From about 1525 onward, the Renaissance gradually gave way to mannerism, a reaction of the irrational against the rational. The classical, calm, and restful balance of the previous era was now replaced by self-conscious, artificial, and nervously stylized depictions of the unreal and the mystical.

Among Spain's greatest mannerist painters was Luis de Morales (1520–86) from Extremadura. Morales became known for his plain, dark backgrounds, mystical elements, and versatility in painting the same subjects with many variations. Our Lady, for example, teaches the Christ Child to read or write, plays with him, or, wearing a wide-brimmed hat, holds him to her neck. His *Ecce Homo* series shows Christ as the man of sorrows, holding a reed, tied to a column, mocked, or carrying the Cross. Morales brought the Venetian manner to Spain, which emphasized sketchiness, effects at a distance, and colorism. One of his most personal creations is *The Penitent St. Jerome* (1569), in El Escorial.

Indeed, in the mid-1500s, the Real Monasterio de El Escorial — the monastery-palace built by Philip II — became a hotbed of Italian inspiration. Philip commissioned the first Italian artists to paint for his palace in 1567. Several Spaniards were also invited: Sánchez Coello (d. 1588) painted a *St. Catherine,* eight pairs of saints, and a *St. Sebastian;* Luis de Carvajal (1534–1607) painted other pairs of saints; and Juan Fernández Navarrate (d. 1579), called "El Mudo" because he was deaf, created several works (*Beheading of Santiago, Adoration of the Shepherds*) in the style of the Venetian Titian.

One of the most Italianized painters of the time was Pablo de Céspedes (1538–1608), whose treatment of anatomy and contrasts in lighting were influential. His foremost work is the *Altar of the Last Supper* in Córdoba's cathedral.

But perhaps the most famous 16th-century artist was Doménikos Theotokópoulos, known to the world simply as El Greco (1541–1614). Born in Crete and trained in Italy, he came to Spain imbued with the values of both the Byzantine and the Western worlds. He appeared on the Spanish scene around 1576, bringing with him the influence of Venetian art. El Greco's manner of lengthening human figures and his vibrant colors give his paintings their great religious intensity. By refusing to let himself be regimented, he became one of the world's most formidable geniuses, while still managing to maintain his artistic independence.

Although a good many of his figures are derived from mannerist forms, El Greco broke with the lines and anatomical proportions of the Italians; his paintings combine spirituality and pomp, ecstasy and factual description. And although his coloring has Venetian origins, he added flashes of colors, achieved by dipping cloths in the pigments or by directly applying them with his fingers. El Greco painted not for painting's sake, but to use his art as a vehicle for his ideas. He eschewed tricks and careful finishing in favor of intense expression.

El Greco's *View of Toledo* is one of the most famous mannerist paintings. Because he saw Toledo as a city of the spirit, he depicted it as a blossoming light-green landscape filled with petrified, ghostly white and blue-gray buildings, where violent, dramatic emotion charges the atmosphere. Most of El Greco's paintings are in Spain, including what many consider his masterpiece, *The Burial of the Count de Orgaz,* which can be seen in the Church of Santo Tomé in Toledo.

THE SEVENTEENTH CENTURY

The death of Philip II and the accession to the throne of Philip III in 1598 led to sweeping changes in Spain, which were reflected in the arts. From the reign of Philip III on, Spanish sculpture is almost entirely religious. After the first decade of the 17th century, allegory, mythology, and grotesques no longer had a place. There was very little tomb or portrait sculpture, and relief carving lost its importance. The Spanish artist became concerned instead with the devotional and spiritual. Glass eyes, eyelashes and wigs made of human hair, and even costumes of real fabric were widely used to facilitate the beholder's identification with the divine. This was an art meant to arouse people's piety.

It was also an isolated art. Unlike their Renaissance and Mannerist predecessors, the great sculptors of the baroque did not study in Italy but stayed at home. Influences from abroad reached them secondhand. This baroque era, a period that unfolded during the *Siglo de Oro,* or Golden Age, became known for its stern realism and contrasts of light.

The baroque had an ambivalent quality as well. It was in one way oriented toward heaven and in another, toward earth. Jusepe de Ribera, Velázquez, and Zurburán proclaimed the dignity of the individual — a particularly Spanish contribution to the style. No longer was the individual neglected in favor of the ideal, as had been the case with Mannerism. For Velázquez and Ribera, all people had spiritual value as human beings.

Between 1620 and 1650, still life, otherwise known as *bodegón,* paintings flourished. Valencia and Toledo became the main centers for this new style, and Francisco Ribalta (1555–1628) and Jusepe de Ribera (1591–1652) two of the main trend setters. For Ribera, like El Greco, the aim was spiritual. He was a fertile inventor of new themes, and was popular for painting biblical stories and portraits. Ribalta's famous *Vision of St. Francis* and Ribera's *Martydom of St. Bartholomew* are in Madrid's *Prado Museum.*

Painting and sculpture became a bit more somber from about 1640 to 1660. The loss of Portugal, the Catalan rebellion, and the death of the queen in 1644, had a sobering effect on the nation. Late baroque — a style rich in the imaginative and the theatrical — arrived after 1660, when Philip IV and his son Carlos II generously patronized the arts.

Francisco de Zurbarán (1598–1664) was one of the principal painters for the king and a follower of Ribera's style. Known in 17th-century Spain and far into 18th-century Spanish America for the immense spiritual power in his paintings, Zurbarán gave objects life, treating them with a refreshing tenderness and respect. His contribution to the baroque lies in the way he combined the haunting power of mysticism with realism and ascetic simplicity. During his lifetime, the Sevillian school of baroque sculpture was at its height, and some of the altars that he and other contemporary artists painted contained gilded images carved in wood.

But by far the greatest painter of the epoch was the Sevillian Diego Rodríguez de Silva y Velázquez (1599–1660). To many, he is the greatest painter Spain ever produced. Early in life, he was appointed court painter to the court of Philip IV. There he remained for most of his life, painting a marvelous collection of portraits of the royal family. In 1658, the king bestowed on him the title of Knight of St. James. Velázquez's popularity was due in large part to his use of light both to illuminate and to define the space around his figures and to his preoccupation with the character of his subjects. As a result, his canvases convey an aura of luminous realism. He carefully developed his compositions, using free, imprecise brushstrokes and subtle colors to relate the figures to each other and achieve a harmonious whole.

Among his masterpieces, all in the *Prado,* are *The Surrender of Breda, Philip IV,* and his most famous painting — which has a room to itself — *Las Meninas* (The Maids of Honor). This last, a group portrait of the family of Philip IV set within a complex interior, draws the viewer immediately into the scene. Through the use of mirrored images, Velázquez painted himself painting the little Infanta, her attendants, and her royal parents. In its brushwork and palette, its mastery of atmospheric perspective, and its sensitive portrayal of human nature, the canvas is the summation of a career.

The 17th century was also influenced by the style of Bartolomé Esteban Murillo (1617–82). Like his contemporaries, Murillo developed compositions on the basis of Flemish, French, German, or Italian prints. He also came under the influence of Ribera and Velázquez. What differentiates his work from others is the truthful and relaxed gestures of his figures. His *Family Group,* painted around 1660, shows how deftly the artist reached into the life of his people: Murillo's subjects are always strong and vitally human, the very essence of Spanish painting.

THE EIGHTEENTH CENTURY

In the early years of the 18th century, most artists in Spain were either French or Italian. With the rise of neo-classicism in the second half of the century, the desire to establish rules for artistic creation led to the formation of the first Spanish art academy — the Royal Academy of St. Ferdinand of Madrid — in 1752. Others soon followed in various cities throughout the country. One of the academy's founders was the prolific sculptor Luis Salvador Carmona (d. 1767) whose work was more baroque than neo-classical in style. Despite the ruling classes' indifference to sculpture in general and the neo-classicists' preference for plain marble, the art of polychrome wood sculpture continued for several decades.

Eighteenth-century painting focused on portraiture and frescoes. The main center was Madrid, followed by Seville, Valencia, and Granada. The Bohemian Anton Raphael Mengs, who lived and worked in Spain for 10 years, influenced the work of native artist Francisco Bayeau y Subias (1734–1795) who painted some noteworthy frescoes in Saragossa, Toledo, and Madrid. Two brothers who enhanced the churches of Madrid with their paintings were Luis (1715–1764) and Antonio (1729–1793) González Velázques. A genre painter of note was Luis Menéndez de Rivera (1716–1780).

The greatest activity and the greatest influence of the time, however, came from one artist: Francisco José de Goya y Lucientes (1746–1828). The work of Goya represents an entire chapter in the history of Spain. His production was immense: some 500 paintings, 1,000 drawings, and more than 275 watercolors and lithographs. Because he worked during a critical moment in Spanish history — a period of transition from an optimistic era influenced by the Enlightenment to one marked by the failure and misery of the French invasion — he became the spokesman of the political and philosophical changes that took place beginning late in the 18th century. His work personified the very heart and soul of the people.

Goya's first paintings — mostly tapestry cartoons and portraits — were lighthearted and full of colorful optimism. But an illness in 1792 changed his life and his art forever. He became deaf, isolated from the world, and withdrawn within himself. The monsters, witches, robbers, prostitutes, and murderers that suddenly appeared in his work had a symbolic value that Goya used to attack the sociopolitical structure of his time. This same satiric intent showed up later when he began to paint portraits. In one of his most famous, *The Family of Charles IV,* the artist avoided symmetry and included himself at the easel, much as Velázquez had done in *Las Meninas.* The harmony of the figures and the warm colors make the painting a brilliant work. But what truly makes it noteworthy is Goya's depiction of the royal family as a remarkably unattractive and dull-looking group, a marked departure from the usual flattering royal portraits.

Two of Goya's other famous works are the *Clothed Maja* and the *Naked Maja,* painted around 1796–98. In both works, Goya's careful and glossy brushwork heightened the sensuous appeal of his mysterious subject — and prompted charges of obscenity. In marked contrast to these are two of the paintings that portray the artist's reaction to the invasion of Napoleon and his troops, *The Second of May* and *The Executions of the Third of May*. Out of his revulsion for war, Goya created works whose impact is as powerful today as it was then.

THE NINETEENTH AND TWENTIETH CENTURIES

The shadow of the great 18th-century painters reached into the 19th century, profoundly affecting the attitudes of its painters and sculptors. Some, such as Eduardo Rosales, developed a dark cast to their work; the work of others was airy and almost frivolous. Joaquín Sorolla y Bastida (1863–1923) brought a Mediterranean brightness to French Impressionism in his paintings of beaches bathed in light. Like his ancestors before him, he added Spanish touches to the currents of European art. Historical paintings were a big favorite of the Royal Academy. Romanticism had its Spanish adherents, and the artist Mariano Fortuny (1838–1873) represents both. A new school of landscape painting showed affinities with French Impressionism: Aureliano de Beruete (1845–1912) and Darío de Regoyos y Valdés (1857–1913) are two names of note.

In sculpture, the neo-classic work of Damián Campeny (1771–1855) predominated at the beginning of the century. A Catalan, his *Lucretia* is in the *Museum of Modern Art* in Barcelona. By the end of the century, realism — with a marked tendency toward the sentimental anecdote — prevailed. Several representatives of this school are Venancio Vallmitjana, Augustín Querol, and Mariano Benlliure.

Twentieth century art turned to the influences of Paris. Famous Spanish members of the Paris School include Juan Gris (1887–1927), Joan Miró (1893–1974), Pablo Picasso (1881–1973), and Salvador Dalí (1904–89). José Gutiérrez Solana (1886–1945) and Ignacio Zuloaga (1870–1945), on the other hand, were known for their scenes of everyday life. José María Sert y Badia (1874–1945) decorated the Cathedral of Vich in Catalonia, his best-known work, as well as the Barcelona Town Hall and the Palace of the League of Nations in Geneva, Switzerland. Many of these men were responsible for a whole new movement in European art.

The greatest of all and the most influential artist of the 20th century was Pablo Picasso. Born in Málaga, Picasso attended the Barcelona Art School, where he proved himself an extraordinarily gifted young man. He then settled in Paris in 1904 and 3 years later painted his landmark work, *Les Demoiselles d'Avignon,* with its flat planes, rigid geometric forms, and subdued colors, inaugurated the style known as Cubism.

Thirty years later, Picasso was commissioned to paint a mural for the Spanish Pavilion at the *1937 International Exhibition* in Paris. When during Spain's Civil War, Generalísimo Francisco Franco called in German planes to bomb the little market town of Guernica, Picasso had his theme. The result was *Guernica,* an enormous gray, black, and white mural, composed as a triptych, like the altar pieces of earlier centuries. In the tradition of Goya's anti-war paintings, however, *Guernica* is a savage cry against the horrors of war. For many years the painting hung in New York, but in 1981, after negotiations with the post-Franco Spanish government, it was returned to its homeland. It now hangs, temporarily, in the Casón del Buen Retiro, an annex to the *Prado* in Madrid.

Cubism was the most significant of all the early-20th-century movements. Its aim — to show an object not as it is but in its totality as the mind's eye perceives it — complemented the evolution of abstract art. Aside from Picasso, the movement also numbered his countryman Juan Gris among its followers. Gris created familiar objects made of polychromatic abstract shapes. Touches of red and yellow, in honor of his native flag, added a political note. His work influenced Matisse to adopt some Cubist techniques. From 1922 on, Gris created stage sets for the now-legendary Diaghilev ballets.

Surrealism became the next step, further exploring the depth of unconscious thought. There is no moral constraint in Surrealistic art; it is dedicated wholly to the imagination. Joan Miró (1893–1983), who lived in Paris from 1920 to 1940 and later divided his time between Paris and Spain, was one of the forerunners of this new movement. Primarily known for his painting of rounded, animal-like outlines in black, white, and red, he is said to have defined the term "surreal" as "more real than real." Miró was drawn to the poetry of Surrealism; even paintings that are completely abstract contain signs and symbols that seem to have a profound personal meaning.

Although Miró may have defined the movement, it was Salvador Dalí who perfected it. Dalí, another Spaniard transplanted to Paris, was famous in his day for his flamboyant life-style. His is another kind of Surrealism, full of realistic, though unnervingly distorted, objects that are meant to portray scenes from the unconscious. Dalí was influenced by the naturalism of Vermeer and the pre-Raphaelites, and by architect Antoni Gaudí's suggestive forms. By basing his paintings on dream consciousness, he was able to shock and challenge reality with his wild interpretations of life. Perhaps his best-known work is *The Persistence of Memory* (1931), with its bent and draped wristwatches.

After the Spanish Civil War, several schools of painting and sculpture developed. They included the Catalan group Dau al Set, formed by Joan Ponc, Antonio Tàpies, Modesto Cuixart, and Juan José Tharrats; the landscapes of Benjamin Palencia; and the neo-figurative group, which brought together Antonio Clavé, Pancho Cossío, Daniel Vásquez Díaz. Tàpies, born in Barcelona in 1923, is the living artist best known today outside of Spain. His large, massive works, with their rough and earthy textures, have brought him recognition as a master of abstract art. Juan Genoves, a contemporary of Tàpies, born in Valenica in 1930, paints in a disturbingly realistic style. His scenes of violence are photographically accurate in detail, yet the anonymity of their scenes and subjects create an ambiguity that induces anxiety in the viewer.

At the turn of the century, Spanish sculpture was in a lyrical and decorative phase. Naturalistic monuments based on the female form were the hallmarks of José Llimona (1864–1934), the most important sculptor of his day. Soon after Llimona's rise, the classicist José Clará (1878-1957) initiated a reaction against Llimona's work. Another important sculptor of the time was Julio González (1876–1942) who, although he worked in France, had a strong influence on the Spanish sculptors in the decades that followed. Pablo Gargallo (1881–1934), a Cubist who worked in iron, was perhaps the most distinctive sculptor of his generation. The abstract sculptor Angel Ferrant (1891–1959) constructed mobiles which were highly original yet recalled the work of Alexander Calder. A younger group of sculptors includes Eduardo Chillida (b. 1924), who forges austere works out of forged iron, and José María Subiarchs (b. 1927), who stresses color and texture in his work.

Spanish art today remains defiant and individualistic, shaped by new values and new political developments. Few other countries are as rich in museums — more than 600 — and ornate expression.

Architecture

"Castles in Spain," we say, but Spanish architecture exults in more than just fabulous castles. From impressive Roman bridges to gorgeous Moorish mosques, from towering cathedrals to quiet hidden churches, a wealth of glorious buildings blankets the cities and countryside of Spain. This is a country where it's possible to see all the major European architectural styles — from Romanesque to modern — of the past 1,000 years and, in addition, something unique: an architecture formed from Spain's sensuality and love of ornamentation, its physical isolation from the rest of Europe, and its 700-year subjugation by the Moors, an architecture that grandly fuses the richness of East and West.

The earliest architectural examples still extant in Spain — mainly bridges and aqueducts — date from the Roman occupation (206 BC–AD 414). Three bridges still stand as tribute to Roman builders — at Alcántara, Salamanca, and Mérida. The one at Alcántara, built by Emperor Trajan in AD 103, is a level roadway, 250 feet long, over six massive granite arches, with a portal over the central pier. The aqueduct at Segovia is even older — built during the reign of Augustus (27 BC–AD 14); composed of 2 tiers of granite arches, it spans a deep valley, 2,700 feet across.

The Romans were succeeded by the Visigoths, whose churches — characterized by the horseshoe arch — provide examples of the pre-Romanesque building style. San Juan Bautista, a stone basilica with three aisles at Baños de Cerrato, near Palencia, is the best example. It was built in 661 to house a sacred spring that is still visible today, neatly tucked away between two horseshoe arches.

Even during the Moors' reign, Galicia and Asturias in the north remained Christian; the architectural style forged by the Asturians used Visigothic designs. The best example is the Church of Santa María Naranco near Oviedo (842–50). Originally a royal hall for Ramiro I of Asturias, the church has outside steps that lead up to the nave. Arches, however, are rounded rather than horseshoe-shaped.

Christian refugees from the Muslim-occupied south migrated north, where they created a building style — part Christian, part Muslim — called Mozarabic. The Church of San Miguel de la Escalada (912–13), near León, is one of the most beautiful examples. Lovely marble columns topped by the palm-leaf capitals characteristic of Mozarabic design separate the five-bay nave from the aisles.

In the south, meanwhile, the Moors were building their own monuments to God and their rulers. The mosque begun in 785 in the magnificent city of Córdoba is their first significant design. Except for a Gothic chapel added after the Christians retook the city, the structure still looks like a 10th-century mosque with its arcade of horseshoe arches, voussoirs of alternating colors, forest of marbled columns, and filigreed walls and ceilings.

The most famous Moorish monument in Spain, however, is the Alhambra, a stunning complex of palace buildings that perches above Granada. Begun in the 13th century but built largely during the 14th century, it includes the lush palace of the Muslim kings, and features two richly decorated courts. The Court of the Lions is surrounded by an arcade of slender columns beneath arches interlaced with intricate geometric patterns.

Despite its beauty, the Alhambra suffered a demeaning fate after the expulsion of the Moors. For centuries, Christians consigned it to use as a debtor's asylum, hospital, and prison, before learning to value its voluptuous aesthetic appeal. Today, the lovely city of Granada itself has been declared a national monument. Written on its walls are these words of De Icaza, spoken by a blind beggar: "Alms, lady, alms! For there is nothing crueler in life than to be blind in Granada."

The Romanesque style, prevalent from 1000 to 1250, reflects the supreme importance of the Roman Catholic church in medieval life. The most celebrated example is the Cathedral of St. James at Santiago de Compostela, begun around 1075. Said to contain the saint's remains, this silver-gray granite sanctuary quickly became an important Christian shrine. Because the pilgrimage to Santiago was, during the Middle Ages, second only to one to Rome or Jerusalem, masses of travelers came this way, and other Romanesque pilgrimage churches were built. A surviving example is San Martín at Fromista, between Burgos and León.

In the Santiago cathedral, it is the interior that is Romanesque. One striking feature is the original Portico de la Gloria (Gate of Glory), with statues sculpted by Master Mateo in 1188. Other examples of the Romanesque are the cathedrals at Zamora, Tarragona, and Avila, the old cathedral at Salamanca, the collegiate church at Toro, and the Cistercian Abbey church at Meira.

Gothic architecture began in France around 1150. It didn't spread to Spain as quickly as to other countries, because of the Muslim occupation and the Spaniards' predilection for the Romanesque. Once it took hold, however, Spain was reluctant to give it up, and the style lasted until about 1600. Gothic building reached its soaring zenith in cathedrals with pointed arches, stone rib vaulting, flying buttresses, slender spires of great height, and massive amounts of stained glass. The best Spanish example is the Toledo Cathedral (begun in 1227), whose glory lies in the rich splendor of the high altar, the beautiful rose window, and the majestic nave. Paintings by two of Spain's greatest artists, El Greco and Goya, hang within.

Late Gothic is displayed in Seville's cathedral, constructed (1402–1520) on the site of the city's mosque, which was torn down to make room for it. Still surviving is the mosque's famous minaret, the Giralda (1172–82). Another late Gothic monument is Salamanca's New Cathedral, designed by Juan Gil de Hontañon and built from 1513 to 1560. Its style — called Plateresque because it resembles *platería*, or silverwork, an important Spanish craft at the time — illustrates the tendency in Spanish architecture toward excessive ornamentation. Other notable examples of Spanish Gothic are the cathedrals of

León, Burgos, Barcelona, Segovia, and Girona, the churches of San Juan de los Reyes in Toledo (the 1477 masterwork of Juan Guas) and St. Paul's in Valladolid, and the Palacio del Infantado in Guadalajara.

Because of Spain's geographic isolation — surrounded on three sides by water and on the fourth by mountains — and the Catholic church's efforts to hold back the tide of humanism, the Renaissance arrived late. Early examples of Spanish Renaissance style still contain elements of the Plateresque in, for example, the ornamentation of the *Hostal de los Reyes Católicos* (1501–11), now a large luxury *parador,* or hotel, near the cathedral in Santiago de Compostela.

At the core, the very heart of Spain, stands El Escorial (1558–84), an enormous, austere, palace-monastery complex. Commissioned by Philip II to commemorate his victory over the French, it was designed by Juan de Herrera and built out of granite blocks from the neighboring Sierra de Guadarrama near Madrid. It is the best example of later, more classical Renaissance architecture. Although many have called it bleak and severe, Philip's aim for his palace was nobility without ostentation. The complex contains a palace, a church, a monastery, a mausoleum, a library, a museum, and 16 courtyards within its foursquare ground plan. Rising above are two bell towers and the high dome of the royal palace, which projects from the eastern façade.

Philip is also responsible, at least indirectly, for another example of late Renaissance architecture — Juan Gómez de Mora's Plaza Mayor in Madrid (1617–20). Once Philip had transformed the small, unimportant city at the center of Spain into its capital, it became worthy of this large, 4-story arcaded square reserved for pedestrians.

If Renaissance architecture did not fully capture the imagination and passion of Spain, the later baroque style, with its extravagant curved shapes, sensuousness, and feeling of movement certainly did. In Spain, it became known as Churrigueresque, after the talented Churriguera family of designers and builders. The most outstanding example is the Transparente, a masterpiece of sculpture and painting behind the altar of the Toledo Cathedral. Completed in 1732, it depicts the Last Supper, the Virgin Mary soaring to heaven, angels, and Christ seated on clouds. The vault above was broken through to allow daylight to illuminate it from behind.

Another marvelous example is the exterior of the cathedral of Santiago de Compostela, begun in 1738, while the only complete baroque cathedral is the Catedral Nueva in the lovely southern seaport of Cádiz, begun in 1722 by Vicente Acero. An important secular example, sometimes called the "Spanish baroque version of Versailles," is La Granja, the royal mountain palace retreat in the Sierra de Guadarrama.

The baroque culminated in the even more ornate rococo, a predominantly French style that is lighter and less sensuous than its predecessor. A leading illustration of the style is the white alabaster entrance portal to the Palacio del Marqués de Dos Aguas in Valencia (1740–44), a riot of decoration that includes nudes, lions, clouds, palm trees, drapery, twisted abstract shapes, and the Virgin and Child.

Following hard on the heels of baroque and rococo — and in reaction to their excesses — was neo-classicism, which represented a return to a pure, restrained, classic style that never had been popular in Spain. Examples are the main façade of the cathedral at Lugo (1769–84) and the interior of the cathedral at Zaragoza (1753–66).

During the 19th century, all styles were revived and little that was original was created. Churches were built in Romanesque and Gothic, public and civic buildings in classical style. One of the most important developments in architecture was new methods of construction. Engineers were using materials such as iron, steel, glass, and reinforced concrete, and mastering mass-production techniques.

At the end of the century, an architect with a unique style emerged to leave an indelible mark on modern Spain and stun the world. Antoni Gaudí (1852–1926) had been working in the neo-Gothic style in Barcelona, restoring medieval monuments, when he began experimenting with his characteristic parabolic curves in the portal arches of the Palacio Episcopal (Episcopal Palace) at Astorga (1887–1913). His masterwork, La Sagrada Familia (the Church of the Holy Family) in Barcelona, was begun in 1882 as a neo-Gothic work.

Gaudí, who became principal architect of the church in 1891, completed various sections of La Sagrada according to his late employer's specifications. In 1893, however, he began incorporating his own designs into the transept façade depicting the Nativity. From World War I on, he devoted himself to the work. The first bell tower was finished in 1921. Five years later, the church still far from complete, Gaudí was struck and killed by a streetcar in front of the building on which he had labored for so long. His body was buried in the crypt. Work was renewed in 1950, using Gaudí's designs. It will not be finished until well into the next century.

La Sagrada is a far cry from its neo-Gothic origins. Gaudí's style is based on a combination of medieval Gothic, Moorish (his parabolic arch recalls the horseshoe arch), and his own rendition of Art Nouveau. Inspired by natural formations, Gaudí created a façade that has been compared to molten lava, melting snow, and a cake left so long in the sun that its frosting has melted; pointed arches hung with outgrowths like stalactites; and towers that appear modeled on dunce caps or on the towers dribbled atop a child's sand castle.

There are two other striking examples of his work in Barcelona, both built between 1905 and 1910 in the Art Nouveau style. One is Casa Batlló, a townhouse with slender, bony columns and a writhing ceramic roof; the other, Casa Milá, a large apartment block with a wave-like façade and balconies whose ironwork resembles seaweed. Gaudí professed two often-repeated principles: "Originality is a return to origins" and "There are no straight lines in nature."

Modern architecture, which developed in Germany between the world wars, did not produce any monuments of merit in Spain because Generalísimo Francisco Franco's totalitarian government preferred a more traditional style. The liberalization of Spanish society since Franco's death, however, has opened exciting possibilities. One of the most interesting new edifices is Madrid's 30-story Bank Building, designed by Francisco Sáenz de Oiza (1980), with cantilevered beams every fifth floor.

With the arrival of *Expo '92* to Seville, permanent additions and changes have been made to that city's architectural landscape. Among them is the *Teatro de la Maestranza,* a new, 1,800-seat opera house located near the legendary Plaza del Toros on the city side of the Guadalquivir River. Reminiscent in design of the neighboring bullring, the theater opened in May of last year. Though many of the pavilions at *Expo* are temporary buildings, Santa María de las Cuevas, the 15th-century monastery on the fairgrounds at Cartuja Island, has undergone major renovations and will house the royal Spanish pavilion during *Expo* (and will serve as a cultural center thereafter). In addition, a group of Madrid architects have developed what ultimately may flower into an original — and wholly Spanish — style.

Traditional Music and Dance

 Spanish music today is a composite of cultural influences that have shaped it over the course of 2 millennia. Long before the Phoenicians, Greeks, Romans, Visigoths, Jews, Moors, Indo-Pakistani Gypsies, Africans, and natives of the New World added their respective grace notes to the national repertoire, Spain had an indigenous tradition of music and dance that is depicted in several of its renowned prehistoric cave paintings. During the Middle Ages, music and dance were popular diversions at Spanish courts, and no fiesta, fair, or public celebration took place that didn't have its share of song and dance. Though flamenco is Spain's most famous musical form, national dances such as the *morisca* — which spread throughout Europe in the 15th century — the *jota,* and the *bolero* are also known beyond the country's borders.

The *jota, fandango, seguidilla,* and *bolero* share a common pattern, major variations residing in the complexity of the dancer's movements. The Aragonese *jota* debuted in the 18th century, gained widespread popularity during the early-19th-century War of Independence, and eventually spread across the entire Iberian Peninsula and to the Balearic and Canary islands. When the *jota* is rendered in a more sensuous Arabic style, it becomes the *fandango,* a word of Bantu origin. From the 15th to 19th centuries, Africans who were brought to Spain as slaves not only embraced the local dance traditions, but stamped upon them their own infectious rhythms, creating such lively dances as the *rumba flamenca.* Each Andalusian community gave the *fandango* its own local twists and turns; it became the *malagueña* in Málaga, the *granadina* in Granada, the *rondeña* in Ronda, and so on.

Similar to the *jota* and *fandango* is the *seguidilla* — born as a song form in the 15th century and reaching the pinnacle of its popularity in the 17th. Originating in La Mancha and developing regional variations as it spread, the dance's joy and exuberance were described by Cervantes in *Don Quixote* as "the gamboling of the soul, the frolicking of laughter, the restlessness of the body, and, finally, the quicksilver of all senses."

The *bolero,* derived from the *seguidilla,* was born in the Spanish *tablaos* (dance cafés) that enlivened the late 18th and early 19th centuries. "Boleros" and "boleras" were originally terms for the professional dancers who performed there. Metrically and rhythmically, the *jota, fandango, seguidilla,* and *bolero* are similar. All are dances for couples and, much like flamenco, are punctuated with interludes of guitar and song. Together, they represent the archetypal Spanish dance.

In Spain, one musical form outshines all others — flamenco. In its fullest sense, flamenco is more than just a song and dance; it is part of a world view that values freedom and movement over possessions, spontaneity over planning and routine. Artistically, it is a seductive blend of technical discipline and fierce passion ignited by the elusive *duende,* that electric moment when emotion finds its most poignant expression in the exquisite grace of a hand, the raspy trill of a voice, or the rapid-fire play of fingers across guitar strings.

Flamenco is the antithesis of rigidity. Thus any routine professional performance of the dance is a betrayal of its basic philosophy — live for the moment, when it comes. Where does this leave the tourist? More often than not, with facsimile flamenco, which, like an imitation gem, may be technically more perfect but lacks the fire and spirit of the real thing. Flamenco, the folk art, is as different from its professional alter ego as a genuine kiss is from one onstage.

A mixture of Byzantine Christian ritual, Jewish liturgical chants, the calls of the Muslim muezzin, and the half-breed Hindu heritage of the Gypsies, flamenco is a pliant art form that has assimilated disparate musical sources. As the ports of Andalusia thronged with New World commerce during the 16th and 17th centuries, people came from all parts of Spain and its overseas colonies to share the wealth, bringing their diverse musical heritages with them. Thus the folk traditions of the north as well as those of immigrants insinuated themselves into a nascent flamenco.

The catalyst that fused this hodgepodge into a coherent musicial tradition was the Inquisition. From the late 15th through early 19th centuries, this brutal attempt at religious conformity drove the nonconforming Jews, Gypsies, and Moors to seek refuge in the Andalusian hills. Here, in the solemn and moving rhythms of their various chants and songs, they described the terrors of persecution, gave voice to their pain, and found solace. Like the African-American's blues, their music was one of despair. It's possible that the very term "flamenco" is a mispronunciation of "felag" and "mengu," Arabic words for "fugitive peasant." Then, after some 200 years of incubation, flamenco emerged as a musical style in its own right in the 18th century, which saw the first recorded use of the word "flamenco" in the musical sense.

Though today dance is flamenco's most salient feature, first there was song and then the guitar. The *cante* (singing) expresses the fear of death, the enigma of sex, and the joy of existence. The voice must be gruff, gravelly, and as abrasive as the torment it laments. Though flamenco verse runs the emotional gamut from ecstasy to despair, anguish is its wellspring, the stuff of the *cante jondo* (literally, "deep song"), which is flamenco at its most moving and profound. It embraces two basic song forms, *soleares* — a Gypsy pronunciation of the Spanish *soledades,* meaning solitude or loneliness — and *siguiriyas.* The verses of the *cante jondo* speak of alienation, isolation — in short, the lot of the non-Christian in a virulently Catholic Spain.

> *In the district of Triana,*
> *On the street of the Inquisition,*
> *They executed Curro Puya,*
> *The finest of our people.*
> *Look at the shame,*
> *You have made me bear,*
> *To go asking for alms from door to door*
> *To buy you freedom.*

> *The horsemen on the corners*
> *With torches and lanterns*
> *Called out:*
> *"Kill him! He's Gypsy!"*
> *To my enemies*
> *May God never send*
> *The black sorrows of death*
> *He has sent me.*
> *Don't hit my father again!*
> *Stop, for God's sake!*
> *The crime you accuse him of*
> *I myself have committed.*

By the 18th century, the Gypsies had become flamenco's zealous custodians, allowing few *payos* (non-Gypsies) to witness it. Then in 1842, when Seville's first *café cantante* presented flamenco to a paying public, the face of flamenco changed forever. Though for Gypsies it remains an informal, impromptu form of expression, in today's *tablaos* or at *Carnegie Hall* it is, first and foremost, entertainment.

Early in the 20th century, the *tablaos* replaced the *cafés cantantes,* and the dance, originally a mere foil to the *cante* and guitar, moved center stage. Today's flashy footwork and provocative undulations repulse the purist, who would travel hundreds of miles to see the authentic Gypsy dance, which relies on the sinuous movements of arms, hands, upper torso, and head rather than the constant clicking of feet and castanets. *Flamenco puro,* in fact, doesn't use castanets because they restrict the grace and movement of the hands. Most flamenco song forms follow a set rhythm, or *compás.* Most common is the 12-beat rhythm with syncopated accent on the 3rd, 6th, 8th, 10th, and 12th beats. The guitar became a regular feature of flamenco in the 18th and 19th centuries. Before, the *compás* had been marked with *palmas* (hand clapping), feet tapping, or knuckles rapping on tables — a practice that continues today.

Every art form has its own language. In the case of flamenco, two key terms are *duende* and *juerga.* Originally, *duende* meant "spirit" or "demon," but its flamenco connotation is more elusive. The Granadan poet Federico García Lorca defines *duende* as the "black sounds" that emanate from human despair. More generally, it is that moment of self-abandonment when performer, music, and emotion become one. Since *duende* is capricious and spontaneous, it is rarely found where flamenco is routinely performed for wages.

Not all flamenco denotes doom and gloom. The *juerga* is a spontaneous flamenco event that may last hours or even days. By turns, everyone participates, if only by shouting encouragement or clapping in *compás.* No *juerga* is complete without its share of *cante intermedio* and *cante chico* songs. The former, though still moving, are less soul-wrenching than the *cante jondo* and include *fandango.* The *cante chico* highlights the sunny side of flamenco, featuring rhythms that are quick and contagious and verses that are light-hearted, often humorous. No wonder the spirited *bulerías,* accompanying *cante chico,* are among the most popular dances at any *juerga.*

Although it's hard to fix the number of song forms in the flamenco repertoire, estimates run from 70 to as many as 500. Among those most frequently found on professional programs are *bulerías, alegrías, farruca, tarantos, tien-*

tos, rumba flamenca, and, of course, *soleares* and *siguiriyas.* Most modern *tablaos* present the *cuadro flamenco* — a group of singers, dancers, and guitarists seated on stage and featured in turn as soloists (much like any *jota, fandango, seguidilla, bolero* — or jazz — performance). There are no leaps, no jumps, no aspirations to become airborne. And the dance, if authentic, is improvised.

Because flamenco melodies are often monotonous, the singers shrill, and the dancing arrogant, even contemptuous, and because flamenco is an intense art, fueled by reserves of deep-seated cultural passion, most people (including many Spaniards) consider it an acquired taste. Born and bred in Andalusia, flamenco's spiritual center still lies within an imaginary triangle marked by the towns of Lucena, Seville, and Cádiz, where the remaining Gypsies not only keep the fires of flamenco burning but consider it their exclusive possession — regarding with disdain and mockery all *payos* who presume to practice this singular art. Though the death knell has been rung for flamenco almost as many times as for the novel, it always springs back, renewed, revitalized, and a little bit different. The *Fundación Andaluza de Flamenco* (Palacio Pemartín, 1 Plaza de San Juan, Jerez de la Frontera) strives to keep flamenco traditions alive through exhibitions and its vast library of books, cassettes, and videotapes that chronicle all aspects of the art.

There are notable *tablaos flamencos* to be seen in Madrid, and Seville, too, has fine professional flamenco. But every August, flamenco can be seen in its proper cultural context in the towns and villages of Andalusia, which blossom with hundreds of flamenco festivals. The *April Fair* in Seville and the *Horse Fair* in Jerez de la Frontera every May also offer homegrown flamenco. All over Spain, *sevillanas,* Seville's flamenco version of the *seguidilla* of La Mancha, are danced in discos and special *sevillanas* clubs; in Seville itself, the clubs along Calle Salado in the Barrio Triana are the places to try to see *sevillanas.* Flamenco performances rarely begin before midnight, and do-it-yourself dance clubs usually catch fire around 1 or 2 AM.

Also part of the Spanish repertoire of musical offerings is the *zarzuela.* Developed in the 17th and 18th centuries, this national light opera, or operetta, is still popular today, though many foreigners find the language barrier a hindrance to their complete enjoyment. Heavily nostalgic and colorful, *zarzuela* is an unusual Spanish art form that takes a sentimental rather than tragic view of the past. From October to June, *zarzuelas* are staged at Madrid's *Teatro de la Zarzuela.*

Late in the 19th century, a movement arose to integrate the folk music and the classical music of Spain. A leading exponent was Manuel de Falla (1876–1946), a Spanish composer who achieved international fame. Among his best known compositions are the ballets *El amor brujo* (Love the Magician) and *El sombrero de tres picos* (The Three-Cornered Hat) and a nocturne for piano and orchestra, *Nights in the Gardens of Spain.*

One of the instrumentalists Falla wrote for was Andrés Segovia, the great Spanish guitarist, who died in 1987. Until Segovia's time, the guitar had not been considered an appropriate instrument for solo concerts, but his brilliant playing changed all that. Like so many fine Spanish musicians of the 20th century, Segovia delighted audiences all over the world with his music, a music rooted in the finest Spanish tradition.

Bullfighting

There's a point in every bullfight that Spaniards call the "moment of truth." It happens just as the matador prepares to thrust his sword between the bull's shoulders. There will be a death — usually the bull's, but sometimes the bullfighter's.

It's also the moment of truth for hundreds of unsuspecting visitors. Many come away from their first bullfight full-fledged aficionados. The more faint-hearted bolt for the door. Animal lovers have been known to send angry letters to the Spanish government. Most Spaniards, however, see this centuries-old tradition either as a highly skilled sport or as a graceful dance performed by a matador who flirts with death at every turn of his cape.

Bullfighting began in Spain's southern and central regions sometime in the 12th century. Bullrings in Béjar, Campofrío, Zaragoza, and Seville are among the oldest in Spain, although those in Ronda and Seville are architecturally the most satisfying and have the greatest historical importance.

During King Philip III's reign, Madrid's Plaza Mayor, or main square, was used for bullfights. The seats of honor were the gold and black balconies of the 5-story red brick and stone buildings that surround the square. Various guilds decorated their balconies with velvet and damask canopies covered by coats of arms. A special section was allotted for the priests who heard the confessions of the men about to enter the bullring.

Today, the *Las Ventas* bullring in Madrid seats 50,000 and is open from mid-April through October. In May, during the *Feast of San Isidro,* Madrid's patron saint, bullfights take place daily.

Seats in most bullrings are sold in a wide range of prices; some are as low as about $3. Patrons buying *sol* (sun) — the cheapest seats — can expect to sit in glaring sunshine the entire time, while *sombra* seats — the most expensive — are in the shade, and *sol y sombra* seats strike a happy medium.

The bullfighting season generally lasts from late spring through the fall. The fights not to miss take place in Pamplona during the first week of July, when the entire town hosts thousands of visitors for the annual *Fiesta de San Fermín,* best known as a week-long, 24-hour drunken bash. In this northern town, visitors can see the best bullfighters and the most raucous bullfights. At 8 AM every day during the fiesta, six bulls race through the narrow, cobblestone streets to the bullring, challenged on the way by Pamplona's most daring — or most foolhardy — young men.

Small towns and villages are not sophisticated about their bullfights. In Chinchón, an hour's drive south of Madrid, the dirt-covered town square turns into an amateur bullring on Sundays during the summer. There, brave young boys practice their skills, and potbellied has-been matadors test their agility and speed. The bulls, though not exceptionally large, are still dangerous.

Bulls are expertly bred for the professional rings. To be chosen to fight, a bull must weigh at least 460 kilos (1,012 pounds) for the permanent, professional rings, less for the smaller rings, and be between 4 and 6 years old. (It will be checked after death to make sure it has at least six permanently developed teeth.)

The *corrida* (bullfight) always lasts about 2 hours and features six bulls. It always starts on time, to a blaring of trumpets and a flourish. A procession of mounted bailiffs, dressed in the uniforms of King Philip's court, opens the ceremony, followed by the matadors and their assistants.

Seated in the stands is the president, who has been officially elected to the post, or a delegate. He oversees the *corrida* and his word is final. Like a conductor with a baton, the president uses different colored handkerchiefs to cue the action. Resting a white one across the railing starts the parade and subsequent *corrida*. A red handkerchief signals that black *banderillas* be stuck into the bull, a green one signals that the bull be returned to the pen, and a blue one gives the bull another turn around the ring.

The president also awards trophies. Taking his cue from the cheering crowd, he will award the victorious matador one bull's ear, but whether he awards the second is solely up to him. Awarding the bull's tail happens rarely and only for an outstanding performance.

The drama begins when the bull charges into the ring, excited and confused — to be met by six *toreros* waving their capes. In its confusion the bull races about the ring in stops and starts. As it does so, its legs are checked and its performance judged to see if it is an equal match for the matador.

Prologue over, the first act begins when a husky *picador* carrying a long *puya* (spiked stick) gallops out on a padded horse. He must stay on the ring's periphery, outside the white circle painted on the ground. When the bull charges, horse and rider are often pushed against the boards. This is desirable since it makes it easier for the *picador* to thrust the *puya* into the *morrillo* (neck muscle) of the bull. This is the first sign of blood. The injury weakens the head, making for a better kill later in the *corrida*.

The stars of the second act are the three *banderilleros*, who each run at the bull with two barbed sticks (*banderillas*) and throw them into the open wound left by the picador.

Now at last, for the third and final act of this bloody drama, the matador, dressed in a dazzling mirrored costume, enters the bullring. The bull is easily enraged. The matador uses his *muleta* (red cape) to taunt it.

Deft use of the *muleta* is an art form. An inept bullfighter is often booed by a crowd well versed in the distinct variations of each move. The most popular move is the *natural,* in which the bullfighter flutters the cape within inches of the bull, awaits a charge that sometimes grazes his leg, then gracefully turns his wrist and body to face the bull as it returns for another charge. In addition to incredible courage, the ability to sense the bull's movements, speed, and idiosyncrasies is what distinguishes an excellent bullfighter from an unpopular bullfighter, or a dead bullfighter.

At last, trumpets sound to tell the bullfighter he has the customary 15 minutes in which to kill the bull. As the sword is withdrawn from the *muleta,* anyone can hear the hiss as the crowd draws in its breath. Slowly, the matador rises to his toes, raises the sword slightly above his head, and charges. He aims for a spot behind the bull's head. If his aim and thrust are successful, the bull drops to the ground. Sometimes the bull twirls in one spot before crumpling.

As the dead bull is dragged away by a team of horses, the matador either struts triumphantly around the bullring receiving cheers of praise and sometimes roses, or is booed out of the bullring for a bad fight in which the spectators believe the bull was not treated well. Whatever the outcome, the bullfight, for all its pomp and ceremony, remains a dangerous, possibly fatal, contest between fragile human beings and an animal formidable enough to have conquered lions and tigers with its horns.

Dining in Spain

 Sangría, paella, gazpacho, and *tapas,* those delectable Spanish contributions to the American table, are just teasers for the dining adventure that awaits the visitor to Spain. Although today's Spain boasts Michelin three-star restaurants — *Zalacaín* in Madrid, *Arzak* in San Sebastián — and trendy European-style establishments with menus that reflect the country's new internationalism, old Spanish hands needn't panic. Those venerable stucco and beam-ceilinged dining places found on every corner are still serving mountainous platters of *mariscos* (seafood), pots of nourishing *sopas* (soups), and bowls of comforting *cocidos* (stews). And the sidewalk cafés are still here, and the jewel-box pastry shops, and those cozy eateries and watering holes, the *taverna, tasca, bodega,* and *bar* — the neighborhood hangouts for coffee, wine, and *tapas* (snacks).

Those who love appetizers will adore the *tapas* bar. The word *tapa* (lid) came into use when bartenders kept flies out of wine glasses by covering them with a saucer or piece of bread and then placed a tidbit of free lunch on top. Although no longer free, *tapas* today cost only about $2 to $3 a plate. (For a larger portion, order a *ración.*)

Every *tapas* bar features the ultimate Spanish appetizer, a joint of prosciutto-like *jamón serrano* (air-dried mountain ham) to be razored out in paper-thin shavings. Ranged along the counter will be a dozen to 50 earthenware *cazuelas,* serving dishes filled with plump green olives and a mind-boggling assortment of sautéed or sauced seafood — crayfish, shrimp, clams, oysters, mussels, crab, squid, octopus, and roe — as well as cold fish, egg, and vegetable salads; cheeses and sausages; tripe and other varieties of meats; fried or marinated fish; and sea creatures such as snails and barnacles that fall into the "enjoy but don't ask" department.

Although Americans sometimes confuse Spanish and Mexican cuisine, the two are actually quite distinct — even though both use the potatoes, tomatoes, peppers, avocados, beans, and chocolate that 16th-century Spanish explorers discovered in the New World. Spanish-speaking travelers who learned the language in Mexico can be in for some linguistic surprises, though, such as discovering the very different meaning given the word *tortilla.* Unlike the sturdy maize pancake that Mexicans wrap around beans and meat, a Spanish *tortilla* is a deep-dish potato omelette that can be served warm at mealtime or sliced cold for snacks.

Spanish cooking, smoothed by fruity olive oils, doesn't call for the hot-pepper *salsa* of the Mexican kitchen. And despite a love affair with garlic, Spanish food is often as mild as American home cooking. (An exception is any dish labeled *al pil pil,* which means it comes in olive oil spiked with garlic and tongue-searing dried red peppers.) If anything, it's sweetness that runs through Spanish cuisine, thanks to the honey, almonds, hazelnuts, sesame, cinnamon, and aromatic spices introduced by the Moors.

The chance to drink reasonably priced Spanish wines, most of which never reach the United States, is a plus. Besides the fun of discovering young local wines — which change virtually from village to village — connoisseurs will appreciate the chance to taste the famous sherries from Jerez: the dry *finos* and *manzanillas,* the medium dry *amontillados,* and the sweet *olorosos.* Spain's greatest wines, aged red riojas from the north around Logroño compare with burgundies and bordeaux, while younger valdepeñas wines farther south are a popular "little" wine.

The Penedés region near Barcelona produces light reds and whites but is best known as the home of *cava,* Spanish champagne. A Common Market agreement forbids Spanish vintners from labeling their wine *champaña,* so they call it *cava* for the limestone caves where the wine is stored. In Barcelona, *champañerías* (champagne bars), offering dozens of *cava* bottlings, are in vogue. In the apple growing area of Asturias, *sidra* — dry, sparkling hard cider, quaffed in a restaurant or in a *sidrería* (cider bar) — is the "wine" of choice, especially when downed with the local *fabada asturiana* (bean and sausage stew). Ice-cold *cerveza* (beer) is popular everywhere, as is mineral water: *agua con gas* (sparkling), or *sin gas* (without bubbles).

Spain's dining hours can be troublesome to the visitor with only a few days to adjust to the late hours of the Mediterranean, but understanding Spain's flexible restaurant options makes it easier to cope. Spaniards begin their day with a cup of the richest, most flavorful coffee in Europe — *solo* (black) or *con leche* (with milk) — along with *panecillos* (rolls) or a thick slice of *pan* (bread). For a continental breakfast, order a *café completo,* which most hotels include in the room price. There's an extra charge for a bacon-and-eggs American-style *desayuno* (breakfast).

In mid-morning the working population stokes up on *tapas* or sweet rolls at the local bar. This staves off hunger until the *comida,* the leisurely main meal of the day, which begins at 2 PM and lasts at least 2 hours. On weekends, whole families — toddlers to grandparents — settle around big restaurant tables for the afternoon meal. Travelers on the go, however, can grab a quick lunch by dropping into a bar for a *bocadillo* (sandwich), a hard roll filled with selections from the *tapas* platters. *Cafeterías,* American-style coffee shops for malts, burgers, and sandwiches, are now prevalent in Spain, and *auto-servicios,* self-service places, are handy for fast, if perfunctory, fill-ups.

Afternoon tea (*merienda*) fills up the *pastelerías* (sweet shops) late in the day, and by 7 PM the after-work crowd is three deep at the *tapas* bar, tossing back a *fino* (dry sherry) or a *caña* (beer by the glass) and spearing tidbits from shared plates. *Tapas,* too time-consuming for the home cook, are restaurant fare in Spain.

La cena (dinner) completes the culinary day. Most restaurants start serving at 10 PM, though some, especially hotel dining rooms, open earlier to accommodate tourists. If anyone is wondering how the Spanish can eat so much yet stay so slim, the answer is that they can't — and don't. The convivial folks around the bar at 7 o'clock are probably making a meal out of *tapas* before going home to a light supper (a good ploy for travelers, too). The late-night restaurant crowd usually turns out to be a mix of friends out for the evening, businessmen entertaining clients, Spanish travelers, and foreign tourists.

Spanish restaurant menus are à la carte; both lunch and dinner offer the same choices. A typical menu might categorize its offerings like this: *Entremeses* (starters) — either *tapas*-like appetizers or soup, generally *sopa de ajo* (chunks of ham and hard-boiled egg in garlic-chicken broth) or a cold tomato gazpacho. A listing for *verduras y ensaladas* (vegetables and salads) will feature *patatas fritas* (French fries) and seasonal vegetables served family style, while *tortillas* can be found listed under *huevos* (eggs); they can come with a variety of fillings — *jamón* (ham), *gambas* (shrimp), *chorizo* (sausage), but a *tortilla española* will be filled with potatoes and onions, while a *tortilla francesa* is a plain omelette.

The entries listed under *pescados* (fish) may be hard to figure out because so many of the fish come exclusively from local waters. But diners will always find old standbys like *merluza* (hake), *salmonetes* (red mullet), *lenguado* (sole), *trucha* (trout), and either *chiperones* or *puntillitos* (both baby squid). Meat and poultry dishes are generally grouped together under *carne y ave* or *asados* (from the broiler). For beef, look for *filete, solomillo,* or *entrecote* (tender beef filets — the word *buey* for beef is understood). *Puerco* (pork) is Spain's most plentiful meat, so *lomo* (loin of pork) is often a good bet. Many *pollo* (chicken) and *ternera* (veal) choices are offered as well.

Postres (desserts) invariably feature *fruta del tiempo* (fresh fruit) and *frutas en alimbar* (home-style canned fruits in syrup); *helados* (ice creams); flan, a small round cushion of caramelized custard, or one of its even richer relations such as *tocino de cielo;* and *quesos* (cheeses), notably the aged sheep's milk, *manchego,* which, accompanied by *membrillo* (quince jelly), is often served for dessert. Some restaurants, particularly *parador* dining rooms, dress up dessert menus with cookies and candies made by local nuns. Despite the wealth of rich honey-, nut-, and egg-based sweets — or because of them — Spaniards often finish off big meals with plain *zumo de naranja* (orange juice).

To dine at reasonable cost, choose the fixed-price, three-course *menú del día,* which the law requires all eating places — from checkered tablecloth *1 tenedore* (one-fork) *mesones* to white-tablecloth *5 tenedores restaurantes* — to provide. These meals will cost less than the restaurant's comparable à la carte selections. The fork rating, by the way, is based on ambience, service, and the range of menu offerings, not on the quality of the food.

Though many regional specialties have become countrywide, even worldwide favorites, nothing can replace the mystique of eating regional food on its home ground. The local cooking of Castile is king, for example, even in cosmopolitan Madrid, which has its full share of regional and international restaurants. This is the place to sample *cocido madrileño,* a stick-to-the-ribs stew served in three courses — the broth, then the meats, then the vegetables. Madrid and surrounding towns are also famous for *lechazo* (baby milk-fed lamb) and *cochinillo* (suckling pig), spit-roasted to crispy perfection outside, while the meat underneath melts on the fork.

Barcelona, Catalonia's seaside capital, has the best *zarzuela de mariscos,* a seafood stew of shrimp, mussels, prawns, squid, crab, and clams in a tomato-saffron sauce. And a wonderful light lunch is a heaping platter of grilled or sautéed mussels, crayfish, shrimp, barnacles, and crab, accompanied by country bread rubbed with fresh tomato, garlic, and olive oil. But unless money is no object, don't order *langosta* (rock lobster) or *bogavante* (clawed lobster). Lobster is sky-high throughout Europe.

For another Catalan specialty, try *romesco de peix* (fish stew) with its piquant *romesco* sauce, thickened with ground almonds and bread crumbs, and order one of the typical Catalan meat and fruit combinations such as *filet de bou amb fruits sec* (tenderloin of beef with dried fruit). And for the intrepid, there's the local way with snails, as in *conejo con caracoles* (rabbit-snail stew). The dessert of choice is *crema catalana,* creamy custard beneath a caramelized sugar crust.

If there's one thing Spaniards agree on, it's respect for Basque cooking. The word *vasco* (Basque) crops up in restaurant names everywhere. Many of the best cooks (including the owner of the three-star *Zalacaín*) come from Basque Country, which is known for its hundreds of all-male, members-only cooking clubs. It's hard to go wrong in any San Sebastián restaurant. Try the local fisherman's soup, *marmitako,* made with bonito, potatoes, peppers, and tomatoes. Order *bacalao a la vizcaina,* salt cod baked with dried sweet peppers. (Northern Spain shares the Portuguese passion for salt cod.) And, for those who feel daring, there's the popular Basque appetizer *angulas* (match-stick baby eels in a garlic-olive marinade).

The luxuriant rice-paddy country travelers notice along the east-central coastline should signal Valencia, and a stop for paella. This communal pan of creamy short-grained saffron rice, crusty from a wood-burning fire, is served all over Spain in varying delectable combinations of seafood, sausage, poultry and vegetables. But the Valencians invented it. Purists among them will declare that without snails, it's not the real thing.

Maybe it's Andalusia's balmy outdoor dining that captures gourmet fancies. Perhaps it's *tapas*-hopping in Seville or sampling sherry in Jerez or cooling off with an icy pitcher of sangria laced with orange slices. The surprising variety in gazpacho alone is worth exploring: In Seville, it's the familiar tomato and cucumber soup; in Córdoba, *salmorejo,* a thick tomato purée; in Málaga, white garlic-almond broth with sweet seedless grapes.

Andalusia's *pescadito frito* (deep-fried fish) — greaseless frying is an art form here — and its potato chips sizzling in vats of olive oil right on the street are typical southern treats. Andalusians will crunch on anything, even piles of deep-fried thread-like *chanquetes* (tiny whitefish). As befits the birthplace of the *corrida,* Andalusia also serves up a rib-sticking *rabo de toro* (bull-tail stew). Hearty *habas con jamón* (casserole of lima beans and mountain ham) is especially good in spring, when the local beans are soft and sweet. And *urta a la roteña* (a fish called *urta,* unique to Andalusian waters, in a tomato and red pepper sauce) is also worth trying.

The adventure of dining in Spain can reveal itself in the humblest, least expected spots. A case in point is the local *churrería* — a place to stop for the universal treat of hot chocolate and *churros* (crullers). Best on a brisk evening but irresistible anytime except when it's really hot, the slender bread-stick-length crullers are deep-fried in vats, often in the shop window, and served warm with cups of rich, hot chocolate for dunking. Little wonder that simple snacks like this can slip into so many visitors' gastronomic pantheons.

THE CITIES

BARCELONA

Seeing a circle of men and women move in simple, slow steps to the music of flute and drum around a sun-drenched square on a Sunday afternoon provides an almost visceral understanding of Barcelona and its people. This regional dance, the *sardana* — once described by a poet as a dance "of people going forth holding hands" — is indicative of the sense of community and passion for music that is typical of Barcelona.

The *sardana* appears to happen spontaneously. People walking back from mass or a Sunday stroll begin to linger in the cathedral square. Seemingly from nowhere, a band gathers and begins to play what sounds like rhythmic dirges. People set aside purses, prayer books, and hymnals, then join hands to form large circles. Slowly, the circles revolve as the dancers step out the intricately counted measures on tiptoe, and soon they are caught up in the intensity of the music. They hold their hands high; some close their eyes. The music continues in melodic tones. Then, almost abruptly, the *sardana* is over. The dancers nod to their neighbors, gather up their belongings, and continue on their way home.

Witnessing this, you will see the soul of Barcelona, the strong communal feeling that tempers Catalonia's legendary individualism. Not only has Barcelona long been a great Mediterranean port and Spain's "Second City," but it also has long been the capital of the Catalan people, a stronghold of Catalan nationalism in more repressive times, the locus of Catalan representation vis-à-vis the government of Madrid in freer ones. There always has been a strong regional identity and pride here. After the death of Francisco Franco in 1975, the native Catalan language, no longer suppressed, quickly regained its place as the dominant one of the region. Streets and place names were changed back from Castilian to Catalan, and with the democratic constitution of King Juan Carlos, the region of Catalonia — encompassing the provinces of Barcelona, Gerona (Girona in Catalan), Lérida (Lleida), and Tarragona — was designated one of the country's 17 *comunidades autónomas* (autonomous communities).

Given its position across the Pyrenees from France, on the Mediterranean Sea south of the Costa Brava (literally, "wild coast"), Barcelona has a history and language that link it as much to France as to Spain. Catalan, the lilting language of the region, is derived from the French *langue d'oc,* or Provençal, and is spoken in French Catalonia as well.

The history of Barcelona dates back to 218 BC, when Hamilcar Barça, a powerful Carthaginian (and Hannibal's father), founded Barcino. The Romans developed the town, throwing up walls, parts of which can still can be seen. The Visigoths fought over it in the 5th century, the Moors in the 8th century, and in 801 it was the turn of Charlemagne, who included it in the Spanish March — a Frankish province serving as the dividing line between Christian Europe and Muslim Spain. During the 9th and 10th centuries, local lords, the Counts of Barcelona, became strong enough to establish their independence and drive the Moors from the lands to the south, and by 1100 Barcelona had dominion over all of Catalonia. When Ramón Berenguer IV, a 12th-century Count of Barcelona, married an Aragonese heiress and became King of Aragon, the city became the capital of the combined Catalonian and Aragonese kingdom. It grew to be a major force in the Mediterranean before it was assimilated into the new Spain of Ferdinand and Isabella at the end of the 15th century.

At one point, it was said that "every fish in the Mediterranean wore the red and yellow stripes of the kingdom led by Catalonia." Barcelona was a major Mediterranean power, a force whose might can be felt even today in the medieval streets of the city's old Gothic quarter, the Barri Gòtic. During the 1400s, Barcelona rivaled Genoa and Venice in Mediterranean trade. But although Columbus (Colón in Castilian, Colom in Catalan) sailed from here on his historic voyage, the discovery of the New World proved disastrous for Catalonia. As trade moved from east to west, Seville, Cádiz, and other Spanish ports on the Atlantic rose in importance, and Barcelona declined.

Thereafter, the question of Catalan autonomy became a consistent theme in Barcelona's history, and the city and region often picked the wrong team in making a stand against the rest of Spain. They rose up against the Spanish crown during the Thirty Years War in the 17th century and failed in an attempt to set up an independent nation. In the early 18th century, they backed the Hapsburgs in the War of the Spanish Succession, prompting the victorious Bourbons to put an end to what Catalonian autonomy remained. Only in the late 19th and early 20th centuries did Barcelona begin to recoup. Success in industry fostered a cultural revival — the *Renaixença* — and a newfound sense of Catalan identity. Architects such as Antoni Gaudí and his contemporaries designed and raised buildings of astonishing creativity in new city quarters — in fact, Barcelona was as much a center of Art Nouveau as Paris or Vienna, but here the style was called *modernisme.* Catalan and non-Catalan artists such as Joan Miró, Pablo Picasso, and Juan Gris, attracted by the city's life and color and the spirit of its people, made it a meeting place. Political radicalism flourished, and Barcelona became the capital of a short-lived autonomous Catalan government set up in 1932. Then, during the Spanish Civil War, it became the seat of the Republican government from November 1937 until its fall to Franco's Nationalists in January 1939.

Today, Barcelona, the most European of Spanish cities, is big, rich, and commercial. Catalans are famous throughout Spain for their business acumen, and young people seeking commercial advancement are drawn here from all parts of the Iberian Peninsula. Barcelona is the publishing and literary capital of Spain, as well as its major port and second-largest city (pop. 1,755,000). Government offices, boulevards, and fountains here are large and pompous exhibitions of civic pride; Catalans walk the city streets with a swagger and a confidence that boasts, "We are different, better educated, more culturally aware, and much better off than the rest of Spain." It is no coincidence that Barcelona has the highest literacy rate in Spain, and can claim to be the only city where the patron saint's day is celebrated with gifts of books to friends. "There's a bookshop and a bank on every block," they claim, and bellhops and shoeshine boys often are buried in books that on closer inspection turn out to be French, German, or English classics, rather than Spanish mystery novels.

The seaport atmosphere is felt throughout the city, but it is most apparent in the area closest to the waterfront. With all the charms of the rest of the city, the harbor remains a focal point: a place to watch the comings and goings of cruise ships and tankers; to hire motorboats or other pleasure craft for cruises along the coast; to photograph the 200-foot monument to Christopher Columbus or merely to be part of the bustle of the docks.

Barcelona has become a favored destination for Europeans who like their big cities to have more than just a cathedral and an art museum. Scores of good restaurants attest to the Barcelonan love of good food and the variety of the regional dishes. Chic designer fashion boutiques (the city police uniforms were designed by couturier Antoni Miró!) attract visitors, as do some of the finest modernist buildings in Europe, including not only the works of Gaudí but also the Palau de la Música Catalana, which attests to the Catalan love of music in this city where many people belong to choral societies and choirs, and the young usually join societies to learn regional dances such as the *sardana.*

Recent Catalan prosperity has restored the ancient, revamped the old, and forged the new. And it's third time lucky for the city that was turned down as host for both the 1924 and 1972 *Olympic Games,* as it readies itself to host the *1992 Summer Games.* In addition to being a feast of sport, the games have triggered a massive clean-up and rebuilding: Working class areas like Vall d'Hebron have new sports facilities, and the 200-acre formerly decayed waterfront has been transformed into the Olympic Village, and will remain as a living community after the world's athletes have left. In addition, the city is spending over $100 million on the construction of 20 new hotels and has built a new, $150 million terminal at El Prat Airport that is capable of handling over 12 million passengers a year. These and other multibillion-dollar projects, however, are not geared to the requirements of the *Olympics* alone, but are designed to be permanent, expanding the city's tourism and sports facilities for the post-*Olympic* 21st century, referred to locally as "Barcelona 2000."

But all the *Olympic*-inspired construction is hardly the essence of Barcelona. You'll realize this if you are fortunate enough to be walking through the Barri Gòtic some evening at dusk, and hear voices softly singing a medieval madrigal as though the spirits of the past were alive. Just pause and savor the moment: You will have found the true spirit of Barcelona.

BARCELONA AT-A-GLANCE

SEEING THE CITY: There are excellent panoramic views of Barcelona, its harbor, the foothills of the Pyrenees, and the Mediterranean from the top of Tibidabo, a 1,745-foot hill on the northwest edge of the city. Covered with pines, it's topped with an amusement park, a church that is lit up at night, and, to celebrate the upcoming *Olympics,* a needle-like 800-foot-tall telecommunications tower, symbolic of Barcelona's perception of itself as "the city of the future." To get to Tibidabo, take the *FFCC* train to Avinguda del Tibidabo, change to the *tramvia blau* (blue tram), and take it one stop to Peu del Funicular, where you can take the funicular to the *Tibidabo Amusement Park*. Check the park's opening hours with the tourist office before setting out, however, because it's not open every day and it closes fairly early. At other times (or if you're interested more in the view than the park anyway), do as the locals do and get off after the tram ride and walk across the square to the smart but pricey restaurant, *La Venta* (Plaça Dr. Andreu; phone: 212-6455). Or stop for drinks at one of the bars (the *Mirablau* has panoramic picture windows). At night, the lights of the city below create a spectacular sight.

SPECIAL PLACES: The city's oldest buildings of historic and artistic interest are located in the Barri Gòtic, the old medieval heart of Barcelona, an area that is crisscrossed by alleyways weaving among ancient palaces, churches, and apartment blocks. When the walls of the old city were pulled down during the 19th century, Barcelona expanded north and west into the Eixample (Ensanche in Castilian — literally "enlargement"), a grid pattern of wide streets and boulevards. Avinguda Diagonal and Gran Via de les Corts Catalanes, modern Barcelona's major streets, cut across this chessboard, which is the city's special pride because of the unparalleled late 19th- and early-20th-century architecture found here, including Gaudí's most interesting works. To the south of the Barri Gòtic and the Eixample is Montjuïc, called the "Hill of the Jews" because a Jewish cemetery once was located here. This is the city's playground, a sports and recreation area and the site of the *1992 Olympic* complex. Buildings put up to house exhibitions for the *1929 World's Fair* still scale its slopes, and at the summit, a huge castle overlooks the sea.

BARRI GÒTIC

Catedral de Barcelona – Barcelona's cathedral, dedicated to Santa Eulàlia, the 4th-century Barcelona-born martyr who is the city's patron saint, is an excellent example of Catalan Gothic architecture. It was begun in 1298 on the site of an 11th-century Romanesque cathedral that one of the Counts of Barcelona, Ramón Berenguer I, had founded to replace an even earlier church damaged by the Moors. It was largely finished in the mid-15th century, except for the façade and two towers, which were not constructed until the end of the 19th century, although they follow the original plans. The interior is laid out in classic Catalan Gothic form, with three aisles neatly engineered to produce an overall effect of grandeur and uplift. The church is comparatively light inside, with the flickering of thousands of votive candles adding a cheery note, and on the saint's day, February 12, it is full of flowers.

In the enclosed choir are beautifully carved 14th- and 15th-century wooden stalls; the coats of arms painted on them, dated 1518, belong to the Knights of the Golden Fleece, who met here that year. The Grand Master of the group, Holy Roman Emperor Charles V, included the Kings of Hungary, France, Portugal, Denmark, and Poland in this "club," and Henry VIII of England had a stall on the emperor's right. Note also the *trascoro,* the white marble choir screen that forms the back of the choir, beautifully carved in the 16th century with scenes from the saint's life. Her remains are in an impressive white alabaster tomb in the crypt, which is down the stairs in front of the massive High Altar. Also buried in the church are the founder of the Romanesque cathedral, Ramón Berenguer, and his wife, Almodis, in plush-covered caskets on the wall to the side of the High Altar (look up). The chapel of St. Benedict (the third one beyond the caskets) is among the more notable of many in the cathedral; it contains the nine-panel Altarpiece of the Transfiguration by the 15th-century Catalan artist, Bernat Martorell. The fourth chapel before the caskets houses another of the cathedral's treasures, the 15th-century polychrome tomb of St. Raymond of Penyafort. The adjoining cloister is a homey surprise. Reached through the cathedral, through the Santa Llúcia chapel, and through doors from the street, it is an oasis of greenery, full of palm trees and inhabited by numerous pigeons and a gaggle of geese who reside beside fountains and a pool. Off the cloister, in the chapter house, is the small *Museu de la Catedral,* containing, among other exhibits, *La Pietat,* a 15th-century painting on wood by Bartolomé Bermejo. The cathedral is open daily from 7:30 AM to 1:30 PM and from 4 to 7:30 PM; the museum is open from 11 PM to 1 PM. Admission charges to the enclosed choir and to the museum. Plaça de la Seu (phone: 315-3555).

Palau de la Generalitat (Palace of Government) – This 15th-century Gothic structure was the seat of the ancient Catalonian parliament and now houses the executive branch of Catalonia's autonomous government. Inside are a 15th-century Flamboyant Gothic chapel, the Chapel of St. George, with splendid 17th-century vaulting, the 16th-century Saló de Sant Jordi (St. George Room), in which the most important decisions of state have been handed down over the centuries, and other notable rooms. Unfortunately, this is a working building and is not at present open to the public, but arrangements can be made to see it, weekends only, by appointment. Contact the Protocolo (public relations) office. Plaça de Sant Jaume (phone: 301-8364).

Casa de la Ciutat (City Hall) – Like the Palau de la Generalitat across the square, this structure, also known as the Ajuntament, is another fine example of Gothic civil architecture. The façade on the square is 19th-century neo-classical, however. Walk along the Carrer de la Ciutat side to see the building's original 14th-century Flamboyant Gothic façade. Since this, too, is a working building and closed to the public, its interior, including the restored Saló del Consell de Cent (Chamber of the Council of One Hundred) and the Saló de Sesion (Session Chamber), can be seen on weekends and by appointment only. Plaça de Sant Jaume (phone: 302-4200).

Palau Reial Major (Great Royal Palace) – The former palace of the Counts of Barcelona, who later became the Kings of Aragon. Built in the 14th century, it actually is a complex of buildings, of which one large room, the Saló del Tinell, a magnificent banquet hall, is the nucleus. Legend has it that on his return from the New World, Christopher Columbus was presented to King Ferdinand and Queen Isabella here. The room is closed to the public unless there is a concert or exhibition; then it is worth the price of admission just to see it and the stylized painting of the Catholic Monarchs sitting on the palace's great steps, surrounded by the heroic Columbus and the American Indians he brought home on his return voyage. Plaça del Rei.

Museu d'Història de la Ciutat (Museum of City History) – The city's history museum, at the opposite end of Plaça del Rei, is housed in the Casa Clariana-Padellàs, a 16th-century Gothic merchant's house that actually was moved stone by stone from a nearby street and rebuilt on the present site. Begin a tour in the basement, where pathways thread through an actual excavated section of Roman Barcelona, past remains of houses, storerooms, columns, walls, and bits of mosaic pavement. Upstairs rooms contain paintings, furniture, and municipal memorabilia, including the 16th-century Gran Rellotge, one of the six clocks that have occupied the cathedral bell tower. The museum also incorporates part of the Palau Reial Major: that is, the 14th-century Capella de Santa Agata, which is bare except for the *Altarpiece of the Epiphany,* painted in 1465 by Jaume Huguet. Open Tuesdays through Saturdays from 9 AM to 8:30 PM, Sundays from 9 AM to 1:30 PM, and Mondays from 3:30 to 8:30 PM. Admission charge. Entrance on Carrer del Veguer (phone: 315-1111).

Museu Frederic Marès – Set up in another part of the Palau Reial Major, this is an important collection of medieval art, particularly medieval sculpture, donated to the city by the museum's namesake, a prominent local sculptor. The painted wooden religious statues, peculiar to this part of Spain, are outstanding. On the upper floors, a display of artifacts ranging from costumes and combs to pipes and purses invites visitors to discover what everyday life was like in old Catalonia. Open Tuesdays through Saturdays from 9 AM to 2 PM and from 4 to 7 PM, open mornings only on Sundays; closed Mondays. Admission charge. 5-6 Plaça de Sant Iu (phone: 325-5800).

Museu Picasso – Housed in the beautiful 15th-century Palau Agüilar, which is of nearly as much interest as the master's works, this is not strictly within the Barri Gòtic, although it's quite near. A lovely Gothic-Renaissance courtyard opens to the roof, surrounded by tiers of galleries arcaded with pointed arches and slender columns. Lithographs and early works from the artist's years in Málaga and Barcelona (1889–1905) constitute most of the collection, but there are a few special pieces. One is the large exhibition of 44 variations of *Las Meninas,* the famous Velázquez painting in Madrid's *Prado.* Also notice examples of Picasso's warm and unpretentious ceramic work, including brightly painted plates and jugs. Open Tuesdays through Sundays and holidays from 10 AM to 8 PM; closed Mondays. Admission charge. 15 Carrer de Montcada (phone: 319-6310).

Palau de la Música Catalana – Also not far from the Barri Gòtic, although very distant from it spiritually, this is quintessential modernism, the Catalan variation on the Art Nouveau theme. Designed by Lluís Domènech i Montaner and built from 1905-1908, this concert hall is every bit as colorful as anything designed by the more famous Gaudí, but it's also less bizarre and, therefore, in the opinion of many, more beautiful — Gaudí himself is said to have likened it to what heaven must be like. The interior of the auditorium, topped by a stained glass dome, covered with mosaics, and rife with ceramic rosettes, garlands, and winged pegasuses, can be seen only by attending a performance. Those not wishing or unable to get tickets can amble in with the crowd and admire the foyer, itself a lovely space full of brick pillars that rise to ceramic capitals decked with ceramic rosettes. There's an elegant bar in the middle adorned with more stained glass. In summer, when there are no concerts, don't fail to walk by the equally colorful exterior. Carrer d'Amadeu Vives (phone: 301-1104).

EIXAMPLE

Passeig de Gràcia – Running from Plaça de Catalunya to Plaça de Juan Carlos I, where it is cut off by Avinguda Diagonal, this is the widest boulevard in the grid-patterned enlargement that grew up in the 1860s and 1870s after Barcelona's old walls were torn down. Lined with boutiques, banks, hotels, cinemas, and art galleries, it links the Barri Gòtic to what once was the old village of Gràcia, and it provides a pleasant backdrop for a stroll. Characteristic of the street are the *fanals-banc,* combined lampposts and mosaic benches designed by the modernist architect Pere de Falqués and dating from 1900. Of much greater interest, however, are the modernist buildings located here, three of them in one block alone, between Carrer del Consell de Cent and Carrer d'Aragó, the so-called *mançana de la discórdia* or "block of discord." Locals, shocked by the clashing of avant-garde styles, gave it this nickname, a pun on the word *mançana,* which means both city block and apple — the reference to the mythological apple of discord is the sort of sophisticated joke Barcelonans enjoy.

Casa Lleó-Morera – On the corner of Passeig de Gràcia and Carrer del Consell de Cent, this is one of the three noteworthy modernist buildings occupying the "block of discord." Designed by Lluís Domènech i Montaner and built in 1905, at the peak of the Catalan modernist movement, it has stone balconies carved in flower designs and winged lions. The façade is monochromatic, but step across the street to see the ventilator on top, like an elaborate bonnet with a green, pink, and yellow flowered hat band. The ground floor is occupied by a *Loewe* boutique; upstairs the building houses the headquarters of the Patronat de Turisme. 35 Passeig de Gràcia.

Casa Amatller and Casa Batlló – Making up the remainder of the "block of discord," the Casa Amatller (41 Passeig de Gràcia) was designed by Josep Puig i Cadafalch in 1900 and has a Dutch look, with a stepped-gable front inlaid with tiles and green lacy shutters in its windows. It contrasts dramatically with its neighbor, the Casa Batlló (43 Passeig de Gràcia), which dates from 1904-1906 and is a typical design by Antoni Gaudí, the leader of the modernist movement. With mask-shape balconies, sensuous curves in stone and iron, and bits of broken tile in its upper levels, it's a fairy-tale abode looking for all the world as though it were inhabited by giant mice. Casa Amatller is a library, so it's possible to tiptoe in, but Casa Batlló is closed to the public.

Casa Milá – Only a short way up Passeig de Gràcia, this apartment house, dating from 1906-1910, is regarded as the classic example of Gaudí's modernist architecture. Popularly known as La Pedrera (the "stone quarry"), it seems to be making an almost sculptural attempt to distance itself from the harsh, square lines of its turn-of-the-century neighbors. Notice the intricately swirling ironwork of the balconies, the melting, "soft" sinuousness of the building's horizontal lines as it wraps around the corner. The famous roof terrace has more strange formations covering the chimneys and ventilators. Conducted tours of the rooftop take place Mondays through Fridays at 10 AM, 11 AM, and noon and at 4 and 9 PM; Saturdays at 10 AM, 11 AM, and noon only. There is no charge — just turn up. There is no elevator, but the 6 flights of stairs are worth the effort to see details of doorknobs and banisters en route. 91 Passeig de Gràcia (phone: 215-3398 or 319-7700).

Fundació Antoni Tàpies (Antoni Tàpies Foundation) – Along with the *Museu Picasso* and the *Fundació Joan Miró* on Montjuïc, this is Barcelona's third, and newest, museum dedicated to a single artist. Opened in 1990 in a refurbished 19th-century modernist building designed by Lluís Domènech i Montaner, it houses a major collection of the still-living Catalan artist's works — paintings, drawings, sculpture, assemblage, ceramics — previously stored in warehouses and in private collections, including his own. There is also a research library and space for shows by other contemporary artists, but perhaps the main attraction is the huge Tàpies sculpture of metal wire and tubing on the roof of the building, taking up the entire width of the façade and adding 40-plus feet to its height. It's called *Cloud and Chair,* and you may love this bizarre construction or hate it, but if you're walking along the street, near Passeig de Gràcia, you certainly won't fail to notice it. Open daily from 11 AM to 8 PM; closed Monday. Admission charge. 255 Carrer d'Aragó (phone: 487-0315).

Parc Güell – Constructed between 1900 and 1914, this originally was planned as a real estate development by Gaudí and his friend Count Eusebio Güell, a noted Barcelona industrialist and civic leader. Only two plots of this garden city ever were sold, however (one to Gaudí himself), and the city purchased the property in 1926. It now is a public park. Two gingerbread-style houses — entry pavilions intended as the porter's lodge and an office building — flank the entrance gate; between them a staircase sweeps up to a "hall" or "forest" of mock-classical columns that would have been the development's marketplace. They support a raised plaza covered with gravel and entirely edged with an undulating bench whose backrest is a mosaic quilt of colored ceramic tiles. This extraordinary outdoor space originally was meant to be a recreation center, which is more or less the function it serves today. Also within the park is the *Casa-Museu Gaudí* (Gaudí House-Museum), installed in the house in which the architect lived from 1906 to 1926 (it was designed by another architect, Francesc Berenguer); on display are personal objects, including his bed, and furniture designed by Gaudí and others — most interestingly, some of the original built-in closets from Casa Milá and a large sliding door from Casa Battló. The park is open during daylight hours; the museum is open from 10 AM to 2 PM and from 4 to 6 PM; closed Saturdays. Admission charge to the museum. Bus No. 24 up Passeig de Gràcia leads to the Carretera del Carmel entrance, which is close to the museum, and also not far from the main entrance (with pavilions) located at Carrer de Llarrad and Carrer d'Olot.

La Sagrada Familia (Church of the Holy Family) – Antoni Gaudí was killed in a tram accident in 1926 before he could complete this religious edifice, his most famous and controversial work. One of Spain's most extraordinary buildings (its full name is Temple Expiatori de la Sagrada Familia), it still is essentially a building site, unencumbered by a roof. Begun in 1884, the church originally was designed by Francisco del Villar in the neo-Gothic style. When Gaudí was commissioned to take over the project in 1891, he changed the design considerably. Of the two façades and eight towers that are complete, only the famous Nativity Façade, on the Carrer de Marina side, was finished when Gaudí died. Carved to suggest molten stone, it has four tall spires, blue-green stained glass windows, and a porch filled with sculpted figures, including the Virgin Mary, Joseph, and the infant Christ above the main portal. The Passion Façade, on the Carrer de Sardenya side, was begun in 1952. Still to come are a central dome, to rise more than 500 feet and represent Christ, along with several smaller domes representing the Virgin Mary and the Evangelists. Work continues slowly, and few expect the church's completion before the middle of the 21st century. Take the elevator (or the stairs) up the Nativity side to the dizzy heights of the spires for views of the city and close-ups of the amazing architectural details. Steps go even higher, but beware if you suffer from vertigo! The audiovisual show in the *Museu Monogràfic*, located in the crypt (which also was finished at the time of Gaudí's death), traces the history of the church, as do the architect's models. Open daily, June through August, from 8 AM to 9 PM; September through May, from 9 AM to 7 PM. Admission charge, plus an additional charge for the elevator (which keeps shorter operating hours than the site as a whole). Plaça de la Sagrada Familia; entrance on Carrer de Sardenya (phone: 255-0247).

MONTJUÏC

Fonts Lluminoses – These illuminated fountains, designed for the *1929 World's Fair,* look like Hollywood special effects. Colored lights play on jets of water that rise and fall to music broadcast by loudspeakers — all against a backdrop of the Palau Nacional, which was the Spanish pavilion for the same fair. It sounds like kitsch, but it's quite a show! The fountains are in operation in summer on Thursdays, Saturdays, and Sundays from 9 PM to midnight (with music from 10 to 11 PM), and in winter on Saturdays and Sundays from 8 to 11 PM (with music from 9 to 10 PM). No shows from January through March. Between Plaça d'Espanya and Montjuïc.

Poble Espanyol (Spanish Village) – Also built for the *1929 World's Fair* and revitalized (as is everything else in the city) for this year's *Olympics,* this is a 5-acre model village whose streets and squares are lined with examples of traditional buildings from every region of Spain, most of them re-creations of actual structures. There is a Plaza Mayor, a Calle de la Conquista, and a Plaza de la Iglesia, just as might be found in any Spanish town or city, and numerous restaurants, bars, and nightspots. A walk through "town" illustrates the diversity of Spanish architecture and offers a chance to see traditional artisans at work; their carvings, pottery, glass, leather, and metalworks are sold in the village's 35 shops. The grounds are open daily from 9 AM until the wee hours, closing at 2 AM Sundays and Mondays and at 4 AM the remaining days, but note that shops, restaurants, and other enterprises within the village keep their own, shorter hours. Admission charge. Avinguda del Marqués de Comillas (phone: 325-7866).

Museu d'Art de Catalunya (Museum of Catalonian Art) – The museum's home is the massive imitation Renaissance-baroque Palau Nacional that was the Spanish pavilion in the *1929 World's Fair.* It has been undergoing a complete remodeling of its interior, and currently only a small portion of the main treasures is on display in the one section that remains open. The rest of the msueum was closed at press time, and is expected to reopen after the *Summer Olympics.* Often referred to as "the *Prado* of Romanesque art," the museum contains a splendid collection of Romanesque panel paintings and sculpture, in addition to its chief treasure, a series of frescoes removed from small churches of the Pyrenees region. The museum also is renowned for its Gothic holdings, as well as for canvases by such greats as Velázquez, Zurbarán, and El Greco. Open from 9:30 AM to 2 PM; closed Mondays. No admission charge. Mirador del Palau, Parc de Montjuïc (phone: 223-1824).

Fundació Joan Miró (Joan Miró Foundation) – Set up in an ultramodern building designed by Josep Lluís Sert, the late Catalan architect, this is a light, airy tribute to Catalonia's surrealist master, who also was an outstanding sculptor and weaver, as his *Tapis de la Fundació* demonstrates. Numerous painted bronze sculptures are displayed on terraces of the museum's upper level; in the galleries are works in various styles and mediums, including a haunting *Self Portrait,* which the artist began in 1937 and did not finish until 1960. The museum hosts frequent special exhibitions, and also has a library and well-stocked art bookstore. Open Tuesdays through Saturdays, from 11 AM to 8 PM; Sundays and holidays, from 11 AM to 2:30 PM. Admission charge. Plaça Neptú, Parc de Montjuïc (phone: 329-1908).

Museu Arqueològic (Archaeological Museum) – Exhibits include relics found in the excavation of the Greco-Roman city of Empúries nearby, various jewels and miniatures, and other remnants of Spain's prehistoric cultures, as well as a fine collection of Greek, Carthaginian, and Roman statues and mosaics. Open Tuesdays through Saturdays, from 9:30 AM to 1 PM and from 4 to 7 PM; Sundays, from 9:30 AM to 1 PM; and holidays, from 10 AM to 2 PM. Admission charge. Carrer de Lleida (phone: 423-2149).

Anell Olímpic (Olympic Ring) – Montjuïc has been designated the principal site for this year's *Summer Olympics,* which are scheduled to take place from July 25 to August 9. The sports facilities within the *Olympic Ring* include the main, 70,000-seat *Estadi Olímpic* (Olympic Stadium), a complete restructuring of a stadium originally built for the *1929 World's Fair.* The opening and closing ceremonies and track and field events will be held here; tours begin at the Marathon Entrance between 10 AM and 3 PM on weekends (phone: 424-0508). Also within the ring are the new 17,000-seat domed *Palau d'Esports Sant Jordi* (St. George Sports Palace), by the Japanese architect Arata Isozaki; the *Piscines Municipals B. Picornell* (B. Picornell Municipal Pools), open-air pools with seating for 5,000; and baseball, rugby, and practice fields, all within walking distance of one another. There are numerous bicycle and jogging paths, too, and they are such popular exercise sites that it may seem the whole city is getting in shape for the *Olympics.*

Museu Militar (Military Museum) – From time immemorial there has been a fortress at the top of Montjuïc, and the castle occupying the spot today, built largely in the 17th century and expanded in the 18th, has been restored and pressed into service as a museum. The belvedere on the grounds provides stunning views of Barcelona — of the port below and across the city to Tibidabo. On display inside are military uniforms, toy soldiers, models of forts, and a collection of 17th- to 19th-century guns. The castle can be reached by road as well as aboard the Montjuïc *telèferic,* a cable car that takes over where the Montjuïc funicular leaves off (see *Getting Around*) and carries passengers up and over the *Parc d'Atraccions de Montjuïc* (Montjuïc Amusement Park) to the top of the mountain, where the castle, the belvedere, and a panoramic restaurant are located. The museum is open Tuesdays through Saturdays from 10 AM to 2 PM and from 4 to 7 PM, Sundays and holidays from 10 AM to 7 PM. Admission charge. The *telèferic* is in operation daily in summer, on Saturdays, Sundays, and holidays in winter. Parc de Montjuïc (phone: 329-8613).

ELSEWHERE

La Rambla – This is the city's favorite — and liveliest — promenade, brimming with activity. Originally a drainage channel, it runs from the harbor to Plaça de Catalunya, changing its name en route (Rambla dels Caputxins, Rambla de Sant Josep, Rambla de Canaletes, and so on). Traffic moves up one side and down the other, and in the middle is a wide, tree-lined pedestrian esplanade. A brisk 20-minute trot would cover it all, but the whole idea is to take it much more slowly, examining the flower stands, thumbing through the books at the book stalls, reading a favorite newspaper or magazine at a sidewalk café, or merely strolling and chatting with friends. Look for the sidewalk mosaic by Miró at the Plaça de Boquería; stroll to the nearby Mercat de Sant Josep (St. Joseph's market, better known as the Boquería); and be sure to visit the *Gran Teatre del Liceu,* one of the world's great opera houses, at the corner of La Rambla and Carrer de Sant Pau. The no-expenses-spared restoration confirms this as one of the world's largest and most majestic auditoriums. Tours are conducted September through June, Mondays through Fridays, from 11:30 AM to 12:15 PM. Admission charge. Also see Gaudí's first major work, the Palau Güell, 3 Carrer Nou de la Rambla (phone: 317-3974), a few steps off La Rambla and now serving as the *Museu de les Arts de l'Espectacle* (Museum of Theater Arts), open from 10 AM to 1 PM and from 5 AM to 7 PM; closed Sundays and holidays. Admission charge. Just off the port, the triangle between La Rambla and the Avinguda del Paral-lel, with its little alleyways, is known as the Barri Xinès, literally "Chinese district," but is actually the red-light district. These areas, however, are reputedly being cleaned up for the *Olmypics.*

The Waterfront – Barcelona's historic seagoing tradition has made it one of the most important cities on the Mediterranean, one that today serves as a nearly compulsory port of call for major international cruise ships. But its industrial waterfront only lately has been cleaned up and reclaimed for the pleasure of the people. The Moll de la Fusta, the quay where the Barri Gòtic meets the harbor, now boasts a pedestrian promenade, palm trees, and park benches, as well as several outdoor restaurants and bars known as *chiringuitos.* Most locals consider most of these restaurants too expensive to patronize, so just stop in for a drink.

Monument a Colom (Columbus Monument) – At the harbor end of the La Rambla, anchoring one end of the Moll de la Fusta, this is the tallest tribute in the world to the noted explorer. It was erected in 1886 and consists of a statue of Columbus standing atop an orb atop a pillar, pointing seaward. Take the elevator to the top floor for an extraordinary view. Open late June to late September from 9 AM to 9 PM daily; the rest of the year, open Tuesdays through Saturdays from 10 AM to 2 PM and from 3:30 to 6:30 PM; Sundays and holidays from 10 AM to 7 PM. Admission charge. Plaça Porta de la Pau.

Museu Marítim (Maritime Museum) – The old low, stone buildings with the gables behind the Columbus Monument are examples of medieval Catalan industrial architecture. They were built in the 14th century as the Drassanes Reials (Royal Shipyards); ships that carried the red-and-yellow Catalan flag to the far corners of the world were launched from these yards years before Columbus's bold discovery. Fittingly, the city's *Maritime Museum* now occupies the yards. On display are old maps and compasses, ships' figureheads, models of ancient fishing boats, freighters, and other vessels, and a full-size reproduction of the *Real,* the galley that was Don Juan de Austria's victorious flagship in the Battle of Lepanto in 1571. Open Tuesdays through Saturdays from 9:30 AM to 1 PM and from 4 to 7 PM; Sundays and holidays from 10 AM to 2 PM. 1 Plaça Porta de la Pau (phone: 301-1871).

Barceloneta – The lively "Little Barcelona" district is a long finger of land lying across Barcelona harbor, between the city and the Mediterranean. The Passeig Nacional, lined with bars and every kind of eating establishment imaginable, forms the area's waterfront promenade on the city side. Behind it, a grid of streets strung with laundry drying from balconies and encompassing a few leafy plazas stretches to the beach on the Mediterranean side, the Platja de la Barceloneta. The area is famous for its numerous tiny seafood restaurants — in summer, tables are put right on the beach and dining goes on into late evening. Somewhat to the north is Vall d'Hebron, a massive redevelopment zone that is the site of the new Olympic Village. To reach Barceloneta, walk all the way around the waterfront past the Moll d'Espanya, take the subway to the Barceloneta stop and walk from there, take any of several buses, or take the Barceloneta *teléferic.*

Parc de la Ciutadella – This open space was created just over 100 years ago for the *Universal Exhibition of 1888.* It's popular with Barcelonans, not just for the park itself, but for the added attractions such as the zoo (phone: 309-2500) and the Palau de la Ciutadella, which houses the Parlament de Catalunya. Next door is the *Museu d'Art Modern* (phone: 319-5728 or 310-6308), devoted to Catalan artists little known outside the region. The museum is open Tuesdays through Saturdays from 9 AM to 7:30 PM, Sundays until 2 PM, and Mondays from 3 to 7:30 PM. No admission charge. The zoo is open from 10 AM to 5:30 PM daily. Admission charge.

■**EXTRA SPECIAL:** The Sierra de Montserrat lies 40 miles (64 km) northwest of Barcelona, in the geographical and spiritual heart of Catalonia. The many legends that surround Montserrat, which inspired Wagner's opera *Parsifal,* undoubtedly arose from the strangely unreal appearance of these impressive mountain peaks. Tucked within is the Benedictine monastery whose Marian shrine has attracted pilgrims for over 700 years. *La Moreneta* (The Black Madonna), a polychrome statue of the Virgin Mary, represents the spiritual life of the province and is central to Catalan unity. Legend has it that St. Luke carved the statue and presented it to St. Peter in Barcelona in AD 50. Actually, the tall, slim carving dates from the 12th century. The Virgin sits impassively in a small chamber above the main altar of the monastery's basilica, accepting pilgrims' reverential kisses on her out-stretched right hand, which holds a sphere of the world. The basilica is open daily from 8 AM to 8 PM. No admission is charged, but a donation is welcome. The monastery's famous *Escolania,* a boys' choir claiming to be the oldest in the world, sings at 1 PM each Sunday and on special occasions. There is also a museum at the site, open daily from 10 AM to 2:30 PM and from 3:30 to 6 PM. Admission charge (phone: 835-0251). From the monastery, paths and funiculars lead to the Santa Cova, the cave where the statue is supposed to have been found, and to the isolated hermitages of Sant Miguel, Sant Joan, and Sant Jeroni. The belvedere at the latter, 4,061 feet above sea level, provides views that stretch from the Pyrenees to the Balearic Islands and are as breathtaking as they are vertiginous.

SOURCES AND RESOURCES

TOURIST INFORMATION: Brochures, maps, and general information are available from the Patronat Municipal de Turisme de Barcelona (Barcelona Tourist Bureau, 35 Passeig de Gràcia; phone: 215-4477), open Mondays through Fridays, from 9 AM to 2:30 PM and from 3:30 to 5:30 PM. There are also tourist information offices at 658 Gran Via de les Corts Catalanes (phone: 301-7443), open Mondays through Fridays from 9 AM to 7 PM and Saturdays until 2 PM; and in the Barri Gòtic (at the Ajuntament, Plaça de Sant Jaume; phone: 318-2525), open Mondays through Fridays from 9 AM to 9 PM, Saturdays until 2 PM. The informa-tion offices at the Moll de la Fusta (phone: 310-3716) and at Barcelona Sants Central Railway Station (phone: 250-2592) are both open daily from 8 AM to 8 PM, while the office at El Prat Airport international arrival hall (phone: 325-5829) is open Mondays through Saturdays from 9:30 AM to 8 PM, Sundays until 3 PM. The "Casacas Rojas," red-jacketed tourist guides who patrol popular areas such as the Barri Gòtic, the Passeig de Gràcia, and La Rambla, supply on-the-spot information from approximately mid-June to mid-September.

The US Consulate is at 33 Via Laietana (phone: 319-9550).

Local Coverage – The tourist offices provide good free maps and brochures. The weekly *Guía del Ocio* and monthly Barcelona city magazine, *Vivir en Barcelona,* both available at newsstands, provide comprehensive listings of museums, nightspots, restaurants, and other attractions, although not in English (the latter does include some information in English in high-season editions). Watch the news in English on TV3 during the summer. Alternatively, dial 010 for Barcelona Information, a telephone "what's on" service where English-speaking operators occasionally can be found.

TELEPHONE: The city code for Barcelona is 3. If calling from within Spain, dial 93 before the local number.

GETTING AROUND: Airport – Barcelona's airport for both domestic and international flights is El Prat (phone: 379-2762), located 7½ miles (12 km) southwest of the city, or about 30 minutes from downtown by taxi; the fare ranges from about $15 to $20. Trains run between the airport and Barcelona Sants Central Railway Station, connecting with the subway lines, every 20 minutes; the trip takes 15 minutes and the fare is approximately $1. *Iberia's* shuttle (*Puente Aereo*) has flights to and from Madrid every hour throughout the day. There is an *Iberia* office at 30 Passeig de Gràcia (phone for domestic reservations: 301-6800; for international reservations: 302-7656; for information: 301-3893).

Boat – Ferries operated by *Trasmediterránea* leave Barcelona for the Balearic Islands daily in summer, less frequently in winter. The company is located at 2 Via Laietana (phone: 319-8212); departures are from the Moll de Barcelona pier near the Columbus Monument. *Golondrinas,* or "swallow boats," making brief sightseeing jaunts in the harbor (out to the breakwater and back) depart from directly in front of the monument from 10 AM to 8 PM in summer and from 10:30 AM to 1 PM and from 3 to 5 PM in winter. The trip takes only about 15 minutes; buy the ticket from the office at the water's edge (phone: 310-0342).

Bus – Although more than 50 routes crisscross the city, the system is easy to use, since stops are marked with a map of each route that passes there. The best deal for the visitor is *Bus Cien,* the No. 100 bus that constantly circles around 12 well-known sites such as the cathedral, the Sagrada Familia, and so on. The flat-rate full-day ticket (bought on the bus) lets you get on and off as often as you like, and also entitles the bearer to a discount at museums ($3 for 1 day, $8.50 for 3 days, $12.50 for 5 days). The route operates only in high season, however, from approximately mid-June to mid-September. At other times, buy the 10-ride ticket (T-1, or Targeta Multiviatge) for 380 pesetas (about $3.50). It's valid on all buses as well as on the subway, the funicular to Montjuïc, and the *tramvia blau* (blue tram) to Tibidabo. (A T-2 ticket is good for the subway, the funicular, and the *tramvia blau,* but not for the bus.) Buy the ticket at the public transport kiosk in Plaça de Catalunya (where the *Guía del Transport Públic de Barcelona* also is available) or at any subway station. After boarding the bus (enter through the front doors), insert the ticket in the date-stamping machine. For city bus information, call 336-0000.

Long-distance domestic and international buses also serve the city. For information on tickets and departure points, phone 336-0000 or 241-1990.

Car Rental – Cars are useful for day trips outside Barcelona, but usually are more trouble than they are worth for touring within the city. All the major international and local car rental firms have offices at the airport.

Funiculars and Cable Cars – In addition to the funicular to Tibidabo (see *Seeing the City*), there is a funicular making the climb from the Paral-el subway stop up to Montjuïc, where it connects with the Montjuïc *telèferic,* a cable car that swings out over the *Montjuïc Amusement Park* and makes one interim stop before depositing passengers at the castle, belvedere, and restaurant at the top. The funicular, cable car, and amusement park are in operation daily in summer; in winter, only on Saturdays, Sundays, and holidays. Both the T-1 and T-2 tickets are valid on the funicular, but neither is valid on the cable car, which requires an extra fare. Another *telèferic* connects Barceloneta with Miramar, at the foot of Montjuïc, making an interim stop at the Torre de Jaume I on the Moll de Barcelona. The trip is a spectacular one across the harbor — passengers swing out over the cruise ships and hang over the water as though in a slow-moving airplane. Rides begin at 10 AM in summer and 11 AM in winter; T-1 and T-2 tickets are not valid.

Subway – A "Metro" sign indicates an entrance to Barcelona's modern, clean subway system. There are four lines (*L1, L3, L4,* and *L5*), all easy to use. Individual rides cost 65 pesetas (about 60¢), but the 10-ride ticket (T-2, or Targeta Multiviatge) is a better buy for multiple trips; it costs 325 pesetas (about $3) at any subway station, and is valid on the funicular to Montjuïc and the *tramvia blau* as well, but not on the buses.

Taxi – Taxis can be hailed while they cruise the streets or picked up at one of the numerous *paradas de taxi,* taxi ranks, throughout the city. For *Radio Taxi,* call 300-3811. During the day, *Lliure* or *Libre* in the window indicates that a cab is available; at night, a green light shines on the roof. The city is divided into various fare zones, and fares generally are moderate.

Train – Barcelona is served by trains operated by *RENFE* (Spanish National Railways) and by trains operated by *Ferrocarrils de la Generalitat de Catalunya* (*FFCC*). There are four railway stations, all undergoing long-term refurbishment as part of the *Olympic* face-lift. Local, national, and international departures constantly are being changed, so it is vital to check and double-check before any journey. The stations are Estació Central Barcelona Sants, at the end of Avinguda de Roma, the main station for long-distance trains; Estació de França, on Avinguda Marqués de l'Argentera; Estació Passeig de Gràcia, on Passeig de Gràcia at Carrer d'Aragó; and Estació Plaça de Catalunya. For fare and schedule information, contact *RENFE* at Barcelona Sants or call the 24-hour-a-day information service (phone: 490-0202).

LOCAL SERVICES: Dentist – Ask the US Consulate or your hotel concierge for recommendations.

Dry Cleaner – *Tintorería Guilera,* 10 Santa Rosa (phone: 218-9141).

Limousine Service – *International Limousine System,* 47 Ronda Sant Pere (phone: 229-1388; contact Miguel Regol Font).

Medical Emergency – *Hospital de la Santa Creu i de Sant Pau* (167 Sant Antonio María Claret; phone: 347-3133 or 348-1144); ambulance (phone: 311-2121 or 302-3333).

Messenger Service – *Mensajerías Barcelona Express,* 4 Carrer de Berlín (phone: 322-2222).

National/International Courier – *DHL International,* 332-334 Carrer de Entença (phone: 321-4561; for pickup, 321-7316).

Office Equipment Rental – *Rigau,* rents typewriters (Gran Via de les Corts Catalanes; phone: 318-7040); *Exit* rents audiovisual equipment (58 Carrer de Numancia; phone: 322-3166).

Pharmacy – *Farmacia Valls* (314 Carrer del Consell de Cent; phone: 317-1944). Pharmacies operate on a rotating basis 24 hours a day; check newspapers for listings.

Photocopies – There are photocopy shops all over town.

Post Office – Central de Correus, open weekdays from 8 AM to 10 PM; Saturdays from 9 AM to 2 PM; Sundays and holidays from 10 AM to noon. Plaça Antoni López (phone: 318-3831).

Secretary/Stenographer (English-Speaking) – *TEASA* (168 Carrer de Bailén; phone: 257-4709 or 257-3589; contact Carmen Trias); *OTAC* (45-47 Carrer de Sepúlveda; phone: 325-2546; contact José Luís Laborda).

Tailor – *Baleta,* 21 Passeig de Gràcia; phone: 301-0304).

Telex – Central de Correus, open 24 hours a day. Plaça Antoni López (phone: 318-3831).

Translator – *TEASA* (168 Carrer de Bailén; phone: 257-4709 or 257-3589; contact Carmen Trias); *OTAC* (45-47 Carrer de Sepúlveda; phone: 325-2546; contact José Luís Laborda); *Rosario Tauler de Canals* (50 Passeig de Sant Joan; phone: 301-7181).

Other – Convention facilities: *Palacio de Congresos* (Convention Center), at the Barcelona Fair Grounds, features every meeting and convention facility, including an auditorium that holds 1,200 (Av. María Cristina; phone: 423-3101). Convention information: *Barcelona Convention Bureau,* providing information for meetings and conventions at restaurants and historical sites around the city (35 Passeig de Gràcia; phone: 215-4477). Men's formalwear rental: *Trajes Etiqueta* (7 Plaça d'Adriá; phone: 201-9260); *Diagonal 523* (phone: 205-4956).

SPECIAL EVENTS: Although religious holidays and saints' days are occasions for numerous festivities in Barcelona, this year will be highlighted by the *1992 Summer Olympics* (see below). April 23 is the *Festa de Sant Jordi* (Feast of St. George), patron saint of Catalonia. Flower stands overflow with roses, and bookstalls on La Rambla are bustling, because this is the day for lovers, and its gifts are a flower and a book. Bonfires, fireworks, dancing, and revelry mark the nights before the feast days of *Sant Joan* (St. John) and *Sant Pere* (St. Peter), on June 23 and 28 respectively. On Thursdays from June through September, the Guardia Urbana (City Police) don scarlet tunics and white plumed helmets for a riding exhibition at 9 PM at the Pista Hipica La Fuxarda, Montjuïc. September 11 is Catalonia's national day, *La Diada,* while September 24 is the *Festa de la Mercè* (Feast of Our Lady of Mercy), honoring the city's patron saint; the week building up to it is fun, noisy, exhausting, full of folk dancing, fireworks displays, and general gaiety, which includes teams of men forming *castellers* (human pyramids). *Christmas* is heralded by the 2-week *Fira de Santa Llúcia,* when stalls selling greenery, decorations, gifts, and the figures for *Christmas* crèches, are set up in front of the cathedral and the Sagrada Familia. One of the traditional figures on sale strikes an impudent pose — to say the least.

■ **1992 Summer Olympics:** Barcelona has spent the past 3 years vigorously preparing itself for the *Summer Olympics.* From July 25 to August 9 the city will be bustling with activity, from archery, basketball, and badminton to equestrian competitions, judo, swimming, and yachting. The **Opening Ceremony** is on July 25 at the *Montjuïc Olympic Stadium.* **Closing Ceremonies** are set for August 9, at the *Montjuïc Olympic Stadium.*

Package Ticket Sales in the US are available through *Olson Travel World,* Olympic Division, PO Box 1992, El Segundo, CA 90245 (phone: 213-615-0711 or 800-US4-1992; fax: 213-640-1039).

MUSEUMS: Barcelonans love museums, and the city has many more to be proud of than those listed in *Special Places.*

Museu dels Autómates (Museum of Automatons) – A display of mechanical dolls and animals. Open only when the amusement park in which it is located is open: Thursdays and Fridays from noon to 2 PM and from 3 to 5:45 PM; Saturdays, Sundays, and holidays from noon to 3 PM and from 4 to 7:45 PM.

Admission charge to the park includes the museum. Parc del Tibidabo (phone: 211-7942).

Museu del Calçat Antic (Shoemakers' Museum) – Antique shoes, including 1st-century slave sandals and 3rd-century shepherd's footwear, and a collection of famous people's shoes. Open Tuesdays through Sundays and holidays from 11:30 AM to 2 PM. Admission charge. Plaça Sant Felip Neri (phone: 9302-2680).

Museu de la Ciència (Science Museum) – A popular, hands-on kind of place with changing exhibitions (e.g., "The Return of the Dinosaurs"); permanent rooms illustrating optics, the universe, mechanics, perception; and a planetarium. Open Tuesdays through Sundays and holidays from 10 AM to 8 PM. Admission charge. 55 Carrer Teodor Roviralta, off Avinguda del Tibidabo (phone: 212-6050).

Museu del Futbol Club Barcelona (Barcelona Soccer Museum) – Trophies and videos highlighting the local soccer club's illustrious history — one of the most popular attractions in town. Open Tuesdays through Fridays from 10 AM to 1 PM and from 4 to 6 PM, mornings only on Saturdays and holidays. Admission charge. *Estadi Camp Nou,* Carrer Arístides Maillol (phone: 330-9411).

Museu Monestir de Pedralbes (Pedralbes Monastery and Museum) – A 14th-century Gothic church known for stained glass windows, choir stalls, and an unusual 3-story cloister. Open Tuesdays through Sundays from 9:30 AM to 2 PM. No admission charge. 9 Baixada del Monestir (phone: 203-9282).

Museu de la Música – An odd collection of antique musical instruments. Open Tuesdays through Sundays from 9 AM to 2 PM. No admission charge. 373 Avinguda Diagonal (phone: 217-1157).

Museu Taurí (Museum of Bullfighting) – A collection of bullfighters' costumes — suits of light — and other memorabilia. Open daily from April through September from 10 AM to 1 PM and from 3:30 to 7 PM. Admission charge. 749 Gran Via de les Corts Catalanes (phone: 245-5803).

Palau Reial de Pedralbes (Pedralbes Royal Palace) – Mainly Italian antiques including fans, Murano chandeliers, and tapestries, housed in the former palace of Alfonso XIII; also a collection of ceramics (previously housed at the Palau Nacional on Montjuïc) is impressive for its range — from early Moorish and Catalan ware through 18th-century tiles and even contemporary designs. Open Tuesdays through Fridays from 10 AM to 1 PM and from 4 PM to 7 PM, Saturdays, Sundays, and holidays from 10 AM to 1:30 PM. No admission charge. 686 Avinguda Diagonal (phone: 203-7501).

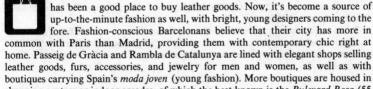

SHOPPING: Barcelona has been a textile center for centuries, and it always has been a good place to buy leather goods. Now, it's become a source of up-to-the-minute fashion as well, with bright, young designers coming to the fore. Fashion-conscious Barcelonans believe that their city has more in common with Paris than with Madrid, providing them with contemporary chic right at home. Passeig de Gràcia and Rambla de Catalunya are lined with elegant shops selling leather goods, furs, accessories, and jewelry for men and women, as well as with boutiques carrying Spain's *moda joven* (young fashion). More boutiques are housed in shopping centers or indoor arcades, of which the best known is the *Bulevard Rosa* (55 Passeig de Gràcia), which has shops selling everything from clothing and hats to unusual jewelry and paper goods. Also located here is the government-sponsored *Centre Permanent d'Artesania* (phone: 215-7178 or 215-5814), where changing exhibitions of crafts by contemporary Catalan artists and artisans are held. What's on display is for sale, although it can't be taken away until the show closes. For crafts, however, don't fail to visit the *Poble Espanyol,* the model village on Montjuïc, where there are some 35 stores featuring pottery, carvings, glassware, leather goods, and other typical folk crafts made by artisans from every region of Spain. Also visit the Ribera-El Born quarter around the *Picasso Museum* on Carrer de Montcada, known as the artists' and craftsmen's quarter. There are two *El Corte Inglés* stores (Plaça de Catalunya; phone: 301-3256; and 617 Avinguda Diagonal; phone: 322-0012). Part of the Spain-wide department store chain, they're known for quality in everything from Lladró porcelain and leather gloves to other clothing, records, and books; best of all, they are open during the long Spanish lunch hour. In general, department stores are open from 10 AM to 8:30 PM; smaller shops close between 2 and 4:30 PM. All are closed — the sign says *Tancat* in Catalan — on Sundays.

As for the markets, a visit to at least one is a colorful must, whether the daily *Boquería* food market just off La Rambla, where the fresh, tempting produce puts big city supermarkets to shame, or one of the weekly meeting places for enthusiasts of coins, stamps, or bric-a-brac. Bargain hard at *Els Encants*, the flea market at Plaça de les Glòries Catalanes (Mondays, Wednesdays, Fridays, and Saturdays, dawn until dusk); spend Sunday mornings in Plaça Reial among the stamp and coin collectors (10 AM to 2 PM) or at Ronda Sant Antoni, leafing through old books (10 AM to 2 PM.) Plaça del Pi hosts an antiques market on Thursdays from 9 AM to 8 PM.

Artespanya – A high-quality choice of Spanish crafts, from handmade glass to tables and chairs. 75 Rambla de Catalunya (phone: 215-2939).

Adolfo Domínguez – Menswear from one of Spain's internationally recognized designers. 89 Passeig de Gràcia (phone: 215-7638).

Camper – Women's shoes and handbags, the latest in styles and colors. 248 Carrer Muntanyer (phone: 201-3188).

Francesc Tasies i Ginesta – Handmade rope-soled espadrilles; an old-fashioned craft brought up to date by the use of contemporary colors and designs. 7 Carrer d'Avinyó (phone: 301-0172).

Groc – The second-floor salon where trendy designer Tony Miró sells his chic and expensive ladies' evening and daywear. Will make-to-order in 15 days, but 20% is added to ready-to-wear prices. 103 Rambla de Catalunya (phone: 216-0089).

Jean Pierre Bua – Fashion by young designers, from Catalunya and elsewhere in Europe. Look for Roser Marcé's "modern classics" for men and women. 469 Avinguda Diagonal (phone: 439-7100).

Jorge Juan – Well-priced women's shoes and handbags in distinctive designs. 125 Rambla de Catalunya (phone: 217-0840).

Loewe – A branch of Spain's best-known and most expensive purveyor of fine leather goods. 35 Passeig de Gràcia (phone: 216-0400).

Matrícula – The latest in men's and women's clothing and accessories from Yamamoto and Rifat Ozbek, among other names. 12 Carrer del Tenor Viñas (phone: 201-9706).

Margarita Nuez – Elegant women's clothing in the finest fabrics. 3 Carrer de Josep Bertránd (phone: 200-8400).

Tema – Fashions by Spanish designers Manuel Piña, Jesus del Pozo, and Jorge Gonsalves (a favorite of Queen Sofía). 10 Carrer Ferrán Agulló (phone: 209-5165).

Trau – Where society girls go for posh glad rags. 6 Carrer Ferrán Agulló (phone: 201-3268).

2 Bis – Amusing "popular art" pieces, including overweight terra cotta bathing beauties and papier-mâché infantas; also, some serious glassware and plates. Near the cathedral, at 2 Carrer del Bisbe (phone: 315-0954).

Vigares – A small, but good selection of leather goods at tempting prices (including riding boots for not much more than $100). 16 Carrer de Balmes (phone: 317-5898).

 SPORTS AND FITNESS: For the last few years, Barcelona has been busy preparing for its role as host to the *1992 Summer Olympic Games* (see *Special Events*), and at press time, more than 100,000 volunteers from all over Spain were busy assisting the Barcelona Olympic Organizing Committee in its task. But the city already boasted many major facilities, including the 120,000-

seat *Camp Nou Stadium,* Europe's largest, and the *B. Picornell Municipal Pools* on Montjuïc, before construction of the new *Olympic Ring* facilities began. Other possibilities for the sports-minded include the following:

Bullfighting – Catalans claim to abhor bullfighting and, in fact, most of the spectators in the arena are Spaniards who have moved to the area — or tourists. The gigantic *Plaça Monumental* (Gran Via de les Corts Catalanes) has fights on Sundays from April to late September at 5 PM (6 PM if it's very hot). Additional fights are on Thursdays in August. Advance tickets are available at 24 Gran Via de les Corts Catalanes, at the corner of Carrer d'Aribau (phone: 245-5803). The city's other bullring, *Les Arenes,* at the other end of the same avenue, is now used for pop shows and exhibitions.

Fitness Centers – *Squash Diagonal* (193 Carrer de Roger de Flor; phone: 258-0809) has a pool, sauna, and gym, in addition to squash courts. *Sport Dyr* (388 Carrer de Castillejos; phone: 255-4949) has four gyms, including weight room, sauna, and massage. A gym for women only (2 Avinguda de Roma; phone: 325-8100) also offers a sauna, a swimming pool, and a solarium, as well as aerobics sessions and beauty treatments.

Golf – There are several golf courses around Barcelona, including the *Real Club de Golf El Prat* (10 miles/16 km southwest of town near the airport; phone: 379-0278), which is the best course, used by the European pro tour; *Club de Golf Sant Cugat* (Sant Cugat del Vallès 12½ miles/20 km away and hard to find in the hilly suburbs to the west; phone: 674-3908); and *Club de Golf Vallromanes* (15½ miles/25 km along the Masnou-Granollers road; phone: 568-0362).

Jogging – Parc de la Ciutadella, near the center of town, has a good track. The paths surrounding Montjuïc also are popular jogging spots.

Soccer – The *Olympics* notwithstanding, soccer is the major passion. The *Futbol Club (F.C.) Barcelona* embodies the spirit of Catalonia, especially when the opponent is longtime rival *Real Madrid.* The world's greatest stars are signed up to play for the club, and infants are enrolled as club members from birth. More than 120,000 fans regularly attend home games, played at the *Estadi Camp Nou* (Camp Nou Stadium), which also will host the *Olympics* soccer final. *Espanyol,* the other, less popular, "major league" club in town, plays at *Sarrìa Stadium.*

Swimming – Take a dip in the waters that will host the *Olympic* swimming events at *Piscines Municipals B. Picornell* (on Montjuïc, near the main stadium; phone: 325-9281). Although the locals go to Barceloneta to the beach, the water is really rather polluted and it's not recommended to swim near the city.

Tennis – Courts may be available at the *Real Club de Tenis Barcelona* (5 Carrer de Bosch i Gimpera; phone: 203-7758) or *Real Club de Tenis de Turó* (673 Avinguda Diagonal; phone: 203-8012).

 THEATER: The city has a strong theatrical tradition in Catalan, but it still embraces foreign playwrights such as Shakespeare and Chekhov. At the *Teatre Lliure* (Free Theater; Carrer Leopold Alas; phone: 218-9251), Fabia Puigserver's cooperative troupe is so dynamic that language is no barrier when the works are familiar. Another Catalan troupe, the *Companiya Flotats,* led by Josep María Flotats, whose repertoire tends to be lighter, though still socially aware, has moved into the new national theater, part of the Plaça de les Arts complex which has been built near the Plaça de les Glòries Catalanes. Experimental theater can be seen in the impressive *Mercat de les Flors* (59 Carrer de Lleida; phone: 426-1875), the old Flower Hall built on Montjuïc for the *1929 World's Fair.* Higher up the hill, the *Teatre Grec* (phone: 243-0062), an open-air amphitheater, hosts a festival every June and July, with classic Greek tragedies and other works. Popular musicals and vaudeville-type shows are at the *Apolo* (59 Avinguda del Paral-lel; phone: 241-4006) and the *Victoria* (65 Avinguda del Paral-lel; phone: 241-3985). The sporting side of the *Olympics* begins this summer, but Barcelona began preparing the cultural calendar back in 1988. Many companies from around the world are making an appearance. The *Gran Teatre del Liceu* (facing La Rambla with the box office at 1 Carrer de Sant Pau; phone: 318-9122) hosts opera and ballet with international stars as well as local favorite Montserrat Caballé (for more information, see *Special Places*).

MUSIC: Barcelona is a music center year-round. From November through May, opera and ballet dominate, but there is a festival of some sort every month, from medieval music in May to the *International Music Festival* in October. Two new concert halls have been built in the Plaça de les Arts complex, located near Plaça de les Glòries Catalanes. The *Palau de la Música Catalana* (just off Via Laietana, at the corner of Carrer de Sant Pere Mès Alt and Carrer d'Amadeu Vives; phone: 301-1104) is a gem of Art Nouveau style by architect Lluís Domènech i Montaner. The *Orquestra Ciutat de Barcelona* (Barcelona Municipal Orchestra) can be heard here, among other groups.

NIGHTCLUBS AND NIGHTLIFE: Barcelona has plenty of action, but beware while roaming through the most popular after-dark centers, since the city also has its share of muggers and purse snatchers. Be wary of thieves on motorcycles and minibikes, who snatch purses from pedestrians and out of cars parked or stopped at traffic signals. The city's pubs, bars, and cafés begin to fill up between 10 and 11 PM, but these establishments merely serve as a warm-up for the clubs and discotheques, which open even later and only kick into high gear at 1 or 2 AM. A Las Vegas–style nightclub, *Scala Barcelona* (47 Passeig de Sant Joan; phone: 232-6363) presents elaborate dinner shows and dancing. For flamenco, try *El Cordobés* (35 Rambla; phone: 317-6653), *Andalucía* (27 Rambla; phone: 302-2009), and *El Patio Andaluz* (242 Carrer d'Aribau; phone: 209-3375). Shows are continuous from 10 PM to 3 AM, but really get going after midnight, when the performers and the audiences are warmed up. Popular discotheques include *Bikini,* which features rock and Latin beats (571 Avinguda Diagonal; phone: 230-5134); the *Up and Down,* with loud music downstairs and a restaurant and a more "sophisticated" club upstairs (179 Carrer de Numancia; phone: 204-8809); and *Studio 54,* a weekends-only favorite, boasting lots of elbow room and the best light show in town (64 Avinguda del Paral-el; phone: 329-5454). For hot jazz, try the live jams at *La Cova del Drac* (30 Carrer de Tuset, phone: 216-5642). The *Gran Casino de Barcelona* (Sant Pere de Ribes, 26 miles/42 km from the city near the seaside town of Sitges; phone: 893-3666). You have to be over 18, with a passport for identification, to enjoy the dining and gambling in a 19th-century setting.

BEST IN TOWN

CHECKING IN: Barcelona always has been short on hotel space; not surprisingly, the drive has been to double the number of beds available in time for the this year's *Summer Olympics.* Five thousand new hotel rooms have been added to the city's previous 14,000-room-plus hotel capacity. These are meant not only to accommodate *Olympics* visitors, but also to serve as permanent expansions that will meet the demands of tourism into the 21st century. The *Arts* hotel, a brand-new establishment managed by the Ritz-Carlton Company is opening in May in the Olympic Village area on the waterfront, and will offer every imaginable amenity. In an already noisy city, the sounds of *Olympic*-inspired construction have become an added intrusion, so ask for a quiet room. Note that with the *Olympics* in town, prices are rocketing. Expect to pay more than $350 a night for a double room at a hotel listed below as very expensive (a category that, in Barcelona, includes only the *Ritz* — not to be confused with the aforementioned Ritz-Carlton–managed property), between $150 and $250 for a double room at a hotel listed as expensive, $100 to $130 at one listed moderate, and less than $100 at an inexpensive hotel. All telephone numbers are in the 3 city code unless otherwise indicated.

Ritz – Built in 1919, this deluxe aristocrat boasts a new face, and once again lives up to its reputation for superb service in an elegant, charming atmosphere. A favorite meeting place — especially during afternoon tea, which is served in the lounge with a string quartet softly playing — this is the hotel of choice of many international celebrities. All 314 rooms have high ceilings and air conditioning. There also is a fine restaurant. Amenities include 24-hour room service; 8 meeting rooms that hold from 20 to 500 people; an English-speaking concierge; foreign currency exchange; English-speaking secretarial services; audiovisual equipment; photocopiers; a translation service; and express checkout. 668 Gran Via de les Corts Catalanes (phone: 318-5200; fax: 378-0148; telex: 52739 RITZOTEL). Very expensive.

Almirante – This small, modern hostelry is in the center of the city near the cathedral. There are 80 oversize rooms with luxury bathrooms and TV sets. Amenities include 24-hour room service; 6 meeting rooms for up to 80; an English-speaking concierge; foreign currency exchange; English-speaking secretarial services; a photocopier; and translation services. 42 Via Laietana (phone: 319-9500). Expensive.

Avenida Palace – Polished brass and fancy carpets lend a tasteful, Old World atmosphere to this deluxe property. The 229 rooms are air conditioned, cheerful, and quiet, with color television sets and mini-bars. The public areas are adorned with sedate paintings, fine reproductions, and interesting antiques. There is a gymnasium and a sauna; 5 meeting rooms that hold up to 300; an English-speaking concierge; foreign currency exchange; English-speaking secretarial services; audiovisual equipment; photocopiers; computers; translation services; 24-hour room service; and express checkout. The staff is well trained and extremely attentive. 605 Gran Via de les Corts Catalanes (phone: 301-9600; fax: 318-1234; telex: 54734 APTEL E). Expensive.

Barcelona Hilton – Relatively new, with 300 rooms, including several executive floors, of which one is reserved exclusively for women. The business center with 15 meeting rooms for up to 1,000, English-speaking concierge, foreign currency exchange, English-speaking secretarial services, audiovisual equipment, photocopiers, computers, translation services, plus the health club all confirm that this is aimed at the business market. There also is 24-hour room service and express checkout. 589 Avinguda Diagonal (phone: 410-7499; fax: 322-5291; telex: 99623). Expensive.

Calderón – Another longtime Barcelona favorite with the business crowd, but with a bright new image. The generously proportioned 244 rooms are air conditioned, and most have been equipped with the conveniences and services frequent business travelers expect. There are 10 meeting rooms; an English-speaking concierge; foreign currency exchange; English-speaking secretarial services; audiovisual equipment; photocopiers; translation services; and express checkout. The rooftop swimming pool, sauna, and sun terrace command a splendid view of the city. 26 Rambla de Catalunya (phone: 301-0000; fax: 317-3157; telex: 99529 or 51549). Expensive.

Colón – A recently renovated old favorite in the Barri Gòtic, right in front of the cathedral. Clean, pleasantly decorated, it has 166 air conditioned, high-ceilinged rooms, including 10 on the sixth floor with terraces (3 of these — two doubles and a single — face the cathedral). Amenities include 24-hour room service; 1 meeting room for up to 100 people; an English-speaking concierge; foreign currency exchange; and translation services. 7 Avinguda de la Catedral (phone: 301-1404; fax: 317-2915; telex: 52654, callback COLONOTEL). Expensive.

Condes de Barcelona – Modernist outside and modern inside, it's in a striking Art Nouveau building that was transformed into a luxury hotel in the mid-1980s, and proved so popular that it is already undergoing an expansion. The 180 air conditioned rooms and suites contain all the expected amenities. Its location in the heart of the Eixample is ideal, the *Brasserie Condal* restaurant, excellent. There are 5 meeting rooms with a capacity of 20 to 225 people; an English-speaking concierge; foreign currency exchange; English-speaking secretarial services; audiovisual equipment; photocopiers; and translation services. 75 Passeig de Gràcia (phone: 487-3737; fax: 216-0835; telex: 51531). Expensive.

Derby – Older sister to the *Gran Derby,* this is an elegant establishment done up in hushed colors, with diffused lighting and impressive wood trim and ornamentation. The 116 air conditioned rooms have private baths; those on the top floor have large terraces. There are 3 meeting rooms for up to 50 people; an English-speaking concierge; foreign currency exchange; English-speaking secretarial services; a photocopier; and translation services. The intimate piano bar adds an extra special touch. Affiliated with Best Western. 21 Carrer de Loreto (phone: 322-3215; fax: 410-0862; telex: 97429 DEHO). Expensive.

Diplomatic – Dedicated to businesspeople with its excellent conference facilities, this modern 213-room establishment is conveniently located near the Pedrera and the Passeig de Gràcia shops. There is 24-hour room service, 5 meeting rooms that hold up to 500 people; an English-speaking concierge; foreign currency exchange; English-speaking secretarial services; audiovisual equipment, photocopiers; computers; translation services; and express checkout. 122 Pau Claris (phone: 317-3100; fax: 318-6531; telex: 54701, callback DIPLOTEL). Expensive.

Duques de Bergara – Stepping into the foyer, you'll find yourself 100 years back in time. Marble floors, pillars, cut-glass mirrors, and molded ceilings make this a charming hotel, located next to the Plaça de Catalunya. The 56 rooms are modern and stylish. Amenities include 24-hour room service; 2 meeting rooms; an English-speaking concierge; foreign currency exchange; English-speaking secretarial services; and photocopiers. 11 Bergara (phone: 301-5151; fax: 317-3442; telex: 98717 APHO-E). Expensive.

Gran Derby – An apartment hotel, with 43 air conditioned suites and duplexes, each containing a sitting room, color television set, bar, and refrigerator. Facilities include 4 meeting rooms seating up to 100; an English-speaking concierge; foreign currency exchange; English-speaking secretarial services; photocopiers; computers; and translation services. The very fashionable marble decor and the helpful staff make up for a somewhat inconvenient location away from the city center. 28 Carrer de Loreto. (phone: 322-2062; fax: 410-0862; telex: 97429 DEHO). Expensive.

Majestic – A Barcelona classic affiliated with Best Western, with 335 air conditioned rooms endowed with color television sets, in-room English-language movies, built-in hair dryers, and mini-bars. There also is a gymnasium, sauna, and rooftop swimming pool, plus 24-hour room service; 9 meeting rooms; an English-speaking concierge; foreign currency exchange; English-speaking secretarial services; audiovisual equipment; and photocopiers. The location, in the heart of the Eixample (opposite the *Condes de Barcelona*), amid restaurants, shops, and Art Nouveau buildings, couldn't be better. 70 Passeig de Gràcia (phone: 215-4512; fax: 215-7773; telex: 52211, callback MAJESTICOTEL). Expensive.

Meliá Barcelona Sarrià – Near Plaça de Francesc Macià, this is a favorite with businesspeople. All 312 rooms are air conditioned and have king-size beds. The executive Piso Real floor features its own concierge. There is 24-hour room service; 9 meeting rooms; an English-speaking concierge; foreign currency exchange; English-speaking secretarial services; audiovisual equipment; photocopiers; and translation services. 50 Avinguda de Sarrìa (phone: 410-6060; fax: 321-5179; telex: 51033 or 51638 HMBS, callback MELIA BARNA). Expensive.

Presidente – Recently renovated, this 161-room modern, luxury establishment is located away from the center of town but is, nevertheless, busy with businesspeople, film stars, and personalities. There is 24-hour room service; 3 meeting rooms holding up to 150; an English-speaking concierge; foreign currency exchange; English-speaking secretarial services; audiovisual equipment; photocopiers; and translation services. 570 Avinguda Diagonal (phone: 200-2111; fax: 209-5106; telex: 52180, callback HUSA). Expensive.

Princesa Sofía – Big, bustling, and modern, this convention-oriented hotel has an indoor swimming pool, a gym, a sauna, and restaurants. It could be anywhere in the world, but is out near the university and the *Camp Nou Stadium*. The 514 air conditioned rooms, decorated in contemporary style, have large, tile bathrooms, direct-dial telephones, color television sets, and mini-bars. Other amenities include 24-hour room service; 28 meeting rooms; an English-speaking concierge; foreign currency exchange; English-speaking secretarial services; audiovisual equipment; photocopiers; computers; translation services; and express checkout. Plaça de Pius XII (phone: 330-7111; fax: 330-7621; telex: 51683 or 51032). Expensive.

Ramada Renaissance – Previously the grand old *Manila* and now upgraded to a big (210-room), imposing member of the international group, providing expected standards of comfort and service including 24-hour room service; an English-speaking concierge; foreign currency exchange; English-speaking secretarial services; audiovisual equipment; photocopiers; computers in its business center; translation services; 10 meeting rooms; and express checkout; the Renaissance Club rooms on the top 4 floors are the top accommodations, featuring Minitel computer terminals. Ideally located near the Barri Gòtic, it has 2 restaurants. 111 Rambla (phone: 318-6200). Expensive.

Regente – This gem among Barcelona's smaller establishments is located on a quiet extension of La Rambla. The 78 rooms are comfortable, with private baths and color television sets, as well as smartly decorated: Door handles, wall panels, windows, and other fixtures reflect an Art Nouveau affinity. Facilities include a rooftop pool, a meeting room for up to 120; an English-speaking concierge; foreign currency exchange; English-speaking secretarial services; photocopier; private garage; and a cozy bar. 76 Rambla de Catalunya (phone: 215-2570; fax: 487-3227; telex: 51939). Expensive.

Gala Placidia – An economical apartment complex, it has 28 suites with sitting rooms (fireplaces, too), dining areas, and refrigerators, in addition to the small bedrooms. 112 Via Augusta (phone: 217-8200; telex: 98820 HGPL). Moderate.

Oriente – Right on the Rambla, so reserve a room at the back. Built in 1842, with fancy public rooms, its Old World charm has worn a bit, but its central location just about compensates. 140 rooms. 45 Rambla (phone: 302-2558; fax: 412-3819; telex: 54134, callback LIHOTEL). Moderate.

Rialto – In the heart of the Barri Gòtic, this simple but stylish place has 128 rooms, all air conditioned. 42 Carrer de Ferrán (phone: 318-5212; fax: 315-3819; telex: 97206 ATT. H. RIALTO). Moderate.

Espanya – A budget hotel with an Art Nouveau dining room in a 19th-century building. It has antique plumbing, but it's clean, with 84 rooms on the edge of the Barri Gòtic. 9 Ronda de Sant Pau (phone: 318-1758; telex: 50574). Inexpensive.

Gaudí – Renovated and rather bare, but handy for Montjuïc, the port, and the Barri

Gòtic. There are 71 rooms; those on the top floor have great views of Montjuïc and the cathedral. 12 Carrer Nou de la Rambla (phone: 317-9032; telex: 98974 HGPL) Inexpensive.

EATING OUT: Catalans take pride in their regional cuisine, which is more sophisticated and closer to French cooking than that of the rest of Spain. Portions are generous and meals are quite frequent: Coffee and a pastry for breakfast, an omelette or a ham-and-cheese sandwich between 11 and noon, a late lunch, a round of *tapas* (see below) later in the day to take the edge off the appetite, and an even later dinner, beginning at 10 or 10:30 PM. (In the heat of summer, and on weekends, this could be 11 PM!) As Catalan self-pride has mushroomed, so have Catalan-style restaurants, exploiting the richness of the Mediterranean fish, as well as bountiful local orchards, fields, and vineyards inland. Try the *sarsuela,* a soup or stew of lobster, crayfish, squid, mussels, and whitefish of various types. The most basic Catalan dish is *escudella i carn d'olla,* a hearty stew of sausage, beans, meatballs, and spices. The ubiquitous caramel custard, *crema catalana,* made with eggs, milk, sugar, and cinnamon, usually concludes a meal. Check for the daily special — *menú del día,* usually a three-course meal with bread and wine — which restaurants are required to offer at a set price. Expect to pay $75 or more for a dinner for two in restaurants classified as expensive, $35 to $65 in the moderate range, and under $30 in the inexpensive places. *Note:* During the *Olympics,* some August closings may be waived. All telephone numbers are in the 3 city code unless otherwise indicated.

Agut d'Avinyó – A favorite for both lunch and dinner, this beautiful multilevel restaurant in the Barri Gòtic has whitewashed walls, oak plank floors, and antique furnishings. Its traditional Catalan food — especially the duck with figs — is excellent. The award-winning owner-hostess, Mercedes Giralt, lends her considerable charm to it all. Closed Sundays, *Holy Week,* and the month of August. Reservations necessary. Major credit cards accepted. 3 Carrer de la Trinitat (phone: 302-6034). Expensive.

Azulete – Imaginative international dishes are served here, and the house, with its gardens and fountain, is a delight. The dining room of this former mansion is actually a glass-enclosed garden, with tables arranged around a decorative pool, surrounded by lush vegetation. Specialties include tiny medallions of pork, crowned with mushroom purée, and broiled *lubina* (sea bass) with fresh dill. For dessert, try figs with strawberry-scented honey. Closed Saturdays at lunch, Sundays, holidays, the first 2 weeks in August, and from *Christmas* through *New Year's.* Reservations advised. Major credit cards accepted. 281 Via Augusta (phone: 203-5943). Expensive.

Beltxenea – When he opened it on the premises of the former *Ama Lur* restaurant, owner-chef Miguel Ezcurra was reviving the tradition of Basque cooking in Barcelona. His new approach to the typical dishes of northwest Spain makes a change from Catalan food. Fish in spicy sauce is a specialty. Closed Sundays, Saturday lunch, and *Easter.* Reservations necessary. Major credit cards accepted. 275 Carrer de Mallorca (phone: 215-3848). Expensive.

El Dorado Petit – Owner Luis Cruañas is a star in a city where eating is a serious pastime. Influenced by the simplicity of Italian cooking, he gave Catalan dishes a lighter touch, relying on the high quality of fresh, local produce. The result is a sophisticated restaurant, with dishes that constantly tempt even regular customers: delicate carrot and champagne soup; black rice, Palafrugell-style; rockfish filets with a tomato *coulis* and shallot vinaigrette; partridge stuffed with prunes and chestnuts; fresh roasted goose liver with sherry vinegar; all followed by homemade ice cream and petits fours. The Catalan white wines, rioja reds, and local sparkling *cavas* complement one of Spain's finest dining experiences. Closed August 8–27.

Reservations essential. Major credit cards accepted. 51 Carrer de Dolors Monserdá (phone: 204-5153). Expensive.

Florián – Rosa Grau cooks while her husband, Javier, minds the front, where pictures line the walls. Pasta with sea urchin sauce, ravioli stuffed with four cheeses, and red mullet with black olives are examples of Rosa's flair with local products. Closed Sundays, *Holy Week,* 2 weeks in August, and *Christmas.* Reservations necessary. Major credit cards accepted. 20 Carrer de Bertrán i Serra (phone: 212-4627). Expensive.

Jaume de Provença – Innovative chef Jaume Bargues reacts well to what's available at the market. Frequent specialties include crab lasagna, sea bass stuffed with fresh salmon, and pigs' trotters with roquefort cheese sauce. Closed Sunday nights and Mondays, *Holy Week,* the month of August, and 2 weeks in September. Reservations necessary. Major credit cards accepted. 88 Carrer de Provença (phone: 230-0029). Expensive.

Neichel – Strictly French, like the owner-chef, whose efforts have won two Michelin stars (there's no more highly rated restaurant in town) and a dedicated local following. The constant flow of inventive new dishes has put exotic little parcels of raw and smoked salmon with caviar, and salads of lobster with mustard vinaigrette on the menu along with more straightforward sea bass with a mousseline of truffles, monkfish in clam sauce, and pigeon with lentils and bacon. Add a selection of 30 desserts from the trolley, fine Spanish wines, and excellent service, and this is a place for a celebration. Closed Sundays, holidays, *Christmas* week, *Holy Week,* and the month of August. Reservations necessary. Major credit cards accepted. 16 *bis* Avinguda de Pedralbes (phone: 203-8408). Expensive.

Quo Vadis – Muted paneling, soft lights, and harmonious decor provide a pleasing ambience at this top establishment. Service is solicitous and the highly original international cuisine is excellent. Closed Sundays. Reservations advised. Major credit cards accepted. 7 Carrer de Carmen (phone: 317-7447). Expensive.

Reno – Another impressive kitchen that uses local recipes in a classic way, its specialties include sole with freshwater crayfish, hake with anchovy sauce, and roast duck with honey and sherry vinegar. The *Menú Reno* offers a sampling of the house's most popular dishes. Open daily, year-round. Reservations advised. Major credit cards accepted. 27 Carrer de Tuset (phone: 200-9129). Expensive.

Arcs de Sant Gervasi – One of Barcelona's newer favorites, in the bustling neighborhood near Plaça de Francesc Macià. Try the gratin of eggplant, ham, and tiny shrimp, or the slices of rare duck with zucchini mousse and sliced pears. Open daily. Reservations advised. Major credit cards accepted. 103 Carrer de Santaló (phone: 201-9277). Moderate.

Blau Mari – A chic new spot on the Barcelona waterfront, featuring fresh fish, seafood, and paellas. Open daily. Reservations unnecessary. Major credit cards accepted. Moll de la Fusta (phone: 218-9222). Moderate.

Brasserie Flo – The atmosphere is Parisian; the meat dishes, especially the barbecue, are outstanding. A favorite place for café society, in jeans or black tie, it's open late for the after-theater crowd. Open daily. No reservations. Major credit cards accepted. 10 Carrer de les Jonqueres (phone: 317-8037). Moderate.

Casa Isidre – The morning market determines the selection of standard-setting Catalan dishes in this Barcelona landmark, once a favorite of Joan Miró. There also is an intelligently stocked wine cellar. Only 10 tables, so reservations are essential and should be made *at least* 2 days in advance. Closed Sundays, holidays, *Christmas* week, *Holy Week,* and during the month of August. Major credit cards accepted. 12 Carrer de les Flors (phone: 241-1139). Moderate.

Los Caracoles – At first glance this bustling, jovial place looks like a tourist trap, but the good solid Catalan cooking is most impressive. Try *los caracoles* (snails);

the langostinos are fresh and delicious. Open daily. Reservations necessary (but, even so, you'll have to wait during rush hours). Major credit cards accepted. 14 Carrer dels Escudellers (phone: 302-3185). Moderate.

La Dorada – On an average day, this popular eatery serves 1,200 meals! The dining room is fitted with nautical relics, which complement the menu of mostly seafood dishes (and the recipes are more national than regional). Among the favorites are Galician scallops and *sarsuela* (seafood stew). Service is deft and, despite the crowds, never rushed. Closed Sundays. Reservations advised. Major credit cards accepted. 44 Travessera de Gràcia (phone: 200-6322). Moderate.

Senyor Parellada – Located near the *Museu Picasso,* this refined and ambitious restaurant serves traditional Catalan cooking at very reasonable prices. Try the *escalivada,* a cold salad of red peppers, onions, eggplant, and thin slices of cod; or breast of duck with tarragon vinegar. Closed Sundays and holidays. Reservations advised. Major credit cards accepted. 37 Carrer Argenteria (phone: 315-4010). Moderate.

Set Portes – Near the waterfront and a Barcelona favorite since it opened in 1836, it still retains its original decor and charm. Catalan cuisine, including great seafood and homemade desserts, is served in abundant proportions, and the large dining rooms are packed on weekends. Open daily. Reservations advised. Major credit cards accepted. 14 Passeig Isabel II (phone: 319-2020). Moderate.

La Bona Cuina – The decor looks a bit like a modernist parlor, with walls paneled in dark wood, lace curtains at the windows, and a huge Art Nouveau mirror, all gold swirls with a golden peacock on top, dominating the room. In the Barri Gòtic, behind the cathedral, it unabashedly caters to tourists, but delivers good food (Catalan, especially fish and seafood) and good value. Open daily. Reservations advised. Visa accepted. 12 Carrer Pietat (phone: 315-4156). Moderate to inexpensive.

La Cuineta – Under the same management as *La Bona Cuina* and quite close by in the Barri Gòtic, this is set up in 17th-century wine vaults. Open daily. Reservations advised. Visa accepted. 4 Carrer Paradis (phone: 315-0111). Moderate to inexpensive.

Can Costa – Only the freshest of fish and seafood is served at this delightful establishment, one of a number of restaurants side by side on the Barceloneta beachfront. The fish and vegetables are piled high on tables on the sidewalk, and guests walk past the hubbub of the kitchen to a large room open to the sea. In summer, the tables and benches spill out onto the sand. Open daily. No reservations. Major credit cards accepted. 12 Platja de Sant Miguel, Barceloneta (phone: 315-1903). Inexpensive.

Les Corts Catalanes – A wonderful vegetarian delicatessen, located 1 block from the Passeig de Gràcia, serving everything from vegetable lasagna to cheese or spinach empanadas (pot pies). Open daily. No reservations. Visa accepted. 603 Gran Via de les Corts Catalanes (phone: 301-0376). Inexpensive.

Egipte – Very popular and definitely bohemian, serving students and artists. It's located behind the *Boquería* market, so order the dish of the day for the freshest food in town. Closed Sundays, Mondays, and religious holidays. No reservations. Visa accepted. 12 Carrer de Jerusalén. Second location at 79 de la Rambla (phone: 317-7480). Inexpensive.

Quatre Gats – The third incarnation of the popular Barri Gòtic café. The original, which opened in 1897, was a hangout for artists and writers of the Catalan modernist movement, and Picasso had his first show here. There's café society ambience still: Art Nouveau lamps, wrought-iron and marble tables, potted palms, and candelabra on the baby grand. The menu is a limited one of unpretentious Catalan dishes (try the *Especial 4 Gats* salad for a new twist on diet food). Open daily. No reservations. Visa accepted. 3 Carrer de Montsió (phone: 302-4140). Inexpensive.

 TAPAS BARS: The Catalans did not invent *tapas*, the Spanish equivalent of hors d'oeuvres; it's said the Andalusians did. But they've become as adept as the rest of the Spaniards at the *tapeo*, which consists of making the rounds of *tapas* bars, downing a drink at each, and sampling these delicious snacks — the Spanish version of the treasure hunt, some might say. Barcelona has numerous *tapas* bars, the most colorful of which are located along La Rambla and in the area surrounding the *Picasso Museum*. Some of the more popular choices are beyond this zone, however, including *Flish Flash*, well off the beaten tourist path (25 Carrer de la Ciutat de Granada; phone: 237-0990), where more than 70 types of tortillas attract a good crowd. *Jamón Jamón* (off Plaça de Francesc Macià at 4 Carrer del Mestre Nicolau; phone: 209-4103) serves what its name (which means "Ham Ham") implies — and it serves the best, from Jabugo. *Mundial* (1 Plaça Sant Agustín; phone: 331-2516) specializes in seafood. *Belvedere* (in a quiet alleyway off Passeig de Gràcia, 3 Passatge Mercader; phone: 215-9088) offers a nice terrace and a wide selection. At *Bodega Sepúlveda* (173 Carrer de Sepúlveda; phone: 254-7094), the proprietor's own wine accompanies cheese in oil and little salads. The *Cava de Olimpia* (10 Carrer de Loreto; phone: 239-1073), near the *Derby, Gran Derby,* and *Meliá Barcelona Sarrìa* hotels, takes its name from *cava,* the Spanish answer to champagne. It's part of a recent vogue of *xampanyerias* where corks are popped at reasonable prices.

BURGOS

Lying between the Spanish *meseta* (plateau) and the foothills of the Cantabrian and Iberian cordilleras, about 150 miles (240 km) due north of Madrid and 95 miles (152 km) due south of the Atlantic coast at Santander (as well as half the way between Barcelona and Santiago de Compostela on Spain's east-west axis), is Burgos. It occupies a position that has made it an important crossroads for centuries, and thrives in a setting that — combining tableland and mountain, wheatfields and pine woods — is particularly characteristic of inland Spain. Although a relatively young city, dating from the 9th century, and a quiet and pleasant one, Burgos nevertheless boasts a rich and colorful history.

The earliest historic reference to Burgos was in 884, when Alfonso III of León chose the Castilian Count Diego Rodríguez Porcelos to build a castle and settlement on the Arlanzón River as an outpost for troops fighting on the Moorish frontier. By 950, Fernán González, another Castilian count, had grown powerful enough (through the consolidation of several small fiefdoms) to declare himself independent of the kingdom of León and establish the county of Castile, making Burgos his capital. When the county of Castile became the kingdom of Castile, Burgos became its capital, and remained so until 1087, when Alfonso VI moved his headquarters to Toledo.

Burgos is probably best known for its most famous native son, Rodrigo Díaz de Vivar, Spain's national hero, more commonly known as El Cid Campeador, a much romanticized hero who was born in the tiny village of Vivar, just north of Burgos, and became a legend of the Reconquest. Following his victory over the Moors in 1081, El Cid was expelled from Castile by Alfonso VI, who was jealous of the soldier's popularity and distrusted him, even though the hero was married to Doña Jimena, the king's cousin. As an exiled soldier of fortune, El Cid joined the forces of the Moorish King of Zaragoza, and subsequently fought *against* the same Christian forces he had once led. His sympathies soon switched again, and in 1094 he led 7,000 Christian knights to a stunning victory over the Moors at Valencia. The Moors, however, had their revenge in 1099, at Cuenca, where the legendary hero met his death. His brave widow held Valencia until 1102, when she burned the city before it was overrun by the Moors, then returned to Castile with her husband's remains.

El Cid was eventually immortalized in the great, anonymous 12th-century Castilian epic poem *El cantar del mío cid,* a tender but mostly fictional account of the often ruthless mercenary's exploits. Today, he and Doña Jimena are buried side by side in the Cathedral of Burgos, after centuries of peaceful rest in the Monastery of San Pedro de Cardeña, several miles east of town. A simple tombstone pays tribute to El Cid's loyal horse, Babieca, reputedly buried here. The hero's presence still pervades the city, as well as Spanish history and literature, and the striking statue of him in the Plaza de Miguel Primo de Rivera, sword thrusting, cape to the wind, bears an inscription that reads: "His death caused much mourning among Christians and great joy to his enemies."

While El Cid was making the name of Burgos known to the Moors of the medieval world, the city also was gaining equal renown among medieval Christians as a major stopping point for pilgrims on their way to the shrine of St. James in Santiago de Compostela. This great mass movement had begun in earnest in the 10th century, and as it grew, so did Burgos. The cathedral, begun and completed for the most part in the 13th century, became the city's focal point, and over the years has come to be recognized as one of the world's most important landmarks of Gothic architecture and sculpture. The cathedral is a living testament to the wealth of Burgos in the 13th century, when a powerful group of sheep farmers, known as the Mesta, generated an unprecedented amount of commerce by selling their merino wool, both locally and abroad. Burgos was a center of the wool trade, a fact that is recalled even by its name, which derives from the "burghers," or middle class merchants, who gave rise to the towns of the Middle Ages.

Burgos remained prosperous through the 16th century, and then began to decline. Only in this century did it return to the fore, this time infamously, as the capital of the Civil War regime of Generalísimo Francisco Franco. In 1936, the Nationalist Party was spawned in Burgos, where it was said that "even the stones are nationalist," and soon after, again in Burgos, Franco was proclaimed head of the Spanish government and commander-in-chief of the armed forces. Yet despite adverse historical circumstances and its share of warfare, Burgos has retained a wealth of artistic relics that few Spanish cities or provinces can boast. The 13th, 14th, and 15th centuries were periods of extraordinary splendor, during which the construction of churches, monasteries, and homes grew under the influence of bishops and abbots and with the patronage of kings and noblemen. During the 15th and 16th centuries, the city achieved further spectacular development, thanks in part to its economic wealth, which attracted corps of painters, sculptors, and architects.

BURGOS AT-A-GLANCE

SEEING THE CITY: The best way to get a panoramic view of Burgos is to walk or drive up to the remains of the old castle, which is just above the cathedral. To reach it on foot, begin in Plaza de Santa María, just in front of the cathedral, take the steps up to the Iglesia de San Nicolás, and turn left onto Calle Fernán González; at the triumphal arch, take the stairs leading upward to the top. The castle is nothing but a ruin, having been blown up by departing Napoleonic troops in the early 19th century, but it's possible to climb carefully to the top of the walls (although it's not encouraged), then sit down and behold Burgos, majestically spread out below.

SPECIAL PLACES: The major sights are clustered in the Old Town, a relatively small area on one side of the Arlanzón River. Its central features are the arcaded Plaza Mayor (Plaza de José Antonio on some maps), just west of which, at the foot of the castle hill, is the impressive Gothic cathedral, which dominates the entire city. South of the cathedral is the Plaza del Rey San Fernando; from it, the Arco de Santa María, a massive gate with semicircular towers, opens onto the beginning of the Paseo del Espolón, one of the most beautiful and pleasant riverside promenades in Spain. Just in front of the gate, the Arlanzón is crossed by the Puente de Santa María (Santa Maria Bridge). The main sights of Burgos are within easy walking distance of this core, although most people will want to take public transportation to the Monasterio de las Huelgas and the Cartuja de Miraflores (Convent of Miraflores).

Cathedral – The cathedral in Burgos is the third-largest in Spain, following those of Seville and Toledo, but it was the country's first great Gothic cathedral. Begun in 1221 on the order of King Ferdinand III (the Saint) and Bishop Mauricio, who laid the cornerstone on July 20 of that year (curiously, no one knows which stone it is), the structure was largely designed by Master Enrique, who also built the Cathedral of León. The first mass was said 9 years later, although the church was not finished for several more centuries. Construction fell into two distinct periods, and two Gothic styles are evident. The main body of the church, mostly completed in the 13th century, is in a simpler Gothic style than that represented by such 15th-century additions as the two west front spires, by Juan de Colonia, or the Capilla del Condestable (Constable's Chapel), by Simón de Colonia. Both of these latter are wondrously Flamboyant Gothic. Yet while the cathedral's plan was originally based on French models, and both French and German architects collaborated in its construction, its design and decoration are in the finest Spanish tradition.

The difference between the two styles can be seen in the cathedral's main (west) façade, which faces Plaza de Santa María (from where it is also evident that the cathedral was built on sloping ground). The two towers bracketing the rose window date from the 13th century, while the lacy openwork spires above them are the masterpiece of the 15th-century architect from Cologne. The door in the main façade is known as the Puerto del Perdón (Door of Forgiveness), but before going inside, walk down to the Plaza del Rey San Fernando, from where a flight of stairs leads up to what is considered the most beautiful of the church's four entrances, the Puerta del Sarmentál, or Sarmental Door, in French Gothic style. (Note the tympanum, with carvings of each of the Four Evangelists writing at their desks.) The remaining splendid portals are the Puerta de la Coronería on the church's north side (Calle Fernán González), with a 13th-century bas relief of Christ in Judgment between the Virgin Mary and St. John, and, nearly adjoining it, the Puerta de la Pellejería, a 16th-century Plateresque design by Francisco de Colonia, Juan's grandson.

Inside, the cathedral stands as an overwhelming testament to the strength of the church. The massive columns rising to the vaulted dome at the crossing of the transept appear to stretch to the heavens, and the dome — colorless, opaque glass in an eight-pointed star shape amid ornate Plateresque stone carving — is as jewel-like as a giant rhinestone pin. In the floor under the dome is the tomb of El Cid and his wife, Doña Jimena, sandwiched between the 16th-century Renaissance Capilla Mayor (Main Chapel, or High Altar) and altarpiece (the Infante Don Juan, one of Alfonso X's sons, and other members of the royal family are in tombs at the foot of the altar) and the 16th-century Renaissance choir, with walnut stalls carved by Felipe Bigarny. Both the choir and the high altar are surrounded by a giant grille. The gilded staircase off to one side (north) here, a 16th-century Renaissance design by Diego de Siloé, is one of the church's treasures. So, too, is the series of extraordinarily expressive sculptured scenes around the back of the altar, depicting the death of Christ, the central ones also carved by Felipe Bigarny.

The cathedral has 19 chapels, not all of which are on view at any given time. Foremost among them is the octagonal Capilla del Condestable, behind the Main Chapel. A striking example of 15th-century Flamboyant Gothic, it contains a very ornate gilt altar, in front of which are the tombs, with Carrara marble effigies, of Don Pedro Fernández de Velasco, the Constable of Castile, and his wife, Doña Mencía de Mendoza y Figueroa; above them is a lovely star-shaped cupola of blue and purple stained glass. In the small room just off the chapel is a painting of Mary Magdalene, attributed to Leonardo da Vinci (it's behind closed cupboard doors — ask the attendant to open it). Another noteworthy chapel is the Capilla del Santísimo Cristo (the first to the right upon entering the church), which contains a much-venerated ancient figure of Christ, made by St. Nicodemus, according to legend; the figure of wood and buffalo hide, also known as the Christ of Burgos, has real hair, wears a skirt, and stands on five ostrich eggs. Two more chapels not to be missed are the Capilla Santa Tecla (directly across from the Santísimo Chapel), with an exceedingly lavish 18th-century gilt baroque altarpiece, by Alberto Churriguera, and the Capilla Santa Ana (next door to the Santa Tecla Chapel), with a wonderful 15th-century altarpiece by Gil de Siloé and Diego de la Cruz.

Also noteworthy are the cloister doors, beautifully carved. They lead into the 13th-century cloister, built on 2 levels, and adjoining chapel and chapter house, which function as the cathedral museum. Here the treasures include the 16th-century *Christ at the Column* sculpture by Diego de Siloé, considered a masterpiece of Spanish expressionism, and the silver carriage that transports the gold monstrance in the city's *Corpus Christi* procession. One of the cathedral's lighter facets is the famous 16th-century Papamoscas (Flycatcher), a clock with automated figures high up above the central aisle. On the hour, a figure to the right rings a bell causing the Flycatcher's mouth to open in a grimace (catching flies in the summer, hence the name). It's hard to see, especially if there's no gawking crowd gathered to direct the gaze, so stand just inside the main door of the cathedral, with your back to the door, and look way up to the left; the clock is set between the two arches of the clerestory windows. The cathedral is open daily, from 9:30 AM to 1 PM and from 4 to 7 PM. Admission charge to the cloister. Plaza de Santa María (phone: 204712).

Iglesia de San Nicolás – An unusual, mostly 15th-century Gothic church just up the stairs from the Plaza de Santa María, it has a magnificent altarpiece by Francisco de Colonia, dating from 1505. Carved in stone are some 48 scenes from the Bible and from the life of the saint, made up of hundreds of figures, some of them polychrome (decorated in several colors). On either side of the altar and on the sides of the church are haunting Gothic tombs. The church also contains some interesting 16th-century Flemish paintings. Don't spare the 100 pesetas for illumination — it's well worth it. Open Mondays from 9 AM to 2 PM and 5 to 9 PM, Tuesdays through Fridays from 6:30 to 8 PM, Saturdays from 9 AM to 2 PM and 6:30 to 8 PM, and Sundays and holidays from 9 AM to 2 PM and 5 to 6 PM. Calle Fernán González.

Arco de Santa María – When Burgos was a walled city, this was its main gateway, fed by the main bridge over the Arlanzón River. It dates from the 14th century (although there was an earlier, 11th-century gate here), and was remodeled in the 16th century. Pictured in its niches are some famous figures from local history: Count Diego Rodríguez Porcelos, the city's 9th-century founder, flanked by judges, on the lower level; Count Fernán González, the 10th-century founder of the County of Castile, flanked by the Holy Roman Emperor Charles V and El Cid, the city's mercenary hero, on the upper level. Plaza del Rey San Fernando.

Museo Arqueológico (Archaeological Museum) – Set up in the Casa de Miranda, a 16th-century mansion which features an elegant 2-story courtyard with a fountain in the center, the collection embraces finds from prehistoric times through the present day, and presents the changing ages in an easy-to-digest fashion through displays of burial sites, tools, jewelry, weapons, and household items. Roman artifacts include ceramics, weapons, glass bowls, and household items. There also is an interesting presentation on the region's Roman road system, complete with aerial photos that trace the old routes, and a small display of Visigothic items. The medieval section houses the Gothic tomb of Juan de Padilla, the Franciscan missionary, and an 11th-century Moorish ivory casket. Open Mondays through Fridays, from 10 AM to 1 PM and from 4:45 to 7:15 PM; Saturdays, from 11 AM to 1 PM. Admission charge. 13 Calle Miranda (phone: 265875).

Museo Marceliano Santa María – The museum occupies the former Augustinian Monastery of San Juan, now fully restored and converted into a palace of the arts. The upstairs houses 165 works by the local 19th- and 20th-century Impressionist painter, including portraits and colorful landscapes of the surrounding countryside. Downstairs is display space for the local art shows that are held here throughout the year; the exhibitions are set up around the enclosed arcades of the cloister, an interesting juxtaposition of modern art and Gothic vaulting. Open Tuesdays through Saturdays, from 10 AM to 2 PM and from 5 to 8 PM; Sundays, from 10 AM to 2 PM. Admission charge. Plaza de San Juan (phone: 205687).

Casa del Cordón – A fine example of secular, rather than ecclesiastic, Gothic architecture of the 15th century, it was built by the same Constable of Castile who lies buried in a chapel of the cathedral; it takes its name from the Franciscan *cordón* that is the decorative motif of its carved façade. The plaque next to the door identifies it as the building where, in April 1497, the Catholic Monarchs met Christopher Columbus after his return from his second trip to the New World. Beautifully restored, the building belongs to the bank that financed its restoration and is open to the public during banking hours, Mondays through Fridays from 9 AM to 2 PM. Plaza de Calvo Sotelo.

Estatua del Cid (El Cid Statue) – This statue of the Burgalese hero astride Babieca, his faithful steed, is so centrally located that visitors come upon it again and again as they explore the city. A contemporary work (1954) in bronze, it bristles with energy, as its subject certainly must have, and its assertiveness never fails to impress. Plaza de Miguel Primo de Rivera.

ENVIRONS

Monasterio de las Huelgas – What originally was a royal summer palace was converted into a Cistercian convent for nuns of aristocratic and royal lineage by Alfonso VIII and his English wife, Eleanor, in 1187. This eventually became one of the most important and powerful convents in Europe, and also served as a pantheon of the Castilian dynasty. The buildings and the artworks they contain reflect a wealth of changing architectural styles and influences from Romanesque and Mudéjar to Renaissance and Plateresque, although the church has a rather simple façade with a square tower. Inside, note the unique 16th-century revolving pulpit that allowed the priest to address both sides of the church, which is divided in two by a wall that turns out to be, when seen from the other side, a carved polychrome Renaissance-style altarpiece. This magnificent piece, surmounted by a 13th-century Deposition, is in the central nave of the church, where the tombs of the founders are also located. Tombs of other royal personages, as well as other wonderful altarpieces, are in the side aisles. Beyond are cloisters, rooms with stone ceilings carved Moorish-style, but with the castle of Castile as the main motif, a small room with a wonderful wooden *artesonado* ceiling, and, at the end, the *Museo de Telas Medievales* (Museum of Medieval Textiles). On display here, among other things, are garments found in the only one of the church's tombs left unsacked over the centuries, that of Don Fernando de la Cerda (1225–75), son of Alfonso X; included are his *birrete* (cap), his *saya* (tunic), his *manto* (cloak), and *cinturón* (sash), along with other articles. Also on display is the restored Moorish banner captured at the decisive Battle of Las Navas de Tolosa, in 1212, when Christian forces finally gained the upper hand against their Arab foes.

All of the above can be seen, unfortunately, only on a fast guided tour, which is conducted only in Spanish. Open Tuesdays through Saturdays, from 11 AM to 1:15 PM and from 4 to 5:15 PM; Sundays and holidays, from 11 AM to 1:15 PM. Admission charge. Located in a residential district about 1 mile (1.6 km) west of the city center. Avenida del Monasterio de las Huelgas (phone: 201630).

Cartuja de Miraflores (Convent of Miraflores) – This is another sight out of town that should not be missed. In the mid-15th century, King Juan II gave the land here to the Carthusians to build a monastery, which he chose as the final resting place for himself and his second wife, Isabel of Portugal — parents of Queen Isabella of Castile. He died in 1454 and work on the church was carried out largely by their daughter, in the late Gothic style that came to be known as Isabeline; it was not finished until 1488. Visitors to the church pass through a grating into the Coro de los Hermanos (Brothers' Choir), with Renaissance choir stalls beautifully carved (1558) with reliefs of saints by Simón Bueras, then through the Felix Coeli Porta into the Coro de los Padres (Fathers' Choir), with Gothic choir stalls carved (1489) with arabesques by Martín Sánchez. Ahead, a wrought-iron grille surrounds the dual tomb of the king and queen, which consists of an intricately sculpted alabaster base in the shape of an eight-pointed star, with reclining figures of the monarchs on top. It hardly seems possible that this lacy extravaganza could have been carved in one lifetime, yet it was the work of the sculptor Gil de Siloé. He was called away from his work at the cathedral to do the job, and also completed the extraordinary exercise in filigree virtuosity against the adjacent wall — the tomb of the Infante Don Alfonso, Isabella's brother, who was "accidentally" dropped off the Alcázar walls in Segovia in 1468, allowing Isabella to become heiress to the Spanish throne. Even more astonishing is that the same Siloé, with the help of Diego de la Cruz, was responsible for the church's magnificent, immense wood altar-piece, whose sculptured, polychromed, and gilded biblical scenes are crowded with figures. Note the Last Supper, in the lowest row to the left, where it appears that the menu included the typically Castilian roast lamb (along with somebody's head on a platter); in the scene to the left of that is King Juan II (Queen Isabel is in a corresponding position to the far right).

Further treasures in the church include the *Annunciation* by Pedro Berruguete on the wall next to the Infante's tomb, the Flemish triptych on the wall facing the same tomb, and the Madonna with an unusually sweet-faced Child above the door marked Clausura. Open Mondays through Saturdays, from 10:15 AM to 3 PM and from 4 to 8 PM; Sundays and holidays, from 11:20 AM to 12:30 PM and from 1 to 3 and 4 to 6 PM. No admission charge. Located a little over 2 miles (3 km) east of the center, the monastery is best visited by car, taxi, or, in July and August, by bus, but it's easy to walk back, since the return is down a slight incline along a paved path the whole way — at a brisk pace it takes about 45 minutes to the city center. If walking *to* the monastery, just cross to the southern side of the river and follow Paseo de la Quinta east.

■**EXTRA SPECIAL:** There are promenades all along the river in Burgos, on both sides. The Paseo del Espolón, however, which runs from the Arco de Santa María to the Plaza de Miguel Primo de Rivera, is truly a treat. A walkway lined with park benches and topiary bushes, a parallel allée of sycamore trees, a sprinkling of fountains, a gazebo, and statues — along with a fair share of the milling citizenry — are all to be found here. Next to this, the river, with its wide grassy banks and overhanging willows, presents so bucolic a picture for a provincial capital that the visitor almost expects to see cows grazing at the water's edge. With such a place to carry it out, it's not surprising that the *paseo* — the communal stroll — is still an important part of Burgalese life, so why not join the crowd?

The medieval town of Briviesca, just 25 miles (40 km) northeast of Burgos on the main highway (N1), is well worth a visit. The 14th-century Colegiata de Santa María (Church of Colegiata de Santa María), with its exquisite Renaissance façade, is a fine example of Christian Castillian architecture. The interior, with three Gothic aisles, contains interesting religious wood paintings. The town is also the site of the San Martin church, built in the 15th century, and the 16th-century Santa Clara church; both draw large crowds of religious art enthusiasts. Treat yourself to lunch at the 14th-century *El Concejo* inn (14 Plaza Mayor, Briviesca; phone: 591686) where roast lamb is the specialty.

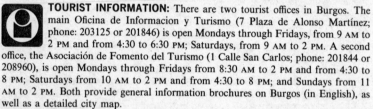

SOURCES AND RESOURCES

TOURIST INFORMATION: There are two tourist offices in Burgos. The main Oficina de Informacion y Turismo (7 Plaza de Alonso Martínez; phone: 203125 or 201846) is open Mondays through Fridays, from 9 AM to 2 PM and from 4:30 to 6:30 PM; Saturdays, from 9 AM to 2 PM. A second office, the Asociación de Fomento del Turismo (1 Calle San Carlos; phone: 201844 or 208960), is open Mondays through Fridays from 8:30 AM to 2 PM and from 4:30 to 8 PM; Saturdays from 10 AM to 2 PM and from 4:30 to 8 PM; and Sundays from 11 AM to 2 PM. Both provide general information brochures on Burgos (in English), as well as a detailed city map.

Local Coverage – *Diario de Burgos*, the local Spanish-language daily newspaper, contains schedules of activities and events in and around the city.

TELEPHONE: The city code for Burgos is 47. If calling from within Spain, dial 947 before the local number.

GETTING AROUND: Walking is the easiest and most enjoyable way to get around in Burgos. Most of the major sights are within a relatively compact area. A car, taxi, or bus, however, will be useful for excursions to the sights in the environs and beyond.

Bus – Burgos has a good city bus system, with stops at or near the major sights and most hotels. A bus for the Monasterio de las Huelgas departs approximately every half hour from Plaza de Miguel Primo de Rivera, stopping at several bridges en route before turning away from the river; take the bus marked Barrio del Pilar. In July and August, there also is service connecting the center with the Cartuja de Miraflores approximately every hour; take the bus marked Fuentes Blancas from the same plaza. Burgos's main station for long-distance buses is at 4 Calle Miranda (phone: 205575), just across the river from the Arco de Santa María. There is daily service to León, Santander, Madrid, Soria, and San Sebastián; schedules are printed in the *Diario de Burgos*, and are often more convenient than those for the trains.

Car Rental – There are several choices: *Hertz* (10 Calle Madrid; phone: 201675); *Avis* (5 Avenida Generalísimo Franco; phone: 205813); and *Azteca* (Avenida General Vigón; phone: 223803).

Taxi – Taxis are available at stands throughout the city, or they can be flagged on the streets. To call a cab, try dialing 203055, 203088, or 262862, which correspond to centrally located cabstands at Plaza Santo Domingo de Guzmán, Calle Conde de Jordana, and Plaza de Vega respectively.

Train – The train station (Plaza de la Estación; phone: 203560) is across the river, at the end of Avenida Conde de Guadalhorce, a 15-minute walk from the cathedral. Burgos is on the main rail line connecting Irún and Madrid, with daily service to Pamplona, Vitoria, Bilbao, Valladolid, and other towns and cities. There also is less frequent service to Zaragoza, Palencia, León, and La Coruña. Tickets can be bought at the station or at *RENFE*'s downtown office (21 Calle Moneda; phone: 209131), open weekdays, from 9 AM to 1 PM and 4 to 7 PM.

 SPECIAL EVENTS: There are two particularly festive occasions that fill up the town. The first, *Corpus Christi,* in late May or early June, and *Curpillos,* the day following it, are marked by picturesque processions. (The banner captured at the Battle of Las Navas de Tolosa used to be paraded through town as part of the latter festivities, but since its restoration it no longer leaves the Monastery of Las Huelgas, where it's on display.) The second occasion, the *Feast Day of St. Peter and St. Paul,* on June 29, is an excuse for a week of celebration known as the *Fiesta de Burgos,* featuring parades, bullfights, sports competitions, and folkloric performances, and a host of other activities that can include anything from mime, ballet, and concerts to model airplane contests and fireworks. Detailed information on these events can be obtained from the tourist information offices.

 SHOPPING: Burgos is not known for any particular craft, food delicacy, or other product that might constitute the perfect souvenir, but it does have a variety of shops befitting its status as a solid provincial capital. The main shopping district spreads from the cathedral to the Plaza Mayor and up to Plaza de Alonso Martínez, including the streets between Calle Santander and Calle Lain Calvo. The major department store chain represented is *Galerías Preciadas* (two entrances: 4 Calle Almirante Bonifaz and 9 Calle Moneda; phone: 205846). In general, shopping hours are from 10 AM to 2 PM and 5 to 8 PM.

Cacharreria – A wide variety of handicraft work in tin and copper. 16 Calle La Puebla (no phone).

Con Rey – Costume jewelry with personality, mainly a Spanish one. 19 Calle Lain Calvo (phone: 260209).

Garden – One of the best clothing stores in town, selling everything from shoes to bags, belts, and overcoats, with departments for men, women, and young people. Plaza de Miguel Primo de Rivera (phone: 206990).

Hijos de Felix Sebastian – Fine leather boots and wineskins. 8 Calle Merced (phone: 206661).

José Ruiz – A wide selection of shoes for men and women. 28 Plaza Mayor (phone: 260215).

Serrano – Another of the town's top shops for men's and women's clothing, but it's mostly for men and mostly British styles. This is where the Burgalese buy their Burberry's and Barbours. 4 Calle Santander (phone: 203668).

Vaquero – Handbags, wallets, briefcases, belts, umbrellas, plus cuff links and costume jewelry. 7 Calle Almirante Bonifaz (phone: 204791).

You – Men's and women's clothing, including cocktail dresses and formal wear, dressy and pricey. 15 Calle Vitoria (phone: 206444).

Zara – A budget clothing store (men, women, children); they do a land-office business, with price tags already converted into major international currencies, including US dollars. Corner of Calle Condestable and Calle Vitoria (phone: 201617).

SPORTS AND FITNESS: The major public sports and recreation complex, *El Plantió* (Calle Vitoria; phone: 220001), has tennis courts and a municipal swimming pool. Open daily, from 10 AM to 9 PM.

Fishing – With the disappearance of the river crayfish, trout has become the most important catch in Burgos and its surrounding areas. There are 500 miles of rivers containing trout in the province. The Arlanzon River yields trout and barbel.

Hunting – Wild boar abound in the oak, holm oak, and beech forests of the Burgos countryside, and roe deer is commonly sighted in the National Game Reserve of the Sierra de la Demanda. For information about hunting licenses, enquire at the tourism information center, 7 Alonso Martínez Plaza (phone: 203125 or 201846).

NIGHTCLUBS AND NIGHTLIFE: Nightlife in Burgos is best described as lively and very youth oriented, with most of the activity centered around the bars and cafés of the Old Town. Calle de la Llana de Afuera, behind the cathedral, is a center of activity, where the overflow bar and café crowds usually spill out onto the street. Popular discotheques include *Pentágono* (2 Calle Conde de Jordana; phone: 202834); *Roma* (11 Calle San Pablo; phone: 265964); *La Finca* (Paseo de la Isla; phone: 234810); *Armstrong* (13 Calle Clunia; phone: 227266); and *Trastos* (9 Calle Huerto del Rey; phone: 246598).

BEST IN TOWN

CHECKING IN: Burgos offers an excellent selection of hotels in various price ranges, most within a short walk of the cathedral. Expect to pay $85 or more for a double room at a hotel listed as expensive (more than $125 for the very expensive listing), $50 to $85 at a moderately priced hotel, and less than $50 at an inexpensive one. All telephone numbers are in the 47 city code unless otherwise indicated.

Landa Palace – The best in the Burgos area and one of Spain's best hotels, this hostelry is a world of its own. Set 2 miles (3 km) from the city center on the road to Madrid, it's a self-contained establishment (indeed, for some guests, Burgos begins to pale in interest) of 42 rooms and suites decorated with antiques, some of them in the stone tower of a 14th-century castle. An indoor/outdoor swimming pool is reached down a circular stone staircase, its indoor portion protected by soaring, skylighted Gothic vaulting, and the restaurant (see *Eating Out*) is a room of equally Gothic splendor. Carretera Madrid–Irún, Km 236 (phone: 206343; fax: 264676; telex: 39594). Very expensive.

Almirante Bonifaz – Noted for its high standards of comfort and service, it has 79 air conditioned rooms (with private baths, color television sets, radios, and telephones), a bar-cafeteria, even a bingo room. Centrally located, in the midst of banks and stores, it's a good choice for businesspeople as well as leisure travelers. 22 Calle Vitoria (phone: 206943; fax: 202919; telex: 039430). Expensive.

Condestable – One of the grand old dames of Burgos, a favorite with bullfighters (among others), also centrally located on one of the main business streets. Some of the 82 rooms retain the Old World elegance — ornate beds, overstuffed chairs, wallpaper that takes you back in time — that made the hotel's reputation; others have been modernized with off-white walls and modern furniture in blond woods. 8 Calle Vitoria (phone: 267125; fax: 204645; telex: 39572). Expensive.

Mesón del Cid – This Best Western–affiliated property occupies a lovely 15th-century house directly opposite the cathedral. The 30 rooms are well appointed, with a rustic, old-fashioned look and private bathrooms with brass fittings, but their biggest strength is that most of them are graced with an excellent head-on view of the cathedral's western façade. Only the public areas are air conditioned, there are a few steps to negotiate out front, and parking can be a problem, but the hotel will provide a garage for an added charge. The restaurant is a longtime Burgos favorite (see *Eating Out*). 8 Plaza de Santa María (phone: 208715; fax: 269460). Expensive.

Cordón – The 35 rooms are large, comfortable, and clean, and the location is favorable. There is no restaurant, but some of Burgos's best eating places are just steps away. Staff members speak little English, which may or may not be a problem. 6 Calle de la Puebla (phone: 265000; fax: 200269). Moderate.

Corona de Castilla – This modern facility offers 52 well-maintained rooms and a decent restaurant, but it is located across the river in a rather dull part of town, about a 10-minute walk from the cathedral. Ask for a room in the rear, which will be much quieter than one overlooking the street. 15 Calle Madrid (phone: 262142; fax: 208042; telex: 39619). Moderate.

Fernán González – Just across the bridge from the Arco de Santa María, overlooking the river. The 64 rooms are quiet and comfortable, the overall decor a medley of dark woods and fascinating antiques pleasantly tucked into virtually every nook and cranny. There's a dining room for guests, a somewhat old-fashioned space, plus a bright, beautiful à la carte restaurant — a blend of the modern with ancient stairways and balconies. 17 Calle Calera (phone: 209441). Moderate.

Conde de Miranda – Across the bridge from the Arco de Santa María and attached to the bus station, making it convenient for bus travelers (the area is safe at all hours). Nothing fancy, but the 14 rooms have private baths and offer simple yet comfortable furnishings. 4 Calle Miranda (phone: 265267). Inexpensive.

Norte y Londres – Centrally located, the 55 rooms here are clean and comfortable, offering lots of Old World charm and decor. Count on the friendly staff to provide good service. 10 Plaza de Alonso Martínez (phone: 264125). Inexpensive.

EATING OUT: Among their other culinary treats, Burgos and the surrounding Castilian provinces are renowned for traditional lamb and pork dishes, especially *cordero asado* (roast suckling lamb) and *cochinillo asado* (roast suckling pig). For starters, try Burgos soup, a tasty broth made of chopped lamb and crayfish tails. Other local favorites include *olla podrida* (stew), *picadillo de cerdo* (finely chopped pork), fresh trout, sausages, *chanfaina a la cazuela* (hash), *caracoles* (snails), and *callos a la burgalesa* (tripe). Candied egg yolks are a well-known sweet. Dinner for two with wine will cost $60 or more in restaurants listed as expensive, $30 to $60 in moderate restaurants, and $30 or less at inexpensive ones. All telephone numbers are in the 47 city code unless otherwise indicated.

Casa Ojeda – Some say they've had the meal of their lives here, while others say the price is too high for the quality of the food. The establishment, however, going strong since 1910, is big enough to encompass all opinions: a traditional, regional restaurant upstairs, a popular and appealing *tapas* bar-*cafetería* downstairs, and a fancy-food store next door. The decor is charming, the ambience everything it should be, the experience worth the cost. Restaurant closed Sunday evenings (but the snack bar stays open). Reservations advised. Major credit cards accepted. Entrances at 5 Calle Vitoria and on Plaza de Calvo Sotelo (phone: 209052). Expensive.

Los Chapiteles – Enjoy *tapas* in the bar before settling down at one of the heavy, dark tables in the smartly rustic dining room. The menu is a regional one, stressing various grilled lamb and pork dishes. Closed Wednesdays and Sunday evenings. Reservations necessary. Major credit cards accepted. 7 Calle General Santocildes (phone: 205998). Expensive.

Fernán González – This dining spot in luxurious surroundings has fast won a good reputation for its imaginative food and excellent wine cellar. Specialties include French beans with truffles and foie gras, sole cooked in a shellfish sauce, and Burgos cabbage with pork knuckles. Closed during the month of August. Reservations advised. Major credit cards accepted. 17 Calle Calera (phone: 209441). Expensive.

Landa Palace – Burgos's finest restaurant is in the hotel of the same name, 2 miles (3 km) from the center of town. It specializes in local Castilian dishes, and is perhaps best known for lamb baked in a wood-fired oven. But guests can choose from a full menu of other meat and fish dishes. The food is wholesome, the portions of good size, the service a study in Spanish exuberance — and the dining room itself is a lovely Gothic room with a 12-foot-high chandelier hanging from the center of the vaulted ceiling. Open daily. Reservations advised. Visa and MasterCard accepted. Carretera Madrid–Irún, Km 236 (phone: 206343). Expensive.

Mesón del Cid – Within the splendor of the 15th-century building housing the *Mesón del Cid* hotel, this Burgos tradition features a downstairs bar and several dining rooms on the upper levels that convey a feeling of medieval rusticity, along with excellent views of the cathedral. The fare includes sumptuous salads, fish, and steaks. Try the *solomillo* (sirloin) or the chef's special *merluza* (hake). Closed Sunday nights and February. Reservations advised. Major credit cards accepted. 8 Plaza de Santa María (phone: 205971). Expensive to moderate.

Ribera del Duero – In the center of town, serving traditional Castilian fare in two elegant, antiques-filled dining rooms at the top of a beautiful winding staircase. Closed Sundays and some holidays. Reservations necessary on weekends. Visa and MasterCard accepted. Plaza Santo Domingo de Guzmán (phone: 208513). Expensive to moderate.

Mesón de los Infantes – Pleasantly tucked into a corner just downhill off the Plaza del Rey San Fernando, serving more fine Castilian specialties such as *olla podrida* and *lentejas medievales,* "medieval lentils." There are tables outdoors for summer dining. Open daily. Reservations advised. Major credit cards accepted. Calle de Corral de los Infantes (phone: 205982). Moderate.

Rincón de España – Another choice spot for fine regional cuisine, which is served in an elegant dining room decorated with ceramic tiles on a culinary theme, or, weather permitting, on the large, awning-covered terrace looking over at the cathedral. The service is pleasant, and though this has the perfect location to draw busloads of sightseers, it is packed with both locals and lucky visitors who happen on a good thing. Closed Mondays. Reservations necessary. Visa accepted. 11 Calle Nuño Rasura (phone: 205955). Moderate.

Angel – Small, frequented by locals, it's up behind the cathedral, with its main dining room built against a section of the old city wall. Its own white stucco walls are accented with handsome wrought-iron lighting fixtures and coatracks, simple but attractive. Castilian cooking and fish dishes are the fare. Closed Sundays. Reservations advised. No credit cards accepted. 36 Calle Fernán González (phone: 208608). Moderate to inexpensive.

El Buen Vantar – Also up behind the cathedral; pass the unpretentious bar and head downstairs to the dining room, which is actually outdoors, covered by an awning. This is a popular place with the lunchtime crowd, due to its picturesque setting, and also cool at night, when part of the awning is rolled back to reveal the stars. The food is regional, well prepared, and very reasonable — a find. Closed Mondays at lunch. Reservations advised. No credit cards accepted. 41 Calle Fernán González (phone: 206116). Moderate to inexpensive.

Bonfin Self-Service – Located at the base of the stairs that descend from the west front of the cathedral. This cafeteria-style eatery has a wide range of entrée choices, as well as simple salads and sandwiches. A good choice for a quick meal between sightseeing stops. Open for lunch and dinner daily. No reservations or credit cards accepted. Calle Cadena y Eleta (phone: 206193). Inexpensive.

Hermanos Alonso – Simple food and surroundings, favored by the student crowd. The chicken, veal, and lamb dishes, all very good, are served in large helpings. Closed Thursdays. No reservations or credit cards accepted. 5 Calle de la Llana de Afuera (phone: 201711). Inexpensive.

TAPAS BARS: Burgos has literally hundreds of *tapas* bars, as well as many cafés and restaurants that also serve *tapas*. *Casa Ojeda* (5 Calle Vitoria; see *Eating Out*) and *Bar La Cabaña Arandina* (12 Calle Sombrereria; phone: 261932), on a pedestrian street leading from Plaza Mayor, are considered by many to be the best *tapas* bars in town. Both offer huge selections, which include *boquerones, pinchos* of meat, fish, or mushrooms, calamari, mussels, sausage, *tortillas,* pickled vegetables, and much more. Another favorite is *Bodega Riojana* (9 Plaza de Alonso Martínez; phone: 260719), a crowded corner eatery with a counter and a few tables where an amazing variety of edibles is consumed, including some in miniature casseroles called *cazuelitas.*

CÓRDOBA

The low-slung city of Córdoba sprawls along a sleepy, shallow stretch of the Guadalquivir River, 90 miles (143 km) upstream from Seville and 103 miles (165 km) northwest of Granada. For a traveler, it is the vital northern apex of the cultural, historical, and geographic triangle formed by the three great medieval Andalusian capitals, and of the three, it is Córdoba that best preserves its Moorish legacy. The city's incomparable treasure, the Mezquita or Great Mosque, is a forest of stone pillars and arches so vast that a full-blown cathedral, built by Christian conquerors who ripped out the heart of the mosque to accommodate it, seems lost in the shadowy aisles. Strange bedfellows, the mosque and cathedral are a fascinating expression of the amalgam of Moslem and Christian elements that is Spain.

The Mezquita, one of the greatest attractions in Spain, stands in the Judería, a quarter of the city where the pattern of narrow winding streets has not changed since Córdoba flourished as the capital of all Iberia under the rule of the opulent Umayyad caliphs, from the 8th to the 11th centuries. Judería, literally the Jewish district, is the name given to this intriguing Old Town, where Arabs and Jews once lived side by side. It still holds the former homes of two of the world's greatest thinkers, the Jewish philosopher-physician Maimonides and the Arab philosopher-mathematician Averroës, a few blocks from each other.

At the height of its splendor under the Arabs, who had wrested the territory from the Visigoths in 711, Córdoba was not merely the capital of all Iberia. It was also a city second in luxury and power only to glittering Constantinople. A pilgrimage to its Great Mosque is said to have equaled a journey to Mecca. Chroniclers of the day wrote of a city of half a million people, with 300,000 homes and palaces, 700 mosques, and hundreds of ritual baths. The same city that in Roman times had been home to Seneca the Elder and his son Lucius Annaeus Seneca, tutor of Nero, but which had declined under the Visigoths, became once again, under the Arabs, a center for scholars, scientists, and philosophers. It had the first university in Europe, a library with 400,000 hand-copied volumes, and legendary pleasure palaces. The silverwork and tooled leathers from its workshops were world famous. The tinseled silk veils produced for the caliph's wives were sheer enough to be drawn through the hoop of a silver earring.

The glory days of the Arabs in Córdoba lasted until 1031, when political infighting among the leaders led to the disintegration of the caliphate of Córdoba. Seville then became the capital of the Iberian Peninsula.

Today, Córdoba is a quiet provincial city of 300,000, its economy sustained by mining from the nearby *sierra* (mountains) and by agriculture from the surrounding *campiña* (plains). Conveniently compact, it has clearly defined old and new sections, which makes it an easy town to tour. Exploring its historic districts absorbs most of any visitor's time, but exploring its broad, tree-lined boulevards and up-to-date central core is a pleasant plus.

There are comfortable hotels, though too few of them, which leads too many visitors to make do with an afternoon stopover at the Mezquita on a trip between Seville and Madrid. Córdoba is worth a stay of at least 2 days, if only for the chance to drive out to the nearby excavations of the Medina Azahara, a country palace and royal city built by a 10th-century caliph. It takes time to browse Córdoba's famous flower-filled patios, to explore the Judería, to loll in Queen Isabella's gardens in the Alcázar, to watch the black-and-white cows grazing on the marshy river islands by the Roman Bridge. And those interested in Renaissance churches, palaces, and monuments will be occupied for several days. All the while, the romantic can fuel their dreams by sleeping and eating in centuries-old buildings that now serve as hotels and restaurants in the heart of the Judería. In Córdoba, if you so choose, you truly can live in the past.

CÓRDOBA AT-A-GLANCE

 SEEING THE CITY: The bell tower of the Mezquita is the best place to take the measure of Córdoba. It's open every day, and though there's a fee to climb it in addition to the Mezquita's admission charge, it's worth it, especially because the tower affords a bird's-eye view of the Mezquita's roof with the cathedral rising out of it. Bordering the Mezquita to the north and northwest are the humble tile roofs of the Judería, enclosed on the west by restored Arab walls. The bridge near the foot of the Mezquita is the Puente Romano (Roman Bridge), leading over the Guadalquivir to the Torre de la Calahorra, a 14th-century fortress, and to working class suburbs on the south side of the river. Running west along the near riverbank are the golden walls and gardens of the Alcázar. They end near the Puente San Rafael, the city's main approach bridge, which feeds traffic into the major north-south avenues, Paseo de la Victoria and Avenida República Argentina. The big oblong green space enclosed by these two boulevards is the Jardines de la Victoria, a flower-filled park that holds the annual May fair. Farther north is the Plaza de las Tendillas, Córdoba's downtown hub; beyond, the residential El Brillante district rises gently toward the hills. North and east of the Mezquita are the beautiful Renaissance church towers, monasteries, and palaces that proliferated after the 13th-century Christian Reconquest, as well as 11 columns of an excavated Roman temple right beside the prizewinning modern white marble building that houses Córdoba's City Hall.

SPECIAL PLACES: Though its easygoing atmosphere is easy to love, Córdoba's casual attitude toward opening and closing times, especially for the less-visited attractions, can disrupt the best-made tourist plans. Be sure to check on hours and days of opening when you arrive, because they seem to change more frequently than in larger cities. Generally, summer hours are mornings from 9:30 or 10 AM to 1:30 or 2 PM and afternoons from between 4 and 6 PM to 7 or 8 PM. (Afternoon times begin earlier in winter.) Museums are closed on Sunday afternoons and Mondays. Because of the city's compact layout, all the sights below, except the Medina Azahara and others situated in the environs, are within walking distance of each other. Unless it's a terribly hot summer day, do it all on foot.

CITY CENTER

La Mezquita (Great Mosque) – This 1,200-year-old masterwork by a succession of caliphs covers so much ground that after the Reconquest, not even the construction of an enormous Catholic cathedral dead in its center could totally destroy the impact of its "forest" of pillars and red-and-white candy-striped Moorish horseshoe arches marching into the hazy distance. In fact, as seen from the Puerta de las Palmas (Palm Door), which leads into the mosque proper from the forecourt, the Patio de los Naranjos (Orange Tree Court), the phantasmagoric rows of columns stretching in every direction seem mercifully to screen out the florid cathedral in their midst. A sensible way to conduct a visit is to leave the cruciform Gothic-Renaissance church section for last and concentrate first on the ancient mosque.

Note that the now-murky mosque was originally open to light and air on all sides. When Abd-er-Rahman I built the first section in 785, on the site of a demolished Visigothic Christian church — which, in turn, had been built on the foundations of a Roman temple — each row of marble columns ran straight out to its own row of orange trees in the forecourt. It was only after King Ferdinand III conquered Córdoba in 1236 that the Christians closed in the mosque and lined the walls with Catholic chapels. Much later, in the 16th century, they tore out more than 60 of its columns to erect a proper cathedral in its heart. At the same time, the mosque's minaret was rebuilt as a bell tower.

Abd-er-Rahman I's original square mosque, 240 feet on each side, was enlarged on three occasions — in 848, 961, and 987 — as Córdoba grew in size and importance in the Muslim world. By the 10th century, it covered its present 6 acres. More than 800 pillars stood along its aisles, for the most part antique classical pillars, some left from the previous Visigoth Christian church and Roman temple on the site and others taken from structures as far away as Italy, France, North Africa, and Constantinople. Since these secondhand columns were of unequal lengths, the builders raised the brick and marble flooring of the mosque and "planted" the columns at various depths to maintain a uniform height (an average of 13 feet) on which to support the arches. This illusion of pillars growing right out of the floor combines with a profusion of leafy Corinthian capitals to underscore the forest image.

The addition made to the mosque by Alhakem II in 961 — the southwest corner, containing 10 rows of exquisite alternating rose and blue marble columns and the most dazzling of its holy shrines — represents the high point in caliphate art. Here, against the south wall, is the holy Mihrab, a glistening alcove indicating the direction of Mecca. Framed by an arch of golden and polychrome Byzantine mosaics that radiate outward like a sun, it was the repository of a bejeweled Koran copied by a caliph's own hand and anointed with his blood. A huge scallop shell of white marble, symbol of the goddess Venus, forms the ceiling of its inner dome. Just in front of it, on the site of a former *mihrab,* is the Mudéjar Capilla Villaviciosa (Villaviciosa Chapel), whose stalactite ceiling and plaster lacework are visible only through a locked grille.

The much-maligned cathedral — which even the Holy Roman Emperor Charles V, who authorized its construction, deplored after seeing how it had disfigured the mosque (he regretted the destruction of something "unique" to make way for something "commonplace") — has some magnificent details. Its 18th-century mahogany choir stalls by Sevillian sculptor Pedro Duque Cornejo are among Europe's most elaborate. Its 240-pound 16th-century monstrance (a vessel used during Mass) by Enrique de Arfe was first carried through the streets for the city's Corpus Christi parade in 1518. The big hanging lamp before the altar is a fine example of 17th-century Cordoban silverwork.

The Puerta del Perdón (Pardon Door), next to the bell tower on Calle Cardenal Herrero, is the main entrance to the mosque, although at present visitors enter at the ticket gate on Calle Magistral González Francés. Before going in, be sure to make a full circuit of its crumbling walls to see all the old mosaic-decorated entranceways (some long since blocked up). The plant-filled balcony near the Pardon Door is the outdoor chapel of the Virgen de los Faroles, whose lanterns (*faroles*) are aglow at night. The Mezquita is open daily from 10:30 AM to 1:30 PM and from 4 to 7 PM. Admission charge; there is a separate fee to climb the bell tower. Calle Cardenal Herrero (phone: 470512).

Judería (Jewish Quarter) – North and west of the Mezquita, Córdoba's Judería, the Old Town, is a medieval warren of whitewashed houses, some still standing from caliphate times. Many of these precious relics are now the residences of middle-class and wealthy Cordobans, and the neighborhood is no longer Jewish or Arab. About a third of a mile of restored town walls, lighted till dawn, runs beside a moat and gardens along Calle Cairuán, at the neighborhood's western edge. A bronze statue of Seneca stands at the northern end of the walls, beside the Puerta de Almodóvar, a gate that once protected the city with an iron portcullis and is the principal western entrance to the Judería; farther south, a marble figure of Averroës stands near a smaller entrance on Calle de la Luna.

Sinagoga (Synagogue) – Pass through the Puerta de Almodóvar and turn right down Calle de los Judíos to one of only three synagogues in Spain to survive the Inquisition. (Toledo has the other two, which are grander.) Note the niche where the holy scrolls were kept and the 14th-century Mudéjar plasterwork along the upper walls and balcony where the women were sequestered during worship. Open Tuesdays through Saturdays from 10 AM to 2 PM and from 6 to 8 PM; open 10 AM to 1:30 PM on Sundays. Admission charge. Calle de los Judíos (no phone).

Museo Municipal de Arte Taurino (Municipal Museum of Bullfighting Art) – The city maintains this display in the 12th-century home of Maimonides (whose seated statue is nearby in the Plaza de Tiberiades). Most of the museum is devoted to bullfighting: room after room of posters, photos, swords, trophies, suits of light (jeweled suits for toreadors), and stuffed heads of bulls that were dispatched by such famous Córdoba-born *toreros* as Lagartijo, Guerrita, Manolete, and El Cordobés. Individual superstars have whole rooms devoted to their costumes (some bloodstained) and personal possessions, including their furniture. The crafts section of the museum, a small exhibit of fine Cordoban silver and leatherwork, is almost an afterthought. Open Tuesdays through Saturdays from 9:30 AM to 1:30 PM and from 5 to 8 PM; open mornings only on Sundays. Admission charge. Plazuela de Maimónides (phone: 472000).

El Zoco (Marketplace) – Across the street from the synagogue and adjoining the bullfighting museum is a 16th-century building complex surrounding a large cobblestone courtyard. Once an Arab *souk,* or marketplace, now it's a crafts market and, in summer, a setting for flamenco dancing. The artisans who work here with silver, ceramics, leather, and other materials, in ateliers provided by the city, welcome visitors to browse or buy. Open daily except Mondays. Calle de los Judíos.

Calleja de las Flores (Alley of Flowers) – The loveliest lane in the Judería offers a postcard view of the Mezquita bell tower framed by flowers. It's just northeast of the Mezquita, reached from Calle Bosco off Calle Cardenal Herrero.

Casa del Indiano (The Indian's House) – Near the Puerta de Almodóvar and also known as the Casa de las Ceas, this was once a great Arab palace, but now only its 15th-century façade remains. Walk through the portal to see a small, upper-crust residential enclave of new Andalusian houses installed in the area once occupied by the palace proper. Calleja del Indiano.

Alcázar de los Reyes Cristianos (Fortress of the Catholic Monarchs) – Unlike the Alcázar of Seville, much of the beauty of this fortress is in its outer walls and three remaining towers rather than in the interior living quarters. Ferdinand and Isabella were in residence during the later stages of their conquest of Granada, but the Alcázar, begun by Alfonso XI in 1328 on the site of an older Arab fortress, has been a prison for most of its grim history. King Boabdil of Granada was held captive here, the local headquarters of the Inquisition was located here until the 19th century, and then the Alcázar became a provincial prison, which it remained until it underwent restoration after the Spanish Civil War. Upon entering the complex under the archway of the Torre de los Leones (Tower of the Lions), turn left into the clean-lined Gothic palace, where a few significant reminders of past glories are displayed, including a sword of Toledo steel that belonged to the 11th-century Castilian hero El Cid and an exquisitely carved marble sarcophagus with scenes of Roman Córdoba. Magnificent Roman murals from the 1st century line the walls of the royal salon, now used for concerts; down steep stairs are the crumbling walls of underground Moorish baths, with typical Arab star-shaped skylights.

The fortress's centerpiece, the Patio Morisco (Moorish Court), endowed with twin pools and an ivy-covered grotto, leads to the Arab-walled Alcázar gardens, a romantic spot filled with more pools, fountains, rose gardens, and orchards. At the far end, a statuary group re-creates the meeting here in 1492 when the Catholic Monarchs gave Christopher Columbus the go-ahead for his auspicious voyage. Before leaving the Alcázar, walk the ramparts and climb the three stone towers remaining from the original four: The Torre de los Leones is the oldest and most interesting because of its Gothic dome, but the other two, El Río (River) and Homenaje (Homage), also command sweeping views. The Alcázar is open daily from 9:30 AM to 1:30 PM and from 5 to 8 PM; gardens are lighted on summer evenings until midnight. Admission charge. Camposanto de los Mártires (phone: 472000).

Puente Romano (Roman Bridge) – Just along the river from the Alcázar and easily recognized by its 16 characteristic arches, this was built by the Roman emperor Augustus in the 1st century BC, although few traces of the original structure remain after centuries of destruction and rebuilding. The restored 16th-century triumphal arch, Puerta del Puente, guards the main Córdoba side of the bridge and is flanked by the Triunfo de San Rafael column, one of a dozen homages to the city's guardian archangel. Another statue of the saint (this one 17th century) stands at the bridge's halfway point, its base blackened by wax from candles burned by passing worshipers. What's left of the Arabs' old water-powered stone flour mills can be seen in the river, whereas the giant wooden waterwheel on the Alcázar side is a replica of one that used to scoop up river water to irrigate the fortress gardens.

Torre de la Calahorra (Calahorra Tower) – In the 14th century, King Henry II constructed this stone fortress at the south end of the Puente Romano to ward off attacks by his hated half brother, Peter the Cruel, who built the Alcázar of Seville. The well-preserved tower, designed in the shape of a cross, was erected over an old Arab fort. It's now a city historical museum with a slide show of Córdoba and Andalusia that is shown at 11 AM, noon, 1, 3, and 4 PM. Open daily from 10 AM to 6 PM. Admission charge. Puente Romano (phone: 293929).

Museo Arqueológico (Archaeological Museum) – Scheduled to reopen this year after extensive restoration, both the beautiful old multi-patioed 16th-century palace and its important collection, beginning with stones from neolithic times, are reasons to see this museum, a short walk northeast of the Mezquita. The history of Andalusia is written in its Roman and Moorish treasures. Some of the most appealing objects, such as the famous stylized bronze stag, come from the ruins of the Medina Azahara outside Córdoba. Open Tuesdays through Saturdays from 10 AM to 2 PM and from 5 to 8 PM; open mornings only on Sundays. Admission charge. Plaza Jerónimo Páez (phone: 471076).

Plaza del Potro – This famous square east of the Mezquita takes its name from the diminutive statue of a rearing colt (*potro*) atop the 16th-century fountain in its center. The austere plaza, with its big, rough, gray paving stones, is walled in by the former Hospital de la Caridad (Charity Hospital) on one side and by an old inn, the *Posada del Potro*, on the other, and looks just as it must have when it rang with the cries of cattle traders and hummed with the gossip of travelers in the 16th and 17th centuries. Cervantes mentioned the big white *posada* in *Don Quixote* — it's where Sancho Panza endured the blanket toss. Now it functions as a cultural center, featuring a program of changing exhibitions.

Museo de Bellas Artes (Museum of Fine Arts) – The museum, with its blue-tile trim and black wrought-iron grilles recently restored, stands at the end of a manicured sculpture garden reached through the archway of the 15th-century Hospital de la Caridad. Goya's portrait of Queen María Luisa is the star of a creditable collection of statues and paintings, including works by such famous painters as Murillo, Zurburán, and Córdoba's own Valdés Leal. Open Tuesdays through Saturdays from 10 AM to 2 PM and from 6 to 8 PM; open 10 AM to 1:30 PM on Sundays. Admission charge. Plaza del Potro (phone: 473345).

Museo Romero de Torres – Scheduled to reopen this year after an extensive face-lift. Most visitors are mystified as to why the entire frescoed building, part of the *Museo de Bellas Artes* complex, should be devoted to the works of the saccharine 1920s painter Julio Romero de Torres. Apparently Córdoba feels some affection for the man who grew up in the *Museum of Fine Arts*, where his father was the curator. His romantic portrayals of Gypsy women and especially his *Naranjas y Limones* (Oranges and Lemons), a portrait of a topless beauty, are the big draw. Open Tuesdays through Saturdays from 10 AM to 1:30 PM and from 4 to 6 PM; open mornings only on Sundays (in July, August, and September, closed all afternoons). No admission charge. Plaza del Potro (phone: 471314).

Plaza de la Corredera – This drab 16th-century plaza north of Plaza del Potro, entirely enclosed by brick-porticoed apartment buildings, faintly resembles Madrid's Plaza Mayor, but there's no other like it in southern Spain. Once the main square of Córdoba and the scene of bullfights, jousts, and races, it now comes alive as an outdoor market from early morning to 2 PM daily except Sundays.

Plaza de las Tendillas – The heart of downtown Córdoba, this is a huge square on a gentle hill, lined with banks, cafés, and shops. The figure astride the horse in the center of the fountain is Queen Isabella's vaunted general, El Gran Capitán, Gonzalo Fernández de Córdoba, who conquered the kingdom of Naples for the Spanish crown. At the northern end of the square, Avenida Cruz Conde leads down to the city's main shopping area; at the southern end, Calle Jesús y María leads to the Mezquita.

Cristo de los Faroles (Christ of the Lanterns) – Don't miss this towering 18th-century stone crucifix surrounded by wrought-iron lanterns in a stark, narrow square. It's particularly moving at night when the lanterns are lit. Inside the small, white church on the square — the Iglesia de los Dolores (Church of the Sorrows) — is Córdoba's most venerated virgin, the tearful, gold-crowned Virgen de los Dolores, displayed above the altar against a background of glowing blue light. Plaza de los Dolores.

Palacio-Museo de Viana (Viana Palace-Museum) – This enchanting ancestral palace of the Marqués de Viana, with a dozen breathtaking patios and 52 lavish rooms (of nearly 100) on view, is one of the best-kept and most efficiently managed attractions in Córdoba. A brochure in English describes a self-guided tour of its magnificent interconnected patio gardens, which are its star feature; a smartly uniformed guard leads visitors through the house itself, which is a complete museum of the aristocratic Andalusian lifestyle, fully furnished and decorated with the family's collections of china, silver sculpture, tapestries, paintings, equestrian trappings, swords, guns, coins, and tiles — just as though the family still lived there. Allow about 2 hours to see both house and gardens. Open from 9 AM to 2 PM (from 10 AM to 2 PM on Sundays); closed Wednesdays. Admission charge. Plaza de Don Gome (phone: 482275).

ENVIRONS

Medina Azahara – A dry, olive-dotted Sierra foothill 4 miles (6 km) west of Córdoba is the site of the extensively excavated and delightfully restored pleasure palace and city built by Abd-er-Rahman III for his favorite wife, Azahara, in 936. This archaeological mother lode, a place that once rivaled the Mezquita for beauty and mystery, runs down the hillside from the entrance at a small museum at the top. Clearly marked paths descend through a terraced town that once housed 20,000 royal retainers and served as the seat of Cordoban government for 70 years until Berber mercenaries, who had been called in to defend it, burned it to the ground. No expense was spared in laying out its royal palace, great mosque, 400 houses, army barracks, royal mint, gardens, fishponds, orchards, fountains, heavy fortifications, and ornate gateways, spread over 275 acres. The arches of the mosque, palace, and other buildings were supported by 4,000 ornamented columns of rose, azure, onyx, white, and mustard marble. After its destruction, the city was fair game for scavengers, so today its marbles are found in later palaces in Andalusia, including the Alcázar in Seville. The imposing early 15th-century Convento de San Jerónimo de Valparaíso (which can be visited by applying to the caretaker) on the mountain above the Medina also uses its stones. Nevertheless, there seem to be enough fragments left to keep restorers at work piecing the city together forever.

Excavation began in 1914 and proceeded fitfully until recent years, when the pace was stepped up. Much of what the visitor sees are foundations and ruined shells of buildings; but the magnificent, colonnaded Dar al-Mulk, or royal apartment complex, with delicate plasterwork, intricate stone carving, and majestic proportions, has already been roofed over and is being meticulously reconstructed. Medina Azahara (phone: 234025) is open Tuesdays through Saturdays from 10 AM to 2 PM and from 6 to 8 PM; open from 10 AM to 1:30 PM on Sundays. Admission charge. To reach the site by private car or cab, take Avenida de Medina Azahara out of town to the C431 highway. (Inquire at the tourist office for possible special bus service.)

Las Ermitas – Scattered in the hills 8 miles (13 km) northwest of town are a baker's dozen Christian hermits' cells known as Las Ermitas. Their existence may go back as far as the 4th century, although the hermits who occupied them to live a life of solitary self-sacrifice were organized into an order only in the 17th century. (They weathered even Córdoba's Moorish days, flourishing with the blessing of the Muslim caliphs.) The community finally died out in the 1950s, and the cells have fallen into disrepair, but the site is still evocative. The grounds are reached via Avenida del Brillante. (The tourist office can supply driving directions.) Admission by voluntary donation.

■**EXTRA SPECIAL:** Don't be shy about gazing into Córdoba's flower-filled patios. It's a local custom. The gorgeous patios are considered an official asset of the city, which has built an annual 2-week festival around them (see *Special Events*). If the door to the forecourt is open, that's an invitation to look through the wrought-iron *cancela* (grille) into the family's private world, fragrant with geraniums, roses, carnations, orange and lemon trees, sweet basil, and jasmine. No two patio landscapes are alike; some of the most sophisticated are studies in greenery, masonry, and ceramics, rather than color. You'll find some outstanding beauties in the Judería around Plaza de Juda Levi, especially at 6 Calle Albucasis, where one of the most visited patios in town displays walls studded with pots of blazing geraniums. Take Calle Buen Pastor (be sure to stop at No. 2) and continue to Calle Leiva Aguilar. There's another cluster of prizewinners across from the Alcázar gardens, on Calle San Basilio and surrounding streets. Ask at the tourist office for a patio tour map.

SOURCES AND RESOURCES

TOURIST INFORMATION: The Oficina Municipal de Turismo (Municipal Tourist Office), in the heart of the Judería (Plaza de Juda Levi; phone: 472000), is open from 9 AM to 2 PM weekdays, 10 AM to 1 PM on Saturdays. A blackboard outside lists the city's principal sights and hours of opening, as well as special events. The Oficina de Turismo de la Junta de Andalucía, just west of the Mezquita (10 Calle Torrijos; phone: 471235), has information on all of Andalusia and is open from 9:30 AM to 2 PM and from 5 to 7 PM weekdays, 9:30 AM to 1:30 PM on Saturdays. Both offices have helpful English-speaking personnel, which is fortunate, because Córdoba lags badly in up-to-date tourist literature, especially in English. When buying a map or local guidebook, look for the one with the most recent printing date. Older maps and books, still being sold, show prominent streets and plazas with their names from the Franco era, which can add to the already considerable confusion caused by winding streets, many with hard-to-spot street names and house numbers. Since there is no satisfactory guidebook for the Mezquita (a lifelong study in itself), a local guide schooled in the subtle complexities of this fascinating structure is recommended. Licensed English-speaking guides can be hired at the entrance or at guide headquarters (2 Calle Torrijos; phone: 474274). A half-day bus and walking tour of the city (buses can't enter the Judería) is offered by *Viajes Vincit* (1 Calle Alonso de Burgos; phone: 472316).

Local Coverage – The local daily read by Cordobans is the *Córdoba*. The weekly *El Mercadillo,* also in Spanish, carries listings of theatrical and special events.

TELEPHONE: The city code for Córdoba is 57. If calling from within Spain, dial 957 before the local number.

GETTING AROUND: Airport – Córdoba's municipal airport, 5½ miles (9 km) from town, has an extremely limited flight schedule since most people arrive by bus, train, or car. For flight information, check with *Iberia,* 3 Ronda de los Tejares (phone: 471227 or 472695).

Bus – Green-and-white city buses cover the town. Tourists rarely use them, however, because it's possible to walk almost everywhere and taxi fares for Córdoba's short distances between sights are low. There is no central bus terminal for intercity buses and no central information number. The tourist office has up-to-date schedules; otherwise, for information on buses to Madrid and Barcelona, call 290158; for Seville, call 472352; for Málaga and Granada, call 236474.

Car Rental – Among the firms represented are *Avis* (at the airport and at 28 Plaza de Colón; phone: 476862); *Hertz* (at the airport and at the railroad station; phone: 477243); and *Europcar* (at the airport and at *Hotel Los Gallos Sol,* 7 Avenida de Medina Azahara; phone: 232011). Convenient parking for the Mezquita and the Judería can be found along the Paseo de la Victoria (a street attendant collects a small fee) or at the river at Plaza del Triunfo, where there's a guarded lot.

Horse and Carriage – A popular way to see the Judería, though coaches can't enter some of its alleyways. Drivers are entertaining guides. *Coches de caballo* are for hire around the Mezquita and the Alcázar.

Taxi – Call for a cab (phone: 470291) or hail one in the street.

Train – The railroad station is on Avenida de América. Tickets can be purchased downtown at the *RENFE* office (10 Ronda de los Tejares). For train information, call 478721.

SPECIAL EVENTS: The famous *Fiesta de los Patios* fills the city with visitors during the first 2 weeks in May. Everyone goes from one private patio to another admiring walls literally covered with gorgeously planted flowerpots, and prizes are awarded for the best displays. At the same time, public plazas are decked with flowers and flowered crosses. This is followed by the annual *Feria de Nuestra Señora de la Salud — Feria* for short — held the last week in May. Córdoba's fair is especially festive because of its location in the heart of town: The lineup of *casetas*, private tents for entertaining, and the midway Ferris wheel, merry-go-round, and snack stands run the length of the Jardines de la Victoria; flamenco contests, pop and classical concerts, ballet, parades, fireworks, and displays of Cordoban horsemanship fill the streets with action; and the sounds of stamping and clapping ring out along with the twang of guitars from El Zoco, where Gypsies dance throughout the summer. Since May is also Córdoba's bullfight season, advance hotel reservations for this action-packed month are a must.

SHOPPING: With prices on most goods generally high, the things to look for are local products, notably silver filigree jewelry and fine tooled leather. Silver shops with affordable filigree jewelry can be found around the Mezquita and especially along Calle Deanes, as can a jumble of souvenir stands selling toreador dolls, fans, caftans, brass trays, embossed leather wallets, handbags, and hassocks. Consider a stop at Córdoba's finest leather shop, *Meryan* (2 Calleja de las Flores; phone: 475902) — more like visiting a museum than shopping, unless you're prepared for a serious purchase. The artistic hand-embossed and tinted leather (*guadamecil*) goods are done in the Renaissance style (with some designs derived from classical paintings), the handwork is painstaking and magnificent, and prices on the larger pieces run into the thousands. Wander up and down the stairs in this centuries-old mansion, whose gardens once extended down to the mosque, to inspect leather chairs, chests, wall hangings, maps, picture frames, and even some wooden pieces, and ask to see the workshops surrounding the serene white marble patio. The more affordable leather bags and wallets that many visitors end up buying here are of excellent quality but not made by the shop. Silversmiths and leather workers are also among the craftsmen (there are woodworkers, weavers, ceramists, and others) selling their wares in *El Zoco,* the municipal crafts market opposite the synagogue in the Judería. The latest addition to this old complex is the avant-garde *Arte Zoco* cooperative art gallery facing Calle de los Judíos (phone: 204033). The *Librería Sefarad* (4 Calle Romero, Judería; phone: 296262) houses Spain's only shop devoted to Sephardic Jewry, including folk songs and books in Ladino — the old Spanish dialect spoken by Spanish Jews before their expulsion from the country during the Inquisition.

For general purchases and boutique fashions, shop the Avenida Cruz Conde area off Plaza de las Tendillas. The city's major department store, the British-owned *Galerías Preciados* (32 Ronda de los Tejares; phone: 470267), is another place for general shopping; it has a convenient cafeteria, too.

SPORTS AND FITNESS: Bullfighting – May is the season at the *Plaza de Toros* (Gran Vía del Parque), although there are occasional *corridas* during the rest of the year. Arrange for tickets through your hotel.

Golf – The *Club de Golf Los Villares* (5½ miles/9 km) north of town via

Avenida del Brillante; phone: 474102) has an 18-hole course, a practice course, a restaurant, a swimming pool, and tennis courts. Visitors may use the facilities; reservations can be made directly or through the Patronato Provincial de Turismo (Provincial Tourist Office; 1 Calle Pérez de Castro; phone: 202377).

Horseback Riding – Try the *Club Hípico,* Carretera Santa María de Trassiera (phone: 271628).

Jogging – Beautiful suburban roads await guests of the *Parador de la Arruzafa* (see *Checking In*); for those staying in town, there's early-morning jogging in the Jardines de la Victoria.

Soccer – The *Club de Fútbol de Córdoba* plays at the *Estadio Arcángel* (Calle Venerable Juan de Santiago) — but Córdoba hasn't been proud of its home team lately.

Swimming – Short of a quick trip to the Costa del Sol, the best bet is to book one of the few hotels in Córdoba equipped with a pool. The great ones are at the *Meliá Córdoba, Las Adelfas,* and the *Parador de la Arruzafa;* the pool at *Los Gallos Sol* is small for laps. The *Club de Golf Los Villares* also has a swimming pool (see above).

Tennis – The *Parador de la Arruzafa* and *Las Adelfas* have tennis courts for guests. Another option is the *Club de Golf Los Villares* (see above), which can be used by non-members.

 THEATER AND MUSIC: Plays (some by national touring companies), dance performances, and classical, flamenco, and pop concerts come to the recently refurbished, century-old *Gran Teatro* (Avenida del Gran Capitán; phone: 480237 and 480644). American and British films in original-language version are just about the only entertainment offered in English and are arranged by the Fundación Pública Municipal. In summer, the municipal orchestra gives Sunday concerts in the Alcázar gardens. Check the weekly *El Mercadillo* for listings or consult the daily newspaper.

 NIGHTCLUBS AND NIGHTLIFE: Except during the *Feria* in May, Cordobans stick pretty close to home at night. Nevertheless, count on finding life after dark in the center at Plaza Ignacio Loyola, off Avenida Menéndez y Pelayo, where, in fair weather, yellow and white café umbrellas sprout in front of the Iglesia San Hipólito. You can do your own *sevillanas* to live combos under orange and white polka dot paper lanterns at the crowded *La Caseta* (4 Plaza Ignacio Loyola; phone: 412967), which also offers dinner and *tapas,* flamenco shows, and disco. Go late for the shows — from 10 PM to 4 AM, although this lively spot is open earlier (closed Sundays). Or have snacks, wine, or beer at the contemporary little pubs, bars, and *bodegas* (liquor shops selling drinks) along the square. For disco, try the neon and red-plush ambience of *Contactos* (8 Calle Eduardo Dato; phone: 292466), or the sleek *Saint-Cyr* (4 Calle Eduardo Lucena; phone: 292440), in the basement of a downtown office building.

Bar hopping is a good way to end a day in the Judería. Join the neighborhood people at the hospitable bar in *Casa Rubio* (5 Puerta de Almodóvar; phone: 290064) or enjoy *tapas* and beer in its postage-stamp patio (closed Wednesdays). Then cross the street (there's no number, but you'll see the sign), for the minuscule and impeccable *Casa Salinas* (phone: 290846), a longtime musicians' hangout, and munch the house specialty, *pescaítos fritos* — *tapas* of crisp fried fish. At the Calle de la Luna entrance to the Judería, Cordobans dance *sevillanas* within the 150-year-old, 3-foot-thick walls of *Mesón de la Luna* (Calle de la Luna) and at *Mesón Murillo* (just across the way). There's also a convivial crowd to be found at the venerable *Bar Mezquita* (24 Calle Cardenal Herrero), across from the front of the mosque.

BEST IN TOWN

CHECKING IN: Córdoba's charms are centered around the Judería, so try for one of the atmospheric hotels there. If they're all booked, don't despair — the city is so compact that even a hotel in the modern section is close to the center. But remember to book early for the month of May, when the *Patio Festival,* the *Feria,* and the bullfighting season make Córdoba's extremely tight hotel situation even tighter. The hotels noted are all air conditioned. Expect to pay from about $100 to $150 for a double room in those listed as expensive, from $70 to $100 in those listed as moderate, and from $35 to $70 in the inexpensive ones. All telephone numbers are in the 57 city code unless otherwise indicated.

Adarve – This white-on-white arcaded palace provides grace and comfort enough to please a caliph. An updated Moorish villa just across the street from the Mezquita, it has 103 rooms, but it seems much smaller and more intimate. The central courtyard, containing discreetly splashing fountains and one perfect orange and one perfect loquat tree, is enchanting. Some rooms have French doors opening onto the courtyard; others face the weathered walls of the mosque. There's a coffee shop, but for lunch and dinner, the *Adarve,* like its sister hotel, the *Maimónides,* uses the *Bandolero* restaurant (see *Eating Out*) adjoining the latter. There also is a garage. 15 Calle Magistral González Francés (phone: 481102; fax: 474677). Expensive.

Las Adelfas – This new establishment is splendidly located near the *Parador de la Arruzafa* (see below) on a gentle hill overlooking the city. The façade is South American–colonial. Inside, it is brightly lit and spacious; paintings and sculpture adorn every space, lending an artistic air. It has 101 rooms, a restaurant, a pool, tennis courts, and conference rooms. Paseo de la Arruzafa (phone: 277420; fax: 272794). Expensive.

Husa Gran Capitán – An efficient international commercial property filled with tour groups. It's on the outskirts across from the railroad station (double window glass muffles the noise), but still only a short cab ride to the Judería and a comfortable haven when closer places are booked. It has 99 rooms, a restaurant, and a garage. 5 Avenida de América (phone: 470250; fax: 474643). Expensive.

Maimónides – Across the street from the Mezquita (but on the opposite side from its glossier sister hotel, the *Adarve*), it is characterized by dignified but somber elegance, with Renaissance Spanish decor. There are 152 comfortable rooms; only breakfast is served, but the *Bandolero* restaurant is two steps across a narrow alley from the lobby (see *Eating Out*). Garage. 4 Calle Torrijos (phone: 471500; fax: 483803). Expensive.

Meliá Córdoba – The city's "grand hotel" lacks architectural flair, but has an ideal location at the head of the Jardines de la Victoria, outside the Arab walls but just a 3-minute walk away, and only about 10 minutes on foot from the modern downtown area. It offers a big-hotel lobby and good concierge service, 106 well-appointed rooms, a cocktail lounge, the elegant *Restaurante del Palacio,* boutiques, and a large swimming pool in an exceptional garden setting. No garage, but street parking is possible to find except during the May festivals. Jardines de la Victoria (phone: 298066; fax: 298147). Expensive.

Parador de la Arruzafa – The former garden of date palms (*arruzafa*) of Abd-er-Rahman I, first builder of the Mezquita, is the expansive country club setting of Córdoba's government-run *parador,* although the structure itself is of fairly recent vintage. Located 2 miles (3 km) from town, it has terraces overlooking spacious lawns and gardens leading down to a big swimming pool and tennis courts. Many of the 94 rooms have balconies. Cab service is available. Avenida de la Arruzafa (phone: 275900; fax: 280409). Expensive.

Albucasis – Close to the Mezquita, this delightful little property occupies an old mansion that has been stylishly restored in Mudéjar fashion. Spotlessly clean, with friendly service, it has 15 rooms and a charming patio, and it's popular among visiting university staff. Breakfast only. 11 Calle Buen Pastor (phone: 478625). Moderate.

Cisne – Simple but sparkling, this hostelry is near the railroad station, a short cab ride to the Judería; it has 44 rooms, and a restaurant. 14 Avenida Cervantes (phone: 481676). Moderate.

Los Gallos Sol – Just a short cab ride from the Old Town is a comfortable 7-story high-rise with upbeat, colorful decor, a token rooftop swimming pool, and a popular lobby cafeteria. Many of its 115 simple, tweedy rooms face a charming avenue; others have patio views. Old hands will recognize it as the former *El Cordobés,* once owned by the famous bullfighter but updated by new owners about a decade ago. 7 Avenida de Medina Azahara (phone: 235500; fax: 231636). Moderate.

Boston – Tidy and comfortable, this little *hostal* of 40 rooms overlooks the hubbub of Plaza de las Tendillas. No restaurant. Reserve early. 2 Calle Málaga (phone: 474176). Inexpensive.

Marisa – A simple refuge with 28 rooms in a prime location across from the shrine of the Virgen de los Faroles at the Mezquita. Breakfast, but no restaurant. 6 Calle Cardenal Herrero (phone: 473142). Inexpensive.

El Triunfo – This 44-room *hostal,* right by the river at the foot of the Mezquita, is one of the best small hotels in the Old Town. A TV set blares in the tiny, crowded lobby during soccer season, the restaurant charges popular prices (see *Eating Out*), and European tourists keep it filled. Reserve early. 79 Calle Cardenal González (phone: 475500; fax: 486850). Inexpensive.

 EATING OUT: Córdoba's most intriguing restaurants and *tapas* bars cluster around the Mezquita, although there are also some well-frequented places in the modern city that are convenient to hotels outside the Judería. As elsewhere in Andalusia, the local cuisine is Arab influenced, but here the Arab accent comes to the fore in dishes rich in almonds, honey, figs, candied fruits, oranges, pine nuts, and sweet, fragrant Arab flavorings. Then there are the dishes Cordobans say they originated, among them *salmorejo,* a thick, waterless tomato gazpacho. The city's most famous culinary contribution is *pastel cordobés,* sometimes called *tarta Manolete,* a flat, round pastry with a honey-sweetened *cabello del angel* (angel hair) pumpkin filling. It's on most dessert menus and in pastry shops. Be sure to taste the local montilla-moriles wines, ranging from dry white *finos* to sweet Pedro Ximenez dessert wines. The Montilla-Moriles wine country to the south produces twice as much sherry-like wine, made by the *solera* system, as is made in Jerez.

Expect to pay $65 or more for a 3-course meal for two with local wine at restaurants listed as expensive, from $35 to $65 at those listed as moderate, and under $35 at those listed as inexpensive. Restaurants in all categories have tourist menus that are relatively inexpensive. All telephone numbers are in the 57 city code unless otherwise indicated.

Mesón Bandolero – Rough brick arches, furnishings in tooled leather and old wood, tables set with hammered-brass service plates — this is a restaurant on a grand scale. It's set in an old palace where Averroës lived, and it has, besides the lavish indoor dining rooms, a spacious canvas-shaded patio where songbirds in filigree cages sing among the four palm trees. The menu is elegant international, with local touches such as *rabo de toro* (oxtail stew), *ensalada de perdiz en* *escabeche* (marinated partridge salad), and *anguilas a pil-pil* (baby eels with garlic and oil). Next door to the *Maimónides* hotel. Open daily. Reservations advised. Major credit cards accepted. 8 Calle Medina y Corella (phone: 414245). Expensive.

Oscar – You'll be off the tourist track here at the city's leading seafood restaurant. Take a seat in the pocket-size plaza in front of the restaurant, inside at the *tapas* bar loaded with crab and rock lobster, or in dark, cozy dining rooms. Closed Sundays and August. Reservations advised. Major credit cards accepted. 6 Plaza de los Chirinos (phone: 477517). Expensive.

El Bosque – An indoor-outdoor suburban dining spot on the sloping road to the *Parador de la Arruzafa* (see *Checking In*). Well-heeled Córdoba congregates here — for a *copa* (glass of wine) while the lights of the city below are coming on, or for an elegant dinner later. Open daily. Reservations unnecessary. Major credit cards accepted. 134 Avenida del Brillante (phone: 270006). Expensive to moderate.

El Caballo Rojo – Consistently well-executed regional dishes, served by patient, red-jacketed waiters accustomed to foreigners, make this big, friendly place across from the mosque the most popular spot in Córdoba for first-time visitors. (It's also probably Andalusia's most famous restaurant.) Bypass the ground-floor bar and head upstairs to the bright dining rooms, where Andalusian specialties are displayed on a big buffet, and while sipping your complimentary aperitif of the local dry white montilla wine, ponder the choices: thick *salmorejo* (gazpacho), *sopa de ajo blanco* (milk-white garlicky gazpacho with chopped apples, raisins, and ground almonds), *rape mozárabe* (monkfish with raisins and brandy), *cordero a la miel* (lamb shanks in honey sauce). A 4-foot-high dessert trolley bears flan and other delights, but if you haven't tried *pastel cordobés*, this is the place. Open daily. Reservations advised. Major credit cards accepted. 28 Calle Cardenal Herrero (phone: 475375). Expensive to moderate.

Seneca – Across the river from the touristy side of town, this classic-style eatery has more of a Castilian than an Andalusian air about it. Meat cooked in wood-fired ovens in view of guests is a specialty. Reservations advised. Major credit cards accepted. Avenida de la Confederación (phone: 204020). Expensive to moderate.

Almudaina – Elegant Andalusian dining, in one of the intimate lace-curtained salons of a 15th-century palace or in the brick-lined, glass-roofed central courtyard. Try the *solomillo al vino tinto* (pork loin in wine sauce) or *merluza en salsa de gambas* (hake with shrimp sauce), and for dessert, order the chef's renowned tropical fruit sorbet or the *pudín de limón y almendras* (semi-frozen lemon-almond crème). The restaurant, across from the Alcázar, is owned by the well-respected *Ciro's* in the business section (see below). Closed Sunday nights. Reservations necessary. Major credit cards accepted. 1 Plaza Camposanto de los Mártires (phone: 474342). Moderate.

Azahar – Vaguely Arab in style, and in vogue, it's often crowded with discerning locals. Roast meats are a specialty, but try the excellent *crema de cangrejos al brandy* (crab purée with brandy sauce). Open daily. Reservations necessary. American Express and Visa accepted. 10 Avenida de Medina Azahara (phone: 414387). Moderate.

El Churrasco – When it comes to that one big meal in Córdoba, this low-key place gives the showier *El Caballo Rojo* a run for its money. Locals join tourists in this unassuming house on a Judería side street, tempted by the patio dining, the sumptuous *tapas* bar, and the signature dish, *churrasco* (charcoal-grilled pork loin in savory sauce), plus other grilled meat and fish dishes. Closed Thursdays and August. Reservations necessary. Major credit cards accepted. 16 Calle Romero (phone: 290819). Moderate.

Ciro's – It offers the same menu and the same prices as its sister restaurant, *Al-*

mudaina, but in a sophisticated international setting that draws Córdoba's expense-account diners. Downstairs there's a lively informal café. Open daily. Reservations advised. Major credit cards accepted. Along the park at 23 Paseo de la Victoria (phone: 290464). Moderate.

Pic-Nic – Small and simple, but extremely popular and highly regarded by locals. The menu is imaginative, and it's a casual place to taste typical Andalusian food without much protocol. Closed Sundays. Reservations advised. Visa and MasterCard accepted. 16 Ronda de los Tejares (phone: 482233). Moderate.

El Burlaero – The modest outdoor dining court and cozy restaurant here are easiest to find by walking through *El Caballo Rojo* to the outdoor staircase in back and turning right up the stairs. A budget sleeper, this place serves simple, well-prepared Cordoban cooking, well suited to a light lunch. Open daily. Reservations unnecessary. No credit cards accepted. The restaurant's front entrance is at 5 Calleja La Hoguera (phone: 472719). Moderate to inexpensive.

El Triunfo – The small restaurant of this *hostal* near the Mezquita is as good a buy as the rooms upstairs. Especially at lunchtime, its menu of *platos combinados* is a smart choice over the rival *mesones* that besiege you with handbills touting tourist specials; most of them are too cheap to be good. Open daily. Reservations unnecessary. No credit cards accepted. 79 Calle Cardenal González (phone: 475500). Inexpensive.

GRANADA

Of all the fabled landmarks in the world, none stands in a more gorgeous setting than the magnificent Alhambra, the hilltop fortress-palace of the Nasrid kings, the last Muslim rulers of Spain. Snow-capped peaks of the nearby Sierra Nevada form a natural tapestry behind its golden walls, and below, a mosaic of Granada's Moorish-Christian towers spreads like a magic carpet over a fertile plain. Granada has much more to offer than the Alhambra alone, but even if visitors were to tour only the Alhambra's multitude of pleasures — for this is not a single building, but a complex of palaces, gardens, towers, gates, courtyards, and other structures whose exquisite decoration sums up the meaning of the word "arabesque" — the city would be worth the trip. This once-remote Arab stronghold, now just a 2-hour drive from the tourist-laden Costa del Sol, is Spain's second-biggest attraction after the *Prado* in Madrid.

In its Roman days and up through the early Muslim period, Granada languished on history's sidelines. But the city came into its own during the 13th century, when the Moors began to lose their grip elsewhere in Andalusia. Córdoba fell to Christian rule in 1236, Seville in 1248. But Granada, which had become the capital of the Nasrid kingdom of Granada (which included the present-day provinces of Granada, Almería, and Málaga) in 1238, would hang on under Moorish rule for approximately another 250 years. As the city became the last surviving Islamic capital in Spain, Moors by the thousands streamed into it, transforming it into a thriving center of artists and craftsmen. The royal Alhambra was their masterpiece. Through ensuing centuries, this wonder of the world cast its spell over writers, painters, and musicians, including the American author Washington Irving and two of Granada's most famous sons, the composer Manuel de Falla and the writer-poet Federico García Lorca.

The final triumph in the Christians' 781-year struggle to regain Moorish-held Spain took place on January 2, 1492, when the last Muslim king, Boabdil, handed over the keys to the city to Ferdinand and Isabella and rode tearfully off into the mountains with the queen mother, Ayesha. ("You weep like a woman for what you could not defend as a man" were her immortal words of consolation to her son.) The Catholic Monarchs installed their thrones in the Alhambra and set about remaking the city in the Christian image, creating the architectural mix that is still in evidence. Isabella ordered the construction of the cathedral and its Capilla Real, the finely wrought Royal Chapel, where the marble tombs of the royal pair, as well as her crown and jewel box, can be seen today. Muslim mosques were converted to Christian uses. Unfortunately, many fine Moorish buildings have been destroyed, but a walk through the twisted, narrow streets of the Albaicín, an old Arab neighborhood on a hill across from the Alhambra, gives a pretty good idea of what the city once was like.

Granada continued to flourish into the 16th century, then sank back into relative obscurity once again. Today, a city of about 265,000, it depends economically on its rich agricultural valley, as well as on nonindustrial enterprises such as banking, education, and tourism. A big boost to the latter will come this year. While the rest of Spain, and especially Seville, celebrates the 500th anniversary of Columbus's discovery of America, Granada will be celebrating the 500th anniversary of the Christian Reconquest as well. During the past few years, many museums and monuments have been renovated in anticipation of expanded world attention.

Sightseeing in Granada is delightful. The absence of heavy manufacturing sections and the existence of only a scattering of garish modern buildings in the busy downtown area confer a small-town, open-air feeling to the streets. And the large student population at the University of Granada keeps the town young. Then there are Granada's famous Gypsy women, those entrepreneurs in housedresses and sweaters pressing carnations and fortunes on passersby at the cathedral and on the Alhambra hill. Begging and wheedling are their chosen livelihood, and everyone seems to accept that. *Granadinos* shoo them off with a firm "no," but visitors don't get off so easily. "*Tu te vas a casar hombre alto*" (you will marry a tall man), they call to a passing tourist, grabbing her hand. And if you cross their palms with coins, they shout "*papel, papel*" (paper)! Your fortune, whether you want it or not, costs whatever the traffic will bear. (Only a "*vamos a la policía*" turns them off.) The Gypsy population played such a colorful part in history here that Granada is more accepting of their ways than Seville. Proposals to license them have come to nothing; posting official rates at the Alhambra has been suggested, though many *granadinos* say that wouldn't change a thing — nor would they want it to.

GRANADA AT-A-GLANCE

SEEING THE CITY: This is a city of many views, but the "postcard" picture of the Alhambra set against mountains that are snow covered most of the year is from Plaza San Nicolás in the Albaicín. Within the Alhambra walls, the Torre de la Vela in the Alcazaba (see below) affords a panorama of city, plains, and mountains.

SPECIAL PLACES: Granada is divided neatly into upper and lower towns. Two prominent hills facing each other across the narrow gorge of a river — the Río Darro — compose the upper city. On the southern hill are the Alhambra and the adjoining Generalife (the summer palace and gardens of the Nasrid kings). On the northern hill is the old Arab quarter, the Albaicín, now a fascinating residential district. An even taller satellite hill leads off from the Albaicín to the dusty Sacromonte Gypsy district, a warren of small white houses trailing out to a rocky mountainside pockmarked with abandoned Gypsy caves.

The main descent from the Alhambra is a narrow road, Cuesta de Gomérez, that drops directly down to the Plaza Nueva, where the lower city begins. The plaza is the eastern end of the principal east-west artery, Calle de los Reyes Católicos, which meets the principal north-south artery, Gran Vía de Colón, at the circular Plaza de Isabel la Católica. A much-photographed bronze statue of the enthroned Queen Isabella offering the Santa Fé agreement to Columbus graces this major intersection; the document, named for the nearby town where it was signed, authorized the epochal voyage to the New World. Calle de los Reyes Católicos then continues west, passing within a few short blocks of the cathedral, the Capilla Real, and other downtown sights, en route to Puerta Real, the hub of the city's business, shopping, and hotel and restaurant district.

Note that the opening hours listed below for Granada's monuments, churches, and museums are for the months of March through September; winter afternoon hours generally are shorter. Times are subject to change.

THE ALHAMBRA COMPLEX

Spain's last remaining fortress-palace built for a Moorish sovereign stands atop the Alhambra hill, girded by more than a mile of ramparts that appear in the distance like a golden shield. (To the medieval Arabs, however, the rust-colored local soil used to build the fortress gave it a more coppery tinge — the name Alhambra comes from the Arabic for "red fort.") Behind these walls is what amounts to a royal city, at the core of which is the Alhambra's crown jewel, the Casa Real (Royal Palace) — actually a series of three palaces leading from one to the other as if they were one building. Within their fountained courtyards and fanciful halls, whose scalloped mirador (balcony) windows frame vistas of the Albaicín and Sacromonte, the sultans conducted state business, housed their families and harems, and lived a fairy-tale lifestyle. Fierce leaders in treacherous times, their perquisites at ease included such niceties as sherbets made of snow brought to their tables by runners from the Sierra Nevada.

Mohammed ben al-Ahmar, a Nasrid sultan who moved his court here from the neighboring Albaicín hill in 1238, began the royal headquarters, but building continued under other rulers for much of the following century. Then, in 1492, the last Moorish ruler, Boabdil, surrendered the city to Ferdinand and Isabella, who raised their standard over the Alhambra and moved in. Their grandson, the Holy Roman Emperor Charles V, added a palace of his own in the 16th century, but during later centuries, the Alhambra was abandoned for long periods. Vagabonds and Gypsies built bonfires and stabled animals in it, and in the early 19th century, Napoleon's forces inflicted heavy damage on it. Washington Irving, writing about it in *The Alhambra* (1832) after a stint as an attaché in the US Embassy in Madrid (he was later Ambassador to Spain), finally focused world attention on this neglected treasure and started it on its long road to recovery.

Except for the limited use of marble in such features as pillars and fountains, the Moors had spun their magic out of perishable wood, plaster, and ceramics. Most of the present plasterwork veiling, colorful mosaic patterns, and *artesonado* (inlaid wood) ceilings are skillful reproductions based on descriptions, drawings, and remnants of the original designs. Restoration and excavation constitute an ongoing project, which accounts for the closing of areas from time to time. An Alhambra visit takes at least one full day (on the run), and it's wise to arrive at opening time, because as the day progresses, the lines of people waiting to walk through the palaces get longer — these famous rooms and courtyards are surprisingly small.

The main approach to the fortress is via the steep Cuesta de Gomérez and through the Puerta de las Granadas (Pomegranate Gate), which signals the entrance to the Alhambra's cool, elm-forested grounds. The gate, added by Charles V, is topped by three stone pomegranates, the symbol of Granada (although the city's name is of Arabic derivation and does not come from the Spanish word for pomegranate, *granada*). Visitors next pass through the Puerta de la Justicia (Justice Gate), a towering horseshoe arch erected by the original Moorish builders and completed with a statue of the Virgin after the Reconquest. This is the Alhambra's main entrance, leading to the Puerta del Vino (Wine Gate), where the ticket office is located. Beyond, bordering the Plaza de los Aljibes (Square of the Cisterns), are the fortifications of the Alcazaba and the Arab royal palaces (Casa Real). The Alhambra admission ticket includes visits to these two, as well as the Generalife, which is outside the Alhambra walls; Charles V's palace, which is within the walls, can be entered without paying any admission charge, although there is a separate charge for its museums.

Alcazaba – The oldest part of the Alhambra, this rugged medieval fortress had been part of the hill's defenses for centuries before construction began on the royal palaces across the square. Climb the most spectacular of its towers, the Torre de la Vela (Watch Tower), for a view directly down into the Plaza Nueva and out as far as the Sierra Nevada. When the Catholic Monarchs moved into the Alhambra, they hoisted their standard over this tower and installed a bell, which tolls each year on January 2 to commemorate the day in 1492 when the Moors lost their last foothold in Spain.

Mexuar – This is the first of the three palaces that make up the Casa Real. From the outside, it appears to be a simple stucco residence, but it was actually the headquarters of the sultan's ministers. The first main council chamber, the Hall of the Mexuar, was converted to a chapel in the 17th century (Chapel of Philip V), thus the coat of arms of Castile beneath the Moorish ceiling of marquetry and plaster restorations. The room is a tame introduction to the splendors of the Alhambra, but its dazzling mirador suggests the mesmerizing world to come, and the spectacle builds as visitors pass through another council chamber, the Cuarto Dorado (Golden Room), to the Patio del Mexuar, one of the palace's smallest but most admired spaces. Its intricate plaster-lace wall with twin tile-rimmed doorways under a deep *artesonado* overhang is actually the north façade of the next building, the Comares Palace.

Palacio de Comares (Comares Palace) – This was the royal palace proper, named for the stained glass that once decorated its windows. Its centerpiece is the Patio de los Arrayanes (Court of the Myrtles), graced with an oblong fishpond running its length between symmetrical myrtle hedges. The tower with the balconies at one end of the pool (to the right upon entering the patio) is a remnant of a seraglio that was partially destroyed to make room for Charles V's palace behind it. Opposite is the Torre de Comares, plainer because it was part of the Alhambra's fortifications. The Sala de la Barca (Hall of Benediction), which forms an antechamber to the latter tower, has a wonderfully intricate inlaid cedar ceiling, a re-creation of the original, which burned in the last century (the ceiling is shaped like an inverted boat, although the name of the hall comes from an Arabic word for "blessing," not from the Spanish *barca* for "boat"). Beyond, inside the tower, is the magnificent Salón de Embajadores (Hall of the Ambassadors), the Moorish kings' throne room. Perfectly square, and clothed in lacy plaster arabesques and brilliant mosaics, this is the largest room in all three palaces. Its domed *artesonado* ceiling is a geometric depiction of the firmament comprising more than 8,000 separate pieces of painted wood.

Palacio de los Leones (Palace of the Lions) – The final palace, built around the famous Patio de los Leones (Court of the Lions), was the royal residence. The court's 124 slim marble columns, each with a subtly different design carved into its capital, are said to represent a palm oasis in the desert (such as Granada seemed to the Moors after centuries in North Africa). In the center is a fountain, its basin supported by 12 gray marble lions, possibly representing the hours of the day, the months of the year, or the signs of the zodiac. At one time, it is said, water flowed from the mouth of a different lion each hour of the day. The lions no longer spout, but the fountain is filled, as are the four narrow channels (representing the four rivers of paradise) that run across the pebbled courtyard floor. The channels were designed to carry used household water from fountains in the living quarters surrounding the court, and on at least one occasion — when Boabdil's father ordered a mass beheading of suspected traitors belonging to a faction of nobles called Abencerrajes — the water ran red. The heads were thrown into the fountain of what came to be known as the Sala de los Abencerrajes, the room to the right upon entering the patio (it has a big rust stain in its fountain). Note the room's stalactite plasterwork ceiling with high inset windows, then go directly across the courtyard to the Sala de las Dos Hermanas (Hall of the Two Sisters), which has an even more extravagant dome. This room, named for two marble slabs set in the floor near the entrance, was reserved for the sultan's wife and inhabited at one time by Boabdil's mother, Ayesha. Off the room is the Sala de los Almeces (Room of the Windows), with the jewel-like Mirador de Lindaraja, or Mirador de Daraxa, the sultana's private balcony. The windows are low to the ground so the queen could gaze into her private cypress garden, the Patio de Lindaraja, from a couch of floor pillows. At the far end of the Court of the Lions is the Sala de los Reyes (Hall of Kings), surprising for its three 14th-century ceiling paintings done on leather by Christian artists.

Downstairs from the Court of the Lions, the Patio de Lindaraja leads to the sumptuous Sala de Baños (Royal Baths), where the sultan surveyed his women from balconies. Small, loosely fitted, star-shaped windows in the ceiling let in light and allowed steam to escape. Washington Irving's furnished rooms (open by special request), where he began his book about the Alhambra, are upstairs in the Patio de la Reja (Window-Grill Patio).

Alhambra Gardens – The Jardines de Partal (Partal Gardens), which occupy an area that once held the kitchen garden of the palace servants and contain the Torre de las Damas (Ladies' Tower), with a delicate porticoed mirador at its base, are passed upon leaving the royal palaces. From here, visitors can choose their own path among the lily pools, fountains, waterfalls, and flower beds that parallel the fortress wall and its succession of towers. Or, by following the fortifications to a footbridge across a narrow gorge, they can proceed directly to the Generalife. (This can also be reached from outside the Alhambra through a ticket gate at the parking lot off Avenida de los Alixares.)

Generalife – The Generalife — the word (pronounced Hay-nay-rah-lee-fay) derives from the Arabic for "Garden of the Architect" — was the summer home of the Nasrid rulers. Though the remnants of its simple white palace and pavilions are appealing, the main attractions are indeed the colorful terraced flower gardens, the pools, and the miradors from which the potentates could catch the country breezes while keeping an eye on the Alhambra below. Changes have been made by various proprietors, but many of the garden plans, fountains, and water channels are as they were. The sunken amphitheater was built in the 1950s to accommodate Granada's annual *International Festival of Music and Dance* (see *Special Events*); the maze of *caminos* (walkways), walled in by cypresses sheared and shaped into colonnades and arches, was replanted in the 1930s. The Patio de la Acequia (Patio of the Canal) within the palace walls, however, is an ancient plant-filled paradise with rows of fountain jets sending arcs of dancing waters over a long, narrow pool. Next to this is another original courtyard, the Patio de los Cipreses (Cypress Patio), where a sign next to a limbless cypress trunk proclaims the tree to be more than 500 years old and a witness to a stolen kiss between Boabdil's unfaithful wife and her lover. Running down the hillside is the Escalera de las Cascadas (Waterfall Staircase), with water running through channels cut into its stone banisters.

Palacio de Carlos V – The Holy Roman Emperor Charles V, who so loved Granada that at one point he planned to hold court here, built himself a grandiose Italianate palace right next to the delicate medieval Moorish palaces in the Alhambra. This majestic interloper, designed by Pedro Machuca, a student of Michelangelo, has been admired for its beautiful proportions and hated for its unsuitable location from the very start. The perfectly square exterior hides a spectacular circular 2-story courtyard open to the sky — a dome in the style of the Pantheon in Rome was originally intended. Inside are two museums. The *Museo Hispano-Musulmán* (Museum of Hispano-Muslim Art) contains fragments of original marble and tile from the Alhambra and other ancient city buildings, as well as jewelry and ceramics. Its most famous possession is the blue Jarrón de la Alhambra, a graceful amphora that was displayed for many years in the Sala de las Dos Hermanas. The *Museo Provincial de Bellas Artes* (Provincial Fine Arts Museum) contains painting, sculpture, and stained glass primarily by Granadan artists from the 15th to the 20th centuries. A prized work is a Limoges enameled portrayal of the Crucifixion that once belonged to Isabella's Gran Capitán, who conquered the kingdom of Naples. The *Museo Hispano-Musulmán* (phone: 226279) is open from 10 AM to 2 PM; closed Saturdays and Sundays. The *Museo Provincial de Bellas Artes* (phone: 224843) is open from 10 AM to 2 PM; closed Mondays. There is an admission charge to both museums (separate from the Alhambra's charge — see details below).

Parador San Francisco – Also within the walls of the Alhambra is the 15th-century Convento de San Francisco, founded by Ferdinand and Isabella and their temporary burial place while their mausoleum downtown was being readied. The convent is now a member of the government-run *parador* chain; non-guests are free to visit or dine in the restaurant (phone: 221443).

Hours for the Alhambra complex are daily from 9:30 AM to 8 PM from March through September, and from 9:30 AM to 6 PM October through February. Visits to the illuminated complex can be made Tuesdays, Thursdays, and Saturdays from 10 PM to midnight, April through September, and from 8 to 10 PM Saturdays only the rest of the year. Admission to the Alhambra (phone: 227527), including the Alcazaba, is combined with admission to the Generalife (phone: 222616), and the ticket is good for 2 days, allowing the bearer to return to see unvisited parts of the complex. The *Parador San Francisco* (see *Best in Town*) and the Palace of Charles V can be seen without paying the admission charge, although there is a charge for the museums in the palace.

ELSEWHERE IN THE UPPER CITY

Casa-Museo Manuel de Falla – The composer's charming whitewashed house on the Alhambra hill has been kept as it was during his lifetime. A typical Granadan villa, or *carmen,* it has a bright blue front door and a garden awash with roses. De Falla's piano, furniture, manuscripts, photos, and mementos are on display. Open from 10 AM to 2 PM and from 4 to 6 PM; closed Mondays. Admission charge. Across from the *Alhambra Palace* hotel on Antequerela Alta (phone: 229421).

Albaicín and Sacromonte – These are Granada's oldest neighborhoods, dating back to medieval times. The Moorish rulers lived on the Albaicín hill before establishing their palaces on the hill across the way, and even after the Reconquest, Moors continued to populate this Old Quarter. Now a residential area in the early stage of gentrification, it can be reached by a fascinating walk from Plaza Nueva up the Carrera del Darro, which becomes Paseo del Padre Manjón before turning left up the Cuesta de Chapiz. En route, it passes several landmarks: El Bañuelo (Moorish Baths; 33 Carrera del Darro), officially visitable at no charge all day but sometimes closed anyway; the ornate 15th-century Casa de Castril (housing the *Museo Arqueológico,* open from 10 AM to 2 PM; closed Mondays; 41 Carrera del Darro; phone: 225640); the 16th-century Convento de Santa Catalina de Zafra (43 Carrera del Darro); and, farther along on Cuesta de Chapiz, the Casa del Chapiz, a quintessential *carmen* serving as a college of Arab studies. Make a right turn at Camino del Sacromonte to climb the dusty streets, lined with sunbaked houses, into the Sacromonte Gypsy district, or continue along the Cuesta de Chapiz into the heart of the Albaicín. The long, steep road is rough going, especially on a hot summer day, but you can't go wrong by choosing any route either up or down through the neighborhood's narrow streets of red-roofed houses and walled gardens.

LOWER CITY

Capilla Real (Royal Chapel) – This Gothic-Plateresque treasure, downtown Granada's greatest attraction, is Ferdinand and Isabella's mausoleum. The cathedral beside it did not yet exist when the royal couple began their final resting place in 1504 — and because the chapel was not yet complete at their deaths (Isabella died before the year was out, her husband in 1516), the two were buried initially at the Convento de San Francisco (now the *parador*) at the Alhambra. They were moved when the new chapel was completed by their grandson and successor, the Holy Roman Emperor Charles V, in 1517. Visitors enter through the Lonja (Exchange House), an adjoining building on Calle de los Oficios, the narrow pedestrian street alongside the cathedral.

Note the graceful frieze on the chapel's façade, one of many decorative variations on the royal initials and crest that appear throughout the building. Inside, a wrought-iron *reja* (grille) crafted by Bartolomé de Jaén separates the nave of the cruciform chapel from the apse. Bronze figures on the grille's gilded Corinthian columns represent the Apostles; the royal coat of arms is centered above the lintel; and the band across the top shows scenes from the Inquisition. Behind the grille is an elaborate carved wood altarpiece, with scenes from the conquest of Granada, including Boabdil's farewell, along its base. To the right (as you face the altar) are the recumbent Carrara marble figures of Ferdinand and Isabella, sculpted by Domenico Fancelli of Florence in 1517; to the left are marble effigies of Juana la Loca and Felipe el Hermoso (Joan the Insane and Philip the Handsome — the parents of Charles V), sculpted by Bartolomé Ordóñez in 1520. Stairs at the royal feet lead to a crypt containing four lead caskets where the royal remains actually lie — plus a smaller one for a royal grandchild.

Isabella's prodigious collection of paintings, many by Flemish masters, as well as church vestments, Ferdinand's sword, Isabella's scepter, her ornate jewel chest, and her surprisingly dainty filigree crown are on display in the chapel's sacristy. Be sure to look above the exit doorway on leaving the chapel: There's a copy of a famous painting documenting Boabdil's surrender to Isabella, who is wearing the very same crown. Open daily from 10:30 AM to 1 PM and from 4 to 7 PM. Admission charge. Calle de los Oficios (phone: 229239).

Catedral – After the lush, dark intimacy of the Capilla Real, the cathedral's white interior, flooded with light from high stained glass windows, overwhelms with a stark grandeur. Begun in 1523, it was originally meant to be Gothic in style, but during the 150 years of its construction, under principal architects Diego de Siloé and Alonso Cano, a Renaissance church took shape. Given its highly built-up downtown setting, a helicopter would be useful to give an idea of this monumental building as a whole, but do walk around it, taking in Cano's 17th-century main façade, on the west along Plaza de las Pasiegas, and the Puerta del Perdón, a notably elaborate side entrance facing north on Calle de la Cárcel. The visitors' entrance at Gran Vía de Colón leads to the ambulatory around the golden Capilla Mayor, or chancel, where a 150-foot dome is ringed by a double tier of stained glass windows and by enormous scenes from the Life of the Virgin painted by Cano. Notice the polychrome figures at prayer on either side of the main arch: These are Ferdinand and Isabella, who commissioned the cathedral to celebrate the Reconquest but died before they saw a stone placed. Farther back in the nave are twin 18th-century organs, their pipes fanning out over the central aisle in the Spanish fashion. Numerous glittering side chapels grace the church, so be careful not to miss the extravagantly carved and gilded Capilla de Nuestra Señora de la Antigua (or Capilla Dorada) on the north wall. Even the gorgeous draped "damask" canopy above the Virgin is carved wood. Open daily from 10:30 AM to 1 PM and from 4 to 7 PM. Admission charge. Gran Vía de Colón (phone: 222959).

Alcaicería (Silk Market) – At one time, the old Moorish silk market in Granada covered an entire quarter and was among the most important markets in the Muslim world. It burned down in the 1800s, but a small part of it near the cathedral has been rebuilt as a tiny 3-street tourist bazaar crammed with gaudy souvenir shops and stands whose merchandise spills out into the paths of the shoppers. Reach it from Calle Zacatín.

Plaza de la Bib Rambla – This big, busy square, where the Moors once thronged for tournaments and horse shows, is now bright with flower stalls, and café tables and their umbrellas. All Granada pauses here, near the cathedral, for *tapas,* beer, or platesful of *churros* — long, skinny crullers just made for dipping into cups of thick hot chocolate.

Corral del Carbón (House of Coal) – A Moorish horseshoe arch leads into the gray stone courtyard of this building, which originally was an inn — the Grand Hotel of 14th-century Arab Granada — and subsequently a warehouse, a theater, and an apartment house. Now it houses Granada's branch of *Artespaña,* the government-run handicrafts company that has shops throughout Spain. 40 Calle Mariana Pineda (phone: 224550).

Monasterio de San Jerónimo (Monastery of St. Jerome) – The first monastery to be founded in Granada after the Reconquest, this huge establishment has both a private and a public cloister, the latter a magnificent space with double tiers of arcaded ambulatories surrounding an orange grove. The 16th-century monastery church, where Isabella's Gran Capitán was originally buried before the altar, is one of Diego de Siloé's greatest buildings. Open daily from 10 AM to 1:30 PM and from 3 to 6 PM. Admission charge. 9 Calle Rector López Argüeta (phone: 279337).

Iglesia de San Juan de Dios (Church of St. John of God) – Widely considered Granada's most beautiful place of worship because of its dazzling gilded chancel, this 18th-century baroque church is part of a complex that includes the 16th-century Hospital de San Juan de Dios. (The latter still functions as a hospital, but have a look at its frescoed courtyards and magnificent staircase with *artesonado* ceiling.) Open daily from 9 to 11 AM and from 6:30 to 9 PM. Calle San Juan de Dios (phone: 275700).

Nuestra Señora de las Angustias (Our Lady of Perpetual Sorrows) – This charming Renaissance church in the downtown shopping district honors the city's patron saint. The church's carved wood statue of the Virgin, bearing Christ in her arms, is carried through the city during *Holy Week.* Open daily for Mass. Carrera de la Virgen (phone: 226393).

La Cartuja (Carthusian Monastery) – The daily routine of the monks is dramatically documented in the well-preserved refectory, capitular hall, and other common rooms of this great 16th-century religious center. The depictions of martyrdom, painted by a monastery friar, Juan Sánchez Cotán, are bloodcurdling. In contrast, the monastery church is enchanting. The sacristy, an 18th-century addition, is an airy surprise: White rococo plasterwork is paired with brown and white marble whose colors are swirled like a chocolate sundae. The interior doors are marvels in marquetry, and the polished cedarwood vestment chests lining the walls are inlaid with silver and mother-of-pearl. In the apsc of the church are four statues surrounding a magnificent coral-colored marble altar — the folded and draped velvet and silk canopies are actually carved and painted wood. On the northern outskirts of town, about 10 minutes by cab (or take the No. 8 bus). Open daily from 10 AM to 1 PM and from 3 to 6 PM. Admission charge. Camino de Alfácar (phone: 201932).

SOURCES AND RESOURCES

TOURIST INFORMATION: The city's Oficina de Turismo has an official home (10 Plaza de Mariana Pineda; phone: 226688), while the provincial office is off Plaza de la Bib Rambla (2 Calle Libreros; phone: 225990). Both offices are open from 10 AM to 1:30 PM and from 4 to 7 PM; closed Saturday afternoons and Sundays. An English-speaking staff can answer questions, but printed information in English is sketchy. At the Alhambra, on the other hand, information services are excellent. Visitors are provided with well-annotated maps of the Alhambra and Generalife, and there is a selection of books for sale. Tour guides for both the Alhambra and downtown attractions are headquartered in the ticket building at the Puerta del Vino entrance (phone: 229936).

Local Coverage – For those who read Spanish, three local papers — *El Ideal, El Día de Granada,* and the *Granada 2,000* — are sources of local and national news, information on entertainment and cultural events, and the *fútbol* scores. The weekly *El Faro* also contains an entertainment guide.

TELEPHONE: The city code for Granada is 58. If calling from within Spain, dial 958 before the local number.

GETTING AROUND: Those traveling by car won't have to park it for the duration of their stay, because Granada, unlike other ancient Andalusian cities, is fairly easy to navigate. Those without a car will find that the city's big red buses go everywhere, although except for hard climbs up the Alhambra and Albaicín hills, you'll probably prefer to walk anyway.

Airport – Granada Airport is 10½ miles (17 km) west of the city (phone: 446411 or 447081). *Iberia* has an office in town (2 Plaza de Isabel la Católica; phone: 227592).

Bus – City bus routes are well marked at stops in the downtown area. The most useful ones for visitors are No. 2, which goes to the Alhambra and the Generalife, and No. 7, which goes to the Albaicín. Fare is 60 pesetas (exact change not required). Intercity buses depart from several terminals, depending on the line operating the service. The Alsina Graells Sur station (97 Camino de Ronda; phone: 251358), serving other points in Andalusia and Madrid, is the main one; the *Bacoma* line terminal in front of the train station (Avenida de los Andaluces; phone: 281883) is the departure point for buses to Murcia, Alicante, Valencia, and Barcelona. *Bonal* buses (Avenida de la Constitución; phone: 273100), go to the Sierra Nevada ski slopes.

Car Rental – *Avis* (31 Calle Recogidas; phone: 252358; and at the airport; phone: 446455), *Hertz* (46 Calle Recogidas; phone: 251682), and *Europcar* (Plaza de Mariana Pineda, Edificio Cervantes; phone: 295065) are among the firms represented.

Taxi – Hail one on the street or call *Radio-Taxi* (phone: 151461) or *Tele-Taxi* (phone: 280654).

Train – The train station is located some distance north of the center on Avenida de los Andaluces. Tickets can be bought there or at the *RENFE* office (at the corner of Calle de los Reyes Católicos and Calle Sillería; phone: 223119). For all train information, call 271272.

SPECIAL EVENTS: Granada's most unique celebration, the *Día de la Toma* (Day of the Capture), on January 2, commemorates the day in 1492 when the Muslim ruler, Boabdil, turned the city over to Ferdinand and Isabella, thereby completing the Christian Reconquest of Spain. Granada marks the day with a parade and the tolling of the Alhambra bell, as the flag of the Catholic Monarchs hangs from City Hall. On May 3, *Cruces de Mayo* (Crosses of May), there is dancing in the streets and plazas, which are bedecked with crosses covered with spring flowers, but this is only a prelude to a much bigger event, *Corpus Christi,* observed in May or June, when the church rolls out a glittering holy procession displaying the monstrance Isabella gave the cathedral and costumed *granadinos* ride horseback through downtown traffic. The fiesta goes on for 10 days, complete with bullfights, a flamenco festival, and a sprawling fair with blazing midway. In another vein, Granada's renowned annual *Festival Internacional de Música y Danza,* 3 weeks bridging June and July, celebrated its 40th anniversary last year and is still going strong (see *Theater and Music*).

SHOPPING: The booty includes ceramics, particularly the typical blue-and-white Fajalauza pottery (which took its name centuries ago from the city gate where the potteries clustered); marquetry items — boxes, trays, and other wooden objects inlaid with wood, shell, or ivory; woven rugs and blankets, some in the traditional style of the Alpujarra region; jewelry; copper pots; leather bags; and some of Spain's finest guitars, sold from stock or made to order (which may take anywhere from a week to several months). Crafts and souvenir shops are concentrated at a few popular tourist locations, so shopping is easy. Downtown, visitors browse the Alcaicería, off Calle Zacatín. In the vicinity of the Alhambra, fine craftsmen, as well as frankly-souvenir shops, line the lower section of the Cuesta de Gomérez approach. The Albaicín is also a good place for shopping. The two major nationwide department store chains both have branches in Granada: *Galerías Preciados* (13 Carrera del Genil; phone: 223581) and *Hipercor* (97 Calle Arabial; phone: 292161). Note that on pleasant weekends, the promenade along Carrera del Genil turns into an outdoor bazaar, blossoming with booths selling paintings, leatherwork, ceramics, jewelry, and souvenirs.

Antonio González Ramos – A standout for marquetry objects. 16 Cuesta de Gomérez (phone: 227062).

Artespaña – The Granada outlet of the nationwide, government-operated company displays local and regional crafts and furniture in a handsome 2-story showroom at the rear of the courtyard in the Corral del Carbón. Calle Mariana Pineda (phone: 224550).

Cerámica Aliatar – Local designs in ceramics. 18 Plaza de Aliatar (phone: 278089).

Cerámica Arabe – A fine selection of typical Fajalauza platters and bowls (but the store doesn't ship). 5 Plaza San Isidro (phone: 201227).

Convento de Santa Catalina de Zafra – Cookies and sweet cakes made by the sisters, on sale year-round. Knock at the convent door when you're touring the Albaicín. 43 Carrera del Darro (phone: 221927).

Eduardo Ferrer Castillo – The craftsman who taught most of the other guitar makers in Granada. 26 Cuesta de Gomérez (phone: 221832).

Eduardo Ferrer Lucena – Fine craftsmanship in leather. 19 Calle del Agua, Albaicín (phone: 279056).

Talabar – Elegant leather handbags and wallets. 2 Puente Verde (phone: 286786).

Tejidos Artísticos Fortuny – Handwoven bedspreads, rugs, and drapes. 1 Plaza Fortuny (phone: 224327).

V. Molero Martínez – Another outstanding shop for marquetry. 8 Calle Santa Rosalia (phone: 111356).

SPORTS AND FITNESS: Bullfighting – Though the *corrida* has lost popularity here, the season of Sunday bullfights runs from mid-March to October, with daily events during *Corpus Christi* in May or June. The *Plaza de Toros* (Avenida de Doctor Olóriz) is near the soccer stadium. Tickets can be purchased downtown on Calle Escudo del Carmen behind the Ayuntamiento (City Hall) from 5 to 9 PM on the day of the bullfight.

Hiking – Follow the joggers to the Parque de Invierno (see below). Serious hikers can follow the route of the snow carriers who brought ice from the mountains to the Alhambra. The tourist office has trail maps.

Jogging – To jog along nearby mountain roads lined with olive groves, take the No. 2 bus beyond the Alhambra to Cementerio (the hilltop cemetery at the end of the line) for the entrance to the Parque de Invierno, the city's favorite outdoor recreation and picnic area.

Skiing – The ski slopes at Solynieve (phone: 249100), the southernmost ski resort in Europe, are less than an hour's drive (about 20 miles/32 km) southeast of Granada along a well-tended mountain road. At 11,000 feet, Solynieve's snows never melt; up-to-date facilities include cable cars, chair lifts, ski shops, restaurants, and hotels, as well as the *Parador de Sierra Nevada* (phone: 480200), with broad terraces and cheery fireplace, bar, and restaurant, above the town. For bus transportation from Granada, call *Bonal* buses (phone: 273100); for slope, weather, and highway conditions, call 480153.

Soccer – Consult the newspaper for game schedules during *fútbol* season at Granada's *Estadio de los Cármenes,* Avenida de Madrid.

Swimming – Because the city is so close to resort towns of the Costa del Sol, few of the hotels have pools. Those planning to swim have a choice of two hotels, *Los Alixares* and *Los Angeles,* both of which have pools for guests only. *Piscina Neptuno* (phone: 251067), part of the *Neptuno* sports complex downtown on Calle Arabial, has two pools open to the public.

Tennis – Courts are for rent at *Pistas Tenis Neptuno* (phone: 251067), part of the *Neptuno* sports complex on Calle Arabial.

THEATER AND MUSIC: One of Granada's several cinemas, the *Cine Teatro Isabel La Católica* (Puerta Real), doubles as a theater for plays and other theatrical events — check the newspapers for what's on if your Spanish is up to it. Gypsy *zambras,* flamenco *tablaos,* and jazz are part of the music scene (see *Nightclubs and Nightlife*), as are classical concerts at the *Auditorio Manuel de Falla* (Paseo de los Mártires, near the Alhambra; phone: 228288). The auditorium, rebuilt after a fire and acoustically acclaimed, also is the principal indoor venue for the city's renowned *Festival Internacional de Música y Danza,* which runs from late June through early July. For the 3 weeks of the festival's duration, Granada is treated to a round-robin of daily performances not only indoors but also in the courtyard of the Palace of Charles V and in the outdoor theater at the Generalife. Among those doing the honors are ensembles such as the *Spanish National Orchestra* and the *Spanish National Ballet,* plus orchestras, ballet companies, chamber groups, and soloists from around the world. For an advance schedule of events, contact the festival office (Casa de los Girones, 1 Ancha de Santa Domingo, Granada 18009; phone: 225441) or branches of the National Tourist Office of Spain in the US.

NIGHTCLUBS AND NIGHTLIFE: Granada's biggest nighttime draw — and its biggest disappointment — are the *zambras,* Gypsy song-and-dance fests put on in cave dwellings hollowed out of the Sacromonte hill. Not so many years ago, the Gypsies danced for their own pleasure, but the shows have now deteriorated into tawdry commercial ventures complete with neon signs, barkers, cover charges, and women and children in tatty polka-dot ruffles stomping around to strident guitars. There's more emphasis on selling souvenir fans and castanets than on artistry, but the caves themselves are interesting — long, narrow rooms with rows of wooden chairs lined up against walls covered with copper pots and photos of legendary dancers. A nightclub bus tour run by *Viajes Meliá* (44 Calle de los Reyes Católicos; phone: 223098) goes to several caves and is one way to see them; another is to have a taxi drive slowly along the Camino del Sacromonte while you choose one that intrigues you. Don't be tempted to wander around alone after dark in this impoverished neighborhood.

For something closer to a Seville-style *tablao* (flamenco song and dance performance), book the show at *La Reina Mora* (Mirador de San Cristóbal; phone: 278228 or 202006), in the Albaicín. *Jardines Neptuno,* a garden nightclub (downtown on Calle Arabial; phone: 251112), has flamenco and regional dance and song, as does *El Curro* (5 Lavadero de las Tablas; phone: 283537), while *El Patio* (downtown on Calle Pedro Antonio de Alarcón; phone: 209259) is the place to show your own flamenco style on the dance floor. Because it's near the university, Calle Alarcón — in the section from Calle Martínez de la Rosa to Callejón de Gracia — has wall-to-wall discotheques, jazz clubs, bars, and burger, pizza, and fried-fish places jammed with young people.

A more sophisticated disco scene prevails at the *Club Cadí* in the *Luz Granada* hotel (18 Avenida de la Constitución) and at *Granada-10* (13 Calle Cárcel Baja). Or try *Oxford 2* (25 Calle del Gran Capitán) or *Distrito 10* (5 Calle del Gran Capitán). Go late. The watering holes around the Campo del Príncipe provide nightlife or *tapas* nearer the Alhambra. Among them, the 2-story *Patio Rossini Quesería Bar* (15 Campo del Príncipe) is particularly charming. (Ask for a *tabla variada,* a cheese board that also includes pâtés, hams, sausages, and olives — priced by weight.) And don't fail to have at least one drink on the terrace of the *Alhambra Palace* hotel (2 Calle Peña Partida), with a view of the city lights glistening at your feet.

BEST IN TOWN

CHECKING IN: Choosing a hotel in Granada means deciding between the forested heights of the historic Alhambra hill and the "real life" of the city below. The hilltop choice offers rustic charm, inspiring views, a feeling of the distant Moorish past, and easy walking access to the Alhambra itself. A downtown hotel means a better acquaintance with Granada's Renaissance period and a greater selection of shops and restaurants. Either way, it's hard to go wrong. Fast, efficient transportation shuttles visitors freely between upper and lower Granada for a full range of sightseeing, shopping, and dining. Expect to pay $115 and up for a double room in a hotel listed as expensive, from $65 to $100 in a moderate hotel, and less than $65 in an inexpensive one. All telephone numbers are in the 58 city code unless otherwise indicated.

Alhambra Palace – A grand old baronial establishment on the Alhambra hill. This beet-red leviathan is an easy stroll to the Alhambra entrance, and many of its 121 high-ceilinged, old-fashioned (but air conditioned) rooms have a view of the city from token balconies. The huge lobby and lounges, with plaster curlicues and tiled dadoes aping the real Alhambra, provide a meeting place for locals and visiting dignitaries. The concierge and staff snap to attention when approached, and there's a palatial dining room with buffet and from-the-menu dining. 2 Calle Peña Partida (phone: 221468; fax: 226404; telex: 78400). Expensive.

Luz Granada – This 174-room businesspeople's hotel stands on the sweeping

Avenida de la Constitución, somewhat out of the way for Alhambra-bound tourists. It offers the comforts of air conditioning, an international restaurant, an American-style cocktail lounge, boutiques, and a discotheque. 18 Avenida de la Constitución (phone: 204061; fax: 293150; telex: 78424). Expensive.

Parador San Francisco – Its 39 air conditioned rooms — within the very walls of the Alhambra — are the most sought-after accommodations in the government-run *parador* chain. Ferdinand and Isabella were originally buried in this former 15th-century convent, and one of the courtyards here has a monument marking the spot. The wait for rooms is from 6 months to a year, depending on the season, but cancellations do come up; ask for a room in the old wing. The restaurant serves Andalusian specialties (see *Eating Out*). In the Alhambra (phone: 221443; fax: 222264; telex: 78792). Expensive.

Princesa Ana – With a white marble and peach-colored interior, this luxurious oasis has 61 air conditioned rooms and is down the street from the *Luz Granada* and a couple of blocks from the railroad station. Popular with European business executives. 37 Avenida de la Constitución (phone: 287447; fax: 273954). Expensive.

Meliá Granada – The city's largest hotel, within a stone's throw of the downtown sights. There are 221 air conditioned rooms, a restaurant, cocktail lounge, coffee shop, and lobby boutiques. 7 Calle Angel Ganivet (phone: 227400). Expensive to moderate.

Los Alixares – The last hostelry up the Alhambra hillside above the Generalife is a charmless modern structure without Andalusian flavor, but it does have a swimming pool and sun deck, and European tour groups love it. The 148 air conditioned rooms (plus a restaurant) are a short cab or bus ride from downtown Granada. Avenida de los Alixares (phone: 225506; telex: 78523). Moderate.

Los Angeles – This place requires a short — but steep — hike to the Alhambra. There may be no connection between the name and the hotel's resemblance to a deluxe LA motel, but the flashy balconies and big heated swimming pool fairly scream Hollywood. The 100 air conditioned rooms are furnished in a comfortable modern fashion. 17 Cuesta Escoriaza (phone: 221424; telex: 78562). Moderate.

Kenia – A favorite with old Granada hands, this 16-room gem occupies a gracious old mansion at the foot of the Alhambra hill, near the Campo del Príncipe. The owner has furnished the lobby and parlor with family antiques, and each guest's plan for the day gets his personal attention. There's also a charming restaurant. 65 Calle Molinos (phone: 227506). Moderate.

Victoria – The silver dome and Parisian façade of this graceful dowager have been a landmark at the bustling Puerta Real for more than a century. The 69 air conditioned rooms were renovated, but the lavish period chandelier and potted palms in the tiny lobby remain, as does the aristocratic turn-of-the-century ambience that keeps the restaurant and bar popular with *granadinos*. Though the traffic is noisy, the downtown location is great, with easy bus access to the Alhambra. 3 Puerta Real (phone: 257700; telex: 78427). Moderate.

Washington Irving – On the Alhambra hill. The building's namesake never actually lived in this century-old hostelry, but the roster of early travelers who have slept here is impressive. The somber lobby and spartan accommodations (68 rooms) need remodeling, but not the Mudéjar dining room, a treasure. The location, at a crossroad leading to the Alhambra entrance in one direction and up to the Generalife in the other, is hard to beat. 2 Paseo del Generalife (phone: 227550; telex: 78519). Moderate.

Guadalupe – By the side of a steep road across from the upper entrance to the Generalife, this modest hostelry is high enough above the city to give guests a country feel. There are 43 air conditioned rooms and a small restaurant; bus to downtown. Avenida de los Alixares (phone: 223423; fax: 223798; telex: 78755). Inexpensive.

 EATING OUT: The fruitful fields and orchards surrounding the city, the game-rich mountains nearby, and the waters of the Mediterranean not far away 'make Granada's menus as notable for their prime ingredients as for the excellent food preparation. One of the most famous local dishes, for instance, is *habas con jamón,* a simple casserole of locally grown fava beans with ham. Most cooks won't use the prized ham from Trévelez, dried in the crisp Sierra Nevada air, but if you want to be your own judge in the ongoing contest between Trévelez lovers and aficionados of Seville's Jabugo ham, try slivers of Trévelez for *tapas,* with a fresh local wine (huétor, huescar, or albondón are names to note) or with one of the Jerez wines, plentiful here. Granada's tables are also laden with an outstanding selection of game, especially during hunting season, and with plenty of fresh seafood from the port of Motril. Then there's the famous local sweet tooth, derived, some say, from the Moorish delights that influence so much of modern Andalusian cooking. The city's convent kitchens are famous for their egg-yolk-based and sugared cookies and candies — some restaurants serve full platters purchased from the nuns. Expect to pay $55 and up for a three-course meal for two with local wine in any restaurant listed below as expensive, from $35 to $55 in a moderate one, and from $25 to $35 in an inexpensive place. All telephone numbers are in the 58 city code unless otherwise indicated.

Alacena de las Monjas – A sophisticated restaurant blending nouvelle cuisine niceties and old Arab recipes to produce an elegant dining experience that's hard to match anywhere. Tuxedo-clad waiters serve in the gleaming whitewashed cellar of a 16th-century house as guests nibble on crusty Arab breads and choose such dishes as *pimientos rellenos de bacalao en salsa de azafrán* (peppers stuffed with salt cod in saffron sauce) and *cordero Alacena de las Monjas* (lamb shank in a prune, carrot, and wine sauce), all more delicate than in the traditional Arab versions. An old Arab dessert, *cogollo de lechuga con miel de caña,* or hearts of romaine lettuce with orange slices in a burnt sugar sauce, is among the fascinating offerings, but there's also the house *tarta,* an airy cheesecake topped with honey and *crème anglaise.* Closed Sundays. Reservations necessary. Major credit cards accepted. 5 Plaza del Padre Suárez (phone: 224028). Expensive.

Baroca – Granada's business establishment favors the topflight international cooking here — salmon and avocado terrine, chef's salad, medallions of venison — but the local dishes are excellent, too. Closed Sundays and August. Reservations advised. Major credit cards accepted. 34 Calle Pedro Antonio de Alarcón (phone: 265061). Expensive.

Cunini – Pass through the long bar and choose your meal from the tempting fish market display. Well-heeled *granadinos* come here for the food, not for atmosphere or solicitous service (neither is to be found in this restaurant's plain, pine-paneled rooms). The menu lists almost a hundred fish and shellfish dishes, in addition to meats. For starters, try the *ensalada de hueva,* a cold fish roe salad, or the *pipirrana de chanquetes,* matchstick-size baby fish in tomato vinaigrette. Closed Sunday evenings. Reservations advised. Major credit cards accepted. 9 Pescadería (phone: 263701). Expensive.

Ruta de Veleta – This luxurious roadhouse restaurant on the way to Solynieve is worth the 4½-mile (7-km) trip. Feast on first-rate pheasant, partridge, roast suckling pig, and a cornucopia of other Spanish and international dishes, and enjoy the finest old rioja wines. Even the dining room ceiling, hung with row upon row of ceramic mugs in the typical blue-and-white floral pattern of Granada, is sensational. Closed Sunday evenings. Reservations advised. Major credit cards accepted. 50 Carretera de la Sierra, Cenes de la Vega (phone: 486134). Expensive.

El Corral del Príncipe – The outdoor tables crowded (especially on Sunday mornings) with homegrown yuppies mark the entrance to one of Granada's most spectacular eating places — a remodeled movie palace whose Andalusian interior is lavish with Moorish brass chandeliers and urns. The full range of Granadan cuisine is available. There's also a bar with lots of action, dancing on the former theater stage, and a late-night flamenco show. Open daily. Reservations advised. Major credit cards accepted. Campo del Príncipe (phone: 228088). Expensive to moderate.

Sevilla – Brigitte Bardot, El Cordobés, and Andrés Segovia have eaten here, and the menu is printed in three languages — you get the idea. But the food is tasty and authentic. Dine in one of the tiled dining rooms or on the narrow terrace, actually an alley, across from the frescoed walls of La Madraza, the old Arab university. Granadan specialties include *cordero a la pastoril* (spicy shepherds's lamb stew), *rape a la granadina* (monkfish in a shrimp, pine-nut, and mushroom sauce), and a dessert of *nueces con nata y miel* (the Arab-inspired nuts with cream and honey). Closed Sunday evenings. Reservations advised. Major credit cards accepted. 12 Calle de los Oficios (phone: 221223). Expensive to moderate.

Alcaicería – Three dining rooms with separate entrances grouped around a small patio are all part of the same restaurant in the silk market. The kitschy imitation of Alhambra tilework and plaster lace seems just right for this tourist enclave. English-speaking waiters help diners choose among the Granadan specialties. Open daily. No reservations. Major credit cards accepted. Placeta de la Alcaicería (phone: 224341). Moderate.

Casa Manuel – Ring the doorbell to gain admission to this old mansion in a neighborhood of elegant hillside residences. The walk down the long front hall to the dining rooms, the china-filled antique sideboards, and the informal, home-style cooking, with desserts baked by the owner's wife, make you feel more like a guest than a customer. Closed Sundays. Reservations unnecessary. No credit cards accepted. Calle Blanqueo de San Cecilio, off Campo del Príncipe (phone: 229617). Moderate.

Chikito – Choose indoor dining in a historic building, once a meeting place for Federico García Lorca and the El Reconcillo band of intellectuals, or pick the restarant's shady outdoor café across the street. Shoppers and businesspeople keep both spots filled. Try the *zarzuela de pescado* (seafood casserole), or selections from the outstanding *tapas* bar. Closed Wednesdays. Reservations unnecessary. Major credit cards accepted. 9 Plaza del Campillo (phone: 223364). Moderate.

Los Manueles – Trévelez hams hang over the noisy bar in this friendly *taberna* in an alley off Calle de los Reyes Católicos. Spaniards and foreigners alike flock to the tile and wrought-iron accented dining rooms, seemingly untouched since the place opened more than 60 years ago. (The chef is set in his ways, too: He doesn't, for instance, serve after-dinner coffee — go to a *cafetería,* says he.) The menu runs to Andalusian specialties. Open daily — and great in summer when the tables spill outdoors. Reservations unnecessary. No credit cards accepted. 4 Calle Zaragoza (phone: 223415). Moderate.

Mesón Antonio – Anyone in town from October through June should make a beeline for this homey eatery — and be hungry. After finding the humble house off Campo del Príncipe (even cab drivers have to inquire), go through the patio and upstairs to a simple dining room with an open kitchen. There, before cavernous wood-burning ovens, Antonio delivers sizzling platters of gratinée leeks, beef tongue in tomato sauce, and roast lamb, while his wife fries potatoes and stirs an intense seafood bisque at the range. Antonio also serves reasonably priced, fine old rioja wines. A bonus is that the couple speaks excellent English. Closed Sunday evenings and July, August, and September. No reservations. No credit cards accepted. 6 Calle Ecce Homo (phone: 229599). Moderate.

Parador San Francisco – A leisurely three-course lunch in the *parador*'s spacious dining room — within view of the rose gardens and the Generalife hill beyond — is a delightful way to break a visit to the Alhambra. The menu is repeated at dinner. Open daily. Reservations unnecessary. Major credit cards accepted. At the Alhambra (phone: 221443). Moderate.

Polinario – The buffet on the patio or a *bocadillo* (sandwich) and beer at the bar make for a quick lunch just outside the Alhambra. The cooking and ambience don't merit raves, but the location is convenient. Closed evenings. No reservations. No credit cards accepted. 3 Calle Real de la Alhambra (phone: 222991). Inexpensive.

MADRID

When King Philip II proclaimed Madrid the capital of Spain and all her colonies in 1561, he said that he chose it because of the "healthy air and brilliant skies" and because, "Like the body's heart, it is located in the center of the Peninsula." Philip was right. Madrid's air is delightfully dry and invigorating. Its "Velázquez skies" that so inspired the court painter are dramatically bright, with more than 3,000 hours of sunshine annually. As a result of Philip's proclamation, what had been an insignificant Castilian town of 17,000 suddenly burst into being as the cosmopolitan nucleus of the Spanish Empire — upon which, in those days, the sun never set. One of Europe's youngest capitals, Madrid grew fast, as if making up for lost time. A comment by a Spanish poet in 1644 continued to be true until just a few decades ago: "Each day, new houses are being built, and those that used to be on the outskirts are now in the middle of the town."

Today, the city has blossomed into a glamorous metropolis of 4.3 million, and it thrives on its own vitality. More than ever, it is ebullient, outgoing, fun-loving, proud, stylish, and creative, a city intensely lived in and adored by its varied mosaic of inhabitants. Throughout its history, a great proportion of its residents have been born elsewhere in Spain, a country of various and diverse cultures. Yet soon after their arrival, they feel "adopted" and become as genuinely *madrileño* as native sons and daughters.

According to a saying as meaningful to *madrileños* as the Cibeles Fountain, "the next best place after Madrid is heaven, but with a peephole for looking down at it." The city has a way of enticing foreigners as well. Visitors invariably feel at home in Madrid — much more so, of course, if they speak Spanish. Another popular saying, often seen on bumper stickers, boasts that Madrid is "*el pórtico al cielo*" ("the gateway to heaven"). The city is, in fact, the highest capital in Europe — 2,135 feet above the sea level of the Mediterranean at Alicante, affirmed by a plaque at Puerta del Sol.

Despite its high-tech, high-fashion, streamlined skyscrapers up the Castellana, and its unparalleled flurry of activities as 1992's European Cultural Capital — designated as such by the European Economic Community (EEC) — Madrid still endearingly refers to itself as a "town," or *villa*. Its official name during the 16th century was the "Very Noble, Loyal, Heroic, Imperial, and Distinguished Village and Court of Madrid, Capital of Spain," or, simply, "Villa." The City Hall, for example, is Casa de la Villa, the modern concert-theater-exhibition center is *Centro Cultural de la Villa*, and the summer-long program of concerts, fairs, and entertainment is called "*Veranos en la Villa.*"

Madrileños love to be out on the streets, where walking or strolling — the *paseo* — is an activity in itself, rather than just a means of getting somewhere. And they enjoy crowding together. In spring, summer, and fall, thousands of outdoor *terrazas* (cafés), set up on sidewalks and in squares and parks, teem day and night with convivial people chatting, eating, drinking, gossiping (locals love to gossip), and simply looking at each other. There's always eye contact and usually a friendly or witty greeting — *madrileños* also admire a quick wit — even to those who are just buying a newspaper.

Madrid's artistic-creative surge of the late 1970s and early 1980s — *la movida* — sparked a rebirth of indoor and outdoor café society. Stylish *madrileños* congregate at *terrazas* along Paseo de Recoletos and the Castellana from dusk until practically dawn. Crowded late-night, Spanish-style pubs, specializing in high-decibel rock or soothing classical music, line Calle de las Huertas, one of the liveliest streets in the old part of town. Amazingly, this street is also occupied by the early-17th-century Convent of the Trinitarias, where cloistered nuns live and embroider, and where Miguel de Cervantes is buried. In the typical old section of Lavapiés, entire families gather to eat, drink, and chat with their neighbors at simple restaurants with sidewalk tables. The *tertulia,* an age-old Madrid custom, brings experts and devotees together for informal discussions about their favorite subjects. Visitors will surely find *tertulias* about theater or literature at the *Café Gijón,* art at the *Círculo de Bellas Artes* lounge, and bullfighting and breeding at the bar of the *Wellington* hotel, to name a random few.

When it's time for the midday *aperitivo* around 1 PM (when stores, offices, and many museums close), thousands of *tapas* bars, *tabernas,* and swank cafés become jammed for a couple of hours until lunchtime, when they suddenly empty and the restaurants fill up. Around 4 or 5 PM (when the stores, offices, and museums reopen), the restaurants become vacant — it's customary to go somewhere else for coffee or cognac — and the bars and cafés are reactivated. They reach another peak when it's *aperitivo* time again, around 8 PM (as stores, offices, and museums close for the day), before dinner around 10 PM, when the restaurants fill up once more. Then it's time for a movie, concert, theater performance, jazz at a café, or simply a stroll.

Madrid boasts the longest nights of any Spanish city — even though in midsummer the sun doesn't set until almost 11 PM. Discotheques don't get started until 1 or 2 AM, and at many, the action continues until 7 AM. Then it's time for a typical Madrid breakfast of thick hot chocolate with *churros* (sticks or loops of crisp fried dough), elbow to elbow with others just beginning their day. Nevertheless, *madrileños* don't mistake their city for a vacation spot and are fully aware that it is indeed a place for hard work.

There are many Madrids. In fact, the city is sometimes referred to in the plural — *los madriles* — because of its various facets. In addition to nocturnal Madrid, daytime Madrid, and seasonal Madrid, there are different architectural and historical Madrids.

Not much remains of medieval Moorish Madrid, and even less is known — although legends abound. In 852, the Emir of Córdoba, Muhammad I, chose the strategic ravine top above the Manzanares River (where the Royal Palace now stands) as the site for a fortified Alcázar (castle) to guard the route between Toledo and Alcalá de Henares against the reconquering Christians. The Moors described their settlement alongside the Alcázar as "a village bordered by the Manzanares River on one side and the brilliant sky on the other." They called it Magerit (later mispronounced as Madrid by Castilians), meaning delicious and "plentiful flowing water," not for the meager water of the Manzanares, but for water from the nearby Sierra de Guadarrama. (This water from the Lozoya River continues to supply the city, and is also the brand name of a bottled mineral water).

Magerit began to grow, and the Moors built and rebuilt walls to enclose it, keeping up with its random expansion. Fragments of these old walls, as well as sections of underground passageways to the Alcázar, have been uncovered as recently as the 1970s — a major site can be seen at Cuesta de la Vega, near the Royal Palace. Other well-preserved remnants of medieval Moorish Magerit are the house and tower of the Lujanes family and the adjacent Periodicals Library building, both at Plaza de la Villa; the Mudéjar tower of the Church of San Nicolás de los Servitas, slightly to the north of the plaza; the equally Mudéjar tower of the Church of San Pedro el Viejo, on the site of what may have been the original mosque of the Moorish Quarter (La Morería), to the south of the plaza; and the Morería itself, a zone of winding alleys around Plaza del Alamillo.

In 1083, King Alfonso VI and his Christian troops reconquered Madrid and took up residence in the Alcázar. The *madrileño* melting pot expanded with the subsequent influx of Christians into what then became medieval Christian Madrid, and more walls were built to surround it.

The city really began to take shape when King Philip II of the Hapsburg House of Austria raised its rank to capital of Spain and moved the throne and court from Toledo. During his reign (1556–98) and those of his 17th-century successors, what is known as Madrid de los Austrias, or the Madrid of the Hapsburgs, was built. This is the charming and picturesque section of Old Madrid around the Plaza Mayor. As the nobility built mansions, the clergy founded churches, convents, monasteries, and hospitals, and merchants, artisans, and innkeepers set up shop. Hapsburg Madrid grew into a labyrinth of meandering narrow cobblestone streets and tiny squares lined with severe buildings of stone, brick, and masonry, topped by roofs that blended into a burnt-red "sea of tiles." The Spanish Empire was at its zenith, and the *siglo de oro* (Golden Age) of Renaissance literature flourished in Hapsburg Madrid. Streets, squares, and statues bear the names of Cervantes, Lope de Vega, Tirso de Molina, Quevedo, and Calderón de la Barca, all of whom lived here.

The city continued fanning southward, creating such delightful *barrios* (neighborhoods) as Lavapiés and Embajadores, lively with *tabernas, mesones* (inns), vendors, organ-grinders, and artisans. The *castizo* (genuine) and uniquely *madrileño* personality of these barrios and their colorful people were the inspiration of many of the 18th- and 19th-century *zarzuelas* (traditional Spanish musical dramas), *La Verbena de la Paloma,* for example, that are presented outdoors during the summer at La Corrala, located in the heart of this *castizo* Madrid at Plaza Agustín Lara. (Lara, a Mexican composer who had never been to Madrid, wrote the city's unofficial anthem, "Madrid, Madrid, Madrid.") Anyone visiting Madrid during the first half of August should be sure to stroll around these *barrios castizos* to see *madrileños* of all ages bedecked in traditional costumes, dancing the graceful *chotis* in the streets, and enjoying the *verbenas* (fairs).

When the Hapsburg dynasty died out at the end of the 17th century, King

Philip V, grandson of France's King Louis XIV, was the chief claimant to the throne of Spain. After a war of succession, he established the Bourbon dynasty as the legitimate heir to the kingdom in 1770. The Bourbon monarchs began the new century by setting out to create a splendid new European capital worthy of their neo-classical French models. When the Alcázar burned down, Philip V commissioned top architects (Spaniard Ventura Rodríguez and Italian Francesco Sabatini) to replace it with a grandiose palace comparable to Versailles. Systematic expansion to the east of old Hapsburg Madrid, with wide avenues and large squares laid out in geometric configuration, transformed Madrid into a model city of the Enlightenment — the Madrid de los Borbones, or Madrid of the Bourbons. The city's urban renewal, embellishment, and social progress culminated with the reign of *madrileño* King Carlos III, "the Construction King of the Enlightenment," known affectionately as the "King-Mayor." Carlos commissioned Juan de Villanueva to design the neo-classical *Natural Science Museum,* which later became the *Prado Museum,* and the adjacent Botanical Gardens. The exquisite tree-lined Paseo del Prado, with its Neptune, Apollo, and Cibeles fountains by Ventura Rodríguez, and the monumental Puerta de Alcalá (then marking the eastern end of the city) are among the legacies of Carlos III.

The steady progress of the city and the country foundered, however, in 1808, when Napoleon was encouraged to invade Spain because of the weakness of Carlos IV, the next Bourbon king. The French succeeded in the invasion after ruthlessly executing Spanish resisters on the night of May 2, a tragedy immortalized by Goya in his famous paintings now in the *Prado.* At the Plaza de la Lealtad on Paseo del Prado, a memorial obelisk with an eternal flame commemorates *el dos de mayo.*

Napoleon forced the crowning of his brother, Joseph Bonaparte, as King of Spain. "Pepe Botella" (Bottle Joe), as he was called (either for his drinking habits or for having put a tax on liquor), in his quest for open space for ongoing urban renewal, tore down picturesque chunks of Hapsburg Madrid, including much of the Retiro Park Palace and a church in the small Plaza de Ramales that contained the grave of Velázquez. But the Spanish War of Independence led to the expulsion of the French and the return to the throne of a Bourbon king, Fernando VII, in 1813.

In the last third of the 19th century, Romantic Madrid spread farther northward. Aristocratic palatial mansions graced the elegant Salamanca district, where today some of Madrid's finest shops and boutiques line Calles Serrano and Velázquez. Paseo del Prado extended north to become Paseo de Recoletos and, still farther north, Paseo de la Castellana. By the early 20th century, a transportation problem arose: There was no street connecting the new outlying districts of Salamanca and Argüelles. The solution was to chop through part of Old Madrid and construct a new thoroughfare, the Gran Vía.

The instability of the monarchy during the early 20th century led to further political upheaval. Alfonso XIII finally abdicated in 1931 to avoid a civil war. But the Socialist Republican government's decentralization plan and reform measures aroused strenuous right-wing opposition, which resulted in insurrection and, in 1936, the Spanish Civil War. Much of Madrid, which remained aligned with the Republican government, was blown to pieces at the hands of Generalísimo Francisco Franco's Nationalist forces. During the nearly 40 years of Franco's dictatorship, Madrid's spirit and creativity were stifled. Franco's death in 1975, the restoration of the monarchy, and the institution of a representative, democratic government brought about a dramatic multifaceted surge of activity ranging from construction to culture. As if making up for those 40 years of lost time, *madrileños,* with their newfound affluence and freedom of expression, have made their city one of Europe's most energetic and trendsetting, in art, fashion, music, and theater. The late Mayor Enrique Tierno Galván, whose irrevocable moniker is "The Best Mayor of Madrid, inspired his fellow citizens with such an affection for the city's own traditions and lore, promoted the arts with such enthusiasm, and fomented the *movida madrileña* with such verve that he became a revered figure — so much so that after his death in 1986, a *zarzuela* was written about him.

During this momentous year for Spain — the multifarious celebrations of the 500th anniversary of the discovery of America — Madrid plays a leading role worthy of its designation as 1992's European Capital of Culture. Sharing the spotlight with Barcelona, capital of Catalonia and host of the *1992 Summer Olympics,* and with Seville, capital of Andalusia and site of *Expo '92,* Madrid is enjoying another "golden age" with 366 days and nights (it's leap year!) of nonpareil scheduled cultural and entertainment events, and the culmination of major permanent city projects. A new logo identifies Madrid '92: a Gothic "M" outlined with a circle and a square, based on the 500-year-old design by Dürer.

The Triángulo del Arte (Triangle of Art) encompasses, within a 1-kilometer area, the newly reopened *Centro de Arte Reina Sofía-Museo Nacional de Arte Moderno y Contemporáneo,* now a premier museum of modern and contemporary art; the refurbished *Prado Museum,* with a series of special exhibitions; and the *Prado*'s *Palacio de Villahermosa* annex, remodeled and reopened this year to permanently exhibit the Thyssen-Bornemisza Collection, considered to be the world's second most important private art collection after that of the Queen of England. Next to the new *Auditorio Nacional* on Calle Principe de Vergara, the brand-new *Museo de la Ciudad* (Museum of the City) exhibits testimonials to the evolution of Madrid. Flanking the Plaza Mayor (Main Square), where major spectacles are being staged throughout the year, the 17th-century *Casa de la Panadería* has been refurbished and opened as a cultural center. The 19th-century Palacio de Linares in the Plaza de Cibeles has just been restored and converted into the *Museo de América* (Museum of America), a cultural and diplomatic center devoted to Spain's relationship with Latin America. Commemorating Columbus's discovery, a spectacular 302-foot-high permanent monument in the form of an armillary sphere (an old astronomical instrument) has been erected in the new Valdebernardo section southeast of downtown. Opening in initial phases are sections of the *Convention and Exhibit Center* of Campo de las Naciones, a vast, multifaceted urban project near Barajas International Airport geared for the year 2000. After 5 years of renovation and transformation, the *Teatro Real* will reopen (hopefully at the end of this year) as one of Europe's premiere opera houses.

And Madrid finally has a completed cathedral. The Catedral de la Almudena, named for the patroness of the city and under construction now for an entire century, is being completed this year and will be the oldest "new" cathedral in Europe, located in the Plaza de la Armería facing the Royal Palace.

Madrileños who can't stand being away from home can zoom to Seville for the day on *RENFE*'s new bullet train that makes the trip in less than 3 hours to visit *Expo '92*. They also can board one of *Iberia*'s *Puente Aereo* (Air Bridge) 1-hour flights — as frequent as 10 minutes apart — to take in the *Olympics* in Barcelona, and return home in time to stroll around Old Madrid where organ grinders still play on the cobblestone streets.

MADRID AT-A-GLANCE

SEEING THE CITY: For a wonderfully romantic view of Madrid, watch the sun set from the 25th-floor roof garden and pool of the *Plaza* hotel. The sharp "Velázquez sky," portrayed in the artist's famous paintings, is usually tinted with a golden hue. Looking over the "sea of tile" rooftops, visitors will see a fine view of the Royal Palace and, to the north, the distant Sierra de Guadarrama. The hotel's terrace and pool are open daily during the summer months. Admission charge. 2 Plaza de España (phone: 247-1200).

SPECIAL PLACES: The bustling Puerta del Sol, "kilometer zero" of the Spanish road network, and the Plaza de Cibeles traffic circle are two focal points at the heart of Madrid, which actually lies within the city's southwestern area. The Atocha railroad station and traffic circle mark the southern extremity of this zone, the Royal Palace and Parque del Retiro form its western and eastern borders respectively, and Plaza de Colón marks its northern limit. One major tree-lined avenue, with three names, bisects the entire city from top to bottom. Its southern section, between Atocha and Plaza de Cibeles, is called Paseo del Prado. From Cibeles north to Plaza de Colón, its name is Paseo de Recoletos. At Plaza de Colón, it becomes the long Paseo de la Castellana, which runs through modern Madrid to the north end of the city beyond Plaza de Castilla and the Chamartín railroad station. The two major east–west arteries are Calle de Alcalá and the Gran Vía; the latter angles northwest to Plaza de España.

For a basic overview, take a half-day motorcoach tour of the city or an excursion to surrounding sights with *Julía Tours* (68 Gran Vía; phone: 541-9125); *Pullmantur* (8 Plaza de Oriente; phone: 541-1805); or *Trapsatur* (23 Calle San Bernardo; phone: 542-6666). *Julía Tours* also can be booked in the US through their US representative *Bravo Tours* (182 Main St., Ridgefield Park, NJ 07760; phone: 800-272-8764). The best way to see Madrid, however, is by walking; many picturesque areas can be seen only on foot. Rest assured that, at least in the center of the city, things are much closer than they seem from the inside of a motorcoach or taxi. A good stroll, for starters, is from Puerta del Sol to Plaza Mayor, then downhill to Plaza de Oriente. Good maps of the city are provided free of charge at the tourist offices. Keep in mind that most museums close on Mondays, some close at midday, and smaller ones for the entire month of August.

Plaza Mayor – Oddly enough, this grandiose main square, which is closed to vehicular traffic, is easily missed if you don't aim for it and enter through one of the nine arched entryways. Built during the 17th century by order of King Philip III, it is the quintessence of Hapsburg Madrid — cobblestones, tile roofs, and imposing austere buildings. Before the king commissioned Juan Gómez de Mora to "straighten it out," the perfectly rectangular, perfectly flat plaza shared the irregularity of the surrounding architectural chaos. After its completion, the plaza became the stage for a wide variety of 17th- and 18th-century spectacles — audiences of over 50,000 witnessed hangings, burnings, and the decapitation of heretics, as well as canonizations of saints (such as St. Teresa and St. Isidro, Madrid's patron saint), jousting tournaments, plays (including those of Lope de Vega), circuses, and even bullfights. The 477 balconies of the surrounding buildings served as spectator "boxes" — not for the tenants, but for royalty and aristocrats. Beautifully refurbished, the Plaza Mayor is still lively, but with tamer entertainment — strolling student minstrels (*la tuna*), other amateur musicians, artists, and on-the-spot portrait painters selling their works, as well as summer concerts and ballets, and outdoor cafés for watching it all. Myriad shops, many over a century old, line the arcades around the plaza. On Sunday mornings, philatelists and numismatists set up shop in the arcades, to the delight of stamp and coin collectors. Visitors can easily lose their sense of direction inside this vast enclosure, so it's helpful to know that the bronze equestrian statue of Philip III in the center is facing east (toward the *Prado Museum*). The legendary Arco de Cuchilleros entrance is at the southwest corner.

Puerta del Sol – This vast oblong plaza is the bustling nerve center of modern Madrid life. Ten streets converge here, including the arteries of Alcalá, San Jerónimo, Mayor, and Arenal. The name of the square, "Gate of the Sun" in English, comes from a long-disappeared medieval city wall carved with a sunburst. On the south side, the 18th-century Comunidad government building, originally the Central Post Office, is topped by a clock tower. At midnight on *New Year's Eve,* thousands gather here to hear the clock strike and swallow one grape at each stroke to ensure 12 months of good fortune during the new year. Near the curb in front of the building's main entrance, a famous (yet inconspicuous) emblem in the sidewalk marks "kilometer zero," the central point from which all Spanish highways radiate, and from which their distance is measured. Directly across the plaza stands the venerated bronze statue of the *Oso y el Madroño* (the bear and the madrona berry tree), the symbol and coat of arms of Madrid since the 13th century.

Museo Nacional del Prado (Prado Museum) – One of the world's supreme art museums, the *Prado* is a treasure house of over 4,000 universal masterpieces, most of which were acquired over the centuries by art-loving Spanish monarchs. The wealth of Spanish paintings includes famous works by El Greco (including the *Adoration of the Shepherds*), Zurbarán, Velázquez (including *The Spinners* and *Maids of Honor*), Murillo, Ribera (including the *Martyrdom of St. Bartholomew*), and Goya (including his renowned *Naked Maja* and *Maja Clothed*). On the ground floor, a special section is devoted to the tapestry cartoons designed by Goya for the palace-monastery at San Lorenzo de El Escorial (see *Extra Special*) and to his extraordinary *Disasters of War* etchings, which represent his thoughts and comments on Spain's War of Independence. Visitors also will find Goya's stunning *Second of May* and *Third of May* canvases. Vast rooms are devoted to Italians Fra Angelico, Botticelli, Raphael, Correggio, Caravaggio, Titian, Tintoretto, and Veronese. Other rooms display paintings by Flemish and German masters such as Rubens, van der Weyden, Hieronymus Bosch (including *The Garden of Earthly Delights*), Memling, Dürer, and Van Dyck. From the Dutch are works by Rembrandt, Metsu, and Hobbema. French art is represented by Poussin, Lorrain, and Watteau, and the English by Reynolds, Gainsborough, and Lawrence.

The neo-classical *Prado* building was originally a natural science museum, conceived by Carlos III, the Enlightenment "King-Mayor," who ordered its construction by architect Juan de Villanueva. In 1819, King Fernando VII converted it into a museum to house the royal art collection. A bronze statue of Velázquez stands before the main façade, a statue of Goya at the north façade, and one of Murillo at the south side. In addition to the main *Prado*, or Villanueva building, the museum also includes two annexes. One, the Casón del Buen Retiro, resembles a small Greek temple, and is just up a hill from the Goya statue. It was once the stately ballroom of the 17th-century Royal Retiro Palace complex, which was destroyed during the French occupation of Madrid. It now contains, up the stairs, the *Museum of 19th-Century Spanish Painting* and, on the other side, facing the Parque del Retiro, with a separate entrance, a wing devoted to Picasso's monumental *Guernica*, which portrays the horrors of the Spanish Civil War and the devastating bombardment of that Basque town. The other annex, the splendid *Villahermosa Palace*, is diagonally across Plaza Cánovas del Castillo (the square with the Neptune Fountain) from the main building. Its spacious interior has been redesigned to house a major portion of the vast Thyssen-Bornemisza Collection, here on long-term loan, and which many consider the most important privately owned art collection in the world.

The *Prado* long ago outgrew its walls. Thus, the main building underwent a major refurbishment program, opening some 2 dozen remodeled rooms to display works previously in storage or on loan to other Spanish museums. Expansion plans for additional exhibit space include the acquisition in the mid-1990s of the nearby 17th-century Salón de Reinos building, which currently houses the *Museo del Ejército* (Army Museum). Still in the planning stages is the final relocation of *Guernica*, and the drawings related to it, to the *Queen Sofía Art Center-National Museum of Modern and Contemporary Art* which is devoted to contemporary art.

The *Prado* collection is so vast that it is impossible to savor its wonders in a single visit. If time is limited, it is best to select a few galleries of special interest, or enlist the services of the extremely knowledgeable government-licensed free-lance guides at the main entrance. The guides are more readily available in the early morning, and their fee is about $15 per hour. Reproductions from the *Prado*'s collection, postcards, and fine arts books are sold at the shop inside the museum. There also is a bar-restaurant on the premises. The *Prado* is open Tuesdays through Saturdays, from 9 AM to 6:45 PM; Sundays, 10 AM to 1:45 PM. Closed holidays. One admission charge grants access to the main building and the annexes. Paseo del Prado (phone: 420-2836).

Palacio Real (Royal Palace) – The Moors chose a strategic site overlooking the Manzanares River to build their Alcázar, or castle-fortress. After the 11th-century Reconquest, Christian leaders renovated it and moved into it, and Philip II made it the royal residence after proclaiming Madrid the capital of Spain in 1561. During the reign of Philip V, Spain's first Bourbon monarch, the Alcázar was destroyed by fire on *Christmas Eve,* 1734. The king then commissioned top Spanish and Italian architects to construct a glorious new palace in neo-classical style on the very same rugged steep site. It took 26 years to build the colossus of granite and white limestone, with walls 13 feet thick, over 2,800 rooms, 23 courtyards, and magnificently opulent interiors. "King-Mayor" Carlos III finally became the first royal resident. The east façade faces the grand Plaza de Oriente; at the north side are the formal Sabatini Gardens; and down the slopes on the west side is the Campo del Moro — 20 acres of forest, manicured gardens, and fountains, now a public park. The palace's main entrance is on the south side, through the tall iron gates leading into an immense courtyard called the Plaza de la Armería (armory), a setting for the pageantry of royal occasions. The imposing structure at the courtyard's south end is the Catedral de la Almudena, honoring the patroness of the city. Under construction for nearly a century, it will finally be completed this year, making it the oldest *new* cathedral in the world!

The palace is seen by guided tour, with different sections shown on different tours; both Spanish- and English-speaking National Patrimony guides lead the tours. Note that the King and Queen of Spain live in the Palacio de la Zarzuela, on the outskirts of Madrid, but the Palacio Real still is used for official occasions and is closed to the public at those times, which are not always announced in advance. Normally, opening hours are Mondays through Saturdays, from 9:30 AM to 5:15 PM; Sundays and holidays, from 9:15 AM to 2:15 PM. Admission charge. Plaza de Oriente (phone: 248-7404).

Plaza de Oriente – To the disappointment of Asian tourists, its name in Spanish simply means East (*oriente*) Square, because it faces the east façade of the Royal Palace (which also is sometimes referred to, in turn, as the Palacio de Oriente). Across the plaza from the palace is the *Teatro Real* (Royal Theater), which, after a major 2-year revamping of its interior, is scheduled to reopen this year as one of Europe's finest opera houses. In the center of the plaza stands the 9-ton bronze equestrian statue of King Philip IV, based on a drawing by Velázquez. Philip's horse is rearing up, supported solely by its hind legs, posing an equilibrium problem for Florentine sculptor Pietro Tacca. He consulted none other than the illustrious Galileo, whose solution was to make the front end of the statue hollow and the rear end solid.

Centro de Arte Reina Sofía-Museo Nacional de Arte Moderno y Contemporáneo (Queen Sofía Art Center-National Museum of Modern and Contemporary Art) – This gargantuan 18th-century building was Madrid's Hospital General de San Carlos until 1965. Following a tremendous reconstruction project, the building was inaugurated in 1986 as a museum devoted to contemporary art, named in honor of the present Queen of Spain. Following a long-term program of expansion within its already vast space, the museum reopened in November 1990 (after a 22-month closure) to take its place among the world's leading contemporary art galleries and modern art museums. The entire collection of the former *Museo Español de Arte Contemporáneo* (Spanish Contemporary Art Museum) was transferred here, and comprises 3,000 paintings, 9,000 drawings, and 400 sculptures, including works by Picasso, Miró, Dalí, Gris, and Julio Gonzáles. In addition to its still-growing permanent collection, it contains the most important contemporary art libraries in Spain with state-of-the-art computerized braille reading facilities, as well as videos (*videoarte*), photography collections, research facilities, and workshops. Throughout the year, several prominent exhibitions are scheduled at *CARS* (the museum's much-needed acronym) and at its two landmark annexes in Retiro Park, the *Palacio de Velázquez* and *Palacio de Cristal*. Open from 10 AM to 9 PM; closed Tuesdays. Admission charge. 52 Calle Santa Isabel (phone: 467-5062).

Plaza de Cibeles – Dominating Madrid's favorite traffic circle is the fountain and statue of the Greek fertility goddess Cibeles, astride her chariot drawn by two rather friendly looking lions. A Madrid custom requires that visitors "say hello to La Cibeles" upon arrival in town. Almost drowning out the vision of the Cibeles Fountain with its massiveness, the wedding-cake, turn-of-the-century Palacio de Comunicaciones (now the city's post office) on the plaza is so imposing that *madrileños* often refer to it as "Our Lady of Communications." Both Cibeles and the monumental arches of the Puerta de Alcalá (Alcalá Gate) up the street at Plaza de la Independencia are 18th-century endowments of the Bourbon "King-Mayor" Carlos III. On the southwest side of Plaza de Cibeles is the Banco de España; on the northwest side, the Palacio de Buenavista, which houses the Ministry of Defense.

Parque del Retiro (Retreat Park) – During the early 17th century, it was a royal retreat and the grounds of both a royal palace complex and a porcelain factory, then on the outskirts of town. Now Madrid's public park, right in the city, the Retiro covers 300 peaceful acres of forest, manicured gardens, statuary, fountains, picnic grounds, and cafés. It is a delightful place for strolling, jogging, a horse-and-carriage ride, or a boat ride around the lake, which is overlooked by the huge semicircular monument to King Alfonso XII. Art exhibitions are held at the park's Palacio de Cristal, a 19th-century jewel of glass and wrought iron, and at the Palacio de Velázquez, named for its architect, not for the painter. During the summer, at 10 PM and midnight, classical and flamenco concerts are staged in the Cecilio Rodríguez Gardens (Menéndez Pelayo entrance), and the outdoor cinema (entrance on Alfonso XII) features Spanish and foreign (including US) films. The park's loveliest entrance is through the wrought-iron gates at Plaza de la Independencia, also referred to as the Puerta de Alcalá.

Plaza de la Villa – One of Madrid's most charming squares, its architectural diversity makes it especially interesting. Dominating the west side, the 17th-century neoclassical Casa de la Villa, also called the Ayuntamiento (City Hall), was designed by Juan Gómez de Mora, the same architect who planned the Plaza Mayor. Adding to the *madrileño* atmosphere, its carillon chimes the hour with *zarzuela* melodies and plays 20-minute concerts every evening. Along the back of the square is the 16th-century Plateresque Casa de Cisneros palace, built by the nephew and heir of the cardinal regent of the same name. On the east side are the old Periodicals Library, with a large Mudéjar doorway, and the massive medieval Lujanes Tower, one of the oldest in Madrid and full of legends (one of its prisoners was King Francis I of France). Separating these two structures, the tiny Calle de Codo (Elbow Street) angles down to the tranquil Plaza del Cordón, which is surrounded by historic noble mansions. The bronze statue in the center of Plaza de la Villa honors Admiral Alvaro de Bazán, who fought — as did Cervantes — against the Turks in the Battle of Lepanto in 1571. The City Hall's splendid museum collection is open to the public every Monday (except holidays), from 5 to 7 PM, with free tours escorted by guides from the Madrid Tourist Board. Plaza de la Villa (phone: 588-0002).

Museo de la Real Academia de Bellas Artes de San Fernando (Museum of the San Fernando Royal Academy of Fine Arts) – Housed in a splendid 18th-century palace just east of the Puerta del Sol, the academy's permanent collection comprises some 1,500 paintings and over 800 sculptures. There are works by El Greco, Velázquez, Zurbarán, Murillo, Goya, and Sorolla, to name a few, as well as by Italian and Flemish masters. The only painting of George Washington in Spain is here; the portrait commemorates the Treaty of Friendship between Spain and the US. Closed to the public for 12 years, the museum reopened in 1986 and is gradually regaining the international renown it deserves — not only for its permanent collection, but for prestigious scheduled exhibitions held throughout the year. Open Tuesdays through Saturdays, from 9 AM to 7 PM; Sundays and Mondays, from 9 AM to 2 PM; during the summer, 9 AM to 2 PM daily. Admission charge. 13 Calle de Alcalá (phone: 532-1546).

Convento de las Descalzas Reales (Convent of the Barefoot Carmelites) – Behind its stark stone façade is an awesomely opulent interior filled with an astonishing wealth of artistic treasures and ornamentation bestowed by kings and noblemen. Princess Juana of Austria, sister of Philip II, opened this convent of the Royal Barefoot Carmelite Nuns in 1559. It welcomed disconsolate empresses, queens, princesses, and *infantas,* including Juana's sister María, Empress of Germany. The grandiose stairway is a breathtaking example of *barroco madrileño,* every centimeter lavishly decorated with frescoes and carved wood. Art treasures include works by El Greco, Zurbarán, Titian, and Sánchez Coello, as well as Rubens tapestries. From the windows of the upper floor is a lovely view over the tranquil rooftop garden, where the cloistered nuns still grow their vegetables just as they have for centuries, unaffected by the bustling Gran Vía just 1 block north, or the gigantic *El Corte Inglés* department store practically alongside. Visitors are escorted by resident Spanish-speaking National Patrimony guides; tours in English should be arranged in advance through the *Office of Museums* (phone: 248-7404). Hours vary according to the season, and are limited because the cloistered nuns often use the museum sections in their daily life; in general, however, opening hours are Tuesdays through Saturdays, from 10 AM to 1:30 PM. The admission charge includes the tour. Plaza de las Descalzas Reales (phone: 248-7404).

Convento de la Encarnación (Convent of the Incarnation) – Built by order of Queen Margarita of Austria, wife of King Philip III, this Augustinian convent was blessed in 1616. Designed in the severe classical style by Juan Gómez de Mora, its façade gives no clue to the bounteous religious and secular art treasures inside. The dazzling reliquary room displays some 1,500 religious relics contained in priceless gold and silver urns and jeweled cases. Among them, a legendary vial contains the blood of St. Pantaleón, which is said to liquefy every year on his birthday, July 27. A contrasting neo-classical 18th-century church designed by Ventura Rodríguez is set back in the center of the convent façade, and a statue of Lope de Vega graces its peaceful front garden. Like the Descalzas Reales, this is an active cloistered convent, and individuals and groups must be escorted by resident guides; tours in English can be arranged in advance through the *Office of Museums* (phone: 248-7404). Open Tuesdays through Saturdays, from 10 AM to 1:30 PM. The admission charge includes the tour. Plaza de la Encarnación (phone: 247-0510).

Museo Municipal – Devoted to the history of Madrid, this fine museum will enhance any visitor's awareness of the city's evolution, culture, and personality. It is filled with art, furnishings, porcelains, photographs, engravings, and meticulously detailed maps and models of the city during the 17th, 18th, and 19th centuries. The museum building, declared a National Monument in 1919, was originally an 18th-century hospital, and its elaborately ornate Churrigueresque-style entrance is in itself a worthwhile sight. Open Tuesdays through Saturdays, from 10 AM to 2 PM and 5 to 9 PM; Sundays, from 10 AM to 2:30 PM. Admission charge. 78 Calle Fuencarral (phone: 522-5732).

Mercado Puerta de Toledo – What used to be Madrid's old Central Fish Market (*mercado*) has been transformed into a sparkling showcase of fine Spanish handicrafts, art, antiques, jewelry, fashion, and interior design — everything from soup to nuts, in fact, since the premises include *El Abanico Gastronómico,* a combined restaurant and store featuring fine foods and wines from every region of Spain. Within the complex, the *Café del Mercado* is a lively nightspot. The market also is the setting for concerts, recitals, and art and photography exhibitions. Regularly scheduled video projections include a "bird's-eye view" of Madrid past and present. At the courtyard entrance is a functional Monument to Time: a giant sculptured combination sundial and lunar clock, considered the world's largest. The market is adjacent to the Puerta de Toledo, one of the ancient city gates, dominated by a 19th-century neo-classical triumphal arch. Joseph Bonaparte initiated construction of the arch; ironically, its completion celebrated the ousting of the French in the War of Independence, and the "welcome back" of Bourbon King Fernando VII. Open daily with dining, drinking, and entertainment going on into the wee hours. No admission charge. 1 Ronda de Toledo (phone: 266-7200).

Jardín Botánico (Botanical Garden) – The garden was designed in 1774 by Juan de Villanueva, the same architect who designed the *Prado Museum,* whose south façade it faces. Twenty manicured acres contain some 30,000 species of plants and flowers from Spain and throughout the world. Carlos III commissioned the project as part of his urban refurbishment program. By his order, therapeutic and medicinal plants and herbs were distributed free to those in need. Between the *Prado* and the entrance to the garden is the small Plaza de Murillo, which has a bronze statue of the 17th-century painter and the "Four Fountains" of mythological triton cherubs playing with dolphins. Open daily, from 10 AM to 7 PM (later in summer). Admission charge. On Paseo del Prado at Plaza de Murillo (phone: 420-3568).

Real Fábrica de Tapices (Royal Tapestry Factory) – Established early in the 18th century, this factory-museum continues to use authentic traditional techniques in producing handmade Spanish tapestries and rugs. In addition to the permanent collection, visitors can see the workshops and watch master artisans at work weaving tapestries from cartoons by Goya and other artists, knotting luxuriant rugs, or doing intricate restoration work. Rugs and tapestries can be purchased by special order, and they can even be custom-made from the customer's own design. Open Mondays through Fridays, from 9:30 AM to 12:30 PM; closed August. Admission charge. 3 Calle Fuenterrabía (phone: 551-3400).

Museo del Ejército (Army Museum) – Everything imaginable related to battle throughout Spain's history is here in an amazing array of over 27,000 items — uniforms, armor, cannon, swords (including one belonging to El Cid), stupendous collections of miniature soldiers, and portraits of heroines and heroes (such as Cervantes, when he lost his hand in the Battle of Lepanto). Downstairs, a curious collection of damaged carriages and automobiles whose illustrious passengers were assassinated en route recounts Madrid's turbulent political history. It's all chockablock within the vast and lavishly baroque interior of one of the two surviving buildings of the 17th-century Royal Retiro Palace complex (the other is the adjacent Casón del Buen Retiro, which the museum's pleasant bar overlooks). Whatever your interests, this is well worth seeing — while it lasts. Plans have been laid for the ever-expanding *Prado Museum* to take over this palatial building, and for the collection to be moved in the mid-1990s to a new venue at the Ministry of Defense complex in the Moncloa district. Open from 10 AM to 2 PM; closed Mondays. Admission charge. 1 Calle Méndez Núñez (phone: 531-4624).

Museo Arqueológico Nacional (National Archaeological Museum) – The star among the Iberian and classical antiquities is the enigmatic *Dama de Elche,* a dramatic Iberian bust of a priestess, or perhaps an aristocrat, estimated to have been sculpted during the 4th century BC. Also on display are basket weavings and funeral objects of early Iberians, as well as neolithic, Celtic, ancient Greek, Roman, and Visigothic artifacts and handicrafts. In the garden at the entrance is an underground replica of the famous Altamira Cave and its prehistoric paintings. Open Tuesdays through Saturdays, from 9:30 AM to 8:30 PM; Sundays and holidays, from 9:30 PM to 2:30 PM. The admission charge includes entrance to the *National Library* (see below), at the opposite side of the same building. 13 Calle Serrano (phone: 577-7912).

Biblioteca Nacional (National Library) – With over 6 million volumes, this is one of the world's richest libraries, truly a researcher's paradise. It was inaugurated in 1892 to commemorate the quadricentennial of the Discovery of America. Statues of Cervantes, Lope de Vega, and other illustrious Spaniards of letters stand at the classical columned entrance. Scheduled and seasonal exhibits of publications and graphics are held in the ground floor galleries. Open Tuesdays through Saturdays, from 10 AM to 9 PM; Sundays and holidays, 10 AM to 2 PM. The admission charge includes entrance to the *National Archaeological Museum* at the opposite side of the same building. 20 Paseo de Recoletos (phone: 575-6800).

Casa de Campo – Once the private royal hunting grounds, this 4,300-acre forested public park on the right bank of the Manzanares River is a playground for *madrileños* and visitors alike. It has a zoo (complete with a panda), picnic and fair grounds (important trade fairs and conventions are held here), and a giant amusement park, *Parque de Atracciones,* with rides and entertainment at an outdoor theater rife with a spirited carnival atmosphere. Other highlights include a concert stadium, an all-encompassing sports complex, a small lake, and the bullpens of La Venta de Batán (for bullfight practice and previews of the bulls). The park is easily reached by bus, metro, taxi, or the *teleférico* (cable car) that runs from Paseo del Pintor Rosales in Parque del Oeste (not far from Plaza de España). The zoo is open daily, April through September; Saturdays, Sundays, and holidays only, October through March. The amusement park is closed in winter and closed Mondays the rest of the year. Admission charge to attractions. Casa de Campo (phone: 463-2900).

Basílica de San Francisco el Grande – A few blocks south of the Royal Palace, this neo-classical church is one of the largest and most richly decorated in Madrid. Another project of King Carlos III, it was designed by the city's finest 18th-century architects. Six side chapels (the first on the left was painted by Goya) line its circular interior, which is topped by a cupola 108 feet in diameter. The museum inside the church contains a wealth of religious art. Museum hours are Tuesdays through Saturdays, from 11 AM to 1 PM and 4 to 7 PM; closed holidays. Admission charge to the museum. Plaza de San Francisco (phone: 265-3800).

■**EXTRA SPECIAL:** Some 30 miles (48 km) northwest of Madrid, the colossal monastery-palace of El Escorial symbolizes the grandeur of the Spanish Empire during its 16th-century Golden Age. King Philip II ordered its construction on a foothill of the Sierra de Guadarrama to commemorate Spain's victory over France at St.-Quentin, Flanders, and also to serve as a pantheon for his father, Holy Roman Emperor Charles V, and himself. It took more than 1,500 workmen 21 years to complete this extraordinary, austere monument designed by Juan de Herrera. The gray granite edifice, with hundreds of rooms and thousands of windows, is a sight never to be forgotten. The guided tour includes visits to the royal apartments, the museums (with paintings by Titian, Ribera, Velázquez, Tintoretto, Dürer, Lucas Jordan, and others), the library (with 40,000 priceless volumes and 4,700 manuscripts), the basilica, the royal pantheon with its tombs of Spanish monarchs, and the adjacent pantheon where their progeny are entombed. To reach the monastery-palace by car, take the N-VI national highway northwest to Guadarrama, then head south on C600; or take the more scenic country route, C505. There is frequent train and bus service between Madrid and the contiguous town of San Lorenzo de El Escorial, which is charming and well worth seeing. Open from 10 AM to 1 PM and 3 to 6 PM; closed Mondays. Admission charge (phone: 890-5903).

Nearby, to the north, is the Valle de los Caídos (Valley of the Fallen), an astonishing memorial to those who died in the Spanish Civil War. A huge basilica containing the tombs of soldiers from both sides has been hollowed into a mountain. Generalísimo Francisco Franco, who ordered the monument's construction, also is buried here. A granite cross stands 500 feet in the air atop the mountain peak. Open Tuesdays through Sundays, 10 AM to 6 PM. No admission charge, but there is a small parking fee (phone: 890-5611).

SOURCES AND RESOURCES

 TOURIST INFORMATION: Information, maps, and brochures can be obtained from the Oficina Municipal de Turismo (Municipal Tourist Office; 3 Plaza Mayor; phone: 266-5477). Information on the city, the rest of the province, and all of Spain also is available from the tourist information office of the Comunidad de Madrid (Province of Madrid, 2 Duque de Medinaceli; phone: 429-4951), near the *Palace* hotel. Other information offices run by the province are at Torre de Madrid, Plaza de España (phone: 541-2325), at Barajas Airport, and at the Chamartín train station.

The US Embassy is at 75 Calle Serrano (phone: 576-3400 or 3600).

Local Coverage – *ABC* and *El País,* among Spain's most important Spanish-language dailies, cover local, national, and international events, plus arts and entertainment listings. The *Guía del Ocio* ("Leisure Guide"), in Spanish, is the most complete weekly guide to restaurants, entertainment, culture, and sports.

TELEPHONE: The city code for Madrid is 1. If calling from within Spain, dial 91 before the local number.

GETTING AROUND: Airport – Aeropuerto de Barajas, 10 miles (16 km) from downtown Madrid, handles both international and domestic flights. It is about a 20-minute taxi ride from the center of the city, depending on traffic; the fare will run about $15. (Note that taxis charge an additional 50¢ for picking up passengers at the airport, as well as another 25¢ per bag. There also is a 50¢ surcharge for all rides at night (11:30 PM to 6 AM) and all day on Sundays and holidays. Public buses run every 15 minutes between the airport and the air terminal in the center of the city under Plaza de Colón; the buses are yellow and are marked "Aeropuerto." The main *Iberia Airlines* office is at 130 Calle Velázquez (phone for domestic reservations: 411-1011; phone for international reservations: 563-9966). *Iberia*'s *Puente Aereo* (Air Bridge) runs 1-hour flights to Barcelona, leaving every 10 minutes.

Bus – Excellent, bus service is available throughout Madrid. Normal service operates from 6 AM to midnight; between midnight and 6 AM, there is service every 30 minutes from Plaza de Cibeles and Puerta del Sol. Signs clearly marking the routes are at each bus stop. Individual bus tickets are bought from the driver and cost 115 pesetas per ride. Discounted "bonobus" passes, good for ten rides, cost 450 pesetas, and can be bought at *Empresa Municipal de Transportes* (*EMT*) kiosks all over the city including one on the east side of Puerta del Sol and another at the south side of Plaza de Cibeles; upon boarding the bus, insert the pass into the date-stamping machine behind the driver. For information on the city bus system, call *EMT* at 401-9900. Madrid has no central bus station from which long-distance buses depart, but the Estación Sur de Autobuses (17 Calle Canarias; phone: 468-4200), serving Andalusia and other points south, is the largest of several.

Car Rental – All major international and Spanish firms are represented; most have offices at Madrid's Aeroporto de Barajas, and some at Chamartín and Atocha train stations. Agencies in the city include *América* (23 Calle Cartagena; phone: 246-7919); *Atesa* (59 Gran Vía; phone: 247-0202; and 25 Calle Princesa; phone: 241-5004); *Avis* (60 Gran Vía; phone: 247-2048; and in the airport terminal under Plaza de Colón; phone: 576-2862); *Europcar* (29 Calle Orense; phone: 445-9930; and 12 Calle García de Paredes; phone: 448-8706); *Hertz* (88 Gran Vía; phone: 248-5803; and in the *Castellana Inter-Continental* hotel (49 Paseo de la Castellana; phone: 319-0378); and *Ital* (31 Calle Princesa; phone: 241-9403).

Subway – Madrid's metro is efficient and clean and in operation from 6 AM to 1:30 AM. Stops along all ten lines are clearly marked, and color-coded maps are easy to read. Tickets are purchased from machines and inserted into electronic turnstiles, or they're bought at pass-through booths. (Do not discard the ticket until the end of the ride.) Discounted ten-ride tickets also are available (410 pesetas); buy these at metro stations. For subway information, call 435-2266.

Taxi – Metered cabs are white with a diagonal red line. If a cab is available, it will have a windshield sign that says *libre* and an illuminated green light on its roof. Fares are moderate. Taxis can be hailed on the street, picked up at cabstands, or summoned by phone: *Radio-Teléfono Taxi* (phone: 247-8200); *Radio-Taxi* (phone: 404-9000); *Tele-taxi* (phone: 445-9008).

Train – The two major stations of the *RENFE* (Spanish National Railway) are Chamartín at the north end of Madrid and Atocha at the south end. Both serve long-distance trains, as well as commuter trains to surrounding areas (*cercanías*). West of Plaza de España, a third station, Principe Pío (also called Estación del Norte), serves some lines to northern Spain. *RENFE*'s main city ticket office is located at 44 Calle de Alcalá (phone: 429-0518 for information; 429-8228 for reservations). Tickets also can be purchased at the train stations and at *RENFE's* Nuevos Ministerios and Recoletos stations.

On Saturdays and Sundays from May through October, *RENFE* operates a series of tourist trains offering 1- and 2-day excursions to nearby places of interest. Museum entrance fees, guided tours, motorcoach sightseeing, and, in some cases, meals are included in the cost of the transportation; hotel accommodations are included in the 2-day packages, which travel to more distant destinations. The specially named 1-day excursion trains head for Aranjuez (*Tren de la Fresa,* or "Strawberry Train"); Toledo (*Ciudad de Toledo*); Avila (*Murallas de Avila*); Sigüenza (*Doncel de Sigüenza*); and the Piedra River and Monastery in Aragon (*Monasterio de Piedra*). The cost is approximately $15–$20, with discounts for children under 12. Trains departing on 2-day excursions, leaving Saturday mornings and returning Sunday nights, make trips to Cáceres (*Ciudad Monumental de Cáceres*); Burgos (*Tierras del Cid*); Cuenca (*Ciudad Encantada de Cuenca*); Valladolid (*Cuna del Descubrimiento*); Salamanca (*Plaza Mayor de Salamanca*); Soria (*Camino de Soria*); Zamora (*Románico de Zamora*); and Palencia (*Camino de Santiago Palentino*). Prices range from about $70 to $135, depending on the train and choice of hotel. *RENFE*'s new bullet trains make the trip to Seville in less than 3 hours. Reservations should be made in advance at *RENFE* offices or through one of the many travel agencies scattered throughout Madrid. (Check the list of destinations for additional cities upon arrival in Madrid, because the innovative tourist train idea has been so successful that new destinations are added each season.)

 LOCAL SERVICES: Dentist (English-Speaking) – Ask at the US Embassy (phone: 576-3400 or 576-3600) or your hotel concierge.

Dry Cleaner – *El Corte Inglés* department store, also does laundry. 3 Preciados (phone: 532-1800).

Limousine Service – *American Express* makes arrangements with English-speaking drivers. 2 Plaza de las Cortes (phone: 429-5775).

Medical Emergency – *British American Hospital* (1 Paseo de Juan XXIII; phone: 234-6700); *Red Cross Central Hospital* (22 Av. Reina Victoria; phone: 233-3900; Emergency, phone: 233-7777); *La Paz Hospital* (Paseo de la Castellana; phone: 734-2600). The national police emergency number is 091; the municipal police is 092.

Messenger Service – *Mensajeros Express,* 5 Calle Berlín (phone: 255-3300).

National/International Courier – *DHL International* (17 Torres Quevedo, Polígono Fin de Semana; phone: 747-7711); *Federal Express* (13 Calle Arrastari, Polígono Las Mercedes; phone: 329-0460).

Office Equipment Rental – *El 7,* for typewriters (39 Hortaleza; phone: 522-5943); *Telson,* for audiovisual equipment (64 Pradillo; phone: 413-4463).

Pharmacy – To find the all-night pharmacy closest to your hotel, call the 24-hour pharmacy hotline 098. Pharmacy hours also are listed in the newspapers; look under "Farmacias de Guardia."

Photocopies – There are shops throughout the city. Outstanding is *Prontaprint,* open Mondays through Fridays 10 AM to 7 PM. Two locations: 15 Jacometrezo, just off the Gran Vía, between Plaza Callao and Plaza Santo Domingo (phone: 248-9958) and 56 María de Molina (phone: 411-0823).

Post Office – The main post office is Palacio de Comunicaciones at Plaza de la Cibeles (phone: 521-4004 or 521-8195). Hours vary according to the service provided; stamps can be purchased from 9 AM to 10 PM.

Secretary/Stenographer (English-Speaking) – *Intercom English SA* (19 General Martínez Campos; phone: 445-4751); *CADRESSA* (33 General Margallo; phone: 270-3077).

Tailor – *Galeote M. Córdova* (10 Manuel de Falla; phone: 457-7539); *Fernando Hervas* (27 Príncipe; phone: 429-6331).

Telex – *Palacio de Comunicaciones* (Plaza de la Cibeles; phone: 521-4004 or 521-8195); *Telefónica* will receive and hold telexes sent to 41663 or 41664. They can be picked up as a type of general delivery. The telex department is open from 9 AM to 9 PM daily (Plaza Colón; phone: 410-3186).

Translator – *CADRESSA* (33 General Margallo; phone: 270-3077); *Siasa* (134 Paseo de la Habana; phone: 457-4891); *Intercom English SA* (19 General Martínez Campos; phone: 445-4751).

Other – Convention facilities: *Palacio de Congresos* (99 Paseo de la Castellana; phone: 555-1600 or 555-4906) has 2 auditoriums that can be joined for a total capacity of 2,684 people, an amphitheater for up to 900, 8 meeting rooms for up to 320, audiovisual equipment, closed-circuit TV, cafeteria, banquet hall, and private dining rooms for 100; total capacity is 10,000 people. *Casa de Campo* has facilities on its fairgrounds and in its auditorium space for hundreds of stands, and the meeting hall has a capacity for 608; located on the outskirts of Madrid (for information: *Auditorio del Recinto de la Casa de Campo,* Avenida Portugal; phone: 463-6334). The *Madrid Convention Bureau* offers full assistance for every aspect of meeting and convention arrangements (69 Mayor; phone: 588-2930).

Communications services: *Telefónica* (locations at 30 Gran Vía, Plaza de las Cibeles, and Plaza Colón. Long-distance calls can be paid by Visa or MasterCard. The Gran Vía location is open 24 hours; the offices at Gran Vía and Colón have AT&T "USA Direct" phone service for collect or phone credit card calls to the US).

Tuxedo rental: *Cornejo* (2 Magdalena; phone: 239-1646).

 SPECIAL EVENTS: Madrid has a distinctive, exuberant way of celebrating Spain's national holidays, as well as its own year-long calendar of local fairs and festivals. And the city's cultural calendar will be extra full for the next 12 months because of Madrid's designation as the European Cultural Capital of the Year. *Madrileños* go all out for *Carnaval* frolic, frocks, and parades in February, ending on *Ash Wednesday* with the allegorical *Entierro de la Sardina* (Burial of the Sardine). The *International Festival of Theater and Film* is held in April. On the *Second of May,* at Plaza 2 de Mayo in the Malasaña district, processions and events commemorate the city's uprising against the massacring French, which Goya portrayed so dramatically. But even more *madrileño* are the *Fiestas de San Isidro* — 10 days of nonstop street fairs, festivals, concerts, special daily bullfights, and more, all in celebration of Madrid's patron saint, whose feast day is on May 15. (This age-old tradition of picnics and merrymaking at the Meadows of San Isidro alongside the Manzanares River also was depicted by Goya.) On June 13, the *Verbena de San Antonio* (St. Anthony's Fair) takes place at the shrine of San Antonio de la Florida, with outdoor singing and dancing and traditional drinking from the fountain. It's also customary to throw pins into the holy water; young "spinsters" dip in, and their chances for acquiring a mate depend on the number of pins that stick in their hands.

Madrid is extra-lively during the summer, despite the mass exodus by summer vacationers. During July, August, and early September, the city government presents *Veranos en la Villa* (Summers in the "Village"), 2-plus months of countless cultural events featuring international superstars and local talent — ballet, symphonic music, opera, jazz, rock, pop, salsa, *zarzuelas,* films, and many diverse exhibitions — in open-air and theater settings throughout the city. Fitting in neatly with all this are colorful *verbenas* (street parties) honoring the feast days of three of Madrid's most popular saints: San Cayetano (August 3), San Lorenzo (August 5), and La Virgen de la Paloma (August 15). In the *barrios castizos* (authentically typical neighborhoods, such as Lavapiés, Embajadores, Puerta de Toledo), *madrileños,* from toddlers to great-grand-parents, dress in the traditional attire of *chulos* and *chulapas* reminiscent of 19th-century *zarzuelas.* They gather at lively street fairs to eat, drink, and dance the *chotis* and *pasodoble,* enjoying musical groups, folk music performances, organ-grinders, processions, *limonada* (not lemonade, but a kind of white-wine sangria), and their own innate ebullience. The world-class *Madrid International Jazz Festival* is held in late October and/or early November. From October to the beginning of December, the *Fiesta de Otoño* (Autumn Festival), also organized by the city government, presents an abundance of concerts and performances by top international and Spanish companies at Madrid theaters and concert halls. November 9 celebrates the day of Madrid's patroness, La Virgen de la Almudena. During the *Christmas* season, the city is bedecked with festive lights, and the Plaza Mayor fills with countless stands selling decorations, figurines for Nativity scenes, candies, wreaths, and *Christmas* trees. On *New Year's Eve,* throngs gather at the Puerta del Sol to swallow one grape at each stroke of the clock at midnight, wishing for 12 months of good luck in the new year. The *Christmas* season lasts until *Epiphany,* January 6, on the eve of which children delight at the *Cabalgata de los Reyes,* the procession through the city streets by the gift-giving Three Wise Men. As if all of this weren't enough, each barrio expresses its individual personality with its own fiestas and *festivales* throughout the year.

MUSEUMS: Many museums are described in *Special Places* (above). Included in the following list of additional museums are certain churches that, because of their high artistic quality, should not be overlooked. Note that the *Museo de América* (America's Museum; 6 Avenida Reyes Católicos), housing Latin American crafts and folk art along with pre-Columbian artifacts, currently closed for restoration, is scheduled to reopen this year (possibly in a new location). Also closed for restoration, but scheduled to reopen this year, is the *Casa-Museo de Lope de Vega* (Lope de Vega House-Museum, 11 Calle Cervantes; phone: 239-4605), consisting of the home and garden of Spain's great Golden Age dramatist; it ordinarily is open Tuesdays and Thursdays only, from 10AM to 2 PM, and closed in summer. Admission charge. Keep in mind that the hours of many museums may vary during the summer, and smaller museums may be closed during July and August. The *Office of Museums* will be able to supply the latest information (phone: 248-7404).

Basílica de San Miguel – An unusual 18th-century church with an air of Italian baroque in its convex façade and graceful interior. Open daily. 4 Calle de San Justo.

Catedral de San Isidro – This imposing 17th-century church was *temporarily* designated the Cathedral of Madrid in 1885, pending the completion of the Catedral de la Almudena — which has been under construction for over a century. The entombed remains of St. Isidro, patron saint of Madrid, and those of his wife, Santa María de la Cabeza, sit on the altar. Open daily. 37 Calle Toledo.

Círculo de Bellas Artes (Fine Arts Circle) – Several galleries of this art, design, and photography center display works by students and prominent teachers. Open daily; exhibits and events are scheduled at varying hours; pick up a monthly program at the tourist office. Admission charge to most exhibits. 42 Calle de Alcalá (phone: 531-7700).

Estudio y Museo Sorolla (Sorolla Studio and Museum) – The house in which Joaquín Sorolla, the Valencian Impressionist "Painter of Light," lived, worked, and died in 1923. Contents include a collection of his works; the studio and library remain intact. Open from 10 AM to 3 PM; closed Mondays. Admission charge. 37 Calle General Martínez Campos (phone: 410-1584).

Fundación Casa de Alba (House of Alba Foundation) – The magnificent 18th-century Palacio de Liria, former residence of the Duchess of Alba, containing the family's priceless private collection of art, tapestries, archives, and furnishings. Admission (free) must be requested well in advance by writing to: Fundación Casa de Alba, 20 Calle Princesa, 28008 Madrid (phone: 247-5302).

Iglesia y Convento de San Jerónimo el Real (Church and Convent of San Jerónimo) – This giant Gothic temple overlooking the *Prado* was built by order of King Ferdinand and Queen Isabella in 1503. It is closed for massive renovation, and is not scheduled to reopen until the mid-1990s. 19 Calle Ruiz de Alarcón.

Museo Cerralbo – The palatial 19th-century mansion of the Marqués de Cerralbo houses an important collection of art, antiques, ceramics, tapestries, and ancient artifacts. Outstanding among the paintings are works by El Greco, Ribera,

Velázquez, Zurbarán, and Van Dyck. Open from 10 AM to 2 PM and 4 to 6 PM; closed Mondays and in August. Admission charge. 17 Calle Ventura Rodríguez (phone: 247-3647).

Museo de la Ciudad (Museum of the City) – This brand-new museum exhibits testimonials to the evolution of Madrid. 140 Calle Principe de Vergara. For more information, call 588-6500.

Museo de Escultura Abstracta al Aire Libre (Outdoor Museum of Abstract Sculpture) – Contemporary Spanish sculptures permanently placed in a pedestrian area on the Castellana, under the Calles Eduardo Dato–Juan Bravo overpass. Open continuously; no admission charge. Paseo de la Castellana (no phone).

Museo de Figuras de Cera (Wax Museum) – An international gallery of historic personages, including celebrity bullfighters and such fictional Spanish notables as Don Quixote and Sancho Panza. Open daily, from 10:30 AM to 1:30 PM and 4 to 8 PM. Admission charge. Centro Colón (phone: 308-0825).

Museo Lázaro Galdiano – Named for its founder, whose palatial mansion houses his extraordinary collection of art, jewelry, ivory, and enamel. Open from 10 AM to 2 PM; closed Mondays and in August. Admission charge. 122 Calle Serrano (phone: 261-6084).

Museo Nacional de Artes Decorativas (National Museum of Decorative Arts) – Four floors of furniture, porcelains, jewelry, Spanish tiles and fans, a full Valencian kitchen, and handicrafts from the 16th through 19th centuries. Open Tuesdays through Fridays, from 10 AM to 3 PM; Saturdays and Sundays, from 10 AM to 2 PM; closed in summer. Admission charge. 12 Calle Montálban (phone: 521-3440).

Museo Nacional Ferroviario (National Railroad Museum) – Madrid's first train station, Estación de las Delicias, now is a museum complete with intact antique trains, royal cars, and other predecessors of the modern railroad. From May through October, the restored 19th-century "Strawberry Train" (*Tren de la Fresa*) departs here on 1-day excursions to Aranjuez. Open Tuesdays through Saturdays, from 10 AM to 5 PM; Sundays and holidays, from 10 AM to 2 PM. Admission charge. 61 Paseo de las Delicias (phone: 227-3121).

Museo Naval (Maritime Museum) – Models of ships and ports, nautical instruments, and maps, including Juan de la Cosa's historic *mapa mundi,* the first map to include the New World, drawn in 1500. Open from 10:30 AM to 1:30 PM; closed Mondays and in August. Admission charge. 2 Calle Montálban (phone: 521-0419).

Museo Panteón de Goya (Pantheon of Goya, also called Ermita de San Antonio) – Goya painted the magnificent religious frescoes on the dome and walls of this small 18th-century church, which was to become his tomb. Open Tuesdays through Fridays, from 10 AM to 1:30 PM and 4 to 7 PM; weekends and holidays, from 10 AM to 1:30 PM. No admission charge. Glorieta de San Antonio de la Florida (phone: 542-0722).

Museo Romántico (Romantic Museum) – Paintings, furniture, and decor of 19th-century Madrid, housed in an 18th-century mansion. Open Tuesdays through Saturdays, from 10 AM to 6 PM; Sundays, from 10 AM to 2 PM. Closed August. Admission charge. 13 Calle San Mateo (phone: 448-1071).

Museo Taurino (Bullfighting Museum) – An important collection of bullfighting memorabilia, including photographs, celebrity bullfighters' "suits of lights," and even taxidermic trophies of ears, tails, and entire bulls. Open Mondays through Fridays, from 9 AM to 3 PM; during bullfighting season (May through October), open Sundays, closed Mondays. Admission charge. Plaza de Toros Monumental de las Ventas, 237 Calle de Alcalá (phone: 255-1857).

Templo de Debod – A gift from the Egyptian government in the 1970s, this 2,500-year-old Egyptian temple was shipped to Madrid in 1,359 cases and reassembled, towering over a reflecting pool. Theater and music performances are held here in summer. Open daily, from 10 AM to 1 PM; holidays, from 10 AM to 3 PM. No admission charge. Parque del Oeste.

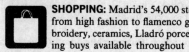

SHOPPING: Madrid's 54,000 stores and shops offer everything imaginable, from high fashion to flamenco guitars. Handicrafts, fine leather goods, embroidery, ceramics, Lladró porcelains, art, and antiques are among the enticing buys available throughout the city. Everything goes on sale twice a year — after *Christmas* (which in Spain means January 7, the day after *Epiphany*) and during the summer. The big summer sales (*rebajas*) begin in July, and prices are reduced even more during the first 3 weeks of August. Shops generally open at 9:30 AM, close from 1:30 to 4:30 PM for lunch and the siesta, and close for the night at 8 PM. The huge flagship stores of Spain's two major department store chains are next to each other in the pedestrian shopping area between the Gran Vía and Puerta del Sol: *El Corte Inglés* (3 Calle Preciados; phone: 532-8100) and *Galerías Preciados* (1 Plaza de Callao; phone: 522-4771). Unlike most retailers, they remain open during the lunch and siesta hours, and they provide special services for tourists, such as English-speaking escorts to accompany shoppers and coordination of shipping services to hotel or home. Branch stores of *El Corte Inglés* are at 56 Calle Princesa, 76 Calle Goya, and 79 Calle Raimundo Fernández Villaverde (the biggest of all, just off the Castellana). Branches of *Galerías Preciados* are at 10-11 Calle Arapiles, 87 Calle Goya, 47 Calle Serrano, and at the *Madrid 2 Shopping Center* (also known as *La Vaguada*) in northern Madrid.

Near the two department stores, four stores specializing in fine china, porcelain (especially Lladró), and Majórica pearls, line the Gran Vía: *Souvenirs* (11 Gran Vía, near Calle de Alcalá; phone: 521-5119); *Vinvinda* (44 Gran Vía, near Plaza de Callao; phone: 213-0514); *Regalos A.R.* (46 Gran Vía; phone: 522-6869); and *La Galette* (67 Gran Vía, near Plaza de España; phone: 248-8938). Window shopping is a favorite pastime along Calle Serrano, which is full of elegant boutiques and galleries; the Plaza Mayor area is another place to look for appealing shopping opportunities.

Other places to browse or buy include the rebuilt *Mercado Puerta de Toledo* (see *Special Places*), where over 150 shops, boutiques, and galleries are stuffed with the finest in Spanish handicrafts, art, fashion, antiques, jewelry, housewares, and food products. Easy-to-operate computer terminals reveal what and where everything is in this sparkling complex, which is all under one roof (1 Ronda de Toledo; phone: 266-7200). *La Galería del Prado* (phone: 429-7551), a recent addition to the *Palace* hotel (7 Plaza de las Cortes), is a glamorous assembly of 38 top fashion boutiques, art galleries, jewelers, and gift shops, as well as a fancy food shop, a beauty salon, bookstore, and a buffet-style restaurant. Still another shopping mall, in modern Madrid, just off the Castellana, is *Moda Shopping* (40 Avenida General Perón), with over 60 establishments selling everything from high fashion to sporting goods, and with plenty of restaurants and bars to enjoy during shopping breaks.

El Rastro, Madrid's legendary outdoor flea market, (open Sundays and holiday mornings only) spreads for countless blocks in the old section of the city, beginning at Plaza de Cascorro and fanning south to Ronda de Toledo. Hundreds of stands are set up to sell everything from canaries to museum-piece antiques, and bargaining, preferably in Spanish, is customary. (Guard wallets and purses from pickpockets.) Open daily, year-round, is the *Cuesta de Moyano*, a stretch of Calle de Claudio Moyano (along the south side of the Botanical Gardens) with a string of bookstalls selling new, used, and out of print "finds" of everything imaginable that's been published.

Adolfo Domínguez – The boutique of the innovative Spanish celebrity designer, whose daring women's fashions set the "wrinkles (in the fabric, that is) are beautiful" trend. 4 Calle Ortega y Gasset (phone: 276-0084).

Antigua Casa Talavera – Authentic regional handcrafted ceramics and dinnerware from all over Spain form an overwhelming display in this small, family-owned shop just off the Gran Vía, near Plaza de Santo Domingo. 2 Calle Isabel la Católica (phone: 247-3417).

Artespaña – Government run, with a wide range of handicrafts and home furnishings from all over Spain. 3 Plaza de las Cortes, 14 Calle Hermosilla, 33 Calle Don Ramón de la Cruz, and *Centro Comercial Madrid 2–La Vaguada* (phone for all locations: 413-6262).

Ascot – An excellent women's boutique selling haute couture and ready-to-wear fashions by María Teresa de Vega, who clothes some of Madrid's most beautiful people. 88 Calle Serrano (phone: 431-3712).

El Aventurero – A small bookstore specializing in guidebooks, maps, books on the art of bullfighting, and outstanding "coffee-table" tomes on Spanish subjects, with an ample selection in English, too. Just off Plaza Mayor at 15 Calle Toledo (phone: 266-4457).

Boutique Granada – A small shop selling leather goods of the highest quality. 12 Calle de Vergara (phone: 241-0746).

Canalejas – Top-quality men's shirtmakers, specializing in the classic European formfitting cut. 20 Carrera de San Jerónimo (phone: 521-8075).

Casa de Diego – Founded in 1858, this old-time store makes hand-painted fans — and frames for displaying them — as well as canes and umbrellas. Two locations: 12 Puerta del Sol (phone: 522-6643), and 4 Calle Mesonero Romanos (phone: 531-0223).

Casa Jiménez – Another classic store specializing in fans and *mantones de manila,* fine lace shawls. 42 Calle Preciados (phone: 248-0526).

Casa del Libro – Madrid's biggest book store. 29 Gran Vía (phone: 521-1932). A brand-new branch, on 4 floors, is at 3 Calle Maestro Vitoria (phone: 521-4898).

Cortefiel – Leading men's and women's fashions and accessories are carried at 40 Calle Serrano (phone: 431-3342). Branches at 178 Paseo de la Castellana (phone: 259-5713) and 27 Gran Vía (phone: 247-1701) specialize in men's fashions only, while those at 146 Paseo de la Castellana (phone: 250-3638) and 13 Calle Preciados (phone: 522-6567) cater exclusively to women.

El Corte Inglés Record Department – The latest in Spanish classical, pop, and flamenco music on record, tape, and compact disc, as well as a complete selection of every other type of recorded music. They even carry *sevillanas* dance lessons on videocassette. Across the street from the main store at 3 Calle Preciados (phone: 532-8100).

Elena Benarroch – Stylish designs in women's furs. This well-known furrier also has a shop in New York. 24 Calle Monte Esquinza (phone: 308-2816).

Gil, Sucesor de Anatolín Quevedo – Spanish and international celebrities purchase work-of-art shawls, mantillas, and embroidery at this generations-old establishment. 2 Carrera de San Jerónimo (phone: 521-2549).

Gritos de Madrid – A fine ceramics shop owned by master craftsman Eduardo Fernández, and featuring his works. He is responsible for the restoration of Madrid's interesting hand-illustrated tile street signs, and his famous ceramic mural of 17th-century Madrid hangs in the City Hall's museum collection. 6 Plaza Mayor (phone: 265-9154).

Joaquín Berao – Fine jewelry by the young Spanish designer — earrings, bracelets, rings, and pendants in ultramodern designs. 13 Calle Conde de Xiquena (phone: 410-1620).

Lepanto – Fashions, luggage, and accessories, in leather. 3 Plaza de Oriente (phone: 242-2357).

Loewe – Fine leather fashions for men and women, as well as accessories and luggage. At several locations: 8 Gran Vía, 26 Calle Serrano, and at the *Palace* hotel; a shop at 34 Calle Serrano carries men's fashions exclusively (phone for all locations: 435-3023).

Maty – For dance enthusiasts: authentic regional (including flamenco) costumes for men, women, and children, and dance shoes and boots as well. 2 Calle Maestro Vitoria (phone: 479-8802).

Seseña – Always in style in Spain, capes are becoming the "in" thing for evening-wear everywhere, and this store, founded in 1901, manufactures a fine line for men and women. (It also instructs clients on the fine art of wearing a cape.) 23 Calle Cruz (phone: 531-6840).

SPORTS AND FITNESS: Basketball – Madrid plays host to much of the finest basketball in Europe. The city is represented by such teams as *Real Madrid* and *Estudiantes* and also is the home of the Spanish National and Olympic squads. The most important games are played at the *Palacio de Deportes* (99 Calle Jorge Juan; phone: 401-9100), and at the *Polideportivo Magariños* (127 Calle Serrano; phone: 262-4022).

Bullfighting – Although not universally appreciated, bullfighting is the most renowned sport of Spain — Spaniards insist it is an art — and the largest bullfighting ring in Madrid is *Plaza de Toros Monumental de las Ventas,* which seats 22,300 people. There also is a smaller ring, *Plaza de Toros de Carabanchel,* near the Vista Alegre metro stop. The season runs from mid-May through October. Tickets may be purchased the day of the event at a counter at 3 Calle Vitoria (near the Puerta del Sol), at the bullring, or through a hotel concierge.

Fishing – There are fishing reserves along the Lozoya, Madarquillos, Jarama, and Cofio rivers not far from Madrid. They are populated mostly by trout, carp, black bass, pike, and barbel. The Santillana reservoir is particularly good for pike. For season and license information, contact the *Dirección General del Medio Rural,* 39 Calle Jorge Juan (phone: 435-5121).

Fitness Centers – Madrid has 27 municipal gymnasiums; for information on the one nearest your hotel, call 464-9050.

Golf – The Madrid area boasts several excellent private golf courses, such as the two 18-hole courses at the *Real Club de la Puerta de Hierro* (Avenida Miraflores; phone: 316-1745); the 18-hole and 9-hole courses at the *Club de Campo Villa de Madrid* (Carretera de Castilla; phone: 207-0395); the Jack Nicklaus–designed 18-hole course of the *Club de Golf La Moraleja* (7 miles/11 km north of town along the Burgos–Madrid highway; phone: 650-0700); and the 18 holes of the *Nuevo Club de Golf de Madrid* (at Las Matas, 16 miles/26 km west of town via the Carretera de La Coruña; phone: 630-0820). The *Federación Española de Golf* (9 Calle Capitán Haya; phone: 555-2682) has details on most of the area's facilities; hotels also can provide information regarding the use of the clubs by non-members.

Horse Racing – The *Hipódromo de la Zarzuela* (4 miles/7 km north of the center, along Carretera de La Coruña) features Sunday-afternoon races during spring and fall meetings. Buses for the track leave from the corner of Calles Princesa and Hilarión Eslava (phone: 207-0140).

Jogging – Parque del Retiro and Casa de Campo both have jogging tracks.

Skiing – *Puerto de Navacerrada,* a mountain resort (just 37 miles/60 km north of Madrid; phone: 852-1435) has 12 ski runs and 6 lifts.

Soccer – One of Spain's most popular teams, the capital's *Real Madrid,* plays its home games at the *Estadio Santiago Bernabéu* (1 Calle Concha Espina; phone: 250-0600), while its rival, *Atlético de Madrid,* takes the field at the *Estadio Vicente Calderón* (6 Paseo Virgen del Puerto; phone: 266-4707).

Swimming – Many hotels have pools, but Madrid also has 150 public swimming pools, including those indoors and outdoors at *Casa de Campo* (Avenida del Angel; phone: 463-0050). Another nice pool is at *La Elipa* (Avenida de la Paz; phone: 430-3358), which also has an area set aside for co-ed nude sunbathing. For information on other municipal pools, call 463-5498.

Tennis – Among the hundreds of public and private tennis courts in town are the 35 courts at the *Club de Campo Villa de Madrid,* Carretera de Castilla (phone: 207-0395), and the 28 courts of the *Club de Tenis Chamartín* (2 Calle Federico Salmón; phone: 250-5965).

THEATER: Theater productions are in Spanish. Anyone fluent and interested in the Spanish classics should check the *Guía del Ocio* for what's on at the *Teatro Español* (25 Calle del Príncipe; phone: 429-6297), which stages the classics of the Golden Age; at the nearby *Teatro de la Comedia* (14 Calle del Príncipe; phone: 521-4931), where the *Compañía Nacional de Teatro Clásico* (National Classical Theater Company) also puts on a fine repertoire of classic Spanish plays, as well as modern ones and foreign adaptations; and at the *Teatro Nacional María Guerrero* (4 Tamayo y Baus; phone: 319-4769), still another venue for both modern plays and classics of the Spanish and international repertoires. For the strictly modern and avant-garde, there's the *Centro Nacional de Nuevas Tendencias Escénicas* (National Center of New Theater Trends), housed at the *Sala Olimpia* (Plaza de Lavapiés; phone: 237-4622). Madrid is a city of film buffs, but if you feel like taking in a film and your Spanish is not good enough for the latest Almodóvar, note that foreign films usually are not dubbed into Spanish — look for "V.O.," meaning *'versión original"* in the ad. *Cine Doré,* known as the Filmoteca Española (3 Calle Santa Isabel; phone: 227-3866), has all the avant-garde foreign films; *Alphavilla* (14 Calle Martín de los Heros; phone: 248-4524) is another possibility. Ballets, operas, and *zarzuelas* (or operettas — some *zarzuelas* resemble musical comedy, others light opera), present fewer difficulties for nonspeakers of Spanish. Check listings for the restored *Teatro Nuevo Apolo Musical de Madrid* (1 Plaza Tirso de Molina; phone: 369-0637), home base for director José Tamayo's *Nueva Antología de la Zarzuela* company; *Teatro Lírico Nacional de la Zarzuela* (4 Calle Jovellanos; phone: 429-8225), which also hosts opera, ballet, and concerts, in addition to traditional *zarzuela;* and the *Centro Cultural de la Villa* (Plaza de Colón; phone: 575-6080), which presents both theater and *zarzuela.*

MUSIC: Bolero and fandango are the typically Castilian dances and flamenco is Andalusian, but it is the latter most tourists want to see and hear, so there are numerous excellent flamenco *tablaos* (cabarets) in Madrid. Some of the best are *Corral de la Morería* (17 Calle Morería; phone: 265-1137); *Café de Chinitas* (7 Calle Torija; phone: 248-5135); *Torres Bermejas* (11 Calle Mesonero Romanos; phone: 532-3322); and, *Venta del Gato* (about 5 miles/8 km outside Madrid on the road to Burgos, 214 Avenida de Burgos; phone: 776-6060). *Café Central* (10 Plaza del Angel; phone: 468-0844) offers live music nightly (jazz, classical, salsa, or folk) as well as late dinner. Madrid's main hall for classical concerts is the new *Auditorio Nacional de Música* (146 Calle Príncipe de Vergara; phone: 337-0100), the home of the *Orquestra Nacional de España* and the *Coro Nacional de España* — the *Spanish National Orchestra* and the *Spanish National Chorus.* At present, the *Teatro Real,* formerly the city's premier concert hall, at Plaza de Oriente, is being converted into the *Teatro de la Opera,* scheduled to open late this year. Classical music also can be heard at several other locations, including the *Fundación Juan March* (77 Calle Castelló; phone: 435-4250). For a list of theaters presenting *zarzuela,* Spain's traditional form of operetta, see *Theater* above.

NIGHTCLUBS AND NIGHTLIFE: Nightlife in Madrid can continue all night. Cover charges at cabarets and nightclubs include one drink, dancing, and floor shows that are becoming more risqué by the minute. Top choices include *Scala-Meliá Castilla* (43 Calle Capitán Haya; phone: 571-4411) and *Florida Park* (in the Parque del Retiro; phone: 573-7804). For a night of gambling, dining, dancing, and entertainment, the *Casino Gran Madrid* has it all (it's 20 minutes from downtown at Torrelodones, with free transportation from 6 Plaza de España; phone: 856-1100). The latest dance rage in Madrid is the *sevillanas*. *Madrileños* have adopted the delightful dance music of their Andalusian cousins as their own and, by popular demand, *sevillanas* music plays at many discos; dozens of *salas rocieras* — nightclubs dedicated to dancing and watching *sevillanas* — attract teens, married couples, and diplomats alike. Among the best are *El Portón* (25 Calle Lopez de Hoyos; phone: 262-4956), *Al Andalus* (19 Calle Capitán Haya; phone: 556-1439), *La Caseta* (13 Calle General Castaños; phone: 419-0343), and *Almonte* (35 Calle de Juan Bravo; phone: 411-6880). *La Maestranza* (16 Calle Mauricio Legendre, near Plaza de Castilla; phone: 315-9059) features star *sevillanas* performers in its floor shows and also serves outstanding Andalusian cuisine. Some discotheques and boîtes run two sessions a night, at 7 and 11 PM until the wee hours. Among the more popular are *Pachá* (11 Calle Barceló; phone: 446-0137) and *Joy Eslava* (11 Calle Arenal; phone: 266-3733), where ballroom dancing is now the fad. Striptease shows are the attraction at *Alazán* (24 Paseo de la Castellana; phone: 435-8948). There's late dining and an energetic downstairs disco at *Archy* (11 Calle Marqués de Riscal; phone: 308-2736), while the latest gathering spot for the glitterati is *Teatriz* (15 Calle Hermosilla; phone: 577-5379). The *Cervecería Alemana* (6 Plaza Santa Ana; phone: 429-7033), a tavern that's an old Hemingway hangout, remains a favorite nightspot. In the *Mercado Puerta de Toledo*, the *Café del Mercado* swings with late-night live jazz, and salsa dancing starts at 2 AM on weekends (1 Ronda de Toledo; phone: 265-8739); *Cock* (16 Calle Reina; no phone) draws an avant-garde set. *Madrileños* love to *pasear*, or stroll along the streets, and from April through October thousands of *terrazas* — outdoor cafés lining plazas, parks, and avenues — are jumping with nocturnal activity. Late revelers usually cap the evening with thick hot chocolate and *churros* at *Chocolatería de San Ginés* (in the alley behind San Ginés church), open all night.

BEST IN TOWN

 CHECKING IN: Modern Madrid boasts over 50,000 hotel rooms, with accommodations ranging from "grand luxe" to countless *hostales* and *pensiones*. Reservations are nonetheless recommended, especially between May and September and during such special events as national and local festivals, expositions, and conventions. And, because of the city's designation as this year's European Capital of Culture, accommodations will be at an even greater premium. Expect to pay $550 or more a night for a double room in a hotel listed as very expensive, from $170 to $300 in an establishment listed as expensive, from $65 to $160 in a moderately priced hotel, and $50 or less in an inexpensive one. All telephone numbers are in the 1 city code unless otherwise indicated.

Ritz – The epitome of elegance, luxury, and Belle Epoque grace, this impeccably maintained classic opened in 1910. It was built at the behest of King Alfonso XIII, and its construction and decoration were overseen by César Ritz himself. No two of the 156 air conditioned rooms and suites are alike, but all are adorned with paintings, antiques, and tailored handwoven carpeting from the Royal Tapestry Factory. Jacket-and-tie attire is appropriate for men in the bar and the exquisite *Ritz* restaurant, one of Madrid's finest (see *Eating Out*). The casual *Ritz Garden Terrace* also offers delightful dining, cocktails, and *tapas*. Business facilities include 24-hour room service, meeting rooms for up to 500, English-speaking concierge, foreign currency exchange, secretarial services in English, audiovisual equipment, photocopiers, computers, cable television news service, translation services, and express checkout. 5 Plaza de la Lealtad (phone: 521-2857; fax: 232-8776). Very expensive.

Santo Mauro – This exquisite addition to Madrid's supreme echelon of *gran lujo* hotels was inaugurated last year in what was originally the turn-of-the-century palatial mansion of the Duques de Santo Mauro, and later became the Philippine Embassy. Centrally located in the elegant Almagro-Castellana section, the French-style building was faithfully restored to its original style. The new interior decor, however, created by Madrid's hottest designers, is the last word in Art Deco. There are public salons and a stately patio-garden. Although there are only 36 rooms, mostly suites, all feature a compact disc and cassette stereo system and satellite TV (VCRs are available on request). Other facilities include 24-hour room service, a sauna, indoor swimming pool, summer terrace restaurant, and in the mansion's original library, the *Belaqua* restaurant (see *Eating Out*). Business facilities include 24-hour room service, English-speaking concierge, foreign currency exchange, photocopiers, translation services, and express checkout. 36 Zurbano (phone: 319-6900; fax: 308-5417). Very Expensive.

Villa Magna – Taken over by Hyatt hotels in 1990, this 194-room property has had a sterling reputation since its construction in the early 1970s. The modern, yet stately, building of glass and marble is set amid landscaped gardens in the heart of aristocratic Madrid. A multimillion-dollar remodeling project added unequaled luster — and technology — to the spacious, air conditioned rooms; high quality personal service enhances the hotel's casual elegance. The *Champagne Bar* boasts one of Europe's finest selection of bubbly beverages, and the, *Villa Magna* restaurant is celebrated for its imaginative specialties (see *Eating Out*). Richly decorated private salons accommodate meetings and banquets. Business facilities include 24-hour room service, meeting rooms for up to 250, English-speaking concierge, foreign currency exchange, secretarial services in English, audiovisual equipment, photocopiers, computers, cable television news service, translation services, and express checkout. 22 Paseo de la Castellana (phone: 578-2000; fax: 575-3158, for reservations; fax: 575-9504, to reach hotel guests). Very expensive.

Villa Real – Among Madrid's newer establishments, its design and atmosphere embody Old World grace; marble, bronze, and handcrafted wood, works of fine art and antique furnishings create a seignorial interior decor. All 115 luxurious rooms and suites are air conditioned and feature satellite television sets, mini-bars, and 3 or more high-tech telephones. Elegantly furnished top-floor duplexes have 2 bathrooms — 1 with a sauna, the other with a Jacuzzi — and large private balconies overlooking the Spanish Parliament Palace, the Neptune Fountain, and the *Prado Museum's* Villahermosa Palace. There is 24-hour room service and a friendly, competent staff. The hotel's choice setting — between Paseo del Prado and Puerta del Sol — couldn't be better. Business facilities include 24-hour room service, meeting rooms for up to 300, English-speaking concierge, foreign currency exchange, secretarial services in English, audiovisual equipment, photocopiers, computers, cable television news service, translation services, and express checkout. 10-11 Plaza de la Cortes (phone: 420-3767). Very expensive to expensive.

Apart-Suites Foxá – Sparkling new and near the Chamartín train station and Plaza de Castilla, this apartment-style hostelry in two adjacent buildings features 282 well-furnished suites that accommodate up to four people (the separate living rooms have sofa beds). Breakfast is included in the room rate. Amenities include air conditioning, color TV sets, a parking garage, a restaurant, and a coffee shop. Business facilities include 24-hour room service, meeting rooms for up to 400, English-speaking concierge, foreign currency exchange, secretarial services in English, audiovisual equipment, photocopiers, computers, cable television news service, translation services, and express checkout. Foxá 25 and Foxá 32 (phone: 733-7064; fax: 314-1165). Expensive.

Apart-Suites Orense – Near the *Convention Center* and the Castellana, this modern apartment-style property, under the same management as the above *Apart-Suites Foxá,* has 141 suites with color TV sets, air conditioning, a restaurant, and a coffee shop. Business facilities include 24-hour room service, meeting rooms for up to 400, English-speaking concierge, foreign currency exchange, secretarial services in English, audiovisual equipment, photocopiers, computers, cable television news service, translation services, and express checkout. Orense 38 (phone: 597-1568; fax: 597-1295). Expensive.

Barajas – The raison d'être of this 230-room hotel is its proximity to Madrid's Barajas International Airport. All rooms are air conditioned and have color television sets. Guests can enjoy the garden swimming pool, bar, restaurant, and health club. Half-day rates are available for meetings or jet-lag therapy. Free transportation is provided to and from the airport terminals. Business facilities include 24-hour room service, meeting rooms for up to 675, English-speaking concierge, foreign currency exchange, secretarial services in English, audiovisual equipment, photocopiers, computers, cable television news service, translation services, and express checkout. 305 Avenida Logroño (phone: 747-7700). Expensive.

Castellana Inter-Continental – Opened in the early 1950s as the *Castellana Hilton,* this has been a traditional favorite of Americans traveling to Madrid for business or pleasure. Its 310 air conditioned rooms, all containing modern accoutrements, are large and nicely decorated in pleasant pastels. Adjacent to the stately, marble-pillared lobby are car rental, airline, and tour desks, boutiques, a health club, and a business services department. *Los Continentes* restaurant and *La Ronda* piano bar are pleasant for meeting and eating. Business facilities include 24-hour room service, meeting rooms for up to 350, English-speaking concierge, foreign currency exchange, secretarial services in English, audiovisual equipment, photocopiers, computers, cable television news service, translation services, and express checkout. 49 Paseo de la Castellana (phone: 410-0200; in the US, 800-327-5853; fax: 319-5853). Expensive.

Eurobuilding – An extremely well designed modern complex off the northern section of the Castellana near the *Convention Center* and *Estadio Santiago Bernabéu.* Within the complex, in addition to the 421-room hotel building, the *Eurobuilding 2* tower comprises 154 apartment-style units. All rooms and apartments are air conditioned. There also are 2 swimming pools, a health club, a hair salon, stores, and 4 restaurants. Business facilities include 24-hour room service, meeting rooms for up to 900, English-speaking concierge, foreign currency exchange, secretarial services in English, audiovisual equipment, photocopiers, computers, cable television news service, translation services, and express checkout. 23 Calle Padre Damián (phone: 457-1700). Expensive.

Holiday Inn Madrid – Typical of the US Holiday Inn chain, this modern and busy establishment with 344 air conditioned rooms, has a swimming pool, health club, gymnasium, shopping arcade, and restaurants. A perfect place for anyone who wants to be near the Azca shopping and commercial complex, the *Convention Center, Estadio Santiago Bernabéu,* and the Castellana. Business facilities include meeting rooms for up to 450, English-speaking concierge, foreign currency exchange, secretarial services in English, audiovisual equipment, photocopiers, computers, cable television news service, translation services, and express checkout. 4 Plaza Carlos Trías Bertrán (phone: 597-0102). Expensive.

Meliá Castilla – Nearly 1,000 air conditioned rooms in a modern high-rise just off the Castellana in northern Madrid's business section. Facilities and meeting rooms cater primarily to executive travelers. There also is a swimming pool, gymnasium, sauna, shopping arcade, several restaurants and bars, and the *Scala Meliá Castilla*, a Las Vegas–style nightclub. Business facilities include 24-hour room service, meeting rooms for up to 800, English-speaking concierge, foreign currency exchange, secretarial services in English, audiovisual equipment, photocopiers, computers, cable television news service, translation services, and express checkout. 43 Calle Capitán Haya (phone: 571-2211; fax: 571-2210). Expensive.

Meliá Madrid – Ideally located near the Plaza de España and very well run. The 266 air conditioned rooms in this gleaming white, modern building are tastefully decorated in various styles, and have color television sets. The dining room, grill, bar, and *Bong Bing* discotheque are popular meeting places. There also is a gymnasium, sauna, and conference facilities complete with state-of-the-art audiovisual equipment. Business facilities include 24-hour room service, meeting rooms for up to 380, English-speaking concierge, foreign currency exchange, secretarial services in English, audiovisual equipment, photocopiers, computers, cable television news service, translation services, and express checkout. 27 Calle Princesa (phone: 541-8200; fax: 541-1988). Expensive.

Miguel Angel – Conveniently located on Paseo de la Castellana, this 304-room property combines modern luxuries with classic decor; 17th-, 18th-, and 19th-century paintings, tapestries, and furniture decorate the lobby and suites. Most rooms have balconies, and all offer color television sets. Facilities include a health club, with sauna, Jacuzzi, gymnasium, and heated, indoor swimming pool. Guests can enjoy fine food at the *Florencia* restaurant, afternoon tea and cocktails at the *Bar Farnesio*, and dinner, dancing, and live entertainment at the *Boite Zacarías* restaurant. Business facilities include 24-hour room service, meeting rooms for up to 650, English-speaking concierge, foreign currency exchange, secretarial services in English, audiovisual equipment, photocopiers, computers, cable television news service, translation services, and express checkout. 31 Calle Miguel Angel (phone: 442-8199). Expensive.

Monte Real – Located in a tranquil residential district about 20 minutes from the city center, this luxurious establishment is near the *Puerta de Hierro Golf Club*. All 77 rooms are air conditioned and have color television sets. Facilities include a swimming pool, sauna, lovely gardens, a restaurant, and a bar. Business facilities include meeting rooms for up to 350, English-speaking concierge, foreign currency exchange, secretarial services in English, audiovisual equipment, photocopiers, computers, translation services, and express checkout. 17 Calle Arroyo del Fresno, Puerta de Hierro (phone: 316-2140). Expensive.

Palace – Inaugurated in 1920, this aristocratic Madrid landmark was, like the *Ritz*, built by personal order of King Alfonso XIII. Its Old World Belle Epoque elegance and decor are faithfully maintained, while the utmost of modern facilities makes for true luxury in the spacious 518 air conditioned rooms and suites. Located in the heart of the city, the hotel overlooks the Neptune Fountain and Paseo del Prado. The lobby, embellished with trompe l'oeil painting, leads to the elegant, cozy lounge, which is topped by an immense painted-glass rotunda — an inviting setting for cocktails or informal dining at *El Ambiqú*, with a musical backdrop of piano and violin until 2 AM.. A recent addition, on the ground floor, is the *Galería del Prado*, a collection of 38 fine boutiques, galleries, and shops, as well as *La Plaza*, a self-service restaurant. Business facilities include 24-hour room service, meeting rooms for up to 1500, English-speaking concierge, foreign currency exchange, secretarial services in English, audiovisual equipment, photocopiers, computers, cable television news service, translation services, and express checkout. 7 Plaza de las Cortes (phone: 429-7551; fax: 429-8655). Expensive.

Wellington – Classic and nicely located in the Salamanca district, with fine boutiques, galleries, and the Parque del Retiro practically at the doorstep. The owner raised brave bulls; a stuffed triumphant one, named Cucharito, resides in the lounge amid the antique tapestries. Bullfighters, breeders, and aficionados stay and congregate here. All of the spacious 258 rooms are air conditioned, with color television sets. In summer, the outdoor swimming pool and the garden, with its restaurant, bar, and health club, are lively gathering spots. Business facilities include 24-hour room service, meeting rooms for up to 250, English-speaking concierge, foreign currency exchange, secretarial services in English, audiovisual equipment, photocopiers, computers, translation services, and express checkout. 8 Calle Velázquez (phone: 575-4400; fax: 576-4164). Expensive.

Suecia – Expansion of this Swedish-managed (hence its name) hotel has added modern rooms and suites within the same building, but the original ones are still well maintained and very comfortable. All 67 rooms, old and new, are air conditioned, with color television sets, mini-bars, and safes. Hemingway lived here, enjoying the great advantage of the location — on a quiet street just west of Paseo del Prado, around the corner from Calle de Alcalá. Smoked salmon and smorgasbord are main attractions in the *Bellman* restaurant. Business facilities include meeting rooms for up to 150, English-speaking concierge, foreign currency exchange, secretarial services in English, audiovisual equipment, computers, and translation services. 4 Calle Marqués de Casa Riera (phone: 531-6900; fax: 521-7141). Expensive to moderate.

Tryp Fénix – This Madrid aristocrat has been refurbished and reborn and once again is considered among the city's finest. Ideally situated on the tree-lined Castellana at Plaza de Colón, it has 216 air conditioned rooms and up-to-the-minute amenities enhanced by an air of sparkling elegance. Business facilities include 24-hour room service, meeting rooms for up to 200, English-speaking concierge, foreign currency exchange, secretarial services in English, audiovisual equipment, photocopiers, computers, translation services, and express checkout. 2 Calle Hermosilla (phone: 431-6700). Expensive to moderate.

Alcalá – Right on the north edge of Parque del Retiro and Plaza de la Independencia, in the genteel Salamanca district, it is within easy walking distance of fine shops and restaurants on Calle Serrano, as well as the *Prado* and other museums. All 153 air conditioned rooms have color television sets. The restaurant serves enticing Basque specialties. Business facilities include meeting rooms for up to 60, English-speaking concierge, foreign currency exchange, secretarial services in English, audiovisual equipment, photocopiers, computers, and translation services. 66 Calle de Alcalá (phone: 435-1060; fax: 435-1105). Moderate.

Arosa – Although it's on the bustling Gran Vía, it has the charm, peaceful mood, and personalized service of a small luxury establishment. The 126 air conditioned rooms, no two exactly alike, are tastefully decorated; luxurious bathrooms feature built-in hair dryers, fabulous showers in the bathtubs, and other treats, such as soothing bath salts. The atmosphere is delightful in the bar, lounge, and restaurant. Doormen at the small, elegant side-street entrance know guests by name. Business facilities include English-speaking concierge, foreign currency exchange, and translation services. 21 Calle de la Salud (phone: 532-1600; fax: 531-3127). Moderate.

Carlton – A complete renovation has raised the comfort level here. In a unique location — the southern part of central Madrid — it is near the Atocha train station complex, as well as within easy walking distance of the *National Museum Queen Sofía Art Center* and, a little farther north, the Botanical Gardens and the *Prado*. All of the 133 air conditioned rooms have color television sets. Business facilities include 24-hour room service, meeting rooms for up to 200, English-speaking concierge, foreign currency exchange, secretarial services in English, audiovisual equipment, photocopiers, computers, and translation services. 26 Paseo de las Delicias (phone: 239-7100; fax: 227-8510). Moderate.

Chamartín – The single advantage of this 378-room property is the fact that it is located within the modern Chamartín train station complex at the north end of the city. All rooms are air conditioned, have color television sets, and offer excellent views. Business facilities include meeting rooms for up to 525, English-speaking concierge, foreign currency exchange, secretarial services in English, audiovisual equipment, photocopiers, translation services, and express checkout. Estación de Chamartín (phone: 733-7011). Moderate.

Emperador – Centrally located right on the Gran Vía. All 232 rooms are air conditioned and have color television sets. Unusual among the many hotels in the immediate area, it boasts a rooftop garden with a swimming pool and excellent views of the city. Business facilities include 24-hour room service, meeting rooms for up to 200, English-speaking concierge, foreign currency exchange, secretarial services in English, audiovisual equipment, photocopiers, computers, and translation services. 53 Gran Vía (phone: 413-6511). Moderate.

Escultor – Conveniently located near the Castellana in a quiet residential area, its 82 air conditioned, apartment-style units offer separate sitting rooms with color television sets, complete kitchens, and mini-bars. Business facilities include meeting rooms for up to 250, English-speaking concierge, foreign currency exchange, secretarial services in English, audiovisual equipment, photocopiers, computers, and translation services. 5 Calle Miguel Angel (phone: 410-4203). Moderate.

Mayorazgo – Excellent service and 200 well-appointed, comfortable, air conditioned rooms just a step from the central Gran Vía. The decor provides a retreat to a pleasant Castilian past. Business facilities include meeting rooms for up to 300, English-speaking concierge, foreign currency exchange, secretarial services in English, audiovisual equipment, photocopiers, computers, and translation services. 3 Calle Flor Baja (phone: 247-2600; fax: 541-2485). Moderate.

Plaza – Located within the gigantic Edificio España landmark building of the early 1950s, this hotel with 306 rooms (all air conditioned) is usually swarming with tour groups. The 26th-floor swimming pool and terrace restaurant offer marvelous panoramic views of the city. Business facilities include 24-hour room service, meeting rooms for up to 500, English-speaking concierge, foreign currency exchange, secretarial services in English, audiovisual equipment, photocopiers, computers, and translation services. 2 Plaza de España (phone: 247-1200). Moderate.

Reina Victoria – After acquisition by the Tryp hotel chain and a total remodeling of its interior in 1990, this Madrid classic is once again worthy of its royal namesake (wife of King Alfonso XIII and grandmother of the present King Juan Carlos). Built in 1923 and designated a building of National Historic Interest, its unaltered 6-story façade, elaborate with pilasters, turrets, wrought-iron balconies, and bay windows, dominates the entire west side of the picturesque Plaza Santa Ana, a prime Old Madrid location. The 201 rooms and suites all have modern amenities (at less than regal prices). The *Bar Taurino* revives the hotel's decades-old tradition as a rendezvous for bullfighters, breeders, and aficionados. Business facilities include meeting rooms for up to 500, English-speaking concierge, foreign currency exchange, secretarial services in English, audiovisual equipment, photocopiers, computers, and translation services. 14 Plaza Santa Ana (phone: 531-4500). Moderate.

Serrano – Small and tasteful, refined and immaculate, on a quiet street between the Castellana and the boutique-lined Calle Serrano. Its marble-floored lobby is comfortably furnished and richly decorated with antiques (including a large 17th-century tapestry) and huge arrangements of fresh flowers. All 34 rooms are air conditioned and have color television sets. No restaurant, but snacks and sandwiches are available at the bar. Business facilities include English-speaking concierge, foreign currency exchange, and translation services. 8 Calle Marqués de Villamejor (phone: 435-5200). Moderate.

Tryp Ambassador – This restored 6-story noble mansion was converted into a fine 181-room hotel only recently. It has all the latest conveniences, and its unique location, close to the *Teatro Real* opera house, and also to Plaza de Oriente and the Royal Palace, makes it especially appealing. The restaurant serves Spanish and international fare. Business facilities include 24-hour room service, meeting rooms for up to 290, English-speaking concierge, foreign currency exchange, secretarial services in English, audiovisual equipment, photocopiers, computers, translation services, and express checkout. 5 Cuesta Santo Domingo (phone: 541-6700) Moderate.

Carlos V – Conveniently located, with 67 air conditioned rooms, right in the lively pedestrian area between the Gran Vía and Puerta del Sol, near the Convento de las Descalzas Reales and *El Corte Inglés* department store. Business facilities include English-speaking concierge and foreign currency exchange. 5 Calle Maestro Vitoria (phone: 531-4100; fax: 531-3761). Moderate to inexpensive.

Don Diego – A well-kept *pensión* near the Parque del Retiro in Madrid's lovely Salamanca district. The 58 rooms are nicely furnished, and several have ample balconies. There is a television lounge and a bar that serves sandwiches and breakfast. 45 Calle Velázquez (phone: 435-0760). Moderate to inexpensive.

Galiano – A converted mansion, complete with marble floors, antique paintings, tapestries, and carved-wood furniture in the lobby and lounge. On a tranquil side street just off the Castellana and Plaza de Colón, it has 29 comfortable singles, doubles, and suites. Breakfast and color television sets are optional. There is an English-speaking concierge. 6 Calle Alcalá Galiano (phone: 319-2000). Moderate to inexpensive.

Puerta de Toledo – Away from major hotel clusters, it is located on the fringe of picturesque Old Madrid, facing the Triumphal Arch of the Puerta de Toledo and near the new Mercado Puerta de Toledo. Its 160 rooms are air conditioned, comfortable, and well maintained. 4 Glorieta Puerta de Toledo (phone: 474-7100). Moderate to inexpensive.

Jamic – A small pension centrally located across the street from the *Palace* hotel and near the *Prado.* 4 Plaza de las Cortes (phone: 429-0068). Inexpensive.

Lisboa – This well run residential *hostal* has 23 rooms, all with private baths and telephones, plus maid service, a television lounge, and an elevator. The location is terrific: just off the Plaza Santa Ana in charming Old Madrid, yet a short walk to the *Palace,* the *Ritz,* and the *Prado.* English is spoken and credit cards are accepted. Fine restaurants of all price ranges line the street. 17 Calle Ventura de la Vega (phone: 429-9894). Inexpensive.

 EATING OUT: *Madrileños* eat the main meal of their day during the work break from 2 to 4 PM. An early-evening snack (*merienda*), such as wine and those typically Spanish tidbits called *tapas, chocolate con churros,* or coffee and sweets takes the edge off appetites until a light supper is eaten after 10 PM. For those who can't adjust to the Spanish schedule, there are always *cafeterías* and snack bars, and many restaurants start serving dinner at about 8:30 PM to accommodate non-Spaniards. Restaurants listed below as very expensive will charge $175 or more for a dinner for two with wine; similar fare will cost $90 to $150 at restaurants listed as expensive, between $40 and $80 at moderate eateries, and $35 or less at inexpensive ones. Most restaurants offer a set menu (*menú del día*), a complete meal for an economical price. Some restaurants include the 6% Value Added Tax in their menu prices. Check beforehand whether the menu says *IVA incluido* or *IVA no incluido.* All telephone numbers are in the 1 city code unless otherwise indicated.

Horcher – Operated for generations by the Horcher family, this remains one of Madrid's most elegant dining places, serving continental fare with an Austro-

Hungarian flavor. Dining here is an indulgence that should include such delicacies as *chuletas de ternasco a la castellana* (baby lamb chops), endive salad (with truffles), and crêpes Sir Holten for dessert. Diners might even try the classic goulash. Closed Sundays. Reservations are necessary for lunch and dinner. American Express, Visa, and Diners Club accepted. 6 Calle Alfonso XII (phone: 522-0731). Very expensive.

Jockey – A Madrid classic, intimate and elegant, and a recipient of the National Gastronomy Award. The continental cuisine is superb, as are traditional dishes such as *cocido madrileño,* a multi-faceted savory stew, the broth of which is served as a side dish. Other specialties include *perdiz española* (partridge), *lomo de lubina* (filet of sea bass), and *mousse de anguila* (eel mousse). Closed Sundays and August. Reservations necessary. Major credit cards accepted. 6 Calle Amador de los Ríos (phone: 319-1003). Very expensive.

Ritz – The sumptuous restaurant of the luxurious *Ritz* hotel, serving French cuisine befitting the Limoges dinnerware and Louis XV silver service. Chamber music adds to the regal rapture. Open daily for breakfast, lunch, and dinner. Reservations necessary. Major credit cards accepted. (The separate *Ritz Garden-Terrace* offers more casual dining, or simply afternoon tea or *tapas.*) 5 Plaza de la Lealtad (phone: 521-2857). Very expensive.

Villa Magna – The remodeling of Madrid's *Villa Magna* hotel has placed its restaurant among the city's finest. Cristóbal Blanco, the prize-winning chef, designs such nouvelle delicacies as grilled scallops with caviar in basil sauce, while the china on which they are served was designed by Paloma Picasso. The *Champagne Bar* dispenses 252 French and Spanish vintages. (By the way, those precious place settings — plates plus silverware — cost $600 each, so be careful!) Open for breakfast, lunch, and dinner. Reservations necessary. Major credit cards accepted. 22 Paseo de la Castellana (phone: 261-4900). Very expensive.

Zalacaín – Probably the finest restaurant in all of Spain, it was the first in the country to win three Michelin stars and still shares that honor only with *Arzak,* in San Sebastián. It serves highly imaginative Basque and French haute cuisines, particularly seafood, and the service — by loyal employees who adore owner Jesús Oyarbide — is perfection. Luxurious decor, gleaming silverware and glasses, fresh flowers, and an irresistible dessert cart all contribute to the dining experience. Closed Saturdays for lunch, Sundays, August, *Easter Week,* and holidays. Reservations necessary (call at least 2 days in advance). American Express, Visa, and Diners Club accepted. 4 Calle Alvarez de Baena (phone: 261-4840). Very expensive.

La Basílica – Once an old baroque church, this is now a baroque and elegant restaurant. Sophisticates enjoy international, nouvelle, and Spanish cuisines in the see-and-be-seen main dining room or in secluded alcoves. It's located on a narrow street in Old Madrid, near Plaza Mayor. Closed Saturdays at lunch and all day Sundays. Reservations essential. Major credit cards accepted. 12 Calle de la Bolsa (phone: 521-8623). Expensive.

Belagua – When it reopened last year in the new *Santo Mauro* hotel, this renowned eatery already had an elite *madrileño* following from its previous location in the *Sanvy* hotel. The same Basque-Navarre fare that has long attracted locals is served in the sophisticated atmosphere of the restored library of a turn-of-the-century French palatial mansion, redecorated in glowing Art Deco. Traditional specialties include monkfish and spider crab stew, entrées with oxtail, pig's feet, lobster, or blood sausage, not to mention the exquisite desserts. Open daily; Sundays exclusively for hotel guests. Reservations advised. Major credit cards accepted. 36 Zurbano (phone: 319-6900). Expensive.

Cabo Mayor – The owner and chef both have won the National Gastronomy Award, and for good reason: Their fresh seafood from the province of Santander is imaginatively prepared, and the vegetable dishes are superlative. If it's on the menu, try the *cigalas y langostinos con verduras al jerez sibarita* (crayfish and prawns with green vegetables in sherry sauce). Closed Sundays, the last 2 weeks of August, *Christmas Week, New Year's Week,* and *Easter Week.* Reservations advised. American Express, Diners Club, and Visa accepted. 37 Calle Juan Ramón Jiménez (phone: 250-8776). Expensive.

El Cenador del Prado – Favored by aficionados of nouvelle cuisine and artistically decorated in a style reminiscent of an elegant conservatory, allowing indoor dining under the stars. Try *patatas a la importancia con almejas* (potatoes with clams) or the *pato al vinagre de frambuesas* (duck with raspberry vinegar). Politicians from the nearby Spanish Parliament may be at the next table. Closed for lunch on Saturdays and all day Sundays. Reservations necessary. Major credit cards accepted. 4 Calle del Prado (phone: 429-1561). Expensive.

La Dorada – Fresh seafood of every imaginable variety is flown in daily from the Mediterranean to this mammoth establishment, which serves Andalusian fare. (There also are two *Doradas* in Seville, one in Barcelona, Marbella, and another in Paris.) Particularly noteworthy is the fish baked in a crust of salt, an Andalusian practice that results, surprisingly, in a dish that's not salty. Closed Sundays and August. Reservations are essential, as this place is always crowded — and you'll enjoy the food even more if you reserve one of the private dining rooms. Major credit cards accepted. 64-66 Calle Orense (phone: 270-2002). Expensive.

Fortuny – Relatively recent on Madrid's restaurant scene, it soon established its place among the preferred, with outstanding international haute cuisine. Housed in an aristocratic 19th-century mansion, it offers private dining rooms for banquets or intimacy. There also is a terrace with a waterfall, for outdoor summer dining. Closed Sundays and holidays. Reservations necessary. Major credit cards accepted. 34 Calle Fortuny (phone: 308-3268). Expensive.

La Gamella – The owner-chef-host is Richard Stephens, an American who also is an instructor at Madrid's Alambique School of Gastronomy. His intimate restaurant here, in the building in which philosopher José Ortega y Gasset was born, is dedicated to new Spanish cuisine — and it's one of Madrid's best. The creative appetizers and main dishes — try the *pastel de chorizo fresco y pimientos rojos* (Spanish sausage and red pepper quiche), the irresistible desserts, and the fine wine list add up to an adventure in taste, and the *colorista* design and art of the decor enhance the experience. A private dining room downstairs seats 10. Closed Sundays, holidays, and August. Reservations advised. Major credit cards accepted. 4 Calle Alfonso XII (phone: 532-4509). Expensive.

Gure-Etxea – One of the best for Basque dishes in Madrid, serving specialties such as *porrusalda* (leek and potato soup with cod) and a variety of fish dishes. Both the atmosphere and the service are pleasant. Closed Sundays and August. Reservations advised. American Express and Visa accepted. 12 Plaza de la Paja (phone: 265-6149). Expensive.

Lhardy – A *madrileño* institution since 1839, and the decor, atmosphere, and table settings haven't changed much since then. One specialty in the upstairs dining rooms and private salons is *cocido madrileño,* the typical stew. At *merienda* time in the late afternoon, the street-entrance restaurant and stand-up bar fill with regulars who serve themselves the *caldo* (broth) of the *cocido* from a silver tureen, and also enjoy finger sandwiches, canapés, cold cuts, pastries, cocktails, or coffee. Closed Sunday and holiday evenings and the month of August. Reservations essential for the private dining rooms. Major credit cards accepted. Carrera de San Jerónimo (phone: 521-3385). Expensive.

O'Pazo – The morning catch from the Cantabrian Sea — lobster, hake, turbot, endemic sea bass, and varieties of shellfish — is flown in wiggling fresh and prepared with loving care to delight the clientele, who fill the place for both lunch and dinner. Closed Sundays and August. Reservations advised. MasterCard and Visa accepted. 20 Calle Reina Mercedes (phone: 253-2333). Expensive.

Paradís Madrid – Barcelona's well-known eatery opened a branch here last year (after establishing one in New York City) in a turn-of-the-century mansion alongside Plaza de las Cortes. The menu is primarily Catalán-Mediterranean — mushrooms served in several delicious ways (one stuffed with duck liver), five variations of *bacalao* (cod), and a "catch of the day." A separate menu entitled "Homage to the Great Chefs" features original dishes of illustrious Basque (Juan Mari Arzak) and Catalán (Santi Santamaría) chefs. For *tapas* and typical Catalán *pan con tomate* (bread spread with tomato), the *Bodiguilla* bar serves until 1:30 AM. Closed for Sunday dinner. Reservations advised. Major credit cards accepted. 14 Marqués de Cubas (phone: 429-7303). Expensive.

Platerías – Its intimate low-key elegance in the heart of Old Madrid creates a pleasant atmosphere for enjoying authentic Spanish dishes, such as *callos madrileños* (succulent tripe, Madrid style), *chipirones* (cuttlefish in its own ink), and remarkable vegetable plates. Closed Sundays. Reservations advised. Major credit cards accepted. 11 Plaza Santa Ana (phone: 429-7048). Expensive.

Príncipe de Viana – Fine seasonal Basque-Navarrese specialties are served in a relaxed, elegant atmosphere. Closed Saturdays for lunch, Sundays, and from mid-August through the first week of September. Reservations advised. American Express and Visa accepted. 5 Calle Manuel de Falla (phone: 259-1448). Expensive.

La Trainera – Another favorite of seafood lovers. The owner prizes his flown-in catch and serves fish and shellfish as nature intended. No fishing village in the world can compete with the grilled sole served here. Closed Sundays and August. Reservations advised. MasterCard and Visa accepted. 60 Calle Lagasca (phone: 276-8035). Expensive.

Café de Oriente – Anything from *tapas* to French haute cuisine can be enjoyed here in a delightful *madrileño* atmosphere. It is an ideal place for afternoon tea or cocktails at a sidewalk table overlooking the square and the Royal Palace or inside the café (reservations unnecessary); for fine Castilian dining downstairs in the vaulted 17th-century Sala Capitular de San Gil (reservations advised); or for superb French-Basque cuisine in the adjacent restaurant (reservations advised) or one of the private dining rooms frequented by royalty and diplomats (reservations essential). Closed Mondays for lunch, Sundays, and August. Major credit cards accepted. 2 Plaza de Oriente (phone: 247-1564). Expensive to moderate.

El Abanico Gastronómico – The "Gastronomic Fan" is a combination restaurant and food shop located within the *Mercado Puerta de Toledo* (see *Special Places*). Regional cuisines, wines, and delicacies from all over Spain are the stock in trade. Open from 11:30 AM to midnight; closed Mondays. Reservations unnecessary. No credit cards accepted. 1 Ronda de Toledo (phone: 576-0009). Moderate.

Antigua Casa Sobrino de Botín – Also known as *Casa Botín,* this is one of Madrid's oldest restaurants — founded in 1725. It is famous for its Castilian-style roast suckling pig and baby lamb, one of which is usually featured on the *menú del día.* Lunch and dinner each seem to fall into two "shifts," with the early-eating tourists first, followed by *madrileños,* whose normal dining hours are after 2 and 9 PM, respectively. Open daily. Reservations unnecessary. Major credit cards accepted. 17 Calle Cuchilleros (phone: 266-4217). Moderate.

Café Gijón – This 100-year-old Madrid institution is a traditional meeting and greeting place for intellectuals and artists, who gather here to enjoy good food and conversation. During the summer, the sidewalk café is one of the city's liveliest.

Open daily. No reservations. Visa and MasterCard accepted. 21 Paseo de Recoletos (phone: 532-5425). Moderate.

El Callejón – A bust of Hemingway and walls chockablock with celebrity photos attest to those who have enjoyed the friendly atmosphere and home-cooked food here in the past. An informal Old Madrid place, it serves a different regional specialty each day of the week, but *callos madrileños* is always on the menu, and *tapas* abound. Open daily. Reservations unnecessary. Major credit cards accepted. 6 Calle Ternera (phone: 531-9195). Moderate.

Casa Lucio – This casual restaurant has become an institution among the elite (and that includes members of the royal family), who enjoy fine Spanish food — especially seafood. Its location in Old Madrid adds to the flavor. Closed Saturdays for lunch and during August. Reservations essential. American Express and Visa accepted. 35 Calle Cava Baja (phone: 265-3252). Moderate.

Casa Paco – The steaks served in this old tavern are excellent. Other specialties include typical *madrileño* dishes. Closed Sundays and August. No reservations. Visa accepted. 11 Calle Puerta Cerrada (phone: 266-3166). Moderate.

La Chata – This totally typical *mesón* bears the nickname of Madrid's adored Infanta Isabel (the only child of Queen Isabel II), who is depicted on the wonderful hand-painted tile façade by artist Eduardo Fernández. Delicious morsels are served at the *tapas* bar, and the small restaurant specializes in roast suckling pig and lamb dishes. Closed Sunday evenings and Wednesdays. No reservations or credit cards accepted. 25 Calle Cava Baja (phone: 266-1458). Moderate.

El Cuchi – The Spanish link of Mexico's famous *Carlos 'n' Charlie's* chain, with specialties of both worlds served by a gregarious staff. It's casual, and jammed with humorous paraphernalia. One of its claims to fame: "Hemingway never ate here." Open daily. Reservations unnecessary. Major credit cards accepted. 3 Calle Cuchilleros (phone: 255-4424). Moderate.

Los Galayos – A typical tavern serving fine Castilian roast suckling pig and lamb, with a *tapas* bar and an outdoor café right alongside the Plaza Mayor. Open daily. Reservations unnecessary. Major credit cards accepted. 1 Plaza Mayor (phone: 265-6222). Moderate.

La Galette – Outstanding vegetarian and non-vegetarian dishes and Viennese pastries are served in a delightful atmosphere at a good location in the elegant Salamanca district. Its popularity makes reservations essential. Closed Sundays. MasterCard and Visa accepted. 11 Calle Conde de Aranda (phone: 276-0641). Moderate.

El Ingenio – This unpretentious, family-run restaurant is decorated with Don Quixote and Sancho Panza memorabilia, and its menu delights diners who fall into either category of physique. The seafood is impeccably fresh since it is flown in from the Bay of Biscay, and the pork, lamb, and beef are all locally farm-grown. Closed Sundays and holidays. Reservations unnecessary. Major credit cards accepted. Just off the Plaza de España at 10 Calle Leganitos (phone: 541-9133). Moderate.

La Maestranza – Andalusian in its cooking, atmosphere, and decor, with great *sevillanas* music groups playing for professional dancers and the customers who know this Andalusian folk dance, which has become Madrid's latest rage. Closed Sundays. Reservations advised. Major credit cards accepted. 16 Calle Mauricio Legendre (phone: 315-9059). Moderate.

El Mentidero de la Villa – Inventive French cuisine by Japanese chef Ken Sato, in a delightful modern-art decor. Specialties include *rollo de primavera con puerros y gambas* (spring rolls with leeks and shrimp). Closed Sundays. Reservations advised. Major credit cards accepted. 6 Calle Santo Tomé (phone: 419-5506). Moderate.

La Mesa Redonda – A small eatery on one of Old Madrid's most charming little streets. Its American owners serve the best *Thanksgiving* dinner in town. Other specialties include beef bourguignon and stews. Dinner only; closed Sundays. Reservations unnecessary (except for *Thanksgiving*). No credit cards accepted. 17 Calle Nuncio (phone: 265-0289). Moderate.

La Plaza – Within the sparkling new *Galería del Prado* at the *Palace* hotel, amid the exquisite boutiques and galleries, this combination buffet-style and self-service restaurant dispenses enticing salads, entrées, and pastries. Serve yourself a multi-course meal or just a snack, to eat in a choice of surrounding settings. The adjacent bar serves cocktails and coffee. Closed Sundays. No reservations or credit cards accepted. 7 Plaza de las Cortes (phone: 429-7551). Moderate.

Posada de la Villa – Although the 3-story building is relatively new, this authentic eatery dates back to 1642, when it was originally a *posada* (inn) for out-of-towners. It has retained its tradition of hospitality and still offers fine typical dishes such as *cocido madrileño* and roast pig and lamb. Closed Sunday evenings. Reservations unnecessary. Major credit cards accepted. 9 Calle Cava Baja (phone: 266-1860). Moderate.

La Quinta del Sordo – The façade of this award-winning restaurant is adorned with fine hand-painted tile mosaics. Its name means "house of the deaf man," referring to the place where Goya lived in Madrid. Reproductions of Goya art and memorabilia add to the decor. An array of fine Castilian dishes offers memorable dining in a pleasant atmosphere. Closed Sunday evenings. Reservations unnecessary. Major credit cards accepted. 10 Calle Sacramento (phone: 248-1852). Moderate.

Riazor – An unpretentious turn-of-the-century establishment with a cordial atmosphere, fine traditional fare, and a cornucopia of hot and cold *tapas* served with verve at the bar. The upstairs dining room has panels adjustable to fit a size range of banquet parties. Open daily. Reservations unnecessary, except for groups. Visa accepted. Located 1 short block south of Plaza Mayor at 19 Calle Toledo (phone: 266-5466). Moderate.

Taberna del Alabardero – A Madrid classic, this was the tavern of the Royal Palace guards (*alabardero* means "halberdier," or a soldier armed with a halberd — a 15th- and 16th-century weapon combining a pike and an ax). There is a wonderful *tapas* bar, and succulent Spanish and Basque dishes are served in cozy dining rooms reminiscent of 19th-century Madrid. Open for lunch and dinner daily. Reservations unnecessary. Major credit cards accepted. (Father Lezama, the famous and popular Basque priest-restaurateur-owner, also has a version of this restaurant in Washington, DC.) 6 Calle Felipe V (phone: 541-5192). Moderate.

Foster's Hollywood – It's a *restaurante americano*, complete with a variety of hamburgers and barbecued spareribs. But far from being a *yanqui* fast-food joint, this small chain of pleasant restaurants offers good service and atmosphere. Open daily at all locations. No reservations. Major credit cards accepted. Several locations: 1 Calle Magallanes (phone: 488-9165); 3 Calle Apolonio Morales (phone: 457-7911); 1 Calle Tamayo y Baus (phone: 231-5115); 16 Calle del Cristo (phone: 638-6791); 14-16 Avenida de Brasil (phone: 455-1688); 80 Calle Velázquez (phone: 435-6128); and 100 Calle Guzmán el Bueno (phone: 234-4923). Inexpensive.

El Granero de Lavapiés – Good vegetarian food in one of Old Madrid's most typical neighborhoods. No reservations or credit cards accepted. 10 Calle Argumosa (phone: 467-7611). Inexpensive.

Mesón Museo del Jamón – Any restaurant with 4,000 hams dangling from its ceiling and draping its walls deserves the name "Ham Museum," and there are four such pork paradises in central Madrid. Fine hams from the regions of Jabugo, Murcia, Salamanca, and Extremadura are served in various ways, including sandwiches, at the stand-up bars and at dining tables. Also featured are an array of cheeses, a great deli, and roast chicken. Any dish can also be prepared to take out. No reservations or credit cards accepted. 6 Carrera San Jerónimo (phone: 521-0340); 72 Gran Vía (phone: 541-2023); 44 Paseo del Prado (phone: 230-4385); and 54 Calle Atocha (phone: 227-0716). Inexpensive.

La Salsería – Befitting its name, this small bar with an outdoor café specializes in sauces — 15 kinds, served in the holes of a conveniently held artist's palette, in the center of which are ruffled fried potatoes for dipping. Try *spaghetti a la siciliana* as well. Closed Mondays. No reservations or credit cards accepted. Across the traffic circle from the Mercado Puerta de Toledo. 2 Calle Ronda de Toledo (phone: 266-0890). Inexpensive.

Taberna de Antonio Sánchez – Genuinely typical of Old Madrid, it has been a venerated favorite ever since it was founded by a legendary bullfighter more than 150 years ago. The small, unpretentious dining rooms are charming, the realm of wonderful food — seafood, Spanish cuisine, salads, and desserts — served with care. Closed Sunday evenings. No reservations. Visa accepted. 13 Calle Mesón de Paredes (phone: 239-7826). Inexpensive.

TAPAS BARS: The uniquely Spanish snacks known as *tapas* probably originated in Seville, when a slice of ham or a piece of bread was discovered to be a convenient *tapa* (lid) to keep flies out of a glass of wine. Today, the drink departs little from the time-tested standard, but the inventiveness of the Spanish chef knows no bounds when it comes to *tapas*. The definition embraces everything from a little plate of green olives through an array of cheeses, sausages, hams, seafood, eggs, and vegetables that have been sliced, diced, wrapped, filled, marinated, sauced, sautéed, or otherwise cooked for hot or cold consumption, to a variety of tidbits swallowed raw and naked as nature made them. *El tapeo* (enjoying *tapas*) is a way of life in Spain, especially in Madrid, where there are literally thousands of places to do so. Practically every bar (not to be confused with pubs or *bares americanos,* which are for drinks only) serves *tapas,* as do *tabernas, mesones, tascas, cervecerías,* and even *cafeterías.* And most establishments specializing in *tapas* also have a few tables or even dining rooms in addition to their stand-up bar. Toothpicks and fingers are the most common utensils; shrimp, langostine, mussel, and clam shells, olive pits, napkins, and almost everything else are dropped on the floor, which is swept and scoured after each surge (from 1 to 3 PM and 7 to 9 PM, more or less — usually more).

A *chato* (glass of wine) or *caña* (draft beer) customarily is served with a free *tapita.* If you want more and if the vast array of *tapas* on display is overwhelming, just point to what you want. If you prefer a larger portion, ask for a *ración,* which can be a small meal in itself. Don't pay until you've completely finished; the bartender probably will remember everything you consumed, even if you don't. He'll deliver your change on a saucer; leave a few *duros* (5-peseta coins) as a tip, and always say *gracias* and *adiós* when you depart.

Tapas bar hopping is at its best in the central and old sections of Madrid. One of the city's best is *La Trucha* (with two locations, both just off Plaza Santa Ana: 3 Calle Manuel Fernández y González; phone: 259-1448; and 6 Calle Nuñez de Arce; phone: 532-0882). They're jammed at *tapa* time, and with good reason: Everything from bull tails to succulent red pimentos, as well as *trucha* (trout), is served with gusto (closed Sunday nights, and they take turns for July and August vacations). Nearby, the *Cervecería Alemana* (6 Plaza Santa Ana; phone: 429-7033) is, despite its name ("German Beer Parlor"), thoroughly *madrileño,* which is why the ubiquitous Hemingway frequented it and artists, intellectuals, and students continue to flock here. Among the *tapas* are good hams, sausages, and cheeses (closed Tuesdays and August). Around Puerta del Sol are *Casa Labra* (12 Calle Tetuán; phone: 532-1405), which was founded in 1860 and has been jam-packed ever since — among the specialties is fluff-fried *bacalao* (cod) that melts in the mouth, and *Mejillonería El Pasaje* (3 Pasaje de Matheu; phone: 521-5155), which deals in mussels exclusively, fresh from Galicia, served in any quantity, and prepared in various delicious ways. *La Torre del Oro* (26 Plaza Mayor; phone: 266-5016) is a lively Andalusian bar appropriately decorated with stunning bullfight photos and memorabilia (including a mounted earless bull's head), with recorded *sevillanas* music adding to the ambience; the *tapas* include such delicacies as baby eels and fresh anchovies, fried or marinated. In the same vicinity, *Valle del Tietar* (5 Calle Ciudad Rodrigo; phone: 248-0511), in the northwest arcade entrance to the plaza, offers *tapas,* Avila style, with suckling pig and kid specialties, while *El Oso y el Madroño* (4 Calle de la Bolsa; phone: 532-1377) is as *madrileño* as its name, which refers to the "bear and the madrona tree" on the city's coat of arms; the nonstop hand-cranked hurdy-gurdy and jovial local clientele make for authentic atmosphere. *El Shotis* (11 Calle Cava Baja; phone: 265-3230) is south of Plaza Mayor. Named after Madrid's traditional 19th-century couple's dance (which you'll hear playing on the jukebox, this unpretentious tavern is as typical as can be (closed Mondays and August). Elsewhere, there's *Monje Cervecería* (21 Calle del Arenal; phone: 248-3598), a showcase of fresh seafood, and lamb sweetbreads as well, and *La Mi Venta* (7 Plaza Marina Española; phone: 248-5091), where a friendly neighborhood atmosphere prevails and fine hot and cold *tapas* and *raciones* are served, with select hams as the specialty. At *Bocaito* (6 Calle Libertad; phone: 532-1219), north of the Gran Vía and Calle de Alcalá, animated *tapas* makers behind the bar prepare a limitless selection of outstanding treats, and giant Talavera ceramic plates on the walls are painted with fine reproductions of Goya's "Wine Harvest." Adjacent is a deli and small dining room with communal tables.

PAMPLONA

The ultimate expression of Pamplona's gusto is the renowned *Fiesta de San Fermín*, held annually from July 6 through 14 in honor of the city's native-born patron saint, who was martyred in 287. Without any doubt it is Spain's wildest and wackiest event, highlighted by the famous *encierros*, or "running of the bulls" through the town streets, and by attendant nonstop revelry. The fiesta, also known as the *Festival de los Sanfermines*, originated in the 17th century and was immortalized by Ernest Hemingway in his first novel, *The Sun also Rises* (known as *Fiesta* in Spain), a story of 1920s expatriates who come to Pamplona from Paris for the party. The book's vivid descriptions have drawn millions to the city over the years, and in deference to his place in the fortunes of the city, there is a statue of the writer on Paseo Hemingway, next to the *Plaza de Toros*.

Pamplona, capital of the ancient Pyrenean kingdom of Navarre got its name from the Roman general Pompey, who camped here with his troops on a hillside above the Arga River in the winter of 75–74 BC. Long known as the Gateway to Spain, because it lies at the junction of two mountain passes through the Pyrenees from France, the city (with a population of 185,000) now serves as the capital of the region of Navarre, one of Spain's 17 autonomous communities, and has grown beyond the core of the Old Town and its massive fortress walls.

The city was occupied by the Visigoths in the 5th century, by the Franks in the 6th century, and by the Moors in the 8th century. The Basques, with the help of Charlemagne, drove the Moors out in 750. Charlemagne remained, however, and soon after he sacked the city and tore down its defensive walls. In an act of patriotic revenge, Basque forces annihilated the rear guard of Charlemagne's army, led by the legendary Roland, in the Roncesvalles Pass in 778, an event later romanticized in the epic poem *Song of Roland*. Sancho III of Navarre made the city the capital of his kingdom in the year 1000, and so it remained until 1512, when the forces of King Ferdinand and Queen Isabella destroyed a second set of walls and occupied the city in the process of annexing Navarre to Castile. In the same century, during a battle to recapture the city, a young army captain named Iñigo López de Loyola (who ultimately became known to the world as St. Ignatius of Loyola) was seriously wounded and endured a lengthy convalescence here. He began to study religion, and in the 1530s founded the Society of Jesus, the Catholic religious order whose members are called Jesuits. Still later in the century, Philip II began a third set of walls, turning Pamplona into the most heavily fortified city in northern Spain.

Today, visitors put on their walking shoes and meander through the cobblestone streets of the old section of the city — "the palpitating heart of Pamplona" — as they call it, still partly surrounded by the historic fortress walls and filled with old noble mansions, convents, and churches. The central point of the town is the Plaza del Castillo, which offers a suggestion of Pamplona's somewhat confusing diversity of architectural styles. Fascist classic, Art Nouveau, and chrome and glass mix; arcades only make it partway around the plaza, and streets enter at odd, irregular angles. The lack of architectural consistency carries over to the city's churches. The mostly Gothic cathedral bears an unusual classical Greco-Roman façade of the baroque era; the church of San Saturnino, a former fortress, is a composite of Gothic and Romanesque; while the exterior of the Church of San Nicolás is that of a medieval castle with Gothic embellishments.

What is consistent, however, is the strong bond among the people of Pamplona, and their independent spirit. When Charlemagne came down from the north to drive out the Moors, the *pamplonicos* welcomed him with open arms as a liberator, but when his desire to be a conqueror revealed itself, they quickly changed their attitude toward him. It also was in Pamplona that the Fueros, a bill of rights similar to the Magna Carta, was signed in the 13th century, guaranteeing the people of Navarre independence from Castilian monarchs, and imposing a system of justice that is still practiced today.

Neighbors of the strongly separatist Basque Country, the *pamplonicos* nonetheless maintain a tolerance for political and cultural differences. They also balance hard work with hard play. Culturally, Pamplona is the home of the University of Navarre run by the rightest Catholic movement, Opus Dei, and the government-run Public University of Navarre, which opened in 1991, as well as various other professional and private institutes and schools. *Pamplonicos* are generally warm, friendly people who, like their city, are cordial and hospitable to visitors.

PAMPLONA AT-A-GLANCE

SEEING THE CITY: The most spectacular view of Pamplona is from the roads descending the Pyrenees over the Roncesvalles and Puerto de Velate passes from France. As you approach the city limits, the fortress walls rise powerfully over the hilltop city and are topped by the spires of the cathedral and the clustered Old Town. The wide green belt of parks, gardens, and tree-lined avenues that surrounds the Old Town adds contrast, making the immense walls appear even more spectacular.

SPECIAL PLACES: Pamplona is composed of an Old Town surrounded by modern suburbs. Just about everything a visitor will want to see is located in the old section, which is a compact area of extremely narrow, picturesque streets that can be traversed on foot in less than 15 minutes. It's best to park your car on one of the streets surrounding it, preferably around the shaded bullring, near the Plaza del Castillo, and walk. Pamplona's modern suburbs, more than mere residential areas, are centers of life complete with bars, restaurants, shops, nightclubs, and discotheques. The suburb of San Juan, west of the Old Town, is considered the most desirable place to live.

Plaza del Castillo – An elegant, arcaded square, shaded by the intertwining boughs of carefully pruned trees. At the southwest corner of the plaza is the Palacio de la Diputación Foral. Built in 1847 and enlarged in 1932, it is the seat of the regional government (open to the public, but because it is a working building, the timetable for visits is variable; no admission charge). The tree-lined Paseo de Sarasate, Pamplona's main promenade, begins at the south end of the plaza and runs past the Monumento de los Fueros, commemorating the region's 13th-century bill of rights.

Cathedral – Pamplona's cathedral stands at the northern tip of the Old Town, hard against the ramparts. Built on the foundations of a 12th-century Romanesque church, it is basically 14th- and 15th-century Gothic, but it has a west façade that is a baroque, Greco-Roman fantasy. The work of architect Ventura Rodríguez, this was constructed over the original Gothic portals in the late 18th century. The effect of stepping through a baroque façade to find a soaring Gothic church on the inside is strange, to say the least. The major work in the otherwise bare cathedral is the alabaster tomb of King Carlos III, the founder of the cathedral, and his wife, Queen Leonor of Castile — a 15th-century Flemish work carved with figures of the couple and a relief of hooded men and lamenting women. Besides various chapels and altarpieces (the 15th-century altarpiece in the ambulatory chapel is notable), there is a beautiful Gothic cloister, with lacelike stonework over the arches and delicately carved doorways. The 14th-century Puerta Preciosa (Precious Doorway), on the cloister's south side, has a tympanum carved with scenes of the life of the Virgin. The *Diocesan Museum*, housed in the former monks' kitchen and refectory, contains polychrome sculptures of sacred figures and other religious relics. The cathedral is open daily from 10:30 AM to 1:30 PM and from 4 to 7 PM; the museum is open daily, May through October 15 only, from 10:30 AM to 1:30 PM; admission charge to the museum. Plaza de la Catedral.

Ayuntamiento (Town Hall) – This stunningly ornate baroque building is noted for its 18th-century façade topped with allegorical statues. Not open to the public. Plaza Consistorial.

San Saturnino – A block away from the Town Hall, this 12th-century Romanesque church, extended by 13th-century Gothic additions, was constructed within former city fortifications, two defensive towers of which were converted into bell towers. The beautiful main portal is decorated with Gothic arches supported by columns whose capitals are embellished with scenes from the childhood of Christ and the Passion. Inside, notice the dark stained glass windows, as well as the dome, more becoming to an American state capitol, which provides the only light. Open daily, from 8 AM to 1 PM and from 4:30 to 7 PM. Calle Mayor.

San Nicolás – At the edge of the Old Town, this 13th-century, partly Romanesque church looks more like a fortified castle, complete with tower and fortress walls. The tower now has a spire on one of its corners, and the fortress walls have Gothic flourishes. The interior resembles a castle throne room, with wooden floors and starkly bare walls, but a few altars are worthy of closer inspection. Open daily, from 8 AM to 1 PM and from 4:30 to 7 PM. 10 Paseo de Sarasate.

San Lorenzo – Beside the Parque de la Taconera (Taconera Park), this church is home to the heart and soul of Pamplona — the baroque chapel of San Fermín, the town's patron saint. Unfortunately, the quarters for this soul are relatively soulless, and the chapel is, indeed, the only reason to visit. The statue of the saint that is paraded through town on the first day of the renowned *Fiesta de San Fermín* is positioned in the chapel under a marble pavilion. Open daily, from 8 AM to 1 PM and from 4 to 8 PM. Corner of Calle Mayor and Calle Taconera.

Museo de Navarra – The 16th-century Hospital de la Misericórdia once occupied this site and its Plateresque portal remains. The building was reopened by Spain's Queen Sofía in May 1990, after extensive renovations. Among the region's artistic treasures housed here are Roman mosaics, capitals from Pamplona's long-gone 12th-century Romanesque cathedral, paintings from the Gothic through the Renaissance periods, murals, a Goya portrait of the *Marqués de San Adrián* that is considered one of the painter's finest works, and luxurious 19th-century furniture. An 11th-century Moorish ivory casket consisting of 19 ivory plaques adorned with scenes from the lives of the caliphs is among the more interesting pieces. Open Tuesdays through Saturdays, 11 AM to 2 PM and 5 to 7 PM; Sundays, 11 AM to 2 PM. Admission charge. Calle Santo Domingo.

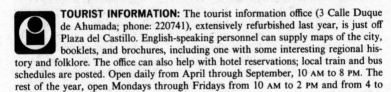

SOURCES AND RESOURCES

TOURIST INFORMATION: The tourist information office (3 Calle Duque de Ahumada; phone: 220741), extensively refurbished last year, is just off Plaza del Castillo. English-speaking personnel can supply maps of the city, booklets, and brochures, including one with some interesting regional history and folklore. The office can also help with hotel reservations; local train and bus schedules are posted. Open daily from April through September, 10 AM to 8 PM. The rest of the year, open Mondays through Fridays from 10 AM to 2 PM and from 4 to 7 PM, Saturdays from 10 AM to 2 PM; closed Sundays.

Local Coverage – The *Diario de Navarra* and *Navarra Hoy* discuss local and regional events.

TELEPHONE: The city code for Pamplona is 48. If calling from within Spain, dial 948 before the local number.

GETTING AROUND: Airport – The Noaín airport is 3 miles (5 km) south of town via the N121 highway toward Zaragoza. A taxi from the airport to virtually anywhere in Pamplona costs from $10 to $14. There is daily direct air service to Madrid, Barcelona, and Santander. The airport (phone: 317512) will provide information.

Bus – An excellent city bus system crosses the town and all areas of interest, including the out-of-the-way train station (take bus No. 9). Buses to Roncesvalles, Burguete, and Estella depart daily before 7 AM from the main station for long-distance buses, Estación de Autobuses de Pamplona, 2 Calle Conde Oliveto (phone: 223854).

Car Rental – *Hertz* (in the *Tres Reyes Hotel,* Calle Jardines de la Taconera; phone: 223569; and at the airport; phone: 318255); *Avis* (29 Monasterio de la Oliva; phone: 170068).

Train – Pamplona is on the main line connecting San Sebastián, Zaragoza, and Barcelona, with service twice daily in both directions. The train station (phone: 126981) is on Calle Rochapea, 1½ miles (2 km) from the center of town. To reach it, take the No. 9 bus, which runs every 15 minutes from Paseo de Sarasate. A taxi will cost about $6. There is a *RENFE* ticket office (8 Calle Estella; phone: 227282).

SPECIAL EVENTS: The *Fiesta de San Fermín* takes place annually from July 6 through 14 and is Pamplona's claim to fame. Popularized by Ernest Hemingway in *The Sun Also Rises,* the festival (aka the *Festival de los Sanfermines*) was also extensively described in *The Drifters* by James Michener. This 24-hour-a-day party reaches the intensity levels of a mystical experience, or a Keystone Cops movie, depending on one's orientation. The fun begins at noon on the 6th, when a bottle of champagne is uncorked at the Town Hall — the opening shot of a day full of ceremony, pageantry, and parades including one to the Chapel of San Fermín in San Lorenzo. The first running of the bulls (*encierro*) from the bull corral by the river to the bullring takes place at 8 AM the next morning (July 7), and the bulls are then run every morning through July 14; every evening at 6:30 PM bullfights take place in the *Plaza de Toros* bullring. Hundreds of brave and/or crazy men run in front of the bulls each morning in the traditional costume of white shirt and pants, red beret, bandanna, sash, and a rolled-up newspaper. Women are traditionally discouraged from participation, but no one will stop them. Indeed, a couple of determined women were among those injured during the 1990 runnings.

The route from the bull corral to the bullring is 1.8 miles. At 8 AM, a *chupinazo*, or signal rocket, is launched as a warning to the participants, most of whom immediately start to run. Seconds later, another rocket is launched, signaling the release of the bulls and the start of the *encierro*. If the bulls are not in a tight herd, a third rocket is fired to warn the runners of a separated or stray bull, more dangerous because it is overly excited, disoriented, or on the rampage. The six bulls that are run each morning are outstanding specimens, the same that appear — once they've caught their breath — in the ring at the afternoon bullfights. For the running, they are accompanied by a small herd of calves and steers to help keep them bunched up and, therefore, a bit less dangerous.

The side streets along the course over which this mad, run-for-your-life dash takes place are planked up, funneling both runners and bulls from the corral to the ring. The smarter runners plot out every step of the route so that when the bulls catch up, they know where to find shelter. Some just make a mad dash for the bullring in a desperate attempt to outrun the bulls. Santo Domingo, the street leading from the corral, is filled with such seasoned veterans; some bait the bulls and even run toward them! Santo Domingo leads toward Plaza Consistorial and into Doña Blanca de Navarra, a treacherous *S* curve with few places to hide. Estafeta (Suicide Alley), a long and narrow canyon, follows (fraught with peril because of the squeeze), leading to the Paseo Hemingway and the ramp into the bullring. Vantage points for spectators are hard to obtain after about 7 AM, by which time the route is thoroughly jammed.

The *encierro* lasts only a few minutes. Once the bulls reach the ring, they are quickly penned, although the festivities continue inside the ring as the runners and other amateur matadors (equipped with blankets, sheets, newspapers, and other homemade capes) do "battle" with the assorted escort calves and steers. Despite all the fun, the element of risk is always present; serious injuries and even fatalities are not uncommon.

At 6:30 PM, the bullfights begin, with the bravest bulls (possibly even angrier than usual because of the morning's trauma), some of Spain's best matadors, and high-level enthusiasm from one of the rowdiest crowds in the country. For many spectators, the real show is not the bullfights but the antics of the *peñas* in the stands, who spend the entire time spraying each other with champagne, flour, powdered sugar, and *sangría*. Tickets for the bullfights are sold almost a year in advance, but 10% are held back and sold at the bullring each evening for the next day's fights. Get in line at about 5 PM if you hope to get one of these tickets; otherwise, deal with the dozens of scalpers who ring the arena each afternoon.

Hotel space is a virtual impossibility for foreigners during *San Fermín*. The tourist office will arrange accommodations with local families; many of these are excellent bargains. For those interested in participating in the bull run, it's a good idea to get friendly with someone who has been through the routine previously. Take a few minutes to discuss the run with a seasoned veteran and decide upon a strategy. Americans tend to congregate at the *Bar Txoco* in Plaza del Castillo (on the corner nearest the bullring) and at the *Windsor Pub* in front of *La Perla* hotel (see *Checking In*). Local officials are inclined to discourage foreigners from participating in the *encierro*, because (they say) they can't run fast enough and usually get run over by the bulls or the other runners. Postcards and photos posted throughout the town showing gory scenes of bull's horns sticking through runners are usually enough to dissuade foreigners with only a casual interest in participating. Many who simply wish to watch the festivities are encouraged to make arrangements to see it from the balcony of a pension or a private house, or to watch it on television (the runs are broadcast live throughout Spain).

Additional *San Fermín* festivities are focused in the Old Town, including parades of papier-mâché giants and bands from Pamplona and neighboring towns. Bars remain packed throughout the day and night. The only lull takes place between noon and 5 PM, when the hot sun makes wandering through the streets uncomfortable. This afternoon respite also serves as a time to recharge for the late-night partying that awaits.

SHOPPING: With the exception of leather wineskins, which are sold in every shop in town, Pamplona is not noted for any particular locally made products. There is, however, a Pamplona food specialty — coffee-, vanilla-, and milk-flavored toffees called *pastillas.* There also is an anise-flavored Basque liqueur, *pacharán,* that is worth a try. A top brand is Etxeko, which comes in a black bottle. Pamplona has only one department store, *Unzu,* located in the center of town (7 Calle Mercaderes). The store is well stocked, and prices are somewhat lower than those of the boutiques surrounding it. The most fashionable, newest, and most spacious shops are in Pamplona's New Town, off Avenida Carlos III. The Old Town area just to the west of the Plaza del Castillo, on Calles San Nicolás, San Miguel, Comedias, and Zapatería, is another shopping district, but the shops — selling everything from perfume, shoes, dresses, shirts, and watches to cosmetics, candy, linen, yarn, and yard goods — are smaller and more pedestrian. General shopping hours are from 9:30 AM to 1:30 PM and from 4:30 to 7 PM, but may vary from shop to shop.

Casa Azagra – The choice for pure saffron. 26 Calle Zapatería (phone: 222355).

Cristal – Trendy fashions in bright colors and at reasonable prices. 37 Calle Castillo de Maya (phone: 240542).

Eduardo Rey – Top quality menswear by top European designers. Good range of cashmere, silk, and furs. 6 Calle Arrieta (phone: 210783).

María Alonzo – Women's European designer fashions. 22 Calle Gorriti (phone: 238871).

Venta Berri – A complete range of Navarre handicrafts and food products, including ceramics, crystal, tapestries, embroidery, chocolates, cheeses, and wines. 56 Calle Zapatería (phone: 210024).

SPORTS AND FITNESS: Among the most popular sports is jai alai, a form of pelota, played in frontóns, or courts, throughout the region. Mountaineering and cycling also are widely practiced in the area.

Fishing – The rivers around Pamplona and the outlying areas boast an abundance of salmon, trout, barbel, tench, carp, eels, and freshwater crabs. Be sure to check on any local or seasonal regulations before casting.

Golf – The 9-hole *Club de Golf Ulzama* course is located in the town of Guerendian, in the Ulzama Valley, 13 miles (21 km) south of Pamplona. Call for information on tee times and greens fees (phone: 313162).

Jogging – The best area for jogging in Pamplona is around the city walls in the vicinity of the cathedral.

Swimming – Pamplona's most popular public swimming spot is the municipal pool at *Aranzadi,* just north of the city walls (open daily, June through September, from 10:30 AM to 9 PM; admission charge). The *Tres Reyes* hotel (see *Checking In*) has a heated pool for the use of guests.

THEATER: There is no major resident theater company in Pamplona. The Escuela Navarra de Teatro (5 Calle San Agustín; phone: 229239) is a theater school that stages various performances and occasionally hosts visits by theater companies from Barcelona and Madrid. Almost all performances are in Spanish.

NIGHTCLUBS AND NIGHTLIFE: Pamplona has some of the most active nightlife in Spain, centered around the city's many bars. At about 7 PM, the citizenry empties into the streets for the evening *paseo* (stroll). Soon after, everyone converges on the bars for *tapas,* and children joyfully play around sidewalk café tables. This camaraderie continues until approximately 10 PM, when many head off for dinner, and then picks up again around midnight. Weeknights are naturally much quieter than weekends; on Saturday nights, bars, cafés, and discotheques stay packed until the wee hours.

The most popular discos are in the San Juan district, just outside the Old Town walls. Try *Reverendos* (5 Calle Monasterio de Velate), a private club that will admit anyone dressed in the latest trend, or *Disco Impacto* (Avenida Bayona), another favorite. *O.N.B.* (outside San Juan on Calle Abejeras) is a dual disco with rooms for both trendy young people and single professionals. Two top San Juan district pubs are the *Opera* and *Baby* (the latter is an abbreviation of its longer name — *Conocerte es Amarte Baby* — "To Know You Is to Love You, Baby"). For live music, try the *Boulevard Jazz Bar* (6 Plaza Reyes de Navarra), around the corner from the *Ciudad de Pamplona* hotel.

BEST IN TOWN

CHECKING IN: For a thriving industrial town, Pamplona has very few hotels. Note that during the *Fiesta de San Fermín,* hotels are allowed to double their normal high-season rates, which can make a stay a very expensive proposition. Many families rent space in their homes at this time — ask at the tourist office about such accommodations. Normally, expect to pay $100 or more for a double room in a hotel listed as expensive, $65 to $95 for a room in a hotel listed as moderate, and $60 or less in an inexpensive one. All telephone numbers are in the 48 city code unless otherwise indicated.

Europa – Recently opened, this luxurious establishment is an extension of the better-known restaurant of the same name (see *Eating Out*), located just off the Plaza del Castillo. Its 25 rooms, all air conditioned, have TV sets and marble bathrooms. 11 Calle Espoz y Mina (phone: 221800; fax: 229235). Expensive.

Iruña Park – This large, modern hostelry with 225 rooms, complete with television sets and private gardens, caters to conventioneers and boasts a wide range of facilities, including a restaurant and bars. Ronda de Ermitagaña (phone: 173200; fax: 172387). Expensive.

Tres Reyes – The best Pamplona has to offer, set in a park between the Old Town and the San Juan district. All 180 rooms are air conditioned and comfortable. There is also a heated swimming pool and a good restaurant, and the service is excellent. Perfect for shelter from the storm of *San Fermín,* but be prepared to pay for it. Jardines de la Taconera (phone: 226600; fax: 222930). Expensive.

Ciudad de Pamplona – This modern establishment with 117 rooms has all the amenities, but its distance — a 25-minute walk from the center of town — is too far out of the way for easy exploring. 21 Calle Iturrama (phone: 266011; fax: 173626). Moderate.

Nuevo Maisonnave – A traditional favorite, offering 152 comfortable rooms, centrally located in the Old Town on a quiet street (one that remains relatively quiet even during *San Fermín*). This place is similar to the *Tres Reyes* but lacks its pool and some of its amenities. Air conditioning is limited to the public rooms. 20 Calle Nueva (phone: 222600; fax: 220166). Moderate.

Orhi – Located across from the Plaza de Toros, this smaller, 55-room hotel is a 5-minute walk from the Plaza del Castillo. 7 Calle Leyre (phone: 228500; fax: 228318). Moderate.

La Perla – On the Plaza del Castillo, this 67-room hostelry is a favorite during *San Fermín* as it overlooks Calle Estafeta, the longest straightaway of the *encierro*. Unfortunately, it offers little else. 1 Plaza del Castillo (phone: 227706). Moderate.

Yoldi – The 48 rooms here are modern and comfortable. For years, this establishment has been the choice of visiting matadors, and it is the place where all the aficionados gather to discuss the bullfights during *San Fermín*. Located on a quiet street, a short walk from the bullring and the Plaza del Castillo. 11 Avenida San Ignacio (phone: 224800; fax: 212045). Moderate.

Eslava – A small, old, 28-room hotel in the Old Town. The rustic wood-beamed rooms all have private baths. Some offer beautiful views over the city walls and into the valley beyond. 7 Plaza Virgen de la O (phone: 222270; fax: 225157). Inexpensive.

EATING OUT: Pamplona is not a diner's paradise, but it does offer some interesting dishes that combine the heartiness of the mountains with the traditional fare of northern Spain. The local cuisine is Basque, which means plenty of grilled meats, stews, and fresh fish from nearby mountain streams and the Atlantic. Favorites include local *trucha* (trout), cooked and served whole with a slice of salty smoked ham slotted into it; and *merluza* (hake). Lamb might be baked in a wood-fired oven, chopped up and soaked in a sauce, or served simply as chops. During *San Fermín*, the bulls killed in the previous day's fights are served up in a wonderful stew. Dinner for two, including wine, will cost $70 or more in restaurants listed as expensive, $40 to $70 at restaurants listed as moderate, and $35 or less at inexpensive ones. All phone numbers are in the 48 city code unless otherwise indicated.

Europa – An opulent dining room, considered the home of nouvelle cuisine in Pamplona, as well as of excellent roquefort filet steaks. Closed Sundays. Reservations necessary, especially during *San Fermín*. Major credit cards accepted. 11 Calle Espoz y Mina (phone: 221800). Expensive.

Hartza – One of two restaurants in Pamplona boasting a Michelin star. It offers traditional regional food, including fish, game, wild mushrooms, and fresh seasonal produce. Try the *merluza de la casa* or *besugo a la bermeana* (sea bream). Closed Mondays, mid-July to mid-August, and *Christmas* week. Reservations advised. American Express, Diners Club, and Visa accepted. 19 Calle Juan de Labrit (phone: 224568). Expensive.

Josetxo – Famous for 30 years for its Basque dishes, this is another local leader with a Michelin star. Specialties include *sopa crema de cangrejos* (cream of crab soup), highly praised trout and rabbit dishes, hake with salmon sauce, and *lubina* (sea bass), grilled or in a white wine sauce. Closed Sundays and August. Reservations advised. Major credit cards accepted. 1 Plaza Príncipe de Viana (phone: 222097). Expensive.

Las Pocholas – Among the best Pamplona has to offer, a place for dishes such as vegetable stew, bull's tail stew, lobster with garlic sauce, and other traditional fare.

The restaurant's official name is *Hostal del Rey Noble,* but everyone in town knows it as *Las Pocholas.* Closed Sundays and August. Reservations necessary. Major credit cards accepted. 6 Paseo de Sarasate (phone: 222214). Expensive.

Sarasate – A comfortable eating house of the the first order, run by the Leránoz family. The menu includes excellent game and vegetable dishes, plus traditional Navarre fare. Closed Sundays. Reservations advised. American Express and Visa accepted. 12 García Castañon (phone: 225102). Expensive.

Casa Angel – A favorite for lunches, the grill here is renowned for its excellent meat dishes, such as *solomillo a la prusina* (broiled filet of beef) and *salchicha* (small sausages). Other specialties include fried peppers and traditional Basque fare. Open daily. Reservations advised. No credit cards accepted. 43 Calle Abejeras (phone: 243962). Expensive to moderate.

Casa Otano – On the second floor over the bar of the same name, it serves one of the best all-purpose menus in town, featuring traditional local dishes. Closed Sunday afternoons. Reservations advised. No credit cards accepted. 5 Calle San Nicolás (phone: 225095). Expensive to moderate.

Don Pablo – Across from the *Tres Reyes* hotel, with a menu of both French and Spanish dishes and a modern atmosphere of smoked glass and chrome. Try the *berenjena* (eggplant) specials (in season), *merluza* (hake), and *lenguado a la romana* (filet of sole). Closed Sunday evenings. Reservations necessary. Major credit cards accepted. 19 Calle Navas de Tolosa (phone: 225299). Expensive to moderate.

Aralar – Baby lamb cooked in an open, wood-fired oven is the specialty here, accompanied by a bottle from the excellent wine list. Closed Wednesday afternoons. Reservations advised. American Express and Visa accepted. 12 Calle San Nicolás (phone: 221116). Moderate.

Casa Mauleon – The main dining room resembles a wine cellar with giant barrels lining the walls, and if you're lucky, you may have a serenade by locals singing up a storm during *San Fermín.* Excellent meals are served at lunch and dinner — try the stuffed peppers. Closed Sunday evenings. Reservations advised. No credit cards accepted. 4 Calle Amaya (phone: 228474). Moderate.

Erburu – Tucked in one of the back streets of the Old Town, it's hard to find but worth the search. Try the *liebre con ajo* (rabbit with garlic) or any of the other local specialties. This is a crowded but friendly place. Closed Mondays. No reservations or credit cards accepted. 19 Calle San Lorenzo (phone: 225169). Moderate.

Marceliano – A favorite with foreigners during *San Fermín,* since Hemingway was rumored to have stayed and dined here. Join the pilgrimage and order a plate of the best bull stew in Pamplona. Closed Mondays. Reservations advised. No credit cards accepted. 7 Calle Mercado (phone: 221426). Moderate.

Estafeta – A self-service, cafeteria-style restaurant — a welcome sight for a low-budget meal. The food is acceptably prepared and the surroundings are clean and pleasant. Closed Sunday evenings. No reservations or credit cards accepted. 57 Calle Estafeta (phone: 222605). Inexpensive.

TAPAS BARS: It seems that *tapas* bars in Pamplona are spaced every 50 feet throughout the Old Town, especially along Calle San Nicolás and Calle San Gregorio. *Cordovilla* (Calle Navarrería) is well known for its *pimientos fritos, calamares fritos,* and *tortillas,* while *Bar Noé* (9 Calle de las Comedias) has excellent *tapas* ranging from peppers and pâtés to fish salads. The bars around Plaza del Castillo also serve great *tapas.* One popular spot is the *Windsor Pub* (at the *La Perla* hotel), which features seafood *tapas* including small crabs, langoustines, shrimp, and squid in its own ink.

SALAMANCA

The golden glow of Salamanca lingers long after you have left this city of amber sandstone. The splendid Plateresque, Renaissance, and baroque façades of the buildings in the historic section of town — made of soft, fine, easy-to-work *piedra arenisca* — have, with age, acquired a warm distinctive patina that grows ever richer with the passing centuries. No wonder the city long has been nicknamed "Little Rome."

Unlike many another town in Spain, including nearby Madrid, Salamanca has remained reasonably free of the deleterious effects of modern architecture and mass tourism. As the home of one of the world's most ancient universities, it has conducted itself through the ages with dignity — so much so that its magnificent monuments and academic structures can seem somewhat imposing to visitors. But Salamanca is really an intimate, lively place, with an army of students to nip any nascent pompousness in the bud.

From 217 BC, when the Romans constructed a bridge of 26 arches across the Tormes River, and throughout the Middle Ages, Salamanca enjoyed an enviable position along important trade routes. Later, after the foundation of the famed university in the 13th century, the steady influx of merchants bent on business was matched by a steady stream of students. Today, although the Roman Bridge is open to pedestrian traffic only, it still seems to echo with the sounds of its commercial heyday, while the tradespeople of old have been largely replaced by a global society of culture seekers drawn to the city's numerous architectural and intellectual legacies. The university, true to its long-standing tradition, continues to attract a sizable foreign student body that lends a cosmopolitan air to this otherwise staunchly Castilian town.

While the Phoenicians were busy establishing Cádiz in the south, the area of Salamanca was inhabited by Iberian tribes who left their mark with the enormous carved stone bulls, or *verracos,* that are seen throughout the province (there is one in the middle of the Roman Bridge). Beginning about 900 BC, the Celts from the north, mingling with the Iberians of the central plateau, created two Celt-Iberian tribes known as Vettons (primarily herdsmen) and Vacceos (primarily farmers).

The next great shift in Salamanca's fortunes came at the hands of Hannibal, who conquered the city in 220 BC during the Second Punic War. Soon after, under the Romans, it became an important communications center. A long, peaceful, and prosperous Roman reign was brought to a contentious halt with the arrival of Germanic tribes in the 5th century. Under the Vandals and Visigoths, and then the Islamic Moors, Salamanca fell into relative obscurity. After its reconquest from the latter in 1085, the area was resettled by an ethnic mix of Franks, Castilians, Portuguese, Jews, Galicians, and some English.

The University of Salamanca was established in 1218, making it — with

Paris, Bologna, and Oxford — one of Europe's oldest universities. It achieved great renown and garnered tremendous intellectual respect for its role in reintroducing the world to the works of the ancient Greek and Muslim philosophers, translated into Latin and Old Spanish by the university's Muslim, Jewish, and Christian scholars. Favored by kings and popes, the university reached its peak of prestige during Spain's Golden Age; John, the son of the Catholic Monarchs, was one of its students. Early in the 16th century, 8,000 of Salamanca's 20,000 residents were university students. Cervantes, St. John of the Cross, and other famed historic personages studied, taught, or spent time in Salamanca, the prime intellectual breeding ground of the period. Delicate and elaborately detailed, the Plateresque façade of the university in the Patio de Escuelas is a symbol of the spirit and wealth of those times.

With the waning of Spain's Golden Age during the 17th century, Salamanca shared in the decline of Castilian cities, a condition that lasted throughout the 18th century. At the turn of this century, when Miguel de Unamuno was university rector, the city had only 25,000 inhabitants; but despite the tremendous political upheavals of 20th-century Spain, Salamanca has regained some of its earlier momentum and today boasts a population of over 169,000, as well as burgeoning hordes of annual visitors. Present-day Salamanca society is clearly divided into students and non-students, who, for the most part, studiously avoid each other. The university — which is not what it used to be — has its classrooms and facilities spread throughout the city, and most after-class socializing takes place in the city's numerous bars. Meanwhile, the *salamanqueses* go about their business largely indifferent to the cultural legacy handed down to them through the centuries. It is left to visitors, then, to "Ooh!" and "Aah!" at the city's golden splendor.

SALAMANCA AT-A-GLANCE

SEEING THE CITY: The best view of the city is from the *Parador de Salamanca* (see *Checking In*), located on a hill south of the city and across the Tormes River. On Saturdays, Sundays, and holidays, many of the monuments are illuminated for several hours after nightfall. The spires of the city's side-by-side cathedrals and the dome and towers of La Clerecía dominate the scene.

SPECIAL PLACES: Salamanca's streets are often narrow and winding, with many one-way thoroughfares, but the Centro Ciudad (City Center) signs leading into the core of town are excellent, and for those arriving by car, there's no trouble driving right to the heart of the city. Once there, it is best to proceed on foot, as all the main sights are concentrated compactly in the *zona monumental* (monument zone), largely between the Plaza Mayor and the river. Visiting hours for the city's sights are erratic, to say the least, and subject to change without notice. No standard hours are set, so each monument sets its own, which vary with the season and other unpredictable factors. It is best to check with the tourist information office (39 Gran Vía; phone: 243730) for current hours, though even those may not turn out to be completely accurate.

CITY CENTER

Plaza Mayor – Deemed by many to be the most beautiful plaza in all of Spain, this harmonious construction, in a muted baroque style, measures roughly 63,500 square feet and, despite all appearances, is trapezoidal, not rectangular. Arcades housing boutiques, souvenir stores, pastry shops, and assorted bars and eateries surround it at ground level; above the arches all around rise 3 stories of balconies, interrupted only by the façade of the Town Hall, which juts out and up to break the uniformity. Begun in 1729 and completed 34 years later, the plaza was originally built as an enclosed market area and arena for public fiestas. Once used for bullfights, it is still the heart of town and the focal point of the festivities of the *Feria de Salamanca,* celebrated every year during the second 2 weeks in September. It's hard to imagine that at one time in the 1960s, cars were allowed into the square. Fortunately, it belongs to pedestrians again.

Catedral Vieja (Old Cathedral) and Catedral Nueva (New Cathedral) – These stand adjacent to one another, though they are 4 centuries apart in age. Visitors ordinarily enter the old structure through the new one. The Catedral Nueva was begun in 1513 and was in use by 1560, although it wasn't consecrated until 1733. Conceived in a Gothic vein — one of the last Gothic churches in Spain, in fact — in actual construction it also drew from the Renaissance and baroque vernaculars. Outside, the church bristles with more than 400 Gothic spikes, and the main doorway, facing Calle Cardenal Playdeniel, is a prime example of the Plateresque stone carvers' art, with biblical scenes in high relief and ornamental borders so richly detailed they tax the eye. Inside, the New Cathedral is notable for the ornate wooden choir stalls, 18th-century baroque works by the Churriguera brothers, and for the two organs; for the Cristo de las Batallas, which is a famous 11th-century Romanesque crucifix said to have been carried into battle by El Cid (this comparatively tiny statue is in the center of an ornate Churrigueresque golden altarpiece in the central chapel behind the Capilla Mayor); and for the Capilla Dorada, located near the entrance to the old cathedral, its walls plastered with small statues of saints, angels, prophets.

The Catedral Vieja, down a flight of stairs off the south aisle of the new one, dates from the 12th century, its plan, columns, capitals, and external arches in Romanesque style, its internal arches and vaults in Gothic. Simpler and more fortress-like than its replacement, the church's monochromatic interior is enlivened by an extraordinary 15th-century main altarpiece made up of 53 panels, painted by Nicolás Florentino, narrating the lives of Christ and the Virgin Mary. Above it, against a dark background, is a Last Judgment by the same painter, and in the center of the altarpiece is the 12th-century image of Nuestra Señora de la Vega, the city's patron. Among the rooms around the adjoining cloister, be sure to note the 12th-century Talavera Chapel, used at one time for Mozarabic rite masses and topped with a distinctive Romanesque-Mudéjar dome; the 14th-century Santa Barbara Chapel, where university examinations once were held and where candidates for the degree customarily spent the night before finals praying; and the Santa Catalina Chapel and Salas Capitulares (Chapter Rooms), set up as a museum. Most of the exterior of the Old Cathedral is obscured by the new one, but before leaving the complex entirely, walk around back to the Patio Chico (Small Courtyard), from where the older church's strange-looking Torre del Gallo (Rooster Tower), covered with scale-like stones, is visible. Open daily from 9 AM to 2 PM and from 4 to 6 PM; closed Sunday afternoons in winter. There is an admission charge to the Old Cathedral (which includes the cloister chapels and museum off the Old Cathedral). Plaza de Anaya (phone: 217476).

Universidad (University) – The university's facilities are dispersed through the city, but the core of its "campus" is just around the block from the cathedrals. Here, at one end of the Patio de Escuelas, is the university building, erected during the reign of the Catholic Monarchs, that bears the most famed Plateresque façade in Spain. It's a real beauty, considered the apogee of this ornamental genre, and one of Salamanca's enduring landmarks. Immediately inside is a courtyard ringed by classrooms — compare a modern one with the Aula Fray Luis de León, where rough benches have been left as they were in the 16th century. A couple of doors beyond it is the interesting Paraninfo Room, featuring Belgian tapestries and a portrait of King Carlos IV by Goya. Note the beautiful painted ceilings all around the courtyard, and especially the ceiling of the university foyer (opposite the visitors' entrance), a lacy Moorish one of star shapes in dark wood. A beautiful staircase with carved balustrade leads to the upper level of the courtyard, topped by another fine coffered Mozarabic ceiling. (The university's old library, a repository of over 40,000 volumes and 3,000 manuscripts, is located up here, but it is no longer open to visitors.)

At the opposite end of the Patio de Escuelas is the Escuelas Menores (Minor Schools), marked by another Plateresque façade and a beautiful interior courtyard, on the far side of which is a room containing a fresco of the zodiac by Fernando Gallego known as *Cielo de Salamanca* (Salamancan Sky — recently reopened following restoration). Both the main university building and the Escuelas Menores are open from 9 AM to 2 PM and from 4 to 8 PM Mondays through Saturdays (closed Sunday afternoons) in summer; winter hours are Mondays through Fridays from 9:30 AM to 1:30 PM and from 4 to 6 PM, Saturdays from 9:30 AM to 1:30 PM, and Sundays from 11 AM to 1 PM. One admission charge for both buildings. Patio de Escuelas (phone: 219708).

Museo de Bellas Artes/Museo de Salamanca (Fine Arts Museum/Salamanca Museum) – Through the door adjacent to the Escuelas Menores and under the 15th-century roof of the former house of Dr. Alvarez Abarca, Queen Isabella's physician, the museum has an eclectic display of paintings and sculptures, both Spanish and foreign, old and modern. Open weekdays from 8 AM to 3 PM and weekends from 10 AM to 2 PM, except when there are temporary exhibitions, which are open from 7 to 9 PM weekdays and from 10 AM to 2 PM weekends. Admission charge. Patio de Escuelas (phone: 212235).

Convento de San Esteban (Convent of St. Stephen) – This 16th-century church, part of a Dominican convent, is just down Calle Tostado from Plaza de Anaya. It sports another of Salamanca's stunning Plateresque façades, this one described by some as a tapestry in stone because of its elaborate depictions of the martyrdom of San Esteban and the crucifixion of Christ. Inside is a sumptuous, late-17th-century golden altarpiece by José Benito de Churriguera, in the upper reaches of which is a *Martirio de San Esteban* (Martyrdom of St. Stephen) painted by Claudio Coello. To the side of the church is the beautiful 2-story Claustro de los Reyes (Kings' Cloister), the only one of the convent's three cloisters that is open to the public. From its second story, a door opens into the church's *coro alto,* from which the view of the altarpiece is breathtaking. Open daily, from 9 AM to 2 PM and from 4 to 5:30 PM. Admission charge. Plaza Santo Domingo (phone: 215000).

Convento de las Dueñas – Nearly next door to San Esteban, the 15th-century Moorish-style structure here was a private home before it was donated to a group of *dueñas* (nuns, or pious women of high social standing living in community). Only the five-sided, 16th-century Renaissance cloister is open to visitors, but it's a real treat. Whereas most of the rich stone carving in Salamanca is too distant or too much in the dark to be easily seen, the elaborate capitals of the cloister's upper tier are only slightly above eye level, so their charming, amusing, and grotesque human and animal figures can be brought into sharp focus. The nuns who run the convent also make sweets, which they sell at the *Despacho* (shop) in a corner of the entry courtyard. Open daily from 10 AM to 1 PM and from 4 to 6 PM from April through September; from 10:30 AM to 1 PM and from 4 to 5:30 PM from October through March. Admission charge. The

Despacho is open from 10 AM to 1 PM and from 4 to 7 PM. Plaza del Concilio de Trento (phone: 215442).

Casa de las Conchas (House of Shells) – One of the more famous buildings in Salamanca, it dates from the 15th century and incorporates Moorish, Gothic, and Renaissance elements. Unfortunately, it's not open to the public, but the façade, covered with the carved seashells that give the building its name, is noteworthy. They were the symbol of the Pimental family, one of whose members was the bride of the building's owner, a member of the Maldonado family, whose symbol, the fleur de lys, is on the coat of arms above the door. Note, too, the Gothic window grilles. Corner of Rua Antigua and Calle de la Compañía.

In addition to the Casa de las Conchas, there are a number of other monuments in Salamanca that are pure façade with interiors that are either off-limits or merely mundane. Be sure to give a passing glance to the Clerecía (or Real Clerecía de San Marcos), a huge 17th-century collegiate church on the corner opposite the Casa de las Conchas, and to the Palacio de Monterrey, a characteristic Spanish Renaissance palace of the early 16th century at the Plaza de Monterrey end of Calle de la Compañía.

ENVIRONS

Alba de Tormes – About 11 miles (18 km) southeast of Salamanca is the village of Alba de Tormes, just over a medieval bridge with 22 arches crossing the Tormes River. Turn left at the end of the bridge and park beside the unfinished Basílica de Santa Teresa. Then walk up between the basilica and the Iglesia de San Pedro (with the red brick bell tower) to the Plaza de Santa Teresa, where the Convento de Madres Carmelitas Descalzas and the Iglesia de Santa Teresa are the goals of a steady influx of faithful pilgrims. The church is primarily Renaissance, with Gothic and baroque flourishes. The marble vault above the altar bears the mortal remains of St. Teresa of Avila, who founded the convent, and died here in 1582. On either side of the altar is a reliquary, one containing an arm and the other the heart of the beloved saint. At the back of the church, opposite the entrance door, is a grating that affords a glimpse of the cell where she died. To see the relics and the cell illuminated, apply at the Centro Teresiano Información across the plaza, open Mondays through Fridays, from 10 AM to 1 PM and 4 to 8 PM. The center also houses a small museum exhibiting mementos of St. Teresa's life, and photos of Pope John Paul II's visit to Alba de Tormes in 1982, the 400th anniversary of the saint's death.

Béjar – This old Moorish fortress town is set in the spectacular Sierra de Béjar, 45 miles (74 km) southeast of Salamanca (on CN-630). Ruins of the old Arab walls surrounding the town still remain, and the city's monuments span several hundred years from Moorish constructions in the 11th century to the baroque Plaza Mayor (Main Square). The nearby Sierra de Béjar and Sierra de Candelaria ranges are popular with Spanish mountaineers.

■ **EXTRA SPECIAL:** The *Casa-Museo Unamuno* (Unamuno House-Museum), the 18th-century house where the renowned scholar, poet, and philosopher Miguel de Unamuno lived from 1900 to 1914 (while he was rector of the University of Salamanca), is now an intimate museum containing his notebooks, library, and many of his most prized personal possessions, including drawings, paper birds, a large crucifix, a small deck of cards (he enjoyed playing solitaire), and his brass bed. Open weekdays from 4 to 6 PM, weekends from 11 AM to 1 PM. Admission charge. (Note — the museum is not to be confused with the house Unamuno moved into when he was no longer university rector, which is at 6 Calle Bordadores and not open to the public.) 25 Calle de los Libreros (phone: 214817).

SOURCES AND RESOURCES

TOURIST INFORMATION: The main tourist information office (39-41 Gran Vía; phone: 268571) is open weekdays, from 9:30 AM to 2 PM and from 4:30 to 7 PM; Saturdays, from 9:30 AM to 2 PM. Information is also available at the Oficina de Información kiosk (in the eastern wall of the Plaza Mayor; phone: 218342). It's open Mondays through Saturdays, from 10 AM to 1:30 PM and from 5 to 7 PM; Sundays and holidays, from 11 AM to 2 PM. Both outlets can provide current information regarding hours and admission fees, as well as maps, brochures, and detailed information on local accommodations in all price ranges. For a detailed city map, go to *Librería Cervantes* (11-13 Calle Azafranal; phone: 218602), one of Salamanca's top bookshops, and ask for a *callejero*.

Local Coverage – *El Adelanto* and *La Gaceta Regional* are local dailies in Spanish, covering local, provincial, national, and international news and events. The monthly *Lugares,* distributed free of charge, is the best source for information on nightlife and entertainment in Salamanca.

TELEPHONE: The city code for Salamanca is 23. If calling from within Spain, dial 923 before the local number.

GETTING AROUND: Salamanca is a small, compact city, and all the sights are within walking distance of one another, so getting around is a simple matter. Sites are easy to find, too, at least in the *zona monumental,* which is a good thing, because the buildings of Salamanca were renumbered in 1989. For some time to come, brochures and other published materials probably will be full of wrong street numbers. In this chapter, every effort has been made to supply the correct number — but even when the visitor is armed with the correct address, it can be difficult to determine which number beside any given doorway is the correct one.

Bus – The bus station (33 Calle Filiberto Villalobos; phone: 236717) is a short distance from the center of town. Schedules are printed in *El Adelanto* and *Lugares.* There is frequent daily service to Zamora, Madrid, Avila, Seville, Barcelona, and León, as well as to nearby Alba de Tormes.

Car Rental – Major rental companies include *Hertz* (131 Avenida de Portugal; phone: 243134; and 23 Calle General Sanjurjo; phone: 232554) and *Avis* (49 Paseo de Canalejas; phone: 257430; and 3 Plaza Madrid; phone: 251632). Local car rental firms include *Castilla* (49 Paseo de Canalejas; phone: 257430); *Prado Martín* (5 Plaza de Santo; phone: 242549); and *Sánchez González* (163 Avenida de Portugal; phone: 220396).

Taxi – There are two taxi stands by the Plaza Mayor, one on Calle del Corrillo, and the other on Plaza del Poeta Iglesias, in front of the *Gran* hotel. Taxis can be hailed throughout the city, or by radio service (phone: 254444 or 250000).

Train – The Salamanca train station (Paseo de la Estación; phone: 220395) is a short cab ride from the city center. There is a *RENFE* office (10 Plaza de la Libertad; phone: 212454). Frequent daily service goes to Madrid, Avila, Valladolid, Barcelona, and Porto, Portugal.

SPECIAL EVENTS: In mid-July, the city sponsors the *Verano Cultural de Salamanca,* a week-long series of silent movies, contemporary Spanish cinema, singers, and theater groups from Spain and abroad. The *Feria de Salamanca,* held annually during the second 2 weeks in September, features music, costumes, parades, various theatrical events, and almost daily bullfights.

MUSEUMS: In addition to those described in *Special Places,* Salamanca's museums include the following:

Convento y Museo de las Ursulas – The small museum — a room adjoining the Ursulas church — contains painting, sculpture, and *artesonado* ceilings; the church contains the alabaster tomb of the convent's founder. Open daily from 9:30 AM to 1 PM and from 4 to 6 PM. Admission charge. Calle las Ursulas (phone: 219877).

Museo de Historia de la Ciudad y Museo Diocesano (Museum of City History and Diocesan Museum) – Various stones of archaeological and architectural interest, plus items associated with local composer Tomás Bretón (1850–1923), in the former; the latter, upstairs, has several late-15th-century paintings by Fernando and Francisco Gallego, and a triptych of St. Michael by Juan de Flandes. Open Tuesdays through Saturdays, from 10 AM to 1:30 PM and from 5 to 8 PM. Admission charge. Plaza de Juan XXIII (phone: 213067).

SHOPPING: Most of the more interesting shops are in the Plaza Mayor and the surrounding streets to the north, although there is almost nothing sold in Salamanca that isn't also available almost anywhere else in Old Castile. Stores are generally open from 10 AM to 1:30 PM and from 5 to 7 or 8 PM.

Escarlata – The most avant-garde clothes shop in town. 9 Calle Padilleros.

Feres – Lladró porcelain and Majórica pearls. 27 Plaza Mayor (phone: 215913).

Handy-Craft – Belts, ceramics, baskets, and assorted international handicrafts. 53 Rua Mayor (phone: 263395).

Oscar – Mantillas, fans, flamenco paraphernalia, and other Spanish souvenirs. 15 Plaza Mayor (phone: 213636).

Segurado – Traditional Spanish souvenirs and novelty items. 10 Plaza Mayor (phone: 212362).

SPORTS AND FITNESS: Salamanca's modern sports complex, *Pabellón Deportivo* (Parque de la Alamedilla; phone: 234069), has a swimming pool, ice skating rink, and basketball and handball courts. Call for availability information and costs. The city also has a variety of gymnasiums and fitness clubs that are open to the public for a fee. Contact the tourist office for further information.

Fishing – Trout fishing in the Tormes, Francia, Mayas, Frio, Quilames, and Batuecas rivers requires a license and the payment of a fee, with the season usually running from March through October. There are no special restrictions or requirements for non-residents. For more information, contact the *Consejeria de Agricultura,* Ganadería y Montes, (Sección de Montes), 28-30 Calle Alfonso de Castro (phone: 232600).

Hunting – Some hunting areas are restricted to Spaniards only, while others have very strict rules and regulations for all would-be hunters. Small game includes hare, rabbit, partridge, and turtledove; bigger game consists of wild boar, mountain goats, and deer. For more information, contact the *Consejeria de Agricultura,* listed above.

Squash – The *Kata Squash Club* (79 Avenida de Alemania; phone: 259689) rents courts and also has a well-equipped gymnasium.

Swimming – Besides the *Pabellón Deportivo* (see above), both the *Complejo Torres*

(Carretera de Madrid; phone: 215754) and the Parque Sindical (Carretera de Fuentesanco) have swimming pools open to the public for an admission charge.

 THEATER AND MUSIC: During the academic year, theatrical performances take place under the auspices of the university, and concerts also are presented by the university, by the *Sociedad de Conciertos,* and by other organizations. The stage at the university's *Teatro Juan del Enzina* (phone: 214274) hosts many of the theatrical events, while the *Paraninfo Room* and the university chapel are used for concerts. The *Teatro Bretón* (Plaza Bretón; phone: 269844), one of several movie theaters in town, is also used for concerts. During the July and September festivals, events proliferate.

 NIGHTCLUBS AND NIGHTLIFE: Although there is a disco scene, nightlife in Salamanca usually involves more traditional pursuits, such as hanging out at a bar with friends or, in good weather, people watching at an outdoor café in Plaza Mayor. At the northeast corner of the plaza, the *Café Novelty,* Unamuno's former haunt, has been going strong since 1905; the Art Nouveau details of its doors and mirrors, its black wrought-iron and brass railings, still give it plenty of character. Two bars offer live jazz performances during the university year (October through May) — *Corrillo* (1 Cerrada del Corrillo, at the edge of Plaza Mayor; phone: 269111) and *Mezcal* (9 Cuesta del Carmen; phone: 213077). Discos come and go, but among those with staying power are *María* (36 Avenida Mirat), *Limón y Menta* (18 Calle Bermejeros), and *Hindagala* (Plaza de la Reina).

BEST IN TOWN

 CHECKING IN: Considering its rather modest size, Salamanca has an impressive array of lodgings, ranging from student pensions and *hostales* to large, full-service hotels. The tourist information office offers a listing of hotels it has inspected and graded, complete with prices and details on facilities with private bath. Expect to pay $90 to $130 for a double room with private bath in hotels classified as expensive, $50 to $85 for a moderate room, and less than $50 for an inexpensive one. All telephone numbers are in the 23 city code unless otherwise indicated.

Gran – Just off the Plaza Mayor's southeastern corner, its lobby is a spacious local gathering place and its 100 rooms just have been redone in a traditional style, with dark wood furnishings — all in all, the feeling is one of substance and comfort. Rooms have private baths (large, marble ones), soundproofed windows, TV sets, and air conditioning; the hostelry has 2 bars and the *Feudal* restaurant, featuring regional dishes. 6-9 Plaza del Poeta Iglesias (phone: 213500; fax: 213501; telex: 26809). Expensive.

Monterrey – Sister to the *Gran* hotel, it's not far from the Plaza Mayor, although it's located beyond the *zona monumental.* The lobby, with upholstery in pale green velvet contrasting nicely with reddish wood, is attractive; the 85 rooms and 4 suites are not quite as nicely furnished as those of its sister, but are air conditioned. A pleasant café, spacious public rooms, and the fine *El Fogón* restaurant. 21 Calle Azafranal (phone: 214400; fax: 923214; telex: 27836). Expensive.

Parador de Salamanca – The local *parador,* just across the Tormes River from the city, offers modern facilities and conscientious service that are the best in town. The 94 double rooms, 10 singles, and 4 suites are all centrally heated and air conditioned, with private bath and direct-dial telephones. There is also a coffee shop, a dining room, an outdoor swimming pool, a garden, and ample parking. 2 Calle Teso de la Feria (phone: 268700; fax: 215438; telex: 23585). Expensive.

Rector – This small, elegant, and exclusive hostelry is ideally located next to the Old Cathedral. With only 25 rooms, all air conditioned and with private baths, this place exudes a calm, intimate atmosphere. No restaurant but breakfast is served daily in the guestrooms or in the breakfast room. 8 Rector Esperabé (phone: 218482). Expensive.

Regio – Located 2½ miles (4 km) south of town, on the N501 highway heading toward Avila, its 121 rooms are centrally heated and air conditioned, with private bath. Facilities include a cafeteria, the *Lazarillo de Tormes* restaurant, an Olympic-size pool and a children's pool, 2 bars, and gardens. Carretera de Salamanca, Santa Marta (phone: 200250; fax: 200144; telex: 22895). Expensive to moderate.

Emperatriz – Housed in one of Salamanca's medieval buildings in the heart of town, its 24 newer rooms have full, private baths, whereas some of the original 38 rooms have showers only. The halls are rather dark and forbidding, but the rooms are comfortable and clean, if somewhat spartan. 44 Calle de la Compañía (phone: 219200). Moderate.

El Zaguan – This clean and pleasant 15-room hotel is located just off the Plaza Mayor. All doubles have full, private baths; singles have showers, no bathtubs. 7-9 Calle Ventura Ruiz Aguilera (phone: 214705). Moderate.

Estefania – Located in a narrow, central street (a cross street of the Rua Mayor), this pension offers 20 beds. Some doubles have complete baths, and a number of rooms have only sinks. 3 Calle Jesús (phone: 217372). Inexpensive.

EATING OUT: The traditional roast suckling pig and lamb of Castile are also the staples of Salamanca's finest restaurants. Sausages such as *farinato* and *morcilla* are local specialties, more typically served in *tapas* bars than in full-fledged eateries. Another local dish is *chanfaina,* a hearty country stew made with rice, spring lamb, chicken, and chorizo (spicy Spanish sausage). While regional wines appear on most menus, they are generally considered inferior to the better riojas. Dinner for two with wine will cost $60 to $85 in expensive restaurants, $30 to $55 in those listed as moderate, $25 or less in inexpensive ones. All telephone numbers are in the 23 city code unless otherwise indicated.

Chez Victor – The napkins here are beautifully embroidered and the bread is served warm and crisp. Owner-chef Victoriano spent 13 years perfecting his craft in France; thus, his innovative cuisine has a decidedly French accent — as well as Salamanca's only Michelin star. The fare changes with the seasons, but year-round standards include *raviolis rellenos de marisco* (ravioli stuffed with seafood), *ragú de salmón y alcachofas* (salmon and artichoke stew), and *tarta de cebolla* (savory onion tart). The ice cream and sorbets in unusual flavors are homemade and served on attractive wafers. Closed Sunday evenings, Mondays, and August. Reservations advised in June and July. American Express and Visa accepted. 26 Calle Espoz y Mina (phone: 213123). Expensive.

Nuevo Candil – The decor and menu are typically Castilian, with such dishes as *tostón* and *lechazo pierna asado* (two variations of suckling pig), *truchas del Tormes* (Tormes trout), and *sopa de rabo de buey* (oxtail soup). The restaurant is the offspring of *El Candil* (see *Tapas Bars*), a quarter of a century old and located 100 yards or so away. Closed Mondays. Reservations unnecessary. Major credit cards accepted. 1 Plaza de la Reina (phone: 219027). Expensive.

El Botón Charro – Tucked away in a narrow alley off the Plaza del Mercado, the attraction is a nouvelle twist to traditional Castilian cuisine. Closed Sundays.

Reservations unnecessary. Visa accepted. 6-8 Calle Hovohambre (phone: 216462). Expensive to moderate.

Châpeau – This stylish Castilian establishment has gained fame for its old-fashioned style of cooking in wood ovens. Specialties include stuffed red peppers, scallops baked in light pastry, and the traditional roast suckling pig. Closed Mondays and during the month of August. Reservations advised. Major credit cards accepted. 20 Calle Gran Vía (phone: 271883). Expensive to moderate.

La Posada – Located next to the Torre del Aire, its regional specialties include *alubias con codornices o con almejas* (beans with quail or clams) and assorted game in season; or try the chef's suggestions of the day. Open daily; closed for 3 weeks in August. Reservations unnecessary. No credit cards accepted. 1 Calle Aire y Azucena (phone: 217251). Moderate.

Río de la Plata – Small, charming, and usually very crowded, this eatery is a block from the Plaza Mayor. In addition to Castilian dishes, the kitchen excels at seafood. Good homemade desserts and fine wines. Closed Mondays and July. Reservations unnecessary. No credit cards accepted. 1 Plaza del Peso (phone: 219005). Moderate.

El Bardo – The clientele here consists mainly of students. The menu could best be termed "national" rather than regional, and the set meals are particularly economical. Closed Mondays and October. Reservations unnecessary. No credit cards accepted. 8 Calle de la Compañía (phone: 219089). Inexpensive.

El Dorado – Near the Plaza del Mercado, with a reputation for marvelous service and solid home-style cooking. Closed Tuesdays. Reservations unnecessary. No credit cards accepted. 3 Calle del Clavel (phone: 217212). Inexpensive.

 TAPAS BARS: A standard feature of Salamanca's social scene. Visit a few and call it a meal. Calle Prado has a string of them, including *Gran Tasca* (3 Calle Prado), *Marín* (5 Calle Prado), and *Bar Mi Vaca y Yo* (11 Calle Prado). So does Calle Ventura Ruiz Aguilera (better known to locals as *la calleja* — the alley). Outstanding here is *El Candil* (10 Calle Ventura Ruiz Aguilera). Also try *Plus-Ultra* (Calle del Concejo, off Plaza Mayor). There is often someone playing guitar in these and other *tapas* bars, and sometimes even a group of musicians from the university.

SAN SEBASTIÁN

Its cafés serve the best croissants south of the Pyrenees, it is the only city in Spain without a bullring, and it has no naughty red-light district — not even a business area. Its avenues are broad and tree-lined, its shops luxurious and chic, and its climate is more Atlantic than Mediterranean. No, this is not the Spain of the Costa del Sol, nor of clamorous cities such as Madrid, Barcelona, or even its Basque neighbor, Bilbao. And yet if you ask any traveler to name his two favorite cities in Spain, one of them is bound to be San Sebastián (probably with Seville), in the same way that most Europeans cite San Francisco and New York as the two cities they'd most like to visit in the United States.

Set around one of Europe's finest natural bays, the Bahía de la Concha (Bay of the Shell), this most elegant turn-of-the-century Belle Epoque beach resort is protected from northerly winds by two mountains that rise up on either side of the town — Mt. Urgull and Mt. Igueldo — while Santa Clara Island in the middle of the shell-shaped bay takes strength out of the breakers that crash in from the vast Bay of Biscay. The wide, curved Playa de la Concha, one of the most beautiful beaches in Spain, is topped by an exquisite promenade of ornate railings and impressive buildings, and the walkways on either side of the Urumea River are another taste of 19th-century elegance in this otherwise modern, tidy, and pretty city that has the calming effect of a small town. San Sebastián is surprisingly small (pop. 180,000) and unrushed, even in midsummer, when there isn't a spare hotel room to be had.

The first recorded mention of San Sebastián was in 1014, when a donation was made by King Sancho el Mayor to a monastery here. In 1200, the new castle on Urgull fell to King Alfonso VIII of Castile. San Sebastián joined the Sea Brotherhood with other coastal towns in 1294 and established trade relations with England and Brittany. Harbor construction began in 1450; in the Middle Ages, the city's inhabitants were well known for the whaling and cod fishing that took them as far as the Newfoundland banks. San Sebastián became a port for a much larger area than the surrounding province of Guipúzcoa, and from its wharves, oil and wine were shipped to the rest of Europe. Indeed, by the 18th century, the city had a special cacao trading deal with Caracas, Venezuela. With the growth of Bilbao along the coast, however, the city's importance as a port declined, and today its seafaring activities are limited to a little anchovy, sardine, and tuna fishing.

Just 12 miles (19 km) from the French border, San Sebastián has a definite Francophile air about it. Its affinity to the French caused it to be burned to the ground for the 12th — and so far, last — time on August 31, 1813. On that date the Duke of Wellington's combined British and Portuguese forces looted and destroyed the town as Napoleon's troops, after 5 years of occupation, fled to the border toward the end of the Peninsular War. The local residents decided to rebuild the town, and in 1814 the four cornerstones of the Plaza de la Constitución in the center of the Parte Vieja (Old Town) were laid. The Old Town, a cramped warren of narrow streets packed with bars and restaurants adjacent to the old fishing port on the city's eastern promontory, was the first part of San Sebastián to be rebuilt. Its bustling streets, bordered by the Alameda del Boulevard, the estuary of the Urumea River, Mt. Urgull, and the port, are where locals and visitors today gather every evening for the pre-dinner *poteo,* a wine or two with *tapas.*

By the 1840s, the Old Town had been rebuilt and San Sebastián was quietly reestablishing itself as the major town on the Spanish coast between France and Bilbao. But it wasn't until 1845 that the place began to take off as a vacation spot. That year, Queen Isabella II spent the summer in San Sebastián, heralding the city's role as a high class holiday resort. It soon became the summer residence of the royal court, the government, and much of the aristocracy. In 1863, a decision was made to demilitarize the town by demolishing the city walls. This allowed urban expansion to boom in the 1860s, and the first buildings in the residential and shopping districts were raised as the glorious line of promenade buildings above La Concha began taking shape. By the 1870s, San Sebastián was the summer home for many European aristocrats, in 1887 La Concha was awarded the title of royal beach, and in 1902 a municipal company was established to promote the city and build a grand hotel. By this time, San Sebastián had been a Spanish pioneer in installing a tram system, electric street lighting, and telephone service.

On July 8, 1912, Queen María Cristina opened the grand hotel named after her. The hotel became King Alfonso XIII's winter residence, and members of many European royal families spent long periods there. Completely restored during the 1980s — and at an astronomical cost — it is still reputed by many to be the best hotel in northern Spain, and with the majestic *Victoria Eugenia Theater* standing alongside it on the Paseo República Argentina, overlooking the Urumea and the sea, it forms a marvelous monument to the Belle Epoque for which San Sebastián is still renowned. This lavish period reached its zenith just after World War I as money poured into the city from some of Europe's richest families, refugees of a war-ravaged continent. By the 1950s, tourist tastes had changed. The nobility joined mere mortals farther south, where sunshine is a much surer commodity. Today, San Sebastián is packed in July and August with visitors from France, Italy, and the rest of Spain, and is especially busy during the international jazz and film festivals in July and September.

Visitors should not be surprised to find the walls of the Old Town daubed with graffiti, because San Sebastián is in the midst of Basque Country — known as the Pais Vasco to the Spanish, as Euskadi to the Basques themselves. The graffiti extols the justice of the Basque fight for self-determination and the violence of the armed separatist organization ETA, and are a clear sign of the Basque political upheaval. Over 600 people have died since democracy was restored in 1977, putting San Sebastián — known to its inhabitants by its Basque name, Donostia — on the front pages of Spanish newspapers for all the wrong reasons. The Old Town and the Alameda del Boulevard are the scenes of occasional clashes between radical separatists and riot police. The City Council is dominated by anti-Spanish Basque nationalist parties, which on paper at least makes this one of the most revolutionary cities in Europe. This blend of the elegant and the radical adds to San Sebastián's charm, and locals are keen to tell visitors that they are different from "the Spanish." ETA terrorism, when it takes place, is directed against the security forces, and tourists have nothing to fear from the political situation — unless they are caught in a police charge! In any case, street fighting is rare away from the Old Town.

The province of Guipúzcoa, one of the three provinces making up the Basque Country, is the smallest province in Spain and the Basque province that has best preserved its historic customs. The extremely complex Euskera language is spoken by at least 50% of the *donostiarras,* as the city folk are known, and by up to 90% in neighboring towns. This is crucial to the local sense of "national identity," or Basqueness, which is evident during the many fiestas held throughout the year. Traditional Basque music is played on three-holed tin whistles known as *txistus,* and on small drums. Basque folkloric dancing is animated and ceremonial. Rural sports, whose aim is to demonstrate speed and strength rather than skill, are an integral part of Basque culture; pelota, or jai alai, is well known outside the Basque region.

Less well known internationally, except to those who pay more than the usual amount of attention to gastronomy, is San Sebastián's reputation for excellent food. The city is acknowledged as the birthplace of the new Basque cooking, a culinary culture that emerged in earnest about 15 years ago. But the city's reputation as a culinary center goes back more than 100 years, when the first gastronomic societies were founded. Developed in the days when local fishermen cooked and ate on the quayside as soon as they landed with their catch, the societies then founded places with kitchens, where they could enjoy their food and company in comfort. Over the years, the societies and their style of cooking became more sophisticated, and many classic Basque dishes were born in men-only kitchens of San Sebastián where, the men say, they have more time than the housewife to pamper the food and cultivate the sauces. Most of the 1,000 societies in the Basque Country, and the best-known ones in San Sebastián's Old Town, now allow women in to dine at certain hours, but they are still *never* allowed in the kitchens.

The societies' dining rooms are for members and guests only (inquire at the tourist office about the chances of being invited), but San Sebastiían's restaurants offer some of the best food in Spain, second only to the restaurants of Madrid in terms of the total number of Michelin stars they have won. And to build up an appetite, it's hard to do better than an early evening stroll along the Paseo de la Concha above the beach and an hour of *poteo* (happy hour) in the Old Town. Even if the city's streets and avenues were not so charming, San Sebastian's natural setting, around the deep, still bay and enclosed by low undulating hills, would ensure its reputation for unusual beauty.

SAN SEBASTIÁN AT-A-GLANCE

SEEING THE CITY: San Sebastián is so small and compact that the entire city can be seen within 20 minutes of walking up Mt. Igueldo or Mt. Urgull. Contemplated from above, San Sebastián is a soothing experience. The bay and beaches could hardly be shaped more perfectly, and the relative newness of the city is evident in the way the avenues and streets are laid out in straight lines. Urgull is the lower vantage point and, therefore, the more accessible. The hill is crisscrossed by wooded and winding paths that can be joined where the Old Town meets the fishing port, or from the Paseo Nuevo, the promenade that begins beyond the aquarium and skirts the hill. Below is the tiny fishing port, brightly colored and more touristic than industrial, with its fish restaurants. Then there's the splendid La Concha, backed by 2 miles of elegant hotels and apartment blocks; no building is higher than 7 stories, giving the promenade a special aesthetic cohesion. A rocky promontory separates the Playa de la Concha from the next beach, Playa de Ondarreta, and beyond it is the higher Mt. Igueldo.

Mt. Igueldo is best ascended by car, by the bus that leaves every few minutes from the Boulevard (marked Igueldo), or by the funicular that leaves from the end of Ondarreta Beach. The hill dominates the western end of the city, and it offers wonderful views of the Basque coast toward Zarauz and Guetaria. There is an amusement park and an extremely good camping site at the top of the hill, with excellent views inland. And the view of the city is superb: the bay, Ondarreta beach and La Concha's semicircle of fine golden sand, the fishing port, the Old Town, and the central shopping and residential area, which is dominated by the Buen Pastor (Good Shepherd) Cathedral.

SPECIAL PLACES: La Concha Beach is the pearl in the San Sebastián oyster, and together with its promenade dominates the city — except at night, when the Old Town and the fishing port at La Concha's eastern end take over. South of the Old Town and La Concha is the charming shopping and residential area, bordered to the east by the Urumea River. This area (from the Alameda del Boulevard to Plaza de Guipúzcoa, on past Avenida de la Libertad to Plaza de Bilbao and the cathedral) is placid and pleasant, not much more than 100 years old. Indeed, because most of the city was built within the past 130 years — even the "Old Town" is 19th century — San Sebastián is short on historical monuments. Every single sight, monument, and museum can easily be exhausted in a day — even more reason for a calm and unhurried visit.

IN THE CITY

Playa de la Concha – This superb beach is the symbol of San Sebastián and undoubtedly the most famous stretch of sand in Spain. When the tide is out, several acres of fine sand are exposed. In the winter, soccer tournaments are held here, with several games being played simultaneously. In the summer, it is a family beach, thankfully free of hordes of radio-blasting rowdies. Meet the tide as it comes in and watch the fish swim around your legs. The promenade above the beach — Paseo de la Concha — is equally delightful, with ornate balustrades and richly ornamental lampposts reflecting the refined tastes of the Belle Epoque. It's an ideal place for leisurely strolls, with periodic pauses to gaze at the crowds on the beach below. Extending westward beyond a small rocky outlet is Ondarreta Beach, also clean and excellent, but smaller than La Concha and without its peerless shell shape. At the end of Ondarreta is *El Peine del Viento* (The Comb of the Wind), a work of modern art, by the local sculptor

Eduardo Chillida, formed by three large, pincer-shaped metal objects protruding from lumps of rock.

La Parte Vieja – The Old Town is not architecturally significant, apart from a handful of buildings that survived the burning of the city in 1813, but it is the market-place and social center of San Sebastián. Its narrow, straight streets are packed with bars, taverns, specialty shops, restaurants, and gastronomic societies. Popular among locals as well as visitors, it is virtually a "tourist trap"-free area. The arcaded Plaza de la Constitución, with the former City Hall at one end, stands in the center. Bullfights used to be held in the square, but the only remaining evidence of that are the numbered balconies where spectators once gathered. The city's two most important churches are survivors of the 1813 fire. The Gothic Church of San Vicente (Calle Narrica) is San Sebastián's oldest building, dating from 1570. Its interior is somber but impressive, with three naves, an octagonal apse, and large buttresses, all crowned with a tall presbytery that covers the altarpiece. At the other end of the Old Town is the graffiti-covered baroque Church of Santa María (Calle 31 de Agosto; phone: 423124). Completed in 1764, it has a richly ornate porch and central pillars supporting its lofty vaults. The statue of the Virgen del Coro (Virgin of the Choir), the city's patroness, is venerated at the main altar.

Museo de San Telmo – The early-16th-century building opposite the Church of San Vicente began as a Dominican monastery (1530–1830), became an artillery barracks in 1836, and was finally converted into a beautiful museum in 1932. Of greatest interest is the section dedicated to Basque ethnography, with paintings, statues, farming uten-sils, fossilized skeletons, and spinning tools to make flax, linen, and canvas. Artist José María Sert painted a series of works on the subject of Basque mythology especially for the museum; there also are three paintings by El Greco. The building's cloister is Renaissance with columns, semicircular arches, and ribbed vaults. Open in summer, Mondays through Saturdays from 9 AM to 9 PM, Sundays from 9 AM to 1 PM; in winter, Mondays through Saturdays from 9:45 AM to 1 PM and 3:30 to 7 PM, Sundays from 10 AM to 1 PM. Admission charge. Plaza de Zuluaga (phone: 424970).

City Hall – One of the most impressive Ayuntamientos (City Halls) in Spain, brim-ming with exquisite decor and marble staircases, this twin-towered building was erected as the *Gran Casino* worthy of San Sebastián's growing European status after the Second Carlist War (1876). The City Council donated 22,960 square feet of land where La Concha and the Boulevard met, facing the Old Town. The casino opened in 1887 and instantly became the center of business activity and progress in the city. Among other things, the casino financed the Alderdi-Eder Gardens, which brighten the area around City Hall with their characteristic squat tamarind trees with umbrella-shaped branches, offering protection from the frequent showers. A ban on gambling in 1924 closed the building until 1947, when the City Council moved in. City Hall is open to the public during office hours; no admission charge. Calle Ijentea.

Aquarium – Officially known as the *Oceanographical Museum* or the Palace of the Sea, the aquarium is a 3-story building that opened in 1928 where the harbor meets the foot of Mt. Urgull, near the beginning of the Paseo Nuevo. The ground floor is an aquarium with many types of marine fauna on view; the first-floor *Oceanographical Museum* boasts collections of shells, fish, seabirds, seaweed, crustacea, and coral, as well as the skeleton of the last whale to be caught in local waters, in 1878; the second floor houses the *Naval Museum*, with documents and models pertaining to the Basque Country's seafaring tradition. Open daily, from 10 AM to 1:30 PM and 3:30 to 7:30 PM (summers until 8 PM); closed Mondays from mid-September through mid-May. Admis-sion charge. Paseo Nuevo (phone: 421905).

Castle of Santa Cruz de la Mota – Around the ruins of the castle on top of Mt. Urgull are the remains of several rusting cannon left by Napoleon's troops when the Duke of Wellington stormed the town in 1813. It's hard to believe that they have been lying in their original locations for nearly 180 years, and haven't been carted off to some museum in London or Madrid. Within the castle are three modern chapels topped by a nearly 100-foot statue of Christ, visible from anywhere in the city. Mass is held on Sundays in one of the chapels. About half way up Mt. Urgull, as you climb from the *San Telmo Museum,* is the unkempt British Cemetery, containing the tombs of about 25 British troops who died in San Sebastián during the First Carlist War in the 1830s. Mt. Urgull.

Urumea River – The real delight here consists of the walks along either side of the river as it flows into the Bay of Biscay. The Urumea is spanned by three Parisian-style bridges of great charm for lovers of the Belle Epoque ornate. The 1905 Puente María Cristina, which leads from the residential area at Plaza de Bilbao to the main France–Madrid railway station, is especially flamboyant, with tiered turrets at either end. The Puente Santa Catalina, nearer to the sea, takes traffic over to the uninteresting Gros district, where there is a third San Sebastián beach (not recommended). The Puente Zurriola de Kursaal is just yards from the sea, near the *Victoria Eugenia Theater* and the *María Cristina* hotel. These buildings, erected early in this century, have both undergone lavish refurbishing in the past decade and form a stunning unity beside the bridge with its huge lampposts, especially when floodlit at night. On either side of the river, along the Paseo República Argentina or the Paseo de Francia, the 10-minute stroll offers a pleasant alternative to La Concha. The large modern sculpture dominating the outcrop between the Zurriola de Kursaal Bridge and the Gros Beach is the work of local sculptor Néstor Basterretxea; called the *Dove of Peace,* it is 23 feet high and weighs 4 tons.

Catedral Buen Pastor – San Sebastián's largest church, the 250-foot-high ogival-style Good Shepherd Cathedral was inaugurated in 1897. A neo-Gothic structure with striking exterior flying buttresses and a belfry that opens to a central nave, it stands in a large square in the modern quarter. It made headline news on the 10th anniversary of the outbreak of the Spanish Civil War (July 18, 1946), when Basque nationalist Joseba Elósegui, a senator at the time of his death in 1990, climbed to the top and raised the then-banned Basque flag. Open daily, from 7:30 AM to 12:30 PM and from 5 to 8:30 PM. Plaza del Buen Pastor (phone: 464516).

Palacio Miramar – The English-style Miramar Palace stands on a low hill overlooking La Concha and Ondarreta, with the residential district of Antiguo behind it. Funded by Queen María Cristina and opened in 1893, the palace fell into decline and was closed during the 1931–36 Republic and the 1936–39 Civil War. Purchased by the City Council in 1971, it was recently renovated but is still closed to the public. The expansive lawns, however, are open to the public from 9 AM to 9 PM in summer and from 10 AM to 5 PM in winter. No admission charge.

Palacio de Ayete – Built by the Duke of Bailen in 1878, the Ayete Palace was the summer residence of King Alfonso XII and Queen María Cristina until the Miramar Palace was constructed. Set back from the bay on the Ayete estate, amid 243,000 square feet of beautiful parkland, the palace was also the summer residence of Generalísimo Francisco Franco from 1940 until his death in 1975, and the site of his cabinet meetings every summer. The palace is closed to the public, but the lush forest trails are worth a stroll. Open summers, from 10 AM to 8:30 PM; winters, from 10 AM to 5 PM. No admission charge.

ENVIRONS

Monte Igueldo – A trip to the heart of Mt. Igueldo affords some idyllic panoramas of the dramatic coastline of the Bay of Biscay and the Guipúzcoan countryside, not to mention a chance to sample some traditional local cider, second in fame and quality only to that from Asturias. Take the steep road to the Igueldo campsite and turn right, down a narrow lane opposite the *Bar Gure-etxea.* After a mile, there is the *Bar Asador Nícolas,* a simple *sidrería* (cider house) that has stupendous views over the haystack-dotted countryside, with the sea visible beyond. A liter of the excellent local cider costs just $1.50, and the best brewing months are February through April.

Fuenterrabía – Known as Hondarribia in Euskera (the Basque language), this beautiful town lies 14½ miles (23 km) east of San Sebastián, and overlooks the French town of Hendaye, from which it is divided by the Bidasoa River. Not surprisingly, Fuenterrabía was a fortress town for centuries, and historians have lost count of the number of sieges it suffered. So many Castilian kings honored it for fighting off French attacks that the town bears an official title meaning "very noble, very loyal, very courageous, and always very faithful." (Most medieval towns were lucky to have a simple "loyal" or "noble" conferred on them.) The town's Nagusi Kalea (Main Street) is straight out of the Middle Ages, and the nearby narrow streets are flanked by Renaissance and baroque mansions with huge carved eaves and wrought-iron balconies. The town is dominated by an 11th-century fortress that was restored by the Holy Roman Emperor Charles V in the 16th century and now serves as the *Parador El Emperador* (Plaza de Armas del Castillo; phone: 642140). The only *parador* in Guipúzcoa, it has 16 rooms overlooking the French border, and is in itself an excellent reason for visiting Fuenterrabía.

■**EXTRA SPECIAL:** Stand anywhere on or near the beach from Mt. Urgull to Mt. Igueldo at 11 PM on any night during the *Aste Nagusia* (Great Week) fiestas, around August 15, for San Sebastián's renowned fireworks displays. The fiestas coincide with the *International Fireworks Competition,* when manufacturers from many countries compete for the coveted first prize. San Sebastián's fireworks week is regarded by Spaniards as the best in Europe — although Monaco and Cannes might have a different opinion. What makes San Sebastián's celebration so wonderful is the unique setting: A 40-minute display might take in Mt. Igueldo to the left, Santa Clara Island in the middle, and Mt. Urgull to the right, all marvelously floodlit. Find a spot early — after 10:30 it's usually impossible to get a good vantage point.

SOURCES AND RESOURCES

TOURIST INFORMATION: There are two very helpful tourist offices, a short walk from one another. The Centro de Atracción y Turismo (CAT), run by the City Council (on Calle Reina Regente, next door to the *Victoria Eugenia Theater;* phone: 481167). The office is open Mondays through Fridays from 9 AM to 2 PM and 3:30 to 7 PM, Saturdays from 9 AM to 2 PM. This office is responsible for the promotion of San Sebastián and Guipúzcoa only, and has excellent information on local fiestas, rural sports, and so on. At the eastern end of La Concha is the Oficina de Turismo del Gobierno Vasco (13 Calle Andia; phone: 426282), run by the Basque Autonomous Government. It is open Mondays through Fridays from 9 AM to 1:30 PM and 3:30 to 6:30 PM, Saturdays from 9 AM to 1:30 PM. Many of the English-language tourist brochures available at both locations are poorly translated, but this should not present any major problem in understanding them.

Local Coverage – The best newspapers for local news in San Sebastián are the moderate *Diario Vasco,* the radical nationalist *Egin,* and the moderate nationalist *Deia.* The best place to buy international newspapers is the kiosk in front of the Banco de Bilbao, near the La Concha end of Avenida de la Libertad.

TELEPHONE: The city code for San Sebastián is 43. If calling from within Spain, dial 943 before the local number.

GETTING AROUND: Any point in San Sebastián is easily reached on foot, except for the top of Mt. Igueldo, which can be reached by taxi or the bus marked Igueldo from the Boulevard.

Airport – San Sebastián Airport is in nearby Fuenterrabía, but it handles only domestic flights (phone: 642144). The nearest international airport is Bilbao's Sondika Airport.

Bicycle – Bicycles can be rented from *Mini* (10 Calle Escolta Real; phone: 211758), for between $5 and $10 per day.

Bus – City buses stop running at around midnight. It's best to buy a *bonobus,* a card allowing 10 trips for about $4); a single journey costs 65 pesetas (about 60¢). Several different bus companies offer service within the Basque Country and beyond. Their offices are on or around the Plaza de Pío XII. Ask for details at either of the tourist offices.

Car Rental – The major car rental companies with offices in San Sebastián are *Atesa* (2 Plaza Zaragoza; phone: 425976); *Avis* (2 Calle Triunfo; phone: 461556); *Diago* (9 Calle Aguirre Miramón; phone: 283701); *Europcar* (60 Calle San Martín; phone: 461717); and *Hertz* (2 Calle Marina; phone: 461084).

Taxi – Taxis are not plentiful. The main stands are located on the Alameda del Boulevard by Calle Mayor and at 31 Avenida de la Libertad, or call 420340.

Train – All trains from the French border crossing of Hendaye-Irún, 12 miles (19 km) away, stop at San Sebastián's Estación Norte, just over the María Cristina Bridge by the Paseo de Francia (phone: 283599), on their way to Madrid. A second station, the Estación Amara, of the narrow-gauge *FEVE* line linking San Sebastián with Bilbao, is by the Paseo de Errondo (phone: 450131). For visitors with children, a miniature tourist train called the *Txu-Txu* leaves City Hall and trundles around the Old Town and the promenade daily every half hour from 11 AM to 2 PM and 4 PM to 9 PM, with commentary in several languages.

SPECIAL EVENTS: Beyond any doubt, San Sebastián enjoys more than its fair share of riotous carnivals and fiestas, beginning with one of Spain's great undiscovered festivals, the January 19 and 20 *Tamborrada* (Festival of Drums). January 20 is *St. Sebastián's Day,* and for 24 hours beginning at midnight on the 19th, the Old Town is filled with young and old dressed as 19th-century soldiers, bakers, and chefs, all banging *tambores* (drums) to mark the annual recurrence of a tradition that began in the early 19th century — although nobody knows exactly how or why. The festivities start on the 19th, with a hearty feast in one of the gastronomic societies or restaurants, and go on to include over 40 *tamborrada* processions, but the two most important are the adults' procession at midnight on the 19th in the Plaza de la Constitución, and the children's procession — with 4,000 children — at midday on the 20th outside City Hall.

The next important event is the *International Jazz Festival,* or *Jazzaldia,* during the second half of July, conveniently following the *Fiesta de San Fermín* and the running of the bulls in nearby Pamplona. The *Aste Nagusia* (Great Week) of carnivals around August 15 involves much more than incredible nightly fireworks displays: Basque sports, processions, folkloric displays, gastronomic competitions, and even pro-independence alternative events are included. The last 2 weeks of August offer the *Classical Music Fortnight,* after which the *Basque Fiestas,* with the emphasis on the promotion of Euskera, the Basque language, begin on the first Sunday in September. Also in September, the first two Sundays, are the famous *Regatas de Traineras* (fishing-boat rowing races), which have been held on La Concha bay since 1879. Tens of thousands gather to watch and wager money on teams from every town and village along the Basque coast, and in the week between the races, to participate in Basque sports — tree chopping, rock lifting, pelota, oxen dragging rocks — as well as folkloric dancing, improvised poetry and theater performances in Euskera, basket making, and so on. The most prestigious annual event is San Sebastián's *International Film Festival,* during the second half of September, now one of the premier events of its type in Europe.

SHOPPING: San Sebastián is one of the wealthiest cities in Spain, and perhaps more important, its proximity to France gives it a certain snobbery when it comes to taste and style — not to mention price. Probably the most distinctive local feature is the Basque beret, or *txapela,* but these are going out of fashion and, in many cases, have a "country yokel" air about them. Note that San Sebastián does not have any department stores and has few supermarkets. Its two central food markets, very colorful and interesting, are *Mercado La Brecha* (at the river end of the Boulevard) and *Mercado San Martín* (on Calle Urbieta, 2 blocks from La Concha). The best shopping streets are Avenida de la Libertad, Calle San Marcial, Calle Loyola, and the square surrounding the Buen Pastor Cathedral. Shopping hours are generally from 9:30 AM to 1:30 PM and 3:30 to 8 PM. Most stores and shops are closed Sundays; some close Monday mornings as well.

Auzmendi – Very trendy clothes for men and women by the best known local designer. 28 Avenida de la Libertad (phone: 420204).

Ayestarán – Excellent handmade shoes and leather bags, at reasonable prices. 29 Avenida de la Libertad (phone: 424060).

Bárbara – Exquisite and very expensive gold jewelry sold behind an unimposing wood exterior. 23 Calle Guetaria (phone: 422680).

Casa Basarte – The best selection of genuine *txapelas* (Basque berets) in town. Also a good range of leather goods. 18 Calle San Jerónimo (phone: 426096).

Delgado – The oldest and one of the best clothing shops in San Sebastián, a family-run affair dating from 1899. Much of the material is now imported from Italy, but the conservatively styled menswear is still made on the premises. 43 Avenida de la Libertad (phone: 426625).

Elizondo – Sports shop with the latest equipment for windsurfing, surfing, sailing, skating, and basketball (including NBA badges and coaching manuals). Calle Arrasate, corner of Paseo de los Fueros (phone: 424097).

Juguetería Antón – Basically a toy shop, but with an amazing collection of Spanish jigsaw puzzles. Designs range from Goya paintings to Moorish tiles, containing up to 8,000 pieces. 21 Calle San Jerónimo (phone: 425017).

Ramón Hernández – Exclusive gentlemen's and ladies' outfitters, with expensive imported and local styles. 23 Avenida de la Libertad (phone: 426849).

Sanfor – The best leather and fur store, featuring beautiful coats, bags, and accessories. 21 Calle Hernani (phone: 421657).

SPORTS AND FITNESS: Bicycling – Cycling is an important sport in the Basque Country. In honor of this, and for the first time in its history, the *Tour de France* — the world's premier bicycle race — will begin this year's competition from San Sebastián's *Anoeta Stadium.* The race starts on July 6.

Boating – Rowing is a Basque passion, especially when the vessel is a large *trainera,* or fishing boat. The tradition dates from the days when fishermen used to row back into harbor, usually against a fierce cross wind. There are many events throughout the year, but don't miss the *Regatas de Traineras* at La Concha (see *Special Events*) on the first two Sundays in September.

Fishing – Fishing from the rocks and even surf casting are popular. The tourist offices can provide exact information.

Golf – The 18-hole course at the *Real Club de Golf de San Sebastián* is 14½ miles (23 km) east of the city in Fuenterrabía (phone: 616845). The 9-hole *Real Club de Golf de Zarauz* is 16 miles (26 km) to the west in Barrio de Mendilauta (phone: 830145).

Horse Racing – San Sebastián's racetrack (in the town of Lasarte, about 4 miles/6 km south of the city) is the only one in Spain to hold summer races. Indeed, there is only one other racetrack still in use in Spain: Madrid's winter-and-spring-only track. For more information, contact the *Sociedad Hipódromo de San Sebastián,* 2 Plaza de Zaragoza (phone: 421002).

Pelota – A pelota court is called a frontón, and there are many in the city. The most popular is the *Frontón de Anoeta,* in the excellent indoor sports complex of the same name (phone: 455917). From a spectator's point of view, the most exciting form of pelota is the very fast *cesta punta,* played with a curved wicker basket used to whip the ball off the wall at lightning speeds.

Soccer – San Sebastián's *Real Sociedad* was one of the shock teams of the 1980s in the Spanish League. After winning nothing since its formation in 1909, it won the coveted league title in 1981 and 1982, the *Spanish Cup* in 1987, and was league runner-up on two other occasions. The club plays its home games in the 28,000-seat *Atotxa Stadium,* located behind the Estación Norte.

Swimming – La Concha is obviously the first choice, for its beauty, fine sand, and safe waters. Even on rough days, Santa Clara Island tames the mightier waves, although they are often big enough for reasonable surfing. Ondarreta beach is also very good, and popular among locals. Gros Beach, the smallest, is dirty and unattractive. There are indoor pools in the La Perla building (Paseo de la Concha; phone: 461258), and at the *Piscina de Tenis Ondarreta* (Plaza de Ondarreta; phone: 218136). All indoor facilities have an admission charge.

Tennis – Courts are available for rent at the *Real Club de Tenis* (Paseo de Ondarreta; phone: 215161) just behind the beach.

 THEATER AND MUSIC: The grand *Teatro Victoria Eugenia,* with its richly decorated ceiling, dome, and spacious foyer, opened just 11 days after the neighboring *María Cristina* hotel in 1912. Home of theater, classical music, ballet, and opera in San Sebastián, as well as the *International Film Festival,* which has been held here every September since 1953, the theater (Calle Reina Regente; phone: 481160) is also the home of the *Classical Music Fortnight* in late August. July's *International Jazz Festival* is held in the pavilion at the *Anoeta Sports Complex* and the open-air Plaza de Trinidad in the Old Town. *Anoeta* is also the venue for major rock concerts, since San Sebastián, together with Madrid and Barcelona, is a "must" on the European tours of many US and British groups.

 NIGHTCLUBS AND NIGHTLIFE: A good night out in San Sebastián involves a hearty Basque meal followed by drinks in one of the numerous late-night bars in the Old Town or in one of the classier pubs in the streets close to La Concha. There are no nightclubs or shows as such, but the discotheques vary from wild and teenage to somewhat more sedate. The best known is *Discoteca Ku* (in Barrio de Igueldo, halfway toward the campsite; phone: 212051), open from midnight to dawn for the super-cool. There are three very lively discotheques along the Paseo de la Concha, virtually on the beach: *La Perla* (phone: 460439), *Bataplán* (phone: 460436), and *La Rotonda* (phone: 428095). The *Be Bop Bar* (3 Paseo de Salamanca) is a piano bar with occasional live jazz performances, not far from the *Victoria Eugenia Theater.* The city's hippest music bars are grouped on Calle San Bartolomé — the best are *Zacro* (17 San Bartolomé); *Rask* (No. 21); *Kokolo* (No. 34); *Twickenham* (No. 36); and *El Cine* (No. 23). The *Casino Gran Kursaal* (in the *Londres y de Inglaterra* hotel, but not affiliated with it) is open Mondays through Fridays, from 6 PM to 2 AM; Saturdays and Sundays, from 6 PM to 3 AM. The entrance fee is about $7.

BEST IN TOWN

CHECKING IN: By Spanish standards, San Sebastián's hotels are expensive. Although the city has probably the best hotel in northern Spain, some of the "high-quality" hotels are either slightly tatty or characterless. What saves many is their immediate proximity to the beach. Another problem is the shortage of accommodations — there are only 2,600 hotel beds in the city and only 6,000 in the whole of Guipúzcoa province. It is very difficult to find vacancies in July and August, and impossible during September's *International Film Festival.* Expect to pay $120 or more for a double room at an expensive hotel, $70 to $110 at a moderate one. All telephone numbers are in the 43 city code unless otherwise indicated.

María Cristina – The queen of Spain's North Atlantic coast, this turn-of-the-century holiday residence for European royalty and aristocracy underwent a major refurbishing in 1987, in which all its Belle Epoque glory was restored. The 139 rooms and public areas are graced with exquisite upholstery, gold-plated metalwork, inlaid Cuban mahogany, Ceylon rosewood marquetry, and Pakistani onyx baths, plus a wonderful location overlooking the Urumea River estuary and the Bay of Biscay. The place is filled with actors and film directors during the *International Film Festival,* held next door at the *Victoria Eugenia Theater.* Its *Restaurante Easo* is excellent, and there are afternoon tea concerts. Paseo República Argentina (phone: 424900; fax: 423914). Very expensive.

Costa Vasca – A good uphill walk away from Ondarreta Beach, this establishment has 203 modern rooms and ranks as San Sebastián's largest property. It does have some style, however, and the service is very good. There is also an attractive restaurant. 15 Avenida Pío Baroja (phone: 211011; fax: 212428). Expensive.

Londres y de Inglaterra – Still glorious despite its slightly faded elegance, this dignified survivor of the 19th century lies in the coveted central section of the Paseo de la Concha, overlooking the beach. It offers unbeatable views of Mt. Urgull and Mt. Igueldo, not to mention the bay. In addition to 135 rooms, there's a restaurant, and the street-level glass-fronted *Swing Bar* — a great place to sip a drink and watch the world stroll by — is a definite bonus. The *Casino Gran Kursaal,* though not affiliated with the hotel, is also located here. 2 Calle Zubieta (phone: 426989; fax: 420031). Expensive.

San Sebastián – Located on the main road to Bilbao and Madrid, so expect plenty of noise if your room faces the road. With 92 rooms from which to choose, however, it shouldn't be too difficult to avoid this problem. Close to Ondarreta Beach. 20 Avenida de Zumalacárregui (phone: 214400; fax: 217299). Expensive.

Monte Igueldo – A car is essential, because this 125-room hostelry is a good drive up Mt. Igueldo. Its rooms offer wonderful views; unfortunately, the atmosphere is less festive than at other hotels in the city. Mt. Igueldo (phone: 210211; fax: 215028). Expensive to moderate.

Codina – Brash and characterless from the outside, the 77 rooms are surprisingly quite pleasant. Close to the *San Sebastián,* with which it shares the traffic noise problem and the proximity to Ondarreta beach. 21 Avenida de Zumalacárregui (phone: 212200; fax: 212523). Moderate.

Europa – A charming 19th-century building converted into a hotel, it's just 60 yards from La Concha. Some of the 60 rooms have large balconies facing the beach. 52 Calle San Martín (phone: 470880; fax: 471730). Moderate.

Niza – Located on the La Concha promenade, its obvious strong point is the view of the bay. This is a pleasant, informal place, with 41 comfortable rooms and a good restaurant. 56 Calle Zubieta (phone: 426663; fax: 426663). Moderate.

EATING OUT: In broad terms, the gastronomic pleasures of San Sebastián can be divided into traditional Basque fare and the more modern Basque cooking, which began in earnest in the mid-1970s and is prepared by chefs who are heirs to a unique tradition that owes much to the city's proximity of France. The Basque Country is still fairly agricultural, with rich soil split into small holdings — a true market economy where fresh produce is available every day (including several kinds of vegetables that can't be grown farther north in Europe). Fresh seafood is available every day, too, and in San Sebastián itself, seafood reigns supreme. Among the delicacies peculiar to the area are *kokotxas,* gelatinous hake gills, which until fairly recently were considered waste by local fishermen and were cut from the fish and thrown back into the sea. But apart from having a particular taste and texture now praised by locals, they are perfect for the slow, patient cultivation of the thick sauces essential to much of Basque cooking. *Kokotxas* are rarely eaten by themselves; a good combination is *merluza con kokotxas y almejas* — hake, hake gills, and clams in a lemon, oil, and parsley sauce. Another Basque favorite is *angulas,* tiny silvery elvers, or young eels, a must on special occasions. Most restaurants serve *cogote de merluza,* baked hake head. Another local specialty is *txangurro,* spider crab baked in its own shell. Dinner for two, including wine, will cost upwards of $75 in an expensive restaurant, between $45 and $70 in a moderate restaurant, and below $40 in an inexpensive one. All telephone numbers are in the 43 city code unless otherwise indicated.

Akelarre – Owner-chef Pedro Subijana, a winner of the National Gastronomy Prize, is a legend of culinary creation whose cooking, blending the traditional with the new, has earned this place two Michelin stars. The restaurant is picturesquely situated on the slopes of Mt. Igueldo, in a splendid building offering memorable views. Try *morcilla envuelta en hoja de berza sobre puré de alubias rojas* (black pudding wrapped in cabbage leaf on a red bean purée). A long-standing favorite here has been *lubina a la pimienta verde* (sea bass with green pepper). Salmon is served in many excellent combinations, and the unparalleled selection of home-made pastries is also renowned. Closed Sunday nights, Mondays, and October. Reservations necessary well in advance. Major credit cards accepted. Barrio de Igueldo (phone: 212052). Expensive.

Arzak – Juan Mari Arzak, who can boast three Michelin stars (a rarity outside of France), is in his own league at the top. Arzak led the new Basque cuisine revolution in 1976 and has created one of Spain's finest restaurants in the large house where he was born, just outside San Sebastián on the road to France. His best known creation is *krabarroka* (scorpion fish pâté). Try *consumé de buey con cigalas y caviar a los aromas a perifollo y estragón* (ox consommé with Norway lobster and caviar in a chervil and tarragon sauce). Closed Sunday nights, Mondays, 2 weeks in June, and November. Reservations necessary well in advance. Major credit cards accepted. 21 Calle Alto de Miracruz (phone: 285593). Expensive.

Casa Nicolasa – The most conservative and serious of San Sebastián's restaurants, reflected in the austere elegance of the decor. But the traditional food is excellent, prepared by master chef José Juan Castillo and served by his wife, Ana María. Situated on the edge of the Old Town by the *Mercado La Brecha,* it is a haven of time-honored dishes where Basque raw materials dominate. Closed Sundays and Monday nights (except in August and September). Reservations necessary. Major credit cards accepted. 4 Calle Aldamar (phone: 421762). Expensive.

Panier Fleuri – Classic cuisine with a French Basque taste, in the hands of the third generation of the Fombedilla family, now led by Tatús, a marvelous woman who has won the National Gastronomy Prize and who takes enormous care to see that her food has an exquisite aroma. Try *becada asada* (roast woodcock). The wine cellar is legendary, with many rare and vintage samples. Closed Sunday nights, Wednesdays, the first 2 weeks in June, and *Christmas.* Reservations necessary. Major credit cards accepted. 1 Paseo de Salamanca (phone: 424205). Expensive.

Patxiku Kintana – Patxiku was a champion pelota player, and emblems of the sport are used to enliven an otherwise stark decor. He is a huge cheery Basque, and this place in the heart of the Old Town often rocks with his laughter. His mother, Maritxu, and wife, Pepita Echevarría, help "Patxi" elaborate a traditional menu with many innovations. Try *vieiras con salsa de algas al armagnac* (scallops with seaweed and brandy sauce). Closed Tuesday nights, Wednesdays (except in August), *Christmas,* and *Easter.* Reservations advised. Major credit cards accepted. 22 Calle San Jerónimo (phone: 426399). Expensive.

Juanito Kojua – Thick, wooden beams help create a homey, warm atmosphere in this delightful Old Town establishment, and the waitresses provide discreet, efficient service. The food is traditional, unpretentious, and very well prepared, especially the fish. Try *cola de merluza rellena de txangurro* (hake tail stuffed with spicy spider crab). Closed Sunday nights. Reservations advised. Visa accepted. 14 Calle Puerto (phone: 420180). Moderate.

Rekondo – The grilled fish and meat here are works of art created by Txomin Rekondo, former bullfighter-turned-restaurateur. The wine cellar, into which diners are welcome (and encouraged to visit), is the largest of any restaurant in Spain — boasting over 200,000 bottles. Try *mendreska de bonito* (grilled tuna steak) and *revuelto de anchoas con espinacas y chalotes* (anchovies, spinach, and shallots scrambled with eggs). There is a wonderful open-air dining patio — but watch out for giant crickets and other flying insects in the summer! Closed Wednesdays (except in July and August) and November. Reservations advised. Major credit cards accepted. Paseo de Igueldo (phone: 212907). Moderate.

Urepel – Don't be put off by the drab exterior. Inside, a friendly atmosphere awaits, where only the freshest food from that day's market is available. Chef Tomás Almandoz has created an impeccable menu of traditional Basque food, as well as novelties from across the border, such as *escalopines de oca* (goose filets). In fact, there is usually goose or duck on the menu, which is unusual in San Sebastián. Closed Sundays, Tuesday nights, July, *Christmas,* and *Easter.* Reservations necessary. American Express, Diners Club, and Visa accepted. 3 Paseo de Salamanca (phone: 424040). Moderate.

Alotza – An intimate family atmosphere awaits diners in this Old Town bar-restaurant, where the food is on a par with many more highly rated establishments. The *pimientos rellenos de txangurro* (peppers stuffed with spider crab) and *cola de merluza a la donostiarra* (hake tail in rich green sauce) are delicious. Closed Mondays. Reservations unnecessary. No credit cards accepted. 7 Calle Fermín Calbetón (phone: 420782). Inexpensive.

Basarri – Noisy and crowded, it is one of the many no-nonsense, value-for-money establishments in the Old Town. Join a table of singing Basques enjoying *merluza* *a la koskera* (baked hake). Closed Mondays. No reservations. No credit cards accepted. 17 Calle Fermín Calbetón (phone: 425853). Inexpensive.

Morgan Jatetxea – A very informal Old Town eating spot, it has a canteen atmosphere with long tables. This is a young people's hangout, but the food is good. Try *hojaldre de puerros con bacon* (puff pastry with leeks and bacon) and the selection of fine homemade pastries. Reservations unnecessary. No credit cards accepted. 7 Calle Narrica (phone: 424661). Inexpensive.

TAPAS BARS: The best of San Sebastián's *tapas* bars include *La Espiga* (43 Calle San Marcial; phone: 290307); *Negresco* (5 Calle Zubieta; phone: 460968); *La Cepa* (7 Calle 31 de Agosto; phone: 426394); *Ganbara* (21 Calle San Jerónimo; phone: 422575); *Astelena* (1 Calle Iñigo; phone: 426275); and *Haizea* (8 Calle Aldamar; phone: 425710).

SANTIAGO DE COMPOSTELA

During the Middle Ages, it is estimated that anywhere from 500,000 to 2,000,000 visitors a year poured into this city in northwestern Spain. They arrived from all over Europe — from as far away as Scandinavia and Britain, from Italy, Germany, and France. Many who came were guided en route by what is considered to be the world's first guidebook, written in 1130 by a French monk. Though they may have set out alone, they eventually became duos, trios, bands, and masses traveling together across the continent, and the exposure to other cultures fostered by this movement of peoples eventually had enormous influence on medieval thought, art, and architecture. But what prompted so many to leave home and hearth and face months — even years — of every hardship from bad water to brigands, was intensely personal — a miracle in this life, the prospect of removing half an eternity from their stay in purgatory, glory thereafter.

Santiago became an object of pilgrimage because of its possession of the remains of St. James (Santiago in Spanish), one of the 12 Christian apostles. As its fame grew throughout the Middle Ages, it became, along with Jerusalem and Rome, one of Christendom's three holiest cities. Yet the founding of this city in the heart of green Galicia, far removed from the crossroads of the continent, and its rise to prominence among the Catholic faithful are based on legend, or at least circumstantial evidence. James, also known as James the Great, son of Zebedee, martyred by Herod in Judaea in AD 44, had allegedly visited northern Spain to proselytize. Though his remains were said to have been returned to Spain by his followers, the location of the grave was unknown until 813, when it was discovered by a peasant who had been led to the spot by a bright shining star — the name Compostela refers to a field (*campo*) of stars (*estrellas*). To house the remains, a church was erected over the site by Alfonso II of Asturias, and it was later replaced by a second church built by Alfonso III (which was burned down by the Moors in the 10th century), and by the third and present church, begun in the 11th century.

The discovery of the relics of St. James served as a unifying force for all European Christians, and in particular for Christians in northern Spain, who, thus inspired, redoubled their efforts to throw out the Moors. Stories of the Reconquest are filled with accounts of Christian knights who claimed they were spurred on to victory by visions of St. James, leading them on horseback, striking down the infidel hoards with a sweep of his lightning-fast sword. St. James began to be referred to as Matamoros, the Slayer of Moors. Scholars may argue vociferously about whether or not James ever went to Spain in the first place, but even if he had never been there in reality, the belief in his presence had a tremendous influence on Spanish history. With the discovery of the tomb, Christian Spain found its patron saint.

The famous Way of St. James (Camino de Santiago), the pilgrims' route to Santiago, is one of the world's oldest tour routes, marked by the churches, monasteries, hospitals, and hospices (the latter the hotels of the day) set up to accommodate them as they moved toward their destination. (For further details of the history of St. James and the pilgrimages, see *Pilgrims' Route,* DIRECTIONS.) The route remained heavily traveled until the 16th century, when, in 1589, Sir Francis Drake attacked La Coruña, and the Bishop of Santiago de Compostela removed the relics from the church for safekeeping, as a result of which they disappeared for 3 centuries. This effectively put an end to pilgrimages until the relics were found again in 1879 and the pilgrimages resumed. Today, pilgrims and the city still do the saint honor, and in *Jubilee* years — years when his holy day (July 25) falls on a Sunday (the next one is in 1993) — the celebrations are especially intense.

Santiago's center of attraction is its cathedral, begun in the 11th century, but not finished until the 13th century. It can be seen from plazas on all sides, the largest of which is the Plaza del Obradoiro, or the Plaza de España. The magnificent Obradoiro façade, an 18th-century creation of Fernando Casas y Novoa, is richly ornate, sculpted in a blend of straight and curved lines characteristic of the baroque style. Also wonderful to behold are the 12th-century Romanesque Gate of Glory, the Romanesque Goldsmith's Door, and the 17th-century Puerta Santa, or Holy Door, which is open only in *Jubilee* years. Beyond the cathedral, the city's narrow streets and dozens of other, smaller churches, monasteries, and convents, as well as bars, shops, and old merchant houses, are appealing. There is a mystical feel to the place, church bells constantly chiming.

But Santiago also is the site of one of Spain's earliest and most important universities, which means that it has something of the flavor of a modern, earthy university town, with tiny pubs, Celtic music, and nonstop conversations on the affairs of the world. Most of the 30,000-odd students live in the new districts of Santiago, however, districts that surround the Old Town but are well separated from it by broad avenues. Thus, in many ways, it seems that life in the Galician capital (pop. 106,000) hasn't changed at all. The feeling of a lived-in museum is heightened when its inhabitants empty into the streets to discuss the ramifications of life, using Gallego, the local dialect, which closely resembles Portuguese and is spoken interchangeably with Spanish. Though still remote, Santiago is as much a focus of tourism as ever, even if today's pilgrims come as much to see the sights as to see their souls.

SANTIAGO AT-A-GLANCE

SEEING THE CITY: There are two favorite vantage points from which to view Santiago. The walkway along the Coto de Santa Susana, a hill that rises across from the cathedral, offers a wonderful panoramic view. For an evocative look at the city from the midst of its clustered buildings, the choice is the balcony off the cathedral cloister, which looks out over the roofs of the town and down the bustling Calle del Franco.

SPECIAL PLACES: The main commercial streets — Calle del Franco, Rúa del Villar, and Rúa Nueva — radiate from the right front of the cathedral and are exquisite examples of medieval thoroughfares, lined with opulent houses with elegantly sculpted façades and intricate ironwork. Behind the cathedral are the historic streets that for centuries led pilgrims — many of them on their knees — into Santiago at the completion of their long journey. Also behind the cathedral is the bustling town marketplace, packed with fish, meat, fruit, and vegetable stands, open every morning except Sundays.

Cathedral – The goal of one of the world's primary pilgrimages, the cathedral was built on the site of a Roman graveyard and the foundations of Alfonso II's 9th-century basilica housing the remains of St. James. All but St. James's tomb were destroyed by Al-Mansur, the Moorish leader, in 997. The present structure was begun around 1075, and was largely completed in the 13th century. The relics of St. James, the object of devotion of centuries of pilgrims, are buried under the high altar.

The cathedral is basically a baroque shell around a Romanesque interior. The Obradoiro façade, the cathedral's western front, faces the Plaza del Obradoiro (Square of Goldwork; also called the Plaza de España) and is considered among the most beautiful cathedral façades in Christendom. Towering above a broad flight of steps (completed in 1606), the Obradoiro façade was designed by Fernando Casas y Novoa and completed in 1750; it is a baroque masterpiece of decorative flourishes and merging curves and lines. The two bell towers, Torre de la Carraca and Torre de las Campanas, were completed in the 17th and 18th centuries, respectively.

The Puerta de las Platerías, facing south onto Plaza de las Platerías, is the cathedral's famous Goldsmith's Door, 12th-century Romanesque. The Puerta Santa, or Holy Door (also known as the Puerta del Perdón, or Pardon Door), because it is open only in *Jubilee* years, faces east onto Plaza de la Quintana, and dates from 1611; the 17th-century Torre del Reloj flanks it. The north façade, facing Plaza de la Azabachería (or Plaza Inmaculada), contains the Puerta de la Azabachería, rebuilt by Ventura Rodríguez in 1765–70.

Illuminated only by candles and occasional shafts of sunlight, the cathedral's interior is a magnificent world of Romanesque opulence and hushed reverence. Just inside the Obradoiro entrance is the Pórtico de la Gloria (Gate of Glory), essentially an older, Romanesque façade within the baroque one, carved by the renowned sculptor Master Mateo between 1168 and 1188. An unsurpassed sculptural masterpiece of the original Romanesque cathedral, the Gate of Glory has three arched doorways, one each for the main nave and side aisles, and more than 200 carved figures. Its overall harmony is magical, yet it also demands careful examination. The central column of the main doorway, carved as a Tree of Jesse, rises to a figure of the seated St. James. It is customary for pilgrims to touch the marble pillar upon their safe arrival, and after centuries, smooth holes in the form of the hand's five fingers have been worn into the marble. At the base of the pillar, kneeling and facing the high altar, is a sculpted self-portrait of Master Mateo. Many pilgrims tap their head against his, hoping to receive some of his genius. Above, on the central arch, are the 24 old men of the Apocalypse surrounding Christ; they hold instruments, one of which (the central one) is a Galician *zanfona,* found only in Celtic regions of the world. The left arch bears a grouping of statues depicting the imprisoned ten tribes of Israel, and Adam and Eve on either side of Christ. On the right arch is the Last Judgment. Angels protect the "blessed" on the left side of the arch, while the "damned" are devoured by devils to the right. Note the local flavor — one of the "damned" is eating an *empanada* (Galician flat pie with meat or fish filling), while another squeezes a drink from a wineskin, symbolizing gluttony.

The remaining focus of the interior is the high altar, a dazzling creation in silver and gold backed by another statue of St. James. The altar is built atop the crypt of St. James, and the faithful can climb down the stairs to pay their respects. Many pilgrims also climb up behind the altar to embrace the statue and kiss the saint's mantle. The cathedral museum, divided into three sections, contains the usual ecclesiastic paraphernalia, in addition to a collection of tapestries showing everyday life in the Middle Ages, archaeological artifacts, and the *botafumeiro* (giant incense burner), which is swung like a bell through the transept during the most important services and celebrations. The portico off the museum offers excellent views of the town and of the Plaza del Obradoiro. The cathedral is open daily from 8 AM to 8 PM; museum hours are 10 AM to 1:30 PM and 3:30 to 7:30 PM. Admission charge to the museum. Plaza del Obradoiro.

Hostal de los Reyes Católicos – This magnificently decorated 15th-century former royal hospital and pilgrims' *hostal,* located in the Plaza del Obradoiro next to the cathedral, is now one of Spain's most memorable hotels (see *Checking In*). Designed by Enrique de Egas, a favorite architect of King Ferdinand and Queen Isabella, the building so captured the interest of the Catholic Monarchs that they personally made decisions about its interior details, such as where to install fireplaces and what wood to select for the floors. Completed in the 17th century, its highlights include an exquisite Plateresque entrance and four 16th- and 18th-century cloistered courtyards with lovely fountains. Also notice the central chapel's wrought-iron designs and beamed ceilings. The complex can be toured with a personal guide; it's also normally included as part of wider group tours of Santiago. Admission charge. Plaza del Obradoiro (phone: 582200).

Monasterio de San Pelayo de Ante-Altares – A colossal monastery located directly behind (east of) the cathedral. Originally founded by Alfonso II, the present structure dates back to the late 17th century and contains a small church with a baroque altarpiece flanked by altars bearing the story of the life of the Virgin Mary. There is also a small museum. Open from 10 AM to 1 PM and 4 to 6:30 PM. Admission charge to the museum. Vía Sacra.

Casa de la Parra – Next to San Pelayo and named for a bunch of grapes, this 17th-century baroque mansion is now an art gallery, featuring exhibitions of contemporary works in revolving 25-day displays. Exhibits include paintings, ceramics, sculpture, and videos, sometimes in combination. Open from noon to 2 PM and 7 to 9:30 PM; closed Sundays. No admission charge. Vía Sacra.

Monasterio de San Martiño Pinario – Originally dating from 912, this multi-styled monastery features three majestic 17th- and 18th-century cloisters and a church with a wide central nave and an ornate baroque altarpiece by Casas y Novoa. The supporting altarpieces are as ornate as the main altar, behind which are some of the most beautiful choir stalls imaginable, carved with scenes from the birth, life, and death of Christ, as well as the death of the Virgin Mary and her assumption into heaven. Until 1993, it will house a major exhibition of Galician arts from prehistoric times to the present day with sculptures, jewelry, and artwork collected from houses and museums throughout Galicia. Open daily, from 10 AM to 1 PM and 4 to 7 PM. Admission charge. Plaza Inmaculada, with the church opening onto Plaza San Martiño.

Santa María la Real del Sar – This 12th-century Romanesque collegiate church appears odd in that it is not large, yet has giant 18th-century flying buttresses supporting its walls. The need for them becomes apparent inside. It seems the church was built on soft, sandy soil, and the columns began to slip as the weight of the ceiling bore down over the years. From an interior perspective, they appear to be falling outward — thus the buttresses to keep the church stable. About half a mile (1 km) south of the Old Town. Open from 10 AM to 1 PM and 4 to 6 PM. Admission charge. Calle de Castrón d'Ouro.

SOURCES AND RESOURCES

TOURIST INFORMATION: Santiago's Oficina de Turismo (43 Rúa del Villar; phone: 584081) can provide general information and an excellent glossy brochure on the city that includes a detailed map. During the annual *Feast of St. James,* the tourist office also distributes a guide to events. Open weekdays, from 10 AM to 2 PM and 4 to 7 PM; Saturdays, from 9 AM to 2 PM.

Local Coverage – The local newspaper is *El Correo Gallego,* a daily publication written in Spanish with the occasional article in the Galician dialect.

TELEPHONE: The city code for Santiago is 81 If calling from within Spain, dial 981 before the local number.

GETTING AROUND: Santiago is very concentrated. Most pubs, restaurants, and shops are within a relatively small, walkable area.

Airport – The Santiago airport is in Labacolla, 7 miles (11 km) east of the city via the C547 highway. Buses to Santiago leave the airport eight times a day, coinciding with flight schedules. Buses to the airport leave from the entrance of the *Iberia* office (25 Calle Calvo Sotelo) in the new part of town. To reserve bus tickets, call *Iberia*'s airport office (phone: 597550), or stop in at the ticket office at the above address. (For additional airport information call 574200 or 572024; for *Iberia* reservations, call 574200.)

Bus – Santiago's city bus routes connect various points of the Old Town, but there is little cause to use them, as the town is so compact. The fare is about 65¢. The central bus station is located on Calle San Cayetano (phone: 587700). There is frequent daily service to Madrid, Barcelona, La Coruña, Vigo, Pontevedra, and San Sebastián.

Car Rental – Rental companies include *Hertz* (145 Avenida de Lugo; phone: 583466; and at the airport; phone: 598893), *Avis* (10 Calle República de El Salvador; phone: 561444), and *Budget/Autour* (in 3 Calle General Pardiñas; phone: 586496).

Taxi – Call one of the city cabstands for a taxi (your hotel will know the nearest one). There are two main, midtown taxi stands (Avenida de Figueroa; phone: 585973; and Avenida General Franco; phone: 561020). Late-night service is available from the Plaza Galicia stand (phone: 561028).

Train – The Santiago train station (phone: 596050) is about a 10-minute walk down Avenida General Franco from the Old Town — or take the No. 14 bus. There is frequent, daily train service to Madrid, La Coruña, San Sebastián, Irún, Pontevedra, Vigo, and Porto, Portugal.

SPECIAL EVENTS: Santiago's major annual celebration is the *Fiesta del Apóstol* (Feast of the Apostle, or Feast of St. James), which takes place on July 25. The actual festivities are played out between July 15 and month's end, with the main events occurring from July 23 through July 26. Galician folkloric shows, competitions, special theater presentations, daily concerts, and a jazz festival consisting of performances by major international groups in the Plaza del Toral are among the attractions. A spectacular fireworks display is held in front of the cathedral on the eve of the feast day (July 24), and the day itself is marked by a high mass in the morning, street bands, special theater, and an orchestral presentation in the Plaza del Obradoiro. The swinging of the *botafumeiro* (giant incense burner) across the cathedral transepts during the mass on July 25 is televised live throughout Spain. During *Jubilee* years, established by papal bull in the 12th century, the St. James celebrations are particularly intense, the cathedral's Puerta Santa is open, and pilgrims who visit the shrine receive special grace. These days occur when July 25 falls on a Sunday, which happens in a sequence of every 6, 5, 6, and 11 years. The next *Jubilee* year will be 1993.

MUSEUMS: Besides the attractions listed in *Special Places,* Santiago boasts a number of other churches, monasteries, and religious buildings, some housing small museums. Two worth visiting are the *Museo de Povo Gallego* and the *Museo Municipal,* both set up in the Convento de Santo Domingo and containing various ethnographic illustrations of rural Galician life. Open Mondays through Saturdays, from 10 AM to 1 PM and 4 to 7 PM. Admission charge. Calle de Santo Domingo (phone: 583620).

SHOPPING: Santiago's main shopping district is located in the New Town on Calles General Pardiñas, República de El Salvador, Alfredo Brañas, and Montero Rios. The Old Town's most popular street for shopping is Calle Caldereria, which runs parallel to Rúa Nueva. A wide variety of street vendors operate along Rúa Nueva, and there is a weekly Sunday market at Plaza de Abastos, next to the Convent of San Agustín. Many shops are worth browsing. General shopping hours are Mondays through Fridays from 9:30 AM to 1:30 PM and 4:30 to 7 PM, Saturdays from 9:30 AM to 2 PM, but may vary from shop to shop.

Antigüedades Sajonia – Featuring antiques, glassware, jewelry, and fine furniture. 22 Calle Gelmírez (phone: 582830).

Confitería Mora – One of the best-known pastry shops in town, a good place to buy a *tarta de Santiago.* Rúa del Villar (phone: 581014).

Fernando Mayer – Very good old European prints and paintings. 6 Plaza de las Platerías (phone: 582536).

Retablo – Fine antiques and artworks. 1 Plaza de la Quintana (phone: 582526).

Sargadelos – One of the best places for Galicia's unique Sargadelos ceramics. Rúa Nueva (phone: 581905).

Tenda – Another shop specializing in fine antiques, ceramics, and jewelry. 23 Calle Gelmírez (phone: 582520).

Xanela – Creative local souvenirs, including tiny, hand-carved cathedrals, ceramic dolls, and religious medallions. 14 Rúa Nueva (phone: 584171)

SPORTS AND FITNESS: Golf – The private, 9-hole *Real Aero Club* golf course is located near the airport. Non-members and visitors are permitted to play on a space-available basis. Call in advance for information (phone: 592400).

Swimming – A public pool is available in the *Santa Isabel Sports Complex* (just south of the Old Town; phone: 581209). There is also a public swimming pool at the university (phone: 584216). Both facilities charge a small admission fee.

Tennis – The university has tennis courts (phone: 584795). Call well in advance for information on availability and to book court time.

THEATER AND MUSIC: There are no regularly scheduled theater or musical seasons in Santiago, but frequent cultural events are held at the *Auditorium of Galicia,* whose full name is the *Palacio de la Opera, Exposiciones y Congresos.* Like most Spanish university towns, there is a student *tuna* group, which performs in Plaza del Obradoiro and surrounding squares. Members of the *tuna* wear student capes, and when they are not serenading a woman, their songs tend to be indelicate.

NIGHTCLUBS AND NIGHTLIFE: Santiago is packed with pubs, bars, and discotheques. A night on the town might consist of *tapas* (see *Eating Out* and *Tapas Bars*) from 6 PM to 8 PM, dinner from 9 PM to midnight, and a combination of pubs and discos from 11 PM to 3 AM. Among the popular pubs in the Old Town, mostly found around the walls of the San Pelayo monastery, are *O'Galo d'Ouro* (14 Calle de Conga), which provides a cozy atmosphere in a series of small rooms built into medieval horse stables, and *Modus Vivendi* (1 Plaza de Feixoo), small and also occupying old stables; in the far back room an ancient watering trough is used as a table and the ribbed horse ramp still leads customers down to lower levels. A small pub with no advertised name at 22 Calle de San Pelayo de Antes-Altares is also worth testing. Farther around the monastery, at *Paradiso Perdito* (3 Calle San Pelayo), customers walk down a stairway where thousands of students have carved their names. *La Casa de las Crechas* (3 Vía Sacra) is a Celtic music pub where the bartenders and waitresses speak only Gallego — at any moment both the upstairs and downstairs rooms may be filled with the sound of impromptu musicians playing a reel or two on fiddle, tin whistle, and guitar. Popular discotheques include *Discoteca Araguaney* (at the *Araguaney* hotel, 5 Calle Alfredo Brañas; phone: 595900); *Discoteca Kilate* (Calle Santiago de Guayaquil); and *Discoteca Black* (in the *Peregrino* hotel, Avenida Rosalía de Castro; phone: 591850).

BEST IN TOWN

CHECKING IN: As the destination of Christianity's third most important pilgrimage and a major university town, Santiago boasts hundreds of places to stay, ranging from luxurious hotels to tiny pilgrim's *hostals,* although the options shrink when only those with private bathrooms and locations within walking distance of the monumental area of town are considered. A double room will cost $110 or more in a hotel listed as expensive, from $65 to $100 in a moderate one, and $55 or less in an inexpensive one. Since the summer weather is generally mild, air conditioned rooms are relatively nonexistent. All telephone numbers are in the 81 city code unless otherwise indicated.

Araguaney – A modern, luxurious, 62-room hotel in the heart of the New Town. It's a popular choice of visiting businesspeople, with a heated swimming pool and a discotheque, but its plain structure doesn't make any particular architectural statement. 5 Calle Alfredo Brañas (phone: 595900; fax: 590287). Expensive.

Parador Los Reyes Católicos – One of Spain's great *paradores,* its architecture alone helps to place it among Europe's finest properties. The building itself is a tourist attraction (see *Special Places*), with 136 elegant rooms surrounding four splendid Renaissance courtyards. The *Peregrinos* restaurant is magnificent, although the international cuisine doesn't match the splendid setting. The location is excellent, with the front door opening right onto Plaza del Obradoiro, adjacent to the cathedral. 1 Plaza del Obradoiro (phone: 582200; fax: 563094). Expensive.

Compostela – Another old establishment in a great location, just across the street from one of the main entrances into the Old Town. The 99 rooms have all the amenities (telephones, color TV sets, room service), although the hotel could use some sprucing up and a bit of brightness. 1 Avenida General Franco (phone: 585700 or 563269). Moderate.

Gelmírez – Located between the railway station and the Old Town, it's a clean, modern, soulless creation, the second-largest (138 rooms) in town after the *Peregrino.* Service must be extracted from the staff. 92 Avenida General Franco (phone: 561100; fax: 563269). Moderate.

Peregrino – A rather nondescript modern hotel, some distance from the center of town, it has 148 plain rooms and a restaurant. But it does have two major advantages: good, quick service and an excellent, large pool. Avenida Rosalía de Castro (phone: 521850 or 521777). Moderate.

Rey Fernando – A pleasant, modern place close to the train station, with a charming staff and a comfortable TV lounge. The 24 rooms are bright and functional, and the surrounding streets are lively during the school year, without being noisy. 30 Calle Fernando III El Santo (phone: 593550). Moderate.

Windsor – Santiago's most popular *hostal,* this pleasant establishment remains full almost year-round, so book well in advance. The 50 rooms are spotless, the lobby glistening, and service is always rendered with a smile. 16 Calle República de El Salvador (phone: 592939). Moderate.

Mapoula – Another *hostal* in the Old Town, a few steps from the Plaza Galicia. The 10 rooms are all nicely furnished and have private baths; the proprietor takes a personal interest in her guests. 10 Calle Entremurallas (phone: 580124). Inexpensive.

Universal – At the top of Santiago's inexpensive list, in an excellent location across the street from the Old Town, and across the square from the *Compostela* hotel, it has direct-dial phones, beds, showers, breakfasts, and low-priced laundry service. There are 54 rooms. 2 Plaza Galicia (phone: 585800). Inexpensive.

EATING OUT: Galician cooking manifests the region's Celtic influences and its proximity to the sea. One specialty is the *empanada,* a flat potpie filled with anything from salami and mushrooms to squid and octopus or rabbit with hot peppers. Another favorite is *pulpo* (octopus), which might be served simply, with potatoes and onions, or chopped up, salted, and topped with a tangy pepper sauce to be enjoyed with beer or wine as a *tapa.* Still another specialty is *caldo gallego,* a hearty vegetable soup made with beef or ham broth. Shellfish is prepared in many styles with a variety of sauces. Fish is generally baked, broiled, or sautéed, and then combined with potatoes, onions, peppers, and asparagus. Dinner for two with wine will cost $65 or more in restaurants listed as expensive, $35 to $55 in moderate restaurants, and $30 or less in inexpensive ones. With its large student population, Santiago can be one of the least expensive places to eat in Spain. Many restaurants regularly offer inexpensive student lunch and dinner specials, consisting of an appetizer, entrée, fruit, bread, and wine, all in generous portions. Another inexpensive way to dine is to find a restaurant serving *platos combinados* — prearranged groupings of appetizers and entrées, such as salad, pork with peppers, and potato croquettes, or soup, veal, or steaks with potatoes — which cost $5 to $7 per plate. All telephone numbers are in the 81 city code unless otherwise indicated.

Anexo Vilas – Under the same management as *Vilas* (see below), serving similarly superb Galician dishes — the food here may even be a touch better. The menu is virtually identical to that of its sister restaurant, so expect to savor some of the best cooking northwestern Spain has to offer. Closed Mondays. Reservations necessary. Major credit cards accepted. 21 Avenida Villagarcía (phone: 598387). Expensive.

Don Gaiferos – There's a rivalry of sorts between *Vilas* and *Don Gaiferos* for the best cooking in town, and diners are the winners. This has a beautiful Old Town location in three stone-arched rooms, a wonderful regional atmosphere and excellent Galician food. Closed Sunday evenings and from *Christmas* through early January. Reservations advised. Major credit cards accepted. 23 Rúa Nueva (phone: 583894). Expensive.

Retablo – Featuring local and continental cuisine, superbly prepared and served in an elegant, mauve-colored dining room by the light of brass chandeliers. Closed

Sundays. Reservations advised. Major credit cards accepted. 13 Rúa Nueva (phone: 565950). Expensive.

Vilas – One of the shrines of Galician cooking and certainly one of Santiago's best restaurants, it's an unassuming place, with simple decor, but it has been turning out excellent food since early this century. A long bar with photographs of Spanish soccer heroes leads to dining rooms adorned with oil paintings, white tablecloths, barrels, and a bookshelf full of wine bottles. Try any of the fish dishes, including *sardinas "Mama Sueiro"* (sardines with sweet peppers and garlic). Closed Sundays. Reservations necessary. Major credit cards accepted. 88 Avenida Rosalía de Castro (phone: 591000). Expensive.

La Arzuana – One of Santiago's most popular restaurants, it is normally packed with locals. The dining room opens out to a vine-covered patio. Specialties include seafood creations made with clams, mussels, and shrimp. Open daily. No reservations or credit cards accepted. 40 Calle del Franco (phone: 581198). Moderate.

Mesón La Cigala de Oro – Very popular with the locals, who feast on filling and appetizing dishes including giant prawns, roast veal, and Santiago almond tart. Closed Mondays. No reservations or credit cards accepted. 10 Calle del Franco (phone: 582952). Moderate to inexpensive.

Casa Manolo – This small spot tucked into a small street near the town market is a local institution. Galician specialties are served up as fast as you can order; the fixed-price menu has over a dozen appetizer and entrée choices; portions are enormous. Closed Sundays. No reservations or credit cards accepted. 27 Rúa Traviesa (phone: 582950). Inexpensive.

 TAPAS BARS: The Old Town's *tapas* bars are primarily concentrated on Calle del Franco and Rúa del Villar. Here, bar after bar can be found serving seafood *tapas,* such as small clams, sardines, and octopus with spicy peppers and salt, along with beer and wine, including traditional country wine — something like a new wine, not fully fermented — served in small bowls called *tazas* (it can also be ordered in larger bowls called *cuncas,* the size of a soup bowl). The tiny *Bar Negreira* (75 Rúa del Villar; phone: 580740) is frequented by virtually everyone in town — stay long enough and you'll have a chance to meet journalists, lawyers, shop owners, students, and probably the mayor. At *Bar Buraquiño* (Calle Entremurallas) *tapas* and *tazas* are served out of the windows into the narrow street (it seems that as much wine is spilled onto the marble windowsills as makes it into the cups).

SEGOVIA

Occupying a rocky perch high above two deep valleys, between the northern slopes of the Sierra de Guadarrama and the high, flat tableland of Castilla y León, Segovia has a city center that reaches an altitude of 3,280 feet. Many compare its overall silhouette to that of a ship, with the Alcázar rising high in the west like a prow above the confluence of the Eresma and Clamores rivers. Its proximity to Madrid, only 57 miles (91 km) to the southeast, makes it a favorite retreat for both foreign travelers and Spaniards themselves, who often come out from the capital for the day to savor its scenic charm, historic sights, and outstanding food.

The Romans endowed the city with its greatest marvel: a 2,000-year-old aqueduct that rises almost 100 feet above the Plaza del Azoguejo, where the bulk of the city's traffic passes through the same slender arches that once watched Roman chariots trundle by. The aqueduct is incredibly well preserved, although it no longer performs its duty of delivering water to the upper reaches of the city. Two Roman roads also converged in Segovia, further attesting to its importance during that era when it was a strategic military town. With the incursion of the Visigoths in the 6th century, a gradual decline began, subsequently accelerated by 200 years of Muslim rule. Then, revitalized by the Reconquest, Segovia greatly enhanced its prestige in 1474 when Isabella la Católica (the Catholic) was proclaimed Queen of Castile in the Plaza Mayor. Decline set in again, however, after the Comuneros uprising of 1520–21, when the *comunidades* (autonomous cities) of Castile, led by Juan de Padilla of Toledo and Juan Bravo of Segovia, revolted unsuccessfully against the absolutism of the Holy Roman Emperor Charles V.

At the turn of the 20th century, two artists — one painter and one poet — focused their creative attentions upon Segovia and Castile. The painter, Ignacio Zuloaga, was a master at capturing Segovia's special light and the earthy quality of its inhabitants. The poet, Antonio Machado, an Andalusian who lived for more than a decade in a house on Calle de los Desamparados that is now a small museum, proclaimed his enchantment with the region in a book of poems entitled *Campos de Castilla*.

Today, resting largely on its historic laurels, Segovia's population of just over 50,000 depends greatly on a steady stream of visitors from the capital for its continuing prosperity. And many return again and again — it is one of Spain's most beautiful cities and the roast suckling pig is the city's greatest gastronomic lure. Most Sundays throughout the year, the Plaza Mayor bristles with exuberant throngs honing their appetites on aperitifs and *tapas* in anticipation of the succulent, sweet pork nestled beneath crisp, brown skin. Later, those who can, walk off their extravagance with a stroll through the narrow streets of the city center, making their way from the Alcázar to the cathedral to the Roman Aqueduct, past Romanesque churches, buildings covered with the *esgrafiado* designs that are characteristic of Segovia, and numerous spots from which to admire panoramic views.

SEGOVIA AT-A-GLANCE

SEEING THE CITY: Approximately 1¼ miles (2 km) north of Segovia along the N601 highway leading to Valladolid, the *Parador de Segovia* offers a marvelous view of the entire city. On Saturday and Sunday nights, the aqueduct and cathedral are illuminated.

SPECIAL PLACES: The major monuments of Segovia are within the confines of the old walled city. Although the walls, which date from the time of the Reconquest, are barely in evidence today, three of the original seven gates — San Cebrián, Santiago, and San Andrés — still stand, and it is the wall that gives the old part of Segovia its ship shape. If the Alcázar is considered to be the prow of the ship, then the Roman Aqueduct is the stern. The cathedral and Plaza Mayor are roughly amidship. Segovia is known for its remarkable collection of Romanesque churches. They, and numerous other monuments are within the walls, but a number of remaining sights are beyond and below the walls on the starboard side, on both sides of the Eresma River. As with most medieval cities in Spain, driving in the old part of town is a tortuous affair. Come by car or a taxi to the Plaza Mayor, then explore the area within the walls on foot.

WITHIN THE WALLS

Alcázar – This Disneyesque castle-palace at the western end of town perches above the confluence of the Eresma and Clamores rivers. In fact, Walt Disney used it as a model for the castle in *Snow White and the Seven Dwarfs.* Built during the 12th and 13th centuries on top of an older fortress, it was enriched and enlarged in the 15th and 18th centuries with numerous magnificent chambers. In 1474, Princess Isabella set forth from the Alcázar to be crowned Queen of Castile in Segovia's Plaza Mayor; a painting commemorating that event today hangs in the castle's Sala de la Galera. The Alcázar also was the site of Philip II's fourth marriage — this one to Anne of Austria. Also in the 16th century, the Torre del Homenaje (Tower of Homage, also known as the Tower of Juan II), covered with the typically Segovian *esgrafiado* decoration suggestive of Moorish times, was used as a state prison. King Carlos III installed the Artillery Academy in the Alcázar in the 18th century, and in 1862, a fierce fire gutted the place. Rebuilt in a romantic vein, it has a simplistic charm that is still magical and elegant. Of special interest are the Mudéjar ceilings and tilework and the authentic period furnishings. The 360° view of the Castilian countryside from the top of the Tower of Juan II is worth the 152 steps up, but you can get a good view of sights outside the city walls from the garden in front of the Alcázar. Open daily from 10 AM to 7 PM (until 6 PM from October through March). Admission charge. Plaza del Alcázar (phone: 430176).

Cathedral – Deliberately built in the late Gothic style at a time when Renaissance structures were in vogue (1515 to 1558), the cathedral was, by order of the Holy Roman Emperor Charles V, constructed on a higher and more secure site than the cathedral it replaced, which had been destroyed in the revolt of the Comuneros. Though known as the "Lady of the Spanish cathedrals" because of its elegance, slender lines, and restrained austerity, its treasures are not comparable to those of the cathedrals of León or Salamanca. Among them are the Flamboyant-style choir stalls and cloister, both brought from the old cathedral; the 16th-century carving of *La Piedad* by Juan de Juni in the Capilla Santo Entierro (the first chapel to the right as you enter the church — a *Deposition* by Ambrosio Benson is in the same chapel); and the altarpiece in the Capilla Santiago (next to the museum entrance). Also note the chapels around the apse, which are quite different in feeling from the rest, painted in pale rococo colors. The museum contains an 18th-century gold carriage used in *Corpus Christi* processions, with the cathedral's silver monstrance on top. A collection of 17th-century Flemish tapestries in the Sala Capitular, which has a richly carved ceiling, completes the list of notable exhibits. Open daily from 9 AM to 7 PM in summer; from October through May, open from 9:30 AM to 1 PM and from 3 to 6 PM weekdays, and from 9:30 AM to 6 PM weekends and holidays. Admission charge to the cloister, museum, and Sala Capitular. Plaza Mayor (phone: 435325).

Plaza de San Martín – This square, at the heart of the walled city, is bordered by old mansions, including the Casa del Siglo XV (House of the 15th Century), often mistakenly identified as the house of Juan Bravo, a 16th-century Segovian who was one of the leaders of the Comuneros' Revolt and whose statue presides over the lower level of the square. The tower off to one end is the 14th-century Torreón de Lozoya, and the portico running along a side belongs to the 11th-century Iglesia de San Martín, the most centrally located of numerous Romanesque churches in Segovia.

Casa de los Picos – A late-15th-century Renaissance mansion, distinguished by the pyramidal stones adorning its façade, is now home to the Escuela de Artes Aplicadas y Oficios Artísticos (School of Applied Arts and Artistic Pursuits). As a result, the visitor often is rewarded with student displays and other somewhat unusual exhibitions. Calle Juan Bravo (phone: 430711 or 428198).

Roman Aqueduct – This landmark is one of Europe's finest examples of Roman architecture. Built some 2,000 years ago to carry water to the upper reaches of the city from the Acebeda River, in the Guadarrama Mountains to the east. Originally over 10 miles (17 km) long, its main section of 167 arches remains amazingly intact, extending almost half a mile from the bullring into the upper section of town. The arches become double-tiered where the aqueduct crosses through the Plaza del Azoguejo, reaching its maximum height of 95 feet. An astounding feat of engineering, the aqueduct was constructed of hand-shaped fitted granite blocks set together without any mortar, clamps, or joints. Today, instead of Roman chariots, automobiles drive through the central arches that tower over the Plaza del Azoguejo. Climb the steps to the side of the square for the best longitudinal view of the arches stretching into the distance and the sea of red tiles created by the city rooftops. At the very top, go through the wall, under an arch, and around to the lookout point. Plaza del Azoguejo.

BEYOND THE WALLS

Iglesia de la Vera Cruz – Across the Eresma River just northwest of the city, this early-13th-century church was constructed by the Knights Templars in the late Romanesque style. Its shape, with 12 sides, is unusual in Spain, and was modeled after the Holy Sepulchre in Jerusalem. Inside is a 2-story circular room (a sort of church-within-a-church), a 13th-century carved wooden Christ above the central apse, and the Lignum Crucis chapel in the base of the tower. Open from 10:30 AM to 1:30 PM and from 3:30 to 7 PM in spring and summer (until 6 PM in fall and winter); closed Mondays. Admission charge. Carretera a Zamarramala (phone: 431475).

Monasterio del Parral – Founded by Henry IV in the mid-15th century and given to the Spanish order of St. Hieronymus, the monastery is another monument located across the Eresma River, half a mile (1 km) north of the city. The church, a blend of Gothic, Renaissance, and Plateresque elements, was designed and begun by Juan Gallego at the end of the century, but its façade was left unfinished. The monastery was abandoned after the suppression of religious orders in 1835, but it has been restored and is once again occupied by the Hieronymus brothers/priests (Jerónimos in Spanish). Notable are the polychrome altarpiece carved by Juan Rodríguez and the alabaster tombs of the Marqués de Villena and his wife, also carved by Rodríguez. Ordinarily, the monastery is open daily from 10 AM to 12:30 PM and from 4 to 6 PM (admission by donation), but at press time it was closed for repairs, with the date of its reopening uncertain. Calle del Marqués de Villena (phone: 431298).

Convento de San Antonio el Real – This also was founded by Henry IV during the mid-15th century, but as a country house; later it was given to the Franciscans and the Poor Clares, who inhabit it today. In the church is a wonderful original Mudéjar ceiling over a huge, lavishly gilt main altarpiece, plus three smaller altarpieces, including one with a remarkable 15th-century Flemish rendering of Calvary in three-dimensional carved wood. A nun takes visitors around the cloister and adjoining rooms, where there are more original *artesonado* ceilings and, set in the walls, several small Flemish Calvary scenes in painted terra cotta. Open weekdays from 10 AM to 1 PM and from 4 to 6 PM (Sundays and holidays from 11 AM). Admission charge to the cloister. To reach the convent, follow the Roman aqueduct from behind the *Mesón Cándido* side of Plaza del Azoguejo; when it ends, with arches about waist high, the convent is only a short distance away. Calle San Antonio el Real (phone: 420228).

Iglesia de San Millán – One of the most beautiful of Segovia's Romanesque churches, it stands in full view in an open square between the aqueduct and the bus station. It was built during the 12th century and has four apses, three doorways, two 13th-century porches, and a remodeled 11th-century Mozarabic tower that dates from a previous structure on the spot. Open during services. Avenida Fernández Ladreda.

ENVIRONS

Palacio Real de la Granja de San Ildefonso – Seven miles (11 km) along the N601 highway toward Madrid stands La Granja, a royal palace built by Philip V, the first Bourbon King of Spain, grandson of Louis XIV of France; it is surrounded by meticulously manicured gardens. Construction began in 1721, on land acquired from the Hieronymite monks of El Parral, who had operated a farm, or *granja,* here. The result was the most impressive example of 18th-century architecture in Spain, more European than Spanish in feeling, however, since the French-born king and his Italian wife, Isabella Farnese, employed architects schooled in the Hapsburg tradition. Unfortunately, a fire in 1918 destroyed the private quarters of the royal family and damaged much of the remaining structure. Extensive restoration has re-created the public and official areas, which remained in use through the days of Alfonso XIII (who reigned until 1931). Visitors see room after room with marble floors, painted ceilings, lace curtains, tapestries, and crystal chandeliers — most of the latter outstanding works produced by the nearby Fábrica de Cristal de La Granja. Included are the throne room, Philip and Isabella's mausoleum, and in the former private quarters, reconstructed rooms serving as a *Tapestry Museum* to accommodate a priceless collection of 16th-century tapestries. Visits to the palace are by guided tour only, usually conducted in Spanish (although an English- and French-speaking interpreter is available), but you can wander at will through the lovely Versailles-style gardens behind the palace, a wonderland of fountains, pools, statues, tree-lined avenues, and water flowing from high ground to low ground through a series of stepped pools known as the Great Cascade. The gardens are open daily all year, from 10 AM to 8 PM in summer (until 6 PM in winter). The palace keeps the same hours year-round, open from 10 AM to 1:30 PM and from 3 to 5 PM; Sundays and holidays, from 10 AM to 2 PM; closed Mondays. The fountains, dependent on rainwater, normally are turned on only a couple of days a week (Thursdays and Sundays in 1990), from late March through early July. Admission charge to the palace. San Ildefonso (phone: 470019).

Palacio de Riofrío – Heading back to Segovia from La Granja on N601, look for the sign and turnoff marked Riofrío. Follow the road 4 miles (6 km) and pass through the intersection following the second sign marked Palacio y Bosque de Riofrio. Continue another 4 miles (6 km) and turn left at the intersection for SG724. A guard signals the entrance to a protected parkland where an amazing multitude of friendly fallow deer greets you along the road leading the last few miles to the palace. (Save your admission ticket to show to the guard on your way out.)

The rather plain exterior of this 18th-century peach-colored palace with lime-green shutters belies the elegance that awaits within. It was built by Isabella Farnese, who feared that she might be ousted from La Granja by the new king, her stepson, after Philip V's death, and it was originally conceived as a hunting palace for her own son. It later served as a residence for Alfonso XII, grandfather of Juan Carlos, the present king. Notice the striking series of draped doorways that create uniquely colorful, curtained corridors; the chandeliers (mostly of Spanish construction); several tapestries by Goya and Bayeu; and the furnishings and decorations from the days of Alfonso XII. Since the palace was never completely outfitted, the northern wing has been given over to a *Museo de la Caza* (Museum of the Hunt), complete with reproductions of hunting paraphernalia from the prehistoric to the modern era. There is also an elaborate array of dioramas depicting animals of Spain in their respective habitats — among them the chamois, ibex, capercaillie, golden eagle, wild boar, pheasant, and lynx. Several rooms are also dedicated to hunting trophies acquired by members of the local nobility. Open from 10 AM to 1:30 PM and from 3 to 5 PM (until 2 PM on Sundays and holidays); closed Tuesdays. All visits to the palace are by guided tour only (in Spanish usually, but an English- and French-speaking guide is available); admission charge (phone: 470019).

SOURCES AND RESOURCES

TOURIST INFORMATION: The tourist information office (10 Plaza Mayor; phone: 430328) has a variety of helpful brochures, current information regarding hours and admission fees, and general information on accommodations in all price ranges. Open Mondays through Fridays from 9 AM to 2 PM, Saturdays from 10 AM to 2 PM; during the summer it stays open until 4 or 5 PM. In addition, a *caseta* (trailer), usually parked at the aqueduct, serves as a mobile tourist office with flexible hours. It is usually open on Sundays and holidays when the other office is closed (phone: 440205).

Local Coverage – *El Adelantado de Segovia* is the city's daily Spanish-language newspaper. The *Guía Semanal de Segovia* and the related *Guía Provincial de Segovia,* available free in hotels and at the tourist office, provide up-to-the-minute information on what's happening in the city and province, respectively. The monthly *Guía Gastronómica de Segovia* provides listings and information, by area, on the city's restaurants, *tascas,* bars, and nightlife, as well as on historic sites. Though written in Spanish, most of the material is decipherable by non-Spanish-speaking readers. Also look for a copy of the English edition of *Segovia — Patrimonio de la Humanidad* (Segovia — Heritage of Mankind), complete with suggested itineraries and detailed historic, cultural, and artistic information.

TELEPHONE: The city code for Segovia is 11. If calling from within Spain, dial 911 before the local number.

GETTING AROUND: Segovia is a small city, and most of its sights can be easily visited on foot. Seeing sights on the edge of town, however, will require a car or taxi.

Bus – City buses ply the streets daily from 7 AM to 11 PM, stopping at most of the major attractions. The Estación de Autobuses (phone: 427725), Segovia's main bus station for long-distance buses, is located on Paseo de Ezequiel González, corner of Avenida Fernández Ladreda (reachable from Plaza Mayor by the No. 3 bus marked Puente de Hierro). There is daily service to and from Madrid, Avila, Valladolid, and other towns and villages throughout the province of Segovia. Buses for La Granja, 20 minutes away, also depart from here. Bus schedules can be found in the *Guía Provincial de Segovia*.

Car Rental – *Avis* has an office at 123 Calle Zorilla (phone: 422584).

Taxi – A taxi almost always can be found in the Plaza Mayor; another stand is in Plaza del Azoguejo. Radio-dispatched cabs also are available (phone: 436680 or 436681). If you are going to a site outside the city, be sure to arrange a pick-up time with the driver.

Train – Segovia's train station, Estación de Ferrocarril *RENFE* (phone: 420774), is located on Plaza Obispo Quesada, reachable by bus No. 3 from Plaza Mayor. There is daily service to Madrid, Medina del Campo, and Valladolid. Schedules of service to Madrid are in the *Guía Provincial de Segovia*.

MUSEUMS: In addition to those described in *Special Places*, the museums below may be of interest. Note that the *Zuloaga Museum*, dedicated to the famous local ceramist Daniel Zuloaga (a relative of Ignacio Zuloaga) and set up in the former Iglesia de San Juan de los Caballeros, which he acquired in 1905 and used as a workshop, is closed for restoration.

Casa-Museo Antonio Machado (Antonio Machado House-Museum) – The simple old house that was the home of the poet from 1919 to 1932, with his kitchen, dining room, and bedroom complete with washstand, chamber pots, and wrought-iron bed. Open Tuesdays through Sundays from 4 to 7 PM (to 6 PM in winter). No admission charge. 5 Calle de los Desamparados (phone: 436649).

Museo Provincial de Bellas Artes (Provincial Fine Arts Museum) – A collection of local paintings from the 15th, 16th, and 17th centuries, including the *Conversion of St. Paul* by Francisco Camilo, displayed in a reconstructed 16th-century house. Open from 10 AM to 2 PM and from 4 to 6 PM (Sundays, mornings only); closed Mondays. Admission charge. 12 Calle de San Agustín (phone: 431585).

SHOPPING: Because Segovia is popular with day-trippers from Madrid, its shopping opportunities tend to consist mostly of souvenirs and mementos. The usual assortment of wineskins, castanets, T-shirts, fans, and mantillas blossoms around all the major sights, and along Calle Marqués del Arco near the cathedral.

El Alfar – Ceramics and souvenir items. 22 Calle del Roble (phone: 424215).

Artesanía Monjas Dominicas – Reproductions of antique figures, such as those found in Renaissance altarpieces, made (of resin) and sold by nuns; prices range from $20 to $150 for an angel with wings, up to $2,000 for a large Nativity scene. Convento de Santo Domingo, Calle Capuchinos Alta (phone: 433876).

La Casa del Siglo XV – Glassware, porcelain, leather goods, jewelry, records and tapes, and toys. 32 Calle Juan Bravo (phone: 434531).

Mi Piel – High-quality leather goods — belts, handbags, suitcases. Centro Comercial Almuzara, 6 Calle Juan Bravo (phone: 426141).

La Suiza – Lladró porcelain, crystal, silver, and other souvenirs. 14 Plaza Mayor (phone: 430334).

SPORTS AND FITNESS: There are two popular ski areas in the Guadarramas near Segovia. Both La Pinilla (35 miles/56 km to the northeast) and Navacerrada (17 miles/27 km south) offer a wide range of skiing opportunities and various accommodations. Consult the tourist information office for details.

 THEATER AND MUSIC: Madrid is too close for Segovia to have become a theater- or concertgoer's dream. Nevertheless, the *Teatro Juan Bravo* (Plaza Mayor; phone: 431228) manages to maintain a fairly full schedule of drama, ballet, and orchestral, chamber, and popular music concerts.

 NIGHTCLUBS AND NIGHTLIFE: Although there are no nightclubs of note, Segovia has an ebullient nightlife. *Oky* (1 and 3 Carmen) is a popular disco where, as in other Spanish cities, ballroom dancing — tango, rumba, and even salsa — is back in style. Here, an added touch is Segovia's own version of the folkloric and energetic *jota.* On weekends *segovianos* enjoy the *verbena* (street fair) set up in the Plaza Mayor, where the "in place" is the new *Ave Turita* bar. During summer months, Plaza San Martín is especially lively with its three outdoor cafés: *El Gimnasio, El Ojo,* and *El Narizotas.*

BEST IN TOWN

 CHECKING IN: Depending on the season, expect to pay $90 to $150 for a double room with private bath in hotels classified as expensive, $50 to $90 for a moderate one, and less than $50 for an inexpensive one. All telephone numbers are in the 11 city code unless otherwise indicated.

Los Arcos – Modern and cheerful, it's located outside the walls near the Church of San Millán and the Roman aqueduct, within walking distance of the rest of the prime sights. There are 59 rooms with bath or shower and air conditioning (some facing the city's steepled skyline); the *Cocina de Segovia* restaurant and 2 bars. Parking is available. Affiliated with Best Western. 24 Paseo de Ezequiel González (phone: 437462; fax: 428161). Expensive.

Infanta Isabel – Opened last year, this luxury property occupies a thoroughly remodeled 19th-century mansion located alongside the main square, facing the Town Hall. Its 31 air conditioned rooms have satellite television, radios, direct-dial telephones, and mini-bars The headboards and nightstands are all hand-painted and decorated by a local artist. There is a meeting room for up to 26 people, a cafeteria, a breakfast room, and room service. No. 1 Isabel la Católica (phone: 443105; fax: 433240). Expensive.

Parador de Segovia – In a modern tile-roof brick building, this government-run *parador* with two lake-like outdoor pools and a spa-like indoor pool sprawls over a lush garden-forest setting called El Terminillo. Most of the spacious public areas and 80 guestroom balconies offer a spectacular panoramic view of the Guadarrama Mountains and the Segovia skyline — the Alcázar, the cathedral, and the aqueduct. Facilities also include air conditioning, central heating, a sauna, a tennis courts, a bar, and a restaurant (see *Eating Out*). About 1½ miles (2 km) along the road to Valladolid. Carretera de Valladolid (phone: 430462; fax: 437362). Expensive.

Los Linajes – Within the walls of the Old City, this hotel retains an 11th-century façade that was part of a palace belonging to the Falconi family, and it has charming public rooms arranged around a minuscule inner courtyard. The 55 rooms offer panoramic views, have complete bath, color television sets, and central heating. 9 Calle Dr. Velasco (phone: 431201; fax: 431501). Moderate to expensive.

Acueducto – In a prime location near the aqueduct, this 20-year-old hostelry has 78 spacious rooms with all amenities including air conditioning and color satellite television, as well as a good restaurant and convention facilities. 10 Padre Claret (phone: 424800; fax: 428446). Moderate.

Las Sirenas – Located in the center of the city, on the main shopping street, right in front of the San Martín church, this pleasant, older hostelry has beautiful wood furnishings throughout its 39 rooms, all of which have private baths. Ask for an exterior room, the best of which overlook the church. 30 Calle Juan Bravo (phone: 434011). Moderate.

Plaza – A fine, affordable *hostal,* with 28 rooms. All the doubles have complete private baths and telephones; some singles have a sink or a sink and shower only. The *José María* restaurant (see *Eating Out*) is located next door. 11 Calle Cronista Lecea (phone: 431228). Inexpensive.

 EATING OUT: Segovia is a favorite spot for *madrileños* (residents of Madrid) to spend a Sunday and indulge in what is reported by many to be some of the finest *cochinillo* — roast suckling pig — in Castile. A *horno de asar* (roasting oven) sign outside announces a "roast" restaurant serving this specialty; so does the poor naked piglet on a platter that is usually displayed in the window. Expect such places to be crowded on weekends, even in low season, when business might otherwise be slow. *Cochifrito,* a local variation of the pervasive suckling pig, is fried with garlic and parsley. The hearty, flavorful *sopa castellana,* a soup of ham, paprika, bread, and poached eggs, is another local specialty, well worth sampling. Dinner for two with wine will cost $60 to $85 in an expensive restaurant, $30 to $55 in a moderate one. All phone numbers are in the 11 city code unless otherwise indicated.

Mesón de Cándido – Located at the foot of the aqueduct and equally a beacon for visitors, as evidenced by the photos of famous people who have dined here and the guestbooks with their autographs. But unlike many other high-profile restaurants, this one offers good food as well as excellent service. The traditional dishes of Segovia, including *cochinillo,* are here, accompanied by a fine ribera del duero house wine. The building, with parts dating from the 15th century, has been classified as an official historic monument, and the restaurant, in operation since the 1860s, has walls adorned with hand-painted plates, copper pots, and other memorabilia. The economical fixed-price menu is famed throughout Spain. Open daily. Reservations advised on weekends. Major credit cards accepted. 5 Plaza del Azoguejo (phone: 428103). Expensive.

Mesón Duque – The sign outside still boasts of the Maestro Asador de Segovia (Segovia's Master Roaster) title won in 1895. Situated on a street running between the aqueduct and the Plaza Mayor, this is *Cándido*'s main competitor. Its ambience is classic Castilian, and it is noted for its *cochinillo, judiones de la Granja* (white bean stew), and various beef and veal dishes. Open daily. Reservations advised on weekends. Major credit cards accepted. 12 Calle Cervantes (phone: 430537). Expensive.

Parador de Segovia – A cut above the quality of conventional *parador* cooking, this restaurant offers a fine view of Segovia to go along with the *sopa castellana,* sweetbreads, salmon, *merluza* (hake), *perdiz* (partridge), roast lamb, *cochinillo,* and fresh crayfish and trout from the Eresma River. Outside of town, 1¼ miles (2 km) along the road to Valladolid. Open daily. Reservations advised on weekends. Major credit cards accepted. Carretera de Valladolid (phone: 430462). Expensive.

El Bernardino – Another traditionally decorated place for sampling the Castilian mainstays, it has plates and paintings on the walls, a beamed ceiling, and a rough-hewn look that extends to the stuffed head of a boar on a pillar. There are set menus in several reasonable price ranges. Open daily; closed in January. Reservations advised on weekends. No credit cards accepted. 2 Calle Cervantes (phone: 433225) Moderate.

Casa Amado – The decor is less elaborate than that of some of Segovia's other establishments, but the food surpasses the lackluster ambience. Besides the Castilian standards, specialties include many fine fish dishes and a memorable *cordero leachal al ajillo* (suckling lamb with garlic sauce). Good bread, fine flan (custard), and attentive service complete the offering. Closed Wednesdays and October. Reservations advised on weekends. No credit cards accepted. 9 Avenida Fernández Ladreda (phone: 432077). Moderate.

José María – Segovia's most popular place for Sunday lunch and *tapas* throughout the week — with good reason: The food is extremely good, the service friendly, and the house wine a fine ribera del duero red. Besides *cochinillo* and *cochifrito,* specialties include *ancas de rana rebozadas* (breaded frog's legs), homemade *morcilla* (blood sausage), and, for dessert, *pastel de frambuesa con nueces* (raspberry cream with walnuts). Closed November. Reservations advised for Sunday lunch, or go early. Major credit cards accepted. 11 Calle Cronista Lecea (phone: 434484). Moderate.

SEVILLE

For a city that had no opera house until just last year, Seville has been the stage for more than its share of operatic heroes and heroines. The temptress Carmen, the famous barber of Seville, and Don Giovanni, the musical equivalent of the legendary Don Juan, all played out their high drama and romantic nonsense in its winding alleys, secluded patios, jasmine-scented gardens, and fountain-filled plazas. And no one has ever taken down the set. Carmen's cigarette factory, Escamillo's bullring, the wrought-iron balconies where Don Juan trysted — even, some claim, the barbershop — are all still in place, waiting for the curtain to go up each morning on the friendly, fun-loving southern city that epitomizes all we envision when we think of sunny Spain.

After Madrid, Barcelona, and Valencia, Seville, a university center with a population of 700,000, is Spain's fourth-largest city. It also is the capital of the eight-province Autonomous Region of Andalucía, which includes the province of Seville with a population of 1½ million. Seville also is one of Spain's loveliest cities, and it works at preserving the fascinating Roman-Arabic-Judaic-Christian past that made it so. Traditional Andalusian colors are faithfully maintained on traditional Andalusian buildings — white walls to deflect the southern heat, gold trim to echo the ocher earth. Golden sand (*alvero*) is trucked in 20 miles from the hills of Carmona to be used ornamentally in local gardens, and the famous Seville orange trees, loaded with bitter fruit that the city contracts with marmalade-makers to harvest, shade the town's tiled sidewalks. Restaurants, hotels, and shops lean to fanciful Moorish arabesque details, colored tiles, and white-walled beam-ceilinged interiors, while computerized 20th-century businesses hide behind the Plateresque façades and wrought-iron gates of Renaissance palaces. Splashing fountains, tiled benches, leafy plazas, and patios with canvas awnings are, as for centuries past, the everyday amenities of a city on the doorstep of Africa, with summer temperatures reaching up to 112F.

Beginning in spring, Seville (Sevilla in Spanish) lives in its streets. *Semana Santa* (Holy Week) fills them with 7 nights of religious pageantry. On its heels, the *Feria* (April Fair) is a week of nonstop revelry, and even after it's over, the fun goes on: Teenagers strum their guitars at café tables, the rattle of castanets sounds from around a corner, a group at the *tapas* bar breaks out in steady, wordless, syncopated flamenco clapping, and 10-year-old *señoritas* in brilliant polka-dot dresses dance the *sevillanas* in the plaza. All the while, horses and carriages clip-clop through city traffic.

It takes a somewhat selective focus to isolate a view this romantic of any modern city. But the face of Seville has a brand new look this year following the extensive construction, renovations, and transportation improvements made for *Expo '92* (see *Extra Special*), the world's fair celebrating the 500th anniversary of Christopher Columbus's big discovery. With the arrival of the

6-month extravaganza comes a new sophistication in Seville, making the city a prime tourist spot and a competitor in the European tourism market.

Seville has successfully survived some far more traumatic renovations in its time. Since its earliest days, conquerors — Phoenicians, Greeks, Carthaginians — prized it for its river, a 70-mile-long highway to the sea. Spain's only inland port city was taken by the Romans in 205 BC and made the capital of the province of Baetica, their name for what we now call Andalusia. They called the river the Baetis, a name that survives as Calle Betis, the riverfront street of clubs and cafés in the Triana district, across the Guadalquivir from the bullring. (The name Guadalquivir, Arabic for big river, comes from the Moors, who arrived centuries later.)

With the waning of the Roman Empire in the 5th century, Seville was ruled by the Vandals and then by the Visigoths, but the character of the city that is seen today dates largely from the 8th century, when the Moors crossed the Strait of Gibraltar to begin their fruitful 500-year reign. After takeovers by several successive Moorish contingents, the city enjoyed a flourishing 100 years under the Almohads, Moorish conquerors who arrived in the mid-12th century and fostered an unprecedented climate of intellectual, artistic, and commercial cooperation among the resident communities of Christians, Arabs, and Jews. Skilled engineers, they built up the port and repaired the city's fortifications, silent testimony of which remains in the outer walls of the Alcázar, the clean-lined Torre del Oro, and the lower portion of the Giralda tower, survivors of the Almohad reign.

Though Seville fell to Ferdinand III (the Christian king who later became a saint) in 1248, the Moorish influence continued for at least 2 centuries. It can be seen inside the Alcázar walls, in the ornate 14th-century palace of King Pedro el Cruel (Peter the Cruel), which was built by Mudéjar workmen (Moors who continued to live and work in Spain after the Christian conquest) using traditional Arab design.

Columbus's voyage to the New World was the beginning of Seville's most glorious period. The Catholic Monarchs, Ferdinand and Isabella, established their headquarters for New World exploration and trade in the Alcázar, and Columbus's return up the Guadalquivir inspired successful trips by Ferdinand Magellan and Amerigo Vespucci, who sailed out from the Torre del Oro. The golden age of Seville was under way — though not for the city's ill-fated Jews, who were forcibly converted, slain, or driven from their homes in the Judería (the present Barrio de Santa Cruz) by the Royal Inquisition.

During the 16th and 17th centuries, Seville was the richest and most powerful city in Spain, filled with Renaissance palaces, churches, and monasteries decorated with frescoes and paintings of native sons Bartolomé Esteban Murillo and Juan de Valdés Leal and of adopted son Francisco de Zurbarán, who was born in a village nearby. (Seville-born Diego Velázquez left early for the court in Madrid, and his hometown is seriously deficient in his works.) Ironically, the river that earned the city its earlier acclaim was the same conduit that would turn its economic tides. With the gradual silting up of the Guadalquivir, which once had been navigable all the way to Córdoba, the city's fortunes turned down sharply, and Cádiz, perched on the Atlantic, took over Seville's lucrative trade.

Today, with the river long since restored, Seville is once again a major port, shipping minerals, manufactured goods, and agricultural products. As prospects of a smash-hit *Expo* escalate from day to day, city fathers expect that besides attracting more international commerce, the world's fair will build tourism for Andalusia's chain of Moorish masterpiece cities: Córdoba and Granada, as well as Seville. If there's time to see just one of these treasures, Seville, the largest, is the best choice. Once you've been here, you'll agree, *"Quien ha visto Sevilla ha visto maravilla"* — to see Seville is to see a wonder.

SEVILLE AT-A-GLANCE

 SEEING THE CITY: The core of Seville sprawls along the east bank of the Guadalquivir River. The most breathtaking city view and best orientation point is from the top of the Giralda Tower, 307.8-feet high. Abutting the cathedral, La Giralda is as symbolic of Seville as the Eiffel Tower is of Paris. Enter at the Plaza Virgen de los Reyes. Classic horse-drawn open carriages (*calesas*) provide a delightful way to see the city. They can be hired here alongside the cathedral, and stops include the Plaza de España, María Luisa Park, Murillo Gardens, and Torre del Oro. The cost, about $25 per hour, includes the driver's expressive explanations — in English — of the sights. Half-day motorcoach city tours, and excursions to surrounding sights can be arranged through your hotel concierge.

 SPECIAL PLACES: Spain's fourth-largest city does look big from the top of the Giralda Tower, but except for the *Expo '92* site on Cartuja Island across the Guadalquivir from the northern part of town, visitors spend most of their time on the east bank of the river in the compact area of an Old Town that once huddled inside the city walls. Most touristic highlights are concentrated around or between the city's two most central bridges, the mid–19th-century Eiffel-esque Isabel II Bridge, commonly known as La Puente de Triana, and the San Telmo Bridge to the south. Closer to the former are the old *Maestranza* bullring, the new *Maestranza Opera House,* downtown shopping streets, and the *Museo de Bellas Artes* (Museum of Fine Arts). Near the San Telmo Bridge are María Luisa Park, the University (previously the old tobacco factory), and the Torre del Oro. Clustered in the middle, a few blocks "inland," are Seville's four greatest treasures: the cathedral; the adjoining Giralda Tower; the Alcázar; and the winding streets of the Barrio de Santa Cruz.

Across the Guadalquivir on the west bank, between the two bridges, is the Barrio de Triana with its own colorful personality. Once a Gypsy haven, it still resounds with flamenco music from *tabernas* (dance studios), even in special evening masses at the San Jacinto church. Countless *sevillanas* lyrics sing praise to Triana including the classic song that Federico García Lorca put on paper for posterity, entitled "Sevil-lanas." Next door to Triana, the Barrio de los Remedios with its flamenco cabarets attracts nocturnal locals as well as visitors (see *Nightlife*).

North of the Triana Bridge are motor-vehicle and pedestrian-only bridges crossing the river to La Cartuja Island, site of *Expo '92.*

Public attractions are open from 9:30 or 10 AM to 1:30 or 2 PM and from around 4 or 5 PM to 7 or 8 PM; some hours change with the seasons. Museums tend to be open mornings only; closing days tend to be Sundays or Mondays. Check with the tourist office (phone: 422-1404) for the most up-to-date hours. Although it is usual for many places to close during July and August, this year will be an exception because of the events surrounding *Expo '92.*

■ **Warning:** For all its present upward mobility, Seville still has a bad record when it comes to theft. Most *sevillanos* pride themselves on their friendliness and hospitality, and one way they show it is with constant warnings about the wave of pickpocketing and purse snatching, usually by gangs of youths from the suburbs. As in any big city, women should keep money in a pocket, not a purse. Men should keep track of their wallets. Never put purses down in a café or on the seat of the car beside you, and nothing you wouldn't want to lose should ever be left in a parked car. As for the Gypsies outside the cathedral, enjoy their shenanigans, but be cautious. Many simply want to charge outrageous sums to tell your fortune, but others will distract you with chatter and jostling while an accomplice goes to work on your wallet. Crimes against foreigners here are usually for profit, not bodily harm. Be prudent, not fearful.

CITY CENTER

Reales Alcázares (Alcázar, or Royal Palace) – Although surrounded by rough Almohad walls that would lead anyone to expect a military compound within, King Pedro's delicate Mudéjar palace, built by Moorish craftsmen at a time when this had been a Christian city for over a century, is the most wondrous and beguiling building in Seville. Work on the palace began in 1350, on the site of the previous Moorish fortress, and ended abruptly in 1369, when the king, known as Pedro el Cruel — Peter the Cruel to the English-speaking world — was done in by a brother. (Pedro himself had earned his reputation by murdering his half brothers as well as a Granadan potentate he had invited to the palace for dinner — the ruby he stole from his guest, after spearing him, is now the center stone in the British crown.) Unlike the Alhambra in Granada, which deteriorated during years of abandonment and has required massive restoration, the Alcázar compound was kept pretty much in shape by Spanish royalty, who used it as a residence into our own century, adding upper stories and new wings. There's even one remnant of the earlier Almohad palace, the fragile Patio del Yeso, which is closed to the public.

Pass through the narrow Puerta del León (Lion's Gate), the entrance to the Alcázar, and Pedro's palace is directly across the Patio de la Montería (Hunter's Court). Once inside the palace, bear in mind that the intricately pierced and curlicued decorations clinging to the upper walls like lacy veils are merely plaster, molded and sculpted to look like marble, as are the dizzying carved stalactite clusters. The Mudéjars were masters at disguising mundane materials, piecing dazzlingly painted ceramic tiles, or *azulejos,* into mosaics of star forms and zigzag ribbons, and using wood for gorgeous *artesonado* ceilings that are carved, gilded, coffered, and inlaid in an infinite variety of geometric patterns. They also displayed their inner feelings in disguise: The graceful Arabic script worked into their decorations for the walls of the Christian king are prayers from the Koran.

The best way to see the palace is to wander at random through the clusters of courtyards and chambers, so typical of Moorish palaces, although the visit begins at the colonnaded Patio de las Doncellas (Court of the Maidens), with its multi-lobed arches resting on sets of twin marble columns. This was the center of official palace life and it leads to the great, square Salón de Embajadores (Ambassadors' Hall), where Pedro betrayed his guest and where the Holy Roman Emperor Charles V (King Carlos I of Spain) was wed to Isabella of Portugal. The salon's complex, colored and faceted cedarwood cupola, resting on vaults of gilded plasterwork, is the palace masterpiece. Not to be missed is the graceful Puerta de los Pavones (Peacock Arch), a surprising note, since Moorish designs usually derive from botanical and geometric forms, rarely from animal life. Among the dozens of other splendid royal rooms, a universal favorite is the Patio de las Muñecas (Dolls' Court), which was the hub of the palace's living quarters; to ensure privacy, only blind musicians played here. Look for the two little dolls' faces carved into a marble column. Notice, too, the marble capitals, each different, brought from the ruins of the Medina Azahara near Córdoba.

For a trip back to the Age of Discovery, return to the Patio de la Montería and enter Queen Isabella's 15th-century addition. Here, in the Cuarto del Almirante (Admiral's Apartment), she established the Casa de Contratación, headquarters for New World exploration and commerce. The austere rooms hold such New World mementos as a model of the *Santa María,* 15th-century navigators' maps, and an altarpiece, Virgen de los Navegantes, in which Columbus is among the figures beneath the Virgin's cloak. Stairs at the rear lead to royal apartments, including Isabella's Gothic chapel, the Oratorio de los Reyes Católicos, which has a famous tiled altar by Niculoso Pisano finished in 1504, the year of Isabella's death. Another wing, added by Charles V, is entered through Pedro's palace. Filled with an exceptional series of Flemish tapestries woven with silk, gold, and wool, chronicling the Holy Roman Emperor's triumphs in his Tunisian campaign of 1535 (a 16th-century equivalent of a war photographer, Jan Vermayan, had gone along to sketch it), it's also the wing that leads to the overgrown palace gardens, a sight straight out of the Arabian Nights (see below). The Alcázar is open Tuesdays through Saturdays from 10:30 AM to 5:30 PM, Sundays and holidays from 10:30 AM to 1:30 PM. Admission charge includes the gardens. Plaza del Triunfo (phone: 421-4971).

Jardines del Alcázar (Alcázar Gardens) – Moorish, Renaissance, and modern gardens are all part of the Alcázar complex. Charles V erected the monumental pink stone wall with recessed frescoes that backstops the terrace and the outsize lily pond (the statue in the center of the pond is of Mercury). Steps lead down to the baths of María de Padilla, King Pedro's mistress (whose apartment can be seen in the palace). There's a choice of paths through flower-filled gardens past the Charles V Pavilion (geraniums sprout from the roof), past an orange tree supposed to have been in existence in Pedro's day, to a myrtlewood maze, palm groves, rose gardens, and a fountain where ducklings bathe. In an upper garden, a narrow, tiled trough carries a stream of water downhill from terrace to terrace. Engineers for *Expo '92,* borrowing from this old Arab "air conditioning" system, are able to lower temperatures on the fairgrounds at least 10 degrees by circulating cold water under the plazas. Opening hours are the same as for the Alcázar, above, and the admission charge to the Alcázar includes the gardens.

Plaza de Toros de la Real Maestranza de Caballería (Seville's Bullring) – The giant crimson door of Seville's bullring swings open on *Easter Sunday* to begin the bullfight season, which runs until October. The quintessentially Spanish spectacle of the *corrida,* or bullfight, is quintessentially Andalusian — modern bullfighting began in the Andalusian town of Ronda, near Seville, in the 18th century — and while the bullring in Madrid may be larger, Seville's *Maestranza,* built in the 1760s, is more beautiful. An appearance here is a must for all of the world's greatest matadors. The *corridas,* with sparkling pageantry and the inevitable moment of truth, are held Sunday and holiday afternoons at 6:30 PM (daily during the *Feria*). Buy tickets well in advance, ranging, in peak season, from about $25 in the sun to $150 in full shade (remember, the summer sun is still blazing at 7 PM in the south of Spain), at the ring, at the *Agencia Teatral* (phone: 422-8229), or in bars along Calle Sierpes. Paseo de Colón (phone: 422-3506).

Cathedral – Seville's Gothic cathedral, the third-largest Christian church in Europe after St. Peter's Basilica in Rome and St. Paul's Cathedral in London, hunkers down along Avenida de la Constitución, displaying three carved, arched portals — but not the soaring façade that might be expected. Go around to the Plaza del Triunfo visitors' entrance. There, at the south transept, the 19th-century tomb of Christopher Columbus, his coffin borne by life-size figures representing the Kings of Aragon, Navarre, Castile, and León, stands just inside the door. The cathedral was begun in 1402 as a grandiose symbol of Christian Seville at a time when Granada was still to be in Muslim hands for another 90 years. The Great Mosque of the Almohads, on the same site, had already been serving as a Christian church (many of Seville's churches are former mosques) when the church fathers decided to demolish it. And at record speed — only 104 years — this 380-foot-long, 250-foot-wide, and 184-foot-high vaulted and buttressed behemoth rose in its place. Only the mosque's most exquisite minaret (the present Giralda tower) was saved to become the cathedral's spire.

The enormous sweep of the cathedral is hard to appreciate because bulky choir stalls and a soaring Capilla Mayor (Main Chapel), or chancel, block the center aisle, and the Flemish stained glass windows are set so high that their light barely penetrates the shadows. A magnificent three-sided gold *reja* (grille) encloses the chancel and its 70-foot-high carved wooden *retablo* (altarpiece), the largest in Spain. The 45 niches, with over 1,000 figures in scenes from the lives of Christ and the Virgin, took Flemish sculptor Pieter Dancart 10 years to finish. It's here that ten young boys in red-and-white tunics and cocked hats click their castanets in the ritual dance of the *seises* (sixes, even though there are ten dancers) on church holidays. Behind the choir there's a stone marking the tomb of Columbus's son, Hernando, rewarded by burial here because he donated the 3,000-volume family book collection, some with his father's margin notes, to the cathedral library. At the apse stands the domed 16th-century Capilla Royal (Royal Chapel) with a *reja* showing Ferdinand III, conqueror of Seville and later sainted, receiving the keys to the city. His well-preserved body, displayed to the public on the *Feast of San Fernando* (May 30) and on the anniversary of the day he reconquered the city from the Moors (November 23), lies in a silver tomb at the feet of the city's patron saint, the Virgen de los Reyes, or Virgin of the Kings. (Both she and the Virgen de la Macarena, in the Basílica de la Macarena across town, are so popular here that when Spaniards anywhere meet a woman named Reyes or Macarena, they assume she's from Seville.) King Pedro and his mistress, María de Padilla, are in a crypt below the chapel.

Masterpieces by Murillo, Valdés Leal, Zurbarán, and Jacob Jordaens are in the ill-lit St. Anthony Chapel, although they may be moved to a brighter location by next year. Look closely at Murillo's *Vision of St. Anthony,* to make out the fine line where restorers pieced it back together after thieves, in 1874, cut out the figure of the saint. (It was recovered in New York City 3 months later.) Two more Murillos are in the Sacristía Mayor (Treasury) along with the crown, studded with more than 1,000 colored stones, that is worn by the Virgen de los Reyes for her processon on August 15. Also in the treasury are a 650-pound silver monstrance by Juan de Arfe, which is carried in the *Corpus Christi Day* procession, and a cross said to have been made from the first gold Columbus brought back from the New World. Murillo's *Holy Family,* and works by Leal, Zurbarán, Titian, and Goya are in the Sacristía de los Calices (Chalice Treasury), and Murillo's *Immaculate Conception* is in the oval Sala Capitular (Chapter House). On the north side of the cathedral is the Patio de los Naranjos (Orange Tree Court) with remnants of the original fountain of ablutions and the bronze-sheathed Puerta del Perdón (Door of Forgiveness) from the Great Mosque. Open Mondays through Fridays from 11 AM to 5 PM, Saturdays from 11 AM to 4 PM, and Sundays from 2 to 4 PM. Admission charge. Plaza del Triunfo.

La Giralda (Giralda Tower) – On a clear day, it's possible to see the olive groves around Seville in a 360-degree view from this 20-story bell tower, the same one from which the muezzin called the faithful to prayer when it was the minaret of the Great Mosque. Its ingenious *sebka* rhomboid brick patterning so pleased the Christians that they spared the tower and used it for their new cathedral. The four huge golden spheres, called the Apples of Yanmur, with which the Almohads had topped their tower in the 12th century (and which reflected beams of sunlight across the countryside), are no longer extant. Instead, the 307.8-foot tower is topped with a belfry, lantern, and an almost 12-foot high revolving statue representing the Faith, all additions of the 16th century. The statue, known locally as the *Giraldillo,* serves as a weather vane (*giralda* in Spanish, hence the name of the tower). There's no elevator, but the climb is easy, via 35 inclined ramps and some stairs, designed to be ridden up easily on horseback. Windows along the way present gargoyle-framed previews of the full panorama. Conversely, the towering Giralda is an orientation point visible from all over Seville, and is brilliantly illuminated at night. Hours are the same as for the cathedral, above, and the admission charge to the cathedral includes La Giralda.

Barrio de Santa Cruz (Santa Cruz Quarter) – Hugging the walls of the Alcázar is the old Jewish quarter, or Judería, a medieval neighborhood of narrow, winding streets, handkerchief-size plazas dotted with café tables, whitewashed houses where geraniums spill from wrought-iron balconies, and flower-filled patios glimpsed from beyond fanciful gates. Seville's Jewish community flourished here for generations under the Moors but vanished in the 15th century after the Inquisition. Later the area became the playground of the aristocracy, and today it still attracts the Spanish well-to-do. One convenient way to begin a tour is by turning right upon leaving the Patio de Banderas at the exit of the Alcázar and walk up Romero Murube. Turn right again at the Plaza de la Alianza and head up Calle Rodrigo Caro into the lovely pebble-paved Plaza de Doña Elvira, where there are inviting benches under the orange trees. From here, any street will lead to one or another of the barrio's loveliest places.

Plaza de Santa Cruz – Though it is on the outer edge of the barrio, near an entrance to the Barrio de Santa Cruz at the Jardines de Murillo (Murillo Gardens), this tiny square is its heart. The 17th-century filigreed, wrought-iron Cruz de la Cerrajería (Cross of the Locksmithy), which once stood downtown on Calle Sierpes, has been its centerpiece since the 1920s. Murillo's ashes are buried in an unmarked place in the square. (One of his famous paintings, *The Last Supper,* is in the nearby 17th-century baroque Church of Santa María la Blanca.)

Casa de Murillo (Murillo's House) – Seville's favorite son lived his last years in this typical old Barrio de Santa Cruz house, now furnished with period pieces (not Murillo's own) and five of his lesser paintings. The visit is especially interesting if the caretaker has time to take you around. Open Tuesdays through Sundays, from 10 AM to 2 PM. Admission charge. Calle de Santa Teresa (phone: 421-7535).

Hospital de la Caridad (Charity Hospital) – The name may not be appealing, but this 17th-century baroque masterpiece shouldn't be missed, if only because the man-about-town who founded it was the model for Don Juan. Saddened by the death of his wife or repentant over past peccadilloes (both stories circulate), the aristocratic Miguel de Mañara became a monk and used his wealth to build this hospital for the indigent, where the elderly can still be seen taking their ease among the tropical plants in the ocher- and rose-walled patios. He also financed the adjoining church, San Jorge, worthy of a visit for its rich ornamentation, with great golden twisted columns before the altar, beneath which Mañara is buried, and for its trove of Murillos and Valdés Leals. Good lighting here lets the viewer closely examine Murillo's massive canvases of *Moses Striking Water from the Rock* and the *Miracle of the Loaves and Fishes.* The most talked about paintings, though, are two by Valdés Leal over the entrance door and on the wall just opposite. His macabre *Finis Gloria Mundi* and *In Ictu Oculi* don't spare the corpses, maggots, and skulls in delivering their message about man's mortality. Open Mondays through Saturdays from 10:30 AM to 1 PM and from 3:30 to 6 PM,, Sundays and holidays from 10 AM to 12:30 PM. Admission charge. Near the Torre del Oro. 3 Calle Temprado (phone: 422-3232).

Torre del Oro (Tower of Gold) – Seville's most romantic symbol, on the banks of the Guadalquivir, was once one of 64 defensive towers built along the city wall (remnants of the wall can be seen near the Basílica de la Macarena, in the northeast section of town). Dating from 1220, its clean lines are typical of the simple but forceful Almohad style that produced the Alcázar walls and the Giralda. The tower is 12-sided and was originally faced with ceramic tiles finished in gold, an Andalusian specialty. The tiles have disappeared, but when it's illuminated at night, the Torre del Oro still glows. It has served as a prison and a storehouse for New World gold, and it once secured a chain that stretched to a twin tower (no longer in existence) on the opposite shore, enabling toll collectors to stop ships entering the port. Now the tower contains a small maritime museum and provides a nice view. Open Tuesdays through Saturdays from 10 AM to 2 PM, Sundays from 10 AM to 1 PM. Closed Mondays and holidays. Admission charge. Paseo de Colón (phone: 422-2419).

Archivo General de Indias (Archive of the Indies) – Juan de Herrera, the same architect who planned the 16th-century Escorial monastery near Madrid for Philip II, designed this building to house the old Lonja (Stock Exchange). In the 1660s, the building housed the Seville Academy, the art academy founded largely by Murillo. Today it's the repository of documents on Spain's role in New World exploration, conquest, and commerce. A majestic red marble stairway leads to a great L-shaped gallery where carved shelves of mahogany brought from Cuba hold some 43,000 cardboard files filled with an estimated 80 million original documents. Some 400,000 priceless papers, which include correspondence between Columbus and Queen Isabella, are locked away in air conditioned storage. Only researchers with university credentials may examine the documents (successful hunts for sunken treasure in the New World have begun here), but anyone will get the idea from the displays of drawings, charts, letters, account books, and royal decrees in the many glass cases along the center. Open from 10 AM to 1 PM for visitors; 8 AM to 1 PM for researchers; closed Sundays and holidays. Between the cathedral and the Alcázar. Avenida de la Constitución (phone: 421-1234).

Plaza Nueva – A short walk north from the cathedral along Avenida de la Constitución leads to Seville's central city square, with the block-long Renaissance Ayuntamiento (City Hall) fronting it and a bronze horseman (Ferdinand III) in the middle. Another entrance to the Ayuntamiento is around the back, on Plaza de San Francisco, the scene of Inquisition *autos-da-fé,* as well as tournaments, bullfights, and political rallies.

Museo de Bellas Artes (Fine Arts Museum) – Still farther north, near the Córdoba train station, this is a superb museum whose collection of international art from the 16th through the 20th centuries — with an especially fine selection of paintings by Murillo, Zurbarán, Valdés Leal, and other Spanish artists — is second only to that of the *Prado* in Madrid. It has been closed for renovation, although a few rooms reopened in 1990 (putting some of the more prized Spanish Old Masters back on view), however, the full museum is expected to open again this year. It is housed in the 17th-century baroque Convent of La Merced, whose patios, cloisters, and chapel — and façade the color of the oranges on the trees outside — are works of art in themselves. Open Tuesdays through Sundays from 9:30 AM to 3 PM. Admission charge. 9 Plaza del Museo (phone: 422-0790).

Universidad de Sevilla (University of Seville) – The monumental Royal Tobacco Factory that Bizet used as the setting for the first act of his opera *Carmen* has been part of the University of Seville since the 1950s. It still hints of its past at its main entrances, carved with bas reliefs of tobacco plants, Indians, galleons, and the faces of Columbus and Cortés. The largest building in Spain after the Escorial, it is worth walking through at least some of it for a look at student life in the vast graffiti-covered halls and courtyards. Just south of the *Alfonso XIII* hotel. Calle San Fernando.

Parque María Luisa (María Luisa Park) – The San Telmo Palace, whose colorful baroque façade can be seen behind the *Alfonso XIII* hotel, was built as a naval college and now is used as a seminary. During the 19th century, however, it belonged to María Luisa, sister of Queen Isabella II, and the present María Luisa Park, the Bois de Boulogne of Seville, was the palace grounds. The park was given to the city in the early 1900s, and the extravagant period buildings in it were built for the *1929 Iberoamerican Exposition*. Cars have been banned from the park for the past decade, leaving room for jogging, bicycling, and sightseeing by horse and carriage. In summer, all Seville strolls its long, forested allées. In winter, sun worshipers crowd into the open Plaza de España, at its eastern edge.

Plaza de España – Practically at the entrance to María Luisa Park, along Avenida Isabel la Católica, is a grandiose, semicircular plaza surrounded by a Renaissance-style government office complex, originally built for the 1929 exposition. The canal that follows the semicircle of the plaza is so long that rowboats can be rented for mini-excursions. Take time to walk over the canal's beautiful all-tile bridges and to browse the alcoves — each highlights one of Spain's 50 provinces with a lively tiled mural — set into the curving plaza wall.

Plaza de América – At the far end of the park, in a beautifully laid-out area of palm-shaded terraces, rose gardens, lily ponds, and splashing fountains, stand three more stunning buildings left from the exposition. The one in the center houses Andalusia's government headquarters; the other two are the *Museo Arqueológico* (see below) and the *Museo de Arte y Costumbres Populares* (phone: 423-2576), a folk museum with exhibits of regional life (open Tuesdays through Sundays from 10 AM to 2 PM). Parque María Luisa.

Museo Arqueológico (Archaeological Museum) – This museum, in a Plate-resque-style exposition building, contains a definitive collection of artifacts from excavations in western Andalusia. Don't miss the Roman section, which has statues, jewelry, and coins found in the ruins of the ancient city of Itálica (see below), just outside Seville. Open Tuesdays through Sundays, from 10 AM to 2 PM. Admission charge. Plaza de América (phone: 423-2405).

Casa de Pilatos (House of Pilate) – A trip to this 16th-century mansion, the last of the great private houses in Seville open to visitors, is an entrée to the splendid lifestyle of an Andalusian nobleman of days long past. The Marqués de Tarifa, who finished it in 1540, is supposed to have been inspired by the house of the Roman emperor in Jerusalem, but his architects didn't spare Mudéjar, Plateresque, and Gothic glories. The ceiling of the grand staircase has been compared to the Alcázar and the tiled walls and patios are sensational. There's also a collection of Roman sculpture. Open daily, from 9 AM to 6 PM. Admission charge. In the ancient San Esteban eastern part of town. 1 Plaza de Pilatos (phone: 422-5208).

ENVIRONS

Itálica – The impressive ruins of this Roman city, founded at the end of the 3rd century BC by the Roman general Scipio Africanus, are about 5 miles (8 km) northwest of Seville, just outside the town of Santiponce. The birthplace of Hadrian and Trajan, its main attraction is the colossal amphitheater, said to have held 25,000 spectators. Digging, begun in 1971, was recently completed down to the last pit for wild animals. There are also largely intact mosaic floors, baths, temple remains, and a museum (although major finds are in the *Museo Arqueológico* in Seville). The Roman amphitheater is the stage for dance festivals, and there will be a special festival this year as part of the *Expo* program. When special events are not on the schedule, hours, from April through September, are Tuesdays through Saturdays from 9 AM to 6:30 PM, Sundays from 9 AM to 3 PM; the rest of the year, open Tuesdays through Saturdays from 9 AM to 5:30 PM, Sundays from 10 AM to 4 PM. Admission charge. Buses leave every 30 minutes from Calle Marqués de Paradas in Seville, near the Córdoba train station (phone: 439-4900 or 439-2784).

■**EXTRA SPECIAL:** *EXPO '92:* The apogee of Spain's multifarious celebrations of the 500th anniversary of Columbus's discovery of America is Seville's colossal *Expo '92* (April 20 to October 12). It ranks as a Class I *Universal Exposition,* the highest category of world's fair — and the last to be scheduled in this century.

The *Expo '92* site is the 538-acre Cartuja Island in the Guadalquivir River, just "offshore" from northern downtown Seville, accessible by new bridges, taxi, automobile, bus, water taxi, aerial tramways, helicopter, and horse-drawn carriages. Visitors can walk from downtown Seville to *Expo* by crossing the new Puente de la Cartuja pedestrian bridge at Plaza de Armas, or they can take the cable car at the plaza that travels to and through the site, connecting to the monorail that encircles the area. The other new pedestrian bridge, La Barqueta, is farther up the river in the northern part of the city. Motor vehicles can cross on the Calatrava, the Chapina, and other bridges that lead to both sides of Cartuja Island where there is parking for 40,000 cars and 1,100 buses. The world's fair complex includes some 96 restaurants, 70 bars, 51 shops, 10 banks, 10 tourist information offices, three monorail stations, and three cable car stations.

A record 103 nations, 22 international organizations, and 24 multinational companies, as well as each of Spain's 17 autonomous regions, are participating in the festivities following the theme of "The Age of Discoveries." The event is celebrating mankind's ingenuity, creativity, and thirst for knowledge, and our discoveries of Planet Earth, outer space, and human consciousness. Exhibits highlight innovations in mathematics, physics, chemistry, biology, and the social sciences through the past 5 centuries, as well as delineating the frontier fields of our own time — data processing, telecommunications, genetic engineering, medicine, and space exploration.

Before the advent of *Expo '92,* the barren Cartuja Island site was inhabited only by the 15th-century Carthusian Monastery of Santa María de las Cuevas, where Columbus lived and prepared for his voyages, and the adjacent 19th-century ceramics factory, both now impeccably restored to comprise the lavish Royal Pavilion of Spain. Visitors experience "time travel" in the Spanish government's four theme pavilions: *Discovery, The Fifteenth Century, Navigation,* and *The Future.* The $50-million United States Pavilion, with the theme "Rediscover the USA," showcases all 50 states and every ethnic background that comprises the country, as well as additional exhibits by *NASA* and the *Smithsonian Institution.* Amid the overwhelming schedule of events, each country celebrates its own *National Day* (see box). The United States's big bash will be on the *Fourth of July.* Visitors also will get a taste of the folklore of each of Spain's regions through productions of each area's own traditional fiestas and festivals.

Some 55,000 performances are scheduled day and night throughout the 6-month "cultural fiesta" (see *Theater and Music*). Major operatic productions in Seville's new *Maestranza Opera House* include *Carmen, The Barber of Seville,* and other milestones inspired by the city.

Entrance tickets to *Expo '92* and hotel accommodations can be arranged through US travel agents and tour operators. *Expotourist Services* (Isla de la Cartuja, Seville 41010; phone: 446-1992) provides general information and brochures. The official *Expo '92* reservations center for hotel accommodation is *Coral* (Isla de la Cartuja, Seville 41010; phone: 429-0092). For more information, see *Checking In.*

Below is an abbreviated list of some of the highlights of *Expo '92.* All 103 nations participating will celebrate a *National Day,* as will all 17 regions of Spain.

DATES TO REMEMBER

Opening date: April 20, 1992
Special Day of Madrid: May 2, The Palenque
The National Day of France: May 6, The Palenque
The Special Day of The European Communities: May 9, The Palenque
The National Day of the United Kingdom: May 21, The Palenque
The National Day of Portugal: June 10, The Palenque
The Special Day of the United Nations: June 26, The Palenque
The National Day of Canada: July 1, The Palenque
The National Day of the United States: July 4, The Palenque
The National Day of Spain: October 12, The Palenque
Closing date: October 12, 1992

SOURCES AND RESOURCES

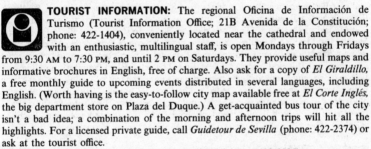

TOURIST INFORMATION: The regional Oficina de Información de Turismo (Tourist Information Office; 21B Avenida de la Constitución; phone: 422-1404), conveniently located near the cathedral and endowed with an enthusiastic, multilingual staff, is open Mondays through Fridays from 9:30 AM to 7:30 PM, and until 2 PM on Saturdays. They provide useful maps and informative brochures in English, free of charge. Also ask for a copy of *El Giraldillo,* a free monthly guide to upcoming events distributed in several languages, including English. (Worth having is the easy-to-follow city map available free at *El Corte Inglés,* the big department store on Plaza del Duque.) A get-acquainted bus tour of the city isn't a bad idea; a combination of the morning and afternoon trips will hit all the highlights. For a licensed private guide, call *Guidetour de Sevilla* (phone: 422-2374) or ask at the tourist office.

The US Consulate is at 7 Paseo de las Delicias (phone: 423-1885).

Local Coverage – Daily newspapers widely read in Seville are *El Correo de Andalucía* and provincial editions of the daily *ABC* and *El País.* Visitors rely on the monthly *El Giraldillo,* available free in shops and hotels, as well as at the tourist office. For information on art, entertainment, dining, and nightlife, the weekly *Revista del Ocio* leisure magazine has it all in Spanish, but the names and addresses are easily understood.

TELEPHONE: The city code for Seville is 5. If calling from within Spain, dial 95 before the local number. Note that all Seville phone numbers now have seven digits and begin with a 4. Many brochures and other printed materials still give old numbers with fewer than seven digits. To convert these to the new system, simply preface them with a 4.

GETTING AROUND: It's possible to walk almost anywhere in the city, but the summer heat and the duration of most tourist visits, too short for a leisurely pace, may make a bit of help desirable.

Airport – Seville's recently revamped and expanded Aeropuerto San

Pablo (phone: 451-0677) is 8 miles (13 km) from town. There is frequent airport bus service. Cab fare for the 20-minute ride should be around $15.

Bus – Bright orange buses go everywhere in the city. Pick up a route map at the tourist office or in front of the *Inglaterra* hotel in Plaza Nueva, where city routes begin. Fare is 75 pesetas (about 83¢ — exact change not required); discounted 10-trip tickets, 415 pesetas (about $4.60), are available in Plaza Nueva and at kiosks elsewhere. The tourist office also has schedules of intercity buses, which leave from the Estación de Autobuses (Central Bus Station), 1 Prado de San Sebastián (phone: 441-7111).

Car Rental – International rental companies represented include *Hertz* (3 Avenida República Argentina; phone: 427-8887; and at the airport); *Avis* (15 Avenida de la Constitución; phone: 421-6549; and at the airport); and *Europcar* (32 Calle Recaredo; phone: 441-9506; and at the airport).

Horse and Carriage – The way to go. During the *Feria,* even the locals do it. Rates, regulated by the city, run about $20 per hour. Choose your *calesa* from the lineup around the cathedral square or at María Luisa Park.

Taxi – Since distances are short, fares in town average under $4. Drivers legitimately charge extra for bigger pieces of luggage and for travel after 10 PM and on holidays. Hail cabs on the street or call *Radio-Taxi* (phone: 458-0000) or *Tele-Taxi* (phone: 462-2222).

Train – The sparkling new state-of-the-art Santa Justa train station, designed for *Expo '92* and for the 21st century, was inaugurated last fall on Avenida Kansas City (in turn, Seville's US sister city boasts a replica of La Giralda). A generally expanded and speedier rail network now radiates from Seville all across the peninsula. *RENFE*'s (Spanish National Railway's) new high-speed bullet trains now zoom between Seville and Madrid in 2¾ hours! (The little old San Bernardo station near Plaza España still handles local trains.) If you're planning to head to Seville's famous neo-Mudéjar Plaza de las Armas train station (also known as Estación de Córdoba), it's good to know that as of last year it is no longer a train station. The refurbished landmark building now houses offices and an important art exhibition center; the tracks leading to it have been replaced by a riverside promenade facing the *Expo '92* site on Cartuja Island. Near the old train station, however, a new aerial tramway crosses the river, running through the fair site all the way to its north end. Schedules and tickets can be obtained from the *RENFE* office (29 Calle Zaragoza; phone: 441-4111), near Plaza Nueva.

 SPECIAL EVENTS: This year's extravaganza is *Expo '92* (see *Extra Special* for details). In addition, every year two world-famous festivals make springtime prime time. The city is mobbed for both events, with hotels booked a year in advance, restaurant tables at a premium, and rates for horse and carriage doubled. But you get a lot of Seville for the money. During the emotion-packed *Semana Santa* (Holy Week), which begins on *Palm Sunday,* members of the city's more than 50 *cofradías* (brotherhoods) — religious organizations with origins in 16th-century guilds — take to the streets each evening in candlelit processions. Robed and hooded in traditional penitential garb, they are followed by *costaleros* (porters) staggering under the weight of elaborate gilt and bejeweled *pasos* (floats) bearing statues of Christ or the Virgin Mary that are carried to the cathedral and back to their own parish churches. The most popular images, such as the beloved Virgen de la Macarena, crying crystal tears, bring out a mixture of mourning and revelry in the crowd as spectators fall into step behind the penitents, break into flamenco laments called *saetas,* and root for their favorite floats.

By the time *Semana Santa* ends on *Easter Sunday,* Seville is ready to begin dressing for the riotous *Feria* (April Fair), which opens 2 weeks later. Across the river, near Los Remedios, workers already are putting up rows of green- and white-striped *casetas* (little tents) where families, companies, and clubs hold open house or private fiestas around the clock during the 6 days of celebration. The fair began in the mid-19th century as a rural livestock market, but it has gussied itself up considerably since then: Andalusia's high-stepping horses, in tassels and bells, go through their paces, and brightly costumed groups parade around town in flower-decked coaches. There are nightly *corridas,* fireworks, amusements, and dancing — mainly *sevillanas* — in the streets.

 MUSEUMS: Most of the museums of interest to visitors are discussed in *Special Places.* In addition, Seville has the *Museo de Arte Contemporáneo* (5 Calle Santo Tomás; phone: 421-5830). A repository of Spanish art of the 20th century in an 18th-century building, it's open Tuesdays through Fridays from 10 PM to 7 PM, and Saturdays and Sundays from 10 AM to 2 PM. Admission charge.

 SHOPPING: Anyone looking for the across-the-board bargains of a few years back will do better shopping at home, but anyone coveting a gorgeous hand-embroidered, silk-fringed shawl that would be hard to find elsewhere has come to the right place. Seville has Andalusia's largest selection of mantillas, fans, hand-embroidered linen and shawls (if prices sound too low, make sure it's not machine embroidery), flamenco dresses, castanets, and guitars. Plenty of the above can be found in colorful shops around the cathedral and in the Barrio de Santa Cruz. For more, plus shoes and handbags, go downtown, and don't miss Calle Sierpes. Seville's favorite pedestrian street, tiled in rose and blue, winds downtown for about 5 blocks between Plaza de San Francisco, behind the Ayuntamiento, and Plaza la Campana, an intersection of several streets near Plaza del Duque (some maps give its full name, Plaza del Duque de la Victoria). Nearby are tiny Calle Rosario and Calle Muñoz Olive, lined with boutiques selling Italian and French fashions. Seville's two big downtown department stores, *El Corte Inglés* (Plaza del Duque) and *Galerías Preciados* (Plaza de la Magdalena) are good fallback stops because they don't close for siesta — and they're good bets for a quick, inexpensive lunch. The latter has an upstairs coffee shop serving burgers and malts as well as Spanish snacks and luncheon specials, wines, and cocktails; the cafeteria in the former store offers similar values but is much more crowded. (*El Corte Inglés* is also strong on guidebooks and maps.)

Other possibilities include a leather crafts and jewelry fair that takes place daily except Sundays on Plaza del Duque opposite *El Corte Inglés,* a Sunday morning crafts fair downtown at Alameda de Hércules, and a Sunday morning stamp and coin market at Plaza del Cabildo. The picturesque Triana food market occupies tumbledown stalls under the Triana Bridge across the river, and the indoor *El Arenal* food market is near the bullring at Calle Pastor y Landero (both markets are open mornings and closed Sundays).

La Alcazaba – Delicate hand-painted ceramic tiles and platters from Seville and other regions, including the lovely florals from Valencia. Near the Alcázar exit. 1A Calle Joaquín Romero Murube (phone: 421-8088).

Artesanía Textil – Mantillas, silk shawls, embroidered linen, fans, and everyday leather coats and jackets for men and women, sold in a factory-to-customer atmosphere near Plaza del Cabildo. 33 Calle García de Vinuesa (phone: 422-1606). Also in the Barrio de Santa Cruz at 4 Plaza de Doña Elvira (phone: 421-4748).

Artespaña – Part of the Spain-wide, government-sponsored chain, selling arts and crafts from all over the country — and they pack and ship. Near *El Corte Inglés.* 2 Plaza de la Gavidia (phone: 422-1865).

Bolsos Casal – Medium-priced handbags and luggage. There are several branches downtown; a helpful sales staff can be found at 73 Calle Sierpes (phone: 422-6055).

El Caballo – Andalusian horsemen come to this shop near the bullring for the finest leather boots, saddles, hunting gear, traditional riding suits, and flat, wide-brimmed hats. 14 Calle Adriano (phone: 422-2047).

Casa Rubio – Exquisite lacy, hand-painted fans. 56 Calle Sierpes (phone: 422-6872).

Cerámica Santa Ana – A large selection of ceramics at good prices. In Triana. 31 Calle San Jorge (phone: 433-3990).

Convento de San Leandro – It's impossible to buy more authentic *yemas* (dainty sweets of egg yolk and sugar) than the ones made by the nuns here. Near the Casa de Pilatos. 1 Plaza de San Ildefonso (phone: 422-4195).

Juan Feronda – Mantillas, shawls, flamenco dresses, linen; several stores, but the best selection is at the one near La Giralda. 18 Calle Argote de Molina (phone: 422-8467).

Loewe – The ultimate in luxury leather (women's handbags begin at around $350), wallets, attaché cases, luggage, and couture by a fifth-generation Madrid firm, with some items up to 30% less than at US branches. 12 Plaza Nueva (phone: 422-5253) and at the *Alfonso XIII* hotel (phone: 422-1371).

Martian – Hand-painted ceramics of the highest quality. 74 Calle Sierpes (phone: 421-3413).

El Postigo Artesanía – Not a single shop but a group of boutiques in a 3-story arcade; made-to-measure flamenco dresses, religious art, antiques, contemporary jewelry, ceramics, paintings, and leather goods. Calle Arfe at Plaza del Cabildo (phone: 421-3976).

Sevillarte – A beautiful selection of hand-painted ceramics. 66 Calle Sierpes (phone: 421-2836).

Vértice – Guidebooks and maps in Spanish and English, as well as books on Spanish art and history. In the Barrio de Santa Cruz. 24 Calle Mateos Gago (phone: 421-1654).

SPORTS AND FITNESS: *Expo '92* will leave a legacy of sports facilities on its Cartuja Island site including a state-of-the-art track and field complex, and the *Seville Rowing Center* on the Guadalquivir River.

Boating – Clubs along the right back of Guadalquivir, including *El Náutico* (phone: 445-4777) offer facilities for sailboating, rowing, and canoeing. Also, look for the "Barcos" sign along the river in the vicinity of Plaza de Cuba.

Bullfighting – The *Maestranza* bullring (see *Special Places*) is the setting for Seville's bullfights and is the oldest and possibly most beautiful bullring in Spain. The season opens on *Easter Sunday* and runs until October. Tickets are sold at the ring, at the *Agencia Teatral* (phone: 422-8229), or in bars along Calle Sierpes. Paseo de Colón (phone: 422-3506).

Horse Racing – Seville's racetrack is the *Hipódromo del Club Pineda* (Avenida de Jerez; phone: 461-1400). The club offers horseback riding facilities and instruction, a 9-hole golf course, and a swimming pool. Races take place on Sundays from October through February or March.

Jogging – María Luisa Park in the cool of the morning is the place to run.

Soccer – The city's two first division teams are *Real Betis,* based at the *Benito Villamarín* stadium, and *Sevilla,* which plays at the *Sánchez Pizjuán* stadium. The season runs from September to the beginning of May.

Swimming – The *Alfonso XIII, Meliá Sevilla, Doña María,* and other hotels have pools; if yours doesn't, try the *Municipales Chapina* (Avenida Cristo de la Expiración; phone: 433-3654), one of several municipal pools in town.

Tennis – Hotel concierges sometimes can arrange guest sessions at private tennis facilities such as the *Betis Tenis Club,* Calle San Salvador (phone: 423-1028).

THEATER AND MUSIC: The brightest stars in the galaxy of entertainment will be shining in Seville during the 6-month-long *Expo '92* (April 20 to October 12). A schedule of over 55,000 live performances will be spread over 16-hour-long days in Cartuja Island's pavilions, gardens, and avenues, and over a dozen new entertainment venues including the *Expo Theater, Expo Cinema* (with a gargantuan 3,100-square-foot outdoor screen), *Cartuja Auditorium,* the *Palenque-Marquee, Cinema Street,* and "Expo-night" spectaculars on the high-tech manmade lake. On the city side of the river, parks, plazas, and theaters will be glowing more than ever with the world's most popular music, theater, dance companies, and entertainment stars.

In addition to stellar bullfighters and the bravest bulls, the *Maestranza* bullring is the setting for the Andalucía Pavilion's "How the Andalusian Horses Dance," featuring the amazingly balletic *Royal School of Equestrian Art* (home-based in nearby Jerez de la Frontera), every Saturday throughout *Expo.* The refurbished *Lope de Vega Theater* (Avenida María Luisa Park; phone: 423-1835), originally built for the *1929 Iberoamerican Exposition,* and its new *Expo Theater* (Cartuja Island) will co-present a series of the best in world theater. The former stages traditional works and the latter avant-garde. This also is the year in which Seville will be the apogee of the flamenco performing arts world with its festival of the *Biennal de Arte Flamenco,* held at various venues throughout the city.

And, at last, Seville has its own opera house! The *Teatro de la Maestranza* (5 Nuñes de Balboa; phone: 456-0520; fax: 456-0698), was inaugurated last May to join the ranks of Europe's best. It will kick off *Expo* with a grand production of Bizet's *Carmen* (co-starring Spanish tenor Plácido Domingo) which, along with other Seville-inspired works — Rossini's *The Barber of Seville,* Verdi's *La Forza del Destino,* Beethoven's *Fidelio,* Donizetti's *La Favorita,* Mozart's *Marriage of Figaro* and *Don Giovanni,* as well as quintessentailly Spanish *zarzuelas* — will be on the marquee into the 21st century.

 NIGHTCLUBS AND NIGHTLIFE: Seville keeps the flamenco flame burning nightly in rousing song and dance cabarets called *tablaos,* even more authentic than those of Madrid, especially since flamenco is Andalusian (and Seville is Andalusia's capital). The *tablao*'s handful of dancers, guitarists, and singers, some young and sleek, some mature and hefty (looks matter less than ability and *duende* — raw emotion), run through a repertoire of stylized songs and dances that express Gypsy sorrows, loves, and joys. The show usually begins with a sometimes virtuoso duet by guitarists seated on a small and simple wooden stage and ends in a whirlwind of ruffles and the thunder of guitar strings, handclaps, and footwork. Tickets, which can usually be reserved through hotels, cost around $30, one glass of wine included; depending on the season, there are two or three shows a night. *Los Gallos* (11 Plaza de Santa Cruz; phone: 421-6981), a romantic little theater in the Barrio de Santa Cruz, has a well-known troupe. *El Arenal* (7 Calle Rodo; phone: 421-6492), in a cobbled alley near the river, puts on a stirring, authentic *tablao* and also offers a dinner show for about $40. *El Patio Sevillano* (11 Paseo de Cristóbal Colón; phone: 421-4120) offers a program that includes flamenco, folk dance, and classical guitar. Do-it-yourself flamenco can be sampled by joining the locals on the floor of one of the *sevillanas* discos called *salas rocieras* on the Barrio de los Remedio's earthy Calle Salado. If you don't know how to dance *sevillanas* (Seville's own folk dance, related to flamenco), just watch and enjoy. Go after 1 AM, when the young crowd begins warming up to dance at *Canela Pura,* a modest storefront pub (9 Calle Salado), or drop in at nearby *Tres Faroles* (8A Calle Salado) or at *La Garrocha* (11 Calle Salado).

For a less folkloric change of pace, save an evening for the little Euro-style bars, pubs, and outdoor cafés between Calle Virgen de Africa and Calle Virgen de las Montañas near *La Dorada* restaurant in Los Remedios. For international disco, the action is at *Holiday* (downtown at 73 Calle Jesús del Gran Poder, in the former red-light district); *El Coto* (in the *Lebreros Hotel,* 118 Calle Luis Montoto); or *Río* (Calle Betis), where you can cruise a whole gaggle of riverside clubs. Go late.

BEST IN TOWN

CHECKING IN: As the capital of Andalusia, Seville attracts business and government travelers as well as tourists, so there's a wide selection of hotels. With an estimated 300,000 daily visitors to *Expo,* hotel rooms in Seville proper figure to be scarce, and visitors may want to opt for accommodations on the Costa del Sol (which has 600,000 additional rooms). Other Andalusian cities also are connected to Seville by new rapid trains and superhighways. Madrid is only 2¾ hours away via *RENFE*'s new bullet train. The "Open City Program" has made 60,000 beds available in government-approved private residences in Seville and its immediate environs at rates 25% to 50% less than 2- or 3-star hotels. Contact *Exhibit* (37-A Avenida República Argentina, Seville 41011; phone: 428-2936). Rates usually are lowest during the hot summer months, when Spaniards are taking their own vacations at the beach. Prices are much higher during *Semana Santa* and the *Feria* and will remain high while *Expo* reigns. With a few exceptions, our choices are confined to those most suitable for leisure travelers; unless otherwise noted, all are within reasonable walking distance of the central area including the cathedral, Alcázar, and the Barrio de Santa Cruz. All have some English-speaking personnel, and their concierges or desk clerks are generous with advice to help guests get around the city. Hotels have air conditioning unless otherwise noted, and breakfast is available even when there is no formal restaurant. Expect to pay from $125 to $250 for a double room in hotels listed as expensive, from $75 to $125 for those listed as moderate, and from $30 to $75 for the inexpensive ones. All telephone numbers are in the 5 city code unless otherwise indicated.

Alfonso XIII – It makes no difference that this handsome Spanish palace is a reproduction, built in 1929 for the *Iberoamerican Exposition.* Even a caliph could be fooled by its *azulejo*-lined hallways, ultra-spacious guestrooms (149), regal lobby, white marble courtyard, and Moroccan garden with a big swimming pool and poolside bar. Unsurpassed for location, Seville's grande dame (now part of the CIGA chain) not only is a hop, skip, and jump from the Alcázar, but also central enough to let a visitor walk downtown in one direction and to María Luisa Park in the other. Its restaurant is the elegant continental *Itálica.* It also has tennis courts. 2 Calle San Fernando (phone: 422-2850; in the US, 800-221-2340; fax: 421-6033). Very expensive.

Príncipe de Asturias – This new supreme-luxury establishment bears the title of the son of the present King Juan Carlos I, heir to the throne of Spain. (Prince of Asturias is a title comparable to Prince of Wales.) While Seville's noble *Alfonso XIII* hotel, named after and inaugurated by the great grandfather of the Prince of Asturias, was built for the *1929 Iberoamerican Exhibition,* this place, inaugurated last July, was built for *Expo '92.* It stands in the center of the fair's Cartuja Island site, near Spain's Royal Pavilion, facing the Guadalquivir, and is a short walk from the center of Seville across La Barqueta pedestrian bridge. Designed in three ultramodern circular modules, there are 303 luxurious rooms and suites with every imaginable amenity, plus tennis courts, a swimming pool, health and fitness center, conference and business facilities, and 2 restaurants. During *Expo,* the hotel will be occupied by heads of state and dignitaries. Isla de la Cartuja (phone: 446-0565 or 446-0092). Very expensive.

Casas de la Judería – Just the thing for anyone who wants to go native, in a very upscale sort of way. Tucked in the historic heart of the Barrio de Santa Cruz, near Plaza Santa María la Blanca, these furnished luxury apartments occupy a group of refurbished 3-story buildings that once belonged to the Duke of Bejár, patron and benefactor of Cervantes. Each of the 35 units — 1 to 3 bedrooms — has a fully equipped kitchen, direct dial telephones, and satellite television; some have terraces and private elevators, and some even have Andalusian-style patios with a fountain. No restaurant, but breakfast is served. Callejón de Dos Hermanas (phone: 441-5150; fax: 442-2170). Expensive.

Inglaterra – Its very central location makes this sleek, remodeled old-timer a convenient headquarters for an in-depth visit to the city. (All buses stop at its front door.) The big, comfortable, contemporary salon is an after-work gathering spot for downtown bankers and businessmen. Rooms (116 of them, some with terraces on the square) have modern furnishings; service is efficient, the concierge desk is helpful, and there is a sunny second-floor restaurant. 7 Plaza Nueva (phone: 422-4970; fax: 456-1336). Expensive.

Meliá Sevilla – The jazziest of the newer hotels in town is in an L-shaped high-rise apartment and shopping complex near María Luisa Park. The bright white marble atrium lobby, decidedly trendy café scene, choice of restaurants, disco, and swimming pool, and the adjoining boutiques could hold up any sightseeing. Decor in the 366 rooms is ultramodern. 3 Avenida de la Borbolla (phone: 442-2611; fax: 442-1608). Expensive.

Tryp Colón – A luxurious rival to the *Alfonso XIII,* this is an old hotel that's been completely redone, right down to the white sofas and the restored antique glass dome in the upstairs lobby. Because the property — with its 204 rooms and 14 suites — is handy to the bullring, it is the traditional headquarters for touring toreros, and a bullfighting theme prevails in the fine *El Burladero* restaurant (see *Eating Out*). Located in the middle of downtown. 1 Calle Canalejas (phone: 422-2900 or fax: 422-0938). Expensive.

Husa Sevilla – Facing a small square in the Triana district, this place is in a new building, but one that is true to traditional Sevillian style — pastel stucco façade, wood-beamed ceilings, potted plants, hand-painted tiles, and marble accents. It has 116 rooms and 16 suites (all soundproof), a bar, café, and a restaurant, and it's only a few blocks back from the river, a 15-minute walk across the Triana Bridge to the core of the city. 90 Pagés del Corro (phone: 434-2412; fax: 434-2107). Expensive to moderate.

Macarena Sol – Casablanca kitsch describes the mirror-trimmed Andalusian façade and rattan-furnished lobby-bar patio complete with fountain. Across from the old Roman and Moorish walls and the Basílica de la Macarena, this 327-room hostelry is a taxi ride away from the center of town. Now, however, its location has become prime because of its proximity to Cartuja Island (the *Expo '92* site) — a short walk across the new, nearby La Barqueta pedestrian bridge. There is a good restaurant, busy cafeteria, shops, and an executive floor with special services and amenities. 2 Calle San Juan de Ribera (phone: 437-5700; fax: 438-1803). Expensive to moderate.

Pasarela – Near the *Meliá Sevilla* but closer to the park, this one is small (82 rooms), modern, efficient, and a current favorite with Spanish business travelers. No restaurant. 11 Avenida de la Borbolla (phone: 441-5511; fax: 442-0727). Expensive to moderate.

América – An affordable, efficient, modern businessman's hotel in the heart of the downtown shopping district, across from the *El Corte Inglés* department store. It has 100 rooms, motel decor, a cafeteria, and no atmosphere, but the service is good and it's close to Calle Sierpes, the *Museo de Bellas Artes,* and the Triana Bridge. 2 Calle Jesús del Gran Poder (phone: 422-0951; fax: 421-0626). Moderate.

Bécquer – On a lovely café-lined street 2 blocks from the Triana Bridge and only a short walk to the *Maestranza Bullring,* shopping, and the *Museo de Bellas Artes.*

It offers a wood-paneled lobby, big-hotel service, and 126 average rooms. No restaurant. 4 Calle Reyes Católicos (phone: 422-2172; fax: 421-4400). Moderate.

Doña María – Every morning this intimate, luxurious little place gets calls from people hoping for cancellations. The location (one door up from the cathedral square), the combination of period charm and up-to-date convenience, the romantic decor in the 61 rooms (all one-of-a-kind), and the little rooftop swimming pool in the shadow of La Giralda make it the number one small hotel choice. No restaurant. 19 Calle Don Remondo (phone: 422-4990; fax: 421-9546). Moderate.

Puerta de Triana – It shares the same attractive, convenient location as the *Bécquer* across the street, but it costs even less, and many of the 65 rooms have balconies on the avenue. Despite the postage-stamp lobby with the soft-drink machine and blaring TV set, it's an outstanding buy. 5 Calle Reyes Católicos (phone: 421-5401; fax: 421-5401). Moderate to inexpensive.

Goya – This *hostal* (inn) is one of those too-good-to-be true bargains: a narrow house with gaily striped awnings in the Barrio de Santa Cruz, 20 shipshape rooms, a charming upstairs garden — and budget-minded guests congratulating one another on finding it. No air conditioning; no restaurant. Write early for reservations. 31 Calle Mateos Gago (phone: 421-1170). Inexpensive.

EATING OUT: The capital of Andalusia sets a fine table, although all of the city's dazzling *tapas* bars (see below) may keep you from sitting down to it. The star of restaurant menus haute or lowly is sweet Atlantic seafood from Huelva. Try baby fish and eels, batter-dipped and deep-fried to airy crispness, as in *fritura;* bass baked in a tomato casserole as in *urta a la roteña;* shrimp sautéed in olive oil and hot red peppers as in *gambas al pil pil;* or hake simply pan-fried in a bit of olive oil as in *merluza a la plancha.* Delicious cured country ham is found everywhere in Spain, but the local mahogany-colored *jamón de Jabugo,* found in better *tapas* bars, is the best. Other dishes to try are Seville's favorite, *huevos a la flamenca* (baked eggs with asparagus and peas), and, in cold weather, *rabo de toro* (oxtail stew), or, in warm weather, gazpacho, the cold tomato and cucumber soup. No wine is made in Seville, so the "local" wine comes from Jerez, Andalusia's sherry and wine capital. When a dry sherry aperitif is in order, ask for a *fino* or for the very special dry, amber-colored *manzanilla* from Sanlúcar de Barrameda. Or try a big pitcher of cooling sangria laden with orange and lemon slices.

Seville's restaurants observe the traditional long lunches, closing in late afternoon and opening again around 8 PM for early-bird diners. (If you crave a sandwich in between, drop by an American-style cafeteria or ask for a *bocadillo* — a sandwich on a hard roll — anywhere you see *tapas.*) Menus with English translations are the rule, and many economy restaurants compete for tourists by displaying photographs of their popular dishes. Expect to pay from $60 to $100 for an average three-course meal for two with house wine in a restaurant listed below as expensive (the *menú de la casa* could run less), from $20 to $60 in a moderate restaurant, and under $20 in an inexpensive one. Opening days and hours change from time to time and some places usually close for at least a month's summer vacation. However, during *Expo '92,* some summer closings may not take place. Call before you go. All telephone numbers are in the 5 city code unless otherwise indicated.

La Albahaca – Gracious dining prevails in this stately old mansion that a famed Spanish architect built for himself in the Barrio de Santa Cruz. Dine late on such delicacies as *perdiz del coto en cazerola* (partridge casserole) or *lubina al hinojo* (a type of sea bass with fennel) and attend the midnight *tablao* at *Los Gallos* right next door. Closed Sundays. Reservations necessary. American Express, Diners Club, and Visa accepted. 12 Plaza de Santa Cruz (phone: 422-0714). Expensive.

Egaña-Oriza – A chic, Basque-owned bastion of nouvelle cuisine, it's *the* place to be seen in Seville. It enjoys a glamorous greenhouse setting against a wall of the Alcázar Gardens (a small section of the wall, a national monument, is actually inside the entrance). Out front, café tables have a good view of the adjoining Murillo Gardens, the flashy fountain in Plaza San Juan de Austria, and promenading *sevillanos*. The menu runs to elegant innovations such as *gazpacho con langostinos de Sanlúcar* (gazpacho with Sanlúcar prawns) or *solomillo con mousse de foie a las uvas de Corintio* (steak with foie gras in a grape sauce). Closed Sundays and August. Reservations essential for lunch or dinner. Major credit cards accepted. 41 Calle San Fernando (phone: 422-7211). Expensive.

Enrique Becerra – Most visitors never take the trouble to find this elite little gem hidden away on a narrow street off the Plaza Nueva. Besides the cozy dining room on the main floor, there are private dining salons upstairs (two people can reserve the smallest one for themselves). Friendly waiters offer advice about the chef's highly personalized menu. Closed Sundays at lunch. Reservations advised. Major credit cards accepted. 2 Calle Gamazo (phone: 421-3049). Expensive.

La Isla – Though locals are put off by its formality, the restaurant's high-backed, black-lacquer chairs and salmon tablecloths make a relaxing setting in which to enjoy extraordinarily fresh seafood flown in from Galicia. Select a personal favorite from the refrigerated window display on the street. This is a comfortable place to spend the afternoon after a hard day in the Alcázar across Avenida de la Constitución. Closed August. Reservations advised. Major credit cards accepted. 25 Calle Arfe (phone: 421-5376). Expensive.

Ox's – A typical Basque *asador* (barbecue restaurant) specializing in the finest quality charcoal-grilled meats, fish, and some Sevillian specialties. It's a local favorite, on a par in its way, with *Egaña-Oriza,* which used to share the building. Closed Sundays and August. Reservations advised. American Express, Diners Club, and Visa accepted. 61 Calle Betis (phone: 427-9585). Expensive.

El Burladero – The name refers to the bullfighter's protective barrier at the entrances to the arena, and the taurine theme here is carried all the way from photographs of past heroes such as Juan Belmonte and Rafael El Gallo on the walls to cattle-brand designs woven into the damask tablecloths. And, since it's in the elegant *Colón* hotel, tuxedoed waiters serve with a style that attracts a top-drawer clientele — stop in at the bar and watch the city's yuppies networking. The menu, largely continental, includes regional specialties from all over Spain, among them the Andalusian *bacalao al horno con patatas* (baked salt cod with saffron and potatoes) and *pochas con almejas* (white kidney beans with clams). Open daily. Reservations necessary. American Express, Diners Club, and Visa accepted. 1 Calle Canalejas (phone: 422-2900). Expensive to moderate.

La Dorada – This big, bright, seafood restaurant — with waiters and waitresses in snappy nautical uniforms, and a doorman in captain's garb — was the model for *La Doradas* in Barcelona and Madrid. Order the specialty, *dorada a la sal,* sea bream baked in a crust of rock salt, which is cracked open at tableside to release the tender, sweet, steaming fish, or the *fritura malagueña* (tiny baby eels, baby squid, and red mullet, none longer than a little finger, dipped in batter and fried to a crunch). Closed Sundays and August. Reservations advised. Major credit cards accepted. 6 Calle Virgen de Aguas Santas (phone: 445-5100). Expensive to moderate.

Figón del Cabildo – The decor of heavy plaster, brick, and wood beams is the perfect setting for Sevillian specialties in this popular spot across Avenida de la Constitución from the cathedral. Try *berenjenas gratinadas con jamón y langostinos* (eggplant with ham and crayfish) or *sopa de picadillo* (consommé with egg yolk and ham). Closed Sunday evenings. Reservations advised. Major credit cards accepted. Plaza del Cabildo (phone: 422-0117). Expensive to moderate.

El Rincón de Curro – Anyone will tell you that this comfortable restaurant (another place where white plaster and dark wood beams predominate) in Los Remedios is the best place in town for meat dishes, although there's a good seafood menu, too. Food critics have singled out the *cochinillo asado a la segoviana* (roast suckling pig) and the *chuletón de buey al plato caliente* (steak sizzling on a hot clay plate). Closed Sunday evenings and August. Reservations necessary. Major credit cards accepted. 45 Calle Virgen de Luján (phone: 445-0238). Expensive to moderate.

Hostería del Laurel – This place has a come-on that's better than its food — Don Juan supped here (or at least the man who inspired the legend did). Nevertheless, an acceptable menu of Andalusian standards, served in country dining rooms hung with bunches of garlic and dried laurel, makes it a pleasant lunch stop in the Barrio de Santa Cruz. (The large ruined wall across the way belongs to the Hospital de los Venerables Sacerdotes, a 17th-century home for old priests that is noted for its patio and church, but closed for renovation at present.) Open daily. Reservations advised. American Express and Visa accepted. 5 Plaza de los Venerables (phone: 422-0295). Moderate.

Mesón Don Raimundo – If there's time for only one meal in Seville, have it in this restaurant, in a convent ruin in the Barrio de Santa Cruz. A long, dark alley overgrown with vines leads to capacious dining rooms decorated with massive Arab cooking vessels and farm utensils; a cozy barroom is patterned in tiles clear to the ceiling. Ask owner Raimundo Fernández for advice on the dishes he's adapted from old Arab-Spanish cookbooks: The baby lamb roasted over grape vines is especially good in the fall. Also try his *sopa de almejas con piñones* (clam soup with pine nuts) and the *pato mozárabe (*duck stuffed with apples, honey, nuts, and sultanas). Closed Sunday evenings. Reservations advised. American Express, Diners Club, and Visa accepted. 26 Calle Argote de Molina (phone: 422-3355). Moderate.

La Raza – This pretty terrace-restaurant in a park setting serves typical Andalusian food and drink and is most festive on a Friday or Saturday when there's music. Open daily. Reservations unnecessary. Major credit cards accepted. It's just inside the entrance to María Luisa Park (phone: 423-2024). Moderate.

Río Grande – Located in Triana, the best time here is evening, when the Torre del Oro across the river is bathed in lights. Dine indoors in the formal peach-walled Salon Reina Sofía or catch the river breeze on the broad terrace. There's a paella that's rich with goodies, perfect gazpacho, and *salteado de ternera a la sevillana* (diced veal with local green olives, carrots, and potatoes). Everyone should eat here once, or at least come for *tapas* at the long bar in the building across the patio. Open daily. Reservations necessary. American Express, MasterCard, and Diners Club accepted. 70 Calle Betis (phone: 427-3956). Moderate.

Taberna Dorada – Newer and snappier than most Seville seafood spots, this place attracts the young set. Closed Sundays and August. Reservations advised. Major credit cards accepted. 18 Calle José Luis de Casso (phone: 465-2720). Moderate.

Bodega El Diamante – A chain of *buffets libres* (all you can eat, self-service), not only a great buy, but also a way to eat quickly and without language problems. There's more than one, but this location generates so much traffic that the food is fresher and hotter. Load up on paella, *ensalada rusa* (potato salad with vegetables and mayonnaise), fried fishsticks, fish salads, hard-boiled eggs in mayonnaise, sliced tomatoes, fried eggplant, green and red peppers, and fresh fruit, but leave the *salchichas* (rubbery hot dogs) alone. Closed Sundays. No reservations. Visa and MasterCard accepted. 10 Avenida de la Constitución (no phone). Inexpensive.

Las Escobas – It claims to be Seville's oldest restaurant, having fed the likes of Lope de Vega, Miguel de Cervantes, and Lord Byron, and the elaborately carved bar and oak-paneled ceiling are convincing, despite the remodeling it has undergone. Of all the competing little eateries lined up on the streets north of the cathedral, this is the most pleasant place for *platos combinados* (economy specials), paper tablecloths notwithstanding. Open daily. Reservations unnecessary. No credit cards accepted. 62 Calle Alvarez Quintero (phone: 421-4479). Inexpensive.

 TAPAS BARS: *Tapas* originated in Andalusia. In fact, it is said that they were invented in Seville when, in the old days, wine or sherry was served with a free slice of ham covering the glass like a lid (*tapa*) in order to keep flies from diving into the wine. Another version explains that they were served on the house to drivers to dilute the effects of the wine, keeping them sober on the road. Whatever the truth, the selection of *tascas* (*tapas* bars) in Seville is bountiful and the camaraderie of *tasca* hopping, chowing down enough tidbits of seafood, hams, sausages, cheeses, and marinated vegetables to hold you between meals, is irresistible. A larger portion of a particular *tapa* is called a *ración* and can be a small meal in itself. Follow the crowd and you'll find it beating a path to the door of *Modesto* (5 Calle Cano y Queto, next to the Murillo Gardens), where the *acedías* (deep-fried baby sole) and *pimientos aliñados* (red and green peppers in a spicy marinade) are the talk of the town. Upstairs, there's a moderately priced restaurant. At *Sanlúcar-Mar* (in a tower at the far end of the Triana Bridge), a cozy basement restaurant and small upper dining terraces are among the choices, but the selection of *tapas* at the inviting U-shaped glass-and-brass bar on the main floor is so spectacular that you'll want to make a meal right there — or take *tapas* on a terrace that looks straight down the river with the city gleaming on both sides. (Dining is expensive to moderate here, but for the *tapas,* as elsewhere, figure about $2 to $5 for each little dish, depending on what you order.) Also at the end of the bridge, just down the steps from *Sanlúcar-Mar,* is a little sailors' bar, *Kiosko de las Flores,* where the young crowd chugs beer along with plates of big green olives into the night. Not far away are *El Puerto* (on Calle Betis, next door to the *Río Grande* restaurant), with a multilevel terrace right on the river — you serve yourself from a cafeteria bar — and a sit-down restaurant indoors; and *La Albariza Bodega* (6 Calle Betis), where upended black wine barrels serve as tables. Order plates of dry *serrano* ham, aged *manchego* cheese, olives, and sausages from the counter in back and stand around a barrel with a *copa* (glass of wine). Back across the river, in the Barrio de Santa Cruz (next to the *Hostería del Laurel* restaurant in Plaza de los Venerables), is the venerable *Casa Román,* a *tasca* that looks like a rustic country store (there's a deli counter up front). It serves the finest Jabugo ham in town — at around $11.50 per 100-gram portion (just short of a quarter pound). People who can — and can't — afford it meet here for a *fino* and *jamón* — it's the great leveler. You also can order to go, and choose from among their selection of other excellent but much less expensive hams.

TOLEDO

The very first glimpse of Toledo, whether its spires are piercing a winter mist or pointing heavenward toward a vibrant blue sky, confirms that it was not some newfangled city in Ohio that gave rise to the hackneyed exclamation "Holy Toledo!" This *is* the place — the original.

Even today, the Catholic Primate of Spain is based here, and within the old Arab ramparts that El Cid reclaimed, dozens of churches and convents stand atop older places of worship, holy archaeological heaps hidden beneath their foundations. History and legend glower from their very stones. The local Carpetani tribe of the Celt-Iberians lived here before the Romans founded the city of Toletum in 193 BC. Imperial coins were minted here, and a since-vanished aqueduct tapped the Tagus River. There are still traces of the Roman Circus on the north side of town, and the looming Alcázar, riddled by Civil War machine-gun fire, is built over the site of a 3rd-century Roman encampment. Later, Toledo became the seat of power for the Visigothic kingdom, which ultimately stretched into France during the 6th and 7th centuries. Leovigild, the Visigothic king, held council with his advisers near where the Cristo de la Luz hermitage now stands. The few relics from this era are displayed in the *Visigothic Museum* in the Church of San Román.

Known to the Moors as Tulaytulah, Toledo was required to pay tribute to the caliphs in Córdoba, but considerable autonomy was granted because it had put up so little resistance against the initial Arab invaders in 712. Toledo flourished, far removed from the intrigues and infighting of Al-Andalus to the south, and over the next 3 centuries grew into a city of silk and steel where clergy, merchants, and the military peacefully coexisted. Toledo's intimate courtyards, its characteristic covered passages bridging upper stories across alleyways, and its crooked streets, like narrow streams cutting through a mountain ravine, are all of obvious Moorish legacy. Its population of 200,000 was almost four times what it is today, and a prominent Jewish community — which was well established back in Visigothic times — throve alongside the Moors and Mozarabic Christians.

Even when King Alfonso VI and El Cid recaptured the city for Christendom in 1085, a cosmopolitan tolerance endured. During its first century as Spain's Christian capital, Toledo constantly fortified its walls and towers in readiness for war, but workaday life within the ramparts went largely uninterrupted. Before the full weight of the Catholic church pressed down to obliterate or banish the competition during the Spanish Inquisition, three religions enriched the lives of Toledo's citizenry. Christians, Muslims, and Jews cooperated in intellectual exchange and trade, and for nearly 5 centuries, Toledo enjoyed a reputation throughout the Mediterranean as a center of learning. Alfonso the Wise, King of Castile, grew up in this heady cultural mix and founded the influential School of Translators here during the 13th century.

Under his rule, Castilian Spanish became the official language, replacing Latin. His court of Jewish scholars made esoteric Greek and Arabic science (as well as the Islamic and Jewish religions) accessible to the people of northern Europe. Alchemists studied and worked alongside mathematicians and philosophers. Prosperity brought commissions for exquisite Mudéjar buildings; plaster ceilings as intricately carved as filigree complement sumptuously patterned tile and brick walls. Much of this craftsmanship still can be seen in Toledo's chapels, synagogues, hospitals, and palaces. High taxes, especially aimed at the wealthy Jewish merchants who worshiped at 12 different temples in the city, helped fund civic projects in the kingdom's capital. However, an abrupt pogrom in 1355 and the 1391 massacre at the Santa María la Blanca Synagogue were early warnings that Toledo's tolerance would not last, regardless of local traditions.

While the clergy in Toledo grew extremely potent, they were not always too pious to be expedient. Despite the persecutory efforts of Torquemada, the grand inquisitor, it was clear that Arab craftsmen were a mainstay of the city's livelihood. So on December 18, 1499, 4,000 Moors were baptized in Toledo by Cardinal Jiménez de Cisneros. Any Jew who refused the rite had already been killed or banished from Spain. The new Moorish converts kept up their swordsmithery and tile work, but concentrated on embellishing the interiors of the churches and monasteries. The convent Church of San Juan de los Reyes received special attention, intended as the eventual mausoleum for the Catholic Monarchs, King Ferdinand and Queen Isabella. Later events overtook this advance planning, and lavish tombs at Granada's cathedral now hold the pair. Isabella, who died in 1504, ultimately chose Granada as her burial site in order to commemorate the proudest moment of her reign: not the discovery of the New World, but the transformation of her present one, by the final act of the Reconquest — ousting the Moors from their last stronghold on the Iberian Peninsula, the Alhambra in Granada.

After Isabella's death, aging King Ferdinand ruled from Toledo; well-married daughter Juana was branded La Loca (the mad), unfit to reign. Cardinal Cisneros, the undisputed power behind the throne, took over the kingdom openly for a brief period after Ferdinand died in 1516, but the arrival of Juana's son, the Hapsburg heir to the throne, greatly diminished the cardinal's personal authority. Toledo became an imperial city when the new king, Carlos I of Spain, inherited the mantle of Holy Roman Emperor in 1519 and became Charles V. His double-headed eagle was unfurled, and from Toledo he also commanded Naples, Sicily, Sardinia, Germany, Franche-Comté, and the Low Countries, as well as the American lands newly plundered by the conquistadores. Great resentment quickly grew against the king and his court of foreigners. What rankled was his insistence on absolute rule, thwarting aspiring local nobles and church officials who were politically sophisticated. Tax hikes, which now would finance the European empire rather than go through the accustomed channels, were the final straw. Toledo's Juan de Padilla joined with Juan Bravo of Segovia in a local citizens' revolt, known as the Comuneros uprising. Both leaders were executed in 1521 when their rebellion was crushed, but they set the tone for Charles V's reign. Far-flung wars and revolts would continually strain his patience and his treasury, even with its unprecedented influx of Aztec gold and Inca silver.

Cervantes hailed Toledo as that "rocky gravity, glory of Spain and light of her cities," and it became the focus of Spain's golden age of literature. But that didn't stop Philip II, son of Charles V, from snubbing the arrogant clergy and moving the capital up the road to Madrid just 5 years after he assumed the throne in 1556, as his father prepared to retire to a monastery. Nevertheless, with the political distractions removed, Toledo remained the spiritual center of Spain, perched on a granite spire in the midst of the country. Traditionally, retiring Spanish cardinals can choose wherever they wish to hang up their official hats for the last time, and the number of odd tasseled scraps that are even now suspended like red velvet bats from unlikely spots in the vaulting of Toledo's cathedral attest that the city is still the cardinals' prize pick.

Distancing himself from the established church, King Philip II aimed to build from scratch a somber state retreat that might override the centuries of pious greed in Toledo. His palace-cum-mausoleum north of Madrid was meant to be a grand statement, a counter-reformation in stone. Eager artists from all over Europe competed for commissions at El Escorial, but one Cretan painter, Doménikos Theotokópoulos, soon fell from Philip's favor and was dismissed. He set up his studio in Toledo, where he became known simply as El Greco.

It is El Greco's skewed vision of Toledo, with its roiling clouds over elongated figures and startling clashes of color in almost geometric composition, that most visitors come to see. Indeed, the skyline has not changed measurably since he completed his *View over Toledo*. There are paintings galore: the *Burial of the Count of Orgaz* in the Church of San Tomé is held as a masterpiece, as is *El Expolio*. The artist's adopted hometown has no shortage of his work. In fact, El Greco has become such a significant local money-maker that the relentless promotion is off-putting. One might be tempted to take Philip's side and dismiss El Greco as a minor talent whose draftsmanship cannot compare with such masters as Titian or Rubens. For those inclined to adopt this line of thought, canvases are there for side-by-side comparison. Certainly, though, El Greco shattered the painterly conventions of his time, and the best of his work is breathtaking. Some art historians claim his use of color influenced a much later genius, Paul Cézanne.

Toledo's new status as a mere provincial capital and the fact that far more politically significant prizes were within striking distance spared this city from the worst of the battles that ravaged Spain in succeeding generations. But the Spanish Civil War was fought here with full fury. The huge restored Alcázar, which dominates the highest ground in Toledo and was once rebuilt by Charles V as a royal residence, was besieged for a grim 2 months in the summer of 1936. Franco's Nationalist forces held out against the Republicans despite blasts of dynamite that collapsed much of the fortress, formerly the most prestigious military academy in the nation.

The residents of contemporary Toledo are as long-suffering as any earlier forces inside the Alcázar. Hordes of visitors come daily to gawk at the city's treasures, inevitably getting lost in the tangle of narrow alleyways. The citizens resolutely provide directions, in response to queries in countless languages, and rarely lose their courtesy. When the last tour bus pulls away at dusk and the onslaught subsides, Toledo comes into its own. This is the best time to explore, finding the way back by remembering the coats of arms carved in stone on the buildings. The tackiest souvenir windows appear almost as comic relief, a balance to the weight of history.

TOLEDO AT-A-GLANCE

SEEING THE CITY: For an overall perspective, drive along Carretera de Circunvalación, which follows the banks of the Tagus River which surrounds Toledo like a moat. As the road climbs the hillsides, it passes close to a little hermitage called Virgen del Valle, and provides a sweeping view of the city. Close by is an outcropping called Cabeza del Moro (Moor's Head). Anywhere on the hillside offers a good view. Just to the left is the *Parador Conde de Orgaz* (see *Checking In*), the best place to watch the sunset, a drink in hand on the patio, with all of Toledo stretched out below. Just above the Alcántara Bridge is the Castillo de San Servando, a monastery revamped as a school, which offers a panorama from a different angle. For a more intimate view over Toledo's tiled rooftops and spires, climb the cathedral's belfry. A door on Calle Hombre de Palo (Straw Man Street) opens onto stairs in the cloisters that ascend the tower. *Miradero* literally means "lookout," and from this area, not far above the Puerta del Sol on the Cuesta de las Armas, informal cafés offer a fine vantage point out over the river and beyond. From nearly any strategic spot along the old walls, there is a sentry's view of the surrounding countryside.

SPECIAL PLACES: Toledo has so many points of interest that tourists would be hard-pressed to view even the exteriors of all historically important monuments on a single visit. If time is especially limited, pick up the free brochure from the tourist office at the Puerto de la Bisagra and follow its "essential itinerary," which is arranged in a very convenient sequence. Even though Toledo is quite small, its steep streets and dead ends can make monuments seem very far indeed. Be aware that Spanish visiting hours are erratic. To make the most of a visit, try to take the time to experience each place fully, rather than rush around checking off sites on a list and remembering nothing more than a blur.

Alcázar – Reconstruction atop reconstruction, this foursquare fortress has always been one of Toledo's key landmarks. Despite numerous sackings, torchings, and even bombings, this strategic building has been regirded, patched up, and continually put back into service. The Moors refashioned the Visigothic citadel built over an old Roman fort on the site, and El Cid reputedly served as the city's first governor here. The present structure dates from the time of Charles V, who converted it into a palace, though most of it is now a product of reconstruction. The north façade, with its Plateresque portal, was designed by Alonso de Covarrubias, as was the east façade, which is by far the oldest. Since the Imperial Court left the building almost 500 years ago, it has been wracked by misfortune. The palace became a state prison in 1643, and German, British, and Portuguese troops burned it in 1710, during the War of the Spanish Succession. After restoration by Cardinal Lorenzana, it stood only 35 years before French troops gutted it during the Peninsular War. It later reemerged as the national military academy, though it suffered another blaze at the hands of careless cadets and again had to be overhauled. Its worst days were during a Civil War siege in 1936, when a band of Nationalists, together with over 600 women and children, holed up inside for 2 months.

Republican bombs again reduced it to ruins. The dungeons are worth a visit, to see items like the motorcycle rigged to grind meal for the besieged. The emphasis on the ultimate Falangist victory brings out raw emotion in visiting Spaniards, and most who come to the *Museo de Asedio* (Siege Museum) are uncompromisingly rightist. There also is a reconstruction of Queen Blanca's medieval prison cell (Peter I locked her up here while he consorted with his mistress; no wonder he was nicknamed "the Cruel"). Open from 9:30 AM to 1:30 PM and from 4 to 6:30 PM; closed Mondays. Admission charge. Calle Capuchinos (phone: 223038).

Cathedral – For such an enormous building, the cathedral can be surprisingly difficult to locate. On approach, it seems to disappear. The site, like so many in Spain, was formerly occupied by a mosque, but it is not elevated, and in the time elapsed since construction began in the early 13th century, other buildings have boxed it in. In the main (or west) façade, between the tower and the dome, are three lovely Gothic portals: Most of the parish would choose the middle Puerta del Perdón (Gate of Pardon) over the Puerta del Juicio (Gate of Justice) to the right and the Puerta del Infierno (Gate of Hell) to the left. The Puerta del Perdón has a tympanum showing one of Toledo's favorite miracles, said to have occurred on the very spot. The Virgin Mary descends to San Ildefonso, who wrote in ardent defense of her virginity, and presents him with the robes for his next mass. The 14th-century Puerta de Reloj (also called de la Chapinería, or Clock Gate), in the north wall, is the cathedral's oldest, and is lavishly adorned with Gothic pointed arches and ornaments. The Puerta de los Leones (Lions' Gate), on the south, is the most flamboyant, with its great bronze doors. The modern entrance is a plain doorway to the left of the Puerta de Mollete, just off Calle Hombre de Palo.

Inside, the architectural styles run the gamut from Gothic to Mudéjar to flagrant rococo. The wrought-iron screens are magnificent, and 800 stained glass windows from the 15th and 16th centuries help light the vast space. Yet even the glorious rose window looks ordinary next to a bizarre skylight that directs a single celestial beam onto the altar. Known as the Transparente, the altar was created in 1732 by hacking through the ambulatory's vaulting and the wall of the Capilla Mayor (Main Chapel). Narciso Tomé then embellished it all and created a bit of baroque heaven by confecting a swirl of saints and chubby angels that peer from the cathedral stones. Some are paintings with three-dimensional appendages, innovations that have remained controversial throughout the centuries. The polychrome retable is exquisitely carved, and the walnut choir stalls are also exceptional. Panels above them show deep relief carvings of the battles fought in 1492 at Granada, made just 3 years after the event. In contrast to this fervent depiction of the infidels' defeat, one Muslim has a place of honor on the right pier of the main altar. This pacifist Moorish leader, Abu Walid, dissuaded the enraged King Alfonso X from taking retribution against an upstart bishop who, against the king's wishes, had desecrated the mosque that used to stand here. The sacristy contains a wealth of paintings, including 27 by El Greco, as well as works by Velázquez, Titian, Van Dyck, and Goya. The Capilla Mozárabe, beneath a dome designed by El Greco's son, is the only place on earth that still follows the ancient rituals of the Visigoths; it is kept locked between masses. The treasury (*tesoro*) displays the gold and silver Arfe monstrance, which is always hefted through the streets during *Corpus Christi*. Standing 10 feet high and weighing 450 pounds, this elaborate reliquary incorporates gold from Columbus's first shipload back from the New World. The cathedral is still very much an active church, and visitors often encounter a mass or a lavish wedding party in progress. Open daily, from 10:30 AM to 1 PM and from 3:30 to 6 PM (7 PM in summer). Admission charge to the sacristy, treasury, choir, chapterhouse, and King's Chapel. Plaza Mayor (phone: 222241).

Iglesia de Santo Tomé – This unremarkable 14th-century Mudéjar church is crowded with visitors because of one painting, El Greco's *El Entierro del Conde de*

Orgaz (Burial of the Count of Orgaz). The famous canvas was painted some 250 years after the funeral of the count, who had funded the church's first major reconstruction. The scene is split into heaven and earth, with a row of mourners marking the divide. Their faces are portraits of prominent citizens, all in 16th-century dress. El Greco's own face is supposedly just above that of the young St. Stephen, and the boy in the foreground is the painter's son, Jorge. The monogram on his pocket handkerchief is El Greco's signature. The count's ascent to heaven is conveyed by the strong use of color, but any sense of joy or release in death is oddly absent. Each brushstroke is laden with the austere yet fervent faith of 16th-century Castile. Open Tuesdays through Saturdays, from 10 AM to 1:45 PM and from 3:30 to 5:45 PM (6:45 PM in summer); Sundays, from 10AM to 1:45 PM. Admission charge. 1 Plaza Conde (phone: 210209).

Taller del Moro (Moor's Workshop) – This almost palatial 14th-century building was once used as a workshop by Moorish masons completing cathedral commissions. Displays are mostly of carpentry and tiles, and the Mudéjar style of the building is exemplary in itself with its *artesonado* ceilings and plasterwork. Open Tuesdays through Saturdays, from 10 AM to 2 PM and from 4 to 7 PM; Sundays, from 10 AM to 2 PM. Admission charge. Calle Taller del Moro (phone: 227115).

Casa y Museo del Greco (El Greco House and Museum) – The name is a misnomer, for El Greco never lived precisely here, but this was certainly his old neighborhood and this house indeed belonged to his landlord. Admirably restored to its 16th-century state, the house is charming due to the small scale of the furnishings, especially the tiny kitchen. The courtyard and garden are very pleasant, and a fine collection of the painter's later works, particularly bold portraits of the apostles, is worth a look. An early version of *St. Peter Repentant* is considered of the highest artistic merit, and *St. John,* with a dragon inside his cup, looks peculiarly sinister. Two works by Zurbarán are also noteworthy. Open Tuesdays through Saturdays, from 10 AM to 2 PM and from 4 to 6 PM (7 PM in summer); Sundays, from 10 AM to 2 PM. Admission charge. 3 Calle Samuel Ha-Levi (phone: 224046).

Sinagoga del Tránsito (El Tránsito Synagogue) – This major synagogue was founded in 1366 by Samuel Ha-Levi, Peter the Cruel's Jewish treasurer. Rich cedar carvings on the 12-foot-high *artesonado* ceiling and lacy Mudéjar plasterwork incised with Hebrew inscriptions and stars of David show that he spared no expense. Long after he was put to death, the warrior Knights of Calatrava revamped part of the synagogue as a monastery, but preserved many of the original trappings. The *Sephardic Museum* installed here opened in 1971; its exhibits include a marble pillar from the 1st or 2nd century, with carved Hebrew inscriptions, alongside silver manuscript cases, robes and wedding costumes, amulets, and elaborate objects used in Jewish festivals. Detailed explanations are included for Spaniards understandably ignorant of Jewish customs after a 500-year absence. Open Tuesdays through Saturdays, from 10 AM to 2 PM and from 4 to 6 PM (7 PM in summer); Sundays, from 10 AM to 2 PM. Admission charge. Calle Samuel Ha-Levi (phone: 223655).

Sinagoga de Santa María la Blanca – This architectural gem, built in 1180, was the primary Jewish synagogue in Toledo, and was later converted into a church by the Knights of Calatrava. The façade is rather drab, but inside, horseshoe arches and delicately carved columns shimmer with diaphanous whiteness. The polychrome altarpiece was added in the 16th century. Demoted to a mere barracks in 1791 until a general commanded its make-over into a quartermaster's store and saved it from further abuse, the synagogue has been remarkably restored to its original Almohad-period splendor. Open daily, from 10 AM to 2 PM and from 3:30 to 6 PM (7 PM in summer). Admission charge. Cuesta de los Reyes Católicos (phone: 228429).

Monasterio de San Juan de los Reyes – The outside walls of this grandiose monastery are hung with chains once worn by Christian slaves in Moorish Granada and brought here, after they gained their freedom, in testament to a faith that fueled the final Christian victory of the Reconquest. Inside, the great church is done in soaring Isabeline style, and incorporates Mudéjar and Gothic touches with Renaissance art. Construction, undertaken in 1476, continued through the 16th century, when Covarrubias designed the northern portal, and was not completed until the early 17th century. Although originally planned as the mausoleum of King Ferdinand and Queen Isabella, the monastery became an important center for the Franciscan order. Heraldry is heavy-handed, even on the stained glass windows. The initials F&Y (for Fernando and Ysabel) are repeated constantly between the shields of Castile, León, and Aragon, the pomegranate of Granada, and the royal yoke and arrows motif. The Flemish architect Juan Guas designed most of the interior, with its massive round columns and the great shields supported by haloed eagles, each eyeing the altar. The cloister has graceful arches and decorated tracery on the gallery, under a Mudéjar ceiling celebrating the Catholic Monarchs. A pine and an orange tree are the focal points for the simple courtyard. On the second floor, beneath the arches, 18th-century restorers added whimsically irreverent gargoyles and waterspouts. Open daily, from 10 AM to 1:45 PM and from 3:30 to 6 PM (7 PM in summer); closed *Christmas* and *New Year's Day*. Admission charge. Cuesta de los Reyes Católicos (phone: 223802).

Hospital de Santa Cruz – Cardinal Pedro González de Mendoza initiated plans for this elaborate orphanage and hospital just off Plaza de Zocodover in the early 16th century, and the project was completed by Queen Isabel after this death. Designed by Enrique Egas, with a façade and patio by Covarrubias, the building now houses the *Museum of Fine Arts,* the *Museum of Applied Arts,* and the *Provincial Museum of Archaeology,* showcasing swords and scimitars, ceramics, vestments, bits of furniture, tapestries, and paintings, including 22 by El Greco. Off the lovely Plateresque patio is an archaeology exhibit of mostly Roman finds. A display of prehistoric items is in the basement. The intricate ceiling, lavish stairways, and spacious rooms are typical of 16th-century hospitals where pleasant surroundings were vital to the cure. Open Tuesdays through Saturdays, from 10 AM to 6 PM; Sundays from 10 AM to 2 PM. Admission charge includes entrance to the San Román Visigothic museum (see below). 3 Calle Cervantes (phone: 221402).

Museo de los Concilios y de la Cultura Visigótica (Museum of the Councils and Visigothic Art) – It was here in the heights of the city that the Visigothic kings held several councils of the Western church. A 13th-century Mudéjar church, the Iglesia de San Román, now occupies the site, and it has been turned into a museum — the sole museum of Visigothic art and artifacts in Spain. The collection of votive crowns, bronze brooches, Maltese crosses, and funerary inscriptions from the period seems rather paltry, however, but the church merits a close look for its architecture alone. Mudéjar horseshoe arches are balanced on Arabic columns, with carved capitals from Visigothic, Byzantine, and Mozarabic artisans. Late Romanesque frescoes, preserved on the walls, show strong Moorish influence. Open Tuesdays through Saturdays, from 10 AM to 2 PM and from 4 to 7 PM; Sundays, from 10 AM to 2 PM. Admission charge includes entrance to the Santa Cruz Hospital. Calle San Clemente.

Posada de la Hermandad (Inn of the Brotherhood) – The entrance of this former prison is marked by two archers with crossbows, supporting a wooden coat of arms. The Holy Brotherhood based here was a paramilitary order founded during the Reconquest to police lines of access between Andalusia and central Spain. It was an early precursor to today's Civil Guard — with its odd black patent leather hats — which was formed in 1844. After the brotherhood was disbanded in the 19th century for abuse of its privileges, the building became an inn. Despite an intricate ceiling in the immense Sala de Juntas, the overriding atmosphere is unsettling. The dank basement resembles a quintessential medieval torture chamber. Temporary exhibits are held here frequently. Open Mondays through Fridays, from 10 AM to 2 PM and from 4 to 8 PM (9

PM in summer); Saturdays and Sundays, from 10 AM to 8 PM (9 PM in summer). Admission charge. 6 Calle de la Hermandad (phone: 214150).

Cristo de la Luz (Christ of the Light) – Also known as the Mezquita, this minuscule "mosque," perhaps intended originally as a sepulchral chamber, is one of the most venerable Moorish buildings on the Iberian Peninsula. Near the Puerta del Sol, it was erected on top of Visigothic ruins and later became a Mudéjar church. Kufic characters in the brickwork spell out the name of Muza Ibn Ali, the architect, and give the dedication date as 980. Nine domes rise from the bays, each different, as though the designer were flaunting his versatility. Delicate horseshoe arches inside are supported by more ancient Visigothic capitals, and paintings in the Mudéjar annex, though worn, are rare surviving examples of Toledan Romanesque art. (The few others are displayed in the *San Román Visigothic Museum.*) Cristo de la Luz is shrouded in legend; according to one, El Cid's charger fell to its knees here during a post-Reconquest victory parade and refused to rise until a Visigothic crucifix, with a votive candle still flickering, was miraculously uncovered in a bricked-up niche. Opening hours are erratic, depending on the doorkeeper's whim. No admission charge. Calle Cristo de la Luz.

Hospital de Tavera – This large 16th-century hospital located outside the city gates contains Cardinal Juan Pardo de Tavera's extensive collection of paintings and also features apartments furnished by the Duchess of Lerma in a lavish 17th-century style. The cardinal's magnificent tomb and the family crypt for the Dukes of Medinaceli are in the chapel off the double patio. Impressive portraits by Titian, including the huge *Portrait of Charles V,* hang in the vast dining hall, but Ribera's odd *Bearded Woman* is stashed in a side room, camouflaged by bland cityscapes on either side. Upstairs are works by Tintoretto, Zurbarán, and, of course, El Greco. His last canvas, the *Baptism of Christ by St. John,* is enormous and serves as a sampler of all his trademarks: Vivid clothing stakes out geometric zones on the picture, but the lines of the angel hailing a dove pull the composition together. Drapery on another angel is lighted like a thunderbolt, which points down to a most omnipotent-looking God robed in bright white. Open daily, from 10:30 AM to 1:30 PM and from 3:30 to 6 PM. Admission charge. Calle Baja (phone: 220529).

Circo Romano (Roman Circus) – Not much remains of the Roman arena, only a few mosaics and a reconstructed building outside the gates north of town. Still, this is a pleasant place to stroll after the cramped and twisting streets of the city, and it size (original capacity 20,000) hints at the strength of the Roman settlement, Toletum. Off Avenida de la Reconquista.

ENVIRONS

Montes de Toledo – South and west of Toledo, along either the C401 road or the N401 highway and the local routes branching off of them, rise the harsh uplands that were long celebrated in troubadors' couplets. These were trysting spots for Moorish princesses and caballeros locked in doomed romances, and later they became the haunts of bandits. There are villages and dusty hamlets here, but they are unobtrusive. Streams interlace the scrubby bush cover of rock roses, heather, and cork oaks. The area is best explored by car. Picnickers should be aware of the wild variety of game, mostly in the heights: deer, wild boar, lynx, foxes, and even wolves. Much of the land is private hunting ground, particularly in the southern stretches near Los Yébenes, but there are prehistoric sites scattered throughout the area. Calancho, Los Navalucillos, and Hontanar all boast curious megalithic relics. Ciudad de Vascos, near Navalmoralejo, is an ancient Hispano-Moorish ghost town protected by a fortress. Odd stone boars or bulls — *verracos* — that have grazed in the rubble of forgotten fields since early Celtic tribes lived in Castile can be seen at the Castillo de Bayuela and Torecilla de la Jara. Driving over these rough roads past crumbling castles feels like time travel. Guadalerzas is spanned by an impressive late Roman aqueduct with 24 arches. One of the prettiest valleys, heading west toward the higher sierra behind Guadalupe, is Robledo del Mazo, where the locals still wear traditional straw hats decorated with baubles and tiny mirrors.

Route of the Castles – The area surrounding Toledo is littered with castles, mostly constructed during the time of the Reconquest when Spanish Christians took back land occupied by Moorish invaders from North Africa. About 8 miles (13 km) southwest of Toledo (local road 401) lies Guadamur, a small town dominated by a magnificent 15th-century castle that was restored in the 19th century. The rooms, occupied for a time by Queen Juana the Mad and her son, the future Emperor Charles V, are furnished with Spanish period furniture. Leaving Guadamur and continuing south, take the first right-hand turn toward San Martin de Montalban. Go past San Martin de Montalban; the next right turn will bring you to the hamlet of Melque, which contains one of the most beautiful and least known castles in Spain, a jewel of Moorish-Christian (Mozárabe) architecture. The Melque castle, which also shows traces of Visigoth influence, boasts one of the largest pointed Gothic military arches ever built. Close to the castle lie the ruins of two Roman dams, further examples of the historic wealth of the region. Other noteworthy monuments on this southwest circular route are the Gothic-Renaissance chapel at Torrijos, the 15th-century castle at Maqueda, and the turreted edifice at Escalona on the banks of the Alberche River.

Illescas – Though this town looks forgotten in the highway dust, with only a slender Mudéjar tower lifting it off the flats, it was an influential midway point in the 16th century between the old court in Toledo and the new one in Madrid. As the chief town of the region of La Sagra, located 21 miles (34 km) north of Toledo, Illescas figures in the Golden Age of Spanish literature, but its main claim to fame is five splendid El Greco canvases displayed in the Hospital de la Caridad, which was built by Cardinal Cisneros. Open Mondays through Saturdays, from 9 AM to 2 PM and from 4 to 7 PM. Admission charge.

■**EXTRA SPECIAL:** Talavera de la Reina and Puente de Arzobispo are traditional ceramic centers for the whole of Spain and are an easy day's excursion from Toledo via C502. Talavera is the largest city in the province, so don't expect a quaint potter's village. This is not a heritage city like Toledo, for modern industries have penetrated the thick ramparts, and biweekly livestock fairs are the major social events. On the fringes of the city, just past the main park, is the Hermitage de la Virgen del Prado. This is a showcase for the famous *azulejos,* distinctive blue and yellow glazed picture tiles, which date back to the 14th century and were the preferred decor for the finest palaces and monasteries. Pottery from Talavera, with its multi-color designs, can be distinguished from the Puente de Arzobispo school, which relies on the more subdued green-on-white style. Browse along the main street, where vendors sell shelf after shelf of platters, vases, and bowls inspired by these classic designs.

Continuing west on the N-V highway, just past Oropesa, is a turnoff to Lagartera, the village where the best La Mancha embroidery originates. Every cottage has its own display of the free-form floral stitching, which decorates silk hangings, tablecloths, peasant bonnets, and full skirts. Advertising is understated, inscribed on shiny tile plaques. In summer, the women working outdoors in the clear light provide an excellent photo opportunity. With luck, a wedding party may be in progress, allowing a glimpse of heirloom finery in full flower.

To reach Puente de Arzobispo, popular for its green-toned pottery, double back through Oropresa and drive south for 9 miles (14 km) to a fortified bridge across the Tagus River. A 14th-century archbishop had the bridge built to protect pilgrims trekking to the shrine at Guadalupe, hence the name: Puente de Arzobispo.

Shops and vendors in the village sell ceramics for less than the equivalent items would cost in Toledo, but since quality here is consistently high, there are no astonishingly inexpensive wares. Valdeverdeja, a smaller and prettier village, lies just 4½ miles (7 km) to the west and sells distinctive unglazed red earthenware. Return to Toledo through Talavera (the quickest route), or loop down on local roads through the Montes de Toledo for a leisurely drive back.

SOURCES AND RESOURCES

 TOURIST INFORMATION: The Oficina de Turismo (just outside the Puerta de la Bisagra; phone: 220843) provides brochures and an excellent foldout map — indispensable for negotiating the winding streets. The Provincial Tourist Office (11 Plaza de Zocodover; phone: 221400) has detailed information about touring the surrounding villages. Both are open Mondays through Fridays, from 9 AM to 2 PM and from 4 to 6 PM; Saturdays, from 9 AM to 1:30 PM.

Local Coverage – Understanding Spanish is a must for gleaning information from the local press. The local daily newspaper, *La Voz del Tajo,* has good entertainment and dining listings. Regional editions of the Catholic national daily, *Ya,* also cover local events. More esoteric topics are explored in *Toletum,* published sporadically by Toledo's Academy of Fine Arts and Historical Sciences. *Castilla–La Mancha* is the provincial monthly magazine.

 TELEPHONE: The city code for Toledo is 25. If calling from within Spain, dial 925 before the local number.

 GETTING AROUND: The visitor's own two feet are the best bet in a town full of dead ends, blind corners, twisting cobbled alleys, and very steep hills. If a car is available, it's a good idea to park in one of the eight covered garages within the walled precinct, as far uphill as possible, and then wander.

Bus – There is a bus station, Nueva Estación de Autobuses, on the ring road around Toledo (Carretera de Circunvalación; phone: 226307). Two companies — *Continental* (4 Calle Geraldo Lobo; phone: 227360) and *Galiano* (Paseo de Miradero; phone: 223641) — offer frequent daily service to Madrid and other towns in La Mancha. Buses depart for and return from Madrid every half hour from 6:30 AM to 10 PM on weekdays. On Sundays and public holidays, the half-hourly service commences at 8:30 AM and ends at 11:30 PM.

Car Rental – Like most medieval towns, Toledo is meant for pedestrians; car rental is not advisable. With the exception of *Avis* (Paseo de Miradero; phone: 214535), the international firms do not have offices in Toledo, but operate out of Madrid, an hour's drive away. Local agencies include *López Salazar* (Avenida Plaza de Toros; phone: 220615) and *Maroto Iglesia* (4 Calle Don Diego; phone: 224347).

Taxi – Toledo's two taxi stands are located on Cuesta de Alcázar and Cuesta de la Vega. Roving taxis with an illuminated green light can be hailed as they pass or called (phone: 221968).

Train – Frequent train service to Madrid takes slightly longer than the bus journey. Trains depart for Madrid every 90 minutes from 6:15 AM to 9:50 PM. The return service is from 8:45 AM to 8:55 PM. The train station is located across the Puente de Safont (on Paseo de la Rosa; phone: 223099). There is a *RENFE* office (7 Calle Sillería; phone: 221272).

 SPECIAL EVENTS: *Semana Santa,* or *Holy Week,* has subdued beauty in Toledo when the Procession of Silence winds through the streets on *Good Friday.* A more boisterous procession, the carrying of the Virgen del Valle around the hillsides near her hermitage on the far side of the river, occurs during the local *Romeria,* on *May Day* afternoon. Enormous excitement is unleashed each May or June when the town dresses up in folk costume for *Corpus Christi* and the precious Arfe monstrance from the cathedral treasury is unlocked and carried through the city streets. The monstrance is made of 40 pounds of pure gold and 400 pounds of silver. Wild thyme and rosemary underfoot scent the parade. For 8 centuries, this has been Toledo's ultimate celebration (and one of the most important in Spain), always scheduled for the Thursday of the 9th week after *Holy Week.* Check with the tourist office for full details and the traditional parade route. Fireworks light the August skies during the *Fiesta de la Virgen del Sagrario,* held annually from August 14 through 20. This fiesta solicits the Virgin's protection for the coming year, and part of the festivities are set inside the cathedral cloisters.

 MUSEUMS: Besides those mentioned in *Special Places,* Toledo has other museums, listed below. In addition, there are over 40 churches and convents in the city, along with seven palaces, containing collections of sculpture and precious paintings that would demand special mention anywhere else. Amid such a surfeit of art and historic relics, a visitor often can stumble onto treasures merely by investigating what is behind a promising-looking doorway.

Museo de Armas Blancas de la Real Fábrica de Armas (Royal Arms Factory Museum of Hand Weaponry) – The Royal Arms Factory itself, dating from 1783, is on the outskirts of town. It is now a military installation manufacturing modern weaponry and is closed to the public, but its comprehensive collection of traditional swords, shields, and lances, including the weapons of such personages as El Cid and Boabdil, is on display on the patio of the Alcázar. Open from 9:30 AM to 1:30 PM and from 4 to 6:30 PM; closed Mondays; admission charge to the Alcázar includes entrance to the museum. Calle Capuchinos (phone: 221673).

Museo de Arte Contemporáneo – Installed in the distinguished Casa de las Cadenas, the museum contains works by contemporary Spanish artists, including Alberto Sanchez, who lived and worked in exile in Moscow until his death in 1962. Prohibited throughout Generalísimo Francisco Franco's regime, his paintings now fill two rooms of their own. Open Tuesdays through Saturdays, from 10 AM to 2 PM and from 4:30 to 6:45 PM; Sundays, from 10 AM to 2 PM. Admission charge. Calle de los Bulos (phone: 220615).

 SHOPPING: The swordsmiths of Toledo were renowned in more swash-buckling days, and it was no idle fear to dwell on the consequences of being run through with sharp Toledo steel. Knives of all sorts and even suits of armor on sale today continue this tradition. Damascene, the Moorish art of inlaying gold, copper, or silver threads on a matte black steel background, is also a thriving craft. Souvenir shops throughout the city offer an amazing range of items, some quite mysterious in their function, all decorated in the distinctive black-and-yellow inlaid patterns. Most traditional are the small sewing scissors that snap threads in the sharp beak of a gilded stork, but there is a vast choice of earrings, bangles, cuff links, tie tacks, letter openers, picture frames, and decorative platters. Good, handcrafted damascene is expensive; machine-made items cost less than half the handmade price. Also available is pottery, sold in shops and along the roadside, and generally of high quality, although it's not strictly local. Still, unless a specific trip is planned to the neighboring ceramic centers of Puente de Arzobispo or Talavera de la Reina (see *Extra Special*), Toledo's shops offer a wide selection. Highly caloric marzipan, some of it prepared by nuns, is definitely a local specialty, another one celebrated throughout Spain. The small forms of sweet almond paste, a Moorish legacy, are a traditional *Christmas* treat, though available year-round.

Bargaining is not unheard of in Toledo, but it is best to haggle only if seeking a discount for buying a number of items. If this is the case, be sure to pay in cash. Bargaining ruthlessly and then pulling out a credit card is an invitation to ridicule. With the waves of day-trippers from Madrid, many merchants have little time for dickering over prices, whereas others in quieter shops view it as entertainment. Of the many stores and shops in Toledo, the following are of particular interest:

Casa Bermejo – A source of top-quality Toledo damascene, including that made by Santiago Sanchez Martin (see below). 5 Calle Airosos (phone: 220346).

Casa Telesforo – Some of the best marzipan in town. 17 Plaza de Zocodover (phone: 223379).

Confitería Santo Tomé – More marzipan — marginally less expensive than that of *Casa Telesforo* and a close match for quality. 5 Calle Santo Tomé (phone: 223763), with a branch at 11 Plaza de Zocodover (phone: 221168).

Santiago Sanchez Martín – A damascene artisan who has been inlaying 24-carat gold by hand on the most special pieces for 40-plus years. This is his workshop, featuring 40 different models of mirror frames, jewelry, decorative pitchers, and other items. 18 Calle Río Llano (phone: 227757).

Suárez – A wide range of damascene items; personalized shields with your own family crest can be made up, if you supply the design. 19 Paseo de los Canónigos (phone: 225615).

 SPORTS AND FITNESS: Fishing – The best fishing in the Tagus River, which forms a natural moat around Toledo, is in the river basin, far from the city. Near Finisterre Dam, about 28 miles (45 km) southeast of the city, black bass have been introduced. In other reservoirs where fishing is encouraged, carp and large pike abound. Fishing permits are available from the Valencia office of *ICONA* (*Instituto Nacional para la Conservación de la Naturaleza;* 6 Plaza San Vicente; phone: 222158); or call *Caza y Pesca* (phone: 213124). The standard permits are issued for a year, so ask for the special visitor's license, valid for 2 weeks.

Flying – Anything from a hang glider to a propeller plane is a possibility in the skies over Toledo, where unseen assets beckon pleasure pilots from all over Europe. Steady updrafts and less-predictable waves and slopes in the air occur when La Mancha's miles of broad plateau suddenly rear up as a range of mountains, producing almost a washboard effect. The *Royal Aero Club of Toledo* (20 miles/32 km from the city in Mora de Toledo; phone: 300194) specializes in gliding. The *Ocaña/Toledo Aerodrome*, regional headquarters for the Civil Aviation Authority, offers instruction in gliding, ultra-lights, ballooning, skydiving, and powered flight. Some courses include lodging (for more information, call 130700 or 130769). Pilots must have foreign licenses validated before taking off.

Hunting – The season for small game (partridge, rabbit, hare, quail, dove, and so on) runs from the third Sunday in October through the first Sunday in February. Stalking of larger game starts in September, and the waterfowl season continues through March. The most plentiful hunting grounds are on the highest slopes of the Montes de Toledo. Any area signposted *coto* is a hunting reserve in one of four categories: common use, local, private, or national. Hunters must have a license from their own country, as well as a seasonal permit and insurance. Obtain a customs permit for shotguns and rifles before entering Spain. A separate permit is also required for leaving the country. For more information, contact *Caza y Pesca* (phone: 213124) or visit *ICONA*'s office (6 Plaza San Vicente; phone: 222158).

Swimming – Swimmers can use several public pools in town, but the biggest and cleanest (aside from the guests-only facility at the *Parador Conde de Orgaz*) is at the Circo Romano campground (21 Calle Circo Romano; phone: 220442), just north of the old walls. There is an admission charge, plus a weekend surcharge.

Tennis – Arrangements can be made to use courts at the private *Club de Tenis de Toledo* (Calle Navalpino, Km 49; phone: 224278). Admission charge.

Windsurfing – The sport is forbidden in many of the manmade lakes, but when the Cazalegas Reservoir is full, sailing and windsurfing are popular. Contact the tourist office for further details.

THEATER: The *Teatro de Rojas* (4 Plaza Mayor; phone: 223970) has been carefully restored to its 19th-century grandeur. Details regarding any classical Spanish production to be staged here are available from the box office or through the tourist office. Usually, however, this lovely venue is used as a cinema for dubbed foreign movies.

MUSIC: Sacred music is the norm in Holy Toledo, and can be heard at vespers services at most of the 40-odd churches throughout the city.

NIGHTCLUBS AND NIGHTLIFE: The clue to nightlife in Toledo is to be part of *la movida,* the movement, or the action, and not to stay in any one place too long. Most people stop for a drink or two, then move on to another café or pub. In summer, the open-air terraces near the ramparts come alive. The youngest crowd gravitates to the sundry establishments along Calle Chapinería, Calle Sillería, and Callejón Barrio Rey, while a more sophisticated scene takes place beneath the arcades of the Plaza de Zocodover and the adjoining streets. *La Sal que Esta* (Calle de la Sal) attracts young professionals who scrutinize each other without mercy. Discos tend to be quite provincial and young. The brashest one in town is *Sithon's* (4 Calle Lucio). *Mascara* (in the *Galería del Miradero*) is the trendiest, while *Gris Disco* (Carretera Toledo–Avila, Km 2.5) is the most self-conscious.

BEST IN TOWN

CHECKING IN: Considering the number of tourists who traipse through town, Toledo seems a bit short on lodgings. This is because the vast majority of visitors are here just for the day. But quite a few are enticed to stay the night, so good hotel rooms can be at a premium. Expect to pay $100 and up for a double room in a hotel listed as expensive and $60 to $90 at a moderate one. All telephone numbers are in the 25 city code unless otherwise indicated.

Parador Conde de Orgaz – The stunning view of Toledo is the focal point here, and though inconveniently distant from the center of town, the 77 well-equipped, air conditioned rooms feature color television sets and private baths, and provide guests with their own skyscapes just outside the picture window. Modern design incorporates traditional architectural styles of the region, and decorations include lovely provincial ceramics. The restaurant serves regional specialties, at a price, and there is an outdoor swimming pool. Advance reservations are recommended.

Paseo de los Cigarrales (phone: 221850; fax: 225166; telex: 47998). Expensive.

María Cristina – Situated within the walls of the former Hospital de San Lázaro near the bullring, it offers 65 air conditioned rooms with private baths and all modern conveniences. A popular spot for business meetings and banquets, the place has a lively Spanish atmosphere, yet remains comfortable and peaceful nonetheless. Honeymooners can book a special suite under the dome of the ancient chapel. The vast dining room of the restaurant *El Abside* resembles a Moorish tent (see *Eating Out*). 1 Calle Marqués de Mendigorría (phone: 213202; telex: 42827). Expensive to moderate.

Alfonso VI – Comfortable lodgings directly in front of the Alcázar. All 88 air conditioned rooms have color television sets and private baths, and the public areas are done up in austere Castilian style, which contrasts with the bright commercial gallery near the lobby. 2 Calle General Moscardó (phone: 222600; fax: 214458). Moderate.

Almazara – A particularly tranquil spot, with splendid views and friendly service. All 21 rooms have color television sets and private baths. Well worth the 2-mile (3-km) detour outside town, though it is only open from mid-March through October. 47 Carretera Piedrabuena (phone: 223866). Moderate.

Cardenal – This 18th-century cardinal's palace in the shade of the city ramparts is now a *hostal,* evocative of a grand age. All 27 rooms are air conditioned, with private baths. The overall atmosphere is elegant and distinguished, but the service can be a bit desultory. The place is best known for the meals served in its 2-tiered garden (see *Eating Out*). 24 Paseo de Recaredo (phone: 224900; fax: 222991). Moderate.

Carlos V – A very proper, modern establishment, offering views over the cathedral from many of its 55 rooms. The quiet plaza is deceptive, however, for music often blares from the noisy bar next door. 1 Calle Trastamara (phone: 222100 or 222104; telex: 47245). Moderate.

Los Cigarrales – This pleasant 29-room country house on the far side of the Tagus River has excellent views of Toledo. Each room is air conditioned and decorated with wooden beams and glazed tiles. The management is friendly. 12 Carretera de Circunvalación (phone: 220053; fax: 215546). Moderate.

Los Guerreros – The 13 clean and comfortable rooms are air conditioned and have private baths, and the extremely friendly management and staff makes this *hostal* a favorite with students. Quite a distance from the city's principal sites. 8 Avenida de la Reconquista (phone: 211807; fax: 228811). Moderate.

Imperio – Modern efficiency in the medieval midst of Toledo. Despite the somewhat charmless, simple rooms (21, all with private baths), this place is a good value. 7 Calle Cadenas (phone: 227650). Moderate.

Santa Isabel – Centrally located and a few steps from the cathedral, this small 15th-century converted inn is an intimate, popular spot. Soberly decorated, it has 22 rooms, all with private bathrooms, but no air conditioning. An attraction is the spacious interior patio where guests can while away the evenings with a cool drink. Most rooms provide an excellent view of surrounding historic buildings. 24 Calle Santa Isabel (phone: 253136). Moderate.

Sol – A central location and pretty terrace distinguish this 14-room hostelry, not to mention its resident hairdresser and doctor. 15 Calle Azacanes (phone: 213650). Moderate.

EATING OUT: La Manchan cuisine is not particularly distinguished, other than the basics: a good sharp cheese and a hearty red wine. It is based on ingredients from a harsh land of shepherds and hunters. Be prepared to eat *perdiz estofada* (marinated partridge) at room temperature; it won't be served piping hot. Toledan-style partridge, stewed in red wine, is less tart. Roast lamb is usually a good bet, and crisp grilled *chuletas* (lamb chops) can be exquisite. In season, venison, hare, and game birds are served with originality and pride. Low-cost meals are scarce in this city, where restaurants raise prices for tourists too tired to look for something else. An à la carte, three-course dinner for two with wine will cost $70 or more in a restaurant listed as expensive, $40 to $65 in a moderate restaurant, and $35 or less in an inexpensive one. The *menú del día,* or daily special, is almost always the most reasonably priced option and usually includes wine and bread along with at least two courses. All telephone numbers are in the 25 city code unless otherwise indicated.

Asador Adolfo – The chef has a light touch with some of the heavy Manchegan classics such as *perdiz en paté,* served with white beans. The seafood and roast meats are also excellent, and the wine made from the brujidero grape, *Priorato de Ucles,* is a very special treat. Closed Sunday evenings. Reservations advised. Major credit cards accepted. Situated near the cathedral, this 14th-century building can be hard to find, hidden away on a corner shared by 7 Calle Hombre de Palo and 6 Calle La Granada (phone: 227321). Expensive.

Aurelio – The flagship of Toledo's sole "chain" establishment has traditional ambience with antique pottery on the wall, and presents the most time-honored Castilian recipes. Aurelio Montero is one of Toledo's classic chefs. Like his father, he keeps a watchful eye on the authentic Castilian cuisine. Partridge and sea bream are the house specialties, but save room for the *arroz con leche* (rice with milk), a far cry from ordinary rice pudding. Closed Tuesdays. Reservations advised. Major credit cards accepted. 8 Plaza del Ayuntamiento (phone: 227716). Expensive.

Cardenal – In an elegant 18th-century palace tucked up against the city walls, this is worth seeking out even if you are bedding down somewhere less grand. It is linked with the celebrated Madrid restaurant *Botín,* and clients are eager eaters. In fine weather, dine alfresco in the split-level garden. Roast lamb and suckling pig, Castilian specialties, rival the partridge *a la toledana.* Fresh asparagus and strawberries are a must in the spring. Open daily. Reservations advised. Major credit cards accepted. 24 Paseo de Recaredo (phone: 220862). Expensive.

El Abside – Quite offbeat, by Toledan standards, with an adventurous crowd. The ancient Moorish tower adjacent to the *María Cristina* hotel has been revamped as a spacious and bright dining room; the bright blue decor and painted Moorish patterns are as festive as a nomad's party tent. The cuisine is imaginative, but the nouvelle touch can be a bit shaky. Try the almond soup and duck with honey-orange sauce. Various Arab-Sephardic dishes provide a choice for vegetarians, not always easy in Castilian restaurants, which cater to carnivores. Open daily. Reservations advised. Major credit cards accepted. 1 Calle Marqués de Mendigorría (phone: 213202). Expensive to moderate.

La Botica – Located in the heart of the city, this stylish place has a more formal dining room upstairs, along with a cafeteria and outdoor terrace for those who want to people watch. Cosmopolitan variations of Castilian standards and innovative dishes like eggplant and shrimp gratin are served with flair. Fresh fruit sherbets provide a light finish. Open daily. Reservations unnecessary. Visa accepted. 13 Plaza de Zocodover (phone: 225557). Expensive to moderate.

Casa Aurelio – Sister to *Restaurante Aurelio,* serving excellent cream of crab soup, partridge, quail, sirloin, and other traditional Castilian dishes in a somewhat less formal atmosphere. Closed Wednesdays. Reservations advised. Major credit cards accepted. 6 Calle Sinagoga (phone: 222097). Moderate.

Chirón – A comfortably air conditioned dining place that serves the Toledo standards: partridge, thick slabs of potato omelette, homemade crusty bread, and *manchego* cheese. Open daily. Reservations advised. No credit cards accepted. Paseo de Recaredo (phone: 220150). Moderate.

La Cubana – Cross the Tagus River at the Puente de Alcántara for filling dishes that taste just that much better when eaten on the open-air terrace. There also is a wood-paneled indoor dining room. Open daily, except the first 2 weeks in September. Reservations unnecessary. Visa accepted. 2 Paseo de la Rosa (phone: 220088). Moderate.

Hierbabuena – A romantic spot where diners eat by candlelight beneath an intricate Mudéjar ceiling. Latecomers may be seated in a slightly musty side chamber, which is plainly a whitewashed cave. Service is elegant yet friendly. Game (when in season) and duck in plum sauce are the house specialties. Closed Sunday evenings and all day Mondays. Reservations advised. Visa accepted. 9 Calle Cristo de la Luz (phone: 223463). Moderate.

Mesón Aurelio – A sister to the formal *Restaurante Aurelio* and the less formal *Casa Aurelio,* this casual place serves traditional Castilian dishes plus partridge, quail, and steaks. Closed Mondays. Reservations advised. Visa accepted. 1 Calle Sinagoga (phone: 221392). Moderate.

Venta de Aires – An old and famous Toledo establishment. As many locals as tourists eat here for the typical Toledo fare: marinated partridge, *tortilla* (potato omelette), garlic soup, and the regional *manchego* cheese. The marzipan is made on the premises. A large tree-shaded terrace is wonderful for summer dining. Closed Mondays. Reservations unnecessary. No credit cards accepted. 25 Calle Circo Romano (phone: 220545). Moderate.

Sinaí – Although this street in the Judería (old Jewish quarter) is solemnly named for the Catholic Monarchs, who drove both Jews and Moors from Spain, kosher and Moroccan dishes are the wave of the present here. Couscous or tangerine steaks makes an unusual and pleasant change of pace from tepid partridge. The restaurant plays host to an annual *Passover* feast. Open daily, but closes at 6 PM. Reservations unnecessary. Visa accepted. 7 Cuesta de los Reyes Católicos (phone: 225623). Moderate to inexpensive.

El Nido – Bustling with students and hungry tourists. The fixed-price *menú del día* here makes this lively place the best deal in town. But be forewarned: The house wine is ghastly. Closed Mondays. Reservations unnecessary. No credit cards accepted. 5 Plaza de la Magdalena. Inexpensive.

 TAPAS BARS: Several *tapas* bars line the narrow streets just off the Plaza de Zocodover, particular Cállejon Barrio Rey. *Bar Ludeña* (in Plaza de la Magdalena, just below Barrio Rey) is a colorful place offering a wide variety of *tapas,* snacks, and inexpensive meals. *Los Cuatro Tiempos* (5-7 Calle Sixto Ramón Parro) has a downstairs *tapas* bar featuring a splendid ceramic decor. *La Tarasca* (6 Calle Hombre de Palo) is an overpriced restaurant that nevertheless serves good *tapas,* which are less expensive when eaten standing at the bar.

VALENCIA

Valencia is known the world over as the home of paella, possibly the most international of all Spanish dishes, and rightly so. But this city, an agricultural capital that is Spain's third-largest, offers far more than fish, sausage, and rice. A character in Ernest Hemingway's *For Whom the Bell Tolls,* describing the town during a bullfight fiesta more than a half a century ago, put it like this: "Never have I seen so many people. Never have I seen cafés so crowded. For hours it would be impossible to get a seat and it was impossible to board the tram cars. In Valencia, there was movement all day and all night."

And so there is today. Like nowhere else in Spain, the residents of Valencia took to the Arabs' love for flame and fireworks, still evidenced in the city's *fallas,* riotous celebrations that draw tens of thousands of visitors every March. The cafés of the old city bustle with people year round, and the economy thrives. The city has, as its local cheerleaders say, *mucha marcha* — lots of life.

But Valencia is a pearl that must be sought out among the swine. The Old City is surrounded by a depressing sprawl of working class housing blocks, and most prospective visitors pass it by in favor of the better known sites to the north and south. Only once you enter the Old City, clustered along an elbow of the Turia River, will you find the architecture, museums, and unusually rich historical heritage of what once was one of Spain's most powerful kingdoms.

Valencia lies at the heart of the *huerta,* a fertile crescent of alluvial plain that is irrigated according to a complex system begun some 2,100 years ago. Water has transformed the area into an agricultural paradise: a flat, rich plain covered with millions of orange trees, ubiquitous market gardens, flower nurseries, and nut tree orchards. "The soil never rests in these *huertas,* crops succeed each other without interruption," a Spanish naturalist enthused almost 200 years ago, and farmers today are still harvesting as many as four crops a year from their fields. Everything depends on the precious water of the Turia River, and the elected judges of Valencia's Water Tribunal have been meeting every Thursday since the Middle Ages outside the cathedral to settle disputes. The proceedings are open to the public and are held in Valencian, a dialect of the Catalan language; decisions are recorded only in the local farmers' memories.

The Romans founded Valentia in 137 BC, although Greeks, Phoenicians, and Carthaginians coasted this area and traded with the native Iberians long before. The city eventually fell into the hands of the Visigoths and, in the 8th century, the Arabs, who invaded the peninsula from northern Africa. It was the Arabs who gave the region some of its most lasting features — its orange groves, the palm trees that line its avenues, the glazing techniques that made its ceramics famous, tremendous improvements to the irrigation system still in use today, fireworks, silk, and rice, which is grown in paddies to the south. But the favor was not to be repaid: In succeeding centuries, Catholics would raze all Moorish landmarks, leaving only an Arab bathhouse that cannot be visited today. The first of the Catholic "liberators" was El Cid, the legendary hero who took the town in 1094 and died here 5 years later. Following his death, his brave wife, Doña Jimena, was unable to hold the city, and it slipped back under Arab control for another 150 years.

Valencians regard King Jaime I of Aragon, known as the Conqueror, as their true liberator. Following a 5-month siege, the warrior-king marched into the city in triumph one September day in 1238, granting its Christian inhabitants special rights, or *costums,* in return for their allegiance to the crown of Aragon. But toward the end of the Middle Ages, the kingdom of Valencia entered a dark period. The Black Death ravaged the city twice. A violent pogrom in Valencia's old Jewish quarter, around the Plaza Virgen, set off further popular attacks on Jews and converted Moors. Vicente Ferrer, a brilliant but bigoted Valencian cleric who was later sainted and made patron of his native city, delivered virulent anti-Semitic diatribes and helped frame discriminatory laws aimed at religious minorities. When the Spanish Inquisition came to the city in 1482, at least 100 Valencians were burned at the stake for refusing to convert. This sad story of religious intolerance and narrow-mindedness would be completed about 130 years later, when the expulsion from Spain of converted Moors deprived the kingdom of 170,000 of its most skilled artists, craftsmen, and traders.

The Bourbons came to rule Spain in the early 18th century via the War of the Spanish Succession — a war in which Valencia, along with Aragon and Catalonia, made a fatefully bad choice, backing the Hapsburg favorite. The city paid for its mistake with the Nueva Planta decree of 1707, stripping it of its ancient rights and generating resentment that still exists today. The kingdom became a province; its viceroy, a captain general sent from Madrid.

For better or for worse, Valencia has since been involved in just about every war and rebellion in Spain, winning a gritty reputation for independence and liberal-mindedness. In 1808, led by one Father Rico, the populace stormed the city arsenal and rose bloodily against Napoleon's occupying troops; Marshal Louis Gabriel Suchet managed to restore French rule only 4 years later. Over the following decades, Valencia was a hothouse of conspiracies, plots, and failed uprisings, notably the Republican-inspired insurrections of 1856 and 1864. A rebellion during the Revolution of 1868 was settled only with an artillery bombardment of the city.

True to its liberal past, Valencia fought on the losing side during the Spanish Civil War, wringing crops from the overworked *huerta* to feed the starving population of besieged Madrid. For most of 1937, with the war going badly in Madrid, Valencia became the Republican capital. It was shelled and bombed until, as the war came to a close in March 1939, it finally fell to Generalísimo Francisco Franco's troops. In the decades of repression that followed, the local language was almost stamped out; but after Franco died, it made a strong comeback and is now widely spoken.

All this bad luck in war and rebellion appears to have done little to dampen the spirits of the typical Valencian. He seems a hardy fellow, a citified dirt farmer who has seen all manner of catastrophes come and go. Kick the pavement in Valencia, the saying goes, and an artichoke springs up. The city today does have the feel of an overgrown agricultural capital of 750,000, despite its heavy industry and sprawling development. Valencia had its age of glory, but in the last few centuries it certainly has not produced many of Spain's leading artists or intellectuals.

Still, exceptions make the rule, and Valencia boasts one exceptional and famous 20th-century writer: Vicente Blasco Ibáñez, an intellectual and Republican politician who died before the Civil War. To English speakers, he is probably best known for *Blood and Sand,* possibly the finest novel ever written on bullfighting (from an opponent's point of view); it was later made into movies starring Rudolph Valentino (1922) and Tyrone Power (1941). He also wrote the novel *The Four Horsemen of the Apocalypse.* Some of the city's best-known artists include Joaquín Sorolla y Bastida (1863–1923), a Spanish Impressionist who loved to paint sunlight, and the sculptor Mariano Benlliure y Gil (1862–1947), the best known of a family of prolific artists.

One of the great attractions of Valencia is precisely that it is not a major tourist attraction. With its furniture, ceramics, and many other industries, and the industrial port of El Grao that serves it, it can be off-putting to the casual passerby. But once its many charms are discovered, it is seen as a particularly Spanish place. Valencians are less affected than most by the onslaught of coastal tourism in recent decades, so they are more apt to be generous in that most valuable of foreign-exchange earners — a genuine desire to show the visitor why their city deserves a second look.

VALENCIA AT-A-GLANCE

SEEING THE CITY: For those who don't mind a grueling, 207-step climb, a perfect view of the city can be had from El Miguelete, Valencia's most popular monument, the 14th-century octagonal bell tower of the cathedral, on the Plaza de la Reina. Clustered around the tower are all the principal buildings of the Old City, and the visitor sees a vista of bridges over the Turia River bed, blue-domed churches, and the fertile *huerta* stretching beyond the ends of the city's streets. Although they are now seldom used in chorus, El Micalet (as the tower is fondly known to Valencians in their native language) used to ring all 12 of its named bells a half hour before the city's gates were locked for the night (they were also sounded to regulate the irrigation of the *huerta*). Under no circumstances was anyone allowed in after the doors swung shut, giving rise to the Spanish expression *quedarse a la luna de Valencia,* literally, to be left in the moonlight of Valencia — out in the cold. The tower is open daily, from 10:30 AM to 12:30 PM and from 5 to 6 PM. Admission charge. Enter through the cathedral.

SPECIAL PLACES: Valencia's last set of city walls was torn down in 1865, but almost all of the city's main monuments and museums are within the relatively small area it once enclosed. The area is defined to the north by the bed of the Turia River, which has been rerouted farther away from the city to solve the chronic flooding that had long plagued the old section, and on the west, south, and east by Avenida de Guillem de Castro, Calle de Xàtiva, and Calle Colón, respectively. A major shopping, restaurant, and hotel district, however, lies southeast of the old section, in the blocks just beyond Calle Colón. In the city's port of El Grao, 2½ miles (4 km) to the east, and especially on the Levante beach just north of it, there are dozens of popular seafood restaurants, as well as some interesting turn-of-the-century Spanish Modern buildings, reminiscent of Art Deco.

Cathedral – Angled oddly into a corner of the Plaza de la Reina, the Old City's main square, the Seo Metropolitan Cathedral is a mixture of styles, as reflected in its three portals, which are Romanesque, Gothic, and baroque (it is outside the Gothic Apostle's Door that the Water Tribunal meets on Thursdays). Begun in 1262 on the site of a mosque razed by the Catholic conquerors, the cathedral also is rather eclectic inside. The architectural highlights are the Gothic dome and the chapter house. The main altarpiece depicts the life of Christ in six sections, including birth and crucifixion panels. The main chapel contains the pulpit used by San Vicente Ferrer to give some of his apocalyptic orations, and one of the leading Spanish candidates for the "true" Holy Grail — a much-revered agate cup, set with emeralds and pearls on a base of pure gold. The church also boasts some fine paintings, including the *Baptism of Christ* by Juan de Juanes, but the real art treasures are housed in the *Museo de la Catedral*, which contains works by Zurbarán, Juan de Juanes, and others. Notice also the Goya murals, one of which depicts San Francisco de Borja surrounded by devilish creatures as he exorcises a dying man. The cathedral and its museum are open Mondays through Saturdays, from 10 AM to 1 PM and from 4:30 to 6 PM; Sundays for mass only. Admission charges for the museum and tower. Plaza de la Reina (phone: 331-8127).

Basílica de la Virgen de los Desamparados (Basilica of the Virgin of the Forsaken) – An arcade connects the cathedral to this elliptical building, which was completed in 1667 and is said to have been the first mental asylum in the world. The basilica was founded by a priest who called for donations in a sermon after seeing a madman beaten in the streets; the institution later became responsible for burying dead travelers found on roads outside the city. Today, the structure contains fine frescoes by Antonio Palomino on the interior of the dome, and a sculpted image of the Virgin of the Forsaken, the patroness of Valencia, that was supposedly sculpted by angels. On the second Sunday in May (*Virgin's Day*), and on *Corpus Christi*, the Virgin is carried throught nearby streets in processions marked by showers of rose petals and other flowers. Plaza de la Virgen.

Museo Provincial de Bellas Artes (Provincial Fine Arts Museum) – Many people come to this first-rate art museum, one of Spain's best (but least-visited), simply to see the small, brooding self-portrait painted by Velázquez in 1640. While this is the museum's single unquestioned gem, its most interesting display is the collection of Valencian religious "primitives" of the 14th, 15th, and 16th centuries. It is remarkable just how graphic much of this work was before centuries of further "refinement" drained altarpieces and other types of painting of much of their naive vigor. Blood gushes from Christ's sword wound into a goblet in one painting; the Lactating Virgin spouts milk from her swollen breasts into the mouth of the infant Christ in another. Downstairs, there are early Iberian and Hispano-Roman artifacts, including an altar to a pagan Roman emperor, Claudius Gothicus, on which some rebellious Christian chiseled the words "Christus Magis" — Christ is More. There is also a small treasure of works upstairs by Francisco Ribalta (who died in Valencia in 1628), Ribera, Murillo, El Greco (*St. John the Baptist*), Van Dyck, Hieronymus Bosch, and Goya, who once taught at the Fine Arts Academy that runs the museum. There are several rooms dedicated to 19th- and 20th-century Valencian artists, the most interesting of which display works by Ignacio Pinazo and Sorolla. Open Tuesdays through Saturdays, from

10 AM to 2 PM and from 4 to 6 PM; Sundays, from 10 AM to 2 PM. Admission charge. Located just across the Real Bridge. 9 Calle de San Pío V (phone: 360-5793).

Jardines del Real (Royal Gardens) – Also just across the Real Bridge and next door to the fine arts museum, this small paradise of rose gardens, bougainvillea, palms, mimosas, jacarandas, cypress, and myrtle trees also has a diminutive but pleasant zoo. The gardens are open daily, from 8 AM to sundown; the zoo is open daily, from 10 AM to sundown. Admission charge for the zoo. Calle de San Pío V (phone: 362-3512).

La Lonja de la Seda (Silk Exchange) – In a city known for its Gothic architecture, this structure in the heart of the Old City is the undoubted highlight of the genre. The Valencian Père Compte completed La Lonja in 1498, leaving a nearly hidden plaque boasting that construction took just 15 years and exhorting merchants to honesty. In addition to an array of gargoyles, the façade also features a series of fantastic and often erotic small figures: centaurs playing flutes, orgies, a monkey and a hare, naked men clasping great clubs, a miser trapped by the devil — even a squatting man defecating. The first room is the main Silk Exchange, a great vaulted hall supported by 24 twisting columns reminiscent of massive hanks of silk; on Fridays from 1 to 3 PM, fruit wholesalers hold auctions reminiscent of 16th-century silk fairs here. Next to this hall is the tower of La Lonja, said to have once served as a prison for bankrupt silk merchants. A remarkable circular stairway, with no central support, leads from a courtyard of orange trees to an upstairs hall famous for the elaborately gilded and carved wooden ceiling that looks down on otherwise sober surroundings. Open Tuesdays through Fridays, from 10 AM to 2 PM and from 4 to 6 PM; Saturdays and Sundays, from 10 AM to 1 PM. No admission charge. Plaza del Mercado (phone: 331-6158).

Mercado Central (Main Market) – One of the finest — and largest — market buildings in Spain is made additionally delightful by the colors and smells of the products of the *huerta,* along with the glazed *azulejo* tiles showing Valencian citrus fruits and vegetables. Built in 1928, the market is a fine example of Valencian modernism, and is visually similar to a turn-of-the-century railroad station, with glass skylights supported by an elaborate framework of iron girders. Open Mondays through Saturdays, the market offers a quick taste of modern Valencian life. Plaza del Mercado.

Palacio del Marqués de Dos Aquas – The amazing façade of this 18th-century rococo palace was designed by the painter Hypólito Rovira, who died in a Valencian mental asylum in 1740. Its main entrance is a riotous alabaster fantasy of crocodiles, Cupids, a Virgin with Child, and two men spilling jugs of water — the "two waters" of the Marqués de Dos Aguas. The building, which was once even wilder, with paintings on the plasterwork that have since been destroyed, now houses the *Museo Nacional de Cerámica,* Spain's leading ceramics museum. The gilded and tiled interior of the building, a kind of Hollywood version of a European palace, is a showcase of centuries of excellent pottery from the outlying towns of Paterna, Alcora, and Manises, beautifully glazed work that was widely sought across Europe in the late Middle Ages. In other rooms, there are works by Picasso, a Valencian tiled kitchen, and pottery from other regions of Spain and abroad. Finally, downstairs, is the marquis's fairy-tale carriage. Open Tuesdays through Saturdays, from 10 AM to 2 PM and from 4 to 6 PM; Sundays, from 10 AM to 2 PM. Admission charge. 2 Calle Poeta Querol (phone: 351-6392).

Real Colegio del Patriarca – This Renaissance collegiate church, founded in 1610 by San Juan de Ribera, the Archbishop of Valencia, is memorable for the severity of its lines and its lack of exterior embellishment. The first thing seen upon entering is a huge alligator nailed to the wall — the so-called Dragon of the Patriarch. Legend has it that the beast devoured dozens of Valencians before being slain by a brave Jew who, in order to escape a death sentence for previous crimes, devised an ingenious suit of armor to do the deed; historians claim that the beast was sent as a gift by the Viceroy of Peru in 1606, and hung by the patriarch as a symbol of silence. Besides the church and a lovely arcaded courtyard, the complex houses the *Museo del Patriarca,* a rich little museum containing paintings by El Greco, Rogier van der Weyden, Juan de Juanes, Ribalta, and others. Open daily, from 11 AM to 1:30 PM. Admission charge to the museum. 1 Calle de la Nave (phone: 351-4176).

Museo Fallero – This small museum is crammed with *ninots* — the satirical papier-mâché figures that ordinarily are burned in effigy at midnight on *St. Joseph's Day* (March 19) as part of the *falla* celebrations for which Valencia is famous. Each year a selection committee votes to save the best one from the flames, and this museum is a repository of such *ninots indultas,* or figures "pardoned" at the last minute. Big-busted women, "typical" Valencians, politicians, and a girl on a swing representing Spain's young democracy are just a few of the cartoon-like, lampooning figures preserved here since 1935, along with exceptionally colorful and historic *falla* posters. Open Tuesdays through Sundays, from 10 AM to 2 PM and from 4 to 7 PM (closed afternoons in August and September). Admission charge. 4 Plaza de Monteolivete.

Museo Taurino – Almost hidden away in a covered concourse next to the bullring, one of Spain's leading taurine museums is filled with bullfighting memorabilia. The exhibit contains examples of 19th-century bullfighting garb, a savage-looking collection of swords and pics, lances, suits of lights worn by some leading toreros when they were gored, and the stuffed heads of some of the offending beasts. Valencia was for many centuries a leading city for bullfighting, though its reputation has fallen off in recent decades. Open Mondays through Fridays, from 10:30 AM to 1:30 PM. No admission charge. Pasaje Doctor Serra (phone: 351-1850).

Estación del Norte – Many visitors, whether arriving by train or not, take the time to visit this charming railroad station, one of the most beautiful in Europe. Both the interior and exterior are decorated with *azulejo* tiles bearing such Valencian motifs as oranges, the *huerta,* and *barracas,* the region's traditional thatch-roofed houses. The ticket counters and the cafeteria are especially delightful. 24 Calle de Xàtiva (phone: 351-3612).

Torres de Serranos (Serranos Towers) – The 14th-century gate next to the northern Puente Serranos (Serranos Bridge) was fully restored in 1930 and remains an imposing fortified arch. From 10 AM to 2 PM Tuesdays through Saturdays, the towers can be climbed for an excellent view of Valencia and the old Turia River bed, which is slowly being converted into a lengthy concourse of gardens. A second gate remaining from the medieval walls is the 15th-century Torres de Quart, nearby on Avenida de Guillem de Castro. Like a proud old warrior, it still bears the scars of French cannonballs from the War of Independence, known as the Peninsular War. Admission charge.

Instituto Valenciano de Arte Moderno/IVAM (Valencian Institute of Modern Art) – Hard by what remains of the Old City walls (in fact, a vestige of the medieval ramparts protrudes into one of the galleries), not far from the Torres de Quart, this is one of a crop of new museums in Spain devoted exclusively to modern art. Opened in 1989 with much fanfare, the collection is housed in two locations — an ultramodern stone-and-glass building called the Centre Julio González and, nearby (and in complete contrast), a restored 13th- to 16th-century Carmelite convent called the Centre del Carme. Besides the permanent collection of some 1,400 pieces (paintings, drawings, and sculpture by Julio González, a lifelong friend of Picasso form the nucleus), the Centre Julio González has an auditorium, restaurant-bar, and a bookshop, and is host to a year-round schedule of changing exhibitions and special cultural events that are international in scope. Both buildings are open Tuesdays through Sundays from 11 AM to 8 PM; admission charge, except on Sundays. Centre Julio González, 118 Avenida de Guillem de Castro; Centre del Carme, 2 Calle Museu (phone for both: 386-3000).

Palau de la Musica – Across the Aragón Bridge from the Old City, Valencia's concert hall, built in the now-dry bed of the Turia River in 1987, is a rather bizarre mix of reflecting pools, palm trees, small temple-like structures, and a main building that resembles an exceptionally swank greenhouse. It is known to locals as the "microwave" because of its initial lack of air conditioning, and its designers also failed to include a system to clean its vast glass surfaces — leading the city to hire mountaineers to do the job. 1 Plaza del Rey (phone: 360-3356, for information; 361-5212, for tickets).

ENVIRONS

Manises – The town of Manises has been a major pottery center since the Middle Ages, when its fame reached far and wide and emissaries from the richest courts of Europe vied to buy its fine wares. Although it suffered centuries of eclipse as Spanish tastes turned to the Toledan city of Talavera de la Reina, Manises today, while otherwise unattractive, is packed with ceramics factories and retail shops, many of which sell good reproductions of pieces in Valencia's *Museo Nacional de Cerámica* at bargain prices. Manises is about 4½ miles (7 km) from Valencia, and is well served by city buses.

Sagunto – In 219 BC, the first inhabitants of this fortified rocky ridge, the Iberians, set their possessions and themselves afire in a gigantic holocaust rather than surrender to the Carthaginian general Hannibal. The Romans eventually rebuilt the town, and it was successively held by the Visigoths, the Arabs, and, in the 19th century, the French. Today, Sagunto has an impressive 8,000-seat amphitheater, which is, unfortunately, in relatively poor shape, as well as an ancient acropolis, and nearly half a mile of mostly Moorish medieval walls and ramparts. An old Roman forum is marked by a huge broken stone marked with the letters "FORV." The long ridge occupied by the fortifications provides a dramatic, 360-degree view of orange groves, the surrounding mountains, and the Mediterranean. The castle and amphitheater complex is open Mondays through Saturdays, from 10 AM to 2 PM and from 4 to 6 PM (7 PM in summer); Sundays and holidays, from 10 AM to 2 PM. Admission charge. The complex also includes the *Museo Arqueológico,* which contains Roman mosaics and other artifacts. It was closed at press time and not expected to reopen until late this year or in early 1993.

Modern Sagunto has a population of nearly 60,000, and boasts an old Jewish quarter, a supposed Temple of Diana, and other sites. For more information on Sagunto, contact the tourist office (Plaza de Cronista Chabret; phone: 266-2213). Theater performances are frequently staged in the ancient amphitheater, against a panoramic backdrop. For information, call the tourist office or City Hall (phone: 246-1230). Sagunto is 16 miles (26 km) north of Valencia, is easily reached by car, and has frequent bus and train service.

■**EXTRA SPECIAL:** Just 9½ miles (15 km) south of Valencia lies one of Spain's largest and most beautiful lakes, La Albufera, in the center of the Albufera national park. This peaceful, lagoon-like lake, surrounded by rice paddies, is home to more than 250 species of fowl, including European flamingos and other unusual birds, as well as the baby eels and fish that have long attracted local fishermen. The lake is separated from the sea by a thin strand of sand and pine trees between the towns of El Saler and El Palmar. In either of these places, or along the highway connecting them, visitors can easily rent flat-bottom boats from local fishermen. The sunsets from this side of the lake are stupendous, marked by golden yellows and reddish tints and the calls of the waterfowl. In El Palmar, the farther away of the two towns, try the *alli al pebre* (baby eels from the lake fried in a garlic sauce) at the *Racó de l'Olla* (Carretera de El Saler; phone: 161-0072) near the lake, before heading back to the city.

SOURCES AND RESOURCES

TOURIST INFORMATION: There is no shortage of tourist information offices in Valencia, with four run by the city and a large fifth one under the aegis of the regional government. This regional office, the Conselleria d'Industria Comerc y Turisme (48 Calle de la Paz; phone: 352-4000), near the Plaza Alfonso el Magnánimo, can provide information on both the city and the surrounding areas, and also has some good publications. The office is open Mondays through Fridays, from 9 AM to 2 PM and from 5 to 7 PM; Saturdays, from 9:30 AM to 2 PM. The main Municipal Tourism Office is located in Valencia's City Hall (1 Plaza del Ayuntamiento; phone: 351-0417), and is open Mondays through Fridays, from 9:30 AM to 1:30 PM and from 4:30 to 7 PM; Saturdays, from 9:30 AM to 2 PM. The other offices are located in the Estación del Norte (phone: 352-2882); at the airport in Manises (phone: 153-0325); and near the city's northern limits (at 1 Avenida de Cataluña; phone: 369-7932). These offices are open Mondays through Fridays, from 9 AM to 2 PM and from 5 to 7 PM.

Local Coverage – Two small, locally oriented newspapers serve Valencia: *Las Provincias* and *Levante*. *Turia* is a weekly guide to local entertainment, including theater, music, and dining. *Geográfica Valenciana,* a paperback collection of excellent photographs of the region, is sold at the regional tourist office and in local shops. English-language newspapers are easily found in the Plaza del Ayuntamiento and other central squares in the Old City.

TELEPHONE: The city code for Valencia is 6. If calling from within Spain, dial 96 before the local number.

GETTING AROUND: Downtown Valencia is perpetually packed with cars, and on-street parking is nearly impossible, so it's advisable to walk through the Old City, which is relatively small and easily seen on foot. Trips to outlying areas, including the port, can be made by train or bus; but taxis are quick and quite inexpensive.

Airport – The surprisingly busy Valencia Manises Airport (phone: 370-9500), 4½ miles (7 km) northwest of Valencia, near the pottery center of Manises, has flights to most Spanish cities, as well as most major European capitals. Take bus No. 15, which departs the main bus station hourly.

Boat – From Valencia, it's a quick trip to the Balearic Islands of Majorca, Minorca, and Ibiza. *Trasmediterránea* (15 Calle Manuel Soto; phone: 367-6512/0704; and at the port; phone: 323-7580) offers year-round, daily ferry service Mondays through Saturdays, from the port of El Grao to Majorca (less often to the other islands).

Bus – Most of the city bus lines a visitor will want to use depart from the Plaza del Ayuntamiento. Ask for help at the Municipal Tourism Office in the same square or get a schedule at *EMT* (1 Calle Nuestra Señora de Gracia; phone: 352-8399). The long-distance bus station (13 Avenida Menéndez Pidal; phone: 349-7222), which also serves the airport, is a 10-minute walk north of the Old City, across the Glorias Valencianas Bridge. There is frequent daily service to Madrid, Barcelona, Málaga, and other cities and towns.

Car Rental – The leading international and Spanish firms have offices at the airport and downtown. Agencies in the city include *Avis* (17 Calle Isabel la Católica; phone:

351-0734); *Hertz* (7 Calle Segorbe; phone: 341-5036); *Europcar* (7 Avenida de Antic Regne de Valencia; phone: 374-1512); *Ital* (19 Calle Isabel la Católica; phone: 351-6818); *Flycar* (3 Calle San José de Calasanz; phone: 326-7155); and *Furgocar* (12 Calle Linares; phone: 326-5500).

Subway – A recent metro system (or subway) serves the city's west side, but virtually no tourist sites. Fare depends on the distance traveled.

Taxi – Taxis can be hailed on the street or called by telephone (phone: 370-3333 or 357-1313).

Train – Valencia's main railway station for long-distance trains is the Estación del Norte (Calle de Xàtiva; phone: 351-3612), a colorful iron-and-glass building at the foot of the Old City. Tickets also can be bought at the *RENFE* office (2 Plaza Alfonso el Magnánimo; phone: 352-0202). The creaky old narrow-gauge train that goes to the port of El Grao and northwest through the outlying *huerta* to Liria leaves from the Estación Puente de Madera (1 Calle Cronista Rivelles; phone: 347-3750), just across the Turia River bed from the Serranos Towers.

SPECIAL EVENTS: If there's one thing for which Valencia is famous, it's the *Fallas de San José* — those annual eruptions of flame and popular mirth each *St. Joseph's Day,* March 19. A week of flower-bedecked processions, fireworks, bullfights, and all-out partying ends at midnight on the saint's day, when a fantastic array of satirical effigies is set afire in huge towers, as fire trucks prudently stand by. Some of the *ninots,* lovingly crafted over the entire proceeding year, reach 40 feet high. The fiesta dates back to the Middle Ages, when the carpenters' guild used to burn a year's worth of accumulated wood shavings on the feast day of its patron saint. Today, no one is immune to the papier-mâché lampooning — politicians, the church, the rich, and the poor are all fair game. The *fallas* draw huge crowds from Spain and abroad, so hotel reservations are essential. Around the same time of year, *Holy Week* is marked by boats parading in maritime processions. The patroness of the city, the Virgin of the Unprotected, has her day on the first Sunday of May, followed by *Corpus Christi,* when Valencian *rocas,* baroque holy images of great beauty, are rolled through the streets. The city fills up with tourists again during its *Feria de Julio,* a week-long fair in early July that includes topnotch bullfights, music, fireworks, and even a paella contest. And in early October, Valencians — a strange breed in love with all manner of pop, fizzle, and flare — host the *International Pyrotechnic Festival,* a tournament of the world's finest makers of fireworks.

MUSEUMS: Noteworthy museums not mentioned in *Special Places* include the following:

Museo Histórico Municipal – A small but interesting museum containing a collection of paintings and mementos pertaining to the history of Valencia, ensconced in the Ayuntamiento (City Hall). Open Mondays through Fridays, from 9 AM to 1:30 PM. No admission charge. Plaza del Ayuntamiento (phone: 352-5478).

Museo José Benlliure – The former home of one of the city's most famous painters now houses a museum of his work. Benlliure spent most of his life in Italy, but returned to Valencia in his later years and died here in 1937. Open Mondays through Fridays, from 10 AM to 2 PM. No admission charge. 23 Calle Blanquerías, near Portal Nuevo (phone: 331-1662).

Museo Paleontológico – Skeletal remains and other artifacts in the Almudín, a 14th-to-16th-century granary decorated with *azulejos* and curious frescoes. Open Tuesdays through Fridays, from 10 AM to 1 PM and from 4 to 6:30 PM; Saturdays and Sundays, from 10 AM to 1 PM. No admission charge. Note that winter flooding in 1990 caused damage to the museum and reopening was scheduled at press time; check with the tourist office. Calle Almudín (phone: 331-8562).

Museo de la Prehistoria – In the former Bailía Palace, with exhibits of cave paintings, Roman pots, Stone Age and Iberian ceramics, and other archaeological remains of the Valencian region. Open Tuesdays through Sundays, from 10 AM to 2 PM. No admission charge. 36 Calle Corona (phone: 331-7164).

SHOPPING: Valencia thinks of itself as a design center, and this is reflected in the scores of attractive and very upscale boutiques and designer shops found here. Some of the finer shopping streets — Calle de la Paz, Calle Poeta Querol, Calle de Colón, and Calle Sorni — compare favorably with anything found in Madrid or Barcelona. Valencia is also home to some of Spain's best pottery, Manises stoneware (see *Environs* above), and Lladró porcelain; and *azulejos,* the brightly colored ceramic tiles so gloriously developed by the Arabs in Spain, are a local pride and joy. Glassware is also blown and sold in the region. Another indigenous specialty is seen in the painstakingly hand-sewn silk garments that make up traditional Valencian women's costumes — and sell at huge prices. Business hours are generally 9:30 AM to 1:30 PM and 4:30 to 8 PM. The best stores are generally found around the southeastern portions of the Old City.

Altarriba – A remarkable toy store with a wide selection of model trains from around the world, as well as a collection of peculiarly Spanish miniatures. 22 Calle Mar (phone: 332-3024).

Artespaña – A state-run crafts shop featuring fine handmade ceramics, furniture, hand-blown glass, and leather goods at reasonable prices. 7 Calle de la Paz (phone: 331-6403).

Carla – Specializing in fine silk, including garments for women. 4 Calle Bordadores (phone: 331-8430).

El Corte Inglés – Valencia has two branches of the popular national department store chain, offering just about everything; they remain open during the lunch hour and on Saturday afternoons. 26 Calle Pintor Sorolla (phone: 351-2444) and in the *Nuevo Centro Shopping Mall,* 15 Avenida Menéndez Pidal (phone: 347-4142).

Francis Montesinos – Trendy men's and women's fashions by Valencia's best-known designer. 40 Calle Caballeros (phone: 331-2844).

J. Sugrañes – When this atmospheric little shop opened in 1885, its silk dresses, shawls, mantillas, and other items were still worn regularly by Valencia's moneyed damsels; today, the finely crafted, very expensive women's wear made by the Sugrañes family counts as "traditional" finery for fiestas only. 18 Calle de la Paz (phone: 352-6432).

Lladró – The internationally known porcelain maker — the place for those whose tastes run to figurines of forest dryads, small children, and animals. Also, its own line of leather goods. Three locations: Calle Marqués de Sotelo (phone: 351-0937), Calle Poeta Querol (phone: 351-1625), and in the *Nuevo Centro Shopping Mall* (phone: 347-0086).

Loewe – One of Spain's most elegant — and expensive — purveyors of men's and women's clothing, leather goods, luggage, and accessories. Men's store at 7 Calle Poeta Querol (phone: 352-7372); women's store at 7 Calle Marqués de Dos Aguas (phone: 352-4301).

Neri – An exclusive ceramics and kitchenware store, offering some of the finest traditional pottery in the city. 1 Calle Poeta Querol (phone: 351-8961).

SPORTS AND FITNESS: Boating – The *Real Club Náutico* (Royal Nautical Club) offers boat rentals, a sailing school, fishing, scuba diving and snorkeling, and full yacht service. Camino Canal (phone: 367-9011).

Bullfighting – One of the largest rings in Spain is located next to the train station (28 Calle de Xàtiva; phone: 351-9315). *Corridas,* or bullfights, are held for a week during the *fallas* and the July festival, otherwise irregularly.

Golf – There are four golf courses near Valencia. The 18-hole, par 72 *Campo de Golf El Saler* is at the *Parador Luis Vives,* sandwiched between the Mediterranean and the Albufera lagoon 11 miles (18 km) south of Valencia on a strand of pine trees and sand dunes (phone: 161-1186). Also try the 18-hole *Club de Campo del Bosque* (Calle Chiva, phone: 251-1011), 2½ miles (4 km) from town; or the 18-hole *Club de Golf Escorpión* at Bétera, 12 miles (19 km) northwest along the road to Liria (phone: 160-1211). There is also a 9-hole course 7½ miles (12 km) west of town in Manises (phone: 379-0850).

Soccer – Valencia's first-division team is a cause célèbre in the area, with victory liable to provoke flag waving, horn honking parades downtown. Valencia plays at the *Estadio Luis Casanova,* Avenida de Suecia (phone: 360-0550).

Swimming – The beaches just north and south of the port, Playa de Levante and Playa de la Punta, are too polluted to make swimming advisable. There are miles of popular beaches to the south, however, toward El Saler, that are cleaner.

Trinquete – This is a peculiarly Valencian form of that great Spanish sport, pelota (best known to Americans in one of its many forms, jai alai). The crowd sits along one side of the frontón while players bat a calfskin ball over a net with their hands. Afternoon games are played daily except Tuesdays and Sundays at the *Trinquete Pelayo,* 6 Calle Pelayo (phone: 352-6845).

THEATER: There are several theaters in Valencia, but only one has consistently interesting Spanish and European productions: the *Teatro Principal* (15 Calle Barcas; phone: 351-0051). North of the city, in Sagunto, productions are at times staged in the old Roman amphitheater against a spectacular backdrop of the town, the plain, the sea, and the mountains (see *Environs*).

MUSIC: Valencia's futuristic *Palau de la Música* (see *Special Places;* 1 Plaza del Rey; phone: 360-3356 for information, 361-5212 for tickets), east of the Old City across the Aragon Bridge, hosts world class concerts of classical and other music during much of the year. The 19th-century *Teatro Principal* (see *Theater*) holds an opera season, usually in the fall and winter, and hosts occasional jazz, dance, and other festivals.

NIGHTCLUBS AND NIGHTLIFE: As does every large Spanish town, Valencia has a thriving bar scene, although in this city it is unusually scattered. Younger and hipper bars tend to be concentrated around the Plaza del Carmen and Calle Caballeros in the Old City — *Café Lisboa* (35 Calle Caballeros; phone: 332-1764) doubles as a photo gallery. Quite a trek northeast of the Old City, around the Plaza Xuquer, the bars and fast-food joints are popular with students from the nearby university. A truly charming Old City bar, the *Cervecería Madrid* (10 Calle Abadía de San Martín; phone: 352-9671), is owned by Constante Gil, who painted the hundreds of naïve canvases that decorate the place's 2 floors. Nearby, in the Plaza del Ayuntamiento, walk through the front door of the old *Cine Rialto* (phone: 351-5603), a theater that shows foreign films in their original language, into the *Cafetería Rialto* (phone: 351-5603), a perfect spot for a drink. Less chic but more "elegant" bars, aimed at an older crowd, are on Gran Vía Marqués del Turia, east of the Estación del Norte, the main train station. Large, all-night discotheques are found on the highway to El Saler — the *Spook Factory* (Carretera del Saler, Pinedo) is one of the most popular. For those with a taste for the tables, there's the very classic — and expensive — *Hotel-Casino Monte Picayo* (casino phone: 142-1211; hotel phone: 142-0100), a luxury complex featuring every gaming, lodging, and sporting service imaginable. Casino hours are 7 PM to 5 AM nightly. Monte Picayo is 9½ miles (15 km) north of Valencia, on the N-340 highway to Barcelona.

BEST IN TOWN

 CHECKING IN: Valencia generally has no shortage of hotel space — but this rule of thumb does not apply during the March 12–19 *fallas* (see *Special Events*), when reservations are an absolute must. The city also hosts a number of business conventions throughout the year that can suddenly fill several hotels. Parking is a year-round nightmare anywhere close to the Old City, a fact that should be considered when choosing accommodations. The city is among the more economical ones in Spain to visit — its hotel rooms cost less on the whole than those in other large cities that are more firmly established on the tourist track. Expect to pay $85 and up for a double room listed as expensive, $55 to $85 for a moderate room, and $45 or less for an inexpensive one. All phone numbers are in the 6 city code unless otherwise indicated.

Astoria Palace – When Spanish politicians, entertainers, and other celebrities visit Valencia, this is where they stay. Manuel Benítez, "El Cordobés," rode the shoulders of a crowd direct from the bullring into the lobby here; opera diva Montserrat Caballé is a more contemporary visitor. Sumptuously decorated and ideally located on a small square in the heart of the Old City, the hotel manages to retain an atmosphere of personal attention. All of its 207 rooms and 20 suites are air conditioned and have color television sets, radios, and, on request, mini-bars. Other facilities include a restaurant, a convention center, private dining rooms, parking, and a discotheque. 5 Plaza Rodrigo Botet (phone: 352-6737; fax: 352-8078; telex: 62733). Expensive.

Dimar – Functional is the operative word at this 95-room modern establishment, just far enough from the central city to make it a long walk. A pleasant lobby leads to clean and carpeted air conditioned rooms that offer color television sets, mini-bars, and rambling bathrooms. The hotel is only a few steps from a district well known for its upscale boutiques and fine restaurants. As you walk out the front door, listen for the occasional cacophony of thousands of birds gathering in the trees of the Gran Vía. 80 Gran Vía Marqués del Turia (phone: 334-1807). Expensive.

Reina Victoria – Luis Ferreres Soler, the designer of this centrally located 1910-vintage building, was clearly influenced by 19th-century French architecture, but threw in a splash of modernism. Glass encloses corner balconies, the dining room, and the lobby, giving the interior a light and airy feel. Many of the 92 air conditioned rooms offer striking views of the Old City. The bar is dark, woody, and very English; the restaurant and its marble-floored dining room are local favorites. All around, the service here is excellent. Convention facilities are also available. 4-6 Calle Barcas (phone: 352-0487; fax: 352-0487; telex: 064755). Expensive.

Rey Don Jaime – A short taxi ride from the city center, near the *Palau de la Música*, stands this luxurious, spacious, and somewhat impersonal establishment. The lower lobby contains a concourse of shops, a hairdresser, and a sweeping marble staircase that leads up to a sitting room, an English-style bar, and convention and meeting rooms. The restaurant offers both international dishes and reasonable examples of Valencian specialties. Upstairs, the 314 air conditioned rooms are very large and well serviced, the bathrooms, huge. The hotel is primarily a businessperson's place, however, in a somewhat gloomy location outside the life of the Old City. 2 Avenida Baleares (phone: 360-7300). Expensive.

Bristol – Behind a turn-of-the-century brick, stone, and glassed-in façade are 40 pleasant rooms in the center of the Old City. It's a short walk from the *Ceramics*

Museum and other downtown monuments — not to mention the *Cervecería Madrid* (see *Nightclubs and Nightlife*). The service is pleasant and helpful. 3 Calle Abadía de San Martín (phone: 352-1176). Moderate.

Excelsior – Comfortable and pleasant, with a wood-paneled lobby, it's just a few steps from the *Astoria Palace* and costs only half as much. Downstairs, a white brick cafeteria-bar and an elegant little dining room are both enjoyable spots, and the service is good. All 65 rooms have color television sets and clean, comfortable appointments and facilities. 5 Calle Barcelonina (phone: 351-4612). Moderate.

Inglés – The elegant Old World charm here fades rather quickly beyond the lobby and the connected restaurant. The building, which overlooks the *Ceramics Museum* in the heart of the Old City, is the former palace of the Duke and Duchess of Cardona, and is a historical landmark. Its sunlit restaurant is elegant, with classy if slightly stuffy service — an especially pleasant place for a lingering breakfast. All 62 rooms have color television sets. 6 Calle Marqués de Dos Aguas (phone: 351-6426; fax: 3940251; telex: 62228). Moderate.

Llar – Cheerful, helpful service, an ideal location for those who aren't set on staying smack-dab in the Old City, and unusually homey wood-and-plaster rooms. This 50-room establishment is located on the artery of a bustling and upscale shopping district, where designer boutiques and quality department stores compete for the milling crowds, but it is neither noisy nor unpleasantly busy. No more than a 10-minute walk to almost anywhere in the city, less to most places. 46 Calle Colón (phone: 352-8460). Moderate.

Alcázar – Offering 18 quiet rooms just off the Plaza del Ayuntamiento, easily located by a huge and somewhat garish 4-story sign hanging out over the street. The rooms are small and a bit depressing, but it's hard to beat the price. The larger part of the establishment is a 2-story restaurant specializing in popular Valencian and Spanish dishes; the tavern downstairs, hung with hams, is particularly charming. Try the *tapas* and shellfish on display under glass at the bar. 11 Calle Mosén Femades (phone: 351-5551). Inexpensive.

Castelar – At the foot of the Plaza del Ayuntamiento, this family-run property offers 17 clean, comfortable rooms for less than half the price of similar digs across the street at the much larger *Europa*. Each room has running water; the shared bathrooms are well maintained and clean. 1 Calle Ribera (phone: 352-9575). Inexpensive.

EATING OUT: Valencia is home to Spain's most internationally famous dish of all — paella — and the city's restaurants compete vigorously with one another to concoct the most delightful examples of this rice plate. Paella was originally a peasant's dish, rice with whatever happened to be at hand; but today, it can come with shellfish, rabbit, chicken, lobster, snails, eels, and more. Other delicious rice dishes, based like paella on the paddies of the wetlands around the Albufera National Park south of Valencia, include *arroz a banda* (rice with fish, garlic, onion, tomato, and saffron); *arroz en bledes* (rice with stewed cabbage, tomato, red peppers, white beans, and garlic); and *arroz al forn* (rice cooked in an oven casserole with chickpeas, potatoes, garlic, paprika, and sometimes pork ribs). *Fideuà*, a paella in which vermicelli is used in place of saffron rice, is the rage among Valencia's contemporary master chefs, and should be sampled. All vegetables in the region — not to mention the ubiquitous citrus fruits, which are best from December through March — are likely to be excellent, as they come straight from the fertile *huerta* that surrounds the city. Another local delight is *horchata*, a cold, refreshing summer drink made with *chufas* (earth almonds), water, and sugar; the best way to sample it is in the cafeterias and orchards of Alboraya, the village — about 4 miles (6 km) north of

Valencia — where it's made. A local pastry is *mona de pascua,* a spongy *Easter* cake. The region's wines are many, with a tendency to the slightly sweet, but none has so far received much recognition elsewhere. Note that good restaurants in Valencia are not concentrated in the Old City, and several are in the port of El Grao. Expect to pay $80 or more for a meal for two with wine in restaurants listed as expensive, $50 to $80 in moderate restaurants, and $45 or less at inexpensive ones. All telephone numbers are in the 6 city code unless otherwise indicated.

Eladio – Eladio, the Swiss-trained owner, is a master of fish — hake, sea bass, angler, turbot, and sole, which he brings south from the stormy Atlantic waters off his native Galicia. The menu occasionally verges on nouvelle cuisine but generally sticks to European and Galician dishes. Try the *pulpo a la gallega* (Galician octopus), and don't miss the pastries prepared by Eladio's wife, Violette Fontaine. Closed Sundays and August. Reservations necessary. Major credit cards accepted. 40 Calle Chiva (phone: 326-2244). Expensive.

La Hacienda – A few steps outside the city's old east gate, serving Spanish dishes and other selections in an atmosphere of mirrored walls and elegant old furniture. The *rabo de toro a la cordobesa* (oxtail stew, Cordoban style) is renowned, and game, in general, is very good. Closed Saturday afternoons, Sundays, and *Holy Week.* Reservations advised. Major credit cards accepted. 12 Avenida Navarro Reverter (phone: 373-1859). Expensive.

Ma Cuina – Valencians still flock here, but it's no longer considered the best place in town. The Basque and Valencian cooking remains delightful, however, and private dining rooms are still available. Very much worth a visit. Closed Sundays. Reservations advised. Major credit cards accepted. 49 Gran Vía Germanias (phone: 341-7799). Expensive.

Marisquería Civera – Without a doubt, the best shellfish in the city — and that probably goes for the fish, too. There's a galaxy of seafood and vegetable *tapas* laid out on the counters, all absolutely fresh. Closed Mondays and during the month of August. This *marisquería,* or shellfishery, is always busy, so go early or make reservations. Major credit cards accepted. Across the Serranos Bridge, at 11 Calle Lérida (phone: 347-5917). Expensive.

El Gourmet – Consistently fine Spanish and continental food, coupled with excellent service, have made this place one of Valencia's most popular. Try some of chef Jaime Capilla's specialties: *revueltos de berenjenas con gambas* (scrambled eggs with eggplant and shrimp), *merluza con almejas* (hake with clams), and *perdiz moscovita al hojaldre* (Muscovy partridge in pastry), among others. Closed Sundays and mid-August through mid-September. Reservations advised. Major credit cards accepted. 3 Calle Taquígrafo Martí (phone: 374-5071). Moderate.

Lionel – A dining room that is meant to reflect elegant French turn-of-the-century style, it is pleasant but perhaps a bit grandmotherly. Usually good are the homemade soup, croquettes, partridge, and rabbit. The kitchen specializes in duck and turkey dishes, but tends to overcook both. Service is adequate. Closed Saturdays at lunch and Sunday evenings. Reservations advised on weekends. Major credit cards accepted. 9 Calle Pizarro (phone: 351-6566). Moderate.

La Marcelina – In a row of several dozen restaurants lining the beach near the port of El Grao, this is one of the more famous of Valencia's old beach establishments, having made a remarkable comeback recently after years of decline. For more than a century, it has been offering great paellas and, in summer, music on an outdoor terrace. Closed Sundays in summer. Reservations unnecessary except Saturday evenings in summer. Major credit cards accepted. 10 Avenida del Neptuno (phone: 371-2025). Moderate.

Nevada – In 1979, this hidden treasure won the international prize for *fideuà,* and, if anything since then, its offering has improved. An excellent — and exceedingly fairly priced — place to sample Valencian rice dishes. Try *arroz al horno, arroz negro con chipirones* (black rice with squid), or *arroz al marisco* (shellfish and rice). Closed Tuesdays and Sunday evenings (all day Sunday during summer). No reservations or credit cards accepted. In a nondescript residential neighborhood. 53 Avenida Fernando el Católico (phone: 325-5121). Moderate.

La Pepica – This grand old eatery is on the beach next to *La Marcelina* and is known as *the* lunchtime spot for paella and other Valencian rice dishes. Walk past the great open kitchen, hung with hundreds of black paella pans, and into a spacious dining room overlooking a white sand beach (there are outdoor tables in summer). Open daily; closed November. No reservations or credit cards accepted. 6-8 Avenida del Neptuno (phone: 371-0366). Moderate.

La Riuà – *Arroz a banda* (rice with seafood) is Pilar Lozano's specialty, and although only men are supposed to be Valencia's greatest rice chefs, she is an exception. Two different rice dishes are served daily, 12 a week, in a three-level dining room lavishly decorated with glazed tiles and handicrafts and located in the heart of the Old City. Seafood dishes also are very good, and the *menú del día* (menu of the day) is a bargain. Closed Sunday evenings (all day Sunday during summer), *Holy Week,* and August 15 through the first week in September. Reservations advised on weekends. Major credit cards accepted. 27 Calle Mar (phone: 331-7172). Moderate.

L'Estimat – Also in the port of El Grao, specializing in Valencian rice dishes, with its own circle of fans who swear it's the best. Closed Tuesdays and September. Reservations advised. Visa accepted. 18 Avenida del Neptuno (phone: 371-1018). Inexpensive.

Los Madriles – Pablo Martínez opened this small Castilian restaurant in 1964, and it has since become a favorite of Valencia's bullfighting aficionados, serving such Madrid regional specialties as *cocido* (chickpea stew), *cordero al horno* (oven-baked lamb), and *ternera en su jugo* (veal in its own juices). Good rioja wines are served in a humble but charming atmosphere under walls of bullfight posters. Closed Sunday evenings (all day Sunday during summer), August, and *Holy Week.* No reservations or credit cards accepted. 50 Avenida de Antic Regne de Valencia (phone: 374-2335). Inexpensive.

La Montaraza – Spanish cooking with good roast meats and sausages at a fair price. Closed for dinner on Sundays and holidays; in summer, closed all day Sunday. No reservations. Major credit cards accepted. 47 Calle Olta (phone: 373-1653). Inexpensive.

Rue de la Paix – Decent, reasonably priced French cooking that's even less expensive if ordered from the *menú del día*. Closed Saturdays at lunch and all day Sundays. Reservations unnecessary. No credit cards accepted. 18 Calle de la Paz (phone: 351-2610). Inexpensive.

 TAPAS BARS: The best way to sample *tapas* is to go on a *tapeo* — a round-robin tour of *tapas* bars. Valencia's leading *tapas* streets are Calle Mosén Femades, just off the Plaza del Ayuntamiento, and Calles Ribera and Convento Jerusalén. *Taberna Alcázar* (9 Calle Mosén Femades; phone: 352-9575) is a rustic and charming bar in the hotel and restaurant of the same name (the dining room is upstairs and the hotel is next door); its old wooden bar practically groans under the weight of the colorful offering of *tapas*. At *Trocadero* (3 Plaza del Ayuntamiento; phone: 351-7582), another of the city's busier *tapas* spots, try a *ración* (larger than a *tapa*) or one of the rice specialties or the wonderful anchovies in vinegar. Mushroom *tapas* are especially good at *Amorós* (3 Calle Llop; phone: 351-7057), centrally located and sometimes thronged; while *Casa Mario* (3 Calle Roteros; phone:

331-7006), in the offbeat and increasingly interesting Barrio del Carmen near the Serranos Towers, does a terrific job serving shellfish *tapas* and *raciones. Glorieta* (1 Calle General Tovar; phone: 321-2687) is centrally located at the east end of Calle de la Paz. On October 14, 1957, the worst floods in Valencian memory reached a level about 9 feet up the wall in this charming corner bar, lit beautifully by a full-length window. Look up above the bar to the left for the commemorative plaque.

DIVERSIONS

DIVERSIONS

For the Experience

Quintessential Spain

The Iberian Peninsula is like a hypothetical aisle marked "Experience" in a choice-laden supermarket — full of good things that come in a variety of enticing packages. So just as sherry comes in *fino, amontillado, manzanilla,* and *dulce,* flamenco can be either raucous side-street strumming, a tourist sideshow in Granada's Sacromonte Caves, or a whirl-perfect spectacle on a limelighted Madrid stage. Gazpacho can be eaten with a spoon or drunk with a straw, and there are endless varieties of seafood, from the hearty cod stews of the Basque Country to fresh, grilled tuna (with just a squirt of lemon juice) in the Algarve to the elaborate mussel-and-shrimp paella of Valencia. Nor do all Spaniards speak Castilian. There is the "s"-less Andalusian sing-song, a different form of Catalan on each Balearic Island, and the exotic language of the Basques, called Euskera, that isn't related to anything else on this planet.

Iberia's range of flavors comes from its capacity for absorption. One of Spain's most characteristic painters was a Greek (El Greco), the Bourbon dynasty was French, and an American popularized Pamplona's *Fiesta de San Fermín* (in recognition of which the city named a square for him — Plaza Hemingway). The New World sent the old one tomatoes, potatoes, coffee, and the gold that decorated Toledan swords, and made Madrid one of the most powerful cities in Europe. Africa gave Spain an architectural heritage, the microtonal wail of Spanish flamenco, and an often crushing heat that spawned such relaxing institutions as the afternoon siesta, the evening *paseo,* the strategically placed café, and the evening gathering around the motor scooter in a small town square.

Still, there are several things that capture the special spirit of this singular peninsula, and provide a visitor with an insight into its irresistible personality.

OPENING NIGHT AT THE LICEU AND DINNER AT SET PORTES, Barcelona: Thanks to the hosting of the *1992 Olympic Games,* the grimy exterior has been given a face-lift to match the interior of the *Gran Teatre del Liceu,* one of Europe's great opera houses, which gleams with the polish, plushness, and crystal sparkle that was the hallmark of the 19th century. Almost every Spaniard sings, but see if the concierge at your hotel can wheedle tickets to hear homespun pro Plácido Domingo do a slow burn at the Royal Tobacco Factory in *Carmen,* that quintessentially Spanish story of smoldering sex, jealousy, and clicking castanets. The warbles and guitar twangs that float down the alleyways of the Barri Gòtic are reminders that a Spain filled with melody is not just a figment of Bizet's fantasy. When you emerge, it still may be a little early to eat, so join the rest of the city for a languid amble along La Rambla. On a cool, clear night, the pedestrian traffic on this thoroughfare lined with bookstands and birdstalls may be at a standstill, as bench-sitters, browsers, and boulevardiers jostle through the midnight ritual of strolling and stopping and doffing of caps. Wend your way to the waterfront and to *Set Portes* (see *Best Restaurants of Spain,* in this section), where a jovial roar and a tinkling piano fill the huge dining rooms, and the clientele seems to have been sitting at the same leisurely Catalan dinner since the restaurant's opening in 1836. Try the braised partridge, the *zarzuela* (a local, family-size version of bouillabaisse), or the *escalivada* (a cold, roast vegetable platter).

BULLFIGHT IN PAMPLONA, Navarre: This Sunday ritual, heralded by fanfare and pomp, is an assault on all the senses: the ocher turf glaring in the late afternoon sun; the band's tinny blare; the gaudy, spangled costumes of the procession; the *bandilleros'* ballet; the coarse, feverish crowd watering its passion with warm wine squirted from bulging skins; the bull's thundering fury; the graceful arrogance of the matador; the swirl of the fuschia and yellow *muleta,* the flash and plunge of the sword. This celebration of life and death and "grace under pressure," as Hemingway described it, is watched on television in living rooms and bars all over Spain, as a reminder of the time when Christians dueled lions in a Colosseum full of Romans. The president of the corrida (usually a local public official) sits in box seats high above the arena with a group of advisors, and decides when to begin each phase of the event. The matador's artistry and daring determine whether the president, like an emperor decreeing mercy or death for a gladiator with a flick of his thumb, will award him one or two ears. The crowd plays a major role by wildly waving white handkerchiefs at the president indicating their support for the matador. An extraordinary performance will bring two ears and a tail. During the *Fiesta de San Fermín* in July (see "The Best Festivals" in *For the Mind*), each morning the bulls for the day's corrida are sent galloping down narrow, barricaded streets on a 2-mile route to the *Plaza de Toros.* The animals receive a measure of revenge when they manage to gore a handful of the hundreds of brave (or crazy) men — and a few women — who, dressed in the red and white colors of the festival, race before the bulls.

LONELY ARAB CASTLES OF ANDALUSIA: It takes a car, a sharp eye, a love of detours, and a well-stocked picnic hamper to find the romantic, weed-strewn ruins of castles that once guarded every hill and port in Arab Al-Andalus. Perched on cragtops that look stormable only by eagles, these worn, but still stern, battlements formed a Maginot Line along the tense border between the Muslim and Christian worlds of long ago, where the names of towns still bear the epithet *de la frontera* ("on the border"). But this martial past acquires a latter-day peaceful haze if the scant remains are contemplated with the benefit of a bottle of wine, a hunk of *manchego* cheese, some smoky slices of *jamón serrano,* and a handful of Spanish olives. Because the road to the top can be nearly vertical, it's probably best to leave the car in the olive grove or by the cluster of whitewashed houses that invariably cower in the castle's shadow. Count on being alone at the top, except perhaps for a state employee who is likely to be as lonely as the ruins he guards and will be more than happy to point out the storerooms, the water drains, the narrow, L-shaped passageways meant to thwart a battering ram, the direction from which the Christians finally came, the best angle for a snapshot, and the precise plot in the distant cemetery where his grandfather is buried.

TAPAS AND PATIOS, Córdoba, Andalusia: The glare of the southern sun and the heady odor of orange blossoms are everywhere in Córdoba, settling on the city, seeping from the cobblestones, sliding through the painted shutters, making everyone sleepy and sultry and hot. A *tapas* (Spanish smorgasbord) bar is the perfect refuge for sodden sightseers and lounging locals, who gather in the grudging breeze from a creaking electric fan, nursing chilled sangria and gazpacho. Beneath the glass counter are countless accompaniments to a glass of beer — marinated mushrooms, shrimp in garlic sauce, olives seasoned with thyme, fried squid, bits of sausage, roasted sweet peppers with olive oil, smoked ham, spicy meatballs — all available in the mouthful-size portions that make them *tapas* and not a meal. Throughout the day, the floor becomes littered with shrimp tails, toothpicks, and crumpled paper napkins, and when, periodically, the counterman sweeps up this traditional litter, the customers do a distracted dance around the broom that is as much a part of Spanish culinary culture as the *seguidilla* (flamenco song and dance). For those who can bring themselves to step out into the sticky Andalusian summer, occasional cool gusts of comfort come from the patios not quite hidden behind wrought-iron grilles or wooden doors left ajar just enough for one to peer in and breathe deeply. Geraniums, jasmine, and lemon trees lovingly arranged against patterned, tiled walls offer sun-stroked visitors a fresh, perfumed caress. The lushest and most colorful patios win prizes in the city's 2-week *Fiesta de los Patios* in May (see "The Best Festivals" in *For the Mind*).

FLAMENCO IN THE BARRIO DE TRIANA, Seville: The impromptu stomp, strum, snap, clap, and growl gets going around 1 or 2 AM in the working-class district of Triana, with all the spark and ancient pathos of those Gypsy blues. The patrons of the slightly seedy bars along the Calle Betis bring their own guitars and tambourines — the dancing is unrefined and improvised, and the singing is soulful and throaty. Flamenco grew out of a mixture of *sevillanas* liturgical chants, the call of the Moorish muezzin, and plaintive Gypsy folk tunes, catalyzed by the Inquisition into a music of guttural sounds lamenting the fate of the heathen in brutally Catholic Spain. Now that the Word is no longer spread by the pyre, singers moan more about music and lust, and syncopated clapping and flashy footwork have replaced campfire thrumming. But while the high artistry of the song and dance performances — *tablaos* — in the more gentrified Barrio de Santa Cruz, for which foreigners pay a pricey cover charge, can also be heard at *Carnegie Hall,* this, with its rough edges and drinking and picking of pockets, is the real thing.

ON HORSEBACK THROUGH EXTREMADURA: The name means "extreme or remote," and seems apt for the *duro* (tough) region, where the local specialties are black-bull steaks and cured hams made from snake-fed pigs. Ride here in the spring, before the heat has burned away the tapestry of flowers and turned the rich, red soil a cracked and sunbaked brown. At a leisurely canter, you can't help but savor the cork woods and chestnut groves that motorists mostly miss on their way to the hilltop monasteries of Guadalupe and Yuste. And in some parts, you and your mounts will be the only visitors — few cars ever make it up the stomach-churning curves through the forests of Las Hurdes, the northernmost part of Extremadura, populated by rugged mountain people. There is some poetic justice in the stares you will attract as you ride into a dusty shepherd town, for it was Extremaduran peasants-turned-conquistadores who rode the first horses off Spanish galleons and into the New World — and were taken for half-equine gods.

THE ROYALTY TRAIL, Castile-León: Like children romping in a playroom shin-deep in toys, the Kings and Queens of Spain scattered palaces, gardens, and summer retreats all over Castile. They all can be visited, but take it slow, because if you try to retrace the dainty steps of royalty in one whirlwind day, your tour will meld into a sumptuous haze of polished wood and tarnished mirrors and the very chair where Carlos the Somethingth sat. Start at the *Prado,* once the storehouse for the king's art collection, to see court life through Diego Velázquez's keen, cruel eye for the pomposity, frills, and formalities of the 17th century. His portraits of the royal family and paintings such as *Las Meninas* (The Maids of Honor) seem like sociological studies of how the other half a handful lived. The itinerary then spirals out from King Juan Carlos's current throne room in Madrid's Palacio Real, swooping through extremes of opulence: the once suburban, still idyllic Parque del Retiro; the tapestried walls of El Pardo; the passionate austerity of the royal monastery of El Escorial, glowing fervently in its halo of mountains above Madrid; the weave of graveled walks and marble stairways at Aranjuez; the bursting geyser fountain at La Granja de San Ildefonso, outside Segovia.

Paradores

No visit to the Iberian Peninsula is complete without a visit or an overnight stay in a Spanish *parador* or even a manor house. Imagine sleeping where kings and queens slept, walking corridors and chambers where Franciscan monks walked, and dining in elegant rooms where nobles and aristocrats sat down to countless formal meals over the centuries. The Spanish people pride themselves on their rich sense of such traditions, and have impeccably restored and converted ancient landmark castles and monasteries into magnificent hotel accommodations, offering travelers a historic return to the past, complete with modern — and often luxurious — facilities.

Spain's first *parador* (an inn that offers food and shelter to travelers) was introduced west of Madrid in the Sierra de Gredos in 1928, when King Alfonso XIII opened a lodge to be used primarily as a base for hunting excursions. This concept of low-cost accommodation became so popular that it eventually expanded into the world's most successful transformation of long-abandoned national treasures. Of the 86 *paradores* in the countrywide network today, many are restored convents, palaces, and castles, filled with original decorations and antiques. It's not unusual to be escorted past standing figures in coats of armor, or up winding stone staircases past hanging wrought-iron lanterns. Other *paradores* are constructed of gleaming marble and boast the latest modern touches — including indoor and outdoor swimming pools, golf courses, and other sports facilities. All have fine restaurants serving breakfast, lunch, and dinner; most serve regional specialties and carry wine bottled under their own labels. The restaurants are of simple design and usually match the *parador*'s overall decor.

Not all *paradores* are for everyone. About 90% of the rooms are doubles furnished with twin beds. Travelers who want a double bed should request a room with a *cama de matrimonio,* but be advised that normally there are only a few per *parador.* Some *paradores* are low-key, and may be considered too remote (or too dull for a traveler seeking continuous activity). Not every room in every *parador* has a television set or a radio, and many are located on the outskirts of town (requiring a car to get to most sightseeing stops). Travelers unable to climb stairs should inquire about elevators, since some *paradores* do not have easy access to all rooms and public areas.

Reservations for *paradores* in or near major cities such as Toledo, Segovia, and Granada should be made well in advance. Although it is possible to travel through Spain from *parador* to *parador* without reservations, this practice is not recommended. Ask the *parador* concierge to phone ahead to determine availability and to make reservations. Rates are seasonal in the majority of the *paradores,* but also can be one price year-round in the more popular ones. Low season runs from November through March, mid-season is from April through June, and high season is from July through October. Expect to pay between $75 and $150 for a double room. This rate includes breakfast, taxes, and service charges. For more information about the *paradores* of Spain, contact *Paradores del Estado* (18 Calle Velázquez, Madrid 28001; phone: 91-435-9700), or the network's US representative, *Marketing Ahead* (433 Fifth Ave., New York, NY 10016; phone: 212-686-9213).

PARADOR DE ALMAGRO, Almagro, Castile–La Mancha: Don Quixote loved the region of La Mancha, and so will any guest staying in this former 15th-century Franciscan convent. The elegant touches of this 55-room *parador* recall the building's original functions, and it also features 16 courtyards and patios, gardens, a wine cellar, a swimming pool, and a convention hall. Note, however, that the beds are of hammock configuration. From May through October, Almagro's main square becomes an open-air theater for classical works performed by topnotch national and international compa-

nies. The town is also famous for its lace. Information: *Parador de Almagro,* Calle Ronda de San Francisco, Almagro 13270 (phone: 926-860100).

PARADOR ALCÁZAR DEL REY DON PEDRO, Carmona, near Seville, Andalusia: This majestic *parador,* the former 14th-century retreat of King Pedro the Cruel, overlooks the lush green countryside below, where cows graze and farmers plow. The high-ceilinged dining room, with its coats of arms and huge paintings, is fit for a king. There is also a lovely Moorish garden full of colorful tiles and bright yellow seats, an excellent spot to sit and sip a drink of sherry, special to the region. The 59 rooms are immaculate but otherwise routine. Information: *Parador Alcázar del Rey Don Pedro,* Carmona 41410 (phone: 95-414-1010).

PARADOR DE CHINCHÓN, Chinchón, near Madrid: This lovely village, only a half-hour's drive south of Madrid, is primarily known for its anisette liqueur, its *Holy Week* re-creation of the Crucifixion and the Resurrection, and its summer amateur bullfights in the main square. In 1982, the town's 17th-century convent was transformed into a 38-room *parador,* complete with settees, murals, wall tapestries, and other ornate furnishings. There's a wonderful glass-walled circular hallway overlooking a beautiful courtyard — a perfect spot for afternoon tea. The *parador* also boasts a chapel and garden with winding paths, plus a swimming pool and a convention hall. Information: *Parador de Chinchón,* 1 Avenida de Generalísimo, Chinchón 28370 (phone: 91-894-0836).

PARADOR SAN FRANCISCO, Granada, Andalusia: Because Granada's Alhambra Palace is one of the most visited sites in Spain, it's no wonder that this *parador,* located within its sprawling complex, is booked months in advance. The building is a former Franciscan monastery, founded by Queen Isabella (she was even temporarily buried here) when she was in Granada with her husband, King Ferdinand, sending troops against the Moors. The 39-room *parador* has meandering corridors, carved bedroom doorways reminiscent of 18th-century monks' cells, and religious statues. Rich Moorish purples and golds decorate the public rooms. Other features include gardens, a convention hall, and an outdoor café overlooking the Alhambra. The wait for rooms is from 6 months to a year, depending on the season, but cancellations do come up; ask for a room in the old wing. Information: *Parador San Francisco,* Recinto de la Alhambra, Granada 18009 (phone: 958-221440).

PARADOR ZURBARÁN, Guadalupe, Extremadura: Adventurous travelers should take a ride south from Oropesa to the town of Guadalupe to visit the Monasterio de Nuestra Señora de Guadalupe. A reported appearance of the Virgin Mary in 1300 on this site was the reason for the construction of the monastery. A statue of the Virgin (it had been buried in a nearby hillside for nearly 700 years) is enshrined on the altar. Pilgrims and tourists travel hundreds of miles to view the statue, and to examine the extensive collection of art by Francisco de Zurbarán, as well as embroideries, frontals, and precious stones. The 40-room *parador,* once a 15th-century hospice, is next door. The rooms look out over a central courtyard with Moorish-style gardens. Information: *Parador Zurbarán,* 10 Calle Marqués de la Romana, Guadalupe 10140 (phone: 927-367075).

PARADOR DE SAN MARCOS, León, Castile-León: For centuries, Christians making their yearly pilgrimage to Santiago de Compostela used this majestic former hospice as a resting point. Travelers making the trek from Madrid to northern Spain today find this *parador,* with its 16th-century coffered ceiling, Plateresque exterior, and grand staircases, a perfect stop. The 253 rooms make it the largest property in the *parador* network. Facilities include gardens, a nightclub, hairdresser's salon, children's day-care center, and a convention hall. Information: *Parador de San Marcos,* 7 Plaza de San Marcos, León 54001 (phone: 987-237300).

PARADOR VIRREY TOLEDO, Oropesa, near Toledo, Castile–La Mancha: According to legend, this massive medieval stone castle was built by Hercules' army, and later housed powerful Spanish and Moorish lords and kings. Today, it looms over a valley of squat olive trees and small farms. After a rain shower, the sweet smell of hay often wafts upward and into the 44 rooms. A short walk from Oropesa's Plaza Mayor, this *parador* is just 2 miles (3 km) away from the small town of Lagartera, famous for its lacework, where local women still sit outside their homes practicing this centuries-old craft. Information: *Parador Virrey Toledo,* 1 Plaza del Palacio, Oropesa 45560 (phone: 925-430000).

PARADOR DE SALAMANCA, Salamanca, Castile-León: Opened over a decade ago in response to the general mediocrity of this university city's hotels, this modern, multilevel, 108-room *parador* overlooks golden brick Salamanca and offers truly glorious views. Located on the outskirts of town, it features an outdoor swimming pool, a garden, and a convention hall. All rooms have glass-enclosed terraces with cushioned bamboo chairs — an excellent vantage point to watch the sunset, when Salamanca's buildings turn rich shades ranging from golden yellow to crimson. Information: *Parador de Salamanca,* 2 Calle Teso de la Feria, Salamanca 37008 (phone: 923-228700).

PARADOR LOS REYES CATÓLICOS, Santiago de Compostela, Galicia: This magnificently decorated 15th-century former royal hospital and pilgrims' *hostal,* located in the Plaza del Obradoiro next to the cathedral, is now one of Spain's most memorable *paradores.* King Ferdinand and Queen Isabella personally made decisions about its interior details. The 157 elegant rooms, which feature canopied beds, antique desks, and individual safes, surround four splendid Renaissance courtyards and a chapel with a beamed ceiling and wrought-iron grill. There are also shops, a garden, a nightclub, and concert, conference, and exhibition halls. Information: *Parador Los Reyes Católicos,* Plaza de Obradoiro, Santiago de Compostela 15705, Spain (phone: 981-582200).

PARADOR GIL BLAS SANTILLANA DEL MAR, Santillana del Mar, Cantabria: A graceful manor house and former home of the local Barreda-Bracho family, this *parador* affords visitors the experience of typical life in this region centuries ago. The building is made of heavy stone walls and arches, and the 56 rooms feature wood-beamed ceilings, tile floors, gracious rustic furnishings, and spacious patios. Information: *Parador de Santillana del Mar,* 8 Plaza Ramón Pelayo, Santillana del Mar 39330 (phone: 942-818000).

PARADOR DEL GOLF, Torremolinos, Andalusia: This 60-room *parador* is a golfer's paradise. The 18-hole course was designed by Robert Trent Jones, Sr., and it has a resident professional and a well-stocked pro shop. The *parador* is also a favorite of traveling and vacationing families, who enjoy its oceanfront location and its circular swimming pool. There are also tennis courts, a children's playground, a library, and gardens. Information: *Parador del Golf,* Apartado 324, Torremolinos, Málaga 29620 (phone: 952-381255).

The Best Restaurants of Spain

When it comes to dining, Spaniards seem to have it all: Thousands of restaurants throughout the country's 52 provinces feature a vast repertoire of their own delicious specialties — from seafood, meats, and fowl to fruit, vegetables, and fine wines — with all the flavor (and often only a fraction of the calories) found in the dishes of many other European countries. But don't confuse "Spanish food" with hot and spicy Mexican-style dishes: The Spanish are strangers to piquant seasonings. They also insist on *materia prima,* or wholesome, chemical-free ingredients — most dishes are olive oil and garlic based.

Though many regional specialties have become countrywide — even worldwide — favorites, nothing can replace the mystique of eating regional food on its home ground. Castile's local cooking is king, even in cosmopolitan Madrid, but the word *vasco* (Basque) crops up in restaurant names everywhere. Many of Spain's best chefs come from the Basque Country, renowned for its hundreds of all-male, members-only cooking clubs. And then there is paella, the communal pan of creamy, short-grained, saffron-flavored rice, crusty from a wood-burning fire, which is served all over Spain in varying delectable combinations of seafood, sausage, poultry, and vegetables.

Note: Many restaurants may waive their closing dates this year due to the *1992 Summer Olympics.*

ELDORADO PETIT, Barcelona: A proud recipient of the National Gastronomy Award, owner Luis Cruañas made a big hit with his first restaurant of the same name, in Sant Feliu de Guíxols on the Costa Brava, before opening this culinary shrine in the Catalan capital. Situated in one of Barcelona's elite neighborhoods, the restaurant combines local and French dishes in a "new Catalan" style. For starters, try the shrimp salad vinaigrette, or the cold cod salad with cilantro and thyme. Entrées include *bacalao* wrapped in bell peppers, scallops with leeks julienne, salmon lasagna, and goose liver and duck liver pâtés. Dessert specialties include exquisite homemade ice creams and sherbets. There is also a walk-through wine cellar. Closed Sundays and the for 2 weeks in the middle of August. Information: *Eldorado Petit,* 51 Carrer de Dolors Monserdá, Barcelona 08017 (phone: 93-204-5153).

NEICHEL, Barcelona: Owner Jean Louis Neichel serves Catalan specialties with a French flair, among them rare slices of duck breast lavished with juniper and wild raspberries, lobster salad garnished with quail eggs and truffle strips, a wonderful seafood platter of *merluza,* mollusks, and freshwater crab in two tasty sauces, filet of sea bass in cream of sea urchin, fish pot-au-feu with wine, and the best pastry cart in all of Spain. When the taste buds crave something French, this luxurious and elegant restaurant is the place to visit. Closed August, Sundays, holidays, *Christmas Week,* and *Holy Week.* Information: *Neichel,* 16 bis Avinguda de Pedralbes, Barcelona 08034 (phone: 93-203-8408).

SET PORTES, Barcelona: Situated on the waterfront, this Barcelona favorite still retains much of its original decor (including 150-year-old furnishings) and all of the charm of its 1836 debut. Catalan cuisine, including great seafood and homemade desserts, is served in abundant portions, and the large dining rooms are packed on weekends. Try the rice with sardines, among other delicacies. Open daily. Information: *Set Portes,* 14 Passeig d'Isabel II, Barcelona 08024 (phone: 93-319-2020).

LA GAMELLA, Madrid: American owner-chef-host Richard Stephens, also an instructor at Madrid's famed Alambique School of Gastronomy, dedicates his creative flair to new Spanish cuisine. Using choice ingredients, he offers adventures in taste with such dishes as slices of cured duck breast in Belgian endives with walnut oil, for starters, followed by turbot in wild mushroom sauce with a fresh tomato *coulis* and irresistible desserts, all complemented with a fine wine list. Facing Parque del Retiro, in the aristocratic building in which philosopher José Ortega y Gasset was born in 1883, this intimate restaurant is decorated with *colorista* design and art. A private dining room downstairs seats 10. Closed Sundays, holidays, and August. Information: *La Gamella,* 4 Calle Alfonso XII, Madrid 28014 (phone: 91-532-4509).

EL MENTIDERO DE LA VILLA, Madrid: This delightfully intimate restaurant, situated near the famous Convento de las Salesas Reales, just off the bustling Castellana, boasts a charming combination of classic and modern decor, inventive food, and efficient and friendly service. Co-owners Mario Martínez and award-winning Japanese chef Ken Sato provide a creative French menu with a Spanish and Japanese flair. The salads are superb, as are *pato con manzana* (duck with apple) and *rollo de primavera con puerros y gambas* (spring rolls with leeks and shrimp). For dessert, try the home-made chocolate mousse. Closed Sundays. Information: *El Mentidero de la Villa,* 6 Calle Santo Tomé, Madrid 28004 (phone: 91-419-5506).

PRÍNCIPE DE VIANA, Madrid: Owner Iñaki Oyarbide, another of Madrid's top restaurateurs, and the son of *Zalacaín*'s famous proprietor, offers fine seasonal Basque-Navarran specialties (the menu changes from season to season) in a relaxed, elegant atmosphere. Loyal clientele includes the crème de la crème of Madrid's financial community, as well as some of his father's longtime clientele. Reservations should be made at least a day in advance. Closed Saturdays for lunch, Sundays, and mid-August through the first week in September. Information: *Príncipe de Viana,* 5 Calle Manuel de Falla, Madrid 28036 (phone: 91-259-1448).

ZALACAÍN, Madrid: Considered by many to be the finest restaurant in all of Spain, winner of three Michelin stars (only one other establishment in the country has been so honored — see *Arzak* below), it celebrates Basque, French, and highly imaginative haute cuisines, with an emphasis on seafood. Owner Jesús Oyarbide is often on the road to the Rioja, Navarre, and Aragon regions, in search of new products and additions to his wine cellar. Luxuriously decorated, the restaurant shimmers with gleaming glasses, polished silverware, and fresh floral arrangements. Try the fish and shellfish soup, and pigs' feet stuffed with lamb. Daily specials are also served, and private dining rooms are available. Reservations are necessary. Closed Saturdays for lunch, Sundays, August, *Easter Week,* and holidays. Information: *Zalacaín,* 4 Calle Alvarez de Baena, Madrid 28006 (phone: 91-261-4840).

LA HACIENDA, Marbella: Belgian-born owner-chef Paul Schiff fell in love with Marbella, became a Spanish national, opened this lovely Costa del Sol restaurant, and won a National Gastronomy Award. Situated just outside the city in the Urbanización Las Chapas, with an excellent view of the African coast, this serious dining establishment has developed an excellent reputation, based on Paul's interpretations of favorite French dishes. The menu requires close study, but pay extra attention to the lemon swordfish, duck liver with figs, fish mousse, guinea fowl, and red mullet. Closed Mondays, and Tuesdays except in August. Information: *La Hacienda,* Carretera Cádiz-Málaga, Km 193, Marbella 29600 (phone: 952-831116).

AKELARRE, San Sebastián: Venerated champion of new Basque cooking, picturesquely situated on the slopes of Mt. Igueldo overlooking the city. National Gastronomy Award–winning owner-chef Pedro Subijana, a legend of culinary creation, blends the traditional with the new in an always-changing menu; regular patrons customarily consult him for his suggestions of the day. Always outstanding, however, are his herb salads, leg of lamb with mushrooms, *rodaballo* (trout) with nettle sauce, and a fine array of homemade desserts and pastries. Other specialties, from time to time, include *morcilla envuelta en hoja de berza sobre puré de alubias rojas* (blood pudding wrapped in a cabbage leaf on a purée of red beans), and *lubina a la pimienta verde* (sea bass with green pepper). Salmon is also served in many excellent combinations. Make reservations well in advance. Closed Sunday nights, Mondays, and October. Information: *Akelarre,* Barrio de Igueldo, San Sebastián 20008 (phone: 943-212052).

ARZAK, San Sebastián: Truly an institution in the Basque Country, this restaurant is, with *Zalacaín* in Madrid, one of only two restaurants in Spain to have earned three Michelin stars. It won the National Gastronomy Award in 1974 and has been on the crest of the wave ever since. New Basque cuisine is the featured specialty, as well as *nueva cocina* (nouvelle cuisine), which owner-chef Juan Mari Arzak says "is geared for the year 2000." Seafood is the highlight; try *krabarroka* (scorpion fish pâté), *merluza* (hake) in green sauce, *chipirones en su tinta* (squid in its own ink), oyster soup with green asparagus, *consumé de buey con cigalas y caviar a los aromas a perifollo y estragón* (ox consumé with Norway lobster and caviar in a chervil and tarragon sauce), or smoked salmon tartar with caviar. Non-seafood choices include salted baby lambs' brains seasoned with mint and lime. Make reservations well in advance. Closed Sunday nights, Mondays, 2 weeks in June, and November. Information: *Arzak,* 21 Calle Alto de Miracruz, San Sebastián 20015 (phone: 943-278465).

Shopping Spree

No matter where the dollar stands relative to the peseta, the temptation of shopping in Spain is irresistible. Colorful hand-painted tiles and lovingly sewn handicrafts are eye-catching, easily luring the visitor into one of Madrid's 54,000 shops and stores, or through the bric-a-brac in its famous flea market, *El Rastro.* Although there are no great bargains anymore, the quality is high and there's a wide array of leather goods, embroideries, jewelry, fine porcelain, and fashion ranging from very basic handicraft sweaters and clothing to haute couture.

The shopping day often begins around 9:30 AM, when shopkeepers are still hosing down the sidewalk in front of their stores. Most owners take pride in their shops; their business is a very personal affair, and they'll no doubt strike up a conversation with curious browsers. It isn't uncommon, either, for those who opt to ship their purchases back to the US to get a handwritten note from shopkeepers.

Spaniards are traditional strollers. They take to the streets as a pastime, particularly for browsing in the plethora of small specialty shops found in most cities. But the relaxed ambience and 3-hour lunchtime shop closings (except for major department stores) mean careful shopping plans should be made. Shopkeepers are helpful, warm people who take extra time to satisfy customers. Most, however, do not speak English.

While Madrid is charming and a pleasure to shop in, Barcelona is closer to northern European fashion capitals, and has adopted a more cosmopolitan style. Seville is the land of castanets, flamenco, and vivid colors. Spain's designers have a flair for fashion, experiment with styling and color, and have emerged as strong rivals to French and Italian creators. Spanish fashion has become provocatively alluring, yet it keeps a classical line. Spanish porcelain, particularly the Lladró figurines, are collectors' items. Ceramic and porcelain tableware and giftware are well made and exported worldwide. Leather goods are subtle, soft, and a good value. Majórica pearls, made in Spain, carry a worldwide 10-year guarantee. Fine gold jewelry, by law, is 18 karat.

General shopping hours in Spain are Mondays through Fridays, from 9:30 AM to 1:30 PM and from 4:30 to 8 PM; Saturdays, from 9:30 AM to 3 PM. Department stores are open Mondays through Saturdays, from 10 AM to 8 PM. Most shops are closed in August, but department stores remain open year-round.

WHERE TO SHOP

Travelers can find good buys all over Spain, provided they know where to look.

POST-CHRISTMAS AND SUMMER SALES: In Spain, they're called *rebajas* and unlike in the US, they're held only twice a year. Here's the good part: They're universal; practically *all* stores and shops have them. Winter *rebajas* start January 6, which in Spain marks the *Day of the Three Wise Men,* the traditional *Christmastime* gift-giving day. Summer sales start in mid-July and last through the month of August (prices drop even more toward the end of August).

OPEN MARKETS: Never pass up a chance to wander through some of Spain's bustling open markets. It is here that visitors have the opportunity to see the *real* Madrid — people selling their crafts, friends meeting for a meal or a drink, and curious onlookers taking in the vast array of goods and daily bargains. These open markets are a smorgasbord of vibrant colors, overflowing with the song of the people.

Madrid – *El Rastro* (The Thieves Market) is one of Europe's largest and most famous flea markets. It is open year-round on Sundays and holidays from about 9 AM to 2 PM. Beginning at Plaza de Cascorro, *El Rastro* meanders down Ribera de Curtidores to Ronda de Toledo, spilling over into small side streets. Antiques buyers should visit the area's permanent stores, which are open throughout the week, to avoid the massive Sunday crowds. Also on Sunday mornings, at the nearby Plaza Mayor, arcades overflow with stamp and coin dealers.

Barcelona – Spain's most cosmopolitan city has a variety of outdoor offerings throughout the week. From dawn to dusk on Mondays, Wednesdays, Fridays, and Saturdays, *Els Encants,* just off the Plaça de les Glòries Catalanes, hosts a huge flea market with everything from clothes to antiques on display. The Plaça Nova has a weekly antiques market every Thursday. The Plaça Sant Josep Oriol transforms itself into one of Spain's largest open-air painting exhibitions and marketplaces every weekend, and the Plaça Reial features coin and stamp markets on Sunday mornings.

Seville – The city's biggest market sets up its stalls from 10 AM to 3 PM every Sunday along Alameda de Hércules. This is the place for crafts, costume jewelry, antiques, and novelty items. The Plaza del Cabildo (opposite the cathedral) hosts a coin and stamp mart every Sunday morning as well.

DEPARTMENT STORES: Expect to find anything and everything at the department stores in Spain. *El Corte Inglés* ranks at the top of Europe's best department store list. It's desirable for travelers to have an idea about what they wish to purchase before shopping in one of the store's branches (there are 18 throughout the country); otherwise the visitor is almost guaranteed to get lost, as this store is literally a city within a city. Free translators, shoppers' cards (for purchases to be sent to a central depot for pickup), food (take-out and eat-in), a travel agency, currency exchange, hairdresser, ample parking, and, in some stores, international communications centers are among the many special services provided. *El Corte Inglés* even manufactures some of its own designs, and sells them exclusively at prices up to one-third less than fashions of similar quality found in other European capitals. Many of Spain's top designers also sell here. There are four locations in Madrid: 3 Calle Preciados (phone: 91-532-8100); 76 Calle Goya (phone: 91-448-0111); 79 Calle Raimundo Fernández Villaverde, just off upper Paseo de la Castellana (phone: 91-556-2300); and 56 Calle Princesa (phone: 91-542-4800). Barcelona boasts the chain's largest store (in Plaça de Catalunya; 3-301-3256). All *El Corte Inglés* branches remain open during normal afternoon siesta hours.

Spain's other major department store chain, *Galerías Preciados,* offers many of the same services as *El Corte Inglés,* though its offerings are a bit more downscale and less comprehensive. Its "passport service" offers discounts to foreign visitors, in addition to IVA (value added tax) rebates. Specialty items include Spanish ceramics, rugs, glassware, handicrafts, and souvenirs. Branches can be found throughout Madrid, as well as other major cities. The main store is at 1 Plaza de Callao (phone: 91-522-4771) in Madrid. Barcelona has a branch (19 Avinguda Portal de l'Angel).

SPECIAL SHOPPING STREETS AND DISTRICTS: The mixture of old and new, the lively sounds of families and couples linked arm in arm, make strolling through the streets an inviting experience. Stop and savor both the street scenes and the shops that line them.

Madrid – With over 54,000 specialty shops to choose from, shopping in Madrid is varied and fun, and can occupy seemingly endless hours. Start at the maze of streets surrounding Plaza Mayor, the heart of Old Madrid. Most of the small shops here have thrived for hundreds of years. The once-elegant Gran Vía is still a busy shopping street, while the choice and pricier shops, boutiques, and art galleries run along Calles Serrano and Velázquez in the Salamanca District. In both of these areas, explore its side streets and check out some of the lesser known but more charming shops.

More affordable stores are located in the city center around the Puerta del Sol and the adjoining Calle Preciados pedestrian mall, which runs up to the Gran Vía.

Barcelona – The rest of Spain admires the Catalans and their capital city, Barcelona, for their long-standing business and commercial attributes. Most of Spain's textiles are woven in the Catalan region surrounding Barcelona, and because of the strong influence of Spanish designers in the fashion world now, the city is considered to be in the same ranks as Milan and New York. For concentrated shopping, the major streets are the Passeig de Gràcia, Avinguda Diagonal, the Rambla de Catalunya, and Gran Via de les Corts Catalanes.

Córdoba – The busiest area is in the upper part of the city, in the vicinity of Calle Gondomar, Plaza de las Tendillas, and Ronda de los Tejares. The shops surrounding the mosque and in the old Jewish Quarter sell mostly souvenirs and other touristy items.

Granada – The city's old Arab silk market, next to the cathedral, has been reconstructed and now houses mainly souvenir shops. There are numerous small crafts shops in the Albaicín quarter, particularly along the Cuesta de Gomérez, the Plaza Nueva, and the adjoining side streets.

COMMERCIAL CENTERS (SHOPPING MALLS): Visitors will feel right at home in the bright lights, chain stores, and fast-food restaurants of a Spanish shopping mall. Most stay open from 9 AM to 10 PM, 7 days a week, including holidays.

Madrid – *Madrid 2* (Av. Monforte de Lemos), also known as *La Vaguada*, just north of central Madrid, is an enormous 350-shop complex, complete with restaurants, movie theaters, discos, amusement arcades, and parking for 4,000 cars. The *Galería del Prado* is a recent addition to the *Palace* hotel (7 Plaza de las Cortes, Madrid; phone: 91-429-7551) and has a glamorous assembly of 38 top fashion boutiques, art galleries, jewelers, and gift shops, as well as a fancy food shop, a beauty salon, a bookstore, and a buffet-style restaurant. The *Mercado Puerta de Toledo* (at the Puerta de Toledo, on the southwestern edge of the city) is a former fish market, now transformed into a 150-shop showcase for Spain's finest designers in fashion, jewelry, interior design, and antiques.

Barcelona – If there's time for only one shopping excursion, head straight for the elegant *Bulevard Rosa Mall* (55 Passeig de Gràcia). Here, several hundred shops display an elegant flair in items ranging from trendy young fashions to sophisticated jet setter designs. *Diagonal Center* (584 Avinguda Diagonal) is small but brims with good shops.

BEST BUYS

ANTIQUES: Spain is an excellent hunting ground for antiques, with a wide range of dealers, auction houses, and non-commercial institutions that offer many items at bargain prices.

Madrid – In addition to the antiques shops in and around the Plaza Mayor area, Calle del Prado, and Carrera de Jerónimo, where religious antiques shops abound, the magnificent 5-story *Central de Arte Antiquedades* (5 Calle Serrano) houses 50 antiques shops, each with an honored reputation. There are also antiques in *El Rastro*, Madrid's famous flea market (see *Open Markets*).

Barcelona – Most of Barcelona's 150 antiques shops are found in the Barri Gòtic, the old medieval heart of the city. Wonderful pieces from a host of major periods, such as the 12th and 15th centuries and Queen Anne, as well as pieces showing French, Catalan, and English influences, are readily available here. Spain protects its treasures carefully, and reputable dealers will assist visitors with Spanish customs and regulations. Generally speaking, a work of art is considered of cultural and artistic importance if the artist is not living or, if living, his or her prominence is widely accepted. The second floor of the *Bulevard Rosa Mall* (55 Passeig de Gràcia) is dedicated entirely to antiques shops and auction houses.

Seville – Seville's antiques shops are among Spain's best. Some of the more popular shops include *Andrés Moro* (8 Calle Placentines; phone: 95-422-4633); *Lola Ortega* (Plaza del Cabildo; phone: 95-421-8771); *María Dolores Mellado Valencia* (5 Avenida de la Constitución; phone: 95-422-3345); and *Pedro Montelongo* (17 Calle Santa Teresa; phone: 95-421-6353). Seville hosts a special antiques fair every year in April. Contact the *Associación de Anticuarios* (7 Calle Rodrigo Caro; phone: 95-421-6558) for complete details.

BOOKS AND MAPS: Most visitors may not be able to read many of Spain's treasured old books, but it's still fun to browse. Many bookstores have dozens of booths and stalls filled with books from around the world, both old and new; some stores specialize in reduced-rate and secondhand books, old editions, and rare titles. Much of Spanish literature is printed in both Spanish and English; for those interested in learning the language, why not learn while reading one of the classics? Addicted browsers will have to be dragged out of the following bookworm haunts.

Madrid – *México II* (17 Calle Huertas; phone: 91-532-7664) has over 200,000 books from the 16th century to the 18th, as well as drawers full of historical prints and maps. *Casa del Libro* is Madrid's largest bookstore, with 5 floors for browsing at its old location (29 Gran Vía), and another 4 floors at its newer location (3 Calle Maestro Victoria). *Turner English Bookshop* (3 Calle Genova, on Plaza de Santa Barbara; phone: 91-319-2037) stocks an impressive collection of English, French, and Spanish titles. Also visit *La Tienda Verde* (38 Calle Maudes; phone: 1-533-0791), for the best in adventure travel. *El Corte Inglés* department stores also have *librerías*, with fine selections of Spanish- and English-language books. Browsers should walk up the stretch of sidewalk known as the Cuesta de Moyano, along Calle Claudio Moyano, which starts at the south end of Paseo del Prado and borders the Jardín Botánico (Botanical Garden). This virtually permanent book fair is stocked with dozens of stalls of reduced-rate and secondhand books.

Barcelona – It is no coincidence that Catalonia has the highest literacy rate in Spain and can claim to be the only city in the country where the patron saint's day (*St. George's Day,* April 23) is celebrated with gifts of books to friends. In Barcelona, there's a bookshop on every block, and residents are often buried in books that on closer inspection turn out to be French, German, or English classics, rather than Spanish mystery novels. The bookstalls on La Rambla, which bustle each afternoon, are a good place to find an interesting title. *Librería Francesa* (91 Passeig de Gràcia), Barcelona's largest bookstore, also has a nice selection.

Seville – *Cervantes* (5 Calle Azafranal) is one of Spain's largest general bookstores. There is sure to be a title on one of its 7 floors for any who wish to spend an afternoon browsing.

CERAMICS AND TILES: The diversity of Spain's regions is highly evident in the country's wide range of ceramics. The 700-year Arab domination prevails in ceramic designs of the southern regions; wall plates are enameled and trimmed in 24-karat gold. Later, when the English settled in the area around Cádiz, florals and busy scenic designs became the preferred style.

Madrid – *Cerámica El Alfar* (112 Calle Claudio Coello; phone: 91-411-3587) has a large assortment of regional ceramics and earthenware. Glazed-tile reproductions of famous Spanish paintings are a specialty. *La Cerámica Talavera* (113 Claudio Coello) offers a fine selection of wall plates, dinner sets, planters, cups, and other larger items. *Antigua Casa Talavera* (2 Calle Isabel la Católica; phone: 91-247-3417) has an overwhelming display of authentic regional hand-crafted ceramics and dinnerware from all over the country. *Gritos de Madrid* (6 Plaza Mayor; phone: 91-265-9154) has hand-painted tiles, tile art-mosaic decorations, and plates with classic Madrid motifs, signed by master craftsman Eduardo Fernández.

Seville – *La Alcazaba* (1-A Calle Joaquín Romero Murube) carries delicate hand-painted ceramic tiles and platters from Seville and other regions, including the lovely florals from Valencia. *Cerámica Santa Ana* (31 Calle San Jorge) also stocks a large selection of ceramics at good prices.

CURIOSITY SHOPS: A peek into the numerous boutiques and specialty shops should provide ample insight into the Spanish way of life, of both the past and the present.

Madrid – *Musgo* (36 Calle Hermosilla; phone: 91-431-5510) comprises five row houses joined together as one huge store and filled with contemporary clothing and furnishings. *Capas Seseña* (23 Calle Cruz; phone: 91-531-6840) makes a fine line of capes for men and women, from the finest available wool, and has been selling them at this store for almost a century. *Casa Jiménez* (42 Calle Preciados; phone: 91-248-0526) is one of Madrid's oldest shops for custom-made shawls and fans. *Maty* (5 Plaza Comandante las Morenas; phone: 91-541-2016) specializes in flamenco dresses and accessories.

San Sebastián – *Casa Basarte* (18 Calle San Jerónimo) has the best selection of genuine *txapelas* (Basque berets) in town. *Juguetería Antón* (21 Calle San Jerónimo) features an amazing collection of Spanish jigsaw puzzles. Designs range from Goya paintings to Moorish tiles, containing up to 8,000 pieces.

DESIGNER CLOTHING: Spain demonstrates a cosmopolitan flair for fashion, especially in and around the cities and towns close to the French border. Whatever the latest trend, visitors can rest assured that both country's designers are up-to-date.

Madrid – *Molinero Costura* (3 Calle Ayala; phone: 91-575-1157) is the exclusive Valentino representative, featuring his ready-to-wear, haute couture, and evening clothes — all the latest. This sleek and very expensive shop with a marble interior boasts Queen Sofía as a regular client. *Pedro Muñoz* (72 Calle Serrano; phone: 91-431-1661), a shirtmaker and tailor, designs fashions for men only. *Don Algodón* is Spain's answer to *Benetton*. This 30-year-old designer has taken cotton and color to create smashing mix-and-match sportswear. This chain store has nationwide outlets, with its headquarters at 58 Calle Claudio Coello. *Adolfo Domínguez* (4 Calle Ortega y Gasset; phone: 91-576-0084) is the boutique of the innovative Spanish celebrity designer whose daring women's fashions illustrate his "wrinkles (in the fabric, that is) are beautiful" philosophy. *Ascot* (88 Calle Serrano; phone: 91-431-3712) is an excellent women's boutique selling haute couture and ready-to-wear garments by María Teresa de Vega, a favorite designer among Madrid's beautiful people.

San Sebastián – *Delgado* (43 Avenida de la Libertad; phone: 943-426625) is one of the oldest and best clothing shops in town. Founded in 1899, it's still a family-run affair. Much of the material is imported from Italy, but the conservatively styled men's suits, shirts, and ready-to-wear outfits are still made on the premises.

EMBROIDERY AND LACE: In Spain, embroidery prices are determined by the intricacy of the stitch, not by the size of the item. Look carefully: Stitches made by a human hand cannot duplicate themselves over and over, and will therefore lack consistency; the more perfect the stitch, the more likely that an item was machine made.

Madrid – *Casa Bonet* (76 Calle Núñez de Balboa; phone: 91-575-0912) stocks a variety of handmade embroidery, including the beautiful ones from Palma de Mallorca on the island of Majorca. The prices here are very reasonable, whether it's a handkerchief or linens. Also try *Gil, Sucesor de Anatolín Quevedo* (2 Carrera de San Jerónimo; phone: 91-521-2549), a generations-old establishment that has supplied Spanish and international celebrities with high-quality embroidery, including exquisite embroidered silk shawls (*mantones de manila*), for many years.

Toledo – Toledo and the nearby village of Lagartera are famous for their embroidery, lace, and needlework. In Lagartera, the place where the best La Mancha embroidery originates, every cottage has its own display of the free-form floral stitching, which decorates silk hangings, tablecloths, peasant bonnets, and full skirts. Damascene, the Moorish art of inlaying gold, copper, or silver threads on a matte black steel background, is also a thriving craft in Toledo, used on boxes, plates, and swords, as well as in jewelry. *Santiago Sanchez Martín* (18 Calle Río Llano; phone: 25-227757) is named for its owner, a damascene artisan who, after 40 years in the business, still inlays 24-carat gold by hand on the most special pieces. *Bermejo Espadería* (5 Calle Airosos) also carries top-quality Toledo damascene.

FOOD AND WINE: Food shopping in Spain is a pleasure, probably because local customers are so demanding. Everything is fresh — sometimes so fresh that food stores hang unskinned rabbits in their windows. And of course, Spain is famous for its wines — the sherries and riojas.

Madrid – *El Corte Inglés* (see *Department Stores*) has everything, including a well-stocked supermarket with an excellent meat and fish section, its own brand of olive oil, and delicious breads and cakes, most of which are baked on the premises. Also visit *Horno del Pozo* (9 Calle del Pozo), a small shop established in 1830 with a reputation for the best *hojaldres* (puff pastries) in town. Others include *El Gourmet del Palacio* (2 Pavía, Plaza de Oriente); *Chamberi* (61 Calle Alonso Cano); and *Maravilla* (134 Calle Bravo Murillo). *Santa Cecilia* (74 Calle Blasco de Garay) has a fine selection of wines, spirits, liqueurs, beers, and *cavas* (sparkling wines) at reasonable prices. Another good choice for Spanish and foreign wines is *Bolsa de Licores* (13 Calle Infantas).

Granada – *Casa Hita* (7 Carrera del Genil; phone: 958-221322) is the best place in town for local hams and traditional confectioneries.

Toledo – A trip to Toledo is incomplete without a sampling of its famous marzipan. Popular shops include *Barosso* (11 Calle Real del Arrabel); *Casa Telesforo* (47 Plaza de Zocodover; phone: 925-221168); and *Santo Tomé* (5 Calle Santo Tomé and 11 Plaza de Zocodover; phone: 925-223763).

GIFTWARE: In Spain, nothing is as famous as fine Lladró porcelain. The Lladró factory is located in Valencia, along the Mediterranean coastline. There is also a factory store that sells hard-to-distinguish seconds for one-third to one-half off retail (cash-and-carry only).

Madrid – *Fernando Durán* (11 Calle Conde de Aranda; phone: 91-431-3806) is one of the city's most prestigious shops for antique furniture, sculptures, china, and a wide variety of silver products ranging from miniature frames to decorative pieces. *Paulino* (12 Gran Vía and 68 Velázquez) imports giftware from all over Europe and has exclusive, limited editions of Lladró porcelain figures. *Plata Meneses* (3 Plaza de Canalejas; phone: 91-429-4236) is Spain's leading silver manufacturer, featuring a huge line of giftware and place settings, which fill two showrooms.

GUNS: The King of Spain and other aristocrats shop at *Diana Turba* (68 Calle Serrano, Madrid; phone: 91-401-6250), where everything from guns and fishing tackle to clothing is spread out on 2 huge floors. The store will also take care of all the necessary paperwork involved in shipping guns back to the US.

HANDICRAFTS: Handicrafts are ubiquitous in Spain.

Madrid – The Spanish government formed the *Artespaña* group to preserve the country's handicraft traditions and to promote the sale of goods from the finest artisans. These shops sell a wide range of handicrafts and home furnishings from all over Spain. Among several locations is one at 3 Plaza de las Cortes (phone: 91-429-1251).

Barcelona – The *Poble Espanyol* (Spanish Village), on Montjuïc, is a 5-acre exhibition of Spanish art and architecture in the form of a traditional village. Built for the *1929 World's Fair,* it was later transformed into a miniature artisans' community representing the entire country, and has just been revitalized for this year's *Olympics.*

Plan a full day visiting traditional artisans at work; their carvings, pottery, glass, leather, and metalworks are sold in the village's 35 shops.

JEWELRY: There are excellent jewelry bargains in Spain. Look for the famous Majórica pearls, but watch out for imitations. There is only one authentic brand — *Perlas Majórica* — and "Majorca" or "Mallorca" pearls should not be confused with the real thing. Look for the official agency seal and for the unique, 10-year International Certificate of Guarantee that comes with each piece. Sizes run from 4 to 14 millimeters in diameter, in hundreds of combinations. The pearls can be found throughout Spain, but the factory is in Manacor, on the island of Majorca. In Palma, the shop is at 11 Avenida Rey Jaime III.

Madrid – Spanish sculptor and jeweler *Veiga* (22 Gran Vía; phone: 91-521-5506) has created his own distinctive designs, all in bronze. *Aldao* (15 Gran Vía and 43 Calle Velázquez) is a long-established jeweler that makes unique and limited-edition pieces in its own workshop. *Joaquín Berao* (13 Calle Conde de Xiquena) is an imaginative young Spanish designer selling limited-edition earrings, bracelets, and rings in gold, silver, bronze, and titanium in ultramodern designs. *Suárez* (63 Calle Serrano) is one of Madrid's great jewelers. Stones and jewels are mounted in settings of its own design. The store also carries a huge line of international big-name watches.

Córdoba – Cordoban silver filigree pieces are favorite souvenir items. Travelers will find a good selection at the *Zoco Municipal de Artesanía* (Calle de los Judíos; phone: 957-204033) and *José Villar Jiménez* (3 Calle Muro de la Misericórdia; phone: 957-481034).

LEATHER GOODS: Most leather on the Iberian Peninsula comes from sheep and lambs; cows produce a heavier quality skin that's made into jackets and coats. Antelope skin is not available in Spain. There are thousands of stores selling leather jackets, coats, gloves, pocketbooks, wallets, and other items. Generally speaking, shoppers can tell the quality of the leather by the feel. The softer it is, the more expensive. Spain is a good place to buy leather fashions because of its large selection and variety of items.

Madrid – *Loewe* specializes in fine leather fashions for men and women, as well as accessories and luggage. The several locations include 8 Gran Vía, 26 Calle Serrano, a shop at the *Palace* hotel (7 Plaza de las Cortes), and a shop at 34 Calle Serrano that carries men's fashions exclusively. There are also branches in Seville, Granada, Valencia, Bilbao, and Palma. *Manuel Herrero* (7 and 23 Calle Preciados) is also a popular leather outlet, offering a wide selection and good prices. *Lepanto* (3 Plaza de Oriente) overflows with leather jackets, gloves, handbags, belts, briefcases, and accessories. Drawers of leather gloves and handbags line the walls at *Zurro* (16 Calle Preciados and 4 Calle Carmen). Classically styled items made of reptile skins are available at *Vivar* (11 Calle Preciados and 64 Gran Vía). *La Casa de las Maletas* (45 Calle Claudio Coello; phone: 91-431-7765) offers beautifully displayed luggage, shoes, briefcases, pocketbooks, and accessories, all at attractive prices.

Barcelona – *Loewe* (35 Passeig de Gràcia) is the place for handbags and traditional Spanish leather goods. Also check the merchandise at *Camper* (248 Muntanyer) for the latest styles and colors for ladies.

Córdoba – Shopping at *Merian* (2 Calleja de las Flores; phone: 957-225902) is more like visiting a museum, unless the customer is prepared for a serious purchase. The artistic hand-embossed and tinted leather (*guadamecil*) goods are done in the Renaissance style (with some designs derived from classical paintings), the handwork is painstaking and magnificent, and prices on the larger pieces run into the thousands of dollars. Wander up and down the stairs in this centuries-old mansion, whose gardens once extended down to the mosque, to inspect leather chairs, chests, wall hangings, maps, picture frames, and even some wooden pieces, and ask to see the workshops surrounding the serene white marble patio. The more affordable leather bags and wallets that many visitors end up buying here are of excellent quality but not made by *Meryan.*

Seville – Andalusian horsemen come to *El Caballo* (14 Calle Adriano), near the bullring, for the finest leather boots, saddles, hunting gear, traditional riding suits, and flat, wide-brimmed hats.

MUSICAL INSTRUMENTS: Who can resist listening to the beautiful sounds of Spanish guitars? Those in Spain are primarily classical.

Madrid – *Manuel Contreras* (80 Calle Mayor; phone: 91-248-5926) has one of the city's largest collections of guitars and other musical instruments. *Real Musical* (Calle Carlos III) also carries guitars, other musical instruments, and records.

SHOES: Spain offers a wide variety of sleek footwear designs. The leathers used are soft and durable. Women's shoes rarely come in half sizes, but men's do. The Charles Jourdan brand is in many shops and is more reasonably priced than in French stores. Many shoe stores also carry leather accessories. When buying a pair of Spanish shoes, use the size only as a reference; the last of a Spanish shoe sold in Spain is different from the last of a Spanish shoe made for the American market.

Madrid – *Yanko* (40 Gran Vía; phone: 91-532-5328) is famous for its handmade shoes for men and women. *Bravo* (42 Calle Serrano, 31 Gran Vía; phone: 91-522-7300, and 24 Ayala; phone: 91-575-8072) carries the finest in European shoes, particularly good buys on Charles Jourdan styles. Pierre Cardin, Elio Berhanyer, Pertegaz, and many more designer shoes are available at *Los Pequeños Suizos* (68 Calle Serrano), which also carries half sizes, a rarity in Spain.

Barcelona – *Francesc Tasies i Ginesta* (7 Carrer d'Avinyó; phone: 93-301-0172) is noted for handmade, rope-soled espadrilles, the sort of footwear used for dancing the *sardana.*

SPORTING GOODS: Department stores are usually the best bet, carrying everything including equipment and clothing for hunting, camping, surfing, tennis, golf, skiing, fishing, and aerobic workouts.

Most Visitable Vineyards

 Spain has a long-standing wine making tradition, but the practice of opening wineries to the visiting public is still relatively new. Because of this, and the vast profusion of small vineyards, it is advisable to make arrangements in advance. Since the days of the Phoenicians and Greeks, sweet wine has been made in southern Spain. Under the Romans, wine production spread throughout the country and was eventually brought to the Americas along with the Spanish conquistadores.

Today, Spain is the world's third-largest wine producer, with more acreage devoted to vines than in any other European country. Much like Italy, production is fragmented and spread over a wide area, with half of it organized into 850 cooperatives comprising some 200,000 members. Except for the highest elevations, there is virtually no corner of the country that does not produce wine.

Running the full range from the aperitif and dessert wines of Andalusia to the brut *cavas* of the Penedés and a fine assortment of brandies, Spain's viniculture is a vast and varied adventure in good drinking. In addition to the famous rioja reds, Spain produces a large assortment of red wines, the best hailing from the temperate northern climes. East of the Rioja region, Navarre makes full-bodied, fruity red wines from the same Rioja grape varieties; south of the Rioja along the Duero Valley, the Ribera del Duero demarcation is gaining increasing cachet; and Catalonia's Penedès and Lleida areas produce some of the country's best red wines from the native monastrell, ull de llebre, and garnacha grapes, as well as from such acclimatized varieties as the cabernet sauvignon, merlot, and pinot noir. Less sophisticated, but still eminently drinkable, are the reds of the central plateau and the regions around Valencia and Alicante.

Though white wines are produced throughout Spain, those of Rioja and Catalonia have earned international renown. Made from the native viura, malvasi, and garnacha blanca grapes, the rioja whites were formerly matured in oak, but are now mostly cold-fermented in stainless steel to retain the crisp freshness of the fruit. La Mancha now produces a flowery white from the airén grape, and Jerez produces table wines from the palomino sherry grape. In Galicia, the whites have a light, natural efferves- cence.

For free maps, brochures, and other information on Spanish wines, contact *Wines of Spain* (Commercial Office of Spain, 405 Lexington Ave., New York, NY 10174; phone: 212-661-4959). There is no admission fee at any Spanish winery, and all of those mentioned below are accustomed to receiving visitors.

RIOJA: Best known among the Spanish table wines, riojas — emanating from a hilly region on the western side of the Ebro Valley in northern Spain — have been around since Roman times. At the end of the 19th century, when French vineyards were devasted by disease, wine makers from Bordeaux moved here, giving an immense boost to the regional production, which leans toward reds over whites. These wines are similar to a bordeaux or burgundy, but with a higher alcoholic content (between 10 and 12.5%) — which is generally true of most Spanish wines in comparison with those of other European countries. The rioja reds, made from a blend of the native tempranillo, garnacha, mazuelo, and graciano grapes, have a characteristic oaken taste and vanilla aroma. Within the Rioja region are three sub-regions: Rioja Alta, Rioja Alavesa, and Rioja Baja. The wines of the first two, in the hilly west, are considered the best.

The younger wines are labeled either *crianza* or *sin crianza,* meaning with or without aging. The *crianza* wines are aged for no less than 2 years, of which at least a year must be spent in a 225-liter oak cask. *Reservas* and *gran reservas* are the mellow old wines that have spent long years in cask and bottle. Red *reservas* are aged for at least a year in oak casks and 2 years in the bottle, leaving the winery no earlier than the 4th year after vintage. Red *gran reservas* spend no less than 2 years in casks and a minimum of 3 in the bottle, leaving the winery no sooner than the 6th year after vintage. The same production regulations apply throughout Spain, but in the Rioja, the hoary old *bodegas* steeped in tradition still age their reds considerably longer in oak to cultivate the vanilla bouquet and the velvety texture that are their trademarks. Rioja also produces saucy *claretes* (light reds or rosés) and dry whites. There are dozens of vineyards in the Rioja, with the most important ones found in Logroño (the region's capital), Haro, Cenicero, and Fuenmayor.

Bodegas Montecillo – Located in Fuenmayor, 10 miles (16 km) from Logroño, this winery dates from 1874. Visits must be arranged in advance, and a full selection of whites, reds, and rosés is for sale at the *bodega*. The whites are young and fruity; the rosés, slightly matured; and the reds, rounded and pleasant, with good color and aroma. Information: 34 Calle San Cristóbal, Fuenmayor, La Rioja 26360 (phone: 941-440125).

Bodegas Campo Viejo – Visitors to the regional capital will enjoy sampling the wines of this bodega, produced from its own vines and nourished in its vast store of wooden casks. The whites and rosés are young and fruity; the reds, mature, aromatic, and light on the palate. The *reserva* reds are full-bodied and velvety. Visits must be arranged in advance. Information: 3 Calle Gostavo Adolfo Bécquer, Logroño, La Rioja 26006 (phone: 941-238100).

Bodegas Berceo – Established in 1872, this winery in Haro, some 30 miles (48 km) from Logroño, makes fresh, fruity whites and rosés, fruity young reds with good color, and well-rounded *reserva* reds with body and acidity. Visits must be arranged in advance. Information: 38-40 Calle Cuevas, Haro, La Rioja 26200 (phone: 941-670050).

Unión Vitivinicola (Bodegas Marqués de Cáceres) – A mere 20-odd years old, this Cenicero winery, located 14 miles (22 km) from Logroño, has made quite an international name for itself in a very short time. Its whites and rosés are fresh and fruity, and its reds are full-bodied, smooth, and long. Visiting hours are weekdays from 8:30 AM to 6:15 PM. Closed August. Information: *Carretera Logroño,* Cenicero, La Rioja 26350 (phone: 941-454000).

For further information on the region and its wineries, contact either of the following associations: *ARBOR-Agrupación de Artesanos Bodegueros de Rioja* (43 Gran Vía Juan Carlos I, Logroño 26002; phone: 941-225034), or *Grupo de Exportadores de Vinos de Rioja* (6-7 Gran Vía, Logroño 26002; phone: 941-257555).

CATALONIA: This region in the northeast corner of Spain borders the Mediterranean and produces a great variety of wines, the best known among them those of Ampordá (reds and rosés), Alella (dry or sweet whites), and the Penedès (whites and reds). But the pièce de résistance of the region are the champagne-like sparkling wines known as *cavas,* produced in brut, sec, and demi-sec varieties. Since 1872, when Spain produced its first bottle of *cava,* the country has become the largest producer of sparkling wines in the world. Although *cava* is made by the *méthode champenoise,* or champagne method, it is not a budget substitute for champagne, since the native parellada, macabeo, and xarello grapes give it its own distinctive regional characteristics. About 95% of Spanish *cava* comes from the Penedès, with the majority of producers grouped around the town of Sant Sadurní d'Anoia. Information: *Consejo Regulador Vinos Espumoso,* 24-26 Avenida Tarragona, Vilafranca del Penedès, Barcelona 08720 (phone: 93-890-3104).

In the Penedès, which spreads across the south of Barcelona province and the northeast of Tarragona province, table wines are also produced. The careful harvesting and elaboration of base wines to create sparkling wines have given rise to high-quality whites that are fruity and fresh and have an alcoholic strength of between 9 and 13%. The rosés are similar to the whites, and the area also produces light, smooth reds.

Codorníu – Since 1551, the Codorníu family has been producing still wines. In 1872, it produced Spain's first *cava.* Now a national monument welcoming over 250,000 visitors a year, the winery produces more than 45 million bottles of *cava* annually in the world's largest underground wine cellar network — extending 11 miles on 5 levels. These pale yellow sparkling wines have a hint of green, with a smooth, flowery aroma and lovely flavor. The winery is open Mondays through Thursdays, from 8 AM to noon and from 3 to 6 PM; Fridays, from 8 AM to noon. Closed August. Information: Calle Afueras, Sant Sadurní d'Anoia, Barcelona 08770 (phone: 93-891-0125).

Freixenet – This winery has been producing light, fresh, and aromatic *cavas* for just over 100 years. Open Mondays through Fridays, from 9:30 AM to noon and from 3:30 to 5:30 PM. Closed holidays and August. Information: 2 Calle Joan Sala, Sant Sadurní d'Anoia, Barcelona 08770 (phone: 93-890-0700).

JEREZ DE LA FRONTERA: Among the world's most popular aperitif wines, genuine sherry comes only from the region of Jerez de la Frontera at the southern tip of Spain. Produced in great cathedral-like *bodegas,* these wines are continuously blended, the younger and older wines mixing in a series of casks that constitute the *solera.* The result — no vintage sherries and a quality that is absolutely consistent from year to year.

The predominant grape varieties are palomino *fino,* palomino jerez, Pedro Ximénez, and muscatel. The four standard styles of sherries are *finos* (pale, dry, and light, often with a hint of bitter almonds), *manzanillas finas* (driest of all, with the tang of the sea air of their native Sanlúcar de Barrameda), *amontillados* (amber sherries with more depth and body, and a nutty flavor), and *olorosos* (dark and fragrant, dry in their natural state, but often sweetened with Pedro Ximénez wine to achieve the rich, raisiny creams that elegantly top off a meal). In addition, pale cream is a new style — a light, medium sherry with a touch of sweetness.

Before heading down to Jerez, contact Bartolomé Vergara, Director of Public Relations, A.C.E.S. (Asociación de Criadores y Exportadores de Sherry), 3 Calle San Ildefonso, Jerez de la Frontera, Cádiz 11402 (phone: 956-341046).

Pedro Domecq – A maker of wines since 1730, Domecq produces the full range of sherries in its vast facilities. All visits must be arranged through the public relations department, and the winery is closed on Saturdays and August 1 through 20. Information: *Pedro Domecq, S.A.* 1 Calle Colón, Jerez de la Frontera, Cádiz 11400 (phone: 956-330950).

González Byass – Established in 1835, this winery produces *finos, olorosos,* and sweet sherries. It also offers a unique ritual, featuring a mouse that climbs a miniature ladder to sip a daily dram of sherry from a glass set out expressly for it. All visits are by appointment, made through the public relations department. Closed Saturdays and August. Information: *González Byass, S.A.* 12 Calle Manuel María González, Jerez de la Frontera, Cádiz 11400 (phone: 956-340000).

Spas

 The spas of Spain are a slightly different breed from those of the US. Unlike their American counterparts, which are predominantly exercise- and fitness-oriented, Spanish spas take more of a therapeutic approach. They are health resorts in a purer sense, and are monitored by each country's National Health Association. In Spain, *balnearios* (spas) tend to focus on three specific approaches: thalassotherapy, in which ocean water, seaweed, and algae are used for therapeutic purposes; hydrotherapy, using mineral water drawn from natural springs; and mud therapy, which relies on rich volcanic or natural spring sources. Spain has over 90 spa resorts spread throughout its various regions. Some are simple, concentrating solely on relaxation and cures, while others are more elaborate, offering the best in resort, spa, and sports facilities. The *Spanish National Health Association* (23 Calle Martín de los Héroes, 4-D, Madrid; phone: 91-542-9775) provides detailed information about the country's *balnearios.*

BALNEARIO DEL GRAN HOTEL DE LA TOJA, Isla de la Toja, Pontevedra: Built in 1903 and recently renovated, this is one of Spain's finest spa resorts, offering the perfect recipe for stress reduction. Tucked away on a small, secluded island in the Atlantic Ocean off the coast of the northwestern Galician province of Pontevedra, the spa rises in grand majesty from a lush forest. Surrounded by tranquil waters and romantic beaches, it specializes in cures for skin diseases, rheumatism, and respiratory disorders, reduction of stress and tension, and physical rehabilitation. Facilities include thermal baths, vapor inhalation rooms, a thermal swimming pool, mud and bubble baths, a gymnasium, and a sauna. Physiotherapy and massages are also administered. In addition, the 200-room *Toja* hotel offers a wide range of leisure activities and facilities, including tennis, golf, swimming, elegant restaurants, entertainment, and a casino. A 10-day stay is recommended for best results. Information: *Gran Hotel de la Toja,* Isla de la Toja, Pontevedra 36991 (phone: 986-730025).

BALNEARIO VICHY CATALÁN, Caldes de Malavella, Girona: This small, comfortable, and relatively undiscovered traditional spa resort north of Barcelona may be short on elegance, but it makes up for that with its commitment to health. Facilities include pressure baths with controlled jets, bubble baths, massage and pressure jet showers, paraffin mud baths, Finnish and steam saunas, vapor inhalation treatments, a gymnasium, tennis courts, a swimming pool, and a children's playground. Information: *Hotel Balneario Vichy Catalán,* 32 Avenida Dr. Furest, Caldes de Malavella, Girona 17455 (phone: 972-470000).

INCOSOL SPA AND RESORT, Marbella, Costa del Sol: This 9-story, 200-room modern hotel, set along Spain's famous Costa de Sol, has everything. The spa facilities are so wide-ranging that guests could spend a week just sorting through the choices. Treatments include medical checkups and thorough case histories by a resident doctor, obesity treatments, massage, toning, laser therapy, acupuncture, mud baths, a variety of facial treatments, physiotherapy, hydrotherapy, electrotherapy, and more. The spa specializes in helping patients with weight problems, geriatric problems, and beauty care. There is also tennis, golf, squash, and water sports at the nearby beach. Information: *Incosol Spa & Resort Hotel,* Golf Rio Real, Marbella, Costa del Sol 29600 (phone: 952-773776 or 952-771700; in the US, 800-R-WARNER; in Canada, 800-344-6535).

LOUISON BOBET'S THALASSOTHERAPY, Mijas, Costa del Sol: Built in 1986, the *Biblos Andaluz* hotel is one of Spain's most modern and most efficient spa resorts. The Institute of Thalassotherapy's philosophy is based on the medicinal properties of warm sea water; there are up to 18 different treatments using water heated to 99F to penetrate the skin and tone up the body. Other treatments include the application of seaweed to relax muscles and the treatment of circulatory problems, varicose veins, and cramps. The institute also specializes in treating rheumatic illness, body pampering, and overall physical fitness. Accommodations consist of deluxe suites and mini-suites overlooking rolling greens, mountains, and the whitewashed town of Mijas. The hotel was designed to resemble a Moorish palace, complete with patios and long white porticoes; rooms open onto small courtyards filled with fountains, flowers, and orange trees. Many guests come here to play golf on the 2 courses, or to bask in the pleasures of *salud y sol* — health and sun. The 135-room hotel also features 3 restaurants, 5 tennis courts, sightseeing, and entertainment. Information: *Hotel Bilbos Andaluz,* Club de Golf de Mijas, Apt. 138, Fuengirola, Málaga 29650 (phone: 952-476873 or 952-460250); in the US, *Crown International,* 11 W. Passaic St., Rochelle Park, NJ 07662 (phone: 800-628-8929 or 800-323-7500).

VITATOP, Loja, Granada: This modern resort, built in 1986, is a sparkling Moorish wonder, neatly tucked amid a lush Mediterranean forest high up in the Sierra Nevada. Each of the 35 elegantly appointed rooms in *La Bobadilla* hotel offers maximum comfort — all have private terraces and gardens, and huge bathtubs. The spa here is similar to a fitness club, featuring a modern gymnasium with full Nautilus equipment, a heated indoor swimming pool, a Jacuzzi, 2 Finnish saunas, 2 Turkish steambaths, and a solarium. Professional fitness counseling, personal programs, and massages are also available. There is also a beauty salon, 3 restaurants, an outdoor swimming pool, 2 tennis courts, horseback riding, and nearby skiing. Information: *Hotel La Bobadilla,* Finca La Bobadilla, 52 Apartado, Loja, Granada 18006 (phone: 958-321861); in the US, *Marketing Ahead,* 433 Fifth Ave., New York, NY 10016 (phone: 212-686-9213).

TERMAS, Archena, Murcia: The hotel is simple: 69 rooms and 6 suites. Its claim to fame is its mineral water, which features chlorinated, iodized, brominated, and sulfurous properties with regenerative power. The spa specializes in treating rheumatism, respiratory ailments, and obesity. Thermal pools, a fitness center, massage, mud applications, and beauty treatments are also available. Information: *Hotel Termas,* Carretera del Balneario, Balneario de Archena, Archena, Murcia 30600 (phone: 968-670100).

BALNEARIO PRATS, Caldes de Malavella, Girona: This casual spa is situated in a 100-room Catalan-style hotel. The spa specializes in treating rheumatism, arthritis, and other circulatory and respiratory ailments, through the use of hydrotherapy, bubble baths, Scottish showers, underwater massages, sauna, infrared lamp therapy, and paraffin, wax, and clay treatments. Information: *Hotel Balneario Prats,* 7 Plaza Sant Esteve, Caldes de Malavella, Girona 17455 (phone: 972-470051).

For the Body

Great Golf

 The British brought golf to the Iberian Peninsula around the turn of the century, but it was another 50 years before the game acquired any degree of popularity — and then it remained an activity of only the very social or the very rich. Today, an increasing number of foreign golfers have discovered that Spain's 70 or so courses offer the perfect formula for a golfing vacation: a beautiful natural setting, ideal climate almost year-round, and some rather challenging layouts. In Spain alone, the number of golf clubs has quadrupled over the last 2 decades. American visitors will find little problem adjusting to Spanish course configurations; they tend to be designed in the American mold — target golf, with fairly narrow fairways leading to greens surrounded by bunkers and trees.

Most trips to Spain begin in the capital, and championship courses surround Madrid. The most popular courses, however, are found in the south. There are over a dozen courses along the 85-mile stretch of highway between Málaga and Sotogrande on Spain's Costa del Sol, among them the oldest and best known in the land. But some courses have become so overrun that increasing numbers of golfers are turning to the less-crowded courses of northern Spain, where spectacular scenery is often an added attraction. Some of the best are listed below.

Golf fees vary at most resorts. For guests staying at a golf hotel, greens fees usually are included. The cost for 18 holes generally runs about $20. Club rentals start at $6, handcarts at $2, gas or electric carts at $20. Lesson costs vary according to the reputation of the pro and the price level of the resort. Some courses require a valid US handicap certificate. Information: *Royal Spanish Golf Federation,* 9-5 Calle Capitán Haya, Madrid 28020 (phone: 91-555-2682 or 91-555-2757).

LA MANGA CAMPO DE GOLF, Los Belones: The two 18-hole championship layouts offer tantalizing views of the Mediterranean from nearly every tee, and the sights and scenery provide a sort of ancillary hazard. Gary Player has called it the "most superbly maintained course in the world." Information: *La Manga Campo de Golf,* Carretera Cabo de Palos, Los Belones, Cartagena, Murcia 30385 (phone: 968-564511).

GOLF LA TOJA, Isla de La Toja: This 9-hole course lies on an island in the Ría de Arosa, 50 miles (80 km) south of Santiago de Compostela; a bridge links the island to the mainland. At first sight, the course seems rather easy. But looming pines, the adjacent sea, and a constant wind add unexpected pressure. *La Toja*'s club membership totals 250, but some 5,000 golfers tackle its narrow fairways and doglegs every summer. Since it is open year-round, it is possible to avoid the summertime crowds. Information: *Golf La Toja,* Isla de La Toja, Pontevedra 36991 (phone: 986-730726 or 86-730818).

REAL SOCIEDAD HÍPICA ESPAÑOLA CLUB DE CAMPO, Madrid: This 18-hole course, founded in 1932, is 2½ miles (4 km) from Madrid near the right bank of the Manzanares River in Casa de Campo. One of Madrid's best, it hosted the *World Cup* in 1975 and the *Spanish Open* in 1957, 1960, and 1982. The course is characterized by very narrow fairways, flanked by oak trees, which lead to elevated greens protected by bunkers. There also is a 9-hole course. Information: *Real Sociedad Hípica Española Club de Campo,* Carretera de Castilla, Km 4, Madrid 28023 (phone: 91-207-0395).

REAL CLUB DE PUERTA DE HIERRO, Madrid: Founded at the turn of the 20th century, this prestigious club occupies a slope studded with pines and oaks. There are 2 18-hole courses (known as *Course I* and *Course II*), and several holes are crossed by bridle paths. Information: *Real Club de Puerta de Hierro,* Avenida de Miraflores, Madrid 28035 (phone: 91-316-1745).

CLUB DE GOLF LAS LOMAS-EL BOSQUE, Madrid: Built in the early 1970s, this pleasantly rambling 18-hole, par 72 course offers some deceptive challenges. Eleven of its fairways and greens lie against, or very close to, a manmade lake and stream. Information: *Club de Golf Las Lomas-El Bosque,* Villaviciosa de Odón, Apartado 51, Madrid 28003 (phone: 91-616-2170 or 91-616-2382).

CLUB DE CAMPO DE GOLF DE MÁLAGA, Málaga: Just 6 miles (10 km) from Málaga and 4 miles (6 km) from Torremolinos, this 18-hole Costa del Sol seaside course is over half a century old. Studded with eucalyptus trees, it is completely flat; its greens are well defined by bunkers. Information: *Club de Campo de Golf de Málaga,* Apartado 324, Málaga, 29088 (phone: 952-381120 or 952-381121).

GOLF TORREQUEBRADA, Málaga: A stunning 18-hole, par 72 mountainside course, 6,446 yards long. Numerous elevated tees offer fine views of the countryside and the sea. One especially challenging hole requires players to clear the tops of a grove of trees. Alternative (though still tricky) routes are provided where the more obvious challenges may prove too much for less talented players. There is plenty of other activity for non-golfers who have tagged along: The *Torrequebrada* hotel offers tennis, swimming, and a casino. Numerous villas and condominiums built in whitewashed elegance surround the course, giving it a Mediterranean charm unlike other such sites on the Costa del Sol. Information: *Golf Torrequebrada,* Apartado 67, Benalmádena Costa, Málaga 29630 (phone: 952-442742).

GOLF NUEVA ANDALUCÍA, Marbella: Just 5 miles (8 km) from Marbella; two 18-hole courses designed by Robert Trent Jones, Sr. undulate along a river valley below the Sierra Blanca. One course is called *Los Naranjos,* for the orange groves that dot the back 9; the other, *Las Brisas,* was the site of the *1983 Spanish Open.* Both courses are often tormented by wind, and they contain a full complement of water hazards and bunkers. Information: *Golf Nueva Andalucía,* Apartado 2, Marbella, Málaga 29080 (phone: 952-780300 or 952-787200).

GOLF GUADALMINA, Marbella: Part of a resort complex offering 2 courses, tennis, horseback riding, water skiing, a private beach, and 3 swimming pools, this is an ideal destination for golfers with non-golfing family members or friends along. The southern course, along the sea, is largely flat with only an occasional dogleg. The northern course is hilly, with elevated greens, varied bunkers, and water hazards, making it the more challenging of the two. There is a golf pro, pro shop, club and gas cart rental, a driving range, and putting green. The complex offers superb views of the Rock of Gibraltar on the horizon, and the hotel-restaurant offers first-rate Spanish and international fare. Information: *Golf Hotel Guadalmina,* San Pedro de Alcántara, Marbella, Málaga 29670 (phone: 952-781317).

HOTEL BILBOS ANDALUZ, Mijas: This Moorish hideaway is situated in the heart of two 18-hole Robert Trent Jones, Sr. courses. The first course, *Mijas,* a par 72, spreads out before the hotel, offering postcard views of whitewashed Andalusian villages and azure skies. The second course, *Los Olivos,* a par 71, is to the west of the hotel. This gently rolling track requires long shots and considerable technical skill to deal with the numerous water hazards and closely sheltered greens. The hotel organizes its own annual *Challenge Competition* during the first weeks of November. Facilities include 3 swimming pools, horseback riding, 5 tennis courts, a world class spa (see *Spas,* in this section), and shopping excursions. Information: *Hotel Bilbos Andaluz,* Urbanización Mijas Golf, Apartado 138, Fuengirola, Málaga 29080 (phone: 952-476843).

CLUB DE GOLF DE PALS, Playa de Pals: Twenty minutes up the coast from the Costa Brava course (see below), this club by the sea is studded with Mediterranean pines. It hosted the *Spanish Open* in 1972. Now and then, between the dunes, the Mediterranean is visible. Less alluring is the wind, which proves a year-round hazard and blows most defiantly during the *tramuntana,* Catalonia's version of the French mistral — a cold, dry wind that knows no particular season. The small club membership welcomes visitors year-round. Closed Tuesdays from mid-September through June. Information: *Club de Golf de Pals,* Playa de Pals, Girona 17256 (phone: 972-636006).

REAL CLUB DE GOLF DE CERDANYA, Puigcerdá: This 60-year-old club in the Pyrenees is often touted as Europe's finest mountain course. Located 19 miles (30 km) east of the principality of Andorra, the club is a 4-hour drive from Barcelona. Its 18 holes dot a valley, 4,000 feet above sea level, that extends into nearby France. Open year-round, it's primarily a summer and autumn course, but mild weather from January through March often makes for comfortable play during these months as well. The *Chalet de Golf* clubhouse offers simple, comfortable rooms and suites. Accommodations are also available at the nearby *Del Prado* and *Park* hotels. Information: *Real Club de Golf de Cerdanya,* Apartado de Curreus 63, Puigcerdá, Girona 17520 (phone: 972-881338 or 972-880950).

CLUB DE GOLF COSTA BRAVA, Santa Cristina de Aro, Catalonia: The nearest golf course to Barcelona, it is set in a wooded valley a few miles from the Mediterranean and 19 miles (30 km) southeast of Girona. Pines and cork oaks line the fairways of the par 70 course; some holes are quite narrow and sharply doglegged. The clubhouse is a distinctive, well-preserved, 18th-century Catalan country manor. The front 9 has its ups and downs, and snakes through a forest of oaks; the back 9, down in the valley, is relatively flat. The 4th and 18th holes are among Catalonia's best. The Ridaura River, dry for much of the year, cuts across the former; a long par 4 uphill bedevils the latter. Closed Wednesdays. Nearby hotels include the *Costa Brava, Murla Park,* and the *Park Sant Jordi.* Information: *Club de Golf Costa Brava,* Santa Cristina de Aro, Girona 17246 (phone: 972-837052).

REAL GOLF DE PEDREÑA, Santander: This course lies on a peninsula in the middle of a bay, some 15 miles (24 km) east of Santander. Pine, cypress, and eucalyptus trees adorn the challenging 6,277 yards, which require the use of virtually every club in the bag. Severiano Ballesteros, Spain's most famous golfer and international superstar, lives adjacent to the 7th hole. All guests must be accompanied by a member. Information: *Real Golf de Pedreña,* Apartado 233, Santander 39000 (phone: 942-500001 or 942-500266).

PARADOR DEL GOLF, Torremolinos: This 60-room *parador* near Málaga is a golfer's paradise. The 18-hole course — the oldest on the Costa del Sol — was designed in 1925 by English architect Tom Simpson and has a resident pro on the premises. It is popular with vacationing families, thanks in part to its non-golf facilities, which include the ocean, a swimming pool, tennis courts, and a children's playground. Information: *Parador del Golf,* Apartado 324, Carretera de Malaga, Km 3, Torremolinos, Málaga 29620 (phone: 952-381255).

REAL SOCIEDAD DE GOLF DE NEGURI, Vizcaya: Dating from 1911, this par 72 course is one of Spain's oldest. Its front 9 abuts the sea, amid dwindling pines reminiscent of English links. The back 9 features narrow fairways and an occasional dogleg. There are various accommodations nearby. Information: *Real Sociedad de Golf de Neguri,* Apartado de Correos 9, Algorta, Vizcaya 48990 (phone: 944-690200 or 944-690208).

Tennis

In Spain, tennis usually takes a back seat to golf. But many hotels and resorts have tennis facilities, and beginners and experts alike will find an abundance of places to play. Racquets, balls, and courts are easily rented, and a single player can find a partner easily. The majority of tennis facilities are located along the Costa del Sol, which is in the midst of rapid expansion, with more and more emphasis being placed on residential developments — small communities of villas and townhouses clustered around sports facilities and the sea. So far, only the British have truly "discovered" this area, and thanks in part to their inroads, almost everyone speaks English. The Costa del Sol is considerably developed; many have labeled it the Miami of the Mediterranean. There are a number of exclusive areas where the tennis enthusiast can enjoy a vacation amid golden beaches, turquoise waters, and the uniquely Spanish atmosphere of Andalusia.

Most Spanish tennis courts have either an asphalt or clay surface, and traditional tennis whites are preferred — often required. Expect to pay about $5 per hour for court time. In most cases, court time must be reserved in advance. There also is an emphasis on the social aspects of tennis, and visitors will find that many hotels sponsor weekly tournaments and "get acquainted" parties where tennis enthusiasts can meet and mingle. In addition, there are a variety of members-only tennis clubs spread throughout Spain's major cities and resort areas where, for a small additional fee, guests are permitted to play. Also keep in mind that tennis can be fun to watch, and despite its slow start, tennis as a spectator sport — thanks in part to the stocky Spanish sensation, Aranxtha Sánchez-Vicario — is catching on. Spain plays host to a continual series of championship events each year. For details on Spanish tennis tournaments, contact the *Royal Spanish Tennis Federation* (186 Diagonal, Barcelona 08028; phone: 93-201-0844, 93-200-5355, or 93-201-5586); or the *ATP* (4 Sawgrass Village, Suite 240, Ponte Vedra Beach, FL 32082; phone: 904-285-5776).

CAMPO DE TENIS DE LEW HOAD, Mijas, Costa del Sol: Australian Lewis Hoad, the 1956 and 1957 *Wimbledon* champion, first spotted this hilly enclave in 1966, and decided it was the perfect spot to build a tennis ranch. Twenty-five years later, the "ranch" is a favorite spot for both serious players and beginners serious about learning the game. This facility is not a resort, but a full-service tennis center and club, where guests sharpen their skills and socialize with other tennis enthusiasts. The tennis school is run by Manrique Floreal, a professional who teaches the Aussie style, a gentle technique that emphasizes the reception of opponents' serves. Facilities include 8 hard courts (the Spanish refer to this surface as "quick"), which are surrounded by exotic and carefully landscaped gardens, and a well-stocked pro shop. There are weekly singles and doubles tournaments for advanced players. There is also a bar overlooking the courts, a restaurant, changing rooms, sauna, swimming pool, massage facilities, beauty salon, aerobics classes, art exhibits, and occasional concerts. Guests can rent one of the exclusive villas that surround the club, or find accommodations in nearby Fuengirola and Mijas. Information: *Campo de Tenis de Lew Hoad,* Apartado 111, Carretera de Mijas, Fuengirola, Málaga 29640 (phone: 952-474858).

DON CARLOS, Marbella, Costa del Sol: The privacy and excellent facilities here have helped this 212-room resort, located in the heart of a 130-acre private estate of pine woods, exotic flowers, and subtropical gardens, achieve its standing as the official home of the European Women's Tennis Association. Martina Navratilova and Chris Evert are just two of the many top-ranked professionals who have practiced and competed here. Throughout the year, visitors usually can catch a glimpse of a superstar or two either playing or relaxing at the restaurant overlooking the courts. Don't be overwhelmed by the abundance of talent; the mood here is casual and relaxed, and a beginner will feel as comfortable as a pro. There are 11 courts (6 clay, 5 hard; 4 courts are floodlit), between the swimming pool and the sea. In addition, the hotel offers windsurfing, sailing, water skiing, a driving range, horseback riding, a gymnasium, a sauna, and a Jacuzzi — all free to hotel guests. Information: *Don Carlos Hotel,* Jardines de las Golondrinas, Marbella, Málaga 29600 (phone: 952-831140 or 52-831940); in the US, *Utell International,* 119 W. 57th St., New York, NY 10019 (phone: 212-245-7130).

LOS MONTEROS, Marbella, Costa del Sol: One of the most prestigious hotels and sporting resorts on the coast. Set among pine woods and tropical gardens, it makes for an ideal vacation getaway that will keep guests as busy or as relaxed as they wish. There are 10 hard courts, 2 of which are floodlit for night play, as well as 5 squash courts, a paddle tennis court, 2 swimming pools, a terrace bar, pro shop, gymnasium, sauna, massage facilities, beautician, nursery, nightclub, and nearby golf. Guests are automatically considered tennis club members and may use the courts free of charge, subject to availability and club regulations. Information: *Los Monteros Hotel,* Marbella, Málaga 29600 (phone: 952-771700); in the US, *Distinguished Hotels,* c/o Robert F. Warner, Inc., 307 Fifth Ave., New York, NY 10016 (phone: 212-725-4500; outside New York City and in Canada, 800-888-1199).

PUENTE ROMANO, Marbella, Costa del Sol: This self-contained Moorish residence is a city in itself. For the tennis enthusiast, there are 11 courts — 4 hard, 5 clay, and 2 artificial surface (Astroturf) — on which to practice, as well as a large stadium that plays host to many national and international tournaments. Björn Borg was once the pro at the tennis center here; today, former *Wimbledon* champion Manolo Santana sets the tone. In addition to tennis, the resort offers surfing, water skiing, a fitness center, swimming pool, horseback riding, polo, and nearby golf. The 200 rooms and suites are built in pueblo-style Andalusian *casitas,* which overlook tropical gardens and waterfalls. Information: *Puente Romano Hotel,* 204 Apartado de Correos, Marbella, Málaga 29600 (phone: 952-770100); in the US, *Utell International,* 500 Plaza Dr., Secaucus, NJ 07096 (phone: 201-902-7800 or 800-223-9868).

MARBELLA CLUB, Marbella, Costa del Sol: One of the most famous hotels on the coast, and the cornerstone of Marbella. Set in a subtropical garden by the sea, this resort is a fine place to mix tennis and beach life. There are 11 tennis courts, and Manolo Santana serves as the coach. Information: *Marbella Club Hotel,* Carretera de Cádiz, Km 178, Marbella, Málaga 29600 (phone: 952-771300).

SOTOGRANDE, Estepona, Costa del Sol: Set in the enormous Sotogrande complex, where guests have access to some of the best and most varied sports facilities on the coast. The tennis center offers first-rate instruction, and the secluded hotel is peaceful and well looked after by a helpful and attentive staff. All rooms have separate sleeping and living areas, as well as private patios and fountains. Information: *Hotel Sotogrande,* Sotogrande, Carretera 340N, Km 131, Cádiz 11310 (phone: 952-792100).

Sensational Skiing

When most people think of skiing in Europe, they think of Switzerland, Austria, and France. Yet Spain, the second-most mountainous country in Europe, has excellent skiing facilities that seem to be one of the country's best-kept secrets. In the north, there are the Pyrenees, that guard the border with France, and the Cantabrian range near the Galician coast; in the south, the Sierra Nevada range that rises 10,000 feet above the towns and villages of Andalusia; and in the center of the country, the Guadarramas, north of Madrid. In addition, there are ski areas in the provinces of Burgos, Soria, Logroño, and Teruel. Skiing is possible from January through May in the north, and from January through March in the south and lower elevations.

Spain offers novice through advanced skiers the thrills of a lifetime — and once experienced, these hills will not soon be forgotten. Spain is also one of European skiing's bargain capitals; hotels, meals, drinks, equipment, and lift passes are available at prices far below those found in the Alps. Other benefits include an abundance of snow, relatively mild weather conditions, and plenty of sunshine. Some large international resorts such as Tuca-Betrén, Baqueria-Beret, Cerler, and Pal in Andorra have it all — a vast array of runs and lifts, troops of multilingual instructors, a selection of winter sporting opportunities such as ice skating and tobogganing, a horde of shops, shimmering hotels, high-speed nightlife, and the glossy aura of Europe's leisure classes. But there also are numerous cozier, family-oriented villages, many of them linked to a constellation of neighbors by far-reaching networks of chair lifts and cable cars.

Throughout most of the resort regions, those who like their luxury rugged can hire a helicopter for a quick trip up a mountaintop blanketed with glittery virgin powder, and enjoy the subsequent opportunity to carve a solitary trail back down through miles of untracked mountainside. For those whose special pleasure is cross-country skiing, be aware that the sport is beginning to boom here; a wide choice of trails and excursions (and a good supply of the necessary equipment) is readily available. And no matter where you go, there's a very high standard of cooking in the restaurant dining rooms adjacent to the slopes.

Words of caution: If you need an English-speaking instructor from the area's ski school, say so when signing up, or risk having to learn to recognize "Bend your knees" enunciated in all-too-faultless Spanish. Know the local trail markings — green for novice, blue for intermediate, and red for expert. Be prepared for sometimes hair-raising traffic — both on the mountain roads and on the slopes. Since skiing as a mass activity is a Juan-come-lately in Spain, the average level of expertise is lower than is routinely found in Switzerland, France, or Austria, and the traditions of slope safety and etiquette are not always readily apparent. For those familiar with European skiing, be aware that the high and low skiing seasons in Spain are significantly different from those of the better-known Alpine regions. All weekends are designated as high season, with premium prices on hotels, lessons, and lifts. High season also applies to the period from *Christmas* through *New Year's,* and the first week of January. Prices rise again during February and the first 2 weeks of March.

VAL D'ARAN, Lleida (Lérida), Catalonia: Past the orchards and vineyards of Catalonia and up into the Pyrenees Mountains bordering France lies one of the most beautiful alpine valleys in the world — and the ski resorts of Tuca-Betrén and Baqueria-Beret. Tuca-Betrén, the lesser known of the two, offers a wide variety of slopes and trails that will challenge even the most experienced skier. In fact, all of the resort's 18 slopes and trails are marked either advanced or expert. The first trail starts at the 5,000-foot level; the highest peaks overhead top off at 9,000 feet. Eight miles (13 km) away is Baqueria-Beret, one of the most extensive ski resorts in Europe outside the Alps. It is the favorite ski resort of King Juan Carlos and also attracts a predominantly French clientele from north of the border. The facilities and restaurants are more modern and sophisticated here than in Tuca-Betrén. The skiing on the Baqueria side is down tight trails with a dense lift network of T-bars and double chair lifts. The skiing above Beret is in a wide-open bowl served by three strategically placed triple chair lifts. Together, Baqueria-Beret offers 43 slopes and trails, 22 lifts, 2 slalom courses, and helicopter service to the peaks for the thrills of fresh powder. Due to the terrain — steep slopes and wide courses — there is great skiing variety. Of special note is the descent from the peak of Cap de Baqueira, the highest point. Val d'Aran's two distinct segments are separated by a row of natural stone and mortar villages, scenery for which the word "charm" was coined. Much of this area looks the way it did in the 13th, 14th, 15th, and 16th centuries — give or take a few power lines and Seats (Spanish-built Fiats). This area alone has a total of almost 5,000 rooms spread throughout hotels, inns, and quaint *pensiones.* Information: *Oficina d'Información Turística de Baqueira-Beret,* Apartado 60, Calle Viella, Val d'Aran, Lleida 25530 (phone: 973-645050 or 973-645025), or *Oficina d'Información Turística,* Calle Arc del Pont, Lleida 25000 (phone: 973-248120).

EL FORMIGAL, Huesca, Aragonese Pyrenees: Another favorite stomping ground of the current King of Spain and his family, this is just one of five resorts in the area (Astún, Cerler, Panticosa, and Candanchú are the others). Together they constitute one of the most attractive and unspoiled regions in Spain, guaranteed to motivate even the most sedentary to hit the hills. As the westernmost resort in the Pyrenees, El Formigal lacks woodland, but instead boasts great open spaces — perfect for beginners and intermediates. Only 2 of the 24 runs are designated for experts, but most are rated as difficult. The wide-open off-piste possibilities, however, compensate for those strong enough to handle heavy snow. A double chair lift rises out of the town, reaching the mid-station and the main mountain restaurant. From here, beginners can enjoy gentle slopes, intermediates can drop down to the lower gondola station, and experts can take a chair lift or T-bar to the summit and enjoy a 3,000-foot drop back into the village. There is also a slalom course, 6 hotels, and a wide variety of activities, including very lively nightlife. Information: *Oficina de Turismo,* Estación de Formigal, Sallent de Gallego, El Formigal, Huesca 22000 (phone: 974-488125), or *Oficina de Turismo de Huesca,* 23 Calle Coso Alto, Huesca 22022 (phone: 974-225778).

CERLER, Huesca, Aragonese Pyrenees: Larger than El Formigal and closer to the French border, Cerler boasts 5,875 acres of spectacular skiable terrain for skiers of all abilities. The 23 trails, the highest slopes the Pyrenees have to offer, provide plenty of challenges; the majority of the trails are over 3 miles long and are served by 11 chair lifts, and there is also an ice skating rink and a wide variety of other activities, including sledding and swimming. Information: *Oficina de Turismo de Huesca,* 23 Calle Coso Alto, Huesca 22022 (phone: 974-225778).

LA MOLINA, Girona, Catalan Pyrenees: This is one of the oldest ski resorts in Spain, as well as the closest to Barcelona. For this reason, the resort attracts a weekend crowd that usually overwhelms the 17 chair lifts. During the week, however, there are rarely any lines. Only 3 of the 22 trails are listed as difficult, making the resort a favorite for skiers of all abilities. There is also a 3-mile cross-country course, and 3 ramps for ski jumping. The resort was created with skiers specifically in mind, and features modern, self-contained hotels, good restaurants, a smattering of shops, and a group of lively discos and bars. There are also 9 *hostales* located nearby. Information: *Oficina de Turismo,* Carretera 151N, Km 15, La Molina, Girona 17537 (phone: 972-892175), or *Oficina de Turismo,* 12 Calle Ciudadanos, Girona 17000 (phone: 972-325-5829).

SOLYNIEVE, Sierra Nevada, near Granada: This resort is a cluster of concrete buildings huddled above the tree line in the far south of Spain, only 20 miles (32 km) from Granada and 60 miles (96 km) from the coast at Motril. Here, the perpetually snow-covered mountains rise to 11,420 feet. The scenery is inspiring and the snowfields are seemingly endless. Its status as a ski resort, however, is not all that high. The skiing here, though extensive, is tame and not particularly demanding; it will, however, keep advanced beginners and intermediates busy. With its wide, treeless slopes and patient Spanish instructors, Solynieve is perfect for beginning skiers. The resort boasts 19 lifts, which serve some 30 miles of trails. The village itself is rather soulless; even the southern Spanish personality can't seem to help fire up the nightlife. But in the spring, Solynieve does offer dependable snow and the opportunity to ski in the morning and then drive down to the Costa del Sol for an afternoon of sun on the beach or a round of golf — so be sure to pack sunscreen and sunglasses. Information: *Federación Andaluza de Esquí,* 78 Paseo de Ronda, Veleta, Granada 18000 (phone: 958-250706), or *Patronato Provincial de Turismo de Granada,* Calle 32 Arabial, Granada 18000 (phone: 958-223527).

ALTO CAMPO, Santander, Cantabria: This is one of those resorts where the skiing season lasts until late May. The resort lies in the Brana Vieja Valley, sheltered from harsh winds. On a clear day, the distant peak of Tres Mares, the Polaciones Valley, and the heights of the Picos de Europa are visible. The slopes here vary from easy to extremely difficult, making skiing available for enthusiasts of all levels. Information: *Oficina de Turismo,* 1 Plaza Velarde, Santander 39001 (phone: 942-211417 or 942-310756).

ANDORRA: One of Europe's last feudal protectorates, this tiny co-principality, governed nominally by Spain and France, has abundant snow from November through April. Combined with an excellent climate of dry air and sunny skies, this is truly a skiers' paradise. Some of Europe's best inexpensive skiing can be found at the resorts of Pas de la Casa–Grau Roig, Soldeu–El Tarter, Pals, Arinsal, and Ordino Arcalis. Pas de la Casa–Grau Roig, just within the French border, is the oldest resort, and has 18 trails for advanced skiers, a slalom course, and several tame slopes for beginners, as well as 25 lifts and 33 hotels. Soldeu–El Tarter is the largest complex, with 28 slopes (including 5 designed especially for children), a 7½-mile cross-country course, 22 lifts, 20 hotels, and 3 self-contained apartment blocks. Pals features 20 trails, a forest slalom course, 2 children's slopes, and 14 lifts. Arinsal, next to the village of the same name, has 23 slopes ranging from beginner to expert, all served by 15 lifts. Ordino Arcalis is the most dramatically beautiful of Andorra's resorts, offering 16 slopes, 11 lifts, and 4 modern hotels in nearby El Serrat. Information: *Sindicat d'Iniciativa de les Valls d'Andorra,* Carrer Dr. Vilanova, Andorra la Vella, Andorra (phone: 973-820214); in the US, *Tourist Office of Andorra,* 120 E. 55th St., New York, NY 10022 (phone: 212-688-8681).

Horsing Around

 It almost goes without saying that Spain is the land of the horse. It was here that the Moorish invaders crossed the Bab steeds of their homeland with the native Iberian stock that had provided mounts for conquerors from Julius Caesar to Richard the Lion-Hearted. They came up with a noble breed renowned for its sturdy legs, strong back, and agility — the Andalusian.

Raising Andalusian thoroughbreds is still a tradition carried on at over 100 ranches in southwestern Spain. Visits can be arranged through the breeders' association, the *Real Sociedad Española de Fomento del Cría Caballar,* located at the *Hipódromo de la Zarzuela* in Madrid (phone: 91-307-0140). The association also provides a free brochure listing the names and addresses of its members. In addition, there are some 50 other ranches dedicated to preserving the pure Arabian bloodline, reintroduced at the turn of the century. Information: *Asociación de Criadores de Caballos Arabes,* 20 Calle Hermosila, Madrid 28009 (phone: 91-275-9065).

To witness with what grace Andalusian horses lend themselves to classical European and Spanish dressage, a visit to Jerez de la Frontera's *Real Escuela Andaluza del Arte Ecuestre* (7 Avenida Duque Abrantes; phone: 956-303718) is a must. This school was founded in 1972 by Alvaro Domecq, of the local sherry dynasty, who has since retired after years as Spain's top-ranked *rejoneador,* a bullfighter on horseback.

The 35 Spanish mounts are trotted out in their fancy dress gear every Thursday for a 2-hour show entitled "How the Andalusian Horses Dance." During the second week of May, the people of Jerez de la Frontera emerge blinking from their sherry vaults to welcome riding enthusiasts from all over the world for their annual week-long *Horse Fair.* Spanish equestrian specialties on display, along with much dancing, hand-clapping, and *fino*-drinking, include the *acoso y deribo,* in which riders use long blunt poles to isolate one bull from a stampeding herd and overturn it. The colorfully dressed riders then try their hand at *doma vaquera,* or Spanish rustic dressage, performing a series of showy maneuvers that climax when the horses approach at full gallop, then come to a dead halt before the judges' stand. Some extremely flashy carriage driving rounds out the city's tribute to the animal that was originally bred with patient perfectionism by the Carthusian monks, who were based here until the last century.

HORSE TREKKING

"The remembrance of those wild and weary rides through tawny Spain where hardship was forgotten ere undergone," sighed Richard Ford, the grand old man of wandering Hispanophiles, reflecting on the various ambles from Santiago de Compostela to Seville that he made during the 1830s. "Then and there will be learnt golden rules of patience, perseverance, good temper, and good fellowship."

Horse trekking involves day-long trips on the back of a sturdy native horse or pony, and has participants traveling mainly at a walk — partly because most are inexperienced riders, partly because the riding is through dense forests and steep mountain terrain, along narrow trails and roads that don't lend themselves to a faster pace. Absolute novices may be provided with some instruction, but ordinarily it will be at a relatively elementary level. In recent years, a number of agencies specializing in horseback treks have rediscovered the old cattle trails and royal bridle paths of the Middle Ages — all to prove their point that Spain looks very different when observed up close from the back of a congenial quadruped. The following include some of the best Spanish horse trekking centers, which offer trips lasting anywhere from a day to a month. Backup vehicle, insurance, meals, and lodging are usually included.

Rutas a Caballo, Madrid. More than 15 years' experience and numerous repeat clients from the US, Germany, and Switzerland make this a best bet for everyone from serious riders to the merely determined. Popular routes include trails through Segovia, Andalusia, and Coto Doñana. Information: *Rutas a Caballo,* 21 Calle Juan Bravo, Madrid 28006 (phone: 91-576-7629).

Equestrian Tours Almansur, Madrid. One of Spain's most popular trekking centers, catering to the American market. Most of the clientele come back for a second look at Extremadura and the Sierra de Gredos. Information: *Equestrian Tours Almansur,* 3 Glorieta Puente de Segovia, Madrid 28011 (phone: 91-402-1187); in the US, *FITS Equestrian,* 2011 Alamo Pintado Rd., Solvang, CA 93463 (phone: 805-688-9494).

Viajes Geosud, Madrid. Organizes outings to order for groups of 3 to 15 in Almería, the Sierra de Alpujarra of Granada, and northern Navarre. Information: *Viajes Geosud,* 9 Calle Juan de Dios, Madrid 28015 (phone: 91-542-6194).

Viajes Nobel, Madrid. This agency pioneered the practice of bringing riders from abroad to accompany the *Transhumancia* cattle drive (see *Extra Special*). Popular routes include the Sierra de Gredos, Málaga, Avila, and Andalusia. Information: *Viajes Nobel,* 3 Calle Duque de Liria, Madrid 28015 (phone: 91-542-3125).

POST TREKKING/TRAIL RIDING

There's nothing quite as delightful as seeing the Spanish countryside from the back of a horse or sure-footed native pony, heading from ranch to ranch through narrow trails, along abandoned train beds, and down wide sandy beaches — and staying away from the trekking center for up to a week at a time. Post trekking, or trail riding, as this activity is called, is not generally recommended for riders without experience, as it usually involves good horses and a fast enough pace to cover about 25 miles (40 km) a day. Usually a warm camaraderie develops among riders en route, as they traverse the rural miles. Post trekking is also a practically worry-free holiday: There are guides to keep riders going at a reasonable pace, to make sure the group doesn't get lost, and to arrange for the rider's luggage to be transported from one hostelry to the next.

ALMERÍA: Those who think they know the desert probably haven't seen or even imagined anything quite like the arid wastelands of Tabernas, a stretch of mind-boggling barrenness between the Sierra Nevada and Almería's still undeveloped Mediterranean beach resorts. After 3 days riding through a scallop-edged sea of surreal sandstone, where the sun has bleached every color out of the landscape, it's a relief to return to the *cortijo,* or workday ranch, located on the Cabo de Gata Peninsula, and the greenery of its adjacent national park. People can also visit Yuka City, which has kept the corner saloon doors swinging even after the paella-Western boom of the 1970s went bust. Groups require a minimum of three riders; there are no fixed departure dates, and accommodations (an ad hoc combination of inland ranches alternating with hotels on the coast) and itineraries are available by specific arrangement only. Information: *Viajes Geosud,* 9 Calle Juan de Dios, Madrid 28015 (phone: 91-542-6194).

ASTURIAS: Misty, mountainous, gorgeous, and green, Spain's northern coast serves as a gateway to secluded inland valleys settled by a hard-boiled race of cider-swigging mountain men who spend their days tending their cattle and flocks of merino sheep. All this is within a few hours' riding time from Gijón, where excursions of 1 to 3 days lead up into the sierra to the sprawling Valle del Peón, the seven lakes of Saliencia, the Somiedo Wildlife Reserve (full of brown bears, wolves, wild boar, and imperial eagles), and other no-frills natural wonders. Information: *Compañia Asturiana de Rutas y Excursiones,* 8 Plaza Romualde Alvargonzález, Gijón 33202 (phone: 985-341968).

In adjacent Oviedo Province, *Trastur,* a cooperative of youthful trekking enthusiasts, has a setup aimed at a young, casual, and outdoorsy clientele: riding by day and partying determinedly through the night in the log cabin shelters of the *vaquieros,* the Asturian livestock drivers. Their trails lead from the crossroad towns of Tineo and Navelgas, where this rough-and-ready culture is best preserved, then north to the pretty fishing village of Luarca. Arrangements must be made by telephone from the enthusiasts' base in Tineo (phone: 985-806036), and they will pick guests up in Oviedo. In Madrid, call 91-477-9236 to find out when the next outing is scheduled.

AVILA: The Sierra de Gredos is where Madrid's horsey set heads for a taste of real wilderness. The mountains have a certain preeminence for trail riders and boast 7,500-foot peaks, as well as deep ravines clawed out of the landmass by glaciers. Many of the routes also overlap the adjoining Tietar Valley. *Viajes Nobel* (see above) buses clients from Madrid to Navaredonda de Gredos, the starting point for an 8-day trek that leads into the lush Barco de Avila, following roads laid down by Roman legionnaires. One night is spent at a log cabin shelter run by the *Spanish Mountaineering Federation,* so a sleeping bag is necessary. All guides speak English, and departures are scheduled once a month from March through November. Weekend excursions for 1 or 2 days, departing from the *Parador de Gredos,* Navarredonda de Gredos 05635 (phone: 918-348048), are also available throughout the year, except in December.

Another week-long trek is offered by *Gredos — Rutas a Caballo* (13 Calle Guijuelos,

Hoya de Espina, Avila 05001; phone: 918-384110). This trek and other short half-day outings can also be booked in Madrid (phone: 91-576-7629).

In August, when the plains of Extremadura are broiling, *Equestrian Tours Almansur* (3 Glorieta Puente de Segovia, Madrid 28011; phone: 91-402-1187) moves its horses to the northern side of the Gredos range to keep cool. Twice a month, week-long sallies take riders down to visit the walled city of Avila, as well as along the Piedrahita River for a look at the palace of the Dukes of Alba. Another group, *Turismo Ecuestre La Isla,* has 3-day rides from its ranch in Navaluenga to Avila, and week-long trips through the Gredos central highlands and to the remote Lagoons of Gredos. Departures are from May through September (in Madrid, call 91-633-3692).

CÁDIZ: Dusty cattle trails head down the heartland of Andalusia's wild west, where the whitewashed towns all bear the tag *de la frontera* as a reminder that this was where Muslim and Christian Spain fought most furiously for control. The 260-mile (416-km) route starts in Arcos de la Frontera, with 5- to 7-hour stretches in the saddle, then breaks for an unhurried picnic lunch. The trail leads through bull breeding ranches and fields of cultivated sunflowers drooping on their 5-foot stalks, and it ends with a gallop through the Atlantic surf. Stopover specials include a day in Jerez de la Frontera, with a visit to that city's celebrated School of Equestrian Arts, and a canter along the beachside Roman ruins of Bolonia. Provision is made for an occasional afternoon on two legs for a peek at the pueblo or to bask on the beach. Accommodations at the *Arco* ranch, as well as the *hostales* along the way, are clean and comfortable, but not luxurious. Private baths are included — and will be needed. Bring a 10-gallon hat and a canteen of equivalent capacity, as the summer temperatures can hover around 100F.

Rutas a Caballo (21 Calle Juan Bravo, Madrid 28006; phone: 91-576-7629), which pioneered this trek, offers departures every third weekend from March through October, including accommodations and all meals — which are simple and good. A shorter 8-day version that heads to the sea, forsaking the return trek, is also available. *Viajes Nobel* (3 Calle Duque de Liria, Madrid 28015; phone: 91-542-3125) offers essentially the same 8-day route from Arcos to the coast, with similar overnight stops, but offers different weekend departure dates. In May, June, October, and November, *Rutas a Caballo* offers an inland tour of the *pueblos blancos,* the celebrated whitewashed towns of Andalusia, including Arcos de la Frontera, Grazalema, Zahara de la Sierra, and Ronda. It also offers a 1-week variant, the 140-mile(224-km) "Atlantic Sea Tour," allowing for 3 days inland riding and 4 days splashing along the beach as the breakers come rolling in from the Strait of Gibraltar, with Morocco's Atlas Mountains visible on the other side.

COTO CONANA NATIONAL PARK, Huelva: A unique chance to spend a week trotting through the salt marsh and scrub of one of Europe's largest and most ecologically vital wildlife sanctuaries. After picking up riders in Seville, the organizers get one and all saddled up in Arcos de la Frontera. From there, it's a 2-day ride via Jerez de la Frontera to where the land turns swampy and some of more than 150 different species of birds — including flamingos, imperial eagles, and many more birds of prey — can be observed roosting above the deer, lynx, and wild boar that inhabit the 50,000 acres of restricted parkland. Riders and mounts are ferried across the marshes in shallow-draft skiffs. A visit to the shrine of the Virgen del Rocío, which is inundated by pilgrims each May during one of Spain's most colorful outbursts of religious fervor, is also included. Contact *Rutas a Caballo* (21 Calle Juan Bravo, Madrid 28006; phone: 91-576-7629) for details. It offers departures in May, July, September, and November.

EXTREMADURA: The rugged and still-backward land that toughened up Spanish conquistadores such as Cortés and Pizarro opens itself up for reciprocal exploration from the New World on treks ranging from 1 to 3 weeks. The wide-ranging Route of the Conquistadores leaves very little of the region unseen. Riders explore the Monfragüe National Park, a unique sanctuary for migratory birds, the poor but pretty pueblos of the Jerte Valley and La Vera, the Roman city of Mérida, the monasteries of Guadalupe and Yuste, and the historic towns of Cáceres, Trujillo, and Plasencia. Departures are scheduled in early September only, and include 22 days on the trail.

The Monastery of Guadalupe, where Columbus pleaded for cash before King Ferdinand and Queen Isabella, is a 14th-century sanctuary visited by pilgrims from all over the Spanish-speaking world. But its larger mountain setting is a treat seldom seen by anyone, although its deep valleys and dense oak forests make it well worth the 8-day outing, covering 105 miles (168 km). Departures are scheduled for April, May, September, and October.

All of the Extremadura excursions can be booked through *Equestrian Tours Almansur* (3 Glorieta Puente de Segovia, Madrid 28011; phone: 91-402-1187), which offers an excellent selection of Hispano-Arab mounts and provides first class accommodations and meals at the various *paradores* in the region. It also offers a week-long close look at the Tietar River Valley, on the fertile southern flanks of the Gredos mountain range. This route is also trekked by *Viajes Nobel* (3 Calle Duque de Liria, Madrid 28015; phone: 91-541-9517), which shares mounts and facilities at the Dehesa del Roble ranch estate. An American organization that handles excursions is *FITS Equestrian* (2011 Alamo Pintado Rd., Solvang, CA 93463; phone: 805-688-9494 or 800-666-3487). Departures are scheduled from May through November, except in August, when it's simply too hot to trot.

GALICIA: The *Club Equitación de la Espuela* (at Noalla, La Lanzada, outside Pontevedra; phone: 986-731092) can arrange tours around the fjord-like Rías Bajas of Galicia, as well as trips to stately inland manor estates for groups with a minimum of 6 riders. Accommodations include farmhouses, fishermen's cottages, or hotels. Outings are scheduled irregularly, most often around public holidays. Otherwise, group prices can be negotiated by arrangement.

GRANADA: No visit to the Andalusian hinterland would be complete without a side trip to the rugged and impressive Alpujarras Range, where experienced mounts negotiate the sharp precipices through chestnut woods, lavender scrubland, and steep pueblos. Tours of 1 to 10 days on the trail are available year-round; each includes approximately 5 hours of daily saddle time and lodging at village inns along the way. Non-riders can accompany the caravan in a covered jeep-type support vehicle. Information: *Viajes Geosud,* 9 Calle Juan de Dios, Madrid 28015 (phone: 91-542-6194), or *Viajes Granatur,* Granada 18412 (phone: 958-223580), or *Rutas Alternativas,* Bubion 18412, Granada (phone: 958-766146).

Each year, during the first week in August, arrangements can be made through any of the above agencies to take part in a week-long excursion that heads from the outskirts of Granada, through the Sierra Nevada (the second highest mountain range in Europe, after the Alps), and into the High Alpujarras, coming down onto the beaches of the Mediterranean around Almuñecar. Most of the riders taking part bring their own horses, but steeds supplied by the organizers are also available.

LEÓN: Seldom visited — except by hunters out for pheasant or skiers on their way to the nearby ski resorts — the extensive facilities offered by this modern campsite complex 25 miles (40 km) north of the provincial capital include access to up to ten horses and guides for 1- to 3-day sallies into the high sierra, visiting an island saltwater lake, the Valdecortero caverns, the hermitage of Valdorria, and more. This is the place to go for those who wish to do some trout fishing. Information: *Campament-Finca* "La Granja," La Vecilla, León 24001 (phone: 987-741222).

NAVARRE: Riders (a minimum of three) can tour one of the farthest-off-the-beaten-track regions in all the Iberian Peninsula, the northern part of the province of Navarre. The route travels along hidden, willow-shrouded rivers, forests of oak and beechnut, hilly pastureland, and up into the foothills of the Pyrenees, where the Cima de San

Martín, the world's second-deepest canyon, is located. One- and 2-week routes are offered. Accommodations consist of simple village inns, with the odd night spent in a hotel. Horses are 7- to 11-year-old mixed Spanish-English veterans. Information: *Viajes Geosud,* 9 Calle Juan de Dios, Madrid 28015 (phone: 91-542-6194).

SEGOVIA: The royal bridle paths laid down by the 14th-century Castilian sovereigns to tie their precarious kingdom together, along the trails of the *mesta* (medieval sheepherders guild), are the arteries leading straight into the heart of ancient Spain. *Rutas a Caballo* brings the highlands of Old Castile, with its castles, churches, hermitages, rivers, and forests, within easy reach of its home base, a ranch set around a centuries-old water mill, Molino de Rio Viejo, 12 miles (19 km) northwest of the provincial capital.

A 2-week excursion leads through the Sierra de Guadarrama, along the Duratón River canyon, and past the royal summer palace of La Granja, stopping in Sepúlveda, Pedraza, Turegano, and other towns with emblazoned palaces gone to ruin after their medieval glory. Departures are scheduled twice monthly, May through August, and once each during March, April, September, and October. A shorter 8-day version of the same route can be booked any month of the year. One-day and weekend outings from the mill are also offered, in which clients not only get to ride a horse, but also get to eat like one! Information: *Rutas a Caballo,* 21 Calle Juan Bravo, Madrid 28006 (phone: 91-576-7629).

EXTRA SPECIAL

EL TRANSHUMANCIA: This is the big chance for closet cowboys. Every year, Spanish cowpunchers round up their stock from the winter pastures of Extremadura and move 'em on up to the cooler grasslands of the Gredos range in a week-long cattle drive that is one of Europe's largest. Visitors can accompany them as they go off branding them dogies and fording the Tagus River, while sampling a lifestyle that did not end when Clint Eastwood left the rawhide range. But in between the long stretches of prairie, visitors will bed down at the luxury *paradores* of Trujillo and Oropesa, and at other stylish hotels. The roundup takes place around the second week of June, but the number of participants is limited. Bring along a pouch of Bull Durham. Information: *Rutas a Caballo, Viajes Nobel,* and *Equestrian Tours Almansur* (see above).

SPAIN FROM THE SADDLE: A solid month in the stirrups, from Segovia down the royal bridle paths running southeast to the Atlantic coast of Andalusia. The route also passes the foothills of the Sierra de Guadarrama into the barren 4,000-foot-high tableland of Avila province, followed by the evergreen oak forests of Extremadura to Guadalupe, Trujillo, Cáceres, and Mérida, up into the Sierra Morena and through the Guadalquivir River Valley to Seville and Arcos de la Frontera. Information: *Rutas a Caballo* (see above), which offers this tour in June and October.

Best Beaches

Welded to Europe by a thin strip of land reinforced by the Pyrenees Mountains, the Iberian Peninsula seems to have been made to maximize its shoreline. The fantastically varied blends of sea, sand, and civilization range from the bathtub-like waters of the Mediterranean to the shivering shocks of the Atlantic surf, from the lonely and lush, mist-soaked greenery of northwest Spain to the teeming glitz of the Costa del Sol.

One way to choose a beach is by its lack of recognition. Since many of Spain's most popular beach resorts are now being reduced to functional blots encased in concrete, visiting them is as much of a return to nature as going to lunch at a salad bar. Many visitors, therefore, carefully take the time to seek out remote and undiscovered ocean paradises, far removed from the sands of mass tourism. Many others, however, head straight for the crowds. For those unable to avoid the large resorts, but wishing to escape the masses, try a visit in late August or September.

BALEARIC ISLANDS: In an archipelago whose recent history is a catalogue of famous visitors, ranging from the Spanish royal family on Majorca to a generation's worth of hippies on Ibiza, the number of people who share these beaches is in inverse proportion to the time one invests in reaching them. Palma de Mallorca, seemingly everyone's first stop, is a busy port city complete with condos, a cathedral, and convention-size hotels. Miles of sandy beaches stretch to the east; those from Ca'n Pastilla to El Arenal are lined with high-rise hotels, restaurants, and discos, known collectively as the Playa de Palma. To the west lie a cluster of smaller beaches — Cala Major, Palma Nova, Magaluf, and, beyond the Bay of Palma, Paguera. The smaller island of Minorca has miles of solitary pine-ringed beaches, sloping countrysides, and historic ruins, making it a worthwhile trek from even the tiniest town. Its capital is Mahón, whose serried whitewashed houses were given distinguished Georgian make-overs during the island's British colonial days. Just outside town is the Stone Age village of Trepuco, one of the prehistoric mini-Stonehenges that dot the island (another reason 17th-century colonists thought that Minorca should belong to England). Information: *Oficina de Turismo,* 13 Plaza de la Constitución, Mahón, Minorca 07701 (phone: 971-363790).

EL CABO DE GATA, near Almería, Andalusia: At the southeastern tip of Spain, on the edge of the Costa del Sol and squarely in the middle of nowhere, El Cabo de Gata ("the Cape of the Cat") is the place to go to get away from it all — including hotels, paved roads, and vegetation. The dusty, brush-covered desert that turns imperceptibly into beach looks as if it should be accompanied by the twang and whistled tune of a spaghetti (or paella) western. This is indeed where many a parched cowboy squinted into the pretend Texas sun before whipping out his Colt .45. San José is the cape's only (barely) burgeoning resort, but the city of Almería is only a short drive away, and the town of Mojácar (just up the coast, though a long way around by road) clambers quaintly up a hillside a mile or two back from the shore and has a *parador.* Accommodations here are scarce and by no means luxurious, but the food is good and there are some bargain prices to be enjoyed. Information: *Oficina de Turismo,* Calle Hermanos Machado, Edificios Servicios Multiples, Almería 04004 (phone: 951-234705).

CANARY ISLANDS: An hour's water skiing from the coast of the Western Sahara, the volcanic archipelago of the Canaries belongs technically to Spain, geographically to Africa, and physically to the moon. Join a camel caravan through the gray-brown, crater-marked interior of the island of Lanzarote to the Cueva de los Verdes, a 4-mile tube tunneled by flowing lava. Pause for a dinner of suckling pig roasted over jets of heat escaping through the earth's thin crust, and wash it down with wine made from grapes nurtured in the warm, moist ash that covers the ground. Then descend to the coast through cinder-black fields, between towers of hardened lava, to vast stretches of sand, which make this all seem like a desert island. Those seeking less-tortured landscapes and manicured lawns should head for the larger islands of Tenerife or Grand Canary. Information: on Lanzarote, *Oficina de Turismo,* Parque Municipal, Arrecife 35500 (phone: 928-811860); other islands, *Oficina de Turismo,* Parque de Santa Catalina, Las Palmas 35007, Grand Canary (phone: 928-264623).

COSTA BRAVA, Tossa del Mar, Catalonia: The Costa Brava looks like a landscape painted by Cézanne — straight brushstrokes of ocher cliffs rising from the flat blue base to a daub of pine-tree green, the clean horizontals of Tossa's old port, and the vertical slice of a fishing boat's mast. The town lies in one of this weatherbeaten coast's many snug, sandy inlets; these once gave shelter to Phoenician sailors, but now provide exposure to Nordic bathers. Choose from Tossa's three beaches: La Playa Grande, Mar Menuda, and Es Codolar, each as spectacular as the next. If Tossa seems too tame after dark, or its medieval Villa Vella too old, head for Lloret de Mar, a casino-powered resort where young people sizzle till dawn. If even Tossa seems rowdy, the cliff-top *Parador de Aiguablava* (phone: 972-622162) in Bagur offers contemplative views of the see-through water 400 feet below and the sea-floor rocks 40 feet below that. Information: *Oficina d'Información Turística*, 12 Carrer Ciutadans, Girona 17004 (phone: 972-201694), or at the bus terminal on Carretera de Lloret in Tossa (phone: 972-340108).

COSTA CANTÁBRICA, Santander, Cantabria: This elegant city, almost as close to the powdery snow as it is to the powdery sand, is proud of the quality of its double life — its measured off-season pace and its summer pulsation of students, orchestras, and tourists, all drawn by Santander's spectacular beaches, its festivals of music and dance, and its university. Dense crowds and a rather rough Atlantic are the trademarks of the Playa del Sardinero, while the beaches on the bay are graced by ladies and gentlemen who prefer gentler surf. When visiting the nearby Altamira Caves, it may take a while for the medieval town of Santillana del Mar to stop seeming garishly modern and harshly sunlit after emerging from the prehistoric underground dwellings. Only small groups (up to 10 people per day in summer and 35 per day in winter) may take the 20-minute guided tour of the caves. Tour reservations must be made at least 3 months in advance by letter. Specify the number of people in the group and a range of possible dates for a visit. Reservations: *Director, Centro de Investigación y Museo de Altamira* (Santillana del Mar, Cantabria 39330; phone: 942-818003; open October through May, 10 AM to 1 PM and 3 to 6 PM; June through September, 10 AM to 1:30 PM and 3 to 7:30 PM; admission charge). Comillas, some 40 miles (64 km) from Santander, is a quiet, still-aristocratic resort, where visitors are more likely to run across a marquis than a marquee. The wide Playa Comillas, where the titled sunbathe until they achieve the color of expensive leather, ends in a small pleasure port. The nearby Oyambre Beach is twice as long, with half the tourists. Information: *Oficina de Turismo*, 1 Plaza Porticada, Santander 39001 (phone: 942-310708 or 942-310756).

COSTA DEL SOL, Marbella, Andalusia: The Costa del Sol is a glittering avenue of low-slung bathing suits and high-rise prices, and Marbella is the center of Europe's wealthy worshipers of sun and self. The tennis courts and golf courses are world class, but the primary sport here is people watching. The world's wet set finds shelter in the nearby yacht harbor at Puerto Banus, and the smoothness of Estepona's silky water is guarded from the rough and tumble of the Atlantic by the Rock of Gibraltar, visible from the town's wide beachfront. In the other direction, past Málaga (pass it quickly; it is the tourists' Ellis Island), is the town of Nerja, with a *parador*, a cliff-top boardwalk, and a set of spectacular caves scooped out by water flowing through the soft limestone. Information: in Marbella, *Oficina de Turismo;* 1 Avenida Miguel Cano, Marbella 29600 (phone: 952-771442); the rest of the Costa del Sol, *Oficina de Turismo*, 5 Calle Marqués de Larios, Málaga 29015 (phone: 952-213445) and at Málaga Airport (phone: 952-312044).

RÍAS BAJAS, La Toja, Galicia: The Celts once came to green Galicia and gave it their bagpipes, heaths, and a wet Gaelic fog. But when the mist slides off the fjords of the Rías Bajas, it reveals some of the peninsula's most voluptuous coastline, where meadow lanes link small stone churches to shingle-roofed villages, and the people speak Galician, a language of their own. Reachable by bridge from the town of O Grove, La Toja is a dressed-up island off a sensibly shod shore, complete with large, expensive hotels, swimming pools, golf courses, a spa, and a casino. In a region where the specialty is squid cooked in its own ink, O Grove is religious about its seafood. On the second Sunday in October, the town celebrates the *Feast of the Exaltation of Shellfish*. Information: *Oficina de Turismo,* 2 Calle General Mola, Pontevedra 36001 (phone: 986-850814).

SAN SEBASTIÁN: This pearl of a city on an oyster shell–shaped bay situated between two emerald mountains is one of the most popular resorts in northern Spain. It's in the heart of Euskadi (the Basque Country), where people are fiercely independent and proud of being perceived as different from the rest of Spain. Among other things, the Basques play jai alai, instead of tennis, test their machismo in log-rolling competitions, and run with the bulls in Pamplona every July. Believed to be decendants of the original Stone Age residents of the Iberian Peninsula, the Basques speak a language unrelated to Latin or Gaelic, or to any known language in the history of the world. Fortunately, most of them also speak Castilian (Spanish), especially when dealing with tourists. Although the weather can be unreliable in this part of Spain, during most summer months this slice of coast is thickly spread with oiled bodies. At sunset the crowds flow into the streets of San Sebastián's Old Quarter, drifting between *tapas* bars and stand-up counters, and dining on mini-courses of fresh shrimp, dried cod in tomato sauce, and squid in its own ink. Information: *Oficina de Turismo,* 13 Calle Andía, San Sebastián 20004 (phone: 943-426282).

Gone Fishing

With countless miles of sun-soaked Atlantic and Mediterranean coastline, unpolluted waters, and over 200 varieties of fish, Spain is truly an angler's paradise. Deep-sea enthusiasts can wrestle year-round with swordfish, ray, tuna, shark, trout, and snapper, while freshwater anglers can cast for tench, salmon, carp, trout, pike, bass, barbel, and chub. Although there are numerous lakes and rivers for fishing, it is not a wide-open free-for-all. In order to protect and maintain their fish populations, Spain has instituted numerous restrictions for visiting fishermen, as well as for locals. The country has limits on where and when fishing is permitted, as well as various catch limits. These laws are often so dizzying that the effort to obtain permits and satisfy restrictions may not be worth the day spent at sea. A lottery-style drawing is held each fishing season and permits are issued to the winners. If the maximum number of seasonal permits has been distributed before a visitor's arrival, he or she may be out of luck.

Nearly all game-fishing waters in Spain are tightly controlled by the country's various local and regional governments. Some regions do not allow foreigners to fish in their waters, period! Those that do require the appropriate licenses and permits, but bear in mind that these documents do not grant fishermen the right to clean out the ocean, lakes, rivers, or streams. Spain also has strongly enforced catch limits, as well as strict rules regulating minimum sizes, bait and tackle, and Sunday fishing. Sea angling is discouraged, and is considered illegal in some regions; the seas along the Costa del Sol and the Costa Brava are rare exceptions.

Three types of fishing are available in Spain: deep-sea, river and lake, and underwater. Permits are available from the *Instituto Nacional para la Conservación de la Naturaleza (ICONA)* through each of its offices in the various autonomous communities. In Madrid, *ICONA* is located at 35-41 Avenida Gran Vía de San Francisco (phone: 91-266-8200). The permits vary according to the type of fishing to be practiced. Be warned: Most federations have strange hours; some don't open until after 6 PM, and some are open only from 9 AM to noon. Also, many *ICONA* staff members throughout Spain do not speak English. Permits cost about $10 per day, and a passport is required. Salmon and trout permits cost about $2; a license, which is separate, costs about $10. It is advisable to check with a travel agent or the National Tourist Office of Spain in the US before going. The tourist office provides a fishing map called *Pesca* (fishing), which outlines the best available areas. For the particulars once there, check with the *Spanish Fishing Federation* (3 Calle Navas de Tolosa, Madrid 28013; phone: 91-232-8353). Other good sources include the *Promocion de Caza y Pesca* (41 Duque de Sexto, Madrid, 28010 Spain; phone: 91-276-3661); and the *Consejeria de Agricultura y Cooper-ación de la Comunidad Autónoma de Madrid* (60 Calle Orense, Madrid 28020; phone: 91-455-7703). The most rewarding months for angling are March through August.

ANDALUSIA: Outside the cities of Granada and Jaén are some of the country's best spots for catching trout, crab, pike, and cyprinids. Maximum catches allowed range from 10 to 80. The season is best from March 1 through August 15, except along the Guadalquivir, Jándula, Rumblar, and Guadalén rivers in the fishing reserves of Esta-ción, Andújar, San Juan, San Julian, and Rumblar, where people can fish (mostly for cyprinids) year-round. Surrounded by the ranges of the Sierra Morena and the Segura, this is one of the most scenic and enjoyable fishing sites around. Information: *Oficina de Turismo,* 10 Avenida de Madrid, Jaén 23008 (phone: 953-222737).

CANTABRIAN COAST: Wedged between the Basque Country to the east and Gal-icia to the west, this area is one of Spain's most unspoiled. Choose a base in Santander, Oviedo, Pontevedra, or Lugo, and experience the pleasures of medieval living. This natural paradise remains virtually untouched, and visitors will relish in its history, artistry, modesty, and gorgeous beaches. On top of all that, fresh fish is never far away. This is the place for catching salmon and enjoying a meal while overlooking the twinkling waters. Information: *Oficina de Turismo,* 1 Plaza Porticada, Santander 39001 (phone: 942-310708 or 942-310756), or *Consejeria de Ganaderia, Agricultura y Pesca de la Diputación Regional de Cantabria,* 1 Pasaje de la Puntida, Santander 39071 (phone: 942-312969).

CASTILE-LEÓN: Head to Avila, Burgos, or Seville for some of the best angling central Spain has to offer. Restrictions apply a bit more heavily here, to the point where people have to check their days for fishing. Usually, Fridays and Saturdays are all right. Catches are restricted as well; the take-home limit ranges from 6 to 10. Best bets are trout and cyprinids. Information: *Oficina de Turismo,* 4 Plaza de la Catedral, Avila 05001 (phone: 918-211287), or *Oficina de Turismo,* 7 Plaza de Alonso Martinez, Burgos 09003 (phone: 947-203125).

CATALONIA: Most avid fishermen know the areas around Barcelona, Girona, and Lleida as some of the most prolific year-round spots for catching trout, black bass, and cyprinids. Like other areas, strict restrictions apply. Also check out the areas along the Costa Brava. These rough waters are perfect for underwater fishing. Check with *ICONA* or the local tourist office for details. The Catalan Pyrenees are also good for trout and salmon. About half of the 250 lakes in the Pyrenees National Park are stocked with various kinds of trout, and there is at least one good fishing stream in each valley. Information: *Patronat Municipal de Turisme de Barcelona,* 658 Gran Via de les Corts Catálanes, Barcelona 08008 (phone: 93-301-7443 or 93-317-2246; El Prat Airport, phone: 93-325-5829), or *Consejeria de Agricultura, Ganaderia y Pesca de la Generalidad de Catalunya,* 329 Carrer Còrsega, Barcelona 08037 (phone: 93-237-7862).

Freewheeling by Two-Wheeler

Because of the mild climate in Spain, touring by bicycle is easy and the itinerary possibilities are nearly inexhaustible. Visitors who pedal through the Spanish countryside will get to know parts of the country that most vacationers never see. These are the real sights, the hidden enclaves still untouched by tourism. Leisurely bicycle rides pass through tiny fishing villages and medieval towns dotted with Moorish ruins. In Spain, a bike ride can cover a variety of terrain, from the hilly land of olive groves to flat vineyards and lush countryside overflowing with orange and lemon trees. There's an unleashed sense of freedom out on the open road; days are spent exploring, always wondering what lies ahead when climbing over the next hill.

Those who have traveled around Europe by bicycle before will find that a cycling vacation in Spain is slightly more primitive than in most other Western European countries. There is hardly an abundance of sophisticated repair shops, nor even the guarantee of well-surfaced secondary roads (though Spain is getting there). Bicycle rentals are available in both countries, but not omnipresent. Intermediate and diehard cyclists will want to bring their own bicycles and gear. Airlines will generally transport bikes as part of passengers' personal baggage, but they may insist that the entire bike be crated; check with the airline before departure. Also be sure to confirm insurance coverage. And note that when traveling by train in Spain, a bike (like luggage) must be placed in the last car, so make sure that it is properly labeled with name, address, and the stations of origin and destination. A sturdy lock is another sensible precaution.

Some cyclists choose to travel alone through Spain. Others, however, team up with fellow cyclists and soon become fast friends. The natives are so friendly, they will practically apologize if they cannot accompany a rider to his or her destination (many riders often wind up staying in one place longer than they had planned). It does help, however, to have a rudimentary understanding of Spanish, especially when touring the rural routes, as most people in the countryside do not speak English. A pocket dictionary is heartily recommended. As usual, taking along a basic set of tools and spares, including a tire pump, puncture repair kit, tire levers, spoke key, oil can, batteries and bulbs, rag, extra spokes, inner tubes and tires, pliers, and odd nuts and bolts is also a good idea. Traveling with a minimal amount of cash and a credit card is also advised. In addition, take along a good map; Michelin generally has the best. In Madrid, check out the maps and books at *La Tienda Verde* (The Green Shop; 38 Calle Maudes; phone: 91-533-0791), which stocks the best assortment on naturalist tours; books are available in both Spanish and English. In Barcelona, try *Liberia Quera* (2 Carrer Petritxol; phone: 93-318-0743) for good maps and guides of Catalonia.

If the thought of biking alone is less than a satisfactory vacation idea, there are numerous organized bicycle tours in both countries. For information on bicycle tours, see *Camping and Caravanning, Hiking and Biking,* GETTING READY TO GO.

When cycling in Spain, always remember that it is more relaxing and enjoyable to take it slowly and enjoy the country's sights and sounds. After choosing a region, consult the local tourist literature. Then plot out the tour on a large-scale highway map of the country. Base daily mileage on what usually iscovered on the road at home, but be sure to allot time for en route dawdling — chats with the natives, walks through ruined castles, wine and *tapas* at the local bar.

ANDALUSIA: This region's warm year-round climate, well-marked and well-paved roads, and scenery rank it as one of the best places to go biking in Spain. Home to feisty flamenco dancers and sun-splashed villages, Andalusia also boasts three of the country's most fascinating cities: Granada, Córdoba, and Seville. Begin the tour in Granada, with a steep ride up to the Alhambra, a complex of palaces, fortresses, and gardens built during the 13th and 14th centuries. Then meander in Columbus's historic footsteps to Sante Fe, the city where King Ferdinand and Queen Isabel signed the famous agreement sponsoring the explorer's famous voyage. Next, head to Córdoba, one of Spain's oldest cities. Along the way, the route skirts past two rivers, the Marbella and the Guadajoz. The terrain along the route is fairly easy, consisting mostly of gentle downhill slopes and flat land. The road begins to climb just beyond the small village of Torres Cabrera. At the top of the next stretch, the slope of Lobaton (best climbed with a 20–24 gear ratio), awaits a picture-postcard view of Córdoba, which is reached by an easy descent. The main attraction here is the Mezquita, the Arab palace famous for its red-and-white arches. Other Córdoba attractions include its synagogue and its European-style cafés; at the latter, local women casually dance the flamenco. The city's roads are narrow and cobbled, but soon after leaving the city limits, following the Avenida de Medina Azahara, they get better. Heading south toward Seville, the route passes through alternating views of extensive fields and barren wastelands. Occasionally, a fortress pokes its revered head in the distance. Seville is one of the most romantic cities in Spain and one of its most touristic. The roads are well marked, the scenes full of history and intrigue. Visit the old Jewish Quarter and the Santa Cruz barrio, as well as the cathedral and the Alcázar. Always be careful to lock up the bike and take off one of its wheels; unfortunately, caution is necessary here (as in most major Spanish cities), as crime has become an all-too-frequent problem. After Seville, it's a 1-hour ride northeast to Carmona, once a thriving Arab stronghold, to view its famous 14th-century mansions. Stop for lunch at Carmona's *Parador del Rey Don Pedro* (phone: 954-141010), the former palace of the king called Pedro el Cruel (Peter the Cruel). Information: *Oficina de Turismo,* Casa de los Tiros, 19 Calle Pavanezas, Granada 18009 (phone: 958-221022 or 958-225990); *Oficina de Turismo,* 10 Calle Torrijos, Córdoba 14003 (phone: 957-471235 or 957-483112); and *Oficina de Turismo,* 21 Avenida de la Constitución, Seville 41004 (phone: 954-22-1404).

BASQUE COUNTRY: The hilly Basque Country is best known for the town of Guernica, made famous by Pablo Picasso's painting of the same name, depicting the horrors of the Spanish Civil War. It is an interesting area to explore because its culture and its people — even its language — are quite different from the rest of Spain. The area will appeal to cyclists who enjoy diverse geography. The tour rolls past rugged mountains and stony undulations to soft, sloping, wide sandy shores and steep, pine-covered hillsides. In San Sebastián, the road along the *puerto*'s edge travels past some of the best seafood restaurants serving fresh food caught that day. Cycle along the Bilbao coast for some of the finest and most surprising scenery along the North Atlantic Coast. Information: *Oficina de Turismo,* 13 Calle Andía, San Sebastián 20004 (phone: 943-426282).

CASTILE-LEÓN: This is a land of fairy-tale images, including that of El Escorial, King Philip II's somber yet lavish palace-monastery near Madrid; the near-perfect 11th-century walled city of Avila, framed by the snow-capped ridge of the Sierra de Gredos; and Segovia, home to an ancient Roman aqueduct and the Alcázar, a medieval castle that was the model for Snow White's Castle in *Disneyland* in California. This trip pedals past the royal palace and gardens of La Granja de San Ildefonso, often referred to as the Versailles of Spain, and the romantic spiraling cathedrals of Valladolid. Start either in Madrid or at El Escorial, and plan enough time for a visit to the *Valle de los Caídos* (Valley of the Fallen), a spectacular memorial to those who died in the Spanish Civil War. A huge basilica containing the tombs of soldiers from both sides has been hollowed into a mountain. Generalísimo Francisco Franco, who ordered the monument's construction, is also buried here. Information: *Oficina de Turismo,* 10 Calle Floridablanca, San Lorenzo de El Escorial, Madrid 28036 (phone: 91-890-1554); *Oficina de Turismo,* 4 Plaza de la Catedral, Avila 05001 (phone: 918-211387); and *Oficina de Turismo,* 10 Plaza Mayor, Segovia 34001 (phone: 911-430323).

CATALAN PYRENEES: Intermediate pedalers will enjoy the challenge of this region, as it is filled with a number of ups and downs, but the views here are so spectacular that even beginners should give it a try. The area is the home of many of Spain's better ski resorts, including Baqueira-Beret and Tuca-Betrén, and during spring and summer, rich green and yellow fields crisscross the wide valleys and small undiscovered villages. Because of the proximity to France, the French influence on the food and the people here is very obvious. Ask the staff at the tourist office for the map *Valles Superiores del Segre/Ariege,* which covers the High Urgell, Cerdanya, and the Ribes Valley. A favorite tour is through the Aigües Tortes National Park, with the Sant Maurici Lake, just south of Val d'Aran. This national park is a wonderland of crashing waterfalls and serene lakes, which makes for very pleasant bicycling. Information: *Oficina d'Información Turística*, Passeis Avenida del Valira, La Seu d'Urgell, Lleida 25700 (phone: 973-351511).

COSTA DEL SOL: Although this area along Spain's southern coast falls under the jurisdiction of the region of Andalusia, it warrants a special mention. This tour passes through hills that drop off into the gentle surf of the Mediterranean and along roads that coil around the crashing waves. The Costa del Sol officially extends from Tarifa, west of Gibraltar, in the Spanish southwest, to the town of Cabo de Gata, just east of Almería. Those seeking the action and international flavor of some of Europe's most popular and lively beach resorts should pedal into the crowded resorts of Málaga, Marbella, and Torremolinos. Those seeking the scenic but quiet Spanish coast, without the trappings of mass tourism, may prefer the more forgotten towns of Vejar de la Frontera, Salobreña, and Ronda. Throughout the coast, the beaches are great, the weather is perfect, and the resort atmosphere instills that "get away from it all" vacation feeling. One of the best places to enjoy a fiery Andalusian sunset is from the Puente Nuevo in Ronda, where the cliffs glow a soothing orange and red, reflecting the strong Spanish sun. In general, the roads along the Costa del Sol are in fairly good condition and easy to follow. Cyclists traveling in the off-season should prepare to ride west to east, thus avoiding the strong easterly winds. Also not to be missed is the great Rock of Gibraltar. The view is breathtaking along the Straits of Gibraltar all the way to the Moroccan coast. Although the area itself is more British than Spanish (Gibraltar is a British Crown Colony), a visit here offers a chance to view one of the Iberian Peninsula's most famous sights. Information: *Oficina de Turismo*, 5 Calle Marqués de Larios, Málaga 29015 (phone: 952-213445).

COSTA BLANCA: The "White Coast," which extends from Denia down to Torrevieja, is another resort rich in natural beauty that is perfectly conditioned for the cyclist. Like the Costa del Sol, it has its share of unspoiled spots. Venture to Alicante, inlaid with festive red tiles and graced with the famous Castillo de Santa Bárbara, full of secret passageways and tunnels. Nearby, Elche is known for its half-million palm trees, which supply all of Spain with fronds for *Palm Sunday.* Information: *Oficina de Turismo*, 2 Explanada de España, Alicante 03002 (phone: 965-212285).

COSTA BRAVA: This coast is rougher and rockier than its sister resort areas, but just as magnificent. Most people flock here during the summer, so try to visit during the off-season, when it is more tranquil and easier to explore. Be careful, though, as many hotels and restaurants close at the end of the high season. The roads here are well paved, but the terrain is often steep, physically challenging, and, in some spots, even dangerous. This tour is not recommended for novice cyclists. Information: *Oficina de Turismo*, 4 Calle Iglesia, Tossa de Mar, Girona 17320 (phone: 972-340108).

NAVARRESE PYRENEES: There is probably no area in Spain quite as suited for quiet pedaling than this region along the valleys of the Arga and Aragón rivers, where mountain valleys swoop down to the dusty red desert. Begin this itinerary in Sangüesa, an ancient town on the Aragon River, and travel northeast, past the large and austere Cistercian monastery of Leyre, whose ancient church with its 12th-century crypt was the final resting place of the Kings of Navarre. Continue west into the sleepy town of Roncal, with its cobbled streets and stone houses, and the more upbeat town of Isaba, just to the north. Ahead lies Roncesvalles, historically known for the *Song of Roland,* an epic poem that romanticized the defeat of Charlemagne's rear guard during its retreat from Spain. The monastery here marked the beginning of the famous Pilgrims' Route as it entered Spain from France en route to Santiago de Compostela in the northwestern corner of the country. Don't be surprised by the sign warning of cattle on the loose in the valley of Valcarlos, a few miles from the French border, which marks the end of this tour. Information: *Oficina de Turismo,* 2 Calle Mercado, Sangüesa, Navarre 31400 (phone: 948-870329).

Great Walks and Mountain Rambles

Almost any walker will say that it is the footpaths of a country — not its roadways — that show off the local landscape to best advantage. Closer to earth than when driving or even biking, those on foot notice details that might not otherwise come to their attention: valleys perfumed with edelweiss, for instance, or hillsides dotted with medieval villages; sheep gambol in the shade of fig and cork oak trees, and the friendly company of the sun makes the leaves shine and the mountaintops glisten.

The geographic diversity of the Iberian Peninsula makes walking here a wonderful journey full of surprises. Many paths were literally walked into existence by generations of people traveling to work, market, or church, or were carved by medieval pilgrims and advancing or retreating soldiers. Today, there is terrain for walkers and hikers of all abilities — from picnic stroller to fearless alpinist. The high mountain ranges of Spain's Picos de Europa and the Pyrenees, and the green valleys of the Basque Country all make for peaceful, pleasant strolls or climbs. Spain also boasts a number of national parks to explore, while visitors less attracted to wilderness will find villages perched on high, with cobblestone streets, mansions, churches, ruins, and shops that are guaranteed to hold their interest and challenge their feet. Add to this a climate that is generally benign (Spain's southern coast is a Mediterranean paradise year-round), friendly natives, and good food — all the ingredients of a perfect expedition.

Before choosing a specific area of the country for hiking, look at a general road map of Spain that shows physical characteristics, so as not to opt for terrain that is too demanding for one's level of fitness. For those who are sedentary, the choice of a mountainous region would be foolhardy. To make the outing safe and pleasant, it is imperative for hikers to know their own limits. Unless they are very experienced, hikers always should stick to the defined areas — and *always* let someone know the planned destination and time of expected return (leave a note on the car if hiking alone). Those who prefer going as part of an organized tour should contact a local hiking club, a travel agent, or one of the many tour packagers specializing in hiking tours. For information on Iberian hikes, see *Camping and Caravanning, Hiking and Biking,* GETTING READY TO GO.

Since hot weather is not necessarily a welcome companion on a walk, it's best to avoid the southern regions in midsummer. And since it can get warm almost anywhere in Spain between May and September, the wise walker will get most of a day's journey done before midday. Basic hiking essentials should include a sturdy pair of shoes and socks, long pants if headed into heavily wooded areas, a canteen, a hat, sunblock, rainwear, and something warm, just in case. It is always best to dress in layers. Also make sure to wear clothes with pockets, or bring along a pack so that both hands can remain free. Some useful but often overlooked tools include a jackknife, waterproof matches, a map, a compass, and snacks. In the more remote areas, a backpack, sleeping bag and pad, cookstove, food, and other gear are required.

Spain is consistent only in its diversity. There are the extreme peaks of the highlands, the Pyrenees, and the Picos de Europa, and the lowlands of the Basque Country — where, incidentally, the rain does not fall mainly on the plain. The most advisable times of year to hike these areas are late spring and early autumn, when the flora and fauna are at their most vibrant and the temperatures are at their most delightful. Always check the weather in advance. Like the topography, the temperature varies enormously from region to region; the high plains of the center suffer from fierce extremes — stiflingly hot in summer and bitterly cold in winter. The Atlantic Coast, in contrast, has a permanent tendency to dampness and a relatively brief summer. The Mediterranean is warm virtually the entire year.

BASQUE COUNTRY, San Sebastián: The Basque Country is a land of contrasts. Just steps away from its industrial centers sit isolated hamlets, submerged in the silent surroundings of valleys and forests. The most spectacular sight here is the city of San Sebastián, and the green mountains and thundering ocean that surround it. Climb to the top of Mt. Igueldo, at the far side of the bay, for the best view of the countryside and the Atlantic. Information: *Club Vasco de Acampado,* 19 Calle San Marcial Bajo, San Sebastián 20008 (phone: 943-428479), or *Club de Montaña Kresala,* 9 Calle Euskal Erria, San Sebastián 20003 (phone: 943-420905).

CATALAN PYRENEES: Good, fairly gentle trails, coupled with plenty of historic sights and a hospitable nature, make this northeast corner of Spain a sensible choice for the less ambitious walker in need of wayside distractions. By virtue of its location (just across from the border with France), hikers can experience a variety of cultures, languages, and foods. In La Seu d'Urgell, nature buffs will have a field day roaming quiet peaks, scouting for wild mushrooms. Other expeditions lie in the valley of Nuria, where wildflowers and waterfalls dot the landscape. Also popular is the majestic Puigmal peak, rising over 9,500 feet, and the nearby Queranca Lakes. Information: *Oficina d'Información Turística,* Avenida del Valira, La Seu d'Urgell, Lleida 25700 (phone: 973-351511).

AIGÜES TORTES NATIONAL PARK AND SANT MAURICI LAKE, Catalan Pyrenees: This is for the hiker who rejoices in waterfalls and serene lakes. Some 20,000 years ago, a glacier blasted its way through what is now northern Lleida province, leaving behind a panoramic wonderland. The park is reached either from the town of Bo Hi to the west or from Espot, on its eastern edge. The park's tourist office provides numerous hiking suggestions. Of special interest is a 16-mile (26-km) walk that passes the mountain lakes surrounding Estany de la Llosa and enters the valley of Estany de Sant Maurici. Wild goats roaming the area are a frequent sight. Less traveled but equally rewarding is the path leading up to Aigües Tortes. Along the way, the trail passes through the Vall d'Bo Hi, reputedly one of the best places to view Romanesque architecture in the world. The land is predominantly rural and dotted with churches dating from the 12th and 13th centuries. The park is best viewed in late spring, summer, and autumn. Information: *Oficina d'Información Turística,* Arc de Pont, Lleida 25002 (phone: 973-248120).

COVADONGA MOUNTAIN NATIONAL PARK, near Oviedo: Separating the provinces of Asturias and Castile-León, this national park lays claim to the western region of the Picos de Europa and boasts some of the most beautiful scenery, as well as the largest number of annual visitors. It was here, according to legend, that the Virgin Mary interceded with God on behalf of the king, Don Pelayo, and created an invisible shield, ensuring his warriors of victory against the Moors. Today, the park caters to both naturists and religious entourages. The Santa Cueva (Sacred Cave) is where Don Pelayo supposedly prayed to the Virgin. For those seeking solitude, it's best to avoid the park on and around September 8, when the area celebrates the *Day of the Virgin* with numerous festivities. During this period, head instead for the hills and enjoy the real master of the park: the wildlife that inhabits it. The higher you hike, the more likely you are to encounter a fleeting glimpse of a bear, wolf, wildcat, or fox. At the mountain's base are two lakes of glacial origin: El Enol and La Ercina. Both swimming and camping are permitted here. The best times to visit are summer and autumn. The area gets a lot of rain, so be sure to bring the appropriate clothing. Information: *Federación Asturiana de Montañismo,* 16 Calle Melquiades Alvarez, Oviedo 33007 (phone: 985-211099).

NAVARRESE PYRENEES, east of Pamplona: It takes a dedicated hiker to navigate his or her way through this rugged profile of the mountains and the valleys along the Arga and Aragon rivers. In return for the effort, however, the intrepid will get a close glimpse of some vital bits of history. The 24-mile (40-km) route from the Pyrenees through Navarre's mountain passes bisects the river valleys and is the same route used by thousands of 11th- and 12th-century pilgrims on their journey from France to Santiago de Compostela and the shrine of St. James. In Yesa, the route leads past a weathered stone monastery, once a center of power and wealth and the favorite charity and residence of the Kings of Navarre during the Middle Ages. Other remnants of medieval life worth exploring include nearby Tierman, an abandoned town on the shore of Yesa Lake, and Javier Castle, once a fortress and now a Jesuit College. Upon moving west through the mountains, each valley becomes a bit more green and moist. Noteworthy towns along the way include Roncal, Isaba, and Ochagava. Of special note is the town of Roncesvalles, historically known for the *Song of Roland,* the epic poem about Charlemagne's retreat from Spain, and the starting point for many medieval pilgrims. Information: *Oficina de Turismo,* 3 Calle Duque de Ahumada, Pamplona 31002 (phone: 948-220741).

ORDESA AND MONTE PERDIDO NATIONAL PARK, near Jaca, Aragonese Pyrenees: Here, in Spain's northeast, is terrain that will please hikers of all abilities. This is one of the country's most beautiful areas. Its jewel-like gorges and waterfalls, steep mountains flowered with edelweiss, and dazzling forests of pine and beech are enough to encourage even the most sedentary of hikers. The park's finest scenic assets lie near the magnificent Escuain Gorge and the Yago River. There are also four distinct valleys to explore; the visitors' center provides a guided itinerary with recommended routes. The Ordesa area is a walker's paradise, with many routes available. One way to learn more about the park is to buy the red *Cartographic Guide to Ordesa, Vignemale, and Monte Perdido,* about $2 in local bookstores. Although written in Spanish, its maps are easy to understand.

Recommended itineraries include Torla–Ordesa, an easy 8-mile (13-km) hike that winds through beautiful valleys and forests. Cross the bridge below Torla (Puente de la Glera) and follow the trail marked Camino de Turieto. More ambitious hikers may want to undertake the Torla–Gavarnie tour, a 24-mile (38-km) walk to the French town of Gavarnie. Following the valley, turn left at the river fork and continue along the Ara River for about 6 miles (10 km) before reaching the hamlet of San Nicolas de Bujaruelo. The trail goes directly into the mountains, crosses through the 828-foot-high Puerto de Bujaruelo, and descends straight into Gavarnie. For an even more scenic view of the Pyrenees, experienced hikers should take the Valle de Ordesa–Sierra Custodia–Valle de Vio triangle, which winds past thundering waterfalls, pine forests, and alpine valleys. Another challenging adventure is the 44-mile (71-km) Ordesa–Gavarnie trail, which starts near the Ordesa information hut and shoots straight up the steep gorge of the Circo de Salarons.

The Soasa Circle is a more realistic and relatively easy walk through the natural wonders of the Aragonese Pyrenees. Take a hearty lunch, as this walk covers a good 28 miles (45 km). Begin by following the gently sloping Arazas River eastward to the surging Cascada del Abanico. Here, the river roars over the rocks at lightning speeds. For a close view, cross the bridge a few minutes upstream and come back down to the observation point, situated on a huge rock. Continue toward Soasa, past more thundering falls, until the path leaves the forest. Once beyond the Gradas de Soasa (stepped waterfalls), the valley broadens and flattens. The fan-shaped Cascada de Soasa at the far end of the valley jets forth from between two cliffs, and is a welcome resting point. This marks the approximate halfway point of the climb; it is also a perfect vantage point for surveying the sweeping panorama of snow-capped peaks: Monte Arruebo, Monte Perdido, and Pico de Anisclo. Cross the river and follow the semi-hidden path that hems the tree line into mountain goat territory. The mountaintops and meadows blanketed with woolly-leafed edelweiss and multicolored butterflies are inspiring. But don't get too light-footed. The last leg of the excursion is a challenging climb, as the path clambers near jutting rocks and abrupt edges. It tumbles down, down, down, with views of the parking lot below teasing the mind until it is reached in about an hour.

The best areas of the park can usually be covered in 2 to 4 days. Accommodations can be found in the nearby towns of Huesca and Jaca. There is also the *Parador Monte Perdido* in Bielsa, in the province of Huesca (inside the park, at the head of the Pineta Valley; phone: 974-501011). The best time of year to visit the park is from mid-July through late August. Information: *Oficina de Turismo,* 2 Avenida Regimiento de Galicia, Jaca 22700 (phone: 974-360098), or *Oficina de Turismo,* 23 Calle Coso Alto, Huesca 22002 (phone: 974-225778).

PICOS DE EUROPA, near Potes: This stretch of remote territory is especially popular with backpackers and experienced hikers, who take advantage of its numerous trails that transcend the range's jagged profile, valleys, and lower slopes. Always be sure to check weather forecasts before setting off on a hike in this region, as the area is partial to sudden drops in temperature and surprise rainstorms. Note that only well-equipped and very advanced alpinists should attempt to scale the peaks themselves. Accommodations are few and far between here, and most hikers use the nearby town of Potes, along the Deva River, as a base. Quiet and snowbound in winter, Potes becomes a cosmopolitan climber's town in summer. Information: *Federación Asturiana de Montañismo,* 16 Calle Melquiades Alvarez, Oviedo 33007 (phone: 985-211099). Detailed maps, including those published by the Instituto Geográfico Nacional and the Federación Española de Montañismo, are available at *Bustamante,* a photo shop in Potes's main square; each costs about $3.

SIERRA DE GUADARRAMA, near Madrid: This pine-covered mountain range, halfway between Madrid and Segovia, is one of the most beautiful in central Spain. Particularly noteworthy are the alpine village of Cercedilla and the breathtaking mountain pass of Puerto de Navacerrada, the geographic border between Old and New Castile. Cercedilla is a town of picturesque alpine chalets and cow pastures. Its *piscinas* (ponds), set below cascading waterfalls, are a popular summer attraction. The peaks of Puerto de Navacerrada reach 6,102 feet and offer excellent views of the surrounding Castilian plains. Nearby, in the town of Rascafría, take a swim in La Laguna de Peñalara, a beautiful lagoon situated in a valley below the commanding mountain peak. Use either Madrid or Segovia as a base, but be forewarned: The weather here is wild, so dress warmly, even in summer. Information: *Oficina de Turismo,* 1 Calle Princesa, Madrid 28008 (phone: 91-541-2325), or *Oficina de Turismo,* 10 Plaza Mayor, Segovia 34001 (phone: 911-430328).

SIERRA MORENA, near Córdoba: Few travelers know of the Sierra Morena, and even most Andalusians have trouble placing it. Though not one of Spain's more dramatic mountain ranges (its highest peak rises to just over 4,300 feet), it is nonetheless an enjoyable and very mellowing climb. The best time to visit is in March and April, when the flowers are in full bloom. Expect to be given a private performance by armies of frogs and turtles that live along the stream. Most often, they are a hiker's only companions. The Moorish towns of Córdoba and Jaén make the best bases and starting points. Information: *Oficina de Turismo,* 10 Calle Torrijos, Córdoba 14003 (phone: 957-471235), or *Oficina de Turismo,* 10 Avenida de Madrid, Jaén 23008 (phone: 953-222737).

SIERRA NEVADA, near Granada: The tallest range in all of Spain is also the most challenging. Even in summer, the weather is severe, with whipping winds and temperatures that drop considerably at night. The peaks of these mountains, Mulhacén (11,407 feet) and Veleta (11,128 feet), are best tackled as a day trip, using Granada as a base. Particularly rewarding is the 25-mile (40-km) route surrounding Las Alpujarras, the small white villages that line the range's base. Capilera is the closest thing to a tourist center in the area, offering good accommodations and a few other adventurous activities. Those who decide to climb farther than Las Alpujarras should be no less than intermediate climbers, able to handle sudden wind changes and a fair ammount of rough terrain. The region is best tackled in the summer, long after all the snow has melted. Spain's highest peak and ultimate vantage point is Mulhacén, often most accessible after May. The area is noticeably secluded; wild goats and birds are often the only company. Nearby are the town of Trevelez, Spain's highest community, renowned for its ham, and the cozy hamlet of Pitres. An alternative route is a hike up Mt. Veleta. Buses run year-round and climb as high as they can; from mid-June on, they can usually make it clear up the road to a point from where it's a treacherous 3-hour hike to the peak. Under clear skies, the view extends all the way to the Rif Mountains of Morocco. The most detailed map of the region is published by the *Federación Española de Montañismo* ($3), available in both English and Spanish in most of Granada's bookstores. Information: *Oficina de Turismo,* Casa de los Tiros, 19 Calle Pavanezas, Granada 18001 (phone: 958-225990).

TORCAL MOUNTAINS, near Antequera: Some 30 miles (48 km) north of Málaga, and just south of the tidy agricultural-industrial town of Antequera, await two circular trails that will enthrall adventurous hikers who delight in exploring desolate rock gardens. The path marked with yellow arrows is about 8 miles (13 km); the red-arrowed tour covers about 12 miles (19 km). Both feature spectacular vistas of curious rock formations and begin and end in Antequera, at the *refugio* (refuge hut) at the base of the mountain. Information: *Oficina de Turismo,* Palacio de Nájera, Antequera 29200 (phone: 952-841827).

For the Mind

Museums, Monuments, and Ruins

 From paleolithic bison to Picasso's bulls, Spanish painting has always been wildly intense: El Greco's emaciated, longing saints, Goya's *Disasters of War,* Picasso's *Guernica,* Velázquez's portraits of monarchs in armor, rearing their horses against threatening skies. All depict a passion released in religious fury or desperate wars, against a backdrop of deserts, mountains, and gorge-top towns.

A series of conquests, losses, and clever marriages left Roman ruins, Moorish castles, medieval turrets, and sinuous spires sculpted out of the land all over the Iberian Peninsula. Preserved and renovated, or ruined and crumbling, they stand as reminders of a turbulent and fascinating past. The Alhambra stands starkly against the Sierra Nevada, while Cuenca's *Museum of Spanish Abstract Art* hangs 200 feet above the rushing Huécar River, and Segovia's Alcázar is raised on its natural, jagged pedestal above the stark Castilian plain.

Spain has fostered the development of some of the most original artists in Europe. While some of the works of Velázquez, Goya, Picasso, and others have made their way to various museums and art galleries in the US, the bulk of the masters' works remain where they originated; for example, canvases by Murillo and Zurbarán hang in Seville's *Museo de Bellas Artes* (unfortunately, large parts of this *Fine Arts Museum* are closed for renovation until later this year, although a few rooms, displaying the most prized paintings, are open), and El Greco's treasures grace museum walls in Toledo.

A museum can be all the more pleasurable if a few simple guidelines are kept in mind. Rather than one long visit to a large museum, plan several short ones, staying for an hour and taking in no more than a dozen fine works each time. There's no fatigue quite like aching, yawning museum fatigue — which has been described as the dread "museum foot" — and when it has set in, merely sitting in front of a Picasso for 3 minutes will not effect a cure.

WALLS OF AVILA, Castile-León: Avila's ramparts look like a row of sharpened teeth amid the dry stubble of the battlefield-brown plain. The 11th-century walls seem unweathered and brand-new, and the stocky, somewhat rectilinear, 12th-century stone cathedral looms over and leans on them, glaring out at the forbidding mass of the Sierra de Gredos. Construction of the wall began in 1090; it took 10 years and more than 2,000 workers to complete 90 semicircular towers, 9 gates, several posterns, and innumerable battlements along an 8,200-foot perimeter. It may feel as if the only way to get into the city is with a battering ram, but only a walk through a gate in the walls is necessary to see banks and cafés and hear the televised sounds of soccer games blaring through open windows. From the gardens of the *Parador Raimundo de Borgoña,* it's an easy climb up to the battlements for a squint into the distance for an approaching army of Moors. Also patrol the town's perimeter from the outside — though you may find yourself glancing nervously up at the battlements, checking for boiling oil. Information: *Oficina de Turismo,* 4 Plaza de la Catedral, Avila 05001 (phone: 91-821-1287).

FUNDACIÓ JOAN MIRÓ, Barcelona, Catalonia: This museum is a light, airy tribute to Catalonia's Surrealist master and native son, Joan Miró, who was also an outstanding sculptor and weaver — as his 35-foot-long *Tapis de la Fundació* demonstrates. The permanent exhibit spans Miró's life, and a stroll through the galleries illuminates the artist's various styles and mediums — most evident in his *Self-Portrait,* which is, in effect, two pictures on one canvas. Miró's images are surreal, and emphasize his commitment to make even the most ordinary object complex. The museum hosts frequent special exhibitions, and also features a library and a bookstore. Information: *Fundació Joan Miró,* Plaça Neptú, Parc de Montjuïc, Barcelona 08004 (phone: 93-329-1908).

MUSEU D'ART DE CATALUNYA, Barcelona, Catalonia: Perched in a park above Barcelona's busy port, this luminous collection of medieval religious panels, carvings, and walls teems with the tumultuous detail of births, benedictions, and agonized deaths. Dragons are slain, saints martyred, and sinners stirred into infernal cauldrons — all beautifully hung, labeled, and lighted. The collection includes 11th-century frescoes peeled off the walls of small Catalonian mountain churches and reassembled on brand-new apses, making this one of the world's great collections of Romanesque and Gothic art — featuring not just frescoes, but also woodcarvings, ceramics, and everyday utensils of medieval life. Of special note is the Gothic altarpiece by Luis Dalmau (active 1428–60), the *Madonna of the Aldermen of Barcelona,* and the excellent 12th-century wall paintings from San Clemente at Tahull. The museum building itself is a sight to be seen: A huge palace built for the *1929 World's Fair,* it covers nearly 8 acres atop Montjuïc, and offers a spectacular view of the city. Information: *Museu d'Art de Catalunya,* Mirador del Palau, Parc de Montjuïc, Barcelona 08004 (phone: 93-423-1824).

MUSEU PICASSO, Barcelona, Catalonia: Although Pablo Picasso lived in France for 69 years, Barcelona was where he spent his student days, and it occupied a warm spot in his heart throughout his life. The museum was founded in 1963 when Jaime Sabartés, a native of Barcelona and friend of Picasso's, presented his collection of the master's work to the city. Picasso himself donated 58 paintings, including 44 bizarre variations of *Las Meninas,* the famous Velázquez painting in Madrid's *Prado.* Later, he donated more than 800 of his lithographs and early works from his years in Málaga and Barcelona (1889–1905), which constitute most of the collection. Information: *Museu Picasso,* 15 Carrer de Montcada, Barcelona 08010 (phone: 93-319-6310).

TEATRE-MUSEU DALÍ, Figueres, Catalonia: This small town, equidistant from the mountains, the sea, and the French border, was the birthplace in 1904 of the late Surrealist artist Salvador Dalí, one of the most eccentric in a profession famous for eccentrics. His sculptures feature a lobster basking on the receiver of a telephone, and a giant woman standing on the hood of a Cadillac. His paintings offer much of the same: A dog collar doubles as a viaduct, locks of hair curl into fruit, and a chest of drawers with huge, bare human feet ascends into heaven. Dalí worked here until 1982, and lived bedridden in the building's Galatea Tower until his death in 1989. The artist is buried in the museum's inner court, beneath the building's great glass dome. Over 300,000 annual visitors make the museum Spain's second most popular (Madrid's *Prado* ranks number one). Information: *Oficina d'Informació Turística,* Plaça del Sol, Figueres 17600 (phone: 972-503155).

ALHAMBRA, Granada, Andalusia: The mountain snow of the Sierra Nevada and the gleaming whitewash of the Albaicín's medieval houses, reflected in Granada's clear sky, illuminate the Alhambra's frosty plaster filigree with a dazzling ray of white. The green shade of the courtyards and gardens, decked with oranges swaying lusciously within reach, and the cool gurgle of the fountains and pools offer refuge from Andalusia's rugged glare. In the darkening years of their rule, the Moorish sultans retreated behind the fortress's forbidding walls to this maze of lavish rooms, decorated with delicate mosaics of minute colored tiles. This was the palace and harem of the Arab conquerors (its name is a corruption of the Arabic for "red castle"), begun during the 14th century. After the Catholic Monarchs conquered it in 1492, it was left to decay. Restoration began during the late 19th century, and today it retains much of its former splendor. The main complex is made up of four areas: the Alcázar, or royal palace; the 16th-century Palace of Carlos V; the Alcazaba, the oldest portion of the fortress; and the Generalife, the summer palace. There are no guided tours in English, but many of the locals who loiter around the main entrance conduct informal English-speaking tours for a small fee. Don't worry; they are legitimate guides, and though the English-language guidebook is adequate, the Alhambra is so colorful and rich with history that it is a good idea to give these locals a try. The admission charge also includes the treasury and the cathedral museum. Also worthwhile is an illuminated nighttime visit. Information: *Oficina de Turismo,* Casa de los Tiros, 19 Calle Pavenezas, Granada 18001 (phone: 958-225990).

MUSEO NACIONAL DEL PRADO, Madrid: One of the world's supreme art museums, the *Prado* is a treasure house of over 4,000 universal masterpieces, a polychrome smorgasbord of Spanish painting, with a rich dessert of Rembrandts and Raphaels. Try a bit of everything, and come back for seconds: Bosch's grotesque and electrifying *Garden of Earthly Delights,* Goya's frothy scenes from Spanish country life and his creamy *Maja Desnuda,* Rubens's portraits with their cherry-red noses and cheeks, El Greco's wild, wine-tinted skies and religious scenes suffused with a pale, lemon-yellow light. And leave some room for *Las Meninas,* Diego Rodríguez de Silva Velázquez's famous *Maids of Honor,* a portrayal of the court during the 17th century. There is also an impressive collection of the works of the Italian masters Fra Angelico, Botticelli, Raphael, Correggio, Caravaggio, Titian, Tintoretto, and Veronese. The neo-classical *Prado* building originally was a natural science museum, later converted into a museum to house the royal art collection. In addition to the main *Prado,* or Villanueva building, the museum also comprises two annexes, the *Casón del Buen Retiro* and the Villahermosa Palace. The Casón del Buen Retiro is home to the *Museum of 19th-Century Spanish Painting,* as well as *Guernica,* Picasso's epic painting of the Spanish Civil War, which, following the artist's instructions, remained in New York's *Museum of Modern Art* until democracy was restored to Spain after Generalísimo Francisco Franco's death. The Villahermosa Palace is currently being redesigned to house the Thyssen-Bornemisza Collection, on long-term loan to the museum and considered the most important private art collection in the world. The *Prado* collection is so vast that it is impossible to savor its wonders in a single visit. If time is limited, it is best to select a few galleries of special interest, or enlist the services of the extremely knowledgeable, government-licensed free-lance guides at the main entrance. Reproductions from the *Prado*'s collection, postcards, and fine-arts books are sold at the shop inside the museum. Information: *Museo Nacional del Prado,* Paseo del Prado, Madrid 28014 (phone: 91-420-2836).

REAL MONASTERIO DE EL ESCORIAL, San Lorenzo de El Escorial, Madrid: Sixteenth-century Spain was fervently, often brutally, Catholic. Its fire-eyed monarchs had defeated the Moors, hunted down heretics, and banished or killed all the Jews who didn't convert. Their wars were fought with God on their side, and their trips to the New World were equal parts of conquest and conversion. King Philip II built the Real Monasterio de San Lorenzo de El Escorial — El Escorial for short — in thanksgiving for his victory over the French at Saint-Quentin in Flanders in 1557. The lean architecture of this royal and religious complex in the mountains outside Madrid bears the mark of Philip's asceticism, but the collection of works by the likes of Ribera, El Greco, Velázquez, Titian, Veronese, and Bosch in the *Nuevos Museos* (New Museums) is sinfully opulent. The combination of truly royal grandeur with monastic austerity here is unique in the world. The small, monastic chambers in the Palacios (Royal Apartments), from which Philip governed the Spanish Empire for 14 years (1584–98), are in stark contrast to the splendor of the rest of the structure. The monastery also houses the Panteón de los Reyes (Royal Pantheon), which contains the remains of 26 Spanish monarchs. Information: *Oficina de Turismo,* 10 Calle Floridablanca, San Lorenzo de El Escorial 28036 (phone: 91-890-1554).

VALLE DE LOS CAÍDOS (Valley of the Fallen), San Lorenzo de El Escorial, Madrid: North of the Monasterio de San Lorenzo de El Escorial, the *Valley of the Fallen* is a spectacular memorial to those who died in the Spanish Civil War. A huge basilica containing the tombs of soldiers from both sides has been hollowed into a mountain. Generalísimo Francisco Franco, who ordered the monument's construction, is also buried here. A granite cross stands 500 feet in the air atop the mountain peak. Information: *Oficina de Turismo,* 10 Calle Floridablanca, San Lorenzo de El Escorial 28036 (phone: 91-890-1554).

UNIVERSIDAD, Salamanca, Castile-León: Formed from golden stone during the Middle Ages, and now well into its golden years, Salamanca's university is pushing a perky 800 years of age. Accumulated centuries of wisdom have given the buildings a soft, restful glow. On the Patio de Escuelas is the university's original main building, erected during the reign of the Catholic Monarchs and bearing a famed Plateresque façade. The leafy curlicues, twisted gargoyles, imaginary birds, and heraldic animals, seem to have been the work of an army of jewelers. The classrooms are pampered and polished, and the only signs of decrepitude are the eroded pews etched with 16th-century graffiti in the Aula de Fray Luis de León. The lecture hall has been kept as it was when the legendary professor, returning to work after 4 years in the Inquisition's jails, started his first class by saying, *"Decíamos ayer . . ."* ("As we were saying yesterday . . ."). At the opposite end of the Patio de Escuelas is the Escuelas Menores (Minor Schools), which has another Plateresque façade and a beautiful courtyard. Information: *Oficina de Turismo,* 41 Gran Vía, Salamanca 37001 (phone: 923-243730).

CUEVAS DE ALTAMIRA, Santillana del Mar, Cantabria: Tucked beneath the soft green cow pastures that roll down to the cloudy Cantabrian beaches, the caves seem chilly and dank today. But to its Stone Age inhabitants, it must have felt like a cozy place to come home to after a hard day chasing bison. Drawings of running, hunted, wounded animals, painted with blood and mineral pigments and incredibly preserved after 16,000 years, cover the walls and ceilings, earning Altamira the title of the "Sistine Chapel of Primitive Art." No more than 10 people a day may take the 20-minute guided tour of the caves in the summer, no more than 35 in winter, and all tour requests must be made in writing 3 months in advance, specifying group size and a range of possible dates for a visit. Send requests to: *Director, Centro de Investigación y Museo de Altamira,* Santillana del Mar, Santander 39001 (phone: 942-818102 or 942-818003).

ROMAN AQUEDUCT, Segovia, Castile-León: A majestic row of double arches, made only of oiled granite blocks, stretches from the dusty-orange hills above the dry Castilian plain to the hilltop city of Segovia. The aqueduct was built some 2,000 years ago without the use of cranes, pumps, or even mortar, but with that sense of elegance that the Romans brought to even their most functional creations. They cut the granite to a perfect, jigsaw fit, then stacked the blocks into a remarkable feat of engineering to siphon spring water to the city from the Acebeda River. On the eastern side of Segovia, the aqueduct is formed by 166 arches in 2 tiers (the lower level forming prized parking spaces), and is 21,500 feet long and 96 feet high. The most impressive frontal view is from Plaza del Azoguejo, where the aqueduct reaches its highest point. Climb up the stairs on the left side of the plaza for an internal view, and a good look at the fairy-tale city below. Information: *Oficina de Turismo,* 10 Plaza Mayor, Segovia 34001 (phone: 911-430323).

REALES ALCÁZARES, Seville, Andalusia: The mosaics, patios, and wrought-stucco windows, the finely tooled ceilings, and the dizzying, interlocking patterns will make the visitor dream of turbaned sultans reclining on oversize cushions and puffing on elaborate pipes. But it was mainly Spanish royalty that took its ease (or was otherwise engaged) in Seville's Alcázar, which was begun in the 14th century by King Peter the Cruel (he was not always a perfect host) and later expanded by Ferdinand and Isabella and by the Holy Roman Emperor Charles V. For all their furor against the Moors, the Spanish monarchs recognized the Moorish talent for palaces. Thus, this lovely Mudéjar creation, the work of Moorish craftsmen left unexpelled after Seville was reconquered in the 13th century. The lavish interior is similar to Granada's Alhambra, but on a smaller scale. Of special note here are the gardens surrounding the Hall of the Ambassadors, full of cheerful Moorish fountains and colorful tiles. Also not to be missed in Seville (and there really is no way to miss it) is the Catedral de Sevilla across the street, the third-largest church in Europe (after St. Peter's in Rome and St. Paul's in London). Begun in 1402, it took nearly a century to complete. Inside lie hidden treasures, among them the Tumba de Cristóbal Colón (Tomb of Christopher Columbus). Information: *Oficina de Turismo,* 21-B Avenida de la Constitución, Seville 41004 (phone: 95-422-1404).

EL GRECO'S TOLEDO, Castile–La Mancha: Doménikos Theotokópoulos, alias El Greco, was born in Crete, studied in Venice, and painted in Toledo, where he was dubbed "the Greek." Ancient, stylized figures, their bodies twisting in supple Venetian curves and shining with the mystic fervor of Castile, are the painter's trademarks. From a hillside just outside the city, the pile of tangled streets, often threatened by purplish clouds, looks much the same as it did in El Greco's *View of Toledo* in the *Casa y Museo del Greco.* This bite-size museum is an imaginative re-creation of the painter's house, and its collection includes a breathtaking series of portraits of Christ and the Apostles. A single painting with a cast of thousands, *The Burial of the Count of Orgaz,* is in the nearby Church of Santo Tomé. The cathedral sacristy and the *Museo de Santa Cruz* contain another 50 or so El Grecos between them. Toledo's cathedral, the second-largest in Spain (after Seville's), is a storehouse of artwork. Start in the Capilla Mayor, with its glittering altarpiece. Behind the high altar is the *Transparente,* an 18th-century baroque work by Narciso Tomé. Next, behold the *coro* (choir) with its set of stalls carved by Spain's finest sculptor, Alonso Berruguete. Down the winding and narrow Toledo streets are two synagogues, which attest to the fact that this city once was a thriving Jewish community. The 14th-century Sinagoga del Tránsito is a simple building with wonderful Mudéjar decorations. Its *Museo Sefardí* houses a fine collection of Sephardic Jewish manuscripts, inscriptions, and personal ornaments. Nearby, on Cuesta de los Reyes Católicos, is the Sinagoga de Santa María la Blanca, a 12th-century synagogue; it resembles a mosque, and for most of its life has served as a Catholic church. Information: *Oficina de Turismo,* Puerta de la Visagra, Toledo 45003 (phone: 925-220843).

The Performing Arts

Spain overflows with cultural activities, from the colorful flamenco shows to the poignant strains of a classical guitar concert. This is where the famous Don Juan and the barber of Seville were born, as were the works of Cervantes and Calderón de la Barca. But the stage in Spain is not simply a showcase for the traditional and the classical. Since the death of Generalísimo Francisco Franco in 1975, the country has been undergoing a cultural renaissance. The Minister of Culture along with the people in and around Barcelona have been preparing Spain for its role as host of the *1992 Summer Olympic Games* in Barcelona, as well as for Seville's *Expo '92,* the largest of the celebrations scheduled for the 500th anniversary of Columbus's discovery of the Americas. Madrid, in fact, has been declared the Cultural Capital of Europe for 1992 by the Council of Ministers of the European Economic Commission. During any summer, Madrid is *the* city for free cultural events, including international film festivals, theater performances, and concerts. *Guía del Ocio* and *Villa de Madrid,* both available throughout the city, offer the most comprehensive listings of all events, and the information in them is readily understood even by non-speakers of Spanish. Nowhere is the stage grander than at a live concert in the Plaza Mayor. The Plaza de Lavapiés and the Plaza Vila de Paris also host summer shows.

AUDITORIO NACIONAL DE MÚSICA, Madrid: Spain's new center for the performing arts, this "temple of symphonic music" opened in late 1988. Its two soundproof theaters — with 707 and 2,280 seats, respectively — are home to the *Orquestra Nacional de España* (Spanish National Orchestra) and the *Coro Nacional de España* (Spanish National Chorus). Symphonic, choral, chamber, and solo works are presented during a season that stretches from May through October. The hall has a unique layout that brings the audience closer to the orchestra; 20% of the audience is distributed on each side of and directly behind the performers, and the main section is tiered. The separate chamber music hall is semicircular, providing an intimate proximity between the performers and the audience. In addition to its 23 rehearsal halls, private suites, and dressing rooms, the *Auditorio* is equipped with state-of-the-art television broadcast and recording facilities. Information: *Auditorio Nacional de Música,* 146 Calle Principe de Vergara, Madrid 28002 (phone: 91-337-0100).

TEATRO LIRICO NACIONAL DE LA ZARZUELA, Madrid: The *zarzuela* is a Spanish form of light opera, and this is its citadel. The stage also hosts some of the world's greatest operas and performances by the *National Ballet Company.* Information: *Teatro de la Zarzuela,* 4 Calle Jovellanos, Madrid 28014 (phone: 91-429-8225).

TEATRO REAL, Madrid: Long a home for classical music, this performance house was opened in 1850, and following a massive restoration, it is scheduled to reopen late this year as the *Teatro de la Opera,* one of Europe's finest "modern" opera houses, as well as the largest in the world. Outdoor classical music concerts are held on weekends during the summer. Information: *Teatro Real,* Plaza de Oriente, Madrid 28003 (phone: 91-247-1405).

TEATRO NACIONAL MARÍA GUERRERO, Madrid: Full-scale revivals of Spain's great dramas, by the likes of Lope de Vega or Calderón de la Barca, are staged here, as well as examples of the international repertoire. Opened in 1885, this richly decorated, state-subsidized theater presents classic and modern performances from October through June. Information: *Teatro Nacional María Guerrero,* 4 Tamayo y Baus, Madrid 28004 (phone: 91-319-4769).

SALA OLIMPIA, Madrid: This is the place for those whose taste runs to the avant-garde or the experimental. It is the home of the *Centro Nacional de Nuevas Tendencias Escénicas* (National Center of New Theater Trends). Information: *Sala Olimpia,* Plaza de Lavapiés, Madrid 28008 (phone: 91-237-4622).

TORRES BERMEJAS, Madrid: This dinner-theater (dinners are somewhat overpriced) stages what many consider to be the most authentic flamenco show in town. Information: *Torres Bermejas,* 11 Calle Mesonero Romanos, Madrid 28013 (phone: 91-532-3322).

CORRAL DE LA MORERÍA, Madrid: Authentic flamenco dancing is featured in this *tablao* (nightclub), located in a simply furnished cellar in the Caba Baja district of the Old City. Information: *Corral de la Morería,* 17 Calle Morería, Madrid 28005 (phone: 91-265-1137).

GRAN TEATRE DEL LICEU, Barcelona, Catalonia: The city's principal opera house presents about 15 productions a year from the international repertoire. One of

Barcelona's proudest structures, it opened in 1847 and is one of the world's leading stages — and the only facility in Spain that is currently devoted almost solely to opera (with a very small concession made to ballet). The building itself is an attraction. The stage, one of Europe's largest, is especially suited to grand opera. The original gas lamps still line the auditorium's halls, and the foyer is richly decorated with mirrors and columns, which support arches with medallions representing a history of famous composers, singers, and actors. The opera season opens in November. Information: *Gran Teatre del Liceu,* 1 Carrer de Sant Pau, Barcelona 08001 (phone: 93-318-9277; telex: 99750 LICEU E).

PALAU DE LA MÚSICA CATALANA, Barcelona, Catalonia: Just off Via Laietana, near the Barri Gòtic, this dazzling 1908 landmark by the Catalan architect Lluís Domènech i Montaner hosts concerts of all varieties of symphonic and choral music. Worth a look for its grandeur alone, it's a jewel of a concert hall, combining a symphony of artistic notes from Art Nouveau to Moorish revival, executed in a colorful chorus of stained glass, mosaics, and ceramics, into a bewitching stylistic whole known to turn-of-the-century Barcelonans as *Modernisme.* The *Palau* was conceived amid the cultural euphoria that filled Barcelona in 1888, the year of the city's *Universal Exposition* (world's fair). The fair was meant to be a Spanish cultural event, but it actually turned into a display of regional pride as Catalans went out of their way to prove their inherent superiority over their Castilian brothers. One of the primary focuses of the fair was music, so the Catalans raised the idea of a permanent center for secular choral music in their capital city. The *Municipal Orchestra* and visiting orchestras perform here, and every October the *Palau* hosts Barcelona's *International Festival of Music,* featuring classical concerts. Information: *Palau de la Música Catalana,* Carrer d'Amadeu Vives, Barcelona 08005 (phone: 93-301-1104).

BARRIO DE LA JUDERÍA, Córdoba, Andalusia: The fast footwork of flamenco is featured here; just follow the music. Numerous performances are staged nightly at the restaurants in front of the Mezquita. The entertainment is impromptu, and the experience is delightful. Popular spots include *Mesón de la Luna, Restaurante Rafael,* and *Mesón La Muralla.* Information: *Oficina de Turismo,* 10 Calle Torrijos, Córdoba 14003 (phone: 957-471235).

Best Festivals

Festivals, direct descendants of the Greek drama marathons and the first *Olympic* games, are annual celebrations of the pleasures of creating, competing, or just plain existing. They let a visitor cram the best and most of any given experience into the shortest possible time — whether it's auto racing or chamber music, wine tasting or bullfighting.

In Spain, the calendar year is a kaleidoscope of celebration, a constant whirl of dancing, drinking, and devotion. There are festivals to honor saints, bulls, horses, flowers, grapes, and shellfish. There are symphony orchestras and blaring local bands, dancers in ballet slippers and on stilts, and evenings lit by chandeliers or fireworks. The festivals provide a chance for young Spanish men to show off their skills — and the original *machismo* — in climbing poles, wrestling bulls, or standing on each other's shoulders to form Catalonia's six-story *castellers,* or human towers. Each festival bears the trademark of its town, like the stomp, strum, clap, and yodel of Granada's summer flamenco festival, or the flowers and frills of Seville's *Feria de Abril.* Most festivals fall on Catholic holidays — *Carnaval, Corpus Christi,* and *Holy Week* before *Easter* are celebrated everywhere — but many still show traces of their pagan roots — the *Bonfires of San Juan* mark the summer solstice. For a complete listing of events, contact the *National Tourist Office of Spain,* 665 Fifth Ave., New York, NY 10022 (phone: 212-759-8822).

A word of sober caution to those planning to hurl themselves into the merriment at one of Spain's frothiest celebrations: Crowds are very much a part of most festivals, so be prepared for crowded hotels, crowded restaurants, crowded streets, and crowded auditoriums. Advance planning will mitigate much of the discomfort — so reserve rooms ahead of time — but it's still necessary to be prepared mentally for being jostled, for waiting in line, and for paying $2 or more for a can of warm cola — all part and parcel of festival-going.

WORTH A LONG DETOUR

MOORS AND CHRISTIANS, Alcoy, Valencia: The 7-century war of the Reconquest is shrunk every April into a tightly scripted, 2-day game of capture-the-flag. This town near Alicante is first duly conquered by Moors in blackface, wielding scimitars and wearing feathered turbans, embroidered cloaks, and shoes with 6-inch, turned-up points. On the second day, the Christians, firing harquebuses, storm the "castle" erected in the town square for the occasion. The routed infidels flee through the smoke and embers, still carrying their vicious-looking pikes but, in their baubled headgear, fringes, and feather boas, looking more like primitive witch doctors than Moorish warriors. The victors parade triumphantly with their protecting statue of the Virgin, amid the beating of drums and the dull thuds and crackling of fireworks. Not far away, in the coastal town of Villajoyosa, the *Feast of St. Martha* in July features a naval battle at dawn and a Saracen landing on the beach. Information: *Oficina de Turismo,* 2 Explanada de España, Alicante 03002 (phone 65-212285).

LAS FALLAS DE SAN JOSÉ, Valencia: The *cremá,* or bonfire, is a popular means of celebration in the region of Valencia, and the one for St. Joseph is the *crème de la cremá.* Originally planned as a way for local carpenters to get rid of a year's worth of wood chips and sawdust, as well as to honor their patron saint, this tradition spawned an art for the sake of destruction. The city's neighborhoods compete in building hundreds of elaborate *fallas* — giant, satirical floats made of colored papier-mâché and wood. Six-foot cherubs, overweight athletes, and paunchy politicians dance on a fallen *Olympic* torch, and a grimacing globe staggers under the weight of nuclear arms. The week-long rush of bullfights, concerts, and parades begins on March 19 to a thundering chant of "*Fuego*" — "Fire!" — and a burst of fireworks, as the *falleros* light their own constructions and the flames leap into the sky. The fire consumes the sins of the winter and the woes of the world, reducing stock-market crashes to ashes and lust to dust. The next morning, it's back to the drawing board for next year's floats. Information: *Oficina de Turismo,* 46 Calle de la Paz, Valencia 46003 (phone: 96-352-2897).

THE BONFIRES OF SAN JUAN, Alicante, Valencia: After the longest day of the year, the light keeps burning through the short *nit de foc,* or "night of fire." From June 21 through 29, scavenged boards, blocks of wood, shoeboxes, and old upholstery are feverishly assembled into a gigantic tower resembling an oversize, highly flammable Erector Set. Then, in the name of St. John the Baptist, it is burned: a sort of latter-day bonfire of vanities or auto-da-fé. The pyre symbolizes the sins of the town, and the cardboard human figures writhing in the flames look like heretics and witches sacrificed by the Spanish Inquisition. By dawn, the wind has dispersed the cinders and the sunshine has dissolved the lurid lights, but the festival continues with 5 more days of parades and nightly fireworks shows that make the thought of sleep a purely theological quibble. Information: *Oficina de Turismo,* 2 Explanada de España, Alicante 03002 (phone: 965-212285).

ROMERIA DEL ROCÍO, Almonte, Andalusia: As in the grand finale of a Broadway musical, the white covered wagons and little surreys with a fringe on top trundle westward, flanked by extras in wide-brimmed hats and brightly colored, flouncy skirts, dancing to the music of flutes and tambourines. Fifty days after *Easter,* pilgrims pour through the fields and olive groves of Andalusia in a slow stream of flower-festooned horses and beribboned oxen, converging on the rural sanctuary of El Rocío, 40 miles (64 km) from Seville. The festival mixes equal parts of fervor and fun. Pilgrims march silently at night over the candlelit marshes, then break out into foot-stomping, finger-snapping *seguidillas.* The climax comes with the parading of the statue of the *Virgen del Rocío,* hoisted on the shoulders of the faithful in a brilliant scene painted in sun, sweat, and tears. There are no accommodations in El Rocío or in Almonte, so stay in Seville, Cádiz, or Huelva, and try to hitch a ride on a wagon. Information: *Oficina de Turismo,* 5 Calle Vázquez López, Huelva 21001 (phone: 955-257403).

SEMANA SANTA AND FERIA DE ABRIL, Seville, Andalusia: Perhaps one of the most popular fiestas is *Holy Week,* a 7-day celebration in Seville that begins on *Palm Sunday* and lasts through *Easter.* The week is highlighted by some of the most colorful floats around (guaranteed to dazzle even the most weary paradegoer), as well as rows and rows of masked paraders prancing through the streets. When the curtain falls on *Holy Week,* Sevillians disappear into the wings of the city for a brief intermission, to switch from pointed hoods to black felt hats. The plot thins, and *Passion Plays* give way to passionate playing, sober robes are exchanged for ruffled Gypsy dresses, and solemn hymns segue into throaty flamenco warbles. Across the river from the pious Old Town that cleaves to its cathedral lies a fairy-tale city of striped tents and avenues of colored lights. Transportation is by horse and buggy, and traffic noises are the tinkling of harness bells and the clicking of castanets. What began in the 19th century as a local market where peasants bartered grain for plowshares has become a showy convention of Andalusian merrymakers. Be sure to book well in advance; rooms get very crowded during this time of year. Information: *Oficina de Turismo,* 21-B Avenida de la Constitución, Seville 41004 (phone: 95-422-1404).

FERIA DEL CABALLO, Jerez de la Frontera, Andalusia: Jerez is famous for sherry and horses, and even has a museum devoted to both, but for 5 days at the end of April, the horses steal the show. Straight-backed riders in felt hats and embroidered uniforms canter through the streets, and carriage drivers guide harnessed teams through the myriad maneuvers of dressage. All around the city, horses jump, trot, whinny, rear, gallop, spar with bulls, or simply stand still to be admired. The preening white Cartujanos with cottony manes are the graceful stars, descended from the horses the Moors rode during their conquest of Spain, and bred through the centuries at Jerez de la Frontera's Royal School for Equestrian Art. The fair is still faithful to its 13th-century origins as a livestock market; you may have come for the costumes, parades, and bullfights that are part of any Spanish festival, but if in a Walter Mitty life you ever cast yourself as a cowboy, or if you have a weakness for gambling, you just might ride away on a horse. Information: *Oficina de Turismo,* 7 Alameda Cristina, Jerez de la Frontera 11400 (phone: 956-331150), or *Oficina de Turismo,* 1 Calle Calderón de la Barca, Cádiz 11003 (phone: 956-211313).

CARNAVAL, Santa Cruz de Tenerife, Canary Islands: Rooted in an ancient pagan rite, and mixed with the apocalyptic Catholic bingeing before the severity of *Lent,* this *Carnaval* has the flavor of a Spanish *Halloween.* It is celebrated for 12 days in February throughout Spain, but nowhere more extravagantly than on the island of Tenerife, where tradition melds with a Greenwich Village sense of fashion to produce wild parades and costumes that would have made Liberace look staid. It is an orgy of purple makeup, leopard-skin leotards, sequined hats, masks, feathers, capes, and wigs. Ornate carts function as mobile bandstands, stages, and puppet theaters, and the air is filled with strums and songs and wheezing clarinets. Information: *Oficina de Turismo,* 57 Calle de la Marina, Santa Cruz de Tenerife 38001 (phone: 922-285651).

HOLY WEEK AND THE FESTIVAL OF RELIGIOUS MUSIC, Cuenca, Castile–La Mancha: Cuenca froths over the sides of its cliff, leaving a frozen dribble of houses hanging in the gorge above the Huecar River. During *Holy Week,* trumpets echo between the sheer, rock walls — eerie calls from the Middle Ages to the modern world below. Above, austere processions, silent except for the solemn fanfares, wind slowly through the narrow alleys. Penitents carry sculpted and painted scenes from the Passion story, and members of religious brotherhoods march together in the forbidding robes and pointed hoods of the Spanish Inquisition. Each evening, in the church of San Miguel, orchestras and choirs from all over Europe perform recitals of religious music ranging from somber motets to Wagner's mystical *Tannhäuser.* Every year, a new work commissioned for the festival is played here for the first time. Information: *Oficina de Turismo,* 8 Calle Dalmacio García Izcarra, Cuenca 16004 (phone: 966-222231).

FIESTA DE SAN FERMÍN, Pamplona, Navarre: The crowd crackles nervously at dawn around a group of young men dressed in white with scarlet sashes around their waists, who wait with clammy hands and a defiant swagger for the beginning of the *encierro* (bull run). At 8 AM, a rocket is fired from a corral on the outskirts of town, signaling that six fighting bulls have been released from the corral, along with six steers. A second rocket is fired when the last bull leaves the corral. Experienced runners count the minutes between the first and second rockets — a long pause between shots means a bull has left the corral late and in all likelihood has been separated from the herd. That's when the bull becomes aggressive and dangerous.

Within minutes of the first rocket, the bulls, following the steers, shoot through the narrow, winding streets, usually oblivious to the hundreds of runners and the cheering crowd. The goal of the runner is to run in front of the bull for a few glorious seconds, before jumping aside and letting the herd pass. Since the bulls will not charge unless separated from the herd, most of the danger result from tripping and being trampled by the 1500-pound animals.

Soon after all the bulls have left the corral and traveled the streets, they burst into the bullring, and a third rocket is fired to signal that the *encierro* has ended. In the bullring, however, young bulls with sawed-off horns charge the second rank of heroes. Then the day's casualties are counted, and the survivors go off the prepare for the next morning's run and to celebrate with all-night street parties. This celebration of stamina, held from July 6 through July 14 and immortalized by Ernest Hemingway in *The Sun Also Rises,* actually honors San Fermín, who brought Catholicism to Navarre. Information: *Oficina de Turismo,* 3 Calle Duque de Ahumada, 31002 Pamplona (phone: 948-220741).

FEAST OF ST. JAMES, Santiago de Compostela, Galicia: Santiago de Compostela grew famous as a result of the great medieval pilgrimages to the tomb of St. James the Apostle. The *Fiesta del Apóstol* (Feast of St. James), which takes place on July 25, highlights 10 days of festivities; Galician folkloric shows, competitions, special theater presentations, and daily concerts are among the attractions. There is also a jazz festival, consisting of performances by major international groups, in the Plaza de Tournal during the days immediately preceding the feast day. A spectacular fireworks display is held in front of the cathedral on the eve of the feast (July 24), and the day itself is marked by high mass, street bands, special theater, and an orchestral presentation in the Plaza del Obradoiro. Another main event is the swinging of the *botafumeiro* (giant incense burner) across the cathedral transepts. Check with the church for the date — it's well worth the experience. Information: *Oficina de Turismo,* 43 Rua del Villar, Santiago de Compostela 15705 (phone: 981-584081).

A RAPA DAS BESTAS, San Lorenzo de Sabuceno, near Pontevedra, Galicia: For most of the year, horses roam over Galicia's green hills, but on the first weekend of July, an age-old chore becomes a spectacle, as hundreds of horses are rounded up, pounded down the mountainside, and careened into *curros* (corrals). They spend 2 days of imprisonment, eating bales of hay and thinking of the greener grass on the wild side of the fence. The town's young men then wrestle them to the ground and crop their manes or mark their hides with a symbol to identify their owners, afterward releasing them as branded animals. Information: *Oficina de Turismo,* 2 Calle General Mola, Pontevedra 36001 (phone: 986-850841).

EXPO 1992, Seville: The 538-acre Cartuja Island in the Guadalquivir River, is the site of this year's colossal *Expo '92* extravaganza and the culmination of the celebrations of the 500th anniversary of Columbus's discovery of America. From April 12 through the closing ceremonies on October 12, a record 103 nations, 22 international organizations, and 24 multinational companies, as well as each of Spain's 17 autonomous regions are participating in the festivities, which include exhibitions, celebrations of national days, and numerous theater and dance performances. The site includes 96 restaurants, 70 bars, 51 shops, 10 banks, 10 tourist information offices, 3 monorail stations, and 3 cable car stations. For details see Seville, THE CITIES. Information: *Expotourist Services,* Isla de la Cartuja, Seville 41010 (phone: 446-1992).

IF TRAVELING NEARBY

CARNAVAL, Madrid: Prohibited during Generalísimo Francisco Franco's 40-year reign, this nonstop street fiesta is filled with lively parades and dancing from noon until night. The activity takes place from late February to early April and climaxes with the "Encierro de la Sardina" — the "Burial of the Sardine." Information: *Oficina de Turismo,* Torre de Madrid, Plaza de España, Madrid 28008 (phone: 91-541-2325).

CORPUS CHRISTI, Granada, Andalusia: This is Granada's most famous festival, complete with parades and bullfights. The party begins on the Thursday following the 8th Sunday after *Easter.* Information: *Oficina de Turismo,* Casa de los Tiros, 19 Calle Pavanezas, Granada 18009 (phone: 958-225990).

Antiques and Auctions

Antiques bargains abound in Spain for the careful, tireless shopper. It is particularly notable for its antique jewelry, old books, and ceramics, especially the boldly designed 17th-century Talavera polychrome plates, modeled after the Italian works of Faenza and Urbino.

A REPERTOIRE OF ANTIQUES SOURCES

SHOPS AND ANTIQUES CENTERS: There are basically three different types of places to hunt for antiques. At the low end of the scale are the flea markets, where those willing to sift through piles of miscellanea may uncover a true gem, or at least a good bargain. Auction houses are another option that can often yield a good find or two. Antiques shops, however, are usually the best bet. They are convenient; the dealer already has made the rounds through the markets and has purchased the cream of the crop. These shops do tend to be on the expensive side, but the quality is excellent and the selection can't be beat. Antiques hunters are practically guaranteed to find something of interest in one of these shops.

Madrid – As in other European capitals, Madrid's antiques shops are often found clustered in certain areas. Antiques row is the Calle del Prado, near the *Prado* museum. Worth a look is *Luis Rodríguez-Morueco* (16 Calle del Prado; phone: 91-429-5757), and in the *Mercado Puerta de Toledo* (Ronda de Toledo; phone: 91-265-9927), both of which feature treasures from the 16th, 17th, and 18th centuries; objects of interest include fans, boxes, and canes. For more concentrated antiques browsing and buying, try *Centro de Anticuarios Lagasca* (36 Calle Lagasca). It has 11 antiques shops under one roof, including *Luis Carabe* (phone: 91-431-5872), which has an interesting collection of crystal. Also browse along Calle Serrano, where many antiques shops are located; the 5-story *Central de Arte Antiquedades* (5 Calle Serrano) houses 50 shops with honored reputations. For fine ceramics, try *Abelardo Linares* (11 Plaza de la Cortés; phone: 91-432-4962). *Alcocer* (5 Calle Santa Catalina, 68 Calle Pelayo, and 104 Calle Hortaleza) is a fourth-generation antiques dealer specializing in furniture, paintings, and other objects, including antique Spanish silver. The bibliophile also can savor the experience of *Luis Bardon Mesa* (3 Plaza San Martín; phone: 91-521-5514), which counts among its 50,000 volumes masterpieces by authors such as Cervantes, Lope de Vega, and Calderón de la Barca. Also try *Librería del Callejón* (4 Callejón de Preciados; phone: 91-521-7167).

Madrid's old *Central Fish Market* was rebuilt in 1988 and opened as the *Mercado Puerta de Toledo* (Ronda de Toledo), a sparkling cultural and shopping showcase of fine handicrafts, art, jewelry, fashion, interior design, and gastronomy, as well as antiques.

Barcelona – More than 150 antiques shops are spread along the narrow streets of the Barri Gòtic in Barcelona. Major periods as far back as the 12th century are represented. One of the best shops is *Alberto Grasas* (10 Carrer Banys Nous and 10 *bis* Carrer Palla; phone: 93-317-8838), which sells antique paintings, furniture, and decorative objects, principally porcelain. For ceramics, one of the city's top showrooms is *Arturo Ramón* (25 Carrer Palla; phone: 93-302-5974). Its prize possessions include 18th-century furniture, as well as the highly prized ceramics from Manises. Also visit *Bulevard Rosa* (Passeig de Gràcia), with 70 shops. Look out for the monthly *subastas* (sales) at *Sotheby's* (2 Passeig Domingo; phone: 93-215-2149).

Seville – Seville's antiques shops are among Spain's best. Plaza del Cabildo houses antiques shops such as *Antigüedades Lola Ortega* (phone: 95-421-8771). Also try *Segundo Antiguedades* (89 Calle Sierpes; phone: 95-422-5652) and the shops along Calle Placentines.

Toledo – Toledo is a major supplier of furniture to the Spanish market, and has been for many years. Most of the antiques shops are on the Toledo–Madrid highway, within the area just outside the city. Try *Balaguer* (Pasadizo del Ayuntamiento and Calle Puerta Llana); *Linares* (Calle de los Reyes Católicos in front of the San Juan de los Reyes monastery); and the *Olrey* shopping complex (in Olías, about 10 miles/16 km from Toledo on the Toledo–Madrid highway).

FLEA MARKETS AND OTHER SPECTACLES: The heady mixture of rubbish and relic affords collectors the chance to find that special, unrecognized rarity. Try to arrive early, as markets quickly get crowded with other people who have the same idea.

Madrid – The city's biggest flea market, *El Rastro,* is held every Sunday from about 9 AM to 2 PM. Behind the stalls of clothing, accessories, and household furnishings are permanent — and elegant — antiques shops, which generally offer high-quality merchandise. (It's better to shop at these places during the week, when things are not so hectic.) Try *Galerías Piquer* (29 Ribera de Curtidores; phone: 91-227-9545) and *Nuevas Galerías* (12 Ribera de Curtidores; phone: 91-227-2057) for antique glass.

Barcelona – Spain's most cosmopolitan city has a variety of outdoor offerings throughout the week. From dawn to dusk on Mondays, Wednesdays, Fridays, and Saturdays, *Els Encants* (just off the Plaça de les Glòries Catalanes hosts a huge flea market with everything from clothes to antiques on display. The Plaça Nova has a weekly antiques market every Thursday. The Plaça de Sant Josep Oriol transforms itself into one of Spain's largest open-air painting exhibitions and marketplaces every weekend, and the Plaça Reial features coin and stamp markets on Sunday mornings.

Seville – One of Spain's best antiques fairs is held every April in Seville. Information: *Associación de Anticuarios,* 7 Calle Rodrigo Caro (phone: 95-421-6558).

AUCTIONS: As any auction addict knows, this is a sport that combines the fanaticism of the stock market, gambling casino, and living theater. *Subastas* (the Spanish word for auctions) are held mainly in the two largest cities, Madrid and Barcelona, although antiques dealers may be able to tell visitors about some in other parts of the country. Unlike auctions in New York, which usually are quite specialized, Spanish *subastas* offer an assortment of many kinds of objects. Auctions are the perfect answer to rainy day blues, provided newcomers pay attention to these notes:

Don't expect to make a killing. Even Chinese peasant children are hip to the art market today, it seems. But chances of unearthing a real find are better for those who shop at smaller auctions.

Buy the catalogue before bidding. Catalogues often include a list of estimated prices. Those prices are not a contractual commitment, but they do act as a guide for prospective buyers. An elaborate stylistic code hints at the conviction the house may have about the age or authenticity of an item. The use of capital letters, of artists' full names, and of words like "fine," "rare," and "important" all carry positive connotations. The use of a last name only and of words like "style" and "attributed" should serve as warnings.

Visit the pre-sale exhibition carefully, thoroughly, and even repeatedly. There is the pleasure of browsing in a store without a hovering clerk. Even more important is the prospective buyer's chance to examine the offerings. *Caveat emptor* is the prevailing rule at any auction. Serious buyers should have paintings taken down from the wall and ask to handle objects under lock and key. Those who can't be at the sale can leave a commission bid with the auctioneer, or even place a bid by telephone, but if they can't be at the exhibition they should be wary of buying.

Decide on a top bid before the auction begins, and don't go beyond it. Bidding has its own rhythm and tension. The auctioneer becomes a Pied Piper, with buyers winking, blinking, and nodding in time to his or her music. This situation arouses unusual behavior in some people. Suddenly their self-worth is at stake, and they'll bid far beyond what the item is worth — or even what they can afford. A bid may be canceled by promptly calling out "Withdrawn." *Note:* In determining their top price, bidders should remember to add the house commission, which is generally 10%, but can be more, and any value added tax. The following spots warrant prime attention:

Madrid – In Madrid, two international auction houses have branches: *Sotheby's* (8 Plaza de la Independencia; phone: 91-522-2902) and *Christie's* (7 Calle Valenzuela; 91-532-6627). Auctions are conducted at the *Ritz* hotel about five times a year, alternating between paintings and decorative objects. Works by such famous artists as Goya and El Greco may be sold at astronomical prices. Other places in Madrid for *subastas* include *Ansorena* (52 Calle Alcalá; phone: 91-532-8516), where jewelry and *platería* (silver) are auctioned off monthly; *Durán Subastas* (12 Calle Serrano; phone: 91-401-3400), which has about five sessions monthly, divided according to the type of selections; *Fernando Durán* (11 Calle Conde de Aranda; phone: 91-431-3806), which conducts between six and ten events a year at the *Wellington* hotel. Commissions usually range from 12% to 15% above *el precio de adjudicación* (the sale price).

Barcelona – A wide assortment of antiques is auctioned periodically at *Balclis* (227 Carrer del Roselló; phone: 93-217-5607). Best known for quality of goods are the monthly *subastas* held at *Sotheby's* (2 Passeig Domingo; phone: 93-215-2149), *Brok* (167 Carrer de Pau Claris; phone: 93-215-5028), and at *Prestige* (277 Carrer de Valencia; phone: 93-215-6857). Jewelry auctions are held periodically at *Subarna* (257 Carrer de Provença; phone: 93-215-6518).

RULES OF THE ROAD FOR AN ODYSSEY OF THE OLD

Buy for sheer pleasure and not for investment. Treasure seekers should forget about the supposed resale value that dealers habitually dangle in front of amateur clients. If you love an object, you'll never part with it. If you don't love it, let someone else adopt it.

Don't be timid about haggling. That's as true at a posh Madrid shop on Calle Serrano as at *El Rastro* flea market. You'll be surprised at how much is negotiable — and the higher the price the more it has to fall.

Buy the finest example you can afford of any item, in as close to mint condition as possible. Chipped or tarnished "bargains" will haunt you later with their shabbiness.

Train your eye in museums. Museums that specialize in items you collect are the best of all. Take a close look at the famous paintings and sculptures in Madrid's *Prado* museum.

Peruse art books and periodicals — preferably before you go auction hunting. Unfortunately, however, there is a lack of English-language reading material available.

Get advice from a specialist when contemplating a major acquisition. Major auction houses like *Sotheby's* have fleets of resident specialists available for consultation. The Spanish Tourist Office may also be able to offer some assistance.

Sacred Spain

 All over Spain, every invasion, migration, and wave of conversion left its signature in stone, much of which has been all but erased by time and the furor of the Reconquest. As generations of Catholics poked at the hegemony of the Moors, finally pushing them back into North Africa in 1492, they destroyed mosques and erected huge cathedrals in their place. And despite the recently named *calles de la Judería* that crop up in medieval quarters, the statues of Maimonides, and the Star of David pendants for sale in trinket stores, not many traces remain of the thousands of Jews who, until their expulsion or forcible conversion in 1492, lived in Spain for centuries alongside Phoenicians, Romans, Visigoths, Arabs, and Christians.

The ritual drawings of bulls in the caves of Altamira, the small Visigothic Church of Santa María del Naranco in the countryside near Oviedo, the Jewish Cabala school tucked away in an alley in Girona, the grand mosque in Córdoba, the somber palace-monastery of El Escorial — each is an entry in the guestbook of religions come and gone. Here is a sampling of the Church's catholic tastes in architecture, ranging from the severity of Guadalupe to the niceties of Seville, as well as a few reminders of "infidel" times.

LA SAGRADA FAMILIA, Barcelona, Catalonia: The knobby towers reaching twistingly for the sky look like an enormous set of melting candles or the wavy walls of a sandcastle made by some oversize child. La Sagrada Familia is in the great Gothic tradition of Flamboyant swirls, jutting gargoyles, allegorical façades — and lifetimes of construction. The architect Antoni Gaudí's estimate that the completion of his final project would take 200 years may prove to be overly optimistic. Begun over a century ago, this gingerbread church in the middle of the residential neighborhood of the

Eixample still doesn't have four complete walls or a roof. In the basement museum, there is a scale model of the structure as it will be one day, although we may never be able to compare it to the real thing. Information: *Patronat Municipal de Turisme de Barcelona,* 658 Gran Via de les Corts Catalanes, Barcelona 08010 (phone: 93-301-7443 or 93-317-2246).

CATHEDRAL, Burgos, Castile-León: Burgos is a reminder that the center of the world can move. The quiet town that nestles in its cathedral's colossal shadow was once the capital of a kingdom and the stamping ground of the Spanish Superman — El Cid Campeador, whose epic feats of war won him a tomb of honor in the transept. This elegant cathedral's spikes, steeples, and spires stand in memory of Burgos's Gothic glory. From the interior, the windows, the screens, and the light shining through the star-shaped skylight and glinting on the grillwork inside all make the building appear as if it were made mostly of air. Information: *Oficina de Turismo,* 7 Plaza de Alonso Martinez, Burgos 09003 (phone 947-203125).

MEZQUITA, Córdoba, Andalusia: Inside the plain brown wrapper of its walls is a fantasy assortment of fruit-colored columns and candy-cane arches stacked in twos and threes. The biggest treat of all is the *mihrab,* a holy niche iced with colored stucco and stones and topped with a golden cupola. For centuries (from the middle of the 8th to the middle of the 11th), Córdoba was the center of Al-Andalus, the Moorish Western world, and the mosque was spun lovingly out in stages, each addition fulfilling the grandest dreams of a different ruler. But with the Reconquest came the Christian kingdom, which dropped a cathedral in the middle of the mosque and clothed the minaret in a 17th-century bell tower. The new church did not impress the Holy Roman Emperor, who commented: "You have replaced something unique with something ordinary." Information: *Oficina de Turismo* (Plaza de Juda Levi, Córdoba 14003; phone: 957-290740, and 10 Torrijos; phone: 957-471235).

CABALA SCHOOL, Girona, Catalonia: The steep, narrow streets of the Call, climbing away from Girona's ocher reflection in the Onyar River, was home to a medieval Jewish community teeming with merchants and mystics. The Centre Isaac el Cec is named for a blind sage of the *cabala,* a sort of 12th-century teacher of the Jewish brand of mysticism that promised its disciples control over the universe through the mastery of a special force. Few buildings in Spain are unmistakably Jewish, but here a Star of David is laid in the floor of the patio, under the tables of the café that now shares the building with a center for Sephardic studies and an exhibition hall. Information: *Oficina d'Informació Turística,* 12 Carrer Ciutadans, Girona 17004 (phone: 972-201694).

CAPILLA REAL, Granada, Andalusia: For King Ferdinand and Queen Isabella, to die in Granada was a triumph, and the Capilla Real (Royal Chapel) was their eternal gilded trophy. For 7 centuries, Spain had belonged to the Moors, and Granada was their last stand. So when the Catholic Monarchs finally conquered the city, they built a small chapel and filled it with themselves: their swords and crowns, their royal jewels, and priceless gems of Christian art — Italian sculptures, Flemish paintings, and Spanish grillwork. The chapel is a monument to their achievements, faith, and wealth, and their righteous challenge to the Alhambra's decadent dazzle. Information: *Oficina de Turismo,* Casa de los Tiros, 19 Calle Pavanezos, Granada 18009 (phone: 958-225990).

REAL MONASTERIO DE SANTA MARÍA DE GUADALUPE, Guadalupe, near Cáceres, Extremadura: Within the grim fortress walls, standing guard over the rocky dry landscape, is a womb of luxury. In the center, on a golden throne, sits the *Virgen Negra de Guadalupe,* made of carved and painted wood. With her black face and silver hand, she rules over the Catholic Hispanic world. From here, and in her name, tough sons of Extremadura left with stony faces and iron hands to ensure that America became part of that world. It was here that Christopher Columbus signed the contract entitling him to the *Niña,* the *Pinta,* and the *Santa María,* and where he returned with his first cargo of Indians to be baptized in her faith. The Italian painter Luca Giordano, whose stunning paintings of the life of the Virgin cover the walls, must also have been rebaptized — as the paintings are attributed to Lucas Jordan. Information: *Oficina de Turismo*, Plaza Mayor, Cáceres 10003 (phone: 927-246347).

CATHEDRAL, León, Castile-León: With sparer lines and fewer frills than those of Burgos or Seville, León's cathedral looks more French, softened by a Spanish, orangish hue. Step out of the León sun and into its cool interior, where the heavy walls seem like slender frames for the panoramic movie-screen-size windows, whose stained glass saints throw a bejeweled glimmer on the gray, stone floor. The windows are an illustrated catalogue of vices, virtues, and the wages of both, which taught, warned, and admonished illiterate medieval Spaniards — but modern visitors may need a catalogue and a pair of binoculars to understand them. Information: *Oficina de Turismo*, 3 Plaza de la Regla, León 24003 (phone: 987-237082).

SANTIAGO DE COMPOSTELA, Galicia: Pilgrims once trudged through the Pyrenees from all corners of medieval Europe to worship at Santiago de Compostela. The road to Santiago, lined with *hostales*, churches, and shrines, winds through Burgos, León, and Astorga. Today, airlines and air conditioned buses deliver millions of visitors to the soaring granite cathedral that houses the tomb of St. James the Apostle. The cathedral's pride, the Gate of Glory, is the original façade — neither outside nor in, but slipped between the church's baroque envelope and the Romanesque interior. Almost as spectacular are the façade, patios, and Gothic chapel of the *Parador de los Reyes Católicos* (who might be among the few who could afford to stay here). Information: *Oficina de Turismo*, 43 Rua del Villar, Santiago de Compostela 15705 (phone: 981-584081).

CATHEDRAL, Seville, Andalusia: It is somehow symbolic of Spain's religious history that her largest cathedral should be squeezed between a Moorish Alcázar and a once-Arab neighborhood renamed for the Holy Cross, and that its bell tower should be a dressed-up minaret. After the city was reconquered from the Moors, the mosque was razed and its minaret raised by half a dozen stories of bells and columns crowned by a revolving bronze statue of Faith. From the top of the tower, the horizon is filled by the gargoyles, turrets, spires, and buttresses of this cathedral, built to be so large that "those who come after us will take us for madmen." Information: *Oficina de Turismo*, 21 Avenida de la Constitución, Seville 41004 (phone: 95-221404).

JEWISH TOLEDO, Castile–La Mancha: Of the dozen or so synagogues in medieval Toledo's sprawling Jewish quarter, only two still exist, but neither is functioning. Look carefully around the city to find — wedged beneath a sagging windowsill or propping up a crumbling wall — bits of Hebrew writing on a stone from a pillaged synagogue. But when the banker who built the sumptuous Sinagoga del Tránsito was arrested and his house sacked by order of his client, King Pedro I of Castile, the synagogue itself, with praises of the king sculpted into its ornate walls, went miraculously unscathed. Information: *Oficina de Turismo*, Puerta de la Visagra, Toledo 45003 (phone: 925-220843).

Parks, Plazas, and Paseos

Regardless of a visitor's touristic fervor, fatigue will eventually slow the maddest rush from site to sight, forcing a periodic stop for a stretch, a drink, or a snack. Fortunately, the Spanish have made the snack an institution and the stroll a national pastime. They have turned musty quays and dusty castles into sleek spaces specifically for lazing, lounging, and loafing. So when planning a trip, be sure to include a dollop of idleness on the list of musts, and *tapas* (snacks)

and the *paseo* (stroll) at the top of the vocabulary list. Here are some of the lushest parks, the most languid plazas, and the most luxurious *paseos* in Spain.

LA RAMBLA, Barcelona, Catalonia: Even at 2 AM, it seems as if it's always Sunday afternoon here. While the rest of the world sleeps, Barcelona is just finishing a meal and funneling from the alleyways of the medieval Barri Gòtic into this quintessential *paseo*. Running from the harbor to Plaça de Catalunya (with several name changes en route), La Rambla was originally designed as a drainage channel. Now, young mothers take their babies for an after-dinner stroller ride along this tree-lined promenade, their husbands riffle through the bookstalls' offerings of everything from porn to Proust, children paint beards of ice cream on their faces, and grandfathers sit on benches reading tomorrow's newspaper. Phalanxes of foreign sailors moving up from the port meet lines of teenage girls coming arm in arm from the Plaça de Catalunya. The two groups cross and pass each other with giggles and ogles, like a well-rehearsed dance. The birds in their cages tune their chirps to the horns of cars in the narrow traffic lanes squeezed to the sides of this pedestrian highway. Note the sidewalk mosaic by Joan Miró at the Plaça de Boquería; stroll to the nearby *Mercat de Sant Josep* (St. Joseph's Market, better known as the Boquería); or visit the *Gran Teatre del Liceu* (at the corner of La Rambla and Carrer de Sant Pau), one of the world's great opera houses. Information: *Patronat Municipal de Turisme de Barcelona,* 658 Gran Via de les Corts Catalanes, Barcelona 08008 (phone: 93-301-7443 or 93-317-2246).

PARC GÜELL AND PASSEIG DE GRÀCIA, Barcelona, Catalonia: The works of the architect Antoni Gaudí are scattered through Barcelona like candies on a deep-pile rug. Some are brightly colored clumps; others line the city's fringes. Originally planned as a real estate development by Gaudí and his friend Count Eusebio Güell, a noted Barcelona industrialist and civic leader, Parc Güell is a confectioner's pastoral fantasy. At its core, resting on 86 pillars and edged with an undulating stone bench "upholstered" with a mosaic quilt of broken glass and tiles, is a plaza that was meant to be the garden city's marketplace. Only two of the development's houses — the gingerbread cottages flanking the park entrance — were ever built; a third, not designed by Gaudí but his home for the last 2 decades of his life, has been turned into the *Casa-Museu Gaudí,* containing drawings, models, furniture, and other items that belonged to him. South of the park, the Passeig de Gràcia ambles past some impish turn-of-the-century houses that — with their technicolored tiles and curved facades — seem to be laughing at their neighbors' stodgy grayness. Gaudí designed the liquid Casa Batlló, with mask-shaped balconies, swelling wooden doors, delicate tiles, and sensuous curves in stone and iron, and the wavy Casa Milá (popularly known as La Pedrera), with its almost sculptural attempt to distance itself from the harsh, square lines of the adjoining apartment blocks. But he was not the only member of what might be called the Dramamine School: Josep Puig i Cadafalch was responsible for the Casa Amatller, which also contrasts greatly with its neighbors. Parc Güell is open daily from 10 AM to dusk. Information: *Patronat Municipal de Turisme de Barcelona,* 658 Gran Via de les Corts Catalanes, Barcelona 08010 (phone: 93-301-7443 or 93-317-2246).

PLAZA DE SANTA MARÍA, Cáceres, Extremadura: The Arco de la Estrella is like a sound barrier between the contemporary noises of the new city and the quiet of the old. Step through it from the honking of traffic in the Plaza Mayor to the cooing of pigeons in the Plaza de Santa María. From the square — a sunny, cobblestone oasis in a city of dark alleys — Cáceres looks like a classic medieval town. But for all its ancient sternness and looming towers, there is an occasional touch of frivolous grillwork or a patterned frame of tiles around a window. Information: *Oficina de Turismo,* Plaza Mayor, Cáceres 10003 (phone: 927-246347).

PATIOS OF CÓRDOBA, Andalusia: In the narrow streets of the Judería, a quarter that hasn't been Jewish for over 500 years, front doors are left ajar with a purposeful carelessness and a studied pretense of privacy. So lean through the head-wide crack or peer through the convenient gaps in the vines that veil the iron gate, into the preening patios inside. They are tiled oases, green-filled refuges from the Andalusian sun, which bounces glaringly off the whitewashed walls of Córdoba's North African–style houses. They are lovingly tended — water burbles from hoses and laps lavishly onto plants, flowers, and white-and-blue patterned ceramic floors. In a yearly pageant in May, Córdobans shed their coyness, open their doors wide, and bare their patios to the judges who award a city prize to the best. Information: *Oficina de Turismo,* 10 Calle Torrijos, Córdoba 14003 (phone: 957-471235 or 957-483112).

LA GRANJA DE SAN ILDEFONSO, Castile-León: There is a little of Versailles in the purple mountains between Segovia and Madrid. King Philip V began this 18th-century palace as a simple country grange, but foreign architects and landscapers fussed over it until it became a Frenchified weave of fountains, frescoes, and façades. The formal gardens, with a high geyser rising from a pool, flow into less-manicured grounds, where sculpted gods, frogs, and cherubs cavort among the leaves. Open daily, from 10 AM to 8 PM in summer, until 6 PM in winter. (The palace itself keeps shorter hours and is closed on Mondays.) Information: *Oficina de Turismo,* 10 Plaza Mayor, Segovia 34001 (phone: 911-430323).

PARQUE DEL RETIRO, Madrid: If a morning in the *Prado* museum has left you with artache, this civilized swath of nature is a perfect place to soothe a sizzling brain amid the blended smells of cedar and suede. On a sunny Sunday afternoon, all of Madrid comes to jog, hug, gossip, or walk the dog around the lakeside colonnade. The splashing of oars and the rustle of gravel provide a gentle counterpoint to the beating and blaring of the concert bands. The range of shades of the lovingly tended flowers in the Rosaleda, from saffron to cream to vermilion, will create doubt about whether a rose is necessarily a rose. The park has a style to which anyone easily can become accustomed, so indulge in a *coupe royale* — a deluxe ice cream — among statues of kings, a cocktail on the satin-white terrace of the *Ritz* hotel, and dinner at the discreet, patrician *Horcher's* both just outside the gates on Calle Alfonso XII. Information: *Oficina de Turismo,* 1 Calle Princesa, Madrid 28008 (phone: 91-541-2325).

FROM THE BRIDGE TO THE BULLRING, Ronda, Andalusia: The old and new parts of Ronda tilt away from each other like neighborhoods split by a cleaver, tenuously linked by a bridge over a plunging gorge. Stand on the bridge and lean over into a mighty crack in the earth. At sunset, the red rays of sunlight seem to flow under the city, along the bottom of El Tajo. Catch your breath and step back into the newer part of town, toward the oldest bullring in Spain. In early September, Ronda celebrates itself as the birthplace of the modern *corrida* by holding bullfights in the 18th-century *Plaza de Toros.* On quiet days, wander through the *Bullfighting Museum* (open daily, from 9 AM to 7 PM), and wonder why a people on a precipice should invent such a dangerous game. Information: *Oficina de Turismo,* 1 Plaza de España, Ronda 29400 (phone: 952-871272).

PLAZA MAYOR, Salamanca, Castile-León: A golden, ingot-shaped, perfect square. It is a happy place, sunny and carefree, and there can be no better place to sit down and enjoy a cup of coffee. Foreign students sit on the cobblestones and practice their Spanish, while mothers sit on benches and try to keep children, clad in brightly colored overalls, from rolling on the ground. In the evening, bands of students uniformed in black and red breeches, leotards, and puffy sleeves wander through the plaza armed with violins, guitars, and mandolins. They are *la tuna,* occasionally coming to rest around a café table, singing local songs, attracting crowds, and drinking on the house. Like most places in Spain, this 18th-century square wasn't always quite so peaceful; it used to double as the city's bullring. Information: *Oficina de Turismo,* 41 Gran Vía, Salamanca 37001 (phone: 923-243730).

PARQUE MARÍA LUISA AND PLAZA DE ESPAÑA, Seville, Andalusia: This swanky park and elegant plaza out of some fairy-tale colonial city were all that remained when the *1929 Iberian-American Fair* collapsed with the economy. Now communion parties row in canals dug for visitors who never came. Pavilions built for exhibits that never took place stand ready for this year's world's fair *Expo '92*. Stroll down the park's graveled avenues in June and you may become part of some local family's history, caught in the background of a wedding photograph, or simply recover from Seville's drenching heat on a bench protected by a high hedge. Through the leaves, the sunlight spatters on the brick floor and miniature ornamental tiles. Twin baroque towers, ornate lampposts, and bridges with blue and white terra cotta balustrades make the Plaza de España look like a Mexican fantasy of Venice. Information: *Oficina de Turismo,* 21-B Avenida de la Constitución, Seville 41004 (phone: 95-422-1404).

DIRECTIONS

Introduction

The Iberian Peninsula is a land that has been irresistible to travelers and explorers. As far back as 650 BC, foreigners (mostly in the form of invaders back then) were arriving in Spain and discovering its diversity and individuality. During the Age of Discovery beginning in the 15th century, numerous explorers, sailing under the flag of Spain, went in search of other lands to call their own.

Spaniards take enormous pride in their country, and today travelers from all over the world come to enjoy (not conquer) Spain's glorious beaches, challenging mountains, and breathtaking countryside. This year, Spain presents a unique triple treat for visitors as it hosts *Expo '92* (in Seville), the *1992 Summer Olympics* (in Barcelona), and celebrates the 500th anniversary of Columbus's discovery of America — countrywide. As if this were not enough, Madrid has been designated as the European Cultural Capital for 1992.

Until the 1960s, Spain was considered the perfect destination for adventurous travelers since public transportation was limited and primitive at best, and accommodations for visitors were far below other Western European standards. If hitch-hiking and sleeping on the beach were your cup of tea then this was the place to come. But with expanded air travel, improved train and bus services, and increased interest in European travel among young and old alike, Spain became an inexpensive and popular choice for travelers. And as interest grew, facilities for the traveler improved (although visitors today will no longer find prices to be much lower than those in other Western European countries). Spain's diversity of culture — a direct result of numerous invasions by other countries — and its varied topography provide today's traveler with a colorful journey, filled with limitless options for side trips far off beaten paths. From Algerciras to Zaragoza, this land still offers plenty of places to tilt at your own windmills.

In the following pages, we have outlined 13 driving routes that we think best represent — and cover — every corner of this fascinating country. Roads are generally in good repair in Spain, unless otherwise noted, and with few exceptions each route is designed to take between 3 and 5 days. We have even included several delightful day trips from the capital city of Madrid. And if at any point you tire at the wheel, it's possible to break your drive with an occasional ride on a rural railway. Each route includes numerous sightseeing highlights, suggested activities, and places to eat and stay. The *Best en Route* section at the end of each tour offers suggestions for the best hotels, inns, small *hostales,* indigenous *paradores,* and restaurants along the way (hotels are listed first, in order of expense, followed by restaurants).

Our routes are the paths that we think best show off this exciting land from the Pyrenees to the Strait of Gibraltar, plus detailed descriptions and information about the Canary and Balearic islands. It's possible for each traveler to mix and match, or combine routes according to his or her timetable and interests. But if you are pressed for time, you will find that by following a single itinerary, you will get the best taste of what each region of Spain has to offer.

Galicia

Despite Eliza Doolittle's assertion, the rain in Spain does *not* fall mainly on the plain: It falls on Galicia. In fact, Spain's northwestern corner wages a constant battle against the moisture-laden winds that roll in from across the Atlantic, making the region the country's wettest.

Cut off both geographically and culturally from mainstream Spain, Galicia contradicts the country's arid image. Instead of the familiar parched plains of central and southern Spain, its annual 64 inches of rain produce green mountain slopes, a network of blue-green rivers, pine and eucalyptus forests, palm trees, and lush terraces of vines. *Gallegos* rarely go out without umbrellas — even if a natural immunity to a few splashes means they often forget to use them. And in the fishing villages scattered along the coast and beside the *rías* (estuaries, or inlets), where the riverbeds are regularly raked for mussels and clams, the local costume includes an oilskin, over-the-knee galoshes, a pair of rubber gloves, and a resigned grin.

Galicia is also one of Spain's poorest regions. There are no Porsches here, only small domestic vehicles and shaky mopeds. There are also relatively few tractors, compared with the number of bullocks to be seen pulling carts of corn and other produce. And since there are also relatively few foreign visitors, the sight of a tourist car is often enough to stop a peasant in his or her tracks.

Historically, rather than farm in the traditional cooperative manner, the Galicians carved their land into hundreds of small holdings, each consisting of little more than a terra cotta–roofed shack, a few vines, a field of corn, and a donkey. By the turn of this century, as transatlantic travel became more accessible, those who could scrape together the pesetas emigrated to Central and South America. Argentina, in particular, was such a popular destination that, today, there are more *gallegos* in Buenos Aires than in Galicia.

The region was not always so undeveloped and far from the mainstream. During the Middle Ages, this distant corner of Europe was transformed, in the course of only a century or two, from a sleepy backwater into the world's first mass "tourist destination," with one of Christendom's three holiest cities. The metamorphosis began in 813, when a peasant, led to a field by shining starlight, discovered what was thought to be the long-forgotten tomb of St. James, one of the 12 Christian apostles. Over the years, the saint's remains became the object of a pilgrimage ranking second in importance only to one to Jerusalem or Rome, and the chapel built to house the bones grew to be the magnificent Cathedral of Santiago de Compostela, the final jewel in a chain of churches, monasteries, and hospices strung across northern Spain along the Camino de Santiago — the famous Way of St. James. (For further details, see *Pilgrims' Route,* DIRECTIONS.)

At the end of their journey, medieval pilgrims hobbled across the Plaza del

Obradoiro from the cathedral to have their blisters treated in the Hostal de los Reyes Católicos, a hospital and inn built in 1499 by King Ferdinand and Queen Isabella. Pilgrims knocking on the doors today find themselves ushered into cloistered comfort, their luggage whisked away by maroon-coated porters, because the former hospice is now the *Parador Los Reyes Católicos* (phone: 981-582200). Converted into a hotel in 1954, it is not only the flagship of Spanish *paradores,* but also one of the finest hotels in Europe. Seen from the outside, the only concession to modernity appears to be a pair of glass doors slotted into the magnificent Plateresque granite façade that stretches across the entire northern side of the plaza. Within, thick stone walls, heavy wooden furniture, fountains, and patios provide a luxurious retreat for weary travelers.

Buildings in Galicia, it must be said, are either monumental or monumentally ugly. To be sure, the historic centers of towns such as Santiago, La Coruña, Lugo, Pontevedra, and Bayona are archetypical Spain — the Spain of one's imagination. A cathedral, usually modeled on that of Santiago, overlooks a peaceful square shaded by plane trees. Children kick a soccer ball around, old men huddle and talk, black-veiled widows remember times long gone, and the cobbled streets are so quiet that passersby can hear the clatter of coffee cups coming from a bar long before they reach it.

But beyond these oases of aestheticism, grim and granite ugliness prevails. Suburbs in the larger towns consist of characterless and often unfinished apartment blocks; the smaller, one-street towns are strung out in shades of gray; and even vast stretches of otherwise stunning coastline have been marred by tasteless, prefabricated holiday bungalows. There are exceptions, of course, including the *pazos* — the former homes of noble Spanish families, standing aloof in the countryside — and, attached to most small holdings, the *horreos* — distinctive wooden and granite huts, perched on stilts, traditionally used for storing grain.

Many parts of Galicia, however, are free from modern encroachment. In summer, as foreign hordes descend on Spain's southern and eastern coasts and the inland plains suffocate in soaring temperatures, many Spaniards seek refuge along the cool, deserted Galician coastline. From the Eo River, which borders Asturias, around to the Miño River on the Portuguese frontier, the shoreline is rugged and beautiful, as yet uncluttered by vacation homes and attendant businesses.

Galicia consists of four provinces — La Coruña and Lugo to the north, Pontevedra and landlocked Orense to the south — and its deeply indented coastline is divided into two sections. The wild, more exposed Rías Altas (Upper Estuaries) run westward along the coast of the provinces of Lugo and La Coruña, from Ribadeo roughly to the city of La Coruña; and the gentler coves, wooded hills, and fishing villages of the Rías Bajas (Lower Estuaries) run south along the coast of the provinces of La Coruña and Pontevedra, from Muros down to Bayona.

The still and quiet estuaries closely resemble Norwegian fjords or Scottish lochs, while long stretches of palm-fringed sand have yet to experience the commercialization that has altered the shore along much of the Mediterranean. But between the Rías Altas and the Rías Bajas is a stretch of coast called the Costa de la Muerte (Coast of Death), treacherous to sailors through the ages (the roads are none too good, either). It begins at Malpica and comes to an abrupt end at Cabo Finisterre, literally the "end of the land" for medieval man.

Galician cuisine revolves around seafood. Along the coast, entire communities are engaged in milking the sea and rushing the day's (or night's) catch to restaurant tables. Even the smallest restaurant has at least one fish tank full of crabs and lobsters: Window decor is often no more than a huge, refrigerated display packed with regimental lineups of hake, bass, shrimp, crayfish, squid, and octopus. *Gallegos* tired of the sight of fish will probably opt for a plate of *lacón con grelos*. A potage of salted pork and turnip tops, this is Galicia's traditional soul food, and it's usually accompanied by local wine drunk from a white porcelain cup.

Galicia is a wonderful region in which to drive, and the A-9 highway, linking the region's two biggest cities and industrial areas — La Coruña and Vigo, 97½ miles (156 km) apart — is scheduled for completion this year. A well-planned network of freeways, fast and scenic, delves into the remotest corners, backed up by numerous and fairly well maintained country roads. Traffic is light beyond the pinpricks of urbanization, and distances that may look lengthy on a map are covered in a relatively short time. Road signs are excellent, even though several Castilian place-names have been altered by Galician separatists, who demand (thankfully, in a less violent manner than in other areas) that the region be accorded the rights and status of an independent nation.

The route outlined below is a circular one, encompassing significant stretches of both coastline and countryside. It begins in Santiago de Compostela and hugs the coastline from the vicinity of Padrón, southwest of Santiago, to Pontevedra, before continuing due south through Vigo to Bayona. From here it follows the seashore again, at times only yards from the water, before turning east along the Miño River, which forms the border with Portugal (and is known as the Minho in Portuguese), to the frontier town of Túy (where it is possible to walk or drive to Portugal across the bridge spanning the river.) The itinerary then cuts inland from Túy, following the Miño to Orense, keeping to the north bank of the river at first, then to the southern bank, and passing through the Ribeiro vineyard country around Ribadavia. From Orense, the route heads north via the old walled town of Lugo to Ribadeo on Galicia's north coast. Except for an excursion inland to Mondoñedo, the route now stays on the coast, exploring the Rías Altas around the northwest corner of Galicia (and of Spain) to El Ferrol and La Coruña.

Because Galicia is not, relatively speaking, a hotbed of tourism, the choice of accommodations is rather grim. The region's nine *paradores,* particularly the two in Santiago and Bayona, however, are among the notable exceptions. For their price, the *paradores* represent the best value for the money, and their reliably high standards are not only rewarding but almost essential at the end of a long day's drive.

Expect to pay $85 or more for a double room in a hotel or *parador* described as expensive, $60 to $85 in one listed as moderate, and under $60 in one listed as inexpensive. Prices do not include breakfast, but eating out in Galicia is rarely a costly experience. Restaurants listed as expensive charge around $80 for a dinner for two, including wine; a moderate establishment, $50 to $80; and an inexpensive one, under $50.

■**Note:** When two spellings are given (usually in the first reference to a place), the first one is in Spanish, and the second is in Galician, the local, Portuguese-like language.

SANTIAGO DE COMPOSTELA: By some stroke of good fortune, Santiago has remained much as it was in its days as a religious mecca. All streets lead to the cobbled Plaza del Obradoiro (also known as Plaza de España). One of the world's most spacious, majestic squares, it has managed to escape the ubiquitous neon signs, bars, restaurants, and cafés, and instead is snugly protected by four splendid, historic buildings: the cathedral, the College of San Jerónimo, the Town Hall, and the *Parador Los Reyes Católicos,* all built in the same honey-colored granite. The paucity of action in the plaza (beyond the frantic clicking of camera shutters) is more than compensated for down the side streets, particularly Rúa Nueva, Rúa del Villar, and Calle del Franco. Pedestrians in a constant stream pass under the porticoes or sip coffee in the sidewalk cafés — university students clutching clipboards, couples gossiping arm in arm, puzzled visitors poring over maps, and police casually patrolling in blue. (For full details on sights, hotels, and restaurants, see *Santiago de Compostela,* THE CITIES.)

En Route from Santiago de Compostela – Leave the outskirts of Santiago and head 12½ miles (20 km) south to Padrón on N550, an easy, fast main road that cuts through green fields and passes several *pazos* camouflaged behind iron gateways. The majority of these stately manor houses were built along the rivers leading into the Rías Bajas by families who made their fortunes across the Atlantic and returned to invest their newfound wealth. Beyond Padrón, at Ponte Cesures, leave N550 and take the coast road off to the right, signposted Villagarcía de Arousa. As the road hugs the woody southern shores of the Ulla River, leading into the Ría de Arousa, there are fine views across the water — unless it's raining, in which case mist rolls up the valley and settles in a low, dense layer. Lucky travelers will arrive in Villagarcía, 15½ miles (25 km) from Padrón, in time to see the townspeople up to their knees in the estuary, plucking shellfish from the sand flats. The *ría,* like the land in Galicia, has been sectioned off into "plots," and the scene is one of organized chaos as gulls scream, dogs bark excitedly, men chug around in boats, and well-built women hunker down to scour the beds for fish.

Continue on the coast road south, curving around the peninsula to Pontevedra, 34½ miles (55 km) from Villagarcía. En route, a short detour to the right, following the signposts to El Grove (O Grove), leads across a bridge to the island of La Toja (A Toxa), one of the region's few tourist developments — site of large expensive hotels, swimming pools, a spa, and a casino. Out of season, the scene is one of closed shutters, gentle drizzle, and old ladies valiantly trying to sell armfuls of shell necklaces to anyone with a foreign-looking complexion. Signs to Praia da Lanzada lead to the most beautiful beach in Galicia, with long swathes of pale sands, palm trees, and shallow waters. Still on the island, Combarro, a few miles farther, is a lost-in-time fishing village. With its line of waterfront *horreos* (granaries), it has been declared an artistic monument by the locals.

PONTEVEDRA: The streets of this old, charming town are lined with characteristic Galician glazed balconies called *solanas,* built to catch all the available sun but keep out the rain and wind. The town sits above the Pontevedra River, which at its wider points resembles a peaceful lake. There was a time when Pontevedra was a thriving hub for fishermen, merchants, and traders; but by the 18th century the delta had silted up, and sea traffic was forced to use the port at nearby Marín. (Ironically, the closest good beach is also at Marín.)

Concentrate on the Old Quarter, sitting on the doorstep of the *parador*. It's a peaceful mishmash of streets that rarely plays host to visitors. Finding the town's main museum, the *Provincial Museum*, an unmarked, solid granite building on Plaza de la Leña, is a task in itself. The museum (open Mondays through Saturdays, 11 AM to 1:30 PM and 5 to 8 PM; Sundays and holidays, 11 AM to 1 PM) contains maritime exhibits, artifacts from Galician history through the 19th century, and a valuable collection of jewelry. Other sights include Plaza de la Herrería, an arcaded square presided over by the Convento de San Francisco, and the Church of La Peregrina.

CHECKING IN: *Parador Casa del Barón* – Believed to stand on the site of an old Roman villa, like many *paradores* it is a former *pazo;* but during its checkered past it has also been a school, a granary, a masonic lodge, and, lastly, an 18th-century residence owned by the Barons of Casa Goda, who restored it. It has 47 rooms and flower-filled gardens. Plaza de Maceda, Pontevedra (phone: 986-855800; fax: 986-852195). Moderate.

EATING OUT: *Casa Solla* – A top-rate Galician eatery, the shellfish dishes never disappoint, but the chef's strengths are in the traditional stew, meat, and fish dishes. Closed Thursdays and Sunday evenings, and *Christmas.* Reservations advised. Major credit cards accepted. Km 2 on the Pontevedra–El Grave road, Pontevedra (phone: 986-852678). Moderate.

En Route from Pontevedra – Take the A9 freeway southwest 17 miles (27 km) to Vigo. Apart from Santiago, it is here, in the Rías Bajas areas around Pontevedra, Vigo, and Bayona (Baiona), that Galicia welcomes most of its holiday visitors. With a milder and sunnier climate than their northern counterparts, the Rías Bajas are backed by thick pine forests, and the hidden coves and gently shelving beaches make this the only strip of coastline where swimming is a viable (though not very warm) option.

VIGO: On the southern shore of the Ría de Vigo, Spain's largest fishing port is a lively, modern city, as well as a good example of how the deepwater anchorages and shelter of Galicia's coastline have been commercially exploited. Sir Francis Drake sacked the city in 1585 and again in 1589, and in 1702, a combined English and Dutch force attacked a Spanish treasure fleet returning from the Americas, sending many gold-laden galleons to the bottom of the estuary; they have yet to be discovered.

Vigo is a remarkably clean and manicured place, perhaps because hulking transatlantic liners no longer berth at the city's harbor terminal. During the day, visitors can shop for the city's famous *angulas* (eels) at the morning fish auction down near the waterfront, or climb to the heights of Parque del Castro. This superb public park is built around the Castillo de San Sebastián, a 10th-century fortress. The views overlook the estuary and its narrow neck, where the galleons were sunk. For lively nighttime bars, head for the old fishermen's quarter.

The entrance to the Ría de Vigo is sheltered by the Islas Cíes, a cluster of steep, abrupt rock islands with magnificent beaches, rich flora and fauna, spectacular cliff paths, and turquoise water. Passenger boats cross regularly to the islands from the port. Other beaches line the southern shores of the estuary in a practically unbroken strip.

CHECKING IN: *Bahía de Vigo* – A comfortable, 110-room hotel, strategically placed opposite the old transatlantic terminal. Its nautical decor includes portholes in the bar and naval trappings throughout. 5 Avenida Cánovas del Castillo, Vigo (phone: 986-226700; fax: 986-437487). Expensive to moderate.

Ciudad de Vigo – Functional and impersonal, this 126-room hotel, in a pretty part of town, primarily serves local businessmen. 5 Calle Concepción Arenal, Vigo (phone: 986-435233; fax: 986-439871). Expensive to moderate.

 EATING OUT: *El Timón Playa* – With the Islas Cíes and the sea as a backdrop, you'll want to be sure to reserve a table by the window here. The food is simple yet delicious — try the cockle empanada. Closed Sundays. Reservations unnecessary. Major credit cards accepted. 12 Calle Carrasquería (phone: 988-490815). Inexpensive.

BAYONA (BAIONA): A lively tourist town 13 miles (21 km) south of Vigo via C550, Bayona sweeps along the shore at the entrance to the Ría de Vigo. It's a pretty town, as well as a historic one — Bayona welcomed Columbus's return on the *Pinta* in 1493 after his discovery of the Americas — and it has retained many of its medieval features. Much of the long harbor road is lined with nautically themed clothing shops and restaurants; stores on the maze of streets behind the harbor (try *Náutic Mare* on Calle Ramón y Cajal, a clothes shop with branches in Marbella and other chic points south) echo the maritime theme.

The town is dominated by Monte Real, a fortified peninsula across the bay; besides a defensive wall, the peninsula is the site of a 16th-century castle that pokes into the river and is now the the town's *parador* (see below). When the winds get up, and the rain sweeps across the bay (which it frequently does), the waters turn gray and choppy — and the reason for the shipwreck lying on a group of treacherous rocks suddenly becomes clear. A huge statue of the Virgin (known as the Virgen de la Roca), stands on the shoreline to the south of town, looking out to the Cíes Islands.

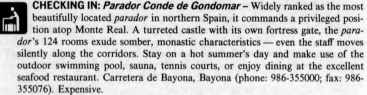 **CHECKING IN:** *Parador Conde de Gondomar* – Widely ranked as the most beautifully located *parador* in northern Spain, it commands a privileged position atop Monte Real. A turreted castle with its own fortress gate, the *parador*'s 124 rooms exude somber, monastic characteristics — even the staff moves silently along the corridors. Stay on a hot summer's day and make use of the outdoor swimming pool, sauna, tennis courts, or enjoy dining at the excellent seafood restaurant. Carretera de Bayona, Bayona (phone: 986-355000; fax: 986-355076). Expensive.

Tres Carabelas – Tucked down the back streets where ancient buildings echo to the sounds of noisy, adolescent-filled bars. Homey and comfortable though basic, with television sets in all 10 rooms. 61 Calle Ventura Misa, Bayona (phone: 986-355133). Inexpensive.

EATING OUT: *O Moscón* – Don't let the name (The Fly) put you off. The lobster tank is on view from the promenade outside, and there is also a display of gigantic crabs, an indication of the extensive range of seafood served here. It is cozy and smart, and features good local dishes; the menu has English translations. Open daily. Reservations advised. Major credit cards accepted. 2 Calle Alférez Barreiro, Bayona (phone: 986-355008). Moderate.

En Route from Bayona – The 19 miles (30 km) along C550 heading south to La Guardia (A Garda) are bleak, but this is where the route is at its most intimate with the white foaming seas, the waves breaking dramatically against giant rocks — sometimes spraying the car windshield. A sharp turn inland at La Guardia brings an equally sharp change in landscape — the gentle Miño River, which forms the frontier with Portugal, replacing the waves and the coastal stone walls and springy turf giving way to woods, scruffy villages, the occasional oxen, and fields of green maize and sinewy bamboo. Follow C550 as it twists eastward along the river 17 miles (28 km) to the frontier town of Tuy (Tui). The town has an attractive historic center, including a 12th-to-13th-century fortress-like cathedral, but it's worth a stop primarily to stroll across the river to Valença do Minho, Portugal, on the Ponte Internacional, the 19th-century suspension bridge designed by Alexandre-Gustave Eiffel, of Paris tower fame.

From Tuy, take the N550 9 miles (14 km) north to Porriño (signposted Redondela and Vigo), then turn east along N120 and continue 34 miles (55 km) to Ribadavia, proof that fast roads don't necessarily compromise dramatic, mountain scenery. Ribadavia is a scruffy but lively market town that heralds the entrance to Ribeiro vineyard country. Thick vines suddenly cover the slopes to the left and right as the road crosses the green waters of the Miño and connects to the rougher N202 which runs along the river's southern bank for 14 miles (22 km) to Orense (Ourense).

ORENSE (OURENSE): The approach to town, thick with dull apartment and office blocks, is suddenly relieved by a beautiful, seven-arched Roman bridge crossing the Miño into the town center. The bridge — the Puente Viejo — was reconstructed during the 13th century to ease the heavy traffic of pilgrims on their journey to Santiago. Orense is primarily an industrial town today, but it has been famous since ancient times for Las Burgas — springs of medicinal drinking water, which rise at around 149F in the center of the Old Town. The 12th-century cathedral is the last of the great western Romanesque churches; the grandiose scale of its nave, aisles, and east end and the sculptures of the Pórtico del Paraíso (Paradise Doorway) have been excelled only by the work of Master Mateo on the Gate of Glory in the cathedral in Santiago de Compostela.

CHECKING IN: *San Martín* – Smack in the Old Town; its 90 rooms are modern and functional. 1 Calle Curros Enríquez, Orense (phone: 988-235690; fax: 988-236585). Moderate.

Padre Fejióo – Close to the Old Town, this 71-room establishment is surrounded by a variety of fine restaurants. 1 Plaza Eugenio Montes, Orense (phone: 988-223100; fax: 988-223100). Inexpensive.

EATING OUT: *San Miguel* – Sample excellent shellfish and Galician dishes on the summer terrace or in the tastefully decorated dining room. Closed Tuesdays. Reservations necessary. Major credit cards accepted. 12 Calle San Miguel, Orense (phone: 988-221245). Expensive.

En Route from Orense – Leaving town, cross the Miño River and head north on N525 to the N540 intersection, 7 miles (11 km) from Orense. Take N540 north 16 miles (26 km) to Chantada, a charming little town known for its Monastery of San Salvador de Asma, an 11th-century Romanesque creation just outside town to the east; recently restored, the monastery's highlight is a collection of old Galician frescoes. Continue north on N540 another 24½ miles (39 km) to Guntín de Pallares, where N540 becomes N640 and continues another 11 miles (18 km) north to Lugo.

LUGO: The center of this provincial capital, one of Galicia's quintessentially Spanish towns, is wholly surrounded by a thick Roman wall, the best-preserved example of its kind in Spain. Join the handful of citizens walking their dogs along the ramparts, and you'll have a bird's-eye view of Lugo's terra cotta roofs and its street life, not to mention of the wall itself — about a mile in length, 30 to 45 feet high, about 15 feet thick, and interrupted at regular intervals by 85 semicircular towers. There are some 10 gates, but the most interesting one is the Santiago Gate, which opens before the Romanesque-Gothic Cathedral de Santa María overlooking Plaza Mayor. Arrive on a sunny Sunday morning and the entire town will be out taking a slow *paseo* (walk) in this tree-lined plaza: little girls in their best dresses and ribbons, old men in somber suits, and smart ladies whispering together, carrying freshly bought cakes oozing cream and dusted with powdered sugar. The outdoor tables of the cafés down one side of the square are packed, and toward lunchtime, as further crowds emerge from morning mass, the Lugo band begins to play on the turn-of-the-century bandstand at the center of the square. The town's gracious 18th-century Town Hall is also located here.

CHECKING IN: *Méndez Núñez* – An upscale but friendly establishment with 100 comfortable rooms, just around the corner from the main plaza. 1 Calle Reina, Lugo (phone: 986-230711; fax: 982-229738). Moderate.

En Route from Lugo – There's not much sign of civilization along N640 as it heads 56 miles (90 km) north to Ribadeo. It rides high, at first, over the green open plain, an occasional cattle farm camouflaged behind huge granite walls. As the road begins to follow the contours of the Eo River, it narrows to a single lane, its regular bends cutting through towering, pine-forested gorges. During the last few miles, watch the picturesque river — which here forms the boundary between the regions of Asturias and Galicia — unfold toward the coast at Ribadeo.

RIBADEO: The sights of this palm-fringed resort town on the Ría de Ribadeo, where the Eo River meets the sea, include the Art Nouveau buildings of the Plaza de España in the town center, as well as a pretty beach. There is a pleasant walk out to the lighthouse on the Eo estuary, to see fishermen taking in their catch and children clambering down the cliffs, as the waves crash against the rocks in the stiff Atlantic breeze. The town is dominated by the Torre de los Moreno, a tower built in 1905, whose copper dome is supported by four draped female figures. The Santa Cruz hill and hermitage, 1¼ miles (2 km) out of town, offers a marvelous view of the coastline. This is the site of the *Xira a Santa Cruz* pilgrimage, held annually on the first Sunday in August, with much traditional dancing and bagpipe music. Notice the bagpiper monument on the hill. Ribadeo's fishermen's quarter is full of *pulperías,* bars dedicated to the eating of octopus and the drinking of fine Galician wine from cups that resemble Chinese tea bowls.

From Ribadeo, a worthwhile excursion can be made inland to the old Galician town of Mondoñedo, 24 miles (39 km) southwest on N634. Mondoñedo's twin-towered 12th-century cathedral is a treasure, and the entire straggling, sleepy farming town is delightfully nestled in a broad-bottomed valley. The cathedral has a carved and painted 15th-century wooden statue, La Virgen Inglesa (English Virgin), rescued from St. Paul's Cathedral in London during the Reformation and brought to Spain, where it was acquired by a Mondoñedo aristocrat. The church also contains a superb, though cluttered and unkempt, museum filled with 12th- and 13th-century objects such as Arab boards, candle holders, sand clocks, and marble images of Christ. Mondoñedo is famous for its sweet, sticky baked goods made from sponge cakes, vermicelli, and almonds.

CHECKING IN: *Parador de Ribadeo* – The local link in the government-run chain, a modern, 47-room hostelry, inspires mixed reviews. Critics note that it's a could-be-anywhere *parador* of endless, shabbily carpeted corridors, bearable in summer but depressing under gray skies. Fans point out its wonderful views across the broad Eo estuary into Asturias. The breakfast display is impressive, but it's worth finding a more atmospheric restaurant in town in the evening. Popular despite the difference of opinion, so reserve rooms well in advance. Calle Amador Fernández, Ribadeo (phone: 982-110825; fax: 982-110346). Moderate.

EATING OUT: *O Xardin* – A 5-minute walk into town from the *parador,* it's the nearest Galicia comes to a bistro-style restaurant-bar. It has a comprehensive menu of fish and meat dishes and a large selection of wines. Closed

February. Reservations advised. Diners Club accepted. 20 Calle Reinante, Ribadeo (phone: 982-110222). Moderate to inexpensive.

En Route from Ribadeo – West of town, the route explores the Rías Altas portion of the Galician coastline, hopping from one long, indented inlet to the next as far as La Coruña (A Coruña). Take N634 out of Ribadeo and follow it 15 miles (24 km) west to Foz, a fishing village and beach resort on the far side of the Ría de Foz. From Foz, C642 continues westward 12 miles (19 km) to Cervo, where a left turn and subsequent signs lead visitors the extra mile or so to the Royal Ceramics factory at Sargadelos. It's a large, futuristic-looking building; the factory makes and sells distinctive plates, jewelry, pots, and figurines (closed during early afternoon siesta).

Return to C642 and head west for 12 miles (19 km) to Vivero (Viveiro), where the scenery improves dramatically. Here, steep cliffs drop down to spectacular panoramas of flat sands and shallow seas, unmarred by hotels, restaurants, boats, or even people. The province of Lugo ends at the Sor River and the Ría de Barqueiro, just beyond Vivero, but C642 continues west to Ortigueira, a fishing town on the Ría de Santa Marta de Ortigueira 22 miles (35 km) west of Vivero, and then to Campo de Hospital. At this point, C642 bends south, while C646 continues west to the most beautiful of the Rías Altas, the Ría de Cedeira. Cedeira itself, 17 miles (27 km) from Ortigueira, is a sleepy, pretty little sardine fishing town built along the banks of the Condeminas River.

El Ferrol (O Ferrol) is a pleasant 24-mile (38-km) drive south of Cedeira on C646. It's set directly across the water from La Coruña — the *gallegos* say that "If you can't see El Ferrol from La Coruña, it must be raining, and if you can, rain is on the way!" It's notable mainly as the birthplace of Generalísimo Francisco Franco (1892–1975). It certainly doesn't score on looks but thrives today as Spain's principal naval base and dockyard. The main shopping area, lined with clothing, footwear, and pastry shops, leads down to a square in front of the Town Hall, and makes for lively *paseos* in the early evening. Also of interest is the 18th-century church of El Socorro, which houses a famous statue of Christ walking on water.

CHECKING IN: *Parador El Ferrol* – A 39-room *parador* in an unlikely position overlooking the docks. Visitors are quite likely to be awakened at 8 AM to the sounds of a pre-recorded trumpet fanfare as sailors perform their ritual flag hoisting ceremony in the mini-square outside the hotel. Calle Almirante Vierna, El Ferrol (phone: 981-356720; fax: 981-356720). Moderate.

LA CORUÑA (A CORUÑA): A 38-mile (61-km) drive around three of the Rías Altas from El Ferrol leads to Galicia's largest city and business center. An important trading post on the ancient tin route, La Coruña is today one of Galicia's largest coastal developments and an active commercial port, its main trade the curing, salting, and tinning of fish. Philip II's Invincible Armada was launched from here in 1588; its defeat resulted in 15,000 deaths and the loss of half the fleet.

The town, which sits on a peninsula jutting out into the Ría de la Coruña, is divided roughly into three sectors: the Old Quarter (around the neck of the peninsula), with its two 12th-century, Romanesque-Gothic churches, Iglesia de Santiago and Santa María del Campo; the modern shopping quarter; and the busy port, bordering the beaches of Orzan and Riazor. The town is noted for its typically Galician 19th-century balconied buildings on the waterfront, but the most important single monument is the 2nd-century Tower of Hercules, the last remaining Roman lighthouse in operation (although in 1791 its original crumbling masonry was encased in modern brickwork).

CHECKING IN: *Finisterre* – On La Coruña's seafront, it has 3 swimming pools, tennis courts, and 127 small but comfortable rooms, the best of which overlook the harbor. Paseo del Parrote, La Coruña (phone: 981-205400). Expensive to moderate.

 EATING OUT: *El Rápido* – Serving excellent grilled shellfish and other seafood specialties for over 40 years. Closed Monday evenings. Reservations necessary. Major credit cards accepted. 7 Calle Estrella, La Coruña (phone: 981-224221). Expensive.

Castile-León (Old Castile)

Rather formidable and stern, the Castilian *meseta* (plateau) is the historical and spiritual heartland that eventually gathered a united Spain around it. After the impetus for the country's protracted Reconquest was born in the early 8th century in Asturias — a remnant of the old Visigothic, and therefore Christian, Spain, and the only part the Moors had failed to conquer — the movement spread southward across León and into the vast, elevated plateau of Castile, where it gained its greatest foothold. A shared commitment to driving the Moors out of Spain forged a firm bond between the kingdoms of Castile and León, one that was politically sealed early in the 13th century when León was united with Castile. Then, in 1469, the region began a rapid rise to prominence when Isabella of Castile wedded her personal and political fortunes to those of Ferdinand of Aragon. By 1479, the couple had become the embryo of the present Spanish monarchy, ruling over a joint kingdom of Aragon and Castile that was the basis of modern Spain. Their union also set in motion the centuries-long and notoriously cruel quest for religious uniformity known as the Spanish Inquisition, first instituted by Isabella in Castile in 1478 and not abolished until the early 19th century.

The singlemindedness of purpose, raw courage of conviction, and unflinching historic vision characteristic of Isabella (called Isabel la Católica — a title she was granted by Alexander VI, a Spanish pope, in 1496) were undoubtedly attributes she absorbed from the hard-edged reality of her native Castile. Virtually ringed by high mountain ranges, the immense Castilian plateau occupies the central part of Spain at an average altitude of 2,600 feet. Here, vast fields stretch long, flat, and often uninterrupted to a dusty horizon. Exposed to everything from scorching hot summers to blustery, bone-chilling winters, this is not a region that pampers its populace. Here, too, religion, ritual, and tradition of the ages keep a firm rein on the imagination.

Castilians are a hearty, no-nonsense lot who, when their security is threatened, often act first and ask questions afterward. Recently, the leader of an extreme right-wing Catholic organization came to visit the Iglesia de Santa Teresa in the small village of Alba de Tormes, not far from Salamanca. Enshrined in the church are two important relics of St. Teresa of Avila — her heart and a portion of bone from her arm. A fray soon broke out between members of the organization and other visitors to the church, and the church deacon, mistakenly believing that the extremist leader was trying to steal St. Teresa's arm bone, rang the church bell to summon the townspeople to the rescue. As rumor of the alleged theft attempt spread, villagers prepared to lynch the man on the spot. When he sought refuge in his car, they pushed it into the Tormes River. Eventually the Guardia Civil of Salamanca was summoned to fish him out. Such is the character of Castile.

Today's autonomous community of Castile-León, the result of the reorganization of the map of Spain following the death of Generalísimo Francisco Franco, encompasses the former kingdom of León and the northern half of the former kingdom of Castile. In all, it comprises 9 provinces: Zamora, León, and Salamanca, which correspond to the former kingdom of León, plus Palencia, Valladolid, Avila, Burgos, Segovia, and Soria, which correspond to the northern half of the former kingdom of Castile. The latter also conforms roughly to the historic region known as Old Castile, or Castilla la Vieja. (The autonomous community of Castile–La Mancha is the latter-day version of the historic region of New Castile, or Castilla la Nueva.)

Before León and Castile joined forces against the Moors early in the 13th century, they had already enjoyed an on-again, off-again arrangement as far as their autonomy was concerned, since the kingdom of León had once before been united with Castile, from 1037 to 1157, and then become independent again until the final reunion in 1230. But after the Reconquest, jockeying for position in the larger entity of a newly unified Spanish kingdom created regional rifts that linger today. There is token resistance, for instance, to the tandem nature of the recently constituted autonomous community of Castile-León. Sporadic graffiti spied in the provinces of León at times crosses out the Spanish name "Castilla" in expressing a desire for independent status, or suggests León get top billing by transposing the names. Throughout the provinces of Castile, on the other hand, the name "León" occasionally is deleted with equally chauvinistic zeal.

At the dawn of the 16th century, with Spain at the height of its power, Castile composed more than half of the Iberian Peninsula, extending from the Pyrenees to Gibraltar. But with the decline of Spain that took place after the defeat of its "Invincible Armada" came the decline of Castile, and the 18th century saw a steady emigration deplete the populations of its most prosperous cities and towns by as much as one-half. Today's autonomous community of Castile-León makes up about one-fifth of modern-day Spain, yet its population barely tops 2,500,000. It remains largely a region of wheat and corn fields, vegetable patches, and dairy and sheep farms, although it is not immune to changes mandated by Common Market membership and the subsequent progress that is sweeping through the peninsula. Still, habits die hard, and customs of vocation, craft, and sentimental allegiance are slow to change. Donkeys are still a common beast of burden, daily masses still draw appreciable numbers of parishioners to local churches, and in scattered villages pottery is still made as it has been for centuries — by women sitting at potter's wheels in the backs of family barns.

A certain cultural and culinary unity binds the nine provinces of Castile-León. This is *la tierra de asados,* the land of roasts — especially lamb and pork. And although the region is at a significant remove from the sea, its rivers provide fine tench, trout, and *ancas de rana* (frogs' legs). Chickpeas, lentils, and assorted varieties of broad beans are the prime ingredients of some tasty, rib-sticking regional stews. A prime hunting ground, this region is also noted for its *liebre* (hare), *codorniz* (quail), *pichón* (pigeon), and *perdiz* (partridge). Among the favored desserts are *leche frita* (fried milk), *almendrados* (almond paste), and *yemas de Santa Teresa* (candied egg yolks).

Castile-León also produces one of the widest ranges of wines in all of Spain — from the robust reds of Toro to the delicate whites of Rueda. With over 50,000 acres devoted to the grape, the region is third within Spain in terms of area planted in vines, and seventh in terms of production. Among the 13 noteworthy wine growing areas in the region, Ribera del Duero, Rueda, and Toro have achieved "Denomination of Origin" status (the equivalent of the French *appelation*). The remaining vinicultural areas are Benavente, Cebreros, Cigales, El Bierzo, Fermoselle, La Ribera del Arlanza, La Ribera del Cea, La Ribera de Salamanca, La Sierra de Salamanca, and Valdevimbre–Los Oteros.

Hunting of both big and small game is a popular sport in this landscape of vast cultivated plains interspersed with occasional mountains and forests. Perhaps most prized among small game is the red partridge, abundant in the provinces of Zamora, Salamanca, Valladolid, Avila, Segovia, Burgos, and Soria. The cereal growing areas of León and Zamora, and the provinces of Palencia, Valladolid, Burgos, Soria, Avila, and Segovia, are prime quail turf, and hare and rabbit abound throughout the region. Among big game, roe deer and boar are readily found in the provinces of Burgos and Soria. The *capra hispánica* (mountain goat), a unique national treasure and prized hunting trophy, is also indigenous to the region; and organized expeditions led by experienced guides provide the greatest assurance of success.

Architecturally, Castile-León is primarily fluent in the Romanesque, Gothic, and Mudéjar vernaculars, which achieve their finest expressions in a profusion of cathedrals, castles, and palaces. Castile derives its name from the abundance of castles that guarded its numerous feudal interests during the Middle Ages. Given the ravages of time and man, however, these structures are notably scarce along the 500-mile (800-km) route described below. The itinerary stays mainly along the plain of what was Castilla la Vieja (Old Castile), before the recent division of Spanish territory into autonomous communities. A stern and sober land, Castile-León demands of visitors a certain immunity to scenic monotony and to a lack of scenic definition. For here the earth is often the color of golden sand — as are the houses and churches that loom infrequently against the blur of a horizon smudged with a golden dust. But that is after the harvest, when the land is spent. In the spring, when the wheat and corn are green, and the fields rich with the promise of succulent vegetables, the scenery becomes less lunar and more lush.

Throughout Castile-León, hotels charging $75 and above for a double room with private bath are classified as expensive, $45 to $75 as moderate, and less than $40, inexpensive. Dinner for two with wine will cost $70 and up in an expensive restaurant, $45 to $70 in a moderate restaurant, and under $40 in an inexpensive one.

The following journey into the Spanish heartland begins in Madrid, which is geographically separated from Castile-León by the Sierra de Guadarrama. For a full report on Madrid, its sights, hotels, and restaurants, see *Madrid,* THE CITIES.

En Route from Madrid – As a point of reference, begin at the Plaza de Cibeles in the heart of Madrid and follow the Gran Vía and its extension, Calle Princesa, out past Moncloa until it becomes the N-VI highway at the edge of the city. Eager suburban development in recent years has blurred the former sharp demarcation between city and country, and nowadays the transition is marked by gradually decreasing numbers of billboards and housing developments as the distant mountains approach.

From Madrid to Avila, via N-VI and C505, is a distance of 69 miles (110 km). Take C505, which branches off from N-VI about 10 miles (16 km) northwest of Plaza de Cibeles. At this point, the city has been left behind, and after crossing a big bridge over the very small Río Guadarrama, the road becomes more rurally curvaceous. After another 11 miles (18 km), just before the bridge crossing the Embalse de Valmayor (Valmayor Reservoir), there is a glimpse of Philip II's palace-monastery of El Escorial straight ahead. The massive yellow walls and crowning cupolas of this eminently conspicuous construction are the architectural manifestation of Philip's own proud, pious, and tormented soul. For the next few miles, his imposing monument ducks in and out of sight, looming ever larger and more insistent until the traveler makes the turn to explore its austere, lugubrious charms. The turnoff occurs 4½ miles (7 km) beyond the reservoir, when the road splits, veering right for San Lorenzo de El Escorial, the village that abuts the palace-monastery, and left for Avila and El Escorial itself (follow signs for "Monasterio de El Escorial," not just for "El Escorial"). About half a mile (1 km) farther on, C505 turns left to Avila, while C600 goes straight for a little over a mile (2 km) to the El Escorial parking lot.

Philip built the monastery-palace in thanksgiving for his victory over the French in Flanders in 1557. Construction went on for 21 years, from 1563 to 1584 — record time for such an extensive edifice — and from 1584 to his death in 1598, this was the isolated residence from which the ascetic king ruled the vast Spanish Empire. The monastery-palace stands in eloquent testimony to the acute religious mania that clouded Philip's mind during his later years, and the combination of truly royal grandeur with austerity evident here is unique. His small, monastic chambers in the Palacios (Royal Apartments) are in stark contrast to the splendor of the rest of the structure. It was here that Philip learned of the defeat of the Armada; and in the adjoining bedroom, where a window overlooks the high altar of the monastery's grandiose, cross-shaped church, that he died. The monastery also houses the Panteón de los Reyes (Royal Pantheon), which contains the remains of 26 Spanish monarchs (all but Philip V and Ferdinand VI), and the *Nuevos Museos* (New Museums), complete with works by Ribera, Velázquez, and El Greco. The Escorial complex (phone: 91-890-5903) is open Tuesdays through Sundays, from 10 AM to 6 PM; admission charge. For further details, see *Madrid Region,* DIRECTIONS.

Head with care back to C505, en route to Avila. (Although well marked approaching El Escorial, the way out of town is not clearly signposted.) The road offers a good view of the towering monastery to the right, then continues to Avila amid mountains that were only a hazy mirage from Madrid, bald mountains with sporadic tufts of trees and assorted evergreens. Ahead, a large sign marks the border of Castile-León, and in particular, the province of Avila; then the road gradually ascends the Castilian plateau to Spain's highest provincial capital (3,600 feet), which appears after the crest of a hill. Follow the Centro Urbano or Centro Ciudad signs into the city.

AVILA: Built on the banks of the Adaja River, Avila is a city whose historical center is surrounded by remarkably well preserved rectangular walls that are most dramatic when viewed in silhouette against the surrounding Castilian plain. To the southwest, the wall divides Avila from an expanse of undeveloped land, but to the northeast, it has failed to contain the city, which has grown beyond its medieval boundaries to a current population of just over 43,000. Construction of the wall began in 1090; it took 10 years and more than 2,000 workers to complete 90 semicircular towers, 9 gates, several posterns, and innumerable battlements along an 8,200-foot perimeter. The result still looks astonishingly new, and many sections of the city that are built up against the wall have an unfinished feel about them. In fact, much of the city seems unfinished — even the modern areas that have leap-frogged the wall, possibly because of the unadorned bluntness of the architecture combined with Avila's elevated vantage point upon a rather bleak, barren *meseta.*

As the birthplace and religious training ground of the famous Santa Teresa de Jesús de Avila, commonly known as St. Teresa, a Carmelite nun who founded a reformed order of Carmelites, the Barefoot (Discalced) Carmelites, Avila has played a strong spiritual role in the evolution of both Castile and Spain. Born in 1515 in what is now the Convento de Santa Teresa (Plaza de la Santa; open daily, 8 AM to 1 PM and 3:30 to 9 PM; no admission charge), St. Teresa took her vows and had the spiritual experiences that paved the way for her canonization in the Monasterio de la Encarnación (Plaza de la Encarnación; open daily, 9:30 AM to 1 PM and 4 to 6 PM; admission charge). Nearby, in the Convento de San José, or Convento de las Madres (Calle del Duque; open daily, from 10 AM to 1 PM and 4 to 7 PM; admission charge) — the first Convent of the Barefoot Carmelite order — St. Teresa first put her religious principles into practice in a place of her own.

Though St. Teresa is not the only reason to visit the town, Avila's other noted sights are also religious in nature. Just inside the Puerta de los Leales is the starkly rectilinear, 12th-century stone cathedral (on Calle Alemaña), a structure that is building-block plain, except for an incongruous inset of ornately carved excess above the multi-arched Gothic entrance. Forming part of the old wall, the cathedral had a military raison d'être, and it shows. Comic relief is at hand, however, in the sets of carved lions surrounding the plaza, their haunches protruding prominently beyond their supporting pedestals. Inside the cathedral are three aisles and a central choir. The museum, housed in the 15th-century Capilla del Cardenal, contains hymnal tomes from the 15th century; silk-embroidered, gold- and lace-adorned garments of the 18th century; a 5-foot tall, 16th-century silver Custodia del Corpus that is paraded through the streets every *Corpus Christi Day* and looks very much like an overgrown, 6-tiered wedding cake ornament; a carved wooden coffin containing the remains of San Segundo, Avila's first archbishop; and a 16th-century Ecce Homo. Just inside the cathedral entrance, the bronze statue of San Pedro is kept shiny at the knees, nose, and hands by the faithful hoping that good fortune will rub off on them. The cathedral is open daily, May through September, 8 AM to 1 PM and 3 to 7 PM; October through April, 10 AM to 1:30 PM and 3 to 7 PM. The museum is open daily, May through September, 10 AM to 1:30 PM and 3 to 7 PM; October through April, 10 AM to 1:30 PM and 3 to 5 PM. Admission charge to the museum. Across the square from the cathedral is the town's tourist office, 4 Plaza de la Catedral (phone: 918-211387).

Avila's Romanesque Iglesia de San Vicente (Plaza de San Vicente; open daily, 10 AM to 1 PM and 4 to 6 PM; admission charge) is just outside the walls on the northeast, through the Puerta de San Vicente. Built between the 12th and 14th centuries, it has an arched loggia of gray stone that clashes in tone and tenor with the amber blocks of the main structure. The main attraction inside is the Sepulcro de los Niños Mártires, recalling the church's founding legend, which holds that three young siblings were martyred on this spot. Of a more welcoming nature is the Iglesia de San Pedro (Plaza de Santa Teresa; open daily, 10 AM to 1 PM and 4 to 6 PM), begun in 1100 as a Romanesque structure and later fitted with Gothic flourishes. Situated outside the walls opposite the Puerta del Alcázar at the far end of the Plaza de Santa Teresa, it contains — since Pope John Paul II's 1983 visit — a mounted "chapel" honoring the "Virgin of Czestochowa, Queen of Poland." The Monasterio de Santo Tomás, on Plaza de Granada, once isolated from the city proper, now stands at the very edge of Avila's urban expansion. Its checkered past includes use as the headquarters of the Inquisition (Tomás de Torquemada, the inquisitor general, lived here), a turn as the summer palace of Ferdinand and Isabella, and an interlude as the seat of a university. The final resting place of Ferdinand and Isabella's son, Prince Juan, today it continues as a Dominican monastery complete with church, cloisters, and choir, as well as an Oriental art gallery in the former royal apartments. The complex is open daily, from 10:30 AM to 1 PM and 4 to 7 PM. Admission charge to the cloister, through which the complex is entered; additional charge for the art gallery.

CHECKING IN: *Palacio de Valderrábanos* – Built as a palatial home by the family of the same name late in the 14th century. Diagonally across from the cathedral, it offers 73 rooms, all with private baths, and 3 suites, one of which is romantically situated in the tower. Lamps with cloth shades and skirted chairs impart a cozy, country feeling. The restaurant, *El Fogón de Santa Teresa,* serves traditional Castilian dishes. 9 Plaza de la Catedral, Avila (phone: 918-211023; telex: 2248). Expensive.

Parador Raimundo de Borgoña – One of the state-run *paradores,* it incorporates the Palacio de Benavides, also known as the Palacio de Piedras Albas, built during the late 15th century. Abutting the northern walls, its 62 rooms (12 of which are of palace vintage) all have private baths. The hostelry's gardens are next to walkways on top of the city walls that offer choice views of Avila and the *meseta* beyond. Local delicacies such as roast suckling pig, as well as more generic Spanish dishes (gazpacho, *truchas fritas con jamón serrano* — fried trout with smoked ham), are served in the dining room. 16 Calle Marqués de Canales y Chozas, Avila (phone: 918-211340; fax: 918-226166). Expensive.

Rey Niño – Built in 1840 as a hotel, it is near the cathedral and has has 24 rooms that are structurally romantic but spare of furnishings. All is clean, and the plumbing is modern. 1 Plaza de José Tomé, Avila (phone: 918-211404). Moderate.

EATING OUT: *Mesón del Rastro* – Castilian cuisine featuring *truchas del Tormes* (trout from the Tormes River) and *mollejas de ternera* (veal sweetbreads), served in a rustic decor. Reservations unnecessary. Major credit cards accepted. 1 Plaza del Rastro, Avila (phone: 918-211218). Moderate.

En Route from Avila – Leaving town by the western gate, cross over the Adaja River and follow the signs for N501 and Salamanca. A half mile (1 km) on, there is a fine panoramic view of Avila at Cuatro Postes, a spot marked by four concrete posts with a cross in the center. The N501 highway covers the entire 61-mile (98-km) distance to Salamanca, passing a scenic potpourri of broad fields marked by rock walls, sporadic outcroppings, occasional outbursts of trees and scrub, wheat fields, grazing sheep, and stands of sunflowers. Here and there, the *meseta* slopes down on either side of the road, giving the impression that the world drops off beyond the dust-hazy horizon. Suddenly, without fanfare, Salamanca materializes in spired splendor to the right.

SALAMANCA: For a complete report on the city and its sights, hotels, and restaurants, see *Salamanca,* THE CITIES.

En Route from Salamanca – The N630 highway from Salamanca to Zamora stretches north for 39 rather unscenic miles (62 km), crossing the border into the province of Zamora about halfway along the route. On the outskirts of town, avoid following the signposts to Zamora Este; continue straight on N630, bear right, and follow the signs for Centro Ciudad.

ZAMORA: A 13th-century Romanesque bridge over the Duero River marks the historic center of Zamora, which rises 2,000 feet on the river's right bank. This is the city where El Cid spent part of his youth and was reportedly knighted. Its most outstanding feature is the cathedral (Plaza del Castillo); built during the 12th century with a few later additions, it has a great dome decorated in a curious Byzantine scalloped pattern. The cathedral museum contains an unsurpassed collection of tapestries, yet another example of the numerous hidden treasures Spain offers to those willing to stray off the beaten track. The ten tapestries on the upper floor are the most splendid, the largest measuring 30 feet in length. Exquisite for their vibrant colors, scrupulous detail, and expert three-dimensional illusion, these 15th-century Flemish masterpieces depict Greek mythological scenes. The remaining, 17th-century tapestries of Hannibal are smaller and would be more impressive than they appear here, if displayed separately. The museum is open daily, 11 AM to 2 PM and 4 to 8 PM, though times are unpredictable. (Out of season, the museum door is closed while the cashier-guide shows small groups around, so wait for the tour to end.) Admission charge. A fine view of the Duero River and the Romanesque bridge that spans it can be appreciated from the Puerta del Obispo, an arched gateway in the city wall behind the cathedral.

A favorite excursion from Zamora is to Pereruela, a small village with a few hundred inhabitants 10 miles (16 km) southwest of town via C527. A handful of families here still make fine ceramic cookware by hand; visitors can see the clay being sculpted and ovens being fired out back by the family barns. Although there are no shops, the goods can be purchased from the source, or from family members displaying their wares along the road.

 CHECKING IN: *Parador Condes de Alba y Aliste* – Installed in the former 15th-century palace of the Count of Alba y Aliste in the city's historic core, this beautiful *parador* offers 27 double rooms with private bath on the second floor of a Renaissance cloister. The property is endowed with a bar, a restaurant, gardens, and a swimming pool. Plaza de Cánovas, Zamora (phone: 988-514497; fax: 988-530063). Expensive.

Dos Infantas – Very pleasant, comfortable, and central, with 68 rooms, 5 of which are a tub shy of a complete bath. 3 Cortinas de San Miguel, Zamora (phone: 988-532875; fax: 988-533548). Moderate.

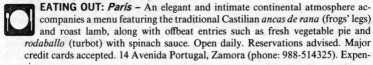 **EATING OUT: *París*** – An elegant and intimate continental atmosphere accompanies a menu featuring the traditional Castilian *ancas de rana* (frogs' legs) and roast lamb, along with offbeat entries such as fresh vegetable pie and *rodaballo* (turbot) with spinach sauce. Open daily. Reservations advised. Major credit cards accepted. 14 Avenida Portugal, Zamora (phone: 988-514325). Expensive.

Serafín – Seafood is the specialty here, along with traditional Castilian and Zamoran fare. Open daily. Reservations advised. Major credit cards accepted. 10 Plaza Maestro Haedo, Zamora (phone: 988-531422). Expensive.

La Posada – Quiet and refined, with local specialties including *mollejas a la zamorana* (sweetbreads in a spicy red sauce) and *lentejas* (lentil soup with garlic-spiced sausage and potato). Closed July 1–15. Reservations advised. American Express and Visa accepted. 2 Calle Benavente, Zamora (phone: 988-516474). Moderate.

En Route from Zamora – There are two ways to reach Benavente. If time is short, take N630 about 37 miles (60 km) north, then follow the Benavente signs to the N-VI highway, which leads to the turnoff for the center of town, another 5 miles (8 km) away from N630.

If time permits, however, take the longer route (a total of 69 miles/110 km), via the town of Toro, which is 20½ miles (33 km) due east of Zamora. Leave Zamora on N122, a road that parallels the Duero River. About halfway to Toro, the *meseta* stretches expansively into the distance on the right, with the Duero marking the boundary between the Tierra del Pan (Land of Bread) to the north and the Tierra del Vino (Land of Wine) to the south. Besides recently having its wine accorded *denominación* (appellation) status, Toro enjoys some historic and artistic distinctions. During the Second Punic War, Hannibal passed through the town; and during the early centuries of the Reconquest, Toro was a frequent battleground between Christian and Muslim forces. The peripatetic St. Teresa also established a convent here; and the Inquisition, one of its cruel tribunals. Follow the signs for Centro Ciudad, and the service road into town. The center is reached through either of two arched gateways. The first is the Puerta de Corredera (Sliding Gate), which leads straight beneath the arch of the 18th-century Torre del Reloj (Clock Tower), past the Plaza de España, and on to the town's main sight, the Church of Santa María la Mayor. The second gateway, Puerta Santa Catalina, is near the tourist information kiosk and a stone statue of an Iberian pig in the center of a small traffic circle. Passing through this gate, follow the street into the Plaza de España and turn left to the church.

The Colegiata de Santa María la Mayor, Toro's highlight, is a 12th-century Romanesque collegiate church (open daily, May through August, 10:30 AM to 1:30 PM and 5 to 7 PM; September through April, noon to 1 PM and 7 to 8 PM — but hours are erratic, and if a guide is not on duty, ask for the priest in charge, who will gladly open the church). The western door, the Puerta de la Majestad, where guided tours begin, is crowned by seven pointed arches and compares favorably with the famed Pórtico de Gloria in Santiago de Compostela's cathedral. The sacristy contains several treasures, among them the well-known Virgen de la Mosca (Virgin of the Fly) — so named because of the fly on her knee — painted by Fernando Gallego. Also notice, in the church itself, the unusual 14th-century statue of a pregnant Virgin, one of a very few in Spain.

The 12th-to-13th-century Romanesque-Mudéjar Church of San Lorenzo (Plaza de España) is another church worth visiting. Sweet and simple, it has a wonderful altar by Fernando Gallego, Plateresque tombs, and a beautiful polychrome mezzanine sagging with the weight of centuries. If the church is locked, ask someone at the tourist information kiosk to open it, but bear in mind that the presence of the tourist board staff is unpredictable.

Leaving Toro through the Puerta Santa Catalina, take N122 west, back toward Zamora, but turn right almost immediately at the sign indicating the road to Pozoantiguo and Castronuevo. After crossing the Valderaduey River and exiting Castronuevo, turn left onto ZA702 toward Villarrín de Campos, some 7½ miles (12 km) away. This entire route crosses the flat wheat fields that earned the area the epithet Tierra del Pan (Land of Bread). Pass Villarrín de Campos and head toward Estación de la Tabla, a mere scattering of warehouses and a granary, then continue on ZA701 toward Granja de Moreruela. This will lead to the right turn back onto N630 toward Benavente.

EATING OUT: *Catayo* – A typical village tavern just off the Plaza de España, serving home-style meals at home-style prices and offering a selection of regional wines from the newly established *denominación* Toro. Open daily. No reservations or credit cards accepted. 7 Calle José María Cid, Toro (phone: 988-690060). Inexpensive.

BENAVENTE: Situated on a promontory near the confluence of the Orbigo and Esla rivers, this town of 11,000 inhabitants offers a stunning view of the Castilian plain to the south and west. Santa María del Azoque, a 12th-century church of very irregular construction, is one of two special sights in town — be sure to walk around it to appreciate the kaleidoscopic effect of its diverse architectural elements. Most striking in its interior are three slender Gothic naves with precisely pointed arches. Open for mass at 9 AM and 7 PM daily, and more frequently on Sundays, the church is best visited just before or after the service.

The town's other special sight is the *Parador Fernando II de León,* on Paseo Ramón y Cajal (see below). Built on the elevated site of the former 12th-century castle-palace of the Counts and Dukes of Benavente, it incorporates a well-preserved, 16th-century Gothic-Renaissance tower that was part of that noble complex. Inside, two engravings of the castle in its heyday and an 1880 photo of it in ruins are on display. Installed in the vestigial tower are a lovely salon and, below that, an impressive bar (open 5 to 11:30 PM) with a new wooden ceiling and rusty chandelier that are remarkable imitations of antiques. Watching the sun set though the bar's oversized windows is a rare treat.

CHECKING IN/EATING OUT: *Parador Fernando II de León* – This lovely *parador* offers 28 double rooms and 2 singles, all with private bath, and many with terraces offering splendid views. The dining room menu features such provincial dishes as *arroz a la zamorana* (rice Zamora-style — a kind of peasant paella with tripe, pig's ear, pig's knuckles, and *chorizo* sausage in a red sauce), as well as sweetbreads with prawns, and more of the town's fine panorama. Major credit cards accepted. Paseo Ramón y Cajal, Benavente (phone: 988-630300; fax: 988-630303). Expensive.

En Route from Benavente – León lies 44½ miles (71 km) north of Benavente via N630. Coming into town, follow the Centro Ciudad signs, cross over the Bernesga River, then turn left and follow the tree-lined boulevard that parallels the river all the way to the *Parador San Marcos.*

LEÓN: This provincial capital traces its origins back to the mid-1st century, when the Romans built a fortification at the confluence of the Bernesga and Torió rivers. Its most remarkable structure is the cathedral, built during the 13th and 14th centuries. One of the most beautiful ever built, it was modeled after the cathedrals at Reims and Amiens in France, and is an exquisite example of Spanish Gothic architecture. Its crowning glory lies not in its stonework, but in its over 16,000 square feet of stained glass,the most dazzling display in Spain. Almost hallucinatory in their effect, the windows, which date from every century since the cathedral's birth, depict religious scenes from the lives of Christ, the Virgin Mary, and the saints, as well as purely ornamental motifs. In a country brimming with stunning cathedrals, the colored shafts of light that slice through the stone-gray gloom here make León's among the most memorable in the land. Its museum, too, stands out for its commendable collections of Roman bronze figures and weapons, neolithic artifacts, and Romanesque statues; also of interest is the exhibit of vintage sketches referred to in the restoration of many of the cathedral's stained glass treasures. The cathedral (Plaza de Regla) is open daily, from 8:30 AM to 1:30 PM and 4 to 7 PM. The museum is open daily, May through

August, from 10 AM to 1:30 PM and 4 to 6:30 PM; September through April, from 10 AM to 1:30 PM and 4 to 7:30 PM. Admission charge to the museum.

About a 10-minute walk from the cathedral is another important León sight, the Romanesque Basilica of San Isidoro, a hybrid house of God born during the 11th century, adorned and cloistered during the 12th, and partially reconstructed and enlarged during the 16th. Regrettably, the later remodeling obliterated much of the original Romanesque, but the basilica's pantheon remains one of the earliest examples of the Romanesque architectural genre in Spain. Here, 22 kings and queens of the old kingdom of León are buried beneath 12th-century frescoes that have prompted many to refer to this as the "Sistine Chapel" of Romanesque art; the pantheon can also boast capitals and a portal carved with scenes from the gospel, the earliest in Spain to be so decorated. A separate room houses the treasury, complete with illuminated Bibles and other fine relics. The church (Plaza de San Isidoro) is open daily, 7 AM to midnight. The pantheon is open daily, May through August, 9 AM to 2 PM and 3:30 to 8 PM; September through April, 10 AM to 1:30 PM and 4 to 6:30 PM. There is an admission charge to the pantheon and treasury, which are seen on tours conducted by multilingual guides.

A third important monument in León, the *Parador San Marcos* (see *Checking In*), is located along the river and built in the Renaissance style. One of León's liveliest and loveliest landmarks, this was formerly the Monasterio de San Marcos, which was donated to the Order of Santiago by the Catholic Monarchs in appreciation of services rendered during the Reconquest. The monastery then became a hospital for pilgrims en route to Santiago de Compostela. During the Renaissance, it blossomed to its present sumptuousness; the *parador* now shares the grounds of the original monastery with the *Provincial Archaeological Museum,* which contains items from the Stone Age to the Renaissance. The adjacent Gothic church with its ornately carved choir stalls was a 16th-century addition. The museum is open daily, from 10 AM to noon and 4 to 6 PM; admission charge.

All of the above sights of León are in the Old Town, which is surrounded by a modern city of high-rises, and which has itself been substantially rebuilt, although its streets still follow the old twists and turns. The tourist office (3 Plaza de Regla; phone: 987-237082) is just across from the cathedral. Not far away is the Plaza Mayor, surrounded by porticoes and, on most days, alive with a market selling fruits and vegetables.

 CHECKING IN: *Parador San Marcos* – One of the most impressive hostelries in the country, in a converted 16th-century monastery that also hosted pilgrims on their way to Santiago, it has 245 majestic double rooms and 7 suites. Most are in a newly built section, but 30 ample rooms in the old structure have vintage decorations. The rooms in the modern addition, as well as the lobby, open onto the monastery's original cloister. The hotel has a fine restaurant. 7 Plaza San Marcos, León (phone: 987-237300; fax: 987-233458; telex: 89809). Expensive.

Quindós – This very comfortable hotel has 96 rooms, each with private bath, direct-dial telephone, and a color television set. Centrally located, only 2 blocks from the *parador,* with a public video salon and a restaurant. 24 Avenida José Antonio, León (phone: 987-236200; fax: 987-242201). Moderate.

Riosol – Functional and comfortable following recent renovations, it has 139 rooms with private baths, direct-dial telephones, and color television sets. This place is across the river from the other hotels. 3 Avenida de Palencia, León (phone: 987-216850; fax: 987-216997; telex: 89693). Moderate.

Don Suero – On the street that runs from San Isidoro to the *parador,* it has over 100 rooms with varying in-room bath facilities; all very clean. 15 Calle Suero de Quiñones, León (phone: 987-230600). Inexpensive.

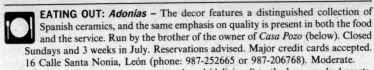

EATING OUT: *Adonías* – The decor features a distinguished collection of Spanish ceramics, and the same emphasis on quality is present in both the food and the service. Run by the brother of the owner of *Casa Pozo* (below). Closed Sundays and 3 weeks in July. Reservations advised. Major credit cards accepted. 16 Calle Santa Nonia, León (phone: 987-252665 or 987-206768). Moderate.

Casa Pozo – From the coarse peasant bread (delicious!) to the homemade desserts, this is a fine restaurant with service to match; it also boasts an extensive selection of rioja wines. Closed Sundays, the first half of July, and December 23 through January 7. Reservations unnecessary. Major credit cards accepted. 15 Plaza San Marcelo, León (phone: 987-223039). Moderate.

El Racimo de Oro – Just off the Plaza San Martín in a 17th-century mansion, this restaurant serves dishes made from good local produce. Walk past the bar and upstairs to the beautiful rustic dining room. Closed Sunday evenings and Tuesdays. No reservations. Major credit cards accepted. 2 Calle Caño Vadillo, León (phone: 987-257575). Moderate.

En Route from León – It is 80 miles (128 km) from León southeast to Palencia via N601 and N610, the latter of which veers off to the left about 42 miles (67 km) into the route at Becilla de Valderaduey.

PALENCIA: Located on the left bank of the Carrión River, Palencia was once a capital of the *vacceos,* a Celtic tribe. Construction of its cathedral spanned 2 centuries (14th to 16th) and took place on the site of a 7th-century Visigothic basilica dedicated to San Antolín, the city's patron saint. This earlier basilica, marked by three arches and a single rectangular Romanesque nave, has become the crypt of the present church and is accessible via a Plateresque stairway. The cathedral museum (admission charge) contains a painting of *San Sebastián* by El Greco, a small sampling of Romanesque statues, and some 15th-century tapestries. Stop in at the Palencia Tourist Office (105 Calle Mayor; phone: 988-720068) for information on other sights in town, which include the Iglesia de San Miguel, where, according to legend, El Cid married Doña Jimena. Its crenelated tower makes it look more like a fortress than a church.

CHECKING IN: *Castilla la Vieja* – Not far from the Plaza Mayor, this place offers all the usual facilities in its 87 rooms, plus a restaurant. 26 Avenida Casado del Alisal, Palencia (phone: 988-749044; fax: 988-747577; telex: 26595). Moderate.

Monclus – Smaller (40 rooms) and less endowed than the *Castilla la Vieja,* but still clean and comfortable; near the Plaza Mayor. 3 Calle Menéndez Pelayo, Palencia (phone: 988-744300). Moderate.

EATING OUT: *Casa Damián* – Featuring Castilian classics and fine duero wines. Closed Mondays and July 25 through August 25. Reservations necessary. Major credit cards accepted. 9 Calle Martínez de Azcoitia, Palencia (phone: 988-744628). Expensive.

Mesón del Concejo – Traditional Castilian fare is served; *chuleta de cervera* (veal cutlet from free-range calves) is a specialty. Open daily. Reservations unnecessary. MasterCard and Visa accepted. 5 Calle Martínez de Azcoitia, Palencia (phone: 988-743239). Moderate.

En Route from Palencia – Valladolid is 29½ miles (47 km) south via N611 and N620. Here the Castilian *meseta* is at its harshest and most alienating. An ambitious irrigation project may soon alleviate some of the dry, dusty monotony, however. Along the way, 9 miles (14 km) south of Palencia, at Baños de Cerrato — near the railway junction of Venta de Baños — is what is reputed to be the oldest church in Spain, the Basílica de San Juan Bautista, built in 661 by the Visigoths.

VALLADOLID: A former capital of Spain, this is where the Catholic Monarchs were married in 1469, where Columbus died in 1506, and where Philip II was born in 1527. For those willing to fight the traffic and battle the lack of coherent signs in this rather unattractive and fairly large (330,000 inhabitants) city, there are several sights worthy of attention. The 15th-century Colegio de San Gregorio (Cadenas de San Gregorio) is noted for its façade, a masterpiece of the Isabeline style, and for its courtyard, wonderfully Plateresque, but above all as the home of one of Spain's most important museums, the *Museo Nacional de Escultura Policromada* (phone: 983-250375). A repository of the types of polychrome wooden sculptures seen in churches all over the country, the museum includes works from the 13th through the 17th centuries. But it is particularly strong in sculptures by Castilian masters of the Renaissance, including Alonso Berruguete, Diego de Siloé, and Juan de Juni, as well as by the later sculptor Gregorio Fernández (open Tuesdays through Saturdays, from 9 AM to 2 PM and 4 to 6 PM; admission charge). The adjacent 15th-century Iglesia de San Pablo (Plaza de San Pablo, open daily, from 9 AM to 1 PM and 4 to 6 PM) is also worthy of note, above all for the ornate façade, its lower level a Gothic design carved by Simon of Cologne, its upper reaches Plateresque. Valladolid's cathedral was designed in the late 16th century by Juan de Herrera, of El Escorial fame, but it was finished much later, according to plans by Alberto Churriguera—note that the upper part of the façade is baroque. The *Museo Oriental,* located in the basement of the Real Colegio Padres Agustinos Filipinos (7 Paseo Filipinos), houses the best collection of Asian art in Spain, consisting, not surprisingly, mainly of works from the Philippines and China (open Mondays through Saturdays, from 4 to 7 PM; Sundays, 10 AM to 2 PM; admission charge). Valladolid's Tourist Office is at 3 Plaza de Zorrilla (phone: 983-351801).

En Route from Valladolid – The itinerary continues southeast on N601 via Cuéllar, to Segovia and back to Madrid. For those not in a hurry, however, a detour of 37½ miles (60 km) round-trip southwest from Valladolid will lead to the small town of Tordesillas, perched some 7,000 feet above the Duero River. A typical Castilian *pueblo* and the place where Juana la Loca, mother of Philip II, was imprisoned until her death, Tordesillas was also the spot where the Spanish and Portuguese met in 1494 to sign the Treaty of Tordesillas, which divided the New World in two, giving all lands west of a line to Spain and all lands east to Portugal, a decision that ultimately resulted in Spanish-speaking Latin America and Portuguese-speaking Brazil. Of less import beyond the confines of Iberia, Tordesillas was also the headquarters of the 16th-century Comuneros revolt. Besides a somewhat austerely attractive Plaza Mayor, the Church of San Antolín is worth a visit if only for the vista of the Duero and the medieval bridge that leads into town. The church museum houses the *Inmaculada* by Pedro de Mena, and an almost life-size representation of the Holy Family attributed to Gregorio Fernández. The palace-cum-monastery known as Santa Clara is a fine example of Mudéjar architecture, with a beautiful Arabic patio — a rarity in these parts. Both are closed Mondays.

Return to Valladolid and pick up the N601 highway south to Segovia. Along the 31-mile (50-km) stretch from Valladolid to the town of Cuéllar, the terrain begins to roll a bit, and welcome hills appear near Santiago del Arroyo. Here and there, too, mesas jut into the horizon, providing scenic pegs upon which to fix one's gaze. Just before Cuéllar, the route passes into the province of Segovia.

CHECKING IN/EATING OUT: *Parador de Tordesillas* – A modern structure barely half a mile from the center of town, this hostelry has 73 rooms, a bar, garden, and swimming pool. Like other *paradores,* its restaurant is of dependable quality and offers a mixture of regional and national dishes and wines. Major credit cards accepted. Carretera Salamanca, Km 152, Tordesillas (phone: 983-770051; fax: 983-771013). Expensive.

CUELLÁR: From the crown of a hill, Cuellár commands an ample panorama, especially from just outside the walls of its 15th-century castle; now home to a school, the castle courtyard can be visited only if it happens to be open (there is no posted schedule).

EATING OUT: *El Rincón Castellano* – Tucked away in a corner of the Plaza Mayor, this cozy restaurant has lots of Castilian charm to complement its fine home-style cooking, featuring the typical Castilian roast baby lamb, tasty *mollejas lechazo* (lamb sweetbreads sautéed with garlic and oil), and an ample *ensalada mesonero* (mixed salad with tuna, eggs, and olives). Open daily. No reservations. Major credit cards accepted. 13 Plaza Mayor, Cuellár (phone: 911-141031). Moderate.

En Route from Cuellár – Stands of trees become more frequent along N601 south toward Segovia, 37½ miles (60 km) away. A little more than halfway there, the vague silhouette of the Sierra de Guadarrama appears in the distance. The entrance into Segovia is dramatic — the cathedral dominates the crest of a hill and the fairy-tale Alcázar perches at the extreme right (western) edge of town.

SEGOVIA: For a detailed report on Segovia and its sights, hotels, and restaurants, see *Segovia,* THE CITIES.

En Route from Segovia – The 55-mile (88-km) stretch of road between Segovia and Madrid via N601 (sometimes posted as CL601) winds through the pines of the scenic Sierra de Guadarrama, where many *madrileños* spend their weekends and the better part of the summer school holidays. Here, too, in the winter they come to ski the slopes around Navacerrada. Puerto de Navacerrada, the mountain pass 17½ miles (28 km) beyond Segovia, is 6,000 feet above sea level and marks the border between the province of Segovia and the Comunidad de Madrid. Several miles beyond the mountain-ringed Embalse de Navacerrada at Villalba, the A6 highway veers off to the left for Madrid, becoming the N-VI highway about 5 miles (8 km) before reaching the capital.

North Atlantic Coast

The Romans could never fully conquer the area, the Visigoths were plagued by perpetual uprisings, the Moors suffered their first setback here as they tried to sweep across the Iberian Peninsula in the 8th century — and the most fearsome plunderers of them all, 20th-century tourists, have so far managed to establish only a handful of beachheads. While the rest of Spain fell under the influence of one marauder after another, the country's northern coast, along the Atlantic Ocean, remained determinedly independent. And for that very reason, it remains truly fascinating.

A Spanish saying has it that "In summer, the rich go south and the wise go north." For south, read constant and often blistering sun, packed beaches, and nonstop flamenco-flavored discotheques. The northern coast, on the other hand, offers thickly forested mountainsides, intensely green hills, and lush valleys and meadows to offset the stormy sea and the wave-battered cliffs. The entire coast from San Sebastián, just 12 miles (19 km) from the French border, to Ribadeo, 272 miles (435 km) to the west, is prone to dampness — from mist and fog, from a fine drizzle called *sirimiri* by the Basques, and from good old-fashioned rain. A filtered light — not the brilliant Castilian sky-blue sunlight seen farther south — glows on this coast. But when the sun shines there are numerous beaches to equal the best of "package-tour Spain" to the south. Many of these beaches are isolated and remote, protected by rugged cliffs, just as this area and its peoples have been throughout history.

Spain's Atlantic coastline edges four traditional regions that have become, in the post-Franco era, four *comunidades autónomas,* or "autonomous communities," and are actually four distinct "countries." Our route covers three of them, ending just inside the fourth. It starts out at San Sebastián, the queen of northern Spain's beach resorts, in the thick of Basque Country, a region known to the Basques themselves as Euskadi, to the rest of Spain as the País Vasco, and to the outside world as the site of 2 decades of political violence in the fight for Basque self-determination. Westward beyond the bustling industrial port of Bilbao, the route leaves the Costa Vasca (Basque Coast) behind and enters Cantabria, the most Spanish of the northern regions, with its attractive coastal capital of Santander. Still farther west, it reaches Asturias, a beautiful, little-visited, emerald-colored region with a coast known, appropriately, as the Costa Verde (Green Coast). It then ends just inside Galicia, another region steeped in history and rich in folklore, which looks and sings like the Irish but speaks like the Portuguese who live to the south. Four languages — Basque (or Euskera), Spanish, Bable (the old Asturian tongue, but barely spoken nowadays), and Gallego, a kind of Spanish-Portuguese — and four peoples.

If the Basques are a mystery to most Spaniards today, they completely stump anthropologists and philologists trying to ascertain the origin of Euskera. It has no apparent linguistic connection with any other language, and nobody knows where the extremely complex tongue came from, but it certainly predates the arrival in Europe of the Indo-European languages some 3,000 years ago. Recent research has tried, with little success, to link Euskera to pre-Indo-European languages such as those still spoken in the Caucasus and among the Berbers of North Africa.

Indeed, there is considerable evidence that the Basques are the last surviving representatives of Europe's aboriginal population. Although the Romans did occupy parts of the Basque region, they had a difficult time of it. Plutarch and others described a poor, warlike people with strong tribal features — which is perhaps why many males from the area were sent to man the Roman garrisons in equally warlike Britain. The Basque Country was the last area of southern and western Europe to be converted to Christianity, and the last region of Europe to construct towns — away from the big cities, many Basques still live in isolated homesteads of fewer than 30 people. In other words, this wild place was one of the last corners of Europe to be civilized.

The Basque homesteads are characteristic flat-roofed, Alpine-style farmhouses known as *caseríos,* where occupants sleep upstairs but share the downstairs with their animals. The Basques' highly individual lifestyle — they were renowned as North Sea whalers until the 18th century, and many of the small fishing ports feature whales on their coats of arms — meant that, much as today, they were little given to central control, especially from outside the region. Not only did this cause potential invaders to give up and leave them alone, but it also meant that they enjoyed a long tradition of great personal liberties at a time when most of Europe lived in serfdom. By the 15th century, these liberties were enshrined in the *fueros,* a body of ancient laws and privileges that the Basques in Spain did not lose until well into the 19th century. A bizarre mystery language, immunity from invasion, life in remote settlements with little or no central government, and the freedoms of the *fueros* all help to explain the current political turmoil, which the visitor cannot fail to recognize when touring the Basque Country, if only because of the abundant street graffiti.

The Basques are the most indomitable of all the Spanish peoples as well as the most fun-loving of those in the north. They enjoy a reputation for being the biggest drinkers and the heartiest eaters in Spain, and for having the best cuisine, whether it's traditional fare or the new Basque cuisine that is all the rage. Basque specialties include such distinctive dishes as *cogote de merluza* (baked hake's head), *kokotxas y almejas* (hake gills and clams in a lemon, oil, and parsley sauce), *angulas* (tiny silvery elvers, or young eels), *bacalao al pil pil* (cod in a Bilbao-style green sauce), *porrusalda* (leek, cod, and potato stew), *marmitako* (fresh tuna, tomato, and potato stew), and *alubias* (beans).

Equally distinctive is the folklore of the region. Rural sports, whose aim is to demonstrate speed and strength rather than skill, are an integral part of the Basque culture. The only Basque sport widely known outside the region is pelota (related to jai alai), but others include wood chopping, grass scything, rock dragging by bulls, and ram butting. Any fiesta will include traditional dances such as the *aurreska* — which honors the Basque flag, or *ikurriña* — and the *espatadanza,* or sword dance. They are accompanied by the simple music of the *txistu,* or three-holed tin whistle, and a small drum.

Cantabria is often referred to as the piece of Spain that separates the Basque

Country from Asturias. The mountainous green region has taken advantage of this slight slur to push its own identity, an alloy of fiery Castile tempered by the damp influence of the Cantabrian mountains. The earliest evidence of human settlement in Spain, about 25,000 to 30,000 years ago, has been found around Santander, the capital of Cantabria. The culture of these early settlers, who crossed the Pyrenees from southern France, peaked around 15,000 BC, which is approximately the date of the most treasured of several caves with prehistoric paintings in northern Spain — those at Altamira, near Santander.

The Romans found life easier in Cantabria than in the Basque Country, and this is the part of the coast with the most Roman remains, including bridges. Documents show that Santander was a busy port in 1068, and the city received a boost early in the 20th century when King Alfonso XIII made it his summer residence. However, Santander never had sufficient charm to rival San Sebastián, and a devastating fire in 1941 destroyed most of the lower Old Town, leaving a legacy of inelegant new buildings.

Westward, and only 25 miles (40 km) inland, are some of Spain's most remarkable mountains, the Picos de Europa. They are just that, peaks — mighty, craggy peaks that rise giddily from the Bay of Biscay to form a buttress that divides Cantabria from Asturias. On the western fringe of the Picos is the National Park of Covadonga, a haunt of bears and wolves that takes its name from the hamlet of Covadonga, site of the battle in AD 718 at which the Christian forces of Pelayo, a Visigothic nobleman, defeated the powerful Moors. Pelayo became the first monarch of the tiny kingdom of Asturias, which at first covered just 1,200 square miles, and which was, for about 200 years, Christianity's only stronghold in Spain.

From the time they crossed into Spain at what is now Gibraltar with 7,000 men in AD 711, it had taken the Moors only 2 years to sweep across the whole of Spain and Portugal and conquer all of it except this outpost in the heart of the Asturian mountains. The significance of the battle of Covadonga in AD 718 is that it marked the beginning of what the Spanish called the "Reconquest" — even though the Moors wouldn't be completely driven out of Spain until 1492! The tough Asturians, who had fiercely resisted the Romans and were subdued only after a 10-year war (29–19 BC) that ended with the presence of Augustus himself, now turned their attention to building churches and hermitages, while the rest of Spain skirmished with the Moorish armies. Many of these early Asturian or pre-Romanesque buildings still stand today, constituting the best and most complete series of 9th-century edifices in Europe.

The Reconquest pushed the Moors southward, and by 914 Asturias had gained control of León, most of Galicia, and the north of Portugal. This power was ceded only when the Asturian kings moved their court south from Oviedo and made León the capital of a combined Asturias-Léon. In 1388, Asturias became a principality, much as Wales is in Great Britain; to extend the analogy, the present heir to the Spanish throne currently occupied by King Juan Carlos, his son Felipe, is the Prince of Asturias.

Much of Asturias today consists of red-roofed villages with their characteristic *hórreos,* or granaries built on stone supports several feet high, scattered over the green carpets of the valleys and meadows. But the storm-ridden sea is the real spectacle, and the uneven coastline exposes increasingly dramatic wave-battered cliffs as the route moves toward Galicia. Local food matches the local character: strong blue cabrales cheese, and a hearty stew of broad beans, pork, and sausages called *fabada,* are downed with cider, *the* drink of Asturias — a popular image of the place is of an apple orchard. Accompanying this is the sound of the region's best-known instrument, the *gaita,* a small bagpipe.

Anyone driving the entire route, including the two or three inland excursions, should allow several weeks to do justice to it. Most of it is sea, fishing village, beach, and mountain, but there is also the bustle and shopping of Bilbao, Santander, Oviedo, or Gijón to add variety. (Bilbao and Avilés, west of Gijón, add a sample of old-fashioned European smokestack industry, too.) From Bilbao westward into Galicia, the route is seconded by a narrow-gauge railway line — *FEVE* — that is a travelers' dream. The *FEVE* line is slow and cumbersome (the state-owned *RENFE* rail network has long since taken over as the region's primary means of ground transportation) but it skirts beaches, runs across estuaries and through limestone gorges, and is often surrounded by forest and hills. For a more comfortable ride, catch the Santiago de Compostela–San Sebastián *El Transcantábrico* luxury train, which takes a leisurely 8 days to travel the entire North Atlantic Coast. A bus leaves from Santiago for El Ferrol where passengers board the train, complete with a full-service restaurant and guided tours of places of interest — Ribeades, Cangas de Onis, Covadonga, Santillara del Mar, Comillas, Oviedo, Santander, and San Sebastián (phone: 985-290104; fax: 985-290820). The main road joining San Sebastián and Galicia, N634, is generally poor, and in summer traffic snarls are common. The only stretches of motorway on the route are A8, from San Sebastián to Bilbao, and A66 and A8, which link Gijón, Oviedo, and Avilés.

The disadvantage of getting away from it all is the generally poor tourist infrastructure. There are few top class hotels or restaurants outside the main cities, and even in town, accommodations are very hard to find in July and August. A double room with bath will cost $145 or more in a hotel listed as expensive, $80 to $135 in a moderate one, and below $75 in an inexpensive one. Dinner for two with wine costs $80 or more at restaurants listed as expensive, $60 to $75 at moderate restaurants, and $45 or less at inexpensive places. But be aware that it is not difficult to find superb cooking at moderately priced restaurants, sometimes right next door to an expensive eating house that charges three times the price. Quality, but not necessarily price, is generally higher in the Basque Country than elsewhere.

■ **Note:** Most place-names in the Basque Country have two spellings. In this chapter, when two spellings are given (usually at the first reference to a place), the first one is Spanish, and the second — often vital for following signs along the route — is Basque.

SAN SEBASTIÁN (DONOSTIA): This most elegant turn-of-the-century Belle Epoque beach resort is set on a fine shell-shaped bay. It is edged by a wide curving beach, which is, in turn, topped by an exquisite promenade of ornate railings and impressive buildings. Mountains on either side of town protect it from northerly winds, and a small island in the bay softens the surf. Home to a famous annual *International Film Festival,* San Sebastián is small (pop. 180,000), and in midsummer there isn't a spare hotel room to be had. For full details on this charming city just 12 miles (19 km) from the French border, see *San Sebastián,* THE CITIES.

En Route from San Sebastián – The chief Basque city and port of Bilbao, just 62½ miles (100 km) to the west, can be reached in an hour on the excellent A8 highway, which skirts undulating deep green Basque hills. But it would be an enormous shame to miss some of the pretty Basque fishing villages, not to mention a chance to sample some fine cuisine. Take A8 out of San Sebastián to reach the first stop, Zarauz (Zarautz), 14 miles (22 km) away. The turnoff, 2 miles (3 km) past the tiny fishing port of Orio, leads right into the town. Zarauz is a booming resort that hugs a magnificent 1½-mile beach. A vacation home for thousands of Basques from inland industrial towns, it has a population of approximately 18,000 year-round — quadruple that in summer. During the Middle Ages, Zarauz was the site of much factional warring, and defensive structures typical of the period sprang up. One of the few surviving is the 15th-century, 3-story Luzea Tower, in the central Kale Nagusia (*kale,* or *kalea,* means street in Basque), with an exterior staircase and 16th-century paintings. The tower's ground floor is now a bank, though the thick stone façade has not been altered. The 16th-century Palacio de Narros stands at the western end of town — the "wrong way around," with its back facing the sea. The 9-hole *Real Club de Golf de Zarauz* (Barrio de Mendilauta; phone: 943-830145), at the eastern end of town by the beach, is one of the Basque Country's best.

The beautiful fishing village of Guetaria (Getaria), 2 miles (3 km) from Zarauz, had Roman origins but was subsequently founded as a country estate by Alfonso VIII in 1209. Guetaria was the birthplace of Juan Sebastián de Elcano, the first man to sail around the world. Regardless of inaccurate schoolbook history, the fact is that Ferdinand Magellan was killed en route in 1521, and Elcano's ship was the only one in the fleet to make it back. The mighty San Salvador church in which he was christened still stands amid a remarkable group of medieval houses. Today, with a population of 2,000, the village is nationally famous for seafood — dishes such as the local *cogote de merluza a la Getaria* (hake head grilled over charcoal in wire holders) and *txangurro al horno* (baked spider crab prepared in its own shell) — and as the home of *txakoli* wine, white and slightly sour, a perfect accompaniment to the seafood. Often compared to a good moselle, the Rolls-Royce of the *txakolis* is the locally produced Txomin Etxániz. Guetaria is also famous for El Ratón (The Mouse), the rodent-shaped islet of San Antón that juts out from the harbor and can be seen for miles from either side of the village.

Zarauz and Guetaria used to be whaling ports, and in 1878 the towns virtually declared war on each other over the disputed catch of a monster whale. The dispute, which still causes heated words today, lasted so long that the whale's meat rotted and its skeleton was donated to San Sebastián's aquarium, where it is still exhibited.

Six miles (10 km) along N634 is Zumaya (Zumaia), a less-attractive version of Zarauz that nonetheless enjoys the best surfing waves in the region. Take the C6317 turnoff southward, 1¼ miles (2 km) beyond Zumaya, for a worthwhile excursion to the Belle Epoque spa resort of Cestona (Zestoa), 6 miles (10 km) inland, and to the Sanctuary of Loyola, between Azkoitia and Azpeitia, another 6 miles (10 km) farther on. The imposing shrine here was built on the site of the home of St. Ignatius of Loyola, the 16th-century founder of the Society of Jesus — the religious order of the Jesuits.

Return through Cestona and join the A8 highway for the 3 miles (5 km) to the turnoff for Deva (Deba). Then, instead of taking N634, which turns inland at Deva, exit at the coastal C6212, a truly scenic road atop a cliff. Past the unattractive port of Motrico (Mutriko), the road leaves the province of Guipúzcoa (Gipuzkoa), one of three provinces making up the Basque Country, and enters Vizcaya (Biskaia), another Basque province (landlocked Alava, or Araba, is the third). The Vizcayan coast is a world of rocks and cliffs, small ports and coves, sheltered beaches, and small industries merging with the sea. The squawking of seagulls and the smell of grilled sardines await at any stop, but nowhere more so than at Ondárroa, the largest Basque fishing port. Nevertheless, the real treasure of Vizcayan fishing villages is Lequeitio (Lekeitio), 8 miles (13 km) farther along a winding road with breathtaking views.

Lequeitio has a beautiful bay and two beaches, and is a typical Basque fishing port. Its vessels are a riot of color, mainly the red, green, and white of the Basque flag, and the wooden balconies and tall, narrow façades of its houses rest on the harbor itself. The 16th-century Santa María church is an impressive example of Vizcaya Gothic. The town is notorious for its September 1 fiesta, which includes a boat race during which competitors pull off the heads of live geese tied to a rope across the bay!

Continue 15 miles (24 km) inland along C6212 to Guernica (Gernika), immortalized by Pablo Picasso's *Guernica,* a nightmarish painting of the world's first major aerial bombing of civilians. German bombers, assisting Generalísimo Francisco Franco in the 1936–39 Civil War, flattened the town in 1937, because of its symbolic value to the Basques, who were fighting on the Republican side. Thousands died, and the town has suffered from unimaginative postwar rebuilding, but it remains the traditional heart of Basque nationalism. It was here, under the Tree of Guernica, that the Basque parliament met throughout the Middle Ages. From the 15th century through most of the 19th century, successive Spanish monarchs were obliged to visit the same oak tree, which still stands outside the Casa de Juntas parliament building, to acknowledge their acceptance of the *fueros* system of privilege. Three miles (5 km) away, just off C6212 at Kortezubi, are the Santimamiñe caves, containing 13,000-year-old paintings.

Take C6315 south from Guernica to the junction with the A8 highway at Amorebieta, then follow the signs for Bilbao, 22½ miles (36 km) from Guernica.

CHECKING IN: Karlos Arguiñano – The well-known restaurant of the same name (see *Eating Out*) recently has been partially converted, adding 12 elegant and well-appointed guestrooms with all amenities. Visa accepted. 13 Calle Mendilauta, Zarauz (phone: 943-130000; fax: 943-830178). Expensive.

Gran Hotel Balneario de Cestona – A grand Belle Epoque spa, with 110 rooms, built in 1900. Facilities include hot thermal baths, meeting rooms, a period conference hall, 4 restaurants, tennis courts, a chapel, and gardens. Closed mid-December through February. Paseo de San Juan, Cestona (phone: 943-147140). Moderate.

Zarauz – The largest hotel along the Basque coast outside San Sebastián, offering 82 rooms, 100 yards from the beach. Facilities include a television lounge, lovely gardens, and a restaurant. 26 Avenida de Nafarroa, Zarauz (phone: 943-830200; fax: 943-830193). Moderate.

EATING OUT: Elkano – Locals say it serves the best grilled fish in Guipúzcoa province, and the most succulent *rodaballo* (turbot) in the Basque Country. Also renowned for its *salpicón de bogavante* (lobster cocktail), *rape entero a la brasa* (whole braised angler), and any northern fish in season. Closed Tuesdays and for the month of November. Reservations advised. Major credit cards accepted. 2 Calle Herrerieta, Guetaria (phone: 943-831614). Expensive.

Kaia y Kaipe – Guetaria is where the chefs prepare fish in wire holders over charcoal grills, and this is a seafood house par excellence. Its name means Upstairs and Downstairs in Basque, so there is dining with a view. Try *txangurro al horno* (spider crab prepared in its shell) and the regional favorite, *cogote de merluza a la Getaria* (charcoal-grilled hake head). Wash it all down with the local *txakoli* white wine. Closed October. Reservations necessary. Major credit cards accepted. 10 Calle General Arnao, Guetaria (phone: 943-832414). Expensive.

Karlos Arguiñano – One of the bright lights of the new Basque cuisine. The food here is vigorously Basque yet surprisingly original, combining recent "discoveries" with traditional fare. Specialties include *liebre con rabo de ternera* (hare with calf's tail) and *sesos de ternera con hongos* (veal brains with mushrooms). Part of the building has been converted into an elegant small hotel. Closed Sunday nights and Wednesdays. Reservations advised. Visa accepted. 13 Calle Mendilauta, Zarauz (phone: 943-130000; fax: 943-830178). Expensive.

Masoparri – Another good fish house, in an old country manor with a terrace facing the sea high above the harbor. Try *bonito a la parrilla* (grilled tuna) or *kokotxas en su gelatina* (hake's gill muscles in gelatin). Closed mid-December through late January. Reservations unnecessary. American Express, Diners Club, and Visa accepted. 1 Calle Sagartzaga, Guetaria (phone: 943-835707). Moderate.

BILBAO (BILBO): It's hard to believe sometimes, as you look up from any part of the city and see green hills beyond the drab apartment blocks, that this is Spain's sixth-largest city and the country's main port, with approximately 570,000 inhabitants (1.4 million in greater Bilbao). Standing on the central Arenal Bridge that spans the Nervión River and looking at the glorious City Hall and its utterly rural backdrop, you'd think you were in some middling river town. But look again. The Gran Vía, Bilbao's chief avenue, boasts gleaming skyscrapers, huge department stores, and elegant clothing shops. And a train ride along the banks of the Nervión estuary to the Bay of Biscay passes scores of dockyard cranes, shipyards, warehouses, factories, wharves, and iron and steel foundries. Bilbao's smokestack industries are in decline, and the air of industrial decay, political tension, and frequent rain make the city less than a touristic glamour spot. But Bilbao does have a great feel to it, the locals are renowned for their friendliness, and the city is packed with good places to eat and drink.

The city was founded in 1300, although it didn't really take off until the Industrial Revolution arrived in the mid-19th century. Then, from the 1860s until World War I, Britain became Bilbao's main trading partner. Even today the city betrays a strong British influence, seen in the way people dress, the architecture, and even in the long list of English managers in charge of the local soccer team, *Athletic Bilbao,* traditionally one of Spain's top three. Touristic interest centers on the Casco Viejo, or Old Quarter, which combines numerous fine clothing outfitters, specialty stores, traditional Basque restaurants, and bars. It is here that locals indulge in two Bilbao customs. One is the *chiquiteo,* the drinking in rapid succession of small wines or beers — no more than a mouthful each — at several bars in double-quick time. The custom has an important social dimension, as does the *copa y puro,* the sipping of a liqueur, usually brandy or an anise-based brew called *patxarán,* and the smoking of a cigar after a hearty lunch. These customs are no longer sexist — Bilbao women take part, too.

The grandiose Santiago Cathedral, in the heart of the Old Quarter, has a cloister built in 1404, although the church was largely rebuilt in the 16th century, after a fire. Nearby is the Plaza Nueva; built in 1830 and enclosed by 64 arches, it houses a flea market on Sunday mornings. *Gorostiaga* (9 Calle Victor; phone: 94-416-1276) is a curious Old Quarter shop where seven generations of the same family have been making hats since 1857; the specialty is the famous Basque beret, or *txapela,* although trilbys and Panama hats are also made. The *Teatro Arriaga* (in the Plaza Arriaga next to the Arenal Bridge just before the Old Quarter; phone: 94-416-3244) was exactly a century old in 1990, and freshly renovated. A delightful building both inside and out amid the industrial grime, its jolly imitation French architecture is in contrast with Bilbao's neo-classical style. (Like the magnificent City Hall, 2 years younger, it is floodlit at night and reflected in the waters of the Nervión.) Two museums are worth a visit. The *Museum of Basque Archaeology, Ethnology, and History* (4 Calle Cruz; phone: 94-415-5423; open Tuesdays through Saturdays, from 10:30 AM to 1:30 PM and from 4 to 7 PM; Sundays, from 10:30 AM to 1:30 PM; admission charge) has a special room devoted to the commercial life of Bilbao since 1500. The ivy-covered *Museum of Fine Arts* (in the English-style Doña Casilda Iturrízar Park; phone: 94-441-9536; open Tuesdays through Saturdays, from 10 AM to 1:30 PM and from 4:30 to 7:30 PM; Sundays, from 11 AM to 2 PM; admission charge) features an extensive collection of Spanish and foreign paintings and sculpture from the Romanesque period to the early 20th century. El Greco, Velázquez, Ribera, Ribalta, Zurbarán, and Goya are represented, as are modern artists, from Gauguin to Sorolla.

Two city center coffeehouses are worthy haunts for an early evening break. The *Café Iruña* (13 Calle Colón de Larreátegui; phone: 94-423-7021), built in 1903, has tiled arabesque decor and imitation carved-wood ceilings; the *Café La Granja* (Plaza Circular; phone: 94-423-0813), opposite the statue to Bilbao's founder, Don Diego López de Haro, has peach-red decor that imparts a genteel feel. (If in doubt, order the *Copa Feliz* — burned rum, banana, cream, and ice cream.) The *Heladería Nossi-Be* (1 Calle Navarra) serves 34 different flavors of ice cream, as well as milkshakes, and is open daily from March through October. *Semana Grande* (Aste Nagusia in Basque, Big Week in English), Bilbao's week-long fiesta, runs from August 15 to 22, and is among the best in Spain. Ask at the tourist office (Alameda de Mazarredo; phone: 94-424-4819) for information — bullfights, rural sports, male-only open-air gastronomy contests, and folk dancing are all part of it.

CHECKING IN: *Ercilla* – Nearly always full, it is the choice of politicians, journalists, bullfighters, and businessmen, as well as conventions of all types, so book well in advance. All 350 rooms have air conditioning and private baths. The *Bermeo* restaurant (see *Eating Out*) is one of the city's best. 37 Calle Ercilla, Bilbao (phone: 94-443-8800; fax: 94-443-9335). Expensive.

***Indautxu* –** Opened in December 1990 with the aim of capturing an elite clientele, this 190-room luxury property has been completely rebuilt within what was an early–20th-century maternity hospital. Its downtown location makes it ideal for a short stay. There is a bar and a restaurant. Plaza Bombero Etxaniz, Bilbao (phone: 94-421-1198; fax: 94-422-1331). Expensive.

***López de Haro* –** A recent, luxury establishment in town, needed more because of the city's growing role as a convention center than for touristic purposes. In the city center, 6 stories high, it's built in the quasi-English classic style of Bilbao, and the 53 rooms have a full range of amenities. The *Club Náutico* restaurant is highly acclaimed. 2 Calle Obispo Orueta, Bilbao (phone: 94-423-5500; fax: 94-423-4500). Expensive.

***Villa de Bilbao* –** Modern and luxurious, with 142 large air conditioned rooms, tennis courts, a heated swimming pool, a discotheque, hair salons, and a restaurant. Pets are welcome. 87 Gran Vía, Bilbao (phone: 94-441-6000; fax: 94-441-6529). Expensive.

***Roquefer* –** A delightful, family-run establishment in the Old Quarter. The 18 rooms are simple, but clean. 2 Calle Lotería, Bilbao (phone: 94-415-0755). Inexpensive.

EATING OUT: *Bermeo* – At the *Ercilla* hotel, and rated as one of Spain's best hotel-restaurants, it is the culinary gathering spot before and after all social, political, sporting, and cultural events. A Basque-Navarrese menu suggests mushrooms, woodcock and partridge with turnip, steamed hake, and oxtail (the latter during the August bullfight week). Closed Sunday nights. Reservations necessary. Major credit cards accepted. 37 Calle Ercilla, Bilbao (phone: 94-443-8800). Expensive.

Guria – Codfish is *the* Bilbao specialty, and they say it is never better than when prepared by Chef Génaro Pildain in his own restaurant. *Bacalao al pil pil* (cod baked in green sauce with peppers) is just one of the succulent dishes served. The menu is traditionally Basque, but the best around. Closed Sundays, the last week of July, and the first week of August. Reservations advised. Major credit cards accepted. 66 Gran Vía, Bilbao (phone: 94-441-0543). Expensive.

Zortziko – The choice for new Basque cuisine in Bilbao, run by Chef Daniel García and his six brothers and sisters, with great attention to detail. The menu is pure poetry: *tartar de salmon en flor al aroma de eneldo* (salmon tartar in a flower shape with dilled mint sauce), *rodaballo asado a la vinagreta tibia y al aroma de genjibre natural* (baked turbot in a vinaigrette sauce with a hint of ginger), and *mousse de polen a la miel de encina* (honey mousse). Closed Sundays and September 1–15. Reservations advised. Major credit cards accepted. 17 Calle Alameda de Mazarredo, Bilbao (phone: 94-423-9743). Expensive.

Aitxiar – Modest but atmospheric, in the Old Quarter, with a charming dining room beyond the bar. Basque favorites include *chipirones en su tinta* (squid in its own ink) and *porrusalda* (leek, onion, and cod stew). Closed Mondays and September. No reservations. No credit cards accepted. 8 Calle María Muñoz, Bilbao (phone: 94-415-0917). Inexpensive.

En Route from Bilbao – The newly improved N634 leads through 8 miles (13 km) of heavily industrial Greater Bilbao towns — Barakaldo, Sestao, Portugalete, and Santurce (Santurtzi) — on the left bank of the Nervión before it hits the countryside and, suddenly, Cantabria. For a last glimpse of the Basque Country and a view of the amazing Puente Colgante (Hanging Bridge), turn into the steep roads leading down to Portugalete.

Just a mile (1.6 km) farther on, Santurtzi is famous for its sardines, grilled in the open air by fisherwomen. Beyond it, the stretch of N634 to Castro-Urdiales, a surprisingly unspoiled fishing town, is particularly bad, but there is no alternative route. Trucks, buses, and cars creep along steep and narrow bends, so the arrival in Castro-Urdiales is a relief. Its harbor is dominated by the dauntingly buttressed 13th-century Gothic church of Santa María and the nearby Knights Templars Castle, complete with lighthouse; in 1814, locals escaped from Napoleon's troops through secret castle passages to waiting British ships. Cave paintings in the vicinity show human presence 12,000 years ago. The town was called Flaviógriga by the Romans, Alfonso VIII granted it special favors in 1163, and it was the regional capital until French troops sacked it during the 18th century and Santander took over. From the broad promenade and gardens on the seafront, the scene often includes the brightly colored sails of windsurfers and little boys fishing for crabs from the harbor steps.

Another 16 miles (26 km) along N634, past the lush green valley of Guriezo and after a spectacular descent into the town of Liendo, is Laredo. Doubtless it once had all the charm of Castro-Urdiales, but a 1960s building boom, and a parallel influx of European tourism, has disfigured the promenade facing the otherwise wonderful La Salvé beach. There is also a marvelous 13th-century Gothic church, Santa María; its exterior is not imposing, but its Bethlehem altarpiece is reckoned to be one of the finest jewels of Flemish sculpture in Spain. The church stands atop the Old Town, whose narrow cobbled streets wind down to the harbor. Laredo's *Battle of the Flowers,* when flower-bedecked carnival floats parade through town, takes place annually on the last Friday in August.

Toward Santander, the road passes through unattractive Colindres and over a steel bridge that spans the Asón estuary, to Solares. Here, just after the pink house with a Sala de Fiestas neon sign, the road divides. Take the N635 turnoff to Santander and follow the signs to the city center.CHECKING IN

El Ancla – An ideal place for families who enjoy spending time on Laredo's crowded beaches. Although close to the beach, it is in the only residential zone away from tall concrete blocks. Excellent service; pleasant garden; 25 rooms. 10 Calle González Gallego, Laredo (phone: 942-605500; fax: 942-611602). Moderate.

EATING OUT: *Risco* – Famed for its traditional Cantabrian cooking and splendid sea views. Zacarías and Inés Puente have perfected *pimientos rellenos de cangrejo* (peppers stuffed with crab), and offer a great selection of Cantabrian cheeses. Reservations advised. American Express, Diners Club, and Visa accepted. 2 Calle La Arenosa, Laredo (phone: 942-605030). Moderate.

SANTANDER: A kind of staid San Sebastián, Santander has tried without real success since the early 1900s to rival the Basque resort. The city even paid for the construction of the English-style Magdalena Palace as a gift to Alfonso XIII and Victoria Eugenia in 1912, in an attempt to give Santander the "royal residence" status that San Sebastián had earlier gained. Although it *was* the royal summer residence from 1913 to 1930, the town (pop. 194,000) never quite knocked San Sebastián off the throne as the queen of northern Spanish resorts, perhaps due to its greater distance from France or to its not having a beach and a bay quite as stunning as La Concha. Or to the terrible fire that destroyed much of it in 1941, leaving it essentially modern and dull — albeit leafy, with a large number of gardens (by Spanish city standards), as well as some very pleasant beaches.

The first surprise, for those entering the city from the east, is the bronze statue of Franco on horseback in the aptly named Plaza del Generalísimo, opposite City Hall. It is the first statue of the autocratic ruler along the entire coast from the French border. Activity in the city center revolves around the porticoed Plaza Porticada, or Plaza de Velarde, where the tourist office (phone: 942-310708) is found. Until 1990, when it moved to a new auditorium on the *Palace of Festivals* site, this was also the home of the annual *International Festival of Dance and Music,* one of Spain's most prestigious, held in August. One block toward the bay from the plaza is the very unattractive cathedral, largely rebuilt after the 1941 fire. It does, however, contain a beautiful high altar and the tiny 13th-century Crypt of Christ, the city's oldest monument, dating back to days — from the 12th to the 16th centuries — when Santander was a booming port. For a while, it was the busiest port in northern Spain, with a near monopoly on the export of Castilian wool to Flanders.

Santander's beauty lies in its beaches, gardens, and promenades. The Paseo de Pereda, which begins at the seaward end of the Plaza Porticada, is a broad, elegant promenade with palm trees and the huge, red arum flowers that dot the city. Notice the *Palacete del Embarcadero,* a small art gallery (admission charge), and the dock from which the only ferry between Spain and Great Britain sails (twice a week, Santander to Plymouth, *Brittany Ferries;* phone: 942-214500 or 942-214272). Farther along, past lines of 5-story glass-balconied houses that escaped the 1941 fire, is Puerto Chico, where dockland Santander ends and pleasure Santander begins. The first building here is the *Royal Maritime Club,* which rises out of the sea on concrete columns in the shape of a ship's upper decks. Beyond it, the road turns away from the sea for a while, then steps lead down to the first great local beach, the Magdalena. Clean and placid, it has a 100-foot backdrop of cliffs and trees (the ivy-covered structure up above belongs to the Royal Tennis Society). At the end of the beach and up the hill is the Magdalena Palace, which was turned into the International Menéndez Pelayo University after the abdication of Alfonso XIII in 1931, and is now famous for summer seminars and language courses for foreign students.

On the other side of the Magdalena promontory is the mile-long El Sardinero beach, dominated by the lavish 1914 Belle Epoque *Gran Casino* at Plaza Italia. One of only two casinos on the coast (the other is at San Sebastián), it is open from 7 PM to 4 AM (5 AM on weekends). Across the bay are the villages of Pedreña and Somo, both with huge, sand-duned beaches. Pedreña is the birthplace of golf pro Severiano Ballesteros and home to the golf course where he developed his skills, the *Royal Pedreña Golf Club* (phone: 942-500266). Also to be seen in Santander are the *Fine Arts Museum* (6 Calle Rubio; phone: 942-239485), which can claim a Goya, and the *Museum of Prehistory* (4 Casimiro Sainz; phone: 942-215050), which has important collections from the Upper Paleolithic period. The best restaurants are located along Calle Hernán Cortés, in the vicinity of Puerto Chico, but for an inexpensive meal and an authentic experience, go to the Barrio Pesquero (Fishing Quarter) — where the Santander working class eats — and choose any one of several fish restaurants with their huge dining rooms, simple decor, and unfussy, yet friendly, service.

CHECKING IN: *Real* – Opened in 1917 during Santander's heyday, when Alfonso XIII spent his summers in the city. Luxurious, set amid terraces and gardens, it retains its early-20th-century architecture and atmosphere. The 124-room hostelry only recently reversed its decades-old policy of closing in winter, and is now open year-round. 28 Paseo de Pérez Galdós, Santander (phone: 942-272550; fax: 942-274573). Expensive.

Bahia – In the city center, facing the bay and close to the ferry quay. This 181-room hotel is spacious if plain, with a good restaurant and several convention rooms. 6 Avenida Alfonso XIII, Santander (phone: 942-221700; fax: 942-210265). Expensive to moderate.

EATING OUT: *Bar Del Puerto* – Not just a bar, nor a fishermen's tavern as it once was, but a restaurant of great renown, especially for its seafood. Upstairs dining overlooks Puerto Chico, with shrubs and hanging plants decorating the façade. Open daily. Reservations necessary. Major credit cards accepted. 63 Calle Hernán Cortés, Santander (phone: 942-213001). Expensive.

Zacarías – Featuring such specialties as *jibiones de huerta* (small peppers stuffed with shellfish) and *maganos encebollados* (squid fried in onions). Open daily. Reservations advised. Major credit cards accepted. 38 Calle Hernán Cortés, Santander (phone: 942-210688). Moderate.

Los Peñucos – One of many excellent homespun fish restaurants in the Barrio Pesquero. Noisy, friendly, and full of locals. Try the *marmita* (tuna stew) and *besugo al horno* (baked sea bream). Open daily. No reservations. No credit cards accepted. 2 Calle Mocejon, Santander (phone: 942-222091). Inexpensive.

En Route from Santander – Santillana del Mar and the Altamira Caves are 19 miles (31 km) to the west. Take N611 out of Santander, through the village of Igollo and into the gently undulating countryside. Eight miles (13 km) down the road is Puente Arce, where a Roman bridge spans the creek-size Pas River. It's another 8 miles (13 km) to the C6316 turnoff for Santillana del Mar.

EATING OUT: *El Molino* – Delightfully situated in gardens beside a creek, with an ancient coat of arms above the entrance, and two low wood-beamed dining rooms. The restaurant, set in a converted 17th-century farmhouse, was made famous by the late, award-winning chef Victcr Merino, and is now in the capable hands of his son, Antonio. Try the Cantabrian fish and clam salad or the sea bream stew with thyme. Closed Mondays. Reservations advised. Visa and Diners Club accepted. Carretera N611, Km 12, Puente Arce (phone: 942-574052). Moderate.

SANTILLANA DEL MAR/ALTAMIRA CAVES: These two treasures — one practically forbidden to all but the chosen few — are unrelated, but less than 2 miles (3 km) apart. Santillana del Mar, which despite its name is nearly 3 miles (5 km) from the sea, is a unique collection of perfectly preserved medieval mansions and palaces strung out along two streets. Jean-Paul Sartre described it as "the prettiest village in Spain." Legend has it that during the 3rd century St. Juliana was murdered by her husband for refusing to renounce her Christian faith and her virginity. Her remains were said to have been brought here during the 8th century by monks who built a small monastery. The village's first name — Sancta Iuliana, after its martyred saint — was in time transformed to Santillana.

The spirit of Cantabria laces the town. The imposing Romanesque houses and mansions lining the dark, ironstone streets are a chunk of the Middle Ages lifted into the 20th century. Happily, the village, with a population just short of 4,000, is a living rural community that does not rely solely on tourism to survive. The locals sell cheese, sponge cake, and fresh milk from their stable doors, and despite the dozens of tourist buses that pour in every day, a medieval air pervades. The original monastery is now the 12th-century Collegiate Church of St. Juliana, with a wonderful façade and high altar complemented by sculptures and carvings added through the centuries. At the other end of the main street is the *Diocesan Museum,* formerly the 16th-century Convent of Regina Coeli, which houses an exceptional collection of painted wooden saints and other religious figures. There are several 16th- to 18th-century mansions to admire, each boasting an impressive coat of arms. Even the relatively humble rural homes, with their solid walls, eaves, balconies, and elegant doorways, are a joy to wander past. One-half mile (1 km) south of the village is a zoo, which is open year-round. Among the usual animals, there also are some European bison, descendants of those depicted in the Altamira Cave paintings.

Often described as the Sistine Chapel of Prehistoric Art, the Altamira Caves — Cuevas de Altamira — contain the best Upper Paleolithic cave paintings in Europe. They are only a short walk southwest of Santillana, along a well-marked road. Unfortunately, it is now extremely difficult to enter; only those with legitimate academic interests are permitted, and entrance applications must be submitted at least 6 months in advance. Discovered by a hunter in 1879, the paintings, which cover a time span from 15,000 to 9500 BC, consist of bison, bulls, boars, and horses etched in red or yellow ocher and delineated in black. They range from 4 to 8 feet high and were in perfect condition when discovered, but they have suffered serious deterioration recently — caused mainly by moisture from the breath of thousands of visitors during recent decades! Now there is a limit to the number of daily visitors (usually 20 are permitted, and these include research students and other non-tourists). There is a museum next to the cave, open Tuesdays through Saturdays, from 10 AM to 1 PM and from 4 to 8 PM; Sundays from 10 AM to 1 PM. Admission charge. To apply for entrance permission, write to Centro de Investigación de Altamira (Santillana del Mar, Cantabria 39330; phone: 942-818005). For information on the other sights of Santillana, visit the tourist office in the town's main square (Plaza de Ramón Pelayo; phone: 942-818251).

CHECKING IN: *Parador Gil Blas* – One of Spain's most exciting *paradores,* this 17th-century converted mansion used to belong to the noble Barreda-Bracho family. In the heart of the complex of medieval stone buildings, it retains all of its original charm and has a fine restaurant. A visit to Santillana del Mar is incomplete without staying in one of its lovely 56 rooms, but make reservations well in advance. 11 Plaza de Ramón Pelayo, Santillana de Mar (phone: 942-818000; fax: 942-818391). Expensive to moderate.

En Route from Santillana del Mar/Altamira Caves – Continue west on C6316 to Comillas, 11 miles (18 km) away. The drive is a beautiful one past unspoiled villages, green meadows, the occasional Romanesque church, and the first sight of the massed backdrop of hills that roll away toward the Picos de

Europa. Comillas is a curious town, fascinatingly gloomy and leafy, dominated by three buildings designed by Barcelona architects in the late 19th century. The huge neo-Gothic Pontifical University, the work of Lluís Domènech i Montaner (who designed Barcelona's Palau de la Música Catalana), can be seen high up on a hill from any spot in the village. The private modernist-style palace of the Marqués de Comillas, designed by Juan Martorell, is on another hill nearer the village's two fine beaches. But the jewel of the ensemble is *El Capricho* (The Whim), on a still lower slope, the only building in Cantabria designed by the inimitable Antoni Gaudí. Built between 1883–1885, *El Capricho* is actually a Moorish-style optical illusion, a bizarre villa whose huge cylindrical tower, topped by a dome half-suspended in the air and supported by squat columns, makes the building look smaller than it is. Closed for some 20 years, it has now been restored and converted into a luxury restaurant (see *Eating Out* below). Bought in January 1991 by a Japanese company, the new owners promise to maintain the unique building as a restaurant and also announced plans to build a hotel and a golf course.

Leaving Comillas, follow the signposts 5 miles (8 km) to La Revilla, where C6316 rejoins N634. Two miles (3 km) on, across the La Maza Bridge, which has been modernized since it first spanned the broad estuary during the 15th century, is San Vicente de la Barquera, and its national monument, the 13th-century Church of Santa María. Six miles (10 km) farther is Unquera, marking the end of Cantabria and the beginning of the Principality of Asturias. Unquera is a good place to stop and sample *corbatas,* a local puff pastry and almond sweet, and a good starting point for a drive into the Picos de Europa — N621 leads through spectacular scenery alongside the Deva River to the town of Potes, 24 miles (39 km) inland. Alternatively, stay on N634 through Unquera and drive 12 miles (19 km) to La Arquera and the AS263 turnoff to the beach resort of Llanes, the first sizable town in Asturias.

EATING OUT: *El Capricho de Gaudí* – This modernist folly, a landmark building designed by Antoni Gaudí, has been restored to its onetime glory and put into service as a deluxe restaurant specializing in Basque and international cooking. There is a bar lounge on the top floor. Closed Mondays and the month of February. Reservations advised. American Express, Diners Club and Visa accepted. Barrio de Sobrellano, Comillas (phone: 942-720365). Expensive to moderate.

Fonda Colasa – A favorite, humble eating house of the old style, with down-home, hearty fare in abundant portions — it's been in the same family since 1890. The meat stews and fish are excellent, and all the desserts are made on the premises. Closed October through April. No reservations. No credit cards accepted. 9 Calle Antonio López, Comillas (phone: 942-720001). Inexpensive.

LLANES: The capital of eastern Asturias, Llanes is often written off as dull. In fact, the town has a delightful Old Quarter, the gentle feel of a typical Asturian fishing port, and about 30 remote and very clean beaches, including Poo, Celorio, and Barros within a few miles to either side — ask at the tourist office (1 Calle Nemesio Sobrino; phone: 985-400164). Llanes is also famous for its August 16 *Fiesta de San Roque,* a day-long binge of folkloric dancing in traditional costumes. The town spreads upward from the tiny sheltered harbor at the foot of picturesque green hills and still retains chunks of its 13th-century ramparts. One segment girds the beer garden of the *El Antiguo* restaurant in Posada Herrera — a wonderful setting in which to enjoy a cold drink on a warm afternoon. Llanes is yet another coastal town with a magnificent church dedicated to Santa María, this one part 14th- and part 15th-century, part Romanesque and part Gothic. It also has a selection of interesting 15th- to 17th-century mansions, boasting their heraldic coats of arms.

CHECKING IN: *Don Paco* – Fairly atmospheric, it has 42 rooms within the walls of a 17th-century palace adjacent to the old ramparts, with a lovely view of the harbor. Closed October through May. Parque de Posada Herrera, Llanes (phone: 985-400150). Moderate to inexpensive.

EATING OUT: *La Bolera* – This small upstairs dining room overlooks the quayside; the food is simple but of the highest quality. Seafood predominates — try *colas de langosta* (lobster tails) or *salmón a la ribereña* (local riverside salmon). Closed Wednesdays in winter. Reservations advised. American Express, MasterCard, and Visa accepted. El Muella, Llanes (phone: 985-401336). Moderate.

En Route from Llanes – Take AS263 signposted to Celorio 3 miles (5 km) away, where it rejoins N634 for a good drive to Ribadesella; the latter is on N632, just after the turnoff at Llovio and some dramatic mist-shrouded mountains that creep to the very edge of the road.

RIBADESELLA: A good base for Picos de Europa excursions, Ribadesella offers a magnificent beach, great hotels, rustic eating houses, a fabulous cave with prehistoric paintings, and *sidrerías* (Asturian cider bars). It is also home to the world's premier canoe festival, the *International Descent of the Sella River,* held annually since 1930 on the first Saturday of August. It attracts 800 participants from many countries and over 200,000 festive spectators, who join in all-night revelry after following the canoeists 11 miles down the river from Arriondas.

The town straddles the broad Sella estuary, crossed by a long, narrow bridge that is actually the N632 highway, from which the locals can be seen fishing for bass, sargo, and red mullet. The "port" side of town brims with bars, restaurants, and shops. The other side is residential, but includes the beach, flanked by two headlands, and the best promenade hotels and mansions, glorious with their creeping purple bougainvillea. At the beach end of the bridge is an odd-looking tourist office (phone: 985-860038; closed in winter), occupying what is, in fact, a converted *hórreo,* one of the ancient granaries that dot the Asturian countryside. Wooden huts erected on 10-foot concrete stilts, they are designed to protect grain from dampness and rodents.

A few hundred yards from the tourist office is the Cave of Tito Bustillo, named for the man who discovered it in 1968. Inside are 15,000- to 20,000-year-old cave paintings that have been pronounced the equal of those at Altamira and France's Lascaux. Three galleries make up the cavern. A vaulted niche in the first has shield-shaped red marks, identified as representing female vulva in an invocation to fertility. In another gallery are a large red horse, deer, reindeer, and a purple and black horse, many over 6 feet tall. A maximum of 400 visitors per day is permitted, so it's best to go in the morning. Open from 10 AM to 1 PM and from 3:30 to 5:15 PM, April 1 through September 30 (closed Mondays in April, May, June, and September; Sundays in July and August). Admission charge, except on Tuesdays.

Ribadesella is also a good place from which to take a ride on the *FEVE* railway. Take this classic rural train, which offers good glimpses of the sea, four stops east to the hamlet of Villahormes, and walk a mile to the deserted beach past cornfields and a tiny chapel. A half-hour stroll along AS263 and you'll find the station, at Nueva, from which to catch the train back to Ribadesella. Another pleasant excursion is to drive west of Ribadesella along N632 about 14 miles (22 km) to Colunga. Turn 2 miles (3 km) down AS256 to the delightful fishing village of Lastres, whose steep, cobbled streets rise dizzily above the old harbor. A final treat before leaving Ribadesella is a taste of the local cider. In any of the quayside *sidrerías,* the waiter will pour the first glass from a bottle raised as high as the right arm can reach, while the left hand holds the glass low at an acute angle so the fine spray splashes on the inside of the glass — "aerating" the drink. No Asturian would pour cider any other way, but even the experts wear rubber boots because of the amount of liquid that splashes to the floor!

CHECKING IN: *Gran Hotel del Sella* – The view from this hotel is an open panorama of the town's beautiful surroundings. The old part was formerly the palace of the Argüelles family. All 82 rooms have private baths. Facilities include a swimming pool and tennis court. Closed October through March. Calle La Playa, Ribadesella (phone: 985-860150). Expensive.

Ribadesella Playa – A simple but very comfortable 17-room mansion overlooking the beach. The murmur of breakers lulls guests to sleep. 34 Calle La Playa, Ribadesella (phone: 985-860715; fax: 985-860220). Moderate.

EATING OUT: *Bohemia* – A new eating house, oozing atmosphere and specializing in traditional Asturian fare. Try the *ensalada templada de bocartes y langostinos* (warm salad with barnacles and prawns), *pixín relleno de centollo* (local white fish stuffed with spider crab), *entrecot al cabrales* (entrecôte with cabrales blue cheese), and *leche frita con arándanos* (fried milk rice with bilberries). Open daily. Reservations advised. American Express, MasterCard, and Visa accepted. 53 Gran Vía, Ribadesella (phone: 985-857649). Moderate.

Mesón Tinín – This old-style cider-tavern restaurant is down to earth and lively. Try the Asturian *fabada* (bean, sausage, and bacon stew). No reservations or credit cards accepted. 20 Calle Caso de la Villa, Ribadesella (phone: 985-860839). Inexpensive.

El Repollu – Small, basic, and family-run, with the finest fish in town. The house cabrales cheese is a powerful experience. No reservations or credit cards accepted. 2 Calle Santa Marina, Ribadesella (phone: 985-860734). Inexpensive.

En Route from Ribadesella – Western Europe's wildest mountains, the Picos de Europa, are only 16 miles (26 km) inland, and for anyone traveling westward along the coast, Ribadesella is the last logical point from which to detour for a visit. To kill two birds with one stone, now is also the time to visit the national shrine of Covadonga, marking the spot where Pelayo defeated the Moors in AD 718, thus beginning the Reconquest. The shrine is set at the edge of the National Park of Covadonga, which occupies the western part of the Picos de Europa, and while it may not be of interest to everyone, it is set in magnificent scenery, with 8,000-foot-high mountains soaring into the sky behind a lush valley. Leave Ribadesella along Oviedo-bound N634 for Arriondas, 11 miles (18 km) away, and from there take the N634 turnoff for Cangas de Onis, which was the first Christian capital of Spain and Pelayo's home after he founded the kingdom of Asturias. Cangas is beautifully positioned: Its famous ivy-covered Roman bridge over the Sella River offers some of the best salmon fishing in Spain. Covadonga, consisting of a small cave, with the image of the Virgin Mary and the tombs of Pelayo and King Alfonso I, as well as a large, late-19th-century pink stone basilica, and a museum, is 5 miles (8 km) ahead, and another 7 miles (11 km) beyond are the two lakes at the center of the national park. The basilica and cave are open daily year-round from 9 AM to 7:30 PM; the museum is open from 10:30 AM to 2 PM and from 4 to 7:30 PM; admission charge to the museum.

Drive back to Arriondas, and turn west onto N634 toward Oviedo. A mile (1.6 km) after Infiesto, take AS255 to Villaviciosa, near the coast. The cider capital of Spain, Villaviciosa has a beautiful Old Quarter and is famous for its jet stone handicrafts. Then, for a different route back to N634, take AS113 out of town and, after about 6 miles (10 km), the turnoff signposted to San Salvador de Valdediós, down a steep lane. The monastery here, better known as El Conventín (Little Convent), is one of a remarkable series of 8th- and 9th-century buildings in the Asturian pre-Romanesque style. The site includes a separate stone chapel deep inside a verdant valley, built during the reign of King Alfonso III (866–911), at the time when Mozarabic influences had been introduced. Note the Cross of Victory, a symbol of Pelayo's feat (the original of which is in Oviedo Cathedral), in the small twin windows of the main façade. Afterward, return up the steep, unpaved climb to AS113, rejoin N634 at Pola, and drive the remaining 5 undistinguished miles (8 km) to Oviedo.

 EATING OUT: *Pelayo* – Not surprisingly, there's a Catholic air to the place. Nestled in a wild setting, a step from the National Park of Covadonga, the menu offers typical Asturian cuisine. Reservations advised. Visa and Master-Card accepted. Covadonga (phone: 985-846000). Moderate.

OVIEDO: The capital of Asturias, 17½ miles (28 km) from the coast, Oviedo forms a geographic triangle with Gijón and Avilés. It is the least grim and industrial of the three, has the most interesting Old Quarter, and can claim genuine historical significance. Early in the 9th century, the city became the capital of the tiny kingdom of Asturias, the Christian outpost of otherwise Muslim Spain. A millennium of history, from the 8th to the 18th centuries, is represented by dozens of buildings in the Old Town, including a handful of remarkable pre-Romanesque structures whose styles were 200 years before their time. Otherwise, Oviedo (pop. 195,000), is fairly nondescript.

The Old Town spreads around the 15th-to-16th-century cathedral, which has a marvelous Gothic tower and one of Spain's best altarpieces. But the real treasure is the tiny Cámara Santa (Holy Chamber), built by Alfonso II (who reigned from 792 to 842) to house relics rescued from Toledo when it fell to the Moors. The chamber, which was incorporated into the later cathedral (and which was damaged by an explosion in 1934 and was actually rebuilt after the Civil War), contains a startling array of priceless objects, including the gold-covered oak cross carried by Pelayo in the battle of Covadonga. Also on display is a cedar wood chest of relics donated in 901 and covered with silver bas-reliefs in 1075. Spain was stunned in 1977 when thieves stayed in the chamber overnight and filled their sacks with the treasure. Luckily, the booty was later recovered and the thieves jailed. Open Mondays through Saturdays, from 10 AM to 1 PM and from 4 to 7 PM; admission charge. Behind the cathedral is the *Provincial Archaeological Museum* (3 Calle San Vicente), one of the most important in Spain, with collections from the paleolithic period onward (open Tuesdays through Saturdays from 10 AM to 1:30 PM and from 4 to 6 PM, Sundays from 11 AM to 1 PM; closed Mondays; admission charge). There are many palaces and mansions in the surrounding streets, but most are closed to the public. The tourist office is in front of the cathedral at 6 Plaza de la Catedral (phone: 985-213385).

Classical music lovers will be happy to know that the *Virtuosos of Moscow Chamber Orchestra* has set up residence in Oviedo, until at least 1994. The 25-member orchestra, led by one-time *Chicago Symphony Orchestra* director and world-renowned violinist Vladimir Spivakov, is sponsored by the Principality of Asturias Foundation. They play frequently at Oviedo's *Teatro Campoamor* in the city center. This year, they are setting up a special international music school for gifted children in nearby Avilés. Ask the tourist office for the latest concert information.

Two miles (3 km) from the city, within 250 yards of each other on Naranco Hill, are two churches that are probably the finest examples of Asturian pre-Romanesque art. Santa María del Naranco and San Miguel de Lillo were both built by Ramiro I during his short 9th-century reign, and the former in particular is regarded as exemplary. Originally built as a palace, it included baths and attached living quarters until it was converted to a church during the 12th century. A rectangular, 2-floor building, it has a complex structure using barrel vaulting with reinforced arches resting on a system of blind arches. From the upper floor, huge open windows offer wide views. Other interesting features include the intricately chiseled stonework depicting hunting scenes, and the Byzantine-style capitals and the open porticoes at both ends, a revolutionary concept at the time. Open Mondays through Saturdays, May to October 15, from 10 AM to 1 PM and from 3 to 7 PM; October 15 through April, from 10 AM to 1 PM and from 3 to 5 PM; admission charge. San Miguel de Lillo, built as a church, is a narrow, elevated building — its height is three times the width of its central nave.

Two minutes from Oviedo's Old Town is San Francisco Park, a huge square of gardens, trees, and fountains — a pleasant refuge from the urban sprawl, right in the city center. Nearby is an excellent gift shop, *Escanda* (5 Calle Jovellanos), where Felipe Prieto makes beautiful leather objects. The third week of September is fiesta time in Oviedo, with celebrations for San Mateo, the local patron saint, on the 21st, and processions, folkloric dancing, and music in honor of Latin America on the 19th.

CHECKING IN: *La Reconquista* – A converted 17th-century orphanage, sumptuously decorated and boasting a baroque façade, it is *the* elite social center of Oviedo. All 139 rooms are air conditioned and have private baths. The bar is a former cloister; there is a good restaurant, conference and banquet rooms, and a concert hall. 16 Calle Gil de Jaz, Oviedo (phone: 985-241100; fax: 985-241166). Expensive.

Gran Hotel España – Stylish yet modern, with impeccable service, this place is geared especially to the business traveler. There are 89 rooms. 2 Calle Jovellanos, Oviedo (phone: 985-220596; fax: 985-220596). Expensive to moderate.

EATING OUT: *Casa Fermín* – Chef Luis Gil has developed a super-Asturian cuisine over the past 23 years, using cider, apples, and local *fabes* beans (the restaurant has been here 70 years). Try the *sopa de puerros y almejas* (leek and clam soup) and *merluza a la sidra* (hake in cider). Closed Sundays except in September. Reservations advised. Major credit cards accepted. 8 Calle San Francisco, Oviedo (phone: 985-216452). Expensive.

Trascorrales – A beautiful wooden building set in a delightful medieval square in the heart of the Old Town, with main, back, and private dining rooms. Try the *perdiz con lombarda y castañas* (partridge with red cabbage and chestnuts) and *crema de manzanas gratinados* (grated apple cream). Closed Sundays and August 15–30. Reservations necessary. Major credit cards accepted. Plaza Trascorrales, Oviedo (phone: 985-222441). Expensive.

En Route from Oviedo – Follow the A66 highway 11 miles (18 km) due north, then join A8 for the remaining 7 miles (11 km) into Gijón.

GIJÓN: Asturias's largest city, Gijón (pronounced Hee-*hon*) has a population of 260,000 and manages to be an active industrial center, a busy port, and a booming summer beach resort all at once. The city dates back to the 13th century, but few historical traces remain. Of chief interest to visitors is the seafaring Cimadevilla district on the Santa Catalina hill, which forms a headland at the western end of the 1½-mile-long San Lorenzo beach. The 15th-century Palacio de Revillagigedo, the *Jovellanos Museum,* the City Hall, and the remains of some Roman baths are the noteworthy structures, found at the entrance to Cimadevilla. Also here is the tourist office (1 Calle Marqués de San Esteban; phone: 985-346046), and an impressive statue of Pelayo, brandishing his victory cross aloft. On the right bank of the River Piles is the interesting and recently refurbished *Museo de las Gaitas* (Bagpipe Museum; in the Pueblo de Asturias; phone: 985-373335), with a collection of bagpipes from all over the world and a workshop (open weekdays, from 10 AM to 7 PM; admission charge). Unlike Oviedo, Gijón *feels* like a city, vital and bustling, whether in the fishermen's cider bars in the Cimadevilla or in the commercial center a short walk away. August is the big month: The *Day of Asturias* is celebrated on the first Sunday with a procession and music, and the *Semana Grande* carnival begins on August 15. The annual *International Trade Fair,* a 2-week exposition of the latest technology, also is held in August.

CHECKING IN: *Hernán Cortés* – Dignified and graceful, in the city center, its 109 rooms feature all the usual comforts. 5 Calle Fernández Vallín, Gijón (phone: 985-346000 or 985-355645). Expensive to moderate.

Parador Molino Viejo – The only *parador* in Asturias (and the only *parador* in Spain with a cider bar), this is a delightful old mill, with 40 rooms, located in a large park close to San Lorenzo beach. Parque de Isabel la Católica, Gijón (phone: 985-370511; fax: 985-370233). Expensive to moderate.

EATING OUT: *Casa Victor* – Regarded as the town's best restaurant for fish, served in tavern-style ambience. Closed Thursdays, Sunday evenings, and November. Reservations advised. Major credit cards accepted. 11 Calle Carmen, Gijón (phone: 985-350093; fax: 985-370233). Moderate.

El Pasaje – A modest establishment facing the harbor, next door to the tourist office. The *merluza a la cazuela* (hake casserole) is excellent. No reservations. No credit cards accepted. 3 Calle Marqués de San Esteban, Gijón (phone: 985-345923). Inexpensive.

En Route from Gijón – Avilés is 15 miles (24 km) to the west. To avoid miles of soulless industrial suburbs and housing estates on the way, and drive through some rolling green Asturian hills, take the A8 highway rather than N362.

AVILÉS: Dominated by heavy industry, Avilés is a major iron and steel producing center that has trebled in size in the past few years (pop. 92,000). The few historical landmarks it possesses are swamped by new housing estates or smokestack scenarios, and the sea, only 2½ miles (4 km) away, is one of Spain's pollution blackspots. But the city does have an Old Quarter (around Galiana, La Ferrería, and Rivero Streets) with a few 12th-century churches and several medieval mansions. The Church of San Nicolás has three 14th- and 15th-century chapels attached to it, and in front of the church of San Francisco there is an ornate 17th-century fountain. On *Easter Sunday* and *Monday,* the city celebrates the *Fiesta del Bollu,* when everybody dons folk costume to eat iced *Easter* buns, drink white wine, and dance to traditional music.

En Route from Avilés – The western Asturian coast is thankfully undeveloped, so there are picturesque villages en route; but good hotels and restaurants are hard to find. Less than 3 miles (5 km) west of Avilés, at the small town of Salinas, which has a splendid, long, horseshoe-shaped beach with a pinewood backdrop, industrial pollution is already left behind. Then the N632 road runs through rolling countryside toward Soto del Barco, after which it crosses the Ría de Pravia estuary. Two miles (3 km) ahead is the turnoff to Cudillero, a typical Asturian fishing village whose steep cliffside is wedged around the harbor. Return to N632 and proceed to Soto de Luiña, a tiny village from which a narrow lane leads to the Cabo Vidio headland, with magnificent coastal views. Then N632 continues past arable farmland, away from the sea, through numerous pretty villages, and into Cadavedo, where a large creaking road sign boasts "Voted prettiest town in Asturias — 1954." Cadavedo hasn't changed much since then, and its large sandy beach appears as clean and fine as ever. Soon after Cadavedo, the N632 rejoins the N634 on the way to Luarca, 45 miles (72 km) from Avilés.

LUARCA: Tucked into an S-shaped cove with a delightful bay and fishing port, unrushed and unpretentious Luarca is a maze of cobbled streets, stone stairways, and beautiful walks. The simple, colorful flowerpots that decorate the whitewashed harbor walls are as near as the place gets to ostentation, except for the stupendously ornate cemetery, with marble burial niches and grand family tombs, which is worth some attention. It's located just before the lighthouse and Atalaya chapel, 20 minutes' walk above the town. Another excellent stroll begins up a stone stairway by the bridge that crosses the town's small river, leading up to the Ermita (Hermitage). Walk 10 minutes beyond the hermitage and you'll come to an old village crammed with ancient *hórreos* (granaries).

Luarca has a fine beach, and is one of the last chances before Ribadeo to enjoy an evening of cider with the locals in a traditional Asturian tavern. Three local celebrations are worth noting. On the last Sunday in July, representatives of a nomadic tribe of Asturian shepherds, the Vaqueiros, participate in the *Vaqueirada,* wearing traditional costumes and playing strange instruments such as the *paye tsa,* a pan with a long handle struck with an iron key. A colorful sea procession takes place on August 15, and August 22 is the *Day of San Timoteo,* Luarca's patron saint. The tourist office (Plaza Alfonso X El Sabio; phone: 985-640083) is open from June through September.

CHECKING IN: *Gayoso* – Old and atmospheric, with wooden balconies; its restaurant a few doors away is very good. The hotel is now open all year, though the restaurant still closes at lunchtime during the summer months. Paseo de Gómez, Luarca (phone: 985-640054). Moderate.

EATING OUT: *Leonés* – Three huge metal chandeliers and rural antiques and cowbells lining the walls evoke medieval images. Try *revuelto de gambas, ajo y espinaca* (scrambled eggs with shrimp, garlic, and spinach) and *sorbete de manzana* (apple sherbet). Open daily. Reservations advised. Major credit cards accepted. El Parque, Luarca (phone: 985-640995). Moderate.

En Route from Luarca – To reach N634, follow the signposts for La Coruña. Ribadeo is 30 miles (48 km) away, past undistinguished Navia and Tapia de Casariago, which has a spacious bay, a picturesque beach, and good surfing. A new bridge over the Eo River leads out of Asturias and into Galicia and, a mile away (1.6 km), Ribadeo. (For a complete description of Ribadeo, see *Galicia,* DIRECTIONS.)

Pilgrims' Route

According to legend, a Spanish peasant was led to a distant field by a single shining star on an otherwise uneventful night in 813. Upon reaching the field, the peasant discovered what he believed to be the tomb of St. James the Apostle. The remains of the saint, martyred in Jerusalem in AD 44, had reportedly been returned by his followers to northern Spain, where he was said to have traveled and proselytized. Over time, the tomb had been forgotten and presumed lost — until 813. Although historians doubt that St. James actually ever entered the region — alive or dead — their down-to-earth testimony has failed to detract from the devotions accorded the site. St. James died centuries before Islam was even conceived, but the repossession of his sacred remains served as an inspirational presence in the war against the Moors, a spiritual device to rival the influence of the prophet Muhammad in the enemy ranks. As a result, the disciple of Jesus was subsequently acclaimed as Matamoros, "Slayer of the Moors." After receiving papal recognition, the town of Santiago de Compostela, where the remains of St. James (Santiago in Spanish) were discovered, became the third most important pilgrimage site in Christendom, after Jerusalem and Rome.

During the first half of the 12th century, Amerique Picaud, a French priest, wrote five volumes of stories connected with St. James, including a detailed guide for pilgrims on the journey to Santiago. This *Pilgrims' Guide* is considered to be the first travel guidebook ever written. It provided information on hospices, churches, difficult portions of the journey, meals and lodging, local customs, where good water could be found and bad water avoided, and the character of the people in each area. Though the Picaud itinerary was not the only one followed, it became known over the centuries as the primary Camino de Santiago (Way of St. James), or the Pilgrims' Route.

The pilgrims, easily identified by the scallop shell (the emblem of St. James) pinned to their cloaks and by their floppy felt hats, believed that completion of the long and arduous journey excused them from half of their allotted time in purgatory. Historically, they proved to have been a melting pot of European cultures, languages and dialects, and architectural tastes. The Pilgrims' Route, as it developed over the centuries, provides one of the most concentrated collections of Romanesque churches and Gothic cathedrals in the world, and the art decorating these religious monuments is a brilliant merging of Moorish, French, Italian, and Spanish influences.

The main Pilgrims' Route runs some 506 miles (810 km) through Spain, crossing the French border near Roncesvalles, in the region of Navarre, and passing through Pamplona, Logroño in La Rioja, and Burgos and León, in the region of Castile-León, on its way to the Galician capital, Santiago. Marked by crucifixes during medieval days, it is designated today by modern signs showing the scallop shell of St. James — the international symbol for pilgrims — stylized in the form of a star. It crosses the extremes of Spanish geography and climate, beginning high in the Pyrenees, then dropping into the fertile foothills and crossing the wide open, dry plains, before rising again over the mountains separating León and Galicia and winding through the hilly, lush green landscape of the Spanish northwest.

Today's pilgrims arrive in Santiago under vastly different circumstances from those of their medieval counterparts. Although 3,000 to 4,000 still arrive on foot each year as genuine pilgrims (who fulfill certain requirements, including mode of travel — on foot, horseback, or by bicycle — and in return receive 3 days' free food and lodging in Santiago), for most visitors the journey is more comfortable. In addition to cars and buses, two luxury trains now travel to and from Santiago. The *Al-Andalus Expreso* moves north from Andalusia in July and August to cover the Pilgrims' Way from Barcelona, Burgos, and León, with guided tours in English in each of these cities. The *El Transcantábrico,* somewhat less *Orient-Express*–like but still splendid, covers the North Atlantic coast from Santiago to San Sebastián via El Ferrol, Luarca, Oviedo, Covadonga, Santillana del Mar, Santander, Guernica, and Zaranz. Modern pilgrims still come primarily to view the massive cathedral and its shrine as sightseers. Judging by the awe-inspired sighs that echo around the Plaza del Obradoiro, they are not disappointed. To round the last corner and come face-to-face with the cathedral's golden granite baroque face, tinged with green lichen, and its magnificently sculpted grand portal and two soaring towers, is to be as inspired as any pilgrim of the Middle Ages. It is, as travel author Jan Morris maintains, "one of the great moments of travel."

A room for two in a hotel listed below as expensive will cost $90 and up; a room in a hotel listed as moderate, between $60 and $90; and in an inexpensive one, $55 or less. A meal for two will run $75 or more in an expensive restaurant, $45 to $70 in the moderate range (the majority of the restaurants), and under $40 in an inexpensive place (also plentiful).

RONCESVALLES: The valley and pass through the Pyrenees here enjoy a certain historical renown because of the *Song of Roland,* an epic poem that romanticized the defeat of Charlemagne's rear guard during its retreat from Spain in 778. Later, the pass became the prime conduit for travelers along the Pilgrims' Route as it entered Spain from France, and in the 12th century King Sancho VII of Navarre (Sancho el Fuerte, the Strong) added an Augustinian monastery to the hospital that had already grown up to serve pilgrims on the Spanish side of the pass. Legend has it that a monk constantly rang a bell to guide pilgrims through the pass. Still in use, the monastery buildings are open to the public. A cloister leads to the entrance of the Colegiata Real (Royal Collegiate Church), one of the first Gothic churches built in Spain, consecrated in 1219, with a nave and two aisles that are beautiful examples of the Romanesque-to-Gothic transition. The church houses the famous *Madonna de Roncesvalles,* a 13th-century cedar figure of the Virgin Mary, clad in silver and adorned with jewels. According to legend, the figure appeared miraculously, pointed out by a red stag with a star shining in its antlers. Also off the cloister is the chapter house, containing the tombs of the monastery's founder, King Sancho, and his wife, Doña Clemencia, and a massive stained glass window depicting the king's victories. The monastery is open daily, from 8:30 AM to 7 PM, depending on when masses are scheduled. An adjoining monastery building houses the small *Roncesvalles Museum,* with artifacts from the

Camino de Santiago or related to it: desks, tapestries, illuminated manuscripts, books on plants, herbs, and philosophy, coins, and letters pilgrims wrote to people back home — a picture of life on the road in the Middle Ages. The museum is open daily, June through September, from 11 AM to 1:30 PM and from 4 to 6 PM (in winter it opens for groups only); admission charge.

Down a road from the monastery is the Chapel of Sancti Spiritus, the oldest building in Roncesvalles, dating from the early 12th century.

CHECKING IN/EATING OUT: *La Posada* – A small, quaint, 11-room hotel. Beautiful and quiet, it is just steps away from the monastery. The restaurant offers high-quality fare. No credit cards accepted. Roncesvalles (phone: 948-760225). Moderate.

En Route from Roncesvalles – Take C135 south about 2 miles (3 km) to Burguete, a picturesque Basque town, where Ernest Hemingway is known to have gone trout fishing. The town has the small Romanesque Church of San Nicolás, and a number of charming hotels and restaurants. Continuing southwest, stay on C135 as it winds along the Arga River to Pamplona. The sights from the road, as it passes over hills and around sharp bends, are spectacular. Ahead are the walls of Pamplona, 29½ miles (47 km) from Roncesvalles; its cathedral and massive fortifications resemble a glowing postcard photo when approached at sunset.

CHECKING IN: *Burguete* – A *hostal* of 22 rooms with bath, across from the ancient church. The owner is an avid fisherman and if you arrive on a day when he was lucky at the stream, you're in for a treat in the dining room — trout so pink you'll swear you're dreaming. Closed December through February. 51 Calle Unica, Burguete (phone: 948-760005). Inexpensive.

Loizu – This 27-room *hostal* with private baths is kept spotless by the owner, who rules over the establishment with an iron hand. It has a restaurant, a long dining room with a rustic, beamed ceiling in which local specialties, including a variety of lamb and trout dishes, are served. Closed December through mid-March. 3 Calle Unica, Burguete (phone: 948-760008). Inexpensive.

EATING OUT: *Marichu* – A grill restaurant serving meat dishes only. Open daily. No reservations or credit cards accepted. 2 Calle Roncesvalles, Burguete (phone: 948-760086). Inexpensive.

Txiki Polit – The area's most picturesque eatery. Dine in either the small, elegant, wood-paneled room with the giant wooden chandelier, in front, or in the long, traditional Basque dining room in the rear. Specialties include mountain trout with smoked ham, and *cordero al chilindrón* (Basque-style lamb). Open daily except Mondays from July through mid-September; open only Saturdays and Sundays the rest of the year. Reservations advised. No credit cards accepted. 42 Calle Unica, Burguete (phone: 948-760019). Inexpensive.

PAMPLONA: For a detailed report on the city, its sights, hotels, and restaurants, see *Pamplona,* THE CITIES.

En Route from Pamplona – Follow N111 southwest for 27 miles (43 km) to Estella. Along the way, the topography changes from relatively mountainous terrain north of Pamplona to rolling plateau land that gradually declines in altitude as it nears the central Spanish plains. For the most part, the road runs parallel to the original Camino de Santiago, passing through wide open fields that erupt into brilliant carpets of sunflowers in the summer. Ruins of old pilgrim hospitals can be found in the town of Cizur Menor, just outside Pamplona, and a stretch of the original route has been preserved in the small village of Zarquiegui. Both are obscure and hard to find, however, even with residents' directions. The first monument of note concerning the pilgrims' progress is the bronze statue of a pilgrim just outside the town of Puente la Reina, 15 miles (24 km) from Pamplona. The statue depicts the traditional pilgrim in flowing cape and wide-brimmed hat, carrying a staff and a gourd for water — an image that is seen repeatedly along the route, particularly in statues of St. James dressed as a pilgrim.

It was in Puente la Reina that a less-traveled pilgrims' road, one that came from Arles (in the Provence region of France) and crossed the Pyrenees via the Somfort Pass, joined the main route (which originated in Paris and descended via Vezelay and Le Puy to the Pyrenees and crossed into Spain via the Roncesvalles Pass). The two trails most likely joined here to take advantage of the bridge that gave the town its name, built across the Arga River in the 11th century. The bridge, with its six arches and peaked central span, stands as strong as ever, one of the best examples of medieval engineering still in existence. The Iglesia del Crucifijo (Church of the Crucifix), a 12th-century Romanesque church that was part of a pilgrims' hospice, was rebuilt in the 15th century and is famous for a Y-shaped crucifix carved with an expressionistic Christ, which is believed to have been brought from Germany by a 14th-century pilgrim.

Continue along N111 to the next significant town, Cirauqui, which clings to the top of a hill overlooking the Salado River and is noted for the San Román church, with an excellent portal. Because the roads leading to town and the streets in town are very steep, drivers should make sure that they are handy with the clutch or have an automatic transmission. In medieval days, the outskirts of Cirauqui were considered a danger spot for pilgrims; the *Pilgrims' Guide* warned of "evil doers" who would encourage pilgrims to water their horses in a nearby stream with bad water. When the horses became ill, the schemers drove off the pilgrims and skinned their steeds.

Back on N111, Estella, 12 miles (19 km) from Puente la Reina, becomes visible after a few more bends in the road.

CHECKING IN: *Mesón del Peregrino* – At the junction of the two pilgrims' routes. The 15 rooms all have private baths, there is a swimming pool, and the restaurant receives rave reviews for its substantial meals (closed Sunday evenings). Carretera Pamplona–Logroño (N111), Km 23, Puente la Reina (phone: 948-340075). Inexpensive.

EATING OUT: *Fonda Restaurante Lorca* – This small, family-run eatery is in the center of Cirauqui, where its upstairs dining room overlooks the town square. The menu is a simple one, featuring chicken and veal entrées. There are some small rooms, but they are recommended only in an emergency. No reservations or credit cards accepted. 54 Calle Mayor, Cirauqui (no phone). Inexpensive.

ESTELLA: Once the seat of the Kings of Navarre, this major stopping point on the Pilgrims' Route is packed with churches. The church of San Pedro de la Rúa (St. Peter of the Way) dominates the entire town. Built during the 12th century, it is Estella's oldest church. A massive portal graces it, and its interior features a mixture of Romanesque and Gothic influences. But its real gem is the small cloister tucked between the church and the towering cliff; its two remaining rows of columns are topped by some of the most intricately carved capitals in Europe, some depicting the life of Christ, but others, in contrast, portraying mythological subjects, with scenes of couples kissing — virtually unheard of in Catholic settings.

The exteriors of Estella's other churches are generally more impressive than their interiors. The Iglesia del Santo Sepulcro (Holy Sepulcher), also in a transitional Romanesque-Gothic style, boasts a Gothic portal with carvings of the Last Supper, the

Virgin Mary, and the Crucifixion. The Church of San Miguel has a magnificent portal with carvings of the Guardian Angels, the Old Men of the Apocalypse, the childhood of Christ, and the Apostles. The Estella Tourist Office (phone: 948-554011) is in the 12th-century Palacio de los Reyes de Navarra (Palace of the Kings of Navarre), one of the oldest secular buildings in Spain, located directly across from the monumental staircase that rises up to San Pedro.

CHECKING IN: *Irache* – Estella's best *hostal,* modern with 74 clean rooms and private baths. The restaurant is uninspiring, but there are plenty of good dining spots nearby. Carretera Pamplona–Logroño (N111), Km 43, Estella (phone: 948-551150; fax: 948-554754). Moderate.

EATING OUT: *La Cepa* – An elegant establishment with a classic wood-carved bar overlooking the main square. The wine list offers extensive selections from the Rioja and Navarre regions. Open daily. Reservations advised. American Express and Visa accepted. 19 Plaza de los Fueros, Estella (phone: 948-550032). Expensive to moderate.

Maracaibo – Across the square from *La Cepa,* it serves excellent regional specialties. Open daily. Reservations advised. No credit cards accepted. 22 Plaza de los Fueros, Estella (phone: 948-550483). Expensive to moderate.

En Route from Estella – The Monasterio de Irache, just 2 miles (3 km) south of Estella along N111, was built in the 12th and 13th centuries and is considered by many to be a particularly beautiful example of the transitional Romanesque-to-Gothic style. It now can be visited once again, after having been closed several years for renovations (open Tuesdays through Fridays from 10 AM to 2 PM and from 5 to 7 PM, Saturdays and Sundays from 9 AM to 2 PM and from 4 to 7 PM; admission charge). Continue southwest on N111 to the town of Los Arcos, 13 miles (21 km) from Estella, where the Iglesia Parroquial de la Asunción (Church of the Assumption) in Plaza Mayor offers a perfect example of baroque excesses. Virtually every inch of the interior walls and domes is covered with gilted decoration, that of the domes in a swirling shell design. The high altar has a 15th-century altarpiece and a fine Gothic statue of the Madonna, while the magnificent choir stalls are also Gothic. Continuing another 4½ miles (7 km), N111 leads to Torres del Río, a town that is beautifully perched on a hillside dropping down to the river. Founded by the Knights of the Holy Sepulcher, it has an interesting octagonal church complete with Moorish decor, including Mudéjar art in the vaulting of the main dome. The route continues another 13 miles (21 km) to Logroño, the only major town in the region of La Rioja.

LOGROÑO: This is the capital of one Spain's main wine producing regions. Rioja wines have long been considered among the best in Europe (they are now enjoying increasing popularity in the US. The Rioja region also grows over 90% of Spain's asparagus. The modern town of Logroño is uninteresting, but the small Old Town at its core holds several religious treasures associated with the Pilgrims' Route. Everything is within easy walking distance of the massive main square. The Rua Vieja and Calle Mayor, the two main arteries of the Old Town, have been traced by countless pilgrims over the centuries. The 15th-century Catedral de Santa María la Redonda is austerely Gothic, set off by twin baroque towers and a baroque façade added in 1742. The Church of Santa María del Palacio, built on the site of the palace of the Kings of Castile, is famous for its eight-sided, pyramid-shaped steeple, originally constructed during the 13th century (the rest of the church is mostly from the 16th to 18th centuries). The portal of the smaller Church of St. Bartholomew, seemingly designed for a grand cathedral, is a fine example of Gothic sculpture, depicting the life of the saint.

CHECKING IN: *Murrieta* – There are more modern and more luxurious hotels elsewhere, but this 113-room hostelry is a good choice for older elegance. Located in the center of town, the *tapas* bars and monuments of the Old Town are only steps away. 1 Calle Marqués de Murrieta, Logroño (phone: 941-224150). Moderate.

***La Numantina* –** Near the main square in the Old Town, this *hostal* offers 17 clean rooms, plus wonderful breakfast pastries imported from across the street. 4 Calle Sagasta, Logroño (phone: 941-251411). Moderate to inexpensive.

EATING OUT: *Asador González* – Also known as *La Chata,* this place serves Logroño's best roast baby goat and baby lamb. Closed Sundays. Reservations advised. Major credit cards accepted. 3 Calle Carnicerías, Logroño (phone: 941-251296). Moderate.

***Mesón Charro* –** The best *chuletas de cordero* (lamb chops) in town are found here, in an informal, picnic-table setting. Closed Mondays. Reservations advised. No credit cards accepted. 12 Calle Laurel, Logroño (phone: 941-224663). Moderate.

En Route from Logroño – Take N232 out of Logroño to N120. From here, the road is very well marked as the Camino de Santiago; the landscape becomes drier, the fertile green of Navarre changing to a dusty brown. Follow N120 west toward Burgos, 70½ miles (113 km) from Logroño. Along the way, three small towns of the Rioja region offer important pilgrim sights. The first is Navarrete, a small town with a large 16th-century church. The next is Nájera, which was at one time the capital of the kingdom of Navarre and which became a main stop on the route when a large bridge was built over the Najerilla River, along with a monastery. The Monastery of Santa María la Real was founded by García, a Navarrese king, in the 11th century, on the site where a statue of the Virgin had been found. Its 15th-century church is notable as a pantheon of 11th- and 12th-century royalty (the 12th-century tomb of Blanca de Navarra is outstanding), and for the particularly intricate Flamboyant Gothic carving of the choir stalls, completed around 1500; the cloister, too, is a fine example of Flamboyant Gothic design. The monastery and church are open daily, from 10 AM to noon and 4 to 7 PM. No admission charge.

Continue to Santo Domingo de la Calzada, the third significant town between Logroño and Burgos, and one of the most important stops on the Pilgrims' Route. The town was named for an 11th-century monk who spent his life helping pilgrims, constructing a bridge across the Oca River for their use, and building a road (his name translates as St. Dominic of the Causeway). Some 300 years later, the same monk reentered church lore when a young man, falsely accused of theft, was sentenced to be hanged. As the sentence was carried out, the young man's parents prayed fervently before the monk's tomb. Passing the gallows, they found their son alive and well, while still hanging by the neck. They immediately raced to the governor and implored him to cut their son down and allow him to live. The governor, understandably, found all of this hard to believe and murmured that if the boy were still alive, then the well-cooked cock could probably crow — which it proceeded to do. The startled governor freed the young man, and to this day, a white cock and hen are kept in the cathedral as a reminder of the miracle. (This miracle, by the way, closely resembles one that occurred in Barcelos, Portugal, and gave rise to the rooster as the Portuguese symbol of good luck; in that story, it was a Galician on his way to Santiago who was falsely accused of stealing.) After this stop, continue west on N120 into the region of Castile-León, driving the remaining 42½ miles (68 km) to Burgos, capital of the province of the same name.

CHECKING IN: *Parador Santo Domingo de la Calzada* – A beautiful *parador* situated in an old pilgrims' hostel that dates back to the 11th century; it has just undergone an extensive restoration. All 35 rooms have private baths.

There are often concerts at the small church next door. 3 Plaza del Santo, Santo Domingo de la Calzada (phone: 941-340300; fax: 941-340325). Moderate.

BURGOS: A onetime capital of the kingdom of Castile, Burgos is associated with the legendary warrior El Cid, who was born nearby. An equestrian statue of the 11th-century hero stands by the Arlanzón River. The city has a lovely riverside promenade, the Paseo del Espolón, supremely conducive to strolling, which begins just outside the city's 14th-century Arco de Santa María gate. A short way inside the gate is the massive 13th-century cathedral, built by King Ferdinand III (the Saint). The city also has two monasteries beyond its Old Town — the Cartuja de Miraflores and the Monasterio de las Huelgas — that are well worth a visit. (For a detailed report on the city, its sights, hotels, and restaurants, see *Burgos,* THE CITIES.)

En Route from Burgos – Follow N120 westward for 19 miles (30 km) to the town of Olmillos de Sasamón, recognizable by the massive castle along the highway, then turn left down the road toward Castellanos de Castro and Castrojeriz. At this point, the Pilgrims' Route temporarily stops running parallel to the national highways and becomes quite convoluted, but the signs for the Camino de Santiago are excellent and easy to follow. About a mile (1.6 km) after the left turn, make a right turn at the sign for Castellanos de Castro. The road winds through fields and between densely planted trees, and actually passes through the ruins of the Convent of San Antonio, under the Gothic arches and past the ornate portal. Soon after, the Castle of Castrojeriz appears in the distance, 11 miles (18 km) from Olmillos.

CASTROJERIZ: A poor pueblo of a place, Castrojeriz has three massive churches. Santa María del Manzano, a 13th-century collegiate church, is just to the left as the Pilgrims' Route enters the village. Now a veritable art museum, it was one of the most important churches along the route until the cathedral in Burgos was completed. The church features a 16th-century stained glass window, four ornate wooden altarpieces carved by Italian craftsmen, and a polychromatic sculpture of the Virgin of the Apple Tree. The town's three other churches, San Juan, Santa Clara, and Santo Domingo, are impressive from the outside (the parish priest or one of his assistants will open them for visitors between *Easter* and October; phone: 947-377036). Castrojeriz's portico-lined main square is surprisingly well maintained for what is otherwise a dusty and forgotten town.

En Route from Castrojeriz – Heading west out of town, be prepared to share the road with herds of sheep that, at times, graze in the area. Follow the local road (marked Melgar) for 16 miles (26 km) to Frómista, an agricultural center boasting perhaps the most beautifully constructed Romanesque church along the route. Built early in the 11th century, San Martín has three perfectly formed naves, ribbed arches, and sculpted capitals on the columns. The exterior has two round towers, small arched windows, and an octagonal cupola, all fashioned to breathtaking excellence. Open daily, from 10 AM to 2 PM and 4 to 8 PM.

The narrow country roads, still well marked as the Camino de Santiago, continue for about 12 miles (20 km) to Carrión de los Condes, another important stop on the Pilgrims' Route. Its two churches feature excellent exterior carvings. The Church of Santa María has crumbling carvings of the Old Men of the Apocalypse and the Three Kings. The Church of St. James, tucked just off the main town square, has a beautiful façade with statues of the Apostles and an even more impressive portal with carvings depicting men at everyday work — an architect with a compass, a sheep shearer with scissors, and a farmer.

At Carrión de los Condes, the Pilgrims' Route returns to N120; follow it about

27 miles (43 km) west to Sahagún. Here, the churches of San Tirso and San Lorenzo are fine examples of early Romanesque brick construction, with interiors bearing extensive Mudéjar decorations. Continue along to the next stop of importance, León, a 42-mile (67-km) drive from Sahagún, reached by heading west along N120 to the N601 intersection, and then taking N601 north into the provincial capital.

LEÓN: For centuries a center of Spanish culture, León, like most of Spain's larger cities, is composed of an Old Town surrounded by a spreading new city of high-rises. The old medieval section has been substantially rebuilt, but still follows the maze-like twists and turns of the original streets. León's crowning jewel is its cathedral. The beauty of this 14th- and 15th-century structure is not apparent outside, but once inside the visitor is overwhelmed by the most dazzling display of stained glass in all of Spain. The Romanesque Basilica of San Isidro, containing a pantheon of kings and queens of the old kingdom of León, is another important building, as is the *Parador de San Marcos* (7 Plaza de San Marcos; phone: 987-237300), a 15-minute walk from the Old Town, at one time a monastery that saw service as a way station for pilgrims. The main square (Plaza Mayor) of the Old Town fills daily with a vast fruit and vegetable market. The surrounding neighborhood is the place where the city's evening *paseo* takes place, and is also the quarter where most of the best restaurants and nightlife are found. For further details on León, see *Castile-León (Old Castile)*, DIRECTIONS.

En Route from León – Take N120 heading west from León 18 miles (29 km) to the village of Hospital de Orbigo, where a famous bridge crosses the Orbigo River. The bridge was the site of a celebrated series of jousts by the love-struck knight Suero de Quiñones, who, to prove his valor to his love, challenged anyone who tried to cross the bridge for 30 days. Together with nine companions whose names are inscribed on the bridge, he took on all comers, breaking over 300 lances in all. His fame spread throughout medieval Europe, and the bridge crossing became known as the Passage of Honor. Eventually Quiñones made the pilgrimage to Santiago de Compostela and placed a gold-plated silver collar around the bust of St. James, which remains in Santiago's Chapel of Relics. Another 10 miles (16 km) west of Hospital de Orbigo along N120 is the town of Astorga, with its medieval city walls, an impressive cathedral, and a palace designed by Gaudí.

EATING OUT: *Il Suero de Quiñones* – Enjoy a drink and the view on the deck overlooking the Passage of Honor Bridge, then try one of the dining room's massive mixed salads or highly recommended lamb chops. Located directly at the end of the bridge. Open daily. No reservations. No credit cards accepted. Hospital de Orbigo (phone: 987-388238). Inexpensive.

ASTORGA: Beautifully situated on a mountain spur 2,850 feet above sea level, Astorga served as a staging point for the final third of the Pilgrims' Route to Santiago. The Romans knew the city as Asturica Augusta, and Pliny the Elder described it as "magnificent." The Cathedral de Santa María, built during the 13th century on the site of an 11th-century church, has bell towers similar to those of León's cathedral, as well as similar massive stained glass windows. Its museum houses noteworthy works of medieval religious art, including an ivory crucifix with small rubies inlaid to represent trickling blood. The cannonballs on the staircase are remnants of the Peninsular War against Napoleon. Take a close look at the four-panel painting of the life of San Antonio Abab. The museum is open daily, from 10 AM to 2 PM and from 4 to 8 PM; no admission charge.

Another sightseeing stop, the Episcopal Palace (Plaza de la Catedral), is a fanciful 19th-to-20th-century mock medieval creation of soaring towers, circular staircases, and an interior where light dances through the rooms. The work of Antoni Gaudí — his most imaginative, spectacular creation outside Barcelona — it was commissioned by the bishop, a fellow Catalonian, after a fire destroyed its predecessor in 1886, but wasn't finished until 1909. The first two floors now house a museum dedicated to the subject of the Pilgrims' Route, the *Museo de los Caminos,* with an extensive collection of statues, paintings, notebooks, and journals from the heyday of the pilgrimage (open from 10 AM to 2 PM and from 4 to 8 PM; admission charge). The third floor houses a permanent exhibition of regional art from the last 2 decades.

CHECKING IN/EATING OUT: *Gaudí* – Astorga's top choice, with a traditional Spanish decor of light walls and dark furnishings. Most of the 35 rooms overlook the fanciful Episcopal Palace, and the restaurant downstairs is one of the best within miles, serving excellent fare in tremendous portions. Major credit cards accepted. 6 Plaza Eduardo de Castro, Astorga (phone: 987-615654). Moderate.

En Route from Astorga – Continue westward on N-VI, the often excellent highway that links Madrid with La Coruña. As the road begins to climb, the views on both sides clearly show how arduous this part of the pilgrimage must have been. Though the highway here doesn't exactly follow the Pilgrims' Route, the smaller C120 does, winding through the Valley of El Silencio, bordered by rugged mountains, and passing the Cross of Iron. The cross is set into a pile of stones, created as a result of a tradition that each passing pilgrim add his own stone. The mountains that line N-VI are marked by giant coal deposits, evidence of the importance of mining in this region of Spain.

After 38 miles (61 km), N-VI drops to the town of Ponferrada, where an 11th-century iron bridge carried pilgrims over the Sil River. The massive Templar castle, overlooking the river, appears spectacular from a distance, but it is little more than a standing outer wall (open from 9 AM to 1 PM and from 3 to 6 PM. Ponferrada does have an excellent example of Mozarabic architecture in the tiny 10th-century Church of Santo Tomás de las Ollas, in which a ring of horseshoe-shaped arches surrounds the altar. The church is up a side road — there's a sign just as the main road enters the town (knock on the door of the adjacent house, where the caretaker lives). Ponferrada marks the beginning of the last stretch of the Pilgrims' Route before it enters the region of Galicia. Follow N-VI 12½ miles (20 km) to the town of Villafranca del Bierzo, with its outstanding *parador.*

VILLAFRANCA DEL BIERZO: The town owes its foundation to French pilgrims, who used the area as a stopover during the 11th century. The medieval buildings here include manor houses that line the famous Calle del Agua, which was known to pilgrims as one of the route's most beautiful streets. The Church of St. James, a typical example of 12th-century Romanesque architecture, boasts an excellent Portal of Forgiveness opening onto the route. Exhausted pilgrims, unable to complete the trek as far as Santiago, could pass through it into the church and receive the same indulgences as those given in Santiago. The town's other churches — all worth a visit — include San Juan en San Fiz, a well-preserved Romanesque building; Santa María de Cluniaco, its floor plan in the form of a Latin cross; and San Nicolás, a 17th-century church that was part of a Jesuit college.

CHECKING IN: *Parador Villafranca del Bierzo* – A modern, 40-room hostelry, at the edge of town, a short walk from most of the ancient buildings. Avenida Calvo Sotelo, Villafranca del Bierzo (phone: 987-540175; fax: 987-540010). Moderate.

EATING OUT: *La Charola* – A real dining experience. For centuries, pilgrims have stopped here to fill up and drink before beginning the most difficult part of the pilgrimage. Today, it's also the sort of place to which truck drivers make a beeline the minute their jobs bring them into the area. Order the *cocido,* the typical stewed meat platter, and a huge tureen of noodle soup will appear, followed by a platter of vegetables, one of garbanzo beans, and one of stewed meats and sausages — guests take what they want, because no one could possibly eat it all. Wash it down with a bottle of wine or *gaseosa* (soda water), and finish with some of the local firewater — *orujo* — in your coffee. Reservations advised. Major credit cards accepted. 19 Calle Doctor Aren, Villafranca del Bierzo (phone: 987-540200). Inexpensive.

En Route from Villafranca del Bierzo – Leave town via N-VI, and the valley immediately narrows. The road zigs and zags as it climbs to enter the region of Galicia through the Puerto de Pedrafita do Cebreiro, 18 miles (29 km) from Villafranca. This is the last major pass to be negotiated before Santiago, and it is at this point that the main highway and the Pilgrims' Route once again part company, as the N-VI takes a more northwesterly course for Lugo and the Pilgrims' Route turns into tiny mountain roads on a more southwesterly course to Santiago. As the road skirts the ridge rising to the summit, almost as a reward for the pilgrims' tenacity, the views to the north are breathtaking, with bright yellow flowers punctuating the green mountains that stretch as far as the eye can see.

O CEBREIRO: The village of O Cebreiro (in Galician — its Castilian spelling is El Cebreiro), not far from the Pedrafita do Cebreiro pass, is an ancient one, with a church and a pilgrims' hospice that were constructed as early as the 9th century, as well as some old reconstructed dry stone huts of Celtic origin. The church became famous following a miracle that was reported around 1300. A priest of little faith was saying mass in the presence of a peasant who had climbed through deep snow and wind to get there. Suddenly, as the priest was musing that it was silly for anyone to brave such weather for only a bit of wine and bread, the Host turned into flesh and the wine into blood. Word of this miracle of the Holy Eucharist spread throughout Europe, and the chalice in which it is said to have occurred is still kept in the church.

CHECKING IN/EATING OUT: *San Giraldo de Aurillac* – Simple accommodations in one of Europe's most mystical locations. The 6 rooms of this *hostal* were built into the original, centuries-old hospice. The restaurant features simple but filling fare. Try the *caldo gallego* (Galician soup), *cocido* (stew), and locally produced cebreiro cheese. No credit cards accepted. O Cebreiro (phone: 982-369025). Inexpensive.

En Route from O Cebreiro – The narrow road continues westward. After Linares, there is a wonderful view to the left of mountain after mountain, all of differing shades of green against a pale sky, eventually fading into the mist. Low stone walls (similar to those in Scotland and Ireland) appear, the sun glistens off shiny slate roofs, and lush ferns line the road. As cattle graze in small roadside pastures, hay wagons, tractors, oxen carts, and cows share the road with cars. In the winter, the vista is of stark, windswept snow punctuated by the forms of naked trees. The tiny towns encountered along these winding roads all have pilgrims in their past, and they have inherited an architecture that is more reminiscent of Ireland than Spain. The village of Triacastela has a pilgrims' jail with interesting graffiti on its walls; farther along, after passing through narrow gorges, the road turns around the massive Monastery of Samos, which goes back to the Middle Ages, although little of its early times remains. The monastery has a small Gothic cloister and a larger neo-classical one, the latter with modern frescoes on its upper level depicting the life of Saint Benedict. The church, built in the 18th century, is purely classical in design. Tours of the monastery take place daily, beginning every half hour from 10:30 AM to 1 PM and from 4 to 6:30 PM. No admission charge.

Sarria is 32 miles (51 km) beyond O Cebreiro. After Sarria, the road, C535, continues westward and about 15 miles (24 km) past Sarria, it crosses the Miño River (Portugal's Minho), which has been turned into a massive lake by a dam. The old village of Portomarín has been lost forever, covered in water, but before that metamorphosis happened, the tower-like church of the Knights of St. John of Jerusalem had been dismantled and rebuilt on a hill behind the new town of Portomarín. It still has a beautiful rose window, and the decoration of its portal, resembling the *Gate of Glory* in Santiago de Compostela, is believed to be the work of Master Mateo.

About 7½ miles (12 km) west of Portomarín, C535 joins N540/N640, the main Orense–Lugo highway. Turn north toward Lugo, but drive only 5 miles (8 km) to the turnoff for C547, which leads to Santiago. Continue about 6 miles (10 km) to the sign marking Vilar de Doñas (just off the main road), a final church of significance along the Pilgrims' Route. The church was a chapter house of the Knights of St. James and a burial place for Galician knights killed fighting the Moors. Its name derives from the frescoes in the apse depicting women with sultry smiles dressed in bonnets and finery. After seeing the church, return to C547 and continue to Santiago de Compostela, which is another 59 miles (94 km) west. (For a detailed report on the city, its sights, hotels, and restaurants, see *Santiago de Compostela*, THE CITIES.)

Catalonia and Andorra

Every year, the beaches of the Costa Brava attract millions of tourists lured by the promise of inexpensive, fun-filled vacations. Most fly to Barcelona or Gerona and head straight for the coast, unaware of the traditional Catalan life that continues in villages, on farms, and in small towns throughout the region, just waiting to be discovered. Barcelona itself is a sophisticated city rich in history, with a lively cultural scene. Tarragona has its Roman heritage. And a few miles away from the high-rise hotels of the best-known resorts there are glorious rocky coves with beautiful beaches and little fishing villages. Inland, the countryside ranges from snow-capped mountains to plains baked red by a fierce sun. The rewards for the visitor include grandiose castles and cathedrals, creepy medieval passages, a 900-year-old nunnery, and a surrealistic art museum.

Not long ago, most tourists had no idea that this region considered itself separate from the rest of Spain. Under Generalísimo Francisco Franco, Catalonia was a province to be subjugated; expressions of nationalism — such as the teaching of the staccato native language — were suppressed. Following Franco's death in 1975, however, things began to change, and Catalonia became one of Spain's 17 autonomous communities, enjoying the equivalent of US statehood. At long last, Catalans had their own *generalitat* (government). With the revival of their language, street signs were changed from Spanish to Catalan, and the red-and-yellow Catalan flag was raised above public and private buildings alike. Throughout the area, roads and public utilities were improved and ancient buildings were restored as Catalan pride manifested itself — a pride that is reflected today in the welcoming of foreigners.

As early as 500 BC, the Greeks were trading along the coast of northeastern Spain, establishing colonies at Empúries and Roses. As elsewhere in the Mediterranean, the Romans soon followed, and by 200 BC Tarragona was the fortress city of an extensive imperial province that stretched across the northern Iberian Peninsula. About 1,000 years later, in 801, Barcelona became the focal point when it was conquered by Charlemagne and turned into the front line of an offensive against the Moors, who controlled the rest of Spain. The demise of the Carolingian Empire at the end of the 9th century led to the founding of the House of Barcelona, which united the counties of what is basically today's Catalonia (plus territory on the French side of the Pyrenees.) This unification was the work of Guifré el Pilós (Wilfred the Shaggy), who had proclaimed himself Count of Barcelona and, legend has it, also was responsible for creating the Catalan flag. While supporting Charles the Bald, Charlemagne's grandson, in battle, Wilfred fought fiercely despite being seriously wounded. Acknowledging this bravery, Charles dipped his fingers in the blood pouring from Wilfred's wounds and drew four gory lines across the count's yellow shield. It's a good story, as legends go, but the first recorded use of the Catalan colors actually came some 200 years later, in 1082. Even that date, however, enables Catalans to boast that their flag is Europe's oldest.

The first usages of "Catalunya" and "Catalan" can also be traced back to the 11th century, when Barcelona was a center of shipbuilding and trade. Later, thanks to the exploits of James the Conqueror, Catalonia became a major Mediterranean force. James reigned from 1213 to 1276 and led the capture of Majorca, Ibiza, and Valencia; his family later continued the expansion, roping in Sicily, Minorca, Athens, Sardinia, and Naples. Catalan power did not last, however. Less than 50 years after its peak, the conquest of Naples in 1423, the marriage of Queen Isabella of Castile and King Ferdinand of Aragon began the unification of Spain, and by the end of the 15th century, Catalonia had lost control of its own affairs and was excluded from the lucrative trade with the newly discovered Americas.

By 1640, the suppression had become so intense that the peasants revolted. But like so many other valiant struggles, the War of the Reapers (1640–52) was in vain; lost was the idea of an independent Catalan republic, along with territories east and north of the Pyrenees, which were ceded to France. All that remained was "Els Segadors" (The Reapers), a marching song that became the Catalan anthem.

The next great upheaval was the War of the Spanish Succession early in the 18th century, with all of Europe embroiled in a battle for the Spanish throne between Archduke Charles of Austria and Philip V of the House of Bourbon. Having allied itself with the archduke, who promised Catalonia her independence, the region again suffered when the victorious Philip stringently repressed the would-be nation. Castilian law ruled; the use of Catalan was forbidden in the courts, and the universities in Barcelona and Lérida were closed. Catalonia was again reduced to a mere province.

It takes more than a defeat or two to keep a Catalan down, however, and by the end of the 19th century, the region was thriving, thanks to the burgeoning Industrial Revolution, centered in Barcelona, which saw the first steam trains chug the 20 miles (32 km) north to Mataró in 1848. Forty years later, the city symbolized the resurgence of a strong and confident Catalonia when it hosted an international *Universal Exhibition*. As the arts flourished anew, so did interest in Catalan as a written language, and poems and novels wound the web of solidarity ever more tightly. At the turn of the century, Barcelona, like Paris, was a hotbed of revolutionary creativity. Pablo Picasso was here, having arrived from his native Málaga at the age of 14; he would spend almost 10 years in the Catalan capital. Architects such as Antoni Gaudí were in the vanguard, adorning new city quarters with buildings of astonishing design — the local version of Art Nouveau, called Modernisme. Later, Joan Miró, Salvador Dalí, Antoni Tàpies, and other artists came to the fore. Barcelona was even the capital of a short-lived Catalan government, set up in 1932.

Unfortunately, the potential of Catalan power posed a threat to centralist forces in Madrid, and during the Spanish Civil War Catalonia made the mistake of backing the "wrong" side. When Franco took power, the Catalan language was once again banned in businesses, churches, the press, and, most wounding of all, in schools. The only place that Catalans could gather in great numbers was at the local soccer club, *F.C. Barcelona*. Boys were (and still are) signed up at birth to become members of the club that epitomizes the Catalan spirit, regularly attracting more than 125,000 aficionados to its games. Famous coaches and superstar players boost fans to a fever pitch, and the *Camp Nou Stadium* rings with wild chants of "Barça, Barça," particularly when the opposition is *Real Madrid*. No wonder the Catalans are proud that they are the hosts of the *1992 Summer Olympic Games* and that their language is one of the "official" languages of the games — a fitting highlight of the quincentennial celebrations marking the famous voyage of Christopher Columbus, who set sail from the Catalan capital in 1492.

Catalonia today spans some 12,370 square miles and is divided into four provinces — Tarragona, Barcelona, Lérida (Lleida in Catalan), and Gerona (Girona in Catalan) — although the significance of these boundaries is purely administrative. What little rivalry exists takes on a good-natured tone, even down to the 38 *comarques* (counties, or districts), each of which produces its own tourist pamphlet extolling local traditions such as the *festa major* (town fair). Every village and town has its own, and there are thousands in all. Around Tarragona, the highlight is the building of *castells dels xiquets* (human towers), with as many as six "stories" of men and boys standing on one another's shoulders. The festival of *Corpus Christi* brings out masked *gegants* (giants) and *capgrossos* (clowns with giant heads) to entertain the crowds, who dance the traditional *sardana* to the sounds of *las coblas* (traditional bands) playing old-fashioned wind instruments. Music plays an important part in Catalan life: not the Moorish wailing of flamenco as in the south, but more "European" folk songs, and there is a strong choral tradition that is unique in Spain. Catalonia's most famous musical son was Pau (Pablo) Casals (1876–1973), who refused to live in Spain while Franco was in power, and made his home in Prades, just over the border in the French foothills of the Pyrenees.

As for customs, warm evenings bring people out into the street for a promenade just as they do elsewhere in the country, but despite the two large bullrings in Barcelona, bullfighting is not popular and the newspapers devote little space to the subject. Catalans have the reputation of being hardworking businesspeople, and are the butt and punchline of numerous jokes and stories that caricature their thriftiness as stinginess. Visitors should not be put off by this image of a fiercely proud and independent people. Since the 1950s, Catalans have used their business acumen to promote tourism, so hospitality is second nature throughout the region. Nor should visitors who speak Spanish be put off by the Catalan language, which is not totally removed from Spanish, although there are words, such as *tancat,* that have no relation to their Castilian counterparts (*cerrado,* or closed, in this case). In fact, at times Catalan is more understandable; the road sign *perill* needs no translation.

Catalan cooking is part of the resurgence of Catalan culture. Traditional recipes are being revived: rabbit with almonds, partridge with grapes, chicken with lobster, and sea bass with thyme and baked squash. Not surprisingly, the cuisine features fish, fresh from the Mediterranean. The catch may be cooked *a la planxa* (grilled) or simmered with peas, tomatoes, and peppers in a *sarsuela;* trout from Pyrenean lakes and rivers is delicious *a l'agredolç,* with vinegar and honey. Confusingly, *truita* means both trout and omelette, so look under the heading *peix* (fish) on the menu, if you want to order seafood. The most famous Catalan specialty, however, is also the simplest: *Pà amb tomàquet* is a slice of bread rubbed with raw tomato and enlivened with olive oil, salt, and pepper. When abroad, homesick Catalans drool at the thought of this snack, washed down with a glass of wine — not rioja, but penedès, a regional wine that nowadays impresses experts around the world. Miguel Torres is perhaps the best-known name, and the family headquarters at Vilafranca del Penedès welcomes visitors for a tour and tasting. For special occasions, Catalans open a bottle of *cava,* their own champagne-style sparkling wine.

The 703-mile (1,125-km) route outlined below begins in Barcelona and heads north for some 41 flat miles (65 km) past the Costa Brava (Wild Coast) shoreline that is the playground of Europe, with some 15 million visitors per year. High-rises and crowded beaches have thoroughly domesticated the wilderness here, ads push British-style pubs, fish-and-chips, and even cups of tea. At Lloret de Mar, the real Costa Brava begins, and the farther north the route goes, the more nature defeats the developers. Pinkish-red rock tumbles down to lime-green water, sandy inlets and bays are shaded by dense umbrella pines and cork oaks, fishing boats can still be found among the yachts. It is an area that has attracted artists to picture-postcard villages, such as Cadaqués, still charming despite being "discovered."

The northern limits of Catalonia today are the Pyrenees, ancient green-gray mountains that provided little to sustain villages in the past, but now offer the golden rewards of skiing. Here, the route crosses the border into the tiny principality of Andorra, with its dramatic mountains, picturesque villages, scenic landscapes, and duty-free shopping. Beyond, the agricultural hinterland beckons, locked between mountain and sea and dotted by walled towns and villages, each more mysterious than the last. Dark with shadows from turrets and towers, arches and cloisters, they conjure up an illusion of medieval life that is broken only by the sputtering cough of a motorbike or the sight of rooftop television antennas.

Roads vary from four-lane highways to small but well-paved country roads. Local truck drivers are surprisingly polite and encourage the passing of their lumbering vehicles. Along the route, a double room can cost $100 or more at a hotel listed as expensive; $55 to $95 at a hotel listed as moderate; and $50 or less at an inexpensive one. Expect to pay $50 or more for a meal for two with wine at restaurants categorized as expensive, $20 to $45 at a moderate restaurant, and $20 or less at an inexpensive one.

■ **Note:** Many place-names in Catalonia have both a Catalan and a Castilian spelling. In this chapter, where two forms exist, the first one given (usually at the first, or most conspicuous, mention of a town) is the Catalan version and the version in parentheses that follows it is Castilian.

En Route from Barcelona – Take the A7 highway north for 60½ miles (97 km) to Girona. After the industrial suburbs of Barcelona, it's a relief to see open countryside; across the fields, small villages sit on hilltops, always with a solid ocher church, sometimes a castle as well. The Tordera River marks the boundary between the province of Barcelona and the province of Girona, and soon the provincial capital looms up on the right. Take the Girona Sur exit and follow signs through the suburbs to the Centre Ciutat (City Center).

GIRONA (GERONA): The ancient part of the city has always been attractive, and recent renovations have enhanced its appeal. The Romans called it Gerunda; the Moors considered it a stronghold, and Christian folklore holds that this was the first spot where St. James and St. Paul rested on their visit to Spain — although they never really visited the Iberian Peninsula. Another legend, this one based on fact, tells of the defense of the city against invading Napoleonic troops in 1809. The governor held out for 7 months before capitulating, earning the city its sobriquet, *Ciudad de los Sitios* (City of a Thousand Sieges).

The best views of Girona are from the ancient stone footbridges across the Onyar River, but the city's main attraction, the cathedral, is located amid the steep, narrow alleys of the Old Town and is reached by an impressive 17th-century flight of 90 steps. Dating from 1316, the cathedral is of Gothic design, with a baroque façade, and it reflects the Catalan love of honest, simple lines. Awesomely vast inside, it has the world's widest Gothic nave (75 feet wide, as well as 200 feet long and 110 feet high), plus splendid 14th-century stained glass windows high in the gray stone walls. The museum contains invaluable illuminated manuscripts, including a *Commentary on the Apocalypse* dated 975, a bible that belonged to King Charles V of France, and the unusual 12th-century *Tapestry of the Creation.* The cathedral and museum are open daily, March through June, from 10 AM to 1 PM and from 3:30 to 7 PM; July through September, from 10 AM to 7 PM; October through November 3, from 10 AM to 1 PM and 3 to 6 PM; and from November 4 through February, from 10 AM to 1 PM; admission charge to the museum (phone: 972-214426).

Another fine example of local architecture is the nearby Sant Pere de Galligants (Plaça Sant Pere), a Romanesque monastery with a 12th-century octagonal tower; the monastery houses Girona's *Archaeological Museum* (open Mondays through Saturdays from 10 AM to 1 PM and from 4:30 to 7 PM; open mornings only on Sundays and holidays; admission charge; phone: 972-202632). Close by, the 12th-century Banys Arabs (Arab Baths) are an unexpected reminder that Girona was a Moorish stronghold for some 300 years; the eight slender columns in the *sala freda,* or cold room, are straight out of the Arabian Nights, although the capitals are Romanesque. The Jewish Quarter (Call Jueu) is a haunting maze of alleys and medieval buildings, and the synagogue in the *Museu d'Isaac el Cec* hosts Sephardic song recitals on Friday evenings in summer. The building is undergoing renovation until 1993, but a small section remains open from 10 AM to 2 PM during the winter; from 10 AM to 7 PM June through September; admission charge; phone: 972-216761). The nearby *Museu d'Art,* in the former bishop's palace, houses an art gallery with an exemplary selection of medieval and 19th- and 20th-century Catalan paintings, and a 15th-century Catalogue of Martyrs. Open Mondays through Saturdays, from 10 AM to 1 PM and 4:30 to 7 PM, mornings only on Sundays and holidays; admission charge; phone: 972-209536).

 CHECKING IN: *Novotel Girona* – Modern, air conditioned, and comfortable, with 81 rooms, a swimming pool and tennis courts, located near the airport, 7½ miles (12 km) from town, just off A17 at exit 8. Riudellots de la Selva (phone: 972-477100; fax: 972-477296; telex: 57238). Moderate.

EATING OUT: *La Roca Petita* – A family-run country eatery near the airport, featuring local Catalan specialties and *canalones* stuffed with foie gras. Closed Tuesdays. Reservations unnecessary. No credit cards accepted. Riudellots de la Selva, Girona (phone: 972-477132). Inexpensive.

En Route from Girona – Follow C255 and the signs for Palamós. Pass Flaça and Corça, where signs advertising ceramics hint of the local industry. Continue another 2½ miles (4 km) to La Bisbal, a town well known for its pottery, where shops and factories line the main street, piled high with platters, umbrella stands, garden ornaments, hand-painted murals, and tiles. From La Bisbal, continue on C255 about 5 miles (8 km), following signs for Begur (Bagur), Palafrugell, and Palamós. Beyond the rise in the road, the Mediterranean appears to the left, dotted by islands — the Islas Medes. Turn left at the sign for Torrent, Pals, and Begur. Pals, a lovely old medieval town, is straight ahead, but follow the signs to Begur.

BEGUR (BAGUR): A small inland town surrounded by beautiful beaches and coves, Begur is at the heart of the Costa Brava — a term, meaning wild or rugged coast, that was coined in the vicinity in a speech by a turn-of-the-century local dignitary. Begur has narrow streets, whitewashed houses, and at the top, an imposing castle dating back to the 11th century and commanding wonderful views of the countryside. South of town, Aiguablava, or Blue Water, is an appropriately named *cala* (cove) and beach; neighboring Fornells rivals it; just north of town are Sa Tuna, Aiguafreda, and Sa Riera. The area is a good base for local excursions and diversions, which include taking a boat to explore the little coves, circumnavigating the Medes islands' nature reserves by glass-bottom boat, or strolling the spectacular Cap Roig botanical gardens. Many of the medieval villages inland, such as Peretallada and Ullastret, are worth a visit. The former, 900 years old, has only 500 inhabitants now, but hides behind impressive sandstone walls (its name means "cut rock"). Ullastret features an 11th-century church and a double wall, much of which has been restored.

CHECKING IN/EATING OUT: *Aiguablava* – Xiquet Sabater, one of the Costa Brava's great characters, has been running this charming seaside place since the late 1940s. All 85 rooms are air conditioned, with private baths, and many have a wonderful view of the sea. Facilities include a swimming pool, tennis courts, nightclub, and 2 bars. The main dining room offers an international menu with Spanish overtones, but there is also a more intimate room serving à la carte Spanish selections. English is spoken. Major credit cards accepted. Located a bit over 2 miles (3 km) southeast of Begur. Playa de Fornells (phone: 972-622058; fax: 972-56000; telex: 622112). Expensive.

Parador Costa Brava – A low, white building, shaded by pine trees, overlooking a beautiful beach; this modern *parador* (the only *parador* on the Costa Brava) has 87 air conditioned rooms, a bar, restaurant, gymnasium, sauna, swimming pool, and convention hall. It's located across the bay from the *Aiguablava* hotel, about 3 miles (5 km) southeast of Begur. Major credit cards accepted. Playa de Aiguablava (phone: 972-622162; fax: 972-622112; telex: 56275). Expensive.

En Route from Begur – Backtrack westward in the direction of Girona and Figueres. Turn off to Pals, go through Regençós, follow signs for Pals and Figueres, then for Pals itself, 4½ miles (7 km) from Begur. Follow signs to the Recinte Gòtic.

PALS: What was once a farming community is now a tourist attraction, thanks in part to restoration that has brought this 14th-century village back to life and earned it two national awards for its efforts. The village church, originally Romanesque but with some Gothic features as a result of later rebuilding, has an 18th-century façade. Climb the Torre de les Hores (Tower of the Hours) — so named because it once had a clock — in the 9th-century castle of Monteáspero, for lovely views of the coast. The Casa Pruna contains some important archaeological finds from the nearby beach, where there is also an 18-hole championship golf course at the *Club de Golf de Pals* (Playa de Pals; phone: 972-633006), and a worthy restaurant (see *Eating Out* below).

EATING OUT: *Sa Punta* – Well known for its simple treatment of fresh seafood, an excellent wine list, and interesting desserts, it enjoys the distinction of a Michelin star. Closed Mondays in winter and from mid-January to mid-February. Reservations advised. Major credit cards accepted. Playa de Pals, Pals (phone: 972-636410). Expensive.

En Route from Pals – Continue north along the main road for 6 miles (9 km) to Toroella de Montgrí, where the square block of the 13th-century castle of Montgrí sits on a bare bump of a hill. Head 9 miles (14 km) for the coastal village of L'Escala, passing through Bellcaire d'Emporda and miles of flat fields where old men still scythe the grass by hand, and on to Empúries. A sign to the Ruines d'Empúries is off to the right.

EMPÚRIES (AMPURIAS): The archaeological site here consists of 8 acres of Greek and Roman ruins undergoing constant excavation (which yielded a notable statue of Aesculapius among other treasures) and reconstruction. The Greeks built the lower town during the 6th century BC, and Julius Caesar later constructed a "new" town for retired soldiers higher on the hill. It's worth the effort to climb up to the former Roman town to inspect the forum and the two houses, with courtyards and rooms paved with black-and-white mosaics (open daily June through September, 10 AM to 2 PM and 3 to 7 PM; October through May, 10 AM to 1 PM and 3 to 5 PM; admission charge; phone 972-770208).

CHECKING IN/EATING OUT: *Nieves-Mar* – An old but comfortable family-run establishment of 80 rooms just south of Empúries. The beachfront location offers ideal views across the Golf de Roses (Bay of Roses); there is also a swimming pool and tennis courts. The restaurant offers a variety of fresh fish, simply prepared, as well as homemade fish soup. Major credit cards accepted. 8 Passeig Marítim, L'Escala (phone: 972-770300). Moderate.

En Route from Empúries – Take the main road north toward Roses (Rosas), skirting the old fishing village of Sant Pere Pescador and then Castelló d'Empúries, a small town with a magnificent 13th- to 15th-century Gothic church. Continue northeast toward Roses, a popular resort town clustered on low hills 6 miles (10 km) around the bay from Castelló, but after the angular, modern development of Ampuriabrava rears up into view and the turnoff for Roses appears, go straight, following signs inland toward Cadaqués and turning left at the Campsa gas station. For the next 10 miles (16 km), the road crosses an open, rock-strewn Wuthering Heights–like moor flecked with rosemary and thyme.

CADAQUÉS: This picture-postcard fishing village, made famous by Salvador Dalí and once the haunt of artists and intellectuals, has remained peacefully quaint, with a harbor, whitewashed houses, narrow lanes, and, in summer, art exhibitions and a music festival. The 18th-century parish church houses a valuable baroque high altar, carved by Pau Costa. A mile away, the cove of Port Lligat boasts Dalí's split-level house — surmounted by what appears to be a giant boiled egg.

CHECKING IN: *Playa Sol* – Standard and modern, offering 50 rooms overlooking the sea. There is also a swimming pool, tennis courts, and a cafeteria. Major credit cards accepted. 3 Carrer Platja Planch, Cadaqués (phone: 972-258100; fax: 972-258054). Moderate.

***Port-Lligat* –** Right next to Dalí's house. Simple but comfortable with 30 rooms, a pool, and restaurant, and a bar. On the beach (phone: 972-258162). Inexpensive.

EATING OUT: *La Galiota* – By far the best in town, boasting a Michelin star. This small place caters to an "artsy" clientele, and serves local seafood dishes and outstanding soufflés. It's very crowded in summer. Closed weekdays from September through May. Reservations advised. Major credit cards accepted. 9 Carrer Narcis Monturiol, Cadaqués (phone: 972-258187). Moderate.

En Route from Cadaqués – Backtrack across the moor and make a right turn onto the local road north toward the village of Vilajuiga. At the entrance to the village, make a sharp right turn at the sign for Monestir de Sant Pere de Rodes. A new road swoops up alongside olives and vines to open, rugged countryside, and after approximately 6 miles (10 km), there's a small parking lot. Park here and walk along the path to the majestic, brooding castle-cum-monastery, built by the Benedictines 1,000 years ago. On an overcast day, the two 90-foot-high towers loom out of the mist, while on a clear day the attractive former fishing village of El Port de la Selva and the entire peninsula are visible some 2,000 feet below — not to mention the town of Cerbère across the French border, the snow-capped Mt. Canigou inland, and the Golf de Roses to the south. The monastery buildings have been restored to reflect the wealth and power of Catalonia in the 10th and 11th centuries. Open daily, from 9 AM to 1:45 PM and from 3 to 6:45 PM. Admission charge.

Return to the main road at Vilajuiga and follow it for 8 miles (13 km) to Figueres, passing the old town of Perelada, which lends its name to the popular, often sparkling, local wines and has a luxury casino, the *Casino Castell de Perelada*, housed in the old castle. It has a good restaurant that is open daily and offers local dishes. Reservations advised (phone: 972-538125).

FIGUERES (FIGUERAS): Serious Spanish guides point out that this was the heart of Catalonia at the time the Moors were expelled, and that Philip V wed Maria Luisa of Savoy here in the Church of Sant Pere in 1701, a marriage that led to the War of the Spanish Succession. But Figueres, in the heart of the Ampurdan plain, is best known as the birthplace of Salvador Dalí (in 1904) and as the home of the *Dalí Museum*. Identified by a beehive logo in the center of town, the museum is housed in a converted movie theater that has been painted pink and decorated with replica boiled eggs and bubble gum. From the piles of old tractor tires in the square outside to the plastic store mannequins inside, the entire display is best described as weird. Dalí worked here until 1982, and lived, bedridden, in one of the building's towers until his death in 1989. He is now buried in the museum's inner court, beneath the building's great glass dome. More than 300,000 visitors annually make the museum Spain's second most popular (Madrid's *Prado* ranks number one), and contribute to the zoo-like atmosphere. It's difficult to take any of it seriously, though a few good paintings can be seen. There is also a complete orchestra (made of plaster of Paris), plenty of interesting murals, dolls hiding in niches, a Cadillac, and an assortment of plastic and metal kitsch of the 20th century. Unfortunately, cameras are not permitted. To avoid the crowds, visit the museum during lunchtime hours. Open daily, October through June, from 11:30 AM to 5:30 PM; July through September, from 9 AM to 8:30 PM; admission charge (phone: 972-505697). The Figueres Tourist Office is at Plaça del Sol (phone: 972-503155).

CHECKING IN/EATING OUT: *Ampurdán* – Adequate and comfortable, it offers 42 rooms in motel-style simplicity on the outskirts of town. The restaurant is the real prize here, rated one of Spain's best (it has a Michelin star). The Mercader family specializes in real Catalan dishes, often pairing meat with fruit. Try the rabbit and prune terrine, or braised venison with quince sauce. Fish is also a good choice, and the local wines are excellent. Reservations essential for the restaurant. Major credit cards accepted. Antigua Carretera de Francia, Km 763, Figueres (phone: 972-500562; fax: 972-509358; telex: 57032). Moderate.

Durán – In the heart of the Old Town, this is a real family-style establishment dating from 1870, with 67 modernized rooms. Like the *Ampurdán,* it is famous for food — whether the delicate fresh salmon in lemon-butter sauce or the hearty stuffed squash, the local ingredients and flavors are outstanding and honest. Try the *sarsuela* (fish stew) or eggplant mousse with fresh tuna. Reservations essential for the restaurant. Major credit cards accepted. 5 Carrer Lasauca, Figueres (phone: 972-501250; fax: 972-502609). Moderate.

Mas Pau – A pretty, old, beamed farmhouse has been converted, and now offers 7 guestrooms. Set in a quiet garden 3 miles (5 km) southwest of Figueres, it also has a swimming pool and an award-winning (including a Michelin star) restaurant to tempt the traveler. Delicious saffron-flavored chicken and lobster, hearty venison, and subtle lambs' brains ravioli are a few of the menu favorites. Restaurant closed Sunday evenings; reservations advised. Major credit cards accepted. Carretera de Olot (phone: 972-546154). Moderate.

En Route from Figueres – Aiming west along C260 toward Olot and Ripoll, the Pyrenees rear to the north as the road curves through pine forests and, in spring, acres of wildflowers — scarlet poppies, golden buttercups, and snowy daisies. The village of Besalú, 15 miles (24 km) from Figueres, is worth a stroll-through. Follow signs to the Centre Vila and park in the large square, El Prat de Sant Pere. Careful renovation has beautified this mostly forgotten village. The church, Curia Reial (Law Courts), Town Hall, and covered marketplace are still in use, in fact, the Curia Reial houses a traditional Catalan restaurant; the Casa dels Cornellà must have been a merchant's house, judging by its courtyard, arches, and cloistered second floor. Cross the irregular arches of the fortified medieval bridge and observe, on the far side of the Fluvià River, the old Jewish quarter, complete with a *mikvah* (ritual bath), one of only a handful still existing in Europe. As a souvenir, purchase a floppy red Catalan cap (*barretina*), made in the town.

Proceed on C150 into a district known as La Gárrotxa, which means "torn earth," a reminder that the newly improved road to Olot, 13 miles (21 km) away, goes through volcanic countryside, though the 40 extinct cones are now overgrown. On the left, a sheer basalt cliff supports the dusty old village of Castellfollit de la Roca (Mad Castle on the Rock), some 200 feet above the abyss.

OLOT: Although this town has succumbed to dreary industrial development and local workshops churn out seemingly endless religious souvenirs, Olot has managed to keep its folkloric traditions alive. Annually, on the second Sunday of July, some 5,000 dancers arrive to weave magical *sardanas,* traditional Catalan folk dances. On September 8, *gegants, nans, i cavallets* (papier-mâché giants, dwarves, and horses) perform dances, and on October 18, the *cena de duro,* "2-cent dinner," instituted in honor of Sant Lluc (St. Luke) in 1314, still includes wine, bread, and rice for a few pesetas. The *Museum of Modern Art,* housed in a 19th-century palace (Carrer Hospici), displays a collection of Catalan art from the Olot School of Art, which was founded in the 19th century and became the workplace of many Catalan who were inspired by the surrounding countryside (open Mondays through Saturdays from 11 AM to 2 PM and from 4 to 7 PM, Sundays and holidays from 9 AM to 2 PM; admission charge; phone: 972-266457). Also admire the elegant modernist façade of the Sola Morales house (38 Carrer Mulleres). The tourist office (Edifici Plaça del Mercat, Carrer Mulleres; phone: 972-260141) is nearby on the same street.

En Route from Olot – Continue west along C150; after about 7½ miles (12 km), the road forks, with a right turn leading to Sant Joan de les Abadesses. The road sign says it's only 8 miles (11 km) to this remote village where a monastery of Benedictine nuns was founded in the 9th century (what is visible today is no earlier than the 11th century, however); Wilfred the Shaggy, the first Count of Barcelona, made his daughter Emma the first abbess. But the drive is a tortuous one, recommended for enthusiasts only, although the peace of the pretty cloisters and convent may be worth the stress and strain. Otherwise, bear left at the fork and head on to Ripoll, 12 miles (19 km) away.

RIPOLL: This town deserves greater recognition of its past role as a torchbearer for civilization. Wilfred the Shaggy, founder of more than one monastery in Catalonia, founded the Benedictine monastery of Santa María here in the 9th century (there had been an earlier establishment that was destroyed by the Moors), and his influence ensured that it would become a center of learning. By the 11th century, under the stewardship of Abbot Oliba, the library was one of the richest in Christendom, housing 246 books, and it was famed throughout Europe as an intellectual meeting place for Christian and Arab philosophers. The town is pretty dreary now, except for the wonderful (but worn) 12th-century carved stone portal that decorates the entrance to the monastery church, considered one of the finest examples of Catalan Romanesque sculpture. In the days when few could read, the seven horizontal bands of biblical and allegorical scenes here constituted a classic comic book: From the monsters fighting at the bottom, past King David and the musicians, the Books of Kings and Exodus, up to the vision of the Apocalypse, the main stories are all shown. A booklet that includes a tracing-paper guide to the 87 pictures is available. During the summer, classical music recitals often take place in the cloisters. The monastery is open in summer, Mondays through Fridays from 10 AM to 2 PM and from 4 to 7 PM; Saturdays, Sundays, and holidays from 10 AM to 7 PM (winter hours are 11 AM to 2:30 PM weekdays, 11 AM to 2 PM and 4 to 6 PM Saturdays and Sundays; admission charge; phone: 972-720013). For further information, contact the tourist office in Ripoll, 3 Plaça de l'Abat Oliba (phone: 972-701109).

En Route from Ripoll – Take N152 due north into the Pyrenees, following the twisting, rocky bed of the Freser River. High cliffs are typical, and tiny, seemingly inaccessible dark-stone villages blend into the hillsides above. Beyond Ribes de Freser, 9 miles (14 km) from Ripoll, the road climbs endlessly (15½ miles25 km) up to Tosas, a village 6,000 feet up, where snow-capped peaks are visible even in summer. A sleepy gas station provides welcome refueling for car, body, and soul, after which, instead of taking the main road to Puigcerdà, make a sharp left turn down to La Molina, a popular ski resort, and follow the new valley road to Puigcerdà. Compared with other towns along the route, Puigcerdà is visually unremarkable, but it does have a dozen ski resorts within 30 miles to keep it busy. Hard by the border with France, it is only 4 miles (6 km) away from Llívia, which is also visually unremarkable, but worthy of note. In 1659, a border dispute in the region was settled when Spain ceded 33 villages high in the Pyrenees to France. Llívia, however, considered itself a *town,* and thus remained a Spanish enclave, totally surrounded by French soil, a few miles from the Spanish border.

Rather than enter Puigcerdà, turn left at the outskirts, taking C1313 southwest in the direction of Bellver de Cerdanya and La Seu d'Urgell. The road leads past the delightful mountain golf course of the *Real Club de Golf de Cerdaña* (phone: 972-880963), goes on through a wide valley dotted with little hill villages, and crosses into the province of Lleida (Lérida). After Bellver, it runs alongside the Segre River, where fishermen stand waist-deep casting for trout, and goes through Martinet, a trout-fishing and hiking center; 20 miles (32 km) beyond Bellver is La Seu d'Urgell.

CHECKING IN/EATING OUT: *Boix* – A comfortable, 34-room hotel by the Segre River, known for its breakfasts — a rarity in Spain — of homemade bread, jam, and local honey and butter. The restaurant is a splendid one (with a Michelin star), serving a French/Catalan menu: crayfish with mushrooms, trout with thyme, chicken in pastry, and duck with truffles, plus an excellent selection of Spanish and French wines. Reservations essential for the restaurant, which is closed Tuesdays off season and for 3 weeks in January. Major credit cards accepted. Carretera Lleida–Puigcerdà, Km 154, Martinet de Cerdanya (phone: 973-515050; fax: 973-515268). Moderate.

Can Borell – Originally meant to be the retirement home of Lola Pijoan and Jaume Guillén, whose friends persuaded the couple to open a restaurant in the old farmhouse in 1977. In a small village up a mountain road between Puigcerdà and Bellver de Cerdanya, with 8 comfortable, rustic rooms available, it has magnificent mountain views. The establishment also serves as a cooking school, where Lola teaches the simple but richly flavored dishes of the Cerdanya. *Conill amb peras i naps* (rabbit with pears and turnips), pigs' trotters with apple sauce, leek tart, and pears poached in the thick black wines of Tarragona are among the specialties. Reservations essential for the restaurant (and for the rooms), which is closed Sunday nights (except in July, August, and September); both hotel and restaurant are closed 1 month during the winter. Call ahead to check opening times. 3 Carrer Regreso, Meranges (phone: 972-880033). Moderate.

Chalet del Golf – The timber clubhouse of the *Real Club de Golf de Cerdaña* has 16 rooms, plus a swimming pool, tennis courts, and a restaurant. Located 3 miles (5 km) southwest of Puigcerdà. Devesa del Golf, Puigcerdà (phone: 972-880962). Moderate.

LA SEU D'URGELL (SEO DE URGEL): This is another ancient town that flourished at the conjunction of two river valleys, in this case the Valira from the north and the Segre from the east. All around are rolling orchards and farmlands — the foothills of the Pyrenees. Boasting a bishop since 527, a cathedral since 839, and two saints (Just and Ermengol), La Seu is both historically rich and more conventionally affluent, but its main claim to fame is the status of its bishop, who, since 1278, has been the joint ruler — or co-prince — of the co-principality of Andorra. The other holder of the title is the President of France. The Catedral de Santa María, rebuilt during the 12th century and again during the 18th century, features the uncluttered openness that appeals to Catalans, and is noted for its façade and its 13th-century cloister. The church museum, *Museu Diocesà d'Urgell,* in a chapel of the cloister, possesses a prized 11th-century illuminated manuscript of the *Apocalypse of St. John the Divine,* written during the 8th century by the priest Beatus of Liébana. Open weekdays from 10 AM to 1 PM and from 4 to 7 PM (October through March, from 9:30 AM to 1:30 PM and from 3:30 PM to 8 PM); Saturdays and Sundays year-round from 10 AM to 1 PM; admission charge (phone: 973-351177). Across from the church is the Carrer Major, with its medieval equivalent of a shopping mall, the great *porxos,* or arcades, that have sheltered vendors from sun and rain for centuries. The market on Tuesdays and Fridays is worth a visit.

CHECKING IN/EATING OUT: *El Castell* – A discreet, delightful, modern crescent of wood and slate, built into the hillside underneath the ruins of a 13th-century fortress about half a mile (1 km) southwest of town, offering lovely views over the town and the valley and across to the Sierra del Cadí. A luxury hotel, member of Relais & Châteaux group, it has 42 rooms and suites with (rare in Spain) king-size beds, as well as a swimming pool. Eat on the terrace or dine magnificently in the *Celler Grill,* which serves regional and national dishes; the wine cellar has a priceless collection of French and Spanish vintages dating back to the 19th century. Reservations essential for the restaurant, which is closed

Mondays; both hotel and restaurant closed from mid-January to mid-February. Major credit cards accepted. Carretera Lleida, Km 129, La Seu d'Urgell (phone: 973-350704; fax: 973-351574; telex: 93610). Expensive.

Parador de Seu d'Urgell – This modern, comfortable *parador* in town offers 84 spacious, air conditioned rooms, a swimming pool, and a restaurant serving French and Catalan specialties. Tapestries are part of the decor, and a 12th-century cloister from a former nearby church has been incorporated into the lobby and reception lounge. Reservations advised for the restaurant. Major credit cards accepted. Carrer Sant Doménec, La Seu d'Urgell (phone: 973-352000; fax: 973-352309). Moderate.

En Route from La Seu d'Urgell – Driving north on C145, it's a quick 6 miles (10 km) to the border of one of the world's smallest countries, the autonomous principality of Andorra.

ANDORRA: A co-principality governed nominally by Spain and France through the Bishop of Urgell and the President of France, Andorra is an independent country of approximately 50,000 inhabitants (only 8,000 natives, the rest mainly Spanish and French immigrants) and a duty-free haven set high in the Pyrenees. Its mere 175 square miles contain a dramatic landscape of scenic lakes, racing rivers, verdant meadows, quaint mountain villages, good ski slopes, and the nation's capital city, Andorra la Vella, the highest in Europe (3,000 feet), where modern, high-rise buildings almost block out the view of the surrounding peaks. According to tradition, the founding of Andorra dates back to the 9th century, when Louis I, the son of Charlemagne, granted a tract of land to the Bishop of Urgell; dual allegiance dates to the 13th century, when later bishops, feeling their rule challenged by French noblemen, agreed to joint control. The country's blue, red, and yellow flag first waved in 1298, at which time Andorrans also accepted an agreement whereby, in even-numbered years, the Spanish bishop would receive the equivalent of $12 as tribute, in addition to six hams, six chickens, and six cheeses. In odd-numbered years, the French prince (originally the Count of Foix) would be presented with a cash tribute of 960 pesetas.

Because the same rules pertain today, Andorra is Europe's last feudal protectorate. French and Spanish authorities oversee the justice and postal systems (all mail is delivered free within Andorra, and peseta or franc denominations of stamps are issued for mail outside the country). But since 1419, the Andorrans also have elected a 24-member Council General and are, therefore, proud to have one of the oldest parliaments in Europe. The semi-independent state suits most Andorrans just fine, and as is evident in the words of the national anthem — "Faithful and free I wish to live, with my Princes as my protectors" — further autonomy is not on the agenda. One reason is that the unique joint political arrangement and the country's related status as a tax-free enclave benefit Andorra economically. Not too long ago, a visit was an adventure back in time. But the past 2 decades have seen the country jump from medieval feudalism to 20th-century prosperity, from a strictly agricultural country to a model of modernization and growth.

One main, winding road cuts diagonally through Andorra, southwest to northeast, and along it traffic creeps in both directions, especially on weekends and during Spanish and French national holidays. At the borders, traffic jams of cars lined up to return to Spain and France can be monumental, caused by conscientious Spanish and French customs agents assessing the value of the duty-free purchases filling every nook and cranny of the departing convoy — cars, luggage, pockets, and purses of sated bargain hunters. One visit to this "supermarket in the sky" is usually enough for most foreign travelers, but the country has positive appeal beyond the shopping. The Pyrenees may not be as dramatic or even as high as the Alps, but they are wider and far more rugged (which explains why Andorra remained a mostly medieval community until this century). Since the country is perched atop the mountains facing south, it has an excellent climate of dry air, brisk in winter and fresh in summer. Most of its villages are deep in the low valley, but in winter, some of Europe's best inexpensive skiing can be found at the resorts of Pas de la Casa, Grau Roig, Soldeu, Tarter, Pals, Arinsal, and Arcalis. In June, the high valleys, as yet untainted by developers, unveil some of the rarest, yet most abundant wildflowers in Europe; carpets of narcissi, orchids, and iris stretching for hundreds of yards are common sights.

Stamp collectors have long appreciated the variety and abundance of Andorra's impressions, though few realize that they are unnecessary for internal mailings. The police force here can be counted on the fingers of a single hand, and as the folksinger Pete Seeger once noted, "The annual defense budget is spent on fireworks!" As a banking center, Andorra's private, numbered accounts are taken a bit more seriously by those with an embarrassment of riches.

As for historic sights, there are some attractive bridges arching across rushing streams, as well as a few tall, square bell towers on Romanesque churches. In Andorra la Vella, the 16th-century Casa de la Vall, which houses the governing Council General, is worth a visit (open Mondays through Fridays, from 10 AM to 1 PM and from 3 to 7 PM; Saturdays, from 10 AM to 1 PM; no admission charge). Outside of the capital, in Encamp, is the *Museu Nacional de l'Automòbil d'Andorra* (64 Avinguda Príncep Episcopal; phone: 9738-32266), displaying a rich collection of antique cars, motorcycles, and bicycles from 1898 through 1950 (open from 10 AM to 1 PM and from 4 PM to 8 PM, with a lunchtime closing; closed Mondays; no admission charge).

Still, shopping is the main attraction, although in many cases the prices are only attractive to the French and the Spanish, thousands of whom cross the border daily to stock up on cigarettes, liquor, electronic equipment, leather goods, and fashions. The best stores are found in Andorra la Vella, whose main streets bustle like the aisles of *Macy's.* To recommend one store over another is futile, since most shops have standard prices and stock only the most marketable merchandise. This may prove less fun for the kind of shopper who loves to compare and haggle over the price, but it is a pleasure for those who know the cost of the item at home and recognize a bargain.

Spanish currency is accepted throughout the tiny principality. While there are no customs or passport formalities for entering Andorra (visitors will have to beg the officials to mark passports with their flowery stamp), remember that lines for re-entering Spain are often very long, especially in late afternoon (a lunchtime escape is probably best). So are the lines at the service stations just within the Andorran border — a mandatory last stop for motorists, since gasoline prices are often one-third less than those of Spain or France. The country's tourist office, Sindicat d'Iniciativa, is located in Andorra la Vella on Carrer Dr. Vilanova (phone: 9738-20214).

Note: to call Andorra from Spain, the area code is 9738; from the US, dial 33 (country code), 628 (area code), and the local number.

CHECKING IN: *Andorra Palace* – The principality's best, offering 140 rooms with excellent mountain views. Modern and comfortable, it has a swimming pool, tennis courts, and a garage (parking in Andorra is a nightmare). Prat de la Creu, Andorra la Vella (phone: 9738-21072). Expensive.

***Mercure Andorra* –** Part of the popular French chain, connected with and under the same management as the *Andorra Palace;* modern, efficient and comfortable, with 70 rooms, an indoor swimming pool, sauna, and garage. 58 Avinguda Meritxell, Andorra la Vella (phone: 9738-20773). Moderate.

EATING OUT: *1900* – The French fare here has made many of Iberia's "top 30" listings, thanks to nouvelle dishes such as scallops with wild mushrooms, *magret de canard* (sliced breast of duck) with raspberry vinegar and beans, woodcock with wild garlic, and chocolate *millefeuilles* (pastry with whipped cream). Located in a spa about half a mile (1 km) east of the capital. Open daily; closed during July. Reservations essential. Major credit cards accepted. 11 Unió, Les Escaldes (phone: 9738-26716). Expensive.

En Route from Andorra – Leaving behind the glamour of the coast, the history of the old cities, and the romance of the mountains, the route now enters territory not often visited by tourists. Backtrack south on C145 to La Seu d'Urgell and continue south on C1313, following the Segre River and snaking through the gray, rugged gorge of Organyà, past Organyà itself (the proud possessor of the oldest document written in Catalan), and past the dammed valley at Oliana, with its reservoir, beehives, and orchards of almonds and apricots. The river, lined with poplars, broadens, streaked with shoals of boulders that have tumbled for miles from the heights of the Pyrenees.

Just beyond Oliana, at Bassella, 32 miles (51 km) south of La Seu d'Urgell, is the intersection with C1410. For those wishing to return to Barcelona, about 90 miles (144 km) from Bassella, this road (via Solsona, Cardona, and Manresa) is a shortcut. Along the way, the *Parador Nacional Duques de Cardona* (in an old castle in Cardona; phone: 93-869-1275), has 65 moderately priced rooms for guests. Otherwise, to continue the itinerary, continue south along C1313 for about 11 miles (18 km) to Ponts, a logging town, and turn left onto the local road to Calaf. After a few minutes, turn right onto the road to Cervera, 21 miles (34 km) from Ponts, driving through rolling wheat fields and past hilltop hamlets, and crossing the main Barcelona-to-Zaragoza railroad tracks.

CERVERA: The town was originally built around a 13th-century castle. Aim for the ancient main street, Carrer Major, which runs along the top of the ridge, with old houses on both sides. Halfway down, a sign points to the Carreró de les Bruixes Segle XIII (Passage of the 13th-Century Witches). The passage, which runs some 400 yards parallel to Carrer Major and underneath the old houses, has been decorated (quite recently) with black cats, moons, witches' brooms, owls, and cobwebs, but is a spooky-enough experience even without these embellishments. Back into the daylight of the Plaça Major, which is a small square with a row of gargoyle-like faces holding up the balconies of the 18th-century Town Hall, wander to the Carrer Major to see the house where the Generalitat de Catalunya was established in 1359, and where, about a century later, King Ferdinand and Queen Isabella's marriage contract was signed. Cervera has literally been bypassed by the 20th century, as the main road between Barcelona and Zaragoza tunnels under the old town, but it was still in the mainstream in the 18th and 19th centuries. When Philip V suppressed all Catalan universities in 1718, he opened a new Castilian/Bourbon university in Cervera. Not surprisingly, it lasted little more than a century, closing down in 1841. The town is also known for its annual *Crist Misteri de Passió* (Passion Play), some 500 years old. A special theater was built for the crowds that flock to Cervera to witness the play, enacted by over 500 local citizens in March and April. The town's tourist office is at 4 Passeig Balmes (phone: 973-531350).

En Route from Cervera – The main road (N11) to Tàrrega, 7½ miles (12 km) away, is fast and straight, but Tàrrega itself can be a bottleneck. In the center of town, take the turn for C240 south toward Montblanch (Montblanc) and Tarragona and follow it through fields and vineyards, with intriguing villages off to either side, some with castles, some with churches. Just beyond Belltall, there is a sharp rise and the land drops away with a lovely panoramic view across the plains of Conça de Barberà. Look for the sign down the hill, off to the right, for Vallbona de les Monges.

VALLBONA DE LES MONGES: Catalonia boasts three great Cistercian abbeys: Vallbona de les Monges (nuns), and Poblet and Santes Creus (monks). Vallbona de les Monges is the least known, yet nuns have lived here without interruption since 1157. Fairly cut off from the rest of the world until a new road was pushed through in 1988, the convent is wedged into the middle of a village (pop. 275) and held up by tons of cement that are being poured into the foundations to keep it from falling down. Nuns in gray tunics and dark blue cardigans answer a bell at the main gate and conduct guided tours that include the church, whose soaring nave and belfry in a transitional Gothic style (12th to 13th century) are worthy of admiration. Only 26 nuns remain, working in the fields, praying, and making souvenirs, which include pottery, dolls for wedding cakes, bookmarks, and bags of herbs. The convent abbess is a simple soul compared to her mighty antecedents, who once had the power to appoint local mayors and raise taxes to fight the king's crusades. Plans for a museum overlooking the cloisters, the wings of which were built successively during the 12th through 15th centuries, are in the works. Open for guided tours daily from 10 AM to 2 PM and 4:30 to 7:30 PM; admission by donation (phone: 973-330266).

En Route from Vallbona de les Monges – Return to the main road (C240) and continue through Solivella to Montblanch (Montblanc), an attractive town with 34 towers along its castellated walls, medieval streets, and handsome squares — worth a stop for a photo. Another 4 miles (6 km) west is the uninspiring town of L'Espluga de Francolí, 3 miles (5 km) above which is the thoroughly inspiring Monastery of Poblet.

POBLET: The celebrated Monasterio de Santa María de Poblet — a combined monastery, castle, and palace — was founded in 1151 by Ramón Berenguer IV, Count of Barcelona, as thanks to God for the recapture of Catalonia from the Moors. Originally, it housed only 12 Cistercian monks, who arrived from France. The number grew to 200 when the monastery was at its peak, when the Kings of Aragon and Catalonia used it as the halfway resting point on their journeys between the capitals of Barcelona and Zaragoza, and more importantly, honored it as as their royal burial place.

The buildings were abandoned when religious orders were suppressed in 1835, but a group of monks reestablished the monastery in 1940. Following 50 years of careful restoration and rebuilding, which finished on schedule in 1990, Poblet is now perhaps the finest monastic complex in Europe. Surrounded by over a mile of walls, guarded by a dozen turrets, it looks more like a castle than an ecclesiastical establishment, but the monks (35 or so) in their white habits and surplices belie the fortified aspect. Visits can include guided tours (conducted in Spanish, Catalan, and French only), which progress through a series of courtyards and gatehouses to the church, the huge, elegant cloister with its beautifully carved capitals, the Royal Pantheon with its alabastar tombs of kings, and the luxurious, pure Gothic palace built by King Martin the Humane in 1392. Although the treasures that were amassed over the centuries were confiscated during the 19th-century suppression, the church's 16th-century alabaster altarpiece remains, almost too rich in contrast with the pure lines of the rest of the structure. In total, some half-dozen kings and queens are buried at the monastery, along with some 40 princes. The complex is open daily, from 10 AM to 12:30 PM and from 3 to 6 PM; admission charge (phone: 977-870030).

En Route from Poblet – Return to Montblanch and take the main Tarragona road (N240) as far as Valls, famous for the strange art of building *castells dels xiquets* (human towers); teams of men and boys from the town compete on June 23, 24, and 25, and on the Sunday following October 21, to see who can build the highest tower. After Valls, follow signs to the left turn for C246 and Vendrell.

Beyond Alío, follow the signs for the third great Cistercian institution, Santes Creus, which appears suddenly over the brow of a hill, about 21 miles (34 km) from Montblanch.

EATING OUT: *Masía Bou* – Huge pottery wine jars mark this eatery, where the waiters and waitresses wear traditional outfits with vests and cummerbunds, which adds to the rustic atmosphere. Specialties include grilled meat dishes and *calçotada,* a local dish consisting of chops, sausages, broiled onions, and gravy that the restaurant has made famous. Weekends are especially busy between October and April. Reservations advised. Major credit cards accepted. Carretera de Lleida, Km 21, Valls (phone: 977-600427). Moderate.

SANTES CREUS: Like the Poblet Monastery, the Monasterio de Santes Creus was founded for the Cistercians by the Berenguer dynasty in the 12th century, in 1157 to be exact. The Kings of Aragon and Catalonia were among its patrons, and the monastery's abbot served as the royal chaplain. Monks no longer live here, so the buildings, situated out in the country with a few houses lining the approach to the main gate, are now used for exhibitions, conferences, and concerts. Inside, the large forecourt is walled in by medieval apartment blocks — onetime servants' quarters. In the middle, a mitred bishop peers down into a coin-filled fountain in front of the church, begun in 1174 and endowed with a beautiful rose window. The cloister was added during the 14th century, followed by the houses for the dependents a century later. There appear to be much earlier influences, however, even Byzantine and Oriental ones, especially on the tomb of King Pere el Gran (1285), which is in the church and resembles an Egyptian bathtub, complete with a drain! The wine-colored porphyry could well have been captured during the Crusades and delivered to the king by his faithful pirate Roger de Llúria, who is buried by his side. In contrast to the chunky pavilion in the cloister garden, the flame-shaped tracery in the cloister itself shows the more elegant English influence brought to this part of Catalonia by the 14th-century architect Reinard Fonoll. Open daily from 10 AM to 1 PM and from 3:30 to 7 PM (to 6 PM from April through September); admission charge (phone: 977-638329).

En Route from Santes Creus – Backtrack south to C246, then west toward Valls to pick up N240, which leads south 12½ miles (20 km) to Tarragona.

TARRAGONA: There are very few "undiscovered" cities in Europe, but Tarragona may well be one of them. A combination of excavation and restoration has revealed just how important the ancient city of Tarraco was to the Roman Empire for over 600 years. Julius Caesar, Augustus, and Hadrian lived here for a time; legend has it that Pontius Pilate was born here. The streets of the Old Town still run where the Roman streets once lay; yet on top of all this, there is a pleasant, large hill city with medieval areas, long avenues, and views out over the ocean. The Passeig Arqueològic (Archaeological Promenade) is literally a walk of about half a mile through the history of Tarragona, around the ancient walls enclosing the highest part of the town. At the base of the walls are the huge Cyclopean boulders laid down by Iberian tribes in the 6th century BC; above these 25-ton megalithic rocks are the Roman walls built by the Scipio brothers in the 3rd century BC, topped by a later Roman dressed stone layer, then a medieval layer, and added during the War of the Spanish Succession, extra English-built ramparts. To interpret all this, a personal multilingual guide is a good investment, as pieces of Roman history crop up in the shadows of medieval houses and modern apartment blocks. The *Museu Arqueològic* (Archaeological Museum), Plaça del Rei, exhibits mosaics, capitals, statues, ancient household utensils, and other local finds. Most famous is the Head of Medusa mosaic, with a stare fit to turn onlookers to stone. Also not to be missed is the jointed ivory doll, which was found alongside its young owner in a 4th-century grave. Open Mondays through Saturdays, from 10 AM to 1:30 PM and from 4:30 to 8 PM (4 to 7 PM in winter); Sundays and holidays, from 10 AM to 2 PM; admission charge (phone: 977-236211 or 977-236206).

Next to the museum is the Pretori Romà (Roman Pretorium), a 2,000-year-old fortress, presumed to have been Pilate's birthplace. Just below, built into the hillside by the beach, is the Roman amphitheater, where excavations have unearthed the remains of what is believed to be a 2nd- or 3rd-century Christian church. Just above the ruins is the Balcon del Mediterráneo (Balcony of the Mediterranean), a cliffside promenade offering excellent views of the sea. A flight of Roman steps leads up to the fortress-like cathedral in the heart of the Old City, built on the site of the former Temple of Jupiter, which subsequently became a mosque under Moorish rule. The construction lasted from the 1150s to 1331; thus, the interior is an intriguing mixture of Romanesque and Gothic, with Plateresque and Churrigueresque additions from the 16th and 18th centuries. The cathedral is noted for its 15th-century Santa Tecla altarpiece at the main altar; the cloister, similar to those at Poblet and Vallbona, has beautifully carved capitals. Open daily, from 10 AM to 1 PM and from 4 to 7 PM.

There are two splendid Roman remains on the outskirts of town. Pont de les Ferreres aqueduct (or Pont del Diable — the "Devil's Bridge"), some 200 feet long and located 2½ miles (4 km) from the center via N240, is a 2-tiered example of Roman engineering from Emperor Trajan's day. The Roda de Barà (Bara's Arch), a 2nd-century triumphal arch, is located 12½ miles (20 km) north of Tarragona via A7. For more information, consult the tourist office in Tarragona (46 Rambla Nova; phone: 977-232143), just off the Rambla Nova.

 CHECKING IN: *Imperial Tarraco* – Tarragona's best, with 170 spacious, modern rooms. Set high atop a cliff, it has spectacular views of the ocean and the ancient Roman amphitheater below. 2 Rambla Vella, Tarragona (phone: 977-233040; fax: 977-216566; telex: 56441). Moderate.

EATING OUT: *Sol Ric* – About half a mile (1 km) from town, it has a country feel, with a terrace under the trees. The fish dishes are outstanding, and the house wines from Priorato are excellent. (They're served in a *porrón,* a Catalan pitcher with a long spout that aims a stream of liquid into the mouth.) Closed Sunday evenings, Mondays, and mid-December to mid-January. Reservations essential. Major credit cards accepted. 227 Via Augusta, Tarragona (phone: 977-232032). Moderate.

En Route from Tarragona – A seaside break from sightseeing is in order, so follow N340, then C246, north along the coast 33 miles (53 km) to Sitges, the prettiest resort on the Costa Dorada (Gold Coast). An alternative route to the same destination would be the faster A7, turning east at Vilafranca del Penedès.

SITGES: A typical Mediterranean seaside resort town, which means that it is both popular and classy, lively and cultured, tacky here and pretty there. The 1½-mile-long sandy beach of La Ribera is backed by a promenade lined with flowers and palm trees, cafés and restaurants, with a church at the north end. The Old Town is made up of little lanes and some magnificent old villas, homes of "Americanos" — Spaniards who made their fortune a century ago in Central and South America and retired here to enjoy the mild climate. Although the town has expanded over the years, there are few apartment blocks and no towering hotels. To the north, beyond La Punta, a 450-berth yacht harbor at Aiguadolç attracts the nautical fraternity. Summer weekends are very crowded, especially in late July and August, but a stay is very pleasant during the week and out of season.

Sitges has three surprisingly good museums. *Museu Cau-Ferrat* (Carrer Fonollar; phone: 93-894-0364) has one of Europe's finest collections of artistic ironwork along with tiled walls and paintings by El Greco, Utrillo, and Santiago Rusiñol, the 19th-century romantic writer-artist (the museum is housed in his former studio). Next door, and functioning as an annex, is the *Museu Maricel de Mar* (phone: 93-894-0364), with sculptures, glass, mosaics, and drawings from the Middle Ages through the baroque period. The *Museu Romàntic* (Carrer Sant Gaudenci; phone: 93-894-2669), also known as *Casa Llopis,* is an 18th-century mansion sumptuously furnished with neo-classical antiques and paintings, as well as a doll collection on the upper floor. Opening hours for all three museums are Mondays through Saturdays, from 10 AM to 1 PM and from 5 to 7 PM (4 to 6 PM from October through May); Sundays and holidays from 10 AM to 2 PM. There are admission charges to all three museums.

Always staging some sort of festival, Sitges has a *Corpus Christi* celebration in early June that features floral carpets made of over 600,000 carnations, which cover the cobbled streets in intricate, sweet-smelling designs. Lawn cuttings from the local golf course form the base; carnation heads mixed with other flowers produce rich patterns from butterflies to soldiers. Since 1950, the *National Carnation Show,* which runs concurrently, has been enlivened with a competition among the streets for the best *catifa de flors* (carpet of flowers), and visitors file along the narrow pavements to admire the highly proficient handiwork. For almost as many years, the first weekend of March has been highlighted by a splendid car rally, featuring vintage automobiles. De Dion-Boutons and Daimlers, Panhards and Bugattis, Fords, Hispanos, and Rolls-Royces put-put from Barcelona to Sitges, carrying ladies and gentlemen dressed in the style of the respective eras.

CHECKING IN: *Calipolis* – Facing the waterfront, this modern establishment bears the brunt of conventions and international visitors year-round. Though somewhat frayed at the edges, the 160 rooms are air conditioned and have private baths; most have terraces overlooking the beach. The *La Brasa* restaurant serves international and regional fare. Major credit cards accepted. Passeig Marítim, Sitges (phone: 93-894-1500; fax: 93-8940764; telex: 53067). Expensive.

***Terramar* –** Isolated at the southern end of town, offering 209 comfortable rooms and plenty of sports facilities, including tennis courts, a golf course, and riding stables. Major credit cards accepted. Passeig Marítim, Sitges (phone: 93-894-0050; fax: 93-8945604; telex: 53186). Moderate.

EATING OUT: *Fregata* – A typically bustling Spanish restaurant, with fabulous views over the water from a clifftop site. Various fish dishes (served in large portions) and a thick fish soup are on the menu. Closed Thursdays. Reservations advised. Major credit cards accepted. 1 Passeig de la Ribera, Sitges (phone: 93-894-1086). Moderate.

***Mare Nostrum* –** Specializing in excellent local fish dishes, superbly prepared, plus a good wine cellar. Closed Wednesdays and from January 15 to February 15. Reservations advised. Major credit cards accepted. 60 Passeig de la Ribera (phone: 93-894-3393). Moderate.

***La Masía* –** Traditional Catalan cooking, with an emphasis on grilled meats, served in an old, rustic *masía,* or farmhouse. Open daily. Reservations advised. Major credit cards accepted. 164 Passeig Vilanova, Sitges (phone: 93-894-1076). Moderate.

En Route from Sitges – For a final side trip before returning to Barcelona, head north through Sant Pere de Ribes into the Penedès wine region. After crossing the main Tarragona–Barcelona freeway, on the very edge of Vilafranca del Penedès, 14 miles (22 km) from Sitges, turn right for the Bodega Torres (22 Carrer Commerç; phone: 93-890-0100). This family wine business (Spain's largest independent one) dates back to 1870, but it is only in the last decade that Torres wines have had an impact on international palates. Miguel Torres studied in

France and returned to revolutionize his father's wine making methods, using stainless steel vats, cold fermentation, and small oak barrels. The combination proved to be a winning one when his 1970 Gran Coronas Black Label won a gold medal in the cabernet class at the *1979 Gault-Millau Wine Olympics* in France, besting a 1970 Château Latour! Guided tours are available by appointment, Mondays through Fridays, from 9 AM to noon and from 3 to 5 PM; ask for Alberto Fornós. The *Museu del Ví* (Plaça Jaume I; phone: 93-890-0582), in the center of town, is dedicated to the history of wine making in the region (open daily, from 10 AM to 2 PM and from 4 to 6 PM; admission charge). Another wine-related excursion is to Sant Sadurní d'Anoia, 7½ miles (12 km) north of Vilafranca, the center of the sparkling wine — *cava* — industry in Spain. Here Cavas Codorníu, on the edge of town, has been making sparkling wine by the champagne method since the 1870s, and the estate buildings, designed by the 19th-century modernist architect Josep Puig i Catafalch (who designed one of the landmark buildings on Barcelona's Passeig de Gràcia), are open for tours (English-language tours are possible) Mondays through Thursdays from 8 AM to 11:30 AM and from 3 to 5:30 PM; Fridays from 8 AM to noon; closed August. No admission charge (phone: 93-891-0125).

CHECKING IN/EATING OUT: *Sumidors* – This rustic, mountain *hostal* just outside of Sant Pere de Ribes has 11 traditionally furnished, stone-walled suites with beamed ceilings, tiled floors, and wooden doors. Facilities include a television salon, swimming pool, sauna, and solarium. The *Carnivor* restaurant, as its name suggests, specializes in grilled meats in large portions. Open daily. Reservations advised. Major credit cards accepted. Sant Pere de Ribes (phone: 93-896-0302). Moderate.

Aragon

Aragon makes up a significant slice of east-central Spain, taking in the central Pyrenees at their rugged best, with deep glacial valleys scoured between the highest peaks. A knot of rivers unravels through rich Aragonese orchards, vineyards, and farms, but especially through high pastures and bleak badlands. The fighting bull has long held the locals in thrall, with taurine strength and power almost magically evoked in petroglyphs daubed by prehistoric cave dwellers.

Thousands of years later, Roman legions came marching through the region on a wide road from Mérida, in the southwest, and built a sizable settlement at Zaragoza. Still later, in far-flung outposts on unassailable ridges, Christian knights clashed with the Moors for almost the entire centuries-long duration of the Reconquest. Yet Moorish customs never were obliterated; instead, they were revitalized and became part of a distinctive regional style. Geometric Mudéjar brickwork persists in tall towers that dominate the skyline like monochrome mosaics. Some are scarred now by Spanish Civil War bullets, but that only adds to the fierce pride of the region.

Since there is no coast in Aragon, many visitors — Spaniards included — dismiss this region as a place to be passed through quickly, a place where they can bear down on the accelerator and make good time in the dark, cruising up to the mountains or over to the seaside in great haste. This lack of recognition may have roots in the region's avaricious past, dating back to its beginnings as a kingdom in 1035. An advantageous alliance that would result in new territory was never spurned. The kingdom of Navarre was an early ally (1076–1134), and a royal wedding in 1137 tied the knot with the powerful Berenguer family, bringing in the potent House of Barcelona and the region of Catalonia. Aragon quietly began to grow with Catalonia, eventually to encompass a swath of land from the southern stretches of Murcia up to Roussillon in France, as well as the Balearic Islands, Naples, and Sicily. Commerce was a driving force, and further alliances were forged through astute matchmaking rather than through military might. Aragonese daughters usually wed well, but the biggest matchmaking coup was the marriage of King Ferdinand II of Aragon, who could claim Castile and León along with his clever bride, the Catholic Queen Isabella. Under their rule, a united Spain extended its reach to the New World. Yet even they reverted to the Aragonese tradition: Daughter Catherine of Aragon was dispatched to England in hopes of gaining a strong ally against France through wedlock. But their son-in-law — who became the notorious King Henry VIII — had a few surprises up his own sleeve.

Aragon enjoys the dubious distinction of having Spain's worst climate. Heating or air conditioning, depending on the season, is absolutely necessary for those heading to the southern part of the region, where summers are unbearably hot and winters can be extremely bitter. Visitors in late spring or early autumn will have few complaints, for the countryside will be at its best. Southeast of Zaragoza there are vineyards and wineries that welcome curious visitors and encourage wine tasting. With few outsiders interfering in village life, many of the local fiestas are still completely traditional. The odd, jig-like *jota* is about as different as could be from the sinuous arching of flamenco, but it is every bit as Spanish; the embroidered aprons and the pretty ankle-laced slippers are instantly recognizable as the peasant dress of Aragon. In September, especially in the southernmost stretches, bull fever hits. *Encierros,* or the running of bulls through the streets into an enclosure, are certainly not unique to Pamplona. Small local variations, minus the Hemingway hype and the hordes of drunken foreigners, occur near harvest time during celebrations of patron saints in the villages close to Teruel.

The route outlined below begins in Pamplona and enters the old kingdom of Aragon at the base of the Pyrenees, then goes south through a dreamscape of strange mounds and past a strategic castle on its way to Huesca. As it continues south, fields give way to wide flats near Zaragoza, the only sizable city in this sparsely populated region. Still farther to the southwest, past Calatayud, stark badlands hold such surprises as the Piedra Monastery, which is blessed with cascades and iris grottoes and looks like some colorful mirage in these raw, red hills. Once past a valley of orchards and vineyards, brick towers in geometric Mudéjar patterns rise above the arid scrub near Daroca and Teruel, at Aragon's southern extreme. From here, the traveler can opt to head for Valencia, on the coast, or turn inland, toward Cuenca and Madrid. Either way, a detour to the medieval town of Albarracín, guarding the heights to the west, is recommended.

Accommodations in Aragon range from expensive, in Zaragoza, where the priciest doubles go for over $80 a night, to many moderate hotels that charge between $40 and $75, down to the unprepossessing inexpensive inns where a room for two costs $35 or less. Weekend rates are almost always higher, even during low season. Dinner for two with wine will cost $80 or more in restaurants listed as expensive, $40 to $75 in moderate restaurants, and under $40 in inexpensive ones.

PAMPLONA: For a detailed report on the city and its sights, hotels, and restaurants, see *Pamplona,* THE CITIES.

En Route from Pamplona – Take the N240 highway southeast. If there's plenty of daylight and more than a couple of hours to spare for the initial leg of the trip, turn right onto C127 after about 25 miles (40 km) and detour through Sangüesa to the historic town of Sos del Rey Católico, the birthplace of King Ferdinand in 1452. This solemn medieval town is the largest of the Cinco Villas de Aragón (Five Towns of Aragon), which were singled out for honor because of their loyalty to King Philip V during the 18th-century War of the Spanish Succession. King Ferdinand spent his childhood in the Palacio de Sada here, and the building, which contains his nursery, is open to visitors, although ongoing restoration work may temporarily put some rooms off-limits (open from 9 AM to 1 PM and from 4 to 6 PM; no admission charge). San Esteban, a 14th-century Romanesque church with fine 13th-century frescoes, carved capitals and columns, and a wooden Virgin, the Virgen del Perdón, is also worth a visit. But it is the overall atmosphere of the town that is most interesting; it's small and beautiful, and a stroll through its narrow cobbled streets leads past intricate grillwork and carved coats of arms on the mansions of aristocratic families.

From Sos del Rey Católico, loop back to N240, and turn right onto the highway. (Those coming directly from Pamplona will already be on N240 and will have just passed a huge reservoir.) At Puente la Reina de Jaca, a signpost indicates the turnoff to Jaca, another 12½ miles (20 km) east along C134.

 CHECKING IN/EATING OUT: *Parador Fernando de Aragón* – Perched on a hill near some remains of the town's ramparts, this *parador* somehow blends in well with the older parts of town, despite a 400-year architectural gap. Built of local wood and stone, it has 65 rooms, all air conditioned. The outdoor terrace off the dining room is a pleasant spot for a long lunch. If they're in season, order the plump white asparagus served with two sauces, the quintessential appetizer of north Aragon (at other times they will be canned). Other typical regional fare, such as *conejo con caracoles* (rabbit with snails) or *pochas con oreja de cerdo* (white beans garnished with pig's ear), may not appeal to squeamish types, but the blend of unusual flavors is quite delicious. Simpler dishes also are available. Closed December and January. Room reservations should be made well in advance. Major credit cards accepted. Sáinz de Vicuña, Sos del Rey Católico (phone: 948-888011). Expensive to moderate.

JACA: This ancient garrison town, on a hill above the left bank of the Aragon River, still has many young soldiers mixed in with visiting mountaineers and tourists. Medieval pilgrims en route to Santiago de Compostela recuperated from their arduous trek over the Pyrenees here, but today this is a principal base for exploring the Aragonese Pyrenees, so most visitors head *toward* the mountains. During the summer, the University of Zaragoza holds courses for foreign students; during the winter, the town bustles with skiers. The tourist office (2 Regimiento de Galicia; phone: 974-360098) has detailed maps for exploring the distant peaks and high valleys, such as Hecho and Anso. In town, Jaca's primary sight is its Romanesque cathedral, completed in 1076. The first important Romanesque building in Spain, the cathedral influenced every artist, architect, and craftsman who entered the country to work on churches during the 11th century. Though partially restored in Gothic and later decorated in Plateresque styles, much of the original Romanesque remains, including the square bell tower, the exterior walls, the main and south portals, and the pillars of the nave. The cathedral and its museum (*Museo Diocesano*) are open daily, from 11 AM to 2 PM and from 4 to 6 PM. Admission charge — 25 pesetas (Plaza San Pedro; phone: 974-360348). Buy some local cream cakes in the heavenly scented *Pastelería Echeta* (Plaza Catedrales; phone: 974-360343), or try the local candies made from pine nuts, known as *besitos* — or "little kisses." The *Palacio del Hielo* ice-skating rink (Avenida Perimetral; phone: 974-361032), Spain's largest, stays open year-round and is the hub of the young social scene. If visiting here in the summer, join in the *Festival Folklorico de los Pirineos* (Folklore Festival of the Pyrenees), held in odd-numbered years in late July or early August; it's a week-long celebration starring traditional dance groups and bands from around the world.

CHECKING IN: *Conde Aznar* – This small, cozy, family-run establishment has 23 rooms, pleasant gardens, an eccentric staff, and an especially good restaurant, *La Cocina Aragonesa* (see below). 3 Paseo General Franco, Jaca (phone: 974-361050; fax: 974-360797). Moderate.

Gran – The prestige hotel in town, with 166 rooms, and a swimming pool open in summer, a bright garden, and tennis courts. Advance booking is recommended during the winter. 1 Paseo General Franco, Jaca (phone: 974-367161; fax: 974-364061; telex: 57954). Moderate.

EATING OUT: *La Cocina Aragonesa* – Regional cooking is done with panache here — the distinguished restaurant of the *Conde de Aznar*. During the fall, order exquisite game dishes such as *rollitos de jabali* (wild boar in puff pastry). Closed Tuesdays, except during high season. Reservations advised. American Express and Visa accepted. 5 Calle Cervantes, Jaca (phone: 974-361050). Moderate.

La Fragua – This converted blacksmith's shop now fires up the flames beneath appetizing pork chops, lamb, and beef. Open daily during high season (closed mid-April to mid-June). Reservations unnecessary. No credit cards accepted. 4 Calle Gil Berges, Jaca (phone: 974-360618). Moderate to inexpensive.

Gaston – A charmingly intimate family place, with a small upstairs terrace. The hearty fare includes stuffed peppers and pigs' trotters. Closed Wednesdays, except in high season, and September 20–30. Reservations unnecessary. Major credit cards accepted. 14 Avenida Primo de Rivera, Jaca (phone: 974-362909). Inexpensive.

En Route from Jaca – Proceed south on C125, following the twisting road past the green Lake Peña. The ruddy formations that loom like sculptures are called Los Malós (The Evil Ones). Take the N240 turnoff to Ayerbe, then follow the rough local road to the village of Loarre and its Castillo de Loarre (Carretera Forestal, Km 5.5; phone: 974-380049). Regarded as one of Spain's most important Romanesque fortresses, this 11th-century castle, built by Sancho Ramírez as a stronghold against the Moors, commands a sweeping view over a broad plain. Perched on its rocky precipice, it is most striking, even in a country famed for its castles. Pay particular attention to its three magnificently restored towers and its Romanesque chapel (open Tuesdays through Sundays, from 9 AM to 1 PM and from 4 to 7 PM; admission charge). Backtrack to N240 and drive east toward Huesca.

EATING OUT: *Venta del Sotón* – One of Aragon's best restaurants, this is 9 miles (14 km) west of Huesca. A huge fireplace sets the atmosphere, and guests are urged to warm themselves further with a vast choice of *aguardientes,* powerful liqueurs. Grilled *chorizo* (sausage) is a good starter, and the menu offers a fine selection of Spanish nouvelle cuisine, which is somewhat experimental but not too gimmicky. There is also a good wine cellar. Closed Tuesdays. Reservations advised. Major credit cards accepted. Carretera N240, Km 227, Esquedas (phone: 974-270241). Expensive to moderate.

HUESCA: A venerable town, marking the start of the rich Ebro plain, Huesca was, in the first century BC, an independent state founded by the Roman Quintus Sertorius, who even founded a school of Latin and Greek here, Spain's first university. The town was swept up in ensuing invasions by the Romans and the Moors, until Peter I of Aragon liberated it from the Moors in 1096 and made it the residence of the Aragonese kings until 1118. During the Spanish Civil War, it was a Franco stronghold and as such, suffered considerable damage. Subsequent restoration and recent prosperity have made the town sprawl, but there is a medieval core to explore. The Gothic cathedral, built from the 13th to the 16th centuries, has a lovely, famous 16th-century alabaster altarpiece by Damián Forment, a sculptor who worked extensively in Aragon in both the Renaissance and Gothic styles.

More than anything, however, Huesca's renown has to do with the bloody Legenda de la Campana (Legend of the Bell), a 12th-century atrocity that is depicted across the street from the cathedral in a painting at the Town Hall. On the pretext of wanting advice from rebellious nobles about how to cast a bell big enough to be heard through the entire kingdom, King Ramiro II lured his rivals into his council room and beheaded them as they filed in one by one. The actual chamber can be visited in the *Museo Arqueológico Provincial* (Plaza de la Universidad; phone: 974-220586), which is set up in a building incorporating part of the 12th-century palace of the Aragonese kings and which also housed a portion of the university during the 17th century. Displays include Gothic frescoes, 13th- through 16th-century Aragonese paintings, architectural exhibits, sculptures, and archaeological finds (open Tuesdays through Saturdays, from 10 AM to 2 PM and from 4 to 6 PM; Sundays, from 10 AM to 2 PM; admission charge — 50 pesetas). Also visit San Pedro el Viejo, the 12th-century Romanesque church (Calle Cuarto Reyes; no phone); King Ramiro spent the last years of his life as a monk here and is now buried in the church's San Bartolomé chapel (open Mondays through Saturdays, from 9 AM to 1:30 PM and from 4 to 6 PM; Sundays, from 10 AM to 1:30 PM; admission charge — 50 pesetas).

CHECKING IN: *Montearagón* – The place to stay for those who are loath to leave the mountains. It's unpretentious, with views back to the Pyrenees, and it's worth the 2-mile (3-km) drive to the outskirts of Huesca to enjoy it. There is a swimming pool and 27 rooms. Carretera Tarragona-San Sebastián (N240), Km 206, Huesca (phone: 974-222350). Moderate.

***Sancho Abarca* –** Near the center of town, close to the principal sites, in a very pretty setting. Management is friendly and the 32 rooms are comfortable. 15 Plaza De Lizana, Huesca (phone: 974-220650). Moderate.

EATING OUT: *Navas* – A comfortable, clubby kind of place, offering shellfish and beef specialties. After coffee and liqueur, they pass out Havana cigars. Reservations advised. Major credit cards accepted. 15 Calle San Lorenzo, Huesca (phone: 974-224738). Moderate.

En Route from Huesca – It's a quick, flat, 45-mile (72-km) run south along N123/N330 to Zaragoza, Aragon's regional capital, with over 750,000 inhabitants.

ZARAGOZA: Seen from the road, the slender towers and imposing domes of Zaragoza's two cathedrals are the only grace notes in a huddle of ugly warehouses, factories, and high-rise apartments. The Ebro River shines through the dusty heart of the city like a great ribbon, and there are some elegant fountains and tree-lined avenues. Don Quixote supposedly balked at entering this city because it had unwittingly welcomed an impostor in his stead, but most other travelers — raiders and traders — have rolled right on through. The tongue twister name (try lisping it the way Spaniards do!) has ancient roots, in a Roman colony founded on the Iberian site of Salduba in 25 BC, called Caesaraugusta. When the Moors conquered the city in 716, they dubbed it Sarakusta. Despite 400 years of Moorish rule, only the Palacio Aljafaría (Plaza del Portillo; phone: 976-435618), constructed in 1030, remains as a testament to their presence. This was built as a pleasure palace for Moorish kings, but its original Arabian Nights architecture has been tampered with, first by the Aragonese kings and then by Ferdinand and Isabella, who claimed it as their throne room, and afterward by the zealots of the Inquisition, who used it as a headquarters. Though it also endured an ignoble stint in the 19th century as an army barracks and most of its interior fixtures have been removed, it has noteworthy *artesonado* ceilings and other Moorish and Gothic ornamentation, as well as a splendid tiny mosque (open Tuesdays through Saturdays, from 11 AM to 1:30 PM and from 4:30 to 6:30 PM; Sundays, from 10 AM to 2 PM; admission charge).

By the time the Reconquest proclaimed the city as the capital of Aragon, Zaragoza was already a rich agricultural center. The local nobility, wary of any sovereign, managed to secure guarantees of autonomy known as *fueros,* and under these conditions, commerce in this crossroads city boomed. The impressive 16th-century La Lonja, or commercial exchange building, has a lovely Gothic vaulted ceiling, with cherubs dancing around the tops of the supporting columns; the building today houses temporary exhibits of local artists (Plaza Catedrales; no phone; open only during exhibitions, from 9 AM to 2 PM).

On either side of La Lonja are Zaragoza's two cathedrals. The Basílica de Nuestra Señora del Pilar, a striking 16th- to 18th-century structure that incorporates elements of previous churches on the same site, has nearly a dozen *azulejo*-covered domes and four towers surrounding a larger, central dome. On the interior of the domes are frescoes, some by Goya. Also inside is a famous 16th-century alabaster altarpiece by Damián Forment and the Capilla de Nuestra Señor del Pilar. The latter is a small church-within-the-church housing a Gothic statue of the Virgin and the sacred jasper pillar that, according to legend, once stood in a Roman temple here, and atop which the Virgin Mary is said to have miraculously appeared before St. James the Apostle in AD 40. The Virgen del Pilar attracts devout pilgrims and is claimed by the Civil Guard as their patroness. During the Spanish Civil War, she was officially appointed Captain General of Zaragoza, and two Republican bombs that clattered off the roof of the cathedral without exploding now hang in the chapel as a reminder of her divine intervention. The cathedral's *Museo del Pilar* (19 Plaza de Nuestra Señora; phone: 976-223334) contains some Goya sketches for the ceiling frescoes, as well as the *joyero de la Virgen* — the jewelry and vestments that constitute her wardrobe. Open daily, from 10 AM to noon and from 3 to 4 PM. Admission charge — 50 pesetas. Zaragoza'a older cathedral, the 14th-century Gothic Catedral de la Seo (Plaza de la Seo; phone: 976-291231 or 976-291238) reopened last year after major renovations.

Zaragozans are a pragmatic lot. They have enraged purists by installing the first roof and lighting system on a bullring, a concession to unpredictable weather. Yet tradition runs strong in the city, and every October 13, the *Fiesta de la Virgen del Pilar,* fervent followers parade the bejeweled statue through the city streets by the light of 350 carriage-borne lamps. American servicemen from the huge air base outside the city are frequent visitors, and consequently a smattering of English is common in many of the local bars.

CHECKING IN: *Gran* – This stately old hotel, with 138 air conditioned rooms, is considered to be Zaragoza's best. 5 Calle Joaquín Costa, Zaragoza (phone: 976-226741; fax: 976-236713; telex: 58010). Very expensive.

Don Yo – Complete luxury without a stuffy staff, and with 180 beautifully appointed rooms — there is usually space on short notice. The *Doña Taberna* restaurant next door is associated with the hotel, but is not exceptional. 4-6 Calle Bruil, Zaragoza (phone: 976-226741; fax: 976-219956; telex: 58768). Expensive.

Conde Blanco – Reasonable rates in an efficient 83-room hostelry, in one of the prettier sections of the city. No dining room, but a cafeteria provides quick snacks. 84 Calle Predicadores, Zaragoza (phone: 976-441411). Moderate.

EATING OUT: *Los Borrachos* – The name translates as "The Drunkards," but it merely celebrates a favorite Velázquez canvas. Despite its ostentatious decor, this is a Zaragoza institution. Fresh game is the specialty, with boar, venison, and game birds on the menu in season. The asparagus soufflé is outstanding; only the homemade ice creams and sherbets surpass it. Service is attentive and the wine cellar is well stocked. Try the deep red cariñena from the local vineyards. Closed Sundays and August. Reservations advised. Major credit cards accepted. 64 Plaza de Sagasta, Zaragoza (phone: 976-275036). Expensive to moderate.

Costa Vasca – Zaragoza's only Michelin star is the glory of this restaurant, where the host is also the chef. Enjoy a customary *tapa* and champagne appetizer before sampling one of the various Basque fish specialties that are served in the very proper dining room. Closed Sundays and *Christmas*. Reservations advised. Major credit cards accepted. 13 Calle Teniente Coronel Valenzuela, Zaragoza (phone: 976-217339). Expensive to moderate.

La Matilde – Run by a single family — a couple, their three sons, plus the sons' wives — this place is informal and trendy. The cooking is adventurous: deep-fried camembert with homemade tomato chutney, exquisite monkfish steamed with clams, and for the brave, a celebrated *mollejas con trufas,* a delicacy made from young bird gizzards and black truffles. The wine cellar is extensive. Closed Sundays and holidays, *Holy Week,* August, and *Christmas*. Reservations advised. Major credit cards accepted. 10 Calle Casta Alvarez, Zaragoza (phone: 976-433443). Expensive to moderate.

En Route from Zaragoza – Leave Zaragoza heading southwest on the N-II highway, a woeful two-lane link to Madrid shared with enormous trucks and impatient long-distance drivers who break their boredom by passing on blind curves. Often a lane will suddenly narrow around construction and other road "improvements." The distant mountains edge in and soon after, the scenery becomes stark. After 54½ miles (87 km), the highway enters the heart of Calatayud, the second largest city in the province of Zaragoza. At first, the city seems to be a dismal cluster of traffic jams and neon signs. Its name is usually said to be an Arabic rendering of "Castle of Job" (Kalat Ayub), but some insist it derives from Kalat-al-Yeud, a Jew who is said to have founded the city. Either way, local pride centers on the town's tawny brick Mudéjar towers. The striking octagonal belfry on the collegiate Church of Santa María la Mayor (Calle de Obispo Arrué), which also has a notable Plateresque façade, is the best example — it once was the minaret of a mosque and it soars above the rooftops of the houses. There is another notable tower on the 12th-century Church of San Andrés (Calle Dato).

Don't linger in Calatayud if it can be helped, but proceed 9 miles (14 km) west along N-II and, just past Ateca, turn off at the sign for Nuévalos and the Monasterio de Piedra. The road goes through folds of scrubby plateau until it twists along the mountainside above the Tranquera reservoir, startlingly blue-green in the arid landscape.

NUÉVALOS: The town itself is extremely small, with just one main street and few facilities. Its main attraction is the *Monasterio de Piedra* south of town, and the public park that surrounds it. The overriding sounds on the approach are the trickles of cascades and a 174-foot waterfall thundering into the green stillness of old woods. This handsome monastery was founded by Cistercian monks from the all-powerful Poblet Abbey in Tarragona in 1194, as a retreat from the court intrigues that royal visitors inflicted on Poblet. By the early 13th century, its construction was well under way, and substantial additions in a range of architectural styles were made over the years. Abandoned in 1835, the monastery itself is now a hotel (see *Checking In*), but the grounds — a true water garden — are open to the public. They are extremely crowded in the summer, when the mists from the cascades are the only antidote to the blazing heat of southern Aragon. Paths weave through mossy rocks and lush gardens, descending slick steps into a damp grotto behind a falling curtain of water. One path leads up to an ancient hermitage perched high on the hillside. Tunnels and stairways date from the 19th century, when Juan Federico Muntadas tamed the overgrown thickets of the deserted monastery to create a remarkable waterscape with an offshoot of the Piedra River. At the end of the park is a trout hatchery, near a natural reflecting pool poised between two steep cliffs. The park and monastery are open weekdays from dawn till dusk and weekends from 9 AM to 6 PM. No admission charge.

CHECKING IN/EATING OUT: *Monasterio de Piedra* – In its present incarnation, complete with a swimming pool and tennis courts, this former monastery would sorely tempt medieval monks to break their vows and indulge themselves in the comforts of one of the 61 modern, air conditioned rooms that have replaced their former cells. Rooms overlooking the inner courtyard are smaller, but more private; others, on the other side, have balconies looking down on the main public pathway, although privacy prevails in the early morning and after dusk. The restaurant is formal and serves tastier meals than the place next door, which dishes up chow for hungry hikers. Make reservations well in advance. Major credit cards accepted. Monasterio de Piedra, Nuévalos (phone: 976-849011; fax: 976-849054). Moderate.

***Las Truchas* –** Don't despair if the great monastery is booked solid, because this friendly *hostal,* with a busy restaurant and outdoor terrace, has 30 comfortable (though unstylish) rooms. There's also a playground, a miniature golf course, a swimming pool, tennis courts, and a convention room. The owners cater to busloads of tourists, so the restaurant's menu is in three languages and features non-regional dishes such as a particularly oily and bland paella. The service, however, is quite friendly and efficient. No credit cards accepted. Carretera de Cillas-Alhama (C202), Km 37, Nuévalos (phone: 976-849040; fax: 976-849137). Inexpensive.

En Route from Nuévalos – Because the direct road to Daroca is so narrow that drivers are likely to get stuck behind frustratingly slow tractors with no place to pass, take the valley road (C202) 16 miles (26 km) *back* to Calatayud. With the rugged hills sheltering vineyards and orchards of peaches, cherries, pears, almonds, and walnuts, the drive can be a sheer joy during spring blossoming. At Calatayud, turn right onto N234 for the final 22 miles (35 km) to Daroca. Pines stipple the hills here, and the town is hidden in a hollow, surrounded by 2 miles of crumbling walls that once boasted 114 fortified towers, many of which still stand. On the banks of the Jiloca River, Daroca was once a Roman military settlement, then saw heavy fighting under the Moors — mainly for control of the province by rival Moorish factions. King Alfonso I of Aragon liberated the town in 1122. Today, Daroca has few visitors, and not much sightseeing to offer aside from the impressive city gates and a few Mudéjar churches, which are currently undergoing restoration. Not much is left of the craft tradition that distinguished the medieval town; what remains is on display in the *Museo del Santísimo Misterio* (Plaza de España; phone: 976-800761), which has distinguished woodcarvings, as well as an interesting alabaster altarpiece showing Flemish influence (open 10 AM to noon and 4 to 6 PM; admission charge). Most of the pottery on sale in town comes from Teruel and Zaragoza, but the best comes from Muel. The 16th-century, barrel-vaulted tunnel, dug half a mile through the mountains to divert floodwaters from the town, is a remarkable example of canny Aragonese engineering, but it's not much of a sight; the 20 spouts on the fountain just outside the town gates are much more impressive.

Drive south along N234 to Teruel, 62 miles (100 km) away, past cultivated fields that stretch to either side, with stark mountains on the distant horizon.

EATING OUT: *El Ruejo* – In the heart of town, this pension is a favorite of young couples and young bullfight fans. Don't be put off by the dingy bar; the place is clean, comfortable, and heated and air conditioned. A spacious dining room up the tiled stairway is very pleasant. The waiter will dissuade diners from any odd, non-regional offerings; listen to him and stick to the most popular foods, which will be the freshest. Pork or lamb is the best bet, accompanied by a glass of the heavy and potent *vino de la tierra*. Reservations unnecessary. No credit cards accepted. 112 Calle Mayor, Daroca (phone: 976-800335). Inexpensive.

TERUEL: The barren, flat-topped hills that surround this old-fashioned town, capital of the province of Teruel, are echoed in the ocher brick of its five Mudéjar towers. In fact, Teruel is considered to have the best examples of Mudéjar architecture in Spain. The city was recaptured from the Moors in 1171, but the Muslim population that remained was soon granted special privileges, allowing it to live in harmony with the Christian amd Jewish inhabitants. The last mosque was still operating in 1502, which shows that the Inquisition got a late start in this arid backwater, giving the Moorish artisans who built and decorated the towers the opportunity to develop their style in peace. The most distinguished are the Torre de San Martín, at the San Martín church (Plaza de Pérez Prado), and the Torre del Salvador, at the church of the same name (on Calle Salvador); both date from the 13th century and both are adorned with porcelain plaques and tiles worked in decorative patterns into already fancy brickwork. A third tower is that of the cathedral, originally 13th century, but rebuilt in the 16th and 17th centuries and in this one, following Civil War damage (inside, there's a notable Mudéjar ceiling). A particularly grim winter during the Civil War in 1937 saw Teruel devastated as the Republicans gained control, only to lose it a fortnight later to the Nationalists. Los Arcos, the 16th-century aqueduct north of town, managed to remain intact despite the heavy shelling and machine gun fire.

Teruel's main square is the Plaza de Torico, which is marked by an unusual fountain. In its center is a statue of a baby bull with a star between his horns, which has become the town's official symbol. Throughout Spain, however, Teruel is best known as the scene of the tragic love affair between Diego de Marcilla and Isabella de Segura, the star-crossed, 13th-century "Lovers of Teruel" — a story reminiscent of *Romeo and Juliet.* Diego, dismissed as an unsuitable suitor by Isabella's father, left town heartsick. Determined to make his fortune in 5 years' time and return to Teruel and marry his love, he came back 1 day late, to a wedding feast: Isabella had been forced to marry a rich local rival. In despair, Diego expired at her feet, and she died of a broken heart at his funeral. A double grave, unearthed in the 16th century, was presumed to be theirs, and they now lie buried in the funerary chapel by another of the city's Mudéjar towers (San Pedro; open daily, from 10 AM to 1 PM and from 5 to 7 PM). Sculpted figures of the two, atop alabaster sarcophogi, reach out to hold hands, and a macabre transparent crypt displays their embracing skeletons. Over the centuries, many Spanish poets, dramatists, and artists have been inspired by the story, which has also made Teruel a favorite destination for honeymoon couples.

CHECKING IN: *Parador de Teruel* – Outside the city limits, a bit over 1¼ miles (2 km) north of town on N234 and in a disappointingly modern building (in regional style, however), it has 60 spacious rooms, surrounded by attractive gardens. Major credit cards accepted. Carretera Teruel–Zaragoza, Teruel (phone: 974-602553; fax: 974-608612). Expensive.

***Reina Cristina* –** The only comfortable establishment in town, it's near the Salvador church and tower and has 62 rooms equipped with the most modern conveniences. The dining room serves regional specialties, along with the standard "international" fare, but demonstrates no particular flair. 1 Paseo del Ovalo, Teruel (phone: 974-606860; telex: 62614). Expensive.

EATING OUT: *El Milagro* – Good home cooking that makes the most of local products is the attraction here. Roasts and mountain-cured ham, or *jamón serrano,* go well with the hearty cariñena wine. Open daily. Reservations unnecessary. Major credit cards accepted. Located just past the *Parador de Teruel,* it also has some modest rooms with showers available. Carretera Teruel–Zaragoza (N234), Km 2, Teruel (phone: 974-603095). Moderate.

En Route from Teruel – To the southeast, N234 leads to Valencia; to the southwest, N420 leads to Cuenca and ultimately back to Madrid. But Albarracín, a village practically plastered against a steep slope 24 miles (38 km) west of Teruel, is worth a detour even for those planning to backtrack to Valencia rather than continue over the mountains to Cuenca. Leave Teruel heading north on N234, following the signs to the airport, and after about 6 miles (10 km), turn off where signposted to Albarracín. The road climbs steadily until it reaches the Guadalaviar River, which threads past a handful of modern apartments on the outskirts of the town.

ALBARRACÍN: This small medieval village rises in a breathtaking vertical sweep to the snaggletoothed battlements that guard its rear, circled by the Guadalaviar River like a natural moat. The town has been independent on two occasions, once in the 11th century as an autonomous Muslim *taifa,* and once in the mid-12th-century as a Christian holdout from the expanding Aragonese kingdom. Its fortifications date from the late 10th century and the 11th century, and exemplify the caliphs' military style. The village has retained its medieval character to such an extent that it has been declared a national monument. Tall, half-timbered houses are daubed in rosy plaster, with balconies made of wrought iron or carved wood. Escutcheons mark the nobler houses, and around each corner is a view on a new level. The museum in the chapterhouse of the 13th-century Catedral de El Salvador contains a collection of rather worn 16th-century Flemish tapestries, but the life-size trout carved from rock crystal is more treasured by the villagers. Despite its isolation, Albarracín has been discovered by intrepid summer crowds.

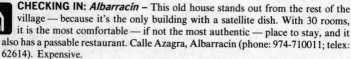

CHECKING IN: *Albarracín* – This old house stands out from the rest of the village — because it's the only building with a satellite dish. With 30 rooms, it is the most comfortable — if not the most authentic — place to stay, and it also has a passable restaurant. Calle Azagra, Albarracín (phone: 974-710011; telex: 62614). Expensive.

EATING OUT: *El Portal* – A welcoming bar serving hot snacks and hearty meals, right in the middle of the village. The impressive doorway has a knocker and handle fashioned as iron lizards. The set menu is filling, and the owner even accepts credit cards. Reservations unnecessary. 14 Portal de Molina, Albarracín (phone: 974-710290). Moderate to inexpensive.

En Route from Albarracín – If the pass over the Montes Universales is open, take the spectacular winding drive through Tragacete and on to the strange formations of the Ciudad Encantada outside Cuenca (see *Castile–La Mancha (New Castile),* DIRECTIONS). Otherwise, return to Teruel via the southern loop, past the three protected caves containing prehistoric petroglyphs of bulls stenciled on the rocks near Abrigos del Callejon. The caves are well marked and can't easily be missed (huge arrows posted on trees and painted on cliffs mark the trails). From Teruel, head toward Valencia on the N234 and E26 highways, both clearly marked. The road passes through a wild area of the southeast corner of Teruel province called the Maestrazgo and soon flattens into the fertile Valencian *huerta*.

Madrid Region

It's not necessary to go as far as Toledo or Segovia to escape the bustle of Madrid or see a bit of Castile. Within an hour's drive of the capital, traffic chaos permitting, it's possible to sample huge fresh strawberries at a green oasis in the dusty plains to the south, to visit the house where Miguel de Cervantes was born in an ancient university town to the east, to view one of the world's great monuments just to the west, or to take in the cool peaks of the Sierra de Guadarrama to the northwest.

At 2,119 feet, Madrid is the highest capital in Europe, but the Sierra de Guadarrama range to the northwest (the setting for much of Ernest Hemingway's *For Whom the Bell Tolls*) is considerably higher. Madrid is often blisteringly hot in summer, and *madrileños* who don't go to the coast head for the hills. This is very important to a city in the geographic heart of Spain, far from any sea. It matters little that the mountain towns are not especially beautiful. Their chief function is as weekend retreats, bases for hiking, and in the case of the higher villages, settings for winter sports. There are also some beautiful scenic views, especially where the mountains overlook a river or a reservoir.

The picture is quite different to the south, where the dusty plains of Castile–La Mancha begin. The countryside is far from exciting, but there are at least two spots in this area worth visiting. One is the delightful little medieval village of Chinchón, today famous for its widely consumed *anís de Chinchón* liqueur. The other is Aranjuez, a onetime royal residence, and still an oasis of luxuriant gardens and abundant vegetation, thanks to the confluence of two rivers here.

Alcalá de Henares to the east has seen better days, but that is not to say it isn't a busy commercial center today. The birthplace of the man who wrote *Don Quixote* conserves many important medieval buildings in the center of town, but the downtown area in general has lost its charm to traffic and industry. Visitors won't have come to Spain to tour a US air base, presumably, but there is one nearby, and it's closing down this year, so now would be the time to see it. In any case, many of the stores in Torrejón de Ardoz, near the base, cater to American tastes.

Without doubt, the greatest cultural treat in the immediate Madrid region is the monumental monastery and palace of El Escorial. Many people have mixed feelings about this bleak place, erected when Spain was the world's most powerful country, while dominated by a Catholic faith that was ruthless and often fanatic. El Escorial was designed to reflect much of this. It is only logical while visiting it to continue a few miles to an even more controversial monument — the Valley of the Fallen, the burial site of Generalísimo Francisco Franco. Like El Escorial, it is hard to deny the fascination of the place, even if it is not the visitor's own cup of tea.

   This chapter has been designed so that, with one exception, these locations can be enjoyed in easily managed day trips. In the case of the Sierra Guadarrama, a 2-day excursion seems more appropriate and leisurely, and a wonderful modern hotel set in a 14th-century monastery (*Santa María de El Paular*) has been selected as a place to spend the night. Apart from this establishment and the *Parador de Chinchón,* no hotels have been recommended in this chapter, as it is assumed that the traveler will be based in Madrid. Both hostelries are categorized as expensive, although in this peripheral area that means much less than it would in the capital — a double room at the *parador* costs about $150 a night, while at the monastery-hotel a double room ranges from about $125 to $150. Along the way, lunch or dinner for two with wine will cost $65 and above in an expensive restaurant, $45 to $60 in a moderate restaurant, and below $40 in an inexpensive one. Note that the Province of Madrid Tourist Office (2 Calle Duque de Medinaceli; phone: 91-429-4951) can be very helpful in furnishing information regarding the sightseeing attractions in the Madrid region.

Day Trip 1: Chinchón and Aranjuez

These two towns are the most beautiful in the southern Madrid region, but in contrasting ways. Chinchón, little more than a village, has hardly changed since the Middle Ages, and it has a splendid medieval Plaza Mayor, one of the most prized in Spain. Aranjuez is a green, spacious oasis in the dusty La Mancha plain, overflowing with luxurious gardens surrounding royal palaces and other mainly 18th-century regal retreats.

   En Route from Madrid – Leave town at the main Atocha railway station in southern Madrid, following the A3 (which becomes the N-III) signs to Valencia. Fourteen miles (22 km) along a freshly improved highway, the Arganda Bridge crosses the Jarama River; immediately afterward is the C300 turnoff to Chinchón, 28 miles (45 km) from Madrid.

CHINCHÓN: To say there is nothing much to Chinchón (pop. 4,100) would be an understatement, but it is nonetheless worth a stop on the way to Aranjuez. The village was founded in 1085, when Alfonso VI reconquered nearby Toledo from the Moors. The village's centerpiece today is the 16th-century Plaza Mayor, an oddly shaped "square" of rickety 3-story arcaded buildings topped with 224 wooden balconies. The village was immortalized in the film *Around the World in 80 Days,* and has been drawing as many as 15,000 visitors per weekend in recent years, many of whom arrive in cars and park in and around the square. That situation, along with the general neglect of the shaky-looking balconies, led to a long-awaited renovation in 1990. At press time the city was building an underground car park, due to be completed this year, leaving the square traffic-free and even more attractive. Since 1502, the square has been the site of bullfights, and it is still occasionally cordoned off for them. The best time is fiesta week, August 13 through 18, but be warned — it is usually scorching hot at that time of the year.
   Try to visit Chinchón during spring or early summer. Sit at one of the many open-air cafés in the Plaza Mayor and enjoy a small glass of the drink for which the village is nationally famous. The *anís* of Chinchón is made with the oily aniseed produced from

locally grown anise, a member of the parsley family, and alcohol. Those who haven't eaten yet should ask for *dulce,* or sweet — the *seco,* or dry, is potent stuff! Speaking of drinks, it was the Marquesa de Chinchón, wife of a 17th-century Viceroy of Peru, who first introduced quinine — a key ingredient of tonic water — to Europe from South America after she had been cured of malaria by the drug, obtained by local Indians from a tree that she named "cinchona" after her hometown. A statue of the marquise is to be placed in the Plaza Mayor this year, in time for the 500th anniversary of the discovery of the Americas.

Chinchón is also famous for its garlic and decorative bread, loaves baked in the shapes of fish, horses, owls, eagles, and other animals. The bread can be bought varnished for decoration or unvarnished to eat. There are several bakeries on the Plaza Mayor — perhaps the widest assortment of strange breads is found at *Luis Ontalva* (25 Plaza Mayor). Most of the other buildings sell garlic or *anís,* or are restaurants. Looming over one side of the square is the parish church, the Iglesia de la Asunción, built between 1534 and 1626, with an *Assumption of the Virgin* by Goya, who often stayed in Chinchón. Just behind the opposite corner is the *Parador de Chinchón* (see below), from which there is a good view of the well-preserved 15th-century castle, with its circular fortified towers; it was sacked along with the rest of the town by Napoleon's troops in 1808.

CHECKING IN: *Parador de Chinchón* – A former 17th-century Augustinian convent that was restored in the 1970s but still preserves its chapel, this *parador* is extremely tranquil. The 38 air conditioned rooms are the height of comfort, and behind the building there are fine terraced gardens with quince trees and goldfish ponds, an open-air swimming pool, and a view of the castle. There is also a bar and a good restaurant. 1 Avenida Generalísimo, Chinchón (phone: 91-894-0836 or 91-894-0908). Expensive.

EATING OUT: *Mesón Cuevas del Vino* – An informal eating place located in converted wine and oil stores. In the basement, notice the 400-year-old caves between huge, centuries-old wine vats. The upstairs dining room is decorated with large, autographed wine jars. Try *alubias de Chinchón* (local haricot beans laced with meaty stock) and *cochinillo asado* (roast suckling pig). Reservations advised. American Express accepted. 13 Calle Benito Hortelano, Chinchón (phone: 91-894-0206). Moderate.

Plaza Mayor – Long a favorite of Madrid's weekend tourists as well as the non-Spanish, this delightful narrow building has 3 floors of small dining rooms, with a lovely balcony on the third. Fresh fish arrives daily and is well prepared; the roast lamb is succulent. Closed Wednesdays. Reservations unnecessary, except for lunch on Sundays. American Express and Visa accepted. 10 Plaza Mayor, Chinchón (phone: 91-894-0929). Moderate.

En Route from Chinchón – The pleasant country road to Aranjuez, 14 miles (22 km) away, passing through the village of Villaconejos, is clearly marked. Apart from the odd gravel quarry and olive grove, there is little to see. As Aranjuez nears, the vegetation thickens and the landscape becomes greener.

ARANJUEZ: Despite a Roman and later an Arab presence, Aranjuez (pronounced Ah-rahn-*hwayth*) is largely a whimsical creation of Spanish monarchs from the 15th to the 18th centuries. However, the lush foliage and respite from the blistering summer heat is a natural phenomenon. Aranjuez (pop. 38,000) lies in the valley formed by the Tagus and Jarama rivers, and the area is fertile and humid. Ferdinand and Isabella, the Catholic Monarchs, first noted its pleasant climate during the 15th century, and late in the 16th century, Philip II ordered buildings to be constructed. But it was the first Spanish Bourbon, Philip V, whose rule spanned the first half of the 18th century, who chose Aranjuez as a royal residence, especially in the spring. His successors, Ferdinand VI and Carlos III, embellished the Royal Palace — the present building dates from 1744, after a fire destroyed much of the palace in 1712 — and built a huge square in front of it and the large, French-modeled Parterre gardens around it. From 1792 to 1803, Carlos IV built a second "palace," the Casa del Labrador, in some ways as beautiful as the first though much smaller, and added the vast landscaped park — Jardín del Príncipe (Prince's Garden) — that surrounds it. The informal Jardín de la Isla, on an island in the river next to the Royal Palace, dates from Philip II's time in the 16th century.

The spacious leafy gardens and long, tree-shaded avenues of Aranjuez are the perfect place for an unhurried stroll. The monarchs wanted to create a Spanish Versailles, and their efforts still attract many visitors. The Royal Palace and the Casa del Labrador are both richly decorated with ornamental fantasies, including priceless gifts from royalty around the world and over the centuries. The palace has hundreds of rooms, the best known being the Porcelain Salon, the former reception hall, whose walls and ceilings are covered with white porcelain by the Italian artist Gricci. The Casa del Labrador (or Peasant's House, so named because a farmworker's home used to stand on the site), in the nearby Jardín del Príncipe, contains an abundance of marble, gold, semi-precious stone, crystal, silk hangings, Roman mosaics, huge chandeliers, and 27 elaborate clocks. The gardens are open daily, from 10 AM to dusk. The Royal Palace and the Casa del Labrador are open daily from 10 AM to 1:30 PM and from 3:30 to 7 PM. A combined ticket allows entry to the palace (the visit here is by guided tour) and the Casa del Labrador; no admission charge to the gardens.

Aranjuez played an important role at the outset of the Peninsular War in 1808, when Carlos IV and Napoleon signed a treaty against Britain. A popular insurrection in the town led to the downfall of the hated minister Godoy, the abdication of Carlos IV in favor of hs son, Ferdinand VII, and the Peninsular War itself. The *Motín,* or Uprising, is celebrated every September during a 5-day annual fair, when thousands of exuberant residents reenact the rebellion in festive style. Napoleon's troops did in fact cause much damage to Aranjuez before the tide turned against them, when the future Duke of Wellington entered the war.

The town is nationally famous for its delicious crops, asparagus and strawberries in particular, and especially during spring and early summer, the roadsides are crammed with stalls selling produce. A meal isn't complete here without a first course of green asparagus and a dessert of strawberries and cream. A popular excursion for *madrileños* is the wonderful *Tren de la Fresa* (Strawberry Train), a 19th-century–style steam train that runs to Aranjuez from Delicias Station in Madrid every Saturday, Sunday, and public holiday from May through mid-October. The ticket (currently about $16) includes visits to the palace and the gardens — and free strawberries on the train. A popular compliment to a girl in Spain is "Your lips are like the strawberries of Aranjuez," but the train's hostesses probably hear it 100 times a day.

EATING OUT: Casa Pablo – Pablo Guzmán has turned his restaurant into a popular haunt over the years, with an extensive menu of Castilian specialties, including fresh fish and game. The walls of the bar and the 2 dining rooms — the larger one is upstairs — are covered with bullfighting posters and photos. Closed August. Reservations unnecessary. No credit cards accepted. 42 Calle Almíbar, Aranjuez (phone: 91-891-1451). Expensive.

La Rana Verde – The *Green Frog* is indeed green, like the town, down to the waiters' jackets, the menu covers, the decor — and even the Tagus River, which flows gently by outside the plentiful windows. Get here early for a riverside table. The place is touristy and large, but with good food — try *espárragos verdes naturales* (fresh green asparagus), *pavo en salsa de almendra* (turkey in almond sauce), and the inevitable *fresones con nata* (strawberries and cream). Open daily. Reservations advised. No credit cards accepted. 1 Calle Reina, Aranjuez (phone: 91-891-1325). Moderate.

En Route to Madrid – For a quick drive 30 miles (48 km) back to Madrid, take the N-IV Madrid–Andalusia highway heading north.

En Route to Toledo – Just south of Aranjuez on N-IV is the N400 turnoff to Toledo, 27 miles (43 km) away along a straight road that follows the Tagus River.

Day Trip 2: Alcalá de Henares and Nuevo Baztán

A person needs a strong interest in history to profit from a journey to Alcalá de Henares, formerly an ancient university center but now little more than a bustling dormitory town for Madrid, 19 miles (31 km) away, with medieval buildings that are choked by permanent traffic jams. The only other place in this region east of Madrid worth visiting is the village of Nuevo Baztán, which has some curiosity value.

En Route from Madrid – Take the A2 highway (it later becomes the N-II) out of northeast Madrid, easily found because it is the route to the well-marked Barajas Airport. This means the traffic is often brutal — especially as this is also the main highway to Barcelona. A few miles before Alcalá de Henares, the highway passes the controversial US air base of Torrejón de Ardoz. After much wrangling with the Spanish government in the 1980s, the Reagan administration agreed to transfer the locally unpopular 401st Tactical Wing of 72 F-16 fighter-bombers to Italy by this year. Of interest is the 16th-century Casa Grande at the entrance to Torrejón on 2 Calle Madrid. This 10,000-square-meter complex of farm buildings, wine cellars, and Spain's only medieval wine press has been converted into restaurants and a museum. Admission charge (phone: 91-675-3900). At Torrejón, travelers might want to take a 7½-mile (12-km) detour south along N206 to the sleepy village of Loeches (pop. 2,100), which was a Moorish fortress and still has a 16th-century church and two convents.

ALCALÁ DE HENARES: The greatest writer in the Spanish language, Miguel de Cervantes, author of *Don Quixote,* was born here in 1547, but the town's history goes back much further. The area around Alcalá de Henares (pop. 150,000) includes several prehistoric, Roman, and Visigothic sites, but unfortunately none is open to the public. A 3,600-square-foot Roman site from the 4th century was discovered in 1988, and it includes an important multicolored mosaic from a villa in the Roman settlement of Complutum, in the Henares River valley. The nearest anyone can get to the remains is the *Museo Tear* (Paseo Juncal; phone: 91-881-3250), an archaeological museum and workshop where students piece together the remains (open Saturdays and Sundays from 10 AM to 2 PM, but it's always best to call in advance; no admission charge). The name of the town, incidentally, comes from the Arabic Al-Qalat, or "fortress" — which fell to the Catholic forces in 1088.

Alcalá's golden age began at the end of the 15th century, when Cardinal Cisneros founded the famous Complutensian University in 1498. For many years the most important in Spain, it published Europe's first polyglot Bible, a six-volume work printed from 1514 to 1517, with side-by-side texts in Hebrew, Greek, and Latin, Chaldee, and

Syriac. Many colleges and convents were built in the next 2 centuries, but the university was moved to Madrid in 1836, and the city has declined in importance and attraction ever since, although there is a new Alcalá University that is an important center of North American studies. The original university complex, the Colegio de San Il-defonso, in the Plaza San Diego (near the main Plaza Cervantes), is now the new university. Its 16th-century Plateresque façade is interesting; the doorway leads into the arcaded Patio de Santo Tomás and the Paraninfo, or auditorium, and on to the adjacent Patio Trilingüe (Courtyard of Three Languages), so named because Greek, Latin, and Hebrew were taught here. (The old university was a renowned language center, and the author of the first Spanish grammar was among its professors.) The university can be visited weekends and holidays, from 11 AM to 2 PM and from 5 to 8 PM; no admission charge. Other monuments of note include the Iglesia Magistral de San Justo, an imposing 17th-century building with a Gothic portal; the 13th- through 16th-century Archbishop's Palace, of several different styles though badly damaged by fire in 1939 (most of the town's churches suffered damage during the 1931–39 Second Republic and Spanish Civil War); and the Capilla de San Ildefonso (2 Calle Pedro Gumiel), where Cardinal Cisneros's 16th-century marble tomb is on display. The *Salon Cervantes* (Calle Santiago), the town's only theater, was built in 1888 and is now open after many years of restoration.

The *Casa de Cervantes* (48 Calle Mayor) is the author's purported birthplace, but is, in fact, a well-reproduced period house and museum. Built in 1956, the house contains original furniture, an arcaded interior patio with eight granite columns holding up wooden balconies, and many old manuscripts and copies of *Don Quixote*. Local authorities are "75% certain" that Cervantes was born in the house that was on this site — what is 100% certain is that the literary genius was born in Alcalá de Henares in 1547 and moved with most of his family to Valladolid when he was 6. The house is open Tuesdays through Fridays, from 10 AM to 2 PM and from 4 to 7 PM; weekends, from 10 AM to 2 PM; no admission charge. The tourist office nearby (Callejón de Santa María; phone: 91-889-2694) is open mornings only (10 AM to 2 PM) daily.

EATING OUT: Hostería del Estudiante – This early-16th-century eating house is part of the original university complex, adjacent to the Patio Trilingüe. A large hall decorated in period style, it has thick beams, whitewashed walls, a tiled floor, and a large chimney contributing to a welcoming atmosphere. The food is typically Castilian. Try *sopa castellana* (bread and garlic soup) and, in mid-afternoon, *chocolate con migas* (hot chocolate with fried bread crumbs). Open daily. Reservations advised during class terms (from October through June approximately). Major credit cards accepted. 3 Calle Los Colegios, Alcalá de Henares (phone: 91-888-0330). Expensive.

San Diego – A pleasant upstairs dining room facing the 16th-century university façade. Try the *churrasco de ternera* (thick steaks served on a grill over hot coals in a metal bowl, so that it slowly cooks on the table while finishing the first course). Reservations unnecessary. No credit cards accepted. 5 Plaza San Diego, Alcalá de Henares (phone: 91-888-3097). Inexpensive.

En Route from Alcalá de Henares – Take N230 south to Nuevo Baztán, 12½ miles (20 km) away, past the villages of El Gurugu and Valverde de Alcalá.

NUEVO BAZTÁN: This semi-derelict village of barely 500 people is undergoing much-needed repairs. Its interest lies in the fact that it was designed during the early 18th century by the leading baroque architect, José de Churriguera, and is the only example of his work in the Madrid region. He was commissioned by Marqués Juan de Goyeneche, a wealthy banker, who wanted to undertake an experiment in town planning, as well as create a local ceramics and decorative glass industry. Churriguera was from the Basque valley of Baztán in the Navarrese Pyrenees near the French border — hence the name. The parish Church of San Francisco Javier and the palace here are noteworthy, but are not expected to regain their full Churrigueresque charm until restoration is completed this year, at which time the European Community hopes to have converted the palace into the International School of Music.

En Route to Madrid – Madrid is 32 miles (51 km) from Nuevo Baztán, via Alcalá de Henares.

En Route to Guadalajara – Another 15½ miles (25 km) along the N-II highway from Alcalá de Henares toward Barcelona is Guadalajara, a historic town; see *Castile–La Mancha (New Castile)*, DIRECTIONS.

Day Trip 3: El Pardo, El Escorial, and the Valley of the Fallen

This trip takes in the foothills of the Sierra de Guadarrama and includes some of the prettier villages — as well as the most popular weekend and summer resorts — in the Madrid region. But for first-time visitors, at least, there is only one real attraction: the Real Monasterio de El Escorial, one of the most famous monasteries in the world. It's both a fascinating and a grim experience, as is the *Valley of the Fallen,* so perhaps a quick side trip to El Pardo will lighten the mood.

En Route from Madrid – Take the A6 Madrid–La Coruña highway out of northwest Madrid; while still in the city's outskirts at Puerto de Hierro, take the C601 turnoff to El Pardo, a few miles ahead through some lovely woods.

EL PARDO: The highlight of the quiet village, 9 miles (14 km) from Madrid, is the delightful El Pardo Palace, a royal residence built in the 16th century on the foundations of a former hunting lodge, partly destroyed by fire in 1604 and enlarged in 1772. Generalísimo Francisco Franco lived here until his death in 1975, and the palace now serves as home to visiting heads of state; when not occupied, it is open to the public. Inside are paintings, frescoes (including some showing the palace's original furnishings), period furniture, and an extensive, fine collection of wall tapestries. Other charming buildings nearby include the Casita del Príncipe (Prince's Cottage), also built in 1772, and the Quinta del Pardo (phone: 91-450-6775), with a collection of 19th-century wallpapers. These two and the palace (when not pressed into service as guest quarters for VIPs) are open Mondays through Saturdays from 10 AM to 12:15 PM and from 4 to 7 PM; 10 AM to 1:40 PM on Sundays; a single admission charge covers all three (phone: 91-376-0329). The Convento de los Capuchinos, on the outskirts of town, contains a magnificent early-17th-century wooden carving of the *Recumbent Christ* by Gregorio Fernández. The royal park preceding El Pardo houses the smaller Palacio de la Zarzuela, also a former hunting lodge, dating from the 17th century and rebuilt during the 18th century. Badly damaged during the Spanish Civil War, it was rebuilt in the 1960s and is now the principal residence of King Juan Carlos and thus closed to the public.

En Route from El Pardo – Back on A6, the turnoff to El Escorial — C505 — is clearly marked at Las Rozas, which is 10 miles (16 km) from Madrid. The road leads to the small town of San Lorenzo de El Escorial, 29 miles (46 km) from Madrid, but way before reaching it, travelers see the enormous rectangular monastery looming in the distance.

EL ESCORIAL: Philip II, the man who sent the "invincible" Spanish Armada to conquer Queen Elizabeth I's England and transferred the Spanish capital from Toledo to Madrid, was a deeply religious ruler of Spain's Catholic Empire at its zenith. The monastery that he built, the Real Monasterio de San Lorenzo de El Escorial, with its patios, palaces, and Pantheon, or Royal Mausoleum, reflects not only that grandeur, but also Philip's Catholic obsession, his grim, austere nature, and his sense of order.

In 1557, Philip had four reasons to order the monastery's construction. First, in that year, his Spanish army defeated the French at the Battle of San Quintín on August 10, the *Day of San Lorenzo* (St. Lawrence). The saint had been martyred on a grill, and the building, the masterpiece of architect Juan de Herrera, is shaped like a gridiron, with the church as its handle. Second, Philip wanted to build a mausoleum for his father, the Holy Roman Emperor Charles V, and his mother, Queen Isabel. Third, he wanted to construct a center of solid religious education. Fourth, he wanted a magnificent summer residence where he could escape from the Madrid heat and go hunting.

El Escorial, however, is more than just a homage to a martyred saint, a mausoleum, a monastery, and a royal residence. It's a church, two palaces, a school, and one of the most important libraries in Spain. But the overall attraction of the place is its ambiguity. It is at the same time a home of splendor and riches, treasures and art, and also a monument of grim, monastic austerity, a place that chills rather than thrills. It was built over 21 years by 3,000 people who worked daily from 1563 to 1584, a feat of great speed for its time. Philip used to like to sit on a slab of sculpted rock above the village, today called Philip's Chair, and watch the work in progress. The main entrance is part of the grand western façade, and just above the doorway are two sculpted grills. There is also a statue of St. Lawrence — the granite is from the local mountains, while his face and hands are made from marble brought from Portugal and southern Spain. Special carts drawn by 40 pair of oxen were built to bring huge granite blocks from the mountains to construct the entrance, which leads into the Kings' Patio, one of El Escorial's 16 courtyards. Granite statues of six Kings of Israel stare down. The left side of the patio is a school, still in use. The monastery is to the right, and in front is the church. A bowl underneath the cross above the church contains a solid gold rock, the only gold in the whole of El Escorial.

Inside the church, the exterior's austerity gives way somewhat to the rich decoration of the high altar, the painted ceilings, and the side chapels. All the paintings are by Italian artists and show events in the life of Christ — except for one that portrays St. Lawrence being grilled! A gilded bronze, marble, and jasper model tabernacle, which took 7 years to make, is outstanding. There are statues here of Philip and three of his four wives; England's Mary Tudor is missing simply because she never visited Spain. One of the chapels contains a beautiful statue of *Christ on the Cross,* made by Benvenuto Cellini in 1562 from one piece of marble. Visitors can even see the "veins" in Christ's legs. Unfortunately, they can also see a chip where the statue was damaged by Napoleon's troops in 1808. Directly below the main altar in the Panteón de los Reyes (or Royal Pantheon), reached by a marble and jasper stairway into the crypt. Here, in black and brown gilded marble tombs, lies every Spanish monarch since the Holy Roman Emperor Charles V (King Charles I of Spain), except Philip V and Ferdinand VI. Also entombed are some of the country's queens, but only those who gave birth to a future king. Next door is the Panteón de los Infantes, where several princes and princesses are buried.

Many sections of El Escorial were added by later monarchs, which explains the varied styles in the Palacios (Royal Apartments). The centerpiece of the earlier, 16th-century Hapsburg Palace is a long room with a single 180-foot fresco depicting a glorious Catholic victory over the Moors. Philip's cell-like bedroom, where he died at age 71 from gout, says everything about the man. It is virtually undecorated, simple and austere, and in it hangs a single portrait of his pallid face, painted when he was already 70. Also in the Hapsburg section of the Palacios are five beautiful inlaid-ebony doors, gifts from Maximilian of Austria, and in one room there is a mighty wooden chair, made especially for Philip's last agonizing trip from Madrid to El Escorial, during which his gout-ridden body was carried for a whole week. When Philip V came from France in 1700, the Bourbon dynasty began, and the 18th century Bourbon Palace is considerably less somber. There are dozens of fine tapestries made at the Royal Factory in Madrid, many showing scenes designed by Goya and Francisco Bayeu, his snootier brother-in-law. Elsewhere, the Biblioteca (Library), above the monastery entrance, has a marvelous Renaissance vaulted ceiling; among its treasures are the personal collection of Philip II, unique Arab and Hebrew manuscripts, the 10th-century Codex Albedensis, St. Teresa of Avila's personal diary, and a Bible lettered entirely in gold. The *Nuevos Museos* (New Museums) contains many works of art by Bosch, Zurbarán, Titian, and many others. The Escorial complex (phone: 91-890-5903) is open Tuesdays through Sundays, from 10 AM to 1:30 PM (to 2 PM September through April) and from 3:30 to 6:30 PM (4 to 6 PM from September through April); admission charge. The tourist office in San Lorenzo de El Escorial is at 10 Calle Floridablanca (phone: 91-890-1554).

EATING OUT: *Charolés* – Traditional Castilian food in traditionally the best place in "monastery town," although recently the menu has shifted its focus more and more to international fare. Try *cocido madrileño* (a mixture of chickpeas, boiled vegetables, and boiled meats) and *berenjenas rellenas con langostinos frescos* (eggplants stuffed with fresh prawns). In summer, dine on the charming open-air terrace. Closed Mondays. Reservations advised. Major credit cards accepted. 24 Calle Floridablanca, San Lorenzo de El Escorial (phone: 91-890-5975). Expensive.

Mesón La Cueva – Situated in a former 18th-century inn, The Cave (in English — and that's what it feels like) is full of atmosphere and charm with antiques adorning the shelves and walls. The usual Castilian specialties and roast meats prevail. Reservations advised. No credit cards accepted. 4 Calle San Antón, San Lorenzo de El Escorial (phone: 91-890-1516). Moderate.

En Route from El Escorial – Take C600 north for 6 miles (10 km) to the turnoff for *El Valle de los Caídos* (Valley of the Fallen). The huge cross is visible a few miles in the distance.

VALLEY OF THE FALLEN: While in a gloomy frame of mind, why not visit a stark place that not only pays homage to the estimated 1 million dead of Spain's 1936–39 Civil War, but also is where thousands of men on the losing side died while building the monument. The *Valle de los Caídos* (phone: 91-890-5544) is a huge basilica carved deep into the granite of a mountain in the forbidding Cuelgamuros Valley. It is topped by an enormous granite cross that stands 495 feet high — as tall as a 33-floor building — on the hill above it.

Everything here is far more austere than El Escorial. The place was ordered built by Generalísimo Francisco Franco as a final resting place for himself and for José Antonio Primo de Rivera, founder of the Spanish Falange, and in honor of the war dead. The crypt contains the coffins of 40,000 soldiers of both sides who were killed in the Civil War, but only prisoners of war from the losing Republican side worked on the monument. The basilica took 10 years, from 1940 to 1950, to construct, and the cross another 9 years — 19 years and thousands of lives in all. Everything was designed to have religious significance — the sculpture of Pity over the entrance is of the Virgin Mary holding Christ. Franco himself chose the tree from which a wooden cross inside the basilica was cut. The dome of the altar under the cross is a mosaic with 5 million pieces, one of the rare examples of gaiety in this dank underground tunnel (open Tuesdays through Sundays from dawn to dusk; admission charge).

En Route to Madrid – Drive back to San Lorenzo de El Escorial and then proceed along C505 to Las Rozas for the final stretch along A6 to Madrid.

En Route to Avila – Thirty-six miles (58 km) west of El Escorial along C505 is the walled city of Avila, the highest provincial capital in Spain. For details on Avila, see *Castile-León (Old Castile)*, DIRECTIONS.

Day Trip 4: Sierra de Guadarrama

This is actually a 2-day trip, with an overnight stop at the converted 14th-century monastery high up in the Sierra de Guadarrama range. The range, which runs along a line about 55 miles (88 km) northwest of Madrid, includes several small towns, peaks at close to 6,560 feet, and limited skiing facilities in the winter. It must be said that none of the towns has much to commend it, and the views are easily surpassed in northern Spain, but the mountains offer an easy and pleasant escape from Madrid's summer heat.

En Route from Madrid – Leave Madrid through the Arch of Triumph at Moncloa in the west of the city and drive past university buildings onto the A6 highway. Twenty-four miles (38 km) away, straddling A6, is Collado-Villalba (at an altitude of 3,000 feet). There is little to see here besides the 16th-to-17th-century Church of Our Lady of Enebral; cross the bridge spanning A6 and get on the old N-VI highway. Six miles (10 km) along is the village of Guadarrama (pop. 6,000), mentioned in Cervantes's classic, *Don Quixote.* It's a busy little place, founded by Alfonso X in 1268 and surrounded by pine, oak, and poplar trees. A handful of 18th-century buildings and an ornate fountain are all that there is to show of its history.

The M710 turnoff for Cercedilla is 200 yards beyond the village, and the old road climbs as it follows the Guadarrama River. Although its population is only 4,000, Cercedilla sprawls over several hills with its weekend chalets, whose development was boosted by the construction of a railway line from Madrid. At 3,900 feet, it is a very popular hiking center. *Madrileños* drive out the 37 miles (59 km) on weekends, go for a 6-hour trek in the hills, and return in the evening. In winter, it is also an important base for skiing at Puerto de Navacerrada, just 8 miles (13 km) away.

Take C607 east out of town to N601, which leads to the village of Navacerrada, 3,945 feet above sea level. Apart from one 17th-century church, the village has nothing noteworthy to offer, except for its surrounding countryside. From Navacerrada, the 2-day trip can be continued along two possible routes. Five miles (8 km) north on C601 is the ski resort of Puerto de Navacerrada, which stands at 6,100 feet at the beginning of the most rugged part of the Sierra de Guadarrama. For those not skiing, there's little point in stopping here for more than a quick look to admire the view at the highest point in the region accessible by road. (The hotels and restaurants are standard fare for a middling ski resort.) But Puerto de Navacerrada is also the point where C604 starts and leads northeast into the mountains, toward El Paular, while N601 begins to descend as it continues northwest.

En Route to Segovia – The N601 highway from Puerto de Navacerrada continues directly northwest to Segovia. For complete details on the city and its sights, hotels, and restaurants, see *Segovia,* THE CITIES.

En Route to El Paular – Take C604 north from Puerto de Navacerrada, signposted to Rascafría. The road is very twisting and the mountains on either side are thickly wooded, with some very pretty sights. The hotel-monastery of *Santa María de El Paular* is 14 miles (22 km) away, over the 6,000-foot-high Puerto de los Cotos pass.

A gentler alternative to El Paular is the long way around from Navacerrada, taking C607 eastward toward Cerceda, 5½ miles (9 km) away, then M611 another 4½ miles (7 km) to Manzanares el Real (pop. 1,800; altitude 2,980 feet). Manzanares el Real is famous for the charming and well-restored 15th-century castle of the Dukes of Infantado, one of Spain's best examples of Castilian military architecture. The castle, with its three cyclindrical towers, is a mixture of Mudéjar and Renaissance-Gothic styles, and it houses a small museum displaying models and documents relating to various Spanish castles. The presence of the adjacent Santillana reservoir enhances the castle's beauty (open Tuesdays through Saturdays, from 10 AM to 2 PM and from 5 to 8 PM; Sundays, from 10 AM to 2 PM; admission charge).

From Manzanares, take M612 for 5 miles (8 km) to Soto del Real, and then M614 another 5 miles (8 km) northward to the pretty town of Miraflores de la Sierra (pop. 2,600). Despite recent expansion as a holiday center, the oldest part around the Plaza España retains a mountain village charm. The 16th-century parish church is of several different styles.

EATING OUT: *Asador La Fuente* – Opened in 1987 in the style of a traditional roast house, it has a 2-story dining room tastefully decorated with tiles, wood, and rustic bricks. There is also a terrace for summer dining. Try *morcilla de Burgos* (Burgos blood pudding) and *buey gallego en parrilla de carbón* (Galician beefsteak grilled over hot coals). Closed Mondays. Reservations necessary on weekends. Major credit cards accepted. 12 Calle Mayor, Miraflores de la Sierra (phone: 91-844-4216). Expensive.

Maito – A comfortable and solid mountain house with a genuine log fire and thick wooden beams. Down-home cooking is featured, with many of the fruits and vegetables coming from the restaurant's own garden. Try *sopa pastora* (garlic and bread soup) and *cochinillo asado* (roast suckling pig). Open daily. Reservations advised. Major credit cards accepted. 5 Calle Calvo Sotelo, Miraflores de la Sierra (phone: 91-844-3567). Moderate.

En Route from Miraflores de la Sierra – Take M6141 16 miles (26 km) away over the twisting, 5,890-foot-high Puerto de la Morcuera pass to the village of Rascafría (pop. 1,300). Less than a mile (1.6 km) away is El Paular, or rather, the hotel-monastery of *Santa María de El Paular* (see below), which is really all there is in El Paular. Both villages lie on C604.

CHECKING IN/EATING OUT: *Santa María de El Paular* – A converted 14th-century monastery, with 58 luxurious air conditioned rooms overlooking an arcaded patio, a fountain, and the surrounding pine forests. It would be hard to find quieter quarters in the Madrid region. There is a heated swimming pool, tennis courts, gardens, and bicycles for rent. The *Don Lope* restaurant is extremely good — try *sopa de cebolla gratinada* (onion soup with grated cheese topping) and *chuletón de Lozoya* (grilled local steaks). Visa, American Express, and Diners Club accepted. El Paular (phone: 91-869-1011; fax: 869-1006). Expensive.

En Route from El Paular and Rascafría – Continue northward on C604 past the village of Lozoya, where the road skirts the beautiful La Pinilla reservoir, to the main N-I highway. Before taking the highway south to Madrid, drive 4 miles (6 km) north to the walled village of Buitrago del Lozoya (pop. 1,300; altitude 3,200 feet), which is actually on a jut of land surrounded on three sides by the Lozoya River. There are some remains of the 10th-century Arab wall, and ruins of a 14th-century castle. The village had been a Roman settlement and later a fortress.

En Route to Madrid – Madrid is 48 miles (77 km) directly south on N-I, which is now in excellent condition, thanks to recent improvements.

Castile–La Mancha (New Castile)

Until fairly recently, it would not have been overstating the case by much to lament that the region extending south and east of Madrid was the one region of Spain that tended to be seen — if it was seen at all — by people on their way to somewhere else. The southeastern quadrant of the central Castilian tableland saw travelers, goods, and, to a large extent, the currents of progress flow along the radial arteries linking Madrid to the bustling, cosmopolitan northeast and to the agricultural heartland of Andalusia. And as they all sliced heedlessly through its 50,000 square miles of territory, the region did very little to draw attention to itself.

No visitor to Spain expects to find the equivalent of a neat series of theme parks laid out one after another, even in regions where culture and landscape make for a fair degree of uniformity. Castile–La Mancha, one of Spain's 17 autonomous communities, consisting of the provinces of Guadalajara, Cuenca, Albacete, Ciudad Real, and Toledo, is nothing more or less than the sum of its parts: topographical remnants administratively lumped together because they did not fit in anywhere else. Take away Albacete and add Madrid itself, and it corresponds to the historic region of New Castile, which was the southern half of the old kingdom of Castile. Nevertheless, southeastern Castile is a place that defies easy categorization, and for that reason, perhaps, it has often struck travelers as the most quintessentially Spanish region of all.

Part of what makes this so are the region's brutal winters and torrid summers. Its 3-tiered landscape — arid mountains, thick-forested river valleys, and endless flat, stultifying plains — is another factor, a compendium of the geographic facts of life that have dominated Spanish history. So is the regions's ample inventory of castles, convents, and palaces left behind from the clash between two cultures evoked by the region's hyphenated name (La Mancha means "the dry lands" in Arabic).

The common thread that unites the area — and recalls the Spain that so fascinated and exasperated 19th-century travelers — is Castile–La Mancha's contemporary socio-economic backwardness. Tilled grain fields, vineyards, and shepherds who brave traffic to maneuver their flocks across the highway are all a reminder that hardscrabble agriculture provides over a third of this vast region's million and a half inhabitants with their only livelihood. Towns and villages of striking charm seemingly cloaked in a sense of doom, little jewels of Renaissance religious architecture boarded up and abandoned, John Deere service signs along the main drag of dusty prairie crossroad towns, woodland streams and glens with strong overtones of the better side of the

Appalachians — all these are part of the picture. Even omitting Toledo from the itinerary, the region's claim on the visitor's attention span is justified by three first-rate towns — Sigüenza, Cuenca, and Almagro — plus some unique swaths of landscape that stand out amid all the empty space that in some curious way manages to bind a vast, diverse region together.

Castile–La Mancha's identity problem is nothing new. The region known to history as New Castile had as its nucleus the southern lands that fell under Christian domination just after the reconquest of Toledo by King Alfonso VI of Castile and León in 1085. These were enlarged by the domains of the harsh-contoured eastern plateau that came under the sway of his successors following the battle of Las Navas de Tolosa in 1212. After the Moors had been duly removed or assimilated, the first to put their stamp on the newly won territories were the Knights of Santiago, the Knights Templars, and the Knights of Calatrava — fighting religious brotherhoods who received land and feudal privileges in payment for services rendered during the Reconquest. The monumental legacy they left behind attests to their might, but their heyday was brief, because the Kings of Castile realized the potential for havoc, should these freewheeling warrior castes become too powerful. So the monarchs whittled away at their potential rivals or suppressed the orders altogether, the fate that befell the Templars in 1310. The last great order of crusading monks to succumb were the Almagro-based Knights of Calatrava, who became victims of medieval Spanish realpolitik in 1495, when Queen Isabella finagled the post of grand master for her husband, King Ferdinand. The Catholic church, whose immense power radiated from Toledo, moved in to fill the vacuum, building lavish cathedrals and grandiose parish churches that have survived even in the most run-down, depopulated towns. Secular control passed to a later generation of noble dynasties that emerged during Spain's 16th-century burst of imperial glory, which is why so much of what is to be seen here is of a late Gothic or Renaissance character.

For years afterward, New Castile remained the breadbasket of central Spain. Agriculture was always the key to the way of life that evolved here, as settlers moved in and set about making a livelihood as best they could. But aside from providing acceptable grazing in the rugged east, and vast plains to the south for the cultivation of grain and, from the 18th century on, wine grapes, New Castile land was never able to sustain a booming economy, especially after new and agriculturally more productive lands had been incorporated into the greater nation unified by King Ferdinand and Queen Isabella. Even during the 16th century, the writer Miguel de Cervantes knew what he was doing when he had his fictitious Don Quixote seek out knightly adventures in the tiny, dreary farm towns of the flatlands, and he succeeded in putting La Mancha on the cultural map of the literary world.

By the time Philip II designated Madrid his capital in the mid-16th century, New Castile had come to rely ever more heavily on a traditional cluster of small-scale skilled industries such as ceramics, ironware, and textiles. But after a short-lived 17th-century boom period, the aftershocks of the Industrial Revolution put these artisans out of business, increasing their sense of economic impotence and social isolation from the rest of Spain. The situation was finally put right in 1977, when the Spanish map was drastically overhauled

2 years after the death of Generalísimo Francisco Franco. Madrid was scooped out to stand on its lofty own, and what was left of New Castile was joined to the adjacent province of Albacete, with which it shared many geographic and demographic characteristics, to form the autonomous community of Castile–La Mancha. New regional authorities began to take inventory of what had come under their administrative purview, following centuries of neglect by a national government that had put its money into resort complexes meant to lure package tourists from northern Europe to the Mediterranean coast. They happily found a region that had a lot more going for it than almost anyone would have given it credit for: a varied and almost entirely untouched landscape, complete with winding rivers and inland lakes, stretching from the arid, rust-colored foothills of Guadalajara to the lush green pine forests, towering granite cliffs, and deep-cut canyons of Cuenca. Even the vast, flat stretches of pokey old La Mancha — the southern part of this region, made up of the province of Ciudad Real, southern Toledo, northwest Albacete, and southwest Cuenca — turned out to possess towns of considerable charm, with extraordinary architectural flourishes in no way inferior to the castles, churches, and convents of the rest of the area. Roman, Visigothic, and Moorish remains are far scarcer than those of the post-Reconquest and Renaissance periods, but they are well worth the trouble of seeking out.

One important point needs to be made. Unlike other parts of Spain, where visitors must pick their way through ugly industrial zones and shabby high-rise apartment blocks to locate the "Old Quarter," this region not only has its monumental jewels fairly intact, but their settings as well. The market towns and villages that form the backbone of this route have not changed much from former times, although they've paid a heavy social and economic price. Many villages have been abandoned altogether, and nearly all the towns along the way seem to be given over to elderly, beret-clad men. Women, strangely enough, remain unseen, and such adolescents as there are still hang around listlessly on the street corners or in the rock 'n' roll bars, waiting for their chance to escape to a factory job in up-to-date, pseudo-Europeanized, un-Spanish Spain.

As might be expected in what formerly was a no-man's-land between two warring cultures, variety is the keynote in the culinary department. In northern Guadalajara, the Castilian taste for tender roast meat — suckling pig, lamb, and baby kid — predominates. Once into Cuenca, the visitor will come across a few dishes unheard-of elsewhere, slow-to-spoil and portable fare created by mule teams and nomadic herdsmen. One such specialty is *ajo arriero,* a creamy paste of mashed codfish and garlic, delicious when spread on Cuenca's excellent bread, which is second only to that of Soria as Spain's best. In both areas, however, pride of place goes to small-game dishes — the ubiquitous partridge, stewed and marinated a dozen different ways, rabbit, and wild boar — and the trout, now mostly fattened in fish farms, but nevertheless inexpensive and not too inferior to its riverbed cousin, and available year-round. La Mancha, where wine and cheese are first and foremost, is an altogether different story. But it, too, has a very tasty and unique menu, which shows its Moorish origins in unusual combinations of flavors: for instance, *migas del pastor* — croutons fried in olive oil, with garlic, ham, fatback, sausage, and grapes — or stewed lamb seasoned with nutmeg, saffron, and white wine. In addition to the millions of gallons of blended table wines produced in Valdepeñas, Daimiel, and Manzanares, a few really choice, fruity young wines have been developed and aged with care. Also, the ubiquitous cheese, *queso manchego,* from ewe's milk, can be fresh from the farm or aged to bring out its strong flavor.

In laying out the following week-long drive through Castile–La Mancha, the entire province of Albacete has been omitted. Although it does have its share of nice touches — the Lagoons of Riudera and Villanueva de los Infantes are beautiful — its features are too similar to what will already have been covered elsewhere. Similarly, the provincial capital of Ciudad Real is simply not worth going that far out of the way to see. (It, and the city of Albacete, rate as two of the dullest towns in Spain.) Autumn is by far the best time to visit, so as to catch the birch trees as their leaves change color. At night, at these altitudes of 800 to 1,200 feet, the temperature can drop drastically — even in summer — so be prepared. And don't come in the winter; even the people who live here aren't too happy about it.

Expect to pay $75 and above for a double room with private bath in hotels classified as expensive, $55 to $75 in moderate hotels, and less than $45 in inexpensive ones. Dinner for two with wine will cost $60 and above in an expensive restaurant, $40 to $60 in a moderate restaurant, and below $35 in an inexpensive one.

En Route from Madrid – Leave the city on the N-II highway heading northeast in the direction of the airport and Zaragoza. Be prepared for hideous traffic and a view of endless factories and warehouses and the automobile plants of Alacalá de Henares. Continue following the Zaragoza signs, giving Guadalajara a wide berth some 35 miles (56 km) along. Then, after about 11 miles (18 km) of what begins to look like real country, and after the 13th-century Templar Castle of Torija is visible on the right, take the turnoff for Brihuega (C201) immediately before the next overpass. Brihuega is a lovely, run-down old town, perched above a dried-up river gorge. It's worth a stop for a cup of coffee, some leg-stretching, and a look at the much-restored 13th-century Romanesque and Gothic Church of Santa María de la Peña and the ruins of the Old City walls, of which two city gates remain. Up the hill, the structure resembling a gigantic bandstand pavilion once served as the Royal Cloth Factory, established by the enlightened King Carlos III during the 18th century. It later became a marvelous French garden, but it has been left unattended for years, growing surrealistically wild. On the way out of Brihuega, a signpost indicates the old road to Sigüenza, forking to the right; take this, to avoid backtracking to the N-II, and follow it through fields that, in season, are a mass of sunflowers. After 11 miles (18 km), turn briefly north onto C204 to rejoin N-II heading for Zaragoza. Almost immediately afterward, exit N-II via the ramp for Sigüenza, and again join C204 north for 16 miles (26 km) into town.

SIGÜENZA: By themselves, a castle and a cathedral do not a medieval town make, but when both dominate the skyline from surrounding hills, they seem equal to the task. The fairly prosperous farmers and artisans who live here, in what once was a major medieval archdiocese (in its heyday before the rest of the region was even properly reconquered by the Christians), confer a pleasant rural bustle. The town is set at an altitude of 3,360 feet, overlooking the Henares River, and inevitably all of the climbing streets lead to the 12th-century cathedral (Plaza de Don Bernardo; open Mondays through Saturdays, from 10 AM to 1 PM and from 5 to 7 PM). Unlike many of its more famous counterparts, where interiors don't live up to exteriors or vice versa, this cathedral is a true beauty, the result of centuries of changing architectural and decorative styles, from the Mudéjar — the star-studded chapter house ceiling — to the Plateresque, all blending together with unusual harmony. Seek out and pay one of the ushers a *duro* (5-peseta coin) or two to unlock and illuminate the side chapel for a look at the town's main attraction, the tomb of the Doncel (Page Boy), who is represented in alabaster as a young man in knightly battle dress, with a sweetly innocent, melancholy expression, reclining on his side and reading from what might as well be a book of love sonnets. Beneath this captivating but mislabeled anonymous sepulchral statue are the remains of Don Martín Vázquez de Arce, who was, in fact, not a page boy but a 25-year-old married man and a full knight in Queen Isabella's service when he died in battle in 1486 during the Granada campaigns.

Other sites in town include an Ursuline convent, a baroque seminary, and the Romanesque Church of San Vicente. The *Diocesan Museum* (opposite the cathedral; no phone; open daily, from 11 AM to 2 PM; admission charge) has a vigorous late El Greco *Annunciation,* as well as Zurbarán's extraordinary *Immaculate Conception,* showing a pre-teen Virgin Mary floating over the city of Seville. (The ineffable sweetness of her expression would have come out as pure saccharine kitsch from the brush of anyone other than such a genius.) A pleasant short walk, through the medieval arch between the cathedral and the Renaissance Plaza Mayor, keeping to the right where the modern bungalows begin, and on up the hill to the cemetery, leads to a great view of the cathedral and Sigüenza's castle, which has been turned into a *parador* (see *Checking In*); both are kept well lit after dark. The streets leading up to the *parador* also reveal crafts shops where hooked rugs, wrought ironware, and decorative mirrors in hammered-copper and hardwood frames are sold. The latter are a particularly good buy, though a bit awkward to carry home. Jesús Blasco's workshop (Calle Cruz Dorada) is the place for hand-sewn goatskin fishermen's boots and wineskins. For further information, try the tourist office at 2 Cardenal Mendoza (phone: 911-391262).

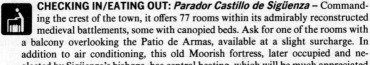

CHECKING IN/EATING OUT: *Parador Castillo de Sigüenza* – Commanding the crest of the town, it offers 77 rooms within its admirably reconstructed medieval battlements, some with canopied beds. Ask for one of the rooms with a balcony overlooking the Patio de Armas, available at a slight surcharge. In addition to air conditioning, this old Moorish fortress, later occupied and neglected by Sigüenza's bishops, has central heating, which will be much appreciated because temperatures can plummet after dark, even in summer. Its huge interior halls make it a favorite place for business conventions. The restaurant offers a fine selection of regional specialties — game in season, fresh river crayfish, and roasts — in a pleasant atmosphere, though it's a bit overpriced. Major credit cards accepted. Plaza del Castillo, Sigüenza (phone: 911-390100; fax: 911-391364; telex: 22517). Expensive.

***El Doncel* –** A comfortable, clean, 16-room *hostal* facing the town's elm-lined promenade. The restaurant specializes in roast kid. No credit cards accepted. 1 Calle General Mola, Sigüenza (phone: 911-391090). Inexpensive.

***El Motor* –** This *hostal* on the town's farthest outskirts has 10 rooms and a restaurant that does a reliable if unexciting job with its mostly international menu, especially steaks. A few concessions to regional cooking occasionally appear. The restaurant is closed Mondays, the last 2 weeks in April, and the first 2 weeks in November. Visa accepted. 11 Calle Calvo Sotelo, Sigüenza (phone: 911-390343 or 911-390827). Inexpensive.

En Route from Sigüenza – It's well worth an extra night in Sigüenza to allow for an excursion into the surrounding mountain towns. All told, the suggested loop that follows entails a detour of 172 miles (275 km), but it can be cut short at more than one point for the return to Sigüenza. From Paseo de la Alameda, head northwest on C114, following signs for Atienza, 19½ miles (31 km) away. Atienza's lordly 12th-century castle will be visible long before the rest of the town comes into view; a closer look reveals four Romanesque churches, red-tiled and half-timbered townhouses, lovely stone columns supporting the Plaza del Trigo, and the 11th-to-13th-century arches of the town walls. At the fork in the road outside of town, make a left onto C101 going south toward Guadalajara. Jadraque lies 20½ miles (33 km) ahead, with its castle on a conical hill towering over lavender-studded fields that feed the bees that make the honey that is the province's main cash crop. Another 12 miles (19 km) ahead on C101 lies the walled town of Hita, famous for the Archpriest of Hita, a renowned 14th-century poet. Early in July, this seemingly abandoned town comes to life for a somewhat overblown but enthusiastic medieval festival, complete with jousting tourneys, colorful folk dancing, and open-air theater performances. Continue south along C101 for 14 miles (22 km) until it rejoins N-II 4 miles (6 km) north of Guadalajara, the provincial capital. Leveled during the Spanish Civil War, Guadalajara does not pretend to be anything other than a high-rise dormitory suburb of Madrid, not worth the bother except to see the 15th-century Palacio de las Infantadas on the Plaza de los Caídos (open daily, from 9 AM to 2 PM and 4 to 9 PM; admission charge) and its diamond-studded façade, and as a possible meal stop. Afterward, if not returning to Sigüenza directly, take N320 east toward Sacedón and Cuenca, but turn onto C200 about 14 miles (22 km) down the road. Soon after, the town of Pastrana rises up on a geologic hump over the surrounding patchwork plains. A pleasant place for a stroll is the steep quarter that once housed Moors from Granada who worked on silk tapestries commissioned by the Dukes of Pastrana. Some of the tapestries are on display at the *Museo Parroquial* in the collegiate church. At lunchtime on weekends and holidays, the nuns who live in the Convento de las Monjas de Abajo serve inexpensive home-cooked meals in the annex ot their 16th-century convent on Calle de las Monjas. Return to Sigüenza by backtracking (the easiest route) on C200 to N320 west and around the Guadalajara bypass to N-II, then heading north.

To continue the route from Sigüenza, proceed south on C204 to N-II, taking it a short 1½ miles (2 km) in the direction of Guadalajara until it meets C204 going south again. Pass Cifuentes and the nuclear power plant at Trillo, to the left. The reactor is cooled by the waters of the Tajo River, which the road does not cross until it is well up into the bluffs overlooking the Embalse de Entrepeñas (Entrepeñas Reservoir). Just outside the town of Sacedón, C204 intersects with N320, which forks sharply left toward Cuenca. For a coffee break, however, bear right for cottage-lined Sacedón, strategically placed on the so-called Sea of Castile, a manmade lake formed by the Entrepeñas Reservoir and the Buendia Reservoir just south of it. (The turnoff to a well-groomed garden and picnic area overlooking the dam is just before the first tunnel.) Then double back along N320, cross over the Guadiela River into Cuenca province, and drive the remaining straight, fast, level road to the intersection with N400 and, a little farther on, the provincial capital, some 59 miles (94 km) from Sacedón and 119 miles (191 km) from Sigüenza.

EATING OUT: *El Castillo* – The reputation of this roadside *hostal* just outside Jadraque is based on the roast kid that comes sizzling from the wood-fired brick oven located around back. Castilian cooking. Open daily. Reservations necessary. MasterCard and Visa accepted. Carretera Guadalajara-Soria, km 46, Jadraque (phone: 911-890254). Moderate.

El Ventorrero – This *mesón* boasts rustic Castilian decor and has been run by the same family since the 1880s. The menu is traditional Castilian, which means excellent roast meats and game. Open daily. No reservations. No credit cards accepted. 4 Calle López de Haro, Guadalajara (phone: 911-212251). Moderate.

CUENCA: A spectacular setting, picturesquely and precariously located "hanging houses," natural wonders, elegant monuments, modern art, and good local food — it's almost impossible to be disappointed by Cuenca. Imagine all the best elements of inland Spain brought together, shuffled, and stacked vertically by a master set designer to produce a showpiece citadel rising from the heart of an otherwise fairly dull provincial capital. The city's medieval Old Town is perched atop a steep escarpment where the Huécar River, a narrow trickle of a stream, intersects with the meandering Júcar River, graced by a bower of birch trees angled like crossed swords over its banks. The town's medieval streets cascade down the escarpment, so exploring it entails just two directions, up or down, and is best done on foot. (For those short of wind, there is a bus that runs every 20 minutes from the new quarter up to the Old Town's main square, the Plaza Mayor de Pio XII, or simply Plaza Mayor.) A preliminary, excellent view of the city as a sculptural ensemble, seen from an outside vantage point, is recommended first, however. Walk behind the cathedral, which edges the Plaza Mayor, past the Casas Colgadas (Hanging Houses), and over the steel footbridge that leads to the opposite side of the Huécar gorge, and the most photogenic side of the Old Town will be directly in front.

The Casas Colgadas are 14th-century houses that, for want of space, were built several stories high and right at the edge of the escarpment, they and their wooden balconies cantilevered out over the gorge itself. Dizzyingly vertical, they are staggered artfully over the cliffside, a masterful feat of 14th-century engineering. Two have been hollowed out, their lath-and-timber innards wonderfully restored to form the *Museum of Spanish Abstract Art* (3 Canonigos), displaying works by modern masters of the non-figurative who settled in Cuenca in the 1950s and 1960s; featured are works by Fernando Zóbel, Luis Feito, Antoni Tàpies, Eduardo Chillida, Antonio Saura, and others (open Tuesdays through Saturdays, from 11 AM to 2 PM and from 4 to 6 PM; Sundays, from 11 AM to 2 PM; admission charge). Across the street, the *Museum of Archaeology* (6 Obispo Valero) displays imperial busts and artifacts from the Roman settlements of Segóbriga and Valeria, as well as remains from the province's Bronze Age (open Tuesdays through Saturdays, from 10 AM to 2 PM and from 4 to 7 PM; Sundays, from 10 AM to 2 PM; admission charge).

Cuenca's cathedral (Plaza Mayor), built in the 12th and 13th centuries with a later façade, is notable for its design, an amalgam of French Gothic and Anglo-Norman styles unique to Spain, and for the mix of baroque and neo-classical elegance lavished on the 18th-century altarpiece and side chapels, as well as a profusion of iron grillwork. Part of the west front was damaged in 1902 when the north tower collapsed, but it has been reconstructed in strict accordance with the original plans (whereas the damaged structure it replaced had not been completed until several hundred years later). The cathedral's *Diocesan Museum* (open daily, from 9 AM to 1:30 PM and from 4:30 to 7:30 PM; admission charge) contains two El Greco canvases, the 12th-century statue of the Virgen del Sagrario, and some interesting Flemish tapestries.

For more spectacular views, over both river gorges and the granite cliffs opposite, take any of the streets going left — uphill — from the Plaza Mayor to the highest part of the rock plinth on which old Cuenca sits. A town map identifying the profusion of ruined convents, churches, and noble palaces along the way is available from the tourist office down in the New City (8 Calle Dalmacio García Izcara; phone: 966-222231). There are three ceramic shops on the Plaza Mayor, but these are stocked with far too much bargain merchandise imported from Andalusia. Since master ceramist Pedro

Mercedes retired a few years ago, the laurels have been passed to Alejandro Fernández Cruz, whose workshop on the Carretera de Madrid almost a mile (1.6 km) outside town is a good place to pick up decorated plates, water jugs, pitchers, and other ceramic knickknacks for reasonable prices. Segundo Santos's small shop (in town on the Plaza Mayor; phone: 966-214038), open only on weekends, is the place to buy lampshades, desk organizers, and notebooks made from his delicate hand-laid paper, a decorative-textured white fashioned from wool scraps and *esparto* grass and stippled with colored threads.

Cuenca is known for its annual *Semana de Música Religiosa,* held the week before *Easter,* with performances packing the Church of San Pablo and other venues, although a new auditorium being built into the Huécar cliffside is expected to become its new home this year. Orchestral and polyphonic choral groups from all of Europe take part in the festival, notable for airing the works of lesser-known Renaissance composers.

CHECKING IN: *Torremangana* – Conveniently located in the humdrum modern town that sprawls at the foot of the Old City. All 155 modern rooms are air conditioned. Comfortable and efficient, it has parking facilities — always at a premium in Cuenca — and its excellent service also argue strongly in its favor. 9 Calle San Ignacio de Loyola, Cuenca (phone: 966-223351; fax: 966-229671; telex: 23400). Expensive.

La Cueva del Fraile – A 16th-century manor house 5 miles (8 km) northwest of town. Built in the corral-style common to La Mancha, it has been so expertly reconstructed it looks completely fake. The combination of thin walls, barking dogs, and noisy Spanish families on bus tours is somewhat of a drawback, but the 54 rooms are generally quiet and always comfortable. The restaurant offers a tasting menu of regional specialties. Closed January and February. Carretera de Buenache, Cuenca (phone: 966-211571; fax: 966-211573). Expensive to moderate.

Posada de San José – This 17th-century house, projecting ever so slightly over the Huécar gorge in the Old Town, was built by a son-in-law of the painter Velázquez and was later put to use as a convent. Subjected to a major restoration in the 1950s, which respected even the uncomfortably low ceiling beams, this is now a 24-room *hostal* (not all with private baths), expertly managed by Jennifer Morter, a transplanted Canadian. As unique as a *parador* without the mini-bars (there is central heating, but no air conditioning), the place is invariably full on weekends, so make reservations well in advance. 4 Calle Julián Romero, Cuenca (phone: 966-211300). Inexpensive.

EATING OUT: *Figón de Pedro* – Owner Pedro Torres put Cuenca on the culinary map with this atmospheric place, located in the heart of the new city. The extensive menu highlights trout, for which Cuenca is deservedly famous, as well as stewed lamb, partridge, and other regional specialties. Closed Sunday evenings. Reservations necessary. Major credit cards accepted. 13 Calle Cervantes, Cuenca (phone: 966-226821). Expensive.

Mesón Casas Colgadas – In a hanging house next door to the *Museum of Spanish Abstract Art,* with a balcony out over the gorge. Under the ownership of Pedro Torres of *Figón de Pedro* fame, the restaurant features a menu very similar to its famous sister, and also boasts a good selection of reasonably priced rioja wines. Closed Monday evenings. Reservations advised. Major credit cards accepted. Calle Canónigos, Cuenca (phone: 966-223509). Expensive.

El Espolon – Devoid of decorative charm and on an unattractive street, it nevertheless serves excellent food. Try fixed-price menu standards such as garlic and egg soup, followed by trout or chicken in garlic sauce; wine and dessert are included. Open daily. No reservations or credit cards accepted. 10 Calle 18 de Julio, Cuenca (phone: 966-211872). Inexpensive.

San Nicolás – Another place to sample the fixed-price menu of regional specialties.

Try *morturelo,* a lumpy, purple-gray concoction of seasoned partridge, rabbit, and lamb's liver — traditional shepherd's food. Open daily; closed mid-November through mid-December. No reservations. No credit cards accepted. 15 Calle San Pedro, Cuenca (phone: 966-212205 or 966-214539). Inexpensive.

En Route from Cuenca – The itinerary continues southwest from Cuenca, but those with the time to spend an extra day in the area and a desire for a change of scenery — trout streams, spectacular birch and pine trees, Appalachia-like mountains glens, and a variety of out-of-the-ordinary natural sights — may wish to pack a picnic lunch and make a detour to the northeast, into the surrounding Serranía de Cuenca mountain range. To make the 94-mile (150-km) detour, take CU920/921, which begins at the small bridge where the Huécar and Júcar rivers converge, and head north along the Júcar for 13 miles (21 km) to the village of Villalba de la Sierra. Bear sharply left there at the sign for Tragacete–Ciudad Encantada. Approximately 200 yards ahead, bear left again, remaining on CU921. Climb up the mountain for 2½ miles (4 km), park at the souvenir stand, and walk up to the Ventano del Diablo, a natural balcony carved by wind and water erosion, which commands a striking view down the 10-mile-long canyon that the Júcar River has gouged out of its limestone bed. Return to the car, continue upward, and take the well-marked road to the right (CU913) to the Ciudad Encantada (Enchanted City). Here the sights are almost as Disneyesque as the name suggests. Centuries of erosion have sculpted the rock into fanciful shapes that resemble everything from balancing seals to gigantic mushrooms. It takes about 40 minutes to walk from end to end (admission charge).

Continuing along CU921 over the Júcar gorge toward Tragacete, the road is narrow but well graded (there are guard rails only on the sharpest curves, but two-way traffic, thankfully, is almost nonexistent). Pass the reservoir and the trout hatcheries of Uña, and follow the road inland, now some 4,600 feet above sea level. At Tragacete, a popular hunting village, turn left at the sign for Nacimiento del Rio Cuervo and continue another 8 miles (13 km) on the rough road to the rest area and picnic grounds. At the Cuervo's source, streams come trickling in a crystal curtain out of the rock face and down a mossy, juniper-framed cliffside. Hiking paths abound.

After viewing the valley at Vega del Coronado, continue along the same road, which now curves back on itself and leads down the other side of the sierra, even more thickly forested with Scotch pine and holm oak. Follow the signs to Las Majadas. Along the way, the El Hosquillo Game Reserve allows 30 visitors per weekend from mid-October through June. Reservations must be made at least 1 week in advance through the National Conservation Agency (ICONA) office in Cuenca (phone: 966-228022). Tours, consisting of a guided excursion in a Land Rover, turn up wild mountain sheep, ibex, wild boar, mouflon, roe deer, fallow deer, and some of the last brown bears in Europe — a must for those with the time and the interest. Returning to the main road, proceed down the mountain about 6 miles (10 km) to the entrance to Las Majadas, a few acres of parkland where erosion has once again produced natural sculptures that rival those of the Ciudad Encantada. From here, the road emerges from the shadows of the pine and holm oaks and circles back to Villalba de la Sierra, then onto CU921 back to Cuenca.

To resume the itinerary, begin at the intersection in front of the tourist office in Cuenca and follow the signs to N400 for Tarancón and Madrid. After 32 miles (51 km), get off the N400 at the Carracosa del Campo exit, and take the poorly paved road to the monastery of Uclés, which becomes visible after 8 miles (13 km). From the outside, this rectangular, 16th-to-18th-century monastery-fortress, once the headquarters of the Order of Santiago, doesn't quite live up to its billing as the "junior Escorial," though it was in fact designed in part by the same architect who designed Philip II's gloomy retreat. Today, the Uclés monastery serves as a church-run boarding school for boys. While class is in session, the women who cook and clean for their charges permit visitors to look at the interesting baroque fountain in the courtyard (incongruously converted into a basketball court) and at the breathtaking Mudéjar refectory ceiling.

Continue along C720/C700 to the N-III Madrid–Valencia highway heading southeast; get off at the Saelices exit, but stay clear of the town and remain on the same road (CU304) for about 4 more miles (6 km). At this point, a turnoff leads to the low-lying mounds that are the remains of the Roman colony of Segóbriga, which flourished briefly but handsomely under the Claudian emperors. The inhabitants did well enough raising cattle and working the extensive selenite deposits nearby to build a considerable amphitheater and a theater for their leisure-time pursuits. Both are substantially intact and still bear ocher traces of Latin graffiti. A small museum (closed Mondays) displays archaeological finds, but the best pieces excavated here have long since been removed to Cuenca. Still, the Roman thermal baths and the Visigothic cemetery are worth a look.

Return to Saelices and the N-III highway, heading southeast in the direction of Valencia for 30½ miles (49 km) to the town of La Almarcha and the turnoff for N420 south. Here, the hills begin to flatten out and give way to the plains of La Mancha. Just ahead (22½ miles/36 km) is Belmonte, and the must-see castle of the Marqués de Villena, attached to the remnants of the Old City walls. This late-15th-century structure, complete with a drawbridge and dungeon, is of a variety uncommon in Spain, built with Renaissance flair as a fortified palace rather than a simply functional military outpost. The caretaker escorts visitors through the curious triangular precincts of this national monument. Though much has sadly decayed, and the inside patio has been done over with 19th-century brickwork, the Mudéjar ceilings and the extraordinary carved-walnut and inlaid-glass cupola suspended over the main bedroom — it once revolved over the room by means of a clockworks' mechanism — are worthy of inspection. The contemporary collegiate Church of San Bartolomé in the center of town is a fine example of noble Renaissance architectural severity combined with the ornamental lavishness of the Gothic interior, well attested by the alabaster funerary sculptures and grillwork.

Back on N420, the landscape is now flat — fields of grapevines, grain, and melons, or vast horizons of empty plains under endless blue skies. The town of Mota del Cuervo, 10 miles (16 km) beyond Belmonte and aptly called "the balcony of La Mancha," provides a handy base from which to sally forth into Don Quixote's old stomping grounds. At the town's crossroads, take N301 north toward Quintanar de la Orden and proceed 10 miles (16 km) to the tile-encrusted *Venta de Don Quijote,* purported to be the inn where the earnest daydreamer was jocularly dubbed a knight by the locals. Make a left at the intersection here, and proceed 3 miles (5 km) to El Toboso, which has cashed in on its fame as the home of Don Quixote's slatternly sweetheart.

CHECKING IN/EATING OUT: *Mesón El Quijote* – A modern, comfortable Best Western affiliate, 10 miles (16 km) from Belmonte, with 36 air conditioned rooms, a swimming pool, beautiful gardens, and 2 restaurants where regional cuisine is in its glory. Specialties include the famous *pisto manchego,* a sort of ratatouille; *chuletas con salsa diabla* (lamb chops with hot sauce); and partridge and quail in spicy casseroles. Major credit cards accepted. 2 Calle Francisco Costi, Mota del Cuervo (phone: 967-180200; fax: 967-180711). Expensive.

EL TOBOSO: This neat little town has been embellished with plaques citing phrases from the Miguel de Cervantes classic to help visitors retrace the steps of Don Quixote, the fictional knight, and his squire, and remind all of his praise of its civic virtues. The House of Dulcinea (Calle José Antonio; phone: 925-197288), once the home of a local lady of loose morals who supposedly was the inspiration for the Cervantes character (she was known to her customers as *la dulce Ana*, or sweet Annie), has been converted into the so-called *Museo de Amor*. On display are an assortment of regional ethnological relics that could have been associated with the region's most famous personage — that is, if he had ever really existed (open Tuesdays through Saturdays, from 10 AM to 2 PM and from 4 to 6:30 PM; Sundays, mornings only; admission charge). The scallop shell over the entrance to the town's disproportionately large 15th-century late Gothic church, which Don Quixote himself commended, indicates that El Toboso once was under the control of the Knights of Santiago.

En Route from El Toboso – Take the local road south to N420 and head west (if setting out after an overnight in Mota del Cuervo, get on N420 directly). Just ahead are the windmills that in the novel unseated the loony Knight of La Mancha, beginning with the eight stalwart structures standing on the ridge above Campo de Criptana. Follow the pictographic signs pointing the way up through the one-way streets for a closer look. On three of the windmills, the gears and milling mechanisms have been maintained, though there is no schedule to indicate when the sailcloth arms will be revolving. Leaflets available at a tiny tourist office around the corner explain the history and function of these devices — which were, in fact, high-tech innovations imported from the Low Countries at the time Cervantes was writing.

Alcázar de San Juan, 7 miles (11 km) from Campo de Criptana, is a crossroads town totally dependent on an enormous oil refinery, and of more interest to the stomach than to the eye (see *Eating Out*). Turn south on C400 to Tomelloso, 19½ miles (31 km) away, a town floating on a sea of wine — it's said to be the world's number one alcohol-producing municipality — and at Tomelloso, turn sharp right onto the local road to Argamasilla del Alba. Stop here at the church, and if you're lucky enough to find someone to open it up, he or she will point out the portrait of Rodrigo Pacheco, a gentleman of the vicinity whose loss of wits and subsequent odd behavior are said to have set Cervantes to musing, "Now, what if . . ." Ring the bell at 8 Calle Cervantes, the unmarked street at the rear left corner of the church, and a caretaker will come out to unlock the Cueva del Medrano, where Cervantes was tossed in jail in 1597, accused of embezzlement during a disastrous stint as a government tax collector. It was apparently from this subterranean small-town hoosegow — "where every discomfort has a seat and every dismal noise its habitation" — that Cervantes passed the time by letting his imagination beget what he called the child of his "sterile and ill-cultivated genius," the literary masterpiece of Spain's Golden Age.

Continue along the local road to Manzanares, 24½ miles (39 km) from Tomelloso. Trucks carrying sugar beets and poultry feed make the going very slow, but the situation improves after the road skirts the silos and melon sheds of Manzanares. Follow the signs for Ciudad Real to reach N430 west, which intersects with N420. Follow the latter for for 2 miles (3 km), passing through the center of the wine-producing town of Daimiel, then take the turnoff for C417, which leads to Almagro, some 15½ miles (25 km) to the south.

EATING OUT: *Caso Paco* – A lunch stop favored by truckers making the all-day haul between Andalusia and central Spain. In addition to regional dishes that will be new to most travelers, there are a few properly prepared fish choices on the menu. Closed Mondays. No reservations. MasterCard and Visa accepted. 5 Avenida Alvarez Guerra, Alcázar de San Juan (phone: 926-540606). Moderate to inexpensive.

ALMAGRO: The landscape is pure Kansas, but visitors will not find a Renaissance jewel of a town like this one anywhere within wishing distance of Wichita. The Order of Calatrava, the oldest and most important Spanish knightly order, established its headquarters here after winning the battle of Las Navas de Tolosa in 1212; the order's squiggly cross emblem can be seen on nearly every one of the historic buildings in town. The 16th-century Monastery of the Assumption of Calatrava, now commonly called the Convento de los Padres Dominicanos, located on the main street, Ejido de Calatrava, should not be missed (open from 9 AM to 2 PM and from 4 to 7 PM; closed Sunday afternoons; phone: 926-860230). The friars in residence happily escort visitors around the extraordinary Renaissance cloister, which surrounds pillars of solid Carrara marble, and the attached Gothic church.

If there appears something distinctly odd about the green, glassed-in balconies propped up by the stone pillars of the elongated 14th-century Plaza Mayor, it's the southern German influence of the Fugger dynasty of banker-princes, who made Almagro their Iberian branch office during the 16th-century New World gold boom that helped keep Holy Roman Emperor Charles V solvent. Their palace, the Palacio de los Fúcares has a stone staircase and assembly hall worth seeing (Arzibispo Cañizares; open daily except Saturdays from noon to 2 PM and from 5 to 9 PM).

Midway along the Plaza Mayor's south portico is the entrance to Almagro's unique *Corral de Comedias,* a theater dating back to the 16th century's Golden Age of Spanish drama. That it has survived at all is thanks to the fact that it was bricked up and forgotten until 1954. If there's nobody on duty to show off the 2-tiered, half-timbered stage, surrounded by linteled galleries and the pit for the groundlings, the tourist office (5 Mayor de Carnicerías; phone: 926-860717) will provide an escort. During the annual *Festival de Teatro Clásico,* held during the first 2 weeks of September, theater companies from all over the Spanish-speaking world muster forces on its creaky stage and perform classics by Calderón de la Barca, Lope de Vega, and their foreign contemporaries such as Shakespeare and Molière. Tickets go on sale in mid-August and sell out quickly. (They also can be reserved through the tourist office.)

A stroll around the heraldic mansions and palaces of the town's oldest quarter offers strong indication that the women of Almagro continue to honor the local tradition of lace making. It's not uncommon to find practitioners sitting in doorways, wooden bobbins flying and clacking in their hands. There are also a few lace shops in the Plaza Mayor, where the markup is negligible. For fine table linen, handkerchiefs, and towels at bargain prices, call on the home/shop of María Carmen Manzano (24 Calle Dominicas; phone: 926-860908). Families from all over Spain also travel to Almagro to stock up on pickled baby eggplants, a regional delicacy packed in the earthenware jugs that are laid out on display in front of every shop in town.

CHECKING IN: *Parador de Almagro* – Formerly a 16th-century convent, this is one of the most charming restoration efforts in the entire *parador* network. The 56 air conditioned rooms are built around no fewer than 16 galleried inner patios. The building abounds in decorative touches that recall its original functions, and its popularity often exceeds its room capacity, so make reservations well in advance. The restaurant is especially good, featuring imaginative variations worked up from regional raw materials, fabulous desserts, and an excellent selection of *reservas* — the *parador* takes top pick from the 25 million liters produced annually at the wine cooperative of nearby Daimiel. Ronda de San Francisco, Almagro (phone: 926-860100). Expensive to moderate.

EATING OUT: *Restaurante Calatrava* – A dining alternative to the *parador,* featuring good, home-cooked Castilian dishes, and specializing in the traditional roast lamb and kid. Closed Monday evenings. Reservations unnecessary. Visa accepted. 7 Calle Bolaños, Almagro (phone: 926-860185). Moderate.

En Route from Almagro – Backtrack north on C417. Upón reaching Daimiel, take the turnoff on the left for the Tablas de Daimiel Nature Reserve. This road crosses the 4-lane N420, then follows a bumpy 7-mile (11-km) path out into the marshlands. After seeing so much of flat and dry old La Mancha, the vast shallow lagoons formed by the confluence of the Guadiana and Gigüela rivers here come as a surprise. Equally surprising is the abundance of migratory waterfowl, notably herons, kingfishers, mallards, terns, cranes, and gulls. Unrestricted hunting and clandestine drainage to irrigate the surrounding farmland almost destroyed the lagoons and their nesting nomads until the area was declared a protected reserve in 1973. Four hiking trails with wooden bridges spanning the bulrushes, reeds, and tiny islands that emerge from the fluvial floodlands have been laid out, allowing for walks that range from 1 to 3 hours. Camouflaged observation posts along the way serve as resting points and allow for close inspection of the winged residents. A free map and helpful English-language brochure are available at the reserve's entrance lodge.

Head back toward Daimiel on the old bumpy road and pick up N420 north to Madrid on the outskirts of town. (Those wanting to stock up on Castillo de Daimiel wine at giveaway prices, however, should stop in at the co-op outlet in town, on Paseo del Carmen.) Puerto Lápice, another crossroads town, lies 21 miles (34 km) ahead; it has possibly made a bit too much of its mention in *Don Quixote* — as the countless signs and statues attest. Follow the N-IV highway, from here on into Madrid, making brief detours from it as required. Ten and a half miles (17 km) north of Puerto Lápice, the highway slices through Madridejos, where a sharp left onto C400 toward Toledo leads to Consuegra, another 4½ miles (7 km) down the road.

EATING OUT: *Venta del Quijote* – Situated in a former farmhouse complete with wooden beams, cartwheels, and huge earthenware wine tuns, this restaurant offers an extensive menu of exceptionally prepared Manchegan dishes and choice wines. A nice patio makes outdoor dining a possibility, weather permitting. The English translations on the menu will probably prove more baffling than enlightening, however. Open daily. Reservations unnecessary. Major credit cards accepted. Carretera Madrid–Cádiz (N-IV), Puerto Lápice (phone: 926-576110). Moderate.

CONSUEGRA: The seven windmills lined up here are hollow shells of their former selves, unlike those in Campo de Criptana, but they are placed in a far more dramatic — and photogenic — setting, high on a cliffside overlooking the entire town and next to the ruins of a windswept 14th-century castle (Don Quixote did not, however, sleep here!). Consuegra is famous for its production of those expensive and irreplaceable reddish threads that make a good paella worth wolfing down. To get just 1 pound of saffron together, it is necessary to pull the stigmas from over 100,000 crocuses. This shortcut to eyestrain is what sustains the economy of Consuegra, evident by the haystack-size heaps of purple petals discarded after an autumn harvest. The *Saffron Festival* falls on the last Sunday in October, complete with folk dancing, wine tasting, and bullfighting, and provides the locals with a chance to whoop it up a bit after the pickers — almost all of whom are women — have finished their laborious task. Unfortunately, visitors can't buy saffron here — it's all sold to out-of-town dealers who toast and package the finished product elsewhere.

En Route from Consuegra – Head back to Madridejos and, once again, take the N-IV highway going north. Make a quick stop in Tembleque, 16 miles (26 km) north of Madridejos, for a glance at the remarkable Plaza Mayor, a graceful, 2-tiered arcade of old beams and plaster, its one entrance crowned by the most un-Spanish-looking 3-story, peaked, gable-like structure. In a town with little else going for it nowadays, if ever, the stunning plaza leaves a most unforgettable impression. The N-IV highway leads next to Ocaña, 19½ miles (31 km) from Tembleque, and then to Aranjuez, another 10 miles (16 km) along (see *Madrid Region*, DIRECTIONS, for more on this town, a favored residence of the Catholic Monarchs and later Spanish royalty). Then traffic jams become a common reminder that Madrid is only 29½ miles (47 km) away. But long before entering the Puerta del Sol, the gruesome industrial suburbs of the capital's southern outskirts might well make the traveler pause — and think about turning around and going back to do it all over again.

Levante: Valencia to Murcia

Almond blossoms and white beaches, verdant orchards and stern mountain ranges, palm trees and sparkling blue water, and at least 300 days of sunshine a year — is it any wonder that the Mediterranean coast south of Valencia has become one of Europe's most popular vacation areas? Or that thousands of expatriates of all nationalities have made it their home?

Roughly speaking, Spain's Levante is the coastal fringe bridging the gap between Catalonia and Andalusia. It includes the three provinces that make up the autonomous community of Valencia (Castellón, Valencia, and Alicante) and the single-province autonomous community of Murcia. From end to end, it is highlighted by striking scenery, lively fiestas, unusual historical sights, and — given the fact that this is the market garden of Spain — distinctive food.

It is the middle section, the Costa Blanca (White Coast), which lies in the province of Alicante, that is the most popular. Every summer, hundreds of thousands of Spaniards and other Europeans flock here to bask in the sunshine and enjoy a wide range of sporting and entertainment activities. Resorts have mushroomed where there were only fishing villages and deserted beaches barely 25 years ago. Those with an aversion to mass tourism need not worry, however, as the region caters to all tastes — from the sophisticated to the mundane. But although it is easy to escape the crowds, it's not advisable to plan a vacation here during July and August, simply because that's when everyone else in the world does — or at least it seems that way. Spring and autumn are fine times to visit; and rainy winter days are usually followed by weeks of dazzling sunshine.

To the people of the Levante, the flood of tourists hardly causes a raised eyebrow, for the region has been a target of invaders throughout its long history. Paleolithic people lived in caves here. Three thousand years ago, the Phoenicians arrived to trade and settle. Later, the Greeks established the colony of Akra Leuka (White Headland) near Alicante. The Carthaginians established a naval base on the site of present-day Cartagena, and after them, the Romans stayed in the region for several centuries. But it was the Moors, who arrived during the 8th century and ruled the region as part of Al-Andalus, who had the most lasting influence, converting the arid but fertile plain between the treeless mountains and the sea into lush *huertas* (orchards and vegetable farms) by introducing an ingenious irrigation system. Remains of *norias,* the giant Moorish water-raising wheels, can still be found on the *huertas* where today, citrus fruits flourish, and thousands of tons of oranges and lemons are exported annually — not to mention dates, tomatoes, and a wealth of other fruits of the earth.

When the Córdoba caliphate collapsed in 1031, warring local leaders struggled for supremacy, and several *taifas,* or kingdoms, were formed. From the early 11th century, the independent Moorish kingdom of Valencia dominated a vast slice of the coast, from Almería to the Ebro River, but the region was racked by war. Toward the end of the century, Spain's legendary warrior El Cid fought long campaigns and wrested it from the Moors, albeit only briefly (1094–99). Only in 1238 was James I of Aragon able to add it to his Christian domain, although it was administered as a separate kingdom until it was added, with the rest of the Aragonese lands, to the kingdom of Castile in the late 15th century. The kingdom of Murcia had a checkered history, at one time acting as intermediary between the Moors and the Christians. Murcia finally came under the rule of the kingdom of Castile in 1243, 5 years after Valencia was conquered by Aragon, but it continued for 2 more centuries as a separately administered kingdom. Today, although the one-province region of Murcia and the much larger region of Valencia are both considered part of the Levante, part of one agricultural land of plenty and both noted for fine beaches (Murcia is attempting to attract more people to its Costa Cálida — Warm Coast), the regions have distinct characteristics, including different languages.

Although Castilian Spanish is the language of Murcia, the language commonly spoken in the region of Valencia is a local version of Catalan, known variously as *valenciano* in Valencia and as *alicantino* in Alicante. Anyone speaking Castilian, French, or any other Latin language will not find this too difficult to read, and anyone attempting to master a few spoken phrases will certainly please the native residents. "Good morning" is *bon dia* and "please" is *per favor*. Place-names often appear in both languages — for example, Alicante is Alacant in the local language; Elche is Elx. But everybody speaks Castilian, too, and since the Costa Blanca is such a popular vacation spot for British tourists, it is easier in some areas to find a speaker of English than of any other tongue.

Gastronomically speaking, this is paella paradise. Because rice is grown here, it forms the basis for scores of dishes. *Paella valenciana* contains both meat and fish, including octopus and mussels, whereas *paella marinera* contains only fish. *Arroz con costra* is prepared with pork and sausage, topped off with a half-dozen eggs. Squid and octopus are also popular local delicacies. Moorish influence is evident when it comes to desserts, with such sticky sweet treats as *turrón* (nougat) and glazed walnuts. *Horchata de chufa,* a chilled mixture of *chufas* (earth almonds), cinnamon, sugar, and water, is a favorite drink. Some good wines are also produced in the region, particularly the hearty jumilla and yecla reds in Murcia.

Many who travel to the region time their journeys to coincide with one of the many reenactments of the epic struggles between Moors and Christians, some of which are the most colorful, exuberant fiestas to be found anywhere in the world. All along the coast, towns and villages spend the entire year preparing for their annual *Moros y Cristianos* battles. Sumptuous Oriental and medieval costumes are worn by the participants as they parade through the streets, each group trying to outdo the other. Lasting several days, these fiestas usually feature the "Moors" capturing a "Christian" stronghold, only to be ousted amid a deafening fusillade of "gunfire." Altogether, more than 70,000 people take part in these historic fiestas and, amid the general revelry, some don't sleep for an entire week. The towns of Alcoy (April 22), Elda (first week in June), and Villajoyosa (July 25), all in the province of Alicante, stage particularly spectacular make-believe battles.

The route outlined below begins in Valencia (for a complete report on this city and its sights, hotels, and restaurants, see *Valencia,* THE CITIES), and heads south to the gracious seaport city of Alicante and on to the inland city of Murcia, with a spur to Cartagena back on the coast before veering southwest toward Granada. From Valencia to Murcia (158 miles/255 km), it's a fast trip if the four-lane A-7 *autopista,* which runs much of the way, is followed. From Murcia, it's 179 miles (286 km) to Granada, over mountainous terrain, most of which is spanned by the much-improved N301 and N342 highways. Those who can't wait to see the glories of the Alhambra can do the Valencia–Granada run in 1 day, but there are abundant reasons to spend at least 4 to 5 days on the journey. By taking the A-7, which runs from Valencia to Alicante, and exiting at appropriate points along the coast, a good deal of time can be saved. For a more leisurely drive, take the N332 from Valencia to Alicante (it follows largely the same coastal route as the A-7). From Alicante to Murcia, the road is the N340.

Along the way, expect to pay $110 or more for a double room in a hotel listed as expensive, $70 to $110 in those marked moderate, and under $60 in an inexpensive one. Restaurants listed as expensive charge around $70 or more for a dinner for two, including wine; a moderate establishment, $45 to $65; and an inexpensive one, under $40.

En Route from Valencia – The most interesting route out of Valencia follows the coast, past long sandy beaches, orange groves, and large rice fields (harvesting, now mechanized, takes place in October). Head south on the A-V15 highway, and follow the signs to El Saler, 6 miles (10 km) south of Valencia. Just past it is La Albufera, Spain's largest lake, renowned for its wildlife and freshwater fish. A pine-fringed sandbar holds back the sea on the left. Follow the local road on the right for 2 miles (3 km) to El Palmar, a village of thatch-roofed cottages on the lake edge, where rustic eateries serve *all i pebre,* a local specialty of eels fried in garlic. Return to A-V15 and proceed to Cullera, 25 miles (40 km) from Valencia; the town is hard to miss, since giant manmade white letters spell out its name on the rocky hill rising above it. A small port town on the Júcar River, Cullera has been dwarfed by dozens of modern apartment blocks on the beaches toward the lighthouse, but it offers magnificent views from its castle ruins. Continue south, via N332 or A-7, some 18 miles (29 km) to Gandía.

EATING OUT: *Les Mouettes* – Enjoy French delicacies such as oyster ragout with leeks and truffles, as well as wines from Bordeaux and the Loire, on a pleasant terrace overlooking the beach (and high-rises). This place is famous among *valencianos* and has earned a Michelin star. Closed Mondays and December 15 through February 15. Reservations advised. Major credit cards accepted. Subida al Santuario del Castillo, Cullera (phone: 96-172-0010). Expensive to moderate.

GANDÍA: A modern town with some fine buildings, Gandía is set inland, surrounded by rice fields and groves of oranges — which are shipped from the harbor formed by the mouth of the Serpis River. It once was the capital of a duchy, which was given by King Ferdinand to the Borgia family (known in Spain as the Borjas) in 1485. Alexander VI, the infamous Borgia pope, father of the equally infamous Cesare and Lucrezia Borgia, was born in Játiva, 25 miles inland, but a later member of the family, the fourth duke, who restored the family's good name by becoming a Jesuit, founding Jesuit missions in the New World and eventually being named a saint — St. Francis Borgia — was born in the family mansion. This, the 16th-century Palacio Ducal (Calle Santo Duque; phone: 96-287-1203), offers an impressive mix of Gothic and Renaissance styles, with a fine patio and staircase, as well as beautifully decorated apartments. Now the property of the Jesuit Order, the building can be visited only on guided tours (conducted in Spanish only), which begin daily at 11 AM and noon and at 6 and 7 PM (May through October; in winter they begin at 4:30 and 5:30 PM); admission charge. Gandía's tourist office is on the Avenida Marqués de Campo (phone: 96-287-4544). Three miles (5 km) from the town lies its port, El Grau, and a vast sandy beach that has succumbed to extensive tourist development. It comes to life at *Easter* and in summer, and most of the hotels are located here.

CHECKING IN: *Bayren I* – Like most others in the area, this comfortable beachfront establishment caters primarily to Spanish vacationers. All 164 rooms are air conditioned, and there is a swimming pool, tennis courts, and in summer, live music and dancing in the gardens. Closed for a month in late November and early December. Paseo de Neptuno, Playa de Gandía (phone: 96-284-0300; fax: 96-284-0653; telex: 61549). Expensive.

Bayren II – This equally comfortable but less-expensive sister of *Bayren I* is just behind its namesake, and offers 125 air conditioned rooms and tennis courts. Closed from November through February. 19 Calle Majorca, Playa de Gandía (phone: 96-284-0700). Moderate.

EATING OUT: *As de Oros* – On the lengthy Gandía beachfront, this eatery is a shrine to the great national obsession for fresh seafood. Sit back and enjoy everything from juicy prawns to succulent squid and grilled mullet, washed down by some of the country's best wines. Fast service is provided by an army of waiters. Closed Mondays and 2 weeks in January. Reservations unnecessary. Major credit cards accepted. Edificio Bonaire, Paseo de Neptuno, Playa de Gandía (phone: 96-284-0239). Expensive.

En Route from Gandía – It's a run of about 20 minutes down the A-7 into the province of Alicante and the pleasant old port town of Denia (take exit 62 at Ondara). Travelers in the mood for an excursion or seeking an entertaining diversion for young children should detour to the *Vergel Safari Park* by taking N332 north at Ondara and proceeding 4 miles (6 km) before turning left (west) onto C3311 toward Pego for the park. Elephants, tigers, zebras, and lions, as well as "singing" dolphins and roller-skating parrots, are on hand (open daily, from 10 AM to 5:30 PM; phone: 96-575-0285; admission charge). To reach Denia from Ondara, take C3311 east.

DENIA: Thanks to its mild climate and excellent beach, Denia has prospered from tourism, yet it has retained its old charm. Founded by the Phoenicians, the town takes its name from a Roman Temple of Diana. The Visigoths made it an episcopal seat, and it later served as the capital of a Moorish kingdom. The 18th-century castle or citadel perched above the town was the scene of a bitter siege during the Napoleonic Wars, when French troops held it for 5 months. Within lies the *Museo Arqueológico,* which contains some noteworthy Roman and Arabic relics unearthed in the area (open daily, from 10 AM to 1 PM and from 3 to 6 PM; admission charge). There are also some interesting 18th-century buildings in the Plaza de los Caídos, including the Church of Santa María and the Town Hall.

Denia is a good base for excursions. There is year-round service to the island of Ibiza via a passenger and vehicle ferry, which departs every evening at 10 o'clock and takes 5 hours; from *Easter* through summer, a passengers-only ferry departs at 7:30 AM and takes 3½ hours. For those in a rush, afternoon hydrofoils make the journey in 90 minutes. Contact *Flebasa* (at the port; phone: 96-578-4011) for details. Another pleasant way to see the Costa Blanca is on the narrow-gauge railroad that runs from Denia to Alicante. The trip takes 2 hours and 20 minutes and the first train leaves at 6:45 AM from Denia. At press time, trains were leaving from the station on Calle Manuel Lattur (phone: 96-578-0445). A new station is due to be completed this year, however, and is located on the same street but farther out of town. For up-to-date information, contact the Denia Tourist Office (9 Patricio Ferrándiz; phone: 96-578-0957).

CHECKING IN: *Los Angeles* – Located in a tranquil setting on an excellent sandy beach, 3 miles (5 km) north of town. All 60 rooms are air conditioned, and facilities include tennis courts. Closed November through mid-March. 649 Playa de las Marinas, Denia (phone: 96-578-0458). Moderate.

EATING OUT: *El Pegolí* – A favorite with seafood lovers. Gaze out from the spick-and-span dining room or the outdoor terrace at the blue Mediterranean and the rocky coastline below while enjoying one of two set menus, which usually include a salad, a plate full of shellfish, a well-grilled fish, wine, bread, and dessert. Closed Sunday evenings and from mid-December to mid-January. Reservations advised. American Express and Visa accepted. Playa de Les Rotes, Denia (phone: 96-578-1035). Moderate.

En Route from Denia – Head south, following the coast road, which offers magnificent views. As it corkscrews up from Denia over the San Antonio headland and winds down through almond trees to Jávea (Xabia in *valenciano*), look for the old windmills that once ground wheat.

JÁVEA: Situated on one of the Costa Blanca's finer bays, between two capes — Cabo de San Antonio and the Cabo San Martín (the latter just around the coast from Cabo de la Nao), this resort town consists of an Old Quarter with narrow streets and stone houses that stands on a rise inland from the fishing and pleasure port. Watchtowers, surviving city walls and gateways, and an old castle contribute to its medieval look. Worth a visit is the *Municipal Museum* (1 Calle Primicias; phone: 96-579-1098), built by King Philip III during the early 17th century. It contains Roman and Punic remains, ceramics, and traditional crafts (open Tuesdays through Sundays, from 10 AM to 1 PM; also open from 5 to 8 PM from June through September; admission charge). The great bulk of Montgó, rising 2,465 feet, shelters Jávea from winter blasts, and the surrounding area has experienced a development boom; thousands of villas have joined the vines and almond trees along the attractive coast of rocky headlands and bays. Jávea's Tourist Office is in the port area (24 Plaza Almirante Bastarreche; phone: 96-579-0736).

CHECKING IN: *Bahía Vista* – A secluded setting on a pine-covered headland 5 miles (8 km) southeast of Jávea proper, with beautiful views over the sea. British run, so there are no language problems, it has 17 rooms, a swimming pool, and a bowling green, plus a restaurant serving international food. Portichol, Cabo la Nao, Jávea (phone: 96-577-0461). Moderate.

Parador Costa Blanca – On Jávea's beautiful bay, 2½ miles (4 km) southeast of the town proper, this is an ideal base from which to explore the area. All 65 rooms are air conditioned; each has a mini-bar and a balcony overlooking the beach. Other facilities include a swimming pool, gardens, and a nearby boat dock. The restaurant features regional food. 2 Playa del Arenal, Jávea (phone: 96-579-0200; fax: 96-579-0308; telex: 66914). Moderate.

EATING OUT: *Chez Angel* – The emphasis here is on French cooking, served in a friendly atmosphere, although it is located in a rather drab shopping center (just under 2 miles/3 km southeast of the Old Quarter.) Try the onion soup and *tournedos calvados,* or Provençal-style lamb. Closed Tuesdays and December 20 through January 20. Reservations unnecessary. No credit cards accepted. Carretera Cabo la Nao, Centro Comercial Jávea Park, Jávea (phone: 96-579-2723). Moderate.

Turpins – Just opposite the *parador* and, therefore, handy for anyone staying there. Stuffed peppers and Dijon chicken are especially recommended dishes on a menu that features international cooking. Closed Sundays and from December 20 through January. Reservations unnecessary. No credit cards accepted. 4 Playa del Arenal, Jávea (phone: 96-579-0713). Inexpensive.

En Route from Jávea – The A134 runs inland to join N332 near Gata de Gorgos, which bills itself as the "Bazaar of the Costa Blanca." The shops along its main street offer baskets, mats, and bags of bamboo, willow, palm leaf, and esparto, some of them made locally. In the nearby hills are the picturesque vineyards of the *Maserof Wine Club* (11 La Mar, Denia), whose members own individual vines and each year receive the wine made from their own grapes. Peter Pateman, the bearded, Falstaffian Englishman who founded the club, loves to talk wine and welcomes visitors to his bodega on Sundays. To reach it from Gata, turn off N332 onto the road to Lliber and Jalón. In Jalón, turn left onto the road signposted Bernia; Maserof is 3 miles (5 km) along on the left. It's best to call the club's Denia office (phone: 96-578-1887) first or write to them at the address above.

Back on N332, the route continues south past eroded ocher hills, the azure sea, and countless almond trees, a breathtaking sight when they are in bloom in February. Just ahead, huge apartment blocks have blossomed on the beaches in the vicinity of Calpe. Fortunately, however, developers have been pushed back from the foot of Peñón de Ifach, now a natural park. Resembling the Rock of Gibraltar, the Peñón soars to a height of over 1,000 feet; a hike up to the top takes about an hour, but no one suffering from vertigo should try it — somebody topples off every year. Take a sweater, as it can be breezy up there.

Continue on N332 to Altea, a charming hillside town perched below the rugged Sierra de Bernia, 20 miles (32 km) from Gata.

ALTEA: The name comes from the Moorish "Altaya," meaning "health for all," and many visitors proclaim this the Costa Blanca's prettiest town. A fortress under the Hapsburgs, it now has modern buildings lining the waterfront, but fortunately, the Old Quarter remains. Narrow streets climb steeply up to the parish church with its blue tile dome, characteristic of churches in the Levante region. In recent years, a number of artists of various nationalities have made their homes here, no doubt seeking inspiration from the surrounding beauty. One of the more pleasant ways to spend a summer evening is to sit in the church square, (Plaza de Calvo Sotelo), high above the Mediterranean, sipping a cool drink and watching the passersby and the stallholders selling their crafts. If you're here on a Sunday afternoon, watch out for *pilota de carrer,* a fiercely competitive game played in the nearby streets by men who whack a small hard ball at one another with their bare hands. Altea's Tourist Office is on the seafront, Paseo Marítimo (phone: 96-584-2301).

EATING OUT: *La Costera* – Swiss specialties are served with a unique flair in this bizarre Old Quarter eatery. Rodolfo, the owner, puts on a hilarious, uninhibited musical show nightly, featuring everything from cossack dancing to flamenco. Open for dinner only. Closed Wednesdays. Reservations advised.

MasterCard and Visa accepted. 8 Costera del Mestre de Música, Altea (phone: 96-584-0230). Moderate.

Bahía – Functional decor and friendly service highlight this family-run establishment, a popular lunchtime favorite, situated between the highway and the sea. Specialties include a variety of tasty rice dishes and excellent *zarzuela* (fish stew). Closed January, *Christmas,* and winter Saturdays and evenings. Reservations advised on weekends. No credit cards accepted. Carretera Alicante, Altea (phone: 96-584-0011). Moderate to inexpensive.

En Route from Altea – Follow N332 south toward Benidorm, 7 miles (11 km) away. If there's time for a pleasant, half-day excursion before entering the city limits, however, make a right turn onto C3318 and drive 7 miles (11 km) to the village of Polop. Once there, turn left onto the small local road that swoops 9 miles (14 km) over the mountains to Guadalest, a medieval village that is one of Spain's most spectacular — and impregnable — fortresses. Built by the Moors, it perches on a crag, accessible only through a 50-foot tunnel cut through the rock. Inside are old women who sit knitting, souvenir shops, and magnificent views of the surrounding countryside. Returning toward the coast, stop in Callosa, locally renowned for its production of honey. Just off C3318, to the north, are the spectacular Algar waterfalls, a good place to cool off on a hot day. Sit in one of the rock pools under a cascade of refreshing water, spilling down some 50 feet from the rocks above. Several of the nearby restaurants have pools, too.

BENIDORM: This is the place for anyone who wants to take a day off from Spain. Formerly a simple fishing village, it has become an international resort town (almost everyone speaks English), cluttered with high-rise buildings and catering mainly to those on inexpensive package tours. Pensioners from all over Europe flock here in winter, and teenagers of all ages take over the place during the summer. Despite its image, Benidorm can still be fun, provided visitors are willing to enter into its easygoing spirit. There are two fine beaches (topless), and the town is immaculately maintained. Jousting tournaments, dog races, discotheques, and bars (the nightlife tends to get a bit wild) are some of the more active attractions. The huge *Benidorm Palace* nightclub (Calle Diputación; phone: 96-585-1661) is the Costa Blanca's answer to the *Folies-Bergères,* complete with bare-breasted dancers and flamenco, while the *Casino Costa Blanca* (Carretera Benidorm–Villajoyosa, N332, Km 115, Villajoyosa; phone: 96-589-0700) packs in gamblers by the busload. This low, off-white building on the main highway between Benidorm and Villajoyosa offers every gambling adventure from roulette to blackjack (admission charge; a passport also is required), and also boasts a small but impressive art gallery. Benidorm's Tourist Office is at 16 Avenida Martínez Alejos (phone: 96-585-3224).

CHECKING IN: *Gran Delfín* – A first-rate establishment on the quieter, southern beach, often busy, but far from the crowded mayhem found at some of Benidorm's other hotels. The 87 spacious and comfortable rooms are air conditioned; there also is a swimming pool, tennis courts, lovely tropical gardens, and a good restaurant. Closed October to *Easter.* Playa de Poniente, La Cala, Benidorm (phone: 96-585-3400; fax: 96-585-3400). Expensive.

Don Pancho – Right in town, the 251 rooms in this popular high-rise are air conditioned, comfortably furnished, and have individual balconies. There also is a swimming pool, lighted tennis courts, and gardens. 39 Avenida del Mediterráneo, Benidorm (phone: 96-585-2950; fax: 96-586-7779; telex: 66630). Moderate.

EATING OUT: *I Fratelli* – Elegant candlelit dining, intimate alcoves, an outdoor patio, and an Italian atmosphere — this is an unexpected find in Benidorm. The pasta is homemade; try the veal marsala with *tagliatelle,* or the duck *à l'orange.* Closed November. Reservations necessary. Major credit cards accepted. 21 Calle Orts Llorca, Benidorm (phone: 96-585-3979). Expensive.

La Pérgola – Masses of greenery give a refreshing air to this restaurant slotted into a cliff. But the dazzling view of Benidorm Bay from the terrace is its most outstanding feature. The international menu includes Basque and French dishes and delicious desserts. Closed December through February. Reservations advised. American Express and Visa accepted. Edificio Coblanca, Calle 25, Barrio Rincón de Loix, Benidorm (phone: 96-583-3800). Expensive.

En Route from Benidorm – Once again, pick up N332 and continue 6 miles (10 km) south to Villajoyosa, a fishing town surrounded by fruit trees and olive groves. The narrow streets of the Old Town lead down to a pleasant palm-lined promenade and houses with colorful, sun-bleached façades. Continue toward Alicante, which is 27½ miles (44 km) from Benidorm; 5 miles (8 km) short of the city, at the small village of San Juan, an opportunity presents itself for a half-day excursion to the Canalobre Caves: Turn right onto N340, and follow the signs for A183, which leads to the village of Busot. The caves are 4½ miles (7 km) beyond, in the stark Cabeco d'Or Mountains. Well-lit walkways lead through vast caverns filled with giant stalagmites and stalactites. The caves are open daily, April through September, from 10:30 AM to 8:30 PM; October through March, from 11 AM to 6:30 PM. Afterward, return toward Busot, but take the first right on the local road to Jijona, noted for its production of *turrón* (nougat), eaten by the ton throughout Spain during the *Christmas* season. *El Lobo* factory (62 Calle Alcoy; phone: 96-561-0225) has a visitors' area, where the tooth-wrenching but delicious product can be sampled (open Mondays through Fridays, from 9:30 AM to 1 PM and 4 to 8 PM). From Jijona, proceed back to San Juan on N340 south and pick up N332 for the remaining drive to Alicante.

CHECKING IN: *El Montíboli* – Located about 2 miles (3 km) south of Villajoyosa, this is an ideal rest stop, safely away from the hubbub found farther north along the coast. It sits on a headland, with magnificent views over the sea, a swimming pool, a private beach, tennis courts, and a well-regarded restaurant (reservations advised). All of the 52 spacious rooms are air conditioned and have mini-bars. Major credit cards accepted. Carretera Benidorm-Alicante (N332), Km 108, Villajoyosa (phone: 96-589-0250; fax: 96-589-3857; telex: 68288).

ALICANTE: This provincial capital (pop. 265,000), capital of the Costa Blanca resort area, is a gracious Mediterranean city dominated by the Castillo Santa Bárbara, which glowers down from a hilltop. Long before the present tourist boom, Alicante was a fashionable wintering place, thanks to its mild climate. Around 200 BC, the Romans had a settlement here known as Lucentum. The same settlement, during 500 years of Moorish rule, was known as Al-Akant. In more recent times, Alicante has been an important port, exporting wine, raisins, and other agricultural products. Palm trees and arid surrounding hills give a hint of Africa to the city, an impression that is strengthened around the port area by the sight of Algerian women in caftans and Senegalese peddlers offering their wares. One of the greatest pleasures is to stroll along the Explanada de España, the promenade that fronts the harbor — an ideal place to relax, sip a drink, and listen to the city band on Sunday mornings. (Don't gaze too intently at the seafront paving, however. The beautiful wavy pattern in marble mosaic may disturb your balance.)

Alicante is a modern city of wide boulevards and numerous shops, but it does have an Old Quarter, a labyrinth of narrow streets lying on the lower slope of the Santa Bárbara hill. And despite the hordes of tourists who alight here to soak up the sun along the local beaches, Alicante remains surprisingly Spanish in character.

The Castillo Santa Bárbara, whose foundations date back 2,200 years, is Alicante's main attraction and should be a sightseer's first stop. The Carthaginians, the Romans, and the Moors each had a base here, before the Spanish kings took over and expanded the structure. What survives is primarily from the 13th to 16th centuries. To reach the castle, walk along Paseo de Gómiz, which continues northeast along the beach from the Explanada, to the 660-foot tunnel penetrating the rock; an elevator takes visitors up to see the dungeons, moats, and battlements which offer splendid views over the city and coast. The castle is open mid-June through September, Mondays through Fridays from 9 AM to 9 PM, Saturdays from 9 AM to 2 PM; October through mid-June, Mondays through Fridays from 9 AM to 7:30 PM, Saturdays from 9 AM to 2 PM. Admission charge.

In the Old Quarter, the *Museo de Arte Siglo XX* (Museum of 20th-Century Art), also known as the *Museo de la Asegurada,* in a fine stone building (3 Plaza de Santa María; phone: 96-521-4578 or 96-521-0022), contains some impressive modern art, with sculptures, paintings, and etchings by the likes of Picasso, Dalí, and Tápies (open Tuesdays through Saturdays from 10 AM to 1 PM and from 5 to 8 PM, Sundays from 10 AM to 1 PM; admission charge). The Iglesia de Santa María, almost opposite the museum, has a wonderful 18th-century baroque façade, although the church, remodeled more than once, dates back to a much earlier period and was built on the site of a mosque.

Head toward the center of town along Calle Jorge Juan to the Ayuntamiento (City Hall), a 17th-to-18th-century palace with a magnificently ornate façade. The rococo chapel and some of the baroque rooms are open to visitors in the mornings (ask the caretaker to open them). Note the brass plaque on the pillar of the main stairway; it's the sea level benchmark from which all of Spain's altitude measurements are calculated. Between the Ayuntamiento and the modern Rambla de Méndez Núñez — which is at the edge of the Old Quarter and is the city's main throughfare — is Alicante's cathedral, San Nicolás (Calle Peñalva), built during the 17th century on the site of a mosque and dedicated to the city's patron saint, Nicholas of Bari. A national monument open during services, it has a severe Renaissance style, with beautifully carved gilded altars. The pedestrians-only Calle Mayor, which runs behind the Ayuntamiento to the Rambla, and the side streets off it, are full of fascinating small shops selling typically Spanish gifts, leatherwear, pottery, and antiques. *Turrones 1880* (9 Calle Mayor; phone: 96-521-9281), which has its own factory and museum at nearby Jijona, proudly boasts that its nougat is the most expensive of all — "because we use only the best almonds and honey." Up a sidestreet from the seafront, *Estudio Rita* (Calle Capitán Meca; phone: 96-520-3404) sells original designs in stoneware, made on the premises.

On Tuesday and Saturday mornings, the *Mercadillo,* a lively open-air market, is held along the Paseo de Campoamor, beyond the Old Quarter to the north of the Plaza de España and the bullring. The *Teatro Principal* (Calle Teatro, 2 blocks west of the Rambla) has concerts and musicals during the winter season, but was closed at press time for renovations. The theater is expected to open again early this year. In summer, nightlife centers on the disco-pubs of the Playa de San Juan, the long beach north of town. Alicante's own local beach, El Postiguet, is even more crowded, but the tiny island of Tabarca, a former haunt of pirates, lies a pleasant boat ride away. It is a good spot for snorkeling, with outdoor restaurants but no accommodations. Trips leave from the harbor along the Explanada, or from Santa Pola (a much shorter sea trip), a fishing port 12½ miles (20 km) to the south. Alicante's Tourist Office (2 Explanada de España; phone: 96-521-2285) can provide schedules.

During the week of June 24, the city goes wild with the unforgettable *Hogueres de San Juan* (Bonfires of St. John). The fiesta includes processions, bullfights, and fireworks, but the climax comes with an arsonist's orgy, the burning of colossal images, sometimes at considerable risk to life and limb, a legacy of pagan midsummer rites.

CHECKING IN: *Sidi San Juan Sol* – Modern and luxurious with a private beach, located 4½ miles (7 km) from the center of town, but close to the area with all the summer action. The 176 air conditioned rooms offer every comfort. Facilities include 2 swimming pools (1 heated), a gymnasium, a sauna, a discotheque, and a shopping arcade. Playa de San Juan, Alicante (phone: 96-516-1300; fax: 96-516-3346; telex: 66263). Expensive.

Gran Sol – A modern skyscraper on the main street in the city center, offering panoramic views from its 26th-floor bar and restaurant. It has 150 straightforward, functional rooms, all with air conditioning and TV sets. 3 Rambla de Méndez Núñez, Alicante (phone: 96-520-3000). Expensive to moderate.

Palas – This pleasant establishment offers old-style charm on the seafront, near the Ayuntamiento (City Hall). Chandeliers and antiques highlight the gracious decor, which caters to a more mature clientele. All 48 rooms are air conditioned and quite comfortable. 5 Calle Cervantes, Alicante (phone: 96-520-9310). Moderate.

EATING OUT: *El Delfín* – Look for the green canopy over the terrace on the Explanada — it marks a spot known for elegant snacking and dining in Alicante, a one-Michelin-star establishment. Downstairs is for simple dishes (and gossip); upstairs, it's mirrors, crystal, and efficient service. There is a broad range of traditional regional and French dishes to choose from (at moderate prices if you stick to the *menú alicantino*). Try the seafood pancake and the *salteado de foie gras, mollejas y pato* (sauté of foie gras, sweetbreads, and duck). Desserts are created from such local fruits as dates and oranges. Open daily. Reservations necessary. American Express, Diners Club, and MasterCard accepted. 12 Explanada de España, Alicante (phone: 96-521-4911). Expensive.

Dársena – An ideal lunch spot overlooking the harbor. More than 20 rice dishes, typical of the region, are served with style. Begin with *bisque de cangrejos al armagnac* (crab soup), and move on to *pastel de atún y espinacas* (tuna and spinach tart). Closed Sunday evenings and Mondays. Reservations advised. American Express, Diners Club, and Visa accepted. Muelle del Puerto, Alicante (phone: 96-520-7399). Moderate.

Nou Manolín – At the justly renowned downstairs bar, order anything from oysters to "grandmother's stew," while sampling some of the fine wines smartly racked above the counter. Upstairs, amid beams and tiles, sample a variety of regional and national dishes, including some of the region's most superb paellas. Closed *Christmas Eve*. Reservations advised. Major credit cards accepted. 4 Calle Villegas, Alicante (phone: 96-520-0368). Moderate.

Quo Vadis – The large bar leads to a cozy, wood-paneled restaurant where diners feast on such local delicacies as *arroz a banda con pescado* (a rice and fish dish). The service is good, the atmosphere agreeable, and the wine cellar well stocked. Closed Mondays and Tuesdays. Reservations unnecessary. American Express, Diners Club, and Visa accepted. 3 Plaza Santísima Faz, Alicante (phone: 96-521-6660). Moderate.

En Route from Alicante – Take N340 and proceed 15 miles (24 km) inland (southwest) to Elche, city of palms, the Lady of Elche, and the Mystery of Elche.

ELCHE: Some 600,000 date palms, originally planted by the Phoenicians, grow around Elche (Elx in the local dialect), which is also important for shoe manufacturing. The irrigation system that waters them was created by the Moors 1,000 years ago. The dates, which grow only on female trees, are harvested from December to March. It's possible to stroll around the Huerto del Cura (Priest's Grove), a palm garden that also features an impressive collection of cacti and tropical flowers (open daily, from 9 AM to 8 PM mid-June to mid-September, to 6 PM the rest of the year; admission charge).

The remarkable 150-year-old *palmera del cura,* or priest's palm, has seven branches sprouting from the same trunk. Look also for the palms dedicated to King Juan Carlos and Queen Sofia — dates from these trees are supplied to the royal palace. Also within the grove is a replica of the *Dama de Elche* (Lady of Elche), a remarkable bust dating back to 500 BC, the original of which is on display in the *National Archaeological Museum* in Madrid. It was discovered in 1897 about a mile (1.6 km) south of Elche in the ruins at La Alcudia, where there now is a museum of Iberian and Roman relics (open daylight hours; closed Mondays; admission charge).

For a spectacular emotional experience, visit Elche in August, when the world's longest-running play is staged in the blue-domed, 17th-century Church of Santa María. The *Misteri d'Elx* (Mystery of Elche), celebrating the Assumption of the Virgin Mary, has been performed by local townspeople for 6 centuries. Although the songs are performed in an ancient form of Catalan, the action is not hard to grasp, and the special effects, including the descent of angels from the lofty dome, are breathtaking. Entry is free (but competition for seats is keen) for the play's first (August 14, 6 PM) and second (August 15, 6 PM) acts. Alternatively, seats can be booked for condensed 1-day performances, staged on August 11, 12, and 13, by writing before July 15 to the Oficina de Turismo (Parque Municipal, Elche, Alicante; phone: 96-545-2747). Telephone after that date to confirm the reservation. A special performance is staged on November 1 in even-numbered years.

CHECKING IN/EATING OUT: *Huerto del Cura* – It would be worth a detour to stay in this tranquil hostelry, which is set amid beautiful gardens in its own palm grove and, in an unusual arrangement, is linked to the *parador* network, although not actually a *parador.* There's a swimming pool and tennis courts; the 70 rooms have TV sets, mini-bars, and air conditioning (important in August). The restaurant, *Els Capellans,* offers regional food and international dishes, and is especially pleasant in summer when tables are set out on the swimming pool terrace. Reservations unnecessary. Major credit cards accepted. Avenida Federico García Sánchez, Elche (phone: 96-545-8040; fax: 96-542-1910; telex: 66814). Hotel, moderate; restaurant, expensive to moderate.

En Route from Elche – Continue along N340, passing more palm groves, through the town of Crevillente to Orihuela, 21 miles (34 km) southwest of Elche in the Segura River Valley. The center of a rich agricultural area, Orihuela has a 14th-to-16th-century Gothic cathedral in which a famous Velázquez canvas, the *Temptation of St. Thomas Aquinas,* is kept under lock and key in the *Diocesan Museum* (open Mondays through Fridays, from 10:30 AM to 1:30 PM and from 4 to 6 PM; phone: 96-530-0638). Velázquez painted the work at the request of Dominican friars, whose 17th-century Monastery of Santo Domingo, later a university and currently a high school, has fine baroque cloisters. Orihuela is the birthplace of Miguel Hernández, a goatherd who became one of Spain's finest poets before dying tragically in Alicante's jail in 1942. His house (Calle Cantos) can be visited on Calle Cantos, but it's best to call the tourist office first (25 Calle Francisco Diez; phone: 96-530-2747).

Still on N340, the road crosses into the province and autonomous community of Murcia; at Monteagudo, it passes a white statue of Christ atop a rocky pinnacle commanding the *huerta,* a jigsaw of tomato, pepper, citrus fruit, and cereal fields. From here, it's only a few miles to the capital.

MURCIA: This pleasant and unhurried city of over 305,000 inhabitants on the Segura River was founded by the Emir of Córdoba in 825 on the remains of a Roman settlement. It enjoyed brief moments of independence under the Moors, but was conquered by King Ferdinand the Holy in 1243 and incorporated into Castile. Fire and

pillage destroyed many of its finest buildings at the start of the Spanish Civil War, but
Murcia later regained its pride when it was made the capital of the autonomous region
of the same name. Most tourists who pass through are on their way to Cartagena or
the coast, so this is a good place for a short respite from summer crowds. The most
important sights are in the older part of town on the north bank of the river. There,
on Plaza Cardenal Belluga, is the mainly Gothic cathedral, begun in the 14th century,
but with a magnificent baroque façade that was not added until the 18th century. Inside,
the Virgen de la Fuensanta, Murcia's patroness, presides over the altar dressed in rich
vestments. The church's Renaissance–baroque bell tower can be climbed for a stirring
view of the city and the surrounding *huerta*. The *Diocesan Museum* (phone: 968-
216344) contains La Fuensanta's gold crown, as well as one of Spain's finest polychrome woodcarvings, depicting in amazingly lifelike detail the penitent St. Hieronymus, by the local sculptor Francisco Salzillo (1707–83). The museum is open daily,
from 10 AM to 1 PM and from 5 to 8 PM; admission charge. More examples of the
sculptor's work can be seen some distance away in the *Salzillo Museum* (1 Calle San
Andrés; phone: 968-291893), which houses some of the woodcarvings that are carried
in Murcia's *Holy Week* processions (see below), as well as a large number of terra cotta
figurines depicting episodes from the Gospels and the daily life of Murcian peasants
(open Mondays through Saturdays from 9:30 AM to 1 PM and from 3 to 6 PM, Sundays
from 10 AM to 1 PM; admission charge).

Just north of the cathedral, on traffic-free Calle de la Trapería, stands the casino
(phone: 968-212255), a 19th-century building that is another of the city's landmarks.
Once a sumptuous private club for wealthier citizens (it never was a gambling den),
it is now a cultural center hosting a changing program of lectures, meetings, and other
events. Marble, molded plaster, carved wood, and crystal chandeliers lend it an august
air — visitors are welcome to look inside (open daily from 9 AM to 11 PM; no admission
charge). North again, the street broadens into Avenida Alfonso X el Sabio, a boulevard
with many sidewalk cafés and a favorite spot for people watching. Many small shops
can be found in the network of narrow pedestrian streets between Calle de la Trapería
and its parallel to the west, the Gran Vía. The local tourist office is on a parallel to the
east, however, at 4 Calle Alejandro Séiquer (phone: 968-213716).

At Alcantarilla, 6 miles (10 km) outside of town on the road to Granada, is the *Museo
de la Huerta* (Carretera de Andalucía; phone: 968-800340), which contains traditional
crafts, costumes, and implements of the region. A huge *noria* (waterwheel), an iron
replica of the wooden one used by the Moors to raise water, stands outside (open from
10:30 AM to 2 PM and 4 to 8 PM; closed Mondays; admission charge).

Murcia celebrates *Holy Week* with great solemnity and pomp in processions of
stunning scope. Over 3,000 people take in a *Holy Wednesday* procession, which
stretches for nearly a mile. Participants include musicians blowing horns so big that
they must be trundled along on wheels. Several of Salzillo's sculptures are borne
through the streets on *Good Friday*. On *Easter Sunday,* a burst of gaiety sweeps the
city with the start of the *Spring Fiesta*. Folk dancing, a jazz festival, and street festivals
fill a week that ends with fireworks and a bizarre pageant known as the *Entierro de la
Sardina* (Burial of the Sardine).

 CHECKING IN: *Siete Coronas Meliá* – This large, modern establishment is
situated opposite the gardens bordering the Segura River. It has an elegant
black-and-white-marble circular lobby, and 108 well-appointed rooms with air
conditioning and color television sets. There is also a garage — important in
Murcia, where parking is a problem. 5 Paseo de Garay, Murcia (phone: 968-
217771; fax: 968-221294; telex: 67067). Expensive.

Hispano II – Close to the cathedral, this modern, family-run establishment has 35
air conditioned rooms with color television sets. The restaurant serves good *tapas*

and excellent regional food. Parking available. 3-5 Calle Lucas, Murcia (phone: 968-216152; fax: 968-216859; telex: 67042). Expensive to moderate.

Rincón de Pepe – Comfortable, tastefully decorated and located in the city center, with 117 air conditioned rooms featuring private baths and mini-bars, as well as a justifiably renowned restaurant (see below). 34 Calle Apóstoles, Murcia (phone: 968-212239; fax: 968-221744; telex: 67116). Expensive to moderate.

 EATING OUT: *Rincón de Pepe* – Its imaginative offerings of typical Murcian dishes have won it a Michelin star. It's possible to dine here in rustic style (beams and barrels) or in modern elegance, and there are several set menus — one with a mighty seven courses. Try the succulent *cordero lechal asado al estilo de Murcia* (roast lamb Murcia style, cooked with apples, pine nuts, and wine), wild partridge in jumilla wine, or the shellfish and truffle salad. Closed Sunday evenings and July 15 through August 15. Reservations necessary. Major credit cards accepted. 34 Calle Apóstoles, Murcia (phone: 968-212239). Expensive.

CARTAGENA: Just 30½ miles (49 km) down the highway (N301) from Murcia is this ancient port city, which encapsulates the Mediterranean coast's turbulent past. Founded by the Carthaginians during the 3rd century BC, called Carthago Nova in its flourishing Roman epoch, pillaged by the Visigoths, independent under the Moors, and sacked by Sir Francis Drake in 1588, Cartagena was the port from which King Alfonso XIII sailed into exile after his 1931 abdication. Because of its deep sheltered harbor, Cartagena is Spain's most important naval base. Ancient ramparts lend a fortress-like air to the city, which is dominated by four hills. The best overall view is from the Castillo de la Concepción, which is now more a park or garden than a fortress, where an Arab-built lighthouse stands. To the west lie the ruins of the 13th-century cathedral, destroyed in the 1936–39 Spanish Civil War. At the port, opposite a monument to sailors who died in the Spanish-American War, is one of the world's first submarines. The 72-foot-long, 85-ton brown-and-gray cigar-shaped craft was built by a local inventor, Issac Peral, in 1888. The impressive City Hall lies close by and at one corner is the tourist office (Plaza del Ayuntamiento; phone: 968-506483). Calle Mayor, the pedestrian mall leading from the plaza, lined with cafés, is an ideal spot for a cup of coffee.

Don't miss the *Museo Nacional de Arqueológica Marítima* (2 miles/3 km) from the center of town, at Faro de Navidad, Puerto de Cartagena; phone: 968-508415); take the Mazarrón road and look for the sign. It is a treasure house of exhibits related to Mediterranean shipping, including ancient amphoras, anchors, jewelry, and a full-size model of a Roman galley (open Tuesdays through Saturdays, from 10 AM to 3 PM; admission charge).

Easter Week attracts many visitors to Cartagena. Particularly impressive are the early-morning processions on *Good Friday*. During the procession from the fishing quarter of Santa Lucía, singers compete to show their mastery of the *saeta*, a spine-tingling flamenco lament. Around dawn, three processions blend together in an emotional encounter and continue as one.

CHECKING IN: *La Manga Club* – A luxurious, British-run, sports-oriented resort located 15 miles (24 km) east of Cartagena on N332. The 47 air conditioned rooms overlook a verdant, carefully landscaped complex, which includes 2 championship golf courses, 13 tennis courts, 2 swimming pools, and a cricket field. There is also horseback riding, scuba diving, and windsurfing. Apartments and bungalows are available. Los Belones, Cartagena (phone: 968-564511). Expensive.

Cartagonova – On a quiet street near the center of town. All 127 rooms are air conditioned and have color television sets. Other facilities include a garage and a restaurant specializing in regional and international dishes. 3 Calle Marcos Redondo, Cartagena (phone: 968-504200; fax: 968-500502). Moderate.

EATING OUT: *Los Habaneros* – Probably Cartagena's best restaurant, with an extensive wine cellar. Service is attentive, the atmosphere relaxing in rooms with wood-paneled pillars. Try the *paletilla de cabrita al horno* (roast kid) or *pollo con langosta* (chicken with prawns). Open daily. Reservations unnecessary. American Express, Diners Club, and Visa accepted. 60 Calle San Diego, Cartagena (phone: 968-505250). Expensive to moderate.

En Route from Cartagena – If returning to Madrid (277 miles/444 km from Cartagena and 247 miles/395 km from Murcia), it's N301 nearly all the way (backtrack through Murcia). If proceeding to Granada, take N332, which weaves southwest over irrigated fields and barren ocher hills for 20½ miles (33 km) to Puerto de Mazarrón, on Murcia's Costa Cálida (Warm Coast), where adjacent beaches have attracted considerable tourist development. From Puerto de Mazarrón, it's a quick 4½ miles (7 km) inland to the town of Mazarrón, from where N332 continues south toward Aguilas, through scenery that becomes increasingly desert-like on approaching the Andalusian province of Almería. Aguilas, an unhurried fishing port dominated by a 16th-century castle, has good beaches but limited accommodations and restaurant facilities. In the surrounding fields, large areas are covered with plastic sheeting designed to retain moisture and allow intensive year-round crop production.

From Aguilas, return inland on the Lorca road, but turn left after 5 miles (8 km) toward Puerto Lumbreras, where an overnight stop can be made. The next morning, head west on N342 to Granada, 127 miles (203 km) from Puerto Lumbreras.

CHECKING IN/EATING OUT: *Parador de Puerto Lumbreras* – A quiet, comfortable, modern *parador* with 60 air conditioned rooms, a swimming pool, and a garage. The restaurant, overlooking a pretty garden, serves local specialties, such as *costillos de cabrito en ajo cabañil* (kid cutlets cooked with garlic, paprika, and wine vinegar) and *berenjenas a la crema con gambas y jamón* (eggplants in a white sauce with prawns and ham). Major credit cards accepted. Carretera N340, Km 77, Puerto Lumbreras (phone: 968-402025; fax: 968-402836). Moderate.

Andalusia and Gibraltar

Andalusia is a name that conjures up images long after the journey has ended. Hooded penitents and the ominous thud of drums during *Holy Week,* a glass of sherry thrust into the visitor's hands by a stranger during *feria,* dark-eyed descendants of Carmen decked out in mantillas and frilly dresses, dusk quietly embracing the Alhambra, a white village clutching a hillside like a determined mountaineer — such memories are the stuff of southern Spain.

Indeed, Andalusia has come to symbolize Spain itself for much of the world. Flamenco can be heard elsewhere, but the staccato hand-clapping and heart-wrenching refrains take on almost mystical qualities when reverberating through the dark alleys of Córdoba and Seville.

Spain's sunshine-swathed southern region — eight provinces in an area about the size of Indiana — is a wild, rugged landscape sprinkled with chalk-white villages, vineyards, and oceans of olive and citrus trees. The shadowy peaks of the Sierra Morena cut it off from the rest of the country to the north, and other ranges, such as the Sierra Nevada, crowned by 11,407-foot-high Mulhacén peak, cross it. Running through the heartland is the broad valley of the Guadalquivir River, carpeted with towns and rich farms since antiquity.

Andalusia is home to the fairy-tale Alhambra palace in Granada, Córdoba's Great Mosque, and the massive Gothic cathedral and evocative Santa Cruz quarter of Seville. Beyond these three "queen cities" are provincial capitals such as wind-whipped Cádiz, where every street leads to the sea, and Jaén, spreading like a white fan at the foot of an awesome fortress. With coastlines on both the Mediterranean Sea and the Atlantic Ocean, this fabled land claims some of Europe's most popular beach resorts. Overbuilding in these areas has become a real problem, but devotees maintain that the coast is still a little piece of earthly paradise, its miles of golden sands covered with acres of golden bodies from every nation.

The invasion of foreigners is nothing new for Andalusia; throughout history it has been a magnet for wandering races. First on the scene were indigenous prehistoric peoples, who left primitive paintings in caves such as La Pileta near Ronda. Waves of settlers called Iberians began arriving from North Africa about 2000 BC, followed by Celts from the north. These Celt-Iberians created the nucleus of the peninsula's permanent population.

Phoenician traders from the eastern Mediterranean planted colonies along the southern shore, including Malaca (Málaga) and Gadir (Cádiz). Founded about 1100 BC, Cádiz is the oldest continuously inhabited city in Europe. The Romans then colonized the region, calling it Baetica, and made it the linchpin of their Iberian empire. Major cities sprouted throughout the Guadalquivir Valley and along the coast.

With the decline of Rome came Vikings, Visigoths, and Vandals, the last a Germanic tribe usually credited with naming the region Vandalusia. When the North African Muslims, called the Moors, began their centuries-long occupation in 711, they called their kingdom Al-Andalus, and the name stuck. Omnipotent caliphs ruled from Córdoba; then, as the Moors were slowly pushed back by the Christian Reconquest, Granada became the last stronghold of medieval greatness. The fall of Granada in 1492 brought all of Andalusia into the newly united nation of Castile and Aragon, later to become modern Spain. It was from Andalusia that Castile ruled its vast colonial empire, and for several centuries treasure-laden galleons unloaded on the banks of the Guadalquivir. All this history left its mark, turning Andalusian cities and towns into vast museums of golden age art and architecture.

But Andalusia is much more than monuments and museums. If Castilians (with the exception of *madrileños*) can be called dignified and sedate, Andalusians are open, gregarious, and dedicated to the art of living life to the fullest. Nowhere is this philosophy more evident than at the seemingly endless Andalusian fiestas, kaleidoscopes of uninhibited singing and dancing, colorful costumes, horse shows, impressive religious rituals, and marathon drinking binges — all rolled into one helluva party!

One warning: Don't be taken in by all the purple prose about Andalusia. There are plenty of dull towns and villages, dirty beaches, barren and ugly stretches of countryside, urban purse snatchers, and awful excuses for roads. But anyone who is selective will discover a seemingly endless variety of travel delights to whet the appetite. And as with those succulent *tapas,* the tasty Spanish hors d'oeuvres that originated here, visitors will invariably find themselves craving one more round.

The driving route outlined below begins at Córdoba, gateway to Andalusia, and continues southwest through the Guadalquivir River valley — farmland for the most part and brutally hot in summer — to Seville, the capital of the region and one of Spain's greatest cities. It then traverses horse-and-sherry country around Jerez de la Frontera and makes its way to Cádiz, on the Atlantic coast, from which it heads southeast, skirting white villages and the Mediterranean coast before arriving at the Rock of Gibraltar, one of the world's great natural landmarks. After turning inland to visit another highlight, the gorge-split town of Ronda, it drops down to the coast again to pass through the touristic Costa del Sol. The route leaves the coast for good near the fairy-tale village of Salobreña, climbing rugged mountains en route to magical Granada, and finally heads north to the lesser-known towns of Jaén and Ubeda, almost untouched by tourism and well worth a visit.

Total highway driving for the route is approximately 612 miles (980 km). Including 2 nights each at the three major cities (Córdoba, Seville, and Granada), the minimum time to allow for the full tour is 15 days.

Accommodations include a few sinfully sumptuous abodes, starting at $100 a night for a double room in the expensive category (very expensive is more than $165). However, there is a wealth of perfectly acceptable, even exceptional, hotels (mostly government *paradores*) in the moderate range, from $65 to $100, and even the occasional inexpensive choice for under $65. Most Andalusian hotels with fewer than three stars (by the government's official classification system) tend to be of the semi-fleabag variety suitable for determined budgeteers only. Expect to pay $75 or more for a meal for two at restaurants rated as expensive; moderate means $45 to $70, and inexpensive less than $45. Prices include a bottle of house wine, dessert, and coffee.

CÓRDOBA: The first stop is time-scarred Córdoba, with its haunting silhouette and sad memories of a millennium ago when it was Europe's greatest city, surpassing such upstarts as Paris and London. The name seems to conjure up foreboding images of taciturn residents, cramped and gloomy streets, and the sad strains of flamenco sung in dramatic overtones. But there's another Córdoba: bright patios brimming with flowers, filigree silver and soft leather, evocative alleys twisting through the old Jewish Quarter, and the Great Mosque, or Mezquita, an incredible forest of jasper and marble columns. For full details on the city's sights, hotels, and restaurants, see *Córdoba,* THE CITIES.

En Route from Córdoba – Take N-IV toward Seville to Carmona, 65½ miles (105 km) southwest across gently rolling countryside known as "the frying pan of Andalusia" because of scorching summer temperatures. Suddenly in the distance loom a series of bluffs, where Carmona has sat perched like a potentate since antiquity, commanding the river plain of the Guadalquivir.

CARMONA: Still partially surrounded by ancient Roman walls, this town has one of the richest histories in Andalusia. Known as Carmo to the Romans, the town straddled the famous Via Augusta, the Roman road that stretched from Cádiz to the north of Spain. In 206 BC, the Roman general Scipio crushed a Carthaginian army nearby. The road into town passes beneath the remnants of a 14th-century fortress — the Alcázar — cleverly transformed into an excellent *parador* (see *Checking In*), and through the 17th-century Puerta de Córdoba (Córdoba Gate; Calle Dolóres Quintanilla), built into the Old Town walls. Once inside, go left up the hill to the *parador* (follow the signs) or follow Calle Santa María de Grácia to the center.

With about 25,000 residents, Carmona is just the right size for strolling — alone through its quiet, white-walled streets or together with everyone else out for the evening *paseo* in the circular Plaza de San Fernando, the town's nucleus. The plaza is lined with wrought-iron lampposts and centuries-old buildings, including the present and former town halls. Within walking distance is the double-arched Puerta de Sevilla from Moorish times; outside stands the Church of San Pedro (Calle San Pedro), with a 17th-century bell tower modeled after the famous Giralda in Seville. The Gothic Church of Santa María (on Calle Martín Lopez) contains the oldest calendar in Spain (6th century), carved on an arch in the Pátio de los Naranjos.

The Roman necropolis about half a mile (1 km) outside town (off the Seville road) shelters several hundred tombs from 2,000 years ago. The Elephant Tomb, named for a statue at its entrance, features dining rooms and a kitchen that once had running water; historians believe that priests must have held some kind of banquet in honor of the deceased. The Servilia Tomb is the size of a villa and has its own pool. The necropolis, which also contains a museum filled with Roman pottery, mosaics, busts, and glass vials, is open from 9 AM to 1 PM and from 4 to 6 PM, except Sunday afternoons and Mondays. Admission charge. For further details, contact Carmona's Tourist Information Office, Plaza de las Descalzas (phone: 95-414-2200 or 95-414-0500).

CHECKING IN/EATING OUT: *Parador Alcázar del Rey Don Pedro* – A Moorish fortress that King Peter the Cruel turned into a luxurious palace in the 14th century, and which later housed Ferdinand and Isabella while they directed the siege of Granada, is the foundation of Carmona's *parador.* Little remains of the original except some walls along the cliff, but architects have brilliantly combined these remnants with modern conveniences. High on a ridge, its 59 air conditioned rooms offer spectacular views, and there is a huge outdoor pool, as well as an impressive vaulted dining hall serving classic Andalusian food. Major credit cards accepted. Carmona (phone: 95-414-1010; fax: 95-414-1712; telex: 72992). Expensive.

En Route from Carmona – Continue on N-IV and drive 24 miles (38 km) into Seville, the "queen" of Andalusia.

SEVILLE: When Madrid became the capital of Spain in the 16th century, it was hardly the richest, the most powerful, or even the best known of Spanish cities. All those superlatives belonged to Seville. For 2 centuries following Columbus's discovery of America, Seville was the chief trading port of an empire. Every ship from Spanish America docked at Seville, and armies of satin-clad bankers and merchants, roguish sailors, and assorted charlatans gave it the raffishness of a frontier boomtown. Much of the grandeur and ambience of those days still survives. Visit Europe's third-largest Christian cathedral, where the bones of Columbus lie in a marble crypt (a must in this quincentennial year of his discovery); climb the stone ramp of the Giralda Tower, built so that a king could ride his horse to the top; and wander by moonlight in the Barrio de Santa Cruz. And if you are visiting Seville between April 20 and October 12, this year, be sure to attend the world's fair — *Expo '92.* For a detailed report on the city's sights, hotels, and restaurants, see *Seville,* THE CITIES.

En Route from Seville – From the center, take N-IV south in the direction of Jerez de la Frontera and Cádiz. Drive 34 miles (54 km) to the junction with C343 near Venta Nueva, turning off toward Espera and Arcos de la Frontera, 22 miles (35 km) away. Rather than go directly into Arcos, take the turnoff to Embalse de Arcos, a lake northeast of town along the road to El Bosque (C344). From this vantage point, Arcos looks like a white pyramid rising from the surrounding plain, with gravity-defying houses welded to a rocky hillside that falls sheer to the river valley below.

ARCOS DE LA FRONTERA: Arcos (*de la frontera* is tacked onto the names of many towns that once stood along the Christian-Moorish boundary) sits on a lofty hill hemmed in on three sides by the Guadalete River. One of its attractions for visitors is its spectacularly situated government *parador,* perched along the edge of a cliff (see *Checking In*). Arcos is also among the most picturesque of a dozen or so whitewashed Andalusian hill towns known as the *pueblos blancos* (white villages) and is included on the Ruta de los Pueblos Blancos (Route of the White Villages), a popular driving route in the region. (A brochure with maps is available from Spanish tourist authorities in the US or in Spain.) Impressive *Easter Week* processions, including the singing of piercing melodies called *saetas* — a kind of *Easter* flamenco — and the running of a lone bull on *Easter Sunday,* are another source of interest.

Legend has it that the town was founded by King Brigo, a grandson of Noah. Known as Medina Arkosh in Moorish times, this seemingly impregnable site was captured by Alfonso X in 1250. Today the sounds of clanging sabers have been replaced by the groans of tourists struggling to reach the Plaza de Cabildo (also known as Plaza de España), the town's main square and the site of both the *parador* and a hair-raising terrace overlooking a valley of neat green fields and orchards. Also on the square is the old Town Hall and the Iglesia de Santa María, a hodgepodge of styles slapped one on another over centuries. (The road up the hill passes right under the church's flying buttresses on the extemely narrow Callejón de las Monjas.) Inside, the supporting columns form a palm vault, and there is an altar of gilt and carved wood. Climb the

386 feet to the top of the bell tower, but try not to arrive at the stroke of 12. (On the way up, a parchment-faced old woman in black, who lives there, asks for a tip.) The views from on high are spectacular: Look for the 18th-century tower of the Iglesia de San Pedro (Plaza de Cabildo) at the other side of the hilltop and for the former castle of the Dukes of Arcos, below and to the right, now occupied by an English aristocrat.

CHECKING IN/EATING OUT: *Parador Casa del Corregidor* – General de Gaulle stayed in this hostelry, formerly a vicar's home. Today it's a pleasing medley of tiles and antiques with 24 air conditioned rooms and a good restaurant that serves local specialties. Major credit cards accepted. Plaza de España, Arcos de la Frontera (phone: 956-700500; fax: 956-701116). Expensive.

En Route from Arcos de la Frontera – Take N342 west 19 miles (30 km) to Jerez, a town steeped in all things Andalusian: bulls, horses, fiestas, and, of course, fine sherry.

JEREZ DE LA FRONTERA: Jerez is the home of Spain's distinctive fortified wine — "sherry," in fact, is an English corruption of the name of the town, from which English, Scottish, and Irish shippers began buying wine as early as the 16th century. The term can legally be given only to wine produced on about 60,000 acres of vineyards lying in a triangle bordered by Seville and Puerto de Santa María (southwest of Jerez) and Sanlúcar de Barrameda (northwest), where the essential white palomino grapes grow. Although Jerez, the main production center and a fairly large town of nearly 200,000 people, does have other points of interest, most visitors get into the spirit of things by touring one of the sherry wineries, or *bodegas,* that are the prime local attraction.

Jerez has some 100 *bodegas* (holding some 125 million gallons of wine), but not all of them are open to the public. The tourist office (7 Alameda Cristina; phone: 956-331150) has details of those that welcome visitors. Among them are the Harvey, González Byass, and Sandeman *bodegas,* but the best of the bunch quite possibly belongs to the Domecq family (3 Calle San Idelfonso; phone: 956-331900), open 10 AM to 1 PM; closed Sundays; no admission charge. Here visitors see the fermentation rooms, mixing tanks, warehouses for aging, and bottling lines, then sample one of the four main sherry varieties — *fino* (extra dry), *amontillado* (dry with fuller body), *oloroso* (medium dry with golden color), and *dulce* (sweet).

Horses run a close second to sherry in the hearts of Jerez residents, so it's not surprising that the outstanding Escuela Andaluza del Arte Ecuestre (Andalusian School of Equestrian Art), a rival to Vienna's renowned Spanish Riding School, is a second major attraction. Although the Jerez school has been open only since 1973, horse breeding and training has been an Andalusian enterprise since Moorish times, and it was the ancestors of these very Hispano-Arab stallions strutting their stuff in Jerez that sired the famous Lippizaners. The "Dancing Horses of Andalusia" perform every Thursday at noon at the school's 1,450-seat arena (Avenida Duque de Abrantes; phone: 956-311111 or 956-311100). Admission charge. Among the show's highlights are the matched team of black horses pulling an old barouche, and the dressage exhibition performed exactingly to baroque music by 12 riders in blue velvet period costumes astride 12 perfectly white horses. If visiting Jerez any other day of the week (except Sundays), go to the school anyway; between 11 AM and 1 PM, visitors may watch a practice session free of charge (at the arena).

Each year, in early September, Jerez hosts the *Fiesta de la Vendimia,* an annual wine harvest festival. An even better time of the year to be in town, however, is during the week-long *Feria del Caballo* (Horse Fair) in May, when aloof aristocrats, the *señoritos,* gather to show off their steeds and horsemanship, and the full impact of the Andalusian twist on the old adage — "wine, women, song, and horses" — can be felt. Each day begins with a promenade of riders, followed by a procession of ornate carriages. There are dressage and jumping competitions, a horse auction, and special *rejoneo* bullfights, when a man on horseback faces the bull. Visitors can test their stamina at scores of *casetas* — open booths overflowing with wine and the seductive rhythms of improvised flamenco.

Jerez has its fair share of historical monuments and churches. Among the best are the 11th-century Alcázar, with Arab baths, located off a large square called the Alameda Vieja (open daily from 10:30 AM to 1 PM; admission charge). Nearby, on the Plaza de Arroyo, is the 18th-century baroque Catedral de San Salvador (La Colegiata), built above an old mosque. Other notable churches include the late Gothic San Miguel and the Santiago, each with finely\carved portals. Better known are the city's secular monuments: the Domecq mansion on Alameda Cristina (across from the tourist office); the home of the Ponce de León family, built by the explorer in 1557; and the Casa del Cabildo, the old Town Hall on the Plaza de la Asunción — today this Renaissance masterwork houses a library and an archaeological museum (closed Sundays; admission charge).

CHECKING IN: Sherry Park – An ultramodern establishment on an elegant, tree-lined avenue — the town's main drag — near the riding school. It has 300 air conditioned rooms, a restaurant, and a swimming pool to help beat the summer heat. 11 Avenida Alvaro Domecq, Jerez de la Frontera (phone: 956-303011; fax: 956-311300; telex: 75001). Expensive.

Avenida Jerez – Less sumptuous than its neighbor across the street, this modern high-rise offers comfort and a good location, if not a lot of atmosphere. There are 95 air conditioned rooms. 10 Avenida Alvaro Domecq, Jerez de la Frontera (phone: 956-347411; fax: 956-337296; telex: 75157). Moderate.

EATING OUT: El Bosque – On the main avenue near the hotel selections, it's said to cater to the local sherry aristocracy. Exotic Andalusian dishes on the menu include such unusual items as a shellfish-and-salmon salad. Closed Mondays. Reservations advised. Major credit cards accepted. 28 Avenida Alvaro Domecq, Jerez de la Frontera (phone: 956-303333). Moderate.

Gaitán – The Domecq family's former cook owns this small place, which is very conveniently located near the tourist office. It features rustic decor, with photos of famous guests on the walls, and a menu of Basque and traditional Spanish specialties. Closed Sunday nights and Mondays. Reservations unnecessary. Major credit cards accepted. 3 Calle Gaitán, Jerez de la Frontera (phone: 956-345859). Moderate.

En Route from Jerez de la Frontera – Leave town on N-IV bound for Cádiz, 22 miles (35 km) away. After 14 miles (22 km), the road to Cádiz veers to the right, while the main highway continues toward Algeciras as N340. Continue through prosaic, resort-style suburbs to the 18th-century Puerta de la Tierra, gateway to the Old Town of Cádiz.

CÁDIZ: From time immemorial, the sea has shaped Cádiz (pronounced *Cah*-dee). For the travel-weary coming from the sunbaked interior, the salty breeze is a soothing tonic; briny port smells and lively sounds jolt heat-deadened senses back to life. It's said to be impossible to get lost here, because every street leads to water: Old Cádiz occupies a club-shaped peninsula that juts out into the Atlantic like the prow of an ocean liner, with the Bay of Cádiz to its back. A narrow isthmus connects it to the mainland. The setting is dramatic, but Cádiz is a bit rough around the edges, with the kind of seedy charm found in such places as Marseilles and Naples — exhilarating or depressing, depending on the visitor's point of view.

A deep, sheltered harbor inspired the Phoenicians to found Gadir around 1100 BC, and every subsequent Mediterranean power made it an important port. The Greeks, for example, arrived about 600 BC, despite Homer's warning that the "Rivers of Hell" lay nearby. After a stint under the Carthaginians, it passed to the Romans, as Gades, and waxed and waned along with the Roman Empire. Much later, the city's role in the discovery and colonization of the New World — and above all as a conduit for trade with the new Spanish possessions — made it wealthy, and it became a favorite of raiding Barbary pirates and English sea dogs such as Sir Francis Drake. When the Guadalquivir River silted up, effectively removing Seville as a competitor, Cádiz became the headquarters of Spain's American fleet, only to slide into obscurity when the country lost its overseas colonies. Today, the port is booming once again.

The best way to get an overview of the town is to drive the loop road that circles the perimeter, skirting a lovely seaside promenade. In fact, travelers will probably want to limit driving to this route alone, because while Cádiz is only a bit smaller than Jerez in terms of population, it has none of that city's sprawl, and negotiating the cramped and confusing streets is extremely difficult. Directly in front of the port on the peninsula's east side is the bustling Plaza San Juan de Dios, site of the imposing City Hall and a dozen or so seafood restaurants with outdoor tables for people watching. (*Gaditanos* — the locals — appear to live on fish, shellfish, and wine, and the number of standup eateries in town, especially in the dank streets around this plaza, is astounding.) Not far away, but on the west side of town, sits the ultra-ornate, golden-domed Catedral Nueva (New Cathedral; in the Plaza de la Catedral), an architectural peacock begun in the early 18th century and finished 116 years later, but still wholly baroque. Outstanding features inside include the choir stalls and, in the museum, the Custodia del Millón, a 17th-century silver monstrance studded with thousands of jewels; in the crypt is the tomb of the Spanish composer Manuel de Falla. The old cathedral, the Iglesia de Santa Cruz (Calle Fray Felix), a 17th-century rebuilding of a church with 13th-century origins, is near the new one.

The city's tourist office (1 Calle Calderon de la Barca, on a corner of the Plaza de Mina; phone: 956-211313) can direct you to the remaining sights in the city. The *Cádiz Museum,* also known as the *Museo de Bellas Artes y Arqueológico,* on the same square, has respectable collections of art, including paintings by Zurbarán and Murillo, and archaeology, especially Phoenician and Carthaginian artifacts. The museum is open from 10 AM to 2 PM; closed Sundays. Admission charge. Another stop might be the 17th-century Oratorio de San Felipe Neri, several blocks away on Calle Santa Inés; the small church is famous as the place where Spain's first liberal constitution was hammered out in 1812; a painting by Murillo hangs above the altar. Next door is the *Museo Histórico Municipal* (Calle Santa Inés), which has a fascinating ivory-and-mahogany scale model of Cádiz as it looked in the 18th century (open from 9 AM to 1 PM and from 4 to 7 PM; closed Mondays; no admission charge). The Oratorio de Santa Cueva (Calle Rosario) contains religious frescoes by Goya.

Strolling through Cádiz is a delight, especially along the seaside promenade with its enormous banyan trees and verdant oases such as the Parque de Genovés, which offers summer concerts and a palm garden. Within the loop of the promenade, the streets and alleys of the Old Town twist and turn like tunnels in a rabbit warren. Just when they become too claustrophobic, however, or a bit too grimy, a sunny, palm-lined square appears. The same streets witness the town's uproarious *Carnavales,* well known throughout Spain. The week before *Lent,* residents go for days without a wink of sleep — singing, dancing madly through the streets, playing odd musical instruments, and rattling nerve-racking noisemakers. A fireworks display signals the end of the carnival celebrations, and the next morning all that remains — besides a citywide hangover — are several tons of confetti and empty wine bottles.

 CHECKING IN: *Atlántico* – A completely refurbished, modern, 6-story hotel that is now a member of the government *parador* chain, albeit an atypical one, without the traditional character of the others. It enjoys an ideal location, overlooking the ocean, and a beautiful pool. Its 173 rooms are air conditioned and have balconies; the dining room serves Andalusian food. 9 Parque de Genovés, Cádiz (phone: 956-226905; fax: 956-214582; telex: 76316). Moderate.

EATING OUT: *El Anteojo* – An excellent location and solid seafood dishes make this place a winner. Closed Mondays. Reservations advised. American Express and Visa accepted. 22 Alameda de Apodaca, Cádiz (phone: 956-274836). Moderate.

El Sardinero – This simple spot is the best of the many seafood restaurants on a square known for good fish. It offers a Basque kitchen — with specialties such as *merluza a la vasca* (hake, Basque-style) — and outstanding *tapas* at the bar. Closed Mondays. No reservations or credit cards accepted. Plaza San Juan de Dios, Cádiz (phone: 956-282505). Inexpensive.

En Route from Cádiz – Head south toward Algeciras. The road, flanked by the Bay of Cádiz and the Atlantic, follows a narrow isthmus dotted with saltworks. After 10 miles (16 km), turn off to the main highway (N340), which travels along — a few miles inland, however — the southern half of the Costa de la Luz. This lesser-known Spanish *costa* stretches along the Atlantic all the way from Huelva near the Portuguese border to wind-pummeled Tarifa, where it meets the Mediterranean. The coastline is relatively unscathed by resort developments, and because of the extra effort necessary to reach it from the main highway, it's still possible to find isolated beaches of golden sand and mobs of seagulls.

VEJER DE LA FRONTERA: This picturesque village is another of Andalusia's "white villages" (and a stop on the Ruta de los Pueblos Blancos). It lords over the landscape 32½ miles (52 km) from Cádiz, just a mile (1.6 km) off the main road. The site is another exceptional one, used as a defensive bastion ever since the days when Romans were fighting Iberians. The Moors, naturally, couldn't pass up a chance to plunk down a hilltop castle, and some of its old walls have been restored. Nearby, the Church of San Salvador (Calle Rosario) is a blending of Gothic and Mudéjar styles, built on the foundations of a mosque. Moorish influence is also evident in the unusually labyrinthine streets weaving up the hill. Trying to drive up to the castle would be a mistake; fortunately, there is a parking lot near the entrance to the village.

CHECKING IN/EATING OUT: *Convento de San Francisco* – A hostelry occupying a former monastery that has been impeccably restored. It's family owned and operated, with one son managing the hotel restaurant, Vejer's best. None of the 25 rooms is air conditioned, but summers are moderate here. MasterCard and Visa accepted. Vejer de la Frontera (phone: 956-451001; fax: 956-451004). Moderate.

En Route from Vejer de la Frontera – The N340 highway south to Tarifa passes a wild and windy landscape, with huge limestone outcroppings and a smattering of whitewashed farmhouses. One of the largest hunks of rock marks Punta Paloma, where the highway turns seaward. The E-5 turnoff for Tarifa comes 28 miles (45 km) from Vejer, and it's another mile (1.6 km) into town.

TARIFA: The town sits at Spain's southernmost point, looking out on the Strait of Gibraltar and, on a clear day, as far as Morocco. Head for the Old Quarter through an ancient portal. Within are the 16th-century Gothic Iglesia de San Mateo and the 13th-century (reconstructed) Castillo de Guzmán el Bueno, still used as an army barracks. The fortress was the scene of a celebrated incident in Spanish history. When the Moors were trying to retake it from the Christians in 1292, they captured the son of the Spanish commander, Alonso Pérez de Guzmán. The lad was brought forward and threatened with death unless the castle's defenders surrendered, but the elder Guzmán threw the Moors his weapon and shouted, "If you need help to murder my son, here is my knife, but we will not surrender." The attack was rebuffed and Guzmán became known as El Bueno (the Good); the son's fate is not clear. The castle is open from 11 AM to 2 PM and from 4 to 10 PM daily during the summer months, on weekends only the rest of the year. Admission charge. Most visitors who come to Tarifa do not come for the sightseeing, however. They come to take the hydrofoil that makes a daily run across the water to Tangier in Morocco. Windsurfing is another big draw — this is considered one of the best spots in Europe for the sport — as are beaches such as Playa Lances. Nordic types now roam the cobbled streets where Moors used to walk.

En Route from Tarifa – Return to N340 and head east toward Algeciras. This part of Andalusia, known as the Campo de Gibraltar, is mainly an industrial and shipping center, of little interest to tourists. Several miles east of Tarifa, however, the famous Rock of Gibraltar — a little piece of the British Empire isolated in the Mediterranean — comes into view. It thrusts up from across the Bay of Algeciras just as mighty and defiant as expected, a point not lost on neighboring Spaniards, who have claimed it for almost 3 centuries.

ALGECIRAS: The Moors arrived in 711 and named their settlement Al-Djezirah. They endured until the mid-14th century; a few scattered remnants of their presence survive west of the present town. A thousand years after the arrival of the Moors, Spanish refugees from Gibraltar arrived to settle the site. Today, this growing port city has little to offer visitors except wonderful views of the Rock. A great many visitors do get the picture, however, since each year more than 3 million passengers use the ferries and hydrofoils that ply the Strait of Gibraltar between Algeciras and both Tangier and the Spanish enclave of Ceuta in North Africa. The city also has a grand old landmark hotel, the *Reina Cristina* (see below), the brainchild of a turn-of-the-century English lord who constructed a railroad across Andalusia. During World War II, the harborside hotel's guests were joined by a number of German spies, who watched ship traffic through the strait from their second-story rooms.

CHECKING IN/EATING OUT: *Reina Cristina* – The pink lady with green shutters, turrets, and a tiled roof manages to blend Victorian and arabesque into a nostalgic hideaway. Built 100 years ago and named for Spain's queen regent, the hotel sits aloof from the rest of Algeciras, with its own terraced gardens, English library, and aging British clientele, who come for the service and the inspiring views of "Gib." It has 135 air conditioned rooms and a traditional, moderately priced restaurant. Major credit cards accepted. Paseo de la Conferencia, Algeciras (phone: 956-602622; fax: 956-603323; telex: 78057). Expensive.

En Route from Algeciras – If headed for Gibraltar, take N340 northeast 8 miles (13 km) to San Roque, then turn off to La Línea de la Concepción, from which the border lies 5 miles (8 km) away. If not visiting Gibraltar, turn off N340 onto C3331 just before San Roque and proceed directly to Ronda.

GIBRALTAR: The self-governing British colony of Gibraltar is only 3 miles long and three-quarters of a mile wide, with approximately 29,000 inhabitants settled mainly in Gibraltar Town, on the Rock's west side. Tiny as it is, the colony is an immense source of bitterness among the Spanish, who consider themselves its rightful owners; their attempts to reclaim it led to the closing of the frontier between Spain and Gibraltar in 1969. For years, the Rock was accessible only by air or sea from the United Kingdom or North Africa. But the steel mesh gates swung open again in February 1985, and the border is now open round the clock. Visitors need only a passport, not a visa, to cross.

Gibraltar's dramatic silhouette owes itself to a geologic cataclysm in some distant era that sent huge chunks of its north and east sides crashing into the sea. This left a sheer 1,400-foot-high face that was famous long before an American insurance ad made it familiar — for the ancients, the Rock was one of the Pillars of Hercules marking the limits of the Mediterranean. When the Moors launched their invasion of Spain from here in 711, they called it Gebel-Tarik (Tarik's Rock), in honor of their leader. The Moorish occupation left its legacy not only in the modern name of this piece of real estate, but also in an old castle and defensive walls and in the arabesque flourishes found in both Catholic and Protestant churches here; the tiled courtyard of St. Mary the Crowned, in fact, once belonged to a mosque.

Spaniards regained this colossal toehold from the Moors, but lost it again to Britain in 1713, after first losing the War of the Spanish Succession. Then came the Great Siege (1779–83), one of innumerable Spanish attempts to retake the mesmerizing hunk of limestone. So many cannonballs have been fired at the Rock that when more turn up during a new building project, residents no longer blink. Indeed, history itself turns up in every nook and cranny. In Trafalgar Cemetery (Prince Edward Rd.), for example, heroes of the famous naval battle fought off Cape Trafalgar (about halfway between Cádiz and Tarifa) are buried near the spot where the body of the fallen Admiral Horatio Nelson was brought ashore. Two men lie in one grave here, both killed by the same cannonball. The *Gibraltar Museum* (off Main St. on Bumbhouse La.; phone: 935-074289) tells the Rock's whole fascinating story and has a 30-foot scale model. It's open from 10 AM to 6 PM; closed Sundays. Admission charge.

Although Gibraltarians are really more Mediterranean than British, both in temperament and language (a strange variety of Spanish with an abundance of English expressions), the British presence is unmistakable, from fluttering Union Jacks and friendly bobbies to photos of the queen and gin-and-tonic urbanity at the yacht club. There's a changing-of-the-guard ceremony every Tuesday at 10 AM at the Governor's Residence on Main Street, as well as other displays of colonial pomp. Main Street itself, the Rock's backbone, is a throbbing half mile of discount shops (there's no VAT here), British retail institutions such as *Marks & Spencer,* and pubs like the *Angry Friar* and *Old Vic's.* Unfortunately, Gibraltar has taken on an increasingly seedy appearance, and traditional hospitality has suffered from the onslaught of visitors since 1985.

Willis's Road, to the east of Main Street, leads past the Moorish Castle, with its square Tower of Homage, built in 1333 (admission charge). From here, Queen's Road climbs to the Upper Galleries, huge tunnels for housing artillery that were carved out by hand during the Great Siege. They are open daily from 10 AM to 7 PM (to 5:30 in summer). Admission charge. Farther up lies the Apes' Den, home of perhaps the world's most famous simians. Gibraltar's official mascots, they are so revered that Churchill vowed to protect them when their numbers dwindled. (According to recent legend, the Rock will remain British as long as the monkeys stay.) Daily feedings take place at 8 AM and 4 PM. Another way to reach the den is via a spectacular cable car ride that goes to the top of the Rock from just below the *Rock* hotel. More information on the sights can be obtained at the Gibraltar Tourist Office in Cathedral Square.

Note: To call Gibraltar from Spain, dial the area code (9567) before the local number (except from La Línea de la Concepción, just across the border in Spain, where you dial only 7 before the local number in Gibraltar); from the US, dial only the country code (350) before the local number.

CHECKING IN: Rock – Like *Raffles* in Singapore, this hotel is a classic of the British colonial genre, with 160 comfortable rooms, good service, and spectacular views. Other amenities are a restaurant with roast beef and Yorkshire pudding on the menu, a saltwater pool, miniature golf, and a nearby casino. 3 Europa Road, Gibraltar (phone: 935-073000). Expensive.

EATING OUT: *Da Paolo* – Located at an attractive yacht harbor between the airport and town, it offers an imaginative menu in Art Deco surroundings. Closed Sundays and all of February. Reservations advised. Major credit cards accepted. Marina Bay, Gibraltar (phone: 935-076799). Moderate.

Spinning Wheel – The convenient location and the recommendation of a loyal following make this a top traditional choice. Lamb dishes are the specialty. Closed Sundays. Reservations unnecessary. Major credit cards accepted. 9 Horsebarrack Lane, Gibraltar (phone: 935-076091). Moderate.

En Route from Gibraltar – Return to San Roque and take C3331 to Ronda, spearing through farmland along the Guadarranque River and into the hills. Several of the towns passed before reaching the classic old Andalusian town of Ronda are included on the Ruta de los Pueblos Blancos, among them picturesque Jimena de la Frontera, draped like a sheepskin on the side of a hill 22 miles (35 km) from San Roque and crowned by a castle. From Jimena, take C341; the road passes golden hills dotted with olive trees, citrus orchards, and clusters of white houses. After a stretch that soars high above a spectacular valley, the village of Gaucín appears, then tiny Algatocín and Benadalíd. The final approach to Ronda, 37½ miles (60 km) from Jimena, provides inspiring scenery, with huge bare slabs of stone thrusting up from the landscape. This is the heart of the Serranía de Ronda range, a traditional retreat for bandits.

RONDA: Its fame rests chiefly on El Tajo, a 400-foot gorge cut by the Guadalevín River that literally splits the town in two. Incredible cliff-hanging houses perch right along the edge of the precipice and look as if they might slide into the abyss at any moment. The 5-foot-high iron grilles on the 18th-century Puente Nuevo, one of three bridges that span the gorge, are all that separate visitors from a horrifying drop. The bridge links two towns and two eras. To the north lies the "new" town, called El Mercadillo, begun around 1500, after Ronda fell to the Christians. Here, a pedestrian street, the Carrera de Espinel, is lined with scores of shops, becoming a vibrant sea of shoppers and strollers each afternoon. At the head of the street is the Plaza de Toros, Ronda's famous bullring. Although bullfights are held only about once a month from May through October, visitors may inspect Spain's most beautiful bullring and its second oldest (1785) daily from 10 AM to 1 PM and from 4 to 7 PM. Admission charge. Don't miss the opportunity, because Ronda is the cradle of modern bullfighting. The local Romero family developed most of the rules and techniques used today, including the introduction of the cape, the killing sword, and the group of assistants to the matador called the *cuadrilla.* Each September, at the *Corrida Goyesca,* aficionados pay homage to a 19th-century family member, Pedro Romero, who killed 5,000 bulls during his career and fought until the age of 90. (Goya immortalized the epoch in several sketches and engravings.) End a tour of the new town by strolling north from the bullring through the Alameda Gardens (Calle Virgen de la Paz), supposedly paid for with fines levied on anyone using foul language in public.

The Old Town, called La Ciudad, is a symphony of cramped streets and wrought-iron balconies brimming with potted geraniums. Here are some of Andalusia's finest aristocratic mansions, such as the twin-turreted 16th-century Renaissance Casa de Mondragón, off the Plaza del Campillo (now a crafts school that is closed to the public). A short walk away is the circular Plaza de la Ciudad, the coolest spot in town on a summer day. Fronting it is a 15th-century church, Santa María la Mayor, with a baroque altar dripping with gilt and a former Muslim mihrab (a niche indicating the direction of Mecca); the church's tower was once a minaret. On the other side of the Old Town (near the bridge off Calle del Comandante Alejandro) are more mansions, including the Casa del Rey Moro, which is the restored home of King Badis, a Moorish ruler who drank wine from the jewel-encrusted skulls of his victims. (Today it's a private home that can't be visited.) Farther down the same street is the 18th-century Palacio del Marqués de Salvatierra (Calle Santo Domingo; closed Thursdays), the home of a Spanish aristocrat complete with Plateresque portal, marble staircase, and Alhambra-style gardens. The house is open daily from 11 AM to 2 PM and from 4 to 6 PM. Admission charge. The Arab baths at the bottom of the same hill are among the finest in Spain. The baths were closed for renovation at press time, but were expected to reopen early this year; check with the tourist office (1 Plaza de España; phone: 952-871272) for opening hours, which vary. Admission charge.

CHECKING IN: *Reina Victoria* – The grand old dowager of Ronda in the Mercadillo section has a gabled roof, English gardens, chandeliers, and dark wood furniture. Its 89 air conditioned rooms are often crowded with tour groups, but it's still a treat in a town with few hotels. 25 Avenida Dr. Fleming, Ronda (phone: 952-871240; fax: 952-871075). Moderate.

EATING OUT: *Don Miguel* – Clinging to one side of El Tajo next to the bridge, this spot offers a stunning outdoor terrace as well as good food. Rabbit in sherry sauce and devilfish with green peppers are on the inventive menu. Closed Mondays. Reservations unnecessary. Major credit cards accepted. 4 Calle Villanueva, Ronda (phone: 952-871090). Moderate.

Pedro Romero – Bullfighting memorabilia give it atmosphere, and the traditional Spanish food is good. Try the *rabo de toro* (oxtail stew). Closed Sunday evenings. Reservations unnecessary. Major credit cards accepted. 18 Calle Virgen de la Paz, Ronda (phone: 952-871110). Moderate.

En Route from Ronda – The tour route of Andalusia proceeds from Ronda to the Costa del Sol. Those on a tight schedule, however (as well as those who eschew the ravages of mass tourism), may want to head directly to Granada. If done in 1 day, this trip involves a fairly strenuous drive of 120 miles (192 km) along routes C341 and N342 via Antequera, a pleasant, medium-size town with dozens of historic churches and a Moorish castle. If traveling at a leisurely pace, stop in Antequera or farther along for a meal or an overnight stay.

To continue the complete Andalusia route, proceed from Ronda south to the Costa del Sol via C339, which drops from about 2,300 feet to sea level in a distance of 30 miles. The landscape along the way is a harsh blending of volcanic rock and red clay, studded with rare *pinsapo* firs, black cork oaks, wild olives, and mauve rock roses.

CHECKING IN/EATING OUT: *La Bobadilla* – This extraordinary, sumptuous resort near Loja, about 20 miles (32 km) east of Antequera, is on the way from Ronda to Granada and is reason enough for anyone to break up this trip. The creation of a German hotelier and designed by a Granadan architect, it's set in the middle of isolated countryside looking much like a typical Andalusian "white village," with everything in authentic Andalusian style: tiled roofs, arches, wrought-iron grilles, a plaza, and as a central gathering place, a chapel with a 30-foot-high, 1,595-pipe organ. Most of the 35 rooms have their own patio or garden, and there is a gymnasium, a sauna, 2 pools, tennis courts, and a stable of horses for riding. Two highly rated restaurants serve meals for the likes of King Juan Carlos, who has been known to pop in. Major credit cards accepted. Finca La Bobadilla, Loja (phone: 958-321861; fax: 958-321810; telex: 78732). Very expensive.

Parador de Antequera – Another option for those en route to Granada. It features a pool and 55 air conditioned rooms, plus a popular restaurant serving regional specialties. Major credit cards accepted. Paseo García del Olmo, Antequera (phone: 952-840061; fax: 952-841312). Moderate.

PUERTO BANÚS AND MARBELLA: The first town on the coast for those who arrive from Ronda is an insignificant resort, San Pedro de Alcántara. Only 2 miles (3 km) east of it, however, is the crown jewel of local tourism, Puerto José Banús, a yacht harbor filled with dozens of pleasant places to stop for a drink or a meal and, quite possibly, to rub elbows with a movie star or an Arab sheik. The Port, as it's known to residents, is home to hundreds of craft of all sizes and pedigrees; Rolls-Royces and Mercedes wait quayside, as their impeccably groomed owners join the evening parade of strollers who come to see and be seen on the promenade. Behind is a modern, quasi-Andalusian fishing village filled with luxury apartments and looking like a giant cardboard cutout.

Puerto Banús is technically part of San Pedro, but in spirit it belongs to Marbella, 5 miles (8 km) east, the fabled resort where the "beautiful people" play — or at least used to play, before package tourism began to drive them away. The golf is great at several local courses; so is the tennis, and the windsurfing and other water sports. Even sunbathing is better here than at other spots on the coast, thanks to a superb climate created by a backdrop of coastal mountains. Dining and nightlife aren't shabby either, although Marbella is not just limousines and popping champagne corks. Having cut its teeth as a Phoenician village called Salduba, it has a rich history. An ancient Arab wall still partially surrounds its Old Town, a traffic-free oasis of cool, cobbled alleys and half-hidden squares brimming with aromatic flowers and fruit trees. Among them, the Plaza de los Naranjos, a truly idyllic spot with orange trees, gurgling fountains, and outdoor cafés, is probably the best of the lot. Also on the square are a statue of King Juan Carlos (where one of Franco once loomed), and the 16th-century Town Hall. The *Museo Arqueológico* has been closed for renovations, but is due to reopen this year at a new location on the Calle Viento.

Other sights in the Old Town are the parish Church of La Encarnación and its clock tower on the Plaza Caridad, and the adjacent Calle Gloria, a tiny street that has become a floral showcase. Nearby Calle Alamo leads to a nice upstairs bar called *The Townhouse*. Just across Avenida Ricardo Soriano from the Old Town lies the Alameda del Parque, a park and promenade with an abundance of vegetation and beautifully tiled benches. Two blocks away is the Mediterranean in all its glory, framed nicely with a promenade, the Paseo Marítimo, and a much smaller, humbler version of Puerto Banús, the Puerto Deportivo. The tourist office (1 Avenida Miguel Cano; phone: 952-771442) can supply further information.

CHECKING IN: *Los Monteros* – One of Spain's most elegant hotels, set in a complete resort complex with few rivals. It caters to the affluent and famous, with prices to match, but it offers superb golf, tennis, horseback riding, 5 swimming pools plus the beachfront, water sports, a health clinic, and the acclaimed *El Corzo* restaurant, boasting one of Andalusia's few Michelin stars. The location, however, a few miles east of Marbella, is a drawback. Urbanización Los Monteros, Marbella (phone: 952-771700; fax: 952-825846; telex: 077059). Very expensive.

***El Fuerte* –** Back down on earth, this older hotel, completely renovated, enjoys a wonderful location amid manicured gardens between Marbella's beach and the Old Town. There are 262 rooms, 2 swimming pools, an illuminated tennis court, and 2 restaurants; ask for an air conditioned room in the new wing. Llano de San Luis, Marbella (phone: 952-771500; fax: 952-824411; telex: 77523). Expensive.

EATING OUT: *Don Leone* – For years the best dining spot at Puerto Banús. It offers solid Italian cooking and an ideal situation for people watching. Open daily; closed from November 20 through December 20. Reservations necessary. American Express accepted. Muelle Ribera, Puerto Banús (phone: 952-811716). Expensive.

***Hostería del Mar* –** At the western edge of town at the beginning of the "golden mile," where Marbella's most expensive real estate is to be found. The menu — Spanish cooking, done with international finesse — features such dishes as sole stuffed with shrimp mousse and squid in ink sauce. Closed Sundays. Reservations advised. Major credit cards accepted. 1A Avenida Cánovas del Castillo, Marbella (phone: 952-770218). Expensive.

Mesón de Pasaje – This impeccably managed little restaurant occupies a friendly old house just off the Plaza de los Naranjos. Continental cooking at reasonable prices means it is often crowded, so reservations are a must. Closed Thursdays and from mid-November through mid-December. Reservations advised. American Express and Visa accepted. 5 Calle Pasaje, Marbella (phone: 952-771261). Moderate.

En Route from Puerto Banús and Marbella – The 16-mile (27-km) stretch of coast between Marbella and Fuengirola, once among the nicest on the Costa del Sol, now bristles with new developments. Fuengirola itself is a place to avoid, which is easy enough to do. Take the bypass (left toward Málaga) just west of town; 2 miles (3 km) farther along, another road heads 4 miles (6 km) into the hills to the pretty little village of Mijas, probably Spain's most photographed white *pueblo*.

MIJAS: It's often mobbed by busloads of sightseers and armies of souvenir hawkers, yet despite all this, Mijas retains a good deal of its original charm. Much of the appeal derives from its spectacular site, welded to the side of a mountain and looking like a stack of sugar cubes against a pine-draped backdrop. From stunning lookout points, a gaze spans much of the coast and the luminous Mediterranean as far as Morocco's foreboding Rif Mountains.

The road splits at the entrance to Mijas; take the left fork to a wide parking area, then walk up the hill to an early Christian shrine, the Santuario de la Virgen de la Pena (after passing the "burro taxi" service — corny but fun). Walk toward the center of town to the Plaza de la Constitución, a shady spot for watching village life. From here, a path leads up past the ultramodern bullring (where seats go for more than $40 a head) to a terraced lookout area called the *cuesta de la villa* (literally, "slope of the town"), where visitors can enjoy that famous view.

CHECKING IN: *Mijas* – The only real hotel in town offers 100 rooms, swimming, tennis, and a hairdresser (but no air conditioning), at slightly inflated prices. Guests pay for the view, which is spectacular. Urbanización Tamisa, Mijas (phone: 952-485800; fax: 952-485805; telex: 77393). Expensive.

EATING OUT: *Mirlo Blanco* – The excellent location and tasty Basque cuisine such as *txangurro* (spider crab baked in the shell) make this an ideal choice. Closed Sundays. Reservations necessary. Visa accepted. Plaza de la Constitución, Mijas (phone: 952-485700). Moderate.

En Route from Mijas – To avoid the congested coast, take the turnoff for Benalmádena just below Mijas (on the road to Fuengirola). After 7 miles (11 km), this narrow road cuts down to Arroyo de la Miel and the fringes of Torremolinos, a package-tour paradise that has seen better days. Another 2 miles (3 km) east of Arroyo, the road joins the Torremolinos bypass road (N340); from here, the destination is Málaga, 7 miles (11 km) away.

MÁLAGA: The center of the Costa del Sol offers more shopping, cultural events, museums — more of everything — than any other place along the coast, but it also has more crime, traffic, noise, and pollution. Because of its busy international airport, the city's name is stamped in millions of passports every year, but most of the visitors who land here go elsewhere to stay. Málaga has been around since the Phoenicians, who founded a settlement to trade in salted fish; the hill overlooking the sinewy harbor was later fortified by every power to rule the Mediterranean. The sweet málaga wine has been famous since antiquity and is still served from 500-liter barrels at murky little *bodegas*. (One of the best is the *Antigua Casa Guardia* on the Alameda.)

The center of town is dominated by the refreshing Paseo del Parque that begins at the Plaza de la Marina (where there is underground parking) and extends eastward. This pedestrian promenade and park, lined with palms and banana trees, features fountains, ponds with geese and ducks, and 3,000 species of luxuriant plants bathed in Málaga's intense light. Fronting it are the lemon-colored Ayuntamiento (Town Hall) and other government buildings. Beyond, to the east, are the bullring (Paseo de Reding; phone: 952-219482); the Paseo Marítimo promenade along La Malagueta Beach; and a nostalgia-tinged district of aging buildings known as El Limonar. Better beaches lie to the east at Baños de Carmen and El Palo.

The Alcazaba, an 11th-century Moorish fortress-palace, is perched directly above the park and reached via Calle Alcazabilla. Although nicely restored, this is something of a "poor man's Alhambra" in terms of historical and architectural interest. The winding approach passes ruins of a Roman amphitheater, horseshoe arches, and walls draped in bougainvillea and wisteria. Peer down the murky hole where Christian prisoners were kept and, in the *Archaeological Museum* in the main building, peruse the collection of artifacts (the statue with an iron peg leg is curious). The Alcazaba is open daily from 10 AM to 1 PM and from 4 to 7 PM. Admission charge. Rearing up to the east is another Moorish fortress, the 14th-century Castillo de Gibralfaro, built on the site of an ancient Greek lighthouse. (It can be reached by a strenuous walk up from the Alcazaba, or by driving a mile east from the Paseo del Parque and then another mile up the hill.) Wander at will around the extensive ramparts and towers, which held off many an attack before the city fell to Christian armies in 1487. Open from 9 AM until dusk; no admission charge.

Málaga's Renaissance cathedral (Calle de Molina Larios in the center of town) has only one of the two towers originally planned because, so the story goes, money was diverted to help the colonials fight the American Revolution. It's quite dark inside, but look for the Corinthian columns as big as giant redwoods and the 17th-century choir stalls, with 100 seats and dozens of saints carved by the famous artisan Pedro de Mena. A small museum with religious artifacts is open daily from 10 AM to 1 PM and from 4 to 5:30 PM. Admission charge. From the cathedral's north side, follow the signs to the *Museo de Bellas Artes* (8 Calle San Agustín; open from 10 AM to 1:30 PM and from 5 to 8 PM; closed Mondays; admission charge). The eclectic collection — 20 rooms full, much of it on permanent loan from the *Prado* — includes paintings by Murillo and Ribera, as well as a small room devoted to the boyhood works of Málaga's most famous son, Pablo Picasso. The house where Picasso was born, in 1881, is 2 blocks away (take a right on Calle Granada) in Plaza de la Merced, whose 19th-century buildings — with green shutters, tile roofs, and peeling yellow paint — retain some of the charm of the epoch. A plaque commemorates the event.

Another throwback to earlier times not far from the museum (take Calle Granada toward the Plaza de la Constitución) is the Pasaje de Chinitas, where the *malagueña* style of flamenco evolved in the mid-19th century. Stroll along this car-free stretch of wrought-iron lamps and cobblestones, then stop for a drink at the *Bodega la Campana,* where the tab is kept with chalk on the bar counter. Or stop for *tapas* — Málaga is known for its *tapas,* and some of the best bars for sampling them are a short hop from the Pasaje de Chinitas. Among them is *Bar Orellana* (3 Calle Moreno Monroy) famous for its *lomo mechado* (loin of pork, veal, or other meat, larded with hard-boiled egg, bacon, and other stuffings, then sliced). The tourist office (4 Pasaje de Chinitas; phone: 952-213445) can recommend many others.

CHECKING IN: *Málaga Palacio* – Although it has slipped from a once loftier position, this 228-room establishment still features baronial-style public rooms, a rooftop pool, and an outstanding location. Ask for an air conditioned room with a view over the Paseo del Parque. 1 Cortina del Muelle, Málaga (phone: 952-215185; telex: 77021). Moderate.

***Parador de Gibralfaro* –** On the south side of the Gibralfaro hill, next to the castle, its location is a mixed blessing. It's a 2-mile (3-km) drive from the center, but the splendid views over the harbor, bullring, and modern lighthouse of Málaga are worth the inconvenience, as is the good restaurant. None of the 12 rooms is air conditioned. Major credit cards accepted. Monte de Gibralfaro, Málaga (phone: 952-221902; fax: 952-221904). Moderate.

EATING OUT: *Antonio Martín* – A traditional favorite, it has a somewhat erratic reputation but a superb location, especially for lunch outside on the terrace. Closed Mondays. Reservations unnecessary. Major credit cards accepted. 4 Paseo Marítimo, Málaga (phone: 952-222113). Moderate.

***La Cancela* –** A pleasant choice, often crowded with tour groups at lunch. Specialties include *fritura malagueña,* or fried seafood, and *ajo blanco,* a cold soup made with garlic. Closed Sundays. Reservations unnecessary. Major credit cards accepted. 3 Calle Denis Belgrano, Málaga (phone: 952-223125). Inexpensive.

En Route from Málaga – Continue 33 miles (53 km) east on N340 to Nerja, passing a nearly continuous wall of resort developments along the way. To reach the center of Nerja, follow the Balcón de Europa signs.

NERJA: This resort town lies at the mouth of the Chillar River, on a sloping site beneath a wall of jagged coastal mountains. Its name comes from the Arabic *narixa,* or "abundant spring." The nicest spot in town is the Balcón de Europa, a palm-shaded promenade jutting dramatically into the Mediterranean. Built in 1885 and named by King Alfonso XIII, it's lined with antique iron lampposts and old cannon, with one side overlooking a pretty beach and some fishing boats. On another side are several cafés with loyal customers and outdoor tables, the place to stop for a cup of *café con leche.* (Locals say the *Alhambra* serves the best coffee and is popular with visiting film crews in town to take advantage of the nearly perfect climate.) Just around the corner sits the parish church, which celebrated its 500th anniversary in 1983. The tourist office (4 Puerta del Mar; phone: 952-521531) is at the entrance to the Balcón.

CHECKING IN: *Parador de Nerja* – A gem in a beautiful setting atop a bluff overlooking the sea, with one of the area's best beaches just a stroll away. It has 73 air conditioned rooms, a nice pool, and a restaurant serving international and Andalusian cuisine. Major credit cards accepted. Calle Rodríguez Acosta, Nerja (phone: 952-520050; fax: 952-521997). Moderate.

EATING OUT: *Casa Luque* – On one of the town's loveliest squares and loaded with atmosphere. The food blends the traditional (rabbit stew) and the innovative (asparagus mousse). Open daily. Reservations advised. American Express and Visa accepted. 2 Plaza Cavana, Nerja (phone: 952-521004). Moderate.

En Route from Nerja – Those who like Andalusian villages may want to detour 4½ miles (7 km) inland along a well-paved road to the *pueblo* of Frigiliana, a stack of white blocks that was once voted Andalusia's prettiest village. Ceramic plaques in the Old Quarter tell a fascinating history. Here, in 1569, about 10,000 Moors dug in for a last stand against the forces of King Philip II. With defeat imminent, hundreds hurled themselves off a cliff rather than be captured — local yarn spinners claim that whitened bones and rusty weapons still occasionally turn up in the hills. Go to the Plaza de la Iglesia, where the old-timers hang out, and drink in the heady scents of orange blossoms, or have a drink and some *tapas* at the *Bar-Café Viritudes,* opposite the bus stop and Civil Guard barracks.

Return to Nerja and head east, stopping 3 miles (5 km) from town, near the village of Maro, to visit the Cuevas de Nerja. These colossal caves, discovered in 1959 by boys trying to trap bats, boast the world's longest stalactite — 295 feet — and prehistoric paintings dating from 20,000 BC. Over the ages, underground water has worn down rocks and built up limestone deposits into bizarre shapes — known as the Tower of Pisa, Pinocchio, and so on — that are tastefully lit for full effect. Other highlights include the Hall of the Elephant's Tusk and its giant fossil embedded in stone, and the Cataclysm Chamber, where an enormous column fell and shattered millennia ago. An outstanding festival of music and dance, with top classical ballet, unfolds every August in the Cascade Chamber. The caves are open daily from 9:30 AM to 9 PM in summer and from 10 AM to 1:30 PM and 4 to 7 PM in winter. Admission charge.

Continue east into the province of Granada. Once a driver's nightmare, the highway is now quite good and very scenic: goatherds leading their flocks over the scrub-covered hills, old watchtowers grasping at hilltops, cliffs plummeting down to the glittering sea, and slender fingers of intensely cultivated land painting swathes of green. Fewer beaches, golf courses, and high rises line this stretch of the Costa del Sol, and the first significant settlement, the fishing village of La Herradura, sitting on a horseshoe-shape bay, is fully 10 miles (16 km) from Nerja. All around are terraced hillsides and orchards of dark green *chimayo,* a tropical fruit. A few miles farther along, Almuñecar appears, its Old Town clinging to a lofty hill. Unfortunately, the ravages of modern development have begun to take their toll on what was once an idyllic spot. Proceed 10½ miles (17 km) farther to Salobreña.

SALOBREÑA: On sunny days, this stunning village is nearly blinding from the endless layers of whitewash slapped on by old women wielding buckets and brushes. In the moonlight it becomes a dream town, rising above a broad plain, peacefully suspended between the stars and the sea. Its Moorish castle, one of Andalusia's most impressive, occupies an impregnable site that must have seemed like a gift from Allah. From the castle, flat-roofed houses spill down the hillside to the plain. It's possible to drive partway up, but park and walk to the top. The final stretch climbs along Calle Andrés Segovia, named for the renowned guitarist who called Salobreña home. Inside the castle, wander the battlements and catch an eyeful of coastal scenery (admission charge).

CHECKING IN: *Salobreña* – This little hideaway, a 2-story, 80-room modern structure perched on a cliff overlooking the Mediterranean, lies 2 miles (3 km) west of the village. There's a nice pool, but no air conditioning. Carretera Cádiz, Km 341, Salobreña (phone: 958-610261; fax: 958-610101). Inexpensive.

En Route from Salobreña – Continue on the coastal road for 2 miles (3 km) to pick up N323 to Granada. The road slices 42 miles (67 km) north through the rugged Sierra Nevada, following the course of the Guadalfeo (Ugly River) and leaving the sensuous world of palm trees and tropical fruit behind. To the east lies a wild region of primitive villages called Las Alpujarras.

Seven miles (11 km) south of Granada a sign is marked Suspiro del Moro. It was from this hill that Boabdil, the last Muslim king in Spain, wept as he took a final look back on his way to exile in Morocco. From here, it's smooth sailing across a fertile plain to the fabled city of the Moors.

GRANADA: At first sight, the city of a thousand and one legends is a disappointing jumble of gray façades and snarling traffic. But Granada's delights are slightly veiled, making discovery more exciting. Among them: the exquisite golden web of filigree work sheltering the tombs of Ferdinand and Isabella in the Royal Chapel and the chalk white Albaicín quarter, huddling beneath one of Spain's great sights, the Alhambra. Despite the incursions of modern life, Granada still evokes images of courtesans in silk gowns and silver slippers. For full details of sights, hotels, and restaurants, see *Granada,* THE CITIES.

En Route from Granada – Leave town on N323 for Jaén, 61 miles (98 km) north, and enter a rolling sea of olive trees ringed by dusty mountains. The road cuts through rough hills to a mountain pass, Puerto de Carretero (3,400 feet high); suddenly, the provincial capital — olive trees at its feet and flanked by gray granite hills and a Moorish castle — appears in the distance. About 6 miles (10 km) before Jaén, another road (N321) veers to the right toward Ubeda. However, if going into Jaén, continue straight ahead on N323.

JAÉN: The capital of the province of Jaén sits at the confluence of the Guadalquivir and Guadalbullon rivers. The site was called Auringis by the Romans and became famous for its silver mines and olives. The Moors called it Geen, "way of the caravans," because it lay on the main route between Andalusia and Castile. The Moors were defeated in 1246, but they left behind the chief reason for a visit to Jaén: a spectacular hilltop fortress — the 13th-century Castillo de Santa Catalina — whose crumbling ruins have been reconstructed and converted into a government *parador.* Located 2 miles (3 km) from the center of town, the castle sits at the end of a steep, winding road that provides magnificent views of the entire area. Besides the *parador* (see *Checking In/Eating Out*), visit the former castle parade ground, ringed by defensive towers, and peek into the keep and the Santa Catalina Chapel. Then walk to the far end of the hill to reach a thrilling lookout spot over the town. From this viewpoint, the 16th-century Renaissance Catedral de Jaén (Plaza de Santa María) looks imposing but a bit odd, its massive façade out of proportion with the surrounding buildings. Begun about 1525 by Andrés de Vandelvira, the cathedral tempts the limits of architectural good taste with its ornate façade, topped with statues of saints. Inside are choir stalls with delicately carved biblical scenes, marble columns, and soaring cupolas. One chapel contains a veil said to have been the one used by St. Veronica to wipe Christ's face, while some Ribera paintings and a bronze candelabrum with 15 arms are on display in the *Museo de la Catedral* (open Fridays through Sundays from 11 AM to 1 PM; admission charge).

For further information on the sights of Jaén, which include the *Museo Provincial* (27 Paseo de la Estación; phone: 953-250320), open in summer from 9 AM to 2 PM Tuesdays through Sundays; during the winter also open 4 PM to 7 PM Tuesdays through Saturdays, and several churches (the Capilla de San Andrés in particular), contact the tourist office (1 Calle Arquitecto Berges; phone: 953-222737).

CHECKING IN/EATING OUT: *Parador de Santa Catalina* – It incorporates much of the original structure of Jaén's Moorish castle and looks like something out of a Hollywood epic, with beamed sitting rooms replete with massive chandeliers, tapestries, armor, and coats of arms. Have lunch in the vast dining room with vaulted ceiling or spend the night in a canopied bed. There are 43 air conditioned rooms. Major credit cards accepted. Castillo de Santa Catalina, Jaén (phone: 953-264411; fax: 953-223930). Moderate.

En Route from Jaén – Double back on N323 about 6 miles (10 km) to the junction of N321, a two-lane road called the Ruta del Renacimiento (Renaissance

Route). Indeed, some of Spain's finest Renaissance architecture lies ahead. Baeza is 30 miles (48 km) from Jaén, Ubeda 35½ miles (57 km).

BAEZA: This sleepy little town looks as though its residents had closed the gates centuries ago and let time pass them by. Forget about the stark white of most Andalusian towns; Baeza's buildings of golden stone look Italian. Because it lies near the border with Castile and was an important frontier town during the Reconquest, Baeza, in 1227, was the first Andalusian town to be retaken by Christian armies. Subsequently, it became a showplace of grand mansions and religious buildings.

A good map for a walking tour is available at the tourist office (Plaza del Pópulo; phone: 953-740444). The office is housed in the Casa del Pópulo, a former courthouse with decorative Plateresque windows and six doors that once opened onto as many notaries' offices; the square was named for the four carved lions that grace the fountain. The Roman figure of a woman is said to be that of Hannibal's wife — her modern head is a replacement for the original, which was cut off during the Spanish Civil War when an anti-clerical mob mistook her for the Virgin. Also on the square is a former slaughterhouse that would be called a mansion in most other towns.

The most interesting part of Baeza surrounds the 16th-century, late Gothic Catedral de Santa María and the square of the same name. The church (open from 10:30 AM to 1 PM and from 5 to 7 PM) has an outstanding main chapel with gilded relief work and a hexagonal pulpit. A silver monstrance that sits behind a painting is an unusual feature: Put in 25 pesetas and the art rolls up, music commences, and the monstrance revolves in dazzling light. Then, just as suddenly, the show ends — until another coin is inserted. Across from the cathedral is the 17th-century Seminario de San Felipe Neri, whose carved main façade is covered with inscriptions written with bull's blood (as was the tradition) by graduates. Nearby is the ornate Palacio de Jabalquinto (Cuesta de San Felipe), built in the early 16th century, with huge studded doors, a harmonious main façade, and an interior patio with marble columns. (Both buildings are open only sporadically.)

CHECKING IN/EATING OUT: *Juanito* – A modest, old-fashioned hostelry on the road to Ubeda, it's better known as a restaurant of classic Spanish cooking, patronized by noble and commoner alike, than as a hotel. (Restaurant reservations advised on weekends.) There's no air conditioning in the 21 rooms. Major credit cards accepted. Avenida Arca del Agua, Baeza (phone: 953-740040; fax: 953-742324). Inexpensive.

UBEDA: Just 5½ miles (9 km) away from Baeza and even more impressive is historic Ubeda, known as the Florence of Andalusia — and with good reason. Its Plaza Vázquez de Molina is the most architecturally harmonious square in Andalusia, an oasis from another time lined with Renaissance monuments to all the glory that was 16th-century Spain. To reach the square, follow the Conjunto Monumental signs into the confusing town center. Along the way, you'll pass the bustling Plaza de Andalucía, with a graceful clock tower, outdoor tables for relaxing, and a bullet-ridden statue of a Francoist general — in short, everything a small Andalusian town square should have.

Several noteworthy buildings front the shaded Plaza Vázquez de Molina. The 16th-century Renaissance Casa de las Cadenas serves as the town hall; its interior patio of slender arches was an elegant touch by architect Andrés de Vandelvira, who designed most of old Ubeda. The square's architectural highlight is the Iglesia de San Salvador, whose massive golden façade and sumptuous interior make it one of the best examples of Spanish Renaissance architecture. Built in the early 16th century as the family chapel and mausoleum for Francisco de los Cobos, secretary of the Holy Roman Emperor

Charles V, it is still privately owned, but a live-in guide shows visitors the ornate altarpiece crowned by a sculpture of the Transfiguration and an enormous wrought-iron grille (open from 10 AM to 1 PM and from 4 to 7 PM; admission charge). The little Iglesia de Santa María, also on the square, stands on the site of a mosque that was demolished after Christians took the Moorish town of Ubbadat in the early 13th century.

The Muslim legacy survives here in the traditional crafts of esparto weaving and pottery making, and the Exposición de Artesanía Ubetense, next to the Casa de las Cadenas, displays green Ubeda ceramics, esparto rugs, and other examples of the best of this timeless craftsmanship. (Later, visit the San Millán district — especially Calle Valencia — to see artisans at work.)

Before the Plaza Vázquez de Molina was completed, a nearby square, the Plaza Primero de Mayo, was the heart of Ubeda; an outdoor market, sports events, and, while the Inquisition reigned, burnings at the stake took place here. On one corner today is the old City Hall, featuring a double row of elegant Gothic arches. Similar touches are found in the Iglesia de San Pablo on the plaza's opposite side, parts of which date from around 1400. Another Ubeda sight, the (former) Hospital de Santiago, a Vandelvira masterpiece, sits on Carrera del Obispo Cobos, far from the historic center. This imposing 16th-century edifice has been called the "Escorial of Andalusia." Note the monumental staircase leading upstairs from the inner courtyard and the woodcarvings in the chapel. Open from 9 AM to 2 PM and from 5 to 8 PM; closed Sundays. No admission charge. The Ubeda Tourist Office is on Plaza del Ayuntamiento (phone: 953-750897).

CHECKING IN/EATING OUT: *Parador Condestable Dávalos* – This time, a 16th-century palace served as inspiration for government architects, who converted it into a comfortable, history-steeped hotel. Antiques and fresh flowers fill the 26 air conditioned rooms (ask for number 12 for the best view). The moderately priced restaurant offers excellent traditional cuisine (reservations unnecessary). Major credit cards accepted. 1 Plaza Vázquez de Molina, Ubeda (phone: 953-750345; fax: 953-751259). Moderate.

En Route from Ubeda – Our Andalusia tour officially ends in Ubeda. Travelers can return to Castile and Madrid via Bailén, 25½ miles (41 km) west on N322, or proceed northeast toward Valencia via Albacete, also on N322.

Extremadura

Far to the west of Madrid, close against the Portuguese border, lies a remote and often rugged region that played a leading role in one of the most important chapters of Spanish history. During the 15th and 16th centuries, this vast, landlocked area exported its sons to the farthest reaches of the earth to chart unfamiliar and hazardous oceans to discover the New World of the Americas. Extremadura was the cradle of the conquistadores, men like Francisco Pizarro, an uneducated swineherd who set off to conquer for the Spanish the land they called Peru and to plunder the gold of the Inca. Pizarro came from Trujillo, today one of the jewels of Extremadura, a small town rich in fine 16th-century palaces built with American gold. Also from Trujillo was Francisco de Orellana, the first European to explore the Amazon, while Vasco Núñez de Balboa, who made the first European discovery of the Pacific Ocean, and Hernando de Soto, who colonized Florida for the Spaniards, both hailed from the southern Extremaduran town of Jerez de los Caballeros. Pedro de Valdivia, who conquered present-day Chile, was born and brought up in Villanueva de la Serena.

Today, the names of Extremadura's towns and cities echo all over Latin America. There are Trujillos in Peru, Honduras, and Venezuela. Medellín, the small Extremaduran citadel that produced Hernán Cortés, the European discoverer of Mexico, can also be found in Mexico itself, as well as in Colombia and Argentina. Numerous other New World sites, including the Caribbean island of Guadeloupe, take their name from the mountain Monastery of Guadalupe, the very place in which Queen Isabella of Spain drew up a contract with Christopher Columbus for his voyage of discovery to America and in which the first American Indians brought back as prisoners were baptized by their conquerors.

The modern-day sons of Extremadura continue to travel far from home, although now they are more likely to go to the big cities of Spain or the more industrially advanced north of Europe than to cross the Atlantic. Life can still be harsh and primitive in this wild corner of the country, and emigration is an attractive option for young people not drawn by the prospect of a life of rustic peace and tranquillity.

For the visitor, however, it is precisely this remoteness that gives Extremadura its appeal. As a region, it does not have the obvious charm of Andalusia, directly to the south. Its towns are not as lively as Madrid or Barcelona. There is no coastline and, consequently, there are none of the sophisticated resorts that can be found on the Costa del Sol or the Costa Brava. It is still largely undiscovered and undeveloped as a tourist spot, and in the towns that do have tourist offices, very few of the staff speak anything but Spanish.

For those who can bear to do without such refinements, the rewards are great. Extremadura is an area of immense natural beauty, with vast expanses of rolling countryside broken only occasionally by little whitewashed *pueblos,* or villages, peopled by shepherds and their families. In the north, the fertile plains of wheat, cotton, and tobacco give way to soft hills and tumbling olive groves, then to the snow-capped peaks of the Gredos and Gata mountain ranges. Farther south, the rich red soil is thickly wooded with pungent eucalyptus trees and holm and cork oaks. In spring and early summer, before the heat has burned the landscape brown, carpets of wildflowers stretch for miles.

Three great rivers bathe the region. The Guadiana is in the south, forming the border with Portugal for part of its length. The calm, slow-flowing Tagus is in the center, its high cliffs dotted with castles. Farther north, where the hills turn into mountains, the tributaries of the Alagon become rushing streams and waterfalls that plunge from huge granite boulders into pools of ice-cold, crystal-clear water.

Eagles, vultures, and buzzards all can be spotted in the more remote corners of the countryside, given a little patience. Storks can be seen everywhere, even in the towns, where they make their giant nests atop the towers and belfries of castles and churches. On the ground there are deer, wild ponies, dozens of species of lizards, and the lynx, now extinct in many parts of Europe.

But all is not wildlife and wide-open spaces. The region is also rich in architecture and history. The towns, especially Cáceres, Trujillo, and Guadalupe, contain palaces and fine churches built by the Spanish nouveaux riches with gold brought back in galleons from their newly discovered territories — fantastic examples of 16th-century one-upmanship. Mérida has a museum housing the finest collection of Roman finds in the whole of Spain — fittingly, since Extremadura was one of the chief colonies of the Romans' vast province of Lusitania, and Mérida, founded during the 1st century BC, was Lusitania's capital. The Visigoths, who came later, also left an important heritage, particularly in finely tooled stonework and jewelry. Again, Mérida has some of the best examples of this early Christian civilization.

During the 8th century, the Arabs arrived from North Africa, and they stayed for 500 years. They left behind them magnificently constructed castle-fortresses, which still dominate many a skyline in the region, as well as countless examples of more decorative architecture using elaborately sculpted friezes and richly designed *azulejos,* the glazed pottery tiles that still face many houses and doorways throughout the region.

Several orders of knights established themselves in Extremadura, making it their role to chase out the Moors and to protect Christian pilgrims on the long and arduous journey north to the sacred shrine of Santiago de Compostela, in Galicia. They controlled vast areas of land, given to them by grateful Spanish nobles in payment for their services. Alcántara, Monfragüe, Mérida, and Cáceres are still steeped in the history of these crusading orders, which wielded immense political and financial power in the late Middle Ages.

During the 19th century, Napoleon's armies tried to turn the plains of Extremadura into a French province. The region was the scene of much fierce fighting before the future Duke of Wellington, allied with the Spanish, came from his fortress stronghold in Portugal to beat the French back over the Pyrenees. Badajoz, near the Portuguese border, was the scene of a particularly brutal battle in 1812, with 5,000 of Wellington's 15,000 troops killed as they tried to storm the French-held ramparts.

The route outlined below enters the northeast corner of Extremadura, turning off the main N-V highway from Madrid just short of the small town of Navalmoral de la Mata and running down through the foothills of the Sierra de Altamira Mountains to the famous sanctuary town of Guadalupe. From there, it continues west to Trujillo, birthplace of two of Spain's most famous conquistadores, southwest to Mérida, with its fine amphitheater and other Roman remains, and west again to Badajoz, a town dominated by the imposing Moorish castle where generations of Muslim kings made their base. The itinerary then proceeds north to Cáceres, richly evocative of Spain's golden age, and on up to Plasencia, a charming town and a good base for trips into the picturesque valleys of the far north of Extremadura. Among these, a visit to the lovely wooded Monastery of Yuste, where the Holy Roman Emperor Charles V spent his last days, is particularly recommended. The total length of the route is between 422 and 453 miles (675/725 km), depending on excursions.

A few words of warning are warranted. The roads in Extremadura are generally good (provided you stick to those recommended in the itinerary) — with one notable exception in the remote Las Hurdes area, which can be explored as an optional detour. Distances are often greater than they seem on a map, however, and gas stations can be few and far between, so allow plenty of time and keep the tank full. Don't rely on renting a car locally, because tourism is still very new here and as yet there are only a few car rental offices in operation.

The food of the region is good and hearty, with lots of game and meat dishes. Extremadura is one of Spain's main cattle raising areas — black bulls are visible everywhere along a drive through the countryside. The bravest ones will end up in the bullring; the others will be used to make big, thick steaks. Lamb and pork are both good, and the strong, deep pink ham is superb. (Extremaduran pigs are reportedly fed on snakes to make the flesh more tender.) Fish such as trout and tench feature widely on most menus. Another favorite meal is braised partridge. The region produces some good wines, including two particularly noteworthy ones: the strong rosé from Cañamero and the justly renowned, full-bodied red named for the Marqués de Cáceres.

Extremadura is particularly rich in *paradores,* the state-run inns usually converted from old monasteries or castles. Staying in them is the best way to get a real taste of the region, but be sure to book well in advance, as they tend to fill up quickly, even outside the high season. As a general guide, the north is likely to prove more captivating than the south, so it's a good idea to allow more time around Trujillo, Cáceres, and Guadalupe when planning. Expect to pay $75 or more for a double room in hotels listed as expensive, from $50 to $75 in moderate hotels, and under $45 in the inexpensive ones. Expensive meals are $50 and up for two; moderate, between $30 and $50; and inexpensive, under $30.

GUADALUPE: Entering Extremadura from the east along the main N-V highway from Madrid, take the well-marked turnoff for Guadalupe to the left, 2 miles (3 km) before Navalmoral de la Mata. The road is narrow and often winding, but the drive is spectacular, through olive groves and chestnut woods and, 2½ miles (4 km) outside Guadalupe, past the exquisite Humilladero Hermitage, a small chapel in a panoramic spot where pilgrims of more impressionable times would fall to their knees at the first sight of the Monasterio de Guadalupe below them. It's not hard to understand why. The crenelated, turreted extravaganza makes a dramatic sight, nestling in the lee of the Guadalupe mountains, the old village that grew up as an adjunct to it hugging its doorstep. The edifice, a mishmash of architectural styles, honors the Virgin of Guadalupe, a small wooden statue reputedly carved by St. Luke and found buried on the site in the 13th century. At first, only a chapel marked the spot; the monastery was founded in the mid-14th century by King Alfonso XI, after he successfully invoked the Virgin's aid in a battle against the Moors in 1340. The conquistadores adopted the shrine as their own and heaped treasures on it from the New World, making it one of the most elaborate and richly decorated monasteries in the whole of Spain. Conquered Inca leaders were brought here to be baptized. Freed Christian slaves left their chains here in votive thanks. Although the monastery was abandoned in the 19th century, then restored and taken over by Franciscan friars in 1908 (it was originally run by Hieronymite monks), it is still, for the Spanish, one of the most important places of pilgrimage in Christendom, as well as a symbol of *hispanidad,* the cultural and linguistic link between Spain and Spanish America.

A guided tour (Spanish language) takes visitors around the complex (open daily, from 9:30 AM to 1 PM and 3:30 to 7 PM; admission charge; phone: 927-367000), including the manuscript room, which houses giant illuminated books of hours, and the sacristy, which has eight paintings by Extremadura's most famous artist, the 17th-century painter Francisco de Zurbarán. The 14th-century church, which was added to in later centuries, has an altarpiece with works by Carducci, Giraldo de Merlo, and Jorge Manuel Theotocópuli, son of El Greco. One of the main features of the monastery is the 15th-century Mudéjar cloister, unmistakably Moorish in influence and faced with glazed colored tiles (there is a smaller, Gothic cloister in the monastery as well). The tour ends with the crowning glory, a visit to the Camarín de la Virgen, where the Virgin reposes on a richly worked altar, a casket to one side of her stuffed full of peseta notes, gifts from grateful or hopeful pilgrims.

CHECKING IN: *Parador Zurbarán* – This imposing 15th-century palace opposite the monastery was founded by one of its priors to take care of pilgrims who came to Guadalupe — in fact, this was the building used for the signing of contracts with explorers setting out for the New World. Today, it is one of the region's most comfortable hotels, with 40 rooms, a swimming pool, and an excellent restaurant serving typical dishes such as *cabrito asado al tomillo* (roast kid with thyme). 10 Calle Marqués de la Romana, Guadalupe (phone: 927-367075; fax: 927-367076). Expensive.

Hospedería Real Monasterio – Housed in the monastery itself and run by the enterprising Franciscan friars. A stay here is an experience — it's not deluxe, but you are in a monastery! The 46 rooms are arranged around the Gothic cloister and furnished with hand-carved monks' tables and chests. Both hotel and restaurant, which serves an excellent fixed-price menu, are extraordinarily reasonable. Plaza Juan Carlos I, Guadalupe (phone: 927-367000; fax: 927-367177). Moderate.

EATING OUT: *El Cordero* – The best restaurant in town, apart from those in the hotels. It's run by the very capable Angelita, whose specialty is *cordero asado,* the roast lamb from which the restaurant takes its name. Open daily. Reservations unnecessary. No credit cards accepted. 11 Calle Convento, Guadalupe (phone: 927-367131). Moderate.

En Route from Guadalupe – Take the road marked Mérida and follow it down through more olive groves, over a gurgling stream on the valley floor, and on to Cañamero, where a stop to taste the deservedly famous local wine would not be a bad idea. But be careful if driving: The pale red liquid is deceptively strong. At Zorita, 32 miles (51 km) from Guadalupe, continue toward Trujillo instead of turning left for Mérida.

TRUJILLO: This enchanting town occupies a special place in Spanish history as the home of some of the most celebrated conquistadores. Francisco Pizarro, who waged war on the Inca to win Peru for Spain, was born here, the illegitimate son of a nobleman. A bronze statue of him astride a fiery steed, ready for battle, dominates the pretty Plaza Mayor in the heart of the Old Town. The statue, an early-20th-century work by the American sculptors Charles Runse and Mary Harriman, has its exact double in Peru's capital city, Lima. Trujillo's two other famous sons were Diego García de Paredes, who founded another Trujillo in Venezuela, and Francisco de Orellana, the first European to explore the Amazon. The Old Town, perched on a granite hill above the modern one, is full of grand 16th-century mansions financed with wealth brought back from the new territories. Of particular interest is the Palacio del Marqués de la Conquista, built by Pizarro's legitimate half-brother Hernando; it still contains busts of the explorer's family. The palace, located on the Plaza Mayor, is open only sporadically; to arrange a visit call the tourist office in the same square (8 Plaza Mayor; phone: 927-320653). The 13th-century Santa María church holds the tombs of some of the town's most prominent nobles, including García de Paredes, and is also noted for its 15th- to 16th-century Gothic altar (ask the tourist office for admittance). Towering over everything is the impressive Arab-built Castillo — a walk up to its ramparts at sunset gives a spectacular view over the town's rooftops. In Trujillo's narrow back streets, its people still live as they always have, the men tending their sheep and goats, and the women doing their washing by hand. In the evening, the main square is an evocative place to sit and sip a glass of sherry before going on to dine at one of the town's several good restaurants.

 CHECKING IN: *Parador de Trujillo* – Beautifully converted from the 16th-century Convent of Santa Clara and tastefully decorated with furniture from that time. Built around a central cloister, it has 46 air conditioned rooms, a small swimming pool, and an excellent restaurant, housed in the old refectory. Try the *morteruelo,* a pâté of chicken, partridge, and rabbit, and the *cochinillo asado,* roast suckling pig. Plaza de Santa Clara, Trujillo (phone: 927-321350; fax: 927-321366). Expensive.

Las Cigüeñas – This modern, air conditioned, 78-room hotel doesn't have the charm of the *parador,* but it's a comfortable alternative if the latter is booked. It's situated on the main highway from Madrid, a mile before Trujillo. N-V, Km 253, Trujillo (phone: 927-321250; fax: 927-321300). Moderate.

EATING OUT: *La Cadena* – Housed in a fine 18th-century palace in the main square, it has whitewashed walls decorated with local ceramics, and serves a very reasonable fixed-price menu. Open daily. No reservations or credit cards accepted. Plaza Mayor, Trujillo (phone: 927-321463). Moderate.

Hostal Pizarro – Also in the main square, this restaurant produces some fine local dishes, including *estofado de perdices,* a partridge casserole, and a good *cordero asado,* roast lamb. Open daily. Reservations unnecessary. American Express and Visa accepted. Plaza Mayor, Trujillo (phone: 927-320255). Moderate.

Mesón La Troya – Concha Alvarez, the delightful old woman who runs this superb restaurant, has been in the business for 50 years and still personally oversees the cooking and the dining room, imaginatively converted from former stables. The food is among the best in Extremadura. Diners receive a complimentary Spanish *tortilla* and a salad as soon as they sit down; other dishes may include *carne con tomate,* beef cooked in a tomato sauce, or *prueba de cerdo,* a wonderfully garlicky pork casserole. Don't be surprised to see the village priest — he eats here every night and has his own table. Open daily. No reservations or credit cards accepted. Plaza Mayor, Trujillo (phone: 927-321364). Inexpensive.

   En Route from Trujillo – Take the N-V highway south in the direction of Mérida. After 36 miles (58 km), turn left at the signpost for Santa Amalia, and after another 4½ miles (7 km), turn right at the signpost for Medellín. The road leads over a magnificent 17th-century bridge on the Guadiana River into Medellín, a little town crowned by a well-preserved medieval castle. Medellín, which gave its name to three other towns in Latin America, owes its fame to Hernán Cortés, born here in 1485. The man who conquered the Aztec empire and colonized Mexico for the Spanish died forgotten in Spain at the age of 62, but a statue of him now dominates his home town's Plaza Mayor. Go to Plaza de España early enough, and you can watch a woman frying *churros* (fritters) in a huge vat of fat — the whole town's breakfast, evidently, judging by the lines forming outside the entrance to her small take-out place next to the tobacco shop. The town has a small but bustling market on Thursday mornings. From Medellín, retrace the route to the main N-V and turn left for Mérida.

   MÉRIDA: Founded by the Romans in 25 BC as Emerita Augusta, a colony for the *emeriti,* or veterans, of the fifth and tenth Roman legions, Mérida quickly grew to be the Spanish Rome, capital of the vast and powerful province of Lusitania. The Roman ruins are among the best in Spain, with pride of place going to the Roman theater, which was built by Agrippa, son-in-law of Emperor Augustus, shortly after the city's foundation and had seating for 6,000. In summer, classical plays and flamenco dances are performed here. Nearby is a Roman amphitheater which held 14,000 spectators. (Both theaters are open daily, from 8 AM to 9:30 PM; admission charge; there's ample parking near the entrance.) The *Museo Nacional de Arte Romano* (National Museum of Roman Art), in a building forming part of the theater complex, not only is acknowledged to be the finest repository of Roman artifacts in Spain, but also has drawn kudos for its design. It incorporates a Roman road, discovered when the museum was being built in the early 1980s, and contains a superb collection of statues, glassware, pottery, coins, and mosaics (open Tuesdays through Saturdays, from 10 AM to 2 PM and 4 to 6 PM; Sundays from 10 AM to 2 PM; Mondays from 4 to 6 PM; admission charge). Two Roman houses near the theaters have been excavated, revealing an intricate water system and some fine mosaics (open from Tuesdays through Saturdays, from 8 AM to 1 PM and 4 to 7 PM; Sundays and holidays, from 9 AM to 2 PM· admission charge). Other Roman remains include an exquisite Temple of Diana, recently restored; the circus, used for chariot racing; the well-preserved Trajan's Arch; the Milagros Aqueduct, the better preserved of two that served the city; and the 60-arched Roman bridge across the Guadiana, the longest bridge ever built in Spain.

   Mérida's past as an Arab fiefdom is best seen in the Alcazaba, a Moorish castle built during the 9th century (open Tuesdays through Saturdays, from 8 AM to 1 PM and 4 to 7 PM; Sundays and holidays, from 9 AM to 2 PM; admission charge). Inside this fortress, note the cistern, a fine example of sophisticated Arab engineering — its construction assured the Moors a constant supply of water from the Guadiana. One last sight not to be missed in Mérida is the Hornito de Santa Eulalia, a shrine dedicated to the little girl who, according to local legend, was baked in an oven (*horno*) in the 4th century, after she spat in the eye of a pagan official rather than renounce Christianity.

 CHECKING IN: *Las Lomas* – A recently built 134-room hotel, complete with air conditioning and a large swimming pool, a mile (1.6 km) out of town on the road (N-V) to Madrid. Carretera Madrid, Km 338, Mérida (phone: 924-311011; fax: 924-300841). Expensive.

***Parador Vía de la Plata* –** The 16th-century building housing this air conditioned, 44-room *parador* was at first a convent and later a prison. In a quiet but still central part of town, it has a markedly Moorish feel about it, with richly tiled floors and a cool, cloistered courtyard. There's a good restaurant, serving Spanish and Extremaduran specialties. 3 Plaza de Queipo de Llano, Mérida (phone: 924-313800; fax: 924-319208). Expensive.

***Emperatriz* –** Right in the heart of town in the main square, this 16th-century palace claims to have offered hospitality to such illustrious guests as the Holy Roman Emperor Charles V, Queen Isabella of Portugal, and Kings Philip II and III of Spain. Now a 41-room hotel, its entrance is a wonderful Moorish galleried foyer faced with intricate tiles. Its restaurant, popular with local folks, serves specialties that include *tencas fritas con limón* (fried tench) and *gazpacho ajo blanco,* an Extremaduran version of the Andalusian iced soup. 19 Plaza de España, Mérida (phone: 924-313111; fax: 924-300376). Moderate.

***Nova Roma* –** A clean, comfortable, modern hotel near the Roman theater, amphitheater, and museum, with 28 rooms, but no restaurant. 42 Calle Suárez Somonte, Mérida (phone: 924-311201; fax: 924-300160). Moderate.

 EATING OUT: *Nicolás* – Starched linen tablecloths and lots of marble grace this restaurant, which serves a good fixed-price menu with regional specialties. Open daily. Reservations unnecessary. American Express and Visa accepted. Calle Félix Valverde, Mérida (phone: 924-319610). Moderate.

***Briz* –** Close to the *Nicolás,* but not as smart. It may not look like much from the outside, but it turns out some fine local dishes, including *perdiz en salsa,* a casserole of partridge, and an interesting appetizer of artichokes and chorizo sausage. It also serves an excellent red house wine. Open daily. Reservations unnecessary. No credit cards accepted. Calle Félix Valverde, Mérida (phone: 924-319307). Moderate to inexpensive.

***Mesón Benito* –** It would be easy to miss this one, since it's tucked away in a small square off Mérida's main street, but that would be a pity, because it's easily the best eatery in town, with good regional cooking, an excellent fixed-price lunch menu that changes every day, and extremely friendly service. The walls are covered with pictures of Extremadura's most famous bullfighters. Very reasonably priced, even in the evening, when the menu goes à la carte. Open daily. Reservations unnecessary. No credit cards accepted. Calle Santa Eulalia, Mérida (phone: 924-315502). Moderate to inexpensive.

En Route from Mérida – Leaving Mérida, take the N-V highway west about 39 miles (62 km) to Badajoz.

BADAJOZ: The most populous city in Extremadura, with 123,000 residents, and capital of the province of Badajoz, one of the two provinces into which the region is divided (the other is Cáceres), Badajoz was once one of the most important Arab strongholds in western Spain, home to Muslim kings who left behind an impressive castle-fortress and massive ramparts. Today, it's hard not to get the impression that the town has seen better days, hardly surprising considering its troubled history. Its frontier position, just 3 miles (5 km) from the Portuguese border, has made it particularly vulnerable, and it has been torn by just about every war fought on the Iberian Peninsula in the past 500 years. One of the worst scenes of carnage occurred in 1812, during the Peninsular War, when 5,000 of the Duke of Wellington's 15,000 troops died here trying to drive Napoleon's occupying forces back toward France. More recently, in the early stages of the Spanish Civil War, Badajoz was the scene of a brutal massacre when Franco's Nationalist forces captured it and then rounded up scores of citizens and herded them into the bullring, where they were summarily executed by machine gun.

Badajoz is not the kind of place in which to spend a great deal of time, but it is fascinating to climb up to the top of the town to get an idea of what it once was. Visit the Alcazaba, the Arab fortress (open daily during daylight hours; admission charge), and take a closer look at the Torre del Apendiz, known locally as the Torre de Espantaperros, or "Dog Scarer Tower." Inside the fortress is the *Museo Arqueológico* (open Tuesdays through Sundays from 10 AM to 3 PM). This vantage point also gives a good view of the Puente de las Palmas, the fine 16th-century bridge that leads across the Guadiana and into town through the crenelated Puerta de las Palmas gate. The area around the Alcazaba is still very Moorish in feeling — a glimpse into the courtyards of some of the houses reveals typically Arabic tiles and ornate columns. Farther down, in the town's main square, Plaza de España, stands a monument to the 16th-century painter Luis de Morales, nicknamed "the Divine," a native of Badajoz. Several of his works can be seen in the *Museo de Bellas Artes* (32 Meléndez Valdez; phone: 924-222845; open Mondays through Saturdays from 8:30 AM to 2:30 PM; admission charge), as well as in the 13th-century Gothic cathedral of San Juan, which stands in the same square. Other works in the cathedral are by Zurbarán and Ribera. The Badajoz Tourist Office is at 3 Plaza de Libertad (phone: 924-222763).

CHECKING IN: Zurbarán – Badajoz has no outstanding hostelries such as the *paradores* of Trujillo, Guadalupe, and Mérida, but this hotel in the city center is an acceptable place to spend a day or two. It has 215 rooms, air conditioning, a big garden, a swimming pool, and a good restaurant. Paseo de Castelar, Badajoz (phone: 924-223741; fax: 924-220142; telex: 28818). Moderate.

Lisboa – A comfortable, modern, 176-room, air conditioned hotel that, as its name suggests, is on the road to Portugal, just under a mile (1km) out of town. 13 Avenida de Elvas, Badajoz (phone: 924-238200; fax: 924-236174; telex: 28610). Moderate to inexpensive.

Río – Close to the *Lisboa* on the way to Portugal and similar in quality and style, with 90 air conditioned rooms. Avenida Adolfo Díaz Ambrona, Badajoz (phone: 924-237600; telex: 28784). Moderate to inexpensive.

EATING OUT: Mesón El Tronco – The only real restaurant in town (although there are several bars and cafés that serve food), and very good it is, too. It offers fixed-price menus, named for the various towns and regions of Extremadura, as well as a lively bar with an excellent range of *tapas*. Closed Sundays. Reservations unnecessary. Major credit cards accepted. 16 Calle Muñoz Torrero, Badajoz (phone: 924-222076). Moderate.

El Sótano – A good place for a quick lunch. The bar has a tempting array of *tapas* — ham, chorizo (sausage), small fried fish — or order something more substantial, such as the *caldereta de cordero,* a typical Extremaduran lamb casserole. Open daily. No reservations. Major credit cards accepted. 6 Calle Virgen de la Soledad, Badajoz (phone: 924-223161 or 924-220019). Inexpensive.

La Panda – Right on the main square, this bar has an upstairs restaurant that serves a daily three-course set menu of exceptional value. Open daily. No reservations. No credit cards accepted. 11 Plaza de España, Badajoz (phone: 924-222152 or 924-220537). Very inexpensive.

CÁCERES: The capital of the province of the same name, Cáceres is 57 miles (91 km) northeast of Badajoz via N523. The city is really in three parts, one of which is an Old Town surrounded by Moorish walls and so superbly preserved that it has served as a backdrop for more than one film that is set in the Middle Ages. A stroll through the sandy-colored maze of narrow streets in this Old Quarter is like stepping back hundreds of years, to the 15th and 16th centuries, when noblemen vied with each other to build more beautiful mansions and palaces with the wealth acquired in their exploits across the Atlantic. Almost every house bears a coat of arms, proudly carved out of the tawny stonework. Until the late 15th century, most of them had battlemented defensive towers as well, but Queen Isabella ordered all but one — that of the Casa de las Cigüeñas (House of the Storks) — to be razed in an effort to put a halt to internecine fighting. The tower stands in the Plaza de las Veletas, and is now a military government office that is closed to the public. All is quiet now, and storks nest everywhere in old Cáceres — atop the Church of San Mateo (Plaza de San Mateo), site of a former mosque, and up on the spire of the Church of Santa María. Step inside this latter church, in the main square of the walled city, to see the tombs of some of Cáceres's most famous citizens, marked with their heraldic crests. Keep an eye out for the 15th-to-16th-century Palacio de Ovando in the same square, for the intricately carved façade on the 15th-century Palacio de los Golfines de Abajo nearby, and, in a corner of the walled city, for the 16th-century Casa de Toledo-Moctezuma, where Juan Caño, a henchman of Hernán Cortés, lived with his wife, a daughter of Montezuma, the last Aztec emperor. The 16th-century Palacio de Godoy is just outside the walls. Still in the Old Town, on Calle de los Condes, a quiet back street, a plaque bears witness to another era in Spanish history. Here, reads the inscription, Generalísimo Francisco Franco was declared the supreme ruler of Spain. The whole effect is made more dramatic by a huge splotch of brown paint that someone has thrown at the plaque.

Near Plaza de San Mateo, the 17th-century Casa de las Veletas (House of the Weather Vanes), site of the onetime Moorish Alcázar, today serves as the town's *Museo Arqueológico* (Plaza de las Veletas; open Tuesdays through Sundays from 9:30 AM to 2:30 PM; admission charge). It incorporates an interesting Arab cistern and houses collections of Celtic, Roman, and Visigothic remains. The Roman colony at Cáceres, founded during the 1st century BC, was one of the five most important in the province of Lusitania. Destroyed by barbarians, it was rebuilt by the Arabs, who called it Cazris, the forerunner of its modern name. The Moors used it as a fortress town from which to embark on other incursions, and built the walls that still stand today, setting them atop Roman foundations.

Besides the walled Old Town at the top, Cáceres has a much more bustling area at the foot of the walls in the vicinity of the Plaza del General Mola; the main square and the location of the tourist office (phone: 927-246347). Much farther down is the sprawling New Town, which houses most of the shops, hotels, and offices. Two miles (3 km) east of town, on a road that climbs steeply up through olive trees to the peak of the Sierra de la Mosca, stands the Sanctuary of Nuestra Señora de la Montaña (Our Lady of the Mountain). From here, there is a spectacular view over Cáceres itself, with the Gredos mountains to the north and the Sierra de San Pedro range to the south.

 CHECKING IN: *Alcántara* – In the new part of town, along with most of the hotels in Cáceres. This one is comfortable and modern, with 67 rooms and air conditioning. No restaurant. 14 Avenida Virgen de Guadalupe, Cáceres (phone: 927-228900; telex: 28943). Moderate.

Extremadura – One of the nicest hotels in town, just opposite the *Alcántara*, with 69 air conditioned rooms, gardens, a swimming pool, and a restaurant. 5 Avenida Virgen de Guadalupe, Cáceres (phone: 927-221604; fax: 927-211095). Moderate.

EATING OUT: *El Atrio* – A chic establishment in the new part of town. It offers haute cuisine and has built up a faithful following. Open daily. Reservations advised. Major credit cards accepted. 30 Avenida de España, Bloque 4, Cáceres (phone: 927-242928). Expensive.

La Malvasia – Also in the new part of town, but serving more regional cooking than *El Atrio*. For dessert, try the *higo chumbo,* as exotic as its name suggests: it's an ice cream made of prickly pear. Open daily. Reservations unnecessary. American Express and Visa accepted. 5 Calle Antonio Silva, Cáceres (phone: 927-244609). Expensive.

El Figón – One of the most popular restaurants in Cáceres, it serves finely cooked local dishes. Open daily. Reservations advised. American Express, Diners Club, and Visa accepted. 14 Plaza San Juan, Cáceres (phone: 927-248194). Expensive to moderate.

La Bodega Medieval – This attractive eatery, hidden away in a quiet alley of the walled Old Town, has painted beamed ceilings and a bottle-lined *bodega* next door, where customers can drink an aperitif and eat *tapas* before dining. On the menu, watch for *perdiz al estilo Alcántara,* a casserole of partridge with mushrooms, red pepper, and juniper berries. Open daily. Reservations advised. Major credit cards accepted. 1 Calle Orellana, Cáceres (phone: 927-245458). Moderate.

En Route from Cáceres – Instead of taking the main road north to Plasencia, head west on N521 toward Valencia de Alcántara, and after 7½ miles (12 km), at Malpartida de Cáceres, turn right onto C523, following it through Brozas to Alcántara. This quiet, peaceful town takes its name from the Arab word for bridge, *al kantara,* specifically referring to the magnificent Roman construction that spans the ravine of the Tagus River just below the town. Alcántara's position close to the Portuguese border has made it an important strategic point throughout history. After the Romans and the Arabs, the military order of the Knights of Alcántara made it their headquarters during the early 13th century, using it as a base for incursions against other Moorish strongholds in the area. The knights' now-crumbling castle can still be seen at the top of the town. Queen Isabella of Spain and her aunt, Beatrice of Portugal, signed a treaty here in 1479, ending years of enmity between the two countries. Napoleon's army occupied the town during the 19th century, billeting troops in the 16th-century Convent of San Benito.

From Alcántara, follow the signs to Mata de Alcántara, and turn left there for Garrovillas. The road passes fields strewn with giant, strangely shaped boulders, clusters of conical stone cattle sheds, and then some wild countryside, relieved only by fig trees and prickly pears, before coming out onto the main N630 highway, where a left turn leads to Plasencia. Along the way, a half-ruined 2nd-century Roman bridge still stands just outside Cañaveral.

PLASENCIA: Its name — derived from the Latin for "may it be pleasing to God and man," which is what Alfonso VIII hoped it would be when he rebuilt it in the 12th century after its recapture from the Moors — suggests that Plasencia is a charming town. With its whitewashed houses, narrow streets, and flowers on almost every wrought-iron balcony, it is that, as well as an ideal base to explore the north of Extremadura, one of the most beautiful corners of Spain as far as natural scenery is concerned. The town is set in a bend of the Jerte River and is crowned by a splendid cathedral, part 13th-century Romanesque and part late 15th-century Gothic, especially dramatic at sunset. The choir stalls, carved by Rodrigo Alemán during the 16th century, depict episodes from the Bible and from daily life in Extremadura — look for the scenes from an old-style bullfight. The area around the cathedral, containing the 13th-century San Nicolás church and, in a quiet plaza dotted with orange trees nearby, the magnificent Church of San Vicente, is the most interesting from a historical point of view. The porticoed Plaza Mayor, the town's main square, is a pleasant place to have a drink and watch the green man on top of the town hall at the north end of the square spring into action to strike the hours. If visiting the town on a Tuesday, note the market, which has been held in Plasencia since the 13th century.

CHECKING IN: *Alfonso VIII* – The only really good hotel in town. Don't be put off by its slightly tatty exterior or by its position on one of Plasencia's busiest streets. Inside, it's comfortable and elegant, with 57 rooms and air conditioning. 32 Calle Alfonso VIII, Plasencia (phone: 927-410250; fax: 927-418042; telex: 28960). Moderate.

EATING OUT: *Nykol's* – A popular place with Plasencians, it serves refined versions of classic Extremaduran dishes. Try the gazpacho with melon and the *solomillo de cerdo crema,* a filet of pork cooked with ham and cheese. Open daily. Reservations advised. American Express and Visa accepted. 8 Calle Pedro Isidio, Plasencia (phone: 927-415850). Expensive to moderate.

Florida – Well-cooked international dishes and a few local specialties are the fare at this restaurant, about a mile out of town on the road to Cáceres. Open daily. Reservations unnecessary. No credit cards accepted. 22 Avenida de España, Plasencia (phone: 927-413858). Moderate.

En Route from Plasencia – Madrid is 160½ miles (257 km) to the east, Salamanca 82½ miles (132 km) to the north, but if there is time to spare, it's worth spending an extra couple of days in Plasencia and using it as a point from which to explore one or more of the stunningly beautiful valleys to the north of town. Each can be taken in as a day trip, with nights spent in Plasencia.

Those visiting in spring or early summer should be sure to drive up the valley of the Jerte River, taking N110 northeast out of Plasencia and passing through the small towns of Navaconcejo, Cabezuela del Valle, Jerte, and Tornavacas. The valley is one of Spain's main cherry growing areas, and in May and June the fields are a profusion of pink and white blossoms.

The Vera Valley, which also runs northeast of Plasencia, is an idyllic spot any time of the year. Here, hidden among chestnut and pine woods, is the Monasterio de Yuste, the Hieronymite monastery where the great Holy Roman Emperor Charles V retired in 1557, and where he died, riddled with gout, in September 1558. The powerful monarch's rooms can still be seen, along with the chapel where he heard mass (guided tours only; open daily from 9 AM to 1 PM and from 4 to 7 PM; admission charge). A restaurant in the monastery serves lunch, but not dinner. To reach Yuste, follow the signs out of Plasencia and drive 28 miles (45 km) along C501 to the turnoff at the village of Cuacos; the monastery is a mile (1.6 km) farther and is well signposted. Before returning to Plasencia, drive to nearby Garganta la Olla and Aldeanueva de la Vera, picturesque mountain villages with cobbled streets and ornately carved overhanging wooden balconies.

The object of the third worthwhile excursion from Plasencia is the rugged area known as Las Hurdes, where some of the most remote and most beautiful scenery of Extremadura is to be found. This region has long been branded as one of the wildest in Spain, a place whose inhabitants, it is rumored, drink bull's blood and practice devil worship. It is certainly one of Spain's more backward areas, with high levels of illiteracy, but it is also one of the most stunning to view. Rolling hills studded with olive trees give way to fir trees and rushing streams, and those traveling early in the morning will see villagers riding their basket-laden mules and donkeys out for a day's work in the fields and women washing clothes in the streams the way their great-grandmothers did.

To reach this area, take the Salamanca road (N630) north from Plasencia and, after 20 miles (32 km), turn left toward Guijo de Granadilla and follow signs for Cerezo and Caminomorisco. It's a good idea, before setting out, to pick up one of the special enlarged maps of the area from the tourist office just off the main square in Plasencia (17 Calle Trujillo; phone: 927-412766). It is almost inevitable for a first-time visitor to get lost at least once, although it hardly matters, as long as there is plenty of time — and gas in the tank. As a rule of thumb, the farther north you go, the more remote and fascinating the villages become. If there is time, the entire circuit can be made, ending in the small mountain town of Hervás — but be warned, it's a long drive and will take the better part of a day. There are *hostales* offering good but basic food and accommodations at Cerezo, Caminomorisco, Nuñomoral, and La Alberca. Better still, make a picnic of slices of local ham and cheese, with fresh bread bought from one of the village *panaderías,* and eat it near a Roman bridge, with your feet dangling in the cool waters of one of the many mountain streams. Hervás is a pretty town, with an interesting and well-preserved Jewish quarter, still much as it was when its original inhabitants, along with the rest of Spain's unconverted Jews, were expelled from the country during the late 15th century.

From Hervás, just a mile or so off N630, it's a 60-mile (96-km) drive north to Salamanca, or a 28-mile (45-km) drive south back to Plasencia.

CHECKING IN/EATING OUT: *Parador Carlos V* – The imposing 15th-century fortified castle where Charles V stayed for several months, while his rooms were being prepared at the Monastery of Yuste, is today a hotel with 53 air conditioned rooms, a garden, a swimming pool, and a first-rate restaurant. Major credit cards accepted. It's 7½ miles (12 km) beyond the monastery in the direction of Jarandilla de la Vera. Carretera de Plasencia, Jarandilla de la Vera (phone: 927-560117; fax: 927-560088). Expensive.

The Balearic Islands

The Balearic Islands, set in the Mediterranean Sea southeast of Barcelona and east of Valencia, have been invaded repeatedly over the centuries, as the Phoenicians, Greeks, Carthaginians, Romans, Byzantines, Vandals, Moors, French, English, and Spanish successively became the dominant Mediterranean power. Today, the invasion continues, sustained by more annual air power than that focused on London during the Blitz and more foreign troops than those that stormed Normandy in the D-Day landings. Today's invasion, however, is one of tourists. While the Balearics (Islas Baleares to the Spanish) are relatively undiscovered by Americans visiting the Continent, as far as the Europeans — and particularly the British and the Germans — are concerned, they are Europe's most popular tourist destination.

Four main islands, aligned in two pairs — Majorca (Mallorca in Spanish) and its smaller neighbor, Minorca (Menorca in Spanish), plus Ibiza and its little sidekick, Formentera — make up the Balearic Archipelago, which also includes several smaller islets. Together, they constitute Spain's Baleares province, with Palma de Mallorca, on Majorca, as provincial capital. Majorca is not only the largest of the islands but also the best known and the most developed in terms of the tourist trade. Minorca is the second-largest island, but its tourist industry lags behind that of the slightly smaller Ibiza. Only in the past few years has Minorca entered the competition in earnest, so it still has plenty of undisturbed countryside and isolated beaches appearing much today as they were decades ago. The smallest island, Formentera, is equally tranquil.

Togetherness notwithstanding, each island has had its own history, although there are some common threads. Evidence that the archipelago was the home of an advanced megalithic civilization abounds, on Majorca and above all on Minorca, in the form of monuments in stone — cylindrical *talayots,* T-shaped *taulas,* and ship-shaped *navetas* — whose exact origins and purpose remain a mystery to scholars. Later, the islanders became mercenaries in the armies of Rome and Carthage; indeed, so renowned were they among the ancients for their skill with a slingshot that the very name of the island group derives from the Greek word for sling. History records that the Romans who captured Majorca in 123 BC used leather skins to protect their ships from the islanders' lead and stone pellets.

Arab incursions began during the 8th century, and by 902 the Moors were securely installed. They remained so, under succeeding dynasties, until James I of Aragon conquered the islands for the Christians, beginning in 1229; about a half-century later, an independent kingdom of Majorca was created (including Montpellier and Roussillon in France as well as the Balearics), which endured until the mid-14th century. Thanks to the islands' position along the main seagoing trading route between northern Italy and northern Europe, these were prosperous times, a virtual Balearic golden age — as Palma's imposing Gothic cathedral, begun in 1230, can testify. Prosperity continued even after the islands reverted to the kingdom of Aragon in 1343 — witness the Lonja, Palma's old stock exchange, which was booming during the 15th century. But early in the 16th century, because of a plague of pirates off their shores, the Balearics were prohibited by the newly united crown of Aragon and Castile from engaging in trade with the New World, a ban that effectively cut them off from Spain's golden age and consigned them to a backwater of history.

The islands are closely tied culturally to the region of Catalonia. Two languages are spoken: Castilian Spanish and the local language, the Balearic dialect of Catalan, which varies slightly from island to island (thus the confusion of many island place-names, spelled one way in Spanish and another in the local language).

Each island has a distinct personality. Majorca (its name, dating back to the Romans, means "the larger") is a microcosm of Spain. On this small island is the very Spanish city of Palma, complete with a massive cathedral and a medieval Old Town. On either side of the capital city are beaches endowed with blocks of high-rise hotels, tourist-oriented restaurants, and late-night discos that stretch for miles, much like areas of the Costa del Sol. Mountains rising ruggedly along the western coast provide roads as narrow and twisting as those found in the Pyrenees and views across the sea as spectacular as those found in Galicia. It is an island of contrasts. In the countryside, only a 10-minute drive from the center of Palma, almond and olive groves blanket the fields, peasants still plow the land with oxen, and black-clad women with weathered hands help with the harvest. Sundials still tell the time in some places; in others, Europe's largest discos seem to be keeping pace with the space-age future. In one port, the world's most luxurious yachts lie at anchor, while in the next, fishermen drag their boats onto the beach after working through the night.

Majorca has been a magnet for writers, painters, and musicians for more than a century. The trend may have begun in the 1830s when the consumptive composer Frédéric Chopin and his mistress, the author who used the pseudonym George Sand, shivered through an unusually cold winter here in the Valldemosa Carthusian Monastery. Despite the aggravation to his already ill health, Chopin was inspired to write some of his finest work. His lover wrote *A Winter in Majorca,* a not exactly flattering account of island life (Majorcan society had not taken kindly to this illicit couple) that was nevertheless enthusiastic about the landscape. It was later translated into English by a 20th-century visitor, the poet and novelist Robert Graves. The author of *I, Claudius* and *The White Goddess,* Graves settled in Deyá and presided over a virtual artists' and writers' colony on Majorca. The steady stream of books they generated spread the word of the island's beauty, creating the mass tourism industry that boomed in the 1960s.

Minorca (whose name means "the smaller") is far less developed than either Ibiza or Majorca. It bears its own gentle charm. If the desire is to disappear for a honeymoon, this is the island to choose. For those who really want to get away from it all and enjoy beaches in solitude, quiet dinners beside cozy fishing harbors, and evenings under the stars, Minorca is the place. The island is easy to explore — no part of it is more than an hour's drive away from another. Yet it has a split personality. At the Mahón end, the unmistakable stamp of almost 8 decades of British occupation during the 18th century caters to predominantly English-speaking visitors. At the opposite end, anchored by the distinctly Spanish town of Ciudadela, Germans fill the bungalows of the tourist villages. Nightlife here is tame by Spanish standards, with only a handful of discos pulsating until dawn. Ancient megaliths and burial grounds — very much a part of the contemporary Minorcan landscape — provide the major distraction from a very lazy beach existence.

Ibiza's history doesn't jump at the visitor the way the castles and cathedrals of Majorca do, nor do cows graze around its ancient ruins as they do on Minorca. The Carthaginians established a colony here during the 7th century BC to exploit the island's salt beds, and the remains of 500 years of this Punic culture — the island's most significant remains of its past — are preserved in museum displays and carved in the hillsides as tombs. Ibiza came to the world's attention relatively recently, as a haven for writers and artists and a refuge for the counterculture in the 1950s and 1960s, and then, as this advance guard was absorbed into the mainstream, as the jet set playground that it is today. Bob Dylan, Bruce Springsteen, *U2*, and Julio Iglesias have all made regular appearances on this small island, and some of them even maintain sprawling hidden villas here. Tucked-away recording studios churn out top-ten albums, and prominent European fashion designers run shops in the narrow streets of the port. Ibiza buzzes with an international energy. Don't bother looking for Spain here. But for those who want to pull out all stops, keep themselves entertained throughout the night, sleep on the beach, and then start all over again, this is nirvana.

Ibiza (pronounced Ee-*bee*-tha) is something Disney might have created had he desired the perfect holiday island. The town of Ibiza tumbles down from a cathedral and rampart that overlook the protected harbor. Narrow streets and stairs wind between picture-perfect whitewashed houses, with views of the more modern city and the bay around every corner. Tiny boutiques hawk gaily colored scarves, T-shirts, and postcards, as well as trendy art. Outside of town, there are hundreds of private coves for swimming — some with fine white sand, others with tiny, water-smoothed pebbles — rather than mile-long beaches. High-rise hotels are limited, and the tourist enclaves blend with the island's natural lines. Nightspots are truly that — coming to life late, with live entertainment and dancing that slows down only with the dawn. Tourism is unabashedly the mainstay of the economy. During the winter months, fewer than a dozen of the island's scores of hotels remain open, and the discos pack up the speakers and lights.

Formentera, counted among the four major islands of the Balearics, is little more than a spit of sand that lies 4 miles across a strait from Ibiza. But those short miles separate two worlds. Undeveloped Formentera is a retreat from the crush of tourists packing Ibiza during the height of summer. Here, a handful of hotels cater to those seeking long sandy beaches and a quiet vacation. Visitors should take a good look as they arrive on the island — what they see is what they'll get. Don't expect any major changes in scenery, though the cliffs at the far end of the island are spectacular. Remember, the point is to relax and lie in the sun. In Formentera, there aren't many distractions from those pursuits.

SOURCES AND RESOURCES

TOURIST INFORMATION: The islands have more than one level of tourist information office (provincial, island, city), although in many cases they occupy the same premises. On Majorca, there's the Balearic Government Tourist Office (located in the arrivals area of the island's Son San Juan Airport; phone: 971-260803) and in downtown Palma (8 Avenida Rey Jaime III; phone: 971-712216). These offices provide excellent maps, listings of hotels, and information on a host of other subjects, including golf courses and deserted beaches. There are also 15 municipal tourism offices (Oficinas Municipales de Turismo) on Majorca, one in each major town. The most important are the two in Palma (11 Calle Santo Domingo; phone: 971-724090; and in a booth on Plaza de España, near the train station; phone: 971-711527). These tourist offices have schedules of events, buses, and trains, restaurant listings, and excellent local maps. The hours of all tourist offices in Palma are from 9:30 AM to 1:30 PM and from 4 to 6 PM; some of the smaller municipal tourist offices are open only in the morning.

On Minorca, the main tourist office (13 Plaza de la Constitución, Mahón; phone: 971-363790) is open from 9 AM to 2 PM; closed Saturdays. The office distributes maps of the island and brochures outlining the historical sights of interest in Ciudadela and Mahón, as well as the island's archaeological sites. On Ibiza, the main tourist office (13 Paseo Vara de Rey; phone: 971-301900) is open from 9:30 AM to 1 PM and from 4 to 6 PM. The office provides a map of the island and of the town of Ibiza that is helpful, although it leaves much to the imagination.

Local Coverage – Those who read a smattering of Spanish should pick up a copy of the *Diario de Mallorca,* which publishes an edition for each island, or of *Ultima Hora,* which provides a good list of activities on Majorca. There is no dearth of information in English, however. The English-language *Majorca Daily Bulletin,* published in Palma and sold at newsstands, is packed with timetables and news about happenings around the island. The *Balearic Times,* a glossy magazine published every 2 months with information on upcoming events, nightlife, and restaurant recommendations, is sold at most magazine stands; *Majorca Today,* also sold at newsstands, outlines activities and events on the islands but without the style of the *Times.* The *Reader,* published monthly and distributed free through hotels and tourist agencies, has comments on tourist activities and plenty of advertisements for upcoming events.

TELEPHONE: The area code for the Balearic Islands is 71. If calling from within Spain, dial 971 before the local number.

CLIMATE: The weather is sparklingly clear, with average high temperatures in the low to mid-80s in July and August, the warmest months, and in the high 50s in January and February, the coldest ones. (Average lows for July and August are in the high 60s to low 70s, and in the mid- to high 40s in January and February.) The temperate climate makes the islands year-round resorts, and even February, when the almonds are in bloom, is beautiful. Note that the swimming season extends from April through October and that the average sea temperature, about 60F in April, rises to about 80F in August. Ibiza and Formentera are a bit warmer than the other two islands, and Minorca is the coolest, although the differences are minimal.

GETTING THERE: The main connection between the islands and the Continent is by air; over 7½ million visitors a year arrive by plane, another 750,000 by ferry boat. Scheduled flights arrive directly from every European capital, along with hundreds of charter flights from cities such as Manchester, England, and Hamburg, Germany. Arriving European flights land most frequently at Son San Juan Airport on Majorca, though there also are direct flights to Ibiza and Minorca. Most European airlines maintain a minimum of one flight a week during the winter; in summer, the frequency is increased.

Inbound flights from Spain are aboard *Iberia* or its subsidiary, *Aviaco*. The greatest number of daily nonstops to Majorca depart from Barcelona (35 minutes flying time) and Madrid (1 hour, 10 minutes); Alicante, Málaga, Valencia, and Vitoria also have nonstop service, in most cases on a daily basis. In addition, there are direct (not nonstop) flights from the Canary Islands. Nonstop service to Minorca is from Barcelona, Madrid, and Valencia, and there is direct sevice from Bilbao and Vigo. Nonstop service to Ibiza departs from Barcelona, Madrid, Valencia, and, in summer, Alicante. (Note that the Balearics are among the 30 Spanish destinations that may be visited by holders of the Visit Spain Airpass, which must be bought in conjunction with a round-trip air ticket between the US and Spain, at least one leg of which must be aboard *Iberia*. See *Traveling by Plane,* GETTING READY TO GO).

The airplane is also the most important form of inter-island hopping, with Palma serving as the hub. *Aviaco* flies several times a day between Palma and Minorca and between Palma and Ibiza, a 30-minute trip in each case. Interestingly, the flights are no more expensive than the same trip by sea.

Car and passenger ferries operated by *Trasmediterránea* (5 Muelle Viejo, Palma; phone: 971-726740) link the islands with Barcelona and Valencia (and Sète, France) and, via hydrofoil, with Alicante. The company has offices in several cities (2 Vía Laietana, Barcelona; phone: 93-3102508; at 15-Bajo Avenida Manuel Soto, Valencia; phone: 96-367-6512 or 96-367-0704; and at 2 Explanada de España, Alicante; phone: 96-520-6011). For Majorca, there are ferries daily throughout the year from Barcelona, 6 days a week from Valencia, and twice a week from Sète, France. For Minorca, there are ferries from Barcelona daily between mid-June and mid-September and then twice a week during the winter; connections between Valencia and Mahón operate only once a week. For Ibiza, there are ferries from Barcelona daily from mid-June to mid-September and then 4 or 5 days a week, depending on the month; ferries from Valencia to Ibiza run once or twice a week. The same company operates a hydrofoil service from Alicante to Ibiza daily year-round. Inter-island service links Palma and Mahón, Minorca, on Sundays, and Palma and Ibiza twice a week year-round by normal steamer and daily in summer by hydrofoil. Travel times for these trips are as follows: Barcelona to Palma, 8 hours; Valencia to Palma, 9 hours; Barcelona to Mahón, 9 hours; Valencia to Mahón, 16 hours (via Palma); Barcelona to Ibiza, 9½ hours; Valencia to Ibiza, 7 hours; Alicante to Ibiza by hydrofoil, 2¾ hours; Palma to Mahón, 6½ hours; and Palma to Ibiza, 4½ hours, or 2 hours by hydrofoil.

Another ferry company, *Flebasa,* connects Denia on the mainland (between Valencia and Alicante) with Ibiza, docking at San Antonio Abad rather than at Ibiza town. Departures are daily year-round, and the trip takes 3 hours. The company has offices in Denia (phone: 965-784200 or 965-784011), Ibiza (phone: 971-342871), Madrid (phone: 91-473-2055), and San Sebastián (phone: 943-394891).

Formentera is reached by ferry from Ibiza daily year-round (about 1 hour).

SPECIAL EVENTS: The Balearic Government Tourist Office distributes a booklet outlining the traditional festivals that take place throughout the year. For the most part, these are small local events and, except for those mentioned below, not of particular interest to visitors. On Majorca, the *Majorca Open Golf Tourna-*

ment is held annually in March at the *Santa Ponsa* course. The *Chopin Festival,* which takes place throughout the month of August, features concerts every Sunday night at the Valldemosa Carthusian Monastery, north of Palma. The *Pollensa Music Festival,* held in August and early September, features classical music on Saturdays in the Convent of Santo Domingo, Pollensa, near the northern tip of the island. (The *Fiesta de Nuestra Señora de los Angeles,* on August 2, during which the Pollensa townfolk reenact a 16th-century battle against invading pirates, is worthwhile for visitors already in the area.) The *Majorca Jazz Festival* brings jazz greats such as Oscar Peterson, Chick Corea, and *Spyro Gyra* to Palma for performances running from mid-November through mid-December.

On Minorca, two music festivals share the season: The *Ciudadela Music Festival* presents classical music in the town square every Monday or Tuesday during July and August, while the *Mahón Music Festival* makes use of the majestic organ of the Santa María church on weekends from late July through mid-September. The *Fiestas de San Juan,* June 23 and 24 in Ciudadela, are the most important of the traditional celebrations: Centuries old, they revolve around horses and include mock jousts and displays of equestrian bravura such as the *jaleo* of prancing horses. Ibiza has two traditional festivals that are small affairs but worthwhile for visitors already on the island: On March 19, the *Fiesta de San José* includes a procession through the streets of the town of Ibiza; during the first week of September, Santa Eulalia del Río celebrates a *Semana Cultural,* with locals dressed in traditional costumes. Formentera islanders in traditional costume parade through San Francisco Javier, the island capital, on July 25 — *Santiago Apóstol* (Feast of Saint James).

SPORTS AND FITNESS: The islands provide opportunities for water sports of all kinds, as well as other spectator and participatory sports.

Golf – There are nine courses — seven on Majorca, one on Minorca, and one on Ibiza. Three of those on Majorca are 18-hole courses: the *Son Vida Club de Golf* (Urbanización Son Vida; phone: 971-237620), about 3 miles/5 km northwest of Palma, the *Club de Golf de Poniente* (Magaluf-Calvía; phone: 971-223615), and *Golf Santa Ponsa* (Calvía; phone: 971-690211), approximately 10 to 12 miles (16 to 19 km) southwest along the Bay of Palma in the Magaluf area. The 9-hole *Club de Golf de Son Parc* (11 Plaza Bastion, Minorca; phone: 971-352250) is about 14 miles (22 km) north of Mahón. On Ibiza, the *Club de Golf Roca Llisa* (phone: 971-304060), at Santa Eulalia del Río, also has 9 holes.

Hang Gliding – Along with parachuting and flying, this sport is available to the public at the *Royal Flying Club* (at the Aeropuerto de Son Bonet, Marratxi, Majorca; phone: 971-600114). Equipment is available for rental.

Horse Racing – On Majorca, racing takes place regularly at the *Son Pardo Hippodrome* (Carretera de Sóller Km 3; phone: 971-254032), and at the *Manacor Hippodrome* (Calle Es Pla; phone: 971-550023). But racing holds an even greater fascination for the islanders of Minorca, where trotting races take place every summer on Sunday at tracks in Mahón and Ciudadela.

Sailing – Virtually every hotel on a beach has facilities where small sailboats can be rented and lessons can be arranged. The main sailing school on Majorca is the *Escola Espanyola de Vela Cala Nova* (National Sailing School of Cala Nova) at San Agustín (phone: 971-402412).

Scuba Diving – Information on scuba diving around Majorca can be picked up at the *Scuba Club* (13 Calle Pedro Alcántara Peña, Palma; phone: 971-463315), or at the *Scuba Club of Santa Ponsa* (84 Vía Rey Jaime; phone: 971-690266).

Tennis – Numerous hotels have their own courts or courts nearby that are open to guests. On Majorca, tennis clubs operating independently of hotels are the *Tenis Club Aeropuerto de Son Bonet* (Marratxi; phone: 971-600114); *Tenis Arenal Son Veri* (1 Calle

Costa y Llobera, El Arenal, Palma; phone: 971-263834); and the *Mallorca Club de Tenis* (Calle Artillería de Montaña, also in Palma; phone: 971-238473).

Windsurfing – Windsurfers (also called board sailers) can be rented at most beach-front hotels.

MAJORCA

The largest of the Balearic Islands is roughly diamond-shaped, measuring approximately 62 miles from east to west and 47 miles from north to south, with about 250 miles of coastline. The northeastern and southwestern sides of the island curve in long beaches and harbors conducive to perfect vacations. The northwestern part of the island is a rugged mountain range — the Sierra de Tramuntana — that drops sharply to the sea, with only Puerto de Sóller offering a small sandy beach and yacht mooring. The southeastern part is rolling farmland strewn with rock walls and stone windmills, with a rocky shore interrupted by a series of sandy coves that have been developed into tourist villages.

The city of Palma de Mallorca — Ciutat de Mallorca in the local dialect — is set on the Bay of Palma on the island's southwest coast. With approximately 300,000 residents, it is home to almost half of the Majorcan population. The city itself is not a beach resort, but miles of sandy beaches stretch to the east of it, with those from Ca'n Pastilla to El Arenal, lined by high rise hotels, restaurants, and discos, known collectively as the Playa de Palma. To the west, newer tourist developments — their high-rise hotels clustered rather than strung along the sea — have been created on smaller beaches at Cala Mayor, Palma Nova, Magaluf, and, beyond the Bay of Palma, at Paguera.

At the northern tip of the island is the town of Pollensa, a few miles inland from Puerto de Pollensa, on Pollensa Bay, which offers excellent swimming and boating. The rugged Cabo de Formentor (Cape Formentor), at the end of the peninsula curving up around the bay, offers spectacular scenery, especially to those who make it to the lighthouse at the end of the road. Just south of Pollensa Bay is Alcudia, where a Roman city once stood (and a ruined Roman theater still stands), and, a mile or so south of the village, Alcudia Bay, lined by a 6-mile beach that is much less developed than the Playa de Palma outside the capital city.

Majorca's mountainous western coast is dotted with small villages that have become retreats for those seeking to leave the crowds behind. Sóller is the largest town in this part of the island, and it, along with Puerto de Sóller a few miles away on the coast, does receive its share of tourists via the train that connects the beach with Palma. A bit to the south is Deya, a medieval-looking town built on a small mound between the sea and towering mountains. Still farther south, the villages of Banyalbufar and Estellenchs hug mountainsides that drop steeply to the sea. Valldemosa, where Chopin and George Sand stayed, lies at one of the few passes through the spine of mountains that separate Palma from the coast.

The bulk of Majorca lies to the east of Palma. Most visitors make their way in this direction to visit the Drach Caves and the Hams Caves, in the vicinity of the village of Porto Cristo on the island's eastern coast. They also stop in the city of Manacor, in the interior, 30½ miles (49 km) due east of Palma, where the island's pearl industry is based. Compared to the coasts, the interior of Majorca is a step back in time. Here, the life of the islanders still revolves around farming, shopkeeping, and early-morning markets, rather than around the housing, feeding, and entertaining of tourists. Inca, 17½ miles (28 km) northeast of Palma on the way to Pollensa and Alcudia, is probably the most interesting interior town. A leatherworking center, it also has the island's largest flea market, in full bustle every Thursday morning.

The real beauty of Majorca's countryside is enjoyed by driving — across the fields, through the mountains, along the coastline. Limit excursions to trips easily completed in a day, since detours to visit unexpected sights constantly crop up. Loop from Palma to Valldemosa, then along the coast to Banyalbufar, Estellenchs, San Telmo, Puerto de Andraitx, Paguers, Magaluf, and back to the city. On another day, go north to Pollensa, then take the narrow road to the tip of Cape Formentor. A visit to a pearl factory in Manacor and to one of the massive caves farther east is another day trip. Or head away from the crowds down to Arenal de la Rapita, a totally undeveloped beach near the southeast corner of the island.

GETTING AROUND: Airport – Flights from Europe, mainland Spain, and the other islands arrive at the Aeropuerto de Son San Juan, 7 miles (11 km) to the east of Palma, or a 10-minute ride from the center and hotels along the Playa de Palma. An airport bus links the terminal with Plaza de España, where the bus and train stations are located; taxis to any hotel in the city will cost less than $10. For airport information, call 971-264162. The *Iberia* office is at 10 Paseo del Borne, Palma (phone: 971-262647 for information and reservations).

Bus – Palma has a well-organized bus system, used primarily by the local population. Two tourist offices (11 Calle Santo Domingo and on Plaza de España) distribute a timetable and route map. (Once a visitor is in the inner city, however, everything is within walking distance.) Buses also link every town on the island, as well as most of the beaches; a schedule is available from a third tourist office (8 Avenida Rey Jaime III). The main bus station in Palma is located on Plaza de España (phone: 971-752224).

Car Rental – The most extensive rental operations are provided by *Avis* (airport; phone: 971-260910 or 971-260911; and on the Palma waterfront at 16 Paseo Marítimo; phone: 971-230720 or 971-230735; as well as many others throughout the island). Some *Avis* offices are seasonal, so check with them for opening dates and hours. *Hertz* has several offices (at the airport; phone: 971-260809 or 971-264495; and on the Palma waterfront, at 13 Paseo Marítimo; phone: 971-234737 or 971-234833). *Europcar* also has two offices (at the airport; phone: 971-263811 or 971-490110; and at 19 Paseo Marítimo; phone: 971-454800 or 454400). In addition, there are many small local car rental operations that, in some cases, are significantly less expensive than *Avis* or *Hertz.* Check with your hotel for the closest one or, perhaps, for one offering hotel guests special discounts.

Ferry – Ferries connect the island with Barcelona (8 hours), Valencia (9 hours), Mahón on Minorca (6½ hours), and Ibiza (4½ hours, 2 hours by hydrofoil). *Trasmediterránea* (5 Muelle Viejo, Palma; phone: 971-726740) is the main source, but the ferries dock farther southwest along the bay at the Muelle de Pelaires. In addition to these basic mainland and inter-island services, numerous smaller companies operate around the island, linking the ports of Andraitx and San Telmo at the southwest corner of Majorca with the small offshore island of Dragonera, Palma with Magaluf, and Alcudia with Formentor. The tourist office provides a complete listing of such sailings.

Taxi – Plentiful, inexpensive, and much more convenient than buses. Call *Aero-Taxi* (phone: 971-267312), *Radio-Taxi* (phone: 971-755440), *Tele-Taxi* (phone: 971-401414), or *Fono-Taxi* (phone: 971-710403).

Tours – Sightseeing tours by motorcoach regularly reach every corner of the island. They can be booked through tour operators or hotels — tour buses call to pick up participants at their hotels every morning. There are some 20 fairly standard, full-day itineraries, such as the tour from Palma to Alcudia Bay, including stops at a local market, the house of Father Junípero Serra in Petra (the Spanish Franciscan, who founded missions in California, was a native Majorcan), and Picafort beach; and the tour to the Drach Caves, with stops at a pearl factory in Manacor.

Train – The island has two railroad lines. One connects Palma with Sóller, one of the most spectacular and picturesque train rides in Europe. Trains leave five times a day from the station on Calle Eusebio Estrada, off Plaza de España, and wind their way to Sóller and then down to the beach at Puerto de Sóller. Another train links Palma with Inca, departing at least every hour from another station next door on Plaza de España.

SPECIAL PLACES: Palma de Mallorca – The city features remains of the Moorish occupation, one of Spain's largest cathedrals, and stately 15th- and 16th-century mansions that attest to the island's onetime mercantile prosperity. The cathedral (La Seu), an immense golden stone Gothic construction with flying buttresses that looms on the seafront like a ship anchored at port, is the city's most important sight. Begun in 1230 and not finished until 1601, it underwent alterations during the early 20th century when Antoni Gaudí, the famed Catalan architect who was restoring it, removed the central choir that blocks the nave of most Spanish cathedrals. The result was a greater feeling of space and an uninterrupted view from the main entrance to the high altar, above which hangs Gaudí's wrought-iron baldachin. The cathedral chapter house contains a small museum, open Mondays through Fridays from 10AM to 12:30 PM and from 4 to 6:30 PM, Saturdays from 10 AM to 1:30 PM; closed Sundays. Admission charge. The cathedral has the same hours and is also open during services.

Palma's cathedral, in Plaza Almoina, stands on high ground at the western edge of the oldest part of the city, which is to the east of the wide, tree-shaded promenade known as El Borne (or Paseo del Borne). Across from the cathedral is the Palacio de la Almudaina, the palace-fortress of the island's Arab rulers, later converted into a royal palace for the Spanish Kings of Majorca (and now used, in part, to house the *Museo del Patrimonio Nacional* — closed Saturday afternoons, Sundays, and Mondays; no phone; admission charge). Only an arch of the Moorish construction is intact, but not too far away, on Calle Serra, are the Baños Arabes (Arab Baths; open 10 AM to 1 PM and from 4 to 6 PM; no phone; admission charge), which — although small and perhaps requiring some imagination to picture veiled women scurrying through the courtyard — remain essentially as they were under the caliphs. (Open daily from 10 AM to 1:30 PM and from 4 to 6 PM; admission charge.) Still in the Old Town, in the Portella quarter behind the cathedral, is the *Museo de Mallorca,* housed in an old mansion at 5 Calle de la Portella; it illustrates island history through a collection of archaeological artifacts, documents, paintings, and sculpture (open from 10 AM to 2 PM and from 4 to 7 PM; closed Sunday afternoons and Mondays; no phone; admission charge). Working your way north, you'll also see the 17th-century Casa Oleza (33 Calle Morey) — known for its inner courtyard — and the 16th-century Gothic and Renaissance Casa Palmer (17 Calle del Sol), before reaching Palma's second most renowned church, San Francisco, on the plaza with the same name. Built during the 13th and 14th centuries and given a baroque facade during the 17th, the church contains the tomb of Ramón Llull, a 13th-century philosopher, poet, theologian, and religious mystic who was born in Palma and martyred in North Africa while trying to convert the Arabs; it has a beautiful cloister attached to it. (Open from 9:30 AM to 1 PM and from 3:30 to 7 PM; closed Sunday afternoons.)

Proceed west from St. Francis to reach the Santa Eulalia church, a fine example of Majorcan Gothic, built from the 13th to the 15th centuries; behind it (at 2 Calle Zavella) is the 18th-century Casa Vivot, another mansion with a notable courtyard. Still farther west, but still in the Old Town on the east side of El Borne, is Palma's 17th-century Ayuntamiento (Town Hall), standing in a beautiful old square, Plaza Cort.

The Lonja, on the seafront west of El Borne, is one of Palma's star attractions. Built during the 15th century as a stock exchange and commercial building for the city's busy trading merchants, it now serves as an exhibition space for art shows (and is thus open irregularly); its secular Gothic design, by Guillermo Sagrera, is open and light, with spiral columns holding up the soaring ceiling. Also on the west side of El Borne is the Casa de los Marqueses de Sollerich (10 Calle San Cayetano), an 18th-century mansion with perhaps the finest courtyard in town.

The attractions beyond the center, on the west side of Palma, should not be missed. One of them, the Castillo de Bellver, an unusual round castle built during the 14th century and beautifully preserved, boasts perhaps the best view of Palma and the surrounding area. The courtyard has 2 levels of arcades, with classical arches ringing the lower level and Gothic arches soaring on the upper level. The rooms are sparsely furnished, but the kitchen has a massive cooking area; the adjoining Tower of Homage, looking like a stone rocket ready for blast-off, housed the dungeons. (Open from 8 AM to 10 PM from April through September, to 6 PM the rest of the year; admission charge.) The other attraction, the Pueblo Español (Spanish Village), located across from the Palacio de Congresos, offers a chance to see all of Spain at a glance. Much like its counterpart in Barcelona, this model village contains reproductions of houses and famous buildings from all parts of Spain. It also offers a chance to see Spanish artisans at work and shops where their handiwork can be purchased. The village is open daily from 9 AM to 8 PM. Admission charge.

ELSEWHERE ON THE ISLAND

La Cartuja de Valldemosa (Valldemosa Carthusian Monastery) – Set in the mountains 11 miles (18 km) north of Palma, this monastery was founded during the 14th century, although the present buildings are from the 17th and 18th centuries. After the Carthusian monks left it during the 18th century, its cells were rented out to guests, including Frédéric Chopin and George Sand, who spent the winter of 1838–39 here. The Cloister of Saint Mary offers beautiful views, and the neo-classical church is decorated with frescoes, an intricately carved choir stall, and rich tapestries. Closed Sundays; no phone; admission charge.

Deya – This lovely old village (Deiá in the local language) enjoys an enchanting setting perched loft-like over the sea and backed by evergreen mountains 17 miles (27 km) northwest of Palma. Its natural beauty lured those who made it an artists' and writers' colony — the poet Robert Graves, who lived here until his death in 1985, was probably its most famous long-term resident. He is now buried in the local cemetery, which also has a splendid view of the area.

Sóller – Almond, lemon, and orange groves surround this town 19 miles (30 km) north of Palma, the largest town on the western side of the island. Like many a settlement on Majorca, the threat of attack from the sea caused it to grow up a few miles inland from its port, Puerto de Sóller, which sits 3 miles (5 km) from the valley on a round, sheltered, beach-lined bay and has become a thriving resort center. Sóller itself has little to see, beyond a cathedral that is among the most elaborate on the island. Most visitors arrive aboard the turn-of-the-century narrow-gauge railroad train from Palma — a wonderfully scenic ride that is well worth the trip — then continue via an extension down to the port for the beach or a bite to eat.

Pollensa – On the northeast coast, 32½ miles (52 km) from Palma, Pollensa (Pollença in the Majorcan dialect), too, is an inland town; Puerto de Pollensa, a fishing village turned resort town, is 4 miles (6 km) away on one of the three largest bays of Majorca, with a big, sweeping beach. On the outskirts of Pollensa is Monte Calvario, a hill crowned by a small chapel reached by car or a climb of 365 steps. In town are the 14th-century parish Church of Nuestra Señora de los Angeles and the 16th-century Santo Domingo convent. Visitors not staying in the area invariably pass through both Pollensa and Puerto de Pollensa en route to Cabo de Formentor, at the extreme tip of the peninsula that forms the northern arm of Pollensa Bay.

Cabo de Formentor – The road from Puerto de Pollensa to Cape Formentor follows the spine of the Sierra de Tramuntana out to sea and provides stunning vistas, particularly at the Mirador d'Es Colomer and at the Formentor lighthouse at the end of the peninsula.

Cuevas de Artá (Artá Caves) – These extensive caves are perhaps the most beautiful of the many on the island, yet they are the least visited. They were first explored thoroughly during the 19th century — and are said to have inspired Jules Verne to write *Journey to the Center of the Earth* — but were known as long ago as the 13th century, when they served as a hiding place for Moors after the Reconquest. Open daily; admission charge. On the east coast of the island at Cabo Vermell, 6 miles (10 km) east of Artá (phone: 971-563293).

Cuevas del Drac (Drach Caves) – The largest of Majorca's caves are just over a mile long and contain a subterranean lake in addition to four chambers full of fanciful formations in limestone. Visits are guided (English-language tours are possible) and include a concert by floating musicians at the end of the tour. Be warned: The crowds are ridiculous during the summer months. Open daily; admission charge. On the east coast of Majorca, just south of Porto Cristo (phone: 971-570002).

Cuevas de Els Hams (Hams Caves) – Virtually next door to the Drach Caves and less impressive, although they are known for the whiteness of their stalactites and stalagmites. Open daily; admission charge. Just west of Porto Cristo (phone: 971-570227).

SHOPPING: Shopping in Palma is concentrated in the city center. Upscale shops, with such names as *Rodier, Gucci,* and *Armani,* tend to be found along Avenida Rey Jaime III. The shopping area that is more likely to be packed with Majorcans and thus with many more bargains is one on the east side of the Paseo del Borne, in small pedestrian streets that climb to the Plaza Mayor and then along Calle Sindicato and Calle San Miguel, which branch out from the square. Leather goods, embroidery, ceramics, and manufactured pearls are all good buys. For general purchases, stop in at *Galerías Preciados* (15 Avenida Rey Jaime III), a branch of the Spain-wide department store chain. Majorca also has a well-organized series of open-air markets. The main vegetable and fish market in Plaza Oliver is in operation daily and is worth a visit if only to see the colorful catch — orange crustaceans, black octopus, fish and shellfish of every other hue. An interesting crafts market takes place on Plaza Mayor on Saturday mornings year-round, and more frequently in summer. Markets in the smaller towns take place once or twice a week; the schedule is printed in the *Balearic Times,* as well as in several tourist office publications. Among the larger markets are the ones in Alcudia on Tuesday and Sunday mornings, in Artá on Tuesday mornings,

Inca on Thursday mornings, Manacor on Monday mornings, Pollensa on Sunday mornings, and Sóller on Saturday mornings. Among the more interesting shops are the following:

Bamuco – Moderately priced leather goods. 19 Palau Reial, Palma de Mallorca (phone: 971-722512).

Casa Bonet – One of the best embroidery shops on the island. 3 Calle Puigdorfila, Palma de Mallorca (phone: 971-722117).

L'Ofre – Better-quality purses and other articles in leather. 28 Paseo del Borne, Palma de Mallorca (phone: 971-223665).

Perlas Majórica – The island's well-known pearls, of the highest quality, organically manmade (of fish scales), at factory prices. 11 Avenida Rey Jaime III, Palma de Mallorca (phone: 971-725268). Pearls can also be bought directly from the factory, open daily, except Sundays, just off the main road in Manacor (48 Vía Romana; phone: 971-725268).

P'tit Percay – More moderately priced leather goods. 2 Avenida Antonio Maura, Palma de Mallorca (phone: 971-210370).

Scherezade – The best place to buy Lladró porcelain. 5 Calle Brossa, Palma de Mallorca (phone: 971-711974).

NIGHTCLUBS AND NIGHTLIFE: The Balearics have a justly deserved reputation for offering some of the wildest nightlife in the world. Not only does Palma dance all night long, but *BCM* in Magaluf, which has a capacity of over 5,000 revelers, is indisputably the world's largest discotheque. Any disco tour of Palma begins in the western part of the city around Plaza Gomila. Here, the stunning glass façade of *Tito's* (phone: 971-237642) faces the sea on the Paseo Marítimo, with another entrance on Plaza Gomila. Glass elevators move party animals between the 4 bars and 5 levels of this extravaganza, and revolving lights present a stunning light show to those on the waterfront. *Alexandra's,* nearby (Plaza Mediterráneo; phone: 971-237810), has the loud music and light shows without the wild setting of *Tito's.* Farther along the bay on the western side of the city, in Cala Mayor, *Pepe's Centre* (322 Avenida Joan Miró; phone: 971-403047) and *Disco Liberty,* just down the road (phone: 971-403644), offer excellent late-night dancing and are packed with tourists from every corner of the Continent. Still farther along the bay, Magaluf, a created resort city about a 30-minute drive to the west of Palma, is the area's main disco scene. Here the mega-disco *BCM* (phone: 971-683869) reigns, hosting some of rock's top stars in live performance; *Alexandra's 2 Disco* packs them in as a good, smaller alternative to *BCM*'s massive madness; and plenty of bars percolate with nonstop parties, complete with giant snake dances rolling from one pub into the next. Majorca's *Casino* (Urbanización Sol de Mallorca; phone: 971-680000), featuring American and French roulette, blackjack, and other games of chance, as well as a restaurant and discotheque, is also out this way (take the Cala Figuera turnoff from the Andraitx road).

The Playa de Palma area along the bay to the east of the city also has its complement of nightspots. Try *Riu Palace* (Calle Laud, El Arenal; phone: 971-265704), Majorca's largest disco until the creation of *BCM,* and *Zorba's* (4 Avenida Son Rigo; phone: 971-266664), which offers open-air disco along the beach.

Downtown Palma can indulge other tastes. For early-evening drinks, there are *tapas* bars lining Calle Apuntadores. Later, a visit to the *Bar Abaco* (1 Calle San Juan; phone: 971-714939), installed in a former Majorcan palace, is a memorable experience. Guests enter a giant room with wide arches over columns, a bar 30 feet long, Oriental carpets, classical statues, café tables, and baskets of fruit spilling across the floor; upstairs patrons chat on couches surrounding a fireplace while others wander through a reconstructed kitchen and gaze into the garden below, where a small pond shimmers in the light of dozens of giant candles. Classical music plays quietly in the background of this sophisticated establishment, where a mixed drink can cost anywhere from $8 to $16.

CHECKING IN: The majority of the hotels on the islands are dedicated to the group tour trade, but accept individual guests should space be available. The hotels listed below have been selected from more than 1,000 that the island has to offer. Prices are for a double room during high season, from June through September and at *Christmas* and *Easter.* Low-season rates can be 25% less. Expect to pay $90 and up in a hotel listed as expensive, from $50 to $90 in a moderate one, and less than $50 in an inexpensive one.

PALMA AND ENVIRONS

Meliá Victoria – At the western side of the bay, it overlooks the entire city, with one of the best views of the harbor. The 167 rooms all have television sets, the buffet breakfast is sumptuous, all the services that could be desired are available, and the location, next to the Plaza Gomila nightclubs, makes it central to Palma nightlife. (The pulsating lights of *Tito's* are next door, so get a room facing the other way to avoid the noise). There are 2 pools and open-air dancing in summer. 21 Avenida Joan Miró (phone: 971-234342; fax: 971-450824). Very expensive.

Bellver Sol – Half the price of the *Victoria* and not far away from it, on the road that rims Palma's harbor. The 393 rooms are simply and sparsely furnished — ask for one with a panoramic view of the yacht harbor. There is a good pool. 11 Paseo Marítimo (phone: 971-238008; fax: 971-284182). Expensive.

Nixe Palace – In the Cala Mayor beach area to the west of Palma, yet still within a 10-minute cab ride of the center. (There's no need to go into Palma for the nightlife, since there's more than enough in Cala Mayor.) This place is right on the beach, as a resort hotel should be, and there is a great pool. The 130 rooms are big and well furnished, in a contemporary style. 269 Avenida Joan Miró, Cala Mayor (phone: 971-403811; fax: 971-403595). Expensive.

Punta Negra – A 61-room hotel with bungalows as well, a pool, and virtually a private beach tucked between the rocks at Palma Nova. Carretera Andraitx, Km 12, Palma Nova (phone: 971-680762). Expensive to moderate.

Aquarium – In Palma Nova, just across the street from the beach and a short walk from the nightlife. A good basic tourist hotel with 109 rooms; closed from November through March. Paseo del Mar, Palma Nova (phone: 971-680308; telex: 69534). Moderate.

Costa Azul – One of the bargains on the road along Palma's harbor. It has 126 simple rooms and an indoor-outdoor pool with sliding glass overhead. This is closer to downtown Palma than it is to the Gomila nightlife quarter. Closed in December. 7 Paseo Marítimo (phone: 971-231940 ; fax: 971-231066). Moderate.

Santa Ana – On the Cala Mayor beach, it has 190 simply furnished rooms, most with terraces overlooking the sea, and a pool. 9 Calle Gaviota, Cala Mayor (phone: 971-401052). Moderate to inexpensive.

La Cala – Sitting side by side with its sister hotel, the *Santa Ana,* on the Cala Mayor beach, it is less than half the size (70 rooms) and a bit less expensive. It, too, has a pool. Closed November through March. 4 Calle Gaviota, Cala Mayor (phone: 971-401612). Inexpensive.

Horizonte Sol – Located at the far western end of Palma, near Porto Pí, this is a basic tourist hotel (200 rooms) but the price is right. It's within a short taxi ride of the Gomila nightlife section and has good views of the bay. 1 Calle Vista Alegre (phone: 971-400661; fax: 971-400783). Inexpensive.

ELSEWHERE ON THE ISLAND

La Residencia – An old mansion turned into a wondrous, low-key hotel with spectacular views over the sea. It's tucked just off the road leading into Deya from Valldemosa, perched high above the Mediterranean, a 15-minute walk from town.

Simple antiques, four-poster beds, and marble floors grace the 31 rooms. There is a swimming pool and tennis. Son Moragues, Deya (phone: 971-639011). Very expensive.

L'Hermitage – Virtually a self-contained resort in a mountain setting off the road from Palma to Sóller, far from the crowds and the beach. Rustic elegance is done as perfectly here as it can be. There are only 20 rooms, with furniture in heavy wood; dining is outside when possible; there are tennis courts, and the swimming pool is surrounded by pines. Carretera de Sollerich Km 8, Orient (phone: 971-613300; fax: 971-613300). Expensive.

Vistamar – A former manor house, this hostelry has 7 double rooms and a suite about 1¾ miles (3 km) from Valldemosa, on the road to Andraitx. It overlooks the sea on one side and is surrounded by olive and almond groves on the other. The restaurant is set on the porticoed terrace, the beds are four-poster, the house full of Spanish art. All is magic when lit at night. Carretera Andraitx, Km 2, Valldemosa (phone: 971-612300; fax: 971-612583). Expensive to moderate.

Ses Rotges – In the northeast corner of the island, it has 24 rooms, beautiful gardens, a pool, and an outdoor restaurant with a rustic lounge. Closed November through March. 21 Rafael Blanes, Cala Ratjada (phone: 971-564345). Moderate.

Miramar – It's as if time had stopped in the 1930s. The 69-room hotel is right on the beach at the far north of Majorca and couldn't be more pleasant. Reserve early. Closed November through March. 39 Paseo Anglada Camarasa, Puerto de Pollensa (phone: 971-531400). Moderate to inexpensive.

Costa D'Or – A small place (42 rooms) just up the road from Deya in Lluch Alcari, with views of the crashing sea below. It's very simple, but the beauty of the spot cannot be improved. Closed November through March. Lluch Alcari (phone: 971-639025). Inexpensive.

Mar y Vent – Set just off the main highway and about 500 feet above the sea, which lies at the end of a long terraced slope dropping steeply in front of the hotel. It has 19 good, simple rooms, a swimming pool, and great food. Closed December through February. 49 Calle Mayor, Banyalbufar (phone: 971-610025). Inexpensive.

EATING OUT: As with any popular tourist destination, restaurants abound in the Balearic Islands. They are as varied as the tourists who frequent them, seemingly bringing their own cooking with them as they come. Though German, Scandinavian, and English dining places easily can be found, there are still scores of restaurants serving up local specialties — fish restaurants and others stressing the lamb, goat, rabbit, chicken, and snail dishes typical of Balearic food. Wines to try are binisalem and felanitx, both from Majorca. Expect to pay $65 and up for a meal for two including an appetizer, main course, dessert, and wine in any restaurant listed as expensive; moderate means between $35 and $65, and inexpensive normally ranges between $25 and $35. Because the island economy is extremely seasonal, be sure to call restaurants to make sure they are open, especially off season.

PALMA AND ENVIRONS

Honoris – An excellent French restaurant in the northeastern part of Palma, near the industrial section. Only a handful of well-heeled tourists manage to make the pilgrimage, but those who are serious about eating and have money to spare should try it for a change of pace. Closed Sundays, holidays, *Holy Week,* and the first 2 weeks of August. Reservations advised. Major credit cards accepted. 76 Carretera Vieja de Bunyola (phone: 971-203221). Expensive.

La Lubina – Long established and one of the best fish places in Palma. Right on the old pier, it is as upscale and pricey as any that can be found in the city proper, with classical music filling the air, white tablecloths, and a hushed atmosphere. Try the grilled swordfish or the grilled fresh fish of the day, but avoid the lobster, since it would probably cost less to fly to Maine to satisfy those cravings. Open daily. Reservations advised. Major credit cards accepted. Muelle Viejo (phone: 971-723250). Expensive.

Porto Pí – Where King Juan Carlos eats when he comes to Palma — which means almost the top prices in town. Honored with a Michelin star, it is located in one of Palma's oldest mansions, and the menu features French Basque cooking. The fresh fish here is said to be some of the best on the island — try it baked in pastry, and then try one of the fabulous desserts. Closed Saturdays at lunch, Sundays, and mid-November to mid-December. Reservations necessary. Major credit cards accepted. 174 Avenida Joan Miró (phone: 971-400087). Expensive.

Caballito del Mar – Hard to beat for moderately priced outdoor eating along the seafront. On sunny days, the setting couldn't be better, and the food is normally well prepared, even with crowds of tourists descending from time to time. Have the fish of the day, perhaps grilled. Closed Sundays. Reservations advised. Major credit cards accepted. 5 Paseo de Sagrera (phone: 971-721074). Moderate.

Casa Eduardo – Come here just for the fish soup. It's located on the pier opposite *La Lubina* and is a "real people's" fish place, priced accordingly. Closed Sundays and Mondays. Reservations unnecessary. No credit cards accepted. 4 Industria Pesquera, on Mollet (phone: 971-721182). Moderate.

Don Peppone – The best Italian food in town. Great antipasti, linguine with shellfish, and osso buco. It's packed with Palma yuppies, who love it when the roof is rolled back to let the sun shine in. Closed Sundays. Reservations necessary. Visa accepted. 14 Calle Bayarte (phone: 971-454242). Moderate.

Gina – This dining spot has a beautiful terrace with a view of the magnificent Lonja. The specialties include *zarzuela de pescado* (fish soup) and chicken Kiev. Closed Wednesdays. Reservations necessary. No credit cards accepted. 1 Plaza de la Lonja (phone: 971-226484). Moderate.

Es Parlament – In an ornate classical setting in the Balearic Autonomous Parliament building, it's particularly famous for its paella. Closed Sundays. Reservations necessary. No credit cards accepted. 11 Calle Conquistador (phone: 971-726026). Moderate.

La Pergola – In the French bistro tradition, this tiny eatery has rustic wood details over whitewashed walls. The owner and chef, a former head chef at the *Waldorf Astoria* in New York, works magic with thin steaks. Open daily. Reservations necessary. Visa accepted. 13 Plaza Atarazanas (phone: 971-714808). Moderate.

Ca'n Juanito – A basic Spanish restaurant with simple, uninspired decor, it serves excellent local dishes such as rabbit, goat, and lamb. Closed Wednesday evenings. Reservations unnecessary. No credit cards accepted. 11 Avenida Aragon (phone: 971-461065). Inexpensive.

Celler Sa Premsa – For those who've dreamed of the perfect Spanish restaurant — bullfight posters on the walls, long wooden tables shared with strangers, and great budget food. This is Palma's largest such dining place (seating for 250), and it's usually full. The roast suckling pig is a reliable choice. Open daily. Reservations advised on weekends. Visa accepted. 8 Plaza Obispo Berenguer de Palou (phone: 971-723529). Inexpensive.

ELSEWHERE ON THE ISLAND

Na Burguesa – Just outside Palma in the small town of Génova (from where it has a marvelous view of the capital). Loud and boisterous, it serves Majorcan dishes, but be prepared to wait for a table. Try the roast shoulder of lamb or the pork loin. Closed Monday evenings. Reservations essential on weekends. Visa accepted. Mirador de Na Burguesa, Génova (phone: 971-402043). Moderate.

Celler Ca'n Amer – An immense room with wine casks surrounding the diners. This has gained fame as one of the best spots on the island for local cooking; unfortunately, the prices have increased as its popularity has soared. Closed Sundays in summer, Saturdays and Sundays at other times. Reservations are essential for those planning to have lunch here on a Thursday, when the market brings an overload of hungry folks into town; at other times, reservations are advised. American Express and Visa accepted. 7 Calle Bruy, Inca (phone: 971-501261). Moderate.

Mandilego – In a small town on the Bay of Alcudia, on the north coast of the island, it offers excellent fish dishes, from swordfish steaks to Mediterranean lobsters. Closed Mondays. Reservations advised. No credit cards accepted. 49 Calle Isabel Garau, Ca'n Picafort (phone: 971-527003). Moderate.

Mesón Ca'n Pedro – One of the shrines of Majorcan cooking, this rustic restaurant is also just outside Palma in Génova. Try the *cabrito* (kid) if any is available. Closed Wednesdays. Reservations necessary. Visa accepted. 4 Calle Rector Vives, Génova (phone: 971-402479). Moderate.

Puig de Sant Miguel – Majorcan specialties are featured at this rambling rustic place in the interior, on the road from Montuiri to Manacor. Try suckling pig or leg of lamb, served on wooden tables surrounded with wagon wheels and local pottery. Closed Tuesdays. Reservations advised. No credit cards accepted. Carretera Manacor–Montuiri, Km 31 (phone: 971-646314). Moderate.

Ses Porxeres – This Catalan eatery is best known for its fantastic appetizers. Order the appetizer plate and a good bottle of wine, and have a feast. In fact, for a party of six, four portions will be plenty. Closed Sunday evenings and Mondays. Reservations advised. Visa accepted. Carretera Palma–Sóller, Km 17, Bunyola (phone: 971-613762). Moderate.

Ca'n Jaime – A simple, tiny, typical restaurant serving excellent food, in the tiny town of Deya. Try the *sopas mallorquinas* (Majorcan soup) and the *arroz brut* ("ugly rice" or "rice in the rough"), and wolf it all down with wine and olives. Closed Mondays. Reservations unnecessary. No credit cards accepted. 13 Calle Archiduque Luis Salvador, Deya (phone: 971-639029). Inexpensive.

Escorca – High in the mountain between Sóller and Pollensa, near the Lluch Monastery, this rustic place with a giant fireplace specializes in roast leg of lamb and goat and has wonderful baked apples. Closed Thursdays. Reservations advised. No credit cards accepted. Carretera Pollensa–Sóller, Km 25 (phone: 971-517095). Inexpensive.

El Guía – A simple Spanish place in Sóller, and a nice place to have lunch after taking the train up from Palma. The food is basic, the seafood excellent. Closed Mondays. Reservations unnecessary. Visa accepted. 3 Calle Castañer, Sóller (phone: 971-630227). Inexpensive.

Es Pouet Francisca – In the western mountains, this place is built against a cliff high above Alaro, on the winding unpaved road to the Castillo de Alaro. The roast lamb and the snails are worth every bit of the effort; the homemade *tinto* (red) wine is dark and heavy. Closed Thursdays and Saturdays for lunch. Reservations unnecessary. No credit cards accepted. Leave Alaro on the road to Orient and look for a small sign indicating Espouet, then turn left and begin the climb. The restaurant is the last building reachable by car (phone: 971-510277). Inexpensive.

MINORCA

The second-largest of the Balearic Islands is the easternmost of the group and also the island farthest from the Spanish mainland. The Romans referred to it as the "smaller one," compared to Majorca, which is about 25 miles to the southwest. Although Minorca is larger than either Ibiza or Formentera, it measures only about 30 miles from east to west and between 6 and 12 miles from north to south. The island is relatively flat — a hilly plateau with its highest point, Monte Toro, rising just over 1,000 feet in the island's center. The absence of a mountain range such as the one on Majorca means that Minorca is without some of the larger island's spectacular scenery. Yet its outline is rugged and irregular, resulting in roughly 125 miles of coastline blessed with countless small coves and beautiful beaches. More and more tourists are beginning to appreciate Minorca's pleasures, but without inundating the island yet, and agriculture, particularly dairy products, remains a major industry, along with the making of shoes and costume jewelry.

Traces of past cultures have all but been destroyed on the island, except for massive megalithic constructions remaining from prehistoric times. Although Majorca has its share, Minorca is dotted with hundreds of these stone monuments, which are of three main types: Called *talayots, taulas,* and *navetas,* they are remnants of a so-called *talayotic* Bronze Age culture that may have begun about 2000 BC and was at its height around 1000 BC. Scholars do not yet fully understand the origins of the civilization that raised these monuments (the nuraghic culture of the Italian island of Sardinia may have been its kin), nor have they been able to fathom the structures' exact function. *Talayots* — circular mounds of stone built on high ground — may have been watchtowers or the houses of chieftains (or the roofs or foundations of such structures). *Taulas,* the form most peculiar to Minorca, consist of one large flat stone set upon another in a T-shape (the name means "table" in the local dialect). Reminiscent of Stonehenge, they are usually found in the center of other vertical stones and may have served a religious purpose. *Navetas,* similar to the conical mounds of the *talayots* but oblong and containing chambers (like the upside-down hull of a ship, whence the name), are thought to have been communal graves. These monuments are found on both government and private land; although some of the sites are easily accessible from the road, others are not.

The largest city on Minorca is its capital, Mahón (population 23,000), a port at the eastern end of the island. Known in the Minorcan language as Maó, it gave the world a favorite local sauce — mayonnaise. The second-largest city and former capital, Ciudadela (Ciutadella in the local language), is at the island's western extreme. The two are starkly different. Mahón shows the influence of 8 decades of 18th-century British rule in its architecture, which sports details such as sash windows and Georgian doors, while the architecture of Ciudadela is classically Spanish. Other towns, such as Alayor, Mercadal, and Ferrerias, are in the interior, along the main road that crosses the island from east to west. Fornells, at one time a fishing village and now a resort town, is on the north coast on a deeply indented bay.

Minorca's beaches are what most visitors come to explore. All are posted with flags due to capricious currents — red signals danger, yellow means caution, and green signifies safety. Son Bou and Santo Tomás, in the center of the southern shore, are the two longest beaches on the island. Cala Santa Galdana, to the west of these, is a beach in a sheltered cove, with very safe and shallow waters, and Cala Blanca, a few miles south of Ciudadela, is a tiny beach surrounded by rocky cliffs. Cala del Pilar, a deserted beach on the north side of the island, is known mainly to locals. To reach it, turn off the main Mahón–Ciudadela road about 3 miles (5 km) past Ferrerias, near the Alputzer farm. Cala Pregonda, east of Cala del Pilar, is also deserted but easier to reach. From Mercadal, take the road northwest toward Ferragut Nou, then walk the last hundred yards to the sea. Es Grao, one of the beaches closest to Mahón, is very shallow, perfect for children. Drive due north from the city to the sea.

 GETTING AROUND: Airport – Charter flights arrive from most European countries, scheduled flights aboard *Aviaco* from mainland Spain and from Palma de Mallorca. Mahón Airport (phone: 971-360150) is 3 miles (5 km) southwest of the city at San Clemente. Expect to pay about $6 for a ride between the airport and downtown Mahón. The *Aviaco* office is at Mahón Airport (phone: 971-369202 for information and reservations).

Bus – Buses depart from Plaza Explanada, Mahón, for Ciudadela a half dozen times a day. Schedules are available from the tourist office (13 Plaza de la Constitución) and are also posted on the square.

Car Rental – A rented car is the recommended means of transportation. The island's main road, between Mahón and Ciudadela, has recently been widened, and traffic is no problem on the other roads, though parking in the center of Mahón is virtually impossible. *Avis* (at the airport; phone: 971-361576; 971-368976; 971-381838 and at 53 Plaza Explanada, Mahón; phone: 971-364778) offers the most convenient rentals and has several other locations. *Hertz* has one office (42 Carrer Gran, Villacarlos; phone: 971-364881 or 971-367822). Scores of smaller car rental agencies exist, many associated with hotels. Check with them if a car is needed for only a day or two. (The tourist office has a complete list of all car rental offices on the island.) Note that the best map of the island is the *Archaeological Map of Minorca,* available in local bookstores. It shows not only the roads, including tiny one-lane streets, but also the names of farms in the countryside — invaluable for those who have lost their way, with no road signs for miles, because farm names are clearly marked across the island.

Ferry – Ferry service connects the island with Barcelona (9 hours), Valencia (16 hours, via Palma de Mallorca), and Palma (6½ hours). Ferries land at Mahón's Estación Marítima. For *Trasmediterránea* information, call 971-362950.

Motor Scooter Rental – Because Minorca is small, many visitors see it by rented motor scooter or motorcycle. Among the scores of agencies are *Motos Ramos* (21 Anden de Levante; phone: 971-366813), *Motos Gelabert* (12 Calle José A. Clavé; phone: 971-360614), and *Motos Kike* (69 Calle Ciudadela; phone: 971-364120), all in Mahón.

Taxi – Cabs do not scurry around the island. Call *Radio-Taxi* in Mahón (phone: 971-367111) or in Ciudadela (phone: 971-382335 or 971-381197).

SPECIAL PLACES: Mahón – Throughout most of its history, the capital of modern Minorca was second in importance to Ciudadela. That changed during the 18th century with the arrival of the British, who found Mahón's long, narrow, deep harbor and port facilities preferable to those at the other end of the island. Mahón, set on a high cliff at the end of the harbor, does not have the wide avenues, majestic buildings, and tree-lined streets of other Spanish capitals, resembling an overgrown fishing village instead. Among the sights is the 18th-century Santa María church, which houses an extraordinary early-19th-century organ that is one of the largest in the world and is considered to be one of the finest (it's the raison d'être of the city's annual summer music festival). Not far away, the marketplace built into the arcaded cloister of a former Carmelite convent is worth a morning visit; otherwise, the town is best enjoyed by wandering through its narrow streets. At night, the port, reached by a steep, winding road called Abundancia, becomes the focus of most nightlife, with dozens of bars and restaurants in the area of the Estación Marítima and several excellent restaurants lining the harbor toward Villacarlos. The British founded this village, southeast of Mahón near the entrance to the harbor, to house the garrison of a nearby fort. Once called Georgetown, it remains even more British in atmosphere than the capital itself.

Trepucó – A 13-foot *taula,* the highest on Minorca, and a *talayot* are located at this easily accessible archaeological site a little over a mile south of Mahón.

Ciudadela – Minorca's second-largest city, at the western end of the island, is blessed with a beautiful location and ornate Spanish architecture that attests to its onetime importance as the former capital. Although it was largely destroyed by the Turks during the mid-16th century and then rebuilt, it has a wonderful Old City center with narrow streets and tiny shops. The Catedral de Santa María, a Gothic church begun during the 14th century, has a crumbling façade, but the interior has been restored and is especially beautiful when the morning light streams through its stained glass window; it contains columns with geometric designs that appear to have come from an old Arab mosque, intricately carved choir stalls, and a delicate cupola over the main altar. Outside the church, Calle Quadrado, lined with arcades and shops, leads to Calle Mayor Borne and to Plaza d'es Borne, Ciudadela's main square. Be sure to walk into the Palacio Saura on Calle Santísimo (south of Calle Quadrado and west of the marketplace) to get a sense of an old Minorcan palace with courtyard, staircase, and dome.

Naveta d'es Tudons – The restored *naveta* at this accessible site 3 miles (5 km) east of Ciudadela, just south of the road to Mahón, is the best preserved, the most important, and the most famous megalithic monument on the island. It is also the *naveta* that looks most like an upside-down ship.

Torre d'en Gaumés – A megalithic settlement covering several acres, it includes *taulas, talayots,* and ancient caves used for habitation; it's easily accessible 2 miles (3 km) south of Alayor, off the road to Son Bou.

SHOPPING: Minorca has a reputation for making excellent leather goods and shoes and is a European leader in the manufacture of costume jewelry. The products of both industries can be bought from factory outlets. Market days on Minorca are Tuesday and Saturday mornings in Plaza Explanada, Mahón, Friday and Saturday mornings in Ciudadela, and Monday and Wednesday mornings in Villacarlos.

Catisa – The island's largest costume jewelry factory. 26 Calle Bellavista, Mahón (phone: 971-364545).

Massa – Upscale silver handicrafts. 36 Sant Ferrán, Mahón (phone: 971-364189).

Patrizia – A prime place for leather goods. 2 Calle Favaller, Ciudadela (phone: 971-380397).

Salord Jovel – A factory outlet that is a good source of leather items. Located in the industrial area along the main road into Ciudadela (phone: 971-382300).

NIGHTCLUBS AND NIGHTLIFE: Nightlife here pales in comparison to that found on Ibiza and Majorca. There are bars and restaurants packed with locals near the Estación Marítima in Mahón and along the harbor to and including the port area of Villacarlos — which is also lively in the evening with crowds enjoying the bars and dining on the wharf. A number of discos do exist. One that is unique is *Cova d'en Xoroi* (no phone), built into a cave on the coast south of Alayor at Cala'n Porter. The cave opens to the sea below a cliff dropping straight to the water. Guests reach the disco via a staircase clinging to the rocks, then strut their stuff on a dance floor 100 feet above the crashing waves. Everything begins slowly after midnight and really begins to cook between 2 and 3 AM.

CHECKING IN: *Biniali* – A small *hostal,* much like a country inn, each of its 9 rooms is furnished differently with antiques. The villa, which also has a pool, is about 3 miles (5 km) south of Mahón, beyond the town of San Luis. Reservations should be made as much in advance as possible. 50 Calle Suestra, San Luis (phone: 971-361724; fax: 971-150352). Moderate.

Club Falco Sol – This is a village complex at the far southwest corner of the island. A self-contained resort, it offers accommodations in a series of bungalows, several restaurants and pools, and nightlife, all a short walk from the sea. Closed from November through April. Reservations by the week are preferred. Playa de Son Xoriguer, Cala'n Bosch (phone: 971-384623; telex: 69509). Moderate.

Port Mahón – A grand old hotel overlooking the port, within a short walk of both the town center and the port area. The 74 rooms are simply furnished; there is a pool. Avenida Fort de l'Eau, Mahón (phone: 971-362600; fax: 971-364362). Moderate.

Rey Carlos III – This modern, 87-room hotel with a swimming pool overlooks the harbor at Villacarlos, only a short walk to the port area that is one of the nightlife centers of Minorca. Closed November through March. Miranda de Cala Corp, Villacarlos (phone: 971-363100; fax: 971-363108). Moderate.

San Jaime – An apartment hotel only about 300 yards from the longest beach on the island, Playa Son Bou. Each of the 53 apartments has at least one bedroom; there is also a restaurant, pool, and tennis court. The beach is very quiet — any nightlife entails a half-hour drive. Closed November through March. Urbanización San Jaime, Playa Son Bou, Alayor (phone: 971-368011). Moderate.

S'Algar – A sprawling low building in the middle of the S'Algar resort development on the coast southeast of Mahón and Villacarlos. The 106 rooms have a bungalow feel, with most opening onto a garden area, and there is a pool. Closed November through March. Urbanización S'Algar, San Luis (phone: 971-361700; fax: 971-350465). Moderate to inexpensive.

Royal – The rooms in this 17-unit apartment hotel are all 1-bedroom with foldout couches. There are a restaurant and bar downstairs, as well as a swimming pool, and it is only a 5-minute walk to the center of Mahón. 131 Calle del Carmen, Mahón (phone: 971-369534). Inexpensive.

EATING OUT: *Casa Manolo* – The premier fish restaurant in Ciudadela, located at the far end of the port with a great view back to the town. The fish is as fresh and the prices are as high as can be found on the island. Open daily. Reservations necessary. Major credit cards accepted. 105-107 Marinas, Puerto, Ciudadela (phone: 971-380003). Expensive.

Jágaro – In the port area of Mahón, it is closed in by French doors, with lush green plants separating the tables. Definitely upscale, but not too overpriced; the chef is proudest of his fresh fish, either grilled or with sauces. Open daily. Reservations advised. Major credit cards accepted. 80 Calle Mártires de Atlante, Mahón (phone: 971-364660). Expensive.

Ca'n Aguedet – Perhaps Minorca's best restaurant for Minorcan cooking. In the center of the island, it's family run and quietly elegant, with whitewashed walls and wicker furniture. For appetizers, sample the eggplant stuffed with shrimp or the stuffed onions, then tuck into the peppers stuffed with fish or the rabbit with figs. Open daily. Reservations necessary on weekends. No credit cards accepted. 23 Calle Lepanto, Mercadal (phone: 971-375391). Moderate.

Ca'n Delio – A favorite among the cluster of several similar restaurants set on the romantic Villacarlos harbor, which crawls with tourists during the summer and is locked tighter than a drum from November through March. Reservations advised. No credit cards accepted. 39 Muelle Cala Fons, Villacarlos (phone: 971-369971). Moderate.

Ca's Quintu – In the center of Ciudadela, this is a good, simple place serving dishes ranging from fish to Minorcan specialties; try the grilled crayfish. Open daily. Reservations unnecessary. No credit cards accepted. 4 Plaza Alfonso III, Ciudadela (phone: 971-381002). Moderate.

Marivent – A marvelous terrace overlooking the harbor recommends it. Upstairs, the dining room, with a marble-top bar in the center, is used mainly in winter. Try any fish specialty. Closed Mondays in summer, Sundays and at lunch on Mondays in winter. Reservations advised. No credit cards accepted. 54 Calle Mártires de Atlante, Mahón (phone: 971-369067). Moderate.

Moli Des Raco – Housed in a converted windmill in Mercadal, on the main road between Mahón and Ciudadela, the Minorcan cooking here is exceptionally popular with locals and plates are heaped with food. Try the lamb or the rabbit and the local wine. Open daily. Reservations necessary. American Express and Visa accepted. 53 Vicario Fluxa, Mercadal (phone: 971-375392). Moderate.

Pilar – Minorcan specialties in the center of Mahón. This is a tiny eatery, and on most nights its dozen tables are filled with islanders lingering over lamb with parsnips and snails with mayonnaise. Closed Mondays. Reservations unnecessary. American Express and Visa accepted. 61 Forn, Mahón (phone: 971-366871). Moderate.

Bar España – The gathering place for the town of Villacarlos, and a good part of Mahón as well. Wide open and crowded even in winter, it offers the most reasonable meals on the island — a bit of everything from steaks and veal to fried squid and steamed mussels. The din remains through the evening. Open daily. Reservations unnecessary. No credit cards accepted. 50 Calle Victori, Villacarlos (phone: 971-363299). Inexpensive.

Los Bucaneros – The most famous of the *chillinguitos* (covered beach restaurants), where crowds eat at long tables just off the sand, it's on the beach in Binibeca, south of Mahón. Great, fresh food is the fare; there is no need for dining protocol. Open in summer only. Reservations unnecessary. No credit cards accepted. Playa de Binibeca (no phone). Inexpensive.

Es Caliu – Hewn beams, stone walls, the sounds and smells of meat searing over an open fire, and rafters hung with gourds, garlic, and hams combine to make this an eating experience. Try the fried peppers as an appetizer before a choice of either steaks or chops. In winter, open only on weekends. Reservations unnecessary. No credit cards accepted. South of Ciudadela, on the road to Cala Blanca (phone: 971-380165). Inexpensive.

IBIZA

The third-largest of the Balearic Islands lives up to its reputation as the jet set playground of Europe. Before the 1950s and 1960s, when this once-obscure island began to evolve into an international artists' colony and concourse for the counterculture, word of its existence had hardly seeped beyond the borders of Spain. Then it became almost a household word — its fame boosted considerably some years back when one of its expatriate residents, Clifford Irving, the self-proclaimed biographer of Howard Hughes, made news in the US. Today, its customary, simple, insular way of life is a thing of the past. The island is home-away-from-home to artists and pseudo-artists, movie stars, rock stars, fashion designers, and other representatives of the world's beautiful people, and while Majorca's tourist industry has been leveling off of late, business in Ibiza is booming. The year round population (about 25,000) of its capital, Ibiza town, increases nearly tenfold in summer, so don't even think of alighting here in high season without a confirmed and reconfirmed hotel reservation. The hippie nomads of only a decade ago have been replaced by both the young rich and the packaged traveler, and the resulting mix has made the island so cosmopolitan it is virtually impossible to label it Spanish.

The Greeks referred to Ibiza and its southern neighbor, Formentera, as the pine-clad islands. Except for the addition of almond, olive, fig, and other fruit trees, the reference still holds. But Ibiza is also known as the Isla Blanca (White Island), thanks to the brilliance of its square, flat-roofed houses, typically Arabic in style and religiously whitewashed each spring. The local architecture reflects a close affinity to North Africa, a legacy not only of 300 years of Moorish rule, but also, in the island's more distant past, of 500 years of colonization by the Carthaginians.

Ibiza is the southernmost of the three largest Balearic Islands and also the closest to the Spanish mainland, which is about 80 miles to the west. It measures approximately 25 miles from east to west and about 12 miles from north to south, with Ibiza town (also known as Eivissa) occupying a hill next to a natural harbor on the southeast coast. The two other main towns are San Antonio Abad (Sant Antoni Abat in the local language) and Santa Eulalia del Río (Santa Eularia del Rio). The former, the epicenter of packaged tourism on the island, with a frenetic nightlife, is 9½ miles (15 km) across the island from the capital on a still better natural harbor. The latter, a pleasant, quieter resort town, is 9½ miles (15 km) up the coast from the capital, at the mouth of the Balearic Islands' only river.

Ibiza's beaches range from those that are backed with hotels and packed with the tourists that occupy them to stretches of fine white sand lining deserted coves. Beach buses and boats connect the more popular ones to town; a car or a yacht or even a pedal boat allows travelers to discover the more secluded ones. The beaches closest to Ibiza town are Playa Talamanca to the north and Playa Figueretas and Playa d'en Bossa to the south, but anyone seeking to avoid the crowds keeps on riding to Las Salinas, the salt flats farther south, where the beaches include Playa Cavallet, one of the island's official nudist strands — although there is some shedding of bathing suits nearly everywhere. Similarly, the hotels of San Antonio Abad hold many more people than can be accommodated on Playa San Antonio, but within easy reach by bus or boat are the beaches of Port des Torrent, Cala Bassa, Cala Conta, and Cala Tarida, all southwest of town. The beach at Santa Eulalia del Río is also unimpressive, but Playa Llonga to the south and the beaches that stretch northward — Playa d'es Cana, Cala Nova, Cala Lena — are some of the best on the island. Along the north coast are the beaches at the resort development of Portinatx and at Puerto de San Miguel.

 GETTING AROUND: Airport – Most visitors arrive by air, aboard both regularly scheduled and charter flights that link the island with mainland Spain and, during the summer, with virtually every major city in Europe. *Aviaco* and

Iberia fly in from mainland Spain; *Aviaco* also provides daily flights from Palma de Mallorca. Ibiza Airport (phone: 97-300-300), 5 miles (8 km) southwest of Ibiza town, is equipped to handle jumbo jets and is within a half-hour's drive of virtually every hotel on the island. The *Iberia* office is at 34 Avenida de España (phone: 971-300954).

Bus – The main bus terminal in Ibiza town is on Avenida Isidoro Macabich. Buses link Ibiza town with San Antonio Abad and Santa Eulalia del Río every half hour during the day. Buses to Portinatx, San Miguel, and the inland villages of San Juan Bautista and San José leave once or twice a day.

Car Rental – A rented car is the recommended form of transportation. *Avis* (phone: 971-302949 or 971-302488) has offices at the airport, as does *Hertz* (phone: 971-300542 or 971-307290). *Avis* also has offices elsewhere on the island (Rincón Verde, Portinatx; phone: 971-333068; Avenida Dr. Fleming, San Antonio; phone: 971-341034; and Apartamentos S'Arenal, Portinatx; phone: 971-333186). *Hertz* has two other offices (Marina Botafoch, Puerto Deportivo; phone: 971-316723; and Area Servicio, Es Codolar; phone: 971-307822).

Ferry – Ferries are operated by *Trasmediterránea* (Avenida Bartolomé Vicente Ramón; phone: 971-301650). *Trasmediterránea* connects Ibiza town's Estación Marítima (phone: 971-314513) with Barcelona (9½ hours), Valencia (7 hours), and Palma (4½ hours); there is also a hydrofoil between Alicante and Ibiza (a 2¾-hour trip) and, in summer only, between Palma and Ibiza (a 2-hour trip). Other ferries, operated by *Flebasa* (phone: 971-342871), connect San Antonio Abad with Denia on the mainland, a 3-hour trip. Ferries to Formentera, operated by *Marítima de Formentera* (phone: 971-320157) and *Transportes Marítimos Pitiusos* (*Transmapi;* Avenida Santa Eularia; phone: 971-314486) leave from Ibiza town and take about an hour.

Taxi – Taxis operate on a system of fixed destination charges, available from every cabbie. In Ibiza town, the main taxi stands are on Paseo Vara de Rey (phone: 971-301794) and at Playa de Ses Figueretas (phone: 971-301676). In San Antonio Abad, call 971-340074; in Santa Eulalia del Río, 971-330063.

SPECIAL PLACES: Ibiza – Sightseeing on Ibiza really means observing the passing scene, although the island does have its complement of more conventional sights. Most are in the capital, which is divided into a medieval upper town, the Dalt Vila, and a lower town that, at least in the area around the harbor, dates mainly from the mid-19th century. In the lower town, the Barrio de Sa Penya, stretching east from the Estación Marítima, is the fishermen's quarter, full of shops, restaurants, bars, and a lively nightlife. The Marina district to the west of it is the business district, with more shops, restaurants, and bars. Ibiza's main street, Paseo Vara de Rey (the tourist office is at No. 13; phone: 971-301900), is on the western reaches of this district, and still farther west stretch the newer zones of the city, brought about by the boom in tourism.

Dalt Vila is picturesque and compact, an oasis of calm far removed from the hubbub of the rest of the island. An ancient cathedral crowns it, and 16th-century walls that have been declared a national monument enclose it. Enter by the main gateway, the Portal de las Tablas, flanked by Roman statues, and climb the winding cobblestone streets to the cathedral — Santa María de las Nieves — which was constructed during the 13th century on a site previously occupied by a mosque, a Roman temple, and, possibly, a Carthaginian one even earlier. Though much restored early in the 18th century, the church retains a 14th-century bell tower, and the panoramic view from the terrace is the best in town.

Also in Plaza de la Catedral is the *Museo Arqueológico* (open daily from 10 AM to noon and from 6 to 8 PM; no phone; admission charge), which contains items unearthed on Ibiza and Formentera and is one of the most important museums in Spain — and in the world — as far as remains of the Punic (Carthaginian) period are concerned.

Another Dalt Vila museum — the *Museo de Arte Contemporáneo* (Ronda Pintor Narcís Puget; open from 11 AM to 1 PM and from 6 to 9 PM during summer months, and from 5 to 7 PM winter months; closed Sundays and holidays; phone: 971-302723; admission charge) — displays contemporary Spanish paintings and sculpture. Visitors whose appetite for pre-Christian artifacts has not been sated should head down to the lower town and to the west of Dalt Vila, to the Punic necropolis of Puig des Molins (Windmill Hill). Because the Carthaginians considered the soil of Ibiza to be especially good for burial purposes, they buried their dead from other colonies here as well, and this necropolis was the largest of several on the island. More than 4,000 tombs were carved into the hillside, and although the graves were pillaged over the centuries, scientific excavations yielded enough to stock the *Museo Monográfico del Puig des Molins,* at the bottom of the hill (31 Vía Romana; phone: 971-301771). The museum is open daily from 10 AM to noon and from 4 to 7 PM. The admission charge includes a visit to the necropolis.

San Antonio Abad – This former fishing village is now the home of most of the resort development on Ibiza. It's set on a beautiful bay, overlooking an uninhabited rock island, Isla Conejera. Most of the town is a product of the tourist boom, but its 14th-century parish church is the island's second-oldest.

Santa Eulalia del Río – The much-photographed fortress-church, set on a hilltop, is the town's main monument. Built during the 16th century, it contains an ornate Gothic altar screen.

NIGHTCLUBS AND NIGHTLIFE: This is hardly dull. To begin with, there's the nightly *paseo* in Ibiza town, when all those who have spent the day naked or nearly so on the beaches play dress up. Tourist office literature refers to Ibiza's "ad-lib" fashion — male, female, and unisex — as full of gaiety, freedom, and fun. In truth, the nightly parade of wild and colorful costumes creates almost a carnival atmosphere. Then there are the discos. For those seeking out the disco scene, the nightlife on Ibiza is among the liveliest anywhere. Whereas on Majorca most visitors seem to stay in one place until dawn, on Ibiza the party is a movable feast, with entire groups of people moving from one hot spot to another as the night works its way toward day. Among the largest and best-known discos is *KU* (Carretera Ibiza–San Antonio, Km 6, in San Rafael; phone: 971-314474), which is mainly open air, with a giant swimming pool set in front of the stage. Name a group and it has probably played here. *Pachá* (Paseo Marítimo in Ibiza town; phone: 971-313612) is not as large as *KU,* but it still holds 2,500 on two dance floors; it opens at midnight. *Amnesia San Rafael* (Carretera Ibiza–San Antonio, Km 5; phone: 971-314136) is for those who still have not had enough after *KU* and *Pachá* have emptied out between 5 and 6 AM. *Gloria's* (Carretera Ibiza–San Antonio, Km 1.5) doesn't even open its doors until 4 AM. For the party animal who drinks but doesn't dance, there are scores of bars in Ibiza town, in San Antonio, and in the back streets of Santa Eulalia, where the loud music and the exotically dressed crowds spill out into the streets. A final alternative is the *Casino de Ibiza* (Paseo Marítimo; phone: 971-304850), open from 10 PM to 5 AM.

CHECKING IN: *Hacienda Na Xamena –* The ultimate in luxury, isolated in its own world, with views that would inspire an eagle. Set atop a cliff in the northern part of the island, 4 miles (6 km) northwest of San Miguel, this 54-room aerie in white Arabic style has indoor and outdoor swimming pools, tennis courts, and a restaurant serving superb food — as well as rooms that open onto terraces above a sheer 500-foot drop to the sea. The beach and village of Puerto de San Miguel are just down the pine-forested hills. Closed from November through March. San Juan Bautista (phone: 971-333046; fax: 971-333175). Very expensive.

Pikes – In the country, a little over a mile (about 1.6 km) south of San Antonio. The 24 rooms are individually decorated, but each has a terrace, telephone, and air conditioning. Many of the international stars performing at Ibiza's discos stay here. There is a swimming pool, a tennis court, a poolside bar, and a good restaurant (see *Eating Out*). Closed from late October or mid-November to mid-February or late March, depending on bookings. Carretera Sa Vorera, San Antonio Abad (phone: 971-342222; fax: 971-342312). Expensive.

Royal Plaza – The best hotel in the town center, it was built in the early 1980s and has 117 rooms, a rooftop swimming pool, and a bar and coffee shop. 27-29 Calle Pedro Francés, Ibiza (phone: 971-310000; telex: 69433). Expensive.

El Corsario – This *hostal* is in the midst of the old section of Ibiza town, with 14 rooms and good views. 5 Calle Poniente, Dalt Vila, Ibiza (phone: 971-301248). Moderate.

Reco des Sol – A reasonable alternative to expensive accommodations in San Antonio, this is a well-run *hostal* with 89 rooms and virtually every amenity. Closed from November through April. 16 Vedra, San Antonio Abad (phone: 971-341104). Inexpensive.

Ses Savines – It's right on the beach and in the thick of the San Antonio nightlife, with a swimming pool, tennis, and 133 rooms normally packed with British tourists. Playa San Antonio, San Antonio Abad (phone: 971-340066). Inexpensive.

EATING OUT: Pikes – In the hotel of the same name are three unique dining rooms furnished with antiques, plus a terraced garden. Virtually every celebrity who visits seems to eat here, but it's possible to dine reasonably if you're careful. Open daily. Reservations essential. Major credit cards accepted. Carretera Sa Vorera, San Antonio Abad (phone: 971-342222 or 971-343511). Expensive.

Sa Punta – The atmosphere is almost that of a greenhouse. Right on the beach at Santa Eulalia, it serves fresh fish and delicious crunchy vegetables. Closed Sunday evenings, Mondays, and from mid-January through February. Reservations advised. Major credit cards accepted. 36 Calle Isidoro Macabich, Santa Eulalia del Río (phone: 971-330033). Expensive to moderate.

El Naranjo – On Santa Eulalia's restaurant row, it is an island favorite. Try the duck with red currants and pepper sauce. Closed Mondays and from mid-December to mid-March. Reservations necessary. No credit cards accepted. 31 Calle San José, Santa Eulalia del Río (phone: 971-330324). Moderate.

S'Oficina – In the heart of Ibiza town, serving excellent Basque cooking. The fish is good, but for a change of pace, try the beef. Closed Sundays and from mid-December to mid-January. Reservations advised. American Express and Visa accepted. 6 Avenida de España, Ibiza (phone: 971-300016). Moderate.

Ca'n Pujol – Right on the beach, with great seafood and paella. No credit cards accepted. Playa Port des Torrent, San Antonio Abad (no phone). Moderate to inexpensive.

FORMENTERA

The sea is visible from every point on Formentera, which is nearly flat as a pancake except for a lump — the 630-foot-high La Mola "mountain" — at its eastern extremity. Set 4 miles south of Ibiza and made up of two islets joined by an isthmus, the island measures only about 12 miles from end to end. Ferries arrive at La Sabina, the island harbor, which is on the north coast between two lagoons, Estang de Peix and Estang Pudent (which translate as "fish" and "stinky" lagoon, respectively). The cluster of sparkling white houses just short of 2 miles (3 km) down the road from the port is San Francisco Javier, the capital, home to less than half the island's population of 4,500. Of the other tiny villages scattered throughout the island, San Fernando, 1¼ miles (2 km) to the east, is the next largest. For the rest, the island consists of pine forests and salt flats, generously fringed with beaches — Playa de Mitjorn, on the southern coast and 3 miles long, is long enough to escape being crowded. Others include Playa d'Es Pujols, north of San Fernando, which attracts a certain amount of business from package tours; Playa de Ses Illetas and Playa de Llevant, on either side of the Trocadors peninsula, which stretches north from La Sabina; and Cala Sahona, on the western side of the island, still reasonably remote.

The Carthaginians are known to have worked the salt pans, but they left no trace of settlement on the island. The Romans left it its name, a corruption of the Latin Frumentaria — from *frumentum,* or "wheat" — since Formentera served as a granary for the Roman camp on Ibiza. The Arabs were here, too, but when they left after the Reconquest, the island was uninhabited for much of the Middle Ages, due to fear of the marauding pirates who regularly sought refuge from the rough seas on its defenseless shores. Only late in the 17th century did homesteaders from Ibiza settle in; today, their descendants fish, work the fields and the salt pans, and cater to tourists. But Formentera is more tranquil than the other three Balearic Islands and likely to remain so, since a shortage of fresh water limits development. There are numerous small *hostales* and a couple of large hotels, but they're heavily booked, so anyone planning to stay the night should be sure to have a reservation.

Ferry service from Ibiza town to the Estación Marítima in La Sabina (phone: 971-322703) is frequent, with two lines — *Marítima de Formentera* and *Transportes Marítimos Pitiusos* (*Transmapi*) — providing up to 11 round trips daily, year-round. A great many visitors, therefore, come over only for the day. One proviso, however: Although the ride across the Es Freus Channel is short (about 1 hour), it's not necessarily sweet, as the sea can be rough and the currents strong. Because ferries are sometimes canceled, make allowance for possible lost time if there's a plane to catch. Taxis line the pier when ferries arrive; they are reasonable, with an entire island tour costing under $25. The island does have bus service, but renting a car or a moped is preferable. *Autos Ibiza,* located in both Ibiza town (phone: 971-314611) and in La Sabina on Formentera (phone: 971-322031), is one of many companies represented. Formentera's Tourist Office (phone: 971-322034), open mornings only, is located in San Francisco Javier.

CHECKING IN: *Iberotel Club la Mola* – This 328-room resort complex provides the best accommodations on the island, right on its longest beach. Built in Spanish village–style, it offers rooms as well as independent villas, and is equipped with 2 swimming pools, facilities for a variety of water sports, tennis courts, a restaurant, bar, and discotheque. Closed from November through April. Playa de Mitjorn (phone: 971-328069). Expensive.

Sa Volta – A small *hostal* (18 rooms) near the beach, in the midst of the hottest nightlife on this quiet island. It has no pool, but there's a restaurant. Playa de Es Pujols (phone: 971-320120). Moderate to inexpensive.

EATING OUT: *Es Muli des Sal* – A small eatery on the sand dunes in the northern part of the island; the fresh fish and lobsters are mouth-watering. Open daily. Reservations unnecessary. No credit cards accepted. Ses Illetas (no phone). Moderate.

The Canary Islands

A cluster of seven major and six minor islands in the Atlantic Ocean, the Canary Island archipelago lies about 65 miles off the northwest coast of Africa. Not for nothing do they call the Canaries the Fortunate Isles. Bathed by the Gulf Stream and ruffled by the trade winds, they are spread out in a line only about 4° north of the Tropic of Cancer, at roughly the same latitude as Florida, and enjoy a spring-like climate throughout the year — with temperatures mostly in the 70s F. Extremes of heat and cold are unknown in this Spanish archipelago, where European, African, and American influences mingle.

Yet physical contrasts are dramatic. Verdant tropical vegetation flourishes near barren fields of hardened lava, while the snow-capped volcano, the 12,200-foot Pico del Teide, Spain's highest peak, looks down on banana plantations. Morocco and the Sahara lie just across the water, but European capitals are only a brief flight away. The Canaries' blend of the exotic and the familiar, their spectacular scenery, and their long hours of sunshine attract ever-increasing numbers of tourists — most of whom never venture too far from the beaches.

There are 13 islands altogether, but only Grand Canary (Gran Canaria in Spanish), Tenerife, Fuerteventura, Lanzarote, La Gomera, El Hierro, and La Palma are of any significant size. Geologically speaking, the islands were born millions of years ago, when volcanic eruptions from the bed of the Atlantic thrust up a string of islands of striking abruptness, each with its own peculiar characteristics. Hundreds of volcanoes dot the Canaries, and one or two are still smouldering. Because of variations in altitude, and thus of climate, some islands have justly been described as miniature continents. On the heights, the vegetation is alpine, and includes Canary pine and broom. On the lower slopes, irrigation of the rich volcanic soils produces an astonishing abundance of tropical and semi-tropical fruits. Scorching African winds from the Sahara, sometimes bearing a dust haze, create desert conditions on the easternmost islands of Lanzarote and Fuerteventura, as well as along the eastern coasts of Grand Canary and Tenerife. But lofty volcanic peaks block clouds rolling in from the ocean and create damp, luxuriant conditions elsewhere.

The Canary Islands were known to the ancient Greeks; Ptolemy, the 2nd-century geographer, situated his first meridian — 0° longitude — at El Hierro, the most remote of the islands. Although legends suggest to some that the Canaries are the remains of the lost continent of Atlantis, history's first recorded visit occurred during the 1st century. According to Pliny the Elder, the Roman historian, it was explorers from Roman Mauritania who first visited the islands. They found them full of wild dogs, two of which they took back to their king, Juba II. Accordingly, Juba dubbed the islands *insulae canariae* — islands of dogs. (The descendants of these original canine inhabitants, a type of mastiff known as *verdino,* still live in the Canaries.) Other sources maintain that the islands got their name from a variety of finch (*serinus canarius*) found living in the trees. And to make the confusion just a little greater, a Berber-speaking tribe known as the Canarii lived in nearby Morocco, and some scholars believe it was they who gave their name to the islands. Whatever the etymology, the mainland Spaniards who conquered the seven cone-shaped volcanic islands during the 15th century adapted the Latin name to Spanish as Islas Canarias.

Acquiring mastery over this domain was not easy. The Spaniards faced fierce resistance from the original inhabitants, the Guanche cave dwellers, who were not conquered until 1496, although the islands had been rediscovered in 1402. Little is known about the Guanches, who were eventually decimated by Spanish armies, bubonic plague, locust-induced famine, and volcanic eruptions. A tall, fair-skinned, light-haired people, they probably were of Phoenician and/or Berber stock. They had no boats, however; so how they reached the islands, and from where, is still a mystery. They were reputedly generous and courageous, qualities put to the test by Jean de Béthencourt, a Norman knight who launched an invasion in 1402 and captured Lanzarote, Fuerteventura, La Gomera, and El Hierro. Conquest of the other islands was completed only after arduous campaigns met by ferocious resistance, and those Guanches not killed off by disease, disaster, or slavery were absorbed into the Spanish culture. Some of their distinctive physical characteristics are still visible in the modern population, and traces of their crude existence remain all over the archipelago in the form of ceramics and leather artifacts, geometric cave paintings, mummies, and remnants of their language (such place-names as Timanfaya and Tenerife were inherited from the Guanches) and traditions, not to mention their food — *gofio* remains an island staple. Today's islanders have a newly awakened interest in their ancestors, in reaction to what they often feel is neglect from distant Madrid. From time to time, throughout the islands, slogans appear on posters and walls saying "*Godos* go home!" — *Godo,* meaning "Goth" (as in Visigoth), is the islanders' name for a mainland Spaniard.

During the 18th and 19th centuries, sugarcane, wine, and the cochineal insect brought wealth to the Canaries. The dye obtained from the insect, which lives off the islands' cacti, was exported in large quantities to Britain and France until the invention of artificial colorings. Later, the Canaries prospered with new products, namely bananas, potatoes, tomatoes, and tobacco. For a long time, trade was monopolized by British firms, which also made the towns of Las Palmas on Grand Canary and Santa Cruz de Tenerife on Tenerife important coaling stations for their ships. The Spanish-American War proved a nervous interlude, as Spain was convinced that the United States was about to seize the Canaries before launching an attack on the mainland. Fortifications were built, and fear of an invasion at times reached panic proportions.

Wealthy Europeans began spending winters in the Canaries during the late 19th century. In 1896, Tenerife had eight hotels, all foreign owned. Today, the tourism industry has grown to the point that 5 million people visit the islands annually. British vacationers arrive in the largest numbers, followed by Germans, Italians, Swedes, and Spaniards from "La Península," as mainland Spain is called. It can be extremely difficult to get a room in the better resorts during high season, from December through *Easter* — even though the Canaries have more than 300,000 hotel beds.

The Canary archipelago is one of Spain's Comunidades Autónomas, the 17 autonomous communities, or regions, that make up the country's administrative framework in the post-Franco era. But since 1927, the islands have been split into two provinces, and there is considerable and ongoing rivalry between the ports of Las Palmas and Santa Cruz de Tenerife. Las Palmas is the provincial capital of the eastern islands: Grand Canary (the most populated), Fuerteventura (a virtual desert), and Lanzarote (which has the most impressive volcanic scenery). Santa Cruz de Tenerife is the capital of the western group: Tenerife (the largest island), La Palma (the green island), La Gomera, and El Hierro. The archipelago has its own parliament, and each island has its own *cabildo* (council) to look after local affairs. The nomenclature of the Canaries appears designed to confuse. There are two places named Santa Cruz, for example: One is the capital of Tenerife, the other the capital of La Palma.

A mixture of cultures influences Canarian food. *Gofio,* a belly-filling paste made of flour, water, and milk, comes from the Guanches. *Sancocho canario* is fresh fish cooked with potatoes and served with *mojo,* an essential Canarian seasoning made with oil, vinegar, garlic, salt, and various spices. *Mojo picón,* however, is a hot seasoning made with peppers; watch out, because it's ubiquitous, and its seemingly benign aroma belies its true, incendiary nature. *Papas arrugadas* (literally, wrinkled potatoes), or boiled potatoes cooked in their skins and served with *mojo,* are a popular snack. Restaurants in the Canary Islands span the culinary spectrum, from sleek international dining spots to funky regional places serving local dishes.

Today's Canary Islanders are peaceful, friendly, artistic people, who make their living farming, fishing (some of the world's richest fishing grounds lie between the Canaries and the African coast), and producing handicrafts — as well as by working at various jobs in the modern resort developments. They speak Spanish with a musical accent reminiscent of Latin America, a region to which many Canarians have emigrated over the years. Their folk music also has a Latin American rhythm; folk groups play flutes, drums, guitars, and the *timple,* a small stringed instrument. The quaint villages of white cottages with red roofs sprinkled throughout the mountainous interior of the volcanic islands make the archipelago inviting to travelers who enjoy exploring unusual places and discovering the distinctive character of each island.

SOURCES AND RESOURCES

TOURIST INFORMATION: The regional Oficina de Turismo for the Canary Islands is headquartered on the island of Grand Canary (Plaza Ramón Franco in the Parque Santa Catalina, Las Palmas; phone: 928-264623) and is open Mondays through Fridays from 9 AM to 1:30 PM and 5 to 7 PM, Saturdays from 9 AM to 1 PM. Tenerife's tourist office in the Palacio Insular (57 Calle de la Marina, Santa Cruz de Tenerife; phone: 922-287254) is open Mondays through Fridays from 8 AM to 5:45 PM and Saturdays from 9 AM to 1 PM; and a second office (3 Plaza de la Iglesia, Puerto de la Cruz; phone: 922-386000) is open Mondays through Fridays from 9 AM to 7 PM and Saturdays from 10 AM to 2 PM. The Patronato de Turismo on Fuerteventura (33 Calle Uno de Mayo, Puerto del Rosario; phone: 928-851400) is open Mondays through Fridays from 9 AM to 2 PM and 4 to 7 PM. The Lanzarote Tourist Office (in the Parque Municipal, Arrecife; phone: 928-811860) is open Mondays through Fridays from 8 AM to 2:30 PM and 5:30 to 7 PM. The La Palma Patronato de Turismo (3 Paseo Marítima, Santa Cruz de La Palma; phone: 922-411641) is open Mondays through Fridays from 8 AM to 3 PM and Saturdays from 9 AM to 1 PM. The El Hierro Patronato de Turismo (1 Calle Licenciado Bueno, Valverde; phone: 922-550302) is open Mondays through Fridays from 8 AM to 5 PM. La Gomera has no tourist office, but information can be obtained from the Cabildo Insular (Island Council; 7 Calle Rosario; phone: 922-859908), open weekdays from 9 AM to 5 PM.

Local Coverage – Three daily newspapers are published in Las Palmas: *Canarias 7, Diario,* and *La Provincia.* In Santa Cruz de Tenerife, *El Día, Diario de Avisos, La Gaceta de Canarias,* and *Jornada* are also published daily. Newsstands throughout the islands carry a wide range of foreign newspapers and magazines, many of which arrive on the day of publication. A number of English-language publications cater to the needs of tourists and expatriate residents. *Canarias Tourist,* a monthly periodical, is sold on the major islands; published in several languages, it offers information on sights and services. *Tenerife Today* provides similar information on Tenerife. The *Island Gazette,* a monthly magazine long published on Tenerife and aimed mainly at long-term visitors and residents, also includes information on Grand Canary. On Lanzarote, the monthly magazine *Lancelot* serves the English-speaking public.

 TELEPHONE: The area code for the islands of Grand Canary, Fuerteventura, and Lanzarote is 28. If calling from mainland Spain (or from the Santa Cruz de Tenerife province), dial 928 before the local number. The area code for the islands of Tenerife, La Palma, La Gomera, and El Hierro is 22. If calling from mainland Spain (or from the Las Palmas province), dial 922 before the local number. No area code is necessary when dialing between islands of the same province. Note that time in the Canaries is 1 hour earlier than on mainland Spain all year.

CLIMATE: The Canaries are tropical islands situated just above the Tropic of Cancer. Their unique geographic features result in an agreeable climate year-round with no dramatic variations in temperature, which average a very comfortable 67 to 83F from the coldest to the hottest months. Even in the winter, it is rarely necessary to wear more than a sweater in the evening. On Grand Canary and Tenerife, the northern and eastern ends of the islands receive more rain than the mostly arid western and southern regions. Clouds often cover the north, while at the same time the south is basking in sunshine. Las Palmas residents admit that the high humidity and heat can be trying in August. The more low-lying Lanzarote and Fuerteventura have a desert-like climate, while La Palma's greenness testifies to its higher amount of rainfall.

GETTING THERE: The Canaries are linked to the Spanish mainland by frequent air service and regular ferry service. *Iberia Airlines* and its associated commuter lines fly direct to the Canaries from several mainland cities, including Barcelona, Madrid, Málaga, and Seville. Frequent daily inter-island flights are provided by *Iberia* and *Binter,* the Canaries' regional carrier.

Trasmediterránea (26-27 Avenida Ramón de Carranza, Cádiz; phone: 956-284311; and 2 Calle Pedro Muñoz Seca, Madrid; phone: 91-431-0700) operates passenger and vehicle ferries several times a week between Cádiz and Santa Cruz de Tenerife, Las

Palmas on Grand Canary, and Arrecife on Lanzarote. The trip from Cádiz to Tenerife takes about 36 hours and costs a minumum of $130 per person, one way. *Trasmediterránea* also has frequent inter-island ferry and hydrofoil service.

SPECIAL EVENTS: Camels, bands, and lavishly dressed islanders participate in the *Cabalgata de los Tres Reyes* (Cavalcade of the Three Kings), which takes place on January 5 or 6 in several towns throughout the islands, most notably Las Palmas and Santa Cruz de Tenerife. Also celebrated on all the islands, and with astonishing exuberance, is February's *Carnaval,* but once again Santa Cruz de Tenerife and Las Palmas break the bank to outdo each other with dazzling and outrageous parades, costumes, and nonstop music and dancing; the fiesta builds to a climax on *Mardi Gras* when, with due solemnity, the image of a sardine (the symbol of *Carnaval*) is laid to rest. *Semana Santa* (Holy Week), from *Palm Sunday* through *Easter Sunday,* is another occasion that is celebrated with appropriate solemnity and processions throughout the islands. Numerous other annual events may be peculiar to a single island or even to a single community, since each town has a fiesta to honor its patron saint, although exact dates can vary from year to year. During the last 2 weeks of April, Tegueste, near La Laguna, Tenerife, combines its *romería* (flower-bedecked oxcart procession) with a show of 15,000 bottles of wine from 20 Spanish *bodegas;* on the same island, in June, for *Corpus Christi* processions, carpets of flowers are arranged on the streets of La Laguna and La Orotava. Early in May, the *Día de la Cruz* (Day of the Cross) is the occasion for one of the year's most lighthearted fiestas, particularly in communities of the island of El Hierro. During September, San Sebastián on La Gomera holds its *Semana de Colón* (Columbus Week) celebrations. September 8 is a big day on Grand Canary, when a colorful procession pays homage to Nuestra Señora del Pino (Our Lady of the Pine) in Teror. Once every 5 years, La Palma holds its *Fiestas Lustrales,* a 2-week festival in Santa Cruz de la Palma in which the highlight is the *Danza de los Enanos* (Dwarfs' Dance); the next celebration will be held in 1995. Finally, to supplement the various regularly occurring music seasons, such as the *Grand Canary Philharmonic Orchestra* series from October to mid-June, the January-to-June concerts by the *Las Palmas Philharmonic Society,* and other music and dance events, Las Palmas hosts the *Festival de Opera* in February and March; in recent years, artists such as Placido Domingo, Montserrat Caballé, and Luciano Pavarotti have appeared here. On Tenerife, there is the *International Festival of Theater and Dance,* from March to June in La Laguna, in addition to the regular *Tenerife Symphony Orchestra* seasons in La Laguna and Santa Cruz and the annual winter and spring concert season in Puerto de la Cruz.

SPORTS AND FITNESS: The Canaries' ideal climate makes the islands an outdoors lovers' paradise. A wide range of sports and fitness facilities are available, and for those preferring to limit themselves to spectator sports, there are such local favorites as stick fighting, which is believed to have been inherited from the Guanches, and *lucha canaria* — a primitive and colorful form of wrestling in which a wrestler wins by forcing any part of his opponent's body, except his feet, to the floor (regular exhibitions and team matches are held). Cock fighting is legal and usually held on Sundays from December to May; the *López Socas Stadium* (Calle Ortiz de Sarate; no phone) is the venue in Las Palmas. The fight is accompanied by excited wagering, and blood flies, but fights usually are stopped before a bird is killed. Soccer is also popular, and anyone catching a clash between Santa Cruz de Tenerife and Las Palmas may wonder whether this isn't a blood sport, too.

Boating – The Canaries have a variety of well-equipped marinas that serve vacationers as well as the yachtsmen who use the islands as a starting point for their transatlantic crossings. Lateen sailing is a Canarian specialty, and regular regattas are held in the summer. Grand Canary's yachting clubs include the *Real Club Náutico de Gran Canaria,* in Las Palmas (phone: 928-266690 or 928-245202), one of Spain's oldest, with a wide range of sports facilities; *Puerto Deportivo de Puerto Rico* (phone: 928-745331), on the southern part of the island, offers sea excursions and yacht rentals; and *Club de Yates Pasito Blanco* (in Maspalomas; phone: 928-762259).

Fishing – Swordfish, stingray, tunny, grouper, conger eel, and giant ray are some of the 1,500 species that thrive in the waters surrounding the Canaries. Craft and equipment rentals are available at most harbors throughout the islands, and fine catches are also possible casting off the islands' many rock cliffs; good catches also often result from little more than an effortless cast into the surf from the beach. Fishing excursions are organized from Puerto Rico on Grand Canary. *Nautisport* (phone: 922-791459) runs shark fishing trips from Los Cristianos quay on Tenerife (about $35 per person, including lunch and drinks), and daily fishing excursions are organized from Los Gigantes harbor, Santiago de Tiede, in southeast Tenerife (phone: 922-867179 or 922-867332). For deep-sea fishing from Corralejo on Fuerteventura, contact *Escualo* in Jandía (phone: 928-852293) or *Pez Velero* (phone: 928-866173).

Golf – Canary Island golf courses offer challenging conditions amid spectacular and unusual scenery. On Grand Canary, the *Club de Golf Las Palmas* (Carretera de Bandama, Km 5; phone: 928-351050), Spain's oldest golf club, offers beautiful sur-roundings 9 miles (14 km) south of Las Palmas on the edge of a volcanic crater, while the greens at *Campo de Golf, Maspalomas* (near the *Maspalamos Oasis* hotel; phone: 928-762581) are carpeted with Bermuda turf. Tenerife's offerings include the 18-hole championship course (plus another 9 holes) at *Club del Sur* (San Miguel de Abona; phone: 922-704555), laid out around lava fields; the *Club de Golf de Tenerife* (La Laguna; phone: 922-250240); and the *Amarilla Golf and Country Club* (Costa del Silencio, Arona; phone: 922-103422).

Horseback Riding – Horses can be rented from a number of hotels and stables throughout the islands. On Grand Canary, try *Picadero del Club de Golf de Bandama* (Carretera Bandama, Posada; phone: 928-351290) or *Picadero del Oasis de Maspalomas* (Playa de Maspalomas; phone: 928-762378), both in Las Palmas. On Tenerife, the *Amarilla Golf and Country Club* (Costa del Silencio, Arona; phone: 922-103422) has an equestrian center.

Jeep Safaris – *Unisafari,* on Grand Canary (21 Calle Dr. Grau Bassas, Las Palmas; phone: 928-277100), is one of several companies running off-road driving safaris through the wilder parts of the islands.

Scuba Diving – Clear, warm water and myriad exotic fish attract scuba divers and snorkelers. One of the best spots for diving lies between the northern tip of Fuerteven-tura and the southern tip of Lanzarote, around the Isla de los Lobos. The *Diving Center Miguel Abella Cerdá* (Apartado 8, Corralejo, Fuerteventura; phone: 928-866243) offers a variety of boat trips and scuba courses with English-speaking instructors and dive masters. On Grand Canary, Heinz Lange, a German expatriate dive master, runs a scuba school in Maspalomas (phone: 928-765244); the *Club Sun Sub* (at the *Buenaven-tura* hotel, Plaza Ansite, Playa del Inglés; phone: 928-761650, ext. 925) offers a variety of courses and reef trips, as does the *Club Canario de Investigaciones y Actividades Subacuáticas* (67 Calle Pío XII, Las Palmas; phone: 928-246810). On Tenerife, try the *Las Palmeras* hotel (Avenida Marítima, Playa de las Américas; phone: 922-790911).

Swimming and Sunning – Sunbathing is *the* "sport" of the Canaries, and many of the islands' beaches (those away from the huge resort areas) are virtually untouched — at least as yet — by mass tourism. Miles of uncrowded golden sands can be found on Fuerteventura (at the northeastern tip and parts of the southern coast) and Lanzarote (on the southern coast). The most crowded of the islands' beaches are on Grand Canary and Tenerife. Topless bathing is more the rule than the exception, and nude bathing is very common in many of the secluded areas. The waters surrounding the islands are a dazzling blue, and are warm enough (an average of 72F) for year-round swimming.

Tennis – Most of the islands' larger hotels and resorts have tennis courts, and many new sports-oriented complexes are springing up. Tennis clubs on Grand Canary include the *Club Sun Sub* (*Buenaventura* hotel, Plaza Ansite, Playa del Inglés; phone: 928-761650, ext. 925); *Club de Tenis Biarritz* (18 Avenida de Bonn, San Agustín; phone: 928-760356); and *Club de Tenis Helga Masthoff* (Carretera de los Palmitos, El Tablero; phone: 928-761436). Clubs on Tenerife include the *Club Britanico de Juegos* (British Sports Club; Carretera de Taoro, Puerto de la Cruz; phone: 922-384823), and *Oceánico Tenis Club* (Carretera de Fuerteventura, Puerto de la Cruz; phone: 922-380018).

Water Skiing – Water skiing schools operate from the more popular beaches on Grand Canary, Tenerife, and Lanzarote.

Windsurfing – Steady breezes make the Canaries an ideal spot for this ever-growing sport. Enthusiasts trek here from all over Europe, and the islands have hosted several world championships over the years. Instruction is available and boards can be rented, for about $30 a day, on many of the islands' beaches. Popular Grand Canary windsurfing schools and centers include the *Mistral Windsurfing Club* (at the *Bahía Feliz Hotel,* Playa de Tarajalillo; phone: 928-763332) and the *Luis Molina Windsurfing School* (Playa del Inglés; phone: 928-761524). El Médano Beach, near Reina Sofía Airport on Tenerife, is a favorite windsurfing site; *Looping Windsurf School* (Costa Teguise; phone: 922-815796) is the place to learn how to windsurf on Lanzarote. The beaches at Corralejo, Cotillo, and Jandía are the best spots for riding the wind and the waves off Fuerteventura.

GRAND CANARY

Grand Canary, the most heavily populated of the Canary Islands, is circular in shape and covers only 592 square miles, but it encompasses a variety of landscapes and climates. When it is cool and cloudy along the northern slopes — where tomatoes, potatoes, sugarcane, and bananas flourish — sunbathers will be soaking up the rays on beaches in the cloudless south. At the same time, chill winds may be sweeping over the island's 6,400-foot central heights, ruffling the upland forests of laurel, pine, and eucalyptus. Sheer ravines cut into the volcanic mountains of the center, and agriculture flourishes because of intricate irrigation schemes. To anyone flying into Gando International Airport, about midway along the island's eastern coast, Grand Canary looks like Mt. Everest rising from the Sahara. The stark, rugged landscape becomes greener upon descent, and it soon becomes possible to distinguish the banana trees, sugarcane, and other cultivation that make each village an oasis. The island has 600,000 inhabitants, most of whom live in the north in the bustling capital of Las Palmas, while ever-increasing numbers of sun-hungry visitors flock to the fine beaches of the southern coast, inspiring ambitious development.

Las Palmas, extending along a strip of seafront at the island's northeastern tip, is the largest city in the archipelago, a major port, tourist resort, and shopping center. It has, besides its 350,000 inhabitants, a large transient population, from globetrotting yachtsmen to African peddlers, from French sailors to windsurfing freaks. An easygoing place, its rhythm of life is determined by the sun. Visitors often spend the day lying in the sun from 8 or 9 AM until 4 or 5 PM. Then, in the cool of the evening, they head for the outdoor cafés, shops, restaurants, and bars of the seafront promenade. Shops remain open until dusk; if clouds or mist interferes with the sun, people stroll or shop — but only until the sun reappears.

In the interior of the island, southwest of Las Palmas along narrow, mountain roads, is Tejeda, standing about 4,800 feet above sea level amid a bleak, volcanic landscape. The setting, described by the Spanish poet Miguel de Unamuno as a "petrified storm," is awesome, but it's not the aspect of nature that most visitors to the Canaries come to see. More soothing is the Maspalomas–Playa del Inglés–San Agustín resort area, sometimes called the Costa Canaria, along the island's southern coast, about 34½ miles (55 km) from Las Palmas and 15½ miles (25 km) from Gando Airport. The area stretches for miles, embracing three resort developments, excellent beaches, and a mini-Sahara of spectacular sand dunes.

GETTING AROUND: Airport – Scheduled flights connect Grand Canary with Alicante, Asturias (Oviedo), Barcelona, Bilbao, Granada, Jerez de la Frontera, Madrid, Málaga, Santiago de Compostela, Seville, and Valencia on the Spanish mainland, as well as with Palma de Mallorca in the Balearics. There are also daily flights to and from Fuerteventura, El Hierro, Lanzarote, La Palma, and Tenerife. Grand Canary's airport, Gando, is located about 14 miles (22 km) from Las Palmas and 15½ miles (25 km) from San Agustín. The No. 60 bus runs hourly to downtown Las Palmas; a taxi ride costs about $20. The *Iberia* office in Las Palmas is at 8 Calle Alcalde Ramírez Bethancourt (phone: 928-372111).

Bus – The central bus station is next to Salcai, Parque San Telmo. *Salcai* (phone: 928-368631) covers the southern part of the island and *Utinsa* (phone: 928-360179) handles the northern part. The most useful line in the city is the No. 1, or Teatro–Puerto route, which runs runs day and night along Calle León y Castillo from the resort area to the historic quarter.

Car Rental – Major rental car companies are *Avis* (in Las Palmas; phone: 928-265572 or 928-265567; Carretera Las Palmas a Mogán; phone: 928-25572; Playa del Inglés; phone: 928-760963; and at Gando Airport; phone: 928-574846); *Hertz* (phone: 928-226497 in Las Palmas; 928-762572 at Playa del Inglés; 928-264576 at the airport); and *Europcar* (24 Calle Los Martínez de Escobar, Las Palmas; phone: 928-275997; Edificio Bayuca, Playa del Inglés; phone: 928-765500; and at the airport; phone: 928-700147).

Ferry – *Trasmediterránea* (Muelle Ribera Oeste, Las Palmas; phone: 928-267766) operates car and passenger ferries between Las Palmas and Cádiz and between Las Palmas and the six other major Canaries, and jetfoils between Las Palmas and the other islands.

Mopeds and Motorcycles – Throughout the island, mopeds (top speed 35 mph) are available for about $10 a day, motorcycles for about $20. Try *Motos Rent-Puig* (4 Calle Montevideo, Las Palmas; phone: 928-274901) or *Med-Ped* (Edificio Barbados, Avenida Tirajana, Playa del Inglés; phone: 928-764434).

Taxi – Taxis in Las Palmas use meters; elsewhere on the island, it is best to agree on a rate with the driver before the trip. Las Palmas has numerous cabstands, as well as radio cabs (phone: 928-762871). For a radio cab in the Maspalomas area, call 928-762871 or 928-760293.

SPECIAL PLACES: Las Palmas – The city stretches from La Isleta peninsula and the Puerto de la Luz area, where cruise liners and merchant vessels dock, south along a narrow isthmus. The Castillo de la Luz, on the Isleta on Calle Juan Rejón, was built in 1494 to protect the town from pirates and other invaders (which included the English fleet of Sir Francis Drake) and has been restored to serve as a cultural center. Just south of the Isleta, on the western side of the isthmus, begins a 2-mile beach, Playa de las Canteras, which gently curves around a sheltered bay caused by a natural depression in the coastline. A rocky reef offshore, shaped rather like an arm, extends almost around the bay, making it as calm as a lake. Running parallel to the beach is the Paseo de las Canteras, a promenade boasting numerous bars, cafés, and restaurants: not just Spanish but also Swedish, Italian, Chinese, Finnish, Mexican, Indian, and German, as well as a few of the sit-down or stand-up, fast-food variety. Most resort hotels are in the vicinity as well. A pleasant way to spend time in this modern area is to go for a walk in Parque Santa Catalina, where Canarian families often come for their evening strolls, to take a drink at one of the cafés and eye the passing scene. To reach the park from the Paseo de las Canteras, walk along Calle Padre Cueto 3 or 4 blocks, turn right, and walk another 2 blocks. Farther south, the public market is a good place for photographing people engaged in the everyday commerce of buying and selling food and other provisions. It occupies an entire block at the corner of Calle Néstor de la Torre and Calle Galicia.

Still farther south are the palm trees and fountains of Parque Doramas, containing a zoo, a swimming pool, the stately old *Santa Catalina* hotel (phone: 928-243040), and the Pueblo Canario. The latter is an unusual replica of a Canarian village, designed by the local painter and sculptor Néstor de la Torre (1888–1938), with a pleasant open-air café, craft shops, and regular folk dancing and singing performances (Sundays from 11:45 AM to 1:15 PM and Thursdays from 5:30 to 7 PM. It also contains the artist's house, now the *Museo Néstor,* displaying paintings and memorabilia (open Mondays, Tuesdays, Thursdays, and Fridays from 10 AM to noon and from 4 to 9 PM, Saturdays from 10 AM to 1 PM; Sundays and holidays, open from 10:30 AM to 1:30 PM; closed Wednesdays; admission charge; phone: 928-245135). Any bus traveling along Calle León y Castillo at Parque Santa Catalina also goes to Parque Doramas. Another park, Parque de San Telmo, is farther south, where the broad, bustling shopping street, Calle Mayor de Triana, begins and leads south to the Vegueta, the city's Old Quarter. Parallel to Triana is the *Casa-Museo Pérez Galdós* (6 Calle Caño; phone: 928-366976; open Mondays through Saturdays 9 AM to 1 PM and from 3 to 6 PM; closed Sundays; admission charge), the former home of a 19th- and 20th-century writer and campaigner against social injustice (open Mondays through Saturdays from 9 AM to 1 PM.)

The Vegueta, the city's historic center, an area of peaceful cobbled streets, old balconied buildings, and pleasant squares, is a short way farther south (but if heading for it directly from the Isleta or Puerto de la Luz area, take a taxi or bus No. 1). Here, fronting the noble Plaza de Santa Ana, where bronze statues commemorate Canarian canines, is the 15th-century cathedral, Gothic in origin, with a later, neo-classical exterior. Among the treasures of this vast volcanic-rock structure are a gold and emerald chalice, donated by King Philip IV, and an 18th-century gold throne, while the cathedral's *Museo Diocesano de Arte Sacro* (31 Calle Doctor Chil) boasts a collection of magnificent Flemish and Castilian paintings. (The museum is open weekdays, except Wednesdays, from 9 AM to 1 PM and 4 to 7 PM; weekends, from 10 AM to 1:30 PM; admission charge; phone: 928-310872.)

Directly across the street from the cathedral is the *Casa-Museo Colón* (1 Calle Colón; phone: 928-311255), the former governors' residence. This dignified mansion housed Christopher Columbus for a short time in 1502 before he headed to the Americas on one of his later voyages. It now functions as a small museum, containing objects of the period of Columbus's explorations, including heavy cannon, faded maps, and models of the explorer's vessels, as well as sculptures and paintings. Open Mondays and Wednesdays through Sundays, from 9 AM to 1 PM. Admission charge. Another museum, nearby, is the *Museo Canario* (2 Calle Dr. Verneau; phone: 928-315600), displaying ceramics and implements of the original island inhabitants. The first floor is riveting — full of glass cases containing hundreds of skulls of the Guanches, some showing evidence of trepannage techniques used in primitive medicine. Most striking are the mummified remains of entire bodies — one, believed to be a king's son, is wrapped in layers of ceremonial skins and rush weavings. Open Mondays through Fridays, from 10 AM to 1 PM and from 3 to 7:30 PM; Saturdays, 10 AM to noon; closed Sundays and holidays. Admission charge.

The North – Cenobio de Valerón, a remarkable archaeological site, is 15½ miles (25 km) west of Las Palmas via the C810 coastal highway. Here the rock is honeycombed with caves where once, it is believed, young daughters of the Guanche nobility were kept as vestal virgins. From nearby Guía, a road zigags inland and back eastward through fertile terraced farmland, verdant with bananas and sugarcane, to Moya and Arucas. The latter, 10½ miles (17 km) out of Las Palmas, has a somber Gothic-style church, built during this century, standing out against the town's white houses — of which there are spectacular views from the observation deck at the top of the nearby Montaña de Arucas. Continue south to Teror, 13 miles (21 km) from Las Palmas, a marvel of traditional, harmonious architecture with wooden-balconied mansions. At its heart, in an 18th-century basilica with magnificent stonework and a fine coffered ceiling, Nuestra Señora del Pino, is the much-venerated statue of Our Lady of the Pine, Grand Canary's patron saint, said to have been found in a pine tree in 1481. The statue is the object of the island's annual pilgrimage on September 8.

The Interior – Drive south on C811 to Tafira, a green residential area overlooking Las Palmas, and follow signs beyond to the *mirador* (belvedere) on Pico de Bandama, a 1,865-foot peak that looks down on a perfect volcanic crater, more than 3,000 feet across and 650 feet deep. Continuing toward Tejeda, at San Mateo, the *Casa-Museo Cho Zacarías* is a rustically charming old house with rooms full of old furniture and implements, and has a restaurant serving simple, moderately priced meals between 1 and 4 PM (closed Mondays; no phone). From San Mateo, a road winds up into pine-woods and stark mountains. At Cruz de Tejeda, 26 miles (42 km) from Las Palmas and more than 4,825 feet above sea level, there are impressive views of a tortured landscape, including a vast amphitheater and the isolated Roque Nublo, a rock said to have been worshiped by the Guanches. The *Hostería la Cruz de Tejeda* (phone: 928-658050), part of the *parador* chain, is a good place to stop for lunch (open daily; moderate).

The South – The Maspalomas–Playa del Inglés–San Agustín resort area lures most of Grand Canary's visitors. At Maspalomas, the southernmost part of the area, are spectacular sand dunes, a 4-mile beach, a sprawl of elegant resort hotels, and a light-house. San Agustín, the northernmost part, with another beach, also has luxury hotels, but tends to be more residential, while between the two, the endless high-rise hotels and apartment blocks of Playa del Inglés (Englishmen's Beach) attract large numbers of visitors on inexpensive packages. Most of the island's sports facilities and a variety of nightlife and other attractions are in this area — there's even a Sioux City (Ciudad del Oueste), a Western show town, where cowboys and Indians fight it out twice daily, and the *Three Stars Saloon* (Calle Cañon del Aguila, San Agustín; phone: 928-762573) serves meals to the twang of country and western music. At Playa del Inglés is Palmitos Park, home of 230 species of exotic birds that roam an area dotted with lakes and palm trees, and home also of hundreds of varieties of tropical butterflies (open from 9 AM to 7 PM; no phone). About a mile (1.6 km) to the west of the Maspalomas lighthouse, Playa Pasito Blanco has a deep-water harbor with a marina where deep-sea charters can be hired. Also west of Maspalomas, just 20 miles (32 km) away, is the Puerto Rico apartment-condominium development, great for families and couples who want to spend a month, a summer, or the entire year in a setting complete with marina, beach, swimming pools, restaurants, shopping, and playgrounds.

SHOPPING: Las Palmas is a well-known shopper's paradise, offering a dazzling variety of products minus the IVA, or value added tax, found on the mainland. Each island does, however, impose its own luxury tax on imports. This means that products at the lower end of the market are less expensive than elsewhere — tobacco and liquor are particularly low-priced — but costlier goods may be no less expensive than on the mainland or elsewhere in Europe. As the European Economic Community gradually removes duties on the internal movement of goods around the Continent, there will be less variation in prices among the Canaries, mainland Spain, and the rest of Europe.

Large stores and small boutiques stock everything from the latest designer clothing to top-quality leatherware, sold at nonnegotiable prices, while in hundreds of shops known as bazaars, it's possible to bargain over the cost of electronic goods, precious and semi-precious stones, jewelry, and local handicrafts. This "negotiation," as it is otherwise called, is highly appropriate, but the shopper has to be good at it to best the Indian, Pakistani, and Lebanese merchants who own most of the bazaars. It's a good idea to know the range of prices of items under consideration throughout the city before actually buying. It's also a good idea to know the price of luxury goods at home; although items such as cameras, computers, and video and sound equipment may be less expensive than in European capitals, they often sell for less in the US, with more possibility of redress if a purchase proves faulty. Be sure to know the exact model number: It can make a big difference in the price. As for crafts, open-worked embroidery is a Canarian specialty; intricately hand-embroidered blouses, table linen, and bedspreads are especially appealing. Make sure the product is authentic, not a mass-produced imitation. Other interesting buys include the *timple*, the small guitar-like instrument featured in island folk music, and pottery — particularly the simple designs made without the use of a potter's wheel. Plenty of shops also sell Chinese silk, Indian marble, liquor, shoes, and souvenir items.

In Las Palmas, the traditional shopping street is Calle Mayor de Triana (or just Triana), while the larger stores and newer boutiques are found on Avenida Mesa y López, near the port. The bazaars are found mostly around the Parque Santa Catalina district. Shops are generally open from 9 AM to 1 PM and from 4:15 to 7:30 PM. The rival Spanish department stores have branches opposite each other: *El Corte Inglés* (18 Avenida Mesa y López; phone: 928-272600 or 928-263000), and *Galerías Preciados* (15 Avenida Mesa y López; phone: 928-233055).

Fataga Artesanía Canaria – The place for high-quality island handicrafts. Pueblo Canario, Las Palmas (phone: 928-243911).

Maya – Stocks everything from jade and porcelain giftware to computers and stereo equipment. 105-107 Calle Triana, Las Palmas (phone: 928-367167 and 928-372049).

Mikel – Ceramics and other gifts. In the Edificio Vera Cruz, just off the Plaza de España, Las Palmas (phone: 928-274606).

Peridis Brothers – Fine display of luxury furs in a modern showroom. 6 Avenida las Canteras, Las Palmas (phone: 928-274376).

Las Perlas – Precious stones, cultured pearls, and gold and silver jewelry. 32 Calle Luis Morote, Las Palmas (phone: 928-269701).

Saphir – A wide selection of Swiss watches, precious stones, cultured pearls, and silver and porcelain gift items. 97 Calle Triana (phone: 928-362388) and 70 Calle Sagasta, Las Palmas (phone: 928-275964).

Voula Mitsakou – A well-known furrier with shops in half a dozen European cities, charging 30% to 50% less for sable, ermine, and other skins at its Canary Island branch. 28 Calle Luis Morote, Las Palmas (phone: 928-267636).

 NIGHTCLUBS AND NIGHTLIFE: Nightlife activity in the Canaries hits its stride in Las Palmas. Although nightspots are not in abundance, there are some discos and a few of the hotels have casinos. For dancing, try *Cupé* (Calle

Nicholás Estèvanez), *Amnesia* (39 Calle Los Martínez Escobar), *Dinos* (in the *Los Bardinos* hotel, 3 Calle Eduardo Benot), *Reina Isabel* (*Reina Isabel* hotel, 40 Calle Alfredo L. Jones, Paseo de las Canteras), and *Toca-Toca* (53 Calle Secretario Artiles). The Las Palmas chic frequent the *Utopia* pub (Calle de Tomás Miller), and the café *Terraza Derby* (Parque de Santa Catalina) also is popular for late nights. *Cuasquías* (Calle Venegas) has a big Las Vegas–type show with music and dancing. The *Santa Catalina* hotel (El Parque Doramas; phone: 928-243040) and the *Tamarindos* hotel (3 Calle Retama, San Agustín; phone: 928-762600) both have casinos.

CHECKING IN: Hotels are concentrated in Las Palmas and the resort area around Maspalomas, where there are also many apartments for rent at reasonable prices. From November through *Easter,* bookings are heavy and reservations are advisable; in summer, rooms generally do not sell out and advance reservations are not needed. After *Easter,* many establishments offer discounts of 20% to 30% off their high-season rates. Most hotels cater to large tour groups — from northern Europe during winter, from Spain in summer. Expect to pay $115 or more for a double room at hotels listed as expensive, between $60 and $100 at a hotel listed as moderate, and under $60 in those listed as inexpensive.

LAS PALMAS

Meliá Las Palmas – Formerly the *Cristina Sol,* this large and luxurious property overlooking Las Canteras beach is a favorite of businesspeople; its conference rooms can accommodate up to 500 people. The 316 air conditioned rooms feature glass-enclosed balconies, color television sets, videocassette players, and mini-bars. There are also 2 swimming pools and a bather's terrace, which overlooks the beach, as well as 2 fine restaurants, a discotheque, and lovely gardens. 6 Calle Gomera, Las Palmas (phone: 928-267600; fax: 928-268411; telex: 95161). Expensive.

Reina Isabel – Relatively modern in decor and furnishings, this is one of the most luxurious establishments on the island, located right on Las Canteras beach. It could stand some renovations, but all 234 rooms are air conditioned and have color television sets, private balconies, and 24-hour room service. There is also a fine restaurant, a popular terrace bar, a rooftop, heated swimming pool (with an adjoining disco), a solarium, and a beachfront nightclub. 40 Calle Alfredo L. Jones, Paseo de las Canteras, Las Palmas (phone: 928-260100; telex: 95103). Expensive.

Santa Catalina – Most of the city's hotels are modern, but this Spanish colonial fantasy, with carved wood balconies, bucks the trend. Spacious and charmingly old-fashioned, it stands in the middle of the flowers of Parque Doramas. Chandeliers light the marble lobby; the terrace, shaded by green-and-white awnings, is an ideal place to relax and sip a cold drink. The 200 rooms are large, with balconies, traditional furnishings, air conditioning, mini-bars, and color television sets (the rooms appear slightly shabby, but ongoing renovations should bring them up to the same high standards as the public spaces). Other facilities include a new casino, a large swimming pool, tennis courts, a miniature golf course, a shopping arcade, and fireplaces in the public rooms. Parque Doramas, Las Palmas (phone: 928-243040; fax: 928-242764; telex: 96014). Expensive.

Los Bardinos – This circular structure near the Parque Santa Catalina offers fine views of the city and the sea. All 215 rooms are air conditioned and have color television sets. Other facilities include a rooftop swimming pool and a disco on the 24th floor. 3 Calle Eduardo Benot, Las Palmas (phone: 928-266100; fax: 928-229139; telex: 95189). Moderate.

Gran Canaria – A 90-room hotel that overlooks the beach and has a pleasant and efficient staff. The simple yet cheerful rooms are air conditioned and have mini-bars. There is also a good restaurant. 38 Paseo de las Canteras, Las Palmas (phone: 928-275078; fax: 928-262420; telex: 96453). Moderate to inexpensive.

Villa Blanca – For those on a tight budget, this 45-room hotel is comfortable, clean, and functional. Located near Las Canteras beach, across the street from the *Reina Isabel*. 35 Calle Alfredo L. Jones, Las Palmas (phone: 928-260016). Inexpensive.

MASPALOMAS AREA

Gloria Palace – An ultramodern luxury behemoth situated between Playa del Inglés and Maspalomas, its 448 air conditioned rooms have mini-bars and sea views. Facilities include 4 pools, a snack bar, a garden restaurant and a rooftop restaurant, 3 tennis courts, a health club, and a casino. Calle Las Margaritas, Maspalomas (phone: 928-768300). Expensive.

Iberotel Maspalomas Oasis – The center of the action, this busy, large, luxury resort in the vicinity of the lighthouse offers guests idyllic surroundings in an oasis on Maspalomas beach. A low-rise establishment amid flowers, palm trees, lawns, and fountains, it has 342 air conditioned, good-size, and stylishly designed rooms. Tennis, archery, a children's nursery, and nightly entertainment are among the facilities. Excellent international food is served in *Le Jardin* grill. This is a popular place with tour groups, and German visitors outnumber English-speaking guests. Plaza Palmeras, Playa de Maspalomas (phone: 928-760170; telex: 96104). Expensive.

Meliá Tamarindos – Surrounded by beautiful gardens, this hotel rivals the best of them in decor, grounds, and facilities. Its 2 swimming pools and beach make it a good place for simple lounging in the sun, although tennis, mini-golf, archery, bowling, and casino gambling are all available. There are 318 air conditioned rooms, several bars, and a disco. The huge, white, cast-concrete object on the hill across the highway with a pole in its center is a sundial, a gift from Sweden — and people can set their watches by it. 3 Calle Retama, Playa de San Agustín (phone: 928-762600; fax: 928-762264; telex: 95463). Expensive.

EATING OUT: Given its cosmopolitan nature, diners on Grand Canary can enjoy a wide range of international dishes, as well as local specialties and various Spanish offerings. Expect to pay $65 or more for a meal for two at places listed as expensive, between $30 and $60 at restaurants in the moderate category, and under $30 at inexpensive ones. Prices do not include drinks, wine, or tips.

LAS PALMAS

Churchill – In an old colonial-style building that houses the *British Club* upstairs, this restaurant features a menu that makes good use of imaginative recipes from a variety of countries. Specialties include pâtés, roast baby lamb, and home-baked pies. Closed Saturday afternoons, Sundays, and holidays. Reservations necessary. Major credit cards accepted. 274 Calle León y Castillo, Las Palmas (phone: 928-249192). Expensive to moderate.

Bodegón – A longtime favorite for Canarian cooking, especially seafood. Try the *cazuela canaria* (fish casserole) or the *sancocho de pescado* (fish stew). Closed Mondays. Reservations unnecessary. No credit cards accepted. Pueblo Canario, Parque Doramas, Las Palmas (phone: 928-242985). Moderate.

El Cortijo – This wood-beamed replica of a Castilian inn serves mighty portions of roast suckling pig, lamb chops, and Segovia sausage in a hearty and informal atmosphere. Open daily. Reservations unnecessary. Visa accepted. 3 Calle Diderot, Las Palmas (phone: 928-275955). Moderate.

Le Français – A few yards from Las Canteras beach, this is a family-run place, tastefully done in simple French style, with colorful flowered tablecloths accenting the whitewashed walls of the dining room. Try the delicious salmon quiche or the sole almondine. Closed Sundays. Reservations unnecessary. Visa accepted. 18 Calle Sargento Llagas, Las Palmas (phone: 928-268762). Moderate.

House of Ming – One of the town's best Chinese restaurants (there are over 20 in all), offering friendly service and picturesque views of the blue Atlantic. Open daily. Reservations unnecessary. Visa accepted. 30 Paseo de las Canteras, Las Palmas (phone: 928-274563). Moderate.

Mesón La Paella – Authentic Catalan cooking and excellent Middle Eastern rice dishes are the specialties in this eatery, one of the few places in the Canaries offering good paella. Closed Saturday evenings, Sundays, and holidays. Reservations unnecessary. Visa accepted. 47 Calle Juan Manuel Durán, Las Palmas (phone: 928-271640). Moderate.

El Pote – A popular spot for cooking in the style of Galicia — the Galician pork chops and Santiago tart make tasty eating. Closed Sundays. Reservations unnecessary. MasterCard and Visa accepted. 41 Calle Juan María Durán, Las Palmas (phone: 928-278058). Moderate.

Tenderete – This restaurant is noted for its careful preparation of typical Canarian dishes, such as *papas arrugadas con mojo* (wrinkled potatoes in a piquant sauce). Fresh flowers on the tables and numerous hanging plants lend a pleasing air to the white-walled dining room (photos testify to the visit here of the Spanish king and queen). Baked fish, pork, lamb, and suckling pig are all good. Open daily. Reservations unnecessary. Major credit cards accepted. 91 Calle León y Castillo, Las Palmas (phone: 928-246957). Moderate.

El Gallo Feliz – Its Danish owner attracts Scandinavians with plates of herring and smoked eel on toast with scrambled eggs. Friendly, fast service in a cozy room. Open evenings only, November through April. Reservations unnecessary. No credit cards accepted. 35 Paseo de las Canteras, Las Palmas (no phone). Inexpensive.

MASPALOMAS AREA

San Agustín Beach Club – This restaurant, with an African decor, enjoys a strikingly contemporary setting overlooking the beach. It's renowned for topnotch and imaginative international fare — and guests can alternate plunges into the pool with open-air dining. Closed during May and June. Reservations advised. Major credit cards accepted. Playa de los Cocoteros, San Agustín (phone: 928-760370). Expensive.

La Toja – On the ground floor of an undistinguished apartment building, but very comfortable and welcoming inside. Seafood is the specialty here. Try the prawn crêpes, dill-marinated salmon, hake, or angler. Closed Sundays for lunch. Reservations unnecessary. Major credit cards accepted. 17 Avenida Tirajana, Playa del Inglés (phone: 928-761196). Expensive to moderate.

Tenderete II – An offshoot of the original Las Palmas establishment, and now under different ownership, it serves good Canarian and seafood specialties. Open daily. Reservations unnecessary. Major credit cards accepted. Just opposite the *Rey Carlos* hotel in the Edificio Aloe, Avenida San Bartolome de Tirajana, Playa del Inglés (phone: 928-761460). Moderate.

TENERIFE

At 793 square miles, the largest of the Canary Islands is only 20 minutes by air west of Las Palmas and is also accessible by flights from Madrid in a little over 2 hours. Legend has it that God put so much effort into creating the beaches of Grand Canary that night fell before he could finish the mountains. When he came to Tenerife, he began with the mountains, and this time darkness fell before he could get around to the beaches. Thus Tenerife has fewer beaches than its neighbor and the sand is black. Still, there is enough to attract the visitor. Towering above Tenerife's mixture of lush vegetation and arid desert is the massive dormant volcano, Pico del Teide, Spain's highest peak at 12,200 feet — the island's name is believed to have evolved from a Guanche word meaning snow-capped mountain.

A somewhat higher rate of rainfall falls on Tenerife than on its neighbors, which explains why it is is sometimes called the "island of eternal spring." Consequently, Tenerife is the archipelago's main agricultural center, producing most of its vegetables. The northern and northwestern corners receive the most rainfall, which encourages forests and colorful vegetation, while the south is arid and desolate. Also in the north are the settlements of long standing: Santa Cruz de Tenerife, the provincial capital; La Laguna, accommodating one of Spain's oldest seats of learning; and Puerto de la Cruz, once important as a fruit- and wine-exporting port and now a prestigious tourism resort. Around southern beaches at Los Cristianos and Playa de las Américas, the all-year sunshine has fostered a development boom, covering tracts of desert with apartments and hotels. These new resorts, and the nearby Reina Sofía Airport, are linked with Santa Cruz by a fast four-lane highway, while another autoroute speeds traffic up to Puerto de la Cruz. Interior roads, in contrast, are narrow, winding, and tiring to drive.

GETTING AROUND: Airport – Tenerife has direct air service with Alicante, Asturias (Oviedo), Barcelona, Bilbao, Granada, Jerez de la Frontera, Madrid, Málaga, Santiago de Compostela, Seville, and Valencia, on the mainland, as well as with Palma de Mallorca in the Balearics. There are also regular connections with Fuerteventura, Grand Canary, El Hierro, Lanzarote, and La Palma. National and international flights arrive and depart from Reina Sofía Airport, on the island's southern coast, about 37½ miles (60 km) from Santa Cruz de Tenerife. Most inter-island flights use Los Rodeos Airport (Aeropuerto del Norte), 8 miles (13 km) from Santa Cruz. *Iberia* has several Tenerife offices (23 Avenida de Anaga, Santa Cruz; phone: 922-288000; Avenida de Venezuela, Puerto de la Cruz; phone: 922-380050; and at the airport; phone: 922-252340). Buses run between Reina Sofía Airport and Santa Cruz, and there are regular buses from between Los Rodeos Airport and Santa Cruz and Puerto de la Cruz. The taxi fare from Reina Sofía to Santa Cruz is about $50, from Los Rodeos, about $12.

Bus – There is frequent bus service to all of the island's major centers. The main bus station in Santa Cruz is on Avenida 3 de Mayo (phone: 922-218122 or 922-219399); in Puerto de la Cruz, on Calle del Pozo, just opposite the post office (phone: 922-382814). At Los Cristianos, buses stop at the main taxi stand opposite the Cepsa gas station (for information, call 922-770606).

Car Rental – Major rental car companies are *Avis* (21 Imelda Seris, Santa Cruz; phone: 922-241294; Avenida de Venezuela, Puerto de la Cruz; phone: 922-384552; at Reina Sofía Airport; phone: 922-770656; and Los Rodeos Airport, La Laguna; phone: 922-259090); *Hertz* (Avenida Anaga, Santa Cruz; phone: 922-274805; Plaza Augustín de Bethancourt, Puerto de la Cruz; phone: 922-384719 or 922-384560; at Reina Sofía Airport; phone: 922-384719; Los Rodeos Airport, La Laguna; phone: 922-384719 or

922-384560; and Playa de las Américas, Grupo Urbania; phone: 922-790861); and *Europcar* (Edificio Portofino, Puerto de la Cruz; phone: 922-381804 or 922-381928; Centro Comercial Teneguia, Calle Jose Campos y Arenas; phone: 922-381777 or 922-380738; Avenida Via Litoral, Playa de las Américas; phone: 922-791150 or 922-791154; and at Reina Sofia Airport; phone: 922-771150).

Ferry – *Trasmediterránea* (59 Calle Marina, Santa Cruz; phone: 922-277300) has regular sailings between Cádiz and Santa Cruz, as well as between Tenerife and many of the other islands. The company also runs a jet foil from Santa Cruz to Las Palmas, Grand Canary (operating 5 to 7 days a week, 3 to 4 times a day), and to Morro Jable, Fuerteventura (5 weekly departures once a day), as well as a new hydrofoil service between Los Cristianos and San Sebastián, on the neighboring island of La Gomera, stopping occasionally at Las Palmas. Regular ferry service between Los Cristianos and San Sebastián is operated by *Ferry Gomera* (Edificio Rascacielos, Avenida 3 de Mayo, Santa Cruz; phone: 922-219244; and Muelle de Los Cristianos; phone: 922-790556). The ferries run three times a day except Tuesdays, when they offer only once-a-day service.

Mopeds and Motorcycles – These can be rented from *Moped Santos* (Playa Azul, Playa de las Américas; phone: 922-791639) for about $80 to $250 per week, $20 to $35 per day; hourly rates are also available.

Taxi – Cabs can be requested by telephone in Santa Cruz (phone: 922-641459 or 922-615111), Puerto de la Cruz (phone: 922-384910 or 922-385818), Playa de las Américas (phone: 922-791407 or 922-791669), and Los Cristianos (phone: 922-790352, 922-795459, or 922-795509).

SPECIAL PLACES: Santa Cruz de Tenerife and the North – Backed by sawtooth mountains, this provincial capital is an important port, with over 200,000 inhabitants and many modern buildings. More Spanish in character and aesthetically more pleasing than Las Palmas, it has no beaches to speak of, and is primarily a city of shops, with boutique-lined Calle del Castillo closed to traffic but filled with hordes of shoppers. Plaza de España, where this pedestrian island begins, is next to the port and is noteworthy for its memorial to the men of Tenerife who died in the Spanish Civil War. Visible from quite a distance, the towering monument also serves as a directional marker for tourists making their way back to the center of town. Just off the Plaza de España, on the third floor of the Palacio Insular, is the *Museo Arqueológico y Antropológico* (5 Calle Bravo Murillo; phone: 922-242090), which has a collection of 100 Guanches mummies, more than 1,000 skulls, and 300,000 bones, as well as a variety of other artifacts of the Canary Islands' original inhabitants. The museum is open Mondays through Saturdays from 9 AM to 1 PM and from 4 to 8 PM, winter months; 9 AM to 2 PM, summer months. Closed Sundays and holidays. Admission charge. North of the port, along Avenida de Anaga, where flame trees and palms provide a pleasant tropical air, is the Castillo de Paso Alto, a 17th-century fortress that now houses a regional military museum (no phone). Among the cannon on display is the one known as "the Tiger," which fired the ball that tore off Admiral Horatio Nelson's right arm when he laid siege to the town in 1797. The museum is open Tuesdays through Sundays from 10 AM to 2 PM.

Five miles (8 km) north of town lies Playa de las Teresitas, which claims to be the world's largest artificial beach; the golden sand covering this mile-long stretch — a pleasant place for sunbathing or a quick snack at one of its many inexpensive restaurants — was imported from the Sahara. From here, the road turns inlánd and corkscrews steeply upward to the Anaga headland, a dramatic area of knife-edge ridges, ravines, and dense evergreen woods. At El Bailadero pass, the picturesquely situated village of Taganana can be seen down below, but the road continues west along the crest of the range to the Pico del Inglés Belvedere, a lookout point 3,300 feet above sea level, from where there is a spectacular view of Pico del Teide rising in the distance. Soon after, the road descends to La Laguna, the university town and former island capital, which has an interesting old section highlighted by the Plaza del Adelantado, the 16th-century Iglesia de la Concepción (recently declared a national monument), and a 20th-century cathedral with a neo-classical façade.

Puerto de la Cruz – West of Santa Cruz, on the rocky Atlantic coast where the lush Orotava valley meets the sea, Puerto de la Cruz is a major resort center (despite the fact that it has no beach worthy of the name), and has been a cosmopolitan place for centuries. The last eruption of El Teide destroyed the harbor at Garachico, 20½ miles (33 km) to the west, giving added importance to the port here. European traders of many nationalities settled in, and wealthy British tourists began arriving to enjoy the mild winter climate during the last century. Today the town has many foreign residents and almost 100 hotels catering to visitors. Banana plantations, tropical fruits, jasmine, and bougainvillea flourish along the steeply terraced coast, behind which El Teide towers, often girded by cloud and covered with snow in winter.

The town has pleasant squares, especially the Plaza de la Iglesia, with its gardens and old buildings. Straw-hatted women in traditional bright embroidered skirts sell flowers near the Ayuntamiento (Town Hall) on Calle de Santo Domingo. Next to this street, Calle de San Telmo, the elegant main thoroughfare, runs along the waterfront, with a bevy of fine shops and hotels to match. Follow San Telmo until it becomes Avenida de Colón. Here, the resort's lack of safe beaches has been made up for by the creation of the Lago de Martiánez leisure complex, a series of beautifully landscaped seawater pools, promenades, and lounging areas set in and around rocky volcanic outcroppings that extend offshore for hundreds of yards. Don't miss it: Besides being a perfect sunbathing spot, the complex, designed by Lanzarote artist César Manrique, includes a gynmasium, a restaurant, bars, and a nightclub. Just opposite, on Avenida de Colón, is the *Café de Paris,* a popular meeting place where patrons eat and drink amid palms, mirrors, and wrought iron, a piano tinkling in the background.

Also visit the Jardín Botánico (Botanical Gardens), located on Carretera del Botánico at the eastern entrance to town. Rated among the world's finest, the gardens were created by order of King Carlos III in 1788, and cover 5 acres with thousands of varieties of tropical plants, including a 200-year-old rubber tree. The gardens (phone: 922-383572) are open daily from 9 AM to 7 PM. Admission charge. Another attraction, at the opposite end of town and reached by a free bus from Playa de Martiánez, is Loro Parque, a tropical park with a dolphin show and 1,300 parrots — some of which ride bicycles and do other tricks in a parrot show (open from 9 AM to 6 PM; admission charge). On Sundays at 11 AM, typical Canaries folk dancing and singing, plus an exhibition of local wrestling, take place in another park, on the grounds of the *Tigaiga* hotel (16 Parque de Taoro; phone: 922-383500).

La Orotava – In a valley of the same name, overlooking Puerto de la Cruz, which is 6 miles (10 km) away and 1,000 feet below, La Orotava occupies a site that was once the capital of a Guanche chief and is among the most compelling settings on the island. One of the oldest towns on Tenerife, it has steep cobbled streets and handsome homes with exquisite balconies, red roofs, and interior patios. The 18th-century Church of the Conception, now a museum, is a highlight, as is *Artesanía La Casa de los Balcones* (3 Calle San Francisco; phone: 922-380629) an arts and crafts center in an old balconied house with a flower-filled patio. Here visitors will find the delicate *calado,* or drawn-thread embroidery, used for everything from handkerchiefs to tablecloths and manufactured by women working at wooden looms. (They speak English and are glad to answer questions.) The annual *Corpus Christi* festival in June is a celebration of the religious fervor, energy, and artistry of the town's residents. Although the feast day is celebrated throughout the Canaries, the festivities are at their most colorful here. Before the procession, the town's squares and streets are covered with carpets made of hundreds of thousands of flower petals — bougainvillea, dahlias, geraniums, carnations — as well as crushed leaves, pine needles, and colorful designs in sand. The largest and most intricate carpet is laid on the Plaza del Ayuntamiento.

Pico del Teide – This is one excursion not to be missed on any visit to the Canaries. Mt. Teide, which towers 12,200 feet above sea level and overlooks a literal sea of clouds, is situated in the Parque Nacional de las Cañadas del Teide (phone: 922-330701), a beautiful forest of heather, evergreens, eucalyptus, and Canarian pine at an altitude of some 6,500 feet. The park is reached via the town and the valley of La Orotava, where corn, chestnuts, and bananas are raised in abundance (open daily during daylight hours; no admission charge). Beyond La Orotava, the road leads to a desolate, treeless amphitheater. This is Las Cañadas, an ancient volcanic crater some 47 miles in diameter, from the center of which surges the great bulk of El Teide, a newer volcano and the tallest mountain in Spain. Las Cañadas is scarred and strewn with boulders; the last eruption in 1798 destroyed a peak that was even larger than El Teide. A cable car takes 35 passengers on a 10-minute journey to the base of the cone. From there it is a 25-minute hike to the edge, from where most of the Canaries — even the coast of Africa — are visible on a clear day. At dawn, the sun touching the mountains creates splendid shadows that blend with the various shades of lava and ash. The stillness and barrenness, intensified by sulfurous fumes filtering out of the volcano's depths, are intensely moving. Those short of breath should take care, as the air is quite rarefied at this altitude. Dedicated climbers can spend the night near the peak at the *Cueva de Hielo,* a mountain shelter (literally, the "Ice Cave"); for less adventurous sorts, there is a lovely *parador* (see *Checking In*) near the cable car. Free guided tours depart the visitors' center at 9:30 AM, 11:30 AM, and 1:30 PM daily (phone: 922-259903). Avoid Sundays and holidays, when the park is crowded. The cable car (phone: 922-383711) runs from 9 AM to 4:30 PM daily and costs about $6 each way.

Icod de los Vinos – West of Puerto de la Cruz, a road winds above sea-whipped rocks and black sand coves to this small town, the center of the island's wine-producing area. The town's proudest possession is the *drago,* Tenerife's oldest dragon tree, said to be more than 1,000 years old. From Icod, a drive through banana plantations leads to the nearby beach resort of San Marcos, amid black cliffs.

SHOPPING: On Tenerife, visitors will find Puerto de la Cruz the area with the most varied goods. In Santa Cruz, the main shopping streets are found in a square zone formed by Calle del Castillo, Calle Valentín Sanz, Calle Emilio Calzadillo, and the ocean; as in Las Palmas, the Indian, Pakistani, Lebanese, and Spanish shopkeepers are willing to negotiate but are not about to give anything away. Clothing, toys, watches, crafts, and lots more, including junk, are sold every Sunday morning at *El Rastro,* the open-air market on Avenida de Anaga in Santa Cruz. A crafts fair is held on the first Sunday of the month along the Garachico promenade, 20 miles (32 km) along the coast from Puerto de la Cruz (in winter, it usually is held in the patio of the San Francisco convent). A shopping center with 50 shops selling a broad range of goods is located under the *Vallemar* hotel, 2 Avenida de Colón, Puerto de la Cruz (phone: 922-384800).

B. Choitram – Carries Lladró porcelain, jewelry, and fine crystal. 3 Calle Sargento Cáceres, Puerto de la Cruz (phone: 922-380420).

Casa Iriarte – Local handicrafts; this fine old galleried house has over 40,000 gift items, including beautiful embroidery and Toledo ware. 21 Calle San Juan, Puerto de la Cruz (phone: 922-383993).

Casa Romy – A typical bazaar, stocking everything from binoculars to semi-precious stones. 2 Calle San Juan, Puerto de la Cruz (phone: 922-380651).

Joyería Purrilos – Fine watches, crystal, and leather goods. 14 Calle Quintana, Puerto de la Cruz (phone: 922-384432).

Mari Petri – Authentic hand-embroidered items, including blouses, shawls, and skirts. Two locations: 4 Calle Obispo Pérez Cáceres, Puerto de la Cruz (phone: 922-381711), and 3 San Antonio, Puerto de la Cruz (phone: 922-387416).

Regalos Eros – A range of gifts, including Lladró porcelain. 22 Calle Santo Domingo, Puerto de la Cruz (phone: 922-380299).

CHECKING IN: Most of Tenerife's best hotels are concentrated in Puerto de la Cruz, where there is a large selection in all price ranges. Phenomenal development has taken place in the southern beach area around Playa de las Américas, where there are numerous apartment blocks, as well as hotels providing accommodations for package tours. Expect to pay $115 or more for a double room listed as expensive, $60 to $100 for a room listed as moderate, and $60 or less for an inexpensive room.

PUERTO DE LA CRUZ

Meliá Botánico – Set amid lush tropical gardens, this 282-room top-of-the-line establishment, with an attentive, English-speaking staff, is just a step away from the Botanical Gardens, about a mile from downtown. Rooms are air conditioned and tastefully furnished, with color television sets, videocassette players, mini-bars, and hair dryers. Other facilities include fine shops, a discotheque, tennis courts, a swimming pool, and a poolside restaurant. Calle Richard J. Yeoward, Puerto de la Cruz (phone: 922-381400; fax: 922-381504; telex: 92395). Expensive.

Meliá San Felipe – A deluxe, seafront hotel with an elegant marble lobby, its 260 air conditioned rooms have wall-to-wall carpeting, modern decor, and views of the sea or mountains. Tennis courts, a large pool, a children's playground, and a lively entertainment program make it a fine resort choice. 22 Avenida de Colón, Puerto de la Cruz (phone: 922-383311; fax: 922-387697; telex: 92146). Expensive.

Parque San Antonio – Those who want to get away from the madding throngs of tourists in Puerto de la Cruz, but wish to be close enough to the center of town to make quick forays, should consider this. Tucked away in a veritable botanical garden all its own, it is merely 5 minutes by bus from the center. All 211 rooms are air conditioned. There is also a restaurant. Carretera de las Arenas, Puerto de la Cruz (phone: 922-384851; telex: 92774). Expensive.

Semiramis – A 15-story property imaginatively built into the cliff edge. All 275 air conditioned rooms have terraces overlooking the ocean, color television sets, videocassette players, mini-bars, and refrigerators; some have complete kitchens. A good dining room, a tropical garden, 3 swimming pools (2 heated), a tennis court, and shops are among the attractions. 12 Calle Leopoldo Cologán, Puerto de la Cruz (phone: 922-385551; fax: 922-385253; telex: 92160). Expensive.

La Paz – Situated in an upscale residential area of Puerto de la Cruz, this 167-room hotel features a tasteful interior with an abundant use of woodwork. All of the rooms are air conditioned and boast an attractive Spanish decor. There is also a swimming pool and tennis courts. The staff speaks English and is most attentive and friendly. Urbanización La Paz, Puerto de la Cruz (phone: 922-385011; telex: 92203). Expensive to moderate.

Marquesa – Historic charm and modern comforts are combined in this 88-room hotel in the old section of Puerto de la Cruz. A leafy patio, a swimming pool, and a popular terrace and restaurant are among the facilities. 11 Calle Quintana, Puerto de la Cruz (phone: 922-383151; fax: 922-386950; telex: 92758). Moderate.

Monopol – This family-run hotel (since 1888) is a world away from the modern and sometimes soulless establishments found on Tenerife. Part of this structure dates back to 1742, and is worth a visit even for those not staying here, to see the charming old patio with its palms and rubber trees and carved wooden balconies. The 92 rooms are well kept. 15 Calle Quintana, Puerto de la Cruz (phone: 922-384611; fax: 922-37031; telex: 92397). Moderate.

ELSEWHERE ON THE ISLAND

Mencey – This charming old yellow building in the heart of the capital is part of the elegant CIGA chain, and by far the finest hotel on Tenerife. Its former grandeur has survived modernization, and the 275 air conditioned rooms have been splendidly refurbished; a new wing with motel-type units also has been added. There are 2 swimming pools, tennis courts, a bar, a poolside buffet, and lovely gardens. 38 Avenida José Naveiras, Santa Cruz de Tenerife (phone: 922-276700; telex: 92034). Expensive.

Bitácora – A relatively new, L-shaped block, a quarter of a mile from the beach but with an attractive pool area. The marble lobby and general spaciousness are pleasant; the 314 rooms all have mini-bars and air conditioning. Playa de las Américas, Arona (phone: 922-791540; fax: 922-796677; telex: 91120). Moderate.

Bouganville Playa – Large and modern, this 481-room property has 3 swimming pools (1 for children), 4 bars, squash and tennis courts, a fitness center, a large sauna, and conference facilities. All rooms are air conditioned and have terraces with sea views. Urbanización San Eugenio, Playa de las Américas, Adeje (phone: 922-790200; telex: 92742). Moderate.

Gran Tinerfe – Open terraces and spacious gardens give a pleasant air to this well-maintained establishment on a black sand beach. The 356 air conditioned rooms are attractively furnished; 52 one-bedroom garden bungalows are also available. There are 3 ocean-fed saltwater swimming pools, tennis courts, and a nightly cabaret show. Playa de las Américas (phone: 922-791200; telex: 92199). Moderate.

Parador de las Cañadas del Teide – Ideal for those seeking tranquillity and fresh mountain air, this place is about an hour by car from Puerto de la Cruz, more than 7,000 feet above sea level. A state-owned *parador,* it sits in the crater of an extinct volcano and offers remarkable views of lava fields and of El Teide, Spain's highest peak. The 16 large, spotlessly clean rooms are furnished in simple rustic style, the beds are comfortable, and there is a swimming pool, a lounge with a fireplace, and a restaurant serving typical Canaries dishes. Reservations are required well in advance. Las Cañadas del Teide (phone: 922-332304). Moderate.

Los Hibiscos – This pleasant low-rise development of 138 studio apartments and 180 hotel rooms surrounds a series of gardens and a swimming pool. Guests use the facilities of the adjacent *Bouganville Playa Hotel.* Urbanización San Eugenio, Playa de las Américas (phone: 922-791462). Moderate to inexpensive.

EATING OUT: Restaurants on Tenerife feature Canarian and international dishes. The better places, with the most extensive menus, are found in Puerto de la Cruz. For typical Canarian fare at good prices, try the smaller eateries in the narrow streets near the Plaza del Charco. Expect to pay $65 or more for dinner for two in restaurants listed as expensive, between $30 and $60 in restaurants listed as moderate, and $30 or less in inexpensive ones. Prices do not include drinks, wine, or tips.

PUERTO DE LA CRUZ

La Magnolia – A light and airy restaurant with garden, serving Catalan and international dishes. Specialties include a delicious *zarzuela* (fish stew) and stuffed partridge. Closed Mondays and May. Reservations advised. Major credit cards accepted. 5 Carretera del Botánico, Puerto de la Cruz (phone: 922-385614). Expensive.

Peruano – Enjoy authentic Peruvian dishes such as *ceviche* (raw fish marinated in lemon juice with onions and hot peppers), as well as traditional Spanish favorites, in an agreeable atmosphere complete with appropriate Latin American music. Open daily. Reservations unnecessary. No credit cards accepted. Calle del Pozo, Puerto de la Cruz (phone: 922-382253). Moderate.

El Pescado – The name means "the fish," and that's what guests will find on the menu, prepared in a variety of intriguing ways. Closed Wednesdays and May through September. Reservations unnecessary. No credit cards accepted. 3-A Avenida Venezuela, Puerto de la Cruz (phone: 922-382806). Moderate.

La Papaya – Each guest is greeted with a complimentary glass of sherry in this converted old Canarian house. Local dishes are the specialty here; be sure to top off the meal with a dish of homemade ice cream. Open daily. Reservations unnecessary. No credit cards accepted. 14 Calle Lomo, Puerto de la Cruz (phone: 922-382811). Moderate to inexpensive.

La Marina – International dishes are served in a nautical setting near the port, with a strong emphasis on fish. Closed Saturdays and from June through mid-July. No reservations or credit cards accepted. 2 Calle San Juan, Puerto de la Cruz (phone: 922-385401). Inexpensive.

Patio Canario – Enjoy local specialties in this rustic Canarian house with a timber and tiled roof, potted plants, and fresh flowers on the tables. Try *conejo en salmorejo* (rabbit in a tasty sauce) or a hearty *potaje canario de verduras* (vegetable soup). Closed Thursdays. Reservations unnecessary. Major credit cards accepted. 4 Calle Lomo, Puerto de la Cruz (phone: 922-380451). Inexpensive.

ELSEWHERE ON THE ISLAND

Las Folías – Situated in a traditionally designed shopping center by the sea, the emphasis here is on fresh raw ingredients. Try the crab salad, roast lamb, or chateaubriand. The dining room provides an intimate atmosphere, aided by soft lamplight. Closed Sundays. Reservations advised. Major credit cards accepted. *Centro Comercial Pueblo Canario,* Playa de las Américas (phone: 922-792269). Expensive.

La Riviera – Snazzy continental dishes are the hallmark of this chic, tastefully decorated restaurant. Closed Sundays and mid-August through mid-September. Reservations advised. Major credit cards accepted. 155 Rambla General Franco, Santa Cruz de Tenerife (phone: 922-275812). Expensive.

La Caseta de Madera – This popular eatery in an old wooden building specializes in Canarian cooking with a Tenerife twist. The emphasis is on seafood, but the daily specials are also worth a try. Closed Saturday evenings and Sundays. Reservations unnecessary. Major credit cards accepted. Calle Regla, Barrio Los Llanos, Santa Cruz de Tenerife (phone: 922-210023). Expensive to moderate.

Mesón del Orgaz – Seafood and Segovia-style roast meats cooked in a wood-fired oven are the specialties of this place, in the same shopping center as *Las Folías.* The dining room boasts a beamed ceiling and plush red seats. Closed Wednesdays in summer. Reservations unnecessary. No credit cards accepted. *Centro Comercial Pueblo Canario,* Playa de las Américas (phone: 922-793169). Moderate.

L'Scala – Near Los Cristianos beach, with an outside terrace, this restaurant serves authentic Castilian dishes, such as roast suckling pig, in agreeable surroundings. Closed Tuesdays. Reservations unnecessary. No credit cards accepted. 7 Calle La Paloma, Los Cristianos (phone: 922-791051). Moderate.

LANZAROTE

An eerie, burnt-out island punctuated by hundreds of extinct volcanoes, Lanzarote is the most physically astonishing of the Canaries. Its scenery is so unusual that people who fly in from Tenerife or Grand Canary invariably describe it as unforgettable. A 1- or 2-day visit is enough to see this awe-inspiring landscape, but many travelers are tempted to linger longer on some of the island's white sand beaches. Set 85 miles northeast of Las Palmas and only 65 miles from the coast of Morocco, Lanzarote has some 300 volcanoes, and petrified seas of lava — known as *malpaís* — writhe across parts of the island. Nevertheless, its farms produce sumptuous melons, figs, onions, and tomatoes, thanks to a remarkable system of cultivation. Local farmers spread *picón* (black volcanic ash) on their fields to absorb and retain moisture, and thus manage to coax an abundant harvest in a land that has no running water and sparse rainfall. They also produce a notable wine from the malvasía, or malmsey, grape, which is grown on vines planted in walled hollows to protect them from the hot, searing winds.

By such ingenuity and persistence, the native population (now 50,000) managed to survive from approximatly the time when the Genoese navigator Lancelotto Malocello landed here in the 14th century (and gave the island its name) until mass tourism hit in the 1980s. Some 700,000 visitors now set foot in this easternmost of the Canaries annually, and many new hotels and apartment blocks have been built, as well as desalinization plants to provide water. Fortunately, new development may be no higher than 3 stories, billboards are banned, and construction is confined to three main zones. Except for Arrecife, the undistinguished, traffic-clogged capital on the island's eastern coast, and these three "artificial" resort areas — Costa Teguise (north of Arrecife), Puerto del Carmen (south of both Arrecife and the airport), and Playa Blanca (still farther south, facing Fuerteventura, where some of the best beaches are) — the island largely retains its magical quality. For this, much credit is due to César Manrique, its native artist, architect, and ecological campaigner, responsible for the development of various island sites.

 GETTING AROUND: Airport – The Aeropuerto de Lanzarote is 4 miles (6 km) from Arrecife. *Iberia* offers direct service between the island and Alicante, Barcelona, Bilbao, Madrid, Málaga, and Seville, as well as inter-island service with Grand Canary, Tenerife, and Fuerteventura. *Iberia*'s Arrecife office is at 2 Avenida Rafael González (phone: 928-810354).

Bus – Bus service throughout the island is provided by *Arrecife Bus* (phone: 928-811546) and *Lanzarote Bus* (phone: 928-812458).

Car Rental – Major rental car companies are *Avis* (Tías; phone: 928-512400; *Club Resort Los Zocos,* Costa Teguise; phone: 928-816439, ext. 377; *Lanzarote Palace* hotel, Playa de los Pocillos; phone: 928-512400; and at the airport, Arrecife; phone: 928-812256); *Hertz* (at the airport; phone: 928-813711; and at the *Gran Hotel Arrecife;* phone: 928-813711); and *Europcar* (at the airport, Arrecife; phone: 928-814440 or 928-802657; *Centro Comercial La Olita,* Teguise; phone: 928-813976; and at the *Centro Comercial,* Punta Limones, Playa Blance; phone: 928-517077 or 928-517078).

Ferry – *Trasmediterránea* ferries sail regularly between Arrecife and Cádiz, as well as to Las Palmas, Grand Canary, Santa Cruz de Tenerife, and Puerto del Rosario, Fuerteventura. In addition, the company operates a jet foil between Playa Blanca and Corralejo and Puerto del Rosario on Fuerteventura. *Alisur,* a *Trasmediterránea* subsidiary, runs a ferry between Playa Blanca, Lanzarote, and Corralejo, Fuerteventura, 4 times daily. In Arrecife, contact *Trasmediterránea* (90 Calle José Antonio; phone: 928-811188) and *Alisur* (1 Calle La Esperanza; phone: 928-814272).

Taxi – Taxis are available on call in Arrecife (phone: 928-811680 and 928-810283) and in Puerto del Carmen (phone: 928-825034). Hiring a car and driver for a tour of the volcanoes costs about $60, while an organized bus tour with guide runs about $40.

SPECIAL PLACES: Las Montañas del Fuego (Fire Mountains) – Between 1730 and 1736, a series of terrifying eruptions devastated the western part of Lanzarote, burying farmland and a number of villages under volcanic debris. This area now makes up the Parque Nacional de Timanfaya. Entering from Yaiza, a village in the south, 14½ miles (23 km) from Arrecife, visitors come to the Echadero de los Camellos, where dromedaries wait to carry visitors on short journeys over the lava (there is a charge for this, in addition to the park admission). The main road through the park winds up a hill known as Islote de Hilario, where subsurface temperatures reach upward of 800F. A simple way to check is by merely touching the ground. Twigs placed in a hollow catch fire within seconds, and when a park ranger pours water down a vent in the earth's surface, a steam geyser instantly erupts. A tour bus cruises "The Route of the Volcanoes" (with commentary in English) for a close view of this lunar-like landscape of total desolation, where virtually no living creature exists. Before departing, try a volcano-broiled steak at *El Diablo,* the park restaurant (see *Eating Out*), where the meat is actually cooked by the earth's natural heat. The park is open daily, from 9 AM to 5 PM. Admission charge. *Note:* Strong footwear is recommended to explore the lava fields, and those with a camera should remember to bring a blower brush to clean off the dust.

The North – An 18-mile (29-km) drive north of Arrecife leads to Jameos del Agua, a beautiful grotto carved out of the black volcanic rock, with a lagoon formed when molten lava met the sea. At one end is an open-air swimming pool, in surroundings beautifully landscaped by the outstanding Lanzarote artist and environmentalist César Manrique. Folk music shows, with dinner and dancing, are held here. The cave is open daily from 11 AM to 8 PM (later for the show); admission charge (phone: 928-835010). Some 300 yards away is the Cueva de los Verdes (Green Cave), the world's largest volcanic tunnel, a place where Guanches and later inhabitants took refuge from invaders. Extending nearly 5 miles to the sea, it was created by cooling lava. Open from 11 AM to 6 PM daily; tours depart on the hour, sometimes with an English-speaking guide; admission charge. At the northernmost tip of the island, 7 miles (11 km) farther along, is the Mirador del Río, a lookout point atop old fortifications where there is a breathtaking view of some of the smaller Canaries — Graciosa, Montaña Clara, and Alegranza.

Returning southward, the road passes Haría, a village of white houses in a green valley dotted with hundreds of palms, and Teguise, the former island capital. Set on top of an extinct volcano, Teguise has a castle, the Castillo de Guanapay, perched on top of the cone and provides another splendid view of some of the smaller Canaries. The island's current capital, Arrecife, is not particularly interesting, but it does have two castles, the 16th-century Castillo de San Gabriel (open from 9 AM to 1 PM and from 3 to 7 PM, closed Saturdays and holidays; admission charge) and the 18th-century Castillo de San José. The latter, renovated by César Manríque, is now the home of the *International Museum of Contemporary Art* (open daily from 11 AM to 9 PM; no admission charge; phone: 928-812321) and of the deluxe *Castillo de San José* restaurant (which stays open until 1 AM — see *Eating Out*). Except for the hotel bars, there is very little nightlife activity.

CHECKING IN: Until very recently, there were only a few spartan pensions on the island, but modern hotels and apartments now offer a wide range of accommodations, primarily in Costa Teguise and Puerto del Carmen. Expect to pay $115 or more for a double room in hotels listed as expensive, between $60 and $100 in hotels listed as moderate, and $60 or less in those listed as inexpensive.

La Gería – An attractive establishment facing the sea, situated 2 miles (3 km) east of Puerto del Carmen. The black marble steps from the lobby lead to a large circular bar and a huge heated swimming pool. All 244 rooms are air conditioned and have color television sets, videocassette players, and terraces with ocean views. Playa de los Pocillos, Puerto del Carmen (phone: 928-510441). Expensive.

Meliá Salinas – Looking like a giant spacecraft newly touched down in a tropical paradise, this former Sheraton property, decorated by César Manrique, offers 310 modern air conditioned rooms, each with a private terrace facing the sea. Outdoor delights include a private beach, free-form pool, large gardens, tennis courts, and the necessary equipment for scuba diving and sailing, in addition to restaurants, bars, massage services, a sauna, a cinema, and a disco. Calle Sur Teguise, Costa Teguise (phone: 928-813040; fax: 928-813390; telex: 96320). Expensive.

Arrecife Gran – A contemporary resort overlooking Arrecife harbor, with a large pool and sun deck, tennis courts, gym, and sauna. Its most unusual feature is a restaurant on an island in the middle of a small lake that can be reached only by boat. The 148 rooms are air conditioned, pleasant, and comfortable, with large terraces. Avenida Mancomunidad, Arrecife (phone: 928-811250; fax: 928-814259; telex: 95249). Moderate.

Los Fariones – Surrounded by tropical gardens, this friendly 237-room hotel fronts a small beach and features a heated swimming pool and tennis courts. The rooms are air conditioned, comfortable, and functional. Urbanización Playa Blanca, Puerto del Carmen (phone: 928-825175; fax: 928-510202; telex: 96351). Moderate.

Teguise Playa – A large new establishment on its own beach, only a short distance from the *Costa Teguise Golf Club,* it boasts 324 air conditioned rooms, all with sea views, and has 2 pools, a bar, and a restaurant. Urbanización, Costa Teguise (phone: 928-816654; fax: 928-810979; telex: 096399). Moderate.

Aparthotel Don Paco and Apartamentos Castilla – This resort complex near the beach, a few minutes drive from Arrecife and the airport, offers 228 spacious rooms and apartments with attractive pinewood fittings, cheerful fabrics, color television sets, and fully equipped kitchens; all have ocean views. Facilities include 2 swimming pools, squash courts, a gymnasium, 2 restaurants, a bar, and a disco. Playa de los Pocillos, Puerto del Carmen (phone: 928-511034 for the hotel, or 928-511618 for the apartments). Inexpensive.

EATING OUT: The tourist influx has spurred the establishment of restaurants offering international dishes, but a few places continue to serve authentic Canaries cooking. Try the local wine, made from the malvasía, or malmsey, grape, grown in the lava fields. The El Grifo Bodega label has been a favorite since 1775. Expect to pay $65 or more for dinner for two in restaurants listed as expensive, between $40 and $60 in restaurants listed as moderate, and $35 or less in inexpensive ones.

Castillo de San José – In the cellar of an old castle that now houses the *International Museum of Contemporary Art,* this is one of the most beautiful restaurants on the island. (Well-known local architect César Manrique was responsible for the renovation.) Open daily. Reservations advised. Major credit cards accepted. A bit over a mile (2 km) northeast of Arrecife on the road to Las Caletas (phone: 928-812321). Expensive.

Malvasía Grill – Bright checkered tablecloths, a rustic atmosphere, and efficient and friendly service make for pleasant dining in this restaurant in the *Los Zocos* resort club. The menu offers a varied sampling of international dishes and a good selection of international wines. Open for dinner only; closed holidays. Reservations advised. Major credit cards accepted. *Los Zocos,* Playa de las Cucharas, Costa Teguise (phone: 928-816436). Expensive.

Acatife – This centuries-old house in the old town of Teguise is the place for international cooking at reasonable prices. Willy, the German owner, also offers island sightseeing flights in his private plane — for an additional charge. Open for dinner only; closed Sundays and Mondays. Reservations unnecessary. Major credit cards accepted. Plaza de la Iglesia, Teguise (phone: 928-845027). Moderate.

La Bohème – Two parrots guard the entrance to the dining room, which is colorfully decorated with plenty of greenery. International dishes are the specialty, served at tables illuminated by cozy lamplight, which adds to the already intimate atmosphere. Open daily. Reservations unnecessary. No credit cards accepted. 51 Avenida de las Playas, Puerto del Carmen (phone: 928-825915). Moderate.

La Marina – Canarian and South American fare highlight the menu in this promenade restaurant with a nautical air. Don't pass up the grilled lamb chops. Closed Tuesdays. Reservations unnecessary. No credit cards accepted. Avenida Marítimo de las Playas, Puerto del Carmen (phone: 928-826096). Moderate to inexpensive.

La Casa Roja – Good, simple seafood dishes are served at this popular place overlooking the little harbor in Puerto del Carmen. Open daily. Reservations unnecessary. No credit cards accepted. 22 Plaza Varadero, Puerto del Carmen (phone: 928-826515). Inexpensive.

El Diablo – A dramatically located eatery, it stands amid the Montañas del Fuego, the island's volcanic Fire Mountains, and offers the unique opportunity to feast on a volcano-broiled steak. Open daily for lunch only. No reservations or credit cards accepted. Parque Nacional de Timanfaya (phone: 928-840057). Inexpensive.

La Era – A palm-shaded patio adds to the charm of this popular eating spot, situated in a 17th-century house in the southern village of Yaiza. The dining room walls are made of 2-foot-thick lava blocks, and the typical Canarian fare is served by a friendly staff, most efficient when tour groups are not around. Open daily. Reservations unnecessary. No credit cards accepted. Yaiza (phone: 928-830016). Inexpensive.

Playa Blanca – There is no menu; excellent seafood dishes depend on the catch of the day. Open daily. No reservations or credit cards accepted. Yaiza (no phone). Inexpensive.

FUERTEVENTURA

The second-largest of the Canary Islands, Fuerteventura, has the longest shoreline, with plenty of spacious, empty beaches, and an arid climate that guarantees year-round sunshine — just the spot for windsurfers, beach bums, sun lovers, fishermen, and those seeking total seclusion. It is the island closest to Africa — only 59 miles offshore — and the dramatic, howling winds and impressive sand dunes never let visitors forget it.

Bare hills formed by extinct volcanoes, flat-roofed houses, and endless beaches are features of this sparsely populated island. There are some 30,000 permanent residents, plus 60,000 goats, a third of which graze wild. Most of the island's population resides in Puerto del Rosario, the capital, located about midway along the eastern coast. Atlantic rollers break against the rocky western coast, while the best beaches extend along the southeast coast, around

Jandía, for instance, and in the north near Corralejo, once a quiet fishing village and now a growing resort. Fishing, from the beaches or a boat, is excellent.

The island can be toured in a day, taking in the rugged interior including Betancuria, a secluded oasis chosen by Béthencourt as the island's original capital in 1404 (the town now has an interesting cathedral). An enjoyable excursion can be made from Corralejo over translucent waters to the offshore Isla de los Lobos.

GETTING AROUND: Airport – Fuerteventura's airport is located 3 miles (5 km) from Puerto del Rosario. *Iberia* (11 Calle Uno de Mayo; phone: 928-851250; airport; phone: 928-851250) has direct service to and from Barcelona, Bilbao, Málaga, Madrid and Seville, as well as Grand Canary, Tenerife, and Lanzarote.

Bus – The main bus station is located at 25 Calle Alfonso XIII, Puerto del Rosario (phone: 928-850951).

Car Rental – Major rental car companies are *Avis* (8 Calle Primero de Mayo, Puerto Rosario; phone: 928-850261; *Hotel Casa Atlántica;* phone: 928-876017; 18 Calle La Oliva, Juan de Austria, Corralejo; phone: 928-866388); *Hertz* (Avenida Generalísimo, Corralejo; phone: 928-866259, 928-866432, and 928-866436; at the airport; phone: 928-866259; *Centro Comercial Tennis Center,* Playa Paraíso, Morro Jable-Jandía; phone: 928-876126; *Centro Comercial,* El Matorral, Morro Jable-Jandía; phone: 928-876138); and *Europcar* (27 Calle El Cosco, Puerto del Rosario; phone: 928-852436 or 928-852438; at the airport; phone: 928-852436; *Centro Comercial Barqueros,* Corralejo; phone: 928-866167; Apartamentos Tinojay, Caleta de Fuste; phone: 928-852436; Complejo Sotavento, Costa Calma; phone: 928-871041; Edificio Esmeraldo Local 1, Jandía; phone: 928-877044).

Ferry – *Trasmediterránea* (46 Calle León y Castillo, Puerto del Rosario; phone: 928-850877) has regular sailings from Puerto del Rosario to Las Palmas, Grand Canary, and Arrecife, Lanzarote, and from Morro Jable (at the southern tip of Fuerteventura) to Santa Cruz de Tenerife. The company also operates a jet foil between Morro Jable and Las Palmas and between Puerto del Rosario and Correlejo and Playa Blanca, Lanzarote. *Ferry Betancuria,* a subsidiary of *Ferry Gomera* headquartered at Edificio Rascacielos (Avenida 3 de Mayo, Santa Cruz de Tenerife; phone: 922-221040), has three daily sailings between Corralejo and Playa Blanca, Lanzarote, while *Alisur* (1 Calle La Esperanza, Arrecife; phone: 928-814272) covers the same route four times daily.

Taxi – Taxis sometimes can be hailed on the streets in Puerto del Rosario, or they can be requested by calling 928-850059.

CHECKING IN: Frenzied construction in recent years has added hundreds of hotel and apartment rooms to previously meager accommodations. Large hotels around Jandía in the south attract mainly German clients; inexpensive apartments are available in Corralejo. Expect to pay $100 or more for a double room listed as expensive, and between $60 and $90 for a room listed as moderate.

Iberotel Tres Islas – This spiffy, recently renovated, luxury establishment on a remote golden sand beach is surrounded by tropical gardens. All 365 rooms are air conditioned, with television sets and mini-bars, and there are three restaurants, a large saltwater swimming pool, tennis courts, and a fitness center. Playas de Corralejo (phone: 928-866000; fax: 928-866154; telex: 96171). Expensive.

Los Gorriones – A member of the Sol chain, this 309-room hotel is situated on a secluded beach in a town in the south of the island. Totally air conditioned, it is functional and comfortable, and includes tennis courts and windsurfing facilities. Playa de la Barca, Gran Tarajal (phone: 928-870850; fax: 928-870825). Moderate.

Parador de Fuerteventura – Standing on the edge of the ocean about 2 miles (3 km) south of the capital, this modern *parador*, 2 decades old, is the most splendid hotel on the island. A pleasant place, with polished wood floors and oil paintings, it has 50 air conditioned rooms, a swimming pool, and a good restaurant. Playa Blanca, Puerto del Rosario (phone: 928-851150; fax: 928-851158). Moderate.

EATING OUT: A moderately priced meal for two on Fuerteventura will cost between $30 and $45. Prices do not include drinks, wine, or tips.

Casa Juan – A rowboat full of ice proudly supports the day's catch in a display at this seafood house, where fried and baked fish are the specialties. Open daily. Reservations unnecessary. No credit cards accepted. 5 Calle General Linares, Corralejo (phone: 928-866219). Moderate.

El Patio – Whitewashed arches, a timber roof, and a floor of old tiles provide a cozy air to this quaint eatery near the harbor. Try the fish stew, the baked kid, and the banana flambé. Closed Mondays. Reservations unnecessary. No credit cards accepted. Calle Lepanto, Corralejo (phone: 928-866668). Moderate.

LA PALMA

One of the few islands to have escaped inundation by tourists, possibly because it is short on good beaches, La Palma has sufficient numbers of other attractions to justify a visit. Shaped like a leaf, it measures approximately 13 miles by 29 miles and is the greenest, and possibly the most beautiful, island of the archipelago. A massive crater, the Caldera de Taburiente, occupies the center of the island, with ravines running down to the rugged coastline. Below the pine-forested heights are intensely cultivated, terraced fields producing tropical and other fruits (as well as tobacco plants, originally imported from Cuba, from which the island's noted cigars are made). The capital, Santa Cruz de la Palma, was once the third most important port of the Spanish empire. Today, with 18,000 inhabitants, it is one of the most pleasant towns in the Canaries. Although facilities and services for tourists are not as well developed on La Palma as on Grand Canary or Tenerife, it does attract good numbers of Europeans who prefer quiet vacations.

GETTING AROUND: Airport – La Palma's small airport is located 5 miles (8 km) from Santa Cruz. *Iberia* (1 Calle Apurón; phone: 922-411345) has direct flights to Barcelona and Madrid, to Grand Canary and Tenerife, as well as to El Hierro in the summer.

Car Rental – Major rental car companies are *Avis* (32 Calle O'Daly and the airport, Santa Cruz de La Palma; phone: 922-411480 or 922-413742); *Hertz* (18 Avenida Puente, and the airport, Santa Cruz de La Palma; phone: 922-413676); and *Europcar* (39 Calle O'Daly, Santa Cruz de La Palma; phone: 922-414338; and at the airport; 922-428042).

Ferry – *Trasmediterránea* (2 Calle Pérez de Brito, Santa Cruz; phone: 922-412415) offers regular sailings to Grand Canary, Tenerife, El Hierro, and La Gomera.

SPECIAL PLACES: Santa Cruz de la Palma – Standing at the foot of a colossal cliff, which is part of an eroded crater, the island capital has an unhurried Old World atmosphere. Along its quiet streets are excellent examples of the architecture of the Canary Islands, with wooden balconies, the Ayuntamiento (City Hall), with a beautiful Renaissance façade, and El Salvador (a 16th-century church with a fine coffered ceiling). Other attractions include the *Museo Naval*, a maritime museum in a life-size replica of Christopher Columbus's *Santa María* (on Calle Barco de la Virgen; no phone; open Mondays through Saturdays from 10 AM to 1 PM and from 4 to 7 PM; admission charge).

La Caldera de Taburiente – A half-hour's drive west of the capital is the Mirador de la Concepción, a wonderful spot from which to gaze down on the coast and Santa Cruz. The road then proceeds upward and through a tunnel, from where a road to the right winds up amid pinewoods to La Cumbrecita, a lookout point offering a breathtaking panorama of the 5-mile-wide crater, a world of tumbled rock, craggy heights, and forest. The crater bottom can be visited by driving along a dirt track from Llanos de Aridane, a town in the island's western interior, up the Barranco de las Angustias, a giant cleft. A rock sacred to the Guanches stands in the crater, and it was here that the last of the original inhabitants held out against the Spaniards. Not far from Llanos is El Time, a cliff whose top affords a tremendous view up the yawning Angustias chasm and down on banana plantations climbing in steps from the ocean. On the northern edge of the crater, at El Roque de los Muchachos, the island's highest point (7,950 feet), stands an astronomical station, built by several European nations. (Permission to visit must be obtained from the Observatorio Astrofísico de Canarias, Edificio Tynabana, Avenida El Puente, Santa Cruz; phone: 922-413510). To reach El Roque, take the Barlovento road out of Santa Cruz and turn left after 2 miles (3 km); it is another 22 miles (35 km) through impressive scenery.

Fuencaliente – In the southern part of the island, near the village of Fuencaliente, stand the San Antonio and Teneguía volcanoes. Teneguía last erupted in 1971, sending molten lava flowing down to the sea. Sulfurous vapors rise from the crater, and water that pours down the fissures shoots back up as steam. Imperturbably, the local people continue farming nearby. If it's wild nights you're looking for, this is not the place to be as little excitement can be found when the sun goes down.

CHECKING IN: A moderately priced double room in a La Palma hotel will cost between $50 and $100; rooms costing less than $50 are considered inexpensive.

Parador de Santa Cruz de la Palma – Occupying a building that is typically Canarian in style, down to the characteristic wooden balconies, in an ideal seafront location. The 32 rooms are very comfortable; the restaurant specializes in international and local dishes. Major credit cards accepted. Avenida Bláz Pérez González; Santa Cruz de la Palma (phone: 922-412340; fax: 922-411856). Moderate.

Marítimo – A relatively new, 4-story, seafront hotel, with 78 air conditioned rooms complete with color television sets, mini-bars, and terraces. 80 Avenida Marítimo, Santa Cruz de la Palma (phone: 922-420222 or 922-416340; fax: 922-414302; telex: 92708). Moderate to inexpensive.

EATING OUT: Expect to pay between $30 and $60 for a meal for two at moderately priced restaurants on La Palma, and under $30 at inexpensive ones. Prices do not include drinks, wine, or tips.

La Fontana – Situated in a modern apartment block just off the beach south of Santa Cruz, this eatery has a bar and terrace, where patrons enjoy such delights as sirloin steaks cooked in whiskey and prawns fried in garlic. Closed Mondays. Reservations unnecessary. Major credit cards accepted. Urbanización Adelfas, Los Cancajos, Breña Baja (phone: 922-434250). Moderate.

El Parral – With its red tablecloths and fresh flowers, this eating spot opposite the Santa Catalina castle is the perfect place to sample baked fresh salmon, followed by strawberries and cream. Closed Mondays. Reservations unnecessary. Visa accepted. 7 Calle Castillete, Santa Cruz de la Palma (phone: 922-413915). Moderate.

San Petronio – As the name suggests, this restaurant on the island's west coast serves high-quality Italian dishes. Closed Mondays. Reservations unnecessary. No credit cards accepted. Llanos de Aridane (phone: 922-462403). Moderate.

La Abuela – Canarian and international specialties are served in this agreeable old tiled house, which has a large fireplace and a worn wooden floor. It stands just below the Mirador de la Concepción, along a rutted road. Closed Mondays. Reservations unnecessary. No credit cards accepted. 107 Buena Vista de Abajo, Breña Alta (phone: 922-415106). Moderate to inexpensive.

LA GOMERA

Although it measures only 146 square miles, this round island rises steeply from a precipitous shoreline to nearly 5,000 feet at its central peak, Mount Garajonay. The craggy seacoast and mountainous terrain make transportation from one valley to the next so difficult that the islanders have developed a whistling language to commmunicate with one another over great distances. Situated about 20 miles across the water from Tenerife's southwestern coast, La Gomera is usually visited as a day trip by tourists vacationing on one of the larger Canary Islands. The only historical events that the island has witnessed were brief visits paid by Christopher Columbus during the early stages of his trips to the New World, though these momentous layovers were made merely to procure water and provisions. Columbus's presence, however, has nonetheless served as a source of great local pride. In San Sebastián, the island's picturesque capital, is Nuestra Señora de la Asunción, where Columbus and his crews heard mass before setting off for parts unknown. The house in which he is said to have slept, called the *Casa de Colón,* is now a museum, and the Torre del Conde (Count's Tower), an old fortress standing near the sea, has been declared a national historic monument. The island's Garajonay National Park, encompassing the peak and surrounding woodlands — some 10,000 acres — is a UNESCO Natural World Heritage Site, home to over 850 species of plants and flowers. A worthwhile excursion out of San Sebastián is to the Valle Gran Rey, a spectacular ravine on the opposite side of the island, reached by hair-raising roads. The island also has several banana plantations, orchards, a fishing village called Playa de Santiago, with a pebble beach, and the whistling Gomerans themselves. Trade winds keep the skies clear and relatively cloudless, making for a crystalline visibility. Beaches are not a luminous white, but consist of black and red volcanic sand.

 GETTING AROUND: Car Rental – Major rental car companies are *Avis* (21 Caseta del Muelle, San Sebastián; phone: 922-870461), *Hertz* (6 Avenida Fred Olsen, San Sebastián; phone: 922-870924 or 922-870751), and *Europcar* (7 Avenida Fred Olsen, San Sebastián; phone: 922-870055).

Ferry – *Trasmediterránea* (35 General Franco, San Sebastián; phone: 922-871300) has regular sailings to Grand Canary, Tenerife, La Palma, and El Hierro, as well as hydrofoil service between San Sebastián and Los Cristianos, Tenerife. *Ferry Gomera* (Avenida Fred Olsen, San Sebastián; phone: 922-871007) has three daily departures between San Sebastián and Los Cristianos (except Tuesdays, when there are two departures).

 CHECKING IN/EATING OUT: *Parador Conde de la Gomera* – Built in the unique Canarian manorial style, this 42-room inn is surrounded by tropical gardens and has fine sea views and a swimming pool — an ideal, tranquil spot for escapists. The dining room serves good food, too. Accommodations on the island are severely limited and the rooms here are much in demand, so make reservations early. Major credit cards accepted. San Sebastián de la Gomera (phone: 922-871100; fax: 922-871116). Moderate.

EL HIERRO

The smallest and least inhabited of the archipelago's major islands, El Hierro is the harshest of all, with black volcanic soil, steep massifs, deep craters, and barren mountains. Its name means "the iron one," and for centuries, this rocky, 107 square miles was another one of those places that civilization regarded as the end of the world. Anyone who is not a connoisseur of solitude and nature in a dramatic mood may still think it is.

The farthest west of the islands, it appears grim and unfriendly from the sea, since its coasts are of black lava dotted with cactus. Clouds often shroud its central area, a plateau 4,900 feet above sea level. Although the lack of springs deterred the first Spaniards to arrive, the population has managed to survive on agriculture and fishing. So poor is El Hierro that the ownership of one tree was a communal affair in times past, with different branches belonging to different proprietors. Much of the population, as is the case with the other islands, emigrated to South America.

About 3,500 of the current 6,000 residents live in the capital, Valverde, the central town of an agricultural area where wine is the major product. Other local products are figs and cheese. The island's interior consists of emerald-green pastures with flocks of sheep that, but for the stone walls, volcanic rock, the rough Castilian tone of the shepherds, and the frequent sunshine, could pass for corners of Ireland.

The island's tiny airport handles *Iberia*'s flights to Grand Canary, Tenerife, Madrid, and Valencia. *Trasmediterránea* (Puerto de la Estaca, Valverde; phone: 922-550129) has regular ferry service to Grand Canary, Tenerife, La Palma, and Gomera. Though El Hierro usually is visited as a day trip by tourists vacationing on one of the larger islands, accommodations are available at the modern, but traditionally styled, 47-room *Parador de El Hierro* (Las Playas; phone: 922-550101), located on a black sand beach 12 miles (20 km) south of Valverde. Moderate.

INDEX

Index

BIRNBAUM TRAVEL GUIDES

Order by phone, toll-free: 1-800-331-3761

Name_____Phone_____

Address_____

City_____State_____Zip_____

Discover the Birnbaum Difference
More Details and Discounts Than Any Other Travel Guide

Get the best advice on what to see and do and where to stay while benefiting from money-saving information from America's foremost travel experts.

Area and Country Guides 1992—$17.00 Each

☐ Canada   ☐ Great Britain   ☐ Portugal
☐ Caribbean   ☐ Hawaii   ☐ South America
☐ Eastern Europe   ☐ Ireland   ☐ Spain
☐ Europe   ☐ Italy   ☐ United States
☐ France   ☐ Mexico   ☐ Western Europe

New Warm Weather Destination Guides 1992—$10.00 Each

☐ Acapulco   ☐ Bermuda   ☐ Ixtapa &
☐ Bahamas   ☐ Cancun/Cozumel/Isla   Zihuatanejo
  (including Turks   Mujeres (including Playa
  & Caicos)   Del Carmen)

New City Guides 1992—$10.00 Each

☐ Barcelona   ☐ London   ☐ Paris
☐ Boston   ☐ Los Angeles   ☐ Rome
☐ Chicago   ☐ Miami   ☐ San Francisco
☐ Florence   ☐ New York   ☐ Venice

Business Guides 1992—$10.00 Each

☐ Europe 1992 for the Business Traveler
☐ USA 1992 for the Business Traveler

Total for Birnbaum Travel Guides	$
For PA delivery, please include sales tax	
Add $4.00 for first Book S&H, $1.00 each additional book	
Total	$

☐ Check or Money order enclosed. Plase make payable to HarperCollins *Publishers*.
☐ Charge my credit card   ☐ American Express   ☐ Visa   ☐ Mastercard
Card no._____ Exp. date_____

Signature_____

Send orders to:
HarperCollins *Publishers*, P.O. Box 588, Dunmore, PA 18512-0588